THE FORTUNES OF

RICHARD MAHONY

THE FORTUNES OF

RICHARD MAHONY

BY

HENRY HANDEL RICHARDSON

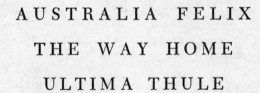

AUSTRALIA FELIX

THE WAY HOME

ULTIMA THULE

With a Foreword by SINCLAIR LEWIS

THE PRESS OF THE READERS CLUB
NEW YORK

PRINTED IN THE UNITED STATES OF AMERICA

FOREWORD

IN 1929 THERE WAS SUCCESSFULLY PUBLISHED a novel called *Ultima Thule*, by a gentleman named Henry Handel Richardson, who is, in private life, a lady named Henrietta Richardson Robertson. The acclaim was in one way unfortunate, because the book was only the final third of a trilogy of novels, of which the first two were called *Australia Felix* and *The Way Home*. The whole thing was a giant structure, as precisely planned as a pyramid, and those who saw only the top could not understand half the implications of what they read.

They were like an unfortunate who has too early glanced at the end of a detective story, and so is uninterested in what comes before. When the trilogy was published complete, under the title of THE FORTUNES OF RICHARD MAHONY, as it is now republished, there were too many readers who supposed that they already knew the whole story, and the trilogy met with not one-tenth of the excitement it merited.

But now, with *Ultima Thule* a little forgotten, we can start all over again, and THE FORTUNES OF RICHARD MAHONY should have supreme honors. For it is not merely an "unusually good novel," or an "important publication," but a book of a certain greatness, of which you actually may use the ordinarily impertinent phrase "you must read it." It is to be ranked with Wells' larger novels, and Dreiser's *Sister Carrie,* and Galsworthy's *The Forsyte Saga,* and Conrad and Lagerlöf and Hamsun, as a truly major work of fiction of the twentieth century.

It is the story of a cultivated doctor, reared in Dublin and Edinburgh, a man noble and upright and skilful and too confoundedly touchy, who tries to contend with the raw rusty Australian frontier of the 1850's and 1860's, during the brutalities of the gold-rushes—which the author makes altogether contemporary. The doctor is bruised and at last broken; he is let down by the very complexities and delicacies of his own mind; but along the way he finds a woman to whom wifehood can be a great profession, and finds, among the hurly-burly of mining-camp life, such friends as the uncombed vegetable man who is to become the great Sir Jake, minister of state.

The characters are impressively real. *The New York Herald Tribune* said truly, "so completely do these people become flesh of your flesh that the details of their experience are hardly less absorbing than your own."

The doctor's woolly practice in the Australian bush, among the tough squatter hamlets, on the red roads that run ruler-straight to the horizon, is not more explicit than the days when, with a sudden fortune from dubious mining-stocks, he tries to return to the damp smugness of an English village and, defeated there by the contempt for a "colonial," he settles too elegantly in a Melbourne mansion, and slips into the shiny marsh of spiritualism.

It is the story, in a different coat, of all of us. We may feel that the author has been spying on us, snaring our secret thoughts and weaknesses and hidden generosities. Dr. Mahony's trick of suddenly wanting to leave a decent home, for no intellectually defensible reason, at whatever cost of rent or contacts or esteem of friends, that emotional compulsion that can be quieted only by up and going, at once—I have known it more times than I would ever confess.

Along with love and triumph, failure and fear and death, all the strong flavors of existence come into the book, unsparingly. There may be readers who will, in anticipation, fear that they will be "depressed." They won't be. Behind everything is the author's unsentimental tenderness.

Americans, most of them, are going to be a little astonished by the parallel of our own pioneering, and the harsher places of our land, with those of Australia. Here, in Mahony's Australia, are our own Californian and Alaskan and Coloradan gold-rushes. Here are our rich pioneers filling pine castles with every known piece of junk that will hold gilt, and their shanty villages that explode into cities, and their too "refined" families. Here are our own dust-bowl and Arizona deserts and ragged mountains. Here is our medley of British and Irish and Germans, loving the Old Country yet, with a bitterness that

Foreword

the citizenry Back Home do not comprehend, resenting their condescension.

The book takes us to Australia. But it also takes us far inside the most impenetrable of all things—a human soul. When it was published, it was ahead of its time. I believe that now it is just at its time.

And the doctor's name must, remember, be pronounced Má-ho-ny, and not, as across the railroad tracks, on the second syllable.

SINCLAIR LEWIS

THE FORTUNES OF

RICHARD MAHONY

BOOK I
AUSTRALIA FELIX

"Every man is not only himself; . . . men are lived over again; the world is now as it was in ages past; there was none then, but there hath been some one since. that parallels him, and is, as it were, his revived self."

RELIGIO MEDICI

[PROEM]

IN A shaft on the Gravel Pits, a man had been buried alive. At work in a deep wet hole, he had recklessly omitted to slab the walls of a drive: uprights and tailors yielded under the lateral pressure, and the rotten earth collapsed, bringing down the roof in its train. The digger fell forward on his face, his ribs jammed across the pick, his arms pinned to his sides, nose and mouth pressed into the sticky mud as into a mask; and over his defenceless body, with a roar that burst his ear-drums, broke stupendous masses of earth.

His mates at the windlass went staggering back from the belch of violently discharged air: it tore the wind-sail to strips, sent stones and gravel flying, loosened planks and props. Their shouts drawing no response, the younger and nimbler of the two—he was a mere boy, for all his amazing growth of beard—put his foot in the bucket, and went down on the rope, kicking off the sides of the shaft with his free foot. A group of diggers, gathering round the pit-head, waited for the tug at the rope. It was quick in coming; and the lad was hauled to the surface. No hope: both drives had fallen in; the bottom of the shaft was blocked. The crowd melted with a "Poor Bill—God rest his

3

soul!" or with a silent shrug. Such accidents were not infrequent; each man might thank his stars it was not he who lay cooling down below. And so, as no more wash-dirt would be raised from this hole, the party that worked it made off for the nearest grog-shop, to wet their throats to the memory of the dead, and to discuss future plans.

All but one: a lean and haggard-looking man of some five and forty, who was known to his comrades as Long Jim. On hearing his mate's report, he had sunk heavily down on a log, and there he sat, a pannikin of raw spirit in his hand, the tears coursing ruts down cheeks scabby with yellow mud, his eyes glassy as marbles with those that had still to fall.

He wept, not for the dead man, but for himself. This accident was the last link in a chain of ill-luck that had been forging ever since he first followed the diggings. He only needed to put his hand to a thing, and luck deserted it. In all the sinkings he had been connected with, he had not once caught his pick in a nugget, or got the run of the gutter; the "bottoms" had always proved barren, drives been exhausted without his raising the colour. At the present claim, he and his mates had toiled for months, overcoming one difficulty after another. The slabbing, for instance, had cost them infinite trouble; it was roughly done, too, and, even after the pins were in, great flakes of earth would come tumbling down from between the joints, on one occasion nearly knocking silly the man who was below. Then, before they had slabbed a depth of three times nine, they had got into water, and in this they worked for the next sixty feet. They were barely rid of it, when the two adjoining claims were abandoned, and in came the flood again—this time they had to fly for their lives before it, so rapid was its rise. Not the strongest man could stand in this ice-cold, subterranean water for more than three days on end—the bark slabs stank in it, too, like the skins in a tanner's yard—and they had been forced to quit work till it subsided. He and another man had gone to the hills, to hew trees for more slabs; the rest to the grog-shop. From there, when it was feasible to make a fresh start, they had to be dragged, some blind drunk, the rest blind stupid from their booze. That had been the hardest job of any: keeping the party together. They had only been eight in all—a hand-to-mouth number for a deep wet hole. Then, one had died of dysentery, contracted from working constantly in water

4

up to the middle; and another had been nabbed in a man-hunt, and clapped into the "logs." And finally, but a day or two back, the three men who completed the night-shift had deserted for a new "rush" to the Avoca. Now, his pal had gone, too. There was nothing left for him, Long Jim, to do, but to take his dish and turn fossicker; or even to aim no higher than washing over the tailings rejected by the fossicker.

At the thought, his tears flowed anew. He cursed the dav on which he had first set foot on Ballarat.

"It's 'ell for white men—'ell, that's what it is!"

"'Ere, 'ave another drink, matey, and fergit yer bloody troubles."

His refilled pannikin drained, he grew warmer round the heart; and sang the praises of his former life.— He had been a lamplighter in the old country, and, for many years, had known no more arduous task than that of tramping round certain streets three times daily, his ladder on his shoulder, his bitch at heel, to attend the little flames that helped to dispel the London dark. And he might have jogged on at this, up to three score years and ten, had he never lent an ear to the tales that were being told of a wonderful country, where, for the mere act of stooping, and with your naked hand, you could pick up a fortune from the ground. Might the rogues who had spread these lies be damned to all eternity! Then, he had swallowed them only too willingly; and, leaving the old woman wringing her hands, had taken every farthing of his savings, and set sail for Australia. That was close on three years ago. For all he knew, his wife might be dead and buried by this time; or sitting in the almshouse. She could not write, and only in the early days had an occasional newspaper reached him, on which, alongside the Queen's head, she had put the mark they had agreed on, to show that she was still alive. He would probably never see her again, but would end his days where he was. Well, they wouldn't be many; this was not a place that made old bones.— And, as he sat, worked on by grief and liquor, he was seized by a desperate homesickness for the old country. Why had he ever been fool enough to leave it? He shut his eyes, and all the well-known sights and sounds of the familiar streets came back to him. He saw himself on his rounds, of a winter's afternoon, when each lamp had a halo in the foggy air; he heard the pit-pat of his four-footer behind him, the bump of the ladder against the prong of the lamp-post. His friend the policeman's glazed stovepipe shone out at the corner; from the distance came the tinkle of the muffin-man's bell, the cries of the buy-a-brooms. He remembered the glowing charcoal in the stoves of the chestnut- and potato-sellers; the appetising smell of the cooked-fish shops; the fragrant steam of the hot, dark coffee at the twopenny stall, when he had turned shivering out of bed; he sighed for the lights and jollity of the "Hare and Hounds," on a Saturday night. He would never see anything of the kind again. No; here, under bare blue skies, out of which the sun frizzled you alive; here, where it couldn't rain without at once being a flood; where the very winds blew contrarily, hot from the north and bitter-chill from the south; where, no matter how great the heat by day, the night would as likely as not be nipping cold: here, he was doomed to end his life, and to end it, for all the yellow sun-shine, more hopelessly knotted and gnarled with rheumatism, than if, dawn after dawn, he had gone out in a cutting north-easter, or groped his way through the grey fog-mists sent up by grey Thames.

Thus he sat and brooded, all the hatred of the unwilling exile for the land that gives him house-room, burning in his breast.

Who the man was, who now lay deep in a grave that fitted him as a glove fits the hand, careless of the pass to which he had brought his mate; who this really was, Long Jim knew no more than the rest. Young Bill had never spoken out. They had chummed together on the seventy-odd-mile tramp from Mel-bourne; had boiled a common billy, and slept side by side, in rain-soaked blankets, under the scanty hair of a she-oak. That was in the days of the first great stampede to the gold-fields, when the embryo seaports were as empty as though they were plague-ridden; and when every man who had the use of his legs—together with the hundreds of new arrivals daily disem-barking—was on the wide bush-track, bound for the north. It was better to be two than one, in this medley of bullock-teams, lorries, carts, and pack-horses, of dog-teams, wheelbarrows, and swagmen, where the air rang with oaths, shouts, and ham-mering hoofs, with whip-cracking, and bullock-prodding; in this hurly-burly of thieves, bushrangers and foreigners, of drunken convicts and deserting sailors, of slit-eyed Chinese and apt-handed Lascars, of expirees and ticket-of-leave men, of Jews, Turks and other infidels. Long Jim, himself stunned by it all: by the pother of landing and of finding a roof to cover him; by the ruinous price of bare necessaries; by the length of this unheard-of walk that lay before his town-bred feet— Long Jim had gladly accepted the young man's company on the road. Originally, for no more than this; at heart, he distrusted Young Bill, because of his fine-gentleman airs, and had intended shaking the lad off as soon as they reached the diggings. There, a man must, for safety's sake, be alone, when he stooped to pick up his fortune. But, at first sight of the strange, wild scene that met his eyes, he had hastily changed his mind. And so the two of them had stuck together; and he had never had cause to regret it. For all his lily-white hands and finical speech, Young Bill had worked like a nigger, standing by his mate through the latter's disasters; had worked till the ladyish hands were horny with warts and corns, and this, though he was doubled up with dysentery in the hot season, and racked by winter cramps. But the life had proved too hard for him, all the same. During the previous summer, he had begun to drink —steadily, with the dogged persistence that was in him—and, since then, he had gone downhill, and his work had grown slovenly. His sudden death had only been a hastening-on of the inevitable. Staggering home to the tent after nightfall, he would have been bound, sooner or later, to fall into a dry shicer and break his neck, or into a wet one and be drowned.

On the surface of the Gravel Pits, his fate was already forgotten. The rude activity of a gold-diggings in full swing had closed over the incident, swallowed it up.

Under a sky so pure and luminous that it seemed like a thinly drawn veil of blueness, which ought to have been transparent, stretched what, from a short way off, resembled a desert of pale clay. No patch of green offered rest to the eye; not a tree, hardly a stunted bush, had been left standing, either on the bottom of the vast shallow basin itself, or on the several hillocks that dotted it, and formed its sides. Even the most prominent of these, the Black Hill, which jutted out on the Flat like a gigantic tumulus, had been stripped of its dense timber, feverishly disembowelled, and was now become a bald protuberance, strewn with gravel and clay. The whole scene had that strange, repellent ugliness that goes with the break-

7

ing-up, and throwing into disorder, of what has been sanctified as final: it belongs, in particular, to the wanton disturbing of earth's gracious green-spread crust. In the pre-golden era, this wide valley, lying open to sun and wind, had been a lovely grassland, ringed by a circlet of wooded hills; beyond these, by a belt of virgin forest. A limpid river, and more than one creek, had meandered across its face; water was to be found there, even in the driest summer. She-oaks and peppermints had given shade to the flocks of the early settlers; wattles had bloomed their brief delirious yellow passion against the grey-green foliage of the gums. Now, all that was left of the original "pleasant resting-place," and its pristine beauty, were the ancient volcanic cones of Warrenheip and Buninyong. These, too far off to supply wood for firing or slabbing, still stood green and timbered, and looked down upon the havoc that had been made of the fair, pastoral lands.

Seen nearer at hand, the dun-coloured desert resolved itself into uncountable pimpling clay- and mud-heaps, of divers shades and varying sizes: some consisted of but a few bucketfuls of mullock, others were taller than the tallest man. There were also hundreds of rain-soaked, mud-bespattered tents, sheds and awnings; wind-sails, which fell, funnel-like, from a kind of gallows, into the shafts they ventilated; flags fluttering on high posts in front of stores. The many human figures that went to and fro were hardly to be distinguished from the ground they trod. They were coated with earth, clay-clad in ochre and gamboge. Their faces were daubed with clauber; it matted great beards, and entangled the coarse hairs on chests and brawny arms. Where, here and there, a blue jumper had kept a tinge of its blueness, it was so besmeared with yellow that it might have been expected to turn green. The gauze neck-veils that hung from the brims of wide-awakes or cabbage-trees, were become stiff little lattices of caked clay.

There was water everywhere. From the spurs and gullies round about, the autumn rains had poured freely down on the Flat; river and creeks had been over their banks; and such narrow ground space as remained between the thick-sown tents, the myriads of holes that abutted one on another, jealous of every inch of space, had become a trough of mud. Water meandered over this mud, or carved its soft way in channels; it lay about in puddles, thick and dark as coffee-grounds; it filled abandoned shallow holes to the brim. The humps of clay and gravel had been worked into a state of glutinous filth, by the thousands of jackbooted feet that crossed and recrossed them, that slipped on them, and squelched in them, and stuck fast.

From this scene rose a blurred hum of sound; rose, and, as it were, remained stationary above it—like a smoke-cloud, which no wind comes to drive away. Gradually, though, the ear made out, in the conglomerate of noise, a host of separate noises, infinitely multiplied: the sharp tick-tick of surface-picks, the dull thud of shovels, their muffled echoes from the depths below. There was also the continuous squeak and groan of windlasses; the bump of the mullock emptied from the bucket; the trundle of wheelbarrows, pushed along a plank from the shaft's mouth to the nearest pool; the dump of the dirt on the heap for washing; the crunching of cart-wheels, and a horse's smacking efforts to get a footing on the slippery ground. Along the banks of a creek, hundreds of cradles rattled and grated; the noise of the spades chopping the gravel in the puddling-tubs, or the Long Toms, was like the scrunch of shingle under waves. The drip and splash of falling water was all-pervading: it was poured from buckets, where wet holes were baling out; from long-handled dippers into buddles and cradles; while here and there it fell, with a splash, from the tall pole of a weegee.— The fierce yelping of the dogs chained to the flag-posts of stores, mongrels, which yapped at friend and foe alike, supplied a note of ear-splitting discord.

But, except for this, it was a wholly mechanical din. Human brains directed operations, human hands carried them out, but the sound of the human voice was, for the most part, lacking. The diggers were a sombre, preoccupied race, little given to lip-work. Even the "shepherds," who, in waiting to see if their neighbours struck the lead, beguiled the time with euchre and "lambskinnet," played moodily, their mouths glued to their pipe-stems; they were tail-on-end to fling down the cards for pick and shovel. The great majority, ant-like in their indefatigable business, neither turned a head nor looked up; backs were bent, eyes fixed, in a hard scrutiny of cradle or tin-dish: it was the earth that held them, the familiar, homely earth, whose common fate it is to be trodden heedlessly underfoot.

Here, it was a loadstone that drew all men's thoughts. And it took toll of their bodies in odd, exhausting forms of labour, which were swift to weed out the unfit.

The men at the windlasses spat into their horny palms and bent to the crank: they paused only to pass the back of a hand over a sweaty forehead, or to drain a nose between two fingers. The barrow-drivers shoved their loads, the bones of their forearms standing out like ribs. Beside the pools, the puddlers chopped with their shovels; some even stood in the tubs, and worked the earth with their feet, as wine-pressers trample grapes. The cradlers, eternally rocking with one hand, held a long stick in the other, with which to break up any clods a careless puddler might have deposited in the hopper. Behind these came the great army of fossickers, washers of surface-dirt, equipped with knives and tin dishes, and content if they could wash out half-a-penny-weight to the dish. At their heels, still others, who treated the tailings they threw away. And, among these last, was a sprinkling of women, more than one with an infant sucking at her breast. Withdrawn into a group for themselves worked a body of Chinese, in loose blue blouses, flappy blue leg-bags, and huge conical straw hats. They, too, fossicked and rewashed, using, in the process, extravagant quantities of water.

Thus the pale-eyed multitude worried the surface, and, at the risk and cost of their lives, probed the depths. Now that deep sinking was in vogue, gold-digging no longer served as a play-game for the gentleman and the amateur; the greater number of these who toiled at it were work-tried, seasoned men. And yet, although it had now sunk to the level of any other arduous and uncertain occupation, and the magic prizes of the early days were seldom found, something of the old, romantic glamour still clung to this most famous gold-field, dazzling the eyes and confounding the judgment. Elsewhere, the horse was in use at the puddling-trough, and machines for crushing quartz were under discussion. But the Ballarat digger resisted the introduction of machinery, for fear of the capitalist machinery would bring in its train. He remained the dreamer, the jealous individualist; he hovered for ever on the brink of a stupendous discovery.

This dream it was, of vast wealth, got without exertion, which had decoyed the strange, motley crowd, in which peers and churchmen rubbed shoulders with the scum of Norfolk Island, to exile in this outlandish region. And the intention of all alike had been: to snatch a golden fortune from the earth; and then, hey, presto! for the old world again. But they were reckoning without their host; only too many of those who entered the country went out no more. They became prisoners to the soil. The fabulous riches of which they had heard tell, amounted, at best, to a few thousands of pounds: what folly to depart with so little, when mother earth still teemed! Those who drew blanks nursed an unquenchable hope, and laboured all their days like navvies, for a navvy's wage. Others again, broken in health, or disheartened, could only turn to an easier handiwork. There were also those who, as soon as fortune smiled on them, dropped their tools and ran to squander the work of months in a wild debauch; and these invariably returned, tail down, to prove their luck anew. And, yet again, there were those who, having once seen the metal in the raw: in dust, fine as that brushed from a butterfly's wing; in heavy, chubby nuggets; or, more beautiful still, as the daffodil-yellow veining of bluish-white quartz: these were gripped in the subtlest way of all. A passion for the gold itself awoke in them, an almost sensual craving to touch and possess; and, to these, the glitter of a few specks at the bottom of pan or cradle came, in time, to mean more than "home," or wife, or child.

Such were the fates of those who succumbed to the "unholy hunger."— It was a like a form of revenge taken on them, for their loveless schemes of robbing and fleeing; a revenge contrived by the ancient, barbaric country they had so lightly invaded. Now, she held them captive—without chains; ensorcelled—without witchcraft; and, lying stretched in the sun like some primeval monster, her breasts freely bared, she watched, with a malignant eye, the efforts made by these puny mortals to tear their lips away.

PART I

[1]

ON THE summit of one of the clay heaps, a woman shot into silhouette against the sky. An odd figure, clad in a skimpy green petticoat, with a scarlet shawl held about her shoulders, wisps of frowsy red hair standing out round her head, she balanced herself on the slippery earth, spinning her arm like the vane of a windmill, and crying, at the top of her voice: "Joe, boys!—Joe, Joe, Joey!"

It was as if, with these words, she had dropped a live shell into the diggers' midst. A general stampede ensued; in which the cry was caught up, echoed, and re-echoed, till the whole Flat rang with the name of "Joe." Tools were dropped, cradles and tubs abandoned; windlasses were left to kick their cranks backwards. Many of the workers took to their heels; others, in affright, scuttled aimlessly hither and thither, like barnyard fowls in a panic. Summoned by shouts of: "Up with you, boys! —the traps are here!" numbers ascended from below, to see the fun, while as many went hurriedly down to hiding, in drive or chamber. Even those diggers who could pat the pocket in which their license lay ceased work, and stood about, with sullen faces, to view the course of events. Only the group of Chinamen washing tail-heaps remained unmoved. One of them, to whom the warning woman belonged, raised his head and called a Chinese word at her; she obeyed it instantly, vanishing into thin air; the rest went impassively on with their fossicking. They were not such fools as to try to cheat the Government of its righteous dues; none but had his license safely folded in his nosecloth, and thrust inside the bosom of his blouse.

Through the labyrinth of tents and mounds, a gold-laced cap could be seen approaching; then a gold-tressed jacket came into view, the white star on the forehead of a mare. Behind the Commissioner, who rode down thus from the Camp, came the members of his staff; these again were followed by a body of mounted troopers. They drew rein on the slope, and, simultaneously, a line of foot police, backed by a detachment of light infantry, shot out, like an arm, and walled in the Flat to the south.

On the appearance of the enemy, the babel redoubled. There were groans and cat-calls. Along with the derisive "Joeys!" the rebel diggers hurled any term of abuse that came to their lips.

"The dolly mops! The skunks! The bushrangers!— Oh, damn 'em, damn 'em! . . . damn their bloody eyes!"

"It's Rooshia—that's what it is!" said an oldish man darkly.

12

But a wit cried: "Git along with yer, matey! It's 'er Gracious Majesty's forty-second-cousin's berfday! . . . an' the swine must 'ave their swill!"

The Commissioner, a horse-faced, solemn man, with brown side-whiskers, let the reins droop on his mare's neck, and sat unwinking in the tumult. His mien was copied by his staff. Only one of them, a very young boy, who was new to the colony and his post, changed colour under his gaudy cap, went from white to pink, and from pink to white again; while, at each fresh insult, he gave a perceptible start, and gazed, dumbfounded, at his chief's insensitive back.

The "bloodhounds" had begun to track their prey. Rounding up, with a skill born of long practice, they drove the diggers before them towards the centre of the Flat. Here, they passed from group to group, and from hole to hole, calling for the production of licenses with an insolence that made its object see red. They were nice of scent, too, and nine times in ten, pounced on just those unfortunates who, through carelessness, or lack of means, or on political grounds, had failed to take out the month's license to dig for gold. Every few minutes one or another was marched off, between two constables, to the Government Camp, for fine or imprisonment.

Now it was that it suddenly entered Long Jim's head to cut and run. Up till now, he had stood declaring himself a free-born Briton, who might be drawn and quartered if he ever again paid the blasted tax. But, as the police came closer, a spear of fright pierced his befuddled brain, and, inside a breath, he was off and away. Had the abruptness of his start not given him a slight advantage, he would have been caught at once. As it was, the chase would not be a long one; the clumsy, stiff-jointed man slithered here, and stuck fast there, dodging obstacles with an awkwardness that was painful to see.— He could be heard sobbing and cursing as he ran.

At this point, the Commissioner, half turning, signed to the troopers in his rear. Six or seven of them shook up their bridles and rode off, their scabbards clinking, to prevent the fugitive's escape.

A howl of contempt went up from the crowd. The pink and white subaltern made what was almost a movement of the arm, to intercept his superior's command.

It was too much for Long Jim's last mate, the youthful

13

blackbeard who had pluckily descended the shaft after the accident. He had been standing on a mound, with a posse of
others, following the man-hunt. At his partner's crackbrained
dash for the open, his snorts of indignation had found words.
"Gawblimy! . . . is the old fool gone dotty?" Now, he drew a
whistling breath. "No, it's more than flesh and blood. . . . Stand
back, boys!" And, though he was as little burdened with a
license as the man under pursuit, he shouted: "Help, help! . . .
for God's sake, don't let 'em have me!" shot down the slope,
and was off like the wind.

His foxly object was attained. The attention of the hunters
was diverted. Long Jim, seizing the moment, vanished underground.

The younger man ran with the lightness of a hare. He had
also the hare's address in doubling and turning. His pursuers
never knew, did he pass from sight behind a covert of tents
and mounds, where he would bob up next. He avoided shafts
and pools as if by a miracle; ran along greasy planks without a
slip; and, where these had been removed, to balk the police, he
jumped the holes, taking risks that were not for a sane man.
Once he fell, but, enslimed from head to foot, wringing wet,
and hatless, was up again in a twinkling. The enemy were less
sure-footed than he, and times without number measured their
lengths on the oily ground. Still, one of them was gaining rapidly on him, a giant of a fellow, with long, thin legs; and, soon,
the constable's foot filled the prints left by the young man's,
while these were still warm. It was a fine run. The diggers
trooped after in a body; the Flat rang with cheers and plaudits.
Even the Commissioner and his retinue trotted in the same
direction. Eventually, the runaway must land in the arms of
the mounted police.

But this was not his plan. Making as though he headed for
the open, he suddenly dashed off at right angles, and, with a
final sprint, brought up dead against a log-and-canvas store,
which stood on rising ground. His adversary was so close behind that a collision resulted; the digger's feet slid from under
him, he fell on his face, the other on top. In their fall, they
struck a huge pillar of tin-dishes, ingeniously built up to the
height of the store itself. This toppled over with a crash, and
the dishes went rolling down the slope, between the legs of the
police. The dog chained to the flagstaff all but strangled him-

self, in his rage and excitement; and the owner of the store came running out.

"Purdy! . . . . you? What in the name of . . . ?"

The digger adroitly rolled his captor over, and there they both sat, side by side on the ground, one gripping the other's collar, both too blown to speak. A cordon of puffing constables hemmed them in.

The storekeeper frowned. "You've no license, you young beggar!"

And: "Your license, you scoundrel!" demanded the leader of the troop.

The prisoner's rejoinder was a saucy: "Now then, out with the cuffs, Joe!"

He got on his feet, as bidden; but awkwardly, for it appeared that, in falling, he had hurt his right ankle. Behind the police were massed the diggers. These opened a narrow alley for the camp officials to ride through, but their attitude was hostile, and there were cries of: "Leave 'im go, yer blackguards! . . . after sich a run! None o' yer bloody quod for 'im!" along with other, more threatening expressions. Sombre and taciturn, the Commissioner waved his hand. "Take him away!"

"Well, so long, Dick!" said the culprit jauntily; and, as he offered his wrists to be handcuffed, he whistled an air.

Here the storekeeper hurriedly interposed: "No, stop! I'll give bail." And darting into the tent and out again, he counted five one-pound notes into the constable's palm. The lad's collar was released; and a murmur of satisfaction mounted from the crowd.

At the sound, the giver made as if to retire. Then, yielding to a second thought, he stepped forward and saluted the Commissioner. "A young hot-head, sir! He means no harm. I'll send him up in the morning, to apologise."

("I'll be damned if you do!" muttered the digger between his teeth.)

But the Chief refused to be placated. "Good day, doctor," he said shortly; and, letting his horse have the spur, he, with his staff at heel, trotted smartly down the slope, followed, till out of earshot, by a mocking fire of "Joes." Lingering in the rear, the youthful sympathiser turned in his saddle and waved his cap.

The raid was over, for that day. The crowd dispersed; its members became orderly, hard-working men once more. The storekeeper hushed his frantic dog, and called his assistant to rebuild the pillar of tins.

The young digger sat down on the log that served for a bench, and examined his foot. He pulled and pulled, causing himself great pain, but could not get his boot off. So he gave it up, and let his hands droop between his knees; he had lost his pipe in the chase. The hum of work resumed rose from the Flat; inside the store, a raucous voice was bargaining over a pound of Glenfield's starch.

But the injured ankle grew ever hotter and heavier. At last he looked back over his shoulder and cried impatiently: "Dick! . . . I say, Dick Mahony! Give us a drink, old boy! . . . I'm dead-beat."

At this, the storekeeper—he was a tall, slenderly built man of some seven or eight and twenty—himself appeared, bearing a jug and a pannikin.

"Oh, bah!" said the lad, when he found that the jug held only water. And, on his friend reminding him that he might, by now, have been sitting in the lock-up, he laughed and winked. "I knew you'd go bail."

"Well! . . . of all the confounded impudence. . . !"

"Faith, Dick, and d'ye think I didn't see how yer hand itched for yer pocket?"

The man he called Mahony flushed above his fair beard. It was true: he had made an involuntary movement of the hand —checked, for the rest, halfway, by the knowledge that the pocket was empty. He looked displeased, and said nothing.

"Don't be afraid, I'll pay you back soon's ever my ship comes home," went on the young scapegrace, who very well knew how to play his cards. At his companion's heated disclaimer, however, he changed his tone. "I say, Dick, have a look at my foot, will you? I can't get this damned boot off."

The elder man bent over the injury. He ceased to show displeasure.— "Purdy, you young fool, when will you learn wisdom?"

"Well, they shouldn't hunt old women, then—the swine!" gave back Purdy; and told his tale.— "Oh, lor, there go six canaries!" For, at his wincing and shrinking, his friend had taken a penknife and ripped up the jackboot. Now, with

16

practised hands, he explored the swollen, discoloured ankle.

When it was washed and bandaged, its owner stretched himself on the ground, his head in the shade of a barrel, and went to sleep.

He slept till sundown, through all the traffic of a busy afternoon.

Some half-a-hundred customers came and went. The greater number of them were earth-stained diggers, who ran up for, it might be, a missing tool, or a hide bucket, or a coil of rope. They spat jets of tobacco-juice, were richly profane, paid, where coin was scarce, in gold-dust from a matchbox, and hurried back to work. But there also came old harridans—as often as not, diggers themselves—whose language outdid that of the males, and dirty Irish mothers; besides a couple of the white women who inhabited the Chinese quarter. One of these was in liquor, and a great hullabaloo took place, before she could be got rid of. Put out, she stood in front of the tent, her hair hanging down her back, cursing and reviling. Respectable women as well did an afternoon's shopping there. These were in no haste to be gone, and sat about on empty boxes or upturned barrels, exchanging confidences, while weary children plucked at their skirts. A party of youngsters entered, the tallest of whom could just see over the counter, and called for shandygaffs. The assistant was for chasing them off, with hard words. But the storekeeper, stepping forward, put, instead, a stick of barley-sugar into each dirty, outstretched hand, and the imps retired, well content. On their heels arrived a digger and his lady-love, to choose a wedding-outfit; and all the gaudy finery the store held was displayed before them. A red velvet dress, flounced with satin, a pink gauze bonnet, white satin shoes and white silk stockings met their fancy. The dewy-lipped, smutty-lashed Irish girl blushed and dimpled, in consulting with the shopman upon the stays in which to lace her ample figure; the digger, whose very pores oozed gold, planked down handfuls of dust and nuggets, and brushed aside a neat paisley shawl for one of yellow satin, the fellow to which he swore to having seen on the back of the Governor's lady herself. He showered brandy-snaps on the children, and bought a polka-jacket for a shabby old woman. Then, producing a bottle of champagne from a sack he bore, he called on those present to give him, after: " 'Er most Gracious little Majesty, God

17

bless 'er!" the: "'Oly estate of materimony!" The empty bottle smashed, for luck, the couple departed arm-in-arm, carrying their purchases in a sack; and the rest of the company trooped to the door with them, to wish them joy.

Within the narrow confines of the tent: where red-herrings trailed over moleskin-shorts, and East India pickles and Hessian boots lay on the top of sugar and mess-pork; where cheeses rubbed shoulders with tallow-candles, blue and red serge shirts, and captain's biscuits; where onions, and guernseys, and sardines, fine combs, cigars, and bear's-grease, Windsor soap, tinned coffee, and hair-oil, revolvers, shovels, and Oxford shoes, lay in one grand miscellany: within the crowded store, as the afternoon wore on, the air grew rank and oppressive. Precisely at six o'clock, the bar was let down across the door, and the storekeeper withdrew to his living-room, at the back of the tent. He changed his coat, and meticulously washed his hands, to which clung a subtle blend of all the strong-smelling goods that had passed through them. Then, coming round to the front, he sat down on the log and took out his pipe. He made a point, no matter how brisk trade was, of not keeping open after dark. His evenings were his own.

He sat and puffed, tranquilly. It was a fine night. The first showy splendour of sunset had passed; but the upper sky was still aflush with colour. And in the centre of this frail cloud, which faded as he watched it, swam a single star.

[2]

WITH the passing of a cooler air, the sleeper wakened and rubbed his eyes. Letting his injured leg lie undisturbed, he drew up the other knee, and buckled his hands round it. In this position, he sat and talked.

He was a dark, fresh-coloured young man, of middle height, and broadly built. He had large white teeth of a kind to crack nuts with, and the full, wide, flexible mouth that denotes the generous talker.

"What a wind-bag it is, to be sure!" thought his companion, as he smoked and listened, in a gently ironic silence, to abuse of the Government.— He knew—or thought he knew—young Purdy inside out.

But, behind all the froth of the boy's talk, there lurked, it

18

seemed, a purpose. No sooner was a meal of cold chop and tea
over, than, brushing aside the proffered advice to go home to
bed, Purdy declared his intention of being present at a meeting of malcontent diggers. Nor would he even wait to wash
himself clean of mud.

His friend reluctantly agreed to lend him an arm. But he
could not refrain from taking the lad to task, for getting entangled in the political imbroglio.— "When, as you know, it's
just a kind of sport to you."

Purdy sulked for a few paces, then burst out: "If only you
weren't so damned detached, Dick Mahony!"

"You're restless, and want excitement, my boy—that's the root
of the trouble."

"Well, I'm jiggered! If ever I knew a restless mortal, it's
yourself."

The two men picked their steps across the Flat and up the
opposite hillside, young Purdy Smith limping, and leaning
heavy, his lame foot thrust into an old slipper. He was, at all
times, hail-fellow-well-met with the world. Now, in addition,
his plucky exploit of the afternoon had blazed a path through
the settlement; and blarney and bravos rained upon him.—
"Golly for you, Purdy, old 'oss!" "Showed 'em the diggers'
flag, 'e did!" "What'll you take, me buck? Come on in for a
drop o' the real strip-me-down-naked!" Even a weary old
strumpet, propping herself against the doorway of a dancing-
saloon, waved a tipsy hand and cried: "Arrah, an' is it yerrself,
Purrdy, me bhoy? Shure an' it's bussin' ye I'd be afther—if me
legs would carry me!" And Purdy laughed, and relished the
honey, and had an answer pat for everybody—especially the
women. His companion, on the other hand, was greeted, by
such as knew him, with a glibness that had something perfunctory in it, and not a touch of familiarity.

The big canvas tent on Bakery Hill, where the meeting was
to be held, was already lighted; and, at the tinkle of a bell, the
diggers, who, till then, had stood cracking and hobnobbing
outside, began to push for the entrance. The bulk of them belonged to the race that is quickest to resent injustice—were
Irish. After them in number came the Germans, swaggering
and voluble; and the inflammable French. English, Scotch and
Americans formed a smaller and cooler, but very dogged group.

At the end of the tent, a rough platform had been erected,

19

on which stood a row of cane seats. In the body of the hall, the benches were formed of boards, laid across from one up-turned keg or tub to another. The chair was taken by a local auctioneer, Carter by name, who, dowered to his own think-ing with the gift of oratory, dedicated the intervals between selling up bankrupts to the political education of the diggers. He was a cadaverous-looking man, with never a twinkle in his eye, and Purdy groaned at the sight of him.

Now, in a lengthy discourse, and with the single monoto-nous gesture of beating the palm of one hand with the back of the other, this Carter strove to bring home to his audience, the degradation of their present political status. The diggers chewed and spat, and listened to his periods with sang-froid: the shame of their state did not greatly move them. They followed, too, with composure, the rehearsal of their general grievances. As they were aware, went on the speaker, the Legislative Council of Victoria was made up largely of Crown nominees; in the election of members the gold-seeking popu-lation, the flower of which it was his privilege to be addressing that evening, had no voice whatsoever. This was a scandalous thing; for the digging constituent outnumbered all the rest of the population put together, thus forming what he would call the backbone and mainstay of the colony. Indeed, he would go further, and term them the blood and marrow of this grand young country. Courage, and an adventurous spirit had led them thither; the labour of *their* hands had raised the colony to its present pitch of prosperity. And yet these same bold and hardy pioneers were held incapable of deciding jot or tittle in the public affairs of their adopted home.— Still unmoved, the diggers listened to this recital of their virtues. But when one man, growing weary of the speaker's unctuous wordiness, dis-charged a fierce: "Why the hell don't you git on to the bloody license-tax?" the audience was fire and flame in an instant. A riotous noise ensued; rough throats rang changes on the ques-tion. Order at length restored, it was evident that the auction-eer's speech was over. Thrown violently out of his concept, Carter struck and struck at his palm in vain; nothing would come. So, making the best of a bad job, he irately undertook not to try his hearers' patience any longer, and sat down in favour of his successor on the programme.

This speaker did not fare much better. The assemblage,

roused, now jolly and merciless, was not disposed to give
quarter; and his obtuseness in dawdling over such high-flown
notions as that population, not property, formed the basis of
representative government, or that taxation without represen-
tation was tyranny, reaped him a harvest of boos and groans.
This was not what the diggers had come out to hear. And they
were as direct as children in their demand for the gist of the
matter.

"A reg'lar ol' shicer!" was the unanimous opinion, expressed
without scruple. While from the back of the hall came the curt
request to him to shut his "tater-trap."

Next on the list was a German, a ruddy-faced man, with
mutton-chop whiskers and prominent, watery eyes. He could
not manage the letter "r." In the body of a word, where it was
negligible, he rolled it out as though it stood three deep. Did
he tackle it as an initial, on the other hand, his tongue seemed
to cleave to his palate, and to yield only an "l." This quaint
defect caused some merriment at the start, but was soon
eclipsed by a more striking oddity. The speaker had the habit
of, as it were, creaking with his nose. After each few sentences,
he paused, to give himself time to produce something between
a creak and a snore—an abortive attempt to get at a mucus
that was plainly out of reach.

The diggers were beside themselves with mirth. Wags
cracked their jokes.

"'E's forgot 'is 'ankey!"

"'Ere, boys, look slippy!—a 'ankey for ol' sausage!"

But the German was not sensitive to ridicule. He had something to say, and he was there to say it. Fixing his fish-like eyes
on a spot high up the tent wall, he kept them pinned to it,
while he mouthed out blood-and-thunder invectives. He was,
it seemed, a red-hot revolutionist; a fierce denouncer of British
rule. He declared the British monarchy to be an effete insti-
tution; the fetish of British freedom to have been "exbloded"
long ago. What they needed, in this grand young country of
theirs, was a "rebublic"; they must rid themselves of those
shackles that had been forged in the days when men were still
slaves. It was his sound conviction that, before many weeks
had passed, the Union Jack would have been hauled down for
ever, and the glorious Southern Cross would wave in its stead,
over a free Australia. The day on which this happened would

be a never-to-be-forgotten date in the annals of the country. For what, he would like to know, had the British flag done for Australia? Had not the Government's most heaven-screaming injustices been committed beneath it? But then what, indeed, had it ever done for freedom, at any time in the world's history? They should read in their schoolbooks, and there they would learn that, wherever a people had risen against their tyrants, the Union Jack had waved, not over them, but over the British troops sent to stamp their rising out!

This was more than Mahony could stomach. Flashing up from his seat, he strove to assert himself above the hum of agreement that mounted from the foreign contingent, and the doubtful sort of grumble by which the Britisher signifies his disapproval.

"Mr. Chairman! Gentlemen!" he cried in a loud voice. "I call upon those loyal subjects of her Majesty who are present here, to join me in giving three cheers for the British flag.— Hip, hip, hurrah! And, again, hip, hip, hurrah! And, once more, hip, hip, hurrah!"

His compatriots followed him though flabbily; and he continued to make himself heard above the shouts of "Order!" and the bimming of the chairman's bell.

"Mr. Chairman! I appeal to you. Are we Britons to sit still and hear our country's flag reviled?—that flag which has ensured us the very liberty we are enjoying this evening. The gentleman who has been pleased to slander it is not, I believe, a British citizen. Now, I put it to him: is there another country on the face of the earth, that would allow people of all nations to flock into a gold-bearing colony on terms of perfect equality with its own subjects?—to flock in, take all they can get, and then make off with it?"—a point of view that elicited forcible grunts of assent, which held their own against hoots and hisses. Unfortunately, the speaker did not stop here, but went on: "Gentlemen! Do not, I implore you, allow yourselves to be led astray by a handful of ungrateful foreigners, who have received nothing but benefits from our Crown. What you need, gentlemen, is not revolution, but reform; not the strife and bloodshed that violence entails, but a liberty consistent with law and order. And this must be accomplished, gentlemen, by peaceful means: by stability, by——"

("You'll never get 'em like that, Dick," muttered Purdy *sotto voce*.)

"Not so much gentlemaning, if *you* please!" said a sinister-looking man, who might have been a Vandemonian in his day. "*Men's* what we are—that's good enough for us."

"'E's a danged sight too ready to tell *us* wot *we* need! Let 'im pull the mote outer 'is own eye first."

Mahony was nettled. The foreigners, too, were pressing him.

"The beam, my good fellow, is what you are endeavouring to say," he gave back sarcastically. Then, turning on his first interrupter: "So I am to believe, sir, am I, what I frequently hear asserted, that there are no gentlemen left on the diggings?"

("Oh lor, Dick!" said Purdy. He was sitting with his elbows on his knees, and now he dropped his face between his hands, and sat clutching his cheeks, as though he had the toothache.)

"Oh, stow yer blatherskite!" said he of the mote and beam.

"Believe what yer bloody well like!" retorted the Vandemonian fiercely. "But don't come 'ere and interrupt our pleasant and h'orderly meetings with *your* blamed jaw."

Mahony lost his temper. "I not interrupt?—when I see you great hulks of men—"

("Oh, lor!" groaned Purdy again.)

"—who call yourselves British subjects, letting yourselves be led by the nose, like the sheep you are, by a pack of foreigners who are basely accepting this country's hospital'ty?"

"Here, let me get out," said Purdy. And, pushing his way along the bench, he hobbled to the platform, where strong arms hoisted him up.

There he stood, fronting the violent commotion that had ensued on his friend's last words; stood bedraggled, mud-stained, bandaged, his cabbage-tree hat in his hand. And Mahony, still on his feet, angrily erect, thought he understood why the boy had refused to wash himself clean, or to change his dress: he had no doubt foreseen the possibility of some such dramatic appearance.

Purdy waited for the hubbub to die down. As if by chance, he had rested his hand on the bell; its provoking tinkle ceased. Now, he broke into one of the frank and hearty smiles that never fail to conciliate.

"Brother diggers!"

The strongly spoken words induced an abrupt lull. The audience turned to him, still thorny and sulky, it is true, but yet they turned; and one among them demanded a hearing for the youngster.

"Brother diggers! We are met here to-night with a single purpose in view. Brother diggers! We are not met here to throw mud at our dear old country's flag! Nor will we have a word said against her most gracious Majesty, the Queen. We're not brutes enough, I hope, to hold *her* responsible for the scurvy tricks of her ministers?— Not us! We're men first, whose business it is to stand up for a gallant little woman, and diggers with a grievance afterwards. Are you with me, boys?— Very well, then.— Now, we didn't come here to-night to confab about getting votes, or having a hand in public affairs—much as we want 'em both, and mean to have 'em, mind you, when the time comes. No, to-night there's only one thing that matters to us, and that's the repeal of the accursed tax!" Here such a tempest of applause broke out that he was unable to proceed. "Yes, I say it again," he went on, when they would let him speak; "the instant repeal! When that's been done, this curse taken off us, then it'll be time enough to parlez-vous about the colour of the flag we mean to have, and about going shares in the government.— But let me make one thing clear to you. We're neither traitors to the Crown, nor common rebels. We're true-blue Britons, who have been goaded to rebellion by one of the vilest pieces of tyranny that ever saw the light. Because we're only diggers, honest, hard-working diggers, they think they can bleed us as they choose. Spies and informers are everywhere about us. Mr. Commissioner Sleuth and his hounds may cry tally-ho every day, if 'tis their pleasure to! To put it shortly, boys, we're living under semi-martial law. To such a state have we free-born men, men who came out but to see the elephant, been reduced, by the asinine stupidity of the Government, by the impudence and knavishness of its officials.— Brother diggers! When you leave the hall this evening, look over at the hill on which the Camp stands! What will you see? You will see a blaze of light, and hear the sounds of revelry by night. There, boys, hidden from our mortal view, but visible to our mind's eye, sit Charley Joe's minions, carousing at our expense, feasting on the fat of the land, washing down each mouthful with good fizz, bought with our hard-earned gold. License-picking, boys, and tips from new grog-shops, and the blasted farce of the Commissariat! We're supposed to be green enough to believe that the Camp hay last year cost a hundred and forty quid the ton; that——"

But, here, Mahony gave a loud fillip of the tongue—in the general howl of execration it passed unheard—rose, and, pushing his way out of the tent, let the flap-door fall to behind him.

[3]

HE RETRACED his steps by the safe-conduct of a full moon, which showed up the gaping black mouths of circular shafts, and silvered the water that flooded abandoned oblong holes to their brim. Tents and huts stood white and forsaken in the moonlight: their owners were either gathered on Bakery Hill, or had repaired to one of the gambling and dancing saloons that lined the main street. Arrived at the store, he set free his frantic dog, and putting a match to his pipe, began to stroll up and down.

He felt annoyed with himself, for having helped to swell the crowd of malcontents, and still more for his foolishness in giving the rein to a momentary irritation. As if it mattered a doit what trash these foreigners talked! No thinking person took their bombast seriously; the authorities, with great good sense, let it pass for what it was—a noisy blowing-off of steam. At heart, the diggers were as sound as good pippins; they sought the redress of a single grievance.

A graver consideration was Purdy's growing fellowship with the rebel faction. The boy was too young, and still too much of a fly-by-night, to have a black mark set against his name. It would be the more absurd, considering that his sincerity in espousing the diggers' cause was far from proved. He was of a nature to ride tantivy into anything that promised excitement or adventure. With, it must regretfully be admitted, an increasing relish for the limelight for theatrical effect—see the cunning with which he had made capital out of a bandaged ankle and dirty dress! At this rate, and with his engaging ways, he would soon stand for a little god to the rough, artless crowd. Did that happen, there would be less hope than ever of his settling down. No, he must leave the diggings—and Mahony

25

rolled various schemes in his mind.— He had it! In the course of the next week or two, business would make a journey to Melbourne imperative. Well, he would damn the extra expense, and take the boy along with him! Purdy was at a loose end, owing to the blocking of the claim he had worked in, and would no doubt rise like a fish to a fly at the chance of getting to town free of cost.— After all, why be hard on him? He was not much over twenty, and, at that age, it was natural enough —especially in a place like this—for a lad to flit like a butterfly, sipping from every cup that took his restless fancy.

Restless? . . . h'm! It was the very word Purdy had flung back at him, earlier in the evening. At the time, he had rebutted the charge, with a glance at fifteen months spent behind the counter of a store. But there was a modicum of truth in it, none the less. The life one led out here was not calculated to tone down any innate restlessness of temperament: on the contrary, it directly hindered one from becoming fixed and settled; or even from feeling the need of such a thing. It was on a par with, for example, the houses you lived in—these flimsy tents and draught-riddled cabins you put up with, "for the time being"—was just as much of a makeshift affair as they. Its keynote was change. Fortunes were made, and lost, and made again, before you could say Jack Robinson; whole townships shot up over-night, to be deserted the moment the soil ceased to yield; the people you knew were here to-day, and gone— ruined, burnt out, sold up, or dead and buried—on the morrow. And so, whether you would or not, your thoughts, your outlook on things, became attuned to the general unrest; you lived in a constant anticipation of what was coming next.— Well, he could own to the weakness with more justification than most. If trade continued to prosper with him, as at present, it would be no time before he could sell out, and joyfully depart for the old country.

In the meantime, why complain? He had much to be thankful for. To take only a small point: was this not Saturday night? To-morrow, the store was closed, and a string of congenial occupations offered: from chopping the week's wood— a clean and wholesome task, which he gladly performed— through the pages of an engrossing book, to a botanical ramble round old Buninyong. The thought of it cheered him. He stooped to caress his two cats, which had come out to bear him the mute and pleasant company of their kind.

What a night! The great round silver moon floated serenely through space, dimming the stars as it made them, and bathing the earth in splendour. It was so light that straight black lines of smoke could be seen mounting from chimneys and open-air fires. The grass-trees which supplied the fuel for these fires spread a pleasant balsamic odour in burning, and the live red patches contrasted oddly with the pale ardour of the moon. Lights twinkled over all the township, but were brightest in Main Street, the course of which they followed like a rope of fireflies, and at the Government Camp on the steep western slope, where, no doubt, as young Purdy had impudently averred, the officials still sat over the dinner-table. It was very quiet—no grog-shops or saloons-of-entertainment in this neighbourhood, thank goodness!—and the hour was still too early for drunken roisterers to come reeling home. The only sound to be heard was that of a man's voice singing *Oft in the Stilly Night,* to the fetching accompaniment of a concertina. Mahony hummed the tune.

But it was growing cold, as the nights were apt to do on this tableland, once summer was past. He whistled his dog, and Pompey hurried out, with a guilty air, from the back of the house, where the old shaft stood that served to hold refuse. Mahony put him on the chain, and was just about to turn in, when two figures rounded the corner of a tent and came towards him, pushing their shadows before them on the milk-white ground.

"'D evenin', doc.!" said the shorter of the two, a nuggetty little man, who carried his arms curved out from his sides, gorilla-fashion.

"Oh, good evening, Mr. Ocock," said Mahony, recognizing a neighbour.— "Why, Tom, is that you? Back already, my boy?"—this to a loutish, loose-limbed lad who followed behind.— "Won't you sit down a minute . . . Mr. Ocock?" The repetition of the name was meant to have a kind of *noli-metangere* effect; but it was also the instinctive glossing-over of a liberty taken: without waiting for permission, the man had seated himself on the log and removed his hat. "You don't of course come from the meeting?"

27

"Not me, indeed!" gave back his visitor with gall, and turned his head to spit the juice from a plug. "I 'ope I've got suthin' better to do as to listen to a pack o' jabberin' furriners settin' one another by th' ears."

"Nor you, Tom?" Mahony asked the lad, who stood sheepishly shifting his weight from one leg to the other.

"Nay, nor 'im eether," jumped in his father, before he could speak. "I'll 'ave none o' my boys playin' the fool up there. And that reminds me, doc., young Smith'll git 'imself inter the devil of a mess one o' those days, if you don't look after 'im a bit better'n you do. I 'eard 'im spoutin' away as I come past—usin' language about the Gover'ment fit to turn you sick."

It was one thing for Mahony himself to be conscious of his responsibility towards his friend; another to hear an outsider take it for granted. He coughed. "I can hardly see that our having once been schoolmates—" he began drily; then broke off, and fell to excusing Purdy. "He's but young yet. After all, youth's youth, sir, and comes but once in a lifetime. And you can't make lads into wiseacres between sundown and sunrise."

"No, by Gawd, you can't!" affirmed his companion. "But I dunno, doc., I think youth's just a fine name for a sort o' piggish mess. What's the good, one 'ud like to know, of gettin' old, and learnin' wisdom, and knowin' the good from the bad, when ev'ry lousy young fathead that's born inter the world starts out again to muddle through it for 'imself, in 'is own way. 'E doesn't want to be 'elped or guided by 'is elders—not 'e! And that things 'as got to go on like this, just the same, for ever and ever—why, it makes me fair tired to think of it. My father didn't 'old with youth: 'e knocked it out of us by thrashin', just like lyin' and thievin'. And it's the best way, too.— Wot's that you say?" he flounced round on the unoffending Tom. "Nothin'? You was only sniffin', was you? You just keep your fly-trap shut, my fine fellow, and make no mousy sounds to me, or it'll be the worse for you, I can tell you. D'you hear?"

"Come, come, Mr. Ocock, don't be too hard on the boy."

"Not be 'ard on 'im? When I've got the nasty galoon on me 'ands again, like this?— Chucks up the good post I git 'im, in Kilmore, without with your leave or by your leave. Too lonely for 'is lordship, it was. Missed the noise o' wimmin's petticoats, 'e did." He turned fiercely on his son. "'Ere, don't you stand starin' there! You git 'ome, and fix up for the night. Now then, wot are you dawdlin' for, pig-'ead?"

The boy slunk away. When he had disappeared, his father again took up the challenge of Mahony's silent disapproval. "I can't 'ardly bear the sight of 'im, doc.—disgracin' me as 'e 'as done. 'Im a father, and not eighteen till June! A son o' mine, who can't see a wench with 'er bodice open, but wot 'e must be arter 'er. . . . No, sir, no son o' mine! I'm a respectable man, I am, and I do me level best to keep a respectable roof over me 'ead."

Mahony gave a soothing assent. "Of course, of course."

"Oh! but they're a sore trial to me, those boys, doc. 'Enry's the only one . . . if it weren't for 'Enry— Johnny, 'e can't pass the drink, and now 'ere's this young swine started to nose arter the wimmin. I try me 'ardest to thrash it out of 'em, but it don't 'elp: they should 'ave tasted the stick long ago."

"There's good stuff in the lads, I'm sure of it. They're only sowing their wild oats."

"They'll sow no h'oats with me."

"I tell you what it is, Mr. Ocock, you need a woman about your place, to make it a bit more homelike," said Mahony, calling to mind the pigsty in which Ocock and his sons housed.

"Course I do!" agreed Ocock. "And Melia, she'll come out to 'er daddy, soon as ever th' old woman kicks the bucket.— Drat 'er! Drat 'er, I say. It's 'er I've got to thank for all the mischief."

"Well, well!" said Mahony, and rising, knocked out his pipe on the log. Did his old neighbour once get launched on the subject of his wife's failings, there was no stopping him. "We all have our crosses."

"That we 'ave. And I'm keepin' you outer your bed, doc., with me blather.— By gum! and that reminds me I come 'ere special to see you to-night. Bin gettin' a bit moonstruck, I reckon,"—and he clapped on his hat.

Drawing a sheaf of papers from an inner pocket, he selected one and offered it to Mahony. Mahony led the way indoors, and lighting a kerosene-lamp, stooped to decipher the letter.

For some weeks, now, he had been awaiting the delivery of a load of goods, the invoice for which had long since reached him. From this communication, carried by hand, he learnt that the drayman, having got bogged just beyond Bacchus's marsh, had decamped to the Ovens, taking with him all he could cram into a spring-cart, and disposing of the remainder for what he could get. The agent in Melbourne refused to be held responsible for the loss, and threatened to prosecute Mahony, if payment for the goods were not immediately forthcoming. Mahony, who here heard the first of the affair, was very indignant at the tone of the letter; and, before he had read it to the end, had resolved to let everything else slide, and to leave for Melbourne early next morning.

Ocock backed him up in this decision, and, with the aid of a great quill pen, stiffly traced the address of his eldest son, who practised as a solicitor in the capital.

"Go you straight to 'Enry, doc. 'Enry'll see you through."

Brushing aside his dreams of a peaceful Sabbath, Mahony made preparations for his journey. Waking his assistant, he gave the man—a stupid clodhopper, but honest and attached —instructions how to manage during his absence, then dispatched him to the township to order horses. Himself, he put on his hat, and went out to look for Purdy.

His search led him through all the drunken revelry of a Saturday night. And it was close on twelve before, having followed the trace from bowling-alley to Chinese cook-shop, from the "Adelphi" to Mother Flannigan's and haunts still less reputable, he finally succeeded in catching his bird.

[4]

THE two young men took to the road betimes: it still wanted some minutes to six, on the new clock in the tower of Bath's Hotel, when they threw their legs over their saddles and rode down the steep slope by the Camp Reserve. The hoofs of the horses pounded the plank bridge that spanned the Yarrowee, and, striking loose stones, and smacking and sucking in the mud, made a rude clatter in the Sunday quiet.

Having followed for a few hundred yards the wide, rut-riddled thoroughfare of Main Street, the riders branched off to cross rising ground. They proceeded in single file, and at a footpace, for the highway had been honeycombed and rendered unsafe; it also ascended steadily. Just before they entered the bush, which was alive with the rich, strong whistling of the magpies, Purdy halted to look back and wave his hat in

30

farewell. Mahony also half-turned in the saddle. There it lay
—the scattered, yet congested, unlovely wood and canvas settlement, that was Ballarat. At this distance, and from this
height, it resembled nothing so much as a collection of child's
bricks, tossed out at random over the ground, the low, square
huts and cabins that composed it being all of a shape and size.
Some threads of smoke began to mount towards the immense
pale dome of the sky. The sun was catching here the panes of
a window, there the tin-foil that encased a primitive chimney.

They rode on, leaving the warmth of the early sun-rays for
the cold blue shadows of the bush. Neither broke the silence.
Mahony's day had not come to an end with the finding of
Purdy. Barely stretched on his palliasse, he had been routed
out to attend to Long Jim, who had missed his footing and
pitched into a shaft. The poor old tipsy idiot hauled up—luckily for him it was a dry, shallow hole—there was a broken
collar-bone to set. Mahony had installed him in his own bed,
and had spent the remainder of the night dozing in a chair.

So, now, he was heavy-eyed, uncommunicative. As they
climbed the shoulder and came to the rich, black soil that
surrounded the ancient cone of Warrenheip, he mused on his
personal relation to the place he had just left. And not for the
first time he asked himself: what am I doing here? When he
was absent from Ballarat, and could dispassionately consider
the life he led there, he was so struck by the incongruity of the
thing, that, like the beldame in the nursery-tale, he could have
pinched himself, to see whether he waked or slept. Had anyone told him, three years previously, that the day was coming
when he would weigh out soap and sugar, and hand them
over a counter, in exchange for money, he would have held
the prophet ripe for Bedlam. Yet here he was, a full-blown
tradesman, and as greedy of gain as any tallow-chandler. Extraordinary, aye, and distressing, too, the ease with which the
human organism became one with its surroundings; it was just
a case of the green caterpillar feeding on the green leaf. Well,
he could console himself with the knowledge that his apparent
submission was only an affair of the surface; he would be able
to re-assert himself, in a twinkling, when the right moment
came. He had struck no roots; and it would mean as little to
his half-dozen acquaintances on Ballarat when he silently vanished from their midst, as it would to him if he never saw one

31

of them again. Or the country either, for that matter!—and he let his eye roam unlovingly over the wild, sad-coloured landscape, with its skimpy, sad-coloured trees. He could not understand those who professed to like it; to him it spoke chiefly of vast distances to be covered; of measureless tracks of bare, stony land, dotted here and there with tiny settlements—the merest pin-heads of civilization.

Meanwhile, they were advancing: their nags' hoofs, beating in unison, devoured mile after mile of the road. It was a typical colonial road; it went up hill and down dale, turned aside for no obstacles. At one time, it ran down a gully that was almost a ravine, to mount straight up the opposite side, among boulders that reached to the belly-bands. At others, it led through a reedy swamp, or a stony water-course; or it became a bog; or dived through a creek. Where the ground was flat and treeless, it was a rutty, well-worn track, between two seas of pale, scant grass.

More than once, Purdy, complaining of a mouth like sawdust, alighted and limped across the verandah of a house-of-accommodation; but they did not actually draw rein till, towards midday, they reached a knot of weatherboard, verandahed stores, smithies and public-houses, arranged at the four corners of two crossroads. Here, they made a substantial luncheon; and the odour of fried onions carried far and wide. Mahony paid his three shillings for a bottle of ale; but Purdy washed down the steak with cup after cup of richly sugared tea.

In the early afternoon they set off again, revived and refreshed. Purdy caught at a bunch of aromatic leaves, and burst into a song; and Mahony. . . . Good God! With a cloudless sky overhead, a decent bit of horseflesh between his knees, and the prospect of a three days' holiday from storekeeping, his name would not have been what it was, if he could for long have remained captious, downhearted. Insufficient sleep, and an empty stomach—nothing on earth besides! A fig for all his black thoughts! The fact of his being obliged to spend a few years in the colony would, in the end, only profit him, by widening his experience of the world and his fellow-men. It was possible to lead a sober, God-fearing life, no matter in what rude corner of the globe you were pitchforked.— And, in this mood, he was even willing to grant the landscape a certain charm. Since leaving Ballan, the road had dipped up

and down a succession of swelling rises, grass-grown and un-
timbered. From the top of these ridges, the view was a far
one: you looked straight across undulating waves of country
and intervening forest-land, to where, on the horizon, a long,
low sprawling range of hills lay blue—cobalt-blue, and painted
in with a sure brush—against the porcelain-blue of the sky.
What did the washed-out tints of the foliage matter, when,
wherever you turned, you could count on getting these marvellous soft distances, on always finding a range of blue-veiled
hills, lovely and intangible as a dream?

There was not much traffic to the diggings on a Sunday.
And having come to a level bit of ground, the riders followed
a joint impulse and broke into a canter. As they began to climb
again, they fell naturally into one of those familiar talks, full
of allusion and reminiscence, such as are only possible between
two of a sex who have lived through a part of their green days
together.

It began by Purdy referring to the satisfactory fashion in
which he had disposed of his tools, his stretcher-bed, and other
effects: he was not travelling to Melbourne empty-handed.

Mahony rallied him. "You were always a good one at striking a bargain, my boy! What about: 'Four mivvies for an alley!'
—eh, Dickybird?"

This related to their earliest meeting, and was a standing
joke between them. Mahony could recall the incident as clearly
as though it had happened yesterday: how the sturdy little
apple-cheeked English boy, with the comical English accent,
had suddenly bobbed up at his side, on the way home from
school, and, in that laughable sing-song of his, without modu-
lation or emphasis, had offered to "swop" him, as above.

Purdy laughed, and paid him back in kind. "Yes, and the
funk you were in for fear Spiny Tatlow 'ud see us, and peach
to the rest!"

"Yes. What young idiots boys are!"

In thought, he added: "And what snobs!" For the breach of
convention—he was an upper-form boy, at the time—had not
been his sole reason for wishing to shake off his junior. Behind
him, Mahony, when he reached home, the door closed of one
of the largest houses in the most exclusive square in Dublin.
Whereas Purdy lived in a small, common house, in a side
street. Visits there had to be paid surreptitiously.

33

All the same, these were frequent—and for the best of reasons. Mahony could still see Purdy's plump, red-cheeked English mother, who was as jolly and happy as her boy, hugging the loaf to her bosom, while she cut round after round of bread and butter and jam, for two cormorant throats. And the elder boy, long-limbed and lank, all wrist and ankle, had invariably been the hungrier of the two; for, on the glossy damask of the big house, often not enough food was set to satisfy the growing appetites of himself and his sisters.— "Dickybird, can't you see us, with our backs to the wall, in that little yard of yours, trying who could take the biggest bite?—or going round the outside: 'Crust first, and though you burst, by the bones of Davy Jones!' till only a little island of jam was left?"

Purdy laughed heartily at these and other incidents fished up by his friend from the well of the years; but he did not take part in the sport himself. He had not Mahony's gift for recalling detail; to him past was past. He only became alive and eager when the talk turned, as it soon did, on his immediate prospects.

This time, Mahony, to his astonishment, had had no trouble in persuading Purdy to quit the diggings. In addition, here was the boy now declaring openly that what he needed, and must have, was a fixed and steadily paying job. With this decision Mahony was in warm agreement, and promised all the help that lay in his power.

But Purdy was not done; he hummed and hawed and fidgeted; he took off his hat and looked inside it; he wiped his forehead and the nape of his neck.

Mahony knew the symptoms. "Come, Dickybird. Spit it out, my boy!"

"Yes . . . er. . . . Well, the fact is, Dick, I begin to think it's about time I settled down."

Mahony gave a whistle. "Whew! A lady in the case!"

"That's the chat. Just oblige yours truly by takin' a squint at this, will you?"

He handed his friend a squarely-folded sheet of thinnest blue paper, with a large purple stamp in one corner, and a red seal on the back. Mahony, opening it, discovered three crossed pages, written in a delicately pointed, minute, Italian hand.

He read the letter to the end, deliberately, and with a growing sense of relief: composition, expression and penmanship,

34

all met with his approval. "This is the writing of a person of some refinement, my son."

"Well, er . . . yes," said Purdy. He seemed about to add a further word, then swallowed it, and went on: "Though, somehow or other, Till's different to herself, on paper. But she's the best of girls, Dick. Not one o' your ethereal, die-away, bread-and-butter misses. There's something *of* Till, there is, and she's always on for a lark. I never met such girls for larks as her and 'er sister. The very last time I was there, they took and hung up . . . me and some other fellers had been stoppin' up a bit late, the night before, and kickin' up a bit of a shindy, and what did those girls do? They got the barman to come into my room, while I was asleep, and hang a bucket o' water to one of the beams over the bed. Then I'm blamed if they didn't tie a string from it to my big toe! I gives a kick, down comes the bucket and half drowns me.— Gosh, how those girls did laugh!"

"H'm!" said Mahony dubiously; while Purdy in his turn chewed the cud of a pleasant memory.— "Well, I, for my part, should be glad to see you married and settled, with a good wife always beside you."

"That's just the rub," said Purdy, and vigorously scratched his head. "Till's a first-class girl as a sweetheart, and all that; but when I come to think of puttin' my head in the noose, from now till doomsday—why, then, somehow, I can't bring myself to pop the question."

"There's going to be no trifling with the girl's feelings, I hope, sir?"

"Bosh! But I say, Dick, I wish you'd just turn your peepers on 'er and tell me what you make of 'er. She's A1 'erself, but she's got a mother. . . . By Job, Dick, if I thought Tilly 'ud ever get like that!—and they're exactly the same build too."

It would certainly be well for him to inspect Purdy's flame, thought Mahony. Especially since the anecdote told did not bear out the good impression left by the letter—went far, indeed, to efface it. Still, he was loath to extend his absence by spending a night at Geelong, where, as it came out, the lady lived; and he replied evasively that it must depend on the speed with which he could put through his business in Melbourne.

Purdy was silent for a time. Then, with a side-glance at his companion, he volunteered: "I say, Dick, I know some one who'd suit you."

"The deuce you do!" said Mahony, and burst out laughing. "Miss Tilly's sister, no doubt!"

"No, no—not her. Jinn's all right, but she's not your sort. But they've got a girl living with 'em—a sort o' poor relation, or something—and that's a horse of quite another colour.— I say, old man, serious now, have you never thought o' gettin' spliced?"

Again Mahony laughed. At his companion's words, there descended to him, once more, from some shadowy distance, some pure height, the rose-tinted vision of the wife-to-be, which haunts every man's youth. And, in ludicrous juxtaposition, he saw the women, the only women, he had encountered since coming to the colony: the hard-working, careworn wives of diggers; the harridans, sluts and prostitutes who made up the balance.

He declined to be drawn. "Is it old Moll Flannigan or one of her darlints you'd be wishing me luck to, ye spalpeen?"

"Man, don't I say, I've *found* the wife for you?" Purdy was not jesting, and did not join in the fresh salvo of laughter with which Mahony greeted his words. "Oh, blow it, Dick, you're too fastidious—too damned particular! Say what you like, there's good in all of 'em—even in old Mother Flannigan 'erself —and 'specially when she's got a drop inside 'er. Fuddle old Moll a bit, and she'd give you the very shift off her back.— Don't I thank the Lord, that's all, I'm not built like you! Why, the woman isn't born I can't get on with. All's fish that comes to my net.— Oh, to be young, Dick, and to love the girls! To see their little waists, and their shoulders, and the dimples in their cheeks! See 'em put up their hands to their bonnets, and how their little feet peep out when the wind blows their petticoats against their legs!" and Purdy rose in his stirrups and stretched himself, in an excess of well-being.

"You young reprobate!"

"Bah!— You've got water in your veins."

"Nothing of the sort! Set me among decent women and there's no company I enjoy more," declared Mahony.

"Fish-blood, fish-blood!— Dick, it's my belief you were born old."

Mahony was still young enough to be nettled by doubts cast

on his vitality. Purdy laughed in his sleeve. Aloud he said:

"Well, look here, old man, I'll lay you a wager. I bet you you're not game, when you see that tulip I've been tellin' you about, to take her up in your arms and kiss her. A fiver on it!"

"Done!" cried Mahony. "And I'll have it in one note, if you please!"

"Bravo!" cried Purdy. "Bravo, Dick!" And, having gained his end, and being on a good piece of road between post-and-rail fences, he set spurs to his horse and cantered off, singing as he went:

> *She wheels a wheelbarrow,*
> *Through streets wide and narrow,*
> *Crying cockles, and mussels,*
> *Alive, alive-oh!*

But the sun was growing large in the western sky; on the ground to the left, their failing shadows slanted out lengthwise; those cast by the horses' bodies were mounted on high spindle-legs. The two men ceased their trifling, and, nudged by the fall of day, began to ride at a more business-like pace, pushing forward through the deep basin of Bacchus's marsh, and on, for miles, over wide, treeless plains, to where the road was joined by the main highway from the north, coming down from Mount Alexander and the Bendigo. Another hour, and, from a gentle eminence, the buildings of Melbourne were visible, the mast-heads of the many vessels riding at anchor in Hobson's Bay. Here, too, the briny scent of the sea, carrying up over grassy flats, met their nostrils, and set Mahony hungrily sniffing. The brief twilight came and went, and it was already night when they urged their weary beasts over the Moonee ponds, a winding chain of brackish water-holes. The horses shambled along the broad, hilly tracks of North Melbourne; warily picked their steps through the city itself. Dingy oil-lamps, set here and there at the corners of roads so broad that you could hardly see across them, shed but a meagre light, and, the further the riders advanced, the more difficult became their passage: the streets, in process of laying, were heaped with stones and intersected by trenches. Finally, dismounting, they thrust their arms through their bridles, and laboriously covered the last half-mile of the journey on foot. Having lodged the horses at a livery-stable, they repaired to a hotel in Little Collins Street. Here, Purdy knew the proprietor, and they were fortunate enough to secure a small room for the use of themselves alone.

[5]

MELBOURNE is built on two hills, and the valley that lies between.

It was over a year since Mahony or Purdy had been last in the capital, and, next morning, on stepping out of the "Adam and Eve," they walked up the eastern slope to look about them. From the summit of the hill, their view stretched to the waters of the Bay, where a forest of masts spoke to the presence of several hundred vessels. The nearer foreground was made up of mud flats, through which a sluggish, coffee-coloured river wound its way to the sea. Beside it, the new railway line was being built, that was to connect Melbourne with Hobson's Bay. On the horizon to the north, the Dandenong Ranges rose storm-blue and distinct, and seemed momently to be drawing nearer; for a cold wind was blowing, which promised rain. The friends caught their glimpses of the landscape between dense clouds of white dust, which blotted everything out for minutes at a time, and filled eyes, nose, and ears with a gritty powder.

When they tired of this, they turned and descended Great Collins Street—a spacious thoroughfare, which dipped into the hollow and rose again, and was so long that, on its western height, pedestrians looked no bigger than ants. The nearer the two came to the heart of the city, the greater grew the confusion around them. Everywhere men were at work, laying gas and drain-pipes, macadamising, paving, kerbing; no longer would the old wives' tale be credited, of the infant drowned in the deeps of Swanston Street, or that of the bullock which sank, inch by inch, before its owner's eyes, in the Elizabeth Street bog. Massive erections of freestone were going up alongside—here a primitive, canvas-fronted dwelling, there one formed wholly of galvanised iron. Fashionable shops, two stories high, stood next tiny, dilapidated weatherboards that had known but a single coat of paint. In the roadway, handsome chaises, landaus, four-in-hands, made room for bullock-teams, eight and ten strong; for tumbrils carrying water, or refuse—or worse; for droves of cattle, mobs of wild colts bound for auction, flocks of sheep on their way to be boiled down for tallow. Stock-riders and bull-punchers rubbed shoulders with elegants in skirted coats and shepherd's-plaid trousers, who adroitly skipped heaps of stones and mortar, or crept along the narrow edging of kerb.

The visitors from up-country paused to listen to a brass band that played outside a horse-auction mart; to watch the shooting in a rifle-gallery. The many decently attired females they met also called for notice. Not a year ago, and no reputable woman walked abroad oftener than she could help: now, even at this hour, the streets were starred with them. Purdy, open-mouthed, his eyes a-dance, turned his head this way and that, pointed and exclaimed. But then, *he* had slept like a log, and, apart from the stiffness inevitable on the ride, and a sense of weight in his injured ankle, felt, in his own words, "as fit as a fiddle." Whereas Mahony had sat his horse the whole night through, had never ceased to balance himself in an imaginary saddle. And when, at daybreak, he had fallen into a deeper sleep, he was either reviewing outrageous females on Purdy's behalf, or accepting wagers to kiss them. He felt, this morning, as if he was one gigantic bruise from top to toe.

Hence, diverting as were the sights of the city, he did not come to them with the naive receptivity of Purdy. It was, besides, hard to detach his thoughts from the disagreeable affair that had brought him to Melbourne. And as soon as banks and offices began to take down their shutters, he hurried off to his interview with the carrying-agent.

The latter's place of business was behind Great Collins Street, in a lane that was reached by a turnpike. Found, with some trouble, it proved to be a rude shanty, wedged in between a Chinese laundry and a Chinese eating-house. The entrance was through a yard, in the middle of which stood a collection of rabbit-hutches, while further back gaped a dirty closet. At the sound of their steps, the man they sought emerged, and Mahony could not repress an exclamation of surprise. When, a little over a twelvemonth ago, he had first had dealings with him, this Bolliver had been an alert and respectable man of business. Now, he was evidently on the downgrade; and the cause of the deterioration was advertised in his bloodshot eyeballs and veinous cheeks. Early as was the hour, he had already been indulging: his breath puffed sour. Mahony prepared to state the object of his visit in no uncertain terms. But his preliminaries were cut short by a volley of abuse. The man accused him point-blank of having been privy to the rascally drayman's fraud, and of having hoped, by lying low, to evade his liability. Mahony lost his temper at this, and vowed that he would have Bolliver up for defamation of character. To which the latter retorted that the first innings in a court of law would be his: he had already put the matter in the hands of his attorney. This was the last straw. Purdy had to intervene and get Mahony away. They left the agent shaking his fist after them, and cursing the bloody day on which he'd ever been fool enough to do a deal with a bloody gentleman.

At the corner of the street, the friends paused for a hasty conference. Mahony was for marching off to take the best legal advice the city had to offer. But Purdy disapproved. Why put himself to so much trouble when he had old Ocock's recommendation to his lawyer-son in his coat pocket? An introduction of this kind would ensure him a better reception than if he went as a stranger to a stranger. And what, in the name of Leary-cum-Fitz, was the sense of making an enemy for life of the old man, his next-door neighbour, and a good customer, to boot?

These counsels prevailed, and they turned their steps towards Chancery Lane, where was to be found every variety of legal practitioner, from barrister to scrivener. Having matched the house-number, and descried the words: "Mr. Henry Ocock, Conveyancer and Attorney, Commissioner of Affidavits," painted black on two dusty windows, they climbed a wooden stair festooned with cobwebs, to a landing where an injunction to: "Push and Enter!" was rudely inked on a sheet of paper, and affixed to a door.

Obeying, they passed into a dingy little room, the entire furnishing of which consisted of a couple of deal tables, with a chair to each. These were occupied by a young man and a boy, neither of whom rose at their entrance. The lad was cutting notches in a stick, and whistling tunefully; the clerk, a young fellow in the early twenties, who had a mop of flaming red hair, and small-slit white-lashed eyes, looked at the strangers, but without lifting his head: his eyes performed the necessary motion.

Mahony desired to know if he had the pleasure of addressing Mr. Henry Ocock. In reply, the red-head gave a noiseless laugh, which he immediately quenched by clapping his hand over his mouth; and, shutting one eye at his junior, he said: "No—nor yet the Shar o' Persia, nor Alphybetical Foster!— What can I do for you, governor?"

"You can have the goodness, sir, to inform Mr. Ocock that I wish to see him!" flashed back Mahony.

"Singin' til-ril-i-tum-tum-dee-ay!— Now then, Mike, me child, toddle!"

With patient reluctance, the boy ceased his whittling and dawdled across the room to an inner door, through which he vanished, having first let his knuckles bump, as if by chance, against the wood of the panel. A second later he reappeared. "Boss's engaged." But Mahony surprised a lightning sign between the pair.

"No, sir, I absolutely decline to state my business to anyone but Mr. Ocock himself!" he declared hotly, in response to the red-haired man's invitation to "get it off his chest." "If you choose to find out when he will be at liberty, I will wait so long—no longer."

As the office-boy had somehow failed to hit his seat, on his passage to the outer door, there was nothing left for the clerk to do, but himself to undertake the errand. He lounged up from his chair, and, in his case without even the semblance of a knock, squeezed through a foot wide aperture, in such a fashion that the two strangers should not catch a glimpse of what was going on inside. But his voice came to them through the thin partition. "Oh, just a couple o' stony-broke Paddy-landers." Mahony, who had seized the opportunity to dart an angry glance at Purdy, which should say: "This is what one gets by coming to your second-rate pettifoggers!" now let his eyes rest on his friend and critically detail the latter's appearance. The description fitted to a nicety. Purdy did in truth look down on his luck. Unkempt, bearded to the eyes, there he stood clutching his shapeless old cabbage-tree, in mud-stained

41

jumper and thread-bare smalls—the very spit of the unsuccessful digger. Well might they be suspected of not owning the necessary to pay their way!

"All serene, mister! The boss'ull take you on."

The sanctum was a trifle larger than the outer room, but almost equally bare; half-a-dozen deed-boxes were piled up in one corner. Stalking in, with his chin in the air, Mahony found himself in the presence of a man of his own age, who sat absorbed in the study of a document. At their entry, two beady grey eyes lifted to take a brief but thorough survey, and a hand with a pencil in it pointed to the single empty chair. Mahony declined to translate the gesture. He remained standing, as did also Purdy, a pace or so in the rear.

Under the best of circumstances, it irked Mahony to be kept waiting. Here, following on the clerk's saucy familiarity, the wilful delay made his gorge rise. For a few seconds he fumed in silence; then, his patience exhausted, he burst out: "My time, sir, is as precious as your own! With your permission, I will take my business elsewhere."

At these words, and at the tone in which they were spoken, the lawyer's head shot up as if he had received a blow under the chin. Again he narrowed his eyes at the couple. And this time he laid the document from him and asked suavely: "What can I do for you?"— He had a big, deep voice, which gave weight to what he said.

The change in his manner, though slight, was unmistakable. Mahony had a nice ear for such refinements, and responded to the shade of difference with the promptness of one who had been on the watch for it. His irritation fell; he was ready, on the instant, to be propitiated. Putting his hat aside, he sat down, and having introduced himself, made reference to Ballarat and his acquaintance with the lawyer's father: "Who directed me to you, sir, for advice on a vexatious affair, in which I have had the misfortune to become involved."

With a "Pray be seated!" Ocock rose and cleared a chair for Purdy. Resuming his seat, he joined his hands, and wound them in and out. "I think you may take it from me that no case is so complicated or unpromising but what we shall be able to find you a way out."

Mahony thanked him—with a tincture of reserve. "I trust you will still be of that opinion when you have heard the facts."

He went on: "Myself, I do not doubt it. I am not a rich man, but, serious though the monetary loss would be to me, I should settle the matter out of court, were I not positive that I had right on my side." To which Ocock returned a quick: "Oh, quite so . . . of course."

Invited to come to particulars, Mahony plunged into his story. Ocock did not interrupt him, let him tell the tale in his own way, himself seeming lost in making notes or designs on the margin of a sheet of foolscap.— He, like his old father, was a short, heavily built man; but there the likeness ended. He had a high, domed forehead, above a thin, hooked nose. His skin was of an almost Jewish pallor. Fringes of straight, jet-black hair grew down the walls of his cheeks and round his chin, meeting beneath it. The shaven upper lip was long and flat, with no central markings, and helped to form a mouth that had not much more shape or expression than a slit cut by a knife in a sheet of paper: there was no need for its owner ever to raise a screening hand. The chin was bare to the size of a crown-piece; and, both while he spoke, and while he listened to others speaking, the lawyer caressed this patch with his finger-tips; so that, in the course of time, it had arrived at a state of high polish—like the shell of an egg.

The air with which he heard his new client out was of a non-committal kind; and Mahony, having talked his first heat off, grew chilled by the wet blanket of Ocock's silence. There was nothing in this of the frank responsiveness with which your ordinary mortal lends his ear. The brain behind the dome was, one might be sure, adding, combining, comparing, and drawing its own conclusions. Why should lawyers, he wondered, treat those who came to them like children, advancing only in so far as it suited them out of the darkness where they housed among strangely worded paragraphs and obscure formulas?— But these musings were cut short. Having fondled his chin for a further moment, Ocock looked up and put a question. And, while he could not but admire the lawyer's acumen, this did not lessen Mahony's discomfort. All unguided, it went straight for what he believed to be the one weak spot in his armour. It related to the drayman. Contrary to custom, Mahony had, on this occasion, himself recommended the driver. And, as he admitted it, his ears rang again with the plaints of his stranded fellow-countryman, a wheedler from the South Country, off whose tongue the familiar brogue had dripped like honey. His recommendation had, he explained, been made out of charity; he had not forced the agent to engage the man; and he now thought it would be a gross injustice, if he alone were to be held responsible.

To his relief, the lawyer did not seem to attach importance to the fact. Shrugging his shoulders, Ocock went on to ask whether any written agreement had existed between the parties. "No writing? H'm! So . . . so!" To read his thoughts was an impossibility; but, as he proceeded with his catechism, it was easy to see how his interest in the case grew. He began to treat it tenderly; warmed to it, as an artist to his work; and Mahony's spirits rose in consequence.

Having selected a number of minor points that would tell in their favour, Ocock took up, and dilated upon, the libellous aspersion that had been cast on Mahony's good faith. "My experience has invariably been this, Mr. Mahony: people who suggest that kind of thing, and accuse others of it, are those who are accustomed to make use of such means themselves. In this case, there may have been no goods at all—the thing may prove to have been a put-up job from beginning to end."

But his hearer's start of surprise was too marked to be overlooked. "Well, let us take the existence of the goods for granted. But, might they not, being partly of a perishable nature, have gone bad or otherwise got spoiled on the road, and not have been in a fit condition for you to receive at your end?"

This was credible; Mahony nodded his assent. He also added, gratuitously, that he had before now been obliged to reclaim on casks of mouldy mess-pork. At which Ocock ceased coddling his chin, to point a straight forefinger at him, with a triumphant: "You see!"— But Purdy, sick and tired of the discussion, had withdrawn to the window, to watch the rain zigzag in runlets down the dusty panes, and hiss and spatter on the sill; Purdy puckered his lips to a sly and soundless whistle.

The interview at an end, Ocock escorted his visitors out. As he did so, he mentioned, in his frigidly urbane way, that he had recently been informed there was an excellent opening for a firm of solicitors in Ballarat: could Mr. Mahony, as a resident there, confirm the report? Mahony regretted his ignorance, but spoke in praise of the Golden City, and its assured

44

future.— "This would be most welcome news to your father, sir. I can picture his satisfaction on hearing it."

Ocock did not reply, and Mahony, who was sensitive to silences, hastened to bridge the gap: "He would, I know, be glad to have your aid with your young brothers. Between ourselves, he finds them hard to manage."

"My father is too severe with those boys," said the lawyer.

"My very words to him!" exclaimed Mahony. Yet, even in saying it, he did not feel by any means sure that he and Ocock meant the same thing. The latter spoke with an utter lack of, warmth—of the tolerance his remark implied.

—"Golly, Dick, that's no mopoke!" was Purdy's comment as they emerged into the rain-swept street. "A crafty devil, if ever I see'd one."

"Henry Ocock seems to me to be a singularly able man," replied Mahony drily. To his thinking, Purdy had cut a poor figure during the visit: he had said no intelligent word, but had lounged lumpishly in his chair—the very picture of the country-man come up to the metropolis—and, growing tired of this, had gone like a restless child to thrum with his fingers on the panes.

"Oh, you bet! He'll slither you through."

"What? Do you insinuate there's any need for slithering . . . as you call it?" cried Mahony.

"Why, Dick, old man. . . . And as long as he gets you through, what does it matter?"

"It matters to me, sir!"

The rain, a tropical deluge, was over by the time they reached the hollow. The sun shone again, hot and sticky, and people were venturing forth from their shelters to wade through beds of mud, or to cross, on planks, the deep, swift rivers formed by the open drains. There were several such cloudbursts in the course of the afternoon; and, each time, the refuse of the city was whirled past on the flood, to be left as an edging to the footpaths, when the water went down.

Mahony spent the rest of the day in getting together a fresh load of goods. For, whether he lost or won his suit, the store had to be re-stocked, without delay.

That evening, towards eight o'clock, the two men turned out of the Lowther Arcade. The night was cold, dark and wet; and they had wound comforters round their bare throats. They were on their way to the Mechanics' Hall, to hear a lecture on Mesmerism. Mahony had looked forward to this all through the sorry job of choosing soaps and candles. The subject piqued his curiosity. It was also the one drop of mental stimulant he could hope to extract from his visit. The theatre was out of the question: if none of the actors happened to be drunk, a fair proportion of the audience was sure to be.

Part of his pleasure this evening was due to Purdy having agreed to accompany him. It was always a matter of regret to Mahony that, outside the hobnob of daily life, he and his friend had so few interests in common; that Purdy should rest content with the coarse diversions of the ordinary digger.

Then, from the black shadows of the Arcade, a woman's form detached itself, and a hand was laid on Purdy's arm.

"Shout us a drink, old pal!"

Mahony made a quick, repellent movement of the shoulder. But Purdy, some vagrom fancy quickened in him, either by the voice, which was not unrefined, or by the stealthiness of the approach, which called up fog-haunted London streets: Purdy turned to look.

"Come, come, my boy. We've no time to lose."

Without raising her pleasant voice, the woman levelled a volley of abuse at Mahony, then muttered a word in Purdy's ear.

"Just half a jiff, Dick," said Purdy. "Oh go ahead!— I'll make up on you."

For a quarter of an hour Mahony aired his heels in front of a public-house. Then he gave it up, and went on his way. But his pleasure was damped: the inconsiderateness with which Purdy could shake him off, when it suited his purpose, always had a disconcerting effect on him. To face the matter squarely: the friendship between them did not mean as much to Purdy as to him; the sudden impulse that had made the boy throw up a promising clerkship to emigrate in his wake—into this he had read more than it would hold.— And, as he picked his muddy steps, Mahony agreed with himself that the net result, for him, of Purdy's coming to the colony, had been to saddle him with a new responsibility. It was his lot for ever to be helping the lad out of tight places. Sometimes it made him feel unnecessarily bearish. For Purdy had the knack, common to sunny, improvident natures, of taking everything that was done for him as a matter of course. The want of delicacy he could show at times, in this respect, was distressing. Yet, in spite of it all, it was hard to bear him a grudge for long together. A well-meaning young beggar, if ever there was one! That very day, for instance, how faithfully he had stuck at his side, assisting at dull discussions and duller purchasings, without once obtruding his own concerns.— And here Mahony, looking back, recalled the conversation they had had on their ride to town. Purdy had then expressed the wish to settle down and take a wife. A poor friend that would be, who did not back him up in this good intention!

As he sidled into one of the front benches of a half-empty hall—the mesmerist, a corpse-like man in black, already surveyed its thinness from the platform, with an air of pained surprise—Mahony decided that Purdy should have his chance. The heavy rains of the day, and the consequent flooding of the Ponds and the Marsh, would serve as an excuse for a change of route. He would go and have a look at Purdy's sweetheart; would ride back to the diggings by way of Geelong.

[6]

IN A whitewashed parlour of "Beamish's Family Hotel," some few miles north of Geelong, three young women, in voluminous skirts and with their hair looped low over their ears, sat at work. Books lay open on the table before two of them; the third was making a bookmark. Two were fair, plump, rosy, and well over twenty; the third, pale-skinned and dark, was still a very young girl. She it was who stitched magenta hieroglyphics on a strip of perforated cardboard.

"Do lemme see, Poll," said the eldest of the trio, and laid down her pen. "You *'ave* bin quick about it, my dear."

Polly, the brunette, freed her needle of silk, and twirled the bookmark by its ribbon ends. Spinning, the mystic characters united to form the words: "Kiss me quick."

Her companions tittered. "If ma didn't know for certain 'twas meant for your brother John, she'd never 'ave let you make it," said the second blonde, whose name was Jinny.

"Girls, what a lark it 'ud be to send it up to Purdy Smith, by Ned!" said the first speaker.

Polly blushed. "Fy, Tilly! That wouldn't be ladylike."

47

Tilly's big bosom rose and fell in a sigh. "What's a lark never is."

Jinny giggled, agreeably scandalized: "What things you do say, Till! Don't let ma 'ear you, that's all."

"Ma be blowed!— 'Ow does this look now, Polly?" and across the wax-cloth Tilly pushed a copybook, in which she had laboriously inscribed a prim maxim the requisite number of times.

Polly, laying down her work, knit her brows over the page. "Well . . . it's better than the last one, Tilly," she said gently, averse to hurting her pupil's feelings. "But still not quite good enough. The f's, look, should be more like this." And taking a steel pen, she made several long-tailed f's, in a tiny, pointed hand.

Tilly yielded an ungrudging admiration. "'Ow well you do it, Poll! But I *hate* writing. If only ma weren't so set on it!"

"You'll never be able to write yourself to a certain person, 'oos name I won't mention, if you don't 'urry up and learn," said Jinny, looking sage.

"What's the odds! We've always got Poll to write for us," gave back Tilly, and lazily stretched out a large, plump hand to recover the copybook. "A certain person'll never know—or not till it's too late."

"Here, Polly dear," said Jinny, and held out a book. "I know it now."

Again Polly put down her embroidery. She took the book. "Plough!" said she.

"Plough?" echoed Jinny vaguely, and turned a pair of soft, crow-like brown eyes on the blowflies sitting sticky and sleepy round the walls of the room. "Wait a jiff . . . lemme think! 'Plough'? Oh, yes, I know. P-l. . . ."

"P-l-o" prompted Polly, the speller coming to a full stop.

"P-l-o-w!" shot out Jinny, in triumph.

"Not *quite* right," said Polly. "It's g-h, Jinny: p-l-o-u-g-h."

"Oh, that's what I meant. I knew it right enough."

"Well, now, 'trough!'"

"Trough?" repeated Jinny, in the same slow, vacant way. "'Trough'? Wait, lemme think a minute. T-r-o. . . ."

Polly's lips all but formed the "u," to prevent the "f" she felt impending. "I'm afraid you'll have to take it again, Jinny dear," she said reluctantly, as nothing further was forthcoming.

48

"Oh, no, Poll. T-r-o-" began Jinny, with fresh vigour. But before she could add a fourth to the three letters, a heavy foot pounded down the passage, and a stout woman, out of breath, her cap-bands flying, came bustling in and slammed the door.

"Girls, girls, now whatever d'ye think! 'Ere's Purdy Smith come ridin' inter the yard, an' another gent with 'im. Scuttle along now, an' put them books away!— Tilda, yer net's 'alf 'angin' off—you don't want yer sweet-'eart to see you all untidy like that, do you?— 'Elp 'em, Polly my dear, and be quick about it!— H'out with yer sewin', chicks!"

Sprung up from their seats, the three girls darted to and fro, like distracted hens. The telltale spelling and copybooks were flung into the drawer of the chiffonier, and the key was turned on them. Polly, her immodest sampler safely hidden at the bottom of her workbox, was the most composed of the three; and, while locks were being smoothed and collars adjusted, in the adjoining bedroom, she remained behind, to look out thimbles, needles, and strips of plain sewing, and to lay them naturally about the table.

The blonde sisters re-appeared, all aglow with excitement. Tilly, in particular, was in a sad flutter.

"Girls, I simply *can't* face 'im in 'ere!" she declared. "It was 'ere, in this very room, that 'e first—you know what!"

"Nor can I," cried Jinny, catching the fever.

"Feel my 'eart, 'ow it beats," said her sister, pressing her hands, one over the other, to her full left breast.

"Mine's every bit as bad," averred Jinny.

"I believe I shall 'ave the palpitations and faint away, if I stop 'ere."

Polly was genuinely concerned. "I'll run and call mother back."

"No, I tell you what: let's 'ide!" cried Tilly, recovering. Jinny wavered. "But will they find us?"

"Duffer! Of course. Ma'll give 'em the 'int.— Come on!"

Suiting the action to the word, and imitated by her sister, she scrambled over the window sill on to the verandah. Polly found herself alone. Her conscientious scrupling: "But mother may be cross!" had passed unheeded. Now, she, too, fell into a flurry. She could not remain there, by herself, to meet two young men, one of whom was a stranger: steps and voices were already audible at the end of the passage. And so, since

49

there was nothing else for it, she clambered after her friends—
though with difficulty; for she was not very tall.

This was why, when Mrs. Beamish flourished open the door,
exclaiming in a hearty tone: "An 'ere you'll find 'em, gents—
sittin' at their needles, busy as bees!" the most conspicuous
object in the room was a very neat leg, clad in a white stocking and black prunella boot, which was just being drawn up
over the sill. It flashed from sight; and the patter of running
feet beat the floor of the verandah.

"Ha, ha, too late! The birds have flown," laughed Purdy, and
smacked his thigh.

"Well, I declare, an' so they 'ave—the *naughty* creatures!"
cried Mrs. Beamish, in mock dismay. "But trust you, Mr. Smith,
for sayin' the right thing. Jus' exackly like birds they are—so
shy an' scared-like. But I'll give you the 'int, gents. They'll not
be far away. Jus' you show 'em two can play at that game.—
Mr. S., you know the h'arbour!"

"Should say I do! Many's the time I've anchored there," cried
Purdy, with a loud guffaw. "Come, Dick!" And, crossing to the
window, he straddled over the frame, and disappeared.

Reluctantly, Mahony followed him.

From the verandah they went down into the vegetable-
garden, where the drab and tangled growths that had outlived
the summer had been beaten flat by the recent rains. At the
foot of the garden, behind a clump of gooseberry-bushes, stood
an arbour formed of a Buddleia. No trace of a petticoat was
visible, so thick was the leafage; but a loud whispering and
tittering betrayed the fugitives.

At the apparition of the young men, who stooped to the low
entrance, there was a cascade of shrieks.

"Oh, lor, 'ow you frightened me! 'Owever did you know we
were 'ere?"

"You wicked fellow! Get away, will you! I 'ate the very sight
of you!"—this from Tilly, as Purdy, his hands on her hips, gave
her a smacking kiss.

The other girls feared a like greeting; there were more
squeaks and squeals, and some ineffectual dives for the doorway. Purdy spread out his arms. "Hi, look out, stop 'em, Dick!
Now then, man, here's your chance!"

Mahony stood blinking; it was dusk inside, after the dazzle
of the sun. At this reminder of the foolish bet he had taken,

he hurriedly seized the young woman who was next him, and embraced her. It chanced to be Jinny. She screamed, and made a feint of feeling mortally outraged. Mahony had to dodge a box on the ears.

But Purdy burst into a horselaugh, and held his sides. Without knowing why, Tilly joined in, and Jinny, too, was infected. When Purdy could speak, he blurted out: "Dick, you fathead!—you jackass!—you've mugged the wrong one."

At this clownish mirth, Mahony felt the blood boil up over ears and temples. For an instant he stood irresolute. Did he admit the blunder, his victim would be hurt. Did he deny it, he would save his own face at the expense of the other young woman's feelings. So, though he could have throttled Purdy, he put a bold front on the matter.

"*Carpe diem* is my motto, my boy! I intend to make both young ladies pay toll."

His words were the signal for a fresh scream and flutter: the third young person had escaped, and was flying down the path. This called for chase and capture. She was not very agile, but she knew the ground, which, outside the garden, was rocky and uneven. For a time, she had Mahony at vantage; his heart was not in the game: in cutting undignified capers among the gooseberry-bushes, he felt as foolish as a performing dog. Then, however, she caught her toe in her dress and stumbled. He could not disregard the opportunity; he advanced upon her.

But two beseeching hands fended him off. "No . . . no! Please . . . oh, *please*, don't!"

This was no catchpenny coquetry; it was a genuine dread of undue familiarity. A kindred trait in Mahony's own nature rose to meet it.

"Certainly not, if it is disagreeable to you. Shall we shake hands instead?"

Two of the blackest eyes he had ever seen were raised to his, and a flushed face dimpled. They shook hands, and he offered his arm.

Halfway to the arbour, they met the others coming to find them. The girls bore diminutive parasols; and Purdy, in rollicking spirits, Tilly on one arm, Jinny on the other, held Polly's above his head. On the appearance of the laggards, Jinny, who had put her own interpretation on the misplaced kiss, pre-

51

pared to free her arm; but Purdy, winking at his friend, squeezed it to his side and held her prisoner.

Tilly buzzed a word in his ear.

"Yes, by thunder!" he ejaculated; and letting go of his companions, he spun round like a ballet-dancer. "Ladies! Let me introduce to you my friend, Dr. Richard Townshend-Mahony, F.R.C.S., M.D., Edinburgh, at present proprietor of the 'Diggers' Emporium,' Dead Hog Hill, Ballarat.— Dick, my hearty, Miss Tilly Beamish, world-famed for her sauce; Miss Jinny, renowned for her skill in casting the eyes of sheep; and, last but not least, pretty little Polly Perkins, alias Miss Polly Turnham, whose good deeds put those of Dorcas to the blush."

The Misses Beamish went into fits of laughter, and Tilly hit Purdy over the back with her parasol.

But the string of letters had puzzled them, roused their curiosity.

"What'n earth do they mean?— Gracious! So clever! it makes me feel quite queer."

"Y'ought to 'ave told us before'and, Purd, so's we could 'ave studied up."

However, a walk to a cave was under discussion, and Purdy urged them on. "Phœbus is on the wane, girls! And it's going to be damn cold to-night."

Once more with the young person called Polly as companion, Mahony followed after. He walked in silence, listening to the rattle of the three in front. At best, he was but a poor hand at the kind of repartee demanded of their swains by these young women; and to-day his slender talent failed him altogether, crushed by the general tone of vulgar levity. Looking over at the horizon, which swam in a kind of gold-dust haze, below the sinking sun, he smiled thinly to himself at Purdy's ideas of wiving.

Reminded he was not alone by feeling the hand on his arm tremble, he glanced down at his companion; and his eye was arrested by a neatly parted head, of the glossiest black imaginable.

He pulled himself together. "Your cousins are excellent walkers."

"Oh, yes, very. But they are not my cousins."

Mahony pricked up his ears. "But you live here?"

"Yes. I help moth . . . Mrs. Beamish in the house."

But as if, with this, she had said too much, she grew tongue-tied again; and there was nothing more to be made of her. Taking pity on her timidity, Mahony tried to put her at ease by talking about himself. He described his life on the diggings, and the straits to which he was at times reduced: the buttons affixed to his clothing by means of gingerbeer-bottle wire; his periodic onslaughts on sock-darning; the celebrated pudding it had taken him over four hours to make. And Polly, listening to him, forgot her desire to run away. Instead, she felt sorry for him, and at the same time could not help laughing at the tales of his masculine shiftlessness. But as soon as they came in view of the others, Tilly and Purdy sitting under one parasol on a rock by the cave, Jinny standing and looking out rather aggressively after the loiterers, Polly withdrew her arm.

"Moth . . . Mrs. Beamish will need me to help her with tea. And . . . and *would* you please walk back with Jinny?"

Before he could reply, she had turned and was hurrying away.

They got home from the cave at sundown, he with the ripe Jinny hanging a dead weight on his arm, to find tea spread in the private parlour. The table was all but invisible under its load; and their hostess looked as though she had been par-boiled on her own kitchen fire. She sat and fanned herself with a sheet of newspaper, while, time and again, undaunted by refusals, she pressed the good things upon her guests. There were juicy beefsteaks, piled high with rings of onion, and a barracoota, and a cold leg of mutton. There were apple-pies and jam-tarts, a dish of curds-and-whey, and a jug of custard. Butter and bread were fresh and new; scones and cakes had just left the oven; and the great cups of tea were tempered by pure, thick cream.

To the two men, who came from diggers' fare: cold chop for breakfast, cold chop for dinner, and cold chop for tea: the meal was little short of a banquet; and few words were spoken in its course. But the moment arrived when they could eat no more, and when even Mrs. Beamish ceased to urge them. Pipes and pouches were produced; Polly and Jinny rose to collect the plates, Tilly and her beau to sit on the edge of the verandah: they could be seen in silhouette against the rising moon, Tilly's head drooping to Purdy's shoulder.

Mrs. Beamish looked from them to Mahony with a knowing

smile, and whispered behind her hand: "I *do* wish those two
'ud 'urry up an' make up their minds, that I do! I'd like to see
my Tilda settled. No offence meant to young Smith. 'E's the
best o' good company. But sometimes . . . well, I cud jus' knock
their 'eads together, when they sit so close, an' say: come, give
over yer spoonin' an' get to business! Either you want one another or you don't.— I seen you watchin' our Polly, Mr. Mahony"—she made Mahony wince, by stressing the second syllable of his name. "Bless you, no—no relation whatsoever! She
just 'elps a bit in the 'ouse, an' is company for the girls. We
tuck 'er in a year ago—'er own relations 'ad played 'er a dirty
trick. Mustn't let 'er catch me sayin' so, though; she won't 'ear
a word against 'em, and that's jus' as it should be."

Looking round, and finding Polly absent from the room, she
went on to tell Mahony how Polly's eldest brother, a ten years'
resident in Melbourne, had sent to England for the girl, on her
leaving school, to come out and assist in keeping his house.
And how an elder sister, who was governessing in Sydney, had
chosen just this moment to throw up her post and return to
quarter herself upon the brother.

"An' so, when Polly gets 'ere—a little bit of a thing, in short
frocks, in charge of the capt'n—there was no room for 'er, an'
she 'ad to look about 'er for somethin' else to do. We tuck 'er
in, an', I will say, I've never regretted it. Indeed, I don' know
now, 'ow we ever got on without 'er.— Yes, it's you I'm talkin'
about, miss, singin' yer praises, an' you needn't get as red as if
you'd bin up to mischief! Pa'll say as much for you, too."

"That I will!" said Mr. Beamish, opening his mouth for the
first time, except to put food into it. "That I will," and he
patted Polly's hand. "The man as gits Polly'll git a treasure."

Polly blushed, after the helpless, touching fashion of very
young creatures: the blood stained her cheeks, mounted to her
forehead, spread in a warm wave over neck and ears. To spare
her, Mahony turned his head and looked out of the window.
He would have liked to say: Run away, child, run away, and
don't let them see your confusion. Polly, however, went con-
scientiously about her task, and only left the room when she
had picked up her full complement of plates.— But she did
not appear again that night.

Deserted even by Mrs. Beamish, the two men pushed back
their chairs from the table, and drew tranquilly at their pipes.

The innkeeper proved an odd, misty sort of fellow, exceedingly backward at declaring himself; it was as though each of his heavy words had to be fetched from a distance. "No doubt about it, it's the wife that wears the breeches!" was Mahony's inward comment. And as one after another of his well-meant remarks fell flat: "Become almost a deaf-mute, it would seem, under the eternal female clacking."

But for each mortal there exists at least one theme to fire him. In the case of Beamish, this turned out to be the Land Question. Before the gold discovery, he had been a bush shepherd, he told Mahony, and, if he had called the tune, he would have lived and died one. But the wife had had ambitions, the children were growing up, and everyone knew what it was, when women got a maggot in their heads. There had been no peace for him till he had thrown up his twelve-year-old job, and joined the rush to Mount Alexander. But at heart he had remained a bushman; and he was now all on the side of the squatters, in their tussle with the Crown. He knew a bit, he'd make bold to say, about the acreage needed in certain districts per head of sheep; he could tell a tale of the risks and mischances squatting involved: "If 'tain't fire, it's flood, an' if the water passes you by, it's the scab or the rot." To his thinking, the government's attempt to restrict the areas of sheep-runs, and to give effect to the "fourteen-year-clause," which limited the tenure, were acts of purblind folly. The gold supply would give out as suddenly as it had begun; but sheep would graze there till the crack of doom—the land was fit for nothing else.

Mahony thought this point of view lopsided. No new country could hope to develop and prosper, without a steady influx of the right kind of population; and this, the colony would never have, so long as the authorities, by refusing to sell them land, made it impossible for immigrants to settle there. Why, America was but three thousand miles distant from the old country, compared with Australia's thirteen thousand, and, in America, land was to be had in plenty at five shillings per acre! As to Mr. Beamish's idea of the gold giving out, the geological formation of the goldfields rendered that improbable. He sympathised with the squatters, who naturally enough believed their rights to the land inalienable; but a government worthy of the name must legislate with an eye to the future, not for the present alone.

Their talk was broken by long gaps. In these, the resonant voice of Mrs. Beamish could be heard, rebuking and directing her two handmaidens.

"Now then, Jinny, look alive, an' don't ack like a dyin' duck in a thunderstorm, or you'll never get back to do *your* bit o' spoonin'!— Save them bones, Polly! Never waste an atom, my chuck—remember that, when you've got an 'ouse of your own!— No, girls, I always says, through their stomachs, that's the short-cut to their 'earts. The rest's on'y fal-de-lal-ing."— On the verandah, in face of the vasty, star-spangled night, Tilly's head had found its resting-place, and an arm lay round her waist.

"I shall make 'im cut off 'is beard, first thing!" said Jinny that night: she was sitting, half-undressed, on the side of a big bed, which the three girls shared with one another.

"Um! Just you wait and see if it's as easy as you think," retorted Tilly from her pillow. Again Purdy had let slip a golden chance to put the decisive question; and Tilly's temper was short, in consequence.

"Mrs. Dr. Mahony! . . . though I do wonder 'ow 'e ever keeps people from saying Ma-*hon*-y," said Jinny dreamily. She, too, had spent some time in star-gazing, and believed she had ground for hope.

"Just listen to 'er, will you!" said Tilly angrily. "Upon my word, Jinny Beamish, if one didn't know you 'ad the 'abit of marrying yourself off to every fresh cove you meet, one 'ud say you was downright bold!"

"*You* needn't talk! Every one can see you're as mad as can be, because you can't bring your old dot-and-go-one to the scratch."

"Oh, hush, Jinny!" said Polly, grieved at this thrust into Tilly's open wound.

"Well, it's true.— Oh, look 'ere now, there's not a drop o' water in this blessed jug again! 'Oos week is it to fill it? Tilly B., it's yours!"

"Serves you right. You can fetch it yourself."

"Think I see myself!"

Polly intervened. "I'll go for it, Jinny."

"What a little duck you are, Poll! But you shan't go alone. I'll carry the candle."

Tying on a petticoat over her bedgown, Polly took the ewer,

and, with Jinny as torch-bearer, set forth. There was still some noise in the public part of the house, beside the bar; but the passage was bare and quiet. The girls crept mousily past the room occupied by the two young men, and, after several false alarms and suppressed chirps, reached the back door, and filled the jug at the tap of the galvanized-iron tank.

The return journey was not so successful. Just as they got level with the visitors' room, they heard feet crossing the floor. Polly started; the water splashed over the neck of the jug, and fell with a loud plop. At this, Jinny lost her head and ran off with the candle. Polly, in a panic of fright, dived into the pantry with her burden, and crouched down behind a tub of fermenting gingerbeer.— And, sure enough, a minute after, the door of the room opposite was flung open, and a pair of jack-boots landed in the passage.

Nor was this the worst: whoever it was did not shut the door again; it remained ajar. Through the chink, Polly shrunk to her smallest—what if one of them should feel hungry, and come into the pantry, and discover her!— Polly heard Purdy say, with appalling loudness: "Oh, go on, old man—don't jaw so!" He then seemed to plunge his head in the basin, for it was with a choke and a splutter that he next inquired: "And what did you think of the little 'un? Wasn't I right?"

There was the chink of coins handled, and the other voice answered: "Here's what I think. Take your money, my boy, and be done with it!"

"Dick!— Great Snakes! Why, damn it all, man, you don't mean to tell me. . . ."

"And understand, sir, in future, that I do not make bets where a lady is concerned."

"Oh, I know—only on the Tilly-Jinny sort! And yet . . . good Lord, Dick!"—the rest was drowned in a bawl of laughter.

Under cover of it, Polly took to her heels and fled, regardless of the open door, or the padding of her bare feet on the boards.

Without replying to the astonished Jinny's query in respect of the water, she climbed over Tilly to her place beside the wall, and shutting her eyes very tight, drew the sheet over her face: it felt as though it would never be cool again.— Hence, Jinny, agreeably wakeful, was forced to keep her thoughts to herself; for, if you lie between two people, one of whom is in a bad temper, and the other fast asleep, you might just as well be alone in bed.

Next morning, Polly alleged a headache, and did not appear at breakfast. Only Jinny and Tilly stood on the verandah of romantic memories, and ruefully waved their handkerchiefs, keeping it up till even the forms of the horses were blurred in the distance.

[7]

His tent-home had never seemed so comfortless.— He ended his solitary ride late at night and wet to the skin; his horse had cast a shoe far from any smithy. Long Jim alone came to the door to greet him. The shopman, on whose doltish honesty Mahony would have staked his head, had profited by his absence to empty the cash-box and go off on the spree.— Even one of the cats had met its fate in an old shaft, where its corpse still swam.

The following day, as a result of exposure and hard riding, he was attacked by dysentery; and, before he had recovered, the goods arrived from Melbourne. They had to be unloaded, at some distance from the store, conveyed there, got under cover, checked off, and arranged. This was carried out in sheets of cold rain, which soaked the canvas walls, and made it doubly hard to get about the clay tracks that served as streets. As if this were not enough—the river in front of the house rose —rose, and in two twos was over its bank—and he and Long Jim spent a night in their clothes, helping neighbours less fortunately placed, to move their belongings into safety.

The lion's share of this work fell on him. Long Jim, who still carried his arm in a sling, was good for nothing but to guard the store and summon Mahony on the appearance of customers. Since his accident, too, the fellow had suffered from frequent fits of colic or cramp, and was for ever slipping off to the township, to procure the spirits in which his employer refused to deal. For the unloading and warehousing of the goods, it is true, old Ocock had loaned his sons; but the strict watch Mahony felt bound to keep over this pretty pair, far outweighed what their help was worth to him.

Now, it was Sunday evening, and for the first time for more than a week, he could call his soul his own again. He stood at

the door, and watched those of his neighbours who were not
Roman Catholics making for church and chapel, to which half
a dozen tinkly bells invited them. The weather had finally
cleared up, and a goodly number of people waded past him
through the mire. Among them, in seemly Sabbath dress, went
Ocock, with his two black sheep at heel. The old man was a
rigid Methodist, and at a recent prayer-meeting had been
moved to bear public witness to his salvation. This was no
doubt one reason why the young scapegrace Tom's almost
simultaneous misconduct had been so bitter a pill for him to
swallow: while, through God's mercy, he was become an ex-
emplar to the weaker brethren, a son of his made his name to
stink in the nostrils of the reputable community. Mahony liked
to believe that there was good in everybody, and thought the
intolerant harshness to which the boy was subjected would defeat its end: it tempted, indeed, to the notion that the old man's
shame was dashed with a secret envy of the sin which thus
easily gained notoriety. Yet it was open to question if clemency would have answered better. "Bad eggs, the brace of
them!" had been his own verdict, after a week's trial of the
lads. One would not, the other apparently could not, work.
Johnny, the elder, was dull and liverish from intemperance;
and the round-faced adolescent, the news of whose fatherhood
had raced the wind, was so sheep-faced, so craven, in the
presence of his elders, that he could not say bo to a battle-
dore. There was something unnatural about this fierce timidity
—and the doctor in Mahony caught a quick glimpse of the
probable reverse of the picture.

But it was cold, in face of all this rain-soaked clay; cold
blue-grey clouds drove across a washed-out sky; and he still
felt unwell. Returning to his living-room, where a small American stove was burning, he prepared for a quiet evening. In a
corner by the fire stood an old packing-case. He lifted the lid
and thrust his hand in: it was here he kept his books. He
needed no light to see by; he knew each volume by the feel.
And after fumbling for a little among the tumbled contents, he
drew forth a work on natural science, and sat down to read.
But he did not get far; his brain was tired, intractable. Lighting his pipe, he tilted back his chair, laid the *Vestiges* face
downwards, and put his feet on the table.

How differently bashfulness impressed one in the case of the weaker sex! There, it was altogether pleasing. Young Ocock's gaucherie had recalled the little maid Polly's ingenuous confusion, at finding herself the subject of conversation. He had not once consciously thought of Polly since his return. Now, when he did so, he found, to his surprise, that she had made herself quite a warm little nest in his memory. Looked back on, she stood out in high relief against her somewhat graceless surroundings. Small doubt, she was both maidenly and refined. He also remembered, with a sensible pleasure, her brisk service, her consideration for others. What a boon it would have been, during the past week, to have had a busy, willing little woman at work, with him and for him, behind the screen! As it was, for want of a helping hand, the place was like a pigsty. He had had neither time nor energy to clean up. The marks of numerous hobnailed boots patterned the floor; loose mud, and crumbs from meals, were swept into corners or under the stretcher-bed; while commodities that had overflowed the shop added to the disorder.— Good Lord, no! . . . no place this for a woman!

He rose and moved restlessly about, turning things over with his foot: these old papers should be burnt, and that heap of straw-packing; those empty sardine and coffee-tins be thrown into the refuse-pit. Scrubbed and clean, it was by no means an uncomfortable room; and the stove drew well. He was proud of his stove; many houses had not even a chimney. He stood and stared at it; but his thoughts were elsewhere: he found himself trying to call to mind Polly's face. Except for a pair of big black eyes—magnificent eyes they seemed to him in retrospect—he had carried away with him nothing of her outward appearance. Yes, stay!—her hair: her hair was so glossy that, when the sun caught it, high lights came out on it—so much he remembered.— From this, he fell to wondering whether her brain kept pace with her nimble hands and ways. Was she stupid or clever? He could not tolerate stupidity. And Polly had given him no chance to judge her; had hardly opened her lips before him. What a timid little thing she had been to be sure! He should have made it his business to draw her out, by being kind and encouraging. Instead of which, he had acted towards her, he felt convinced, like an ill-mannered boor.

He did not know how it was, but he couldn't detach his

thoughts from Polly, this evening: to their accompaniment he paced up and down. All of a sudden he stood still, and gave a short, hearty laugh. He had just seen, in a kind of phantom picture, the feet of the sisters Beamish as they sat on the verandah edge: both young women wore flat sandal-shoes. And so that neatest of neat ankles had been little Polly's property!— For his life he loved a well-turned ankle in a woman.

A minute later, he sat down at the table again. An idea had occurred to him: he would write Polly a letter—a letter that called for acknowledgment—and form an opinion of the girl from her reply. Taking a sheet of thin blue paper and a magnum bonum pen, he wrote:

DEAR MISS TURNHAM,

I wonder if I might ask you to do me a favour? On getting back to Ballarat, I find that the rain has spoilt my store flag. Would you be so kind as to make me a new one? I have no lady friends here to apply to for help, and I am sure you are clever with your needle. If you consent, I will send you the old flag as a pattern, and stuff for the new one. My kind regards to all at the Hotel.

Faithfully yours,

RICHARD TOWNSHEND-MAHONY.

P.S.—I have not forgotten our pleasant walk to the cave.

He went out to the post with it himself. In one hand he carried the letter, in the other the candle-end stuck in a bottle, that was known as a "Ballarat-lantern"; for it was a pitchdark night.

Trade was slack; in consequence, he found the four days that had to pass before he could hope for an answer, exceptionally long. After their lapse, he twice spent an hour at the Post Office, in a fruitless attempt to get near the little window. On returning from the second of these absences, he found the letter waiting for him; it had been delivered by hand. So far, good: Polly had risen to his fly!— He broke the seal.

DEAR SIR,

I shall be happy to help you with your new flag if I am able. Will you kindly send the old one and the stuff down by my

61

*brother, who is coming to see me on Saturday? He is working
at Rotten Gully, and his name is Ned. I do not know if I sew
well enough to please you, but I will do my best.*

I remain,

Yours truly,

Mary Turnham.

Mahony read, smiled, and laid the letter down—only to pick
it up again. It pleased him, did this prim little note: there was
just the right shade of formal reserve about it. Then, he began
to study particulars: grammar and spelling were correct; the
penmanship was in the Italian style, minute, yet flowing, the
letters dowered with generous loops and tails. But surely he
had seen this writing before? It struck him as familiar.— By
Jupiter, yes! This was the hand of the letter Purdy had shown
him on the road to Melbourne. The little puss! So she not only
wrote her own letters, but those of her friends as well. In that
case, she was certainly not stupid; for she was by far the
youngest of the three.

To-day was Thursday. Summoning Long Jim from his seat
behind the counter, Mahony dispatched him there and then to
Rotten Gully, with an injunction not to show himself till he
had found a digger of the name of Turnham. And having
watched Jim set out, at a snail's pace, and murmuring to himself—for he was not accustomed to being ordered about in this
fashion—Mahony went into the store, and measured and cut
off material for the new flag, from two different coloured rolls
of stuff.

It was ten o'clock that night before Polly's brother presented
himself. Mahony met him at the door, and drew him in: the
stove crackled, the room was swept and garnished—he flattered
himself that the report on his habitat would be a favourable
one. Ned's appearance gave him a pleasurable shock: it was
just as though Polly herself, translated into male terms, stood
before him. No need, now, to cudgel his brains for her image!
In looking at Ned, he looked again at Polly. The wide-awake
removed, the same fine, soft, black hair came to light—here,
worn rather long, and curly—the same glittering black eyes,
ivory-white skin, short, straight nose: and an offshoot of Mahony's consciousness wondered, as he gazed, from what quarter this middle-class English family fetched its dark, un-English

strain. All in all, a very comely boy. If there was a fault to find, it was with the mouth. The full red lips did not meet; even in repose there was a perceptible gap between them.

In the beginning, he exerted himself to set the lad at ease. He soon saw, however, that he might spare his pains. Though clearly not much more than eighteen years old, Ned Turnham had the aplomb and assurance of double that age. Lolling back in the single armchair the room boasted, he more than once stretched out his hand and helped himself from the sherry-bottle Mahony had placed on the table. And the disparity in their ages notwithstanding, there was no trace of deference in his manner. Or the sole hint of it was: he sometimes smothered a profane word, or apologised, with a winning smile, for an oath that had slipped out unawares. Mahony could not accustom himself to the foul language that formed the diggers' idiom. Here, in the case of Polly's brother, he sought to overlook the offence, or to lay the blame for it on other shoulders: at his age, and alone, the boy should never have been plunged into this Gehenna.

Ned talked mainly of himself and his doings. But other facts also transpired, of greater interest to his hearer. Thus, Mahony learned that, out of a family of nine, four had found their way to the colony, and a fifth was soon to follow—a mere child this, on the under side of fifteen. He gathered too, that the eldest brother, John, by name, was regarded as a kind of Napoleon by the younger fry. Ned dropped into hyperbole when he spoke of him. At thirty, this John was a partner in the largest whole-sale dry-goods' warehouse in Melbourne. He had also married money, and intended, in due course, to stand for the Legislative Council. Behind Ned's windy bragging—a mere juvenile attempt, no doubt, to dazzle his audience—Mahony thought he discerned tokens of a fond, brotherly pride. If this were so, the affair had its pathetic side; for, from what the boy said, it was evident that the successful man of business held his relatives at arms' length. And, as Ned talked on, Mahony conceived John to himself as a kind of electro-magnet, which, once it had drawn these lesser creatures after it, switched off the current and left them to their own devices. Ned, young as he was, had tried his hand at many trades. At present, he was working as a hired digger; but this, only till he could strike a softer job. Digging was not for him, thank you; what you earned at it hardly repaid you for the sweat you dripped.— His every second word, indeed, was of how he could amass most money with the minimum of bodily exertion.

This calculating, unyouthful outlook was repugnant to Mahony, who liked to see young people throw themselves disinterestedly into whatever they undertook; and, for all his goodwill towards Ned, the longer he listened to him, the cooler he felt himself grow. Another disagreeable impression was left by the grudging, if-nothing-better-turns-up fashion, in which Ned accepted an impulsive offer on his part to take him into the store. It was made on the spur of the moment, and Mahony had qualms about it while his words were still warm on the air, realizing that the overture was aimed, not at Ned in person, but at Ned as Polly's brother. But his intuition did not reconcile him to Ned's lukewarmness; he would have preferred a straight refusal.— The best trait he could discover in the lad was his affection for his sister. This seemed genuine: he was going to see her again—getting a lift halfway, tramping the other twenty odd miles—at the end of the week. Perhaps, though, in the case of such a young opportunist, the thought of Mrs. Beamish's lavish board played no small part; for Ned had a rather lean, underfed look. But this only occurred to Mahony afterwards. Then, his chief vexation was with himself: it would have been kinder to set a dish of solid food before the boy, in place of the naked sherry-bottle. But, as usual, his hospitable leanings came too late.

One thing more. As he lighted Ned and his bundle of stuff through the shop, he was impelled to slip a coin into the boy's hand, with a murmured apology for the trouble he had put him to. And a something, the merest nuance, in Ned's manner of receiving and pocketing the money, flashed the uncomfortable suspicion through the giver's mind that it had been looked for, expected.— And this was the most unpleasant touch of all.

But, bless his soul! did not most large families include at least one poorish specimen?—he had got thus far, by the time he came to wind up his watch for the night. And next day he felt sure he had judged Ned over-harshly. His first impressions of people—he had had occasion to deplore the fact before now —were apt to be either dead white or black as ink; the web of his mind took on no half tints. The boy had not betrayed any actual vices; and time might be trusted to knock the bluster out of him. With this reflection, Mahony dismissed Ned from his mind. He had more important things to think of, chief among which was his own state with regard to Ned's sister.— And during the fortnight that followed, he went about making believe to weigh this matter, to view it from every coign; for it did not suit him, even in secret, to confess to the vehemence with which, when he much desired a thing, his temperament knocked flat the hurdles of reason. The truth was, his mind was made up—had been, all along. At the earliest possible opportunity, he was going to ask Polly to be his wife.

Doubts beset him of course. Night was their favourite time —just when he awakened out of his first sleep. Then, he called himself a fool. How could he suppose that a girl who knew nothing of him, who had barely seen him, would either want or consent to marry him?— And even if—for "if's" were cheap— she did say yes, would it be fair to him to take her out of a comfortable home, away from friends—such as they were!—of her own sex, to land her in these crude surroundings, where he did not know a decent woman to bear her company?— Yet there was something to be said for him, too. He was very lonely. Now that Purdy had gone, he was reduced, for society, to the Long Jims and Ococks of the place. What would he not give, once more to have a refined companion at his side?— Certainly, marriage would postpone the day on which he hoped to shake the dust of Australia off his feet. Life *à deux* would mean a larger outlay; saving not prove so easy. Still, it could be done; and he would gladly submit to the delay, if, by doing so, he could get Polly. Besides, if this new happiness came to him, it would help him to see the years he had spent in the colony in a truer and juster light.— And then, when the hour of departure did strike, what a joy it would be to have a wife to carry with him—a Polly to rescue, to restore to civilization!

He had to remind himself more than once, during this fortnight, that she would be able to devote only a fraction of her day to flag-making. But he was at the end of his tether by the time a parcel and a letter were left for him at the store—again by hand: little Polly had plainly no sixpences to spare. The needlework was perfect, of course; he hardly glanced at it, even when he had opened and read the letter. This was of the same decorous nature as the first. Polly returned a piece of stuff that had remained over. He had really sent material enough for two flags, she wrote; but she had not wished to keep him waiting so long. And then, in a postscript:

Mr. Smith was here last Sunday. I am to say Mrs. Beamish would be very pleased if you also would call again to see us.

He ran the flag up to the top of his forty-foot staff, and wrote:

What I want to know, Miss Polly, is, would you be glad to see me?

But Polly was not to be drawn.

I can only repeat we should all be very pleased.

Some days previously, Mahony had addressed a question to Henry Ocock. With this third letter from Polly, he held the lawyer's answer in his hand. It was unsatisfactory.

Yourself ats. Bolliver. We think that action will be set down for trial in about six weeks' time. In these circumstances we do not think any useful purpose will be served by you calling to see us until this is done. We should be glad if you would call after the action is entered.

Six weeks' time? The man might as well have said a year. And meanwhile Purdy was stealing a march on him, was paying clandestine visits to Geelong. Was it conceivable that anyone in his five senses could prefer Tilly to Polly? It was not.— In the clutch of a sudden fear, Mahony went to Bath's, and ordered a horse for the following morning.

This time, he put the store in charge of a young consumptive, whose plight had touched his heart: the poor fellow was stranded on Ballarat without a farthing, having proved, like many another of his physique, quite unfit for work on the diggings. A strict Baptist, this Hempel, and one who believed hellfire would be his portion if he so much as guessed at the "plant" of his employer's cash-box. He also pledged his word to bear and forbear with Long Jim. The latter saw himself superseded with an extreme bad grace, and was in no hurry to find a new job.

Mahony's nag being in good condition, he covered the distance in a trifle over six hours.

He had evidently hit on the family washing-day. The big boiler in the yard belched clouds of steam; the female inmates of the Hotel were gathered in the out-house: he descried them through the open door, as he rode in at the gate. All three girls stood before tubs, their sleeves rolled up, their arms in the lather. At his apparition, there was a characteristic chorus of cheeps and shrills; and the door was banged to. Mrs. Beamish alone came out to greet him. She was moist and blown, and smelt of soap.

Not in a mood to mince matters, he announced straightway the object of his visit. He was prepared for some expression of surprise on the part of the good woman; but the blend of sheep-faced amazement and uncivil incredulity, to which she subjected him, made him hot and angry; and he vouchsafed her no further word of explanation.

Mrs. Beamish presently so far recovered herself as to be able to finish wiping the suds from her fat red arms.

Thereafter, she gave way to a very feminine weakness.

"Well, and now I come to think of it, I'm blessed if I didn't suspeck somethin' of it, right from the first! Why, didn't I say to Beamish, with me own lips, 'ow you couldn't 'ardly take your eyes off 'er? —Well, well, I'm sure I wish you every 'appiness—though 'ow we're h'ever goin' to get on without Polly, I reely don' know.— Don' I wish it 'ad bin one o' my two as 'ad tuck your fancy—that's all!— Between you an' me, I don' believe a blessed thing's goin' to come of all young Smith's danglin' round. An' Polly's still a bit young—only just turned sixteen. Not as she's any the worse o' that, though; you'll get 'er h'all the easier into your ways.— An' now I mus' look smart, an' get you a bite o' somethin' after your ride."

In vain did Mahony assure her that he had lunched on the road. He did not know Mrs. Beamish. He was forced, not only to sit down to the meal she spread, but also, under her argus eye, to eat of it.

When, after a considerable delay, Polly at length appeared, she had removed all traces of the tub. The hand was cold that he took in his, while he asked her if she would walk with him to the cave.

This time, she trembled openly. Like a lamb led to the slaughter, he thought, looking down at her with tender eyes. Small doubt, that vulgar creature within-doors had betrayed him to Polly, and exaggerated the ordeal that lay before her. When once she was his wife, he would not consent to her remaining intimate with people of the Beamishes' kidney: what a joy to get her out of their clutches! Nor should she spoil her pretty shape by stooping over a wash-tub.

In his annoyance, he forgot to moderate his pace. Polly had to trip many small steps to keep up with him. When they reached the entrance to the cave, she was flushed and out of breath.

Mahony stood and looked down at her. How young she was! . . . how young and innocent! Every feature of her dear little face still waited, as it were, for the strokes of time's chisel. It should be the care of his life that none but the happiest lines were graved upon its precious surface.

"Polly," he said, fresh from his scrutiny. "Polly, I'm not going to beat about the bush with you. I think you know I came here to-day, only to see you."

Polly's head drooped further forward; now, the rim of her bonnet hid her face.

"You aren't afraid of me, are you, Polly?"

Oh, no, she was not afraid.

"Nor have you forgotten me?"

Polly choked a little, in her attempt to answer. She could not tell him that she had carried his letters about with her by day, and slept with them under her pillow; that she knew every word in them by heart, and had copied and practised the bold flourish of the Dickens-like signature; that she had never let his name cross her lips; that she thought him the kindest, handsomest, cleverest man in the world, and would willingly have humbled herself to the dust before him: all this boiled and bubbled in her, as she brought forth her poor little "no."

"Indeed, I hope not," went on Mahony. "Because, Polly, I've come to ask you if you will be my wife."

Rocks, trees, hills, suddenly grown tipsy, went see-sawing round Polly, when she heard these words said. She shut her eyes, and hid her face in her hands. Such happiness seemed improbable—was not to be grasped. "Me? . . . your wife?" she stammered through her fingers.

"Yes, Polly. Do you think you could learn to care for me a little, my dear?— No, don't be in a hurry to answer. Take your own time."

But she needed none. With what she felt to be a most un-maidenly eagerness, yet could not subdue, she blurted out: "I know I could. I . . . I do."

"Thank God!" said Mahony. "Thank God for that!"

He let his arms fall to his sides; he found he had been hold-ing them stiffly from him, every muscle at a strain. He sat down. "And now take away your hands, Polly, and let me see your face. Don't be ashamed of showing me what you feel. This is a sacred moment for us both. We are promising to take each other, you know, for richer for poorer, for better for worse —as the good old words have it.— But I must warn you, my dear, you are not marrying a rich man. I live in a poor, rough place, and have only a poor home to offer you. Oh, I have had many scruples about asking you to leave your friends to come and share it with me, Polly, my love!"

"I'm not afraid. I am strong. I can work."

"And I shall take every care of you. Please God, you will never regret your choice."

They were within sight of the house where they sat; and Mahony imagined rude, curious eyes. So he did not kiss her. Instead, he drew her arm through his, and together they paced up and down the path they had come by, while he laid his plans before her, and confessed to the dreams he had dreamt of their wedded life. It was a radiant afternoon: in the dis-tance, the sea lay deep blue, with turquoise shallows; a great white bird of a ship, her canvas spread to the breeze, was mak-ing for . . . why, to-day, he did not care whether for port or for "home"; the sun went down in a blaze behind a bank of emer-ald green. And little Polly agreed with everything he said—was all one lovely glow of acquiescence. He thought no happier mortal than himself trod the earth.

[8]

MAHONY remained at the Hotel till the following afternoon, then walked to Geelong and took the steam-packet to Mel-bourne. The object of his journey was to ask Mr. John Turn-ham's formal sanction to his marriage. Polly accompanied him a little way on his walk. And whenever he looked back, he saw her standing fluttering her handkerchief—a small, solitary figure on the bare, red road.

He parted from her with a sense of leaving his most precious possession behind, so close had words made the tie. On the other hand, he was not sorry to be out of range for a while of the Beamish family's banter. This had set in, the evening before, as soon as he and Polly returned to the house—pacing the deck of the little steamer, he writhed anew, at the remembrance. Jokes at their expense had been cracked all through supper: his want of appetite, for instance, was the subject of a dozen crude insinuations; and this, though every one present knew that he had eaten a hearty meal, not two hours previously; had been kept up till he grew stony and savage, and Polly, trying hard not to mind, but red to the rims of her ears, slipped out of the room. Supper over, Mrs. Beamish announced in a loud voice that the verandah was at the disposal of the "turtle-doves." She no doubt expected them to bill and coo in public, as Purdy and Matilda had done. On edge at the thought, he drew Polly into the comparative seclusion of the garden. Here, they strolled up and down, their promenade bounded, at the lower end, by the dense-leaved arbour under which they had first met. In its screening shadow, he took the kiss he had on that former occasion been generous enough to forgo.

"I think I loved you, my dear, directly I saw you."

In the distance, a clump of hills rose steep and bare from the waste land by the sea's edge—he could see them, at this moment, as he leant over the taffrail: with the sun going down behind them they were the colour of smoked glass. Last night they had been white with moonlight, which lay spilled out upon them like milk.— Strange old hills! Standing there, unchanged, unshaken, from time immemorial, they made the troth that had been plighted under their shield seem pitifully frail.— And yet. . . . The vows which Polly and he had found so new, so wonderful, were not these, in truth, as ancient as the hills themselves, and as undying? Countless generations of human lovers had uttered them. The lovers passed, but the pledges remained: they put on immortality.

—In the course of their talk, it had leaked out that Polly would not feel comfortable till her choice had been ratified by brother John.

"I'm sure you will like John; he is so clever."

"I shall like every one belonging to you, my Polly!"

As she lost her shyness, Mahony made the discovery that she laughed easily, and was fond of a jest. Thus, when he admitted to her that he found it difficult to distinguish one plump, blonde sister Beamish from the other; that they seemed to him as much alike as two firm, pink-ribbed mushrooms; the little woman was hugely tickled by his masculine want of perception.— "Why, Jinny has brown eyes, and Tilly blue!"

What he did not know, and what Polly did not confess to him, was that much of her merriment arose from sheer lightness of heart.— She, silly little goose that she was, who had once believed Jinny to be the picked object of his attentions!

But she grew serious again: could he tell her, please, why Mr. Smith wrote so seldom to Tilly? Poor Tilly was unhappy at his long silences—fretted over them, in bed at night.

Mahony made excuses for Purdy, urging his unsettled mode of life. But it pleased him to see that Polly took sides with her friend, and loyally espoused her cause.

No, there had not been a single jarring note in all their intercourse; each moment had made the dear girl dearer to him.— Now, worse luck, forty odd miles were between them again!

It had been agreed that he should call at her brother's private house, towards five o'clock in the afternoon. He had thus to kill time for the better part of the next day. His first visit was to a jeweller's in Great Collins Street. Here, he pushed aside a tray of showy diamonds—a successful digger was covering the fat, red hands of his bride with them—and chose a slender, discreetly chased setting, containing three small stones. No matter what household duties fell to Polly's share, this little ring would not be out of place on her finger.

From there, he went to the last address Purdy had given him; only to find that the boy had again disappeared. Before parting from Purdy, the time before, he had lent him half the purchase-money for a horse and dray, thus enabling him to carry out an old scheme, of plying for hire at the city wharf. According to the landlord of the "Hotel Vendôme," to whom Mahony was referred for fuller information, Purdy had soon tired of this job, and, selling dray and beast for what he could get, had gone off on a new rush to "Simson's Diggings" or the "White Hills."— Small wonder then, that Miss Tilly was left languishing for news of him!

Pricked by the nervous disquietude of those who have to do

with the law, Mahony next repaired to his solicitor's office. But
Henry Ocock was closeted with a more important client. This,
Grindle the clerk, whom he met on the stairs, informed him,
with an evident relish, and with some hidden, hinted meaning
in the corners of his shifty little eyes. It was lost on Mahony,
who was not the man to accept hints from a stranger. On the
whole, though, the clerk was respect in person, compared with
the occasion on which he had mistaken Mahony for a needy
digger trying to raise the wind.

The hour was on lunch-time; Grindle proposed that they
should go together to a legal chop-house, which offered prime
value for your money, and where, over the meal, he would give
Mahony the latest news of his suit. At a loss how to get through
the day, the latter followed him—he was resolved, too, to practise economy, from now on. But when he sat down to a dirty
cloth and fly-spotted cruet, he regretted his compliance. The
news Grindle was able to give him, moreover, amounted to
nothing; the case had not budged since last he heard of it.
Worse still was the clerk's behaviour; it made Mahony ashamed
of being seen in his society. For, after lauding the cheapness of
the establishment, Grindle disputed the price of each item on
the "meenew," and, when he came to pay his bill, chuckled
over having been able to diddle the waiter of a penny.

He was plainly one of those who feel the constant need of
an audience. And, since there was no office-boy present, for
him to dazzle with his wit, he applied himself to demonstrat-
ing to his table-companion what a sad, sad dog he was.

"Women are the deuce, sir," he asserted, lying back in his
chair, and sending two trails of smoke from his nostrils. "The
very deuce! You should hear my governor on the subject! He'd
tickle your ears for you.— Look here, I'll give you the tip: this
move, you know, to Ballarat, that he's drivin' at: what'ull you
bet me there isn't a woman in the case? Fact! 'Pon my word
there is. And a devilish fine woman, too!" He shut one eye and
laid a finger along his nose. "You won't blow the gab?—that's
why you couldn't have your parleyvoo with the boss this morning. When milady comes to town, H. O.'s *non est* as long as
she's here. And she with a hubby of her own, too! What 'ud
our old pa say to that, eh?"

Mahony, who could draw in his feelers no further than he
had done, touched the limit of his patience. "My connection

with Mr. Ocock is a purely business one. I have no intention of trespassing on his private affairs, or of having them thrust upon me.— Carver, my bill!"

Bowing distantly, he stalked out of the eating-house and back to the "Criterion," where he dined.— "So much for a maiden attempt at economy!" he thought, with a twist of the lip.

Towards five o'clock, he took his seat in an omnibus that plied between the city and the seaside suburb of St. Kilda, three miles off. A cool breeze went; the hoofs of the horses beat a rataplan on the hard surface; the great road, broad enough to make three of, was alive with smart gigs and trotters.

St. Kilda was a group of white houses facing the Bay. Most were of weatherboard, with brick chimneys; but there were also a few of a more solid construction. Mahony's goal was one of these: a low, stone villa, surrounded by verandahs, in the midst of tasteful grounds. The drive up to the door led through a shrubbery, artfully contrived of the native tea-tree; behind the house stretched vineyard and fruit-garden. Many rare plants grew in the beds. There was a hedge of geraniums that must have been close on fifteen feet high.

His knock was answered by a groom, who made a saucy face: Mr. Turnham and his lady were attending the Governor's ball that night, and did not receive. Mahony insisted on the delivery of his visiting-card—he had had a few cards hurriedly printed off, during the day. And since the servant still blocked the entrance, he added: "Inform your master, my man, that I am the bearer of a message from his sister, Miss Mary Turnham."

The man shut him out, left him standing on the verandah. After a lengthy absence, he returned, and with a: "Well, come along in, then!" opened the door of a parlour. This was a large room, well furnished in horse-hair and rep. Wax-lights stood on the mantelpiece, before a gilt-framed pierglass; coloured prints hung on the walls.

While Mahony was admiring the genteel comfort to which he had long been a stranger, John Turnham entered the room. He had a quiet tread, but took determined strides at the floor. In his hand, he held Mahony's card, and he looked from Mahony to it, and back again.

"To what do I owe the pleasure, Mr. . . . . er . . . Mahony?" he

73

asked, refreshing his memory with a glance at the pasteboard. He spoke in the brusque tone of one accustomed to run through many applicants in the course of an hour. "I understand that you make use of my sister Mary's name." And, as Mahony did not instantly respond, he snapped out: "My time is short, sir!"

A tinge of colour mounted to Mahony's cheeks. He answered with equal stiffness: "That is so. I come from Mr. William Beamish's 'Family Hotel' and am commissioned to bring you your sister's warm love and regards."

John Turnham bowed; and waited.

"I have also to acquaint you with the fact," continued Mahony, gathering hauteur as he went, "that the day before yesterday I proposed marriage to your sister, and that she did me the honour of accepting me."

"Ah, indeed!" said John Turnham, with a kind of ironic snort. "And may I ask on what ground you——"

"On the ground, sir, that I have a sincere affection for Miss Turnham, and believe it lies in my power to make her happy."

"Of that, kindly allow me to judge. My sister is a mere child —too young to know her own mind.— Be seated!"

To a constraining, restraining vision of little Polly, Mahony obeyed, stifling the near retort that she was not too young to earn her living among strangers. The two men faced each other, on opposite sides of the table. John Turnham had the same dark eyes and hair, the same short, straight nose as his brother and sister, but not their exotic pallor. His skin was bronzed; and his large, scarlet mouth supplied a vivid dash of colour. He wore bushy side-whiskers.

"And now, Mr. Mahony, I will ask you a blunt question. I receive letters regularly from my sister, but I cannot recall her ever having mentioned your name. Who and what are you?"

"Who I am?" flared up Mahony. "A gentleman like yourself, sir!—though a poor one. As for Miss Turnham not mentioning me in her letters, that is easily explained. I only had the pleasure of making her acquaintance five or six weeks ago."

"You are candid," said Polly's brother, and smiled without unclosing his lips. "But your reply to my question tells me nothing. May I ask what . . . er . . . under what . . . er . . . circumstances you came out to the colony, in the first instance?"

74

"No, sir, you may not!" cried Mahony, and flung up from his seat; he scented a deadly insult in the question.

"Come, come, Mr. Mahony," said Turnham in a more conciliatory tone. "Nothing is gained by being techy. And my inquiry is not unreasonable. You are an utter stranger to me; my sister has known you but for a few weeks, and is a young and inexperienced girl, into the bargain.— You tell me you are a gentleman. Sir, I had as lief you said you were a blacksmith! In this grand young country of ours, where progress is the watchword, effete standards and clogging traditions must go by the board. What we need here, at the present juncture, is sound and efficient workmen. Grit is of more use to us than gentility. Each single bricklayer who unships serves the colony better than a score of gentlemen."

"In that I am absolutely not at one with you, Mr. Turnham," said Mahony coldly. He had sat down again, feeling rather ashamed of his violence. "Without a leaven of refinement, the very raw material of which the existing population is mostly composed——"

But Turnham interrupted him. "Give 'em time, sir, give 'em time, and let 'em evolve their own upper ten, out of a race bred to the conditions of life here, and equal to it. God bless me, Rome wasn't built in a day!— But to resume. During my residence in Victoria, I have repeatedly had occasion to remark in what small stead the training that fits a man for a career in the old country stands him here. And that is why I am dissatisfied with your reply. Show me your muscles, sir, give me a clean bill of health, tell me if you have learnt a trade and can pay your way.— See, I will be frank with you. The position I occupy to-day, I owe entirely to my own efforts. I landed in the colony ten years ago, when this marvellous city of ours was little more than a village settlement. I had but five pounds in my pocket. To-day, I am a partner in my firm, and intend, if all goes well, to enter parliament. Hence, I think I may, without presumption, judge what makes for success here, and of the right type of man to attain it. He must be ready, sir, to turn his hand to anything that offers; must hold himself too good for no honest job under the sun. Work, hard work, is the key to all doors. So convinced am I of this, that I have insisted on the younger members of my family learning betimes to put their shoulders to the wheel.— Now, Mr. Mahony, I have been open with you. Be equally frank with me. You are an Irishman?"

Candour invariably disarmed Mahony—even lay a little heavy on him, with the weight of an obligation. He made recompense by a light touch of self-depreciation. "An Irishman, sir, in a country where the Irish have fallen, and not without reason, into general disrepute."

Over a biscuit and a glass of sherry, he gave a rough outline of the circumstances that had led to his leaving England, two years previously, and of his dismayed arrival in what he called "the cesspool of 1852."

"Thanks to the rose-water romance of the English press, many a young man of my day was enticed away from a modest competency, to seek his fortune here, where it was pretended that nuggets could be gathered like cabbages— I myself threw up a tidy little country practice. . . . I might mention that medicine was my profession. It would have given me intense satisfaction, Mr. Turnham, to see one of those glib journalists in my shoes, or the shoes of some of my messmates on the *Ocean Queen*. There were men aboard that ship, sir, who were reduced to beggary before they could even set foot on the road to the north. Granted it is the duty of the press to encourage emigration, it nevertheless seems little short of criminal to tempt men, unfit and unwarned, to face such hardships and such a climate as this."

"Let the press be, Mr. Mahony," said Turnham: he had sat back, crossed his legs, and put his thumbs in his armholes. "Let it be. What we need here is colonists—small matter how we get 'em."

Having had his say, Mahony scamped the recital of his own sufferings: the discomforts of the month he had been forced to spend in Melbourne, getting his slender outfit together; the miseries of the tramp to Ballarat on delicate unused feet, among the riff-raff of nations, under a wan December sky, against which the trunks of the gum-trees rose whiter still, and out of which blazed a copper sun, with a misty rim. He scamped, too, his six-months' attempt at digging—he had been no more fit for the work than a child. Worn to skin and bone, his small remaining strength sucked out by dysentery, he had, in the end, bartered his last pinch of gold-dust for a barrow-

load of useful odds and ends; and this had formed the nucleus
of his store. Here, fortune had smiled on him; his flag hardly
set a-flying, custom had poured in, and business had gone up
by leaps and bounds.— "Although I have never sold so much as
half a pint of spirits, sir!" His profits for the past six months
equalled a clear three hundred, and he had most of this to the
good. With a wife to keep, expenses would naturally be heavier; but he should continue to lay by every spare penny, with
a view to getting back to England.

"You have not the intention, then, of remaining permanently
in the colony?"

"Not the least in the world."

"H'm," said John: he was standing on the hearthrug now,
his legs apart. "That, of course, puts a different complexion on
the matter. Still, I may say, I am entirely reassured by what
you have told me—entirely so. Indeed, you must allow me to
congratulate you on the good sense you displayed, in striking
while the iron was hot. Many a one of your medical brethren,
sir, would have thought it beneath his dignity to turn shop-
keeper.— And now, Mr. Mahony, I will wish you good day; we
shall doubtless meet again before very long.— Nay, one moment! There are cases, you will admit, in which a female opinion is not without value. Besides, I should be pleased for you
to see my wife."

He crossed the hall, tapped at a door, and cried: "Emma, my
love, will you give us the pleasure of your company for a
moment?"

In response to this a lady entered, whom Mahony thought
one of the most beautiful women he had ever seen. She carried
a yearling infant in her arms, and with one hand pressed its
pale flaxen poll against the rich, ripe corn of her own hair, as
if to dare comparison. Her cheeks were of a delicate rose pink.

"My love," said Turnham—and one felt that the word was no
mere flower of speech. "My love, here is someone who wishes
to marry our Polly."

"To marry our Polly!" echoed the lady, and smiled a faint,
amused smile—it was as though she said: to marry this infant
that I bear on my arm. "But Polly is only a little girl!"

"My very words, dearest. And too young to know her own
mind."

"But you will decide for her, John."

John hung over his beautiful wife, wheeled up an easy chair, arranged her in it, placed a footstool. "Pray, pray, do not over-fatigue yourself, Emma!— That child is too heavy for you," he objected, as the babe made strenuous efforts to kick itself to its feet. "You know I do not approve of you carrying it yourself."

"Nurse is drinking tea."

"But why do I keep a houseful of domestics, if one of the others cannot occasionally take her place?"

He made an impetuous step towards the bell. Before he could reach it, there came a thumping at the door, and a fluty voice cried: "Lemme in, puppa, lemme tum in!"

Turnham threw the door open, and admitted a sturdy two-year-old, whom he led forward by the hand. "My son," he said, not without pride.

Mahony would have coaxed the child to him; but it ran to its mother, hid its face in her lap.

Forgetting the bell, John struck an attitude. "What a picture!" he exclaimed. "What a picture!— My love, I positively must carry out my intention of having you painted in oils, with the children round you.— Mr. Mahony, sir, have you even seen anything to equal it?"

Though his mental attitude might have been expressed by a note of exclamation, set ironically, Mahony felt constrained to second Turnham's enthusiasm. And it was indeed a lovely picture: the gracious, golden-haired woman, whose figure had the amplitude, whose gestures the almost sensual languor of the young nursing mother; the two children fawning at her knee, both ash-blond, with vivid scarlet lips.— "It helps me," thought Mahony, "to understand the mother-worship of primitive peoples."

The nursemaid summoned and the children borne off, Mrs. Emma exchanged a few amiable words with the visitor, then obeyed, with an equally good grace, her husband's command to rest for an hour, before dressing for the ball.

Having escorted her to another room, Turnham came back, rubbing his hands. "I am pleased to be able to tell you, Mr. Mahony, that your suit has my wife's approval. You are highly favoured! Emma is not free with her liking." Then, in a sudden burst of effusion: "I could have wished you the pleasure, sir, of seeing my wife in evening attire. She will make furore again; no other woman can hold a candle to her in a ballroom.

78

To-night is the first time since the birth of our second child that she will grace a public entertainment with her presence; and unfortunately her appearance will be a brief one, for the infant is not yet wholly weaned." He shut the door and lowered his voice. "You have had some experience of doctoring, you say; I should like a word with you, in your medical capacity. The thing is this. My wife has persisted, contrary to my wishes, in suckling both children herself."

"Quite right, too," said Mahony. "In a climate like this, their natural food is invaluable to babes."

"Exactly, quite so," said Turnham, with a hint of impatience. "And in the case of the first child, I made due allowance: a young mother . . . the novelty of the thing . . . you understand. But, with regard to the second, I must confess I— How long, sir, in your opinion, can a mother continue to nurse her babe without injury to herself? It is surely harmful if unduly protracted? I have observed dark lines about my wife's eyes, and she is losing her fine complexion.— Then you confirm my fears. I shall assert my authority without delay, and insist on separation from the child.— Ah, women are strange beings, Mr. Mahony, strange beings, as you are on the high road to discovering for yourself!"

Mahony returned to town on foot, the omnibus having ceased to run. As he walked—at a quick pace, and keeping a sharp look-out; for the road was notoriously unsafe after dark —he revolved his impressions of the interview. He was glad it was over, and, for Polly's sake, that it had passed off satisfactorily. It had made a poor enough start: at one moment he had been within an ace of picking up his hat and stalking out. But he found it difficult, at the present happy crisis, to bear a grudge—even if it had not been a proved idiosyncrasy of his, always to let a successful finish erase a bad beginning. None the less, he would not have belonged to the nation he did, had he not indulged in a caustic chuckle and a pair of good-humoured pishes and pshaws, at Turnham's expense. "Like a showman in front of his booth!"

Then he thought again of the domestic scene he had been privileged to witness, and grew grave. The beautiful young woman and her children might have served as model for a Holy Family—some old painter's dream of a sweet benign Madonna; the trampling babe as the infant Christ; the upturned face of the little John adoring. No place this for the scoffer! Apart from the mere pleasure of the eye, there was ample justification for Turnham's transports. Were they not in the presence of one of life's sublimest mysteries—that of motherhood? Not alone the lovely Emma: no; every woman who endured the rigours of childbirth, to bring forth an immortal soul, was a holy figure.

And now, for him, too, as he had been reminded, this wonder was to be worked. Little Polly as the mother of his children—what visions the words conjured up!— But he was glad Polly was just Polly, and not the peerless creature he had seen. John Turnham's fears would never be his—this jealous care of a transient bodily beauty. Polly was neither too rare nor too fair for her woman's lot; and, please God, the day would come when he would see her with a whole cluster of little ones round her—little dark-eyed replicas of herself. She, bless her, should dandle them and cosset them to her heart's content. Her joy in them would also be his.— And now, letting his thoughts take wing, he saw them both, her woman's duty done, standing side by side to watch their young brood go forth. They were greyhaired now, and glad to rest, but their love for each other was still fresh and strong.— Oh, God was good, and the world a fair place to live in! The Divine Architect had ordered, not alone the huge, starry field of the heavens, but the narrow river twisting down to the sea, the tender intricacies of the human heart. The same Gracious Will stood revealed in one and all. There *was* a design in Creation!

[9]

HE SAWED, planed, hammered; curly shavings dropped, and there was a pleasant smell of sawdust. Much had to be done to make the place fit to receive Polly. A second outhouse was necessary, to hold the surplus goods, and to do duty as a sleeping-room for Long Jim and Hempel: the lean-to the pair had occupied till now was being converted into a kitchen. At great cost and trouble, Mahony had some trees felled, and brought in from Warrenheip. With them he put up a rude fence round his backyard, interlacing the lopped boughs from post to post, so that they formed a thick and leafy screen. He also filled in the disused shaft that had served as a rubbish-hole, and chose another, further off, which would be less malodorous in the summer heat. Finally, a substantial load of fire-wood carted in, and two snakes that had made the journey in hollow logs dispatched, Long Jim was set down to chop and split the wood into a neat pile. Polly would but need to walk to and from the woodstack for her firing.

Indoors, he made equal revolution. That her ears should not be polluted by the language of the customers, he ran up a partition between living-room and store, thus cutting off the slab-walled portion of the house, with its roof of stringy-bark, from the log-and-canvas front. He also stopped with putty the worst gaps between the slabs. At Ocock's Auction Rooms, he bought a horsehair sofa to match his armchair, a strip of carpet, a bed, a washhandstand, and a looking-glass; and he tacked up a calico curtain before the window. His books, fetched out of the wooden case, were arranged on a brand new set of shelves; and, when all was done, and he stood back to admire his work, it was borne in on him afresh with how few creature-comforts he had hitherto existed. Plain to see, now, why he had preferred to sit out-of-doors rather than within! Now, no one on the Flat had a trimmer little place than he.

In his labours, he had the help of a friendly digger—a carpenter by trade—who one evening, pipe in mouth, had stood to watch his amateurish efforts with the jack-plane. Otherwise, the Lord alone knew how the house would ever have been made shipshape. Long Jim was equal to none but the simplest jobs; and Hempel, the assistant, had his hands full with the store. Well, it was a blessing at this juncture that business could be left to him. Hempel was as straight as a die; was a real treasure—or would have been, were it not for his eternal little bark of a cough. This was proof against all remedies, and the heck-heck of it at night was quite enough to spoil a light sleeper's rest. In building the new shed, Mahony had been careful to choose a corner far from the house, so that Polly's sleep should not be disturbed by the noise as well.

Marriages were still uncommon enough on Ballarat to make him an object of considerable curiosity. People took to dropping in of an evening—old Ocock; the postmaster; a fellow storekeeper, ex-steward to the Duke of Newcastle—to comment on his alterations and improvements. And over a pipe and a glass of sherry, he had to put up with a good deal of banter about his approaching "change of state."

Still, it was kindly meant. "We'll 'ave to git up a bit o' company o' nights for yer lady when she comes," said old Ocock, and spat under the table.

Purdy wrote from Tarrangower, where he had drifted:

Hooray, old Dick, golly for you! Old man, didn't I kick up a bobbery when I heard the news. Never was so well pleased in my life. That's all you needed, Dick—now you'll turn into a first-rate colonial. How about that fiver now I'd like to know? You can tell Polly from me I shall pay it back with interest on the fatal day. Of course I'll come and see you spliced, togs or no togs—to tell the truth my kicksies are on their very last legs —and there's nothing doing here—all the loose stuff's been turned over. There's oceans of quartz, of course, and they're trying to pound it up in dollies, but you could put me to bed with a pick-axe and a shovel before I'd go in for such tom-foolery as that.— Damn it all, Dick, to think of you being cotched at last. I can't get over it, and it's a bit of a risk, too, by dad it is, for a girl of that age is a dark horse if ever there was one.

Mahony's answer to this was a couple of pound-notes: "*So that my best man shall not disgrace me!*" His heart went out to the writer. Dear old Dickybird! pleased as Punch at the turn of events, yet quaking for fear of imaginary risks. With all Purdy's respect for his friend's opinions, he had yet an odd distrust of that friend's ability to look after himself. And now he was presuming to doubt Polly, too. Like his impertinence! What the dickens did he know of Polly!— Keenly relishing the sense of his own intimate knowledge, Mahony touched the breast-pocket in which Polly's letters lay—he often carried them out here with him, to a little hill, on which a single old blue-gum had been left standing; its scraggy top-knot of leaves drooped and swayed in the wind, like the few long straggling hairs on an old man's head.

The letters formed a goodly bundle; for Polly and he wrote regularly to each other, she once a week, he twice. His bore the Queen's head; hers, as befitted a needy little governess, were oftenest delivered by hand. Mahony untied the packet, drew a chance letter from it, and mused as he read. Polly had still not ceded much of her early reserve—and it had taken him weeks to persuade her even to call him by his baptismal name. She was, he thanked goodness, not of the kind who throw maidenly modesty to the winds, directly the binding word is spoken. And he loved her all the better for her wariness of emotion; it tallied with a like streak in his own nature. And this, though, at the moment, he was going through a very debauch of frankness. To the little black-eyed girl who pored over his letters at "Beamish's Family Hotel," he unbosomed himself as never in his life before. He enlarged on his tastes and preferences, his likes and dislikes; he gave vent to his real feelings for the country of his exile, and his longings for "home"; told how he had come to the colony, in the first instance, with the fantastic notion of redeeming the fortunes of his family; described his collections of butterflies and plants to her, using their Latin names. And Polly drank in his words, and humbly agreed with all he wrote, or, at least, did not disagree; and, from this, as have done lovers from the beginning of time, he inferred a perfect harmony of mind. On one point only did he press her for a reply. Was she fond of books? If so, what evenings they would spend together, he reading aloud from some entertaining volume, she at her fancy-work. And poetry? For himself, he could truly say he did not care for poetry . . . except on a Saturday night, or a quiet Sunday morning; and that was, because he liked it too well to approach it with any but a tranquil mind.

I think, if I know you aright, as I believe I do, my Polly, you too have poetry in your soul.

He smiled at her reply; then kissed it.

I cannot write poetry myself, said Polly, but I am very fond of it and shall indeed like very much, dear Richard, to listen when you read.

But the winter ran away, one cold, wet week succeeding another, and still they were apart. Mahony urged and pleaded, but could not get Polly to name the wedding-day. He began to think pressure was being brought to bear on the girl from another side. Naturally, the Beamishes were reluctant to let her go: who would be so useful to them as Polly?—who undertake, without scorn, the education of the whilom shepherd's daughters? Still, they knew they had to lose her, and he could not see that it made things any easier for them, to put off the evil day. No, there was something else at the bottom of it; though he did not know what.— Then, one evening, pondering a letter of Polly's, he slapped his forehead, and exclaimed aloud at his own stupidity. That night, into his reply, he slipped four five-pound notes. *Just to buy yourself any little thing you fancy, dearest. If I chose a gift, I might send what would not be acceptable to you.*— Yes, sure enough, that was it—little Polly had been in straits for money: the next news he heard was that she had bought and was stitching her wedding-gown. Taxed with her need, Polly guiltily admitted that her salary for the past three months was still owing to her. But there had been great expenses in connection with the hotel: it was being added to, for one thing, and whitewashed throughout; and Mr. B. had had an accident to his leg. From what she wrote, though, Mahony saw that it was not the first time such remissness had occurred; and he felt grimly indignant with her employers. Keeping open house, and hospitable to the point of vulgarity—he remembered good Mrs. Beamish's overloaded boards—they were, it was evident, pinchfists, when it came to parting with their money. Still, in the case of a marriage, and that of a little woman who had served them so faithfully! In thought, he set a thick black mark against their name, for their cavalier treatment of his Polly. And extended it to John Turnham, as well. John had plainly made no move to put hand to pocket; and Polly's niceness of feeling had stood in the way of her applying to him for aid. It made Mahony yearn to snatch the girl to him, then and there; to set her free of all contact with such coarse-grained, miserly brutes.

Old Ocock negotiated the hire of a neat spring cart for him, and a stout little cob; and, at last, the day had actually come, when he could set out to bring Polly home. By his side was Ned Turnham. Ned, still a lean-jowled wagesman at Rotten Gully, made no secret of his glee at getting carried down thus comfortably to Polly's nuptials. They drove the eternal forty odd miles to Geelong: each stick and stone by the roadside was fast becoming known to Mahony, and the journey itself remained equally tiresome, whether the red earth rose as a thick red dust, or whether, as now, it had turned to a mud like birdlime, in which the wheels sank almost to the axles. Arrived at Geelong, they put up at a hotel near the wharf, where Purdy awaited them. Purdy had tramped down from Tarrangower, blanket on back, and stood in need of a new rig-out from head to foot. Otherwise, his persistent ill-luck had left no mark on him. The ceremony took place early the following morning, at the house of the Wesleyan minister, the Anglican parson having been called away. The Beamishes and Polly drove to town, a tight fit in a double buggy. On the back seat, Jinny clung to and half supported a huge clothes-basket, which contained the wedding-breakfast. Polly sat on her trunk, by the splash-board; and Tilly, crowded out, rode in on one of the cart-horses, a coloured bed-quilt pinned round her waist, to protect her skirts.

To Polly's disappointment, neither her brother John nor his wife was present; a letter came, at the eleventh hour, to say that Mrs. Emma was unwell, and her husband did not care to leave her. Enclosed, however, were ten pounds for the purchase of a wedding-gift; and the pleasure Polly felt at being able to announce John's generosity helped to make up to her for his absence. The only other guest present was an elder sister, Miss Sarah Turnham, who, being out of a situation at the moment, had sailed down from Melbourne. This young lady, a sprightly brunette of some three or four and twenty, without the fine, regular features of Ned and Polly, but with tenfold their vivacity and experience, caused quite a sensation; and Tilly's audible raptures at beholding her Purdy again were of short duration; for Purdy had never met the equal of Miss Sarah, and could not take his eyes off her. He and she were the life of the party. The Beamishes were overawed by the visitor's town-bred airs, and the genteel elegance of her dress; Polly was a mere crumpled rose-leaf of pink confusion; Mahony too preoccupied with ring and license, to take any but his formal share in the proceedings.

"Come and see you?" echoed Miss Sarah playfully: the knot was tied; the company had demolished the good things laid out by Mrs. Beamish in the private parlour of a hotel, and emptied a couple of bottles of champagne; and Polly had changed her muslin frock for a black silk travelling-gown. "Come and *see* you? Why, of course I will, little silly!"—and, with her pretty white hands, she patted the already perfect bow of Polly's bonnet-strings. Miss Sarah had no great opinion of the match her sister was making; but she had been agreeably surprised by Mahony's person and manners, and had said so, thus filling Polly's soul with bliss. "Provided, of course, little goosey, you have a *spare-room* to offer me.— For, I confess," she went on, turning to the rest of the party, "I confess, I feel inordinately curious to see, with my own eyes, what these famous diggings are like. From all one hears, they must be *marvellously* entertaining.— Now, I presume that *you*, Mr. Smith, never touch at such *rude, out-of-the-world* places, in the course of *your* travels?"

Purdy, who had discreetly concealed the fact that he was but a poverty-stricken digger himself, quibbled a light evasion, then changed the subject, and offered his escort to the steam-packet, by which Miss Sarah was returning to Melbourne.

"And you, too, dear Tilly," urged little Polly, proceeding with her farewells. "For, mind, you promised. And *I* won't forget to . . . you know what!"

Tilly, sobbing noisily, wept on Polly's neck that she wished she were dead, or at the bottom of the sea; and Polly, torn between pride and pain at Purdy's delinquency, could only kiss her several times without speaking.

The farewells buzzed and flew.

"Good-bye to you, little lass . . . beg pardon, Mrs. Dr. Mahony!"— "Mind you write, Poll! I shall die to 'ear."— "Ta-ta, little silly goosey, and *au revoir!*"— "Mind he don't pitch you out of the cart, Polly!"— "Good-bye, Polly, my duck, and remember I'll come to you in a winkin', h'if and when . . ." which speech on the part of Mrs. Beamish distressed Poll to the verge of tears.

But, finally, she was torn from their arms and hoisted into the cart; and Mahony, the reins in his hand, began to unstiffen from the wooden figure-head he had felt like, during the ceremony, and under the whirring tongues and whispered confidences of the women.

"And now, Polly, for home!" he said exultantly, when the largest pocket-handkerchief had shrunk to the size of a nit, and Polly had ceased to twist her neck for one last, last glimpse of her friends.

And then the bush, and the loneliness of the bush, closed round them.

It was the time of flowers—of fierce young growth after the fruitful winter rains. The short-lived grass, green now as that of an English meadow, was picked out into patterns by the scarlet of the Running Postman; purple sarsaparilla festooned the stems of the scrub; there were vast natural paddocks, here of yellow everlastings, there of heaths in full bloom. Compared with the dark, spindly foliage of the she-oaks, the tea-trees' waxy flowers stood out like orange-blossoms—against firs. On damp or marshy ground, wattles were aflame: great quivering masses of softest gold. Wherever these trees stood, the fragrance of their yellow puff-ball blossoms saturated the air; one knew, before one saw them, that they were coming, and, long after they had been left behind, one carried their honeyed sweetness with one; against them, no other scent could have made itself felt. And to Mahony, these waves of perfume, into which they were continually running, came, in the course of the hours, to stand for a symbol of the golden future for which he and Polly were making; and whenever, in after years, he met with wattles in full bloom, he was carried back to the blue spring day of his wedding-journey, and jogged on once more, in the light cart, with his girl-wife at his side.

It was necessarily a silent drive. More rain had fallen during the night; even the best bits of the road were worked into deep, glutinous ruts, and the low-lying parts were under water. Mahony, but a fairish hand with the reins, was repeatedly obliged to leave the track and take to the bush, where he steered a way through trees, stumps, boulders and crab-holes, as best he might. Sometimes, he rose to his feet to encourage the horse; or he alighted and pulled it by the bridle; or put a shoulder to the wheel. But, to-day, no difficulties had power to daunt him; and the farther he advanced, the lighter-hearted he grew: he went back to Ballarat feeling, for the first time, that he was actually going home.

And Polly?— Sitting motionless at her husband's side, her hands folded on her black silk lap, Polly obediently turned her head this way and that, when Richard pointed out a landmark to her, or called her attention to the flowers. At first, things were new and arresting, but the novelty soon wore off; and, as they went on, and on, and still on, it began to seem to Polly, who had never been farther afield than a couple of miles north of the "Pivot City," as if they were driving away from all the rest of mankind, right into the very heart of nowhere. The road grew rougher, too—became a mere worn-down track, scored with ridges and furrows which threw them violently from side to side. Unused to bush driving, Polly was sure, at each fresh jolt, that this time the cart *must* tip over; and yet she preferred the track and its dangers to Richard's adventurous attempts to carve a passage through the scrubs. A little later, a cold south wind sprang up, which struck through her thin silk mantle; she was very tired, having been on her feet since five o'clock that morning; and all the happy fuss and excitement of the wedding was behind her. Her heart sank. She loved Richard dearly; if he had asked her, she would have gone to the ends of the earth with him; but, at this moment, she felt both small and lonely, and she would have liked nothing better than Mrs. Beamish's big motherly bosom, on which to lay her head. And when, in passing a swamp, a well-known noise broke on her ear—that of hundreds of bell-frogs, which were like hundreds of hissing tea-kettles just about to boil—then, such a rush of home-sickness took her, that she would have given all she had to know she was going back, once more, to the familiar little whitewashed room she had shared with Tilly and Jinny.

The seat of the cart was slanting, and slippery. Polly was continually sliding forward, now by inches, now with a great jerk. At last Mahony noticed it. "You are not sitting very comfortably, Polly, I fear?" he said.

Polly righted herself yet again, and reddened. "It's my . . . my feet aren't long enough," she replied.

"Why, my poor little love!" cried Mahony, full of quick compunction. "Why didn't you say so?" And, drawing rein and getting down, he stuffed some of Mrs. Beamish's bundles—fragments of the feast, which the good woman had sent with them —under his wife's feet; stuffed too many, so that Polly drove the rest of the way with her knees raised to a hump in front of her.

All the afternoon they had been making for dim blue ranges. After leaving the flats near Geelong, the track went up and

down. Grey-green forest surrounded them, out of which nob-
bly hills rose like islands from a sea of trees. As they approached the end of their journey, they overtook a large number of heavy vehicles, labouring along through the mire. A
coach with six horses dashed past them at full gallop, and left
them rapidly behind. Did they have to skirt bull-punchers who
were lashing or otherwise ill-treating their teams? Mahony
urged on the horse and bade Polly shut her eyes.

Night had fallen and a drizzling rain set in, by the time they
travelled the last couple of miles that led to Ballarat. This was
worst of all; and Polly held her breath while the horse picked
its way among yawning pits, into which one false step would
have plunged them. Her fears were not lessened by hearing
that, in several places, the very road was undermined; and she
was thankful when Richard—himself rendered uneasy by the
precious cargo he bore—got out and walked at the horse's
head. They drew up before a public-house. Cramped from sitting, and numb with cold, Polly climbed stiffly down, as she
was bidden; and Mahony, having unloaded the baggage,
mounted to his seat again, to drive the cart into the yard. This
was a false move, as he was quick to see: he should not have
left Polly standing alone. For the news of the arrival of "Doc"
Mahony and his bride flew from mouth to mouth, and the loafers who were in the bar turned out to stare and to quiz. Beside
her tumulus of trunks, bag, and bundle, little Polly stood desolate, with drooping shoulders; and Mahony, cursing his want
of foresight, all but drove into the gate-post, which occasioned
a loud guffaw. Nor had Long Jim turned up, as ordered, to
shoulder the heavy luggage. These blunders made Mahony
very hot and curt. Having himself stowed the things inside the
bar, and borrowed a lantern, he drew his wife's arm through
his, and hurried her away.

It was pitch-dark, and the ground was wet and squelchy.
Their feet sank in the mud. Polly clung to Richard's arm, trembling at the rude voices, the laughter, the brawling, that issued
from the grog-shops; at the continual apparition of rough,
bearded men. One of these, who held a candle stuck in a bottle, was accosted by Richard, and soundly rated. When they
turned out of the street, with its few dismal oil-lamps, their
way led them among dirty tents and black pits, and they had
to depend for light on the lantern they carried. They crossed

89

a rickety little bridge, over a flooded river; then climbed a
slope, on which, in her bunchy silk skirts, Polly slipped and
floundered, to stop before something that was half a tent and
half a log-hut.— What! this the end of the long, long journey.
This the house she had to live in?

Yes, Richard was speaking. "Welcome home, little wife! Not
much of a place, you see, but the best I can give you."

"It's . . . it's very nice, Richard," said Polly staunchly; but
her lips trembled.

Warding off the attack of a big, fierce, dirty dog, which
sprang at her, dragging its paws down her dress, Polly waited
while her husband undid the door, then followed him through
a chaos, which smelt as she had never believed any roofed-in
place could smell, to a little room at the back.

Mahony lighted the lamp that stood ready on the table, and
threw a satisfied glance round. His menfolk had done well:
things were in apple-pie order. The fire crackled, the kettle
was on the boil, the cloth was spread. He turned to Polly to
kiss her welcome, to relieve her of bonnet and mantle. But
before he could do this, there came a noise of rowdy voices, of
shouting and parleying. Picking up the lantern, he ran out to
see what the matter was.

Left alone, Polly remained standing by the table, on which
an array of tins was set—preserved salmon, sardines, condensed
milk—their tops forced back to show their contents. Her heart
was as heavy as lead, and she felt a dull sense of injury as well.
This hut her home!—to which she had so freely invited sister
and friend! She would be ashamed for them ever to set eyes on
it. Not in her worst dreams had she imagined it as mean and
poor as this. But perhaps. . . . With a lamp in her hand, she tiptoed guiltily to a door in the wall: it opened into a tiny bedroom with a sloping roof. No, this was all, all there was of it:
just these two miserable little poky rooms! She raised her head
and looked round, and the tears welled up, in spite of herself.
The roof was so low that you could almost touch it; the window was no larger than a pocket-handkerchief; there were
chinks between the slabs of the walls. And from one of these,
she now saw a spider crawl out, a huge black tarantula, with
horrible hairy legs. Polly was afraid of spiders; and, at this, the
tears began to overflow and to trickle down her cheeks. Holding her skirts to her—the new dress she had made with such

pride, now damp, and crushed, and soiled—she sat down and put her feet, in their soaked, mud-caked, little prunella boots, on the rung of her chair, for fear of other monsters that might be crawling on the floor.

And then, while she sat thus hunched together, the voices outside were suddenly drowned in a deafening noise—in a hideous, stupefying din, that nearly split one's eardrums: it sounded as though all the tins and cans in the town were being beaten and banged before the door. Polly forgot the tarantula, forgot her bitter disappointment with her new home. Her black eyes wide with fear, her heart thudding in her chest, she sprang to her feet and stood ready, if need be, to defend herself.— Where, oh where was Richard?

It was the last straw. When, some five minutes later, Mahony came bustling in: he had soothed the "kettledrummers" and sent them off, with a handsome gratuity, and he carried the trunk on his own shoulder, Long Jim following behind with bags and bundles: when he entered, he found little Polly sitting with her head huddled on her arms, crying as though her heart would break.

PART II

[1]

OVER the fathomless grey seas that tossed between, dissevering the ancient and gigantic continent from the tiny motherland, unsettling rumours ran. After close on forty years' fat peace, England had armed for hostilities again, her fleet set sail for a foreign sea. Such was the news the sturdy clipper-ships brought out, in tantalising fragments; and those who, like Richard Mahony, were mere birds-of-passage in the colony, and had friends and relatives going to the front, caught hungrily at every detail. But, to the majority of the colonists, what England had done, or left undone, in preparation for war, was of small account. To them the vital question was: will the wily Russian Bear take its revenge by sending men-of-war to annihilate us, and plunder the gold in our banks—us, months removed from English aid? And the opinion was openly expressed that in casting off her allegiance to Great Britain, and becoming a neutral state, lay young Australia's best hope of safety.

But, even while they made it, the proposers of this scheme were knee-deep in petty, local affairs again. All Europe was depressed under the cloud of war; but they went on belabouring hackneyed themes—the unlocking of the lands, iniquitous license-fees, official corruption. Mahony could not stand it. His heart was in England, went up and down with England's hopes and fears. He smarted under the tales told of the inefficiency of the British troops and the paucity of their numbers; under the painful disclosures made by journalists, injudiciously allowed to travel to the seat of war; he questioned, like many another of his class in the old country, the wisdom of the Duke of Newcastle's orders to lay siege to the port of Sebastopol. And of an evening, when the store was closed, he sat over stale English newspapers and a map of the Crimea, and meticulously followed the movements of the Allies.

But in this retirement he was rudely disturbed, by feeling himself touched on a vulnerable spot—that of his pocket. Before the end of the year, trade had come to a standstill, and the very town he lived in was under martial law.

On both Ballarat and the Bendigo, the agitation for the repeal of the license-tax had grown more and more vehement; and spring's arrival found the digging-community worked up to a white heat. The new Governor's tour of inspection, on which great hopes had been built, served only to aggravate the trouble. Misled by the golden treasures with which the diggers, anxious as children to please, dazzled his eyes, the Governor decided that the tax was not an outrageous one; and ordered license-raids to be undertaken twice as often as before. This defeat of the diggers' hopes, together with the murder of a comrade, and the acquittal of the murderer by a corrupt magistrate, goaded even the least sensitive spirits to rebellion: the guilty man's house was fired, the police were stoned, and then, for a month or more, deputations and petitions ran to and fro between Ballarat and Melbourne. In vain: the demands of the voteless diggers went unheard. The consequence was that, one day at the beginning of summer, all the troops that could be spared from the capital, along with several pieces of artillery, were raising the dust on the road to Ballarat.

On the last afternoon in November, work was suspended

throughout the diggings, and the more cautious among the shopkeepers began to think of closing their doors. In front of the "Diggers' Emporium," where the earth was baked as hard as a burnt crust, a little knot of people stood shading their eyes from the sun. Opposite, on Bakery Hill, a monster meeting had been held and the "Southern Cross" hoisted—a blue bunting that bore the silver stars of the constellation after which it was named. Having sworn allegiance to it with outstretched hands, the rebels were now lining up to march off to drill.

Mahony watched the thin procession through narrowed lids, and with a meditative hand at his beard. In theory, he condemned equally the blind obstinacy of the authorities, who went on tightening the screw, and the foolhardiness of the men. But—well, he could not get his eye to shirk one of the screaming banners and placards: "Down with Despotism!" "Who so base as be a Slave!" by means of which the diggers sought to inflame popular indignation. "If one could," he said, "but induce honest rebels to free their propaganda from melodramatic exaggeration! As it is, those good fellows yonder are rendering a just cause ridiculous."

Polly, standing at his side, from time to time tightened her clasp of his arm. She had known no peace since the previous evening, when a rough-looking man had come into the store, and, with revolver at full cock, had commanded Hempel to hand over all the arms and ammunition it contained. Hempel, much to Richard's wrath, had meekly complied; but it might have been Richard himself; he would for certain have refused; and then. . . . Polly had hardly closed an eye all night, for thinking of it. She now listened, in a deferential silence, to the men's talk; but when old Ocock—he never had a good word to say for the riotous diggers—took his pipe out of his mouth to remark: "A pack o' Tipperary boys spoilin' for a fight—that's what I say! An' yet, blow me, if I wouldn't 'a' bin glad if one o' my two 'ad 'ad spunk enough to join 'em!"—at this Polly could not refrain from saying pitifully: "Oh, Mr. Ocock, do you really *mean* that?" For both Purdy and brother Ned were in the rebel band, and Polly's heart was heavy, because of them.

"Can't you see my brother anywhere?" she asked Hempel, who held an old spyglass to his eyes.

"No, ma'am, sorry to say I can't," replied Hempel. He would willingly have conjured up a dozen brothers, to comfort Polly; but he could not swerve from the truth, even for her.

"Give me the glasses," said Mahony, and swept the line.— "No, no sign of either of those boys. Perhaps they thought better of it, after all.— Listen! now they're singing—can you hear them? The *Marseillaise*, as I'm alive.— Poor fools! Many of them, if I see aright, are armed with nothing more deadly than picks and shovels."

"And pikes," corrected Hempel. "Several are carrying pikes, sir."

"Ay, that's so! they've bin 'ammerin' out bits of old iron all the mornin'," agreed Ocock. "It's said they 'aven't a quarter of a firearm apiece. And the drillin'!— Lord love yer! 'Alf of 'em don' know their right 'and from their left. The troops 'ull make mincemeat of 'em, if they come to close quarters."

"That they'll never do—you can take my word for it."

"Oh, I hope not!" said Polly. "Oh, I do hope they won't get hurt."

Patting her hand, Mahony advised his wife to go indoors and resume her household tasks. And, since his lightest wish was a command, little Polly docilely withdrew her arm, and returned to her dishwashing. But though she rubbed and scoured with her usual precision, bringing the tiny kitchen to the state of perfection it was her pride to keep it in, her heart was not in her work. Both on this day and the next, she seemed to exist solely in her two ears. The one strained to catch any scrap of news about "poor Ned"; the other listened, with an even sharper anxiety, to what went on in the store. Several further attempts were made to get arms and provisions from Richard; and each time an angry scene ensued. Close up beside the thin partition, her hands locked under her cooking-apron, Polly sat and trembled for her husband. He had already got himself talked about, by refusing to back a Reform League that had been founded; and now, her ear glued to a chink, she heard him openly declare to some one that he disapproved of the terms of this League, from A to Z.— Oh dear! If only he wouldn't— But she was careful not to add to his worries by speaking of her fears. As it was, he came to tea with a moody face; and she heard him remark in an undertone to Hempel that, if things went on like this, they would soon be under the

rule of mob law. How Polly did wish, as she made the tea and
served up a dish of buttered toast, that she was just a little
older and wiser. Then, Richard might not have felt bound to
keep her in ignorance, but could have relieved his mind.

The behaviour of the foraging parties growing ever more
threatening, Mahony next day thought it prudent to follow the
general example, and put up his shutters. Wildly conflicting
rumours were in the air. One report said a contingent of Creswick dare-devils had arrived, to join forces with the insurgents;
another, that the Creswickers, disgusted at finding neither firearms nor quarters provided for them, had straightway turned
and marched the twelve miles home again. For a time it was
asserted that Lalor, the Irish leader, had been bought over by
the government; then, just as definitely, that his influence alone
held the rebel faction together. Towards evening, Long Jim
was dispatched to find out how matters really stood. He
brought word that the diggers had entrenched themselves on
a piece of rising ground, near the Eureka lead, behind a flimsy
barricade of logs, slabs, ropes and overturned carts. The Camp,
for its part, was screened by a breast-work of fire-wood, trusses
of hay, and bags of corn; while the mounted police stood or
lay, fully armed, by their horses, which were saddled ready for
action at a moment's notice.

Neither Ned nor Purdy put in an appearance, and the night
passed without news of them. Just before dawn, however, Mahony was wakened by a tapping at the window. Thrusting out
his head, he recognised young Tommy Ocock, who had been
sent by his father to tell "doctor" that the soldiers were astir.
Lights could be seen moving about the Camp, a horse had
neighed—father felt sure they were up to something. He
thought spies might have given them the hint that at least half
the diggers from the Stockade had come down to Main Street
last night, and got drunk, and never gone back.— With a concerned glance at Polly, who was awake and sitting up in bed,
Mahony struggled into his clothes. He must make another effort to reach the boys—especially Ned, for Polly's sake. When
Ned had first announced his intention of siding with the insurgents, he, Mahony, had merely shrugged his shoulders, believing that the young vapourer would soon have had enough
of it. Now, he felt responsible to his wife for Ned's safety: Ned,
whose chief reason for turning rebel, he suspected, was that

a facetious trooper had once dubbed him "Eytalian organ-grinder," and asked him where he kept his monkey.

But Mahony's designs of a friendly interference came too late. The troops had got away, creeping stealthily through the morning dusk; and he was still panting up Specimen Hill, when he heard the crack of a rifle. Confused shouts and cries followed. Then a bugle blared, and, the next instant, the rattle and bang of musketry split the air.

Together with a knot of others, who, like himself, had run forth half dressed into the breathless dawn, Mahony stopped and waited, in extreme anxiety; and, while he stood, the stars went out one by one, as though a finger-tip had touched them. The diggers' response to the volley of the attacking-party was easily to be distinguished: it was a dropping fire, and sounded like a thin hail-shower after a peal of thunder. Within half an hour all was over: the barricade had fallen, to cheers and laughter from the military; the rebel flag was torn down; and the huts and tents inside the enclosure were going up in flames.

Towards six o'clock, just as the December sun, huge and fiery, thrust the edge of its globe above the horizon, a number of onlookers ran up the slope, to all that was left of the ill-fated stockade. On the dust, blood-stains, now set hard as scabs, traced the route by which a wretched procession of prisoners had been marched off to the Camp gaol. Behind the demolished barrier, huts smouldered as heaps of blackened embers; and the ground was strewn with stark forms, which lay about—some twenty or thirty of them—in grotesque attitudes. Some sprawled with outstretched arms, as though crucified to the earth, their sightless eyes seeming to fix the pale azure of the sky; others were hunched and huddled in a last convulsion. And in the course of his fruitless search for friend and brother, an old instinct reasserted itself in Mahony: kneeling down, he began swiftly and dexterously to examine the prostrate bodies. Two or three still lived, the blood gurgling from throat and breast, like water from the neck of a bottle. Here, one had a mouth plugged with shot, and a beard as stiff as though it were made of rope. Another that he turned over was a German he had once heard speak at a diggers' meeting—a windy brag-gart of a man, if he remembered aright, with a quaint impediment in his speech. Well, poor soul; he would never mouth invectives, or tickle the ribs of an audience again. His body was a very colander for wounds.— Altogether, the wounds were bad, very bad. Some had not bled, either. It looked as though the soldiers had viciously gone on prodding and stabbing the fallen.

The wrath of the man whose busines it had once been to preserve life, at any cost, rose in him, in face of this butchery. — Stripping a corpse of its shirt, he tore off a piece of stuff to make a bandage for a shattered leg. While he was binding the limb to a board, young Tom ran up to say that the military, returning with carts, were arresting every one they met in the vicinity. Giving the wounded man a sip from his flask, Mahony, with others who had been covering up and carrying away their friends, hastened down the back of the hill towards the bush. Here was plain evidence of a stampede. More blood-stains pointed the track, and a number of odd and clumsy weapons had been dropped or thrown away by the diggers in their flight.

He went home with the relatively good tidings that neither Ned nor Purdy was to be found. Polly was up and dressed. She had also lighted the fire, and set water to boil, "just in case." "Was there ever such a sensible little woman!" said her husband with a kiss.

The day dragged itself laboriously by, flat and stale after the excitement of the morning. No one ventured far from cover; for the military remained under arms, and detachments of mounted troopers patrolled the streets. At the Camp, the hundred odd prisoners were being sorted out, and the maimed and wounded doctored in the rude little temporary hospital. Down in Main Street, the noise of hammering went on, hour after hour. The dead could not be kept, in the summer heat, must be got underground before dark.

Mahony had just secured his premises for the night, when there came a rapping at the back door. Polly, who was plaiting her hair, sprang up, but Mahony chose to answer the knock himself, and going out of the bedroom, shut the door behind him. But it was not Ned, nor anything to do with Ned. In the yard stood a stranger, who, when the dog Pompey had been chidden and soothed, made mysterious signs to Mahony, and murmured a well-known name. Admitted to the sitting-room, he fished a scrap of dirty paper from his boot. Mahony put the candle on the table and straightened out the missive. Sure enough, it was in Purdy's hand—though sadly scrawled.

Have been hit in the pin. Come if possible and bring your tools. The bearer is square.

Polly could hear the two of them talking in low, urgent tones. But her relief that the visitor brought no bad news of her brother was dashed, when she learned that Richard had to ride out into the bush, to visit a sick man—Mahony made up his mind to tell her no more than this, till his return. However, she buttoned her bodice, and, with her hair hanging down her back, went into the sitting-room to help her husband; for he was turning the place upside down. He had a pair of probe-scissors somewhere, he felt sure, if he could only lay hands on them. And while he ransacked drawers and cupboards, for one and another of the few poor instruments left him, his thoughts went back, inopportunely enough, to the time when he had been surgeon's dresser in the Edinburgh Royal Infirmary. *O tempora, O mores!*—the contrast between then and now made him laugh. He wondered what old Syme, that prince of surgeons, would say, could he see his whilom student raking out a probe from among the ladles and kitchen spoons, a roll of lint from behind the saucepans.

Bag in hand, he followed his guide to where the latter had left a horse in safe-keeping; and having lengthened the stirrups, and received instructions about the road, he set off for the hut in the ranges that Purdy had contrived to reach. He had an awkward cross-country ride of some four miles before him; but this was not what troubled him. The chance-touched spring had opened the gates to a flood of memories; and, as he jogged along, he re-lived, in thought, the happy days he had spent as a student under the shadow of Arthur's Seat, round the College, the Infirmary, and old Surgeons' Square. Once more, he sat in the theatre, the breathless spectator of famous surgical operations; or, as house-surgeon to the Lying-in Hospital, himself assisted in daring attempts to lessen suffering and save life. It was, of course, too late now to bemoan the fact that he had broken with his profession. Yet only that very day, how envy had beset him! The rest of the fraternity had run to and from the tents where the wounded were housed: he, behung with his shopman's apron, had pottered about among barrels and crates. No one thought of enlisting *his* services; another, not he, would set (or bungle) the fracture he had temporarily splinted.

The hut—it had four slab walls and an earthen floor—was in darkness on his arrival, for Purdy had not ventured to make a light. He lay tossing restlessly on a dirty old straw palliasse, and was in great pain; but greeted his friend with a dash of the old brio.

Hanging his coat over the chinks in the door, and turning back his sleeves, Mahony took up the lantern and stooped to examine the injured leg. A bullet had struck the right ankle, causing an ugly wound. He washed it out, dressed, and bandaged it. He also bathed the patient's sweat-soaked head and shoulders; then sat down to await the owner of the hut's return.

As soon as the latter appeared, he took his leave, promising to ride out again the night after next. In spite of the circumstances under which they met, he and Purdy parted with a slight coolness. Mahony had expressed surprise at the nature of the wound caused by the bullet: it was incredible that any of the military could have borne a weapon of this calibre. Purdy was at first unwilling to speak out. Pressed, he admitted that his hurt was a piece of gross ill-luck: he had been accidentally shot by a clumsy fool of a digger, from an ancient holster-pistol.

To Mahony, this seemed to cap the climax; and he did not mask his sentiments. The pitiful little forcible-feeble rebellion, all along but a futile attempt to cast straws against the wind, was now completely over and done with, and would never be heard of again. Or such at least, he added, was the earnest hope of the law-abiding community. This irritated Purdy, who was spumy with the self-importance of one who has stood in the thick of the fray. He answered hotly, and ended by rapping out, with a contemptuous click of the tongue: "Upon my word, Dick, you look at the whole thing like the tradesman you are!"

These words rankled in Mahony all the way home.— But trust Purdy for not, in anger, being able to resist giving him a flick on the raw. It made him feel thankful that he was no longer so dependent on his friendship as of old. Since then, he had tasted better things. Now, a woman's heart beat in sympathetic understanding; there met his, two lips which had never said an unkind word.— He pushed on, with a new zest, reaching home about dawn. And over his young wife's joy at his safe return, he forgot the shifting moods of his night-journey.

It had, however, this result. Next day, Polly found him with his head in one of the great old shabby black books which, to her mind, spoilt the neat appearance of the book-shelves. He stood to read, the volume lying open before him on the top of the cold stove, and was so deeply engrossed that the store-bell rang twice without his hearing it. When, reminded that Hempel was absent, he whipped out to answer it, he carried the volume with him under his arm.

[2]

BUT his first treatment of Purdy's wound was also his last. Two nights later, on again riding out to the ranges, he found the hut deserted; and diligently as he prowled round it in the moonlight, he could discover no clue to the fate of its occupants. There was nothing to be done but to head his horse for home again.— *He* might go on rubbing off the rust, making his mouth water by conning over injuries to the astragalus; some one else would see Purdy's case through.

Polly was more fortunate. Within three days of the fight, Ned turned up, sound as a bell. He was sporting a new hat, a flashy silk neckerchief, and a silver watch and chain. At sight of these kickshaws, a dismal suspicion entered Mahony's mind, and refused to be dislodged. But he did not breathe his doubts —for Polly's sake. Polly was rapturously content to see her brother again. She threw her arms round his neck, and listened, with her big, black, innocent eyes—except for their fleckless candour the counterpart of Ned's own—to the tale of his miraculous escape, and of the rich gutter he had had the good luck to strike.

Meanwhile, public feeling exasperated beyond measure by the tragedy of that summer dawn, slowly subsided. Hesitation, timidity, and a very human waiting on success, had held many diggers back from joining in the final coup; but the sympathy of the community was with the rebels, and, at the funerals of some of the fallen, hundreds of mourners, in such black coats as they could muster, marched side by side to the wild little unfenced bush cemetery. When, too, the relief-party arrived from Melbourne, and martial law was proclaimed, the residents handed over their firearms, as ordered; but an attempt to swear in special constables failed, not a soul stepping forward in support of the government.

There was literally nothing doing during the month the military occupied Ballarat. Mahony seized the opportunity to give his back premises a coat of paint; he also began to catalogue his collection of Lepidoptera. Hence, as far as business was concerned, it was a timely moment for the arrival of a letter from Henry Ocock, to the effect that, "subject of course to any part-heard case," "our case" was first on the list for a date early in January.

None the less, the announcement threw Mahony into the fidgets. He had almost clean forgotten the plaguy affair: it had its roots in the dark days before his marriage. He wished now he had thought twice before letting himself be entangled in a lawsuit. Now, he had a wife dependent on him, and to lose the case, and be held responsible for costs, would cripple him. And such a verdict was not at all unlikely; for Purdy, his chief witness, could not be got at: the Lord alone knew where Purdy lay hid.— He at once sat down and wrote the bad news to his solicitor.

At six o'clock in the morning, some few days later, he took his seat in the coach for Melbourne. By his side sat Johnny Ocock the elder of the two brothers. Johnny had by chance been within earshot during the negotiations with the rascally carrier, and, on learning this, Henry had straightway subpœnaed him. Mahony was none too well pleased with his company: the boy threatened to be a handful. His old father, on delivering him up at the coach-office, had drawn Mahony aside to whisper: "Don't let the young limb out o' yer sight, doc., or get nip or sip o' liquor. If 'e so much as wets 'is tongue, there's no 'olding 'im."— Johnny was a lean, pimply-faced youth, with cold, flabby hands.

Little Polly had to stay behind. Mahony would have liked to give her the trip and show her the sights of the capital; but the law-courts were no place for a woman; neither could he leave her sitting alone in a hotel. And a tentative letter to her brother John had not called forth an invitation: Mrs. Emma

101

was in delicate health at present, and had no mind for visitors.
So he committed Polly to the care of Hempel and Long Jim,
both of whom were her faithful henchmen. She herself, in
proper wifely fashion, proposed to give her little house a good
red-up, in its master's absence.

Mahony and Johnny dismounted from the coach in the early
afternoon, sore, stiff, and hungry: they, with their fellow-passengers, had been flung about the body of the vehicle like
sprats in an ill-packed barrel. They had also broken their fast
merely on half-a-dozen sandwiches, keeping their seats the
while, that the young toper might be spared the sight of intoxi-
cating liquors. Now, stopping only to brush off the top layer of
dust and snatch a bite of solid food, Mahony hastened away,
his witness at heel, to Chancery Lane.

It was a relief to him to find that Ocock was not greatly
put out at Purdy's having failed them.— "Leave it to us, sir!
We'll make that all right." Again, as on the previous visit, he
dry-washed his hands while he spoke, and his little eyes shot
flashes from one to the other, like electric sparks. He proposed
just to run through the morrow's evidence with "our young
friend there"; and, having occasion to rise from his seat, he
gave Johnny a sounding clap on the back—the boy shrank from
him, like a cat that withdraws from under a strange hand. In
the course of the rehearsal Ocock more than once said: "Good
. . . good! Why, sonny, you're quite smart!" This was when
Johnny succeeded in grasping his drift. But at the least hint of
unreadiness, or hesitation, he tut-tutted, and drew his brows
together. And, as this went on, it seemed to Mahony that
Ocock was putting words into the boy's mouth; while Johnny,
intimidated, said yes and amen to things he could not possibly
know. Presently he interfered to this effect. Ocock brushed his
scruples aside. But after a second interruption from Mahony:
"I think, sir, with your permission, we will ask John not to depart from what he actually overheard," the lawyer shuffled his
papers into a heap, and said that would do for to-day; they
would meet at the court in the morning.— Prior to shaking
hands, however, he threw out a hint that he would like a word
with his brother on family matters. And so, for the next half-
hour Mahony paced the street below.

The remainder of the day was spent in keeping Johnny out
of temptation's way. Mahony tried to interest him in the life

of the city, in its monuments, and curiosities. But in vain. The
lad was too apathetic to look about him, and never opened his
mouth. Once only in the course of the afternoon did he offer a
kind of handle. In their peregrinations, they passed a Book
Arcade, where Mahony stopped to turn the leaves of a volume.
Johnny also took up a book, and began to read.

"What is it?" asked Mahony. "Would you like to have it,
my boy?"

Johnny stonily accepted the gift—it was a tale of Red In-
dians, the pages smudged with gaudy illustrations—and put it
under his arm.

At the good supper that was set before him, he picked with
a meagre zest; then fell asleep. Mahony took the opportunity
to write a line to Polly, to tell her of their safe arrival; and
having sealed the letter, ran out to post it. He was not absent
for more than three minutes, but when he came back, Johnny
was gone. He hunted high and low for him, ransacked the
place, without success: the boy had spoken to no one, nor had
he been seen to leave the coffee-room; and, as the clock-hands
were nearing twelve, Mahony was obliged to give up the
search and return to the hotel. It was impossible, at that hour,
to let Ocock know of this fresh piece of ill-luck. Besides, there
was just a chance the young scamp would turn up in the morning. Morning came, however, and no Johnny with it. Outwitted
and chagrined, Mahony set off for the court alone.

Day had broken dim and misty, and, by the time breakfast
was over, a north wind was raging—a furnace-like blast that
bore off the sandy deserts of the interior. The sun was a yellow
blotch in a copper sky; the thermometer had leapt up to a hundred and ten in the shade. Blinding clouds of coarse, gritty
dust swept house-high through the streets: half-suffocated,
Mahony fought his way along, his veil lowered, his handkerchief at his mouth. Outside those public-houses that advertised ice, crowds stood waiting their turn of entry; while
half-naked barmen, their linen trousers drenched with sweat,
worked like niggers to mix drinks which should quench these
bottomless thirsts. Mahony believed he was the only perfectly
sober person in the lobby of the court. Even Ocock himself
seemed to have been indulging.

This suspicion was confirmed by the lawyer's behaviour. No
sooner did Ocock espy him, than up he rushed, brandishing

the note that had been got to him early that morning—now, his eyes looked like little quivering dabs of pitch in his chalk-white face, and his manner, stripped of its veneer, let the real man show through.

"Curse it, sir, and what's the meaning of this, I'd like to know!" he cried, and struck at the sheet of notepaper with his free hand. "A pretty fix to put us in at the last minute, upon my word! It was your business, sir, to nurse your witness . . . after all the trouble I'd been to with him! What the devil do you expect us to do now?"

"The best you can. I understand that's what I pay you for."

Mahony had drawn himself up, and his face went pale under its top-dressing of dust and moisture. To Ocock's gross: "Well, it's your own look-out, confound you!—entirely your own look-out!" he returned a cool: "Certainly," then moved to one side and took up his stand in a corner of the hall, out of the way of the jostle and bustle, the constant going and coming, that gave the hinges of the door no rest.

When, after a weary wait, the time came to enter court, he continued to give Ocock, who had been deep in consultation with his clerk, a wide berth, and moved forward among a number of other people. A dark, ladder-like stair led to the upper story. While he was mounting this, some words exchanged in a low tone behind him arrested his attention.

"Are you O.K., old man?"

"Yes, if our client doesn't give us away. But he has to be handled like a hot—" Here the sentence snapped, for Mahony, bitten by a sudden doubt, faced sharply round. But it was a stranger who uncivilly accused him of treading on his toe.

The court—it was not much more than twenty feet square—was like an ill-smelling oven. Every chink and crack had been stopped against the searing wind; and the atmosphere was a brew of all the sour odours, the offensive breaths, given off by the two-score odd people crushed within its walls. In spite of precautions, the dust had got in: it lay thick on sills, desks and papers, gritted between the teeth, made the throat raspy as a file.

Mahony had given up all hope of winning his case, and looked forward to the sorry pleasure of assisting at a miscarriage of justice. During the speech for the plaintiff, however, he began to see the matter in another light.— Not so much thanks to the speaker, as in spite of him. Plaintiff's counsel was a common little fellow, of ungainly appearance: a double roll of fat bulged over the neck of his gown, and his wig, hastily re-donned after a breathing-space, sat askew. Nor was he anything of an orator: he stumbled over his sentences, and once or twice lost his place altogether, through hitting out at a blow-fly that buzzed between his eyes and the page. To his dry presentment of the case, nobody seemed to pay any heed. The habitués of the court whispered and fidgeted, sidling out from the school bench forms, foolscap in hand, to trickle confidences into one another's ears. The judge, tired of wiping his spectacles dry, leant back and closed his eyes. Mahony believed he slept, as did also some of the jurors, deaf to the citation of Dawes *v.* Peck and Dunlop *v.* Lambert, to many a reference to the Carriers' Act; to the assertion that the carrier was the agent, the goods were accepted, the property had "passed." This "passing" of the property was evidently a strong point; the plaintiff's name itself was not much oftener on the speaker's lips. And it was "Mr. Bolliver" here, and "Mr. Bolliver" there.— "The absconding driver, my Lord, was a personal friend of the defendant's. Mr. Bolliver never knew him; hence could not engage him.— Had this person not been thrust upon him, Mr. Bolliver would have employed the same carrier as on a previous occasion."— And on and on, in the same strain.

Mahony listened intently, his hand at his ear, that organ not being keyed up to the mutterings and mumblings of justice. And for all the dullness of the subject-matter, and counsel's lack of eloquence, his interest did not flag. It was the first time he heard the case for the other side stated plainly; and he was dismayed to find how convincing it was. Put thus, it must surely gain over every honest, straight-thinking man. In comparison, the points Ocock was going to advance shrank to mere legal quibbles and hair-splitting evasions.

Then the plaintiff himself went into the witness-box—and Mahony's feelings became involved, as well. This his adversary!—this poor old mangy grey-beard, who stood blinking a pair of rheumy eyes, and weakly smiling. One did not pit oneself against such human flotsam. Drunkard was stamped on every inch of the man, but this morning, in odd exception to the well-primed crew around him, he was sober—bewilderedly sober—and his shabby clothing was brushed, his frayed collar clean. Mahony, recognising the pitiful bid for sympathy, caught himself thinking: "Good Lord! I could have supplied him with a coat he'd have cut a better figure in, than that."

Bolliver clutched the edge of the box with his two hands. His unusual condition was a hindrance rather than a help to him; without a peg or two, his woolly thoughts were not to be disentangled. He stammered forth his evidence, halting either to piece together what he was going to say, or to recollect what he had just said—it was clear he went in mortal fear of contradicting himself. The scene was painful enough while he faced his own counsel, but, when counsel for the defence rose, a half-hour followed in which Mahony wished himself far from the court.

Bolliver could not come to the point. Counsel was merciless and coarsely jocose, and brought off several laughs. His victim wound his knotty hands in and out, and swallowed oftener than he had saliva for, in a forlorn endeavour to evade the pitfalls artfully dug for him. More than once he threw a covert glance, that was like an appeal for help, at all the indifferent faces. Mahony drooped his head, that their eyes should not meet.

In high feather at the effect he was producing, counsel inserted his left arm under his gown, and held the stuff out from his back with the tips of all five fingers.

"And now you'll p'raps have the goodness to tell us whether you've ever had occasion to send goods by a carrier before, in the course of your young life?"

"Yes." It was a humble monosyllable, returned without spirit.

"Then of course you've heard of this Murphy before?"

"N . . . no, I haven't," answered Bolliver, and let his vacillating eyes wander to the judge, and back.

"You tell that to the marines!" And after half a dozen other tricky questions: "I put it to you, it's a well-known fact that he's been a carrier hereabouts for the last couple o' years or more?"

"I don't know— I sup . . . sup-pose so." Bolliver's tongue grew heavy, and tripped up his words.

"And yet you've the cheek, you old rogue, you, to insinuate that this was a put-up job?"

"I . . . I only say what I heard."

"I don't care a button what you heard, or didn't hear. What I ask is, my pretty, do you yourself say so?"

"The . . . the defendant recommended him."

"I put it to you, this man Murphy was one of the best known carriers in Melbourne, and *that* was why the defendant recommended him—are you out to deny it?"

"N . . . n . . . no."

"Then you can stand down!"—and leaning over to Grindle, who was below him, counsel whispered, with a pleased spread of the hand: "There you are!—that's our case."

There was a painful moment just before Bolliver left the witness-box. As if become suddenly alive to the sorry figure he had cut, he turned to the judge, clasped his hands and exclaimed: "My Lord, if the case goes against me, I'm done . . . stony-broke! And the defendant's got a down on me, my Lord —'e's made up his mind to ruin me. Though 'e knows right enough 'e's in the wrong. Look at him a-setting there—a hard man, a mean man, if ever you saw one! What would the bit of money 'ave meant to 'im! But . . ."

He was rudely silenced and hustled away, to a sharp rebuke from the judge, who woke up to give it. All eyes were turned on Mahony. Under the fire of observation—they were comparing him, he knew, with the poor old Jeremy Diddler yonder, to the latter's disadvantage—his spine stiffened, and he held himself nervously erect. But, the quizzing at an end, he fumbled with his finger at his neck—his collar seemed to have grown too tight.— And outside, the hot blast, dark with dust, flung itself against the corners of the house, and howled, like a soul in pain.

Counsel for the defence made an excellent impression. "Naturally! *I* can afford to pay a better-class man," was Mahony's caustic note. He had fallen to scribbling on a sheet of paper, and was resigned to sitting through an adept presentment of Ocock's shifts and dodges.— But the opening words made him prick up his ears.

"My Lord," said counsel, "I submit there is here no case to go to the jury. No written contract existed between the parties, to bring it within the Statute of Frauds. Therefore, the plaintiff must prove that the defendant accepted these goods. Now I submit to you, on the plaintiff's own admission, that the

107

man Murphy was a common carrier. Your Lordship will know the cases of Hanson *v.* Armitage and various others, in which it has been established, beyond doubt, that a carrier is not an agent to accept goods."

The judge had revived, and, while counsel called the quality of the undelivered goods in question, and laid stress on the fact of no money having passed, he turned the pages of a thick red book with a moistened thumb. Having found what he sought, he pushed up his spectacles, opened his mouth, and, his eyes bent meditatively on the speaker, picked a back tooth with the nail of his first finger.

"Therefore," concluded counsel, "I hold that there is no question of fact to go to the jury. I do not wish to occupy your Lordship's time any further upon this submission. I have my client here, and all his witnesses are in court, whom I am prepared to call, should your Lordship decide against me on the present point. But I do submit that the plaintiff, on his own showing, has made out no case; and that, under the circumstances, upon his own evidence, this action must fail."

At the reference to the witnesses, Mahony dug his pencil into the paper till the point snapped.— So this was their little game! And should the bluff not work. . . ? He sat rigid, staring at the chipped fragment of lead, and did not look up throughout the concluding scene of the farce.

It was over; the judge had decided in his favour. He rose to his feet, with the one wish to get away from the place—and his coat-sleeve swept the dust off the entire length of the ledge in front of him. But before he reached the foot of the stairs, Grindle came flying down to say that Ocock wished to speak to him. Very good, replied Mahony, he would call at the office in the course of the afternoon. But the clerk left the court-house at his side. And suddenly the thought flashed through Mahony's mind: "The fellow suspects me of trying to do a bolt —of wanting to make off without paying my bill!"

The leech-like fashion in which Grindle stuck to his heels was not to be misread. "This is what they call nursing, I suppose—he's nursing *me* now!" said Mahony to himself. At the same time he reckoned up, with some anxiety, the money he had in his pocket. Should it prove insufficient, who knew what further affronts were in store for him!

But Ocock had recovered his oily sleekness.

"A close shave that, sir, a *ve-ry* close shave! With Warnock on the bench, I thought we could manage to pull it off. Had it been Guppy now! . . . Still, all's well that ends well, as the poet says!— And now for a trifling matter of business."

"To what extent am I indebted to you?"

The bill—it was already drawn up—for "solicitor's and client's costs" came to twenty odd pounds. Mahony paid it, then took his leave, and stalked out of the office.

But this was still not all. Once again, Grindle ran after him, and pinned him to the floor.

"I say, Mr. Mahony, a rare joke—gad, it's enough to make you burst your sides! That old thingumbob, the plaintiff, ye know, now what'n earth d'you think 'e's been an' done? Gets outer court like one o'clock—'e'd a sorter rabbit-fancyin' business in 'is backyard. Well, 'ome 'e trots, an' slits the guts of every blamed bunny, an' chucks the bloody corpses inter the street. Oh lor! What do you say to that, eh? Unfurnished in the upper story, what? Heh, heh, heh!"

As Mahony stepped on to the pavement, he was met by a rush of cold air. Within a quarter of an hour, the wind had swung round to the south, the temperature dropped some forty degrees. He paused to button his coat, to expand his lungs in a deep, invigorating breath. And, as he stood, he had a sudden, swift vision of little Polly: he saw her running out to wave her handkerchief in farewell, as she had done—could it actually be only yesterday morning? She had worn a lilac print gown, had looked adorably cool and fresh, in the parched, dusty heat.— But indeed had one ever seen Polly otherwise? In this moment, after the experience he had come through, she seemed to him the embodiment of all that was pure, and clean, and sweet. A wave of homesickness broke over him.— Now, just to be safe back with her once more, in the shelter of his own four walls.

[3]

How truly "home" the poor little gimcrack shanty had become to him, he grasped only when he once more crossed its threshold, and Polly's arms lay round his neck.

His search for Johnny Ocock had detained him in Melbourne for over a week. Under the guidance of young Grindle, he had scoured the city, not omitting even the dens of infamy in the Chinese quarter; and he did not know which to be more saddened by: the revolting sights he saw, or his guide's proud familiarity with every shade of vice. But nothing could be heard of the missing lad; and, at the suggestion of Henry Ocock, he put an advertisement in the *Argus,* offering a substantial reward for news of Johnny, alive or dead.

While waiting to see what this would bring forth, he paid a visit to John Turnham. It had not been part of his scheme to trouble his new relatives on this occasion; he bore them a grudge for the way they had met Polly's overture. But he was at his wits' end how to kill time: chafing at the delay was his main employment, if he were not worrying over the thought of having to appear before old Ocock, without his son. So, one midday, he called at Turnham's place of business in Flinders Lane, and was affably received by John, who carried him off to lunch at the Melbourne Club.

Turnham was a warm partisan of the diggers' cause. He had addressed a mass meeting held in Melbourne, soon after the fight on the Eureka; and he now roundly condemned the government's policy of repression.

"I am, as you are aware, my dear Mahony, no sentimentalist. But these rioters of yours seem to me the very type of man the country needs. Could we have a better bedrock on which to build, than these fearless champions of liberty?"

He set an excellent meal before his brother-in-law, and himself ate and drank heartily, unfolding his very table-napkin with a kind of relish. In lunching, he inquired the object of Mahony's journey to town. At the mention of Henry Ocock's name, he raised his eyebrows and pursed his lips.

"Ah, indeed! Then it is hardly necessary to ask the upshot."

He pooh-poohed Mahony's intention of staying till the defaulting witness was found; disapproved, too, the offer of a reward. "To be paid out of *your* pocket, of course! No, my dear Mahony, set your mind at rest and return to your wife. Lads of that sort never come to grief—more's the pity!— By the bye, how *is* Polly, and how does she like life on the diggings?"

In this connection, Mahony tendered congratulations on the expected addition to Turnham's family. John embarked readily enough on the theme of his beautiful wife; but into his voice, as he talked, came a note of impatience, or annoyance, which

110

formed an odd contrast to his wonted self-possession.— "Yes
. . . her third, and, for some reason which I cannot fathom, it
threatens to prove the most trying of any."— And here he went
into medical detail on Mrs. Emma's state.

Mahony, having heard him out, urged his compliance with
the whims of the mother-to-be, even did they seem extravagant. "Believe me, at a time like this, such moods and caprices
have their use. Nature very well knows what she is about."

"Nature? Bah! I am no great believer in nature," gave back
John, and emptied his glass of madeira. "Nature exists, sir, to
be coerced and improved."

They parted; and Mahony went back to twirl his thumbs in
the hotel coffee-room. He could not persuade himself to take
Turnham's advice and leave Johnny to his fate. For all the distance at which he held his fellow-creatures, he was linked to
them, the meanest not excepted, by a thousand subtle bonds,
of which a nature like Turnham's knew nothing.

And the delay was nearly over. At dawn next morning
Johnny was found lying, in a pitiable condition, at the door
of the hotel. It took Mahony the best part of the day to rouse
him; to make him understand he was not to be horsewhipped;
to purchase a fresh suit of clothing for him: to get him, in
short, halfway ready to travel the following day—a blear-eyed,
weak-witted craven, who fell into a cold sweat at every bump
of the coach. Not till they reached the end of the disagreeable
journey—even a Chinaman rose to impudence about Johnny's
nerves, his foul breath, his cracked lips—did Mahony learn
how the wretched boy had come by the money for his debauch. At the public-house in Main Street where the coach
drew up, old Ocock stood grimly waiting, with a leather thong
at his belt, and the news that his till had been broken open and
robbed of its contents.— With an involuntary recommendation
to mercy, Mahony handed over the culprit, and turned his
steps home.

Polly stood on tip-toe to kiss him; Pompey barked till the
roof rang, making leaps that fell wide of the mark; the cat
hoisted its tail, and wound purring in and out between his legs.
Tea was spread, on a clean cloth, with all sorts of good things
to eat; an English mail had brought him a batch of letters and
journals.— Altogether, it was a very happy homecoming.

When he had had a sponge-down—he wished it was possible

to rid the mind of impressions as easily as the body of dust—and finished tea, over which he listened, with a zest that surprised him, to a hundred and one domestic details: afterwards, he and Polly strolled arm-in-arm to the top of the little hill to which, before marriage, he used to carry her letters. Here, they sat and talked till night fell; and, for the first time, Mahony tasted the dregless pleasure of coming back from the world outside, with his toll of adventure, and being met by a woman's lively and disinterested sympathy. Agreeable incidents gained, those that were the reverse of pleasing lost their sting, by being shared with Polly. Not that he told her everything: he was never for dimming the ingenuous surface of a woman's mind with sordid business concerns; and of the dark side of life he greatly preferred Polly to remain ignorant. Still, as far as it went, it was a delightful experience. In return, he confessed to her something of the uncertainty that had beset him, on hearing his opponent's counsel state the case for the other side. It was disquieting to think he might be suspected of advancing a claim that was not strictly just.

"Suspected! . . . you? Oh, how could anybody be so silly!" said little Polly, and stole a loving glance at her husband. Surely, no one could look at Richard and for a moment doubt his honesty? But, for the case that such people existed, she gave the arm through which hers lay, a tender little squeeze.

For all the fatigues of his day, Mahony could not sleep. And after tossing and tumbling for some time, he rose, threw on his clothing, and went out to smoke a pipe in front of the store. Various worries were pecking at him—the hint he had given Polly of their existence seemed to have let them fairly loose upon him. Of course he would be—he was—suspected of having connived at the imposture by which his suit had been won —why else have put it in the hands of such a one as Ocock? John Turnham's soundless whistle of astonishment recurred to him, and flicked him.— Imagine it! He, Richard Mahony, giving his sanction to these queasy tricks!

It was bad enough, whatever outsiders thought of him, to know that Ocock at any rate had believed him not averse to winning by unjust means. Yet, on the whole, he thought this mortified him less than to feel that he had been written down a Simple Simon, whom it was easy to impose on. Ah, well! At best he had been but a kind of guy, set up for them to let off their verbal fireworks round. Faith, and that was all these lawyer-fellows wanted—the ghost of an excuse for parading their skill. Justice played a negligible rôle in this battle of wits; else not he, but the plaintiff, would have come out victorious.— That wretched Bolliver! . . . the memory of him wincing and flushing in the witness-box would haunt him for the rest of his days. He could see him, too, with equal clearness, broken-heartedly slitting the gizzards of his pets. A poor old derelict—the amen to a life which, like most lives, had once been flush with promise. And it had been his, Mahony's, honourable portion to give the last kick, the ultimate shove into perdition. Why, he would rather have lost the money ten times over!— And once more the old impatience took him, to be done, for ever, with the odious trinity—place, people, and the sordid occupation in which an ugly experience of this kind was just part and parcel of the day's work.

To divert his mind, he began next morning to make an inventory of the goods in the store. It was high time, too: thanks to the recent disturbances, he did not know where he stood. And while he was about it, he gave the place a general clean-up. A job of this kind was a powerful ally in keeping edged thoughts at bay. He and his men had their hands full for several days on end, Polly, who was not allowed to set foot in the store, peeping critically in at them to see how they progressed.— And, after business hours, there was little Polly herself.

He loved to contemplate her.

Six months of married life had worked certain changes in his black-eyed slip of a girl; but something of the doe-like shyness that had caught his fancy still clung to her. With strangers, she could even yet be touchingly bashful. Not long out of short frocks, she found it difficult to stand upon her dignity as Mrs. Dr. Mahony. Besides that, it was second nature to Polly to efface herself, to steal mousily away. Unless, of course, some one needed help, or was in distress, in which case she forgot to be shy. To her husband's habits and idiosyncrasies she had adapted herself implicitly—but this came easy; for she was sure everything Richard did was right, and that his way of looking at things was the one and only way. So there was no room for discord between them. By this time, Polly could laugh over the dismay of her first home-coming: the

113

pitch-dark night and unfamiliar road, the racket of the sere-
nade, the apparition of the great spider: now, all this might
have happened to somebody else, not Polly Mahony. Her dislike of things that creep and crawl was, it is true, inborn, and
persisted; but nowadays, if one of the many "triantelopes" that
infested the roof showed its hairy legs, she had only to call
Hempel, and out the latter would pop, with a broom-stick, to
do away with the creature. If a scorpion or a centipede wriggled from under a log, the cry of "Tom!" would bring the idle
lad next door, double-quick over the fence. Polly had learnt
not to summon her husband on these occasions; for Richard
held to the maxim: "Live and let live." If, at night, a tarantula appeared on the bedroom-wall, he caught it in a covered glass and carried it outside: "Just to come in again!" was
his wife's rueful reflection.— But, indeed, Polly was surrounded
by willing helpers. And small wonder, thought Mahony. Her
young nerves were so sound that Hempel's dry cough never
grated them: she doctored him, and fussed over him, and was
worried that she could not cure him. She met Long Jim's grumbles with a sunny face, and listened patiently to his forebod-
ings that he would never see "home" or his old woman again.
She even brought out a clumsy good-will in the young varmint, Tom; nor did his old father's want of refinement repel
her.

"But, Richard, he's such a kind old man!" she met her husband's admission of this stumbling-block. "And it isn't his fault
that he wasn't properly educated. He has had to work for his
living ever since he was twelve years old."

And Mr. Ocock cried quits by remarking confidentially:
"That little lady o' yours 'as got 'er 'eadpiece screwed on the
right way. It beats me, doc., why you don't take 'er inter the
store and learn 'er the bizness.— No offence, I'm sure!" he made
haste to add, disconcerted by Mahony's cold stare.

Had anyone at this date tried to tell Polly she lived in a
mean, rough home, he would have had a poor reception. Polly
was long since certain that not a house on the diggings could
compare with theirs. This was a trait Mahony loved in her—
her sterling loyalty; a loyalty that embraced not only her dear
ones themselves, but every stick and stone belonging to them.
His discovery of it helped him to grasp her allegiance to her
own multi-coloured family: in the beginning, he had almost

114

doubted its sincerity. Now, he knew her better. It was just as though a sixth sense had been implanted in Polly, enabling her to pierce straight through John's self-sufficiency, or Ned's vapourings, to the real kernel of goodness that no doubt lay hid below. He himself could not get at it; but then, his powers of divination were the exact opposite of Polly's. He was always struck by the weak or ridiculous side of a person first, and had to dig laboriously down to the virtues. While his young wife, by a kind of genius, saw the good at a glance— and saw nothing else. And she did not stint with her gift, did not hoard it up solely for use on her own kith and kin. Her splendid sympathy was the reverse of clannish; it was applied to every mortal who crossed her path.

Yes, for all her youth, Polly had quite a character of her own; and even thus early her husband sometimes ran up against a certain native sturdiness of opinion. But this did not displease him; on the contrary, he would not have thanked you for a wife who was only an echo of himself. To take the case of the animals. He had a profound respect for those creatures to which speech has been denied; and he treated the four-footers that dwelt under his roof, as his fellows, humanising them, reading his own thoughts into them, and showing more consideration for their feelings than if they had been able to speak up for themselves. Polly saw this in the light of an exquisite joke. She was always kind to Pompey and the stately Palmerston, and would as soon have forgotten to set Richard's dinner before him as to feed the pair; but they remained "the dog" and "the cat" to her, and, if they had enough to eat, and received neither kicks nor blows, she could not conceive of their souls asking more. It went beyond her to study the cat's dislike to being turned off his favourite chair, or to believe that the dog did not make dirty prints on her fresh scrubbed floor out of malice prepense; it was also incredible that he should have doggy fits of depression, in which up he must, to stick a cold, slobbery snout into a warm human hand. And when Richard tried to conciliate Palmerston stalking sulky to the door, or to pet away the melancholy in the rejected Pompey's eyes, Polly had to lay down her sewing and laugh at her husband, so greatly did his behaviour amuse her.

Again, there was the question of literature. Books, to Mahony, were almost as necessary as bread; to his girl-wife, on

115

the other hand, they seemed a somewhat needless luxury—less vital by far than the animals that walked the floor. She took great care of the precious volumes Richard had had carted up from Melbourne; but the cost of the transport was what impressed her most. It was not an overstatement, thought Mahony, to say that a stack of well-chopped, neatly piled wood meant more to Polly than all the books ever written. Not that she did not enjoy a good story: her work done, she liked few things better; and he often smiled at the ease with which she lived herself into the world of make-believe, knowing, of course, that it *was* make-believe, and just a kind of humbug.— But poetry, and the higher fiction! Little Polly's professed love for poetry had been merely a concession to the conventional idea of girlhood; or, at best, such a burning wish to be all her Richard desired, that, at the moment, she was convinced of the truth of what she said. But did he read to her from his favourite authors her attention *would* wander, in spite of the efforts she made to pin it down.

Mahony declaimed:

> *'Tis the sunset of life gives us mystical lore,*
> *And coming events cast their shadows before,*

and his pleasure in the swing of the couplet was such that he repeated it.

Polly wakened with a start. Her thoughts had been miles away—had been back at the "Family Hotel." There Purdy, after numerous adventures, had at length betaken himself, his poor leg a mass of suppuration, to be looked after by his Tilly; and Polly's hopes were all alight again.

She blushed guiltily at the repetition, and asked her husband to say the lines once again. He did so.

"But they don't really, Richard, do they?" she said in an apologetic tone—she referred to the casting of shadows. "It would be so useful if they did"—and she drew a sigh at Purdy's dilatory treatment of the girl who loved him so well.

"Oh, you prosaic little woman!" cried Mahony, and laid down his book to kiss her. It was impossible to be vexed with Polly: she was so honest, so transparent. "Did you never hear of a certain something called poetic license?"

No: Polly was more or less familiar with various other forms of license, from the gold-diggers' that had caused all the fuss, down to the special license by which she had been married; but this particular one had not come her way. And on Richard explaining to her the liberty poets allowed themselves, she shifted uncomfortably in her chair, and was sorry to think he approved. It seemed to her just a fine name for wanton exaggeration—if not something worse.

There were also those long evenings they spent over the first hundred pages of *Waverley*. Mahony, eager for her to share his enthusiasm, comforted her each night anew that they would soon reach the story proper, and then, how interested she would be! But the opening chapters were a sandy desert of words, all about people duller than any Polly had known alive; and sometimes, before the book was brought out, she would heave a secret sigh—although, of course, she enjoyed sitting cosily together with Richard, watching him, and listening to his voice. But they might have put their time to pleasanter use: by talking of themselves, or their friends, or how further to improve their home, or what the store was doing.

Mahony saw her smiling to herself one evening; and, after assuring himself that there was nothing on the page before him to call that pleased look to her young face, he laid the book down, and offered her a penny for her thoughts. But Polly was loath to confess to woolgathering.

"I haven't succeeded in interesting you, have I, Pollikins?"

She made haste to contradict him. Oh, it was very nice, and she loved to hear him read.

"Come, honestly now, little woman!"

She faced him squarely at that, though with pink cheeks. "Well, not much, Richard."

He took her on his knee. "And what were you smiling at?"

"Me? Oh, I was just thinking of something that happened yesterday"—and Polly sat up, agog to tell.

It appeared that the day before, while he was out, the digger's wife who did Polly's rough work for her had rushed in, crying that her youngest was choking. Bonnetless, Polly had flown across to the woman's hut. There she discovered the infant, a fat dumpling of a year or so, purple in the face, with a button wedged in its throat. Taking it by the heels, she shook it vigorously, upside-down; and, lo and behold! this had the opposite effect to what she had intended. When they straightened the child out again, the button was found to have passed the danger-point and gone down. Quickly resolved, Polly cut slice on slice of thin bread-and-butter, and with this, she and Mrs. Hemmerde stuffed the willing babe, till full to bursting, it warded them off with its tiny hands.

Mahony laughed heartily at the tale, and applauded his wife's prompt measures. "Short of the forceps, nothing could have been better!"

Yes, Polly had a dash of native shrewdness, which he prized. — And a pair of clever hands that were never idle. He had given her leave to make any changes she chose in the house, and she was for ever stitching away at white muslin, or tacking it over pink calico. These affairs made their little home very spick and span, and kept Polly from feeling dull—if one could imagine Polly dull!— With the cooking alone had there been a hitch in the beginning. Like a true expert, Mrs. Beamish had not tolerated understudies: none but the lowliest jobs, such as raisin-stoning or potato-peeling, had fallen to the three girls' share: and, in face of her first fowl, Polly stood helpless and dismayed. But not for long. Sarah was applied to, for the best cookery-book on sale in Melbourne, and when this arrived, Polly gave herself up to the study of it. She had many failures, both private and avowed. With the worst, she either retired behind the wood stack, or Tom disposed of them for her, or the dog ate them up. But she persevered: and soon Mahony could with truth declare that no one raised a better loaf, or had a lighter hand at pastry than his wife.

Three knocks on the wooden partition was the signal which, if he were not serving a customer, summoned him to the kitchen.

"Oh, Richard, it's risen beautifully!" And Polly, red with heat and pride, drew a great golden-crusted, blown-up sponge-cake along the oven shelf.

Richard, who had a sweet tooth, pretended to be unable to curb his impatience.

"Wait! First I must see . . ." and she plunged a knife into the cake's heart: it came out untarnished. "Yes, it's done to a turn."

There and then it was cut; for, said Mahony, that was the only way in which he could make sure of a piece. Afterwards, chunks were dealt out to every one Polly knew—to Long Jim, Hempel, Tommy Ocock, the little Hemmerdes. Side by side on the kitchen-table, their feet dangling in the air, husband and wife sat, boy-and-girl fashion, and munched hot cake, till their appetites for dinner were wrecked.

But the rains that heralded winter—and they set in early that year—had not begun to fall, when more serious matters claimed Mahony's attention.

[4]

IT WAS an odd and inexplicable thing that business showed no signs of improving.— Affairs on Ballarat had for months past run their usual prosperous course. The western township seemed to grow from day to day, and was straggling right out to the banks of the great swamp. On the Flat, the deep sinking that was at present the rule—some parties actually touched a depth of three hundred feet, before bottoming—had brought a fresh host of fortune-hunters to the spot, and the results obtained bid fair to rival those of the first golden year. The diggers' grievances, and their conflict with the government, were now a turned page. At a state trial, all prisoners had been acquitted, and a general amnesty declared for those rebels who were still at large. Unpopular ministers had resigned, or died; a new constitution for the colony awaited the Royal assent; and pending this, two of the rebel-leaders, now prominent townsmen, were chosen to sit in the Legislative Council. The future could not have looked rosier.— For others, that is. For him, Mahony, it held more than one element of uncertainty.

At no time had he come near making a fortune out of storekeeping. For one thing, he had been too squeamish. From the outset, he had declined to soil his hands with surreptitious grog-selling; nor would he be a party to that evasion of the law which consisted in overcharging on other goods, and throwing in drinks free. Again, he would rather have been hamstrung than have stooped to the tricks in vogue with regard to the weighing of gold-dust: the greased scales, the wet sponge, false beams, and so on. Accordingly he had a clearer conscience than the majority, and a lighter till.— Another reason, he believed, for his mediocre success, was that he had not been enterprising enough. Having once got a roof over his head, he had remained sitfast; he had had neither the *vis* nor the initiative to trapse the country in the wake of new rushes —whether merely from side to side of the great basin of Ballarat, or a hundred miles north to the Ovens—in order that, simultaneously with the pegging-out of the first claim, there should rise, as if by magic, a store equipped with all the necessaries of life.— Even at the legitimate ABC of business, he had proved a duffer. He had never, for instance, learned to be a really skilled hand at stocking a shop. Was an out-of-the-way article called for, ten to one he had run short of it; and the born shopman's knack of palming off, or persuading to, a makeshift, was not his. Such goods as he had, he did not press on people; his attitude was always that of "take it or leave it"; and he sometimes surprised a ridiculous feeling of satisfaction in himself, when he chased a drunken and insolent customer off the premises, or secured an hour's leisure unbroken by the jangle of the store-bell.

Still, in spite of everything, he had, till recently, done well enough. Money was loose, and the diggers, if given long credit when down on their luck, were in the main to be relied on to pay up, when they struck the lead or tapped a pocket. He had had slack seasons before now, and things had always come right again.— This made it hard for him to explain the present prolonged spell of dullness.

That there was something more than ordinarily wrong first dawned on him during the stock-taking in summer. Hempel and he were constantly coming upon goods that had been too long on hand, and were now fit only to be thrown away. Half-a-dozen boxes of currants showed a respectable growth of mould; a like fate had come upon some flitches of bacon; and not a bag of flour but had developed a species of minute maggot. Rats had got at his coils of rope, one of which, sold in all good faith, had gone near causing the death of the digger who used it. The remains of some smoked fish were brought back and flung at his head, with a shower of curses, by a woman who had fallen ill through eating of it.— And yet, in spite of the replenishing this involved, the order for goods he sent to town, that season, was the smallest he had ever given. For the first time, he could not fill a dray, but had to share one with a greenhorn, who, if you please, was setting up storekeeping at his very back-door. And the bulk of the load consisted of articles of female attire, women remaining his most loyal patrons.— A haberdasher! Good God! was this to be his unholy ending? It struck him as ten times worse than that of grocer or general purveyor.

He and Hempel cracked their brains to account for the falling off—or at least he did: afterwards, he believed Hempel had suspected the truth, and had been too mealy-mouthed to speak out. It was Polly who innocently—for of course he did not draw her into confidence—Polly supplied the clue, from a piece of gossip brought to the house by the woman Hemmerde. It appeared that, at the time of the rebellion, his open antagonism to the Ballarat Reform League had given offence all round—to the extremists, as well as to the more wary, on whose behalf the League was drafted. They now got even with him by taking their custom elsewhere.— Mahony snorted with indignation on hearing of it: then laughed ironically. He was now expected not only to bring his personal tastes and habits into line with those of the majority, but to deny his politics, as well. And if he refused to do so, they would make it hard for him to earn a decent living in their midst. Nothing seemed easier to these unprincipled democrats than for a man to cut his coat to suit his job.— Why, he might just as well turn Whig and be done with it! Every child knew that the Whigs had a special talent for acting Mr. Facing-Both-Ways.

He sat over his account-books. The pages were black with bad debts for "tucker." Here, however, was no mystery. The owners of these names—Purdy was among them—had without doubt been implicated in the Eureka riot, and had made off, and never returned.— He struck a balance, and found to his consternation that, unless business took a turn for the better, he would not be able to hold out beyond the end of the year. And even that would mean some contriving. Afterwards, he was blessed if he knew what was going to happen. The ingenious Hempel was full of ideas for tempting back fortune— opening a branch store on a new lead was one of them, or removing bodily to Main Street—but ready money was the *sine qua non* of such schemes, and ready money Mahony had not got. Since his marriage, he had put by as good as nothing; and the enlarging and improving of his house, at that time, had made a big hole in his bachelor savings. He did not feel justified at the present pass in drawing on them anew. For one thing, before summer was out there would be, if all went well, another mouth to feed. And that meant a variety of seen and unforeseen expenses.

Such were the material anxieties he had to encounter, in the course of that winter.— Below the surface, a subtler embarrassment worked to destroy his peace. In face of the shortage of money, he was obliged to thank his stars that he had not lost the miserable lawsuit of a few months back. Had that happened, he wouldn't at present have known where to turn. But this amounted to confessing his satisfaction at having pulled off his case, pulled it off anyhow, by no matter what crooked means; and was a bitter pill for his pride to swallow.— And as if this were not enough, the last words he had heard Purdy say came back to sting him anew. The boy had accused him of judging a fight for freedom from a tradesman's standpoint. Now, it might be said of him that he was viewing justice from the same angle. He had scorned the idea of distorting his political opinions to fit the trade by which he gained his bread. It was a far more serious thing if his principles, his character, his sense of equity, were all to be undermined as well. But if he stayed here, he would end by becoming as blunt to what was right and fair as the rest of them. As it was he was no longer able to regard the two great landmarks of man's moral development—liberty and justice—from the point of view of an honest man and a gentleman.

His self-annoyance was so great that it galvanised him to action. There and then, he made up his mind: as soon as the child that was coming to them was old enough to travel, he would sell out for whatever he could get, and go back to the old country. Once upon a time, he had hoped, when he went, to take a good round sum with him, towards a first-rate English practice. Now, he saw that this scheme had in truth been a kind of Jack-o'-lantern—a marshlight, after which he might have danced for years to come. As matters stood, he must needs be content if, the passage-moneys paid, he could scrape together enough to keep him afloat, till he found a modest corner to slip into. Influence and recommendations were, thanks to the long break in his medical connections, now hardly to be counted on.

His first impulse was to say nothing of this to his wife in the meantime. Why unsettle her?— But he had reckoned without the sudden upward leap his spirits took, once his decision was arrived at: the winter sky was blue as violets again, above him; he turned out light-heartedly of a morning. It was impossible to hide the change in his mood from Polly—even if he had felt it fair to do so. Another thing: when he came to study Polly by the light of his new plan, he saw that his scruples about unsettling her were fanciful—wraiths of his own imagining. As a matter of fact, the sooner he broke the news to her, the better. Little Polly was so thoroughly happy here, that she would need time to accustom herself to the prospect of life elsewhere.

He went about it very cautiously, though; and with no hint of the sour and sorry incidents that had driven him to the step. As was only natural, Polly was rather easily agitated at present: the very evening before, he had had occasion to blame himself for his tactless behaviour.

The way of it was this.— In her first sick young fear, Polly had impulsively written off to Mother Beamish, to claim the fulfilment of that good woman's promise to stand by her, when her time came. One letter gave another: Mrs. Beamish not only announced that she would hold herself ready to support her "little duck" at a moment's notice, but filled sheets with sage advice and old wives' maxims: and the correspondence, which had been languishing, flared up anew. Here, now, came an ill-scrawled, misspelt epistle from Tilly—doleful, too, for Purdy, it appeared, had once more quitted her without speaking the binding word—in which she told that Purdy's leg, though healed, was permanently shortened: the doctor in Geelong said he would never walk straight again.

Husband and wife sat and discussed the news, wondered how lameness would affect Purdy's future, and what he was doing now, Tilly not having mentioned his whereabouts.— "She has probably no more idea than we ourselves," said Mahony.

"I'm afraid not," said Polly with a sigh. "Well, I hope he won't come back here, that's all"; and she considered the seam she was sewing, with an absent air.

"Why, love? Don't you like old Dickybird?" asked Mahony, in no small surprise.

"Oh yes, quite well. But. . . ."

"Is it because he still can't make up his mind to take your Tilly—eh?"

"That, too. But chiefly because of something he said."

"And what was that, my dear?"

"Oh, very silly!"—and Polly smiled.

"Out with it, madam! Or I shall suspect the young dog of having made advances to *my* wife."

"Richard, *dear!*"— Little Polly believed her husband was in earnest, and grew exceedingly confused. "Oh no, nothing like that," she assured him, and with red cheeks rushed into an explanation. "He only said, in spite of you being such old friends, he felt you didn't really care to have him here on Ballarat. After a time, you always invented some excuse to get him away." But now that it was out, Polly felt the need of toning down the statement, and added: "I shouldn't wonder if he was silly enough to think you were envious of him, for having so many friends and being liked by all sorts of people."

"Envious of him? *I?* Who on earth has been putting such an idea as that into your head?" cried Mahony.

"It was 'mother' thought so—it was while I was still there," stammered Polly, still more fluttered by the fact of him fastening on just these words.

Mahony tried to quell his irritation by fidgeting round the room. "Surely, Polly, you might give up calling that woman 'mother,' now you belong to me—I thank you for the relationship!" he said testily. And having, with much unnecessary ado, knocked the ashes out of his pipe, he went on: "It's bad enough to say things of that kind, but to repeat them, love, is in even poorer taste."

"Yes, Richard," said Polly meekly.

But her amazed inner query was: "Not even to one's own husband?"

She hung her head, till the white thread of parting between the dark loops of her hair was almost perpendicular. She had spoken without reflecting in the first place—had just blurted out a passing thought. But even when forced to explain, she had never dreamt of Richard taking offence. Rather, she had imagined the two of them—two banded lovingly against one— making merry together over Purdy's nonsense. She had heard

124

her husband laugh away much unkinder remarks than this. And perhaps if she had stopped there, and said no more, it might have been all right. By her stupid attempt to gloss things over, she had really managed to hurt him, and had made him think her gossipy into the bargain.

She went on with her sewing.— But when Mahony came back from the brisk walk by means of which he got rid of his annoyance, he fancied, though Polly was as cheery as ever and had supper laid for him, that her eyelids were red.

This was why, the following evening, he promised himself to be discreet.

Winter had come in earnest; the night was wild and cold. Before the crackling stove, the cat lay stretched at full length, while Pompey dozed fitfully, his nose between his paws. The red-cotton curtains that hung at the little window gave back the lamplight in a ruddy glow; the clock—it had a loud and rather laboured tick—beat off the seconds evenly, except when drowned by the wind, which came in bouts, hurling itself against the corners of the house. And presently, laying down his book—Polly was too busy now to be read to—Mahony looked across at his wife. She was wrinkling her pretty brows over the manufacture of tiny clothes, a rather pale little woman still, none of the initial discomforts of her condition having been spared her. Feeling his eyes on her, she looked up and smiled: did ever anyone see such a ridiculous armhole? Three of one's fingers were enough to fill it—and she held the little shirt aloft for his inspection. Here was his chance: the child's coming offered the best of pretexts. Taking not only the midget garment, but also the hand that held it, he told her of his resolve to go back to England and re-enter his profession.

"You know, love, I've always wished to get home again. And now there's an additional reason, I don't want my . . . our children to grow up in a place like this. Without companions —or refining influences. Who knows how they would turn out?"

He said it, but in his heart he knew that his children would be safe enough. And Polly, listening to him, made the same reservation: yes, but *our* children. . . .

"And so I propose, as soon as the youngster's old enough to travel, to haul down the flag for good and all, and book passages for the three of us in some smart clipper.— We'll live in the country, love. Think of it, Polly!— A little gabled, red-roofed house, at the foot of some Sussex down, with fruit trees and a high hedge round it, and only the oast-houses peeping over. Doesn't it make your mouth water, my dear?"

He had risen, in his eagerness, and stood with his back to the stove, his legs apart. And Polly nodded and smiled up at him—though, truth to tell, the picture he drew did not mean much to her: she had never been in Sussex, nor did she know what an oast-house was. A night such as this, with flying clouds and a shrill, piping wind, made her think of angry seas and a dark ship's cabin, in which she lay deathly sick.— But it was not Polly's way to dwell on disagreeables: her mind glanced off to a pleasanter theme.

"Have you ever thought, Richard, how strange it will seem when there *are* three of us? You and I will never be quite alone together again.— Oh, I do hope he will be a good baby and not cry much. It will worry you if he does—like Hempel's cough. And then you won't love him properly."

"I shall love it because it is yours, my darling. And the baby of such a dear little mother is sure to be good."

"Oh, babies will be babies, you know!" said Polly, with a new air of wisdom which sat delightfully on her.

Mahony pinched her cheek. "Mrs. Mahony, you're shirking my question. Tell me now, should you not be pleased to get back to England?"

"I'll go wherever you go, Richard," said Polly staunchly. "Always. And of course I should like to see mother—I mean my real mother—again. But then Ned's here . . . and John, and Sarah. I should be very sorry to leave them. I don't think any of them will ever go home now."

"They may be here, but they don't trouble *you* often, my dear, I must say," said Mahony, with more than a hint of impatience. "Especially Ned, the well-beloved, who lives not a mile from your door."

"I know he doesn't often come to see us, Richard. But he's only a boy; and has to work so hard.— You see, it's like this. If Ned should get into any trouble, I'm here to look after him; and I know that makes mother's mind easier—Ned was always her favourite."

"And an extraordinary thing, too! I believe it's the boy's good looks that blind you women to his faults."

"Oh, no, indeed it isn't!" declared Polly warmly. "It's just because Ned's Ned. The dearest fellow, if you really know him."

"And so your heart's anchored here, little wife, and would remain here, even if I carried your body off to England?"

"Oh no, Richard," said Polly again. "My heart would always be where you are. But I can't help wondering how Ned would get on alone. And Jerry will soon be here, too, now, and he's younger still.— And *how* I should like to see dear Tilly settled before I go!"

Judging that enough had been said for the time being, Mahony re-opened his book, leaving his wife to chew the cud of innocent matchmaking and sisterly cares.

In reality, Polly's reflections were of quite another nature.

Her husband's abrupt resolve to leave the colony, disturbing though it was, did not take her altogether by surprise. There were things one could not help seeing: she would have needed to be both deaf and blind not to notice that the storebell rang much seldomer than it used to, and that Richard had more spare time on his hands. Yes, trade was dull, and that made him fidgety.— Now she had always known that someday it would be her duty to follow Richard to England. But she had imagined that day to be very far off—when they were elderly people, and had saved up a good deal of money. To hear the date fixed for six months hence was something of a shock to her.— And it was at this point that Polly had a sudden inspiration. As she listened to Richard talking of resuming his profession, the thought flashed through her mind: why not here? Why should he not start practice in Ballarat, instead of travelling all those thousands of miles to do it?

This was what she ruminated, while she tucked and hemmed.— She could imagine, of course, what his answer would be. He would say there were too many doctors on Ballarat already: not more than a dozen of them made satisfactory incomes; the majority just managed to rub along—or went insolvent. But this argument did not convince Polly. Richard wasn't, perhaps, a great success at storekeeping; but that was only because he was too good for it. As a doctor, he with his cleverness and gentlemanly manners would soon, she was certain, stand head and shoulders above the rest. And then, there would be money galore. It was true, he did not care for Ballarat—was down on both place and people. But this objection, too, Polly waived. It passed belief to her that anybody could actually dislike this big, rich, bustling, go-ahead township, where such handsome buildings were springing up, and every one was so friendly. In her heart of hearts, she ascribed her husband's want of love for it to the "infra dig" position he occupied. If he mixed with his equals again, and got rid of the feeling that he was looked down on, it would make all the difference in the world to him. He would then be out of reach of snubs and slights, and people would understand him better —not the residents on Ballarat alone, but also John, and Sarah, and the Beamishes, none of whom really appreciated Richard.— In her mind's eye Polly had a vision of him going his rounds, mounted on a chestnut horse, dressed in surtout and choker, and hand and glove with the bigwigs of society—the gentlemen at the Camp, the Police Magistrate and Archdeacon Long, the rich squatters who lived at the foot of Mount Buninyong.— It brought the colour to her cheeks merely to think of it.

She did not, however, breathe a word of this to Richard. She was a shade wiser than the night before, when she had vexed him by blurting out her thoughts. And the present was not the right time to speak. In these days, Richard was under the impression that she needed to be humoured. He might agree with her against his better judgment, or, worse still, pretend to agree. And Polly didn't want that. She wished fairly to persuade him that, by setting up here on the diggings, where he was known and respected—or even looked down on, but at least known—he would get on quicker, and make more money, than if he buried himself in some poky English village, where no one had ever heard of him before.

Meanwhile, the unconscious centre of her ambitions wore a perplexed frown.— Mahony was much exercised, just now, over the question of medical attendance for Polly in her illness. The thought of coming into personal contact with a member of the fraternity was distasteful to him; none of them had an inkling who or what he was. And while he was piqued by their unsuspectingness, he at the same time feared lest it should not be absolute, and he have the ill-luck to hit on a practitioner who had heard of his stray spurts of doctoring and written him down a charlatan and a quack. For this reason, he would call in no one in the immediate neighbourhood—even the western township seemed too near. Ultimately, his choice fell on a man named Rogers who hailed from Mount Pleasant, the rise on the opposite side of the valley, and some two miles off. It was true, since he did not intend to disclose his own standing, the distance would make the fellow's fees mount up. But Rogers was at least properly qualified (while the half of those claiming the title of physician were impudent impostors, who didn't know a diploma from the Ten Commandments), of the same *alma mater* as himself—not a contemporary, though, he took good care of that!—and, if report spoke true, a skilful and careful obstetrician.

When, however, in response to a note carried by Long Jim, Rogers drew rein in front of the store, Mahony was not greatly impressed by him. He proved to be a stout, reddish man, some ten years Mahony's senior, with a hasty-pudding face and an undecided manner. There he sat, his ten spread finger-tips meeting and gently tapping one another across his paunch, and nodding: "Just so, just so!" to all he heard. He had the trick of saying everything twice over. "Needs to clinch his own opinion!" was Mahony's swift diagnosis. Himself, he kept in the background. And was he forced to come forward, his manner was both stiff and forbidding, so on tenterhooks was he lest the other should presume to treat him as anything but the storekeeper he gave himself out to be.

A day or so later, who but the wife must arrive to visit Polly! —a piece of gratuitous friendliness that could well have been dispensed with; even though Mahony felt it keenly that, at this juncture, Polly should lack companions of her own sex. But Rogers had married beneath him, and the sight of the pursy upstart—there were people on the Flat who remembered her running barefoot and slatternly—sitting there, in satin and feathers, lording it over his own little Jenny Wren, was more than Mahony could tolerate. The distance was put forward as an excuse for Polly not returning the call, and Polly was docile, as usual; though, for her part, she had thought her visitor quite a pleasant, kindly woman.— But then Polly never knew when she was being patronised!

To wipe out any little trace of disappointment, her husband suggested that she should write and ask one of the Beamish

129

girls to stay with her: it would keep her from feeling the days long.

But Polly only laughed. "Long?—when I have so much sewing to do?"

No, she did not want company. By now, indeed, she regretted having sent off that impulsive invitation to Mrs. Beamish for the end of the year. Puzzle as she would, she could not see how she was going to put "mother" comfortably up.

Meanwhile, the rains were changing the familiar aspect of the place. Creeks—in summer, dry gutters of baked clay—were now rich red rivers; and the yellow Yarrowee ran full to the brim, keeping those who lived hard by it, in a twitter of anxiety. The steep slopes of Black Hill showed thinly green; the roads were ploughed troughs of sticky mire. Occasional night frosts whitened the ground, bringing cloudless days in their wake. Then down came the rain once more, and fell for a week on end. The diggers were washed out of their holes, the Flat became an untraversable bog. And now there were floods in earnest: the creeks turned to foaming torrents, that swept away trees, and the old roots of trees; and the dwellers on the river banks had to fly for their bare lives.

Over the top of book or newspaper, Mahony watched his wife stitch, stitch, stitch, with a zeal that never flagged, at the dolly garments. Just as he could read his way, so Polly sewed hers, through the time of waiting. But whereas she, like a sensible little woman, pinned her thoughts fast to the matter in hand, he let his range freely over the future. Of the many good things this had in store for him, one in particular whetted his impatience. It took close on a twelve-month out here to get hold of a new book. On Ballarat, not even a stationer's existed; nor were there more than a couple of shops in Melbourne itself that could be relied on to carry out your order. You perforce fell behind in the race, remained ignorant of what was being said and done—in science, letters, religious controversy—in the great world overseas. To this day, he didn't know whether Agassiz had or had not been appointed to the chair of Natural History in Edinburgh; or whether fresh heresies with regard to the creation of species had spoiled his chances: did not know whether Hugh Miller had actually gone crazy over the *Vestiges;* or even if those arch-combatants, Syme and Simpson, had at length sheathed their swords.— Now, however, God willing, he would before very long be back in the thick of it all, in intimate touch with the doings of the most wideawake city in Europe; and new books and pamphlets would come into his possession as they dropped hot from the press.

[5]

AND then, one morning—it was spring now, and piping hot at noon—Long Jim brought home from the postoffice a letter for Polly, addressed in her sister Sarah's sloping hand. Knowing the pleasure it would give her, Mahony carried it at once to his wife; and Polly laid aside broom and duster, and sat down to read.

But he was hardly out of the room, when a startled cry drew him back to her side. Polly had hidden her face, and was shaken by sobs. As he could not get her to speak, Mahony picked up the letter from the floor, and read it himself.

Sarah wrote like one distracted.

Oh, my dear sister, how can I find words to tell you of the truly "awful" calamity that has befallen our unhappy brother. Mahony skipped the phrases, and learnt that, owing to a carriage accident, Emma Turnham had been prematurely confined, and, the best medical aid notwithstanding—*John spared absolutely "no" expense*—had died two days later. *John is like a madman. Directly I heard the "shocking" news, I at once threw up my engagement—at "serious" loss to myself, but that is a matter of small consequence—and came to take my place beside our poor dear brother in his great trial. But all my efforts to bring him to a proper and "Christian" frame of mind have been fruitless. I am indeed alarmed to be alone with him, and I tremble for the children, for he is possessed of an "insane" hatred for the sweet little loves. He has locked himself in his room, will see "no one" nor touch a "particle" of nourishment. Do, my dearest Polly, come at once on receipt of this, and help me in the "truly awful" task that has been laid upon me. My nervous system is too much to sustain me unaided. And pray forgive me for using this plain paper. I have had literally no time to order mourning "of any kind."*

So that was Sarah!— With a click of the tongue Mahony tossed the letter on the table, and made it clear to Polly that under no consideration would he allow her to attempt the journey to town. Her relatives seemed utterly to have forgotten her condition; if, indeed, they had ever grasped the fact that she was expecting a child.

But Polly did not heed him.— "Oh, poor, poor, Emma! Oh, poor dear John!"— Her husband could only soothe her by promising to go to Sarah's assistance himself, the following day.

Coaxing her to lie down, he bathed her tear-stained face.— They had been entirely in the dark about things. For John Turnham thought proper to erect a jealous wall about his family life, a wall of impenetrable reserve. What went on behind it was nobody's business but his own. You felt yourself—were meant to feel yourself—the alien, the outsider.— And Mahony marvelled once more at the wealth of love and sympathy his little Polly had kept fresh for these two, who had wasted so few of their thoughts on her.

Polly dried her eyes; he packed his carpet-bag. He did this with a good deal of pother, pulling open the wrong drawers, tumbling up their contents, and generally making havoc of his wife's arrangements. But the sight of his clumsiness acted as a kind of tonic on Polly: she liked to feel that he was dependent on her, for his material comfort and well-being.

They spoke of John's brief married life.

"He loved her like a pagan, my dear," said Mahony. "And if what your sister Sarah writes is not exaggerated, he is bearing his punishment for it in a truly pagan way."

"But you won't say that to him, dear Richard . . . will you? You'll be very gentle with him?" pleaded Polly anxiously.

"Indeed I shall, little woman. But one can't help thinking these things, all the same. You know it is written: 'Thou shalt have none other gods but Me.' "

"Yes, I know. But then this was *just* Emma . . . and she was so pretty and so good"—and Polly cried anew.

Mahony rose before dawn, to catch the early coach. Together with a packet of sandwiches, Polly brought him a small, dull-clothed black mantle.

"For Sarah, with my dear love. You see, Richard, I know she always wears coloured dresses. And she will feel so much happier if she has *something* black to put on." Little Polly's voice was deep with persuasion. Richard was none too well pleased, she could see, at having to unlock his bag again; she feared, too, that, after the letter of the day before, his opinion of Sarah had gone down to zero.

Mahony secured a corner seat; and so, though his knees interlocked with those of his *vis-à-vis,* only one of the eight inside passengers was jammed against him. The coach started; and the long, dull hours of the journey began to wear away. Nothing broke the monotony but speculations whether the driver—a noted tippler—would be drunk before Melbourne was reached, and capsize them; and the drawling voice of a Yankee prospector who told lying tales about his exploits in California, in '48, until, having talked his hearers to sleep, he dropped off himself. Then Mahony fell to reflecting on what lay before him. He didn't at all like the job. Though he was genuinely sorry for John Turnham, his sympathy had not been fired to just that pitch of explosiveness, which alone allowed him to interfere in another's private life. He was not one of your born good Samaritans: he relished intruding as little as being intruded on. Besides, morally to sustain, to forbear with a fellow-creature in misfortune, seemed to him as difficult and thankless a task as any required of one, here below. Infinite tact was essential, the power of putting yourself in the other's place, and, thirdly, a skin thick enough to stand all manner of snubs and rebuffs.— And here he smiled. "Or my little wife's inability to recognise them!"

The tragic suddenness of the death stirred his imagination. He recalled the dead woman as he had seen her for the first, and, as it proved, the last time. In her fair beauty, in her glorious young motherhood, she had seemed to him one of the most favoured of mortals. That was little over a year ago, and now, what living creature whose blood ran red would change with her? She had been rudely thrust forth into the great Uncertainty. . . . Why? For what reason? Was her death designed to break the pride of the man who, it might be, had let his love for her overlap the love due to his Maker? But this would imply that one soul was more precious than another, which was contrary to Christ's teaching. And, in this life, she had had a noble service to render humanity—he knew, indeed, none nobler: that of bearing healthy and beautiful children.— Again was it thinkable that so rare a creature had been fashioned,

133

only in her prime to be destroyed? It was as though a sculptor should pick up his mallet and wantonly shatter the work in which his art had touched perfection. The orthodox would no doubt reply: it was a mark of God's grace that she should be removed from a world of sin, and from the blight of time and decay; but this answer was equally unsatisfying. It took no account of the anguish of parting. How intensely must she have rebelled at being snatched from the arms of husband and children!— And if unconscious, blind to her approaching end, had she been prepared to face her Maker? From what he knew of her, Mahony judged not; he believed that her heart had been set on things temporal: the care of her beauty, social vanities, human loves. Small wonder, indeed, when one came to ponder it, that her adoring husband found it impossible to echo that meekest of utterances: "The Lord gave, and the Lord hath taken away; blessed be the name of the Lord!" Or to bow his head to the knowledge that the radiant being, round whom his life had turned, was now become a mere memory, and, as such, had but the frail houseroom a few poor human hearts could offer her.— Till these, too, forgot, and she died for the second time.

The old, harassing doubts and uncertainties! The difficulty of reconciling the divine benevolence with a cruel deed; the falling back once more on that trite admission of man's impotence: God moves in a mysterious way, His wonders to perform!— Some day, when his lines ran in smoother places, he would grapple with these questions, and get clear about them; so that, did calamity befall him, he might know where he stood. In the meantime, Polly's unreflecting words rang in his ears, and seemed to sum up all that was dark and unanswerable in what had happened.— "But this was *just* Emma. And she was so pretty and so good."

House and garden had lost their air of well-groomed smartness: the gate stood ajar, the gravel was unraked, the verandahflooring black with footmarks. All the blinds were down; the windows looked like so many dead eyes. Mahony's first knock brought no response; at his second, the door was opened by Sarah Turnham herself. But a very different Sarah this, from the elegant and sprightly young person who had graced his wedding. Her chignon was loose, her dress dishevelled. On recognising Mahony, she uttered a cry, and fell on his neck—

he had to disengage her arms by force. Pushing her into the parlour, where his first act was to raise the blind and throw up the window, he seated her on a chair, she passing from tears to a fit of shrill laughter, and back to tears. He spoke severely to her, and declared that he would go away again, if she carried out her intention of swooning.

At last he got her round so far that she could tell her tale, which she did with a hysterical overstatement. She had, it seemed, arrived there just before her sister-in-law died. John was quarrelling furiously with all three doctors, and, in the end, insulted the only one who was left, in such a fashion that he, too, marched out of the house. They had to get the dead woman measured, coffined, and taken away, by stealth; and thereupon, John had locked himself up in his room, and had never been seen since. He had a loaded revolver with him; through the closed door he had threatened to shoot both her and the children. The servants had deserted, panic-stricken at their master's behaviour, at the sudden collapse of the well-regulated household: the last, a nurse-girl, sent out on an errand some hours previously, had not returned. Sarah was at her wits' end to know what to do with the children—he might hear them screaming at this moment.

Mahony, in no hesitancy, now, how to deal with the situation, laid his hat aside and drew off his gloves. "Prepare some food," he said briefly. "A glass of port and a sandwich or two, if you can manage nothing else—but meat of some kind."

But there was not a morsel of meat in the house.

"Then go to the butcher's and buy some."

Sarah gasped, and bridled. She had never in her life been inside a butcher's shop!

"Good God, woman, then the sooner you make the beginning the better!" cried Mahony. And, as he strode down the passage to the door she indicated, he added: "Now control yourself, madam! And, if you have not got what I want in a quarter of an hour's time, I'll walk out of the house again and leave you to your own devices!"— At which Sarah, cowed and shaken, began tremblingly to tie her bonnet-strings.

Mahony knocked three times at the door of John Turnham's room, each time more loudly. Then he took to battering with his fist on the panels, and cried: "It is I, John, your brother-in-law, Mahony! Have the goodness to unlock this door at once!"

There was still an instant of suspense; then heavy footsteps crossed the floor, and the door swung back. Mahony's eyes met a haggard white face set in a dusky background.

"You!" said John, in a slow, dazed way, and blinked at the light. But in the next breath he burst out: "Where's that damned fool of a woman? Is she skulking behind you? I won't see her—won't have her near me!"

"If you mean your sister Sarah, she is not in the house at present," said Mahony; and stepping over the threshold, he shut the door. The two men faced each other in the twilight.

"What do you want?" demanded John, in a hoarse voice. "Have you, too, come to preach and sermonise? If so, you can go back where you came from! I want none of that cant here."

"No, no, I leave that to those whose business it is. I'm here as your doctor"; and again Mahony drew up a blind and opened a window.— Instantly the level sun-rays flooded the room; and the air that came in with them smacked of the sea. Just outside the window a quince-tree, in full blossom, reared extravagant masses of pink snow against the blue overhead; beyond it, a covered walk of vines shone golden-green. There was not a cloud in the sky. To turn back to the musty room from all this lush and lovely life was like stepping down into a vault.

John had sunk into a seat before a secretaire, and shielded his eyes from the sun. A burnt-out candle stood at his elbow; and in a line before him were ranged such images as remained to him of his dead—a dozen or more daguerreotypes, of various sizes: Emma and he before marriage, and after marriage; Emma with her first babe, at different stages of its growth; Emma with the two children; Emma in ball-attire; with a hat on; with a book in her hand.

The sight gave the quietus to Mahony's scruples. Stooping, he laid his hand on John's shoulder. "My poor fellow," he said gently. "Your sister was not in a fit state to travel, so I have come in her place to tell you how deeply, how truly, we feel for you in your loss. I want to try, too, to help you to bear it. For it has to be borne, John."

At this, the torrent burst. Leaping to his feet John began to fling wildly to and fro; and then, for a time, the noise of his lamentations filled the room. Mahony had assisted at scenes of this kind before, but never had he heard the like of the blasphemies that poured over John's lips.— (Afterwards, when he

136

had recovered his distance, he would refer to it as the occasion
on which John took the Almighty to task, for having dared to
interfere in his private life.)

At the moment, he sat silent. "Better for him to get it out,"
he thought to himself, even while he winced at John's scurrility.

When quiet was restored, John having come to a stop
through sheer exhaustion, Mahony cast about for words of
consolation. All reference to the mystery of God's ways was
precluded; and he shrank from entering that sound plea for the
working of Time, which drives a spike into the heart of the
new-made mourner. He bethought himself of the children.
"Remember, she did not leave you comfortless. You have your
little ones. Think of them."

But this was a false move. Like a belated thunderclap after
the storm is over, John broke out again, his haggard eyes
aflame. "Curse the children!" he cried thickly. "Curse them, I
say! If I had once caught sight of them since she . . . she went,
I should have wrung their necks. I never wanted children.
They came between us. They took her from me. It was a child
that killed her.— Now, she is gone and they are left. Keep them
out of my way, Mahony! Don't let them near me.— Oh, Emma
. . . wife!" and here his shoulders heaved, under dry, harsh sobs.

Mahony felt his own eyes grow moist. How paltry, how niggling, in face of this grief, seemed the qualms he had had
about intruding! Whole-heartedly he sprang to make amends.
"Listen to me, John. I promise you, you shall not see your
children again until you wish to—till you're glad to recall them,
as a living gift from her you have lost. I'll look after them
for you!"

"You will? . . . God bless you, Mahony!"

Judging the moment ripe, Mahony rose and went out to
fetch the tray on which Sarah had set the eatables. The meat
was but a chop, charred on one side, raw on the other; but
John did not notice its shortcomings. He fell on it like the
starving man he was, and gulped down two or three glasses
of port. The colour returned to his face, he was able to give
an account of his wife's last hours.— "And to talk is what he
needs, even if he goes on till morning," thought Mahony. He
was quick to see that there were things that rankled in John's
memory, like festers in flesh. One was that, knowing the greys
were tricky, he had not forbidden them to Emma long ago.

But he had felt proud of her skill in handling the reins, of the attention she attracted. Far from thwarting her, he had actually urged her on.— Her fall had been a light one, and at the outset no bad results were anticipated: a slight hæmorrhage was soon got under control. A week later, however, it began anew, more violently, and now all remedies were in vain. As it became clear that the child was dead, the doctors had recourse to serious measures. But the bleeding went on. She complained of a roaring in her ears, her extremities grew cold, her pulse fluttered to nothing. She passed from syncope to coma, and from coma to death. John swore that two of the doctors had been the worse for drink; the third was one of those ignorant impostors with whom the place swarmed.— And again he made himself reproaches.

"I thought to have gone to look for some one else. But she was dying . . . I could not tear myself away.— Mahony, I can still see her. They had stretched her across the bed, so that her head hung over the side. Her hair swept the floor—one scoundrel trod on it . . . trod on her hair! And I had to stand by and watch, while they butchered her—butchered my girl.— Oh, there are things, Mahony, one cannot dwell on, and live!"

"You must not look at it like that. Yet, when I recall some of the cases I've seen contraction induced in . . ."

"Ah yes, if you had been here . . . my God, if you had only been here!"

But Mahony did not encourage this idea; he felt it his duty to unhitch John's thoughts from the past, lead them forward into the future. He now suggested that, the children and Sarah safe in his keeping, John should shut up the house and go away—as far away as possible. To his surprise, John jumped at the proposal, was ready there and then to put it into effect. Yes, said he, he would start the very next morning, and, with no more than a blanket on his back, would wander a hundred odd miles into the bush, sleeping out under the stars at night, and day by day increasing the distance between himself and the scene of his loss.— And now, up he sprang, in a sudden fury to be gone. Warning Sarah into the background, Mahony helped him get together a few necessaries, and then walked him to a hotel. Here, he left him sleeping under the influence of a drug, and next day saw him off on his tramp northwards, over the Great Divide.

John's farewell words were: "Take the keys of the house with you, and don't give them up to me under a month, at least."

He wrung his brother-in-law's hand at parting; otherwise, his manner was a trifle disconcerting. It seemed as though, once spurred to action, he was in a hurry to shake off, to see the last of, his benefactor.

That day's coach was full; they had to wait for seats till the following afternoon. The delay was not unwelcome to Mahony; it gave Polly time to get the letter he had written her the night before.— After leaving John, he set about raising money for the extra fares and other unforeseen expenses: at the eleventh hour, Sarah informed him that their young brother Jerry had landed in Melbourne during Emma's illness, and had been hastily boarded out. Knowing no one else in the city, Mahony was forced, much as it went against the grain, to turn to Henry Ocock for assistance. And he was effusively received—Ocock tried to press double the sum needed on him.— Fortune was no doubt smiling on the lawyer. His offices had swelled to four rooms, with appropriate clerks in each. He still, however, nursed the scheme of transferring his business to Ballarat.

"As soon, that is, as I can hear of suitable premises. I understand there's only one locality to be considered, and that's the western township."— After which, Mahony, whose address was in the outer darkness, repeated his thanks and withdrew.

He found Jerry's lodging, paid the bill, and took the boy back to St. Kilda—a shy slip of a lad this, in his early teens, and with the colouring and complexion that ran in the family. John's coachman, who had shown himself not indisposed—for a substantial sum, payable in advance—to keep watch over house and grounds, was installed in an outbuilding; and next day at noon, after personally aiding Sarah, who was all a-tremble at the prospect of the bush journey, to pack her own and the children's clothes, Mahony turned the key in the door of the darkened house. But a couple of weeks ago, it had been a proud and happy home. Now, it had no more virtue in it than a crab's empty shell.

He had fumed to himself on first learning of Jerry's superfluous presence; but, before they had gone far, he saw that he would have fared ill indeed, had Jerry not been there. Sarah, too agitated that morning to touch a bite of food, was seized, not an hour out, with sickness and fainting. There she sat, her eyes closed, her salts at her nose, or feebly sipping brandy, unable to lift a finger to help with the children. The younger of the two slept, most of the way, hotly and heavily on Mahony's knee; but the boy, a regular pest, was never for a moment still. In vain did his youthful uncle pinch his leg each time he wriggled to the floor. It was not till a fierce-looking digger opposite took out a jack-knife, and threatened to saw off both his feet if he stirred again, to cut out his tongue if he put another question, that, scarlet with fear, Johnny was tamed.— Altogether, it was a nightmare of a journey, and Mahony groaned with relief when, lamps having for some time twinkled past, the coach drew up, and Hempel and Long Jim stepped forward with their lanterns.— Sarah could hardly stand. The children, wrathful at being wakened from their deep sleep, kicked and screamed.

[6]

FOR the first time in her young married life, Polly felt vexed with her husband.

"Oh, he shouldn't have done that . . . no, really he shouldn't!" she murmured; and the hand with the letter in it drooped to her lap.

She had been doing a little surreptitious baking, in Richard's absence, and without a doubt was hot and tired. The tears rose to her eyes. Deserting her pastry-board, she retreated behind the woodstack, and sat down on the chopping-block; and then, for some minutes, the sky was blotted out. She felt quite unequal, in her present condition, to facing Sarah, who was so sensitive, so easily shocked; and she was deeply averse to her fine-lady sister discovering the straitness of Richard's means and home.

But it was hard for Polly to secure a moment's privacy.

"An' so this is w'ere you're 'idin', is it?" said Long Jim snappishly—he had been opening a keg of treacle, and held a sticky plug in his hand. "An' me runnin' my pore ol' legs off arter you!" And Hempel met her on her entry with: "No further bad news, I 'ope and trust, ma'am?"—Hempel always retained his smooth servility of manner. "The shopman *par excellence*, my dear!" Richard was used to say of him.

Polly reassured her attendants, blew her nose, re-read her

letter; and other feelings came uppermost. She noticed how scribbly the writing was—Richard had evidently been hard pushed for time. There was an apologetic tone about it, too, which was unlike him. He was probably wondering what she would say; he might even be making himself reproaches. It was unkind of her to add to them. Let her think rather of the sad state poor John had been found in, and of his two motherless babes.— As for Sarah, it would never have done to leave her out.

Wiping her eyes, Polly untied her cooking-apron, and set to reviewing her resources. Sarah would have to share her bed, Richard to sleep on the sofa. The children . . . and here she knitted her brows. Then, going into the yard, she called to Tom Ocock, who sat whittling a stick in front of his father's house; and Tom went down to Main Street for her, to "Ocock's Auction Rooms," and bought a mattress, which he carried home on his shoulder. This, she spread on the bedroom floor, Mrs. Hemmerde having already given both rooms a sound scouring, just in case a flea or a spider should both be lying perdu. After which, Polly fell to baking again, in good earnest; for the travellers would be famished by the time they arrived.

Towards ten o'clock, Tom, who was on the look-out, shouted that the coach was in, and Polly, her table spread, a good fire going, stepped to the door, outwardly very brave, inwardly all a-flutter. Directly, however, she got sight of the forlorn party that toiled up the slope: Sarah, clinging to Hempel's arm, Mahony bearing one heavy child, and—could she believe her eyes?—Jerry staggering under the other: her bashfulness was gone. She ran forward to prop poor Sarah on her free side, to guide her feet to the door: and it is doubtful whether little Polly had ever spent a more satisfying hour than that which followed.

Her husband, watching her in silent amaze, believed she thoroughly enjoyed the fuss and commotion.

There was Sarah, who was too sick to see anything but the bed, to undress, to make fomentations for, to coax to mouthfuls of tea and toast. There was Jerry to feed and send off, with the warmest of hugs, to share Tom Ocock's palliasse. There were the children . . . well, Polly's first plan had been to put them straight to bed. But when she came to peel off their little trousers, she changed her mind.

141

"I think, Mrs. Hemmerde, if you'll get me a tub of hot water, we'll just pop them into it; they'll sleep so much better," she said . . . not quite truthfully. Her private reflection was: "I don't think Sarah can once have washed them properly, all that time."

The little girl let herself be bathed in her sleep; but young John stood and bawled, digging fat fists into slits of eyes, while Polly scrubbed at his massy knees, the dimpled ups and downs of which looked as if they had been worked in by hand. She had never seen her brother's children before, and was as heartily lost in admiration of their plump, well-formed bodies, as her helper of the costliness of their outfit.

"Real Injun muslin, as I'm alive!" ejaculated the woman, on fishing out their night-clothes. "An' wid the sassiest lace for trimmin'!— Och, the poor little motherless angels!— Stan' quiet, you young divil you, an' lemme button you up!"

Clean as lily-bells, the pair were laid on the mattress-bed.

"At least they can't fall out," said Polly, surveying her work with a sigh of content.

Every one else having retired, she sat with Richard before the fire, waiting for his bath-water to reach the boil. He was anxious to know just how she had fared in his absence, she to hear the full story of his mission. He confessed to her that his offer to load himself up with the whole party had been made in a momentary burst of feeling. Afterwards, he had repented his impulsiveness.

"On your account, love. Though when I see how well you've managed—you dear, clever little woman!"

And Polly consoled him, being now come honestly to the stage of: "But Richard, what else could you do!"

"What, indeed! I knew Emma had no relatives in Melbourne, and who John's intimates might be I had no more idea than the man in the moon."

"John hasn't any friends. He never had."

"As for leaving the children in Sarah's charge, if you'll allow me to say so, my dear, I consider your sister Sarah the biggest goose of a female it has ever been my lot to run across."

"Ah, but you don't really know Sarah yet," said Polly, and smiled a little, through the tears that had risen to her eyes at the tale of John's despair.

What Mahony did not mention to her was the necessity he

had been under of borrowing money; though Polly was aware
he had left home with but a modest sum in his purse. He
wished to spare her feelings. Polly had a curious delicacy—he
might almost call it a manly delicacy—with regard to money;
and the fact that John had not offered to put hand to pocket,
let alone liberally flung a blank check at his head, would,
Mahony knew, touch his wife on a tender spot.— Nor did Polly
herself ask questions. Richard made no allusion to John having
volunteered to bear expenses, so the latter had evidently not
done so. What a pity! Richard was so particular himself, in
matters of this kind, that he might write her brother down
close and stingy—which would be quite wrong. Of course,
John's distressed state of mind might partly serve to excuse
him. But she could not imagine the calamity that would cause
Richard to forget his obligations.

She slid her hand into her husband's, and they sat for a
while in silence. Then, half to herself, and out of a very different train of thought, she said: "Just fancy them never crying
once for their mother!"

*   *   *   *   *

"Talking of friends," said Sarah, and fastidiously cleared her
throat. "Talking of friends, I wonder now what has become of
one of those young gentlemen I met at your wedding. He was
. . . let me see . . . why, I declare if I haven't forgotten his
name!"

"Oh, I know who you mean—besides, there was only one,
Sarah," Mahony heard his wife reply, and therewith fall into
her sister's trap. "You mean Purdy—Purdy Smith—who was
Richard's best man."

"Smith?" echoed Sarah. "La, Polly! Why don't he make it
Smythe?"

It was a warm evening, some three weeks later. The store
was closed to customers; but Mahony had ensconced himself
in a corner of it with a book: since the invasion, this was the
one place in which he could make sure of finding quiet. The
sisters sat on the log-bench before the house; and, without seeing them, Mahony knew to a nicety how they were employed.
Polly darned stockings, for John's children; Sarah was tatting,
with her little finger stuck out at right angles to the rest.
Mahony could hardly think of this finger without a sense of
irritation: it seemed to sum up Sarah's whole outlook on life.

Meanwhile, Polly's fresh voice went on, relating Purdy's fortunes. "He took part, you know, in the dreadful affair on the Eureka, last Christmas, when so many poor men were killed. We can speak of it, now they've all been pardoned; but then, we had to be very careful. Well, he was shot in the ankle; and he will always be lame from it."

"What!—go hobbling on one leg for the remainder of his days? Oh, my dear!" said Sarah, and laughed.

"Yes, because the wound wasn't properly attended to—he had to hide about in the bush, for ever so long. Later on, he went to the Beamishes, to be nursed. But by that time his poor leg was in a very bad state.— You know he is engaged—or very nearly so—to Tilly Beamish."

"What!" said Sarah once more. "That handsome young fellow engaged to one of those vulgar creatures?"

"Oh, Sarah . . . not really vulgar. It isn't their fault they didn't have a better education. They lived right up-country, where there were no schools. Tilly never saw a town till she was sixteen; but she can sit any horse.— Yes, we hope very much Purdy will soon settle down now and marry her—though he left the Hotel again without proposing." And Polly sighed.

"There he shows his good taste, my dear."

"Oh, I'm sure he's fond of Tilly. It's only that his life is so unsettled. He's been a barman at Euroa since then; and the last we heard of him, he was shearing somewhere on the Goulburn. He doesn't seem able to stick to anything."

"And a rolling stone gathers no moss!" gave back Sarah sententiously—and in fancy Mahony saw the cut-and-dried nod with which she accompanied the words.

Here, Hempel passed through the store, clad in his Sunday best, his hair plastered flat with bear's-grease.

"Going out for a stroll?" asked his master.

"That was my h'intention, sir. I don't think you'll find I've left any of my dooties undone."

"Oh, go, by all means!" said Mahony curtly, nettled at seeing his harmless query misconstrued.— It pointed a suspicion he had had, of late, that a change was coming over Hempel. The model employee was a shade less prompt than heretofore to fly at his word, and once or twice seemed actually to be studying his own convenience. Without knowing what the matter was, Mahony felt it politic not to be over-exacting—even mildly to conciliate his assistant. It would put him in an awkward fix, now that he was on the verge of winding up affairs, should Hempel take it into his head to leave him in the lurch.

The lean figure had moved on, and blocked the doorway. Now there was a sudden babble of cheepy voices, and, simultaneously, Sarah cried: "Where have you been, my little cherubs? Come to your aunt, and let her kiss you!"

But the children, who had frankly no great liking for Aunt Sarah, would, Mahony knew, turn a deaf ear to this display of opportunism, and make a rush for his wife. Laying down his book, he ran out. "Polly . . . cautious!"

"It's all right, Richard, I'm being careful."— Polly had let her mending fall, and, with each hand, held a flaxen-haired child at arm's-length.— "Johnny, dirty boy! what *have* you been up to?"

"He played he was a digger, and sat down in a pool— I couldn't get him to budge," answered Jerry, and drew his sleeve over his perspiring forehead.

"Oh fy, for shame!"

"Don' care!" said John, unabashed.

"Don' tare!" echoed his roly-poly sister, who existed but as his shadow.

"Don't-care was made to care, don't-care was hung!" quoted Aunt Sarah, in her severest copybook tones.

Turning his head in his aunt's direction, young John thrust forth a bright pink tongue. Little Emma was not behind-hand.

Polly pumped up, dropping her work to the ground. "Johnny, I shall punish you, if ever I see you do that again. Now, Ellen shall put you to bed, instead of Auntie."— Ellen was Mrs. Hemmerde's eldest, and Polly's first regular maid-servant.

"Don' care," repeated Johnny. "Ellen plays pillers."

"Edn pays pidders," said the echo.

Seizing two hot, pudgy hands, Polly dragged the pair indoors—though they held back mainly on principle. They were not affectionate children; they were too strong of will and set of purpose, for that; but, if they had a fondness for anyone, it was for their Aunt Polly: she was ruler over a drawerful of sugar-sticks, and, though she scolded, she never slapped.

While this was going on, Hempel stood, the picture of indecision, and eased now one foot, now the other, as if his boots pinched him.

At length he blurted out: "I was wondering, ma'am—ahem! Miss Turnham—if, since it is an agreeable h'evening, you would care to take a walk to that 'ill I told you of?"

"Me take a walk? La, no! Whatever put such an idea as that into your head?" cried Sarah; and tatted and tatted, keeping time with a pretty little foot.

"I thought per'aps . . ." said Hempel meekly.

"*I* didn't make your thoughts, Mr. *H*empel," retorted Sarah, laying stress on the aspirate.

"Oh no, ma'am. I 'ope I didn't presume to suggest such a thing"; and with a hangdog air, Hempel prepared to slink away.

"Well, well!" said Sarah double-quick; and ceasing to jerk her crochet-needle in and out, she nimbly rolled up her ball of thread. "Since you're so insistent . . . and since, mind you, there's no society worth calling such, on these diggings. . . !"— The truth was, Sarah saw that she was about to be left alone with Mahony—Jerry had sauntered off to meet Ned, who was expected—and this *tête-à-tête* was by no means to her mind. She still bore her brother-in-law a grudge, for his high-handed treatment of her at the time of John's bereavement.— "As if I had been one of the domestics, my dear—a paid domestic! Ordered me off to the butcher's in language that fairly shocked me!"

Mahony turned his back and strolled down to the river. He did not know which was more painful to witness: Hempel's unmanly cringing, or the air of fatuous satisfaction that succeeded it. When he returned, the couple were just setting out; he watched Sarah, on Hempel's arm, picking short steps in dainty latchet-shoes.

As soon as they were well away, he called to Polly.

"The coast's clear. Come for a stroll."

Polly emerged, tying her bonnet-strings. "Why, where's Sarah? Oh . . . I see.— Oh, Richard, I hope she didn't put on that——"

"She did, my dear!" said Mahony grimly, and tucked his wife's hand under his arm.

"Oh, how I wish she wouldn't!" said Polly, in a tone of concern. "She does get so stared at—especially of an evening, when there are so many rude men about. But I really don't think she minds. For she *has* a bonnet in her box, all the time."— Miss

Sarah was giving Ballarat food for talk, by appearing on her promenades in a hat: a large, flat, mushroom hat.

"I trust my little woman will never put such a ridiculous object on her head!"

"No, never . . . at least, not unless they become quite the fashion," answered Polly. "And I don't think they will. They look too odd."

"Another thing, love," continued Mahony, on whom a sudden light had dawned, as he stood listening to Sarah's trumpery. "I fear your sister is trifling with the feelings of our worthy Hempel."

Polly, who had kept her own counsel on this matter, went crimson. "Oh, do you really think so, Richard?" she asked evasively. "I hope not. For of course nothing could come of it. Sarah has refused the most eligible offers."

"Ah, but there are none here to refuse. And, if you don't mind my saying so, Poll, anything in trousers seems fish to *her* net!"

On one of their pacings, they found Mr. Ocock come out to smoke an evening pipe before his house. The old man had just returned from a flying visit to Melbourne. He looked glum and careworn, but livened up at the sight of Polly, and cracked one of the mouldy jokes he believed beneficial to a young woman in her condition. Still, the leading-note in his mood was melancholy; and this, although his dearest wish was on the point of being fulfilled.

"Yes, I've got the very crib for 'Enry at last, doc.,—Billy de la Poer's liv'ry-stable, top o' Lydiard Street. We sol' poor Billy up yesterday. The third smash in two days, that makes. Lord! I dunno where it'll end."

"Things are going a bit quick over there. There's been too much building."

"They're at me to build, too—'Enry is. But I says no. This place is good enough for me. If 'e's goin' to be ashamed of 'ow 'is father lives, 'e'd better stop away. I'm an ol' man now, an' a poor one. What should I want with a fine noo 'ouse? An' 'oo should I build it for, even if I 'ad the tin? For them two good-for-nothin's in there?— Not if I know it!"

"Mr. Ocock, you wouldn't believe how kind and clever Tom's been at helping with the children," said Polly warmly.

"Yes, an' at bottle-washin', and sweepin', and cookin' a pasty.

147

But a female 'ud do it just as well," returned Tom's father, with a snort of contempt.

—"Poor old chap!" said Mahony, as they passed out of ear-shot. "So even the great Henry's arrival is not to be without its drop of gall."

"Surely he'll never be ashamed of his father?"

"Who knows!— But it's plain he suspects the old boy has made his pile, and intends him to fork out," said Mahony carelessly; and, with this, dismissed the subject. Now that his days in the colony were numbered, he no longer felt constrained to pump up a spurious interest in local affairs. He consigned them, wholesale, to that limbo in which, for him, they had always belonged.

The two brothers came striding over the slope. Ned, in blue serge shirt and corduroys, laid an affectionate arm round Polly's shoulder, and tossed his hat into the air on hearing that the "Salamander," as he called Sarah, was not at home.

"For I've tons to tell you, Poll, old girl. And when milady sits there, turning up her nose at everything a chap says, somehow the spunk goes out of one."

Polly had baked a large cake for her darling, and served out generous slices. Then, drawing up a chair, she sat down beside him, to drink in his news.

From his place at the farther end of the table, Mahony studied the trio—these three young faces which were so much alike that they might have been different readings of one and the same face. Polly, by reason of her woman's lot, looked considerably the oldest. Still, the lamplight wiped out some of the shadows, and she was never more girlishly vivacious than with Ned, entering as she did with zest into his plans and ideas—more sister now than wife. And Ned showed at his best with Polly: he laid himself out to divert her; forgot to brag or to swear; and so natural did it seem for brother to open his heart to sister that even his egoistic chatter passed muster. As for young Jerry, who, in a couple of days, was to begin work in the same claim as Ned, he sat round-eyed, his thoughts writ large on his forehead. Mahony translated them thus: how in the world did I manage to sit prim and proper on the school-bench, when all this—change, adventure, romance—was awaiting me? Jerry was only, Mahony knew, to push a wheelbarrow from hole to water and back again, for many a week to come;

but, for him, it would certainly be a golden barrow, a barrow laden with pure gold, so greatly had Ned's tales fired his imagination.

The onlooker felt odd man out, debarred as he was, by the mass of his profounder experience, from sharing in the young people's light-legged dreams. He took up his book. But his reading—it was about the Diluvium, and how, over the entire continents of Europe and America, the diluvial blocks had travelled in the same direction: "From the north and north-east towards the south-east"—his reading was cut into by Ned's sprightly account of the Magpie rush ("Five thousand tents if there's one, Poll, sprung up overnight!"); by his description of the engine that was at work on the Eureka, and the wooden air-pipes that were being used to ventilate deep-sinkings. There was nothing Ned did not know, and could not make entertaining. He had a seeing eye and a fluent tongue. One was forced, almost against one's will, to listen to him; and so it happened that, on this particular evening, when Ned was neither sponging, nor acting the Big Gun, Mahony toned down his first sweeping judgment of his young relative. Ned was all talk; and what impressed one so unfavourably about him—his grumbling, his extravagant boastfulness—was the mere thistle-down of the moment, puffed off into space. It mattered little, for instance, that he harped continually on "chucking up" his job; or that, each time one saw him, he had some new scheme on hand for making his fortune. Two years had elapsed since he came to Ballarat, and he was still working for hire, in somebody else's hole. He still groaned over the hardships of the life, and still toiled on—and all the rest was just the frothy braggadocio of aimless youth.

[7]

Not twenty-four hours later, Sarah had an accident to her *mâchoire*, and returned posthaste to Melbourne.

"A most opportune breakage!" said Mahony, and laughed.

That day, at the dinner-table, he had given his sister-in-law a piece of his mind. Sarah had always resented the name bestowed on her by her parents, and was at present engaged in altering it, in giving it, so to speak, a foreign tang: henceforth she was to be, not Sarah, but Sara (spoken Sahra). As often as

Polly's tongue tripped over the unfamiliar syllable, Sara gently but firmly put her right; and Polly corrected herself, even begged pardon for her stupidity, till Mahony could bear it no longer. Throwing politeness to the winds, he twitted Sara with her finical affectations, her old-maidish ways, the morning sloth that expected Polly, in her delicate state of health, to carry a breakfast-tray to the bedside: cast up at her, in short, all that had made him champ and fret in silence. Sara might, after a fitting period of the huff, have forgiven him the rest; but the "old-maidish" she could not tolerate.— Directly dinner was over, the mishap to her mouthpiece was made known.

Too much in awe of Mahony to give him tit-for-tat; for, when he was angry, he was very angry, Sara retaliated by abusing him to Polly, as she packed her trunk.

"Manners, indeed! To turn and insult a visitor at his own table, in that fashion! And who and what is he, I should like to know, to speak to me so? Nothing but a common storekeeper. My dear, you have my deepest sympathy. It's a *dreadful* life for you. Of course, you keep everything as nice as possible, under the circumstances. But the surroundings, Polly! . . . and the store . . . and the want of society. *I* couldn't put up with it, not for a week!"

Polly, who sat on the side of the tester-bed, feeling very cast down at Sara's unfriendly departure, shed a few tears at this. For, part of what her sister said was true: it had been wrong of Richard to be rude to Sara while the latter was a guest in his house. But she defended him warmly. "I couldn't be happier than I am; Richard's the best husband in the world. As for his being common, Sara, you know he comes of a much better family than we do."

"My dear, common is as common does; and a vulgar calling ends by vulgarising those who have the misfortune to pursue it.— But there's another reason, Polly, why it is better for me to leave you. There are certain circumstances, my dear, in which, to put it mildly, it is *awkward* for two people of *opposite* sexes, to go on living under the same roof."

"Sarah!— I mean Sara—do you really mean to say Hempel has made you a proposal?" cried Polly, wide-eyed in her tears.

"I won't say, my dear, that he has so far forgotten himself as to actually offer marriage. But he has let me see only too plainly what his feelings are. Of course, I've kept him in his place—the preposterous creature! But all the same it's not *comme il faut* any longer for me to be here."

"Did she say where she was going, or what she intended to do?" Mahony inquired of his wife that night, as she bound the strings of her nightcap.

No, she hadn't, Polly admitted, rather out of countenance. But then, Sara was like that—very close about her own affairs. "I think she's perhaps gone back to her last situation. She had several letters while she was here, in that lady's hand. People are always glad to get her back. Not many finishing governesses can teach all she can";—and Polly checked off Sara's attainments on the fingers of both hands. "She won't go anywhere under two hundred a year."

"A most accomplished person, your sister!" said Mahony sleepily. "Still, it's very pleasant to be by ourselves again—eh, wife?"

An even more blessed peace shortly descended on the house; for the time was now come to get rid of the children, as well. Since nothing had been heard of John, they were to be boarded out, over Polly's illness. Through the butcher's lady, arrangements were made with a trooper's wife, who lived outside the racket and dust of the township, and had a whole posse of little ones of her own.— "Bless you! half-a-dozen more wouldn't make any difference to me. There's the paddock for 'em to run wild in."— This was the best that could be done for the children. Polly packed their little kit, dealt out a parting bribe of barley-sugar, and saw them hoisted into a dray that was to pass the door of their destination.

Once more husband and wife sat alone together, as in the days prior to John's domestic catastrophe. And now Mahony said tentatively: "Don't you think, love, we could manage to get on without that old Beamish woman? I'll guarantee to nurse you as well as any female alive."

The question did not come as a surprise to Polly; she had already put it to herself. After the affair with Sara, she awaited her new visitor in fear and trembling. Sara had at least stood in awe of Richard, and held her tongue before him; Mrs. Beamish prided herself on being afraid of nobody, and on always speaking her mind.— And yet, even while agreeing that it would be well to put "mother" off, Polly drooped her wings. At a time like this, a woman was a woman. It seemed as if even the best of husbands did not quite understand.

"Just give her the hint we don't want her," said Mahony airily.

But "mother" was not the person to take a hint, no matter how broad. It was necessary to be blunt to the point of rudeness; and Polly spent a difficult hour over the composition of her letter. She might have saved her pains. Mrs. Beamish replied that she knew her darling little Polly's unwillingness to give trouble; but it was not likely she would now go back on her word: she had been packed and ready to start, for the past week. Polly handed the letter to her husband, and did not say what she thought she read out of it, namely, that "mother," who so seldom could be spared from home, was looking forward with pleasure to her trip to Ballarat.

"I suppose it's a case of making the best of a bad job," sighed Mahony; and having one day drawn Mrs. Beamish, at meltingpoint, from the inside of a crowded coach, he loaded Long Jim with her bags and bundles. He met her under the shadow of a new, old prejudice. On his way to the coach-office, he had recalled the fact that, at the time of his marriage, the family had made no offer to pay Polly the quarter's salary they owed her.

His grudge was not lightened by his subsequently coming on his wife in the act of unpacking a hamper, which contained half a ham, a stone jar of butter, some home-made loaves of bread, a bag of vegetables, and a plum pudding. "Good God! does the woman think we can't give her enough to eat?" he asked testily.— He had all the poor Irishman's distrust of a gift.

"She means it kindly, dear. She probably thought things were still scarce here; and she knew I wouldn't be able to do much cooking," pleaded Polly. And going out to the kitchen, she untied the last parcel, in which was a big round cheese, by stealth.

She had pulled Mrs. Beamish over the threshold, had got her into the bedroom and shut the door, before any of the "ohs" and "ahs" she saw painted on the broad, rubicund face could be transformed into words. And hugs and kisses over, she bravely seized the bull by the horns, and begged her guest not to criticise house or furnishings in front of Richard.

It took Mrs. Beamish a minute or two to grasp her meaning. Then she said heartily: "There, there, my duck, don't you worry! I'll be as mum as mum." And in a whisper: "So, 'e's got a temper, Polly, 'as 'e?— But this I will say: if I'd known this was all 'e 'ad to h'offer you, I'd 'a said, stop w'ere you are, my lamb, in a comfortable, 'appy 'ome."

"Oh, I *am* happy, 'mother' dear, indeed I am!" cried Polly. "I've never regretted being married—never once!"

"There, there, now!"

"And it's only . . . I mean . . . this is the best we can afford in the meantime, and if *I* am satisfied . . ." floundered Polly, dismayed to hear her words construed into blame of her husband. "It's only that it upsets Richard if people speak slightingly of our house, and that upsets me—and I mustn't be worried just now, you know," she added, with a somewhat shaky smile.

"Not a word will I say, ducky, make yer pore little mind easy about that! Though, such a poky little 'en-coop of a place I never was in!"—and, while tying her cap-strings, Mrs. Beamish swept the little bedroom and its sloping roof, with a withering glance.— "I was 'orrified, girls, simply *'orrified!*" she related the incident to her daughters. "An' I up an' told 'er so—just like me, you know! Not room enough to swing a cat in, and 'im sittin' there at the 'ead of the table, as 'igh an' mighty as a dook! You can thank yer stars, you two, 'e didn't take one of you, instead o' Polly."— But this was chiefly by way of a consolation-prize for Tilly and Jinny.

"An' now, my dear, tell me *everything!*"— With these words, Mrs. Beamish spread her skirts and settled down to a cosy chat on the subject of Polly's hopes.

But, like the majority of her sex, she was an adept at dividing her attention; and, while making delicate inquiries of the young wife, she was also travelling her shrewd eye round the little bed-chamber, spying out and appraising: not one of poor Polly's makeshifts escaped her. The result of her inspection was to cause her to feel justly indignant with Mahony. The idea! Him to rob them of Polly just to dump her down in a place like this! She would never be able to resist telling him what she thought of him.

Here, however, she reckoned without Polly. Polly was sharp enough to doubt "mother's" ability to hold her tongue; and saw

153

to it that Richard and she were not left alone together. And of an evening, when talk languished, she would beg her husband to read to them from the *Ballarat Star*, until, as often as not, Mrs. Beamish fell asleep. Frequently, too, she persuaded him to go out, to take a hand in a newly formed whist club, or to discuss politics with a neighbour.

Mahony went willingly enough; his home was less home than ever, since the big woman's intrusion. Even his food lost its savour. Mrs. Beamish had taken over the cooking, and she went about it with an air that implied he had not had a decent bite to eat, since his marriage.

"There! what do you say to that now? That's something *like* a pudding!" and a great plum-duff was planked triumphantly down in the middle of the dinner-table.— "Lor, Polly! your bit of a kitchen . . . in this weather!— I'm fair dished." And the good woman mopped her streaming face, and could herself eat nothing.

Mahony much preferred his wife's cooking, which took account of his tastes—it was done, too, without any fuss—and he persisted in upholding Polly's skill, in face of Mrs. Beamish's good-natured disbelief. Polly, on edge lest he should openly state his preference, nervously held out her plate.

"It's so good, 'mother,' I must have a second helping," she declared; and then, without appetite in the cruel, midday heat, did not know what to do with the solid slab of pudding.— Pompey and Palmerston got into the way of sitting very close to her chair.

She confided to Richard that Mrs. Beamish disapproved of his evening outings.— "Many an 'usband takes to goin' out at such a time, my dear, an' never gets back the 'abit of stoppin' at 'ome. So just you be careful, ducky!"— This was a standing joke between husband and wife. Mahony would wink at Polly when he put his hat on, and wear it rakishly askew.

As a matter of fact, he quite enjoyed a crack with the post-master, or the town-surveyor, at this juncture. Colonial politics were more interesting than usual. The new Constitution had been proclaimed, and a valiant effort was being made to form a Cabinet; to induce, that was, a sufficient number of well-to-do men to give up time to the service of their country. It looked as if the attempt were going to fail, just as on the gold-fields the Local Courts, by which, since the Stockade, the diggers governed themselves, were failing, because none could afford to spend his days sitting in them. There was also the burning question of vote by ballot. Mahony's neighbours were staunch supporters of this reform. He, with a spice of malice, was fond of quoting Lord John Russell's dictum: "The ballot is essentially un-English."

Yet, however high the discussion ran, he kept one ear turned towards his home. Here, things were at a standstill. Polly's time had come and gone—but there was no end set to their suspense. It was blazing hot now, in the little log house; walls and roof were black with flies; mosquitoes made the nights hideous. Even Polly lost patience with herself when, morning after morning, she got up feeling as well as ever, and knowing that she had to steer through another difficult day.

It was not the suspense alone: the strain of keeping the peace was growing too much for her.

"Oh, *don't* quarrel with her, Richard, for my sake!" she begged her husband one night. "She means so well. And she can't help being like she is—she has always been accustomed to order Mr. Beamish about.— But I wish she had never, never come," sobbed poor Polly.— And Mahony, in a sudden flash of enlightenment, put his arms round his wife, and made humble promises. Not another word should cross his lips! "Though I'd like nothing so well as to throw her out, and her bags and bundles after her. Come, laugh a little, my Polly. Think of the old lady flying down the slope, with her packages in a shower about her head!"

Rogers, M.D., looked in whenever he passed. At this stage, he was of the jocular persuasion.— "Still an unwelcome visitor, ma'am? No little tidbit of news for me to-day?" There he sat, twiddling his thumbs, reiterating his singsong: "Just so!" and looking wise as an owl. Mahony knew the air—had many a time seen it donned to cloak perplexity—and covert doubts of Rogers' ability began to assail him. But then he fell mentally foul of every one he came in touch with, at present: Ned, for the bare-faced fashion in which he left his cheerfulness on the door-mat, when he entered the house; Mrs. Beamish, for the eternal "Pore lamb!" with which she beplastered Polly, and the antiquated reckoning-table she embarrassed them by consulting.

However, this state of things could not last for ever, and, at dawn, one hot January day, Polly was taken ill.

The early hours promised well. But the morning wore on, turned to midday, then to afternoon, and matters still hung fire. While, towards six o'clock, the patient dismayed them by sitting up in bed, saying she felt much better, and asking for a cup of tea.— This drew: "Ah, my pore lamb, you've got to feel worse yet, afore you're better!" from Mrs. Beamish.

It ended in Rogers taking up his quarters there, for the night.

Towards eleven o'clock, Mahony and he sat, one on each side of the table, in the little sitting-room. The heat was insupportable; and all three doors, and the window, were propped open, in the feeble hope of creating a draught. The lamp had attracted a swarm of flying things: giant moths beat their wings against the globe, or fell singed and sizzling down the chimney; winged-ants alighted with a click upon the table; blowflies and mosquitoes kept up a dizzy hum.

From time to time, Mahony rose and stole into the bedroom, where Mrs. Beamish sat fanning the pests off Polly, who was in a feverish doze. Leaning over his wife, he let his finger lie on her wrist; and, back again in the outer room, he bit nervously at his little finger-nail—an old trick of his, when he was in a quandary. He had curtly refused a game of bezique; so Rogers had produced a pack of cards from his own pocket— soiled, frayed cards, which had likely done service on many a similar occasion—and was whiling the time away with "Solitaire." To sit there watching his slow manipulation of the cards, his patent intentness on the game; to listen any longer to the accursed din of the gnats and flies, passed Mahony's powers of endurance. Abruptly shoving back his chair, he went out into the yard.

This was some twenty paces across—from the row of old kerosene-tins that constituted his flower-garden, past shed and woodstack, to the post-and-rail fence. How often he walked it, he did not know; but, when he went indoors again, his boots were heavy with mud. For a brief summer storm had come up earlier in the evening. A dense black pall of cloud had swept like a heavy curtain over the stars, to the tune of flash and bang. Now, all was clear and calm again; the white star-dust of the Milky Way powdered the sky just overhead; and though the heat was still intense, the air had a fragrant smell of saturated dust and rain-soaked earth—he could hear streamlets of water trickling down the hillside to the river below.

Out there in the dark, several things became plain to him. He saw that he had not had any real confidence in Rogers, from the start; while the effect of the evening spent at close quarters had been to sink his opinion to nothing. Why the deuce had he called the fellow in? Examples were plentiful enough of a colonial practitioner botching a promising case. No matter how good a man your ordinary medico might be to begin with, plant him here, in the wilds, and the chances were he would drop behind. Human life, too, was cheaper than in the old country; the hugger-mugger scramble for existence precluded long regrets, dried tears quickly; and, say what you would, this state of things was bound to tell on even a doctor, in the end.— In addition, Rogers belonged to an old school; his method was to sit by and let nature take its course—perhaps just this slowness to move had won him a name for extreme care. His old-fogyism showed up unmistakably in a short but heated argument they had had on the subject of chloroform. He cited such hoary objections to the use of the new anæsthetic in maternity cases, as Mahony had never expected to hear again: the therapeutic value of pain; the moral danger the patient ran in yielding up her will: ("What right have we to bid a fellow-creature sacrifice her consciousness?") and the impious folly of interfering with the action of a creative law.— It had only remained for him to quote Genesis, and the talking serpent!

Had the case been in his own hands, he would have intervened before now. Rogers, on the contrary, was still satisfied with the shape of affairs—or made pretence to be. For, watching lynx-eyed, Mahony fancied each time the fat man propelled his paunch out of the sickroom, it was a shade less surely: there were nuances, too, in the way he pronounced his vapid: "As long as our strength is well maintained . . . well maintained." Mahony doubted Polly's ability to bear much more; and he made bold to know his own wife's constitution best. Rogers was shilly-shallying: what if he delayed too long, and Polly slipped through his hands?— Lose Polly? Good God! the very thought turned him cold. And, alive to his finger-tips with the superstition of his race, he impetuously offered up his fondest dream to those invisible powers that sat aloft, waiting to be appeased. If this was to be the price exacted of him—the price of his escape from exile—then . . . then . . .

To come back to the present, however, he was in an awkward position: he was going to be forced to take Polly's case out of the hands of the man to whom he had entrusted it. Such a step ran counter to all the stiff rules of conduct, the punctilios of decorum, laid down by the most code-ridden profession in the world.

But a fresh visit to Polly, whose pulse had grown markedly softer, put an end to his scruples.

Stalking into the sitting-room, he said without preamble: "In my opinion, any further delay will mean a risk to my wife. I request you to operate immediately."

Rogers blinked up from his cards, surprise writ across his ruddy countenance. He pushed his spectacles to his forehead. "Eh? What?— Well, well . . . yes, the time is no doubt coming, when we shall have to lend Mother Nature a hand."

"Coming? It's come . . . and gone. Are you blind, man?"

Rogers had faced many an agitated husband in his day. "Now, now, Mr. Mahony," he said soothingly, and laid his last two cards in line. "You must allow me to be the judge of that.— Besides," he added, as he took off his glasses to polish them on a red bandana; "besides, I should have to ask you to go out and get some one to assist me."

"I shall assist you," returned Mahony.

Rogers smiled his broad, fat smile. "Easier said than done, my good sir! . . . easier said than done."

Mahony considerately turned his back; and kept it turned. Emptying a pitcher of water into a basin, he began to lather his hands. "I am a qualified medical man. Of the same university as yourself. I studied under Simpson." It cost him an effort to get the words out. But by speaking, he felt that he did ample penance for the fit of techy pride, which, in the first instance, had tied his tongue.

Rogers was dumbfounded.

"Well, upon my word!" he ejaculated, letting his hands with glasses and handkerchief fall to the table. "God bless my soul! why couldn't you say so before? And why the deuce didn't you yourself attend—"

"We can go into all that afterwards."

But Rogers was not one of those who could deal rapidly with the unexpected: he continued to vent his surprise, and to shoot distrustful glances at his companion. He was flurried, too, at being driven forward quicker than he had a mind to go, and said sulkily that Mahony must take full responsibility for what they were about to do. Mahony hardly heard him; he was looking at the instruments laid out on the table. His fingers itched to close round them.

"I'll prepare my wife," he said briskly. And going into the bedroom, he bent over the pillow.— It was damp with the sweat that had dripped from Polly's head, when the pains were on her.

" 'Ere, you girl, get in quick now with your bucket and cloth, and give that place a good clean-up afore that pore lamb opens 'er eyes again. I'm cooked—that's what I am!" and sitting heavily down on the kitchen-chair, Mrs. Beamish wiped her face towards the four points of the compass.

Piqued by an unholy curiosity, young Ellen willingly obeyed. But a minute later, she was back, having done no more than set her pail down inside the bedroom door. "Oh, sure, Mrs. Beamish, and I can't do't!" she cried shrilly. "It's jus' like Andy Soake's shop . . . when they've bin quarterin' a sheep."

"I'll *quarter* you, you lazy trollop, you!" cried Mrs. Beamish, rising to her aching legs again; and her day-old anxiety found vent in a hearty burst of temper. "*I'll* teach you!"—pulling, as she spoke, the floorcloth out of the girl's hand. "Such airs and graces! Why, sooner or later, milady, you've got to go through it yourself."

"*Me* . . . ? Catch me!" said Ellen, with enormous emphasis. "D'yer mean to say that's 'ow . . . 'ow the children always come?"

"Of course it is, you mincing Nanny-hen!—every blessed child that walks. And I just 'ope," said Mrs. Beamish, as she marched off herself with brush and scrubber: "I 'ope, now you know it, you'll 'ave a little more love and gratitoode for your own mother, than ever you 'ad before."

"Oh, lor!" said the girl. "Oh, lor!"— And plumping down on the chopping-block, she snatched her apron to her face and began to cry.

[8]

Two months passed, before Mahony could put Polly and Mrs. Beamish into the coach bound for Geelong.

It had been touch and go with Polly; and for weeks her condition had kept him very anxious. With the inset of the second month, however, she seemed fairly to turn the corner, and from then on made a steady recovery, thanks to her youth, and an unimpaired vitality.

He had hurried the little cradle out of sight. But Polly was quick to miss it, and quite approved of it having been given to a needy expectant mother near by. Altogether, she bore the thwarting of her hopes bravely.

"Poor little baby, I should have been very fond of it," was all she said, when she was well enough to fold and pack away the tiny garments at which she had stitched with such pleasure.

It was not to Mahony's mind that she returned with Mrs. Beamish—but what else could be done? After lying a prisoner through the hot summer, she was sadly in need of a change. And Mrs. Beamish promised her a diet of unlimited milk and eggs, as well as the do-nothing life that befitted an invalid. Just before they left, a letter arrived from John, demanding the keys of his house, and proposing that Polly should come to town to set it in order for him, and help him to engage a housekeeper. A niggardly—a truly "John-ish"—fashion of giving an invitation, thought Mahony, and was not for his wife accepting it. But Polly was so pleased at the prospect of seeing her brother, that he ended by agreeing to her going on to Melbourne, as soon as she had thoroughly recuperated.

Peace between him and Mrs. Beamish was dearly bought, up to the last; they barely avoided a final explosion. At the beginning of her third month's absence from home, the good woman grew very restive, and sighed aloud for the day on which she would be able to take her departure.

"I expec' my bein' away like this'll run clean into a fifty-poun' note," she said one evening. "When it comes to managin' an 'ouse, those two girls of mine 'aven't a h'ounce o' gumption between them."

It *was* tactless of her, even Polly felt that; though she could sympathise with the worry that prompted the words. As for Mahony, had he had the money to do it, he believed he would have flung the sum named straight at her head.

"She must never come again," said Polly to herself, as she bent over the hair-chain she was making as a gift for John. "It *is* a pity, but it seems as if Richard can't get on with those sort of people."

In his relief at having his house to himself, Mahony accepted even Polly's absence with composure. To be perpetually in the company of other people irked him beyond belief. A certain amount of privacy was as vital to him as sleep.

Delighting in his new-found solitude, he put off from day to day the disagreeable job of winding up his affairs, and discovering how much—or how little—ready money he would have, to set sail with. Another thing, some books he had sent home for, a year or more ago, came to hand at this time, and gave him a fresh pretext for delay. There were eight or nine volumes to unpack and cut the pages of. He ran from one to another, sipping, devouring. Finally, he cast anchor in a collected edition of his old chief's writings on obstetrics—slipped in, this, as a gift from the sender, a college-chum—and over it, his feet on the table, his dead pipe in the corner of his mouth, Mahony sat for the better part of the night.

When he could read no more, he let the book fall, and looked before him with unseeing eyes.

The effect of this master-mind on his was that of a spark on tinder. Under the flash, he cursed, for the hundredth time, the folly he had been guilty of, in throwing up medicine. It was a vocation that had fitted him as coursing fits a hound, or housewifery a woman; and his studies had engrossed him utterly, ever since the day on which he had given the humanities the go-by for the dissecting-room. The only excuse he could find for his apostasy was, that he had been caught in an epidemic of unrest, which had swept through the country, upsetting the balance of men's reason. He had since wondered if the Great Exhibition of '51 had not had something to do with it, by unduly whetting people's imaginations; so that but a single cry of "Gold!" was needed, to loose the spirit of vagrancy that lurks in every Briton's blood. His case had perhaps been peculiar in this: no one had come forward to warn or to dissuade. His next relatives—mother and sisters—were, he thought, glad to know him well away. In their eyes he had lowered himself by taking up medicine; to them it was still of a piece with barber's pole and cupping-basin. Before his time, no member of the family had entered any profession but the army.— Oh, that in-

fernal Irish pride! . . . and Irish poverty. It had choke-damped
his youth, blighted the prospects of his sisters. He could remember, as if it were yesterday, the jibes and fleers called forth
by the suit of a wealthy Dublin brewer, who had been attracted—by sheer force of contrast, no doubt—to the elder of
the two swan-necked, stiff-backed Miss Townshend-Mahonys,
with their long, thin noses, and the ingrained lines that ran
from the curled nostrils to the corners of their supercilious
mouths, describing a sneer so deep that, at a distance, it was
possible to mistake it for a smile.— "Beer, my dear, indeed and
there are worse things in the world than beer!" he heard his
mother declare, in her biting way. "By all means take him!
You can wash yourself in it if water gets scarce, and I'll place
my kitchen orders with you." Lucinda, who had perhaps
sniffed timidly at release, burnt crimson: thank you! she would
rather eat rat-bane.— He supposed they pinched and scraped
along as of old—the question of money was never broached
between him and them. Prior to his marriage, he had sent them
what he could; but that little was in itself an admission of failure. They made no inquiries about his mode of life, preferring
it to remain in shadow; enough for them, that he had not
amassed a fortune. Had that come to pass, they might have
pardoned the rude method of its making—in fancy, he listened
to the witty, cutting, self-derisive words, in which they would
have alluded to his success.

Lying back in his chair he thought of them thus, without un-
kindliness, even with a dash of humour. That was possible,
now that knocking about the world had rubbed off some of his
own corners. In his young days, he, too, had been hot and bitter. What, however, to another, might have formed the chief
crux in their conduct—it was by squandering such money as
there was, his own portion among it, on his scamp of an elder
brother, that they had forced him into the calling they despised
—this had not troubled him greatly. For medicine was the profession on which his choice would anyhow have fallen. To ease
the sick, to help new life into the world, had always seemed to
him the noblest career open to man.— And to-night the book
that lay before him had infected him with the old enthusiasm.
He re-lived those days when a skilfully handled case of
placenta previa, or a successful delivery in the fourth position,
had meant more to him than the Charge of the Light Brigade.

162

Book I: *Australia Felix*

Fresh from this dip into the past, this foretaste of the future, he turned, in good heart, to business. An inventory had to be taken; damaged goods cleared out; a list of bad, and less bad, debts drawn up: he and Hempel were hard at work all next day. The result was worse even than he had expected; and he sat down to his evening meal with small appetite. His outlay that summer—ever since the day, in short, on which he had set off to the aid of his bereaved relative—had been enormous. Trade had run dry, and, throughout Polly's long illness, he had dipped blindly into his savings. He could never have said no to Mrs. Beamish when she came to him for money—rather would he have pawned the coat off his back. And she, good woman, was unused to cheeseparing. His men's wages paid, berths booked, the numerous expenses bound up with a departure defrayed, he would have but a scanty sum in hand with which to start on the other side.

For himself he was not afraid; but he shrank from the thought of Polly undergoing privations. So far, they had enjoyed a kind of frugal comfort. But should he meet with obstacles at the outset: if, for instance, patients were laggardly and the practice slow to move, or if he himself fell ill: they might have a spell of real poverty to face. And it was under the goad of this fear that he hit on a new scheme. Why, he asked himself, should he not leave Polly behind for a time, until he had succeeded in making a home for her?—why not leave her under the wing of her brother John? John stood urgently in need of a head for his establishment, and who so well suited for the post as Polly? Surely, if it were put before him, John must jump at the offer! Parting from Polly, and were it only for a little while, would, it was true, be painful; but, did he go alone, he would be free to do his utmost—and with an easy mind, knowing that Polly lacked none of the creature-comforts. Yes, the more he considered the plan, the better he liked it.— The one crease in the sheet of his satisfaction was the thought that, if their child had lived, no such smooth and simple arrangement would have been possible. He could not have foisted a family on Turnham. It was well, no doubt, for us nearsighted mortals, that ultimate decisions did not lie in our hands! At the time, he had been keenly disappointed at his inability to save the infant, yet here he now was, driven to admit that perhaps, after all, things had turned out for the best.

163

Now, he waited with impatience for Polly to return—his reasonable little Polly! But he did not hurry her. Polly was enjoying her holiday. Having passed to Melbourne from Geelong, she wrote:

John is so very kind. He doesn't of course go out yet himself, but I was present with some friends of his at a very elegant soirée. John gave me a headdress composed of black pearls and frosted leaves. He means to go in for politics as soon as his year of mourning is up.

Mahony replied:

Enjoy yourself, my heart, and see all the sights you can.

While into more than one of his letters he slipped a banknote.

For you know I like you to pay your own way as far as possible.

And at length the day came when he could lift his wife out of the coach. She emerged powdered brown with dust, and very tired, but radiantly happy: it was a great event in little Polly's life, this home-coming, and coming, too, strong and well. The house was a lively place that afternoon: Polly had so much to tell that she sat holding her bonnet for over an hour, quite unable to get as far as the bedroom: and even Long Jim's mouth went up at the corners instead of down; for Polly had contrived to bring back a suitable little gift for every one. And, in presenting these, she found out more of what people were thinking and feeling, than her husband had done in all the eight weeks of her absence.

Mahony was loath to damp her pleasure straightway; he bided his time. He could not know that Polly also had been laying plans, and that she watched anxiously for the right moment to unfold them.

The morning after her return, she got a lift in the baker's cart, and drove out to inspect John's children. What she saw and heard on this visit was disquieting. The children had run wild, were grown dirty, sly, untruthful. Especially the boy.— "A young Satan, and that's a fact, Mrs. Mahony! What he

needs is a man's hand over him, and a good hidin' six days
outer seven."

It was not alone little Johnny's misconduct, however, that
made Polly break silence. An incident occurred that touched
her still more nearly.

Husband and wife sat snug and quiet, as in the early days
of their marriage. Autumn had come around, and a fire burnt
in the stove, before which Pompey snorted in his dreams. But,
for all the cosy tranquillity, Polly was not happy; and, time
and again, she moistened and bit at the tip of her thread,
before pointing it through her needle. For the book open before Richard, in which he was making notes as he read, was—
the Bible. Bending over him, to drop a kiss on the top of his
head, Polly had been staggered by what she saw. Opposite the
third verse of the first chapter of Genesis: "And God said, Let
there be light: and there was light," he had written: "Three
days before the sun!" Her heart seemed to shrivel, to grow
small in her breast, at the thought of her husband being guilty
of such impiety. Ceasing her pretence at sewing, she walked
out of the house into the yard. Standing there under the stars,
she said aloud, as if some one, *the* One, could hear her: "He
doesn't mean to do wrong. . . . I *know* he doesn't!"— When she
re-entered the room, he was still at it. His beautiful writing,
reduced to its tiniest, wound round the narrow margins.

Deeply red, Polly took her courage in both hands, and struck
a blow for the soul whose salvation was more to her than her
own. "Richard, do you think that . . . is . . . is right?" she asked
in a low voice.

Mahony raised his head. "Eh?—what, Pollykin?"

"I mean, do you think you ought . . . that it is right to do
what you are doing?"

The smile, half-tender, half-quizzical, that she loved, broke
over her husband's face. He held out his hand. "Is my little
wife troubled?"

"Richard, I only mean. . . ."

"Polly, my dear, don't worry your little head over what you
don't understand. And have confidence in me. You know I
wouldn't do anything I believed to be wrong?"

"Yes, indeed. And you are really far more religious than
I am."

"One can be religious, and yet not shut one's eyes to the

truth. It's Saint Paul, you know, who says: we can do nothing against the Truth, but for the Truth. And you may depend on it, Polly, the All-Wise would never have given us the brains He has, if He had not intended us to use them. Now I have long felt sure, that the Bible is not wholly what it claims to be— direct inspiration."

"Oh, Richard!" said Polly, and threw an anxious glance over her shoulder. "If anyone should hear you!"

"We can't afford to let our lives be governed by what other people think, Polly. Nor will I give any man the right to decide for me what my share of the Truth shall be."

On seeing the Bible closed, Polly breathed again, at the same time promising herself to take the traitorous volume into safekeeping, that no third person's eye should rest on it. Perhaps, too, if it were put away, Richard would forget to go on writing in it. He had probably begun, in the first place, only because he had nothing else to do. In the store, he sat and smoked and twirled his thumbs—not half a dozen customers came in, in the course of the day. If he were once properly occupied again, with work that he liked, he would not be tempted to put his gifts to such a profane use.— Thus Polly primed herself for speaking. For now was the time. Richard was declaring that trade had gone to the dogs, and that his takings had dropped to a quarter of what they had formerly been. This headed just where she wished.— But Polly would not have been Polly, had she not glanced aside for a moment, to cheer and console.

"It's the same everywhere, Richard. Everybody's complaining.— And that reminds me, I forgot to tell you about the Beamishes. They're in great trouble. You see, a bog has formed in front of the Hotel, and the traffic goes round another way and doesn't pass the house, so they've lost most of their custom. Mr. Beamish never opens his mouth at all now, and 'mother' is fearfully worried. That's what was the matter when she was here—only she was too kind to say so."

"Hard lines!"

"Indeed it is.— But about us; I'm not surprised to hear trade is dull. Since I was over in the western township last, no less than six new General Stores have gone up—I scarcely knew the place. They've all got big plate-glass windows; and were crowded with people."

166

"Yes, there's a regular exodus up west. But that doesn't alter the fact, wife, that I've made a very poor job of storekeeping. I shall leave here with hardly a penny in my pocket."

"Yes, but then, Richard," said Polly, and bent over her strip of needlework, "you were never cut out to be a storekeeper, were you?"

"I was not. And I verily believe, if it hadn't been for that old sobersides of a Hempel, I should have come a cropper long ago."

"Yes, and Hempel," said Polly softly; "Hempel's been wanting to leave for ever so long."

"The dickens he has!" cried Mahony in astonishment. "And me humming and hawing about giving him notice!— What's the matter with him? What's he had to complain of?"

"Oh, nothing like that. He wants to enter the ministry. A helper's needed at the Baptist Chapel, and he means to apply for the post. You see, he's saved a good deal, and thinks he can study to be a minister at the same time."

"Study for his grave, the fool!— So that's it, is it? Well, well! it saves trouble in the end. I don't need to bother my head now over what's to become of him . . . him or anyone else. My chief desire is to say good-bye to this hole for ever. There's no sense, Polly, in my dawdling on here. Indeed, I haven't the money to do it. So I've arranged, my dear, with our friend Ocock to come in and sell us off, as soon as you can get our personal belongings put together."

Here Polly raised her head, as if to interrupt; but Mahony, full of what he had to say, ignored the movement, and went on speaking. He did not wish to cause his wife uneasiness, by dwelling on his difficulties; but some explanation was necessary, to pave the way for his proposal that she should remain behind, when he left the colony. He spent all his eloquence in making this sound natural and attractive. But it was hard, when Polly's big, astonished eyes hung on his face.— "Do you think, for my sake, you could be brave enough?" he wound up, rather unsurely. "It wouldn't be for long, love, I'm certain of that. Just let me set foot in England once more!"

"Why . . . why yes, dear Richard, I . . . I think I could, if you really wished it," said Polly in a small voice. She tried to seem reasonable; though black night descended on her at the mere thought of parting, and though her woman's eye saw a hundred objections to the plan, which his had overlooked. (For one thing, John had just installed Sara as housekeeper, and Sara would take it very unkindly to be shown the door.) "I *think* I could," she repeated. "But before you go on, dear, I should like to ask *you* something."

She laid down her needlework; her heart was going pit-a-pat. "Richard, did you ever . . . I mean, have you never thought of . . . of taking up your profession again— I mean here—starting practice here?— No, wait a minute! Let me finish! I . . . I . . . oh, Richard—!" Unable to find words, Polly locked her fingers under the tablecloth, and hoped she was not going to be so silly as to cry. Getting up, she knelt down before her husband, laying her hands on his knees. "Oh, Richard, I wish you would—*how* I wish you would!"

"Why, Polly!" said Mahony, surprised at her agitation. "Why, my dear, what's all this?— You want to know if I never thought of setting up in practice out here? Of course I did . . . in the beginning. You don't think I'd have chosen to keep a store, if there'd been any other opening for me? But there wasn't, child. The place was over-run. Never a medico came out and found digging too much for him, but he fell back in despair on his profession. I didn't see my way to join their starvation band."

"Yes, *then*, Richard!—but now?" broke in Polly. "Now, it's quite, quite different. Look at the size Ballarat has grown— there are more than forty thousand people settled on it now; Mr. Ocock told me so. And you know, dear, doctors have cleared out lately, not come fresh. There was that one, I forget his name, who drank himself to death; and the two, you remember, who were sold up just before Christmas."— But this was an unfortunate line of argument to have hit on, and Polly blushed and stumbled.

Mahony laughed at her slip, and smoothed her hair. "Typical fates, love! They mustn't be mine.— Besides, Polly, you're forgetting the main thing—how I hate the place, and how I've always longed to get away."

"No, I'm not. But please let me go on!— You know, Richard, every one believes some day Ballarat will be the chief city in Victoria—bigger even than Geelong or Melbourne. And then, to have a good practice here would mean ever such a lot of money. I'm not the only person who thinks you oughtn't to let such a chance slip. There's Sara, and Mrs. Beamish—I know, of course, you don't care much what they say; but still—" Polly meant: still, you see, I have public opinion on my side. As, however, once more words failed her, she hastened to add: "John, too, is amazed to hear you think of going home to bury yourself in some little English village. He's sure there'd be a splendid opening for you here. John thinks very, very highly of you. He told me he believes you would have saved Emma's life, if you had been there."

"I'm much obliged to your brother for his confidence," said Mahony drily; "but——"

"Wait a minute, Richard!— You see, dear, *I* can't help feeling myself, that you ought not to be too hasty in deciding. Of course, I know I'm young, and haven't had much experience, but . . . You see, you're *known* here, Richard, and that's always something; in England, you'd be a perfect stranger. And though you may say there are too many doctors on the Flat, still, if the place goes on growing as it is doing, there'll soon be room for more; and then, if it isn't you, it'll just be some one else. And that *does* seem a pity, when you are so clever—so much, much cleverer than other people! Yes, I know all about it; Mrs. Beamish told me it was you I owed my life to, not Dr. Rogers"—at which Mahony winced, indignant that anyone should have betrayed to Polly how near death she had been.— "Oh, I *do* want people to know you for what you really are, and respect you!" said little Polly.

"Pussy, I believe she has ambitions for her husband," said Mahony to Palmerston.

"Of course, I have.— You say, dear, you hate Ballarat, and all that, but have you ever thought, Richard, what a difference it would make, if you were in a better position? You think people look down on you, as it is, because you're in trade. But if you were a doctor, there'd be none of that. You'd call yourself by your full name again, and be as good as anybody. You'd be asked into society, and could write yourself down on the visiting list at Government House, and keep a horse. You'd live in a bigger house, and have a room to yourself, and time to read and write. I'm quite sure you'd make lots of money—you've often said how high the fees are here—and soon be at the top of the tree.— And after all, dear Richard, *I* don't want to go home. I would much rather stay here and look after Jerry, and

169

dear Ned, and poor John's children," said Polly, falling back, as a forlorn hope, on her own preference.

"Why, what a piece of special pleading!" cried Mahony, and leaning forward, he kissed the young flushed face.

"Don't laugh at me. I'm in earnest."

"Why, no, child.— But Polly, my dear, even if I were tempted for a moment to think seriously of what you say, where would the money come from? Fees are high, it's true, if the ball's once set a-rolling. But till then?— With a jewel of a wife like mine, I'd be a scoundrel to take risks."

Polly had been waiting for this question. On hearing it, she sat back on her heels, and drew a deep breath. The communication she had now to make him was the hub round which all turned. Should he refuse to consider it. . . . Plucking at the fringe of the tablecloth, she brought out, piecemeal, the news that John was willing to go surety for the money they would need to borrow for the start. Not only that: he offered them a handsome sum weekly to take entire charge of his children.— "Not here, in this little house—I know that wouldn't do," Polly hastened to throw in, forestalling the objection she read in Richard's eyes. Now did he not think it would be wise to weigh an offer of this kind very carefully? A name like John's was not to be despised; most people in their position would jump at it. "I understand something about it," said the little woman, and sagely nodded her head. "For when I was in Geelong, Mr. Beamish tried his hardest to raise some money and couldn't, his sureties weren't good enough." Mahony had not the heart to chide her for discussing his private affairs with her brother. Indeed, he rather admired the business-like way she had gone about it. And he admitted this; by ceasing to banter her, and by calling her attention to the various hazards and inconveniences the step would entail.

Polly heard him out in silence. Enough for her, in the beginning, that he did not decline off-hand. They had a long talk, the end of which was that he promised to sleep over John's proposal, and to delay fixing the date of the auction till the morning.

Having yielded this point, Mahony kissed his wife and sent her to bed, himself going out with the dog for his usual stroll.

It was a fine night—moonless, but thick with stars. So much, at least, could be said in favour of the place: there was abundant sky-room; you got a clear half of the great vault at once. How he pitied, on such a night, the dwellers in old, congested cities, whose view of the starry field was limited to a narrow strip, cut through house-tops.

Yet he walked with a springless tread. For, in spite of the firm front he had presented to Polly, the canvas door in its battens had scarcely swung to behind him, before he knew that he was not as composed as he had believed. The fact was, certain of his wife's words had struck home; and, in the course of the past year, he had learnt to put considerable faith in Polly's practical judgment. As he wound his way up the little hill, to which he had often carried his perplexities, he let his pipe go out, and forgot to whistle Pompey off butcher's garbage.

Sitting down on a log, he put his chin in his hands. Below him twinkled the sparse lights of the Flat; shouts and singing rose from the circus.— And so John would have been willing to go surety for him! Let no one say the unexpected did not happen. . . . Not that he would greatly care to be beholden to John. He didn't like him well enough. Still, it was generous of him, aye and trusting, too, to make the offer. All said and done, they were little more than strangers to each other, and John had no notion what his money-making capacities as a doctor might be. It was true, Polly had been too delicate to mention whether the affair had come about through her persuasions or on John's own initiative. John might have some ulterior motive up his sleeve. Perhaps he did not want to lose his sister. . . . Or was scheming to bind a pair of desirables fast to this colony, the welfare of which he had so much at heart. Again, it might be that he wished thus to buy off the memory of that day on which he had stripped his soul naked. Simplest of all, why should he not be merely trying to pay back a debt? He, Mahony, might shrink from lying under an obligation to John, but, so far, the latter had not scrupled to accept favours from him; and, comparatively speaking, his sacrifice was bigger than any John could make. But that was always the way with your rich men; they were not troubled by paltry pride; for they knew it was possible to acquit themselves of their debts at a moment's notice, and with interest.— This led him to reflect on the great help to him the loan of his wealthy relative's name would be: difficulties would melt before it. And surely no undue risk was involved in the use of it? Without boasting, he thought he was better equipped, both by aptitude and training, than the ruck of colonial practitioners. Did he enter the lists, he could hardly fail to succeed. And out here even a moderate success spelled a fortune. Gained double-quick, too. After which, the lucky individual sold out and went home, to live in comfort.— Yes, that was a point, and not to be overlooked. No definite surrender of one's hopes was called for; only a postponement. Ten years might do it—meaty years, of course, the best years of one's life—still. . . . It would mean very hard work; but had he not just been contemplating, with perfect equanimity, an even more arduous venture on the other side? What a capricious piece of mechanism was the human brain!

Another thought that occurred to him was that his services might prove of greater use to this new country than to the old, where able men abounded. He recalled the many good lives and promising cases he had here seen lost and bungled. To take the instance nearest home—Polly's confinement. He considered that this had been botched from beginning to end.— Yes, to show his mettle to such as Rogers; to earn respect where he had lived as a mere null—the idea had an insidious fascination. And as Polly sagely remarked: if it were not he, it would be some one else; another would harvest the *kudos* that might have been his. For the rough-and-ready treatment —the blue pills and black draughts—that had satisfied the early diggers had fallen into disrepute; medical skill was beginning to be appreciated. If this went on, Ballarat would soon stand on a level with any city of its size, at home.— But even as it was, he had never been quite fair to it; he had seen it with a jaundiced eye. And again he believed Polly hit the nail on the head, when she asserted that the poor position he had occupied there was responsible for much of his dislike.

But there was something else at work in him besides. Below the surface, an admission awaited him, which he shrank from making. All these pros and cons, these quibbles and hair-splittings, were but a misfit attempt to cloak the truth. He might gull himself with them for a time: in his heart he knew that he would yield—if yield he did—because he was by nature only too prone to follow the line of least resistance. What he had gone through to-night was no new experience. Often enough,

after fretting and fuming about a thing, till it seemed as if
nothing under the sun had ever mattered so much to him, it
could happen that he suddenly threw up the sponge, and
meekly bowed to circumstance. His vitality exhausted itself
beforehand—in a passionate aversion, a torrent of words—and
failed him at the critical moment. It was a weakness in his
blood—in the blood of his race.— But, in the present instance,
he could put forward an excuse for himself. He had not known
—not at least until Polly came out with her brother's magnani-
mous offer—how deeply he dreaded beginning all over again
in England, an utter stranger, without influence or recommendations, and with no money to speak of at his back. He
had worn an air of false courage to himself, while, subconsciously, every nerve had been in revolt, at the prospect of the
humiliations that were in store for him.

But now he had owned up, and there was no more need of
shift or subterfuge: now, it was one rush and hurry to the end.
He had capitulated; a thin-skinned aversion to confronting difficulties, when he saw the chance of avoiding them, had won
the day. He intended—had perhaps the whole time intended—
to take the hand held out to him.— After all, why not? Anyone
else, as Polly said, would have jumped at John's offer. He alone
must argue himself blue in the face over it.— Polly? Well, he
knew one thing: Polly would be a very happy little woman
when she heard of his decision to remain. No parting for them
now! When the time came to go, they would go together. Till
then, she might continue to mother her forlorn clan of relatives
and friends, to her heart's content.

But as he sat and pondered the lengthy chain of circumstance—Polly's share in it, John's, his own; even the part played
by incorporeal things—he brought up short against the word
"decision." He might flatter himself by imagining he had been
free to decide; in reality, nothing was further from the truth.
He had been subtly and slily guided to his goal—led blindfold along a road that was not of his own choosing. Everything and every one had combined to constrain him: his favours to John, the failure of his business, Polly's inclinations
and persuasions, his own fastidious shrinkings. So that, in the
end, all he had had to do was to brush aside a flimsy gossamer
veil, which hung between him and his fate.— Was it straining

a point to see in the whole affair the workings of a Power outside himself—against himself, in so far as it took no count of
his poor earth-blind vision?

Well, if this were so, better still: his ways were in God's
hand. He might leave it at that, with a tranquil mind.— And
after all, what did it matter in the long run, where one strove
to serve one's Maker—east or west or south or north—and
whether the stars overhead were grouped in this constellation
or in that? Their steadfast light was an eternal pledge that one
would never be overlooked or forgotten, traced by the hand of
Him who had promised to note even a sparrow's fall.— And
now, out into the darkness he spoke aloud that ancient and
homely formula, which is man's stand-by in face of the untried,
the unknown.

"If God wills. . . . God knows best."

PART III

[1]

THE house stood not far from the Great Swamp. It was of
weatherboard, with a corrugated iron roof, and might have
been built from a child's drawing of a house: a door in the
centre, a little window on either side, a chimney at each end.
Since the ground sloped downwards, the front part rested on
piles some three feet high—Johnny, brought on a visit of inspection, crawled far underneath—and, from the rutty clay-
track that would one day be a street, wooden steps led up to
the door. Much as Mahony would have liked to face it with a
verandah, he did not feel justified in spending a penny more
than he could help. And Polly not only agreed with him in this,
but contrived to find an advantage in the plainer style of archi-
tecture. "Your plate will be better seen, Richard, right on the
street, than hidden under a verandah."— But then Polly was
overflowing with content. Had not two of the rooms fireplaces?
And was there not a wash-house, with a real copper in it, behind the detached kitchen? Not to speak of a spare-room!—
To the rear of the house, a high paling-fence enclosed a good-
sized yard. Mahony dreamed of a garden, Polly of keeping
hens.

There were no two happier people on Ballarat that autumn than the Mahonys, as they trudged to and fro: down the hill, across the Flat, over the bridge, and up the other side: first, through a Sahara of dust, then, when the rains began, ankle-deep in gluey red mud. And the building of the finest mansion never gave half so much satisfaction as did that of this flimsy little wooden house, with its thin lath-and-plaster walls. In fancy, they had furnished it and lived in it, long before it was even roofed in. Mahony sat at work in his surgery—it measured ten by twelve—Polly at her Berlin-woolwork, in the parlour opposite: "And a cage with a little parrot in it, hanging at the window!"

The preliminaries to the change had gone smoothly enough —Mahony could not complain. Pleasant they had not been: but then, could the arranging and clinching of a complicated money-matter ever be pleasant? He had had to submit to hearing his private affairs gone into by a stranger, to make clear to strangers his capacity for earning a decent income.

With John's promissory letter in his pocket, he had betaken himself to Henry Ocock's office.

This, notwithstanding its excellent position on the brow of the western hill, could not deny its humble origin as a livery-barn—Ocock had plainly no intention of spending money on improvements, in the meantime. The entry was by a yard; and some of the former horse-boxes had been rudely knocked together to provide accommodations.— Mahony sniffed stale dung.

In what had once been the harness-room, two young men sat at work.

"Why, Tom, my lad, you here?"

Tom Ocock raised his freckled face, from the chin of which sprouted some long ragged fair hairs, and turned red.

"Yes, it's me. Do you want to see 'En—" at an open kick from his brother—"Mr. Ocock?"

"If you please."

Waiting was again the order of the day. As he sat, pulling his whiskers, Mahony fretted at himself for having returned to deal with a man who was personally so uncongenial to him. There were lawyers enough on the Flat. Yes, but: "Rogues and liars every one!" And Ocock at least knew who he was—it was not a case of lugging your credentials with you. John, too,

175

whose wishes must be studied under the circumstances, had let drop a hint that Ocock was a rising man.

Informed by Grindle that the "Captain" was at liberty, Mahony passed to an inner room, where he was waved to a chair. In answer to his statement that he had called to see about raising some money, Ocock returned an: "Indeed? Money is tight, sir, very tight!" His face had instantly taken on the blankwall solemnity proper to dealings with this world's main asset.

Mahony did not at once hand over John's way-soothing letter. He thought he would first test the lawyer's attitude towards him in person—a species of self-torment men of his make are rarely able to withstand. He spoke of the decline of his business and his wish to get out of it; of his idea of setting up as a doctor and building himself a house; and, as he talked, he read his answer pat and clear in the ferrety eyes before him. There was a bored tolerance of his wordiness, an utter lack of interest in the concerns of the petty tradesman.

"H'm." Ocock, lying back in his chair, was fitting five outstretched fingers to their fellows. "All very well, my good sir, but may I ask if you have anyone in view as a security?"

"I have. May I trouble you to glance through this?" and Mahony triumphantly brandished John's letter.

Ocock raised his brows. "What? Mr. John Turnham? Ah, very good . . . very good indeed!" The brazen-faced change in his manner would have made a cat laugh; he sat upright, was interested, courteous, alert. ("As if the pair of them were shaking hands over my head!" thought the go-between sorely.)

"Quite in order! And now, pray, how much do we need?" asked the transmogrified lawyer.

Mahony jerked his mind back to the matter in hand.— Unadvised, he had not been able, he said, to determine the sum. So Ocock took pencil and paper, and, prior to running off a reckoning, put him through a sharp interrogation. Under it Mahony felt as though he were in a waking nightmare, in which his clothing was being stripped, piece by piece, off his back. He had to own up to hole-and-corner economies, and whimmy extravagances: those equivalents, in money, of parsimoniously untying string in place of snipping it; of the shudder caused by the contact of steel and fruit. At one moment he stood revealed as mean and stingy, at another as an unpractical spendthrift. More serious things came out, besides. He began to see, under the limelight of the lawyer's inquiry, in what a muddle-headed fashion he had run his business, and how unlikely it was he could ever have made a good thing of it. Still worse was his thoughtless folly in wedding and bringing home a young wife, without, in this settlement where accident was rife, where fires were of nightly occurrence, insuring against either fire or death.— Not that Ocock breathed a hint of censure: all was done with a twist of the eye, a purse of the lip; but it was enough for Mahony. He sat there, feeling like an eel in the skinning, and did not attempt to keep pace with the lawyer, who hunted figures into the centre of a woolly maze.

The upshot of these calculations was: he would need help to the tune of something over one thousand pounds. As matters stood at present on Ballarat, said Ocock, the plainest house he could build would cost him about eight hundred; and another couple of hundred—at the lowest estimate—would go in furnishing; while a saddle-horse might be put down at fifty pounds. On Turnham's letter, he, Ocock, would be prepared to borrow seven hundred for him—and this could probably be obtained at ten per cent. on a mortgage on the house, a further four hundred, for which he would have to pay twelve or fifteen. Current expenses must be covered by the residue of his savings, and by what he was able to make. They would include the keep of the horse, an item this of between fifty and sixty pounds; and the interest that would fall due on the borrowed money, which might be reckoned roughly at a hundred and twenty per annum. In addition he would be well advised to insure his life for five or seven hundred pounds.

The question also came up whether the land he had selected for building on should be purchased or not. He was for doing so, for settling the whole business there and then. Ocock, however, took the opposite view; considering, said he, that the site chosen was far from the centre of the town, Mahony might safely postpone buying in the meanwhile. There had been no government landsales of late, and all main-road frontages had still to come under the hammer. As occupier, when the time arrived, he would have first chance at the upset price; though then, it was true, he would also be liable for improvements.

The one thing he must beware of, was of enclosing too small a block.

Mahony agreed—agreed to everything: the affair seemed to have passed out of his hands. A sense of dismay invaded him while he listened to the lawyer tick off the obligations and responsibilities he was letting himself in for. A thousand pounds! He to run into debt for a sum like this, who had never owed a farthing to anyone! He fell to doubting whether, after all, he had made choice of the easier way; and lapsed into a gloomy silence.

Ocock, on the other hand, warmed to geniality.

"May I say, doctor, how wise I personally think your decision to come over to us?"— He spoke as if Ballarat East were in the heart of the Russian steppes. "And that reminds me. There's a friend of mine. . . . I may be able at once to put a patient in your way."

As they entered the harness-room, there was the noise of a scuffle, and paper rustled and tore.

"Now then, what's up here?" demanded Ocock, sharp as a razor.

"What's up? This, governor!" and Grindle, a trifle red and blown, held aloft a dirty, dog's-eared, paper-covered book— plainly a work of fiction. "So deep in it, boss, you could 'ave knocked 'im down without 'im knowin' it!"

Pale Johnny darted a venomous glance at the speaker—the narrow, slanting look that shoots from the pale little eyes of a snake.

"Indeed!" said Ocock, and stretched his straight mouth in a mirthless smile. "Indeed! So this is the reward I get for giving the young blackguard a chance—his last chance!— Eh? What's that you say, my boy?"

"I said it was a lie—a damned lie!" said Johnny, and worked the palm of one cold, bluish hand over the back of the other.

"The language of the grog-shop, you will observe, Dr. Mahony—the grog-shop, our favourite haunt! Used, sir, under the impression that it is thus one gentleman communicates with another!"— Here, stepping nimbly and noiselessly up behind Johnny, Ocock dealt him half a dozen terrific blows on the ears right and left in quick succession. Blazing red, Johnny slunk from the room.

" 'E wasn't reading," muttered Tom.

178

"And will you, sir, be good enough to hold your tongue till you're spoken to? Feeling the need of a little recreation—is that it? Dull work this, Thomas, eh, after the company we have been accustomed to keep? No petticoats for you to hang round here, my fine fellow!"

Mahony bowed himself out, and walked home in a mood of depression which it took all Polly's arts to dispel.

Under its influence he wrote an outspoken letter to Purdy —but with no very satisfactory result. It was like projecting a feeler for sympathy into the void, so long was it now since the two of them had met, and so widely had his friend's life branched off from his.

Purdy's answer—it was headed "The Ovens"—did not arrive till several weeks later and was mainly about himself.

In a way I'm with you, old pill-box, he wrote. *You'll cut a jolly sight better figure as an M.D. than ever you've done behind a counter. But I don't know that I'd care to stake my last dollar on you all the same. What does Mrs. Polly say?— As for me, old boy, since you're good enough to ask, why the less said the better. A gammy pin is a blankety nuisance to a fellow in a shop like this. One of these days you'll see the old bad half-penny turn up again—the climate here's too damn cooky to suit me. A poor worn old shicer'll come crawling round to your back door to see if you've any cast-off duds you can spare him. Seriously, Dick, old man, I'm stony-broke once more and the Lord only knows how I'm going to win through.*

Not much to be made of this! It was well, thought Mahony, that, before you could receive a reply to an impulsive letter, you were cold to the mood in which you had penned it.— Here, it was easy to read between the lines that his projected change of occupation seemed a mere trifle to Purdy, who was given to changing his job as naturally as he changed his shirt.

In the course of that winter, custom died a natural death; and one day, the few oddments that remained having been sent to auction, to be sold for whatever they would bring, Mahony and his assistant nailed boards horizontally across the entrance to the store. The day of weighing out pepper and salt was over; never again would the tiny jangle of the accursed bell smite his ears. The next thing was that Hempel packed his chattels and departed for his new walk in life. Mahony was not sorry to see him go. Hempel's thoughts had soared far above the counter; he was arrived at the stage of: "I'm every bit as good as you!" which all men reached out here, sooner or later. He had also taken to burning the midnight oil. This kept Polly awake, sniffing for fire, and formed an eternal bone of contention with Long Jim, who shared his mattress.

"I shall always be pleased to hear how you are getting on."

Mahony spoke kindly, but in a tone which, as Polly who stood by, very well knew, people were apt to misunderstand.

"I should think so!" she chimed in. "I shall feel very hurt indeed, Hempel, if you don't come to see us."

—With regard to the other member of the house, she had a talk with her husband one night as they went to bed.

"There really won't be anything for him to do over there, will there? No heavy crates or barrels to move about. And he doesn't know a thing about horses—I think you need a sharp, bright boy for that," said little Polly. "Besides, he does so want to go home. Why not let him? What would you say, dear, to giving him thirty pounds for his passage-money, and a trifle in his pocket? It would make him very happy, and he'd be off your hands for good— Of course, though, just as you think best."

"We shall need every penny we can scrape together, for ourselves, Polly.— And yet, my dear, I believe you're right. There's been little enough for him to do here, and in the new house, as you say, he'll be a mere encumbrance. As for me, I'd be only too thankful never to hear his cantankerous old pipe again. I don't know, now, what evil genius prompted me to take him in."

"Evil genius, indeed!" retorted Polly. "You did it because you're a dear, good, kind-hearted man."

"Think so, wifey? I'm inclined to put it down to sheer dislike of botheration—Irish inertia . . . the curse of our race."

—"Yes, yes, I knoo you'd be wantin' to get rid o' me, now you're goin' up in the world," was Long Jim's answer, when Polly broached her scheme for his benefit. "Well, no, I won't say anythin' against you, Mrs. Mahony; you've treated me square enough. But doc., 'e's always thought 'imself a sight above one, an' when 'e does, 'e lets you feel it."

This was more than Polly could brook. "And sighing and

groaning as you have done, to get home, Jim! You're a silly, ungrateful old man, even to hint at such a thing."

—"Poor old fellow! he's grumbled so long now, that he's forgotten how to do anything else," she afterwards made allowance for him. And added, pierced by a sudden doubt: "I hope his wife will still be used to it, or . . . or else . . . !"

And now the last day in the old house was come. The furniture, stacked in the yard, awaited the dray that was to transport it. Hardly worth carrying with one, thought Mahony, when he saw the few poor sticks exposed to the searching sunlight. Pipe in mouth, he mooned about, feeling chiefly amazed that he could have put up, for so long, with the miserable little hut, his house, stripped of its trimmings, proved to be.

His reflections were cut short by old Ocock, who leaned over the fence to bid his neighbours good-bye.

"No disturbance! Come in, come in!" cried Mahony, with the rather spurious heartiness one is prone to throw into a final invitation. And Polly rose from her knees before a clothes-basket which she was filling with crockery, and bustled away to fetch the cake she had baked for such an occasion.

"I'll miss yer bright little face, that I will!" said Mr. Ocock, as he munched with the relish of a Jerry or a Ned. He held his slice of cake in the hollow of one great palm, and conveyed the pieces he broke off to his mouth, with extreme care.

"You must come and see us, as soon as ever we're settled."

"Bless you! You'll soon find grander friends than an old chap like me."

"Mr. Ocock! And you with three sons in the law!"

"Besides, mark my words, it'll be your turn next to build," Mahony removed his pipe to throw in. "We'll have you over with us yet, never fear!"

"And what a lovely surprise for Miss Amelia when she arrives, to find a brand-new house awaiting her!"

"Well, that's the end of this little roof-tree," said Mahony.— The loaded dray had driven off, the children and Ellen perched on top of the furniture, and he was giving a last look round. "We've spent some very happy days under it, eh, my dear?"

"Oh, very," said Polly, shaking out her skirts. "But we shall be just as happy in the new one."

"God grant we may! It's not too much to hope I've now seen all the downs of my life. I've managed to pack a good many into thirty short years.— And that reminds me, Mrs. Townshend-Mahony, do you know you will have been married to me two whole years, come next Friday?"

"Why, so we shall!" cried Polly, and was transfixed in the act of tying her bonnet-strings. "How time does fly! It seems only the other day I saw this room for the first time. I peeped in, you know, while you were fetching the box. *Do* you remember how I cried, Richard? I was afraid of a spider or something." And the Polly of eighteen looked back, with a motherly amusement, at her sixteen-year-old eidolon.— "But now, dear, if you're ready . . . or else the furniture will get there before we do. We'd better take the short cut across Soldiers' Hill. That's the cat, in that basket, for you to carry, and here's your microscope. I've got the decanter and the best teapot.— Shall we go?"

[2]

AND now, for a month or more, Mahony had been in possession of a room that was all his own. Did he retire into it and shut the door, he could make sure of not being disturbed. Polly herself tapped before entering; and he let her do so. Polly was dear; but dearer still was his long-coveted, treasured privacy.

He knew, too, that she was happily employed; the fitting-up and furnishing of the house was a job after her own heart. She had proved both skilful and economical at it: thanks to her, they had used a bare three-quarters of the sum allotted by Ocock for the purpose—and this was well; for a large number of unforeseen expenses had cropped up at the last moment.— Polly had a real knack for making things "do." Old empty boxes, for instance, underwent marvellous transformations at her hands—emerged, clad in chintz and muslin, as sofas and toilet-tables. She hung her curtains on strings, and herself sewed the seams of the parlour carpet, squatting Turk-fashion on the floor, and working away, with a great needle shaped like a scimitar, till the perspiration ran down her face. It was also she who, standing on the kitchen-table, put up the only two pictures they possessed, Ned and Jerry giving opinions on the straightness of her eye, from below: a fancy picture of the Battle of Waterloo, in the parlour; a print: "Harvey discovering the Circulation of the Blood," on the surgery wall.

From where he sat, Mahony could hear the voices of the children—John's children—at play. They frolicked with Pompey in the yard. He could endure them, now that he was not for ever tumbling over them. Yes, one and all were comfortably established under the new roof—with the exception of poor Palmerston, the cat. Palmerston had declined to recognise the change, and with the immoderate homing-instinct of his kind, had returned night after night to his old haunts. For some time, Mahony's regular evening walk was back to the store— a road he would otherwise not have taken; for it was odious to him to see Polly's neat little appointments going to rack and ruin, under the tenancy of a dirty Irish family. There he would find the animal sitting, in melancholy retrospect. Again and again he picked him up and carried him home; till that night when no puss came to his call, and Palmerston, the black and glossy, was seen no more: either he had fallen down a shaft, or been mangled by a dog, or stolen, cats still fetching a high price on Ballarat.

The window of Mahony's room faced a wide view. The only other two houses on the track stood on the same side as his own, and not a fence, hardly a bit of scrub or a tuft of grass-tree marked the bare expanse of uneven ground, now baked brown as a piecrust by the December sun. He looked across it to the cemetery. This was still wild and unfenced—just a patch of rising ground, where it was permissible to bury the dead. Only the day before—it was the second anniversary of the Eureka Stockade—he had watched some two to three hundred men, with crepe on their hats and sleeves, a black-draped pole at their head, march there to do homage to their fallen comrades. The dust raised by the shuffling of these many feet had accompanied the procession like a moving cloud; had lingered in its rear like the smoke from a fire. Beyond the cemetery was the wide flat road to Creswick's Creek. Drays and lorries crawled for ever laboriously along it, seeming glued to the earth by the monstrous sticky heat of the veiled sun. Further back still rose a number of bald hills—rounded, swelling hills, shaped like a woman's breasts. And behind all, pale china-blue against the tense white sky, was the embankment of the dis-

tant ranges. Except for these, an ugly, uninviting outlook, and
one to which he seldom lifted his eyes.

His room pleased him better. Polly had stretched a bright
green drugget on the floor; the table had a green cloth on it;
the picture showed up well against the whitewashed wall. Behind him was a large deal cupboard, which held instruments
and drugs. The bookshelves with their precious burden were
within reach of his hand; on the top shelf he had stacked the
boxes containing his botanical and other specimens. A chair
stood in front of the table, in readiness for prospective patients.

The first week or so there was naturally little doing: a
sprained wrist to bandage, a tooth to draw, a case of fly-blight.
To keep himself from growing uneasy, Mahony overhauled his
minerals and butterflies, and renewed faded labels. This done,
he went on to jot down some ideas he had, with regard to the
presence of auriferous veins in quartz. It was now generally
agreed that quartz was the matrix; but on the question of how
the gold had found its way into the rock, opinions were sharply
divided. The theory of igneous injection was advanced by
some; others inclined to that of sublimation; there were those
who upheld the hypothesis of an aqueous deposition, and those
who fell back on currents of electricity. Mahony leaned to a
combination of the first two processes, and spent several days
getting his thoughts in order. The while Polly, bursting with
pride, went about on tiptoe, audibly hushing the children:
Uncle was writing for the newspapers.

Still no patients worth the name made their appearance. To
fend off the black worry that might get the better of him, did
he sit idle, he next drew his Bible to him, and set about doing
methodically what he had so far undertaken merely by fits and
starts—deciding for himself to what degree the Scriptures were
inspired. Polly was neither proud nor happy while this went
on, and let the children romp unchecked. At present, it was
not so much the welfare of her husband's soul she feared for:
God must surely know by this time what a good man Richard
was; he had not his equal, she thought, for honesty and up-
rightness; he was kind to the poor and the sick, and hadn't
missed a single Sunday at church, since their marriage. But all
that would not help, if once he got the reputation of being an
infidel. Then, nobody would want him as a doctor. Her one
consolation was, he was safely shut up in his own room. It

should never leak out, if she could help it, what he did there.

Casually begun, Mahony's studies soon absorbed him to the exclusion of everything else.

He had grown up in the cast-iron mould of Irish Protestantism. Of a sober and devout turn of mind, however, he had submitted readily to restriction and coercion; and in his teens himself passed through a crisis of religious fervour.— From this atmosphere he was tossed, as a youthful student, into the freebooting Edinburgh of the forties.

Edinburgh was alive, in those days, to her very paving-stones; town and university combined to form a hotbed of intellectual unrest, a breeding-ground for disturbing possibilities. The patient theorisings of native and foreign scientists, and their hodmannish addition of fact to fact, were now suddenly seen to be pointing to a startling conclusion. Men had, as it were, advanced blindfold to the edge of a precipice; and now, the bandage fallen, they stood and shuddered at their slender footing. The "development theory" was in the air; and a book that appeared anonymously about this time, and boldly voiced, in popular fashion, Maillet's dream, and the Lamarckian hypothesis of a Creation undertaken once and for all, in place of a continuous creative intervention: this book, which opposed natural law to miracle, carried complete conviction to the young and eager; although in truth, it could bring forward no evidence, and was based only on keen observation and a sound common sense. Audacious spirits even hazarded the conjecture that primitive life itself might have originated in a natural way: had not, but recently, an investigator who was causing a powerful voltaic battery to operate upon a saturated solution of silicate of potash, been startled to find, as the result of his experiment, that he had produced numberless small mites, belonging to the species *acarus horridus?* Might not the marvel, electricity, or galvanism, in action on albumen, turn out to be the vitalising force?— To the orthodox zoologist, phytologist, and geologist, such an unholy suggestion savoured of madness; they either took refuge in a contemptuous silence, or condescended only to such a reply as: Had one visited the Garden of Eden during Creation, one would have found that, in the morning, man was not, while in the evening, he was!—morning and evening bearing, of course, their newly established significance of geological epochs. But the famous tracing of the Creator's footsteps, undertaken by a gifted compromiser, was felt by even the most bigoted to be a lame rejoinder. His *Asterolepsis,* the giant fossil-fish from the Old Red Sandstone, the antiquity of which would show that the origin of life was not to be found solely in "infusorial points," but that highly developed forms were among the earliest created—this single prop was admittedly not strong enough to carry the whole burden of proof. No, the immutability of species had been seriously impugned, and bold minds were asking themselves why a single act of creation, at the outset, should not constitute as divine a beginning to life, as a continued series of "creative fiats."

Mahony was one of them. The "development theory" did not repel him. He could see no impiety in believing that life, once established on the earth, had been left to protect itself. Or hold that this would represent the Divine Author of all things as, after one master-stroke, dreaming away eternal ages in apathy and indifference. Why should the perfect functioning of natural law not be as convincing an expression of God's presence, as a series of cataclysmic acts of creation?

None the less, it was a time of crisis, for him, as for so many. For, if this were so, if science spoke true that, the miracle of life set a-going—and was this not miracle enough? —there had been no further intervention on the part of the Creator, then the very head-and-corner stone of the Christian faith, the Bible itself, was shaken. More, much more, would have to go than the Mosaic cosmogony of the first chapter of Genesis. Just as the Elohistic account of creation had been stretched to fit the changed views of geologists, so the greater part of the scriptural narratives stood in need of a wider interpretation. The fable of the Eternal's personal mediation in the affairs of man must be accepted for what it was—a beautiful allegory, the fondly dreamed fulfilment of a world-old desire. The age of the manuscripts must be considered, too; the tremendous room for error in scribe and translator.— And bringing thus a sharpened critical sense to bear on the Scriptures, Mahony embarked on his voyage of discovery. Before him, but more as a warning than a beacon, shone the example of a famous German savant, who, taking our Saviour's life as his theme, demolished the sacred idea of a

Divine miracle, and retold the Gospel story from the stand-point of a destructive rationalism. A savagely unimaginative piece of work this, thought Mahony, and one that laid all too little weight on the deeps of poetry, the mysteries of symbols, and the power the human mind drew from these, to pierce to an ideal truth.— His own modest efforts would be of quite another kind.

For he sought, not to deny God, but to discover Him anew, by freeing Him from the drift of error, superstition, and dead-letterism, which the centuries had accumulated about Him. And he was not to be deterred from his quest by any un-worthy fears of God's displeasure. He conceived of the Almighty as infinitely remote from all such human pettiness. Again, had not God declared, through the mouth of the Adorable Saviour: I am the Way, the Truth, and the Life. A seeking after Truth was thus only a more intense search after Himself, and could in no wise be offensive to Him. Besides, far was it from His servant's mind to wish to decry the author-ity of the Book of Books. Mahony believed it to consist, in great part, of inspired utterances, and for the rest, to be the wisest and ripest collection of moral precepts and examples that had come down to us from the ages. Without it, one would be rudderless indeed—a castaway in a cockleshell boat on a furious sea—and from one's lips would go up a cry like to that wrung from a famous infidel: "I am affrighted and confounded with the forlorn solitude in which I am placed by my philosophy . . . begin to fancy myself in the most deplorable condition imaginable, environed by the deepest darkness."

No, Mahony was not one of those who held that the Chris-tian faith, that fine flower of man's spiritual need, would suffer detriment by the discarding of a few fabulous tales; nor did he fear lest his own faith should become undermined by his studies, and the end of him be—as with several he had known—rank atheism, an utter denial of the Divine Exist-ence. For he had that in him which told him that God was; and this instinctive certainty would persist, he believed, though he had ultimately to admit the whole fabric of Chris-tianity to be based on the Arimathean's dream. It had already survived the rejection of externals: the surrender of forms, the assurance that ceremonials were not essential to salvation, belonged to his early student-days. Now, he determined to send by the board the last hampering relics of bigotry and ritual. He could no longer concede the tenets of election and damnation. God was a God of Mercy, not the blind, jealous Jahveh of the Jews, or the inhuman Sabbatarian of a narrow Protestantism. And He might be worshipped anywhere or anyhow: in any temple built to His Name—in the wilderness under the open sky—in silent prayer, or according to any creed.

In all this critical readjustment, the thought he had to spare for his fellow-men was of small account: his fate was not bound to theirs by the altruism of a later generation. It was a time of intense individualism; and his efforts towards spiritual emancipation were made on his own behalf alone. The one link he had with his fellows—if link it could be termed—was the earnest wish to avoid giving offence: never would it have occurred to him to noise his heterodoxy abroad. Nor did he want to disturb other people's convictions. He respected those who could still draw support from the old faith, and, moreover, had not a particle of the proselytiser in him. He held that religion was either a matter of temperament, or of geographical distribution; felt tolerantly inclined towards the Jews, or the Chinese; and did not even smile at processions to the Joss-house, and the provisioning there of those silent ones who needed food no more.

But just as little as he intermeddled with the convictions of others would he brook interference with his own. These concerned himself and his Maker only; and it was the business of no third persons what by-paths he followed, in his journeying to reach the truth—in his quest after a panacea for the ills and delusions of life. For, call it what he would— Biblical criticism, scientific inquiry—this was his aim first and last. He was trying to pierce the secret of existence—to rede the riddle that has never been solved.— What am I? Whence have I come? Whither am I going? What meaning has the pain I suffer, the evil that men do? Can evil be included in God's scheme?— And it was well, he told himself, as he pressed forward, that the flame in him burnt unwaveringly, which assured him of his kinship with the Eternal, of the kinship of all created things; so unsettling and perplexing were the conclusions at which he arrived.

Summoned to dinner, he sat at table with the mask of a sleep-walker, with stupid hands and evasive eyes. Little Johnny who was, as Polly put it, "as keen as mustard," was prompt to note his uncle's vacancy.

"What you staring at, Nunkey?" he demanded, his mouth full of roly-pudding, which he was stuffing down with all possible dispatch.

"Hush, Johnny. Don't tease your uncle."

"What do you mean, my boy?"

"I mean . . ." Young John squeezed his last mouthful over his windpipe, and raised his plate. "I mean, you look just like you was seein' a enemy. More pudding, Aunt Polly!"

"What does the child mean? An anemone?"

"*No!*" said John, with the immense contempt of five years. "I didn't say anner enemy." Here, he began to tuck in anew, aiding the slow work of his spoon with his more habile fingers. "A enemy's a enemy. Like on de pickshur in Aunt Polly's room. One . . . one's de English, an' one's de enemy."

"It's the Battle of Waterloo," explained Polly. "He stands in front of it every day."

"Yes. An' when I'm a big man, I'm goin' to be a sojer, an' wear a red coat, an' make 'bung'!" and he shot an imaginary gun at his sister, who squealed, and ducked her head.

"An ancient wish, my son," said Mahony, when Johnny had been reproved and Trotty comforted. "Tom-thumbs like you have voiced it since the world—or rather since war first began."

"Don't care. Nunkey, why is de English and why is de enemy?"

But an attempt to answer this question would be like withdrawing the plug from a brimming tank. Mahony shrank from the gush of whats and whys he would let loose on himself.— "Come, shall uncle make you some boats to sail in the washtub?"

"Wiv a mast an' sails an' everyfing?" cried John wildly; and throwing his spoon to the floor, he scrambled from his chair. "Oh yes, Nunkey!—dear Nunkey!"

"Dea Unkey!" echoed the shadow.

"Oh, you cupboard lovers, you!" said Mahony, as, order restored, and sticky mouths wiped, two pudgy hands were thrust with a new kindness into his.

189

He led the way to the yard; and having whittled out for the children some chips left by the builders, he lighted his pipe and sat down in the shade of the house. Here, through a veiling of smoke, which hung motionless in the hot, still air, he watched the two eager little mortals before him add their quota to the miracle of life.

[3]

POLLY had no such absorbing occupation to tide her over these empty days of waiting; and sometimes—especially late in the afternoon, when her household duties were done, the children safely at play—she found it beyond her power to stitch quietly at her embroidery. Letting the canvas fall to her knee, she would listen, listen, listen, till the blood sang in her ears, for the footsteps and knocks at the door that never came. And did she draw back the window-curtain and look out, there was not a soul to be seen: not a trace of the string of prosperous, paying patients, she had once imagined winding their way to the door.

And meanwhile Richard was shut up in his room, making those dreadful notes in the Bible, which it pinched her heart even to think of. He really did not seem to care whether he had a practice or not. All the new instruments, got from Melbourne, lay unused in their casings; and the horse was eating its head off, at over a pound a week, in the livery-barn. Polly shrank from censuring her husband, even in thought; but, as she took up her work again, and went on producing, in wools, a green basket of yellow fruit on a magenta ground, she could not help reflecting on what she would have done at this pass, had she been a man. She would have announced the beginning of her practice, in big letters, in the *Star*, and she would have gone down into the township, and have mixed with people, and made herself known. With Richard, it was almost as if he felt averse to bringing himself into public notice. He had also turned out to be extremely persnickety about encroaching on what he called the preserves of others.

Only another month now, and the second instalment of interest would fall due. Polly did not know exactly what the sum was; but she did know the date. The first time, they had had no difficulty in meeting the bill, owing to their economy in furnishing. But what about this one, and the next again? How were payments to be made, and kept up, if the patients would not come?

She wished with all her heart that she was ten years older. For what could a person who was only eighteen be supposed to understand of business? Richard's invariable answer, did she venture a word, was, not to worry her little head about such things.— He was, besides, very private and peculiar with regard to money; and never took anyone into his confidence.

When, however, another week had dribbled away in the same fashion, Polly began to be afraid the date of payment had slipped his memory altogether. She would need to remind him of it, even at the risk of vexing him. And having cast about for a pretext to intrude, she decided to ask his advice on a matter that was giving her much uneasiness; though, had he been *really* busy, she would have gone on keeping it to herself.

It related to the boy, little Johnny.

Johnny was a high-spirited, passionate child, who needed very careful handling. At first, she had managed him well enough. But that was prior to his five months' boarding-out. Since then, she was sometimes at her wits' end what to do with him. For the chief result of his foster-mother's indiscriminate chastisements had been to drive Johnny into deceitful ways; and the habit of falsehood gained on him daily. Bad by nature, Polly felt sure he was not; she had caught blinks of a disposition that was both generous and lovable. But she could not keep the child on the straight path, now he had discovered that a lie might save him a punishment. He was not to be shamed out of telling it; and the only other cure Polly knew of was whipping. She whipped him; and, by so doing, provoked him to fury.

A new misdeed on his part gave her the handle she sought. Johnny had surreptitiously entered her pantry and stolen a plateful of cakes. When he was taxed with the theft, he denied it, with a smooth tongue. Cornered, he laid, Adam-like, the whole blame on his companion, asserting that Trotty had persuaded him to take the goodies; though fear and bewildered innocence were writ all over the baby's chubby face.

After hearing his wife out, Mahony had the blue-eyed

sinner up before him. But he was able neither to touch the child's heart, nor to make him see the gravity of what he had done: never being allowed inside the surgery, John could now not take his eyes off the wonderful display of gold and purple and red moths, which were pinned, with outstretched wings, to a sheet of cork. He stood o-mouthed and absentminded, and only once shot a blue glance at his uncle, to say: "But if dey're so baddy . . . den why did God *make* lies an' de debble?"—which intelligent query hit the nail of one of Mahony's own misgivings on the head.

No real depravity, was his verdict. Still, too much of a handful, it was plain, for Polly's inexperience. "A problem for John himself to tackle, my dear! Why should we have to drill a non-existent morality into his progeny? Besides, I'm not going to have you blamed for bad results, later on." He would communicate with John there and then, and request that Johnny be removed from their charge.

Polly was not prepared for this summary solution of her dilemma, and began to regret having brought it up; though she could not but agree with Richard that it would never do for the younger child, who was, thus far, candour itself, to be corrupted by bad example. However, she kept her wits about her. Did John take the boy away, said she, she was afraid she would have to ask her husband for a larger housekeeping allowance. The withdrawal of the money for Johnny's board would make a difference to their income.

"Of course," returned Mahony easily, and was about to dismiss the subject.

But Polly stood her ground. "Talking of money, Richard, I don't know whether you remember . . . you've been so busy . . . that it's only about a fortnight now, till the second lot of interest falls due."

"What!—a fortnight?" exclaimed her husband, and, in the act of opening a drawer, he reached out for an almanack. "Good Lord, so it is! And nothing doing yet, Polly . . . absolutely nothing!"

"Well, dear, you can't expect to jump into a big practice all at once, can you? But you see, I think the trouble is, not nearly enough people know you've started." And a little imploringly, and very apologetically, Polly unfolded her artless schemes for self-advertisement.

"Wife, I've a grave suspicion!" said Mahony, and took her by the chin. "While I've sat here with my head in the clouds, you've been worrying over ways and means, and over having such an unpractical old dreamer for a husband. Now, child, that won't do! I didn't marry to have my girl puzzling her poor little brains where her next day's dinner was to come from.— Away with you, to your stitching! Things will be all right, trust to me."

And Polly did trust him, and was so satisfied with what she had effected that, raising her face for a kiss, she retired with an easy mind to overhaul Johnny's little wardrobe. If the child had to go, no one should be able to say he left his uncle's house in any but the best condition.

The door having clicked behind his wife, Mahony's air of forced assurance died away. For an instant he hesitated beside the table, on which a rampart of books lay open, then vigorously clapped each volume to, and moved to the window, chewing at the ends of his beard. A timely interruption! What the dickens had he been about, to forget himself in this fool's paradise, when the crassest of material anxieties—that of pounds, shillings and pence—was crouched, wolf-like, at his door? He had begun merely with the idea of filling up time. But he had failed to reckon with the quiet of his new quarters; with the first real spell of leisure he had had since coming to the colony. He, too, who, did the murmur of voices reach him, or a window rattle, found it hard to string a couple of thoughts together, was capable, under auspicious conditions, of passing, almost, out of the body, so utterly did he become one with the work that gripped him.

As things stood, however, he had taken an unwarrantable liberty with that old hag, Fortune. But in the meantime Polly might rest content. He studied no more.

That night he awakened with a jerk from an uneasy sleep. Though at noon, the day before, the thermometer had registered over a hundred in the shade, it was now bitterly cold, and these abrupt changes of temperature always whipped up his nerves. Even after he had piled his clothes and an opossum-rug on top of the blankets, he could not drop off again. He lay staring at the moonlit square of the window, and thinking the black thoughts of night.

What if he could not manage to work up a practice? . . .

if he found it impossible to make a living? His plate had been on the door for close on two months now, and he had barely a five-pound note to show for it. The scratch patients, the odd tinkerings one had to rely on till one got a footing, had been few and far between. He began to be afraid he had built too much out of the way. But he could not have set up cheek by jowl with an older member of the fraternity, nor have afforded to take possession of a block of land in the township proper. What was to be done?— And here it was that the words Polly had said that afternoon came back to him—came back, with new stress, and plain as the letters in a child's ABC book. "Not nearly enough people know you've started." That was it!— Polly had laid her finger on the hitch. The genteel manners of the old country did not answer here; instead of sitting twiddling his thumbs, waiting for patients to seek him out, it was his business to have adopted the screaming methods of advertisement in vogue on Ballarat. Yes, to have had "Holloway's Pills sold here!" "Teeth extracted painlessly!" "Cures guaranteed!" painted man-high on his outside house-wall. To have gone up and down and round the township; to have been on the spot when accidents happened; to have hobnobbed with Tom, Dick and Harry, in bars and saloons; to have taken a hand at cards with the devil himself, in Bath's Public Room. And in a feverish vision he saw a figure that looked like his own, the centre of a boisterous crowd; saw himself slapped on the back by dirty hands, shouting and shouted to drinks.— He turned, and turned his pillow, to drive the image away.— Whatever he had or had not done, the fact remained that, a couple of weeks hence, he had to make up the sum of over thirty pounds. Again he discerned a phantom self, this time a humble supplicant for an extension of term, brought up short against Ocock's stony visage, flouted by his cocksy clerk; and the wraiths of I.O.U.'s and bills of sale, of bailiffs and auctioneers, danced a grand-chain before the eye of his mind.— Once more, he turned his pillow.— These quarterly payments, which dotted all his coming years, were like little rock-islands studding the surface of an ocean, and telling of the sunken continent below: this monstrous thousand odd pounds he had let himself be induced to borrow. With a possible failure staring him in the face, he felt how recklessly he had acted. Never would he manage to pay off

194

such a sum, and hence never again could he hope to be free
from the incubus of debt. At the end of *this* vista he saw
scandal and ignominy, a shameful bankruptcy.— And, yet
once more, he tossed in his bed, seeking a cool place on the
linen of the pillow.— What if anything should happen to him,
before he had contrived to meet his obligations? God knew,
he was none too robust; and every summer brought its attack
of dysentery. At the thought of dying and leaving Polly not
only penniless, but heir to this burden of debt, he came out
in a cold perspiration. A man with a wife to keep should look,
and look again, before he leapt. With him, not the ground he
stood on, not the roof over his head, could actually be called
his own: he had also been too pushed for money, at the
moment, to take Ocock's advice and insure his life. No doubt,
in the event of his death, John would have pity on Polly and
give her house-room. But the memory of this young community was tenacity itself where money was concerned; and the
odium of her husband's insolvency would stick to Polly ever
after. He would be branded as . . . well, perhaps not exactly
as unprincipled, or a scoundrel; but as one for whom it was
quixotic to have given a pledge: a tyro at his profession; a
fool in the practical conduct of affairs.

The menace of this posthumous shame, and Polly's pitiful
plight, spun itself to a nightmare-web, in which he was the
hapless fly. Putting a finger to his wrist, he found he had the
pulse of a hundred that was not uncommon to him. He got
out of bed, to dowse his head in a basin of water. Polly,
only half awake, sat up and said: "What's the matter, dear?
Are you ill?" In replying to her, he disturbed the children,
the door of whose room stood ajar; and, by the time quiet was
restored, further sleep was out of the question. He dressed
and quitted the house.

Day was breaking; the moon, but an hour back a globe of
polished silver, had now no light left in her, and stole, a misty
ghost, across the dun-coloured sky. A bank of clouds that had
had their night-camp on the summit of Mount Warrenheip
was beginning to disperse; and the air had lost its edge. He
walked out beyond the cemetery, then sat down on a tree-
stump and looked back. The houses that nestled on the slope
were growing momently whiter; but the Flat was still sunk
in shadow and haze, making old Warrenheip, for all its half-

dozen miles of distance, seem near enough to be touched by hand.— But even in full daylight this woody peak had a way of tricking the eye. From the brow of the western hill, with the Flat out of sight below, it appeared to stand at the very foot of those streets that headed east—first of one, then of another, moving with you, as you changed your position, like the eyes of a portrait that remain fixed on you, wherever you go.— And now the sky was streaked with crimson-madder; the last clouds scattered, drenched in orange and rose, and flames burned in the glass of every window-pane. Up came the tip of the sun's rim, grew to a fiery quarter, to a half; till, bounding free from the horizon, it began to mount, and to lose its girth in the pale immensity of the sky.

The phantasms of the night yielded like the clouds to its power: Mahony saw how overstrained his anxiety had been. He was still reasonably young, reasonably sound, and had the better part of a lifetime before him. Rising, with a fresh alacrity, he whistled to the dog, and walked briskly home to bath and breakfast.

But that evening, at the heel of another empty day, his nervous restlessness took him anew. From her parlour, Polly could hear the thud of his feet, going up and down, up and down his room. And it was she who was to blame for disturbing him!

"Yet what else could I do? Things couldn't have gone on as they were."

And meditatively pricking her needle in and out of the window-curtain, Polly fell into a reverie over her husband and his ways. How strange Richard was . . . how difficult! First, to be able to forget all about how things stood with him, and then to be twice as upset as other people. . . .

John demanded the immediate delivery of his young son, undertaking soon to knock all nasty tricks out of him. On the day fixed for Johnny's departure, husband and wife were astir soon after dawn. Mahony was to have taken the child down to the coach-office. But Johnny had been awake since two o'clock with excitement, and was now so fractious that Polly tied on her bonnet and accompanied them. She knew Richard's hatred of a scene.

"You just walk on, dear, and get his seat," she said; and

Mahony gladly obeyed. He had had a bad night again; the
habit of sleep, once broken, was not to be regained at will.
Polly, whom no want of rest could move from her firm young
serenity, dragged the cross, tired child on her hand to the
public-house, where, even at this hour, a posse of idlers hung
about.

And she did well to be there. Instantly on arriving, Johnny
set up a wail, because there was talk of putting him inside
the vehicle; and this persisted, until the coachman, a goat-
bearded Yankee, came to the rescue and said, he was darned
if such a plucky young nipper shouldn't get his way: he'd
have the child tied on beside him, on the box-seat—be blowed
if he wouldn't! But even this did not satisfy Johnny; and while
Mahony went to procure a length of rope, he continued to
prance round his aunt, and to tug ceaselessly at her sleeve.

"Can I dwive, Aunt Polly, can I dwive? Ask him, can I
dwive!" he roared, beating her skirts with his fists. He was
only silenced by the driver threatening to throw him, as a
juicy morsel, to the gang of bushrangers who, sure as blazes,
would be waiting to stick the coach up, directly it entered
the bush.

Husband and wife lingered to watch the start, when the
champing horses took a headlong plunge forward, and, together with the coach, were swallowed up in a whirlwind of
dust. A last glimpse discovered Johnny, pale and wide-eyed
at the lurching speed, but sitting bravely erect.

"The spirit of your brother in that child, my dear!" said
Mahony as they made to walk home.

"Poor little Johnny," and Polly wiped her eyes. "If only
he was going back to a mother who loved him, and would
understand."

"I'm sure no mother could have done more for him than
you, love."

"Yes, but a real mother wouldn't need to give him up,
however naughty he had been."

"I think the young varmint might have shown some regret
at parting from you, after all this time," returned her husband,
to whom it was offensive if even a child was lacking in good
feeling. "He never turned his head. Well, I suppose it's a
fact, as they say, that the natural child is the natural bar-
barian."

197

"Johnny never meant any harm. It was I who didn't know how to manage him," said Polly staunchly.— "Why, Richard, what *is* the matter?" For, letting her arm fall, Mahony had dashed to the other side of the road.

"Good God, Polly, look at this!"

"This" was a printed notice, nailed to a shed, which announced that a sale of frontages in Mair and Webster Streets would shortly be held.

"But it's not our road. I don't understand."

"Good Lord, don't you see that if they're there already, they'll be out with us before we can say Jack Robinson? And then where shall I be?" gave back Mahony testily.

"Let us talk it over. But first come home and have breakfast. Then . . . yes, then, I think you should go down and see Mr. Henry Ocock, and hear what he says."

"You're right. I must see Ocock.— Confound the fellow! It's he who has let me in for this."

"And probably he'll know some way out. What else is a lawyer for dear?"

"Quite true, my Polly.— None the less, it looks as if I were in for a run of real bad luck, all along the line."

[4]

ONE hot morning some few days later, Polly, with Trotty at her side, stood on the doorstep, shading her eyes with her hand. She was on the look-out for her "vegetable man," who drove in daily, from the Springs, with his greenstuff. He was late, as usual: if Richard would only let her deal with the cheaper, more punctual Ah Sing, who was at this moment coming up the track. But Devine was a reformed character: after, as a digger, having squandered a fortune in a week, he had given up the drink, and, backed by a hard-working, sober wife, was now trying to earn a living at market-gardening. So he had to be encouraged.

The Chinaman jog-trotted towards them, his baskets a-sway, his mouth stretched to a friendly grin. "You no want cabbagee to-day? Me got velly good cabbagee," he said persuasively, and lowered his pole.

"No, thank you, John, not to-day. Me wait for white man."

"Me bling pleasant for lilly missee," said the Chow; and

unknotting a dirty nosecloth, he drew from it an ancient lump of candied ginger. "Lilly missee eatee him . . . oh, yum, yum! Velly good. My word!"

But Chinamen to Trotty were fearsome bogies—corresponded to the swart-faced, white-eyed chimneysweeps of the English nursery. She hid behind her aunt, holding fast to the latter's skirts, and only stealing an occasional peep, with one saucer-like blue eye.

"Thank you, John. Me takee chowchow for lilly missee," said Polly, who had experience in disposing of such savoury morsels.

"You no buy cabbagee to-day?" repeated Ah Sing, with the catlike persistence of his race. And as Polly, with equal firmness and good-humour, again shook her head, he shouldered his pole and departed at a half-run, crooning as he went.

Meanwhile, at the bottom of the road another figure had come into view. It was not Devine in his spring-cart; it was some one on horse-back, was a lady, in a holland habit. The horse, a piebald, advanced at a sober pace, and— "Why, good gracious! I believe she's coming here."

At the first of the three houses, the rider had dismounted, and knocked at the door with the butt of her whip. After a word with the woman who opened, she threw her riding-skirt over one arm, put the other through the bridle, and was now making straight for them.

As she drew near, she smiled, showing a row of white teeth, and a dimple in either cheek.—"Does Dr. Mahony live here?"

Misfortune of misfortunes!— Richard was out.

But almost instantly Polly grasped that this would tell in his favour. "He won't be long, I know."

"I wonder," said the lady, "if he would come out to my house, when he gets back? I am Mrs. Glendinning—of Dandaloo."

Polly flushed, with sheer satisfaction: Dandaloo was one of the largest stations in the neighbourhood of Ballarat. "Oh, I'm certain he will," she answered quickly.

"I am so glad you think so," said Mrs. Glendinning. "A mutual friend, Mr. Henry Ocock, tells me how clever he is."

Polly's brain leapt at the connection; on the occasion of Richard's last visit, the lawyer had again repeated the promise to put a patient in his way. Ocock was one of those people, said Richard, who only remembered your existence when he saw you.— Oh, what a blessing in disguise had been that troublesome old landsale!

The lady had stooped to Trotty, whom she was trying to coax from her lurking-place. "What a darling! How I envy you!"

"Have you no children?" Polly asked shyly, when Trotty's relationship had been explained.

"Yes, a boy. But I should have liked a little girl of my own. Boys are so difficult"; and she sighed.

The horse nuzzling for sugar roused Polly to a sense of her remissness. "Oh, won't you come in and rest a little, after your ride?" she asked; and, without hesitation, Mrs. Glendinning said she would like to, very much indeed; and tying up the horse to the fence, she followed Polly into the house.

The latter felt proud this morning of its apple-pie order. She drew up the best armchair, placed a footstool before it, and herself carried in a tray with refreshments. Mrs. Glendinning had taken Trotty on her lap, and given the child her long gold chains to play with. Polly thought her the most charming creature in the world. She had a slender waist, and an abundant light brown chignon, and cheeks of a beautiful pink, in which the two fascinating dimples came and went. The feather from her riding-hat lay on her neck. Her eyes were the colour of forget-me-nots, her mouth was red as any rose. She had, too, so sweet and natural a manner that Polly was soon chatting frankly about herself and her life, Mrs. Glendinning listening with her face pressed to the spun-glass of Trotty's hair.— "Take care, or I shall steal her!" she said once, with a smile. "As a companion for my boy." And added, a trifle disconnectedly: "He is only nine years old; but he can sit almost any horse."

When she rose, she clasped both Polly's hands in hers. "You dear little woman . . . may I kiss you? I am ever so much older than you."

"I am eighteen," said Polly.

"And I on the shady side of twenty-eight . . . you see!"

They laughed and kissed. "I shall ask your husband to bring you out to see me. And take no refusal. *Au revoir!*" and, as she rode off, she turned in the saddle and waved her hand.

For all her pleasurable excitement, Polly did not let the grass grow under her feet. There being still no sign of Richard —he had gone to Soldiers' Hill, to extract a rusty nail from a child's foot—Ellen was sent to summon him home; and when the girl returned with word that he was on the way, Polly dispatched her to the livery-barn, to order the horse to be got ready.

Richard took the news coolly. "Did she say what the matter was?"

No, she hadn't; and Polly had not liked to ask her; it could surely be nothing very serious, or she would have mentioned it.

"H'm. Then it's probably as I thought. Glendinning's failing is well known. Only the other day, I heard that more than one medical man here had declined to have anything further to do with the case. It's a long way out, and fees are not always forthcoming. *He* doesn't ask for a doctor, and, woman-like, she forgets to pay the bills. I suppose they think they'll try a greenhorn this time."

Pressed by Polly, who was curious to learn everything about her new friend, he answered: "I should be sorry to tell you, my dear, how many bottles of brandy it is Glendinning's boast he can empty in a week."

"Drink? Oh, Richard, how terrible! And that pretty, pretty woman!" cried Polly, and drove her thoughts backwards: she had seen no hint of tragedy in her caller's lovely face.— However, she did not wait to ponder; she asked, a little anxiously: "But you'll go, dear, won't you?"

"Go? Of course I shall! A man in my position must be at everybody's beck and call—ride a dozen miles, if need be, to ease an infant's stomach-ache, or lance its gums. Beggars can't be choosers."

Polly was growing used to Richard's emphatic way of putting things, and smiled undisturbed. "Besides, you know, you *might* be able to do something, where other people have failed."

"I hope they'll give you some dinner," she added, as she bustled about, cutting a cabbage-leaf for his hat, and holding out his thin alpaca coat. "But in case they don't I'll have something substantial ready for your tea."

Mahony rode out across the Flat. For a couple of miles his

201

route was one with the Melbourne Road, on which plied the usual motley traffic. Then, branching off at right angles, it dived into the bush—in this case, a scantly wooded, uneven plain, burnt tobacco-brown, and hard as iron.

Here went no one but himself. He and the mare were the sole living creatures in what, for its stillness, might have been a painted landscape. Not a breath of air stirred the weeping grey-green foliage of the gums; nor was there any bird-life to rustle the leaves, or peck, or chirrup. Did he draw rein, and stop the clacking of the hoofs, the silence was so intense that you could almost hear it.

On striking the outlying boundary of Dandaloo, he dismounted to slip a rail. After that, he was in and out of the saddle, his way leading through numerous gateless paddocks, before it brought him up to the homestead.

This, a low white wooden building, overspread by a broad verandah—from a distance it looked like an elongated mushroom—stood on a hill. At the end, the road had run alongside a well-stocked fruit and flower-garden; but the hillside itself, except for a gravelled walk in front of the house, was uncultivated—was given over to dead thistles and brown weeds.

Fastening his bridle to a post, Mahony unstrapped his bag of necessaries, and stepped on to the verandah. A row of French windows stood open; but flexible green sun-blinds hid the rooms from view. The front door was a French window, too, differing from the rest only in its size. There was neither bell nor knocker. While he was rapping with his knuckles on the panel, one of the blinds was pushed aside, and Mrs. Glendinning came out.

She was still in hat and riding-habit; had herself, she said, reached home but half an hour ago. Summoning a stationhand to attend to the horse, she raised a blind and ushered Mahony into the dining-room, where she had been sitting at lunch, alone at the head of a large table. A Chinaman brought fresh plates, and Mahony was invited to draw up his chair. He had an appetite after his ride; the room was cool and dark; there were no flies.

Throughout the meal, the lady kept up a running fire of talk—the graceful chitchat that sits so well on pretty lips. She spoke of the coming Races; of the last Government House Ball; of the untimely death of Governor Hotham. To Mahony,

she instinctively turned a different side out, from that which
had captured Polly. With all her wellbred ease, there was a
womanly deference in her manner to him, a readiness to be
swayed, to stand corrected. The riding-dress set off her handsome figure; and her delicate features were perfectly chis-
elled.— ("Though she'll be florid before she's forty.")

Some juicy nectarines finished, she pushed back her chair.
"And now, doctor, will you come and see your patient?"

Mahony followed her down a broad, bare passage. A number of rooms opened off it, but instead of entering one of
these, she led him out to a back verandah. Here, before a
small door, she listened with bent head, then turned the
handle and went in.

The room was so dark that Mahony could see nothing.
Gradually, he made out a figure lying on a stretcher-bed.
A watcher sat at the bedside. The atmosphere was more than
close, smelt rank and sour. His first request was for light
and air.

It was the wreck of a fine man that lay there, strapped over
the chest, bound hand and foot to the framework of the bed.
The forehead, on which the hair had receded to a few mean
grey wisps, was high and domed, the features were straight,
with plenty of bone in them, the shoulders broad, the arms
long. The skin of the face had gone a mahogany brown, from
exposure, and a score of deep wrinkles ran out fan-wise from
the corners of the closed lids. Mahony untied the dirty towels
that formed the bandages—they had cut ridges in the limbs
they confined—and took one of the heavy wrists in his hand.

"How long has he lain like this?" he asked, as he returned
the arm to its place.

"How long is it, Saunderson?" asked Mrs. Glendinning. She
had sat down on a chair at the foot of the bed; her skirts overflowed the floor.

The watcher guessed it would be since about the same time
yesterday.

"Was he unusually violent on this occasion?—for I presume
such attacks are not uncommon with him," continued Mahony,
who had meanwhile made a superficial examination of the
sick man.

"I am sorry to say they are only too common, doctor,"
replied the lady.— "Was he worse than usual this time,

Saunderson?" she turned again to the man; at which fresh
proof of her want of knowledge, Mahony mentally raised his
eyebrows.

"To say trewth, I never see'd the boss so bad before,"
answered Saunderson solemnly, grating the palms of the big
red hands that hung down between his knees. "And I've
helped him through the jumps more'n once. It's my opinion
it would ha' been a narrow squeak for him this time, if me
and a mate hadn't nipped in and got these bracelets on him.
There he was, ravin' and sweatin' and cursin' his head off,
grey as death. Hell-gate, he called it, said he was devil's-
porter at hell-gate, and kept hollerin' for napkins and his
firesticks. Poor ol' boss! It *was* hell for him, and no mistake!"

By dint of questioning, Mahony elicited the fact that Glendinning had been unseated by a young horse, three days previously. At the time, no heed was paid to the trifling accident.
Later on, however, he complained of feeling cold and unwell,
went to bed, and, after lying wakeful for some hours, had
been seized by the horrors of delirium.

Requesting the lady to leave them, Mahony made a more
detailed examination of his patient. His suspicions were confirmed: there was internal trouble of old standing, rendered
acute by the fall. Aided by Saunderson, he worked with
restoratives for the best part of an hour. In the end, his efforts
were successful; and he had the satisfaction of seeing the
coma pass over into a natural repose.

"Well, he's through this time, but I won't answer for the
next," he said, and looked about him for a basin in which to
wash his hands. "Can't you manage to keep the drink from
him?—or at least to limit him?"

"Nay, the Almighty Himself couldn't do that," gave back
Saunderson, bringing forward soap and a tin dish.

"How does it come that he lies in a place like this?" asked
Mahony, as he dried his hands on a corner of the least dirty
towel; and he glanced curiously round. The room—in size it
did not greatly exceed that of a ship's-cabin—was in a state
of squalid disorder. Besides the stretcher-bed, a deal table, a
couple of chairs, its main contents were rows and piles of
old paper-covered magazines, the thick brown dust on which
showed that they had not been moved for months—or even
years. The whitewashed walls were smoke-tanned, and dotted

with millions of fly-specks; the dried corpses of squashed spiders formed large black patches; all four corners of the ceiling were festooned with cobwebs.

Saunderson shrugged his shoulders. "This was his den when he first was manager here, in old Morrison's time, and he's stuck to it ever since. He shuts himself up in here, and won't have a female cross the threshold—nor yet Madam G. herself."

Having given his final instructions, Mahony went out to rejoin the lady.

"I will not conceal from you that your husband is in a very precarious condition."

"Do you mean, doctor, he won't live long?"— She had evidently been lying down: one side of her face was flushed and marked. Crying, too, or he was much mistaken: her lids were red-rimmed, her shapely features swollen.

"Ah, you ask too much of me; I am only a woman; I have no influence over him," she said sadly, and shook her head.

"What is his age?"

"He is forty-seven."

Mahony had put him down for at least ten years older, and said so. But the lady was not listening: she fidgeted with her lace-edged handkerchief, looked uneasy, seemed to be in a debate with herself. Finally, she said aloud: "Yes, I will." And to him: "Doctor, would you come with me a moment?"

This time, she conducted him to a well-appointed bed-chamber, off which gave a smaller room, containing a little four-poster draped in dimity. With a vague gesture in the direction of the bed, she sank on a chair beside the door.

Drawing the curtains, Mahony discovered a fair-haired boy of some eight or nine years old. He lay with his head far back, his mouth wide open—apparently fast asleep.

But the doctor's eye was quick to see that it was no natural repose. "Good God! who is responsible for this?"

Mrs. Glendinning held her handkerchief to her face. "I have never told any one before," she wept. "The shame of it, doctor . . . is more than I can bear."

Mahony curbed the discourteous retort that sprang to his lips. He said: "Who is the blackguard? Come, answer me, if you please!"

"Oh, doctor, don't scold me . . . I am so unhappy." The

pretty face puckered and creased; the full bosom heaved. "He is all I have. And such a bright, clever little fellow! You *will* cure him for me, won't you?"

"How often has it happened?"

"I don't know . . . about five or six times, I think . . . perhaps more. There's a place not far from here where he can get it . . . an old hut-cook my husband dismissed once, in a fit of temper—he has, oh, such a temper! Eddy saddles his pony and rides out there, if he's not watched; and then . . . then, they bring him back . . . like this."

"But who supplies him with money?"

"Money? Oh, but doctor, he can't be kept without pocket-money! He has always had as much as ever he wanted.— No, it is all my husband's doing,"—and now she broke out in one of those shameless confessions, from which the medical adviser is never safe. "He hates me; he is only happy if he can hurt me and humiliate me. I don't care what becomes of him. The sooner he dies, the better!"

"Compose yourself, my dear lady. Later, you will regret such hasty words.— And what has this to do with the child? Come, speak out. It will be a relief to you to tell me."

"You are so kind, doctor," she sobbed, and drank, with hysterical gurglings, the glass of water Mahony poured out for her. "Yes, I will tell you everything. It began years ago— when Eddy was only a tot in jumpers. It used to amuse my husband to see him toss off a glass of wine like a grown-up person; and it *was* comical, when he sipped it, and smacked his lips. But then, he grew to like it, and to ask for it, and be cross when he was refused. And then . . . then he learnt how to get it for himself. And when his father saw I was upset about it, he egged him on—gave it to him on the sly.— Oh, he is a bad man, doctor, a *bad*, cruel man! He says such wicked things, too. He doesn't believe in God, or that it is wrong to take one's own life, and he says he never wanted children. He jeers at me because I am fond of Eddy, and because I go to church when I can, and says . . . oh, I know I am not clever, but I am not quite such a fool as he makes me out to be. He speaks to me as if I were the dirt under his feet. He can't bear the sight of me. I have heard him curse the day he first saw me. And so, he's only too glad to be able to come between my boy and me . . . in any way he can."

Mahony led the weeping woman back to the dining-room. There, he sat long, patiently listening and advising; sat, till Mrs. Glendinning had dried her eyes, and was her charming self once more.

The gist of what he said was, the boy must be removed from home at once, and placed in strict, yet kind hands. "Let us say, in the house of a clergyman, where he will receive undivided attention."

Here, however, he ran up against a weak maternal obstinacy. "Oh, but I couldn't part from Eddy! He is all I have. . . . And so devoted to his mammy!"

As Mahony insisted, she looked the picture of helplessness. "But I should have no idea how to set about it. And my husband would put every possible obstacle in the way."

"With your permission, I will arrange the matter myself."

"Oh, how kind you are!" cried Mrs. Glendinning again. "But mind, doctor, it must be somewhere where Eddy will lack none of the comforts he is accustomed to, and where his poor mammy can see him, whenever she wishes. Otherwise, he will fret himself ill."

Mahony promised to do his best to satisfy her, and declining, very curtly, the wine she pressed on him, went out to mount his horse, which had been brought round.

Following him onto the verandah, Mrs. Glendinning became once more the pretty woman frankly concerned for her appearance. "I don't know how I look, I'm sure," she said apologetically, and raised both hands to her hair. "Now I will go and rest for an hour. There is to be opossuming and a moonlight picnic to-night, at Warraluen." Catching Mahony's eye fixed on her with a meaning emphasis, she changed colour. "I cannot sit at home and think, doctor. I *must* distract myself; or I should go mad."

When he was in the saddle, she showed him her dimples again, and her small, even teeth. "I want you to bring your wife to see me, the next time you come," she said, patting the horse's neck. "I took a great fancy to her—a sweet little woman!"

But Mahony, jogging downhill, said to himself he would think twice before introducing Polly there. His young wife's

207

sunny, girlish outlook should not, with his consent, be clouded by a knowledge of the sordid things this material prosperity hid from view. A whited sepulchre seemed to him now the richly appointed house, the well-stocked gardens, the acres on acres of good pasture-land: a fair outside, when, within, all was foul.— He called to mind what he knew by hearsay of the owner. Glendinning was one of the pioneer squatters of the district, had held the run for close on fifteen years. Nowadays, when the land round was entirely taken up, and a place like Ballarat stood within stone's throw, it was hard to imagine the awful solitude, to which the early settlers had been condemned. Then, with his next neighbour miles and miles away; Melbourne, the nearest town, a couple of days' ride through trackless bush; a man was a veritable prisoner in this desert of paddocks, with not a soul to speak to but rough station-hands, and nothing to occupy his mind but the damage done by summer droughts and winter floods. No support or comradeship in the wife either—this poor pretty foolish little woman: "With the brains of a pigeon!" Glendinning had the name of being intelligent: was it, under these circumstances, matter for wonder that he should seek to drown doubts, memories, inevitable regrets; should be led on to the bitter discovery that forgetfulness alone rendered life endurable?— Yes, there was something sinister in the dead stillness of the melancholy bush; in the harsh, merciless sunlight of the late afternoon.

A couple of miles out the horse cast a shoe, and it was evening before he reached home. Polly was watching for him on the doorstep, in a twitter lest some accident had happened, or lest he had had a brush with bushrangers: Richard could not be persuaded to carry a revolver; he was convinced that one so lightly weighted as he, with this world's goods, would never be attacked; and, if he were, he said, he preferred to lose his watch and a few coins rather than to risk taking another's life. But there was a further ground for Polly's vigil. "It never rains but it pours, dear!" was her greeting: he had been twice sent for to the Flat, to attend a woman in labor.— And now he had barely time to wash the worst of the ride's dust off him, before he had to pick up his bag and hurry away.

"A VERY striking-looking man! With perfect manners—and beautiful hands."

Polly, her head bent to her sewing, repeated these words to herself, with a happy little smile. They had been told her, in confidence, by Mrs. Glendinning, and had been said, in the first instance, by this lady's best friend, Mrs. Urquhart of Yarangobilly: on the occasion of Richard's second call at Dandaloo, he had been requested to ride to the neighbouring station, to visit Mrs. Urquhart, who was in delicate health. And of course Polly had passed the flattering opinion on; for, though she was rather a good hand at keeping a secret— Richard declared he had never known a better—yet that secret did not exist—or up till now had not existed—which she could imagine herself withholding from him.

For the past few weeks, these two ladies had vied with each other in singing Richard's praises, and in making much of Polly: the next time Mrs. Glendinning called, she came in her buggy, and carried off Polly, and Trotty, too, to Yarangobilly, where there was a nestful of little ones for the child to play with, and a warm welcome from Mrs. Urquhart, whom her condition confined to the house. Another day, a whole brakeful of lively people drove up to the door in the early morning, and insisted on Polly accompanying them, just as she was, to the Racecourse on the road to Creswick's Creek. And everybody was so kind to her that Polly heartily enjoyed herself, in spite of her plain print dress. She won a pair of gloves and a piece of music in a philippine with Mr. Urquhart, a jolly, carroty-haired man, beside whom she sat on the box-seat coming home; and she was lucky enough to have half a crown on one of the winners. An impromptu dance was got up that evening by the merry party, in a hall in the township; and Polly had the honour of a turn with Mr. Henry Ocock, who was most affable. Richard also looked in for an hour, towards the end, and valsed her and Mrs. Glendinning round.

Polly had quite lost her heart to her new friend. At the outset, Richard rather frowned on the intimacy—but then he was a person given to taking odd antipathies that there was no accounting for. As a rule, Polly respected his feelings, even though she could not understand them. But, in this case, it was he who had to yield; for not only did a deep personal liking spring up between the two women, but also a wave of pity swept over Polly, blinding her to more subtle considerations. Before Mrs. Glendinning had been many times at the house, she had poured out all her troubles to Polly, impelled thereto by Polly's quick sympathy and warm young eyes. Richard had purposely given his wife few details of his visits to Dandaloo; but Mrs. Glendinning knew no such scruples, and cried her eyes out on Polly's shoulder. And Polly fought down her instinctive horror at the depths revealed to her, and did her utmost to cheer and console.

But what a dreadful man the husband must be! "For she really is the dearest little woman, Richard! And means so well with every one—I've never heard her say a sharp or unkind word.— Well, not *very* clever, perhaps. But everybody can't be clever, can they? And she's good—which is better. The only thing she seems a teeny-weeny bit foolish about is her boy. I'm afraid she'll never consent to part with him."— Polly said this to prepare her husband, who was in correspondence on the subject with Archdeacon Long, and with John in Melbourne. Richard was putting himself to a great deal of trouble, and would naturally be vexed if nothing came of it. Dear Richard! He expected every one to find it as easy and natural to do right, as he himself.

Polly paid her first visit to Dandaloo with considerable trepidation. For Mrs. Urquhart, who herself was happily married—although, it was true, her merry, red-haired husband had the reputation of being a *little* too fond of the ladies, and though he certainly did not make such a paying concern of Yarangobilly as Mr. Glendinning of Dandaloo—Mrs. Urquhart had whispered to Polly, as they sat chatting on the verandah: "Such a *dreadful* man, my dear! . . . a perfect brute! Poor little Agnes. It is wonderful how she keeps her spirits up."

Polly, however, was in honour bound to admit that, to her, the owner of Dandaloo had appeared anything but the monster report made him out to be. He was perfectly sober, the day she was there, and did not touch wine at luncheon; and afterwards he had been most kind, taking her with him on a quiet little broad-backed mare, to an outlying part of the station, and giving her several hints how to improve her seat. He was certainly very haggard-looking, and deeply wrinkled;

and at table his hand shook so, that the water in his glass ran over. But all this only made Polly feel sorry for him, and long to help him.

"My dear, you *are* favoured! I never knew James make such an offer before," whispered Mrs. Glendinning, as she pinned her ample riding-skirt round her friend's slim hips.

The one thing about him that disturbed Polly was his manner towards his wife: he was savagely ironic with her, and trampled hobnailed on her timid opinions. But then Agnes didn't know how to treat him, Polly soon saw that: she was nervous and fluttery—evasive, too; and once, during lunch, even told a deliberate fib. Slight as was her acquaintance with him, Polly felt sure this want of courage must displease him; for there was something very simple and direct about his own way of speaking; he always went straight to the point.

"My dear, why don't you stand up to him?" asked little Polly.

"Dearest, I dare not. If you knew him as I do, Polly. . . . He *terrifies* me.— Oh, what a lucky little woman you are . . . to have a husband like yours!"

Polly had recalled these words that very morning, as she stood to watch Richard ride away: never did he forget to kiss her good-bye, or to turn and wave to her, at the foot of the road. Each time, she admired afresh the figure he cut on horseback: he was so tall and slender, and sat so straight in his saddle. Now, too, he had yielded to her persuasions and shaved off his beard; and his moustache and side-whiskers were like his hair, of an extreme, silky blond. Ever since the day of their first meeting, at Beamish's Family Hotel, Polly had thought her husband the handsomest man in the world.— And the best, as well. He had his peculiarities, of course; but so had every husband; and it was part of a wife's duty to study them, to adapt herself to them, or to endeavour to tone them down.— And now came these older, wiser ladies and confirmed her in her high opinion of him. Polly beamed with happiness at this juncture, and registered a silent vow always to be the best of wives, that he might never regret his choice.

Not like—but here she tripped and coloured, on the threshold of her thought. She had recently been the recipient of a very distressing confidence; one, too, which she was not at liberty to share, even with Richard. For, after the relief of a thoroughpaced confession, Mrs. Glendinning had implored her not to breathe a word to him—"I could never look him in the face again, love!"— Besides, the affair was of such a painful nature that Polly felt little desire to draw Richard into it; it was bad enough that she herself should know.— The thing was this: once, when Polly had stayed overnight at Dandaloo, Agnes Glendinning, in a sudden fit of misery, had owned to her that she cared for another person more than for her own husband, and that her feelings were returned.

Polly, shocked beyond measure, tried to close her friend's lips. "I don't think you should mention any names, Agnes," she cried. "Afterwards, my dear, you might regret it."

But Mrs. Glendinning was hungry for the luxury of speech— not even to Louisa Urquhart had she broken silence, she wept; and that, for the sake of Louisa's children—and she persisted in laying her heart bare. And here certain vague suspicions that had crossed Polly's mind on the night of the impromptu ball—they were gone again, in an instant, quick as thistledown on the breeze—these suddenly returned, life-size and weighty; and the name that was spoken came as no surprise to her. Yes, it was Mr. Henry Ocock to whom poor Agnes was attached. There had been a mutual avowal of affection, sobbed the latter; they met as often as circumstances permitted. Polly was thunderstruck: knowing Agnes as she did, she herself could not believe any harm of her; but she shuddered at the thought of what other people—Richard, for instance—would say, did they get wind of it. She implored her friend to caution. She ought never, never to see Mr. Ocock. Why did she not go away to Melbourne, for a time? And why had he come to Ballarat?

"To be near me, dearest, to help me, if I should need him.— Oh, you can't think what a comfort it is, Polly, to feel that he *is* here—so good, and strong, and clever!— Yes, I know what you mean . . . but this is quite, quite different. Henry does not expect me to be clever, too—does not want me to be. He prefers me as I am. He dislikes clever women . . . would never marry one. And we *shall* marry, darling, some day— when . . ."

Henry Ocock! Polly tried to focus everything she knew of him, all her fleeting impressions, in one picture—and failed.

He had made himself very agreeable, the single time she had met him; but. . . . There was Richard's opinion of him: Richard did not like him, or trust him; he thought him unscrupulous in business, cold, and self-seeking.— Poor, poor little Agnes! That such a misfortune should just befall her!— Stranger still was it that she, Polly, should be mixed up in it.

She had, of course, always known from books that such things did happen; but then they seemed quite different, and very far away. Her thoughts at this crisis were undeniably woolly; but the gist of them was, that life and books had nothing in common. For, in stories, the woman who forgot herself was always a bad woman; whereas not the harshest critic could call poor Agnes bad. Indeed, Polly felt that even if some one proved to her that her friend had actually done wrong, she would not, on that account, be able to stop caring for her, or feeling sorry for her. It was all very uncomfortable and confusing.

While these thoughts came and went, she half sat, half knelt, a pair of scissors in her hand. She was busy cutting out a dress, and, no table being big enough for the purpose, she had stretched the material on the parlour floor. This would be the first new dress she had had since her marriage; and it was high time, considering all the visiting and going about that fell to her lot just now. Sara had sent the pattern up from Melbourne, and John, hearing what was in the wind, had most kindly and generously made her a present of the silk. Polly hoped she would not bungle it, in the cutting; but skirts were growing wider and wider, and John had not reckoned with quite the newest fashion. So she had to plan and contrive.

Steps in the passage made her note subconsciously that Ned had arrived—Jerry had been in the house for the past three weeks, with a sprained wrist.— And at this moment her younger brother himself entered the room, Trotty throned on his shoulder.

Picking his steps round the sea of stuff, Jerry sat down, and lowered Trotty to his knee.— "Ned's grizzling for tea."

Polly did not reply; she was laying an odd-shaped piece of paper now this way, now that.

For a while Jerry played with the child. Then he burst out: "I say, Poll!" And added, a minute later, since Polly paid no heed to his apostrophe: "Richard says I can get back to work to-morrow."

"That's a good thing," answered his sister, with an air of abstraction: she had solved her puzzle to within half a yard.

Jerry cast a boyishly imploring glance at her back, and rubbed his chin with his hand. "Poll, old girl—I say, wouldn't you put in a word for me, with Richard? I'm hanged if I want to go back to the claim. I'm sick to death of digging."

At this Polly did raise her head, to regard him with grave eyes. "What! tired of work already, Jerry? I don't know what Richard will say to that, I'm sure. You had better speak to him yourself."

Again, Jerry rubbed his chin. "That's just it—what's so beastly hard. I know he'll say I ought to stick to it."

"So do I."

"Well, I'd rather groom the horse than that!"

"But think how pleased you were, at first!"

Jerry ruefully admitted it. "One expects to dig out gold like spuds; while the real thing's enough to give you the blight.—As for stopping a wages-man all my life, I won't do it. I might just as well go home and work in a Lancashire pit."

"But Ned——"

"Oh, Ned! Ned walks about with his head in the clouds. He's always blowing of what he's *going* to do, and gets his steam off that way. I'm different."

But Jerry's words fell on deaf ears. A noise in the next room was engaging Polly's attention. She heard a burr of suppressed laughter, a scuffle, and what sounded like a sharp slap. Jumping up, she went to the door, and was just in time to see Ellen whisk out of the dining-room.

Ned sat in an armchair, with his feet on the chimney-piece. "I had the girl bring in a log, Poll," he said; and looked back and up at his sister, with his cheery smile. Ned was always cold of late; Polly feared the perpetual work underground was beginning to tell on his health. Standing behind him, she laid her hand on his hair. "I'll go and see after the tea." Ned was so unconcerned that she hesitated to put a question.

In the kitchen she had no such tender scruples; nor was she imposed on by the exaggerated energy with which Ellen bustled about. "What was that noise I heard in the dining-room just now?" she demanded.

214

"Noise? I dunno," gave back the girl crossly, without facing her.

"Nonsense, Ellen! Do you think I didn't hear?"

"Oh, get along with you! It was only one of Ned's jokes." And going on her knees, Ellen set to scrubbing the brick floor with a hiss and a scratch that rendered speech impossible. Polly took up the laden tea-tray and carried it into the dining-room. Richard had come home, and the four drew chairs to the table.

Mahony had a book with him; he propped it open against the butter-cooler, and snatched sentences as he ate. It fell to Ned to keep the ball of talk rolling. Polly was distrait to the point of going wrong in her sugars; Jerry highly uneasy at the prospect of coming in conflict with his brother-in-law, whom he thought the world of.

Ned was as full of talk as an egg is of meat. The theme he this day dwelt longest on was the new glory that lay in store for the Ballarat diggings. At present, these were under a cloud. The alluvial was rapidly giving out, and the costs and difficulties of boring through the rock seemed insuperable. One might hear the opinion freely expressed that Ballarat's day as premier gold-field was done. Ned set up this belief merely for the pleasure of demolishing it. He had it at first hand that great companies were being formed to carry on operations. These would reckon their areas in acres instead of feet, would sink to a depth of a quarter of a mile or more, raise washdirt in hundreds of tons per day. It was said that the surface works alone would run into thousands of pounds. One such company, indeed, had already sprung into existence, out on Golden Point; and now was the time to nip in. If he, Ned, had the brass, or knew anybody who'd lend it to him, he'd buy up all the shares he could get. Those who followed his lead would make their fortunes out of it.— "I say, Richard, it'ud be something for you."

His words evoked no response.— Sorry though I shall be, thought Polly, dear Ned had better not come to the house so often in future. I wonder if I should tell Richard why. Jerry was on pins and needles, and even put Trotty ungently from him: Richard would be so disgusted by Ned's blatherskite that he would have no patience left to listen to him.

Mahony kept his nose to his book. As a matter of principle.

He made a rule of believing, on an average, about the half of what Ned said. To appear to pay attention to him would spur him on to more flagrant over-statements.

"D'ye hear, Richard? Now's your chance," repeated Ned, not to be done. "There's a pot o' money in it. A very different thing this, I can tell you, from running round dosing people for the collywobbles. I know men who are raising the splosh to get in, any way they can."

"I dare say you do. There's never been any lack of gamblers on Ballarat," said Mahony drily, and passed his cup to be refilled.

Pig-headed fool! was Ned's mental retort, as he sliced a chunk of rabbit-pie.— "Well, I bet you'll feel sore some day, you didn't take my advice," he said aloud.

"We shall see, my lad, we shall see!" replied Mahony. "In the meantime let me inform you, I can make good use of every penny I have. So if you've come here thinking you can wheedle something out of me, you've made a mistake."— He could seldom resist tearing the veil from Ned's gross hints and impostures.

"Oh no, Richard dear!" interpolated Polly, in her rôle of keeper-of-the-peace.

Ned answered huffily: "'Pon my word, I never met such a fellow as you, for thinking the worst of people."

The thrust went home. Mahony clapped his book to. "You lay yourself open to it, sir! If I'm wrong, I beg your pardon.— But for goodness' sake, Ned, put all these trashy ideas of making a fortune out of your mind. Digging is played out, I tell you. Decent people turned their backs on it long ago."

"That's what I think, too," threw in Jerry.

Mahony bit his lip. "Come, come, now, what do you know about it?" He believed Jerry was weakly echoing his own opinion.

Jerry flushed and floundered, till Polly came to his aid. "He's been wanting to speak to you, Richard. He hates the work as much as you did."

"Well, he has a tongue of his own.— Speak for yourself, my boy!"

Thus encouraged, Jerry made his appeal; and, fearing lest Richard should throw him, half-heard, into the same category as Ned, he worded it very tersely. Mahony who had never given much heed to Jerry—no one did—was pleased by his straightforward air. Still, he did not know what could be done for him just now, and said so.

Here, Polly had an inspiration. "But I think I do. I just remember, Mr. Ocock was saying to me the other day, he must take another boy into the business, it was growing so— the fourth, this will make. I don't know if he's suited yet, but even if he is, he may have heard of something else.— Only you know, Jerry, you mustn't mind *what* it is. After tea, I'll put on my bonnet, and go down to the Flat with you. And Ned shall come, too," she added, with a consoling glance at her elder brother: Ned had extended his huff to his second slice of pie, which lay untouched on his plate.

—"Somebody has always got something up her sleeve," said Mahony affectionately, when Polly came in to him, in walking costume. "None the less, wife, I shouldn't be surprised if those brothers of yours gave us some trouble, before we're done with them."

[6]

In the weeks and months that followed, as he rode from one end of Ballarat to the other—from Yuille's Swamp, in the west, as far east as the ranges and gullies of Little Bendigo—it gradually became evident to Mahony that Ned's frothy tales had some body in them, after all. The character of the diggings was changing before his very eyes. Nowadays, except on an outlying, muddy flat, or in the hands of the retrograde Chinese, tubs, cradle and windlasses were rarely to be met with. Engine-sheds and boiler-houses began to dot the ground; here and there a tall chimney belched smoke, beside a lofty poppet-head, or an aerial trolley-line. The richest gutters were found to take their rise below the basaltic deposits; all the difficulties and risks of rock-mining had now to be faced; and the capitalist, so long held at bay, was at length made free of the field. Companies were springing up, large sums of money being subscribed; and, where these proved insufficient, the banks stepped into the breach with subsidies on mortgages. The population, in whose veins the gold-fever still burned, plunged by wholesale into the new hazard; and under the wooden verandahs of Bridge Street, a motley crew of jobbers and brokers came into existence, who would demonstrate to you, à la Ned, how you might reap a fortune from a claim, without putting in an hour's work on it—without even knowing where it was.

A temptation, indeed! . . . but one that did not affect him.— Mahony let the reins droop on his horse's neck, and the animal picked its own steps among the impedimenta of the bush road.— It concerned only those who had money to spare, and who could afford to let this lie fallow. Months, nay, years must go by, before, from even the most promising of these co-operative affairs, any return was to be expected. As for him, there still came days when he had not a five-pound note to his name. It had been a delusion to suppose that, in accepting John's offer, he was leaving money-troubles behind him; he led the same hand-to-mouth existence as of old. Despite Polly's thrift, their improved style of life cost more than he had reckoned; the patients, slow to come, were slower still to discharge their debts. Moreover, he had never guessed how heavily the quarterly payments of interest would weigh on him. These sums were like yokes, into which, at a given date, he had to thrust his neck. With as good as no margin, with the fate of every shilling decided beforehand, the saving up of thirty odd pounds, four times a year, was a veritable achievement. He was always in a quake lest he should not be able to get it together. No one suspected what near shaves he had— not even Polly. And, so far, he had contrived to scrape through —if by the skin of his teeth. The last time hardly bore thinking about. At the eleventh hour, he had unexpectedly found himself several pounds short. He did not close an eye all night, and got up in the morning as though for his own execution. Then, fortune favoured him. A well-to-do butcher, his hearty: "What'll yours be?" at the nearest public-house waved aside, had settled his bill off-hand. Mahony could still feel the sudden lift of the black fog-cloud that had enveloped him—the sense of bodily exhaustion that had succeeded to the intolerable mental strain.

For the coming quarter-day he was better prepared—if, that is, nothing out of the way happened. Of late he had been haunted by a fear of illness—a misfortune that would be as fatal to his budding practice as an unkempt head to a barber, or ill-fitting clothes to a tailor. The long hours in the saddle did not suit him. He ought to have a buggy, with a hood to it, and a second horse. But there could be no question of this in the meantime, or of a great deal else besides. He wanted to buy Polly a piano, for instance; all her friends had pianos; and she played and sang very prettily. She needed more dresses and bonnets, too, than he was able to allow her, as well as a change to the seaside, in the summer heat. The first spare money he had should go towards one or the other. He loved to give Polly pleasure; never was such a contented little soul as she. And well for him that it was so. To have had a complaining, even an impatient wife at his side, just now, would have been unbearable. But Polly did not know what impatience meant; her sunny temper, her fixed resolve to make the best of everything, was not to be shaken. How sound had been the instinct that led him to her, in the first place!

Well, comforts galore should be hers some day. The practice was shaping satisfactorily. His introduction, through Ocock, at Dandaloo, had proved a key to many doors: folk of the Glendinnings' and Urquharts' standing could make a reputation or mar it, as they chose. It had got abroad, he knew, that at whatever hour of the day or night he was sent for, he could be relied on to be sober; and that, unfortunately, was not the case with some of his colleagues, who, poor souls, had battled through the hardships of a colonial doctor's life, from the beginning. Another thing, he avoided treating his patients indiscriminately as a set of rogues and rascals, or as the scum of the earth—habits which those medicos who had had to do with the riff-raff of the original settlement, now could not break themselves of. And, in addition to this, his fellow-practitioners showed signs of waking up to the fact of his existence. He had been called in lately to a couple of consultations; and the doyen of the profession on Ballarat, old Munce himself, had praised his handling of a difficult case of version.

The distances to be covered—that was what made the work stiff. And, as things stood, he could not afford to neglect a single summons, no matter where it led him. Still, he would not have grumbled, had only the money not been so hard to get in. But the fifty thousand odd souls on Ballarat formed, even yet, anything but a stable population: a patient you attended one day might be gone the next, and gone where no bill could reach him—off on a new "rush," that lay outside the area of the postal service, or, as the result of a glass too much on a dark night, be lying, with a broken neck, at the bottom of one of the many worked-out holes nobody ever thought of filling in. Or again, you suddenly found that your debtor had been sold off at public auction; or that his wooden shanty had gone up in a flare and been reduced to ashes—hardly a night passed without a fire somewhere. In these and like accidents, the unfortunate doctor might whistle for his fee. It seldom happened nowadays that he was paid in cash. The time of lavish open-handedness was over. Money was growing as scarce here as anywhere else. Sometimes, it is true, he might have pocketed his fee on the spot, had he cared to ask for it. But the presenting of his palm professionally was a gesture that was denied him. His natural instinct was rather to put both hands behind his back. And this stand-offishness drove from people's minds the thought that he might be in actual need of money. Afterwards, he sat at home and racked his brains how to pay butcher and grocer. Others of the fraternity were by no means so nice. He knew of some who would not stir a yard towards a bush-patient unless their fee was planked down before them—old stagers these, who at one time had been badly bitten, and were now grown cynically distrustful. Or tired. And indeed who could blame a man for hesitating whether or no, of a pitchdark night in the winter rains, or on a blazing summer day, he should set out on a twenty-mile ride, for which he might never see the ghost of a remuneration?

Reflecting thus, Mahony caught at a couple of hard, spicy, grey-green leaves, to chew as he went: the gums, on which the old bark hung in ribbons, were in flower by now, and bore feathery yellow blossoms, side by side with nutty capsules. His horse had been ambling forward unpressed. Now, it laid its ears flat, and a minute later its master's slower senses caught the clop-clop of a second set of hoofs, the noise of wheels. Mahony had reached a place where two roads joined, and saw a covered buggy approaching. He drew rein and waited.

The occupant of the vehicle had wound the reins round the empty lamp-bracket, and left it to the sagacity of his horse to keep the familiar track, while he dozed, head on breast, in the

corner. The animal halted of itself, on coming up with its
fellow, and Archdeacon Long opened his eyes.

"Ah, good-day to you, doctor!— Yes, as you see, enjoying a
little nap. I was out early this morning."

He got down from the buggy, and, with bent knees, and his
hands in his pockets, stretched the creased cloth of his trousers, where this had cut into his flesh. He was a big, brawny,
handsome man, with a massive nose, a cloven chin, and the
most companionable smile in the world. As he stood, he
touched here a strap, there a buckle, on the harness of his
chestnut—a well-known trotter, with which he often made a
match—and affectionately clapped the neck of Mahony's bay.
He could not keep his hands off a horse. By choice he was his
own stableman, and, in earlier life, had been a dare-devil
rider. Now, increasing weight led him to prefer buggy to saddle; but his recklessness had not diminished. With his left
hand only, he would run his light, two-wheeled trap up any
wooded, boulder-strewn hill, and down the other side, just as
in his harum-scarum days he had set it at felled trees, and, if
rumour spoke true, wire fences.

Mahony admired the splendid vitality of the man, as well
as the indestructible optimism that bore him triumphantly
through all the hardships of a colonial ministry, and made
him the most popular cleric in the diocese of Victoria. No sick
bed was too remote for Long to reach, no sinner sunk too low
to be helped to his feet. The leprous Chinaman doomed to an
unending isolation, the drunken Paddy, the degraded white
woman—each came in for a share of his benevolence. He
spent the greater part of his life in this buggy of his, visiting
the outcasts, and outposts, of civilisation, beating up the un-
baptised, the unconfirmed, the unwed. But his church did not
suffer. One never met him but what he had some fresh scheme
on hand: either he was getting up a tea-meeting to raise money
for an organ; or a series of penny-readings towards funds for
a chancel; or he was training with his choir for a sacred concert. There was a boyish streak in him, too. He would enter
into the joys of the annual Sunday-school picnic with a zest
equal to the children's own, leading the way, in shirt-sleeves,
at leap-frog and obstacle-race; unless, that is, he had been
called far away to lay a foundation-stone, or to support his
Bishop at a consecration. In doctrine, he struck a happy mean

between low-church practices and ritualism, preaching short, spirited sermons, to which even languid Christians could listen without tedium; and, on a week-day evening, he would take a hand at a rubber of whist, or at écarté—and not for love—or play a sound game of chess. A man, too, who, refusing to be bound by the letter of the Thirty-nine Articles, extended his charity even to persons of the Popish faith. He was one of the few to whom Mahony could speak of his own haphazard efforts at criticising the Pentateuch.

The Archdeacon was wont to respond, with his genial smile: "Ah, it's all very well for you, doctor!—you're a free lance. I am constrained by my cloth.— And frankly, for the rest of us, that kind of thing's too—well, too disturbing. Especially when we have nothing better to put in its place. In a community like ours, it's the chief business of religion to be constructive—I'm sure you agree with me in that?"

Doctor and parson—the latter, considerably over six feet, made Mahony, who was tall enough, look short and doubly slender—walked side by side for nearly a mile, the Archdeacon fondling the moist, wide-nostrilled snout that nosed at the hands he carried crossed on his back. The two men flitted from topic to topic, exchanging notes on a long dozen of subjects in the brief time at their disposal: amongst others, the jealous rivalry that prevailed between Ballarats East and West; the installation of a new Grand Master; the seditious uprising in India, where both had relatives; the recent rains, the prospects for grazing. The last theme brought them round to Dandaloo, and its unhappy owner. The Archdeacon expressed the outsider's surprise at the strength of Glendinning's constitution, and the lively popular sympathy that was felt for his wife.

"One's heart aches for the poor little lady, struggling to bear up as though nothing were the matter. Between ourselves, doctor"—and Mr. Long took off his straw hat, to let the air play round his head. "Between ourselves, it's a thousand pities he doesn't just pop off the hooks, in one of his bouts.— Or that some of you medical gentlemen don't use your knowledge to help things on, with a few drops of something."

He let out his great hearty laugh as he spoke, and his companion's involuntary stiffening went unnoticed. But on Mahony voicing his attitude with: "And his immortal soul, sir?

Isn't it the church's duty to hope for a miracle? . . . just as it is ours to keep the vital spark going," he made haste to take the edge off his words. "Now, now, doctor, only my fun! Our duty is, I trust, plain to us both."

It was even easier to soothe than to ruffle Mahony. The bare suggestion of an apology was enough for him. "Remember me very kindly to Mrs. Long, will you?" he said, as the Archdeacon prepared to climb into his buggy. "But tell her, too, I owe her a grudge just now. My wife's so lost in flannel and brown holland that I can't get a word out of her."

"And mine doesn't know where she'd be, with this bazaar, if it weren't for Mrs. Mahony."— Long was husband to a dot of a woman, who, having borne him half a dozen children of his own feature and build, now worked as hard as a parish clerk and a district visitor rolled into one; driving about, in sunbonnet and gardening gloves, behind a pair of cream ponies— tiny, sharp-featured, resolute; with little of her husband's large tolerance, but with an energy that outdid his own, and made her an object of both fear and respect.— "And that reminds me: over at the cross-roads by Spring Hill, I met your young brother-in-law—that poor chap Macguire, who was down with typhoid, is to be sold up to-day. And Jerry told me, if I ran across you, to ask you to hurry home. Your wife has some surprise or other in store for you.— No, nothing unpleasant! Rather the reverse, I believe. But I wasn't to say more.— Well, good-day, doctor, good-day to you!"

Mahony smiled, nodded, and went on his way. Polly's surprises were usually simple and transparent things: some one would have made them a present of a sucking-pig, or a bush-turkey, and Polly, knowing his relish for a savoury morsel, did not wish it to be overdone: she had sent similar chance calls out after him, before now.

When, having seen his horse rubbed down, he reached home, he found her on the doorstep watching for him. She was flushed, and her eyes had those peculiar high-lights in them, which led him jokingly to exhort her to caution: "Lest the sparks should set the house on fire!"

"Well, what is it, Pussy?" he inquired, as he laid his bag down and hung up his wide-awake. "What's my little surprise-monger got up her sleeve to-day?— Good Lord, Polly, I'm tired!"

Polly was smiling roguishly. "Aren't you going into the surgery, Richard?" she smiled, as he headed for the dining-room.

"Aha! So that's it," said he, and obediently turned the handle. Polly had, on occasion, taken advantage of his absence to introduce some new comfort or decoration in his room.

The blind had been let down. He was still blinking in the half-dark, when a figure sprang out from behind the door, barging heavily against him, and a loud voice shouted: "Boh, you old beef-brains! Boh to a goose!"

Displeased at such horseplay, Mahony stepped sharply back —his first thought was of Ned having unexpectedly returned from Mount Ararat, where he had been digging for the past three months. Then, he recognised the voice, his eyes lit up, and he exclaimed incredulously: "*You*, Dicky-bird? You!"

"Dick, old man. . . . I say, Dick! Yes, it's me right enough, and not my ghost. The old bad egg come back to roost!"

The blind was raised; and the friends, who had last met in the dingy bush hut, on the night of the Stockade, stood face to face. And now ensued a babel of greeting, a quick fire of question and answer, the two voices going in and out and round each other, singly and together, like the voices in a duet. Tears rose to Polly's eyes as she listened; it made her heart glow to see Richard so glad. But when, forgetting her presence, Purdy cried: "And I must confess, Dick. . . . I took a kiss from Mrs. Polly. Gad, old man, how she's come on!" Polly hastily retired to the kitchen, to superintend the dishing-up of the dinner.

At table, the same high spirits prevailed: it did not often happen that Richard was brought out of his shell like this, thought Polly gratefully, and heaped her visitor's plate to the brim. His first hunger stilled, Purdy fell to giving a slap-dash account of his motley experiences. He kept to no orderly sequence, but threw them out just as they occurred to him: a rub with bushrangers in the Black Forest, his adventures as a long-distance drover in the Mildura, the trials of a week he had spent in a boiling-down establishment on the Murray: "Where the stink was so foul, you two, that I vomited like a dog every day!" Under the force of this Odyssey, husband and wife gradually dropped into silence, which they broke only by single words of astonishment and sympathy; while the child Trotty spooned in her pudding without seeing it, her round, solemn eyes fixed unblinkingly on this new uncle, who was like a wonderful story-book come alive.

In Mahony's attitude towards Purdy at this moment, there was none of the old intolerant superiority; and the many clashes of opinion and temperament that had vexed the course of their friendship were forgotten. The elder man had been dependent, for so long, on a mere surface acquaintance with his fellows, that he now felt to the full how precious the tie was that bound him to Purdy. Here came one for whom he was not alone the reserved, struggling practitioner, the rather moody man advancing to middle-age; but also the Dick of his boyhood and early youth.

He had often imagined the satisfaction it would be to confide his troubles to Purdy. Compared, however, with the hardships the latter had undergone, these seemed of small importance; and dinner passed without any allusion to his own affairs. And now the chances of his speaking out were but slight; he could have been entirely frank only under the first stimulus of meeting.

Even when they rose from the table, Purdy continued to hold the centre of the stage. For he had turned up with hardly a shirt to his back, and had to be rigged out afresh from Mahony's wardrobe. It was decided that he should remain their guest in the meantime; also that Mahony should call, on his behalf, on the Commissioner of Police, and put in a good word for him. For Purdy had come back with the idea of seeking a job in the Ballarat Mounted Police Force.

When Mahony could no longer put off starting on his afternoon round, Purdy went with him to the livery-barn, limping briskly at his side. On the way, he exclaimed aloud at the marvellous changes that had taken place since he was last in the township. There were half a dozen gas-lamps in Sturt Street by this time, the gas being distilled from a mixture of oil and gum-leaves.

"One wouldn't credit it, if one didn't see it with one's own peepers!" he cried, repeatedly bringing up short before the plate-glass windows of the shops, the many handsome, verandahed hotels, the granite front of Christ Church. "And from what I hear, Dick, now companies have jumped the claims and are deep-sinking in earnest, we're going to make our fortunes like one o'clock."

But on getting home again, he sat down in front of Polly, and said, with a businesslike air: "And now tell me all about old Dick! You know, Poll, he's such an odd fish; if he himself doesn't offer to uncork, somehow one can't just pump him. And I want to know everything that concerns him—from A to Z."

Though taken aback, Polly could not hold out against this affectionate curiosity. Entrenching her needle in its stuff, she put her work away, and complied. And soon to her own satisfaction. For the first time in her married life, she was led to discuss her husband's ways and actions with another person; and, to her amazement, she found that it was easier to talk to Purdy about Richard than to Richard himself. Purdy and she saw things in the same light; no rigmarole of explanation was necessary; a few quite simple words were enough. Now with Richard, it was not so. In conversation with him, one constantly felt that he was not speaking out, or, to put it more plainly, that he was going on meanwhile with his own, very different thoughts. And behind what he did say, there was sure to lurk some imaginary scruple, some rather far-fetched delicacy of feeling, which it was hard to get at, and harder still to understand.

[7]

SUMMER had come round again, and the motionless white heat of December lay heavy on the place. The low little houses seemed to cower beneath it, to hug the ground; and the smoke from their chimneys drew black, perpendicular lines on the pale sky. If it was a misery at this season to traverse the blazing, dusty woods, it was almost worse to be within-doors, where the thin wooden walls were powerless to keep out the heat, and flies and mosquitoes raged in chorus. Nevertheless, determined Christmas preparations went on in dozens of tiny, zinc-roofed kitchens, the temperature of which was not much below that of the ovens themselves; and kindly, well-to-do people, like Mrs. Glendinning and Mrs. Urquhart, drove in, in hooded buggies, with green fly-veils dangling from their broad-brimmed hats, and dropped a goose here, a turkey there, or a pailful of fruit, on their less prosperous friends. They robbed their gardens, too, of the summer's last flowers, arum-lilies and brilliant geraniums, to decorate the Archdeacon's church for the festival; and, under the generalship of Mrs. Long, many ladies spent the whole day in the church, making wreaths and crosses, weaving garlands to drape over the pointed windows, and festoons to encircle the lamps.

No one was busier than Polly. For she wanted to give Purdy, who had been on short commons for so long, a special Christmas treat. She had willing helpers in him and Jerry: the two of them chopped, and stoned, and stirred, while she, seated on the block of the woodstack, her head tied up in an old pillow-case, plucked and singed the goose that had fallen to her share. Towards four o'clock on Christmas Day, they drew their chairs to the table—barring Ned, "poor Ned!" who was miles and miles away—and, with loosened collars, set about enjoying the good things. Or pretending to enjoy them. This was Mahony's case; for the day was no holiday for him, and his head ached from the sun. At tea-time, Hempel, looking very spruce in a long black coat and white tie, arrived to pay a call; and close on his heels followed old Mr. Ocock. The latter, having deposited his hat under his seat and tapped several pockets, produced a letter, which he unfolded and handed to Polly, with a broad grin. It was from his daughter, and contained the news of his wife's death. "Died o' the grumbles, I lay you! An' the first good turn she ever done me." The main point was that Miss Amelia, now at liberty, was already taking advice about the safest line of clipper-ships, and asking for a reply, *by return*, to a number of extraordinary questions. Could one depend on hearing God's Word preached of a Sunday? Was it customary for *females* to go armed as well as men? Were the blacks *converted,* and what amount of clothing did they wear?

"Thinks she's comin' to the back o' beyond, does Mely!" chuckled the old man, and slapped his thigh at the sudden idea that occurred to him of "takin' a rise out of 'er." "Won't she stare when she gits 'ere, that's all!"

"Well, now you'll simply *have* to build," said Polly, after threatening to write privately to Miss Amelia, to reassure her. And imagining the poor young lady's horror, were she set down before the bark-roofed shanty in which her father and brothers pigged it, Polly urged on the old man that it was his bounden duty to make a change. Why not move over west, and take up a piece of ground in the same road as themselves? But from this he excused himself, with a laugh and a spit, on the score that no landsales had yet been held in their neighbourhood: when he *did* turn out of his present four walls, which had always been plenty good enough for him, he wanted a place that 'ud really and truly be his own, and one he could "fit up tidy"; which it 'ud stick in his throat to do so, if he thought it might any day be sold over his head. Mahony winced at this. Then laughed, with an exaggerated carelessness. "Look at me! I've been settled here for more than a year now, and nothing of the kind has happened." If, in a country like this, you waited for all to be fixed and sure, you would wait till Domesday.— None the less, the thrust rankled. It was a fact that he himself had not spent a sou on his premises, since they finished building. The thought at the back of *his* mind, too, was, why waste his hard-earned income on improvements that might benefit only the next-comer? Common sense bid one make the best of things as they were.— The yard they sat in, for instance! Polly had her hens, and a ramshackle hen-house; but not a spadeful of earth had been turned towards the wished-for garden. It was just the ordinary colonial backyard, fenced round with rude palings which did not match and were mended here and there with bits of tin-foil; its groundspace littered with a medley of articles for which there was no room elsewhere: boards left lying by the builders, empty kerosene-tins, a couple of tubs, a ragged cane-chair, some old cases. Wash-lines, on which at the moment a row of stockings hung, stretched permanently from corner to corner; and the whole was dominated by the big round galvanised-iron tank.

On Boxing Day, Purdy got the loan of a lorry, and drove a large party, including several children, comfortably placed on straw, hassocks and low chairs, to the Races, on a course a few miles out. Half Ballarat was making in the same direction; and whoever owned a horse that was sound in the wind, and anything of a stepper, had entered it for some item on the programme. The Grand Stand, a bark shed open to the air on three sides, was resorted to only in the case of a sudden downpour; the occupants of the dust-laden buggies, wagonettes, brakes, carts and drays, preferred to follow events standing on their seats, and on the boards that served them as seats. After the meeting, those who belonged to the Urquhart-Glendinning set went on to Yarangobilly, and danced till long past midnight on the broad verandah. It was nearly three o'clock before Purdy brought his load safely home; and, under the round white moon, the lorry was strewn with the forms of sleeping children.

Early next morning, while Polly, still only half awake, was pouring out coffee, and giving Richard, who, poor fellow, could not afford to leave his patients, an account of their doings—with certain omissions, of course: she did not mention the glaring indiscretion Agnes Glendinning had been guilty of, in disappearing with Mr. Henry Ocock into a dark shrubbery—while Polly talked, the postman handed in two letters, which were of a nature to put balls and races clean out of her head. The first was in Mrs. Beamish's ill-formed hand, and told a sorrowful tale. Custom had entirely gone: a new hotel or public-house had been erected on the new road; Beamish was forced to declare himself a bankrupt; and, in a few days, the Family Hotel, with all its contents, would be put up at public auction. What was to become of them, God alone knew. She supposed she would end her days in taking in washing, and the girls must go out as servants. But she was sure Polly, now so up in the world, with a husband doing so well, would not forget the old friends who had once been so kind to her—with much more in the same strain, which Polly skipped, in reading the letter aloud. The long and short of it was: would Polly ask her husband to lend them a couple of hundred pounds to make a fresh start with, or failing that, to put his name to a bill for the same amount?

"Of course she hasn't an idea we were obliged to borrow money ourselves," said Polly, in response to Mahony's ironic laugh and muttered: "Like her impudence!" "I couldn't tell them that."

"No . . . nor that it's a perpetual struggle to keep the wolf from the door," answered her husband, battering in the top of an egg with the back of his spoon.

"Oh, Richard dear, things aren't quite so bad as that," said Polly cheerfully. Then she heaved a sigh. "I know, of course,

we can't afford to help them; but I *do* feel so sorry for them"
—she herself would have given the dress off her back. "But I
think, dear, if you didn't mind *very* much, we might ask one
of the girls up to stay with us . . . till the worst is over."

"Yes, I suppose that wouldn't be impossible," said Mahony.
"If you've set your heart on it, my Polly! If, too, you can persuade Master Purdy to forgo the comfort of our good feather-
bed. And I'll see if I can wring out a fiver for you to enclose
in your letter."

Polly jumped up and kissed him. "And Purdy is going anyhow. He said only last night he must look for lodgings near
the Police Station." Here a thought struck her; she coloured
and smiled. "I'll ask Tilly first," said she.

Mahony laughed and shook his finger at her. "The best laid
plans o' mice and men! And what's one to say to a match-
maker who is still growing out of her clothes?"

At this Polly clapped a hand over his mouth, for fear Ellen
should hear him. It was a sore point with her that she had
more than once of late had to lengthen her dresses.

As soon as she was alone, she sat down to compose a reply
to Mrs. Beamish. It was no easy job: she was obliged to say
that Richard felt unable to come to her aid; and, at the same
time, to avoid touching on his private affairs; had to disappoint
as kindly as she could; to be truthful, yet tactful.— Polly wrote,
and re-wrote: the business cost her the forenoon.

She could not even press Tilly to pack her box and come at
once; for her second letter that morning had been from Sara,
who wrote that, having decided to shake the dust of the colony off her feet, she wished to pay them a flying visit before
sailing, *"pour faire mes adieux."* She signed herself "Your affectionate sister Zara," and on her arrival explained that, tired
of continually instructing people in the pronunciation of her
name, she had decided to alter the spelling and be done with
it. Moreover, a little bird had whispered in her ear that under
its new form, it fitted her rather *"French"* air and looks, a thousand times better than before.

Descending from the coach, Zara eyed Polly up and down,
and vowed she would never have known her; and, on the way
home, Polly more than once felt her sister's gaze fixed critically
on her. For her part, she was able to assure Zara that she saw
no change whatever in her, since her last visit—even since the

date of the wedding. And this pleased Zara mightily; for, as she admitted, in removing hat and mantle, and passing the damped corner of a towel over her face, she dreaded the ageing effects of the climate on her fine complexion. Close as ever about her own concerns, she gave no reason for her abrupt determination to leave the country; but, from subsequent talk, Polly gathered that for one thing, Zara had found her position at the head of John's establishment—"Undertaken in the first place, my dear, at immense personal sacrifice!"—no sinecure. John had proved a regular martinet; he had countermanded her orders, interfered about the household bills—had even accused her of lining her own pocket. As for little Johnny—the bait originally thrown out to induce her to accept the post— he had long since been sent to boarding-school. "A thoroughly bad, unprincipled boy!" was Zara's verdict. And when Polly, big with pity, expostulated: "But, Zara, he is only six years old!" her sister retorted with a: "My dear, I know the world, and you don't!"—to which Polly could think of no reply.

Zara had announced herself for a bare fortnight's stay; but the man who carried her trunk groaned and sweated under it, and was so insolent about the size of the coin she dropped in his palm, that Polly followed him by stealth into the passage, to make it up to a crown. As usual, Zara was attired in the height of fashion. She brought a set of "the hoops" with her— the first to be seen on Ballarat—and, once more, Polly was torn between an honest admiration of her sister's daring, and an equally honest embarrassment at the notice she attracted. Zara swam and glided about the streets, to the hilarious amazement of the population; floated feather-light, billowing here, depressing there, with all the waywardness of a child's balloon; supported—or so it seemed—by two of the tiniest feet ever bestowed on mortal woman. Aha! but that was one of the chief merits of "the hoops," declared Zara; that, and the possibility of getting still more stuff into your skirts, without materially increasing their weight. There was something in that, conceded Polly, who, as it was, often felt hers drag heavy. Besides, as she reminded Richard that night, when he lay alternately chuckling and snorting at woman's folly, custom was everything. Once they had smiled at Zara appearing in a hat: "And now we're all wearing them."

Another practical consideration that occurred to her she ex-

pressed with some diffidence. "But, Zara, don't you . . . I mean
. . . aren't they very draughty?"

Zara had to repeat her shocked but emphatic denial in the
presence of Mrs. Glendinning and Mrs. Urquhart, both ladies
having a mind to bring their wardrobes up to date. They
agreed that there was much to be said in favour of the appli-
ance, over and above its novelty. Especially would it be welcome at those times when . . . But here the speakers dropped
into woman's mysterious code of nods and signs; while Zara,
turning modestly away, pretended to count the stitches in a
crochet-antimacassar.

Yes, nowadays, as Mrs. Dr. Mahony, Polly was able to introduce her sister to a society that was worthy of Zara's gifts;
and Zara enjoyed herself so well that, had her berth not been
booked, she might have contemplated extending her visit. She
overflowed with gracious commendation. The house—though,
of course, compared with John's splendour, a trifle plain and
poky—was a decided advance on the store. Polly herself was
much improved: "You *do* look robust, my dear!" And—though
Zara held her peace about this—the fact of Mahony's being
from home each day, for hours at a stretch, lent an additional
prop to her satisfaction. Under these circumstances, it was possible to keep on good terms with her brother-in-law.

Zara's natty appearance and sprightly ways made her a favourite with every one—especially the gentlemen. The Epis-
copal bazaar came off at this time; and Zara had the brilliant
idea of a bran-pie. This was the success of the entertainment.
From behind the refreshment-stall, where, together with Mrs.
Long, she was pouring out cups of tea, and serving cheesecakes
and sausage-rolls by the hundred, Polly looked proudly across
the beflagged hall, to the merry group of which her sister was
the centre. Zara was holding her own, even with Mr. Henry
Ocock; and Mr. Urquhart had, for this evening, constituted
himself her right hand.

"Your sister is no doubt a most fascinating woman," said
Mrs. Urquhart, from the seat with which she had been accommodated; and heaved a gentle sigh. "How odd that she should
never have married!"

"I'm afraid Zara's too particular," said Polly. "It's not for
want of being asked."

Her eyes met Purdy's as she spoke—Purdy had come up,

laden with empty cups, a pair of infants' boots dangling round
his neck—and they exchanged smiles; for Zara's latest *affaire
du cœur* was the source of great amusement to them.

Polly had assisted at the first meeting between her sister and
Purdy, with rather mixed feelings. On that occasion, Purdy
happened to be in plain clothes, and Zara pronounced him
charming. The very next day, however, he dropped in, clad in
the double-breasted blue jacket, the high boots and green-
veiled cabbage-tree he wore when on duty; and thereupon
Zara's opinion of him sank to null, and was not to be raised
even by his presenting himself in full dress: white-braided
trousers, red-faced shell jacket, pill-box cap, cartouche box and
cavalry sword.— "La, Polly! Nothing but a common policeman! I never heard tell of such a thing."— In vain did Polly
explain the difference between a member of the ordinary force
and a mounted trooper of the gold-escort; in vain lay stress on
Richard's pleasure at seeing Purdy buckle to steady work, no
matter what. Zara's thoughts had taken wing for a land where
such anomalies were not; where you were not asked to drink
tea with the well-meaning constable who led you across a
crowded thoroughfare, or turned on his bull's-eye for you in a
fog, preparatory to calling up a hackney-cab.

But the chilly condescension with which, from now on, Zara
treated him, did not seem to trouble Purdy. When he ran in
for five minutes of a morning, he eschewed the front entrance,
and took up his perch on the kitchen table. From here, while
Polly cooked, and he nibbled half-baked pastry, the two of
them followed the progress of events in the parlour.

Zara's arrival on Ballarat had been the cue for Hempel's reappearance, and now hardly a day went by on which the lay-
helper did not neglect his chapel work, in order to pay what
Zara called his *"devoirs."* Slight were his pretexts for coming:
a rare bit of dried seaweed for a bookmark; a religious journal
with a turned-down page; a nosegay. And though Zara would
not nowadays go the length of walking out "with a dissenter"
—she preferred on her airings to occupy the box-seat of Mr.
Urquhart's four-in-hand—she had no objection to Hempel keeping her company during the morning: she soon tired of her
woolwork; there was no piano in the house for her to practise
her solfeggios at; and Polly was lost in domestic cares. So, at
eleven o'clock of an empty forenoon Zara was very gracious to

her timid admirer—Hempel had learnt, by now, to cough behind his hand, to use a toothpick—and: "It's not *my* fault, my dear, if the preposterous creature persists in hoping against hope!" She accepted his offerings, mimicked his faulty speech, and was continually hauling him up the precipice of self-distrust, only to let him slip back, as soon as he reached the top.

One day, Purdy entered the kitchen doubled up with laughter. In passing the front of the house, he had thrown a look in at the parlour-window; and the sight of the prim and proper Hempel on his knees, on the woolly hearthrug, so tickled his sense of humour that, having spluttered out the news, back he went to the passage, where he crouched down before the parlour-door, and glued his eyes to the keyhole.

Polly, for Hempel's sake, made protest. "Oh, Purdy, no! What if the door should suddenly fly open?"

But there was a something in Purdy's pranks that a laughter-lover like Polly could never for long withstand. Here, now, in feigning to imitate the unfortunate Hempel, he was sheerly irresistible. He clapped his hands to his heart, showed the whites of his eyes, wept, gesticulated, and tore his hair. Polly, after trying in vain to keep a straight face, sat down and went off into a fit of stifled mirth—and, when Polly did give way, she was apt to set every one round her laughing, too. Ellen's shoulders shook; she held a fist to her mouth. Even little Trotty shrilled out her tinny treble, without knowing in the least what the joke was.

When the merriment was at its height, the front door opened and in walked Mahony. An instant's blank amazement, and he had grasped the whole situation—Richard was always so fearfully quick at understanding, thought Polly ruefully. Then, though Purdy jumped to his feet, and the laughter died out as if by command, he drew his brows together, and without saying a word, stalked into the surgery and shut the door.

In the yard, Purdy, like a schoolboy who had been caned, dug his knuckles into his eyes and rubbed his hindquarters—to the fresh delight of Trotty and the girl.

"Well, so long, Polly! I'd better be making tracks. The old man's on the warpath." And, in an undertone: "Same old grouser! Never *could* take a joke."

"He's tired. I'll make it all right," gave Polly back.

—"It's only his fun, Richard," she pleaded, as she held

out a linen jacket for her husband to slip his arms into.

"Fun of a kind I won't permit in my house. What an example to set the child! What's more, I shall let Hempel know that he is being made a butt of. And speak my mind to your sister about her heartless behaviour."

"Oh, don't do that, Richard. I promise it shan't happen again. It was very stupid of us, I know. But Purdy didn't really mean it unkindly; and he *is* so comical when he starts to imitate people." And Polly was all but off again, at the remembrance.

But Mahony, stooping to decipher the names Ellen had written on the slate, did not unbend. Two at Redan, one at Pennyweight Hill, one some distance out, on the banks of the Gong-Gong. He would have been glad to turn a deaf ear to this last call; for a strong north wind was blowing, beating up a dust that stung like hail.

Then, in the act of copying the addresses into his pocket-book, he let the pencil fall, and sat vacantly staring before him. He had been hurt by what had happened; and in a way all his own. It was not merely the vulgar joke that had offended him; nor yet the fact that Polly had taken part in it. There was still a very girlish side to Polly, for which he was ready to make allowance. No, what rankled was the sudden chill his unlooked-for entrance had cast over the group; they had scattered, and gone scurrying about their business like a pack of naughty children, who had been up to mischief behind their master's back. He was the schoolmaster—the spoilsport. They were all afraid of him. Even Polly.

But here back came Polly herself to say: "Dinner, dear!" in her kindest tone. She also put her arm round his neck and hugged him. "Not cross any more, Richard? I know we behaved disgracefully." Her touch put the crown on her words. Mahony drew her to him and kissed her.

But the true origin of the unpleasantness, Zara, who, in her ghoulish delight at seeing Hempel grovel before her—thus Mahony worded it—behaved more kittenishly than ever at that day's dinner-table: Zara, Mahony could not forgive; and for the remainder of her stay his manner to her was so forbidding that she, too, froze; and, to Polly's regret, the old bad relation between them came up anew.

But Zara was enjoying herself too well to cut her visit short on Mahony's account. "Besides, poor thing," thought Polly, "she has really nowhere to go." What she did do was to carry her head very high in her brother-in-law's presence; to speak at him, rather than to him; and, in private, to insist to Polly on her powers of discernment. "You may say what you like, my dear—I can see you have a *very great deal* to put up with!"

At last, however, the day of her departure broke, and Zara went off amid a babble of farewells, of requests for remembrance, a fluttering of pocket-handkerchiefs, the like of which Polly had never known; and to himself Mahony breathed the hope that they had seen the last of Zara, her fripperies and affectations. To his wife he said: "Your sister will certainly fit better into the conditions of English life."

Polly cried at the parting, which might be final; then blew her nose and dried her eyes; for she had a busy day before her. Tilly Beamish had been waiting, with ill-concealed impatience, for Zara to vacate the spare-room, and was to arrive that same night.

Mahony was not at home to welcome the new-comer, nor could he be present at high tea. When he returned, towards nine o'clock, he found Polly with a very red face, and so full of fussy cares for her guest's comfort—her natural kindliness distorted to caricature—that she had not a word for him. One look at Miss Tilly explained everything, and his respects duly paid he retired to the surgery, to indulge a smile at Polly's expense. Here, Polly soon joined him, Tilly, fatigued by her journey, and by her bounteous meal, having betaken herself early to bed.

"Ha, ha!" laughed Mahony, not without a certain mischievous satisfaction at his young wife's discomfiture. "And the prospect of a second edition to follow later!"

But Polly would not capitulate right off. "I don't think it's very kind of you to talk like that, Richard," she said warmly. "People can't help their looks." She moved about the room, putting things straight, and avoiding his eye. "As long as they mean well, and are good. . . . But I think you would rather no one ever came to stay with us, at all."

Fixing her with meaning insistence, and still smiling, Mahony opened his arms. The next moment Polly was on his knee, her face hidden in his shoulder. There she shed a few tears. "Oh, isn't she dreadful! I don't know *what* I shall do with her.— She's been serving behind the bar, Richard, for more than a year.— And she's come expecting to be taken everywhere, and to have any amount of gaiety."

At coach-time, she told him, she had dragged a reluctant Purdy to the office. But as soon as he caught sight of Tilly: "On the box, Richard, beside the driver, with her hair all towsy-wowsy in the wind!—he just said: 'Oh lor, Polly!' and disappeared, and that was the last I saw of him. I don't know how I should have got on, if it hadn't been for old Mr. Ocock, who was down meeting a parcel. He was most kind; he helped us home with her carpet-bag, and saw after her trunk.— And, oh dear, what do you think? When he was going away, he said to me in the passage—so loud I'm sure Tilly must have heard him—he said: 'Well! that's something like a figure of a female this time, Mrs. Doc. As fine a young woman as ever I see!'"

And Polly hid her face again; and husband and wife laughed in concert.

[8]

THAT night a great storm rose. Mahony, sitting reading after every one else had retired, saw it coming, and, lamp in hand, went round the house to secure hasps and catches: in a recent deluge the girl Ellen had been almost drowned in her bed, through neglecting to fasten her door. This done, he stood at the window and watched the storm's approach. In one half of the sky the stars were still peacefully alight; the other was hidden by a dense cloud; and this came racing along, like a giant bat with outspread wings, and devoured the stars in its flight. The storm broke; there was a sudden shrill screeching, a grinding, piping, whistling, and the wind hurled itself against the house, as if to level it with the ground; failing in this, it banged and battered, making windows and doors shake like loose teeth in their sockets. Then it swept by to wreak its fury elsewhere, and there was a grateful lull, out of which burst a peal of thunder. And now peal followed peal, and the face of the sky, with its masses of swirling, frothy cloud, resembled an angry sea. The lightning ripped it in fierce zigzags, darting out hundreds of spectral fangs, in its craving to reach earth.— It was a magnificent sight.

Polly came running to see where he was, the child cried, Miss Tilly opened her door by a hand's-breath, and thrust a

red, puffy face, framed in curl-twists, through the crack. Nobody thought of sleep while the commotion lasted, for fear of
fire: once alight, these exposed little wooden houses blazed up
like heaps of shavings. The clock-hands pointed to one, before
the storm showed signs of abating. Now, the rain was pouring
down, making an ear-splitting din on the iron roof, and leaping from every gutter and spout. It had turned very cold.
Mahony shivered as he got into bed.

He seemed hardly to have closed an eye when he was wakened by a loud knocking; at the same time, the wire of the
night-bell was almost pulled in two. He sat up and looked at
his watch. It wanted a few minutes to three; the rain was still
falling in torrents, the wind sighed and moaned. Wild horses
should not drag him out on such a night! Thrusting his arms
into the sleeves of his dressing-gown, he threw up the parlour
window.— "Who's there?"— The hiss of the rain cut his words
through.

A figure on the doorstep turned at the sound. "Is this a doctor's? I wuz sent here. Doctor! for God's sake . . ."

"What is it?— Stop a minute! I'll open the door."

He did so, letting in a blast of wind, and a rush of rain
that flooded the oilcloth. The intruder, off whom the water
streamed, had to shout to make himself audible.

"It's me— Mat Doyle's me name! It's me wife, doctor;
she's dying. I've bin all night on the road. Now, for the love
of——"

"Where is it?" Mahony put his hand to the side of his mouth,
to keep his words from flying adrift in the wind.

"Paddy's Rest. You're the third I've bin to. Not one of the
dirty dogs'ull stir a leg! Me girl may die like a rabbit for all
they care."— The man's voice broke, as he halloed further particulars.

"Paddy's Rest? On a night like this? Why, the creek will be
out."

"Doctor! you're from th' ould country, I can hear it in your
lip. Haven't you a wife, too, doctor? Wud you want to see her
die? Then have a bit o' mercy on mine!"

"Tut, tut, man, none of that!" said Mahony curtly. "You
should have bespoken me at the proper time to attend your
wife.— Besides, there'll be no getting along the road to-night."

The other caught the note of yielding. "Sure an' you'd go

238

out, doctor dear, without thinkin' to save your dog if he was drownin'. I've got me buggy down there; I'll take you safe. And you shan't regret it; I'll make it worth your while, by the Lord Harry, I will!"

"Pshaw!"— Mahony opened the door of the surgery, and struck a match. It was a rough grizzled fellow—a "cockatooer," on his own showing—who presented himself in the lamplight, and told his tale. His poor wife had fallen ill that afternoon. At first, everything seemed to be going well; then she was seized with fits, had one fit after another, and all but bit her tongue in two. There was nobody with her but a young girl, whom he had fetched from a mile away. He had intended, when her time came, to bring her to the District Hospital. But they had been taken unawares.— While he waited, he sat with his elbows on his knees, his face between his clenched fists.

In dressing Mahony reassured Polly, and instructed her what to say to people who came inquiring after him; for it was unlikely he would be back before afternoon. Most of the regular patients could be left till then. The one exception, a case of typhoid in its second week, a young Scotch surgeon, Brace, whom he had obliged in a similar emergency, would no doubt see for him—she should send Ellen down with a note, the first thing.— And now, having poured Doyle out a nobbler, and put a flask in his own pocket, Mahony reopened the front door to the howl of the wind.

The lantern his guide carried shed only a tiny circlet of light on the blackness; and the two men picked their steps gingerly along the flooded road. The rain ran in jets off the brim of Mahony's hat, and trickled down the back of his neck. Did he inadvertently put his foot in a hole or a deep wheel-rut, the water splashed up over his jackboots.

Having climbed into the buggy, they advanced at a funeral pace, leaving it to the sagacity of the horse to keep the track. At the creek, sure enough, the water was out, the bridge gone. To reach the next one, five miles off, a crazy cross-country drive would have been necessary; and Mahony was for giving up the job. But Doyle would not acknowledge defeat. He unharnessed the horse, set Mahony on its back, and himself holding to its tail, forced the beast, by dint of kicking and lashing, into the water; and not only got them safely across, but also up the steep sticky clay of the opposite bank.— It was six o'clock and a cloudless morning, when, numb with cold, his clothing clinging to him like wet seaweed, Mahony entered the wooden hut, where the real work he had come out to do began. . . .

Later in the day, clad in an odd collection of baggy garments, he sat and warmed himself in the sun, which was fast drawing up, in the form of a blankety mist, the moisture from the ground. He had successfully performed, under the worst possible conditions, a ticklish operation; and was now so tired that, his chin sinking to his chest, he fell fast asleep.

Doyle wakened him by announcing the arrival of the buggy. The good man, who had had more than one nobbler during the morning, could not hold his tongue, but made still another wordy attempt to express his gratitude.— "Whither me girl lives or dies, it'll not be Mat Doyle who forgits what you did for him this night, doctor!" he declared, as he slashed out unavailingly at one of the many "skeeters" that annoyed him. "An' if ever you want a bit o' work done, or some one to do your lyin' awake at night for you, just you gimme the tip. I don't mind tellin' you now, I'd me shootin'-iron in here"—he touched his right hip—"an' if you'd refused—you was the third, mind you!—I'd have drilled you where you stood, God damn me if I wouldn't!"

Mahony eyed the speaker with derision. "Much good that would have done your wife, you fathead. . . . Well, well, we'll say nothing to *mine*, if you please, about anything of that sort."

"No, may all the saints bless 'er and give 'er health! An' as I say, doctor. . . ." In speaking, he had drawn a roll of banknotes from his pocket, and now he tried to stuff them between Mahony's fingers.

"What's this?— My good man, keep your money till it's asked for!" and Mahony unclasped his hands, so that the notes fluttered to the ground.

"Then there let 'em lay!"

But when, in clothes dried stiff as cardboard, Mahony was rolling townwards—his coachman a lad of some ten or twelve, who handled the reins to the manner born—as they went, he chanced to feel in his coat pocket, and there found five tenpound notes, rolled up in a neat bundle.

The main part of the road was dry and hard again; but all dips and holes were wells of liquid mud, which bespattered the two of them from top to toe as the buggy bumped carelessly in and out. Mahony diverted himself by thinking of the handsome present he could give Polly with this sum. It would serve to buy that pair of gilt cornices, or the heavy gilt-framed pierglass, on which she had set her heart. He could see her, pink with pleasure, expostulating: "Richard! What *wicked* extravagance!" and hear himself reply: "And pray may my wife not have as pretty a parlour as her neighbours?" He even cast a thought, in passing, on the pianoforte, with which Polly longed to crown the furnishings of her room—though, of course, at least treble this amount would be needed to cover its cost.— But a fig for such nonsense! He knew of but one legitimate use to make of the unexpected little windfall, and that was, to put it by for a rainy day. "At my age, in my position, I *ought* to have fifty pounds in the bank!"—times without number he had said this to himself, with a growing impatience. But he had never managed to save a halfpenny. Thrive as the practice might, the expenses of living held even pace with it. He had to keep up appearances, too, nowadays; his debts of hospitality had doubled; nor did it do for his name to be absent from charities and subscription-lists. It was a guinea here, two guineas there, while the new saddle and the medical books he needed, were struck off the list.— And now his brain, having got its cue, started off again on the old treadmill, reckoning, totting up, finding totals, or more often failing to find them, till his head was as hot as his feet were cold. To-day, he could not think clearly at all.

Nor the next day either. By the time he reached home, he was conscious of feeling very ill: he had lancinating pains in his limbs, a chill down his spine, an outrageous temperature. To set out again on a round of visits was impossible. He had to tumble into bed, where he lay helpless.

He got between the sheets with that sense of utter well-being, of almost sensual satisfaction, which only one who is shivering with fever knows. And, at first, very small things were enough to fill him with content: the smoothness of the pillow's sleek linen; the shadowy light of the room, after long days spent in the dusty glare outside; the possibility of resting —the knowledge that it was his duty to rest; Polly's soft, firm hands, which, as she sponged his forehead or administered his self-prescribed doses, were always of the right temperature—

warm in the cold stage, cool when the fever scorched him, and neither hot nor cold when the dripping sweats came on. In the beginning, he lay behind the dimity-curtains of the four-poster, feeling as though he had done for ever with the world and its cares. In this white, still haven, the noise of life came to him like the beating of a muffled drum, and soon died away altogether. And the thought crossed his mind that death itself would not be hard to face, if, when one's hour struck, this sense of aloofness, of detachment from earthly things, prevailed. Wrapped in a dreamless ease, the homing mortal would glide gently down the great River, back into the twilight from which he had sprung.— A further discovery was that only the busy doctor, eternally on the go, eternally, no matter what his own condition, at the beck and call of others, could truly appreciate the luxury of being ill.— But, as the fever declined, and the sweats lengthened, these slight pleasures lost their hold. Then, lying weak and helpless, he was ridden to death by black thoughts. Not only was day being added to day, he meanwhile not turning over a penny; but ideas which he knew to be preposterous insinuated themselves in his brain, and there spread and grew till they had ousted sanity. Thus, for hours on end, he writhed under the belief that his present illness was due solely to the proximity of the Great Swamp; and all that day he lay and cursed his folly, in having chosen just this neighbourhood to build in. Low fever, having once got a grip of its victim, did not readily let go; and he saw his practice cut up, ruined, by continual bouts of ill-health. Had he had the strength to rise, he would then and there have ordered in an army of workmen, bodily to shift the house to another site.— Again, there was the case of typhoid he had been anxious about, prior to his own breakdown: under his *locum tenens,* peritonitis had set in, and carried off the patient. At the time, he had accepted the news from Polly's lips with indifference— too ill to care. But, a little later, the knowledge of what it meant broke over him one morning; and, after that, he suffered the tortures of the damned. Not Brace; he alone would be held responsible for the death; and once more he saw his hopeful practice damaged—destroyed. Perhaps not altogether unjustly, either. Lying there, an easy prey to morbid apprehensions, he began to tax himself with a possible error of judgment. He rebuilt the case in memory, struggled to recall each slight varia-

tion in temperature, each swift change for better or worse; but,
as fast as he captured one such detail, his drowsy brain let the
last but one go, and he had to beat it up anew. During the
night, he grew confident that the relatives of the dead woman
intended to take action against him, for negligence or improper attendance. In all probability, they waited only for him
to be on his feet again, to drag him out into the light of scandal and disgrace.

An attempt he made to speak of these devilish imaginings
to wife and friend was a failure. He undertook it in a fit of
desperation, when it seemed as if only a strong and well-
grounded opposition would save his reason. But this was just
what he could not get. Purdy, whom he tried first, held the
crude notion that a sick person should never be gainsaid; and
soothingly nodded, and sympathised, and agreed, till Mahony
could have cried aloud at such blundering stupidity. Polly
did better; she contradicted him. But not in the right way.
She certainly pooh-poohed his fixed idea of the nearness of
Yuille's Swamp making the house unhealthy; but she did not
argue the matter out, step by step, and *convince* him that he
was wrong. She just laughed at him, as at a foolish child, and
kissed him, and tucked him in anew. And when it came to the
typhoid's fatal issue, she had not the knowledge needed to
combat him with any chance of success. She heard him anxiously out, and allowed herself to be made quite nervous over
a possible fault on his part, so jealous was she for his growing
reputation.

So that, in the end, it was he who had to comfort her.

"Don't take any notice of what I say to-day, wife! It's this
blessed fever. . . . I'm lightheaded, I think."

But he could hear her uneasily consulting with Purdy in
the passage. It was not till his pulse beat normally again,
and he had spirit enough to open a book, that he could smile
at such exaggerated fears. And now, too, reviving health
brought back a wholesome interest in everyday affairs. He
listened, with amusement, to Polly's account of the shifts
Purdy was reduced to, to enter the house unseen by Miss
Tilly. On his faithful daily call, the young man would creep
round by the back door, and Tilly was growing more and
more irate at her inability to waylay him. Yes, Polly was
rather readily forced to admit, she *had* abetted him in his

243

evasions.— ("You know, Poll, I might just as well tie myself up to old Mother B. herself and be done with it!")— Out of sheer pique, Tilly had twice now accepted old Mr. Ocock's invitation to drive with him. Once, she had returned with a huge bag of lollies; and once, with a face like a turkey-cock. Polly couldn't help thinking . . . no, really, Richard, she could not! . . . that, perhaps, something might *come* of it. He should not laugh; but wait and see.

But, as he grew stronger, books and gossip alike palled on him; and the last days of his imprisonment had feet of lead. Many inquiries had been made after him; he could appreciate them now. People had missed their doctor, it seemed, and wanted him back. The wish was mutual; he hankered to see how this case had developed in his absence, and what Brace had made of that. It was a real red-letter day when he could snap to the catches of his gloves again, and mount the step of a buggy.

He had instructed Purdy to arrange for the hire of this vehicle, saddle-work being out of the question for him, in the meantime. And, on his first long journey—it led him past Doyle's hut, now, he was sorry to see, in the hands of strangers; for the wife, on the way to making a fair recovery, had got up too soon, overtaxed her strength and died, and the broken-hearted husband was gone off no one knew where— on this drive, as mile after mile slid from under the wheels, Mahony felt how grateful was the screen of a hood between him and the sun.

While he was laid up, the eternal question of how to live on his income had left him, relatively speaking, in peace. He had of late adopted the habit of doing his scraping and saving, of denying himself wholesale, at the outset of each quarter, so as to get the money due to Ocock put by betimes; while, for current expenses, Doyle's gift had been there to fall back on. His illness had naturally made a hole in this; and now the living momentarily from hand to mouth must begin anew.

With what remained of the sum, he proposed to settle his account at the livery stable. Then, the unexpected happened. His reappearance—he looked very thin and washed-out—evidently jogged a couple of sleepy memories; for, simultane-

ously, two big bills were paid, one of which he had entirely
given up. In consequence, he again found himself fifty
pounds to the good. And, driving to Ocock's office, on term
day, he resolved to go on afterwards to the Bank of Austral-
asia, and there deposit the money.

Grindle, now set off by a pair of flaming "sideboards," and
a manner that aped Ocock's own, himself ushered Mahony
into the sanctum. The latter's little affair was disposed of in
a trice. Ocock was one of the busiest of men nowadays—he
no longer needed to invent sham clients and fictitious interviews—and utilised the few odd minutes it took to procure a
signature, jot down a note, open a drawer, unlock a tin box,
to remark abstractly on the weather, and put a polite inquiry:
"And your good lady? In the best of health, I trust?"

On emerging from the inner room, Mahony saw that the
places formerly filled by Tom and Johnny were occupied by
strangers; and he was wondering whether it would be indiscreet to ask what had become of the brothers, when Ocock
cut across his intention.— "By the way, Jenkins, has that
memorandum I spoke of been drawn up?" he turned to a
clerk.

With a sheet of foolscap in his hand, he invited Mahony
with a beck of the chin to re-enter his room, where he closed
the door. "Half a moment! Now, doctor, if you happen to
have a little money lying idle, I can put you on to a good
thing—a very good thing indeed. I don't know, I'm sure,
whether you keep an eye on the fluctuations of the share-
market. If so, you'll no doubt have noticed the . . . let me say
the extreme instability of those shares known as 'Porepunkahs.' After making an excellent start, they have dropped till
they are now to be had at one-twentieth of their original
value."

As a rule, he did not take much interest in mining matters,
was Mahony's reply. However, he knew something of the
claim in question, if only because several of his acquaintances
had abandoned their shares, in disgust at the repeated calls
and the lack of dividends.

"Exactly. Well now, doctor, I'm in a position to inform you
that 'Porepunkahs' will very shortly be prime favourites on
the market, selling at from double to treble their original

figure—their *original* figure, sir! No one with a few hundreds
to spare could find a better investment. Now is the time to
buy."

A few hundreds! . . . what does he take me for? thought
Mahony; and declined the transaction off-hand. It was very
good of Mr. Ocock to think of him; but he preferred to keep
clear of all that kind of thing.

"Quite so, quite so!" returned Ocock suavely, hitting the
note at once; and he dry-washed his hands, with the smile
Mahony had never learnt to fathom. "Just as you please, of
course.— I'll only ask you, doctor, to treat the matter as
strictly confidential."

"I suppose he says the same to every one he tells," was Mahony's comment as he flicked up his horse; and he wondered
what the extent might be of the lawyer's personal interest in
the "Porepunkah Company." It was quite likely that the
number of shareholders was not large enough to take up the
capital.

Still, the incident gave him food for thought, and only
when it was after hours did he remember his intention of
driving home by way of the Bank.

Later in the day, he came back on the incident, and pondered over his abrupt refusal of Ocock's offer. There was
nothing out of the way in this: he never took advice well;
and, was it forced upon him, a certain inborn contrariness
drove him, nine times out of ten, to go and do just the opposite. Besides, he had not yet learned to look with lenience on
the rage for speculation that had seized the inhabitants of
Ballarat; and he held that it would be culpable for a man of
his slender means to risk money in the great game.— But was
there any hint of risk in the present instance? To judge from
Ocock's manner, the investment was as safe as a house, and
lucrative to a degree that made one's head swim. "Double
to treble their original figure" the lawyer had predicted of
the shares. An Arabian-nights fashion of growing rich, and
no mistake! Very different from the laborious grind of *his*
days, in which, moreover, he had always to reckon with the
chance of not being paid for his services at all. That very
afternoon had brought him a fresh example of this. He was
returning from the Old Magpie Lead, where he had been
called to a case of scarlet fever; and he saw himself covering

246

the same road daily, for some time to come. But he had
learned to adjudge his patients in a winking; and these, he
could swear to it, would prove to be non-payers; of a kind
even to cut and run, once the child was out of danger. Was
he really justified, cramped for money as he was, in rejecting
the straight tip Ocock had given him? And he debated this
moot point—argued his need against his principles—the whole
way home.

As soon as he had changed, and seen his suspect clothing
hung out to air, he went impetuously back to Ocock's office.
He had altered his mind. A small gift from a grateful patient: yes, fifty, please; they might bring him luck.— And he
saw his name written down as the owner of half a hundred
shares.

After this, he took a new interest in the mining sheet of
the *Star;* turned to it, indeed, first of all. For a week, a fortnight, "Porepunkahs" remained stationary; then they made a
call, and if he did not wish to forfeit, he had to pay out as
many shillings as he held shares. A day or two later, they
sank a trifle, and Mahony's hopes with them. There even
came a day when they were not mentioned; and he gave up
his money for lost. But, of a sudden, they woke to life again,
took an upward bound, and, within a month, were quoted at
five pounds—on rumour alone. "Very sensitive indeed," said
the *Star.* Purdy, his only confidant, went about swearing at
himself for having let the few he owned lapse; and Mahony
itched to sell. He could now have banked two hundred and
fifty pounds.

But Ocock laughed him out of countenance—even went
so far as to pat him on the shoulder. On no account was he
to think of selling. "Sit tight, doctor . . . sit tight! Till I say
the word."

And Mahony reluctantly obeyed.

[9]

ALONG with brisk, cool winds and heavy rains, autumn
brought the usual crop of rheums, cramps and dysenteries:
Mahony drove off early, came home late, and snatched
scrappy meals at odd hours. Besides this, a good number of
patients sought him out at the house, after breakfast, and

again after dinner; while, as often as not, a confinement robbed him of part of his night's rest. Not till the cold weather was definitely established, did his time-table grow less exacting.

It was in the course of this winter that John Turnham came to stand as one of the two candidates, for the newly proclaimed electoral district of Ballarat West.

The first news his relatives had of his intention was gleaned from the columns of the daily paper. Mahony lit on the paragraph by chance one morning; said: "Hullo! Here's something that will interest you, my dear," and read it aloud.

Polly laid down her knife and fork, pushed her plate and the chop from her, and went pink with pleasure and surprise. "Richard! You don't mean it!" she exclaimed, and got up to look over his shoulder. Yes, there it was—John's name in all the glory of print. "Mr. John Millibank Turnham, one of the foremost citizens and most highly respected denizens of our marvellous metropolis, and a staunch supporter of democratic rights and the interests of our people."— Polly drew a deep breath. "Do you know, Richard, I shouldn't wonder a bit, if he came to live on Ballarat—I mean if he gets in.— Does Trotty hear? This is Trotty's papa they're writing about in the papers. Perhaps she'll see him soon now, if she's a good girl.— Of course we must ask him to stay with us, Richard."— For this happened during an interregnum, when the spare-room was temporarily out of use.

"Of course we must do nothing of the kind. Your brother will need the best rooms Bath's can give him; and when he's not actually on the hustings, he'll be hobnobbing in the bar, standing as many drinks as there are throats in the crowd," gave back Mahony, who had the lowest possible opinion of colonial politics.

"Well, at least I can write and tell him how delighted we are," said Polly, not to be done.

"Find out first, my dear, if there's any truth in the report. I can hardly believe John would have left us in the dark, to this extent."

But John corroborated the news; and, in the letter Polly read out a week later, he announced the opening of his campaign for the coming month.

I shall feel much obliged to your husband if he will meanwhile exert his influence on my behalf. He is no doubt acquainted professionally with many of the leading squatters round Ballarat, whom he can induce to support my candidature.

"Umph!" said Mahony grumpily, and went on scooping out his egg. "We're good enough to tout for him."— He had been up most of the night, and his temples throbbed.

"Ssh!" warned Polly, with a glance at Trotty. "Think what it means to him, Richard, and to us, too. It will do your practice ever so much good if he gets in—to be the brother-in-law of the Member! We must help all we can, dear."

She was going to drive to Yarangobilly that day, with Archdeacon Long, to see a new arrival Richard had recently brought into the world; and now she laid plans to kill two birds with one stone, entering into the scheme with a gusto that astonished Mahony. Himself living in a perpetual press of business, he envied Polly her woman's leisure with all his heart.— "Upon my word, wife, I believe you're glad to have something to do."

"Will my own papa gimme a dolly? . . . like Uncle Papa?" here piped Trotty.

"Perhaps. But you will have to be a *very* good girl, and not talk with your mouth full, or dirty your pinnies.— Oh, there's a postscript!"— Polly had returned to the sheet, and was gloating over it. "John writes:

Especially must he endeavour to win Lawyer Ocock over to my side. I lay great weight on O.'s support.

Oh, Richard, now *isn't* that unfortunate? I do hope it won't make any difference to John's chances."

Polly's dismay had good grounds. A marked coolness had sprung up between her husband and the lawyer; and, on no account, she knew, would Richard consent to approach Mr. Henry. Some very hot remarks made by the latter had been passed on to her by Mrs. Glendinning. She had not dared to tell Richard the worst.

The coolness dated from an afternoon when Tilly Beamish had burst into the house, in a state of rampant excitement.

"Oh, Polly!—oh, I say!—my dear, whatever do you think? That old cove—old O.—'as actually had the cheek to make me a proposal!"

"Tilly!" gasped Polly, and flushed to the roots of her hair. "Oh, my dear, I *am* pleased!" For Polly's conscience was still somewhat tender about the aid she had lent Purdy in his evasions. The two women kissed, and Tilly cried a little. "It's certainly her first offer," thought Mrs. Polly. Aloud, she asked hesitatingly: "And do you . . . shall you . . . I mean are you going to accept him, Tilly?"

But this was just where Tilly could not make up her mind: should she take him, or should she not? For two whole days she sat about, debating the question; and Polly listened to her with all the sympathy and interest so momentous a step deserved.

"If you feel you could really learn to care for him, dear. Of course it *would* be nice for you to have a house of your own. And how happy it would make poor 'mother' to see you settled!"

Tilly tore the last veil from her feelings, uttered gross confidences. Polly knew well enough where her real inclination lay. "I've hoped against hope, Poll, that a *certain person* would come to the scratch at last." Yes, it was true enough, he had nothing to offer her; but she wasn't the sort to have stuck at that. "I'd have worked my hands to the bone for 'im, Poll, if 'e'd *only* said the word." The one drawback to marriage with "you know 'oo I mean" would have been his infirmity. "Some'ow, Polly, I can't picture myself dragging a husband with a gammy leg always at my heels." — From this, Tilly's mind glanced back to the suitor who had honourably declared himself. Of course, "old O." hadn't a great deal of the gentleman about him; and their ages were unsuitable. " 'E owns to fifty-eight, and, as you know, Poll, I'm only just turned twenty-five,"—at which statement Polly drooped her head a little lower over the handkerchief she was hemming, to avoid meeting her friend's eye. Poor dear Tilly!—she would never see thirty again; and she need hardly have troubled, thought Polly, to be insincere with her. But, in the same breath, she took back the reproach. A woman herself, she understood something of the fear, and shame, and heart-burning, that had gone to the making of the lie. Perhaps, too, it was a gentle hint from Tilly what age she now wished to be considered. And so Polly agreed, and said tenderly: yes, certainly, the difference was very marked.— Meanwhile Tilly flowed on. These were the two chief objections. On the other hand, the old boy was ludicrously smitten; and she thought one might trust her, Tilly B., to soon knock him into shape. It would also, no doubt, be possible to squeeze a few pounds out of him towards assisting "pa and ma" in their present struggle. Again, as a married woman, she would have a chance of helping Jinny to find a husband: "Though Jinn's gone off so, Polly, I bet you'd hardly know her, if you met 'er in the street." To end all, a bird in hand, etc.: and besides, what prospects had she, if she remained a spinster?

So, when she was asked, Tilly accepted, without further humming and hawing, an invitation to drive out in the smart dog-cart Mr. Ocock had hired for the purpose; and Polly saw her off, with many a small private sign of encouragement. All went well. A couple of hours later Tilly came flying in, caught Polly up in a bear's hug, and danced her round the room. "My dear, wish me joy!— Oh lor, Polly, I *do* feel 'appy!" She was wearing a large half-hoop of diamonds on her ring-finger: nothing would do "old O." but that they should drive there and then to the finest jeweller's in Sturt Street, where she had the pick of a trayful. And now Mr. Ocock, all a-smirk with sheepish pride, was fetched in to receive congratulations; and Polly produced refreshments; and healths were drunk. Afterwards, the happy couple dallied in the passage, and loitered on the doorstep, till evening was far advanced.

It was Polly who, in clearing away, was struck dumb by the thought: "But now, whatever will become of Miss Amelia?"

She wondered if this consideration troubled the old man, too. Trouble there certainly was, of some sort: he called at the house three days running, for a word with Richard. He wore a brand-new pair of shepherd's-plaid trousers, a choker that his work-stained hands had soiled in the tying, a black coat, a massive gold watch-chain. On the third visit, he was lucky enough to catch Mahony, and the door of the surgery closed behind them.

Mr. Ocock sat on the extreme edge of a chair; alternately crushed his wide-awake flat between his palms and expanded it again, as though he were playing the concertina; and coughed out a wordy preamble. He assured Mahony, to begin with, how highly he esteemed him. It was because of this, because he knew doctor was as straight as a pound of candles, that he was going to ask his advice on an awkward matter—devilish awkward!—and one nobody had any idea of—except Henry. And Henry had kicked up such a deuce of a row at his wanting to marry again, that he was damned if he'd have anything more to do with him. Besides, doctor knew what lawyers were—the whole breed of 'em! Sharp as needles—especially Henry—but with a sort of squint in their upper story that made 'em see every mortal thing from the point of law. And that was no good to him. What he needed was a plain and honest, a . . . he hesitated for a word, and repeated, "a *honest* opinion." So he had decided on the present step, and he hoped doctor would give him a round answer; for he only wanted to do the right thing, what was straight and above-board. And here, at last, out it came: did "doc." think it would be acting on the square, and not taking a low-down advantage of a female, if he omitted to mention to "the future Mrs. O." that, up till six months back, he had been obliged to . . . well, he'd spit it out short and say, obliged to report himself to the authorities at fixed intervals? Women were such shy cattle, so damned odd! You never knew how they'd take a thing like this. One might raise Cain over it, another only laugh, another send him packing. He didn't want to let a fine young woman like Matilda slip, if he could help it, by dad he didn't! But he felt he must either win her by fair dealing, or not at all.— And now, having got the load off his chest, the old colonist swallowed hard, and running the back of his hand over his forehead, shook to the floor the drops of moisture it had gathered in the transit.

He had kept his eyes glued to the table-leg in speaking, and so saw neither his hearer's involuntary start at the damaging disclosure, nor the nervous tightening of the hand that lay along the arm of the chair. But, had he caught the movements, it would have been only with the fringe of his mind: he was engrossed with himself, with the issue of his

252

courtship; and the effect his words might have on Mahony
was of small account.— The latter sat silent, balancing a
paper-knife. He was fighting down a feeling of extraordinary discomfort—his very fingertips curled under the strain.
It was of no use to remind himself that, ever since he had
known him, Ocock had led a decent, god-fearing life, respected both in his business relations and by his brethren
of the chapel. Nor could he spare more than a glance in
passing for those odd traits in the old man's character,
which were now explained: his itch for public approval;
his unvarying harshness towards the pair of incorrigibles
who weighed him down; his jealous envy of the swiftness
with which evil deeds are noised abroad, compared with
honest endeavour. At this moment Mahony discounted even
the integrity that had prompted the confession. His attitude
of mind was one of: why the dickens couldn't the old fool
have held his tongue? The kindly tolerance, the sense of
good-fellowship, with which he had thus far regarded
Ocock, withered away; his prime instinct was to ward the
latter off, to prevent any further contact between them—
until, at least, he had had time to digest this new fact, and
find his bearings towards it.

Oh, these unbidden, injudicious confidences! How they complicated life and made it difficult! He was pestered with only
too many. As a doctor, he was continually being forced to see
behind the scenes of his patients' lives. And, as if this were not
enough, outsiders, too, must needs choose him for the storehouse of their privacies. Himself he never made a confidence;
but it seemed as though just this buttoned-upness on his part
egged people on, loosened their tongues. The great majority
were blind to the flags of warning he hoisted in looks and
bearing; they innocently proceeded, as Ocock had done, to
throw up insurmountable barriers. He heard a new tone in his
own voice when he replied, and was relieved to know the old
man dull of perception.— For now, Ocock had finished speaking, winding up with the hope that Mahony would mention
no syllable of what he had heard, to his dear little lady; and
sat perspiring with anxiety to learn his fate. Mahony took himself together.— He could and would, in good faith, tender the
sincere advice to let the dead past bury its dead. Whatever
the original fault had been—no, no, please! . . . and he raised

an arresting hand—it was, he felt sure, long since fully atoned. And Mr. Ocock had said a true word: women were strange creatures. The revelation of his secret might shipwreck his late-found happiness. It also, of course, might not—and, personally, Mahony did not believe it would; for Ocock's business throve like the green bay-tree, and Miss Tilly had been promised a fine two-storied house, with bow-windows and a garden, and a carriage-drive up to the door. Or again, the admission might be accepted in peace just now, and later on used as a weapon against him. In his, Mahony's, eyes, by far the wisest and safest course would be, to let the grass grow over the whole affair.

And here, he rose from his seat, abruptly terminating the interview. "You and I, too, sir, if you please, will forget what has passed between us this morning, and never come back on it. Bygones shall be bygones.— How is Tom getting on in the drapery business? Does he like his billet?"

But, none the less, as he ushered his visitor out, he felt that there was a certain finality about the action. It was—as far as his private feelings were concerned—the old man's moral exit from the scene.

On the doorstep Ocock, who seemed to disbelieve his luck in getting off so easily, spun round and laid a knobby hand on Mahony's arm. "An' to 'Enry, too, doc., if you'll be so good, mum's the word! 'Enry 'ud never forgive me, nay, or you eether, if it got to 'is ears I'd bin an' let the cat outer the bag. An' 'e's got a bit of a down on you as it is, for it 'avin' bin your place I met the future Mrs. O. at."

"My good man!" broke from Mahony—and, in these words, which would previously never have crossed his lips, all his sensations of the past hour were summed up. "Has your son Henry the"—he checked himself; "does he suppose I—*I* or my wife—had anything to do with it?"

He turned back to the surgery hot with annoyance. This, too! Not enough that he must be put out of countenance by indiscreet babblings; he must also get drawn into family squabbles, even be held in part responsible for them: he who, brooking no interference in his own life, demanded only that those about him should be as tolerant as he.

It all arose from Polly's indiscriminate hospitality. His house was never his own. And now they had the prospect of John and his electoral campaign before them. And John's chances of success, and John's stump oratory, and the back-stairwork other people were expected to do for him, would form the main theme of conversation for many a day to come.

Mrs. Glendinning confirmed old Ocock's words.

She came to talk over the engagement with Polly, and, sitting in the parlour, cried a little, and was sorry.— But then "poor little Agnes"—Polly always thought of her friend as "little," though she was really a head taller than herself— Agnes cried so easily nowadays. Richard said her nerves had been shattered by the terrible affair of before Christmas, when, in a fit of madness, Mr. Glendinning had tried first to kill her, and then to cut his own throat: since which time the owner of Dandaloo had been a certified lunatic, and the inmate of a private asylum.

Agnes said: "But I told Henry quite plainly, darling, that I would not cease my visits to you, on that account. It is both wrong and foolish to think you or Dr. Mahony had anything to do with it—and after the doctor was so kind, too, so *very* kind, about poor Mr. Glendinning. I can never feel grateful enough to him for taking James to Melbourne himself, and getting him comfortably settled there.— And so you see, dear, Henry and I have had quite a disagreement over it"; and Agnes cried again, at the remembrance. "Of course, I can sympathise with his point of view. . . . Henry is so ambitious. All the same, dearest, it's not quite so bad—is it?—as he makes it out to be. Matilda is certainly not very *comme il faut*— you'll forgive my saying so, love, won't you? But I think she will suit Henry's father in every way. No, the truth is, the old gentleman has made a great deal of money, and we naturally expected it to fall to Henry at his death; no one anticipated his marrying again. Not that Henry really needs the money; he is getting on so well; and I have. . . . I shall have plenty, too, by and by. But you know, love, what men are."

"Dearest Agnes! . . . don't fret about it. Mr. Henry thinks too much of you, I'm sure, to be vexed with you for long. And when he looks at it calmly, he'll see how unfair it is to make us responsible. I'm like you, dear; I can't consider it a misfortune. Tilly is not a lady; but she's a dear, warm-hearted girl, and will make him a good wife.— I only hope though, Agnes,

Mr. Henry won't say anything to Richard. Richard is so touchy about things of that sort."

The two women kissed, Polly with feelings of the tenderest affection: the fact that, on behalf of their friendship, Agnes had actually pitted her will against Mr. Henry's, endeared her to Polly as nothing else could have done.

But when, vigilant as a mother-hen, she sought to prepare her husband for a possible unpleasantness, she found him already informed; and her well-meant words were like a match laid to his suppressed indignation.

"In all my born days, I never heard such impudence!"

He turned embarrassingly cool to Tilly. And Tilly, who had grown partial to his tone of light irony and good-natured chaffing manner, and flattered herself that she had made an equally good impression; Tilly first opened her eyes wide, then tossed her head, flounced, and didn't "care a pin!" Innocent of offence, and quite unskilled in deciphering subtleties, she put her host's sudden change of front down to jealousy, because she was going to live in a grander house than he did. For the same reason he had begun to turn up his nose at "old O.," or she was very much mistaken; and in vain did Polly strive to convince her that here, at least, she was in error.— "Why, I don't know anyone Richard has a higher opinion of!"

But it was a very uncomfortable state of things; and when a message arrived over the electric-telegraph announcing the dangerous illness of Mrs. Beamish, distressed though she was by the news, Polly could not help heaving a tiny sigh of relief. For Tilly was summoned back to Melbourne with all speed, if she wished to see her mother alive.

They mingled their tears, Polly on her knees at the packing, Tilly weeping whole-heartedly among the pillows of the bed. "If it 'ad only been pa now, I shouldn't have felt it half so much," she said sitting up, and blew her nose for the hundredth time. "Pa was always such a rum old stick. But poor ma . . . when I *think* how she's toiled and moiled 'er whole life long, to keep things going! She's 'ad all the pains and none of the pleasures; and now, just when I was hoping to be able to give 'er a helping hand, *this* must happen."

The one bright spot in Tilly's grief was that the journey would be made in a private conveyance. Mr. Ocock had bought the smart gig, and was driving her down himself; driving past the foundations of the new house, out of Ballarat, along the seventy odd miles of road, right up to the door of the mean lodging in a Collingwood back street, where the old Beamishes had hidden their heads.— "If only she's able to look out of the window and see me dash up in my own turn-out!" said Tilly.

Polly fitted out a substantial luncheon-basket, and was keen-est sympathy to the last. But Mahony was a poor dissembler; and his sudden thaw, as he assisted in the farewell prepara-tions, could, Polly feared, have been read aright by a child.

Tilly hugged Polly to her, and gave her kiss after kiss. "I shall *never* forget 'ow kind you've been, Poll, and all you've done for me. I've had my disappointments 'ere, as you know; but p'ra'ps, after all, it'll turn out to be for the best. One o' the good sides to it, anyhow, is that you and me'll be next-door neighbours, so to say, for the rest of our lives. And I'll hope to see something of you, my dear, every blessed day. But you'll not often catch me coming to this house, I can tell you that! For, if you won't mind me saying so, Poll, I think you've got one of the queerest sticks for a husband that ever walked this earth. Blows hot one day and cold the next, for all the world like the wind in spring. And without caring twopence whose corns 'e treads on."— Which, thought Polly, was but a sorry return, on Tilly's part, for Richard's hospitality. After all, it was his house she had been a guest in.

—Such were the wheels within wheels. And thus it came about that, when the question rose of paving the way for John Turnham's candidature, Mahony rigidly drew the line at ap-proaching Henry Ocock.

[10]

JOHN drove from Melbourne in a drag and four, accompanied by numerous friends and well-wishers. A mile or so out of Ballarat, he was met by a body of supporters, headed by a brass band, and was escorted in triumph to the town. They drew up in front of the George Hotel, where, the horses having been led away, John at once took the field, by mounting the box-seat of the coach, and addressing the crowd of idlers that had gathered round to watch the arrival. He obtained an ex-cellent hearing—so Jerry reported, who was an eye and ear-witness of the scene—and was afterwards borne shoulder-high into the hotel.

"Three cheers for Turnham!" were called for and given, as he disappeared from sight; and: "That's our ticket, boys!" bawled a group of miners, to the extreme pride of the candidate's young brother.

Mahony, with Jerry at his heels, called at the hotel in the course of the evening. He found John entertaining a large impromptu party. The table of the public dining-room in the "George" was disorderly with the remains of a liberal meal; napkins lay crushed and flung down among plates piled high with empty nutshells; the cloth was wine-stained, and bestrewn with ashes and breadcrumbs, the air heady with the fumes of tobacco. Those of the guests who still lingered at the table had pushed their chairs back or askew, and sat, some a-straddle, some even with their feet on the cloth. Mahony found an acquaintance in the shape of the Police Magistrate, and took a vacant seat at his side. Instantly a waiter in shirt-sleeves bobbed up at his elbow: "What'll you take?" and set fresh glasses before him. John was confabbing with half a dozen black-coats, in a corner. Each held a wineglass in his hand, from which he sipped, while John, legs apart, did all the talking, every now and then putting out his forefinger to prod one of his hearers on the middle button of the waistcoat. It was some time before he discovered the presence of his relatives; and Mahony had leisure to admire the fashion in which, this corner-talk over, John dispersed himself among the company; drinking with this one and that; glibly answering question after question; patting a glum-faced brewer on the back; and, simultaneously checking over, with an oily-haired agent, his committee-meetings for the following days. His customary arrogance and pompousness of manner were laid aside. For the nonce, he was a simple man among men.

Then he espied them, hurried over, and, rubbing his hands with pleasure, said warmly: "My dear Mahony, this is indeed kind!" to which ensued a rapid inquiry after Polly's health. — "Jerry, my lad, how do, how do? Still growing, I see! We'll make a fine fellow of you yet.— Well, doctor! . . . we've every reason, I think, to feel satisfied with the lie of the land."

But here he was snatched from them by an urgent request for a pronouncement—"A quite informal word, sir, if you'll be so good!"—on the vexed question of vote by ballot. And this being a pet theme of John's, and a principle he was ready to defend through thick and thin, he willingly complied.

Mahony had no further talk with him. The speech over— it was a concise and spirited utterance, and, if you were prepared to admit the efficacy of the ballot, convincing enough —this ended, Mahony quietly withdrew, leaving Jerry, still more inflamed, behind. He had to see a patient at eleven. Polly, too, would probably be lying awake for news of her brother.

As he drew back his braces and wound up his watch, he felt it incumbent on him to warn his wife not to pitch her hopes too high. "You mustn't expect, my dear, that your brother's coming here will mean much to us. He is a public man now, with public duties, and will have little or no time for small people like ourselves.— I'm bound to admit, Polly, I was very favourably impressed by the few words I heard John say," he added.

"Oh, Richard, I'm *so* glad!" and Polly, who had been sitting on the edge of the bed, stood on tiptoe to give him a kiss.

As Mahony predicted, John's private feelings went down before the superior interests of his campaign. Three days passed before he found time to pay his sister a visit; and Polly, who had postponed a washing, baked her richest cakes and pastries, and clad Trotty in her Sunday best each day of the three: Polly was putting a good face on the matter, and consoling herself with Jerry's description of John's triumphs in his tour of the district. How she wished she could hear some of the speechifying! But Richard would never consent; and electioneering certainly did seem, from what Jerry said, to be a very rough-and-ready business—nothing for ladies.— Thus, Polly's delight knew no bounds when John drove up unexpectedly, late one afternoon, between a hard day's personal canvassing and another of the innumerable dinners he had to eat his way through. Tossing the reins to the gentleman who sat next him, he jumped out of the wagonette—it was hung with placards of "Vote for Turnham!"—and gave a loud rat-a-tat at the door.

Forgetting, in her excitement, that this was Ellen's job, Polly opened to him herself, all smiles, and drew him in. "John! How pleased I am to see you!"

"My dear girl, how are you? God bless me, how you've altered! I should never have known you." He held her at arm's length, to consider her.

"But you haven't changed in the least, John. Except to grow younger.— Richard, here's John at last!—and Trotty, John . . . here's Trotty!— Take your thumb out of your mouth, naughty girl!— She's been watching for you all day, John, with her nose to the window."— And Polly pushed forward the scarlet, shrinking child.

John's heartiness suffered a distinct check as his eyes lit on Trotty, who stood as a bit of Dresden china in her bunchy starched petticoats. "Come here, Emma, and let me see you." Taking the fat little chin between thumb and first finger, he turned the child's face up, and kept it so, till the red button of a mouth trembled, and the great blue eyes all but ran over. "H'm! Yes . . . a notable resemblance to her mother.— Ah, time passes, Polly, my dear—time passes!" He sighed.— "I hope you mind your aunt, Emma, and are properly grateful to her?"

Then, abruptly quitting his hold, he swept the parlour with a glance. "A very snug little place you have here, upon my word!"

While Polly, with Trotty pattering after, bustled to the larder to fetch her good things, Mahony congratulated his brother-in-law on the more favourable attitude towards his election policy which was becoming evident in the local press. John's persuasive tongue was clearly having its effect, and the hostility which he had met with at the outset of his candidature, was giving way to more friendly feelings on all sides. He was frankly gratified by the change, and did not hesitate to say so. When the wine arrived, they drank to his success at the polls, and Polly's delicacies met with their due share of praise. Then, having wiped his mouth on a large silk handkerchief, John disclosed the business object of his call. He wanted specific information about the more influential of their friends and acquaintances; and here he drew a list of names from his pocket-book. Mahony, his chin propped on the flaxen head of the child, whom he nursed, soon fell

out of the running; for Polly proved by far the cleverer at
grasping the nature of the information John sought, and at
retailing it. And John complimented her on her shrewdness,
ticked off names, took notes on what she told him; and, when
he was not writing, sat tapping his thick, carnation-red underlip, and nodding assent. It was arranged that Polly should
drive out with him, the next day, to Yarangobilly, by way of
Dandaloo; while for the evening after, they plotted a card-
party, at which John might come to grips with Archdeacon
Long. John expected to find the reverend gentleman rather
a hard nut to crack, their views on the subject of state aid to
religion being diametrically opposed. Polly thought a substantial donation to the chancel-fund might smooth things
over, while for John to display a personal interest in Mrs.
Long's charities would help still more. Then, there were the
Ococks. The old man could be counted on, she believed; but
John might experience some difficulty with Mr. Henry—and
here Polly initiated her brother into the domestic differences
which had split up the Ocock family, and prevented Richard
from approaching the lawyer. John, who was in his most
democratic mood, was humorous at the expense of Henry,
and declared the latter should rather wish his father joy of
coming to such a fine, bouncing young wife, in his old age.
The best way of getting at Mr. Henry, Polly considered,
would be for Mrs. Glendinning to give a luncheon or a bush-
ing-party, with the lawyer among the guests: "Then you and
I, John, could drive out and join them—either by chance, or
invitation, just as you think best."— Polly was heart and soul
in the affair.

But business over, she put several straight questions about
the boy, little Johnny—Polly still blamed herself for having
meekly submitted to the child's removal from her charge—
and was not to be fobbed off with evasions. The unfavour-
able verdict she managed to worm out of John: "Incorrigible,
my dear Polly—utterly incorrigible! His masters report him
idle, disobedient, a bad influence on the other scholars," she
met staunchly with: "Perhaps it has something to do with
the school. Why not try another one? Johnny had his good
qualities, too; in many ways he was quite a lovable child."

For the first time Mahony saw his wife and her eldest
brother together; and he could not but be struck by Polly's

attitude. Greatly as she admired and reverenced John, there was not a particle of obsequiousness in her manner, nor any truckling to his point of view; and she plainly felt nothing of the peculiar sense of discomfort that invariably attacked him, in John's presence. Either she was not conscious of her brother's grossly patronising air, or, aware of it, did not resent it, John having always been so much her superior, both in age and position. Or was it indeed the truth—as he was inclined to believe, on looking back at the visit—that John did not attempt to patronise Polly? That his overbearing nature recognised in her a certain springy resistance, which was not to be crushed? In other words, that, in a Turnham, Turnham blood met its match?

John re-took his seat in the front of the wagonette, Trotty was lifted up to see the rosettes and streamers that adorned the horses, the gentlemen waved their hats, and off they went again at a fine pace, and with a whip-cracking that brought the neighbours to their windows.

Polly had pink cheeks with it all, and even sought to excuse the meagre interest John had shown in his daughter. "He's not used to children; and then Trotty was only a baby in arms, when he saw her last. Besides, I think she reminded him too much of her dear mother. For I'm sure, though he doesn't let it be seen, John still feels his loss."

"I wonder!" said Mahony slowly and with a strong downward inflection, as he turned indoors.

Some weeks later, on the eve of the polling, Polly had the honour of accompanying John to a performance at the Theatre Royale. A ticket came for Richard, too; but, as usual, he was summoned to a troublesome patient at the last moment, and would have to follow when he could. Purdy, who happened to be present, took Polly on his arm and escorted her—not exactly comfortably; for, said Polly, no one who had not tried it knew how hard it was to walk arm-in-arm with a lame person; especially if you did not want to hurt his feelings—Purdy took her to the theatre, helped her to unmuffle and to change her boots, and bore her company till her brother arrived. They had seats in the centre of the front row of the dress circle; all eyes were turned on them as they entered; and Polly's appearance was the subject of audible and embarrassing comment. This continued till, the band having performed its piece, the manager sidled out in front of the curtain, to crave the indulgence of the audience for an actor who was "a trifle indisposed"—he winked as he said it, and there was a general guffaw. Then, the rising of the curtain and the beginning of the play fixed people's attention on the stage.

In every interval John was up and away, to shake a hand here, pass the time of day there; and watching him with affectionate pride, Polly wondered how Richard could ever have termed him "high-handed and difficult." John had the knack, it seemed to her, of getting on with people of every class, and of always finding the right word to say.— But as the evening advanced, his seat remained empty even while the curtain was up, and she was glad when, between the fourth and fifth acts, her husband finally appeared.

On his way to her, at the back of the circle, Mahony ran into his brother-in-law, and John buttonholed him, to discuss with him the prospects of the morrow. As they talked, their eyes rested on Polly's glossy black chignon; on the nape of her white neck; on the beautiful, rounded young shoulders, which, in obedience to the fashion, stood right out of her blue silk bodice. Mahony shifted his weight uneasily from one foot to the other. He could not imagine Polly enjoying her exposed and isolated position, and he disapproved strongly of John's having left her. But for all answer to the hint he threw out, John said slowly, and with a somewhat unctuous relish: "My sister has turned into a remarkably handsome woman!"—words which sent the lightning-thought through Mahony that, had Polly remained the insignificant little slip of a thing John had previously known, she would not have been asked to fill the prominent place she did this evening.

John sent his adieux and excuses to Polly. He had done what was expected of him, in showing himself at a public entertainment, and a vast mass of correspondence lay unsorted on his desk. So Mahony moved forward alone.

"Oh, Richard, there you are! Oh dear, what you've missed! Gustavus Brooke is simply magnificent. I'm sure you'll say equal to Jefferson. I never thought there could be such acting." And Polly turned her great dark eyes on her husband; they were still moist from the noble sentiments of "The True Briton."

The day of the election broke, a gusty spring day, cut up

by stinging hail-showers, which beat like fusillades on the corrugated-iron roofs. Between the showers, the sun shone in a gentian-blue sky, against which the little wooden houses showed up crassly white. Ballarat made holiday. Early as Mahony left home, he met a long line of conveyances heading townwards—spring carts, dogcarts, double and single buggies, in some of which, built to seat two only, five or six persons were huddled. These and similar vehicles drew up in rows outside the public-houses, where the lean, long-legged colonial horses stood jerking at their tethers; and they were still there, still jerking, when he passed again towards evening. On a huge poster the "Unicorn" offered to lunch free all those "thinking men" who registered their vote for "the one and only true democrat, the miners' friend and tyrants' foe, John Turnham."

In the hope of avoiding a crush, Mahony drove straight to the polling-booth. But already all the loafers and roughs in the place seemed to be congregated round the entrance. There they lounged, pipe in mouth, and, after the polite custom of the country, chivied, or booed, or huzzaed those who went in. In waiting his turn, he had to listen to comments on his dress and person, to put up with vulgar allusions to blue pills and black draughts.

Just as he was getting into his buggy John rode up, flanked by a bodyguard of friends; John was galloping from booth to booth, to verify progress, and put the thumbscrew on wobblers. He beamed—as well he might. He was certain to be one of the two members elected, and very likely to top the poll by a respectable majority.

For once Mahony did not grumble at his outlying patients; he was only too thankful to turn his back on the town. It was pandemonium. Bands of music, one shriller and more discordant than the next, marched up and down the main streets —from the fifes and drums of the Fire Brigade, to the kerosene-tins and penny-whistles of mere determined noise-makers. Straggling processions, with banners that bore the distorted features of one or other of the four candidates, made driving difficult; and, to add to the confusion, the schoolchildren were let loose, to overrun the place and fly advertisement balloons round every corner.— And so it went on till far into the night, the dark hours being varied by torchlight processions, fireworks, free fights, and orgies of drunkenness.

The results of the polling were promised for two o'clock the following day.

When, something after this time, Mahony reached home, he found Polly, with the gentle, ox-eyed Jinny Beamish who was the present occupant of the spare-room, at her side, pacing up and down before the house. According to Jerry, who had just run in, news might be expected now at any minute. And when he had lunched, and changed his coat, Mahony, bitten by the general excitement, made his way down to the junction of Sturt Street and the Flat.

A great crowd blocked the approaches to the hustings. Here were the four candidates, who, in attending the issue, strove to look decently unconcerned. John had struck a quasi-Napoleonic attitude: his right elbow propped in the cup of his left hand, he held his drooped chin between thumb and forefinger, leaving it to his glancing black eyes to reveal how entirely alive he was to the gravity of the moment. Standing on the fringe of the crowd, Mahony listened to the piebald jokes and rude wit with which the *vulgus* beguiled the interim; and tried to endure with equanimity the jostling, the profane language and offensive odours, to which he was subjected. Half an hour dragged by before the returning officer climbed the ladder at the back of the platform, and came forward to announce the result of the voting: Mr. John Millibank Turnham topped the poll with a majority of four hundred and fifty-two. The crowd, which at sight of the clerk had abruptly ceased its fooling, drowned his further statements in a roar of mingled cheers and boos, which fought one another for the upper hand. The cheers had it; hats were tossed into the air, and loud cries for a speech arose. John's advance to grip the railing led to a fresh outburst, in which the weakening opposition was quashed by the singing—without the omission of a single verse—of: "When Johnny comes marching home!" and "Cheer, boys, cheer, For home and mother country!"—an incongruity of sentiment that made Mahony smile. And John, having repeatedly bowed his thanks from side to side, joined in, and sang with the rest.

The opening of his speech was inaudible to Mahony. Just behind him stood one of his brother-in-law's most arrant opponents, a butcher by trade, and, directly John began to hold forth, this man produced a cornet-à-piston, and started to blow it. In vain did Mahony expostulate: he seemed to have got into a very wasps'-nest of hostility; for the player's friends took up the cudgels, and baited him in a language he would have been sorry to imitate, the butcher blaring away unmoved, with the fierce solemnity of face the cornet demands. Mahony lost his temper; his tormentors retaliated; and for a moment it looked as though there would be trouble. Then a number of John's supporters, enraged by the bellowing of the instrument, bore down and forcibly removed the musician and his clique, Mahony along with them.

Having indignantly explained, and shaken coat and collar to rights, he returned to his place on the edge of the crowd. The speaker's deep voice—it made one think of brass splashed with oil—had gone steadily on during the disturbance. But indeed John might have been born to the hustings. Interruptions did not put him out; he was brilliant at repartee; and all the stock gestures of the public speaker came at his call: the pounding of the bowl of one hand with the closed fist of the other; the dramatic wave of the arm with which he plumbed the depths, or invited defiance; the jaunty standing-at-ease, arms akimbo; the earnest bend from the waist, when he took his hearers into his confidence. At this moment, he was gripping the rail of the platform as though he intended to vault it, and asserting: "Our first cry, then, is for men, men to people the country; our next, for independence, to work out our own salvation. Yes, my friends, the glorious future of this young and prosperous colony, which was once, and most auspiciously, known as Australia Felix—blest, thrice-blest Australia!—rests with ourselves alone. We, who inhabit here, can best judge of her requirements, and we refuse to see her hampered in her progress, by the shackles of an ancient tradition. What suits our hoary mother-country—God bless and keep her, and keep us loyal to her!—is but dry husks for us. England knows nothing of our most pressing needs. I ask you to consider how, previous to 1855, that pretty pair of mandarins, Lord John Russell and Earl Grey, boggled and botched the crucial question of unlocking the lands—even yet, gentlemen, the result of their muddling lies heavy on us. And the Land Question, though first in importance, is but one, as you know, of many"— and here John, playing on the tips of five wide-stretched fingers, counted off such items as: the want of a law to legalise mining on private property; the reform of the Goldfields' Act;

the endowment of municipalities; the interference of the state in the religious education of children. He wound up with a flaming plea for the creation and protection of purely national industries. "For what, I would ask you, is the true meaning of democracy, in a country such as ours? What is, for us, the democratic principle? The answer, my friends, is conservatism; yes, I repeat it—conservatism!" . . . and thus to a final peroration.

In the braying and hurrahing that followed—the din was heightened by some worthy mounting a barrel to move that "this yere Johnny Turnham" was not a fit person to represent "the constitooency"; by the barrel being dragged from under him, and the speaker rolled in the mud; while this went on, Mahony stood silent, and he was still standing meditatively pulling his whiskers, when a sudden call for a doctor reached his ear. He pushed his way to the front.

How the accident had happened no one knew. John had descended from the platform to a verandah, where countless hands were stretched out to shake his. A pile of shutters leant against the wall, and, in some unexplained fashion, these had fallen, striking John a blow that knocked him down. When Mahony got to him, he was on his feet again, wiping a drop of blood from his left temple. He looked pale, but pooh-poohed injury, or the idea of interfering with his audience's design; and Mahony saw him shouldered and borne off.

That evening there was a lengthy banquet, in which all the notables of the place took part. Mahony's seat was some way off John's; he had to lean forward, did he wish to see his brother-in-law.

Towards eleven o'clock, just as he was wondering if he could slip out unobserved, a hand was laid on his arm. John stood behind him, white to the lips. "Can I have a word with you upstairs?"

Here, he confessed to a knife-like pain in his left side; the brunt of the blow, it seemed, had met him slantways between rib and hip. A cursory examination made Mahony look grave.

"You must come back with me, John, and let me see to you properly."

Having expressed the chief guest's regrets to the company, he ordered a horse and trap, and helping John into it, drove him home.— And that night John lay in their bed, letting out

267

the groans he had suppressed during the evening; while Polly snatched forty winks beside Jinny Beamish; and Mahony got what sleep he could, on the parlour sofa.

[11]

THERE John lay a prisoner for some weeks, a fractured rib encased in strips of plaster. The two women were tireless about his bed. "In your element again, old girl!" Mahony chaffed his wife, when he met her bearing invalid trays.

"Oh, it doesn't all fall on me, Richard. Jinny's a great help—sitting with John, and keeping him company."

Mahony could see it for himself. Oftenest, when he entered the room, it was Jinny's black-robed figure—she was in mourning for her parents; for Mrs. Beamish had sunk under the twofold strain of failure and disgrace, and, the day after her death, it had been necessary to cut old Beamish down from a nail—oftenest it was Jinny he found sitting behind a curtain of the tester-bed, watching while John slept, ready to read to him or to listen to his talk, when he awoke. This service set Polly free to devote herself to the extra cooking; and John was content. "A most modest and unassuming young woman!" ran his verdict on Jinny.

Polly reported it to her husband, in high glee. "Who could ever have believed two sisters would turn out so differently! Tilly to get so . . . so . . . well, you know what I mean . . . and Jinny to improve as she has done. Have you noticed, Richard, she hardly ever—really quite seldom now—drops an h? It must all have been due to Tilly serving in that low bar."

By the time John was so far recovered as to exchange bed for sofa, it had come to be exclusively Jinny who carried in to him the dainties Polly prepared—the wife, as usual, was content to do the hard work! John declared Miss Jinny had the foot of a fay; also that his meals tasted best at her hands. Jinny even succeeded in making Trotty fond of her; and the love of the fat, shy child was not readily won. Entering the parlour one evening, Mahony surprised quite a family scene: John, stretched on the sofa, was stringing cats'-cradles, Jinny sat beside him, with Trotty on her knee.

On the whole, though, the child did not warm to her father.

"Aunty, kin dat man take me away f'om you?"

"That man! Why, Trotty darling, he's your father!" said Polly shocked.

"Kin 'e take me away f'om you and Uncle Papa?"

"He could if he wanted to. But I'm sure he doesn't," answered her aunt, deftly turning a well-rolled sheet of pastry.

And righting her dolly, which she had been dragging upside down, Trotty let slip her fears with the sovereign ease of childhood.

From the kitchen, Polly could hear the boom of John's deep bass: it made nothing of the lath-and-plaster walls. Of course, shut up as he was, he had to talk to somebody, poor fellow; and Richard was too busy to spare him more than half an hour of an evening. Jinny was a good listener. Through the crack of the door, Polly could see her sitting humbly drinking in John's words, and even looking rather pretty, in her fair, full womanliness.

"Oh, Polly!" she burst out one day, after being held thus spellbound. "Oh, my dear, what a splendid man your brother is! I feel sometimes I could sink through the floor with shame at my ignorance, when 'e talks to me so."

But as time went on Mahony noticed that his wife grew decidedly thoughtful; and if John continued to sing Jinny's praises, he heard nothing more of it. He had an acute suspicion what troubled Polly; but did not try to force her confidence.

Then, one afternoon, on his getting home, she came into the surgery looking very perturbed, and could hardly find words to break a certain piece of news to him. It appeared that not an hour previously, Jinny, flushed and tearful, had lain on her neck, confessing her feelings for John and hinting at the belief that they were returned.

"Well, I think you might have been prepared for something of this sort, Polly," he said with a shrug, when he had heard her out. "Convalescence is notoriously dangerous for fanning the affections."

"Oh, but I never *dreamt* of such a thing, Richard! Jinny is a dear good girl and all that, but she is *not* John's equal. And that he can even *think* of putting her in poor Emma's place! — What shall I say to him?"

"Say nothing at all. Your brother John is not the man to put up with interference."

—"He longs so for a real home again, Polly darling," said Jinny, wiping her eyes. "And *how* 'appy it will make me to fulfil 'is wish!— Don't let me feel unwelcome, and an intruder, dear. I know I'm not nearly good enough for 'im, and 'e could 'ave had the choice of ever such handsome women. But 'e 'as promised to be patient with me, and to teach me everything I ought to know."

Polly's dismay at the turn of events yielded to a womanly sympathy with her friend. "It's just like poor little Agnes and Mr. Henry over again," was her private thought. She could not picture John stooping to guide and instruct.

But she had been touched on a tender spot—that of ambitious pride for those related to her—and she made what Mahony called "a real Turnham attempt" to stand up to John. Against her husband's express advice.

"For, if your brother chooses to contract a mésalliance of this kind, it's nobody's business but his own.— Upon my word, though, Polly, if you don't take care, this house will get a bad name over the matches that are made in it! You had better have your spare-room boarded up, my dear."

Mahony was feeling practically rasped by John's hoity-toity behaviour in this connection. Having been nursed back to health, John went about with his chin in the air, and hardly condescended to allude to his engagement—let alone talk it over with his relatives. So Mahony retired into himself—after all, the world of John's mind was so dissimilar to his own that he did not even care to know what went on in it. "The fellow has been caught on the hop by a buxom form and a languishing eye," was how he dismissed the matter in thought.

—"I raise my wife to my own station, Mary. And you will greatly oblige me by showing Jane every possible attention," was the only satisfaction Polly could get from John; and the retort was made in his driest tone.

Before the engagement was a week old, Tilly reappeared— she was to be married from their house on the hither side of Christmas. At first, she was too full of herself and her own affairs to let either Polly or Jinny get a word in. Just to think of it! That old cabbage-grower, Devine, had gone and been and bought the block of land next the one Mr. O. was building on. She'd lay a bet he would put up a house the dead spit of theirs. Did ever anyone hear such cheek!

At the news that was broken to her, the first time she paused for breath, she let herself heavily down on a chair.

"Well, I'm blowed!" was all she could ejaculate. "Blowed . . . that's what I am!"

But afterwards, when Jinny had left the room, she gave free play to a very real envy and regret. "In all my life I never did! Jinn to be Mrs. John! . . . and, as like as not, the *Honourable* Mrs. John before she's done.— Oh, Polly, my dear, why *ever* didn't I wait!"

On being presented to John, however, she became more reconciled to her lot. "'E's got a temper, your brother has, or I'm very much mistaken. It won't be all beer and skittles for 'er ladyship. For Jinn hasn't a scrap of spunk *in* 'er, Polly. She got so mopey, the last year or two, there was no doing anything with 'er. Now it was just the other way round with me. No matter how black things looked, I always kept my pecker up. Poor ma used to say I grew more like her, every day."

And, at a still later date: "No, Polly, my dear, I wouldn't change places with the future Mrs. T. after all, thank you—not for Joseph! I *say!* she'll need to mind her p's and q's."— For Tilly had listened to John explaining to Jinny what he expected of her, what she might, and what she might not do; and had watched Jinny sitting meekly by, saying yes to everything.

There was nothing in the way of the marriage; indeed, did it not take place immediately, Jinny would have to look about her for a situation of some kind; and, said John, that was nothing for *his* wife! His house stood empty; he was very much in love; and pressed for the naming of the day. So it was decided that Polly should accompany Jinny to lodgings in Melbourne, should help her choose her trousseau and engage servants. Afterwards, there would be a quiet wedding—by reason of Jinny's mourning—at which Richard, if he could possibly contrive to leave his patients, would give the bride away. Polly was to remain in John's house while the happy couple were on honeymoon, to look after the servants. This arrangement would also make the break less hard for the child. Trotty was still blissfully unconscious of what had befallen her. She had learnt to say "new mamma," parrot-wise, without understanding what the words meant. And, in the meantime, the fact that she was to go with her aunt for a long, exciting coach-ride, filled her childish cup with happiness.

As Polly packed the little clothes, she thought of the night, six years before, when the fat, sleeping babe had been laid in her arms.

"Of course it's only natural John should want his family round him again. But I *shall* miss the dear little soul," she said to her husband, who stood watching her.

"What you need is a little one of your own to fill her place, wife."

"Ah, don't I wish I had!" said Polly, and drew a sigh. "That would make up for everything.— Still, if it can't be, it can't."

A few days before the set time, John received an urgent summons to Melbourne, and went on ahead, leaving Mahony suspecting him of a dodge to avoid travelling *en famille*. In order that his bride-elect should not be put to inconvenience, John hired four seats for the three of them; but: "He might just as well have saved his money," thought Polly, when she saw the coach. Despite their protests, they were packed like herrings in a barrel—had hardly enough room to use their hands.— Altogether, it was a trying journey. Jinny, worked on by excitement and fatigue, took a fit of hysterics; Trotty, frightened by the many rough strangers, cried, and had to be nursed; and the whole burden of the undertaking lay on Polly's shoulders. She had felt rather timid about it, before starting; but was obliged to confess that she got on better than she expected. A kind old man sitting opposite, for instance— a splitter, he said he was—actually undid Jinny's bonnet-strings, and fetched water for her at the first stoppage.

Polly had not been in Melbourne since the year after her marriage, and was looking forward intensely to the visit. She went laden with commissions; her lady-friends gave her a list as long as her arm. Richard, too, had entrusted her to get him second-hand editions of various medical works, as well as a new stethoscope. Thirdly, she had promised old Mr. Ocock to go to William's Town to meet Miss Amelia, who, even now, was tossing somewhere on the Indian Ocean; and to escort the poor young lady safely up to Ballarat.

Having seen them start, Mahony went home to drink his coffee and read his paper in a quiet that was new to him. John's departure had already eased the strain. Then Tilly had been boarded out at the Methodist minister's. Now, with the exit of Polly and her charges, an unspeakable peace descended on the little house. The rooms lay white and still in the sun, and, though all doors stood open, there was not a sound to be heard but the buzzing of the blowflies round the sweets of the fly-traps. Mahony drew a hearty sigh of relief. He was free to look as glum as he chose of a morning, when he had neuralgia; or to be silent when worried over a troublesome case. No longer would Miss Tilly's bulky presence and loud-voiced re-iterations of her prospects grate his nerves; or John's full-blooded absorption in himself, and poor foolish Jinny's quaver-ing doubts, whether she would ever be able to live up to so magnificent a husband, offend his sense of decorum.

Another reason why he was glad to see the last of them was that, in the long run, he had rebelled at the barefaced way they made use of Polly, and took advantage of her good nature. It was not enough that she should cook for them, and wait on them; he had even caught her stitching garments for the help-less Jinny. This was too much: such extreme obligingness on his wife's part seemed to detract from her personal dignity. He could never have got Polly to see it, though. Undignified to do a kindness? What a funny, selfish idea! The fact was, there was a certain streak in Polly's nature that made her more akin to all these good people than to him—him with his unsociable leanings towards a hermit's cell; his genuine need of an occa-sional hour's privacy and silence, in which to think a few thoughts through to the end. . . .

On coming in from his rounds, he turned out an old linen jacket that belonged to his bachelor days, and raked up some books he had not opened for an almost equally long time. He also steered clear of friends and acquaintances. This was not hard. In Polly's absence they dropped off of themselves—and he mutely paid tribute to his wife's powers of attraction. Should his solitude pall on him—Purdy was away on sick leave, re-covering from a spill from his horse—he would always, he knew, be welcome at the Archdeacon's, for a cup of tea or a game of chess. There were card-tables, too, at the houses of some of his colleagues—though, here, the play was higher than he cared for.

In the meanwhile, he went nowhere, saw no one but his patients. And Ellen, to whose cookery Polly had left him with many misgivings, took things easy. "He's so busy reading, he never knows what he puts in his mouth. I believe he'd eat his boot-soles, if I fried 'em up neat wid a bit of parsley," she reported over the back fence, on Doctor's odd ways.

During the winter months, the practice had as usual fallen off. By now, it was generally beginning to look up again; but this year, for some reason, the slackness persisted. He perceived how lean his purse was, whenever he had to take a banknote from it to enclose to Polly: there was literally nothing doing, no money coming in. Then, he would restlessly lay his book aside, and drawing a slip of paper to him, set to reckoning and dividing. Not for the first time, he found himself in the doctor's awkward quandary: how to be decently and humanly glad of a rise in the health-rate.

He had often regretted having stuck to the half-hundred shares he had bought at Henry Ocock's suggestion; had often spent, in fancy, the sum they would have brought in, had he sold when they touched their highest figure. Such a chance would hardly come his way again. After the one fictitious flare-up, "Porepunkahs" had fallen heavily—the first main prospect-drive, at a depth of three hundred and fifty feet, had failed to strike the gutter—and nowadays they were not even quoted. Thus had ended his single attempt to take a hand in the great game.

One morning he sat at breakfast, and thought over his weekly epistle to Polly. In general, this chronicled items of merely personal interest. The house had not yet been burnt down—her constant fear, when absent; another doctor had got the Asylum; he himself stood a chance of being elected to the Committee of the District Hospital. To-day, however, there was more to tell. The English mail had just come in, and the table was strewn with foreign envelopes and journals. Besides the usual letters from relatives, one in a queer, illiterate hand had reached him, the address scrawled in purple ink on the cheapest note-paper. Opening it, with some curiosity, Mahony found that it was from his former assistant, Long Jim.

The old man wrote in a dismal strain. Everything had gone against him. His wife had died, he was out of work and penniless, and racked with rheumatism—oh, it was "a crewl climat!" Did he stop in England, only "the house" remained to him; he'd end in a pauper's grave. But he believed if he could get back to a scrap of warmth, and the sun, he'd be good for some years yet. Now he'd always known Dr. Mahony for the kindest, most liberal of gentlemen; the happiest days of his life had been spent under him, on the Flat; and if he'd only give him a lift now, there was nothing he wouldn't do to show his gratitude. Doctor knew a bit about him, too. Here, he couldn't seem to get on with folk at all. They looked crooked at him, and just because he'd once been spunky enough to try his luck overseas. Mahony, laying the letter down, pshawed and smiled; then wondered what Polly would say to it. She it was who had been responsible for packing the old man off.

Unfolding the *Star*, he ran his eye over its columns. He had garnered the chief local news, and was skimming the mining intelligence, when he suddenly stopped short, with an exclamation of surprise; and his grip on the paper tightened. There it stood, black on white: "Porepunkahs" had jumped to three pounds per share! What the dickens did that mean? He turned back to the front sheet, to find if any clue to the claim's renewed activity had escaped him; but sought in vain. So, bolting the rest of his breakfast, he hurried down to the town, to see if, on the spot, he could pick up information with regard to the mysterious rise.

The next few days kept him in a twitter of excitement.

"Porepunkahs" went on advancing—not by leaps and bounds, as before, but slowly and steadily—and threw off a dividend. He got into bed at night with a hot head, from wondering whether he ought to hold on, or sell out; and, inside a week, he was off to consult the one person he knew, who was in a position to advise him. Henry Ocock's greeting resembled an embrace— "It evidently means a fortune for him," was his visitor's interpretation—and all the trifling personal differences that had come between them were forgotten, in the wider, common bond. The lawyer virtually ordered Mahony to "sit in," till he gave the word. By this time, "Porepunkahs" had passed their previous limit, and even paid a bonus: it was now an open secret that the drive undertaken in an opposite direction to the first had proved wildly successful; the lead was scored and seamed with gold. Ocock spoke of the stone, specimens of which he had held in his hand—declared he had never seen its equal.

But when the shares stood at fifty-three pounds each, Mahony could restrain himself no longer; and, in spite of Ocock's belief that another ten days would see a *coup*, he parted with forty-five of the half hundred he held. Leaving the odd money with the lawyer for re-investment, he walked out of the office, the possessor of two thousand pounds.

It was only a very ordinary late spring day; the season brought its like by the score: a pale azure sky, against which the distant hills looked purple; above these a narrow belt of cloud, touched, in its curves, to the same hue. But to Mahony it seemed as if such a perfect day had never dawned, since he first set foot in Australia. His back was eased of an immense load; and like Christian on having passed the wall known as Salvation, he could have wept tears of joy. After all these years of pinching and sparing, he was out of poverty's grip. The suddenness of the thing was what staggered him. He might have drudged till his hair was grey; it was unlikely he would ever, at one stroke, have come into possession of such a sum as this.— And the whole of that day, he went about feeling a little more than human, and seeing people, places, things, through a kind of beatific mist. Now, thank God, he could stand on his own legs again; could relieve John of his bond, pay off the mortgage on the house, insure his life before it was too late. And, everything done, he would still have over a thousand pounds to his credit.— A thousand pounds! No longer need he thankfully accept any and every call; or reckon sourly that, if the leakage on the roof was to be mended, he must go without a new surtout.— Best of all, he could now begin in earnest to save.

First, though, he allowed himself two very special pleasures. He sent Polly a message, by the electric-telegraph, to say that he would come down himself to fetch her home. In secret he planned a little trip to Schnapper Point. At the time of John's wedding, he had been unable to get free; this would be the only holiday he and Polly had ever had together.

The second thing he did was: to indulge the love of giving that was innate in him, and of giving in a somewhat lordly way. He enjoyed the broad grin that illuminated Ellen's face, at his unlooked-for generosity; Jerry's red stammered thanks for the gift of the cob the boy had long coveted. It did him good to put two ten-pound notes in an envelope and inscribe Ned's name on it; he had never yet been able to do anything

for these poor lads. He also, without waiting to consult Polly
—fearing, indeed, that she might advise against it—sent off
the money to Long Jim for the outward voyage, and a few
pounds over. For there were superstitious depths in him; and,
at this turn of his fortune, it would surely be of ill omen to
refuse the first appeal for charity that reached him.

Polly was so much a part of himself that he thought of her
last of all. But, then, it was with moist eyes. She, who had
never complained, should of a surety not come short! And he
dropped asleep that night to the happy refrain: "Now she shall
have her piano, God bless her! . . . the best that money can
buy."

PART IV

[1]

THE new house—they had moved into it some few months
later—stood in Webster Street. It was twice as big as the old
one, had a garden back and front, a verandah round three
sides. When Mahony bought it, and the piece of ground it
stood on, it was an unpretentious weather-board, in a rather
dilapidated condition. The situation was good, though—without being too far from his former address—and there was
stabling for a pair of horses. And by the time he had finished
with it, it was one of those characteristically Australian houses,
which, added to wherever feasible, without a thought for symmetry, or design—a room built on here, a covered passage
there, a bathroom thrown out in an unexpected corner, with
odd steps up and down—have yet a spacious, straggling comfort all their own.

How glad he was to leave the tiny, sunbaked box that till
now had been his home. It had had neither blind nor shutter
to keep the light out; and, on his entering it, of a summer midday, it had sometimes struck hotter than outside. The windows
of his new room were fitted with green venetians; round the
verandah-posts twined respectively a banksia and a Japanese-
honeysuckle, which further damped the glare; while on the
patch of buffalo-grass in front stood a spreading fig-tree, which
leafed well, and threw a fine shade. He had also added a sofa

to his equipment. Now, when he came in tired, or with a headache, he could stretch himself out at full length, and close his eyes.— He was lying on it at this very moment.

Polly, too, had reason to feel satisfied with the change. A handsome little Broadwood, with a ruby-silk and carved-wood front, stood against the wall of her drawing-room; gilt cornices surmounted the windows; and from the centre of the ceiling hung a lustre-chandelier that was the envy of every one who saw it: Mrs. Henry Ocock's was not a patch on it, and yet had cost more. This time, Mahony had virtually been able to give his wife a free hand in her furnishing.— And in her new spare bedroom she could put up no less than three guests!

Of course, these luxuries had not all rained on them at once. Several months passed before Polly, on the threshold of her parlour, could exclaim, with an artlessness that touched her husband deeply: "Never, in my life, did I think I should have such a beautiful room!"— Still, as regarded money, the whole year had been a steady ascent. The nest-egg he had left with the lawyer had served its purpose of chaining that old hen, Fortune, to the spot. Ocock had invested and reinvested on his behalf—now it was twenty "Koh-i-noors," now thirty "Consolidated Beehives"—and Mahony was continually being agreeably surprised by the margins it threw off in its metamorphoses. That came of his having placed the matter in such competent hands. By now, he had learned to put blind faith in Ocock's judgment. The lawyer had, for instance, got him finally out of "Porepunkahs" in the very nick of time—the reef had not proved as open to the day as was expected—and pulled him off, in the process, another three hundred odd. Compared with Ocock's own takings, of course, his was a modest spoil; the lawyer had made a fortune, and was now one of the wealthiest men in Ballarat. He had built not only new and handsome offices on the crest of the hill, but also, prior to his marriage, a fine dwelling-house, in extensive grounds, on the farther side of Yuille's Swamp: he drove to business every morning, in a smart turn-out. Altogether, it had been a year of great and sweeping changes. People had gone up, gone down—had changed places like children at a game of General Post. More than one of Mahony's acquaintances had burnt his fingers. Brace, for example, who on occasion had done "locum" for him. The poor fellow, with a young family dependent on him, had dabbled wildly on his own account, come a hopeless cropper, and was now gone to bury himself in some wretched little upcountry hole, never to be heard of again. On the other hand, old Devine, Polly's one-time market-gardener, had made his thousands. There was actually talk of his standing for Parliament, in which case his wife bid fair to be received at Government House.— And the pair of them with hardly an "h" between them!

—From the sofa where he lay, Mahony could hear the murmur of his wife's even voice. Polly sat at the further end of the verandah, talking to Jinny, who dandled her babe in a rocking-chair that made a light tip-tap, as it went to and fro. Jinny said nothing: she was no doubt sunk in adoration of her —or rather John's—infant; and Mahony all but dozed off, under the full, round tones he knew so well.

—In his case, the saying had once more been verified: to him that hath shall be given! Whether it was due to the better position of the new house; or to the fact that easier circumstances gave people more leisure to think of their ailments; or merely that money attracted money: whatever the cause, his practice had of late made giant strides. He was in demand for consultations; sat on several committees; while a couple of lodges had come his way, as good as unsought.

Against this, he had one piece of ill-luck to set. At the close of the summer, when the hot winds were in blast, he had gone down under the worst attack of dysentery he had had since the early days. He really thought this time all was over with him. For six weeks, in spite of the tenderest nursing, he had lain prostrate, and as soon as he could bear the journey had to prescribe himself a change to the seaside. The bracing air of Queenscliff soon picked him up; he had, thank God, a marvellous faculty of recuperation: while others were still not done pitying him, he was himself again, and well enough to take the daily plunge in the sea that was one of his dearest pleasures.— To feel the warm, stinging fluid lap him round, after all these drewthy years of dust and heat! He could not have enough of it, and stayed so long in the water that his wife, sitting at a decent distance from the Bathing Enclosure, grew anxious, and agitated her little white parasol.

"There's nothing to equal it, Mary, this side Heaven!" he declared as he rejoined her, his towel about his neck. "I wish I could persuade you to try a dip, my dear."

But Mary preferred to sit quietly on the beach. "The dressing and undressing is such a trouble," said she. As it was, one of her elastic-sides was full of sand.

Yes, Polly was Mary now, and had been, since the day Ned turned up again on Ballarat, accompanied by a wife and child. Mary was in Melbourne at the time, at John's nuptials; Mahony had opened the door himself; and there, in a spring-cart, he had got his first sight of the frowsy, red-haired woman who was come to steal his wife's name from her.— This invasion was the direct result of his impulsive generosity. Had he only kept his money in his pocket!

He had been forced to take the trio in, and give them house-room. But he bore the storming of his hard-won privacy with a bad grace, and Mary had much to gloss over, on her return.

She had been greatly distressed by her favourite brother's ill-considered marriage. For, if they had not held Jinny to be John's equal, what *was* to be said of Ned's choice? Mrs. Ned had lived among the mining population of Castlemaine, where her father kept a public-house; and, said Richard, her manners were accordingly: loud, slap-dash, familiar—before she had been twenty-four hours under his roof, she was bluntly addressing him as "Mahony." There was also a peculiar streak of touchiness in her nature ("Goes with hair of that colour, my dear!") which rendered her extremely hard to deal with. She had, it seemed, opposed the idea of moving to Ballarat—that was all in her favour, said Mary—and came primed to detect a snub or a slight at every turn. This morbid suspiciousness it was that led Mary to yield her rights in the matter of the name: the confusion between them was never-ending; and, at the first hint that the change would come gracefully from her, Mrs. Ned had burst into a passion. No one had ever asked such a thing of her before! She supposed the truth was, her name was not fine enough for the like of them!—a perversion of the facts that made Mahony throw up his hands at the illogicalness of the female mind.

"It's all the same to me, Richard, what I'm called," Mary soothed him in private. "And don't you think Polly was beginning to sound rather childish, now I'm nearly twenty-four?"

But: "Oh, what *could* Ned have seen in her!" she sighed to herself, dismayed. For Mrs. Ned was at least ten years older than her husband; and whatever affection might originally have existed between them, it was now a thing of the past. She tyrannised mercilessly over him, nagging at him till Ned, who was nothing if not good-natured, turned sullen, and left off tossing his child in the air.

—"We must just make the best of it, Richard," said Mary. "After all, she's really fond of the baby. And when the second comes . . . you'll attend her yourself, won't you, dear? I think somehow her temper may improve, when that's over."

For this was another thing: Mrs. Ned had arrived there in a condition that raised distressing doubts in Mary as to the date of Ned's marriage. She did not breathe them to Richard —though she knew he also must be putting two and two to- gether—for it always seemed to her to make matters of this kind worse, openly to speak of them. She devoted herself to getting the little family under a roof of its own. Through Richard's influence, Ned obtained a clerkship in a carrying- agency, which would just keep his head above water; and she found a tiny, three-roomed house, that was near enough to let her be daily with her sister-in-law, when the latter's time came. Meanwhile, she cut out and helped to sew a complete little outfit ("What she had before was no better than rags!"); and Mrs. Ned soon learned to know on whom she could lean, and to whom she might turn, not only for practical aid, but also for a never failing sympathy in what she called her "troubles."

"I vow your Mary's the kindest-hearted little soul it's ever been me luck to run across," she averred one day to Mahony, who was visiting her professionally. "So commonsense, too— no nonsense about *her!* I shouldn't have thought a gaby like Ned could have sported such a trump of a sister."

—"Another pensioner for your *caritas,* dear," said Mahony, in passing on the verdict. What he did not grieve his wife by repeating were certain bad reports of Ned lately brought him by Jerry. According to Jerry—and the boy's word was to be relied on—Ned had kept loose company in Castlemaine, and had acquired the habit of taking more than was good for him. Did he not speedily amend his ways, there would be small chance of him retaining his present post.

—Here, Mahony was effectually roused by a stir on the verandah. Jinny entered the house to lay down her sleeping babe, and a third voice, Purdy's, was audible. The wife had evidently brought out a bottle of her famous home-brewed ginger-beer: he heard the cork pop, the drip of the overflow on the boards, the clink of the empty glass; and Purdy's warm words of appreciation.

Then there was silence. Rising from the sofa, Mahony inserted himself between blind and window, and looked out.

His first thought was: what a picture! Mary wore a pale pink cotton gown, which, over the light swellings of her crinoline, bulged and billowed round her, and generously swept the ground. A collar and cuffs of spotless lawn outlined neck and wrists. She bent low over her stitching, and the straight white parting of her hair intensified the ebony of the glossy bands. Her broad pure forehead had neither line nor stain. On the trellis behind her, a vine hung laden with massy bunches of muscatelles.

Purdy sat on the edge of the verandah, with his back to Mahony. Between thumb and forefinger he idly swung a pair of scissors.

Urged by some occult sympathy, Mary at once glanced up and discovered her husband. Her face was lightly flushed from stooping—and the least touch of colour was enough to give its delicate ivory an appearance of vivid health. She had grown fuller of late—quite fat, said Richard, when he wished to tease her: a luxuriant young womanliness lay over and about her. Now, above the pale wild-rose of her cheeks, her black eyes danced with a mischievous glee; for she believed her husband intended swinging his leg noiselessly over the sill, and creeping up to startle Purdy—and this appealed to her sense of humour. But, as Richard remained standing at the window, she just smiled slyly, satisfied to be in communion with him over their unsuspecting friend's head.

Here, however, Purdy brought his eyes back from the garden, into which he had been staring, and she abruptly dropped hers to her needlework.

The scissors were shut with a snap, and thrown rather than laid, to the other implements in the workbox. "One 'ud think you were paid to finish that wretched sewing in a fixed time,

Polly," said Purdy cantankerously. "Haven't you got a word
to say?"

"It's for the Dorcas Society. They're having a sale of work.
I want to get it done."

"Oh, damn Dorcases! You're always slaving for somebody.
You'll ruin your eyes. I wonder Dick allows it. I shouldn't—
I know that."

The peal of laughter that greeted these words came equally
from husband and wife. Then: "What the dickens does it matter to you, sir, how much sewing my wife chooses to do?" cried
Mahony, and, still laughing, stepped out of the window.

"Hello!—you there?" said Purdy, and rose to his feet. "What
a beastly fright to give one!"— He looked red and sulky.

"I scored that time, my boy!" and, linking his arm in Mary's,
Mahony confronted his friend. "Afraid I'm neglecting my
duties, are you? Letting this young woman spoil her eyes?—
Turn 'em on him, my love, in all their splendour, that he may
judge for himself."

"Nonsense, Richard," said Mary softly, but with an affectionate squeeze of her husband's arm.

"Well, ta-ta, I'm off!" said Purdy. And, as Mahony still
continued to quiz him, he added in a downright surly tone:
"Just the same old Dick as ever! Blinder than any bat to all
that doesn't concern yourself! I'll eat my hat if it's ever
entered your dull old noodle that Polly's quite the prettiest
woman on Ballarat."

"Don't listen to him, Richard, please!" and: "Don't let
your head be turned by such fulsome flattery, my dear!" were
wife and husband's simultaneous exclamations.

"I shouldn't think so," said Mary sturdily, and would have
added more, but, just at this minute, Jinny came out of the
house, with the peculiar noiseless tread she had acquired in
moving round an infant's crib; and Purdy vanished.

Jinny gazed at her sister-in-law with such meaning—with
such a radiant, superior, yet wistful mother-look—that Mary
could not but respond.

"Did you get her safely laid down, dear?"

"Perfectly, Mary! Without even the quiver of an eyelash.
You recollect, I told you yesterday when her little head touched
the pillow, she opened her eyes and looked at me. To-day there

was nothing of that sort. It was quite perfect;" and Jinny's voice thrilled at the remembrance: it was as if, in continuing to sleep during the transit, her—or rather John's—tiny daughter had proved herself of a marvellous sagacity.

Mahony gave an impatient shrug in Jinny's direction. But he, too, had to stand fire: she had been waiting all day for a word with him about a certain soothing-syrup, which she did not think suited the child. The babe, who was teething, was plagued by various disorders; and Jinny knew each fresh pin's-head of a spot that joined the rash.

Mahony made light of her fears; then, turning to his wife, asked her to hurry on the six-o'clock dinner: he had to see a patient between that meal and tea. Mary went to make arrangements—Richard always forgot to mention such things till the last moment—and also to please Jinny by paying a visit to the baby.

"The angels can't look very different when they sleep, I think," murmured its mother, hanging over the couch.

When Mary returned, she found her husband picking cater-pillars off the vine: Long Jim, odd man now about house and garden, was not industrious enough to keep the pests under. In this brief spell of leisure—such moments grew ever rarer in Richard's life—husband and wife locked their arms, and paced slowly up and down the verandah. It was late afternoon, on a breathless, pale-skied February day; and the boards of the flooring gritted with sandy dust beneath their feet.

—"He *was* grumpy this afternoon, wasn't he?" said Mary, without preamble. "But I've noticed once or twice lately that he can't take a joke any more. He's grown queer altogether. Do you know he's the only person who still persists in calling me by my old name? He was quite rude about it when I asked him why. Perhaps he's liverish, from the heat. It might be a good thing, dear, if you went round and overhauled him. Somehow, it seems unnatural for Purdy to be bad-tempered."

"It's true he may be a bit out of sorts. But I fear the evil's deeper-seated, Mary. It's my opinion the boy is tiring of regular work. Now that he hasn't even the excitement of the gold-escort to look forward to. . . . And he's been a rolling stone from the beginning you know."

"If only he would marry and settle down! I do wish I could find a suitable wife for him. The right woman could make anything of Purdy"; and, yet once more, Mary fruitlessly scanned, in thought, the lists of her acquaintance.

"What if it's a case of sour grapes, love? Since the prettiest woman on Ballarat is no longer free. . . ."

"Oh, Richard, hush! Such foolish talk!"

"But is it? . . . let me look at her. Well, if not the prettiest, at least a very pretty person indeed. It certainly becomes you to be stouter, wife."

But Mary had not an atom of vanity in her. "Speaking of prettiness reminds me of something that happened at the Races last week—I forgot to tell you, at the time. There were two gentlemen there, from Melbourne; and, as Agnes Ocock went past, one of them said out loud: 'Gad! That's a lovely woman.'— Agnes heard it herself, and was so distressed. And the whole day, wherever she went, they kept their field-glasses on her. Mr. Henry was furious."

"If you'll allow me to say so, my dear, Mrs. Henry cannot hold a candle to some one I know—to my mind, at least."

"If I suit you, Richard, that's all I care about."

"Well, to come back to what we were saying. My advice is, give Master Purdy a taste of the cold shoulder, the next time he comes hanging about the house. Let him see his ill-temper didn't pass unnoticed. There's no excuse for it. God bless me! doesn't he sleep the whole night through in his bed?"

Mahony's tone took on an edge as he said this. The broken nights that were nowadays the rule with himself were the main drawbacks to his prosperity. He had never been a really good sleeper; and, in consequence, was one of those people who feel an intense need for sleep, and suffer under its curtailment. As things stood at present, his rest was wholly at the mercy of the night-bell—a remorseless instrument this, given chiefly to pealing just as he had finally managed to drop off. Its gentlest tinkle was enough to rouse him—long before it had succeeded in penetrating the ears of the groom, who was supposed to open. And when it remained silent for a night, some trifling noise in the road would simulate its jangle in his dreams, and cause him to start up, fearing lest some one had been ringing in vain at his door. "It's a wonder I have any nerves left," he grumbled, as the hot, red dawns crept in at the sides of the bedroom-window. For the shortening of his sleep at one end did not mean that he could make it up at

the other. All that summer he had fallen into the habit of
waking at five o'clock and not being able to doze off again.
The narrowest bar of light on the ceiling, the earliest twitter
of the sparrows, was enough to strike him into full consciousness; and Mary was hard put to it to darken the room
and ensure silence; and would be, till the day came when he
could knock off work and take a thorough holiday. This, he
promised himself to do, before he was very much older.

[2]

MARY sat with pencil and paper, and wrinkled her brows.
She was composing a list, and every now and then, after
an inward calculation, she lowered the pencil to note such
items as: three tipsy-cakes, four trifles, eight jam-sandwiches.
John Turnham had run up from Melbourne to fetch home
wife and child; and his relatives were giving a musical card-
party in his honour. By the window, Jinny sat on a low
ottoman suckling her babe; and she paid but scant heed to her
sister-in-law's deliberations: to her it seemed a much more
important matter that the milk should flow smoothly down
the precious little throat, than that Mary's supper should be a
complete success as to quantity. With her free hand she now
imprisoned the two little feet, working one against the other
in slow enjoyment; now felt up the warm little limbs, inside
the swaddling, after the fashion of nursing-mothers.

The two women were in the spare bedroom, which was
dusk, and cool, and dimity-white; and they exchanged remarks
in a whisper; for the lids had come down more than once on
the big black eyes, and now only lifted automatically from
time to time, to send a last look of utter satiation at the
mother-face. Mary always said: "She'll drop off sooner indoors,
dear." But this was not the whole truth. Richard had hinted
that he considered the seclusion of the house better suited
to the business of nursing than the comparative publicity of
the verandah; for Jinny was too absorbed in her task to take
thought for the proprieties. Here, now she sat—she had grown
very big and full since her marriage—in the generous, wide-
lapped pose of some old Madonna.

Mary, thrown entirely on her own judgment, was just saying with decision: "Well, better to err on the right side and

have too much than too little," and altering a four into a five, when steps came down the passage, and John entered the room. Jinny made him a sign, and John, now Commissioner of Trade and Customs, advanced as lightly as could be expected of a heavy, well-grown man.

"Does she sleep?" he asked.

His eyes had flown to the child; only in the second place did they rest on his wife. At the sight of her free and easy bearing, his face changed, and he said stiffly: "I think, Jane, a little less exposure of your person, my dear. . . ."

Jinny, flushing to her hair-roots, began, as hastily as she dared for the sleeping child on her knee, to re-arrange her dress. The quick, red tide slowly retreated from her gentle face; but, when she rose to lay her burden on the bed, there were tears in her eyes.

Mary saw it, and broke a lance on her behalf. "We were quite alone here, John," she reminded her brother. "Not expecting a visit from you." And added: "You know, Richard says it is high time Baby was weaned. Jinny is feeling the strain."

"As long as this rash continues, I shall not permit it," answered John, riding rough-shod, in his usual fashion, over even Richard's opinion. ("I shouldn't agree to it either, John dear," murmured Jinny.) "And now, Mary, let me have a word with you about the elder children. I understand, from Jane, that you are prepared to take Emma back—is that correct?"

Yes, Mary was pleased to say Richard had consented to Trotty's return; but he would not hear of her undertaking Johnny. At eleven years of age, the proper place for a boy, he said, was a Grammar School. With Trotty, of course, it was different. "I always found her easy to manage, and should be more than glad to have her back"; and Mary meant what she said. Her heart ached for John's motherless children. Jinny's interest in them had lasted only so long as she had none of her own; thereafter, she found them troublesome, and intruders; and Mary, who, being childless, had kept a large heart for all little ones, marvelled at the firm determination to get rid of her step-children which her sister-in-law, otherwise so pliable, displayed.

Brother and sister talked things over, intuitively meeting halfway, understanding each other with a word, as only blood relations can. Jinny, the chief person concerned, sat meekly by, or chimed in merely to echo her husband's views.

"By-the-by, I ran into Richard on Specimen Hill," said John, as he turned to leave the room. "And he asked me to let you know that he would not be home to lunch."

"There . . . if that isn't always the way!" exclaimed Mary. "As sure as I cook something he specially likes, he doesn't come in. Tilly sent me over the loveliest little suckling-pig this morning. Richard *would* have enjoyed it."

"You should be proud, my dear Mary, that his services are in such demand."

"I am, John—no one could be prouder. But all the same I wish he could manage to be a little more regular with his meals. It makes cooking difficult; for he has grown finicky about his food. And to-morrow, because I sha'nt have a minute to spare, he'll be home punctually, demanding something nice. — But I warn you, to-morrow you'll all have to picnic!"

However, when the morrow came, she was better than her word, and looked to it that neither guests nor husband went short. Since a couple of tables on trestles took up the dining-room, John and Mahony lunched together in the surgery; while Jinny's meal was spread on a tray and sent to her in the bedroom. Mary herself had time only to snatch a bite, standing. From early morning on, tied up in a voluminous apron, she was cooking in the kitchen, very hot, and floury, and pre-occupied, drawing grating shelves out of the oven, greasing tins and patty-pans, and dredging flour. The click-clack of egg-beating resounded continuously; and mountains of sponge-cakes, of all shapes and sizes, rose under her hands. This would be the largest, most ambitious party she had ever given —the guests expected numbered between twenty and thirty, and had, besides, carte blanche to bring with them any one who happened to be staying with them—and it would be a disgrace under which Mary, reared in Mrs. Beamish's school, could never again have held up her head, had a single article on her supper-table run short.

In all this, she had only such help as her one maidservant could give her—John had expressly forbidden Jinny the kitchen. True, during the morning, Miss Amelia Ocock, a gentle little elderly body with a harmless smile and a promi-

nent jaw, who was now an inmate of her father's house,
together with Zara, returned from England and a visitor at
the Ococks'—these two walked over to offer their aid in setting the tables. But Miss Amelia, fluttery and undecided as
a bird, was far too timid to do herself justice; and Zara spent
so long arranging the flowers in the central épergnes that,
before she had finished with one of them, it was lunch time.

"I could have done it myself while she was cutting the
stalks," Mary told her husband. "But Zara hasn't really been
any good at flowers since her 'mixed bouquet' took first prize
at the Flower Show. To begin with she tried oats, then shivery
grasses, and at each fresh spray she added, she had to walk to
the other end of the room to study the effect.— Of course,
though, it looks lovely now it's done."

Purdy, who dropped in during the afternoon, was more
useful; he sliced the crusts off loaf-high mounds of sandwiches, and tested the strength and flavour of the claret-cup.
Mary could not make up her mind, when it came to the point,
to follow Richard's advice and treat him coldly. She did, however, tell him that his help would be worth a great deal more
to her, if he talked less, and did not always look for an answer
to what he said. But Purdy was not to be quashed. He had
taken it into his head that she was badly treated, in being left
"to slave" alone, within the oven's radius; and he was very
hard on Jinny, whom he had espied comfortably dandling her
child on the front verandah.— "I'd like to wring the bloomin'
kid's neck!"

"Purdy, for shame!" cried Mary outraged. "It's easy to see
you're still a bachelor. Just wait, sir, till you have children of
your own!"

Under her guidance, he bore stacks of plates across the yard
to the dining-room—where the blinds were lowered, to keep
the room cool—and strewed these, and corresponding knives
and forks, up and down the tables. He also carried over the
heavy soup-tureen, in which was the claret-cup. But he had a
man's slippery fingers, and, between these and his limp, Mary
trembled for the fate of her crockery. He made her laugh, too,
and distracted her attention; and she was glad when it was
time for him to return to barracks.

"Now, come early, to-night," she admonished him. "And

289

mind you bring your music. Miss Amelia's been practising up that duet all the week. She'll be most disappointed, if you don't ask her to sing with you."

On the threshold of the kitchen, Purdy set his fingers to his nose in the probable direction of Miss Amelia; then performed some skittish female twists and turns about the yard. "So hoarse, love . . . a bad cold . . . not in voice!" Mary laughed afresh, and ordered him off.

But when he had gone she looked grave, and, out of an oddly disquieting feeling, said to herself: "I do hope he'll be on his best behaviour to-night, and not tread on Richard's toes."

As it was, she had to inform her husband, on his reaching home, of something that she knew would displease him. John had come back in the course of the afternoon, and announced, without ceremony, that he had extended an invitation to the Devines, for that evening.

"It's quite true what's being said, dear," Mary strove to soothe Richard, as she helped him make a hasty toilet in the bathroom. "Mr. Devine *is* going to stand for Parliament; and he has promised his support, if he gets in, to some measure John has at heart. John wants to have a long talk with him here to-night."

But Richard was exceedingly put out. "Well, I hope my dear, that as it's your brother who has taken such a liberty, *you'll* explain the situation to your guests. I certainly shall not. It's one thing for John to invite whom he chooses to his own house, in town; quite another to foist people of this kind on us here. What Henry Ocock will say to his wife being in the company of that woman, I'm sure I can't say. But I do know, there was no need to exclude Ned and Polly from such an omnium-gatherum as this party of yours will be."

Even while he spoke there came a rat-a-tat at the front door, and Mary had to hurry off. And now knock succeeded knock with the briefest of intervals, the noise carrying far, in the quiet street. Mysteriously bunched-up figures, their heads veiled in the fleeciest of clouds, were piloted along the passage; and: "I *hope* we are not the first!" was murmured by each new-comer in turn. The gentlemen went to change their boots on the back verandah, a portion of which had been curtained in; the ladies, to lay off their wraps in Mary's bedroom. And soon this room was filled to overflowing with the large soft abundance of crinoline; hoops swaying from this side to that, as the guests gave place to one another before the looking-glass, where bands of hair were smoothed, and the catches of bracelets snapped. Music-cases lay strewn over the counterpane: and the husbands who lined up in the passage, to wait for their wives, also bore rolls of music. Mary, in black silk, with a large cameo brooch at her throat, and only a delicate pink on her cheeks to tell of all her labours, moved helpfully to and fro, offering a shoe-horn, a hand-mirror, pins and hairpins. She was caught, as she passed Mrs. Henry Ocock, a modishly late arrival, by that lady's plump white hand, and a whispered request to be allowed to retain her mantle. "Henry was really against my coming, dearest. So anxious . . . so absurdly anxious!"

"And pray where's the *H*onourable Mrs. T. to-night?" inquired "old Mrs. Ocock," rustling up to them: Tilly was the biggest and most handsomely dressed woman in the room. "On her knees worshipping, I bet you, up to the last minute! Or else not allowed to show her nose till the *H*onourable John's got his studs in.— Now then, girls, how much longer are you going to stand there preening and prinking?"

The "girls" were Zara, at this present a trifle *passée,* and Miss Amelia, who was still further from her prime; and gathering the two into her train, as a hen does its chickens, Tilly swept them off to face the ordeal of the gentlemen and the drawing-room.

Mary, with Agnes on her arm, brought up the rear. Mr. Henry was on the watch, and directly his wife appeared, wheeled forward the best armchair, and placed her in it, with a footstool under her feet. Mary planted Jinny next her, and left them to their talk of nurseries: for Richard's sake, she wished to screen Agnes from the vulgarities of Mrs. Devine. Herself she saw with dismay, on entering, that Richard had already been pounced on by the husband: there he stood, listening to his ex-green-grocer's words—they were interlarded with many an awkward and familiar gesture—on his face an expression his wife knew well, while one small, impatient hand tugged at his whiskers. ("Felt inclined to ask him, my dear, what his cabbages cost a head!")

But "old Mrs. Ocock" came to his rescue, bearing down

upon him with an outstretched hand, and a howdee-do that could be heard all over the room: Tilly had long ago forgotten that she had ever borne him a grudge; she it was who could now afford to patronise. "I hope I see you well, doctor?— Oh, not a bit of it. . . . I left him at 'ome. Mr. O. has something wrong, if you please, with his leg or his big toe—gout, or rheumatiz, or something of that sort—and 'e's been so crabby with it, for the last day or so, that to-night I said to 'im: 'No, my dear, you'll just take a glass of hot toddy, and go early and comfortable to your bed.'— Musical parties aren't in his line, anyhow."

A lively clatter of tongues filled the room, the space of which was taxed to its utmost: there were present, besides the friends and intimates of the house, several of Mahony's colleagues, a couple of Bank Managers, the Police Magistrate, the Postmaster, the Town Clerk, all with their ladies. Before long, however, ominous pauses began to break up the conversation, and Mary was accomplished hostess enough to know what these meant. At a sign from her, Jerry lighted the candles on the piano, and, thereupon, a fugue-like chorus went up: "Mrs. Mahony, won't you play something?— Oh, do!— Yes, please, do. . . . I should enjoy it so much."

Mary did not wait to be pressed; it was her business to set the ball rolling; and she stood up and went to the piano as unconcernedly as she would have gone to sweep a room or make a bed.

Putting a piece of music on the rack, she turned down the corners of the leaves. But here Archdeacon Long's handsome, weatherbeaten face looked over her shoulder. "I hope you're going to give us the cannons, Mrs. Mahony?" he said genially. And so Mary obliged him by laying aside the *morceau* she had chosen, and setting up, instead, a "battlepiece," that was a general favourite.

"Aha! That's the ticket!" said Henry Ocock, and, sitting back, he rubbed his hands as Mary struck up, pianissimo, the march that told of the enemy's approach.

And: "Boompity-boomp-boomp-boomp!" Archdeacon Long could not refrain from underlining each fresh salvo of artillery; while: "That's a breach in their walls for 'em!" was Chinnery of the London Chartered's contribution to the stock of fun.

292

Mahony stood on the hearthrug, and surveyed the assembly.
His eyes fled past Mrs. Devine, most unfortunately perched
on an ottoman in the middle of the room, where she sat,
purple, shiny and beaming, two hot, fat, red hands clasped
over her stomach. ("Like a heathen idol! Confound the
woman! I shall have to go and do the polite to her.") His
glance sought Mary at the piano, and hung with pleasure on
the slim form in the rich silk dress. This caught numberless
lights from the candles, as did also the wings of her glossy
hair. He watched, with a kind of amused tenderness, how, at
each forte passage, her head and shoulders took their share of
lending force to the tones. He never greatly enjoyed Mary's
playing. She did well enough at it, God bless her!—it would
not have been Mary if she hadn't—but he came of a musical
family: his mother had sung Handel faultlessly in her day,
besides having a mastery of several instruments: and he was
apt to be critical. Mary's firm, capable hands looked out of
place on a piano: they seemed to stand, too, in a sheerly business relation to the keys. Nor was it otherwise with her singing: she had a fair contralto; but her ear was at fault; and he
sometimes found himself swallowing nervously, when she attacked high notes.

"Oh, doctor! your wife *do* play the pianner lovely," said
Mrs. Devine, and her fat front rose and fell in an ecstatic
sigh.

"Richard dear, will you come?" Mary laid her hand on
his shoulder: their guests were clamouring for a duo. Her
touch was a caress: here he was, making himself as pleasant
as he knew how, to this old woman. Arrogant he might be;
yes; but, when it came to doing a kindness, you could rely on
Richard: he was all bark and no bite.

Husband and wife blended their voices—Mary had been
at considerable pains to get up her part—and then Richard
went on to a solo. He had a clear, true tenor, that was very
agreeable to hear; and Mary, in accompanying him, felt quite
proud of his many attainments. Later on in the evening, he
might perhaps be persuaded to give them a reading from Boz,
or a recitation. At that kind of thing, he had not his equal.

But, first, there was a cry for his flute; and in vain did
Mahony protest that weeks had elapsed since he last screwed
the instrument together. He got no quarter, even from Mary

—but then Mary was one of those inconvenient people, to whom it mattered not a jot what a fool you made of yourself, as long as you did what was asked of you. And so, from memory and unaccompanied, he played them the old familiar air of *The Minstrel Boy.* The theme, in his rendering, was overlaid by floral variations, and cumbered with senseless repetitions; but, all the same, the wild, wistful melody went home, touching even those who were not musical to thoughtfulness and retrospect. The most obstinate chatterers, whom neither sham battles, nor Balfe and Blockley had silenced, held their tongues; and Mrs. Devine openly wiped the tears from her eyes.

O, the minstrel boy to the wars has gone!
In the ranks of death you'll find him.

Again and again pealed forth the lament.

While it was going on, Mary found herself seated next John. John tapped his foot in time to the tune, and, at its close, under cover of the applause, remarked abruptly: "You should fatten Richard up a bit, Mary my dear. He could stand it."

From where they sat, they had Richard in profile. At her brother's words, Mary studied her husband critically, her head a little on one side. "Yes, he *is* rather thin. But I don't think he was ever meant to be fat."

"Ah well! we are none of us as young as we used to be," was John's tribute to the power of music. And throwing out his stomach, he leaned back in his chair and plugged the armholes of his vest with his thumbs.

And now, after due pressing on the part of host and hostess, the other members of the company advanced upon the piano, either singly or in couples, to bear a hand in the burden of entertainment. Their seeming reluctance had no basis in fact; for it was an unwritten law that every one who could must add his mite; and only those who literally had not "a note of music in them," were exempt. Tilly took a mischievous pleasure in announcing bluntly: "So sorry, my dear, not to be able to do you a tool-de-rool! But when the *H*onourable Mrs. T. and I were nippers, we'd no time to loll round pianos, nor any pianos to loll round!"—this, just to see her brother-in-law's dark scowl; for no love—not even a liking—was lost

294

between her and John. But with this handful of exceptions, all
nobly toed the line. Ladies with the tiniest reeds of voices,
which shook like reeds, warbled of Last Roses and Prairie
Flowers; others, with more force, but due decorum, cried to
Willie that they had Missed Him, or coyly confessed to the
presence of Silver Threads Among the Gold; and Mrs. Chinnery, an old-young woman with a long, lean neck, which she
twisted this way and that, in the exertion of producing her
notes, declared her love for an Old Armchair. The gentlemen, in baritones and profundos, told the amorous adventures
of Ben Bolt; or desired to know what Home would be Without a Mother. Purdy spiced the hour with a comic song, and,
in the character of an outraged wife, tickled the risibility of
the ladies.

> *Well, well, sir, so you've come at last!*
> *I thought you'd come no more.*
> *I've waited, with my bonnet on,*
> *From one till half-past four!*

Zara and Mrs. Long both produced *Home They brought
her Warrior Dead!* from their portfolios; so Zara good-
naturedly gave way, and struck up *Robert, toi que j'aime!*
which she had added to her repertory while in England. No
one could understand a word of what she sang; but the mere
fitting of the foreign syllables to the appropriate notes was
considered a feat in itself, and corroborative of the high gifts
Zara possessed.

Strenuous efforts were needed to get Miss Amelia to her
feet. She was dying, as Mary knew, to perform her duet with
Purdy; but, when the moment came, she put forward so many
reasons for not complying that most people retired in despair.
It took Mary to persevere. And finally the little woman was
persuaded to the piano, where, red with gratification, she sat
down, spread her skirts, and unclasped her bracelets.

"Poor little Amelia!" said Mary to herself, as she listened
to a romantic ballad, in which Purdy, in the character of a
high-minded nobleman, sought the hand of a virtuous gipsy-
maid. "And he doesn't give her a second thought. If one could
just tell her not to be so silly!"

Not only had Purdy never once looked near Amelia—for

the most part he had sat rather mum-chance, half-way in and out of a French window, even Zara's attempts to enliven him falling flat—but, during an extra loud performance, Tilly had confided to Mary the family's plans for their spinster relative. And: "The poor little woman!" thought Mary again as she listened. For, after having been tied for years to the sick bed of a querulous mother; after braving the long sea-voyage, which, for such a timid soul, was full of ambushes and terrors; Miss Amelia had reached her journey's end only to find both father and brother comfortably wived, and with no use whatever for her. Neither of them wanted her. She had been given house-room first by her father, then by the Henrys, and, once more, had had to go back to the paternal roof.

"It was nothing for Mossieu Henry in the long run," was his stepmother's comment. But she laughed good-humouredly as she said it; for, his first wrath at her intrusion over, Henry had more or less become her friend; and now maintained that it was no bad thing for his old father to have a sensible, managing woman behind him. Tilly had developed in many ways since her marriage; and Henry and she mutually respected each other's practical qualities.

The upshot of the affair was, she now told Mary, that Miss Amelia's male relatives had subscribed a dowry for her. "It was me that insisted Henry should pay his share—him getting all the money 'e did, with Agnes." And Amelia was to be married off to— "Well, if you turn your head, my dear, you'll see who. Back there, helping to hold up the doorpost."

Under cover of Zara's roulades, Mary cautiously looked round. It was Henry's partner—young Grindle, now on the threshold of the thirties. His side-whiskers a shade less flamboyant than of old, a heavy watch-chain draped across his front, Grindle stood and lounged with his hands in his pockets.

Mary made round eyes. "Oh, but Tilly! . . . isn't it very risky? He's so much younger than she is. Suppose she shouldn't be happy?"

"That'll be all right, Mary, trust me. Only give 'er a handle to 'er name, and Amelia 'ud be happy with any one. She hasn't *that* much backbone in 'er. Besides, my dear, you think, she's over forty! Let her take 'er chance and be thankful. It isn't every old maid 'ud get such an offer."

"And is . . . is *he* agreeable?" asked Mary, still unconvinced.

Tilly half closed her right eye, and, on the same side of her face, protruded the tip of her tongue. "You could stake your last fiver on it, he is!"

But now that portion of the entertainment devoted to art was at an end, and the serious business of the evening began. Card-tables had been set out—for loo, as for less hazardous games. In principle, Mahony objected to the high play that was the order of the day; but, if you invited people to your house, you could not demand of them to screw their points down from crowns to halfpence. They would have thanked you kindly, and have stayed at home. Here, at the loo-table, places were eagerly snapped up, Henry Ocock and his step-mother being among the first to secure seats: both were keen, hard players, who invariably re-lined their well-filled pockets.

It would not have been the thing for either Mahony or his wife to take a hand; for several of the guests held aloof. John had buttonholed old Devine; Jinny and Agnes were still lost in domesticities. Dear little Agnes had grown so retiring of late, thought Mary; she quite avoided the society of gentle-men, in which she had formerly taken such pleasure.— Richard and Archdeacon Long sat on the verandah, and, in moving to and fro, Mary caught a fragment of their talk: they were at the debatable question of table-turning, and her mental com-ment as she passed, was a motherly and amused: "That Richard, who is so clever, can interest himself in such non-sense!"— Further on, Zara was giving Grindle an account of her voyage "home," and ticking off the reasons that had led to her return. She sat across a hammock, and daintily exposed a very neat ankle. "It was much too sleepy and dull for *me!* No, I've *quite* decided to spend the rest of my days in the colony. What do you say, Mr. Grindle?"

Mrs. Devine was still perched on her ottoman. She beamed at her hostess. "No, I dunno one card from another, dearie, and don't want to.— Oh, my dear, what a *lovely* party it 'as been, and 'ow well you've carried it h'off! And what a *beauti-ful* drawin'-room you've got 'ere! On'y a lady could 'ave such a tasty room."

Mary nodded and smiled; but with an air of abstraction. The climax of her evening was fast approaching. Excusing herself, she slipped away, and went to cast a last eye over her laden supper-tables, up and down which benches were ranged that had been borrowed from the Sunday School. To her surprise, she found herself followed by Mrs. Devine.

"*Do* let me 'elp you, my dear, do, now! I feel that stiff and silly sittin' stuck up there, with me 'ands before me.— And jes' send that young feller about 'is business."

So Purdy and his offers of assistance were returned, with thanks, to the card-room, and Mrs. Devine pinned up her black silk front. But not till she had freely vented her astonishment at the profusion and delicacy of Mary's good things. "'Ow *do* you git 'em to rise so?— No, I never did! Fit for Buckin'am Palace and Queen Victoria! And all by your little self, too.— My dear, I must give you a good '*ug!*'"

Hence, when, at twelve o'clock, the company began to stream in, they found Mrs. Devine installed behind the barricade of cups, saucers and glasses; and she it was who dispensed tea and coffee, and ladled out the claret-cup; thus leaving Mary free to keep an argus eye on her visitors' plates. At his entry Richard had raised expostulating eyebrows; but his tongue was of course tied.— And Mary made a lifelong friend.

And now, for the best part of an hour, Mary's sandwiches, sausage-rolls, and meat-pies; her jam-rolls, pastries, and lemon-sponges; her jellies, custards, and creams; her blanc and jaune-manges, and whipped syllabubs; her trifles, tipsy-cakes, and charlotte-russes formed the sole theme of talk and objects of attention. And though the ladies picked with becoming daintiness, the gentlemen made up for their partners' deficiencies; and there was none present who did not, in the shape of a heavy and well-turned compliment, add yet another laurel to Mary's crown.

[3]

IT HAD struck two before the party began to break up. The first move made, however, the guests left in batches, escorting one another to their respective house-doors. The Henry Ococks' buggy had been in waiting for some time, and Mrs. Henry's pretty head was drooping with fatigue, before Henry, who was in the vein, could tear himself from the card-table. Mahony went to the front gate with them, to see them off;

then strolled with the Longs to the corner of the road.

He was in no hurry to retrace his steps. The air was balmy, after that of the over-crowded rooms, and it was a fabulously beautiful night. The earth lay steeped in moonshine, as in the light of a silver sun. So snow-white was the radiance that, on emerging from a shadow, one expected it to strike cold. Trees and shrubs were patterned to their last leaf on the ground before them.— What odd mental twist made mortals choose rather to huddle indoors, by puny candlelight, than to be abroad laving themselves in a splendour such as this?

Leaning his arms on the top rail of a fence, he looked across the slope at the Flat, now hushed and still as the encampment of a sleeping army. Beyond, the bush shimmered palely grey—in his younger years he had been used, on a night like this, when the moon sailed full and free, to take his gun and go opossuming there, to the unholy joy of his dog. Those two old woody gods, Warrenheip and Buninyong, stood out more imposingly than by day. The ranges, on the other hand, seemed to have shrunk . . . retreated. The light lay upon them like a visible burden, flattening their contours, filling up clefts and fissures with a milky haze.

"Good evening, doctor!"

Spoken in his very ear, the words gave him a violent start. He had been lost in contemplation, had heard no one approaching; and the address had a ghostly suddenness. But it was no ghost that stood beside him—nor indeed was it a night for those presences to be abroad, whose element is the dark.

Ill-pleased at being disturbed, he returned but a stiff nod; then since he could not in decency greet and leave-take in a breath, he feigned to go on for a minute with his silent study of the landscape. After which he said: "Well, I must be moving. Good-night to you."

"So you're off your sleep, too, are you?" As often happens, the impulse to speak was a joint one. The words collided.

Instinctively Mahony shrank away; the familiar bracketing of his person with another's was distasteful to him. The man who had sprung up thus at his elbow was known to him by sight—and by a reputation that was none of the best. The proprietor of a small chemist's shop on the Flat, he contrived to give offence in sundry ways. For one thing, he was irreligious—an infidel, his neighbours had it—and followed worldly

299

pursuits of a Sabbath, preferring to scour his premises or hoe potatoes instead of attending church or chapel. Though not a confirmed drunkard, he had been seen to stagger and reel in the street, and be unable to answer rationally when spoken to. Also, the woman with whom he lived was not generally believed to be his lawful wife. Hence, the public fought shy of his nostrums, no one dealing at his shop who could go elsewhere. Bankruptcy threatened; it was a standing riddle how he had so far managed to avoid putting up his shutters. More nefarious practices no doubt, said the relentless *vox populi*.— Seen near at hand, he was a tall, haggard-looking fellow of some forty years of age. The muscles on his neck stood out like those of a skinny old horse.

Here, his gratuitous assumption of a common bond drew a cold: "Pray, what reason have you for supposing that?" from Mahony. And without waiting for a reply, the latter again said good-night and turned to go.

His companion shrank under the rebuff—accepted it with a meekness that was distressing to see. "Thought, comin' on you like this, you were a case like my own. No offence, I'm sure," he said humbly. It was plain he was only too well used to getting the cold shoulder. Mahony stayed his steps. "What's the matter with you, man?" he asked. "Aren't you well? There's a remedy to be found, you know, for most ills under the sun."

"Not for mine! The doctor isn't born, nor the drug discovered, that could cure me."

The tone of bragging bitterness grated Mahony anew. Being himself given to the vice of overstatement, he had small mercy on it, in others. "Tut, tut!" he deprecated.

There was a brief silence before the speaker went on more quietly: "You're a young man, doctor, I'm an old one." And he looked old as he spoke; Mahony saw that he had erred in putting him down as merely elderly. He was old, and grey, and down-at-heel—fifty, if a day—and his clothes hung loose on his bony frame. "You'll excuse me if I say I know better'n you. When a man's done, he's done. And that's me. Yes,"— he grew inflated again, in reciting his woes—"yes, I'm one o' your hopeless cases, just as surely as if I was being eaten up by a cancer or a consumption. I tell you there isn't any more use or purpose left in me than in a bit o' chawed orange

300

peel a kid chucks away in the gutter. To mend me, you
doctors 'ud need to start me afresh—from the mother-egg!"

"You exaggerate, I'm sure."

"It's that—knowin' one's played out, with by rights still
a good third of one's life to run—that's what puts the sleep
away. In the daylight it's none so hard to keep the black
thoughts under; first, themselves they're not so daresome;
and then there's one's pipe, and the haver o' the young fry,
and the garden to fossick round in. But night's the time!
Then they come tramplin' along, a whole army of 'em, carryin'
banners with letters a dozen feet high, so's you shan't miss
rememberin' what you'd give your soul to forget. T'every one
his own particular grievance. Mine—what they come scurryin'
to spit at me—is, no future, no prospects, nothin' to hope for;
nothin' any more for as long as I live, but the everlastin'
treadmill of strugglin' to make both ends meet. And so it'll
go on, et cetera and ad lib., till it pleases the old Joker who
sits grinnin' up aloft, to put His heel down—as you or me
would squash a bull-ant or a scorpion."

"You speak bitterly indeed, Mr. Tangye. Does a night like
this not bring you calmer, clearer thoughts?" and Mahony, on
edge at the other's rancour, waved his arm in a large, loose
gesture at the sky.

His words went unheeded. The man he addressed spun
round and faced him, with a rusty laugh. "Hark at that!" he
cried. "Just hark at it! Why, in all the years I've been in this
God-forsaken place—long as I've been here—I've never yet
heard my own name properly spoken. You're the first, doctor.
You shall have the medal. My ears have burnt with it—ached
with it . . . got used to it."

"But, man alive, you surely don't let that worry you? Why,
I have the same thing to put up with every day of my life. I
smile at it." And Mahony believed what he said, forgetting,
in the mood of antagonism such spleen roused in him, the
annoyance the false stressing of his own name could occasionally cause him.

"So did I, once on a time," said Tangye, and wagged his
head sardonically. "But the day came when it seemed the last
straw; a bit o' mean spite on the part o' this hell of a country
itself."

"You dislike the colony, it appears, intensely?"

301

"You like it?" The counter question came tip for tap.

"I can be fair to it, I hope, and appreciate its good sides."— As always, the mere hint of an injustice made Mahony passionately just.

"Came 'ere of your own free will, did you? Weren't crowded out at home? Or bamboozled by a pack o' lying tales?" Tangye's voice was husky with eagerness.

"That I won't say either. But it is entirely my own choice that I remain here."

"Well, I say to you, think twice of it! If you have the chance of gettin' away, take it. It's no place this, doctor, for the likes of you and me. Haven't you never turned on yourself, dumbfounded, and asked yourself what the devil you were doin' here? And that reminds me. . . . There was a line we used to have drummed into us at school—it's often come back to me since. *Coelum, non animum, mutant, quit trans mare currunt.* In our green days, we gabbled that off by rote; then, it seemed to us innocents just one more o' the eel-sleek phrases the classics are full of. Now I take off my hat to the man who wrote it; he knew what he was talkin' about—by the Lord Harry, he did!"

The Latin came out tentatively, with an odd, unused intonation. Mahony's retort: "How on earth do you know what suits me and what doesn't?" died on his lips. He was surprised into silence. There had been nothing in the other's speech, so far, to show that he was a man of any education. Rather the reverse.

Meanwhile Tangye went on: "Of course I grant you it's an antiquated point o' view; but doesn't that go to prove what I've been tellin' you; that you and me are old-fashioned, too —out-o'-place here, out-o'-date? The modern sort, the sort that gets on in this country, is a prime hand at cuttin' his coat to suit his cloth; for all that the stop-at-homes, like the writer o' that line and other ancients, prate about the Ethiopian's hide, or the leopard and his spots. They didn't buy their experience dear, like we did; didn't guess that if a man *don't* learn to fit himself in, when he gets down in such a land as this, he's a goner; any more'n they knew that most o' those who hold it out here—all of 'em at any rate who've climbed the ladder, nabbed the plunder—have found no more difficulty in changin' their spots than they have their trousers. Makes one think they must have been the pick o' the basket, after all.

Anyway, they're topsmen now. And such as us have no earthly
chance against 'em.— Yes, doctor, there's only one breed that
flourishes here, and you don't need me to tell you which it is.
Here they lie"—and he nodded to right and left of him—
"dreamin' o' their money-bags, and their dividends, and their
profits, and how they'll diddle and swindle one another afresh,
soon as the sun gets up to-morrow. Harder 'n nails they are,
and sharp as needles.— You ask me why I do my walkin' out
in the night-time? It's so's to avoid the sight o' their mean
little eyes, and their greedy, graspin' faces."

Mahony's murmured disclaimer fell on deaf ears. Like one
who had been bottled up for months, Tangye flowed on.
"What a life! What a set! What a place to end one's days in!
Remember, if you can, the yarns that were spun round it for
our benefit, from twenty thousand safe miles away. It was the
Land o' Promise and Plenty, topful o' gold, strewn over with
nuggets that only waited for hands to pick 'em up. Such was to
be our agreeable duty, all the labour that was asked of us,
while alongside of it, so to speak, we planted the Union Jack
on a new peak, and so added to the glory of Old England.—
Lies!—lies from beginnin' to end! I say to you this here's the
hardest and cruellest country ever created, and a man like me's
no more good when he gets here, than the muck—the parin's
and stale fishguts and other leavin's—that knocks about a
harbour and washes against the walls. I'll tell you the only use
I'll have been here, doctor, when my end comes: I'll dung
some bit o' land for 'em with my moulder and rot. That's all.
They'd do better with my sort if they knocked us on the head
betimes, and boiled us down for our fat and marrow."

("Not much in that line to be got from *your* carcase, my
friend," thought Mahony, with an inward smile.)

But once more Tangye had paused merely to draw breath.
"What I say is, instead o' layin' snares for us, it ought to be
forbid by law to give men o' my make shiproom. At home, in
the old country, we'd find our little nook and jog along
decently to the end of our days. But just the staid, respectable,
orderly sort I belonged to's the one that's neither needed nor
wanted here. I fall to thinkin' sometimes on the fates of the
hundreds on hundreds of honest, steady-goin' lads, who at one
time or another have chucked up their jobs over there—for
this. The drink no doubt's took most; they never knew before

that one *could* sweat, as you sweat here. And the rest? Well, just accident . . . or the sun . . . or dysentry . . . or the bloody toil that goes by the name o' work in these parts—you know the list, doctor, better'n me. They say the waste o' life in a new country can't be helped; doesn't matter; has to be. But that's cold comfort to the wasted!— No, I say to you, there ought to be an Act of Parliament to prevent young fellows squanderin' themselves, throwin' away their lives as I did mine. For when we're young, we're not sane. Youth's a fever o' the brain. And I *was* young once, though you mightn't believe it; I had straight joints, and no pouch under my chin, and my full share o' windy hopes and illusions. Senseless truck these! To be spilled overboard, bit by bit—like on a hundred-mile tramp a new-chum finishes by pitchin' from his swag all the needless rubbish he's started with. What's wanted to get on here's somethin' quite else. Horny palms and costive bowels; more'n a dash o' the sharper; and no sickly squeamishness about knockin' out other men and steppin' into their shoes. And I was only an ordinary young chap; not over-strong nor over-shrewd, but honest—honest, by God I was! That didn't count. It even stood in my way. For I was too good for this, and too mealy-mouthed for that; and while I stuck, considerin' the fairness of a job, some one who didn't care a damn whether it was fair or not walked in over my head and took it from me. I went from pillar to post. There isn't anything I haven't tried my luck at, and with everything it's been the same. Nothin' prospered; the money wouldn't come—and wouldn't stick if it did. And so here I am—all that's left of me. It isn't much; and by and by a few rank weeds 'ull spring from it, and old Joey there, who's paid to grub round the graves, old Joey will curse and say: a weedy fellow that, a rotten, weedy blackguard; and spit on his hands, and hoe, till the weeds lie there, bleedin' their juices—the last heirs of me . . . the last issue of my loins!"

"Pray, does it never occur to you, you fool, that *flowers* may spring from you?"

The words were out before Mahony could stop them. He bit his lip.

He had listened to Tangye's diatribe in a white heat of impatience, and with the mental reservation—see how carefully he avoids touching on the real root of the evil: his own defects

of character; his well-known weakness; his affronting of the
moral law. But when he spoke he struck an easy tone—nor
was he in any hesitation how to reply; for that, he had played
devil's advocate all too often with himself, in private. An unlovely country, yes, as Englishmen understood natural beauty;
and yet not without a peculiar charm of its own. An arduous
life, certainly, and one full of pitfalls for the weak or the
unwary; yet he believed it was no more impossible to win
through here, and with clean hands, than anywhere else. "I
myself am fortunate enough to number among my personal
friends, men who would be a credit to any country in the
world." To generalise as his companion had done was absurd.
Preposterous, too, the notion that those of their fellow-towns-
men who had gone ahead, carried off the prizes, owed their
success to some superiority in bodily strength . . . or sharp
dealing . . . or thickness of skin. With Mr. Tangye's permission he would cite himself as an example. He was neither a
very robust man, nor, he ventured to say, one of any marked
ability in the other two directions. Yet he had managed to
get the better of the hardships of the life, without, in the
process, sacrificing jot or tittle of his principles; and to-day he
held a position that any member of his profession across the
seas might envy him.

"Yes, but till you got there!" cried Tangye. "Hasn't every
superfluous bit of you—every thought or interest that wasn't
essential to the daily grind—been gradually pared off?"

"If," said Mahony, stiffening, "if what you mean by that
is, have I allowed my mind to grow narrow and sluggish, I
can honestly answer no."

In his heart he denied the charge even more warmly; for,
as he spoke, he saw the great cork-slabs on which hundreds of
moths and butterflies made dazzling spots of colour; saw the
stack of pink blotting-paper, between the sheets of which his
collection of native plants lay pressed; the glass case filled with
geological specimens; his Bible, the margins of which, round
Genesis, were black with his handwriting; a pile of books on
the new marvel, Spiritualism; Colenso's *Pentateuch;* the big
black volumes of the *Arcana Coelistia;* Locke on Miracles: he
saw all these things and more.— "No, I am glad to say I have
retained many interests outside my work."

Tangye had taken off his spectacles, and was polishing them

on a crumpled handkerchief. He seemed about to reply, even made a quick half-turn towards Mahony; then thought better of it, and went on rubbing. A sceptical smile played round his lips.

"And in conclusion, let me say this," went on Mahony, not unnettled by his companion's expression. "It's sheer folly to talk about what life makes of us. Life is not an active force; cannot mould or mar our fates. No, it's we who make what *we* will, of life. And in order to shape it to the best of our powers, Mr. Tangye, to put our brief span to the best possible use, it is necessary never for a moment to lose faith in God or our fellowmen. Never to forget that, whatever happens, there *is* a sky, with stars in it, above us."

"Yes, there's a lot of bunkum talked about life," returned Tangye drily, and settled his glasses on his nose. "And as a man gets near the end of it, he sees just *what* bunkum it is. Life's only got one meanin', doctor; seen plain, there's only one object in everything we do; and that's to keep a sound roof over our heads and a bite in our mouths—and in those of the helpless creatures who're dependent on us. The rest has no more sense or significance than a nigger's hammerin' on the tamtam. The lucky ones o' this world don't grasp it; but we others do; and after all, p'raps, it's worth while havin' gone through with it to have got at *one* bit of truth, however small.— Good night."

He turned on his heel and, before his words were cold on the air, had vanished, leaving Mahony blankly staring. "Well, upon my word!" ejaculated the latter, and rubbed his eyes.

The moonshine still bathed the earth, gloriously untroubled by the bitterness of human words and thoughts. But the night seemed to have grown chilly; and Mahony gave a slight involuntary shiver. "Some one walking over my . . . now what would that specimen have called it? Over the four by eight my remains will one day manure!"

"An odd, abusive, wrong-headed fellow," he mused, as he made his way home. "Who would ever have thought, though, that the queer little chemist had so much in him! A failure? . . . yes, he was right there; and as unlovely as failures always are —at close quarters." But as he laid his hand on the gate, he jerked up his head and exclaimed half aloud: "God bless my soul! What he wanted was not argument or reason, but a little human sympathy." As usual, however, the flash of intuition came too late. "For such a touchy nature, I'm certainly extraordinarily obtuse where the feelings of others are concerned," he told himself as he hooked in the latch.

—"Why, Richard, where *have* you been?" came Mary's clear voice—muted, so as not to disturb John and Jinny, who had retired to rest. Purdy and she sat waiting on the verandah. "Were you called out? We've had time to clear everything away. The boys helped me; Jerry has only just gone. Here, dear, I saved you a plate of sandwiches and a glass of claret. I'm sure you didn't get much supper yourself, with looking after other people."

—He lay wakeful, long after Mary had fallen asleep. The room was close: rolling up the bed-curtain, he tucked it in behind his head, that more air might come to him. Then he turned his pillow, tossed from side to side. The foolish blunder he had made in response to Tangye's appeal rankled in his mind, and would not let him rest. He could not get over his insensitiveness.— And yet there was nothing exactly surprising about it. The adjusting of his mental poise to that of an utter stranger was never an easy job. At a first meeting he was apt either to button up altogether, or else to go to the other extreme, and give himself gratuitously away. As here. How he had boasted, for instance, of his prosperity, his moral nicety, his saving pursuits—he to boast!—when all that was asked of him was a kindly: "My poor fellow-soul, you have indeed fought a hard fight; but there *is* a God above us, and He will recompense you at His own time, take the word for it of one who has also been through the Slough of Despond." And then just these . . . these hobbies of his, of which he had made so much. Now that he was alone with himself he saw them in a very different light. Lepidoptera collected years since were still unregistered, plants and stones unclassified; his own poor efforts at elucidating the Bible waited to be brought into line with the Higher Criticism; Home's levitations and fire-tests called for investigation; while the leaves of some of the books he had cited had never been cut. The mere thought of these things was provocative, rest-destroying; if he went on, he would have to get up there and then and drag his collections down from their dusty hiding-place, on top of the bookshelves. . . . And in a very short time now, the birds, his little enemies would begin. . . . To induce drowsiness he went methodically through the list of his acquaintances, and sought to range them under one or other of Tangye's headings. And over this there came moments when he lapsed into depths . . . fetched himself up again—but with an effort . . . only to fall back. . . .

All the same he seemed barely to have closed his eyes, when the night-bell rang. In an instant he was up and standing in the middle of the room, applying force to his sleep-clogged wits.

He threw open the sash. "Who's there? What is it?"

Henry Ocock's groom. "I was to fetch you out to our place at once, governor."

"But—is Mrs. Henry taken ill?"

"Not as I know of," said the man drily. "But her and the boss had a bit of a tiff on the way home, and Madam's excited-like."

"And am I to pay for their tiffs?" muttered Mahony hotly, withdrawing his head.

"Hush, Richard! He'll hear you," warned Mary, and sat up. "I shall decline to go. Henry's a regular old woman."

Mary, who was lighting the candle, shook her head. "You mustn't do that, Richard; you can't afford to offend the Henrys. And you know what he is—so hasty. He'd call in some one else on the spot, and you'd never get back.— If only you hadn't stayed out so long, dear, looking at the moon!"

"Good God! Mary, is one never to have a moment to one-self? Never a particle of pleasure or relaxation?"

"Why, Richard!" expostulated his wife, and even felt a trifle ashamed of his petulance. "What would you call to-night, I wonder? Wasn't the whole evening one of pleasure and re-laxation?"

And Mahony, struggling into shirt and trousers, had to admit that he would be hard put to it, to give it another name.

[4]

"Hush, dolly! Mustn't cry, and make a noise! Uncle Richard's cross."

Trotty sat on a hassock and rocked a china babe, with all the appurtenant mother-fuss she had picked up from the tending

of her tiny stepsister. The present Trotty was a demure little
maid of some seven summers, and gave the impression of having been rather rudely elongated. Her flaxen hair was stiffly
imprisoned behind a round black comb; and her big blue eyes
alone remained to her from a lovely infancy. ("Poor Emma's
eyes," said Mary.)

Trotty herself kept still as a mouse; for this was Uncle Richard's busy time—half-past eight, on a hot summer morning, and
strange people sat all round the waiting-room—and he was
cross as well. Her increasing years brought with them an increasing reverence for her uncle—even a touch of awe. Not
that he ever actually scolded her; he just went about as if he
didn't see her, and sometimes he pushed aside with his foot
members of the doll-family who were in his way. Aunt Mary
didn't care much for the dolls either—Uncle Jerry was the only
person who asked after their health, and for whom she dressed
them in their best—and Aunty even slapped her now and then
. . . if she put her fingers in the jam, or picked the currants off
the cake's top. "All nasty tricks you've learned since you went
away from *me!*" said Aunt Mary sternly.— Yet Trotty was not
in the least afraid of her aunt; loved her, indeed, with all her
heart, and had done, since that day—already an eternity ago it
seemed—when she had been frightened of the strange, new
railway-train, and, big girl though she was, had had to be
nursed by Aunty the whole way to Ballarat.

Imitative as a monkey, she now went on—with a child's perfect knowledge that it is all make-believe, yet with an entire
credence in the power of make-believe: "Naughty child—*will*
you be quiet? There! You've frown your counterpane off now.
Wonder what next you'll do. I declare I'll slap you soon—you
make me so cross."

Through the surgery-window, these words floated out: "For
goodness' sake, don't bother me now with such trifles, Mary!
It's not the moment—with a whole string of people waiting in
the other room."

"Well, if only you'll be satisfied with what I do, dear, and
not blame me afterwards."

"Get Purdy to give you a hand with Ned's affair. He has time
and to spare." And wetting his finger-tip, Mahony nervously
flipped over a dozen pages of the book that lay open before him.

"Well . . . if you think I should," said Mary, with a spice of doubt.

"I do. I'll leave word, as I pass, for him to come round.— And now go, wife, and remember to shut the door after you. Oh, and tell that woman in the kitchen to stop singing. Her false notes drive me crazy.— How many are there, this morning?"

"Eight—no, nine, if that's another," replied Mary, with an ear to the front door.

"Tch! I'll have to stop then"; and Mahony clapped to the work he had been consulting. A thought that galled him was: "I'll soon have to be taking a back seat now in the profession. Never a minute to keep abreast of the times." But: "That's a good, helpful wife," he said aloud, as Mary stooped to kiss him. "Do the best you can, mavourneen, and never mind me."

—"Take me with you, Aunty!" Trotty sprang up from her stool, overturning babe and cradle.

"Not to-day, darling. Besides, Trotty, why are you here? You know I've forbidden you to be on the front verandah when the patients come. Run away to the back, and play there."

Mary, who had donned hat and shawl, opened her parasol, and went out into the sun. With the years she had developed into rather a stately young woman: she held her head high, and walked with a firm, free step.

Her first visit was to the stable, to find Long Jim—or Old Jim, as they now called him; for he was nearing the sixties, and was plagued with rheumatism. The notice to leave, which he had given the day before, was one of the "trifles" it fell to her to consider. Personally Mary thought his going would be no great misfortune: he had proved but a sorry gardener; he knew nothing about flowers, yet resented instruction; and it had always been necessary to get outside help in, for the horses. If Jim went, they could engage some one who would combine the posts. But Richard had taken umbrage at the old man's tone; had even been nervously upset over it. It behooved her to find out what the matter was.

"I want a change," said Old Jim dourly, in response to her inquiry; and went on polishing wheel-spokes, and making the wheel fly. "I've bin 'ere too long. An' now I've got a bit o' brass

310

together, an' am thinkin' I'd like to be me own master for a spell."

"But at your age, Jim, is it wise?—to throw up a comfortable home, just because you've laid a little past."— "And with your previous bad experiences to warn you," she added, in thought.

"It's enough to keep me. I turned over between four and five 'undred last week in 'Piecrusts.'"

"Oh!" said Mary, taken by surprise. "Then that—that's your only reason for wishing to leave?" And, as he did not reply, but went on swishing: "Come, Jim, if you've anything on your mind, say it out. The doctor didn't like the tone you spoke to him in, last night."

At this, the old man straightened his back, took a straw from between his teeth, spat, and said: "Well, if you must know, Mrs. Mahony, the doctor's not the boss it pleases me to be h'under any more—and that's the trewth. I'm tired of it—dog-tired. You can slave yer 'ead off for 'im, and 'e never notices a thing you do, h'or if 'e does, it's on'y to find fault. It h'aint 'uman, I say, and I'll be danged if I stand it h'any longer."

But people who came to Mary with criticism of Richard got no mercy. She spoke up warmly: "You're far too touchy, Jim —that's what I say. *You* know, if any one does, how rushed and busy the doctor is, and you ought to be the first to make allowance for him—after all he's done for you. You wouldn't be here now, if it hadn't been for him. And then to expect him to notice and praise you for every little job you do!"

But Jim was stubborn. 'E didn't want to deny anything. But 'e'd rather go. An' this day week, if it suited her.

"It's really dreadful how uppish the lower classes get here, as soon as they have a little money in their pocket," she said to herself, as she walked the shadeless, sandy road. But this thought was like a shadow cast by her husband's mind on hers, and was ousted by the more indigenous: "But on the whole, who can blame him, poor old fellow, for wanting to take life easy, if he has the chance." She even added: "He might have gone off, as most of them do, without giving notice at all."

Then her mind reverted to what he had said of Richard, and she pondered the antagonism that had shown through his words. It was not the first time she had run up against this spirit—she had met with it in many quarters—but, as usual, she was at a loss to explain it. Why should people of Old Jim's class dislike Richard as they did?—find him so hard to get on with? He was invariably considerate of them, and treated them very generously with regard to money. And yet . . . for some reason or other they felt injured by him; and thought and spoke of him with a kind of churlish resentment. She was not clever enough to find the key to the riddle—it was no such simple explanation as that he felt himself too good for them. That was not the case: he was proud, certainly, but she had never known any one who—under, it was true, a rather sarcastic manner—was more broadly tolerant of his fellowmen. Hence, she wound up her soliloquy with the lame admission: "Yes, in spite of all his kindness, I suppose he *is* queer . . . decidedly queer," and then she heaved a sigh. What a pity it was! When you knew him to be, at heart, such a dear, good, well-meaning man.

A short walk brought her to the four-roomed cottage where Ned lived with wife and children. Or had lived, till lately. He had been missing from his home now for over a week. On the last occasion of his being in Melbourne with the carrying-van, he had decamped, leaving the boy who was with him to make the return-journey alone. Since then, nothing could be heard of him; and his billet in the Agency had been snapped up.

"Or so they say!" said his wife, with an angry sniff. "I don't believe a word of it, Mary. Since the railway's come, biz has gone to the dogs; and they're only too glad to get the chance of sacking another man."

Polly was louder and untidier than ever; she wore a slatternly wrapper; her hair was thrust unbrushed into its net. But she suffered, no doubt, in her own way; she was red-eyed, and very hasty-handed with her nestful of babies. Sitting in the cheerless parlour, Ned's dark-eyed eldest on her knee, Mary strove to soothe and encourage. But: it has never been much of a home for the poor boy, was her private opinion; and she pressed her cheek affectionately against the little black curly head that was a replica of Ned's own.

"What's goin' to become of us all, the Lord only knows," said Polly, after having had the good cry the sympathetic presence of her sister-in-law justified. "I'm not a brown cent troubled about Ned—only boilin' with 'im. 'E's off on the booze, sure enough—and 'e'll turn up again, safe and sound, like loose fish always do.— Wait till I catch 'im, though! He'll get it hot.

"We never ought to have come here," she went on, drying her eyes. "Drat the place, and all that's in it, that's what I say! He did better'n this in Castlemaine; and I'd pa behind me there. But once Richard sent 'im that twenty quid, he'd no rest till he got away. And I thought, when he was so set on it, may be it'd have a good effect on 'im, to be near you both. But that was just another shoot into the brown. You've been A1, Mary; you've done your level best. But Richard's never treated Ned fair. He's too hard on 'im; I've always said it. I don't want to take Ned's part; he's nothing in the world but a pretty-faced noodle. But Richard's treated 'im as if he was the dirt under 'is feet. And Ned's felt it. That's why he couldn't ever get up any respect for 'imself. Oh, I know whose doing it was we were never asked up to the house, when you'd company. It wasn't *yours*, my dear! But we can't all have hyphens to our names, and go driving round with kid gloves on our hands, and our noses in the air."

Mary felt quite depressed by this fresh attack on her husband. Reminding herself, however, that Polly was excited and over-wrought, she did not speak out the defence that leapt to her tongue. She said staunchly: "As you put it, Polly, it does seem as if we haven't acted rightly towards Ned. But it wasn't Richard's doing alone. I've been just as much to blame as he has."

She sat on, petting the fractious children, and giving kindly assurances: as long as she and Richard had anything themselves, Ned's wife and Ned's children should not want: and, as she spoke, she slipped a substantial proof of her words into Polly's unproud hand. Besides, she believed there was every chance now of Ned soon being restored to them; and she told how Richard was going, that very morning, to invoke Mr. Smith's aid. Mr. Smith was in the Police, as Polly knew, and had influential friends among the Force in Melbourne. By to-morrow, there might be good news to bring her.

Almost an hour had passed when she rose to go. Mrs. Ned was so grateful for the visit and the help, that, out in the narrow little passage, she threw her arms round Mary's neck and drew her to her bosom. Holding her thus, after several hearty kisses, she said in a mysterious whisper, with her lips close to Mary's ear: "Mary, love, may I say something to you?" and the permission granted, went on: "That is, give you a bit of a hint, dearie?"

"Why, of course you may, Polly."

"Sure you won't feel hurt, dear?"

"Quite sure. What is it?" and Mary disengaged herself, that she might look the speaker in the face.

"Well, it's just this—you mentioned the name yourself, or I wouldn't have dared it. It's young Mr. Smith, Mary. My dear, in future don't you have 'im quite so much about the house as you do at present. It ain't the thing. People *will* talk, you know, if you give 'em a handle." ("Oh, but Polly!" in a thunderstruck voice from Mary.) "Now, now, I'm not blaming you—not the least tiddly-wink. But there's no harm in being careful, is there, love, if you don't want your name in people's mouths? I'm that fond of you, Mary—you don't mind me speaking, dearie?"

"No, Polly, I don't. But it's the greatest nonsense—I never heard such a thing!" said Mary hotly. "Why, Purdy is Richard's oldest friend: They were schoolboys together."

"Maybe they were. But I hear 'e's mostly up at your place when Richard's out. And you're a young and pretty woman, my dear; it's Richard who ought to think of it, and he so much older than you. Well, just take the hint, love. It comes best, don't it, from one of the family?"

But Mary left the house in a sad flurry; and even forgot, for a street-length, to open her parasol, using it instead to prod the ground with, as she walked.

Her first impulse was to go straight to Richard. But she had not covered half a dozen yards before she saw that this would never do. At the best of times, Richard abominated gossip; and the fact of it having, in the present case, dared to fasten its fangs in some one belonging to him would make him doubly wroth. He might even try to find out who had started the talk; and get himself into hot water over it. Or he might want to lay all the blame on his own shoulders—make himself the reproaches Ned's Polly had not spared him. Worse still, he would perhaps accuse Purdy of inconsiderateness towards her, and fly into a rage with him; and then the two of them would quarrel, which would be a thousand pities. For, though he often railed at Purdy, yet that was only Richard's way: he was genuinely fond of him, and unbent to him as to nobody else.

But these were just so many pretexts put forward to herself by Mary for keeping silence; the real reason lay deeper. Eight years of married life had left her, where certain subjects were concerned, with all the modesty of her girlhood intact. There were things, indelicate things, which *could* not be spoken out, even between husband and wife. For her to have to step before Richard and say: some one else feels for me in the same way as you, my husband, do, would make her, ever after, unable frankly to meet his eyes. Besides giving the vague, cobwebby stuff a body it did not deserve.

Yet again, this was not the whole truth: she had another, more uncomfortable side of it to face; and the flies buzzed unheeded round her head. The astonishment she had shown at her sister-in-law's warning had not been altogether sincere. Far down in her heart Mary found a faint, faint trace of complicity. For months past—she could admit it now—she had not felt easy about Purdy. Something disagreeable, disturbing, had crept into their relations. The frank, brotherly manner she liked so well had deserted him; besides, short-tempered, he had grown deadly serious, and not the stupidest woman could fail altogether to see what the matter was.— But she had wilfully bandaged her eyes. And if, now and then, some word or look had pierced her guard, and disquieted her in spite of herself, she had left it at an incredulous: "Oh, but then. . . . But even if . . . In that case. . . ." She now saw her fervent hope had been that the affair would blow over, without coming to anything; prove to be just another passing fancy on the part of the unstable Purdy. How many had she not assisted at! This very summer, for instance, a charming young lady from Sydney had stayed with the Urquharts; and, as long as her visit lasted, they had seen little or nothing of Purdy. Whenever he got off duty, he was at Yarangobilly. As it happened, however, Mr. Urquhart himself had been so assiduous in taking his guest about—to picnics, races and lawn-parties—that Purdy had had small chance of making an impression. And, in looking back on the incident, what now rose most clearly before Mary's mind was the way in which Mrs. Urquhart—poor thing, she was never able to go anywhere with her husband: either she had a child in arms, or another coming; the row of toddlers mounted up in steps—the way in which she had said, with her pathetic smile: "Ah, my dear! Willie needs some one gayer and stronger than I am, for company." Mary's heart had been full of pity at the time, for her friend in her woman's lot; and it swelled again now, at the remembrance.

But, oh, dear! this was straying from the point. Impatiently she jerked her thoughts back to herself and her own dilemma. What ought she to do? She was not a person who could sit still, with folded hands, and await events. How would it be if she spoke to Purdy herself? . . . talked seriously to him about his work? . . . tried to persuade him to leave Ballarat. Did he mean to hang on here for ever, she would say—did he never intend to seek promotion?—go in for being a sergeant-major or a superintendent, in another district? But then again, the mere questioning would cause a certain awkwardness. While, at the slightest trip or blunder on her part, what was unsaid might suddenly find itself said; and the whole thing cease to be the vague, cloudy affair it was at present. And, though she would actually prefer this to happen with regard to Purdy than to Richard, yet . . . yet. . . .

Worried and perplexed, unable to see before her the straight plain path she loved, Mary once more sighed from the bottom of her heart.

"Oh dear me! If *only* men wouldn't be so foolish!"

Left to himself, Mahony put away his books, washed his hands, and summoned one by one to his presence the people who waited in the adjoining room. He drew a tooth, dressed a wounded wrist, prescribed for divers internal disorders—all told, a baker's dozen of odd jobs.

When the last patient had gone, he propped open the door, wiped his forehead, and read the thermometer that hung on the wall: it marked 102°. Dejectedly he drove, in fancy, along the glaring, treeless roads, inches deep in cinnamon-coloured dust. How one learnt to hate the sun out here! What wouldn't he give for a cool, grey-green Irish day, with a wet wind blowing in from the sea?—a day, the like of which he had heedlessly wasted hundreds of, in his youth. Now, it made his mouth water only to think of them.

It still wanted ten minutes to ten o'clock; the buggy had not yet come round. He would have five minutes' rest before starting: he had been out the greater part of the night, and, on getting home, had not been able to sleep for neuralgia.— He lay down on the sofa.

When, an hour later, Mary reached home, she was amazed to find groom and buggy still drawn up in front of the house.

"Why, Molyneux, what's the matter? Where's the doctor?"

"I'm sure I don't know, Mrs. Mahony. I've hollered to Biddy half a dozen times, but she doesn't take any notice. And the mare's that restless. . . . There, there, steady old girl, steady now! It's these damn flies."

Mary hurried indoors. "Why, Biddy. . . ."

"Shure and it's yourself," said the big Irishwoman, who now filled the kitchen-billet. "Faith and though you scold me, Mrs. Mahony, I couldn't bring it over me heart to wake him. The pore man's sleeping like a saint."

"Biddy, you ought to know better!" cried Mary, peeling off her gloves, to be ready for action.

"It's pale as the dead he is."

"Rubbish. It's only the reflection of the green blind.— *Richard!* Do you know what time it is?"

But the first syllable of his name was enough. "Good Lord, Mary, I must have dropped off. What the dickens. . . . Come, help me, wife. Why on earth didn't those fools wake me?"

Mary held his driving-coat, and fetched hat and gloves, while he flung the necessaries into his bag. "Have you much to do this morning? Oh, that aut . . . that post-mortem's at twelve, isn't it?"

"Yes; and a consultation with Munce at eleven— I'll just manage it, and no more," muttered Mahony with an eye on his watch. "I can't let the mare take it easy this morning.— Yes, a full day. And Henry Ocock's fidgeting for a second opinion on his wife; thinks she's not making rapid enough progress.— Well, ta-ta, sweetheart! Don't expect me back to lunch." And, taking a short cut across the lawn, Richard jumped into the buggy, and off they flew.

Mary's thoughts were all for him in this moment. "How proud we ought to feel!" she said to herself. "That makes the second time in a week old Munce has sent for him.— But how like Henry Ocock," she went on, with a puckered brow. "It's quite insulting—after the trouble Richard has put himself to.

If Agnes's case puzzles him, I should like to know who will understand it better. I think I'll go and see her myself, this afternoon. It can't be *her* wish to call in a stranger."

Not till some time after, did she remember her own private embarrassment. And, by then, the incident had taken its proper place in her mind—had sunk to the level of insignificance to which it belonged.

"Such a piece of nonsense!" was her final verdict. "As if I could worry Richard with it, when he has so many really important things to occupy him."

[5]

YES, those were palmy days; the rate at which the practice spread and grew astonished even himself. No slack seasons for him nowadays; winter saw him as busy as summer; and his chief ground for complaint was that he was unable to devote the meticulous attention he would have wished, to each individual case.— "It would need the strength of an elephant to do that." But it was impossible not to feel gratified by the many marks of confidence he received. And if his work had but left him some leisure for study, and for an occasional holiday, he would have been content. But in these years he was never able to get his neck out of the yoke; and Mary had to take her annual jaunts to Melbourne and sea-breezes, alone.

In a long talk they had with each other, it was agreed that, except in an emergency, he was to be chary of entering into fresh engagements—this referred, of course, in the first place to confinements, of which his book was always full; and secondly, to outlying bush-cases, the journey to and from which wasted many a precious hour. And where it would have been impolitic to refuse a new and influential patient, some one on his list—a doubtful payer, or a valetudinarian—was gently to be let drop. And it was Mary that arranged who this should be. Some umbrage was bound to be given in the process; but, with her help, it was reduced to a minimum. For Mary knew by heart all the links and ramifications of the houses at which he visited: knew precisely who was related to whom, by blood, or marriage, or business; knew where offence might with safety be risked, and where it would do him harm. She had also a woman's tact in smoothing things over. A born doctor's wife, declared Mahony in grateful acknowledgment. For himself, he could not keep such fiddling details in his head for two minutes on end.

But though he thus succeeded in setting bounds to his activity, he still had a great deal too much to do; and, in tired moments, or when tic plagued him, he thought the sole way out of the impasse would be, to associate some one with himself, as partner or assistant. And once he was within an ace of doing so, chance throwing what he considered a likely person across his path. Whilst attending a coroner's inquest at the "George," he made the acquaintance of a member of the profession who was on his way from the Ovens district—a coach journey of well over two hundred miles—to a place called Walwala, a day's ride to the west of Ballarat. And since he was a pleasant-spoken man, and intelligent—though with a somewhat down-at-heel look about him—besides being a complete stranger to the town, Mahony impulsively took him home to dinner. In the evening they sat and talked in the surgery. The visitor, whose name was Wakefield, was considerably Mahony's senior. By his own account, he had had but a rough time of it for the past couple of years. A good practice which he had worked up in the seaport of Warrnambool had come to an untimely end. He did not enter into the reasons for this. "I was unfortunate . . . had a piece of ill-luck," was how he referred to it. And Mahony, knowing how fatally easy was a trip in diagnosis, a slip of the scalpel, tactfully helped him over the allusion. From Warrnambool, Wakefield had gone to the extreme north of the colony; but the eighteen months spent there had nearly been his undoing. Money had not come in badly; but his wife and family had suffered from the great heat; and the scattered nature of the work had worn him to skin and bone. Again, no second opinion was to be had, within a radius of many miles. The knowledge of this weighed on him so heavily that his health threatened to break down. Hence he was now casting about him for a more suitable place. He could not afford to buy a practice, must just creep in where he found a vacancy. And Walwala, where, he understood, there had never been a resident practitioner, seemed to offer an opening.

Mahony felt genuinely sorry for the man; and, after he had gone, sat and revolved the idea, in the event of Walwala proving unsuitable, of offering Wakefield a post temporarily as

319

assistant. It would help the latter over a tight place, and also provide himself with an opportunity of judging whether or no it was feasible to divide up his work. He went to bed full of the scheme, and broached it to Mary before they slept. Mary made big eyes to herself, as she listened. Like a wise wife, however, she did not press her own views that night, while the idea bubbled hot in him; for, at such times, when some new project seemed to promise the millennium, he stood opposition badly. But she lay awake, telling off the reasons she would put before him in the morning, and, in the dark, she allowed herself a tender, tickled little smile at his expense.

"What a man he is for loading himself up with the wrong sort of people!" she reflected. "And then, afterwards, he gets tired of them, and impatient with them—as, of course, it's only natural he should."

At the breakfast-table, she came back on the subject herself. In her opinion, he ought to think very carefully indeed over what he proposed to do. Not another doctor on Ballarat had an assistant; and his patients would be sure to resent the novelty. Those who sent for Dr. Mahony would not thank you to be handed over to "goodness knows who." He must remember how it was when you went, say, to have a tooth pulled out: if you were fobbed off with any one but the dentist himself, you felt as though you were being cheated out of half your money's worth. Later on, when he had the leading practice in the district, and could ask what fees he liked, it would be different. But, even then, he must take a young man, much younger than himself, and very strong.

"Besides that, Richard, as things are now, the money wouldn't really go so far, would it? And just as we have begun to be a little easy ourselves—I'm afraid you'd miss many comforts you have got used to again, dear," she wound up, with a mental glance at the fine linen and smooth service Richard loved.

Yes, that was true, admitted Mahony with a sigh; and, being this morning in a stale mood, he forthwith knocked flat the card-house it had amused him to build. Himself he had only half believed in it; or believed so long as he refrained from going into prosaic details. There was work for two and money for one—that was the crux of the matter. Successful as the practice was, it still did not throw off a thousand a year. Bad debts ran to a couple of hundred annually; and their improved style of living—the expenses of house and garden, of horses and vehicles, the men-servants, the open house one had to keep—swallowed every penny of the rest. Saving was actually harder than when his income had been but a third of what it was at present. New obligations beset him. For one thing, he had to keep pace with his colleagues and rivals; to make a show of being just as well-to-do as they. Retrenching was out of the question. His patients would at once imagine that something was wrong—the practice on the downgrade, his skill deserting him—and take their ailments and their fees elsewhere. No, the more one had, the more one was forced to spend; and the few odd hundreds for which Henry Ocock could be counted on yearly, came in exceedingly handy. As a rule, he laid these by for Mary's benefit; for her visits to Melbourne, her bonnets and gowns. It also let her satisfy the needs of her generous little heart in matters of hospitality—well, it was perhaps not fair to lay the whole blame of their incessant and lavish entertaining, at her door. He himself knew that it would not do for them to lag a foot behind, in this respect; the results would soon be painfully visible if they did.

Hence, the day on which he would be free to dismiss the subject of money from his mind seemed as far off as ever. He might indulge wild schemes of taking an assistant or partner; the plain truth was, he could not do without even the sum needed to settle in a *locum tenens* for three months, while he recuperated.— Another and equally valid reason was that the right man for a *locum* was far to seek. It would be hurtful to the practice, now that he had worked it up to its present pitch, to hand it over to some well-established medico who had enough to do with his own; and equally foolish to intrust it to a new man, with insufficient experience or a raw manner. The greater number of his patients were women, and kittle cattle to deal with. As time went on, he found himself pushed more and more over into a single branch of medicine—one, too, he had never meant to let grow over his head, in this fashion. For it was common medical knowledge out here that, given the distances, and the general lack of conveniences, thirty to forty maternity cases per year were as much as a practitioner could with comfort take in hand. *His* books for the past year stood at over a hundred! The nightwork this meant was unbearable, infants showing a perverse disinclination to enter this world except under cover of the dark.

His popularity—if such it could be called—with the other sex was something of a mystery to him. For he had not one manner for the bedside and another for daily life. He never sought to ingratiate himself with people, or to wheedle them; still less would he stoop to bully, or intimidate; he was by preference the adviser rather than the dictator. And men did not greatly care for his arm's-length attitude; they wrote him down haughty and indifferent; and pinned their faith to a blunter, homelier manner. But with women it was otherwise; and these also appreciated the fact that, no matter what their rank in life, their age or their looks, he met them with the deference he believed due to their sex. Exceptions there were, of course. Affectation or insincerity angered him; and with the "Zaras" of this world he had scant patience; while among the women themselves, some few—Ned's wife, for example—felt resentment at his very appearance, his gestures, his tricks of speech. But the majority were his staunch partisans; and it was becoming more and more the custom to engage Dr. Mahony months ahead, thus binding him severely fast. And though he would sometimes give Mary a fright, by vowing that he was going "to throw up mid. and be done with it," yet her ambition—and what an ambitious wife she was, no one but himself knew—that he should some day be one of the leading specialists on Ballarat, or a consultant of the first water, seemed not unlikely of fulfilment. If his health kept good. And . . . if he could possibly hold out!

For there still came times when he believed that, to turn his back for ever, on place and people, would make him the happiest of mortals. As long as he had been forced to keep his nose to the grindstone to earn his bread and butter, the idea had left him in peace. Now, it haunted him again. That was perhaps because he had at last grasped the unpalatable truth that it would never be his luck to save: if saving were the only key to freedom, he would still be there, still held fast, and though he lived to be a hundred. Certain it was, he did not become a better colonist, as the years went on. He had learnt to hate the famous climate—the dust, and drought, and brazen skies; the drenching rains, and bottomless mud—to rebel against the interminable hours he was doomed to spend in his buggy. By nature he was a recluse—not an outdoor-man at all. He was tired, too, of the general rampage, the promiscuous connections, and slapdash familiarity of colonial life; sick to death of the all-absorbing struggle to grow richer than his neighbours. He didn't give a straw for money in itself—only for what it brought him. And what was the good of that, if he had no leisure to enjoy it? Or was it the truth that he feared being dragged into the vortex? . . . of learning to care, he, too, whether or no his name topped subscription-lists; whether his entertainments were the most sumptuous; his wife the best-dressed woman in her set?— Perish the thought!

He did not disquiet Mary by speaking of these things. Still less did he try to explain to her another, more elusive side of the matter. It was this. Did he dig deep into himself, he saw that his uncongenial surroundings were not alone to blame for his restless state of mind. There was in him a gnawing desire for change, as change; a distinct fear of being pinned for too long to the same spot; or, to put it another way, a conviction that to live on without change, meant decay. For him, at least. Of course, it was weak to yield to feelings of this kind; at his age, in his position, with a wife dependent on him. And so he fought them—even while he indulged them. For this was the year in which, casting the question of expense to the four winds, he pulled down and rebuilt his house. It came over him one morning, on waking, that he could not go on in the old one for another day, so cramped was he, so tortured by its lath-and-plaster thinness. He had difficulty in winning Mary over; she was against the outlay, the trouble and confusion involved; and was only reconciled by the more solid comforts and greater conveniences offered her. For the new house was of brick, the first brick house to be built on Ballarat (and oh, the joy! said Richard, of walls so thick that you could not hear through them), had an extra-wide verandah, which might be curtained in for parties and dances; and a side-entrance for patients, such as Mary had often sighed for.

As a result of the new grandeur more and more flocked to his door: in consequence, he threw up a couple of lodges. He had once been thankful to get them; now, the work they entailed was poorly paid, compared with the rest of the practice. Besides, the present promised to be a record year, even in the annals of the Golden City. The completion of the railway-line to Melbourne, by way of Geelong, was the outstanding event. Virtually halving the distance to the metropolis in count of time, it brought a host of new people—capitalists, speculators, politicians—about the town. Money grew perceptibly easier. Letters came much more quickly, too; and Melbourne newspapers could be handled, as it were, moist from the press. One no longer had the sense of lying shut off from the world, behind the high wall of a tedious coach-journey. And the merry Ballaratians, who had never feared or shrunk from the discomforts of this journey, now travelled constantly up and down: attending the Melbourne race-meetings; the Government House balls and lawn-parties; bringing back the gossip of Melbourne, together with its fashions in dress, music, and social life.

Mary, in particular, profited by the change; for John Turnham, in one of those "general posts" so frequently played by the colonial cabinet, had turned up Minister of Railways: hence, she could have a "free pass" for the asking. John paid numerous visits to his constituency: came to lay a foundation-stone, with masonic honours; to open the new Town Hall, or a wing of the Hospital: but he was now such an important personage that his relatives did not always get a sight of him. As likely as not, he was the guest of the Henry Ococks, in their new mansion, or of the mayor of the borough. In the past two years, Mahony had only twice exchanged a word with his brother-in-law.

And then they met again.

In Melbourne, at six o'clock on a January morning, the Honourable John, about to enter a saloon-compartment of the Ballarat train, paused, with one foot on the step, and, disregarding the polite remarks of the station-master, who was at his heels, screwed up his rather prominent black eyes against the sun. At the farther end of the train, a tall, thin, fair-whiskered man was peering disconsolately along a row of crowded carriages. "God bless me! isn't that . . . Why, so it is!" And leaving the official standing, John walked smartly down the platform.

"My dear Mahony!—this is indeed a surprise. I had no idea you were in town.

"Why not have let me know you purposed coming?" he inquired, as they made their way, the train meanwhile held up on their account, towards John's spacious, reserved saloon.

("What he means is, why I didn't beg a free pass of him!")

And Mahony, to whom few things were more distasteful than the asking of favours, laid an exaggerated emphasis on his own want of knowledge. He had not contemplated the journey till an hour beforehand. Then, a messenger had come running to say that, the proposed delegate having been suddenly taken ill, he was urgently requested to represent the Masonic Lodge to which he belonged, in Melbourne that same evening, at the Installation of a new Grand Master.

"Ah, then you found it possible to get out of harness, for once?" said John affably, as they took their seats.

"Yes, by a lucky chance I had no case on hand that could not get on without me for twenty-four hours. And my engagement-book I can leave with perfect confidence to my wife."

"Mary is no doubt a very capable woman; I noticed that afresh, when last she was with us," returned John; and went on to tick off Mary's qualities, like a connoisseur appraising the points of a horse. "What a misfortune that she is not blessed with any family!" he added.

Mahony stiffened: this was a point on which he brooked no criticism of his wife. He responded drily: "I'm not sure that I agree with you. With all her energy and spirit, Mary is none too strong."

"Well, well! these things are in the hands of Providence; we must take what is sent us." And caressing his bare chin, John gave a hearty yawn.

The words flicked Mahony's memory: John had had an addition to his family that winter, in the shape—to the disappointment of all concerned—of a second daughter. Mahony offered belated congratulations. "A regular Turnham as to complexion, this time, according to Mary. But I am sorry to hear Jane has not recovered her strength."

"Oh, Jane is doing very well. But it has been a real disadvantage that she could not nurse. The infant is . . . well, ah . . . perfectly formed, of course, but small—small."

"You must send both Jane and the baby to Mary, to be looked after."

The talk then passed to John's son, now a schoolboy in Geelong; and John admitted that the reports he received of the lad continued as unsatisfactory as ever. "The young rascal has ability, they tell me, but no application." John propounded various theories to account for the boy having turned out poorly, chief among which was that he had been left too long in the hands of women. They had over-indulged him. "Mary no more than the rest, my dear fellow," he hastened to smooth down Mahony's rising plumes. "It began with his mother, in the first place. Yes, poor Emma was weak with the boy—lamentably weak!"

Here, with a disconcerting abruptness, John drew to him a blue linen bag that lay on the seat, and, loosening its string, took out a sheaf of official papers, in which he was soon engrossed. He had had enough of Mahony's conversation in the meantime, or so it seemed; had thought of something better to do, and did it.

His brother-in-law eyed him as he read. "He's a bad colour," said the doctor in him. "Been living too high, no doubt."

A couple of new books and a paper-knife were on the seat by Mahony, but he let them lie. He had a tiring day behind him, and the briefest of nights. Besides the masonic ceremony, which had lasted into the small hours, he had undertaken to make various purchases, not the least difficult of which was the buying of a present for Mary—all the little fal-lals that go to finish a lady's ball-dress. Railway-travelling was, too, something of a novelty to him nowadays; and he sat idly watching the landscape unroll, and thinking of nothing in particular. The train was running through mile after mile of flat, treeless country, which was liberally sprinkled with trapstones and clumps of tussock grass. At a distance these could be mistaken for couched sheep. One and all, earth, stones, tuft, were of a yellowish lichen-grey. Here and there stood a solitary she-oak. This, most doleful of trees, with its scraggy, pine-needle foliage, was also bleached to grey. From the several little stations along the line: mere three-sided sheds, which bore a printed invitation to intending passengrs to wave a flag or light a lamp, did they wish to board the train: from these shelters, long, bare, red roads, straight as ruled lines, ran back into the heart of the burnt-up, faded country. Now and then, a moving ruddy cloud on one of them told of some vehicle crawling its laborious way.— Mahony watched till the dust and heat overcame him, and his eyelids fell.

When John, his memoranda digested, looked up, ready to resume their talk—either on a scheme that was under discussion for turning the Great Swamp into a lake, or some other equally striking proof of local enterprise—he found that Mahony had dropped asleep; and, since his first sentence, loudly uttered before he was aware of it, did not rouse the sleeper, he took out his case, chose a cigar, beheaded it, and puffed it alight.

While he smoked, he studied his insensible relative. Mahony was sitting hunched up, in the uncomfortable attitude of one who drops asleep in an upright position: his head had fallen forward and to the side, his mouth was open, his gloved hands lay limp on his knee.

"H'm!" said John to himself, as he gazed. And: "H'm!" he repeated, after an interval.— Then, pulling down his waistcoat, and generally giving himself a shake to rights, he reflected that, for his own two-and-forty years, he was a very well preserved man indeed.

[6]

"Oh, Richard! . . . and my dress is blue!" said Mary distractedly, and sitting back on her heels she let her arms fall to her sides. She was on her knees, and before her lay a cardboard box, from which she had withdrawn a pink fan, pink satin boots with stockings to match, and a pink head-dress.

"Well, why the dickens didn't you say so?" burst out the giver.

"I did, dear. As plainly as I could speak."

"Never heard a word!"

"Because you weren't listening. I told you so, at the time.— Now what *am* I to do?" and, in her worry over the contretemps, Mary quite forgot to thank her husband for the trouble he had been to, on her behalf.

"Get another gown to go with them."

"Oh, Richard . . . how like a man! After all the time and money this one has cost me! No, I couldn't do that. Besides, Agnes Ocock is wearing pink, and wouldn't like it." And Mary, with a forehead full of wrinkles, began slowly to replace the articles in their sheaths. "Of course they're very nice," she added, as her fingers touched the delicate textures.

"They would need to be, considering what I paid for them. I wish now I'd kept my money in my pocket."

"Well, your mistake is hardly my fault, is it, dear?" remonstrated Mary mildly. But Richard had gone off, in a mood midway between self-annoyance and the huff.

Mary's first thought was to send the articles to Jinny, with a request to exchange them for their counterparts in the proper colour. Then she dismissed the idea. Blind slave to her increased nursery that Jinny was, she would hardly be likely to give the matter her personal supervision: the box would just be returned to the shop, and the transfer left to the shop-people's discretion. They might even want to charge more. No, another plan occurred to Mary. Agnes Ocock might not yet have secured the various small extras to go with her ball-dress; and, if not, how nice it would be to make her a present of these. They were finer, in better taste, than anything to be had on Ballarat; and she had long owed Agnes some return for her many kindnesses. Herself she would just make do with the simpler things she could buy in the town. And so, without saying anything to Richard, who would probably have objected that Henry Ocock was well able to afford to pay for his own wife's finery, Mary tied up the box and drove to Plevna House, on the outer edge of Yuille's Swamp.

—"Oh, no, I could never have got myself such beautiful things as these, Mary," and Mrs. Henry let her hands play lovingly with the silk stockings, her pretty face a-glow with pleasure. "Henry has no understanding, dear, for the etceteras of a costume. He thinks, if he pays for a dress or a mantle, that that is enough; and when the *little* bills come in, he grumbles at what he calls my extravagance. I sometimes wish, do you know, Mary, I had kept back just a teeny-weeny bit of my own money. Henry would never have missed it, and I should have been able to pay a small bill for myself now and then. As it is, love, I am sometimes even obliged to have my walking-boots put to Miss Skeffy the dressmaker's account.— But you know how it is at first, love. Our one idea is to hand over everything we possess to our lord and master."

She tried on the satin boots; they were a little long, but she would stuff out the toes with wadding. "If I am *really* not robbing you, Mary?"

Mary reassured her, and thereupon a visit was paid to the nursery, where Mr. Henry's son and heir lay sprawling in his cradle. Afterwards they sat and chatted on the verandah, while a basket was being filled with peaches for Mary to take home.

Agnes Ocock was just as sweet and natural as of old; but
not even the kindly drapery of a morning-wrapper could conceal the fact that she was growing very stout—quite losing her
fine figure. That came of her having given up her riding-exer-
cise. And all to please Mr. Henry. He did not ride himself, and
felt nervous, or perhaps a little jealous, when his wife was on
horseback.

Agnes was still very pretty—though, by daylight, the fine
bloom of her cheeks began to break up into a network of tiny
veins—and her fair, smooth brow bore no trace of the tragedy
she had gone through. The double tragedy; for, soon after the
master of Dandaloo's death, in a Melbourne lunatic asylum,
the little son of the house had died, not yet fourteen years of
age, in an Inebriates' Home. Far was it from Mary to wish her
friend to brood or repine; but to have ceased to remember as
utterly as Agnes had done, had something callous about it;
and, in her own heart, Mary consecrated a fresh regret to the
memory of the poor little stepchild of fate.

The ball for which all these silken niceties were purchased
had been organised to raise funds for a public monument to
the two explorers, Burke and Wills; and was to be one of the
grandest ever given in Ballarat. His Excellency the Governor,
who, shortly before, had come up to lay the foundation-stone
of the monument, would, it was hoped, be present in person.
The ladies had taken extraordinary pains with their dress; and
there had been the usual grumblings at expense on the part of
the husbands; though not a man but wished, and privately
expected *his* wife "to take the shine out of all the rest."

Mary had besought Richard to keep that evening free—it
was her lot always to go out to entertainments under some one
else's wing—and he had promised to do his best. But, a burnt
child in this respect, Mary said she would believe it when she
saw it; and the trend of events justified her scepticism. The
night arrived; she was on the point of adjusting her wreath of
forget-me-nots before her candle-lit mirror, when the dreaded
summons came. Mahony had to change, and hurry off, without
a moment's delay.

"Send for Purdy. He'll see you across," he said as he banged
the front door.

But Mary dispatched the gardener at a run with a note to

Tilly Ocock, who, she knew, would make room for her in her double-seated buggy.

Grindle got out, and Mary, her bunchy skirts held to her, took his place at the back, beside Mrs. Amelia. Tilly sat next the driver, and talked to them over her shoulder—a great big jolly rattle of a woman, who had never had a wish crossed since her marriage, and who ruled her surroundings autocratically.

"Lor, no—we left 'im counting eggs," she answered an inquiry on Mary's part. "Pa's got in a brood of Cochin Chinas, that's the pride and glory of 'is heart. And 'e's built 'imself the neatest little place for 'em you could meet on a summer's day: you *must* come over and admire it, my dear—that'll please 'im, no end. It was a condition I made for 'is going on keeping fowls. They were a perfect nuisance, all over the garden, and round the kitchen and the back, till it wasn't safe to put your foot down anywhere—fowls *are* such messy things! At last I up and said I wouldn't have it any longer. So then 'e and Tom set to work last week, and built themselves a fowl-house and a run. And there they spend their days now, thinking out improvements."

Here, Tilly gave the driver a cautionary dig with her elbow; as she did so, an under-pocket chinked ominously. "Look out now, Davy, what you're doing with us!— Yes, that's splosh, Mary. I always bring a bag of change with me, my dear, so that those who lose shan't have that excuse for not paying up."— Tilly was going to pass her evening as usual at the card-table. "Well, I hope you two'll enjoy yourselves.— Remember now, Mrs. Grindle, if you please, that you're a married woman and must behave yourself, and not go in for any high jinks," she teased her prim little stepdaughter, as they dismounted from the conveyance and stood straightening their petticoats, at the entrance to the hall.

"You know Matilda, I do not intend to dance to-night," said Mrs. Amelia, in her sedate fashion: it was as if she sampled each word before parting with it.

"Oh, I know, bless you! and know why, too. If only it's not another false alarm! Poor old pa'd so like to have a grandchild 'e was allowed to carry round. 'E mustn't go near Henry's, of course, for fear the kid 'ud swallow one of 'is dropped aitches and choke over it." And Tilly threw back her head and

330

laughed. "But you must hurry up, Mely, you know, if you want to oblige 'im."

"Really, Tilly!" expostulated Mary. ("She sometimes *does* go too far," she thought to herself. "The poor little woman!") "Let us two keep together," she said, as she took Amelia's arms. "I don't intend to dance much either, as my husband isn't here."

But, once inside the gaily decorated hall, she found it impossible to keep her word. Even on her way to a seat beside Agnes Ocock she was repeatedly stopped, and, when she sat down, up came first one, then another, to "request the pleasure." She could not go on refusing everybody: it would look, if she did, as if she deliberately set out to be peculiar—a horrible thought to Mary. Besides, many of those who made their bows were important, influential gentlemen; for Richard's sake she must treat them politely.

For his sake, again, she felt pleased; rightly or wrongly, she put the many attentions shown her down to the fact of her being his wife. So she turned and offered apologies to Agnes and Amelia, feeling at the same time thankful that Richard had not Mr. Henry's jealous disposition. There sat Agnes, looking as pretty as a picture, and was afraid to dance with any one but her own husband. And he preferred to play at cards!

"I think, dear, you might have ventured to accept the Archdeacon for a quadrille," she whispered behind her fan, as Agnes regretfully declined Mr. Long.

But Agnes shook her head. "It's better not, Mary. It saves trouble afterwards. Henry *doesn't* care to see it."— Perhaps Agnes herself, once a passionate dancer, was growing a little too comfortable, thought Mary, as her own programme wandered from hand to hand.

Among the last to arrive was Purdy, red with haste, and making a great thump with his lame leg as he crossed the floor. —("I wish I dare venture to give him a hint about it," was Mary's reflection.)

"I'm beastly late, Polly. What have you got left for me?"

"Why, really nothing, Purdy. I thought you weren't coming. But you may put your name down here, if you like," and Mary handed him her programme with her thumb on an empty space: she generally made a point of sitting out a dance with Purdy, that he might not feel neglected; and of late she had

331

been especially careful not to let him notice any difference in her treatment of him. But when he gave back the card, she found that he had scribbled his initials in all three blank lines. "Oh, you mustn't do that. I'm saving these for Richard."

"Our dance, I believe, Mrs. Mahony?" said a deep voice, as the band struck up "The Rats Quadrilles." And swaying this way and that, in her flounced blue tarletan, Mary rose, put her hand within the proffered crook, and went off with the Police Magistrate, an elderly greybeard; went to walk, or be teetotumed through the figures of the dance, with the supremely sane unconcern that she displayed towards all the arts.

—"What odd behaviour!" murmured Mrs. Henry, following Purdy's retreating form with her eyes. "He took no notice of us whatever. And did you see, Amelia, how he stood and stared after Mary? Quite rudely, I thought."

But, at this, Mrs. Grindle was forced to express an opinion of her own—always a trial for the nervous little woman. "I think it's because dear Mary looks so charming to-night, Agnes," she ventured, in her mouse-like way.

Then, Archdeacon Long came up and, dropping into the vacant seat, laid himself out to entertain the ladies.

It was after midnight when Mahony reached home. He would willingly have gone to bed, but having promised Mary to put in an appearance, he changed and walked down to the town.

The ball was at its height. He skirted the rotating couples, seeking Mary. Friends hailed him.

"Ah, well done, doctor!"

"So here you are at last?"

"Still in time for a spin, sir."

"Have you seen my wife?"

"Indeed and I have. Mrs. Mahony's the belle o' the ball," answered a colleague.

"Pleased to hear it. Where is she now?"

"Look here, Mahony, we've had a reg'lar dispute," cried Willie Urquhart pressing up; he was flushed, and decidedly garrulous. "Almost came to blows, we did, over whose was the finest pair o' shoulders—your wife's or Henry O.'s. I plumped for Mrs. M., and I b'lieve she topped the poll. By Jove, that blue gown makes 'em look just like . . . what shall I say? . . . like marble."

"Does fortune smile?" asked Mahony of Henry Ocock as he passed the card-players: he had cut Urquhart short with a nod. "So his Excellency didn't turn up, after all?"

"Not he. Sent a telegraphic communication at the last moment. No, I haven't seen her. But stay, there's Matilda wanting to speak to you, I believe."

Tilly was making all manner of signs to attract his attention.

"Good evening, doctor. Yes, I've a message. You'll find 'er in the cloakroom. She's been in there for the last half-'our or so. I think she's got the headache, or something of that sort, and is waiting for you to take 'er home."

—"Oh, thank goodness, there you are, Richard!" cried Mary as he opened the door of the cloakroom; and she rose from the bench on which she had been sitting with her shawl wrapped round her. "I thought you'd never come." She was pale, and looked distressed.

"Why, what's wrong, my dear? . . . feeling faint?" asked Mahony incredulously. "If so, you had better wait for the buggy. It won't be long now; you ordered it for two o'clock."

"No, no, I'm not ill, I'd rather walk," said Mary breathlessly. "Only please let us get away. And without making a fuss."

"But what's the matter?"

"I'll tell you as we go.— No, these boots won't hurt. And I can walk in them quite well. Fetch your own things, Richard."— Mary's one wish was to get her husband out of the building.

They stepped into the street; it was a hot night, and very dark. Mary, in her thin satin dancing-boots, leaned heavily on Richard's arm as they turned off the street-pavements into the unpaved roads.

Mahony let the lights of the main street go past; then said: "And now, Madam Wife, you'll perhaps be good enough to enlighten me as to what all this means?"

"Yes, dear, I will," answered Mary obediently. But her voice trembled; and Mahony was sharp of hearing.

"Why, Polly sweetheart . . . surely nothing serious?"

"Yes, it is. I've had a very unpleasant experience this evening, Richard—very unpleasant indeed. I hardly know how to tell you. I feel so upset."

"Come—out with it!"

In a low voice, with downcast eyes, Mary told her story. All had gone well till about twelve o'clock: she had danced with this partner and that, and had thoroughly enjoyed herself. Then came Purdy's turn. She was with Mrs. Long when he claimed her, and at once suggested that they should sit out the dance on one of the settees placed round the hall, where they could amuse themselves by watching the dancers. But Purdy took no notice— "He was strange in his manner from the very beginning"—and led her into one of the little rooms that opened off the main body of the hall.

"And I didn't like to object. We were conspicuous as it was, his foot made such a bumping noise on the floor; it was worse than ever, to-night, I thought."

For the same reason, though she had felt uncomfortable at being hidden away in there, she had not cared to refuse to stay: it seemed to make too much of the thing. Besides, she hoped some other couple would join them. But——

"But, Mary . . . wife!" broke from Mahony; he was blank and bewildered.

Purdy, however, had got up after a moment or two, and shut the door. And then— "Oh, it's no use, Richard, I can't tell you!" said poor Mary. "I don't know how to get the words over my lips. I think I've never felt so ashamed in all my life." And, worn out by the worry and excitement she had gone through, and afraid, in advance, of what she had still to face, Mary began to cry.

Mahony stood still; let her arm drop. "Do you mean me to understand, Mary," he demanded, as if unable to believe his ears: "to understand that Purdy . . . dared to . . . that he dared to behave to you in any but a——" And since Mary was using her pocket-handkerchief, and could not reply: "Good God! Has the fellow taken leave of his senses? Is he mad? Was he drunk? Answer me! What does it all mean?" And Mary still continuing silent, he threw off the hand she had replaced on his arm. "Then you must walk home alone. I'm going back to get at the truth of this."

But Mary clung to him. "No, no, you must hear the whole story first." Anything rather than let him return to the hall.— Yes, at first she thought he really had gone mad. "I can't tell you what I felt, Richard . . . knowing it was Purdy— just Purdy. To see him like that—looking so horrible—and

334

to have to listen to the dreadful things he said! Yes, I'm sure he had had too much to drink. His breath smelt so." She had tried to pull away her hands; but he had held her, had put his arms round her.

At the anger she felt racing through her husband she tightened her grip, stringing meanwhile phrase to phrase, with the sole idea of getting him safely indoors. Not till they were shut in the bedroom did she give the most humiliating detail of any: how, while she was still struggling to free herself from Purdy's embrace, the door opened and Mr. Grindle made as if to enter. "He drew back at once, of course. But it was awful, Richard! I turned cold. It seemed to give me more strength, though. I pulled myself away, and got out of the room, I don't know how. My wreath was falling off. My dress was crumpled. Nothing would have made me go back to the ball-room. I couldn't have faced Amelia's husband—I think I shall never be able to face him again,"—and Mary's tears flowed anew.

Richard was stamping about the room, aimlessly moving things from their places. "God Almighty! he shall answer to me for this. I'll go back and take a horsewhip with me."

"For my sake, don't have a scene with him, Richard. It would only make matters worse—far worse," she pleaded.

But Richard strode up and down, treading heedlessly on the flouncings of her dress. "What?—and let him believe such infamy can go unpunished? That, whenever it please him, he can insult my wife—insult *my* wife? Make her the talk of the place? Brand her before the whole town as a light woman?"

("Oh, not the whole town, Richard. I shall have to explain to Amelia . . . and Tilly . . . and Agnes—that's all," sobbed Mary, in parenthesis.)

"Yes, and I ask if it's a dignified or decent thing for you to have to do?—to go running round assuring your friends of your virtue?" cried Richard furiously. "Let me tell you this, my dear: at whatever door you knock, you'll be met by disbelief. Fate played you a shabby trick when it allowed just that low cad of a fellow to put his head in. What do you think would be left of any woman's reputation, after Grindle Esquire had pawed it over?— No, Mary, you've been rendered impossible; and you'll be made to feel it for the rest of

335

your days. People will point to you as the wife who takes advantage of her husband's absence to throw herself into another man's arms; and to me as the convenient husband who provides the opportunity,"—and Mahony groaned. In an impetuous flight of fancy he saw his good name smirched, his practice laid waste.

Mary lifted her head at this, and wiped her tears. "Oh, try not to be so bitter, Richard! . . . you always paint everything so black. People know me—know I would never, never, do such a thing."

"Unfortunately we live among human beings, my dear, not in a community of saints!— But what does a good woman know of how a slander of this kind clings?"

"But if I have a perfectly clear conscience?" Mary's tone was incredulous, even a trifle aggrieved.

"It spells ruin, all the same, in a hole like this, if it gets about."

"But it shan't. I'll put my pride in my pocket and go to Amelia, the first thing in the morning. I'll make it right somehow.— But I must say, Richard, in the whole affair, I don't think you feel a bit sorry for me. Or at least only for me as your wife. The horridest part of what happened was mine, not yours—and I think you might show me a little sympathy."

"I'm far too indignant to feel sorry," replied Richard with gaunt truthfulness, still marching up and down.

"Well, *I* do," said Mary with a spice of defiance. "And not for myself alone. In spite of everything, I feel sorry that any one could so far forget himself as Purdy did to-night."

"You'll be telling me next you have warmer feelings still for him!" burst out Mahony: "Sorry for the crazy lunatic, who after all these years, after all I've done for him, and the trust I've put in him, suddenly, without rhyme or reason, falls to making love to the woman who bears my name?— Why, a mad-house is the only place he's fit for."

"There you're unjust. And wrong, too, Richard," spoke up Mary, urged by a sense of fairness. "It . . . it wasn't as sudden as you think. Purdy has been queer in his behaviour for quite a long time now."

"What in Heaven's name do you mean by that?"

"I mean," said Mary staunchly, though she turned a still

336

deeper red, "I mean what I say.— Oh, you might just as well be angry with yourself, for being so blind and stupid."

"Do you actually mean to tell me you were aware of something?" Mahony stopped short in his perambulations, fixed her, open-mouthed.

"I couldn't help it.— Not that there was much to know, Richard. And I thought of coming to you about it—indeed I did.— I tried to, more than once. But you were always so taken up with other things; I hadn't the heart to worry you. For I knew very well how upset you would be."

"So it comes to this, does it?" said Mahony with biting emphasis. "My wife consents to another man paying her illicit attentions behind her husband's back!"

"Oh, no, no, no!— But I knew how fond you were of Purdy. And I always hoped it would blow over without . . . without coming to anything."

"God forgive me!" cried Mahony passionately. "It takes a woman's brain to house such a preposterous idea."

"Oh, I'm not quite such a fool as you make me out to be, Richard. I've got some sense in me. But it's always the same. I think of you, and you think of no one but yourself. I only wanted to spare you. And this is the thanks I get for it." And sitting down on the side of the bed, she wept bitterly.

"Will you assure me, madam, that till to-night, nothing I could have objected to has ever passed between you?"

"No, Richard, I won't. I won't tell you anything else. You get so angry you don't know what you're saying.— And if you can't trust me better than that—Purdy said to-night you didn't understand me . . . and never had."

"Oh, he did, did he? There we have it! Now I'll know every word the scoundrel has ever said to you—and if I have to drag it from you by force."

But Mary set her lips, with an obstinacy that was something quite new in her. It first amazed Mahony, then made him doubly angry. One word gave another; for the first time in their married lives they quarrelled—quarrelled hotly. And, as always at such times, many a covert criticism, a secret disapproval which neither had ever meant to breathe to the other, slipped out and added fuel to the fire. It was appalling to both to find on how many points they stood at variance.

Some half hour later, leaving Mary still on the edge of the

bed, still crying, Mahony stalked grimly into the surgery, and taking pen and paper scrawled, without even sitting down to it:

You damned scoundrel! If ever you show your face here again, I'll thrash you to within an inch of your life.

Then, bareheaded, he stepped on to the verandah and crossed the lawn, carrying the letter in his hand.

But, already, his mood was on the turn: it seemed as if, in the physical effort of putting the words to paper, his rage had spent itself. He was conscious now of a certain limpness, both of mind and body; his fit of passion over, he felt dulled, almost indifferent to what had happened. Now, too, another feeling—a sense of loss, irretrievable loss—took possession of him, opening up vistas of a desert emptiness, that he hardly dared to face.

But stay! . . . was that not a movement in the patch of blackness under the fig-tree? Had not something stirred there? He stopped; and strained his eyes. No: it was only a bough that swayed in the night air. He went out of the garden, to the corner of the road, and came back empty handed. But, at the same spot, he hesitated, and peered. "Who's there?" he asked sharply. And again: "Is there any one there?" But the silence was unbroken; and, once more, he saw that the shifting of a branch had misled him.

Mary was moving about the bedroom, preparing for rest. He ought to go to her, ought to ask pardon for his violence. But he was not yet come to a stage when he felt equal to a reconciliation; he would rest for a while, let his troubled balance right itself. And so he lay down on the surgery sofa, and drew a rug over him.

He closed his eyes, but could not sleep. His thoughts raced and flew; his brain hunted clues and connections. He found himself trying to piece things together: to fit them in; to recollect. And every now and then some sound outside would make him start up, and listen . . . and listen. Was that not a footstep? . . . the step of one who might come feeling his way . . . dim-eyed with regret? There were such things in life as momentary lapses, as ungovernable impulses—as fiery contrition . . . the anguish of remorse. And, yet once more, he sat up and listened, till his ears rang.

Then, not the ghostly footsteps of a delusive hope, but a hard, human crunching that made the boards of the verandah shake. Tossing off the opossum-rug, which had grown unbearably heavy, Mahony sprang up from his uneasy sleep; was wide awake and at the window, staring sleep-charged into the dawn, before a human hand had found the night-bell, and a distracted voice cried:

"Does a doctor live here? A doctor, I say . . . !"

[7]

THE hot airless night had become the hot airless day: in the garden the leaves on trees and shrubs drooped as under an invisible weight. All the stale smells of the day before persisted—that of the medicaments on the shelves, of the unwetted dust on the roads, the sickly odour of malt from a neighbouring brewery. The blowflies buzzed about the ceiling; on the table under the lamp a dozen or more moths lay singed and dead.— Now, it was nearing six o'clock. Clad in his thinnest driving-coat, Mahony sat in a buggy and watched the man who had come to fetch him, beat his horse into a lather.

"Mercy! Have a little mercy on the poor brute," he said more than once.

He had stood out for some time against obeying the summons, which meant, at lowest, a ten-mile drive. Not if he were offered a hundred pounds down, was his first impetuous refusal; for he had not seen the inside of a bed that night. But at this he trapped an odd look in the other's eyes; and suddenly he became aware that he was still dressed as for the ball. Besides, an equally impetuous answer was flung back at him: he promised no hundred pounds, said the man—hadn't got it to offer. He appealed solely to the doctor's humanity: it was a question of saving a life—that of his only son.— And so here they were.

"We doctors have no business with troubles of our own," thought Mahony, as he listened to the detailed account of an ugly accident. The boy had been on the roof of a shed, had missed his footing, slipped, and fallen some twenty feet, landing astride a piece of quartering. Picking himself up, he had managed to crawl home, and at first they thought he would be able to get through the night without medical aid. But towards two o'clock his sufferings had grown unbearable. God only knew if, by this time, he had not succumbed to them.

"My good man, one does not die of pain alone."

They followed a flat, treeless road, the grass on either side of which was burnt to hay. Buggy and harness—the latter eked out with bits of string, and an old bootlace—were coated with the dust of months; and the gaunt, long-backed horse shuffled through a reddish flour, which, rising, accompanied them as a choking cloud. A swarm of small black flies kept pace with the vehicle, settling on nose, eyes, neck and hands of its occupants, crawling over the horse's belly, and in and out of its nostrils. The animal made no effort to shake itself free; seemed hardened to the pests, indifferent: they were only to be disturbed by the hail of blows which the driver occasionally stood up to deliver. At such moments Mahony, too, started out of the light doze he was for ever dropping into.

Arrived at their destination—a miserable wooden shanty, on a sheep-run at the foot of the ranges—he found his patient tossing on a dirty bed, with a small pulse of 120, while the right thigh was darkly bruised and swollen. The symptoms pointed to internal injuries. He performed the necessary operation.

There was evidently no woman about the place; the coffee the father brought him was thick as mud. On leaving, he promised to return next day, and to bring some one with him to attend to the lad.

For the home-journey, he got a mount on a young and fidgety mare, whom he suspected of not long having worn the saddle. In the beginning he had his hands full with her. Then, however, she ceased her antics, and consented to advance at an easy trot.

How tired he felt! He would have liked to go to bed and sleep for a week on end. As it was, he could not reckon on a single hour's rest. By the time he reached home, the usual string of patients would await him; and, these disposed of, and a bite of breakfast snatched, out he must set anew on his morning round. He did not feel well, either: the coffee seemed to have disagreed with him. He had a slight sense of nausea, and was giddy, the road swam before his eyes. Possibly the weather had something to do with it; though a dull, sunless

morning, it was hot as he had never known it. He took out a
stud, letting the ends of his collar fly.

Poor little Mary! he thought inconsequently: he had hurt
and frightened her by his violence. He felt ashamed of himself now. By daylight, he could see her point of view. Mary
was so tactful and resourceful that she might safely be trusted
to hush up the affair, to explain away the equivocal position
in which she had been found. After all, both of them were
known to be decent, God-fearing people. And one had only
to look at Mary to see that here was no light woman. Nobody
in his senses—not even Grindle—could think evil of that
broad, transparent brow, of those straight, kind, merry eyes.

No, this morning his hurt was a purely personal one. That
it should just be Purdy who did him this wrong—Purdy,
playmate and henchman, ally in how many a boyish enterprise,
in the hardships and adventures of later life. *"Mine own
familiar friend, in whom I trusted, which did eat of my
bread!"*— Never had he turned a deaf ear to Purdy's needs;
he had fed him and clothed him, caring for him as for a well-
loved brother. Surely, few things were harder to bear than a
blow in the dark from one who stood thus deeply in your debt,
on whose gratitude you would have staked your head.— It
was, of course, conceivable that he had been swept off his feet
by Mary's vivid young beauty, by overindulgence, by the
glamour of the moment. But, far from excusing him, this
seemed only to make matters worse. For, if a man could not
restrain his impulses where the wife of his most intimate
friend was concerned. . . . Another thing: as long as Mary
had remained an immature slip of a girl, Purdy had not given
her a second thought. When, however, under her husband's
wing, she had blossomed out into a lovely womanhood, of
which any man might be proud, then she had found favour in
his eyes. And the slight this put on Mary's sterling moral
qualities, on all but her physical charms, left the worse taste
of any in the mouth.

And not content with trying to steal her love, Purdy had
also sought to poison her mind against him. How that rankled!
For, until now, he had hugged the belief that Purdy's opinion
of him was coloured by affection and respect, by the tradition
of years. Whereas, from words Mary had let fall, he saw that
the boy must always have been sitting in judgment on him,

regarding his peculiarities with an unloving eye, picking his motives to pieces: the only equivalent in bitterness he could think of was when the child of your loins, of your hopes, your unsleeping care, turned and rent you with black ingratitude. Yes, everything went to prove Purdy's unworthiness. Only *he* had not seen it, only he had been blind to the truth. And wrapped in this smug blindness, he had given his false friend the run of his home, setting, after the custom of the country, no veto on his eternal presence. Disloyalty was certainly abetted by just the extravagant, exaggerated hospitality of colonial life. Never must the doors of your house be shut; all you had you were expected to share with any sundowner of fortune, who chanced to stop at your gate.

The mare shied with a suddenness that almost unseated him: the next moment she had the bit between her teeth and was galloping down the road. Clomp-clomp-clomp went her hoofs on the baked clay; the dust smothered and stung, and he was holding for all he was worth to reins spanned stiff as iron. On they flew; his body hammered the saddle; his breath came sobbingly. But he kept his seat; and a couple of miles farther on he was down, soothing the wild-eyed, quivering, sweating beast, whose nostrils worked like a pair of bellows. There he stood, glancing now back along the road, now up at the sky. His hat had gone flying at the first unexpected plunge; he ought to return and look for it. But he shrank from the additional fatigue, the delay in reaching home, this would mean. The sky was still overcast: he decided to risk it. Knotting his handkerchief, he spread it cap-wise over his head, and got back into the saddle.

—Mine own familiar friend! And more than that: he could add to David's plaint and say, my only friend. In Purdy, the one person he had been intimate with passed out of his life. There was nobody to take the vacant place. He had been far too busy of late years to form new friendships: what was left of him, after the day's work was done, was but a kind of shell: the work was the meaty contents. As you neared the forties, too, it grew harder and harder to fit yourself into other people: your outlook had become too set, your ideas too unfluid. Hence, you clung the faster to ties formed in the old, golden days, worn though these might be to the thinness of a hair. And then, there was one's wife, of course—one's dear, good wife. But just her very dearness and goodness served to hold possible intimates at arm's length. The knowledge that you had such a confidence, that all your thoughts were shared with her, struck disastrously at a free exchange of privacies. No, he was alone. He had not so much as a dog, now, to follow at heel and look up at him with the melancholy eyes of its race. Old Pompey had come at poison, and Mary had not wished to have a strange dog in the new house. She did not care for animals, and the main charge of it would have fallen on her. He had no time—no time even for a dog!

Better it would assuredly be to have some one to fall back on: it was not good for a man to stand thus alone. Did troubles come, they would strike doubly hard because of it; then was the time to rejoice in a warm, human handclasp. And moodily pondering the reasons for his solitariness, he once more inclined to lay a share of the blame on the conditions of the life. The population of the place was still in a state of flux: he and a handful of others would soon, he believed, be the oldest residents in Ballarat. People came and went, tried their luck, failed, and flitted off again, much as in the early days. What was the use of troubling to become better acquainted with a person, when, just as you began really to know him, he was up and away? At home, in the old country, a man as often as not died in the place where he was born; and the slow, eventless years, spent shoulder to shoulder, automatically brought about a kind of intimacy.— But this was only a surface reason: there was another, that went deeper. He had no talent for friendship; and he knew it; indeed, he would even invert the thing and say bluntly, that his nature had a twist in it which directly hindered friendship; and this, though there came moments when he longed, as your popular mortal never did, for close companionship. Sometimes he felt like a hungry man looking on at a banquet, of which no one invited him to partake, because he had already given it to be understood that he would decline.— But such lapses were few. On nine days out of ten, he did not feel the need of either making or receiving confidences; he shrank rather, with a peculiar shy dread, from personal unbosomings. Some imp housed in him—some wayward, wilful, mocking Irish devil— bidding him hold back, remain cool, dry-eyed, in face of others' joys and pains.— Hence, the break with Purdy was a real calamity. Formed in the plastic days of youth, their brotherly alliance had grown to be an integral part of their lives. The associations of some five-and-twenty years were bound up in it; measured by it, one's marriage seemed a thing of yesterday. And even more than the friend, he would miss the friendship, and all it stood for: this solid base of joint experience; this past of common memories, into which one could dip as into a well; this handle of "Do you remember?" which opened the door to such a wealth of anecdote. From now on, the better part of his life would be a closed book to any but himself: there were allusions, jests without number, homely turns of speech, which not a soul but himself would understand. The thought of it made him feel old, and empty; affected him like the news of a death.— But *must* it be? Was there no other way out? Slow to take hold, he was a hundred times slower to let go. Before now, he had seen himself sticking by a person through misunderstandings, ingratitude, deception, to the blank wonder of the onlooker. Would he not be ready here, too, to forgive . . . to forget. . . ?

But he felt hot, hot to suffocation, and his heart was pounding in uncomfortable fashion. The idea of stripping and plunging into ice-cold water began to make a delicious appeal to him. Nothing surpassed such a plunge, after a broken night. But of late he had had to be wary of indulging: a bath of this kind, taken when he was over-tired, was apt to set the accursed tic a-going; and then he could pace the floor for hours, in agony. And yet . . . Good God, how hot it was! His head ached distractedly; an iron band of pain seemed to encircle it. With a sudden start of alarm, he noticed that he had ceased to perspire—now he came to think of it, not even the wild gallop had induced perspiration. Pulling up short, he fingered his pulse. It was abnormal, even for him . . . and feeble. Was it fancy, or did he really find a difficulty in breathing? He tore off his collar altogether, threw open the neck of his shirt. He had a sensation as if all the blood in his body were flying to his head: his face must certainly be crimson. He put both hands to this top-heavy head, to support it; and in a blind fit of vertigo all but lost his balance in the saddle: the trees spun round, the distance went black. For a second still he kept upright; then he flopped to the ground, falling face downwards, his arms huddled under him.

The mare, all her spirit gone, stood lamb-like and waited. As he did not stir, she turned and sniffed at him, curiously. Still he lay prone, and, having stretched her tired jaws, she raised her head and uttered a whinny—an almost human cry of distress. This, too, failing in its effect, she nosed the ground for a few yards, then set out at a gentle, mane-shaking trot for home.

❋   ❋   ❋   ❋

Found, a dark conspicuous heap on the long bare road, and carted back to town by a passing bullock-waggon, Mahony lay, once the deathlike coma had yielded, and tossed in fever and delirium. By piecing his broken utterances together, Mary learned all she needed to know about the case he had gone out to attend, and his desperate ride home. But it was Purdy's name that was oftenest on his lips; it was Purdy he reviled and implored; and, when he sprang up with the idea of calling his false friend to account, it was as much as she could do to restrain him.

She had the best of advice. Old Dr. Munce himself came two and three times a day. Mary had always thought him a dear old man; and she felt surer than ever of it now, when he stood patting her hand, and bidding her keep a good heart, for they would certainly pull her husband through.

"There aren't so many of his kind here, Mrs. Mahony, believe me, that we can afford to lose him."

But altogether she had never known, till now, how many and how faithful their friends were. Hardly, for instance, had Richard been carried in, stiff as a log and grey as death, when good Mrs. Devine was fumbling with the latch of the gate, an old sunbonnet perched crooked on her head: she had run down, just as she was, in the midst of shelling peas for dinner. She begged to be allowed to help with the nursing. But Mary, though deeply touched, felt it her duty to refuse. She knew how the thoughts of what he might have said in his delirium would worry Richard, when he recovered his senses: few men laid such weight on keeping their private thoughts private, as he.— With regard to herself and the distressing incident of the ball, she had no time now to stop to revolve what people might be saying of her, or whether they thought ill of her or not. In her heart certainly she didn't think they would; for that, she had too firm a belief in people's common sense.

Not to be done, Mrs. Devine installed herself in the kitchen, to superintend the cooking. Less for the patient, into whom at first only liquid nourishment could be injected, than: "To see as your own strength is kep' up, dearie." Tilly swooped down and bore off the child Trotty. Delicate fruits, new-laid eggs, jellies and wines came from Agnes Ocock; while Amelia Grindle, who had no such dainties to offer, arrived to the minute every day at three o'clock, to mind the house while Mary slept. Archdeacon Long was also a frequent visitor, bringing not so much spiritual as physical aid; for, as the frenzy reached its height, and Richard was maddened by the idea that a plot was brewing against his life, a pair of strong arms were needed to hold him down in the bed.— Over and above this, letters of sympathy flowed in; grateful patients called to ask, with tears in their eyes, how the doctor did; virtual strangers stopped the servant in the street with the same query. Mary was sometimes quite overwhelmed by the kindness people showed her.

The days that preceded the crisis were days of keenest anxiety. It cannot however be said that Mary once allowed her heart to fail her. For if, in the small things of life, she built on the ordinary mortal's good sense, how much more could she rely, at such a pass, on the sound judgment of the One above all others. What she said to herself, as she moved tirelessly about the sick room, damping cloths, filling the ice-bag, infiltering drops of nourishment, was: "God is good!"— and these words, far from breathing a pious resignation, voiced a confidence so bold that it bordered on irreverence. Their real meaning was: Richard is still a youngish man, and very clever. He has still ever so much work to do in the world, in curing sick people and saving their lives. God must know this, and cannot now mean to be so foolish as to *waste* him, by letting him die.

And her reliance on the Almighty's far-sighted wisdom was justified. Richard weathered the crisis, slowly revived to life and health; and the day came when, laying a thin white hand on hers, he could whisper: "My poor little wife, what a fright I must have given you!"— For, into Mary, he read the morbid fears of which he, under like circumstances, would have been the prey.

"I think an illness of some kind was due—overdue—with me," he said again, as his recovery made strides.

When he was well enough to bear the journey, they left home for a watering-place on the Bay. There, on an open beach facing the Heads, Mahony lay with his hat pulled forward to shade his eyes, and with nothing to do but to scoop up handfuls of the fine coral sand, and let it flow forth again, like liquid silk, through his fingers. From beneath the brim, he watched the water churn and froth on the brown reefs; followed the sailing-ships, which, beginning as mere dots on the horizon, swelled to stately white waterbirds, and, passing, shrivelled again to dots; drank in, with greedy nostrils, the mixed spice of warm sea, hot seaweed, and aromatic tea-scrub.

But the first week over, his strength came back as rapidly as usual. He now felt well enough, leaning on Mary's arm, to stroll up and down the sandy roads of the township; to open book and newspaper; and, finally, to descend the cliffs for a dip in the transparent, turquoise sea. At the end of a month he was at home again, sunburnt and hearty, eager to pick up the threads he had let fall. And soon Mary was able to make the comfortable reflection that everything was going on just as before.

In this, however, she was wrong; never, in their united lives, would things be quite the same again. Outwardly, the changes might pass unnoticed—though even here, it was true, a certain name had now to be avoided, with which they had formerly made free. But this was not exactly hard to do, Purdy having at once vanished from the scene: they heard at second-hand that he had at last accepted promotion, and gone to Melbourne. And, since Mary had suffered no inconvenience from his thoughtless conduct, they tacitly agreed to let the matter rest.— That was on the surface. Inwardly, the differences were more marked. Even in the mental attitude they adopted towards what had happened, husband and wife were thoroughly dissimilar. Mary did not refer to it, because she thought it would be foolish to re-open so disagreeable a subject. In her own mind, however, she faced it frankly, dating back to it as the night Purdy had been so odious and Richard so angry. Mahony, on the other hand, gave the affair a wide berth, even in thought. For him it resembled a kind of Pandora's box, of which, having once caught a glimpse of the contents, he did not again dare to raise the lid. Things might escape from it that would alter the whole course of his life. But the events of that February night had made such a profound impression on his mind that he, too, dated from it, in the sense of suddenly becoming aware, with a throb of regret, that he had left his youth behind him. And such phrases as: "When I was young," "In my younger days," now rose instinctively to his lips.

Nor was this all. Deep down in Mary's soul there slumbered a slight embarrassment; and she could not get the better of it: it spread and grew. This was a faint, ever so faint a doubt of Richard's wisdom. Odd she had long known him to be, different in many small, and some great ways, from those they lived amongst; but, hitherto, this very oddness of his had seemed to her an outgrowth on the side of superiority—fairer judgment, higher motives. Just as she had always looked up to him as rectitude in person, so she had thought him the embodiment of a fine, though somewhat unworldly, wisdom. Now, her faith in his discernment was shaken. His treatment of her on the night of the ball had shocked, confused her. She was ready to make allowance for him: she had told her story clumsily, and had afterwards been both cross and obstinate; while part of his violence was certainly to be ascribed to his coming breakdown. But this did not cover everything; and the ungenerous spirit in which he had met her frankness, his doubt of her word, of her good faith—his utter unreasonableness, in short—had left a cold patch of astonishment in her, which would not yield. She lit on it at unexpected moments.— Meanwhile, she groped for an epithet that would fit his extraordinary behaviour. Beginning with some rather vague and high-flown terms, she gradually came down, until, with the sense of having found the right thing at last, she fixed on the adjective "silly"—a word which, for the rest, was in common use with Mary, had she to describe anything that struck her as queer or extravagant. And sitting over her fancy-work, into which, being what Richard called "safe as the grave," she sewed more thoughts than most women: sitting thus, she would say to herself, with a half smile and an incredulous shake of the head: "So silly!"

But hers was one of those inconvenient natures which trust blindly or not at all: once worked on by a doubt or a suspicion, they are never able to shake themselves free of it again. As time went on, she suffered strange uncertainties where some of Richard's decisions were concerned. In his good intentions she retained an implicit belief; but she was not always satisfied that he acted in the wisest way. Occasionally, it struck her that he did not see as clearly as she did; at other times, that he let a passing whim run away with him, and override his common sense. And, her eyes thus opened, it was not in Mary to stand dumbly by and watch him make what she held to be mistakes. Openly to interfere, however, would have gone equally against the grain in her; she had bowed for too long to his greater age and experience. So, seeing no other way out, she fell back on indirect methods. To her regret. For, in watching other women "manage" their husbands, she had felt proud to think that nothing of this kind was necessary between Richard and her. Now, she, too, began to lay little schemes, by which, without his being aware of it, she might influence his judgment, divert or modify his plans.

Her enforced use of such tactics did not lessen the admiring affection she bore him: that was framed to withstand harder tests. Indeed, she was even aware of an added tenderness towards him, now she saw that it behooved her to have forethought for them both. But, into the wife's love for her husband, there crept something of a mother's love for her child; for a wayward and impulsive, yet gifted creature, whose welfare and happiness depended on her alone.— And it is open to question whether the mother dormant in Mary did not fall with a kind of hungry joy on this late-found task. The work of her hands done, she had known empty hours. That was over now. With quickened faculties, all her senses on the alert, she watched, guided, hindered, foresaw.

[8]

OLD Ocock failed in health that winter. He was really old now, was two or three and sixty; and, with the oncoming of the rains and the cold, gusty winds, various infirmities began to plague him.

"He's done himself rather too well since his marriage," said

349

Mahony in private. "After being a worker for the greater part of his life, it would have been better for him to go on working to the end."

Yes, that Mary could understand and agree with. But Richard continued: "All it means, of course, is that the poor fellow is beginning to prepare for his last long journey. These aches and pains of his represent the pother of getting ready, the packing and the strapping, etc., without which not even a short earthly journey can be undertaken. And his is into eternity."

Mary, who was making a lace over a pillow, looked up at this, a trifle apprehensively. "Richard! What things you do say! If any one heard you, they'd think you weren't very . . . very religious."— Mary's fear lest her husband's outspokenness should be mistaken for impiety never left her.

Tilly was plain and to the point. "Like a bear with a sore back, that's what 'e is, since 'e can't get down among his blessed birds. He leads Tom the life of the condemned, over the feeding of those bantams. As if the boy could help 'em not laying when they ought!"

At thirty-six Tilly was the image of her mother—or, more exactly, of what her mother would have been, had the latter, at the same age, reached a similar pitch of prosperity. Entirely gone was the slight crust of acerbity that had threatened Tilly in her maiden days, when, thanks to her misplaced affections, it had seemed for a time as if the purple prizes of life—love, offers of marriage, a home of her own—were going to pass her by. She was now a big, stout, high-coloured woman, with a roar of a laugh, full, yet firm lips, and the whitest of teeth. Mary thought her decidedly toned down and improved, since her marriage; but Mahony put it that the means Tilly now had at her disposal were such as to make people shut an eye to her want of refinement: her lavish way of spending money more than condoned her loudness. However that might be, "old Mrs. Ocock" was welcomed everywhere—even by those on whom her bouncing manners grated. She was invariably clad in a thick and handsome black silk gown, over which she wore all the jewellery she could crowd on her person—huge cameo brooches, ear-drops, rings and bracelets, lockets and chains. Her name topped subscription-lists, and, having early weaned her old husband of his dissenting habits, she was a real prop to Archdeacon Long and his church, taking, as she did, the chief and most expensive table at tea-meetings, the most thankless stall at bazaars. She kept open house, too, and gave delightful parties, where, while some sat at loo, others were free to turn the rooms upside-down for a dance, or to ransack wardrobes and presses for costumes for charades. She drove herself and her friends about in various vehicles, briskly and well, and indulged besides in many secret charities. Her husband thought no such woman ever trod the earth, and publicly blessed the day on which he had first set eyes on her.

"After the dose I'd 'ad with me first, 'twas a bit of a risk, that I knew. And it put me off me sleep for a night or two before'and. But my Tilly's the queen o' women—I say the queen, sir! I've never 'ad a wrong word from 'er, since I tuck 'er, an', when I go, she gits every penny I've got. Why, I'm jiggered if she didn't stop at 'ome from the Races t'other day, an' all on my account!"

"Now, then, pa, drop it. Or the doctor'll think you've been mixing your liquors. Give your old pin here, and let me poultice it."

But none the less the sacrifice on Tilly's part had been a very real one; for she adored horse-racing, and missed no meeting that was held for miles round. The old man believed she would end by setting up a racing-stable of her own.— "An' why shouldn't she if she wants to, I'd like to know!"

He had another sound reason for gratitude. Somewhere in the background of his house dwelt his two ne'er-do-well sons; and, from the first, Tilly had accepted their presence uncomplainingly. Indeed she sometimes stood up for Tom, against his father. "Now, pa, stop nagging at the boy, will you? You'll never get anything out of 'im that way. Tom's right enough if you know how to take him. He'll never set the Thames on fire, if that's what you mean. But I'm thankful, I can tell you, to have a handy chap like him at my back. If I 'ad to depend on your silly old paws, I'd never get anything done at all."

And so Tom, a flaxen-haired, sheepish-looking man, of something over thirty, led a kind of go-as-you-please existence about the place, a jack-of-all-trades—in turn carpenter, white-washer, paper-hanger—an expert fetcher and carrier, bullied by his father, sheltered under his stepmother's capacious wing. "It isn't his fault 'e's never come to anything. 'E hadn't half a chance. The truth is, Mary, for all they say to the opposite, men are harder than women—so unforgiving-like. Just because Tom made a slip once, they've never let 'im forget it; they tied it on to 'is coat-tails, for 'im to drag with 'im through life. And Henry's the worst of the lot; only the other day I heard 'im sneer at the lad, as if it 'ad happened yesterday. You'd think, wouldn't you, folks would 'ave enough to do with their own business, without bothering about the other people's? Little-minded I call it.— Besides, if you ask me, my dear, I say it must have been a case of six of one and half a dozen of the other. Tom as sedoocer!—can you picture it, Mary? It's enough to make one split." And, with a meaning glance at her friend, Tilly broke out in a contagious peal of laughter.

As for Johnny—well . . . and she shrugged her shoulders. "A bad egg's bad, Mary, and no amount o' cooking and doctoring 'll sweeten it. But he didn't make 'imself, did 'e?—and my opinion is, parents should look to themselves a bit more than they do."

As she spoke, she threw open the door of the little room where Johnny housed. It was an odd place. The walls were plastered over with newspaper-cuttings, with old prints from illustrated journals, with snippets torn off valentines and keepsakes. Stuck one on another, these formed a layer of loose wallpaper, which entirely hid the former covering, and moved in the draught. Tilly went on: "I see myself to it being kept cleanish; 'e hates the girl to come bothering round.— Oh, just Johnny's rubbish!" For Mary had stooped curiously to the table, which was littered with a queer collection of objects: matchboxes on wheels, empty reels of cotton threaded on strings; bits of wood shaped in rounds and squares; boxes made of paper; dried seaweed glued in patterns on strips of cardboard. "He's for ever pottering about with 'em. What amusement 'e can get out of it, only the Lord can tell."

She did not mention the fact, known to Mary, that, when Johnny had a drinking-bout, it was she who looked after him, got him comfortably to bed, and made shift to keep the noise from his father's ears. Yes, Tilly's charity seemed sheerly inexhaustible.

There was, for instance, the case of Jinny's children.

For, in this particular winter, Tilly had exchanged her black silk for a stuff gown, heavily trimmed with crepe. She was in mourning for poor Jinny, who had died not long after giving birth to a third daughter.

"Died *of* the daughter, in more senses than one!" was Tilly's verdict.

John had certainly been extremely put out at the advent of yet another girl; and the probability was that Jinny had taken his reproaches too much to heart. However it was, she could not rally; and one day Mary received a telegram saying that if she wished to see Jinny alive, she must come at once. No mention was made of Tilly, but Mary ran to her with the news, and Tilly declared her intention of going, too.— "I suppose I may be allowed to see my own sister once more, even though I'm not a *H*onourable?

"Not that Jinn and I ever really drew well together," she continued, as the train bore them over the ranges. "She'd too much of poor pa in 'er. And I was all ma. Hard luck that it must just be her who managed to get such a domineering brute for a husband. You'll excuse me, Mary, won't you?—a domineering brute!"

"And to think I once envied her the match!" she went on meditatively, removing her bonnet and substituting a kind of nightcap, intended to keep her hair free from dust. "Lauks, Mary, it's a good thing fate doesn't always take us at our word. We don't know which side our bread's buttered on, and that's the truth. Why, my dear, I wouldn't exchange my old boy for all the *H*onourables in creation!"

They were in time to take leave of Jinny, lying white as her pillows behind the red rep hangings of the bed. The bony parts of her face had sprung into prominence; her large soft eyes had fallen in, and seemed smaller in their cavernous settings. John, stalking solemnly and noiselessly in a long black coat, himself led the two women into the bedroom, and there left them; they sat down one on each side of the great four-poster. Jinny hardly glanced at her sister: it was Mary she wanted, Mary's hand she fumbled for, while she told her trouble. "It's the children, Mary," she whispered. "I can't die happy, because of the children. John doesn't understand them."— Jinny's whole existence was bound up in the three little ones she had brought into the world.

"Dearest Jinny, don't fret. I'll look after them for you, and take care of them," promised Mary, wiping away her tears.

"I thought so," said the dying woman, relieved, but without gratitude: it seemed but natural to her, who was called upon to give up everything, that those remaining should make sacrifices. Her fingers plucked at the sheet. "John's been good to me," she went on, with closed eyes. "But . . . if it 'adn't been for the children . . . yes, the children . . . I think I'd 'a' done better—" her speech lapsed oddly, after her years of patient practice—"to 'ave taken . . . to 'a' taken"—the name remained unspoken.

Tilly raised astonished eyebrows at Mary. "Wandering!" she telegraphed in lip-language, forming the word very largely and distinctly; for neither knew of Jinny having had any but her one glorious chance.

Tilly's big heart yearned over her sister's forlorn little ones; they could be heard, in their nursery, bleating like lambs for the mother to whom, till now, they had never cried in vain. Her instant idea was to gather all three up in her arms, and carry them off to her own roomy, childless home, where she would have given them a delightful, though not maybe a particularly discriminating up-bringing. But, the funeral over, the blinds raised, the two ladies and the elder babes clad in the stiff, expensive mourning that befitted the widower's social position, John put his foot down on the scheme. To his sister, after Tilly had withdrawn to the hotel she was staying at, he was extremely explicit: "Under no circumstances, my dear Mary, would I permit Matilda to have anything to do with the rearing of my children—excellent creature though she be!"

On the other hand, he would not have been unwilling for Mary to mother them. This, of course, was out of the question: Richard had accustomed himself to Trotty, but would not thank you, she knew, for any fresh encroachment on his privacy. Before she left, however, she had promised to sound him on the plan of placing Trotty as a weekly boarder at a Young Ladies' Seminary, and taking the infant in her place. For it came out that John intended to set Zara—Zara, but newly returned from a second voyage to England, and still sipping like a bee at the sweets of various situations—at the head of his house once more. And Mary could not imagine Zara rearing a baby.

Equally hard was it to understand John's not having learnt

wisdom from his two previous failures to live with his sister. But, in seeking tactfully to revive his memory, she ran up against such an ingrained belief in the superiority of his kindred, that, baffled, she could only fold her hands and hope for the best.

"Besides, Jane's children are infinitely more tractable than poor Emma's," was John's parting shot.— Strange, thought Mary, how attached John was to his second family!

He had still another request to make of her. The reports he received of the boy Johnny, now a pupil at the Geelong Grammar School, grew worse from term to term. It had become clear to him that he was unfortunate enough to possess an out-and-out dullard for a son. Regretfully giving up, therefore, the design he had cherished of educating Johnny for the law, he had resolved to waste no more good money on the boy, but to take him, once he was turned fifteen, into his own business. Young John, however, had proved refractory, expressing a violent antipathy to the idea of office-life.— "It is here that I should be glad of another opinion—and I turn to you, Mary, my dear. Jane was of no use whatever in such matters, none whatever, being, and very properly so, of course, entirely wrapped up in her own children."— So Mary arranged to break her homeward journey at Geelong, for the purpose of seeing and summing up her nephew.

Johnny—he was Jack at school, but that, of course, his tomfools of relations couldn't be expected to remember— Johnny was waiting on the platform, when the train steamed in. "Oh, what a bonny boy!" said Mary to herself, as she was carried past. "All poor Emma's good looks."

Johnny had been kicking his heels disconsolately: another of these wretched old women coming down to jaw him! He wished every one of them at the bottom of the sea. However, he pulled himself together, and went forward to greet his aunt: he was not in the least bashful. And as they left the station, he took stock of her, out of the tail of his eye. With a growing approval: this one at any rate he needn't feel ashamed of; and she was not so dreadfully old after all. Perhaps she mightn't turn out quite such a wet blanket as the rest; though, from experience, he couldn't connect any pleasure with relatives' visits: they were nasty pills that had to be swallowed. He feared and disliked his father; Aunt Zara had

355

been sheerly ridiculous, with her frills and simpers—the boys had imitated her for weeks after—and once, most shameful of all, his stepmother had come down and publicly wept over him. His cheeks still burnt at the remembrance; and he had been glad, on that account, to hear that she was dead: served her jolly well right! But this Aunt Mary seemed a horse of another colour; and he did not sneak her into town by a back way, as he had planned to do before seeing her.

Greatly as Mary might admire the tall fair lad by her side, she found herself at a loss how to deal with him, the mind of a schoolboy of thirteen being a closed book to her. Johnny looked demure, and answered "Yes, Aunt Mary," to everything she said; but this was of small assistance in getting at the real boy inside.

Johnny had no intention, in the beginning, of taking her into his often-betrayed and badly bruised confidence. However, a happy instinct led her to suggest paying a visit to a shop that sold brandy-snaps and gingerbeer; and this was too much for his strength of mind. Golly, didn't he have a tuck-in! And a whole pound of bull's-eye to take back with him to school!

It was over the snaps, with an earth-brown moustache drawn round his fresh young mouth, the underlip of which swelled like a ripe cherry, that he blurted out: "I say, Aunt Mary, *don't* let the pater stick me in that beastly old office of his. I . . . I want to go to sea."

"Oh, but Johnny! Your father would never consent to that, I'm sure."

"I don't see why not," returned the boy, in an aggrieved voice. "I hate figures, and father knows it. I tell you I mean to go to sea!" And, as he said it, his lip shot out, and suddenly, for all his limpid blue eyes and flaxen hair, it was his father's face that confronted Mary.

"He wouldn't think it respectable enough, dear. He wants you to rise higher in the world, and to make money. You must remember who he is."

"Bosh!" said Johnny. "Look at Uncle Ned . . . and Uncle Jerry . . . and the governor himself. He didn't have to sit in a beastly old hole of an office, when he was my age."

"That was quite different," said Mary weakly. "And as for

356

your Uncle Jerry, Johnny—why afterwards, he was as glad as could be, to get into an office at all."

"Well, I'd sooner be hanged!" retorted young John. But the next minute, flinging away dull care, he inquired briskly: "Can you play tipcat, Aunt Mary?" And vanquished by her air of kindly interest, he gave her his supreme confidence. "I say, don't peach, will you, but I've got a white rat. I keep it in a locker under my bed."

A nice frank handsome boy, wrote Mary. *Don't be too hard on him, John. His great wish is to travel and see the world— or as he puts it, to go to sea. Mightn't it be a good thing to humour him in this? A taste of the hardships of life would soon cure him of any such fancies.*

—"Stuff and nonsense!" said John the father, and threw the letter from him. "I didn't send Mary there for her to let the young devil get round her like that." And thereupon he wrote to the Headmaster that the screw was to be applied to Johnny as never before. This was his last chance. If it failed, and his next report showed no improvement, he would be taken away without further ado, and planked down under his father's nose.— No son of his should go to sea, he was damned if they should!— For like many another who has yielded to the wandering passion in his youth, John had small mercy on it, when it reared its head in his descendants.

[9]

HENRY OCOCK was pressing for a second opinion on his wife, who had been in poor health since the birth of her last child.— Mahony drove to Plevna House one morning between nine and ten o'clock.

A thankless task lay before him. Mrs. Henry's case had been a fruitless source of worry to him: by every rule of thumb the lady should long ago have regained her health. She had not done so; and certain suspicions, which he had at first hesitated to admit, had just been rudely confirmed. He saw nothing for it but a straight talk with Henry himself. Hence, the latter's impatience and want of confidence merely forced his hand.

He drove past what had once been the Great Swamp. From

a bed of cattle-ploughed mud, interspersed with reedy water-holes; in summer, a dry and dust-swept hollow: from this, the vast natural depression had been transformed into a graceful lake, some three hundred acres in extent. On its surface, pleasure boats lay at their moorings by jetties and boatsheds; groups of stiff-necked swans sailed, or ducked and straddled. Shady walks followed the banks, where the whiplike branches of the willows, showing shoots of tenderest green, trailed in the water, or swayed, like loose harp-strings, to the breeze.

All the houses that had sprung up round Lake Wendouree had well stocked, spreading grounds; but Ocock's outdid the rest. The groom opening a pair of decorative iron gates, which were the show-piece of the neighbourhood, Mahony turned in and drove past a monster hedge of gum-trees, some sixty or seventy feet high; past exotic firs, Moreton Bay fig-trees, and araucarias; past cherished English hollies, growing side by side with giant cacti. The air was heavy with the fragrance of the pittosporums. A shaded corner held a rockery, where a fountain played and goldfish swam in a stone basin. Before the house, a large oval bed was given up wholly to camellia-bushes; and the white and pink blossoms of these scentless, petrified roses littered the ground. The house itself, of brick, and two-storied, with massive bay-windows, had an ornamental verandah on one side. The drawing-room was a medley of gilt and lustres, mirrors and glass shades; the finest objects from Dandaloo had been brought there, only to be put in the shade by Henry's own additions. Yes, Ocock lived in grand style nowadays, as befitted one of the most important men in the place: his old father once gone—and Mahony alone knew why the latter's existence acted as a drag—he would no doubt stand for Parliament.

Invited to walk into the breakfast-room, Mahony there found—though the hour was well past ten—the family seated at table. A charming scene met his eyes. Behind the urn Mrs. Henry, in be-ribboned cap and morning wrap, dandled her infant on her knee; while Henry, robed in oriental gown and Turkish fez, had laid his newspaper by, to ride his young son on his foot. Mahony refused tea or coffee; but could not avoid drawing up a chair, touching the peachy cheeks of the children held aloft for his inspection, and meeting a fire of playful sallies and kindly inquiries. As he did so, he was sensitively aware that it fell to him to break up the peace of this household. Only he knew the canker that had begun to eat at its roots.

The children borne off, Mrs. Henry interrogated her husband's pleasure with a pretty: "May I?" or "Should I?" lift of the brows; and, gathering that he wished her to retire, laid her small, plump hand in Mahony's, sent a graceful message to "dearest Mary," and swept the folds of her gown from the room. Mahony rose to hold the door open. Henry, watching her from his seat with a well-pleased eye—his opinion was no secret that, in figure and bearing his wife bore a marked resemblance to her Majesty Queen Victoria—Henry admonished her not to fail to partake of some light refreshment during the morning, in the shape of a glass of sherry and a biscuit. "Unless, my love, you prefer me to order cook to whip you up an egg-nog.— "Mrs. Ocock is, I regret to say, entirely without appetite again," he went on, as the door closed behind his wife. "What she eats is not enough to keep a sparrow going. You must prove your skill, doctor, and oblige us by prescribing a still more powerful tonic or appetiser. The last had no effect whatever." He spoke magisterially from the hearthrug, where he had gone to warm his skirts at the wood fire, audibly fingering the while a nest of sovereigns in a waistcoat-pocket.

"I feared as much," said Mahony gravely; and therewith took the plunge.

When some twenty minutes later, he emerged from the house, he was unaccompanied, and himself pulled the front door to behind him. He stood frowning heavily as he snapped the catches of his gloves, and fell foul of the groom over a strap or buckle of the harness, in a fashion that left the man open-mouthed. "Blow me, if I don't believe he's got the sack there!" thought the man to himself, in driving townwards.

The abrupt stoppage of Richard's professional visits to Plevna House staggered Mary. And since she could get nothing out of her husband, she tied on her bonnet and went off hotfoot to question her friend. But Mrs. Henry tearfully declared her ignorance—she had listened in fear and trembling to the sound of the two angry voices—and Henry was adamant. They had already called in another doctor.

Mary came home greatly distressed, and, Richard still wearing his obstinate front, she ended by losing her temper. He knew well enough, she said, it was not her way to interfere, or to be inquisitive about his patients; but this was different; this had to do with one of her dearest friends; she could not sit down and fold her hands; she must know. In her ears rang Agnes's words: "Henry told me, love, he wouldn't insult me by repeating what your husband said of me. Oh, Mary, isn't it dreadful? And when I liked him so much as a doctor!"— She now repeated them aloud.

This was too much for Mahony. He blazed up. "Huh! the confounded mischiefmonger—the backbiter!— Well, if you must know, wife, here you are . . . here's the truth. What I said to Ocock was: I said, my good man, if you want your wife to get over her next confinement more quickly, keep the sherry-decanter out of her reach."

Mary gasped, staring as if she could not believe her ears. Then, she flushed all over, sank on a chair, and let her arms flop to her side. "Richard!" she ejaculated. "Oh, Richard, you never did!"

"I did indeed, my dear.— Oh well, not in just those words, of course; we doctors must always wrap the truth up in silver paper.— And I should feel it my duty to do the same again to-morrow; though there are pleasanter things in life, Mary, I can assure you, than informing a low mongrel like Ocock that his wife is drinking on the sly. You can have no notion, my dear, of the compliments one calls down on one's head by so doing. The case is beyond my grasp, of course, and I am cloaking my own shortcomings by making scandalous insinuations against a delicate lady, who 'takes no more than her position entitles her to'—his very words, Mary!—'for the purpose of keeping up her strength.'" And Mahony laughed hotly.

"Yes, but was it—I mean . . . was it really necessary to say it?" stammered Mary, still at sea. And as her husband only shrugged his shoulders: "Then I can't pretend to be surprised at what has happened, Richard. Mr. Henry will *never* forgive you. He thinks so much of everything and every one belonging to him."

"Pray, can I help that? . . . help his infernal pride? And, good God, Mary, can't you see that, far more terrible than my having had to tell him the truth, is the fact of there being such a truth to tell?"

"Oh yes, indeed I can," and the warm tears rushed to Mary's eyes. "Poor, poor little Agnes!— Richard, that comes of her ever having been married to that dreadful man. And though she doesn't say so, yet I don't believe she's really happy in her second marriage either. There are so many things she's not allowed to do—and she's afraid of Mr. Henry, I know she is. You see he's displeased when she's dull or unwell; she must always be bright and look pretty; and I expect the truth is, since her illness she has been feeling poorly, and has taken to taking things, just to keep her spirits up." Here, Mary saw a ray of light, and snatched at it. "But in that case, Richard, mightn't the need for them pass, as she grows stronger?"

"I lay no claim to be a prophet, my dear," said Mahony drily.

"For, you know, it does seem strange that I never noticed anything," went on Mary, more to herself than to him. "I've seen Agnes at all hours of the day . . . when she wasn't in the least expecting visitors.— Yes, Richard, I do know people sometimes eat things to take the smell away, and all that. But the idea of Agnes doing anything so . . . so low—oh, isn't it *just* possible there might be some mistake? That it isn't as bad as you think?"

"Oh, well, if you're going to imitate Ocock, and try to teach me my business!" gave back Mahony with an angry gesture; and sitting down at the table, he pulled books and papers to him.

Mary repudiated this warmly. "As if such a thing would ever occur to me! It's only that . . . that somehow my brain won't take it in, Richard. Agnes has always been such a dear good little soul—and I've known her for so long now—all kindness. She's never done anybody any harm, or said a hard word about any one, all the years I've known her. I simply *can't* believe it of her, and that's the truth. As for what people will say, when it gets about that you've been shown the door in a house like Mr. Henry's—why, I'm afraid even to think of it!" and, powerless any longer to keep back her tears, Mary hastened from the room.

But she also thought it wiser to get away before Richard had time to frame the request—he was bound to, if she sat there disputing—that she should break off all intercourse with

Plevna House. This, she could never promise to do; and the result might be a quarrel. Whereas if she avoided giving her word, she would be free to slip out now and then to see poor Agnes, when Richard was on his rounds and Mr. Henry at business. But this was the only point clear to her; the rest was a horrid tangle. In standing up for her friend, she had been perfectly sincere: to think ill of a person she cared for, cost Mary an inward struggle. Against this, however, she had an antipathy to set that was stronger than herself. Of all forms of vice, intemperance was the one she hated most. She lived in a country where it was, alas! only too common; but she had never learnt to tolerate it, or to look with a lenient eye on those who succumbed: and whether these were but slaves of the nipping habit; or the eternal dram-drinkers, who felt fit for nothing if they had not a peg inside them; or those seasoned topers who drank their companions under the table, without themselves turning a hair; or yet again those who, sober for three parts of the year, spent the fourth in secret debauches: to none of them had she ever grown inured. Herself she had remained as rigidly abstemious as in the days of her girlhood. And she often mused, with a glow at her heart, on her great good fortune in having found, in Richard, one whose views on this subject were no less strict than her own.— Hence, her distress at her husband's disclosure was caused not alone by grief at Agnes Ocock's backsliding, or by the threatened loss of a dear friendship. She wept out of the horror with which the knowledge filled her.

Little by little, though, her mind worked round to what was, after all, the chief consideration: Richard's action and its probable consequences. And here once more she was divided against herself; did not know what to think. For a moment she had hoped her husband would own the chance of his being in error. But on thinking it over, she saw that this would never do. A mistake on his part would be a blow to his reputation. Besides making enemies of people like the Henrys for nothing. If he had to lose them as patients, it might as well be for a good solid reason, she told herself with a dash of his own asperity. Plainly, she must take sides with one or the other; it was a case of either husband or friend. And though she pitied Agnes from the bottom of her heart, yet there were literally no lengths she would have shrunk from going to, to spare Richard pain or even anxiety. And this led her on to wonder whether, granted things were as he said, he had broken the news to Mr. Henry in the most discreet way. Would it not have lain within his power to avoid a complete break? She sat and pondered this question till her head ached, finding herself up against the irreconcilability of the practical with the ideal, which complicates a man's working life. What she belatedly tried to think out for her husband, was some little common-sense stratagem by means of which he could have salved his conscience, without giving offence. He might perhaps have said that the drugs he was prescribing would be nullified by the use of wine or spirits; even better, have warned Agnes in private. Somehow, it might surely have been managed. Mr. Henry had no doubt been extremely rude and overbearing; but, in earlier years, Richard had known how to behave towards ill-breeding. She couldn't tell why, but he was finding it more and more difficult to get on with people; their foibles seemed to rub him up the wrong way, nowadays; and that made him less tactful and gracious than of old. He certainly had a very great deal to do, and was often tired out. Again, he did not need to care so much as formerly whether he offended people or not—ordinary patients, that was; the Henrys, of course, were of the utmost consequence. Still, once on a time, he had been noted for his fine tact; it was sad to see it thus leaving him in the lurch. Several times of late she had been forced to step in and smooth out awkwardnesses. But a week ago, he had had poor little Amelia Grindle up in arms, by telling her that her sickly first-born would mentally never be quite like other children. To every one but Amelia this had been plain from the outset; but Amelia had suspected nothing, having, poor thing, no idea when a babe ought to begin to take notice, or sit up, or cut its teeth. Richard said it was better for her to face the truth betimes than to spend her life vainly hoping and fretting; that, indeed, it would not be right of him to allow it. Poor dear Richard! He set such store by truth and principle—and she, Mary, would not have had him otherwise. All the same, she thought that in both cases a small compromise would not have hurt him. But compromise he would not . . . or could not.— And as, recalled to reality by the sight of the week's washing, which strained, ballooned, collapsed, on its lines in the yard—Biddy was again letting the clothes get much too dry!—as Mary rose to her feet, she manfully squared her shoulders to meet the weight of the new burden that was being laid upon them.

With regard to Mahony, it might be supposed that, having faithfully done what he believed to be his duty, he would enjoy the fruits of a quiet mind. This was not so. Before many hours had passed, he was wrestling with the incident anew; and, a true son of that nation which, for all its level-headedness, spends its best strength in fighting shadows, he felt a great deal angrier in retrospect than he had done at the moment. It was not alone the fact of his having got his congé. No medico was safe from *that* punch below the belt; and one learned to take it in a philosophical spirit. His chief bitterness was aimed at himself. Once more he had let himself be hoodwinked; had written down the smooth civility it pleased Ocock to adopt towards him, to respect and esteem. The natural vanity of a touchy man! Now that the veil was torn, he saw how poor the lawyer's opinion of him actually was. And always had been. For a memory was struggling to emerge in him, setting strings in vibration. And suddenly there rose before him a picture of Ocock that time had dimmed. He saw the latter standing in the dark, crowded lobby of the courthouse, cursing at him for letting their chief witness escape. He exclaimed aloud at the discovery. There it was! There, in these two scenes, far apart as they lay, you had the whole man. The unctuous blandness, the sleek courtesy was but a mask, which he wore for you just so long as you did not hinder him by getting in his way. That was the unpardonable sin. For Ocock was out to succeed—to succeed at any price and by any means. In tracing his course, no goal but this had ever shone before him. The obligations that bore on your ordinary mortal—a sense of honesty, of responsibility to one's fellows, the soft pull of domestic ties—did not trouble Ocock. He laughed them down, or wrung their necks for them, like so many pullets. And should the poor little woman who bore his name become a drag on him, in her fatal weakness, she would be tossed on to the rubbish-heap with the rest. In a way, so complete a freedom from altruistic motives had something grandiose about it, or would have, could one view it objectively, from a distance. But those who ran up against a nature of this type, and felt unable to fight it with its own weapons, had not an earthly chance.

Thus Mahony sat in judgment, giving rein, for once, to his ingrained dislike for the man he had now made an enemy of. In whose debt, for the rest, he stood deep. Yes, and had done, ever since the day he had been fool enough, like the fly in the nursery rhyme, to seek out Ocock and his familiars in their grimy little "parlour" in Chancery Lane.

But his first heat spent, he soon cooled down, and was able to laugh at the stagy explosiveness of his attitude. So much for the personal side of the matter. Looked at from a business angle, it was more serious. The fact of his having been shown the door by a patient of Ocock's standing was bound, as Mary saw, to react unfavourably on the rest of the practice. The news would run like wildfire through the place; never were such hotbeds of gossip as these colonial towns. Besides this, the man who had been called in to attend Mrs. Agnes, in his stead, was none too well disposed towards him.

His fears were justified. It quickly got about that he had made a gross blunder in his handling of Mrs. Henry's case: all she needed, said the new-comer, was change of air and scene; and forthwith the lady was packed off on a trial trip to Sydney. Mahony held his head high, and refused to notice looks and hints. But he knew all about what went on behind his back: he was morbidly sensitive to atmosphere; could tell how a house was charged as soon as he crossed the threshold. People were saying: a mistake there, why not here, too? Slow recoveries asked themselves if a fresh treatment might not benefit them; lovers of blue pills hungered for more drastic remedies. The disaffection would blow over, of course; but it was painful while it lasted; and things were not bettered by one of his patients choosing just this inconvenient moment to slip his cable—an elderly man, down with the Russian influenza, who disobeyed orders, got up too early, and was carried off by double pneumonia inside a week.— Worry over the mishap robbed his poor medical attendant of sleep, for nights on end.

Not that this was surprising; he found it much harder than of old to keep his mind from running on his patients outside working-hours. In his younger days, he had laid down fixed rules on this score. Every brainworker, he held, must, in his spare time, be able to detach his thoughts from his chief business, pin them to something of quite another kind, no matter how trivial: keep fowls or root round gardens, play the flute or go in for carpentry. Now, he might dig till his palms blistered, it did not help. Those he prescribed for teased him like a pack of spirit-presences, which clamour to be heard. And if some serious case took a turn for the worse, he would find himself rising, in a sweat of uncertainty, and going lamp in hand into the surgery, to con over a prescription he had written during the day.— And one knew where that kind of thing led!

Now, as if all this were not enough, there was added to it the old, evergreen botheration about money.

[10]

THUS far, Ocock had nursed his mining investments for him with a fatherly care. He himself had been free as a bird from responsibility. Every now and again he would drop in at the office, just to make sure the lawyer was on the alert; and each time he came home cheerful with confidence. That was over now. As a first result of the breach, he missed—or so he believed—making a clear four hundred pounds. Among the shares he held was one lot which, up to date, had proved a sorry bargain. Soon after purchase something had gone wrong with the management of the claim; there had been a lawsuit, followed by calls unending, and never a dividend. Now, when these shares unexpectedly swung up to a high level—only to drop the week after to their standing figure—Ocock failed to sell out in the nick of time. Called to account, he replied stiffly that it was customary in these matters for his clients to advise him; thus deepening Mahony's sense of obligation. Stabbed in his touchiness, Mahony wrote for all his scrip to be handed over to him; and, after this, loss and gain hung on himself alone. It certainly brought a new element of variety into his life. The mischief was, he could get to his study of the money-market only with a fagged brain. And the fear lest he should do something rash, or let a lucky chance slip, kept him on tenter-hooks.

It was about this time that Mary, seated one evening in face

366

of her husband, found herself reflecting: "When one comes to think of it, how seldom Richard ever smiles, nowadays!"

They were, for a wonder, at a soirée together, at the house of one of Mahony's colleagues. The company consisted of the inner circle of friends and acquaintances: "Always the same people—the same old job lot! One knows before they open their mouths what they'll say, and how they'll say it," Richard had grumbled as he dressed. The Henry Ococks were not there though, it being common knowledge that the two men declined to meet; and a dash of fresh blood was present, in the shape of a lady and gentleman just "out from home." Richard got into talk with this couple, and Mary, watching him fondly, could not but be struck by his animation. His eyes lit up, he laughed and chatted, made merry repartee: she was carried back to the time when she had known him first. In those days, his natural gravity was often cut through by a mood of high spirits, of boyish jollity, which, if only by way of contrast, rendered him a delightful companion. She grew a little wistful, as she sat comparing present with past. And loath though she was to dig deep, for fear of stirring up uncomfortable things, she could not escape making the discovery that, in spite of all his success—and his career there had surpassed their dearest hopes—in spite of the natural gifts fortune had showered on him, Richard was not what you would call a happy man. No, nor even moderately happy. Why this should be, it went beyond her to say. He had everything he could wish for: yes, everything: except perhaps a little more time to himself, and better health. He was not as strong as she would have liked to see him. Nothing radically wrong, of course; but enough to fidget him. Might not this . . . this— he himself called it "want of tone"—be a reason for the scant pleasure he got out of life? And: "I think what I'll do is, I'll pop down and see Dr. Munce about him one morning, without saying a word to him about it," was how she eased her mind and wound up her reverie.

But daylight, and the most prosaic hours of the twenty-four, made the plan look absurd.

Once alive, though, to his condition, she felt deeply sorry for him, in his patent inability ever to be content. It was a thousand pities. Things might have run so smoothly for him, he have got so much satisfaction out of them, if only he could

have braced himself to regard life in cheerier fashion. But at
this, Mary stopped short . . . and wondered . . . and wondered. Was that really true? Positively, her experiences of late
led her to believe that Richard would be less happy still, if
he had nothing to be unhappy about.— But dear me! this was
getting out of her depth altogether. She shook her head and
rebuked herself, for being fanciful.

All the same, her new glimpse of his inmost nature made
her doubly tender of thwarting him; hence, she did not set
her face as firmly as she might otherwise have done, against
a wild plan he now formed of again altering, or indeed
rebuilding, the house. And this, though she could scarcely
think of it with patience. She liked her house so well as it
stood; and it was amply big enough: there were only the pair
of them, and John's child. It had the name, she knew, of being
one of the most comfortable and best-kept in Ballarat. Brick
for solidity, where wood prevailed, with a wide snowy verandah, up the posts of which rare creepers ran, twining their
tendrils one with another to form a screen against the sun.
Now, what must Richard do but uproot the creepers and pull
down the verandah, thus baring the walls to the fierce summer
heat; plaster over the brick; and, more outlandish still, add a
top story. When she came back from Melbourne, where she
had gone a-visiting to escape the upset—Richard, ordinarily
so sensitive, had managed to endure it quite well, in a little
room to the back, thus proving that he *could* put up with
discomfort, if he wanted to—when she saw it again, Mary
hardly recognised her home. Personally, she thought it ugly,
for all its grandeur; changed wholly for the worse. Nor did
time ever reconcile her to the upper story. Domestic worries
bred from it: the servant went off in a huff because of the
stairs; they were at once obliged to double their staff. To cap
it all, with its flat front unbroken by bay or porch, the house
looked like no other in the town. Now, instead of passing
admiring remarks, people stood stock-still before the gate, and
laughed at its droll appearance.

Still, she would gladly have made the best of this, had
Richard been the happier for it. He was not—or only for the
briefest of intervals. Then, his restlessness broke out afresh.

There came days when nothing suited him; not his fine
consulting-room, or the improved furnishings of the house, or

even her cookery, of which he had once been so fond. He grew dainty to a degree; she scoured the place for piquant recipes. Next, he fell to imagining it was unhealthy to sleep on feathers, and went to the expense of having a hard horse-hair mattress made to fit the bed. Accustomed to the softest down, he naturally tossed and turned all night long, and rose in the morning declaring he felt as though he had been beaten with sticks. The mattress was stowed away in a lean-to behind the kitchen, and there it remained. It was not alone. Mary sometimes stood and considered, with a rueful eye, the many discarded objects that bore it company. Richard, who oddly enough, was ever able to poke fun at himself, had christened this outhouse "the cemetery of dead fads." Here was a set of Indian clubs he had been going to harden his muscles with every morning, and had used for a week; together with an india-rubber gymnastic apparatus, bought for the same purpose. Here stood a patent shower-bath, that was to have dashed energy over him after a bad night, and had only succeeded in giving him acute neuralgia; a standing-desk he had broken his back at, for a couple of days; a homœopathic medicine-chest and a phrenological head—both subjects he had meant to satisfy his curiosity by looking into, had time not failed him.— Mary sighed, when she thought of the waste of good money these and similar articles stood for. (Some day, she would just have them privately carted away to auction!) But if Richard set his heart on a thing, he wanted it so badly, so much more than other people did, that he knew no peace till he had it.

Mahony read in his wife's eyes the disapproval she was too wise to utter. At any other time her silent criticism would have galled him; in this case, he took shelter behind it. Let her only go on setting him down for lax and spendthrift, incapable of knowing his own mind! He would be sorry, indeed, for her to guess how matters really stood with him. The truth was, he had fallen a prey to an utter despondency, was become so spiritless that it puzzled even himself. He thought he could trace much of the mischief back to the professional knocks and jars Ocock's action had brought down on him: to hear one's opinion doubted, one's skill questioned, was the tyro's portion; he was too old now, to treat such insolence with the scorn it deserved. Of course, he had lived the affair down; but the result of it would seem to be a bottomless *ennui,* a *tedium vitæ* that had something pathological about it. Under its influence the homeliest trifles swelled to feats beyond his strength. There was, for instance, the putting on and off of one's clothing: this infinite boredom of straps and buttons—and all for what? For a day that would be an exact copy of the one gone before, a night as unrefreshing as the last. Did any one suspect that there were moments when he quailed before this job, suspect that more than once he had even reckoned the number of times he would be called on to perform it, day in, day out, till that garment was put on him that came off no more; or that he could understand and feel sympathy with those faint souls—and there were such—who laid hands on themselves, rather than go on doing it: did this get abroad, he would be considered ripe for Bedlam.

Physician, heal thyself!— He swallowed doses of a tonic preparation, and restricted himself to a fatty diet.

Thereafter, he tried to take a philosophic view of his case. He had now, he told himself, reached an age when such a state of mind gave cause neither for astonishment nor alarm. How often had it not fallen to him, in his rôle of medical adviser, to reassure a patient on this score! The arrival of middle age brought about a certain lowness of spirits in even the most robust: along with a more or less marked bodily languor went an uneasy sense of coming loss: the time was at hand to bid farewell to much that had hitherto made life agreeable; and for most this was a bitter pill. Meanwhile, one held a kind of mental stocktaking. As often as not, by the light of a complete disillusionment. Of the many glorious things one had hoped to do—or to be—nothing was accomplished: the great realisation, in youth breathlessly chased but never grasped, was now seen to be a mist-wraith, that could wear a thousand forms, but invariably turned to air as one came up with it. In nine instances out of ten, there was nothing to put in its place; and you began to ask yourself, in a kind of horrific amaze: "Can this be all? . . . *this?* For this the pother of growth, the struggles, and the sufferings?" The soul's climacteric, if you would, from which a mortal came forth dulled to resignation; or greedy for the few physical pleasures left him; or prone to that tragic clinging to youth's

370

skirts, which made the later years of many women and not a few men ridiculous. In each case, the motive power was the same: the haunting fear that one had squeezed life dry; worse still, that it had not been worth the squeezing.

Thus his reason. But, like a tongue of flame, his instinct leapt up to give combat. By the gods, this cap did *not* fit him! Squeezed life dry? . . . found it not worth while? Why, he had never got within measurable distance of what he called life, at all! There could be no question of his resigning himself; deep down in him, he knew, was an enormous residue of vitality, of untouched mental energy, that only waited to be drawn on. It was like a buried treasure, jealously kept for the event of his one day catching up with life: not the bare scramble for a living that here went by that name, but Life with a capital L, the existence he had once confidently counted on as his—a tourney of spiritual adventuring, of intellectual excitement, in which the prize striven for was not, he thanked God, money, or anything to do with money. Far away, thousands of miles off, luckier men than he were in the thick of it. He, of his own free will, had cut himself off, and now it was too late.

But was it indeed? Had the time irretrievably gone by? The ancient idea of escape, long dormant, suddenly reawoke in him, with a new force. And, once stirring, it was not to be silenced, but went on sounding like a ground-tone through all he did. At first he shut his ears to it, to dally with side issues. For example, he worried the question why the breaking-point should have been reached just at this moment, and not six months, a year ago. It was mere quibbling to lay the whole blame on Ocock's shoulders. The real cause went deeper, was of older growth. And, driving his mind back over the past, he believed he could pin his present loss of grip to that fatal day, on which he learnt that his best friend had betrayed him. Things like that gave you a crack that would not mend; you must needs treat yourself thereafter with the tenderest care. One effect of the blow had been to undermine his faith in his fellow-men: he now found himself suspicious where he had been credulous; prone to see evil where no evil was. For, deceived by Purdy, in whom could he trust? Of a surety not in the pushful set of jobbers and tricksters he was condemned to live amongst. No discoveries he might make about them would surprise him.— And, once more, the old impotent anger with himself broke forth, that he should ever have let himself take root in such detestable surroundings.

Why not shake the dust of the country off his feet?— From this direct attack he recoiled, casting up his hands as if against the spell of the evil eye. What next—what next! But, exclaim as he might, now that the idea had put on words, it was by no means so simple to fend it off, as when it had been a mere vague humming at the back of his mind. It seized him; swept his brain bare of other thoughts. He began to look worn. And never more so than when he imagined himself taking the bull by the horns, and asking Mary's approval of his wild-goose scheme. He could picture her face, when she heard that he planned throwing up his fine position and decamping on nothing a year. The vision was a cold douche to his folly. No, no! it would not do; marriage forbade such haphazard proceedings. You could not accustom a woman to ease and luxury, and then, when you felt *you* had had enough, and would welcome a return to Spartan simplicity, to an austere clarity of living, expect her to be prepared, at the word, to step back into poverty. One was bound . . . bound . . . and by just those silken threads which, in premarital days, had seemed sheerly desirable. He wondered now what it would be like to stand there free as the wind, answerable only to himself. The bare thought of it filled him as with the rushing of wings.

Once, he remembered, he had been within an ace of cutting and running. That was in the early days, soon after his marriage. Trade had petered out; and there would have been as little to leave behind as to carry with him. But, even so, circumstances had proved too strong for him: what with Mary's persuasions and John's intermeddling, his scheme had come to nothing. And if, with so much in his favour, he had not managed to carry it out, how in all the world could he hope to now, when every mortal thing conspired against him? It was, besides, excusable in your youth to challenge fortune; a very different matter for one of his age.

Of his age!— The words gave him pause. By their light he saw why he had knuckled under so meekly, at the time of his first attempt. It was because he had then been a young man, with the best of his life before him; a few years one way

372

or another did not signify; he had them to spare. Now, each individual year was precious to him; he parted with it lingeringly, unwillingly. Time had taken to flashing past, too; Christmas was hardly celebrated before it was again at the door. Another ten years or so and he would be an old man, and it would in very truth be too late. The tempter voice—in this case also the voice of reason—said: now or never!

But when he came to look the facts in the face, his heart failed him anew, so heavily did the arguments against his taking such a step—and, true to his race, it was these he began by marshalling—weigh down the scales. He should have done it, if it must be, five . . . three . . . even a couple of years ago. Each day that broke added to the tangle, made the idea seem more preposterous. Local dignities had been showered on him: he sat on the Committees of the District Hospital and the Benevolent Asylum; was Honorary Medical Officer to this Society and that; a trustee of the church; one of the original founders of the Mechanics' Institute; vice-president of the Botanical Society; and so on, *ad infinitum*. His practice was second to none; his visiting-book rarely had a blank space in it; people drove in from miles round, to consult him. In addition, he had an extremely popular wife, a good house and garden, horses and traps, and a sure yearly income of some twelve or thirteen hundred. Of what stuff was he made, that he could lightly contemplate turning his back on prizes such as these?

Even as he told them off, however, the old sense of hollowness was upon him again. His life there reminded him of a gaudy drop-scene, let down before an empty stage; a painted sham, with darkness and vacuity behind. At bottom, none of these distinctions and successes meant anything to him; not a scrap of mental pabulum could be got from them: rather would he have chosen to be poor, and a nobody, among people whose thoughts flew to meet his, half-way. And there was also another side to it. Stingy though the years had been of intellectual grist, they had not scrupled to rob him of many an essential by which he set store. His old faculty—for good or evil—of swift decision, for instance. It was lost to him now; as witness his present miserable vacillation. It had gone off arm-in-arm with his health; physically, he was but a ghost of the man he had once been. But the bitterest grudge he bore the

373

life was for the shipwreck it had made of his early ideals. He
remembered the pure joy, the lofty sentiments, with which he
had returned to medicine. Bah!—there had been no room for
any sentimental nonsense of that kind, here. He had long since
ceased to follow his profession disinterestedly; the years had
made a hack of him—a skilled hack, of course—but just a hack.
He had had no time for theory, or for quiet study; all his
strength had gone in keeping his income up to a certain figure;
for fear the wife should be less well dressed and equipped
than her neighbours; or patients fight shy of him; or his
confrères wag their tongues.— Oh! he had adapted himself
supremely well to the standards of this Australia, so-called
Felix. And he must not complain if, in so doing, he had been
stripped, not only of his rosy dreams, but also of that spiritual
force on which he could once have drawn at will. Like a fool
he had believed it possible to serve mammon with impunity,
and for just as long as it suited him. He knew better now. At
this moment, he was undergoing the sensations of one who,
having taken shelter in what he thinks a light and flimsy
structure, finds that it is built of the solidest stone. Worse
still: that he has been walled up inside.

And even suppose he *could* pull himself together for the
effort required, how justify his action in the eyes of the world?
His motives would be Double-dutch to the hard-headed crew
among whom his lot was cast; nor would any go to the trouble
of trying to understand him. There was John. All John would
see was an elderly, and not over-robust man deliberately
throwing away the fruits of year-long toil—and for what? For
the privilege of, in some remote spot, as a stranger and unknown, having his way to make all over again; of being free
to shoulder once more the risks and hazards the operation
involved. And little though he cared for John or any one else's
opinion, Mahony could not help feeling a trifle sore in advance, at the ridicule of which he might be the object, at the
zanyish figure he was going to be obliged to cut.

But a fig for what people thought of him! Once away from
here, he would, he thanked God, never see any of them again.
No, it was Mary who was the real stumbling-block, the opponent he most feared. Had he been less attached to her, the
thing would have been easier; as it was, he shrank from hurting her. And hurt and confuse her he must. He knew Mary as

well—nay, better than he knew his own unreckonable self. For Mary was not a creature of moods, did not change her mental envelope a dozen times a day. And just his precise knowledge of her told him, that he would never get her to see eye to eye with him in this. Her clear, serene outlook was attuned to the plain and the practical; she would discover a thousand drawbacks to his scheme, but nary a one of the incorporeal benefits he dreamed of reaping from it. There was his handling of money, for one thing: she had come, he was aware, to regard him as incurably extravagant; and it would be no easy task to convince her that he could learn again to fit his expenses to a light purse. She had a woman's instinctive distrust, too, of out-of-the-way actions. Another point made him still more dubious. Mary's whole heart and happiness were bound up in this place, where she had spent the flower-years of her life: who knew if she would thrive as well on other soil? He found it intolerable to think that she might have to pay for his want of stability.— Yes, reduced to its essentials, it came to mean the pitting of one soul's welfare against that of another; was a toss-up between his happiness and hers. One of them would have to yield. Who would suffer more by doing so—he or she? He believed that a sacrifice on his part would make the wreck of his life complete. On hers— well, thanks to her doughty habit of finding good everywhere, there was a chance of her coming out unscathed.

Now or never! Here was his case in a nutshell.

Still he did not tackle Mary. For, sometimes, he rehearsed in thought what he would say to her, when the moment came; and imagined her amazed rejoinders. And, did he put himself in her place, a disturbed doubt crept upon him whether it would not, after all, be possible to go on as he was; instead of, as she would drastically word it, cutting his throat with his own hand. And to be perfectly honest, he believed it would. He could now afford to pay for help in his work; to buy what books he needed or fancied; to take holidays, while putting in a *locum* at a guinea per day; even to keep on the *locum*, at a good salary, while he journeyed overseas to visit the land of his birth.— But, at this, another side of him—what he thought of as spirit, in contradistinction to soul—cried out in alarm, fearful lest it was again to be betrayed. Thus far, though by rights coequal in the house of the body, it had been rigidly kept down. Nevertheless, it had persisted, like a bright cold little spark at dead of night: his restlessness of mind, the spiritual malaise that encumbered him, had been its mute form of protest. Did he go on turning a deaf ear to its warnings, he might do himself irreparable harm. For time was flying, the sum of his years mounting, shrinking that roomy future to which he had thus far always postponed what seemed too difficult for the moment. Now, he saw that he dared delay no longer, in setting free the imprisoned elements in him, was he ever to grow to that perfect whole which each mortal aspires to be.— That a change of environment would work this miracle he did not doubt; a congenial environment was meat and drink to such as he, was light and air. Here, in this country, he had remained as utterly alien as any Jew of old who wept by the rivers of Babylon.— And now, like a half-remembered tune, there came floating into his mind words he had lit on somewhere, or learnt on the school-bench— Horace, he thought, but, whatever their source, words that fitted his case to a nicety. *Coelum, non animum, mutant, qui trans mare currunt.* "Non animum?" Ah! could he but have foreseen this—foreknown it. If not before he set sail on what was, after all, to have been but a swift adventure, then at least on that fateful day long past, when, foiled by Mary's pleadings and his own inertia, he had let himself be bound anew.—

Thus the summer dragged by; a summer to try the toughest. Mahony thought he had never gone through its like, for heat and discomfort. The drought would not break, and, on the great squatting-stations round Ballarat and to the north, the sheep dropped like flies at an early frost. The forest reservoirs dried up, displaying the red mud of their bottoms, and a bath became a luxury—or a penance—the scanty water running thick and red. Then the bush caught fire, and burnt for three days, painting the sky a rusty brown, and making the air hard to breathe. Of a morning, his first act, on going into his surgery, was to pick up the thermometer that stood on the table. Sure as fate, though the clock had not long struck nine, the mercury marked something between a hundred and a hundred and five degrees. He let it fall with a nerveless gesture. Since his sunstroke he not only hated, he feared the sun.

But out into it he must, to drive through dust-clouds so opaque that he could only draw rein till they subsided, meanwhile holloaing off collisions. Under the close leather hood he sat and stifled; or, removing his green goggles for the fiftieth time, climbed down to enter yet another baked wooden house, where he handled prostrate bodies rank with sweat, or prescribed for pallid or fever-speckled children. Then home, to toy with the food set before him, his mind already running on the discomforts of his afternoon round.— Two bits of ill-luck came his way this summer. Old Ocock fell, in dismounting from a vehicle, and sustained a compound fracture of the femur. Owing to his advanced age, there was for a time fear of malunion of the parts, and this kept Mahony on the rack. Secondly, a near neighbour, a common little fellow who kept a jeweller's shop in Bridge Street, actually took the plunge: sold off one fine day and sailed for home. And this seemed the unkindest cut of all.

But the accident that gave the death-blow to his scruples was another. On the advice of a wealthy publican he was treating, whose judgment he trusted, Mahony had invested— heavily for him, selling off other stock to do it—in a company known as the Hodderburn Estate. This was a government affair, and ought to have been beyond reproach. One day, however, it was found that the official reports of the work done by the diamond drill-bore were cooked documents; and instantly every one connected with the mine—directors, managers, engineers—lay under the suspicion of fraudulent dealings. Shares had risen as high as ten pounds odd; but, when the drive reached the bore, and, in place of the deep gutter-ground the public had been led to expect, hard rock was found overhead, there was a panic; shares dropped to twenty-five shillings, and did not rally. Mahony was a loser by six hundred pounds, and got, besides, a moral shaking, from which he could not recover. He sat and bit his little-finger nail to the quick. Was he, he savagely asked himself, going to linger on, until the little he had managed to save was snatched from him?

He dashed off a letter to John, asking his brother-in-law to recommend him a reliable broker. And this done, he got up to look for Mary, determined to come to grips with her at last.

[11]

How to begin, how reduce to a few plain words his subtle tangle of thought and feeling, was the problem.

He did not find his wife on her usual seat in the arbour. In searching for her, upstairs and down, he came to a rapid decision. He would lay chief stress on his poor state of health.

"I feel I'm killing myself. I can't go on."

"But Richard dear!" ejaculated Mary, and paused in her sewing, her needle uplifted, a bead balanced on its tip.— Richard had run her to earth in the spare bedroom to which at this time she often repaired. For he objected to the piece of work she had on hand—that of covering yards of black cashmere with minute jet beads—vowing that she would ruin her eyesight over it. So she, having set her heart on a fashionable polonaise, was careful to keep out of his way.

"I'm not a young man any longer, wife. When one's past forty——"

"Poor 'mother' used to say forty-five was a man's prime of life."

"Not for me. And not here—in this God-forsaken hole!"

"Oh, dear me! I do wonder why you have such a down on Ballarat. I'm sure there must be many worse places in the world to live in"; and, lowering her needle, Mary brought the bead to its appointed spot. "Of course you have a lot to do, I know, and being such a poor sleeper doesn't improve matters." But she was considering her pattern sideways as she spoke, thinking more of it than of what she said. Every one had to work hard out here: compared with some she could name, Richard's job of driving round in a springy buggy seemed ease itself. "Besides, you know, dear, I told you at the time, you were wrong not to take a holiday in winter, when you had the chance. You need a thorough change every year to set you up. You came back from the last as fresh as a daisy."

"The only change that will benefit me is one for good and all," said Mahony, with extreme gloom. He had thrown up the bed-curtain and stretched himself on the bed, where he lay with his hands clasped under his neck.

Tutored by experience, Mary did not contradict him.

"And it's the kind I've finally made up my mind to take."

"Richard! How you do run on!" and Mary, still gently

378

incredulous, but a thought wider awake, let her work sink to her lap. "What is the use of talking like that?"

"Believe it or not, my dear, as you choose. You'll see— that's all."

At her further exclamations of doubt and amazement, Mahony's patience slipped its leash. "Surely to goodness my health comes first . . . before any confounded practice?"

"Ssh! Baby's asleep.— And don't get cross, Richard. You can hardly expect me not to be surprised when you spring a thing of this sort on me. You've never even dropped a hint of it before."

"Because I knew very well what it would be. You're dead against it, of course!"

"Now I call that unjust. You've barely let me get a word in edgeways."

"Oh, I know by heart everything you're going to say. It's nonsense . . . folly . . . madness . . . and so on: all the phrases you women fish up from your vocabulary when you want to stave off a change—hinder any alteration of the *status quo*.— But I'll tell you this, wife. You'll bury me here, if I don't get away soon. I'm not much more than skin and bone as it is. And I confess, if I've got to be buried, I'd rather lie elsewhere —have good English earth atop of me."

Had Mary been a man, she might have retorted that this was a very woman's way of shifting ground. She bit her lip and did not answer immediately. After a pause she said: "You know I can't bear to hear you talk like that, even in fun. Besides, you always say so much more than you mean, dear."

"Very well, then, if you prefer it, wait and see! You'll be sorry some day."

"Do you mean to tell me, Richard, you're in earnest, when you talk of selling off your practice here and going to England?"

"I can buy another there, can't I?"

With these words he leapt to his feet, all afire with animation. And while Mary, now thoroughly uneasy, was folding up her needlework, he dilated upon the benefits that would accrue to them from the change. Good-bye to dust, and sun, and drought, to blistering hot winds, and *papier mâché* walls! They would make their new home in some substantial old stone house that had weathered half a century or more,

379

tangled over with creepers, folded away in its own privacy as only an English house could be. In the flower-garden roses would trail over arch and pergola; there would be a lawn with shaped yews on it; while, in the orchard, old apple-trees would flaunt their red abundance above grey, lichened walls.

("As if there weren't apples enough here!" thought his wife.)

He got a frog in his throat as he went on to paint in greater detail for her, who had left it so young, the intimate charm of the home country—the rich, green, dimpled countryside. And not till now did he grasp how sorely he had missed it. "Oh, believe me, to talk of 'going home' is no mere figure of speech, Mary!" In fancy he trod winding lanes that ran between giant hedges: hedges in tender bud, with dew on them; or snowed over with white mayflowers: or behung with the fairy webs and gossamer of early autumn, that were thick as twine beneath their load of moisture. He followed white roads that were banked with primroses and ran headlong down to the sea: he climbed the shoulder of a down on a spring morning, when the air was alive with larks carolling. But, chiefly, it was the greenness that called to him—the greenness of the greenest country in the world. Viewed from this distance, the homeland looked to him like one vast meadow. Oh, to tread its grass again!—not what one knew as grass here, a poor annual, that lasted for a few brief weeks; but lush meadow-grass, a foot high; or shaven emerald lawns, on which ancient trees spread their shade; or the rank growth in old orchards, starry with wild flowers, on which fruit-blossoms fluttered down. He longed, too, for the exquisite finishedness of the mother country, the soft tints of cloud-veiled northern skies. His eyes ached, his brows had grown wrinkled, with gazing on iron roofs set against the hard blue overhead; on dirty weatherboards, innocent of paint; on higgledy-piggledy backyards and ramshackle fences; on the straggling landscape with its untidy trees—all the unrelieved ugliness, in short, of the colonial scene.

He stopped only for want of breath. Mary was silent. He waited. Still she did not speak.

He fell to earth with a bump, and was angry. "Come . . . out with it! I suppose all this seems to you just the raving of a lunatic?"

"Oh, Richard, no. But a little . . . well, a little unpractical. I never heard before of any one throwing up a good income because he didn't like the scenery. It's a step that needs the greatest consideration."

"Good God! Do you think I haven't considered it?—and from every angle? Why, my dear, there isn't an argument for or against, that I haven't gone over a thousand and one times."

"And with never a word to me, Richard?" Mary was hurt; and showed it. "It really is hardly fair. For this is my home as well as yours.— But now listen to me. You're tired out, run down with the heat and that last attack of dysentery. Take a good holiday—stay away for three months, if you like. Sail over to Hobart Town, or up to Sydney, you who're so fond of the water. And when you come back, strong and well, we'll talk about all this again. I'm sure by then you'll see things with other eyes."

"And who's to look after the practice, pray?"

"Why, a *locum tenens,* of course. Or engage an assistant."

"Aha! you'd agree to that now, would you? I remember how opposed you were once to the idea."

"Well, if I have to choose between it and you giving up altogether. . . . Now, for your own sake, Richard, don't go and do anything rash. If once you sell off and leave Ballarat, you can never come back. And then, if you regret it, where will you be? That's why I say don't hurry to decide. Sleep over it. Or let us consult somebody—John, perhaps——"

"No, you don't, madam, no, you don't!" cried Richard with a grim dash of humour. "You had me once . . . crippled me . . . handcuffed me—you and your John between you! It shan't happen again."

"I crippled you? *I,* Richard! Why, never in my life have I done anything but what I thought was for your good. I've always put you first." And Mary's eyes filled with tears.

"Yes, where it's a question of one's material welfare you haven't your equal—I admit that. But the other side of me needs some coddling as well—yes, and sympathy, too. But it can whistle for such a thing as far as you're concerned."

Mary sighed. "I think you don't realise, dear, how difficult it sometimes is to understand you . . . or to make out what you really do want," she said slowly.

Her tone struck at his heart. "Indeed and I do!" he cried in a burst of contrition. "I'm a born old grumbler, mavourneen, I know—contrariness in person! But in this case . . . come, love, do *try* to grasp what I'm after; it means so much to me.'" And he held out his hand to her, to beseech her.

Unhesitatingly, she laid hers in it. "I am trying, Richard, though you mayn't believe it. I always do. And even if I sometimes can't manage it—well, you know, dear, you generally get your own way in the end. Think of the house. I'm still not clear why you altered it. I liked it much better as it was. But I didn't make any fuss, did I?—though I should have, if I'd thought we were only to occupy it for a single year after.— Still, that was a mere trifle compared with what you want to do now. Though I lived to a hundred, I should never be able to approve of this. And you don't know how hard it is to consent to a thing one disapproves of. You couldn't do it yourself, dear! Oh, what *was* the use, Richard, of working as you have done, if now, just when you can afford to charge higher fees, and the practice is really starting to bring in money——"

Mahony let her hand drop, even giving it a slight push from him, and turned to pace the floor anew. "Oh, money, money, money! I'm tired of the very sound of the word. But you talk as if nothing else mattered. Can't you for once, wife, see through the letter of the thing, to the spirit behind? I admit the practice *has* brought in a tidy income of late; but as for the rest of the splendours, they exist, my dear, only in your imagination. If you ask me, I say I lead a dog's life—why, even a navvy works only for a fixed number of hours per diem! My days have neither beginning nor end. Look at yesterday! Out in the blazing sun from morning till night—I didn't get back from the second round, till nine. At ten, a confinement, that keeps me up till three. From three till dawn I toss and turn, far too weary to sleep. By the time six o'clock struck —you of course were slumbering sweetly—I was in hell with tic. At seven I could stand it no longer, and got up for the chloroform bottle; an hour's rest, at any price—else how face the crowd in the waiting-room . . . the liquid butter on the breakfast-table . . . the flies . . . the infernal glare of the roads? And you call that splendour?—luxurious ease? If so, my dear, words don't mean the same thing any more for you and me."

Mary did not point out that she had said nothing of the

kind, or that he had set up an extreme case as typical. She tightened her lips; her big eyes were very solemn.

"And it's not the work alone," Richard was declaring. "It's the place, wife—the people. I'm done with 'em, Mary—utterly done! Upon my word, if I felt I had to go on living among them even for another twelvemonth——"

"But *people* are the same all the world over!" The protest broke from her, in spite of herself.

"No, by God, they're not!" And here Richard launched out into such a diatribe against his fellow-colonists: "This sordid riffraff! These hard, mean, grasping money-grubbers!" as made Mary stand aghast. What could be the matter with him? What was he thinking of, he who was ordinarily so generous? Had he forgotten the many kindnesses shown him, the warm gratitude of his patients, people's sympathy at the time of his illness? Surely he was more to blame than they, that he couldn't manage to fit himself in, here, and be interested in what interested every one else? It wasn't their fault that he happened to be cleverer, and more bookish, and refined. Just for this reason, he ought to have been quicker at understanding them, and, if necessary, at making allowance for them. But the thought never seemed to cross his mind.— Meanwhile he went on: "My demands are of the most modest. All I ask is, to be among human beings with whom I have half an idea in common— men who sometimes lift their noses from the ground, Mary, instead of eternally scheming how to line their pockets, and reckoning human progress solely in terms of £ s. d. No, I've sacrificed enough of my life to this country. I intend to have the rest for myself. And there's another thing, my dear—another bad habit this precious place breeds in us. It begins by making us indifferent to those who belong to us, but who are out of sight, and ends by cutting through our closest ties. And I don't mean by distance alone. I have an old mother still living, Mary, whose chief prayer is that she may see me once again before she dies. I was her last-born—the child her arms kept the shape of. What am I to her now? . . . what does she know of me, of the hard, tired, middle-aged man I have become? And you are in much the same box, my dear; unless you've forgotten by now that you ever had a mother."

Mary was scandalised. "Forget one's mother? . . . Richard!

I think you're trying what dreadful things you can find to say to-day. . . . When I write home every three months!" And provoked by this fresh piece of unreason, she opened fire in earnest, in defence of what she believed to be their true welfare. Richard listened to her without interrupting; even seemed to grant the truth of what she said. But none the less, even as she pleaded with him, a numbing sense of futility crept over her. She stuttered, halted, and finally fell silent. Her words were like so many lassos thrown after his vagrant soul; and this was out of reach. It had sniffed freedom. It *was* free; it ran wild already on the boundless plains of liberty.

After he had gone from the room she sat on, with idle hands. She was all in a daze. Richard was about to commit an out-and-out folly, and she was powerless to hinder it. If only she had had some one she could have talked things over with, taken advice of! But no—it went against the grain in her to discuss her husband's actions with a third person. Purdy had been the sole exception, and Purdy had rendered himself impossible—even if she had known where to find him.

Looking back, she marvelled at her own dullness in not foreseeing that something like this was bound to happen. What more natural than that the multitude of little whims and fads Richard had indulged should culminate in a big whim of this kind? But the acknowledgment caused her fresh anxiety. She had watched him tire, like a fickle child, of first one thing, then another; was it likely that he would now suddenly prove more stable? She did not think so. For she attributed his present mood of pettish aversion wholly to the fact of his being run down in health. It was quite true: he had not been himself of late. But here again, he was so fanciful that you never knew how literally to take his ailments: half the time she believed he just imagined their existence; and the long holiday she had urged on him would have been enough to sweep the cobwebs from his brain.— Oh, if only he could have held on in patience! Four or five years hence, at most, he might have considered retiring from general practice. She almost wept as she remembered how they had once planned to live for that day. Now, it was all to end in smoke.

Then her mind reverted to herself, and to what the break would mean to her; and her little world rocked to its foundations. For no clear call went out to Mary from her native land. She docilely said "home" with the rest, and kept her family ties intact; but she had never expected to go back, unless on a flying visit. She thought of England rather vaguely as a country where it was always raining, and where—according to John—an assemblage of old fogies, known as the House of Commons, persistently intermeddled in the affairs of the colony. For more than half her life—and the half that truly counted—Australia had been her home.

Her home! In fancy Mary made a round of the house, viewing each cosy room, lingering fondly over the contents of cupboards and presses, recollecting how she had added this piece of furniture for convenience sake, that for ornament, till the whole was as perfect as she knew how to make it. Now, everything she loved and valued—the piano, the wax-candle chandelier, the gilt cornices, the dining-room horsehair—would fall under the auctioneer's hammer, go to deck out the houses of other people. Richard said she could buy better and handsomer things in England; but Mary allowed herself no illusions on this score. Where was the money to come from? She had learnt, by personal experience, what slow work building up a practice was. It would be years and years before they could hope for another such home. And sore and sorry as *she* might feel at having to relinquish her pretty things, in Richard's case it would mean a good deal more than that. To him the loss of them would be a real misfortune, so used had he grown to luxurious comfort, so strongly did the need of it run in his blood.

Worse still was the prospect of parting from relatives and friends. The tears came at this, freely. John's children!—who would watch over them, when she was gone? How could she, from so far away, keep the promise she had made to poor Jinny on her death-bed? She would have to give up the baby, of which she had grown so fond—give it back into Zara's unmotherly hands. And never again of a Saturday would she fetch poor little long-legged Trotty from school. She must say good-bye to one and all—to John, and Zara, and Jerry—and would know no more, at close quarters, how they fared. When Jerry married—and his salary, as auctioneer's clerk, already stood at a hundred and eighty—there would be no one to see to it that he chose the right kind of girl. Then Ned and Polly —poor souls, poor souls! What with the rapid increase of their family and Ned's unsteadiness—he could not keep any job long because of it—they only just managed to make ends meet. How they would do it when she was not there to lend a helping hand, she could not imagine. And outside her brothers and sisters, there was good Mrs. Devine. Mary had engaged to guide her friend's tottery steps on the slippery path of Melbourne society, did Mr. Devine enter the ministry. And poor little Agnes with her terrible weakness . . . and Amelia and her sickly babes . . . and Tilly, dear good warm-hearted Tilly! Never again would the pair of them enjoy one of their jolly laughs; or cook for a picnic; or drive out to a mushroom hunt. No, the children would grow up anyhow; her brothers forget her in carving out their own lives; her friends find other friends.

For some time, however, she kept her own counsel. But when she had tried by hook and by crook to bring Richard to reason, and had failed; when she saw that he was actually beginning, on the quiet, to make ready for departure, and that the day was coming on which every one would have to know: then, she threw off her reserve. She was spending the afternoon with Tilly. They sat on the verandah together, John's child, black-eyed, fat, self-willed, playing, after the manner of two short years, at their feet. At the news that was broken to her, Tilly began by laughing immoderately, believing that Mary was merely "taking a rise out of her." But having studied her friend's face, she let her work fall, slowly opened mouth and eyes, and was at first unequal to uttering a word.

Thereafter she bombarded Mary with questions.

"Wants to leave Ballarat? To go home to England?" she echoed, with an emphasis such as Tilly alone could lay. "Well! of all the . . . What for? What on earth for? 'As somebody gone and left 'im a fortune? Or 'as 'e been appointed pillmonger-in-ordinary to the Queen 'erself? What is it, Mary? Whatever's up?"

What indeed! This was the question Mary dreaded, and one that would leap to every tongue: why was he going? She sat on the horns of a dilemma. It was not in her to wound people's feeling by blurting out the truth—this would also put Richard in a bad light—and did she give no reason at all, many would think he had taken leave of his senses. Weakly, in a very un-Maryish fashion, she mumbled that his health was not what it should be, and he had got it into his head that, for this, the climate of the colony was to blame. Nothing would do him but to get back to England, without delay.

"I never! No, never in my born days did I hear tell of such a thing!" and Tilly, exploding, brought her closed fist heavily down on her knee. "Mary! . . . for a mere maggot like that, to chuck up a practice such as 'e's got! Upon my word, my dear, it looks as if 'e was touched 'ere,"—and she significantly tapped her forehead. "Ha! Now I understand. You know I've seen quite well, love, you've been looking a bit down in the mouth, of late. And so 'as pa noticed it, too. After you'd gone the other day, 'e said to me: 'Looks reflexive-like does the little lady nowadays; as if she'd got something on 'er mind.' And I to 'im: 'Pooh! Isn't it enough that she's got to put up with the cranks and crotchets of one o' *your* sect?'— Oh, Mary, my dear, there's many a true word said in jest. Though little did I think what the crotchet would be." And slowly the rims of Tilly's eyes, and the tip of her nose reddened and swelled.

"No, I can't picture it, Mary—what it'ull be like 'ere without you," she said; and pulling out her handkerchief blew snort after snort, which was Tilly's way nowadays of having a good cry.— "There, there, Baby, Aunty's only got the sniffles. Be a little duck, and don't follow suit.— For just think of it, Mary: except that first year or so after you were married, we've been together, you and me, pretty much ever since you came to us that time at the 'otel—a little black midget of a thing, in short frocks. I can still remember 'ow Jinn and I laughed at the idea of you teaching us; and 'ow poor ma said to wait and make sure we weren't laughing on the wrong side of our mouths. And ma was right, as usual. For if ever a clever little kid trod the earth, it was you."

Mary pooh-poohed the cleverness. "I knew very little more than you yourselves. No, it was you who were all so kind to me. I had been feeling so lonely—as if nobody wanted me— and I shall never forget how 'mother' put her arms round me and cuddled me, and how safe and comfortable I felt. It was always just like home there to me."

"And why not, I'd like to know!— Look 'ere, Mary, I'm going to ask you something, plump and plain. 'Ave you really been happy in your marriage, my dear, or 'ave you not? You're such a loyal little soul, I know you'd never show it, if you weren't;

and sometimes I've 'ad my doubts about you, Mary. For you and the doctor are just as different to each other as chalk and cheese."

"Of course I have—as happy as the day's long!" cried Mary, sensitive as ever to a reflection on her husband. "You mustn't think anything like that, Tilly. I couldn't even imagine myself married to any one but Richard."

"Then that only makes it harder for you now, poor thing, pulled two ways like, as you are," said Tilly, and trumpeted afresh. "All the same, there isn't anything I'd stick at, Mary, to keep you here. Don't be offended, my dear, but it doesn't matter half so much about the doctor going as you. There's none cleverer than 'im, of course, in 'is own line. But 'e's never fitted in properly here—I don't want to exactly say 'e thinks 'imself too good for us; but there *is* something, Mary love, and I'm not the only one who's felt it. I've known people go on like anything about 'im behind 'is back: nothing would induce them to have 'im and 'is haughty airs inside their doors again, etcetera."

Mary flushed. "Yes, I know, Tilly, people do sometimes judge Richard very unkindly. For at heart he's the most modest of men. It's only his manner. And he can't help that, now, can he?"

"There are those who say a doctor ought to be able to, my dear.— But never mind him. Oh, it's you I feel for, Mary, being dragged off like this. Can't you *do* anything, dear? Put your foot down?"

Mary shook her head. "It's no use. Richard is so . . . well, so queer in some ways, Tilly. Besides, you know, I don't think it would be right of me to really pit my will against his."

"Poor little you!— Oh! men are queer fish, Mary, aren't they? Not that I can complain; I drew a prize in the lucky-bag when I took that old Jawkins in there. But when I look round me, or think back, and see what we women put up with! There was poor old ma; she 'ad to be man for both. And Jinn, Mary, who didn't dare to call 'er soul 'er own. And milady Agnes is travelling the selfsame road—why, she 'as to cock 'er eye at Henry nowadays, before she trusts 'erself to say whether it's beef or mutton she's eating! And now 'ere's you, love, carted off with never a with-your-leave or by-your-leave, just because the doctor's tired of it 'ere and thinks 'e'd like a change.

There's no question of whether you're tired or not—oh, my, no!"

"But he has to earn the money, Tilly. It isn't quite fair to put it that way," protested her friend.

"Well! I don't know, Mary, I'm sure," and Tilly's plump person rose and sank in a prodigious sigh. "But if I was 'is wife, 'e wouldn't get off so easy—I know that! It makes me just boil."

Mary answered with a rueful smile. She could never be angry with Richard in cold blood, or for long together.

As time went on, though, and the break-up of her home began—by the auctioneer's man appearing to paw over and appraise her furniture—a certain dull sense of resentment did sometimes come uppermost in her. Under its sway, she had forcibly to remind herself what a kind husband Richard was to her; had to tell off his good qualities one by one, instead of taking them, as hitherto, for granted: he did not drink or gamble; he was the soul of honour, and had never caused her a second's uneasiness in respect of other women.— No, her quarrel, she began to see, was not so much with Richard as with the Powers above. Why should *her* husband alone not be as robust and hardy as all the other husbands in the place? None of *their* healths threatened to fail, nor did any of them find the conditions of the life intolerable. That was another shabby trick Fate had played Richard, in not endowing him with more worldly wisdom, and a healthy itch to get on. Instead of that, he had been blessed with ideas and impulses that stood directly in his way.— And it was here that Mary bore more than one of the private ambitions she had cherished for him, to its grave. A new expression came into her eyes, too —an unsure, baffled look. Life was not, after all, going to be the simple, straight-forward affair she had believed. Thus far, save for the one unhappy business with Purdy, wrongs and complications had passed her by. Now, she saw that she could no more hope to escape them than did any one else.

Out of this frame of mind, she wrote a long, confidential letter to John: John must not be left in ignorance of what hung over her; it was also a relief to unbosom herself to one of her own family. And John was good enough to travel up expressly to talk things over with her, and, as he put it, to "call Richard to order." Like every one else, he showed the whites of his eyes at the latter's flimsy reasons for seeking a change. But when, in spite of her warning, he bearded his

brother-in-law with a jocose and hearty: "Come, come, my
dear Mahony! what's all this about? You're actually thinking
of giving us the slip?—doing a bolt, so to speak, to the old
country?" Richard took his interference so badly, became so
agitated over the head of the harmless question, that John's
further words of airy remonstrance died in his throat.

"Mad as a March hare!" was his private verdict, as he shook
down his ruffled plumes. To Mary he said ponderously: "Well,
upon my soul, my dear girl, I don't know—I don't know. You,
of course, possess your husband's confidence to a degree that
I do not. For my part, I am frankly at a loss what to say. Measured by every practical standard, the step he contemplates is
little short of suicidal—suicidal. I fear he will live to regret it.
Though, of course, we must hope for the best."

And Mary, who had not expected anything from John's intervention, and also knew the grounds for Richard's heat—
Mary now resigned herself, with the best grace she could muster, to the inevitable.

[12]

HOUSE and practice sold for a good round sum; the brass
plates were removed from gate and door, leaving dirty squares
flanked by screw-holes; carpets came up and curtains down;
and, like rats from a doomed ship, men and women servants
fled to other situations. One fine day the auctioneer's bell was
rung through the main streets of the town; and both on this
and the next, when the red flag flew in front of the house, a
troop of intending purchasers, together with an even larger
number of the merely curious, streamed in at the gate and
overran the premises. At noon, the auctioneer mounted his
perch and gathered the crowd round him; and soon he had
the sale in full swing, catching head-bobs, or wheedling and
insisting, with, when persuasion could do no more, his monotonous parrot-cry of: "Going . . . going . . . gone!" to the tap of
the falling hammer.

It would have been considered in bad taste for either husband or wife to be seen while the auction was in progress; and
the night before, Mary and the child, with their personal luggage, had moved to Tilly's, where they would stay for the rest
of the time. But Mahony was still hard at work. The job of

winding up, and getting in the money owed him was no light one. For the report had somehow got abroad that he was retiring from practice because he had made his fortune; and only too many people took this as a tacit permission to leave their bills unpaid.

He had locked himself and his account-books into a small back room, where stood also the few articles they had picked out to carry with them: Mary's sewing-table, his first gift to her after marriage; their modest stock of silver; his medical library. But he had been forced to lower the blind, to hinder impertinent noses flattening themselves against the window, and thus could scarcely see to put pen to paper; while the auctioneer's grating voice was a constant source of distraction—not to mention the rude comments made by the crowd on house and furniture, and the ceaseless trying of the handle of the locked door.

When it came to the point, this tearing up of one's roots was a murderous business—nothing for a man of his temperament. Mary was a good deal better able to stand it than he. Violently as she had opposed the move in the beginning, she was now, dear soul, putting quite a cheery face on it. But then Mary belonged to that happy class of mortals who could set up their Lares and Penates inside any four walls. Whereas he was a very slave to associations. Did she regret parting with a pretty table and a comfortable chair, it was solely because of the prettiness and convenience: as long as she could replace them by other articles of the same kind, she was content. But to him each familiar object was bound round by a thousand memories. And it was the loss of these, which could never be replaced, that cut him to the quick.

Meanwhile, this was the kind of thing he had to listen to. "'Ere now, ladies and gents, we 'ave a very fine pier glass —a very chaste and tasty pier glass indeed—a reel addition to any lady's drawin'-room.— Mrs. Rupp? Do I understand you aright, Mrs. Rupp? 'Ere we are then: Mrs. Rupp h'offers twelve bob for this very 'andsome h'article. Twelve bob . . . going twelve. . . . Fifteen? Thank you, Mrs. Bromby! Going fifteen . . . going—going—Eighteen? Right you are, my dear!" and so on.

It had a history, had that pier glass; its purchase dated from a time in their lives when they had been forced to turn each

shilling in the palm. Mary had espied it one day in Plaistows'
Stores, and had set her heart on possessing it. How she had
schemed and plotted, to scrape the money together!—saving
so much on a new gown, so much on bonnet and mantle. He
remembered, as if it were yesterday, the morning on which she
had burst in, eyes and cheeks aglow, to tell him that she had
managed it at last, and how they had gone off at once, arm in
arm, to secure the prize. Yes, for all their poverty those had
been happy days. Little extravagances such as this, or the trifling gifts they had contrived to make each other, had given
them far more pleasure than the costlier presents of later years.

—"The next h'article I draw yer attention to is a sofer,"
went on the voice, sounding suddenly closer; and, with a great
trampling and shuffling, the crowd trooped after it to the adjoining room. "And a very h'easy and comfortable piece o'
furniture it is, too. A bit shabby and worn 'ere and there, but
not any the worse o' that. You don't need to worry if the kids
play puff-puffs on it; and it fits the shape o' the body all the
better.— Any one like to try it? Jest the very thing for a tired
gent gettin' 'ome from biz, or 'andy to pop yer lady on when
she faints—as the best o' ladies will! Any h'offers? Mr. de la
Plastrier"—he said "Deelay-plastreer"—"a guinea? Thank you,
mister. One guinea! Going a guinea!— Now, *come* on ladies
and gen'elmen! D'ye think I've got a notion to make you a
present of it? What's that? Two-and-twenty? Gawd! Is this a
tiddlin' match?"

—How proud he had been of that sofa! In his first surgery
he had had nowhere to lay an aching head. Well worn? And
small wonder! He would like to know how many hundreds of
times he had flung himself down on it, utterly played out. He
had been used to lie there of an evening, too, when Mary came
in to chat about household affairs, report on her day's doings,
and bring order into his untidy books and papers. And he remembered another time, when he had spent the last hours of a
distracted night on it . . . and how, between sleeping and waking, he had strained his ears for the footsteps that never came.

The sofa was knocked down to his butcher for a couple of
pounds, and the crying—or decrying—of his bookcases began.
He could stand no more of it. Sweeping his papers into a bag,
he guiltily unlocked the door, stole out by way of kitchen and
back gate, and got off unobserved.

But, once outside, he did not know where to go or what to do: in his hurry he had neglected to slip a book in his pocket. Leaving the town behind him, he made for the Lake, and roved aimlessly and disconsolately about, choosing sheltered paths and remote roads, where he would be unlikely to have to run the gauntlet of acquaintances. For he shrank from recognition on this particular day, when all his domestic privacies were being laid bare to the public view: in thought, he likened himself to an undetected murderer, who roams the streets while the corpse of his victim is being dissected within-doors. But altogether of late he had fought shy of meeting people. Their hard, matter-of-fact faces showed him all too plainly what they thought of him. At first, he had been fool enough to scan them eagerly, in the hope of finding one saving touch of sympathy or comprehension. But he might as well have looked for grief in the eyes of an undertaker's mute. And so he had shrunk back into himself, wearing his stiffest air as a shield, and leaving it to Mary to parry colonial inquisitiveness.— His wanderings ended at the old cemetery, where, with his chin on his palms, his elbows on his knees, he sat on a sod wall, before him the neglected graves of those diggers who had fallen in the fight for freedom, on the Eureka Stockade.

When he reckoned that he had allowed time enough for the disposal of the last pots and pans, he rose and made his way—well, the word "home" was by now become a mere figure of speech. He came into a scene of the wildest confusion. The actual sale was over; but the work of stripping the house had begun, and the successful bidders were dragging off their spoils. His glass-fronted bookcase had been got as far as the surgery-door. There it had stuck fast; and an angry altercation was going on around it, how best to set it free. A woman passed him bearing Mary's girandoles; another had the dining-room clock under her arm; a third trailed a whatnot after her. To the palings of the fence several carts and buggies had been hitched, and the horses were eating down his neatly clipped hedge. It was all he could do not to rush out and call their owners to account. The level sun-rays flooded the rooms, showing up hitherto unnoticed smudges and scratches on the white-wash of the walls; showing the prints of hundreds of dusty feet on the carpetless floors. Voices echoed in hollow fashion through the naked rooms; men shouted and spat, as they tugged

393

heavy articles along the hall, or bumped them down the stairs. It was pandemonium. Thus a home went to pieces; thus was a page of one's life turned. The death of a loved human being could not, he thought, have been more painful to witness.— He hastened away to rejoin Mary.

There followed a week of Mrs. Tilly's somewhat stifling hospitality, when one was forced, three times a day, to overeat oneself, for fear of giving offence; followed formal presentations of silver and plate from Masonic Lodge and District Hospital, as well as a couple of public testimonials got up by his medical brethren and a body of influential townsmen. But at length all was over: the last good-bye visit had been paid and received, the last evening party in their honour sat through; and Mahony breathed again. He had felt stiff and unnatural under this overdose of demonstrativeness. Now—as always on sighting relief from a state of things that irked him—he underwent a sudden change, turned hearty and spontaneous, joked and laughed with Tilly through breakfast, and rallied the old man, thus innocently succeeding in leaving a good impression behind him. He kept his temper, too, in all the fuss and ado of departure: the running to and fro after missing articles, the sitting on the lids of overflowing trunks, the strapping of carpet-bags, affixing of labels. Their luggage hoisted into a spring-cart, they themselves took their seats in the buggy and were driven to the railway-station; and to himself Mahony murmured an all's-well-that-ends-well. On alighting, however, he found that his greatcoat had been forgotten. He had to get into the buggy again and gallop back to the house, arriving at the station only just in time to leap into the train.

"A close shave that!" he ejaculated, as he sank breathless on the cushions and wiped his face. "And in more senses than one, my dear. In tearing round a corner we very nearly had a nasty spill. Had I pitched out and broken my neck, this hole of a place would have got my bones after all.— Not that I was sorry to miss that cock-and-hen-show, Mary. It was really too much of a good thing altogether."

For a large and noisy crowd had gathered round the door of the railway-carriage to wish the travellers godspeed, among them people to whom Mahony could not even put a name, whose very existence he had forgotten. At sight of them he had felt more disconcerted than obliged; he sniffed an idle curiosity, a lack of anything better to do. Mary, on the other hand, was still tearful at the remembrance of all the kind words said to her, the dozens of hands held out to press hers. It had snowed last gifts and keepsakes, too. Drying her eyes, she set to collecting and arranging these. "Just fancy every one turning up like that, Richard! The railway people must have wondered what the matter was.— Oh, by the way, did you notice —I don't think you did, you were in such a rush—who I was speaking to, as you ran up? It was Jim, Old Jim, but so changed I hardly knew him. He's quite lost his stoop, and was as spruce as could be, in a black coat and a bell-topper. He's married again, he told me, and owns one of the best-paying hotels in Smythesdale. Yes, and he was at our sale, too—he came over specially for it—to buy the piano."

"He did, confound him!" cried Mahony hotly.

"Oh, you can't look at it that way, Richard," Mary made mild remonstrance. "As long as he has the money to pay for it, no one can object. Fancy, he told me he had always admired the 'tune' of it so much, when I played and sang. My dear little piano!"

"You shall have another and a better one, I promise you, old girl—don't fret.— Well, that slice of our life's over and done with," he added, and laid his hand on hers. "But we'll hold together, won't we, wife, whatever happens?"

"Why, of course we shall, dear," said Mary cheerfully; and having taken off her bonnet, she turned to relieve the child of hers.

They had passed Black Hill and its multicoloured clay and gravel heaps, and the train was puffing uphill. The last scattered huts and weatherboards fell behind, the worked-out holes grew fewer, and wooded rises appeared. Gradually, too, the white roads round Mount Buninyong came into view, and the trees became denser. And having climbed the shoulder, they began to fly smoothly and rapidly down the other side.

Mahony bent forward in his seat. "Look, Mary!" he cried eagerly. "There goes the last of old Warrenheip. Thank the Lord, I shall never set eyes on it again. Upon my word, I believe I learnt to think that old hill the most tiresome feature of the place. Yes, I know, I used to admire it. But one can have too much of a good thing. Whatever street one turned into, up it bobbed at the foot. Like a peep-show . . . or a bad dream . . . or a prison wall."

In Melbourne they were the guests of John: Mahony had reluctantly resigned himself to being beholden to Mary's relatives and Mary's friends, to the end of the chapter. At best, living in other people's houses was for him more of a punishment than a pleasure; but for sheer discomfort this stay capped the climax. Under Zara's incompetent rule, John's home had degenerated into a lawless and slovenly abode: the meals were unpalatable, the servants pert and lazy, while the children ran wild—you could hardly hear yourself speak for the racket. Whenever possible, Mahony fled the house. He lunched in town, looked up his handful of acquaintances, bought necessaries—and unnecessaries—for the voyage, and added to his wardrobe. He also hired a boat and had himself rowed out to the ship, where he clambered on board, amid the mess of scouring and painting, and made himself known to the chief mate. Or else he sat on the pier and gazed at the vessel lying straining at her anchor, while quick rain-squalls swept up and blotted out the Bay.

Of Mary he caught but passing glimpses; her family seemed determined to make unblushing use of her as long as she was within reach. A couple of days prior to their arrival, John and Zara had had a violent quarrel; and there and then Zara had for the dozenth time packed her trunks, and left for one of those miraculous situations, the doors of which always stood open to her.

John was for Mary going after her and forcing her to admit the error of her ways. Mary held it would be wiser to let well alone.

"*Do* be guided by me this time, John," she urged, when she had heard her brother out. "You and Zara will never hit it off, however often you try."

But the belief was ingrained in John, that the most suitable head for his establishment was one of his own blood. He answered indignantly: "And why not, pray, Mary, may I ask? Who *is* to hit it off, as you put it, if not two of a family?"

"Oh, John . . ."— Mary felt quite apologetic for her brother. "Clever as Zara is, she's not at all fitted for a post of this kind.

396

She's no hand with the servants, and children don't seem to take to her—young children, I mean. She gets on splendidly with her pupils, of course; they write to her for years after."

"Not fitted? Bah!" said John. "Every woman is fitted by nature to rear children and manage a house."

"They should be, I know," yielded Mary in conciliatory fashion. "But, as you see, with Zara it doesn't seem to be the case."

"Then she ought to be ashamed of herself, my dear Mary— ashamed of herself—and that's all about it!"

Zara, on the same theme, wept into a dainty handkerchief and delivered herself of a rigmarole of complaints, against her brother, the servants, the children. According to her, the latter were naturally perverse, and John indulged them so shockingly that she had been powerless to carry out reforms. Did she punish them, he cancelled the punishments; if she left their naughtiness unchecked, he accused her of culpable indifference. Then, her housekeeping had not suited him: he reproached her with extravagance, with mismanagement, even with lining her own purse.— "While the truth is, John is as mean as dirt! I had literally to drag each penny out of him."

"But what induced you to undertake it again, Zara, in the first place?"

"Yes, what indeed!" echoed Zara bitterly. "However, once bitten, Mary, twice shy. *Never* again!"

But Mary, remembering the bites Zara had already received on this score, was silent.

Even Zara's amateurish hand being thus finally withdrawn, it became Mary's task to find some worthy and capable person to act as mistress to the house and bring up the children. Taking her obligations seriously, she devoted her last days in Australia to conning and penning advertisements, and interviewing applicants.

"Now no one too attractive, if you please, Mrs. Mahony! —if you don't want him to fall a victim," teased Richard, as they retired to rest. "Remember our good John's inflammability. He's a very Leyden jar again, at present."

"No, indeed I don't," said Mary with emphasis. "But the children are the first consideration, Richard. Oh dear! it does seem a shame that Tilly shouldn't have them to look after. I must say I can't understand John in the matter. It would relieve him of so much responsibility. As it is, he's even asked me to make it plain to Tilly that he wishes Trotty to spend her holidays at school."

The forsaking of her brother's poor little motherless flock cut Mary to the heart. Trotty had clung to her, inconsolable. "Oh, Aunty, *take* me with you! *Don't* leave me here! Oh, what shall I do without you?"

"It's not possible, darling. Your papa would never agree. But I tell you what, Trotty: you must be a good girl, and make haste and learn all you can. For soon, I'm sure, he'll want you to come and be his little housekeeper, and take charge of the other children.— Perhaps he would even give his consent to you going to a Seminary in Melbourne. I'll see what I can do."

Sounded on this subject, however, John said drily: "Emma's influence would be undesirable for the little ones."— His prejudice in favour of his second wife's children was an eternal riddle to his sister. He dandled even the youngest, whom he had not seen since its birth, with visible pleasure.

"It must be the black eyes," said Mary to herself; and shook her head at men's irrationality. For Jinny's offspring had none of the grace and beauty that marked the two elder children.

And now the last night had come; they were gathered, a family party, round John's mahogany. The cloth had been removed; the nuts and port were passing. As it was a unique occasion, the ladies had been excused from withdrawing, and the gentlemen left their cigars unlighted. Mary's eyes roved fondly from one face to another. There was Tilly, come over from her hotel: ("Nothing would induce me to spend a night under his roof, Mary!") She sat hugging one of the children, who had run in for the almonds and raisins of dessert. "What a mother lost in her!" sighed Mary once more. There was Zara, so far reconciled to her brother as to consent to be present; but only speaking at him, not to him. And dear Jerry, eager and alert, taking so intelligent a share, thought Mary, in what was said. Poor Ned alone was wanting, neither Richard nor John having offered to pay his fare to town. Young Johnny's seat was vacant, too, for the boy had vanished directly dinner was over.

There was just one jarring note for Mary in the harmony of the evening; and at moments she grew very thoughtful. For the first time Mrs. Kelly, the motherly widow on whom her choice had fallen, sat opposite John at the head of the table; and already Mary was the prey of a nagging doubt. For this person had doffed the neat mourning-garb she had worn on her engagement, and had come forth in a cap trimmed with cherry coloured ribbons. Not only this, she smiled in sugary fashion, and far too readily; while the extreme humility with which she deferred to John's opinion, and hung on his lips, made a bad impression on Mary. Nor was she alone in her observations. After a particularly glaring example of the widow's complaisance, Tilly looked across the table and shut one eye, in an unmistakable wink.

Meanwhile, the men's talk had gradually petered out: there came long pauses in which they twiddled and twirled their wineglasses, unable to think of anything to say. At heart, both John and Mahony hailed with a certain relief the coming break in their relations. "After all, I dare say such a queer faddy fellow *is* out of his element here. He'll go down better over there," was John's final verdict. Mahony's, a characteristic: "Thank God, I shall not have to put up much longer with his confounded self-importance, or suffer under his matrimonial muddles!"

When, at a question from Mary, John began animatedly to discuss the tuition of the younger children, Mahony seized the chance to slip away. He would not be missed. He never was— here or anywhere.

On the verandah, a dark form stirred and made a hasty movement. It was the boy Johnny—now grown tall as Mahony himself—and, to judge from the smell, what he tried to smuggle into his pocket was a briar.

"Oh well, yes, I'm smoking," he said sullenly, after a feeble attempt at evasion. "Go in and blab on me, if you feel you must, Uncle Richard."

"Nonsense. But telling fibs about a thing does no good."

"Oh yes, it does; it often saves a hiding," retorted the boy. And added with a youthful vehemence: "I'm hanged if I let the governor take a stick to me nowadays! I'm turned sixteen; and if he dares to touch me——"

"Come, come. You know, you've been something of a disappointment to your father, Johnny—that's the root of the trouble."

"Glad if I have! He hates me anyway. He never has cared

for my mother's children," answered Johnny, with a quaint air
of dignity. "I think he couldn't have cared for her either."

"There you're wrong. He was devoted to her. Her death
nearly broke his heart.— She was one of the most beautiful
women I have ever seen, my boy."

"Was she?" said Johnny civilly, but with meagre interest.
This long dead mother had bequeathed him not even a memory of herself—was as unreal to him as a dream at second hand.
From the chilly contemplation of her he turned back impatiently to his own affairs, which were burning, insistent. And
scenting a vague sympathy in this stranger uncle, who, like
himself, had drifted out from the intimacy of the candle-lit
room, he made a clean breast of his troubles.

"I can't stand the life here, Uncle Richard, and I'm not going
to—not if father cuts me off with a shilling for it! I mean to
see the world. *This* isn't the world—this dead-and-alive old
country! . . . though it's got to seem like it to the governor, he's
been here so long. You don't think any great shakes of it,
either, do you?— No, it's simply beastly the way he bullies me
—as if it was blue murder to want to leave home for a spell.
He cleared out from his, before he was as old as me. Of course,
there isn't another blessed old Australia for me to decamp to;
he might be a bit sweeter about it, if there was. But America's
good enough for me, and I'm off there—yes, even if I have to
work my passage out!"

Early next morning the Mahonys, fully equipped for their
journey, stood on the William's Town pier, the centre of a
large crowd of relatives and friends. This had been further
swelled by the advent of good Mrs. Devine, who came panting
up, followed by her husband, and by Agnes Ocock and Amelia
Grindle, who had contrived to reach Melbourne the previous
evening. Even John's children had been tacked on, clad in
their Sunday best. Everybody talked at once, and laughed
or wept; while the children played hide-and-seek round the
ladies' crinolines. All eyes were bent on their party, all ears
cocked in their direction; and, yet once again, Mahony's dislike to a commotion in public choked off his gratitude towards
these good and kindly people. But his star was rising: tears
and farewells and vows of constancy had to be cut short, a
jaunt planned by the whole company to the ship itself abandoned; for a favourable wind had sprung up, and the captain

400

was said to be impatient to weigh anchor. And so, the very last
kisses and handclasps exchanged, the travellers climbed down
into a boat already deep in the water with other cuddy-passengers and their luggage, and were rowed out on a choppy sea
to where lay that good clipper-ship the *Red Jacket*. Sitting
side by side, husband and wife watched, with feelings that had
little in common, the receding quay, Mary fluttering her damp
handkerchief till the separate figures were merged in one dark
mass, and even Tilly, planted in front, her handkerchief tied
flagwise to the top of Jerry's cane, could no longer be distinguished from the rest.

Mahony's foot met the ribbed teak of the deck with the liveliest satisfaction; his nostrils greedily drank in a smell of tarry
ropes and oiled brass. Having escorted Mary below, seen to
the stowing away of their belongings, and changed his town
clothes for a set of comfortable baggy garments, he returned
to the deck, where he passed the greater part of the day tirelessly pacing up and down. They made good headway, and
soon the ports and towns at the water's edge were become
mere whitey smudges. The hills in the background lasted
longer. But first the Macedon group faded from sight, then
the Dandenong Ranges, grown bluer and bluer, were also lost
in the sky. The vessel crept round the outside of the great bay,
to clear shoals and sandbanks, and, by afternoon, with the sails
close rigged in the freshening wind, they were running parallel
with the Cliff—"*The* Cliff!" thought Mahony, with a curl of the
lip. And indeed there was no other; nothing but low scrub-
grown sandhills, which flattened out till they were almost level
with the sea.

The passage through the Heads was at hand. Impulsively he
went down to fetch Mary: she had chosen to stay below while
still in the Bay, to arrange the cabin for the seventy to ninety
odd days they expected to have to spend in it. Threading his
way through the saloon, in the middle of which grew up one
of the masts, he opened a door leading off it.

"Come on deck, my dear, and take your last look at the old
place. It's not likely you'll ever see it again."

But Mary, with an eye to future sufferings, was already en-
coffined in her narrow berth.

"Don't ask me even to lift my head from the pillow, Richard.
Besides, dear, I've seen it all so often before."

He lingered to make some arrangements for her comfort, fidgeted to know where she had put his books, his sketching-album, his India ink; then, mounting a locker, he craned his neck at the porthole. "Now for the Rip, wife! By God, Mary, I little thought this time last year I should be crossing it to-day."

But the cabin was too dark and small to hold him. Climbing the steep companion-way, he went on deck again, and resumed his flittings to and fro. He was no more able to be still than was the good ship under him; he felt himself one with her, and gloried in her growing unrest. She was now come to the narrow channel that formed the entrance to this spacious, landlocked harbour. Here, between two converging headlands, the waters of the Bay met those of the open sea. They boiled and churned, in an eternal commotion, over treacherous reefs which thrust far out below the surface and were betrayed by straight, white lines of foam.— Once safely outside, the vessel hove to, to drop the pilot. Leaning over the gunwale, Mahony watched a boat come alongside, the man of oilskins climb down the rope-ladder, and row away.

Here, in the open, a heavy swell was running, but he kept his footing on the swaying boards, long after the last of his fellow-passengers had vanished—a tall, thin figure, with an eager pointed face, and hair just greying at the temples. Contrary to habit, he had a word for every one who passed, from mate to cabin-boy, and he drank a glass of wine with the Captain in his cabin. Their start had been auspicious, said the latter; seldom had he had such a fair wind to come out with.

Then, the sun fell into the sea, and it was night—a fine, starry night, clear with the hard, cold radiance of the south. Mahony looked up at the familiar constellations, and thought of those others, long missed, that he was soon to see again.— Over! That page of his history was turned and done with; and he had every reason to feel thankful. For many and many a man, though escaping with his life, had left youth and health and hope on these difficult shores. He had got off scot-free. Still in his prime, his faculties green, his zest for living unimpaired, he was heading for the dear old Mother Country —for home. Alone and unaided, he could never have accomplished it. Strength to will the enterprise, steadfastness in the face of obstacles, had been lent him from above. And as he stood gazing down into the black and fathomless deep, which sent crafty, licking tongues up the vessel's side, he freely acknowledged his debt, gave honour where honour was due.— *From Thee cometh victory, from Thee cometh wisdom, and Thine is the glory, and I am thy servant.*

The last spark of a coast-light went out. The good ship, buffeted by the rising wind, began to pitch heavily. Her canvas rattled, her joints creaked and groaned, as, lunging forward, she cut her way through the troubled seas that break on the reef-bound coasts of this new, old world.

BOOK II

THE WAY HOME

[PROEM]

. . . qui trans mare currunt.

WHEN, having braved the bergs and cyclones of the desolate South Pacific, and rounded the Horn; having lain becalmed in the Doldrums, bartered Cross for Plough, and snatched a glimpse of the Western Isles: when the homeward bound vessel is come level with Finisterre and begins to skirt the Bay, those aboard her get the impression of passing, at one stroke, into home waters. Gone are alike polar blasts and perfumed or desert-dry breezes; gone opalescent dawns, orange-green sunsets, and nights when the very moon shines warm, the black mass of ocean sluggish as pitch. The region the homing wanderer now enters is alive with associations. These tumbling crested marbled seas, now slate-grey, now of a cold ultramarine, seem but the offings of those that wash his native shores; and they are peopled for him by the salt-water ghosts of his ancestors, the great navigators, who traced this road through the high seas on their voyages of adventure and discovery. The fair winds that belly the sails, or the head winds that thwart the vessel's progress, are the romping south-west gales adrip with moisture, or the bleak north-easters which scour his island home and make it one of the windy corners of the world. Not a breath of balmy softness remains. There is a rawness in the air, a keener saltier tang; the sad-coloured sky broods low, or is swept by scud that flies before the wind; trailing mists blot out the horizon. And these and other indelible memories beginning to pull at his heart-strings, it is over with his long

404

patience. After tranquilly enduring the passage of some fifteen thousand watery miles, he now falls to chafing, and to telling off the days that still divide him from port and home.—

On an autumn morning in the late 'sixties that smart clipper, the *Red Jacket*, of some seven hundred tons burden, entered the English Channel, and having rolled about for a while, for want of a breeze to steady her, picked up a fine free following wind, and forged ahead at a speed of eight and a half knots an hour.

At the eagerly awaited cry of "Land ho!" from the foretop, an excited bunch of cuddy-passengers and their ladies, all markedly colonial in dress and bearing, swarmed to the side of the vessel, and set to raking and probing the distance. Telescopes and spy-glasses travelled from hand to hand, arms were silhouetted, exclamations flew, the female gaze, adrift in space, was gallantly piloted to the sober level of the horizon. And even the most sceptical convinced that the dusky shadow on the water's rim was, in truth, the goal of their journeying, three cheers were called for and given, the gentlemen swung their hats with an "England for ever!" the ladies blew kisses and fluttered their kerchiefs. But, their feelings thus eased, they soon had their fill of staring at what might as well have been a cloud or a trail of smoke; and having settled the wagers laid on this moment, and betted anew on the day and hour of casting anchor, they accepted the invitation of a colonial Crœsus, and went below to drink a glass to the Old Country.

Richard Mahony alone remained, though warmly bidden.

"The pleasure of your company, Mr. Mahony, sir!"

"Mayn't we hope, doctor, for a few words befitting the occasion?"

He had on the whole been a fairly popular member of the ship's party. This was thanks to the do-nothing life one led at sea. For more years than he cared to count he had lived taut as a fiddle-string. Here, on board ship, he had actually known what it was to feel time hang heavy on his hands. In consequence, he had come out of his shell, turned sociable and hearty, taking an interest in his fellow-travellers, a lead in the diversions of the voyage. And the golden weeks of sunshine and sea air having made a new man of him—in looks he resembled a younger brother of the lean and haggard individual who had climbed the ship's ladder—he was able for once harmlessly to enjoy the passing hour. Again: a genuine sea-lover, he had found not one of the ninety odd days spent afloat unbearable; and, in refusing to be daunted—either by the poor, rough food, or the close quarters; or during a hurricane, when the very cabins were awash; or again, in the tropics, when the ship lay motionless on a glassy sea, the cruel sun straight overhead—by making light of inconvenience and discomfort, he had helped others, too, to put a brave face on them. Nobody guessed how easy it came to him. His cheerfulness was counted to him for a virtue, and set him high in general favour; people fell into the way of running to him not only with their ailments, but their troubles; looked to him to smooth out the frictions that were the crop of this overlong voyage. So unusual a state of things could not last. And, indeed, with the vessel's first knot in northern waters, he had become sensitively aware of a cooling-off. Let but a foot meet the shore, and the whole ill-mixed company would scatter to the winds, never to reassemble. Well, he, for one, would not feel that his ties with the colony were broken beyond repair, until this had happened, and he had seen the last of all these boisterous, jovial, kindly, vulgar people.

The liking was chiefly on their part. For though, since setting sail, he had been rid of the big-mouthed colonial boaster, and among runaways like himself, men who were almost as glad as he to turn their backs on Australia—but a single one of the thirty cabin passengers contemplated returning—this was far from saying that he had found in them congenial spirits. They chafed him in ways they did not dream of. The Midases of the party: it was ruled sharply off into those who had amassed a fortune and those who patently had not; none went "home" but for one or other reason; he himself was the only half tint on the palette: these lucky specimens were for ever trumpeting the opinion that the colonies were a good enough place in which to fill your money-bags; whereas, to empty them, you repaired to more civilised climes. And to hear his case—or what might once have been his case—put thus crudely, made Mahony wince. The speakers reminded him of underbred guests, who start belittling their entertainment before they are fairly over their host's door-sill. At the same time he had to laugh in his sleeve. For where, pray, could Monsieur le Boucher and Monsieur l'Epicier undo their purse-strings to better effect, find a society more exactly cut to their shape, than in the Antipodes, where no display was too showy, no banquet too sumptuous, no finery too loud; and where the man who could slap a well-filled pocket was anyone's equal?—Even less to his taste was the group of lean kine. With nothing to show for themselves but broken health and shattered illusions, these men saw the land of their exile through the smoked glasses of hate, and had not a single good word to say for it. Which of course was nonsense.

And so it came about that Mary was sometimes agreeably surprised to hear Richard, if not exactly standing up for the colony, at least not helping to swell the choir of its detractors. This was unending, went round and round like a catch. People outdid one another in discovering fresh grounds for their aversion. Besides the common grievances—the droughts and floods, the dust winds and hot winds, the bare, ugly landscape, the seven plagues of winged and creeping things—many a small private grudge was owned to, and by the most unlikely lips. Here was a burly tanner who had missed the glimmer of twilight, been vexed at the sudden onrush of the dark. Another grumbler bemoaned the fact that, just when you looked for snow and holly-berries: "Hanged if there ain't the pitches and appricoats ripe and ready to tumble into your mouth!"

"An onnatcheral country, and that's the truth."

"The wrong side of the world, say I—the under side."

Quaint home-sicknesses cropped up, too. On board was a skinny little colonist from the Moreton Bay district, with, as the Irish wit of the company had it, "the face of his own granddad upon his shoulders"—who was, that is to say, more deeply wrinkled than the bewrinkled rest. Where this man came from, dirt was not: the little weatherboard houses were as clean when they dropped to pieces as when first run up. He it was who now confessed to an odd itch to see again the grime and squalor of London town: the shiny black mud that served as mortar to the paving-stones; the beds of slush into which, on a rainy day, the crossing-sweepers voluptuously plunged their brooms; the smoke-stained buildings; monuments tarred with the dirt of ages. He wanted to feel his cheek stung by the mixture of flying fodder and dry ordure that whirls the streets, does the east wind go; to sniff the heavy smell of soot and frost that greets the Londoner's nose of a winter morning—even to choke and smother in a London fog. No one smiled.

"Aye, it's what one's born to, that tells, and what one comes back to in the end," nodded a pursy builder, whose gold watch-chain, hung with seals and coins, was draped across his waistcoat like a line of gala bunting. "I knew a man, gents—it's a fact I'm tellin' you!—who could 'a bought out the up-country township he lived in, twice and three times over; and yet I'm blessed if this old Johnny-bono didn't as good as turn on the waterworks, when he spoke o' the pokey old cottage down Devon way, where he'd been young. Seemed as if all the good smells o' the rest o' the world couldn't make up to him for a bit o' peat burnin' on a still winter's evenin'; or new thatch smellin' in the rains; or the softish stink o' the milch-cows' dung in the long wet meadow grass."

That white raven, "the man who was going back," held aloof from the sentimentalists. Was he, however, present at such a sitting, he kept silence, an ambiguous expression on his face. Once only, in a conversation engineered by Mahony out of curiosity, did he speak up. And then it was with a disagreeable overbearing "I left England, sir, six years since, because man isn't a sprite to live on air alone. My father went half-starved all his days—he was a farm-hand, and reared a family o' nine on eleven bob a week. He didn't taste meat from one year's end to another. Out yon"—and he pointed with his cutty-pipe over his shoulder—"I've ate meat three times a day. I've a snug little crib of me own, and a few acres o' land, and I've come home to fetch out me old mother and the young fry. They shall know what it is to eat their fill every day of the seven, and she'll drive to chapel of a Sabbath in her own trap and a black silk gown.— Nay, be sure I haven't loafed around, nor sat with me hands before me. There's not much anyone can learn me in the way of work. But the old country wouldn't either gimme anything to do, nor yet keep me free, gratis and for nothing."— And so on, in a strain dear to the tongues of the lower orders.

These things flitted through Mahony's mind as he stood, chin in hand, elbow on gunwale, gazing over the last stretch of dividing sea. Before him lay an aquarelle of softest colouring, all pale light and misty shadow; and these lyric tints,

these shades and half shades, gripped his heart as the vivid
hues of the south never had. Their very fleetingness charmed.
But a little ago, and the day had been blue and sunny, with
just a spice of crispness in the air to remind one that it was
autumn. A couple of white bales of cloud, motionless overhead, had flung gigantic purple shadows, which lay like
painted maps of continents on the glittering sea. But, the
breeze freshening, the clouds had been set in motion; and
simultaneously the shadow-continents, losing their form, had
begun to travel the surface of the water. A rain-shower was
coming up from the west: it drew a curtain over the sky, and
robbed the sea of its colour. Only in the east did a band of
light persist, above which the fringes of the storm-cloud hung,
sending down straight black rays. And now the squall was
upon them; wind and rain hunted each other over the waves;
the deck slanted, masts and spars whistled, sails smacked and
shrilled.—

In the course of that day the vessel was taken in tow, and
when, towards evening, the downpour ceased, and Mahony
again climbed the companion-way, a very different scene met
his eye. They now, but one of several incoming and out-
going vessels, drove through a leaden sea, which the rain
had beaten flat, reduced to a kind of surly quiescence. Above
them was an iron-grey sky, evenly spread and of a fair height,
the lower clouds having withdrawn to the horizon, where, in
a long, cylinder-like roll, they hung poised on the water's rim.
But this cold and stony aspect of things was more than made
up for. Flush with the ship, looking as though it had just risen
from the waves, was land—was the English shore.

At sight of it, Mahony had a shock of surprise—that thrilled
surprise that England holds for those of her sons who journey
back, no matter whence, across the bleak and windy desert
of the seas. Quite so lovely as this, one had not dared to remember the homeland. There it lay, stretched like an emerald
belt against its drab background, and was as grateful to sun-
tired eyes as a draught of mountain water to a climber's
parched throat. Not a rood of this earth looked barren or unkempt: veritable lawns ran down to the brink of the cliffs;
hedges ruled bosky lines about the meadows; the villages were
bowers of trees—English trees. Even the rain had favoured
him: his first glimpse of all this beauty caught it at its freshest,

grass and foliage having emerged from the clouds as if new painted in greenness.

Another aspect of it struck Mary, who mounted in his wake gloved, shawled and hatted against the evening chills. With an exclamation of pleasure she cried: "Oh, Richard—how pretty! How . . . how *tidy!* It looks like . . . like"—she hesitated, searching her memory for the trimmest spot she knew; and ended—"doesn't it? . . . just like the Melbourne Botanic Gardens."

"It looks too good to be true, my dear."

But he understood what she was trying to say. If the landscape before them was lovely as a garden, it had also something of a garden's limitations. There was an air of arrangedness about it; it might have been laid out according to plan, and on pleasing, but rather finikin lines; it was all exquisite, but just a trifle over-dressed. And as he followed up the train of thought started by Mary's words, he was swept through by a sudden consciousness of England's littleness, her tiny, tight compactness, the narrow compass that allowed of so intensive a cultivation. These fair fields in miniature!—after the wide acreage of the colonial paddock. These massy hedgerows, cutting up the good pasture-land into chequerboard squares!—after the thready rail-and-post fences that offered no hindrance to the eye. These diminutive clusters of houses, huddled wall to wall—compared with the sprawling townships, set, regardless of ground-space, at the four corners of immense crossroads. These narrow, winding lanes and highways, that crawled their mile or so from one village to the near next—after the broad, red, rectilinear Australian roads, that dashed ahead, it might be for the length of a day's journey, without encountering human habitation. These duly preserved morsels of woodland, as often as not, guarded, they too, by a leafy wall, where songsters trilled—compared with the vast and terrible bush, bare alike of bird and man: all these forcible contrasts worked in him, as he stood gazing on the fair natural garden of southern England; and a sensation that was half wonder, half a kind of protective tenderness, called at the same time a smile to his lips and tears to his eyes. In face of this adorable littleness, this miniature perfection, his feelings were those of the nomad son who, weary of beating up and down the world,

turns home at last to rest on the untravelled heart of his
mother. Here, the familiar atmosphere of his childhood laps
him round; and he breathes it greedily—even while he marvels
how time has stood still for the homekeepers, and asks himself
if he can ever again be one of them. All the tempestuous years
of his youth and manhood lie between. He has fought fire-
spueing dragons, suffered shipwreck in Sargasso, bent the knee
at strange shrines. And the sense of an older, tireder wisdom,
which makes of him the ancient, of them the young and untried, completes the breach. How, knowing what he knows,
can he placidly live through the home day, with its small, safe
monotony? How give up for ever the excitement of great risks
taken and met, on grander shores, under loftier skies?

But a truce to such vapourings! Did the man exist that
had it in him to fret and go unhappy, feel pinioned and a
prisoner, while round the cliffs of England, now grey, now
white, now red, danced and beckoned the English sea? For
who, native to these coasts, would renounce, once having
drawn on it, that heritage of vagrancy which has come down
to him through the ages? Amphibian among the peoples, has
he not learnt to adjust his balance to the sea's tumblings,
his sight to its vast spaces?—so that into the English eye has,
with time, come a look of remoteness; the sailor-look, which,
from much scouring of horizons, seems to focus on near
objects with an effort.— And musing thus, Mahony believed
he knew why, for all its smallness, on this little speck of an
island rising green and crumbly from the waves, there should
have bred a mighty race. It was not in spite of its size, but
because of it. Just because the span of the land was so narrow, those whose blood ran high could shove off on the unruly element from their very doorsteps, and whether these
looked north or south, faced sunrise or sunset: the deep-sea
fishers, the great traffickers, the navigators and explorers, the
fighting men of the deep. And with them, so it pleased him to
think, no matter for what point they headed, they bore tidings
of the mother-country, and of her struggles towards a finer
liberty, a nicer justice, that should make of her sons true
freemen; for her a difficult task, because she lay isolate, shut
off by barriers of foam, a prey to hoary traditions, and with no
land-frontier across which seditious influences might slip; and

411

yet for her most needful, seeing that the hearts of her people
were restless, indomitable—had in them something of the un-
ruliness of her seas. And just as these rovers carried out news
of England, so, homing again, either for a breathing-space in
the great tourney, or, old and feeble, to lay their bones in
English earth, they brought back their quota of things seen,
heard, felt, on their Odyssey; a fruity crop of experience; so
that even the chimney-dwellers in England came by a certain
bigness of vision: through the eyes of son or brother they explored outlandish parts, were present at exotic happenings.
And now, his thoughts turning inward, he asked himself
whether even he, Richard Mahony, in his small way, was not
carrying on the great tradition. Having fared forth in his
youth, endured in exile, then heard and obeyed the home-
call, did not he, too, return the richer for a goodly store of
spiritual experience—*his* treasure-trove of life-wisdom—which
might serve to guide others on their road, or go before them
as a warning? And the idea grew, under his pondering. He
saw his race as the guardian of a vast reserve fund of spiritual
force, to which all alike contributed—as each was free at will
or at need to draw on it—a hoard, not of the things themselves,
but of their ghostly sublimates: the quintessence of all achievement, all endeavour; of failure, suffering, joy, pain. And, if
this image held, it would throw light on the obscure purpose
of such a seemingly aimless life as his had been; a life ragged
with broken ends. Only in this way, he must believe, had it
been possible to distil the precious drop of oil, that was *his*
ultimate essence. Not ours to judge of the means used, or in
what our puny service should consist: why to one should fall
the bugles and the glory—the dying in splendour for a great
cause, or the living illustriously to noble issues—to another,
a life that was one long blind stumble, with, for finish, an
inglorious end. Faith bid us believe that, in the sight of the
great Fore-Ordainer, all service was equal. But this we could
not know. The veil—a web of steel, despite its tenuity—was
lowered, and would not rise on the mystery until that Day
dawned, towards which all our days had headed, for which
no man had ever waited in vain. And then, pinched of nostril
and marble-cold, earth's last little posy in our gripless hands,
we should lie supine, and—such was the divine irony of things
—no longer *care* to know.

PART I

[1]

THE ancient little town of Buddlecombe, originally pressed
down the mouth of a narrow valley to the sea, from which
it is protected by rampart and breakwater, has, in the course
of the centuries, scaled the nearer of the two hills that con-
fine it. Nowadays, its streets go everywhere up and down. A
precipitous lane is climbed by the ridge-like steps of an Italian donkey-path; the old town gardens, massively walled, are
built in tiers, so that the apple-trees on the higher levels
scatter their blossoms on the gardens beneath. Coming from
the upland, three driving-roads drop into the town at a bold
gradient; and vehicles, whether they mount or descend, creep
like snails. Half-way down the sheerest of the three, the quaint
little old houses, that set in, oddly enough, just where the
road is steepest, appear to cling shoulder to shoulder, each
a story or a half-story lower than the last, their lines all out
of drawing with age and the insecurity of their foothold; while
those at the bottom of the hill, seen from this point but as a
dimpling cluster of gables, dormers, chimneys, look, till you
are virtually upon them, as if they were standing in the sea.
The roofs of one and all are silvered with the mortar of innumerable repairs, some of their ancient tiles flying off afresh in
every rowdy equinox.

The sea-front is crescent-shaped; and a high, wooded cliff,
which leaves room for no more than a footpath between it
and the surf-rolled shingle, cuts the town in two. The smaller
half, grouped about the harbour, includes the old custom-
house, a couple of ramshackle magazines and their yards, an
ancient inn or two, all bustling places once on a time, when
Elephants' Teeth and Gold Dust were unshipped here, and
the stuffs and linens of England arrived on pack-horses for
transit to France; when, too, much lucrative wine and spirit-
running went on with the French coast. Now, there is little
doing, either here or in the tiny, antiquated storehouses and
weighing-sheds out on the famous old stone quay that crooks
round the harbour. In these sheds children play, or visitors

413

shelter while peeping forth at the great waves which, in stormy weather, toss up over the breakwater; and the storehouses are closed and deserted. A claim to notice, though, they still have. More than one of them is tinted a delicate pink; and the rays of the setting summer sun, catching this, reflect it like a rose in the harbour: which sometimes, half full, lies a pool of melted turquoise; sometimes, during the spring-tides, when the moored boats ride level with the quay, has no more colour in it than an empty glass, or a pure sky before dawn.

To get the best view of the town proper, you must row out beyond harbour and mole, or, better still, swim out, on one of those dead-calm days that every summer brings—days when the yellow cliffs across the bay send down perfect golden shadows in the blue mirror of the sea. Then, lying pillowed on this saltest, most buoyant water, glance back to where, grouped in that perfect symmetry that seems the lost secret of old town-builders, the little place on its gun-cliffs lies curved to the bay. Viewed thus, it looks like a handful of grey shells clustered on a silver shingle—pearl, not stone-grey—for there is no dourness about Buddlecombe: light and graceful of aspect, it might have suffered bodily transport, at the hands of some giant Ifrit, from the French coast over the way. Its silveriness is dashed only by the creeper on the square church-tower—perched, this, too, on the very cliff edge —a creeper which betimes in summer the salt air dyes a blood-red; and by an old jet-black house, tarred and pitched against the breakers which, in a south-west gale, beat to its topmost windows, and hurl roots and branches of seaweed up the slope of the main street.

Above the town the green hillsides are dotted with goodly residences, in which officers on half-pay, and Anglo-Indians in search of clemency, lie snug for the rest of their dormouse days. The houses are as secluded as a foliage of almost tropical luxuriance, or walls well over man's height, with great hedges atop of these, can make them; and the loveliness of their jealously hidden gardens is only to be guessed at from peeps through a door left ajar by a careless errand-boy; from the bold application of an eye to a key-hole; or, in midsummer, from the purple masses of buddleia and the wealth of climb-ing-roses—pink and crimson, yellow and white—that toss over the walls in a confusion of beauty.

414

Book II: *The Way Home*

In this pleasant spot, Richard Mahony had made his home. Here, too, he had found the house of his dreams. It was built of stone—under a tangle of creeper—was very old, very solid: floors did not shake to your tread, and, shut within the four walls of a room, voices lost their carrying power. But its privacy was what he valued most. To the steep road on which it abutted, the house turned a blank face—or blank but for entrance-door and one small window—while, in a line with it, up-hill and down, to conceal respectively flower and kitchen-gardens, ran two arms of massy wall. In addition to this, the front door was screened by a kind of sentry-box porch, open to one side. In this porch was set a tiny glass oval; and here one could stand, secure from rough weather or the curiosity of an occasional passer-by, and watch for mounting postman or expected guest; just as no doubt, fifty odd years before, through this very peep-hole, anxious eyes had strained for news-carrier or outrider bringing tidings of sailor son or soldier husband, absent on foreign service in the Great War.

On stepping over the threshold, you found yourself at once on the upper floor: for so abruptly did the ground on the farther side fall away, that the house was one story to the road, two to the garden. The living-rooms were on the higher level, with a fine view over town and bay—all but one, a snug little oak-panelled parlour on the ground floor; and here it was that, one autumn morning between eight and nine o'clock, the Mahonys sat at breakfast. Although the air of the young day was mild in the extreme, a generous fire burned in the grate and roared up the chimney, entirely putting to shame, with its scarlet vigour, the wraith-like patch of sunshine that lay across the table.

Mary, seated behind the urn, looked very thoughtful; and this was the more marked because, in obedience to the prevailing fashion, she had swept the heavy bands of her hair off cheeks and forehead, and now wore it braided high in a crown. The change threw up the fine, frank lines of head and brow; and atoned for the youthful softness it robbed her of, by adding to the dignity and character of her face.

More than once during the meal she had made as if to speak. But as certainly as she opened her lips, Richard, who was deep in the *Times* of the day before, would either absently hold out his cup to her; or attack the muffin-dish anew;

or, in turning a richly crackling sheet of the paper, exclaim: "Ha! Here we have it! Mr. Disraeli threatens to resign. The poor Queen will be forced to send for that turncoat Gladstone."— And Mary did not wish to spoil his appetite, or interrupt his reading.

But when he had pushed cup and saucer from him, wiped his moustache, and driven back his chair, so that he might fleetly skim the less important columns, she felt justified in claiming his attention.

"Richard, dear—I want to tell you something. What we suspected is true. The Burroughs *have* called in Mr. Robinson. Selina says his gig stood outside their house yesterday for quite a time."

She paused, waiting for a rejoinder that did not come.

"And that's not the most annoying thing, either. He has been sent for to 'Toplands' as well."

After this, she was no longer in doubt whether he heard her. For though he went on reading, his face changed in a way she well knew. To herself she called it "going wrong" —"his face went wrong" was how she put it—and, in the year they had been in England, she had watched what was formerly a casual occurrence turn to almost a habit. Now Richard had always been a very transparent person, showing anger, pride, amusement, all too plainly. But this was something different. It was not so much an expression, as a loss of expression; and it happened when anyone laid a chance finger on some sensitive spot he had believed securely hidden. Put thus out of countenance, he wore an oddly defenceless, even a helpless air; and it distressed her to see him give himself away in front of strangers. Hence, she had a fresh reason for trying to be beforehand with news of a disagreeable nature. In the old days, she had wished to hinder him feeling hurt; now, it was to hinder him showing that he was hurt—which, of the two, she believed he minded more.

In the present case, his sole response was a curt: "Well! . . . fools will be fools," as he turned a page of the paper. A moment later, however, he did what she expected: laid the *Times* down and stalked out of the room.

She threw a motherly glance after him, and sighed. Poor old Richard! She had been bound to tell him, of course; but by doing so she had furnished him with a worry for the whole

day. It was clear he had set his heart on keeping "Toplands";
and now, after consulting him on and off for a couple of
months, the silly people seemed to be going back to that red-
nosed, ungentlemanly Mr. Robinson. She couldn't understand
it. Still, in Richard's place, she would have taken it calmly.
Ten to one, turncoats like these would soon come running to
him again. Time was needed for people here to find out how
clever he was.

Having cleared the breakfast-table, she rang the bell for
the servant to take away the tray. But neither her first ring
nor a second was answered. For at this moment the girl, her
skirts bunched high above a pair of neat prunellas, stood ruefully eyeing the condition of the lower lawn, and wondering
how she could make her master hear, without soiling her boots
or indecently raising her voice.

From the dining-room Mahony had stepped out into the
garden. This was saturated with moisture. During the night
a sea fog had crept up and enmuffled the land; and though, by
now, a watery sun was dissipating the mists—they lingered
only about remote objects, like torn handfuls of cotton wool—
they had left everything drenched and sodden. As he crossed
the grass of the upper lawn, the water came in over the tops
of his carpet-slippers; bushes and shrubs against which he
brushed delivered showers of drops; and gossamer-webs, spun
by the thousand in lovely geometrics that hung whitey-grey
and thick as twine, either shattered themselves on his shoulders, or laid themselves fillet-wise round his brow. At the foot
of the garden he traversed a second lawn, in which his feet
sank and stuck, and climbed three wooden steps set against a
side wall. He had hammered these steps together himself, that
he might have a view to seaward. A small cutting in the end
wall, as well as all the windows of the house, looked to the
town and the row of yellow cliffs beyond. They dated from a
time when a land view of any kind was preferred to that of
the bare and open sea.

Here he now stood and stared at the palely glittering water.
But he did not see it. His mind was busy with the uncomfortable impression left on it by Mary's last statement. At a
stroke this had laid waste the good spirits in which he had
got up that morning; even if, for the moment, it had done
no more than pull him up short, as one is pulled up by a

knot in a needleful of pack-thread, or a dumb note on a keyboard. For the feeling roused in him was no such simple one as mere mortification at the rumoured loss of the big house known as "Toplands"; though the dear soul indoors put it down to this, and he should continue to let her think so. No; there was more behind; and his thoughts raced off after a clue. But only now, when alone with himself, did he get it, and mutter under his breath: "Good Lord! What if this place should prove to be Leicester over again!"

He came no further; for here was it that Selina's prim voice broke on his ear. The girl had followed in his steps to say that Jopson, the liveryman, was at the back door and wished to speak to him. A patient also waited in the passage.

Jopson, a short man of enormous bulk, had been accommodated with a chair, after his drag uphill. He rose at Mahony's approach, but continued to ease his weight against the door-post.

"Sarry, surr, but I ca'an't let 'ee 'ave the mare to-day. 'Er's arff 'er feed.— Sarry, surr. T' others is every one bespoke.— No, surr, mine's t' only livery in the town. One o' the inns *might* let 'ee 'ave a turn-out, of a sart; but I dunno as I'd advise 'ee to go to they. They's almighty partiklar, surr, 'ow their 'arses is drove. 'Twouldn't do to bring one o' them whoam along, winded and h'all of a sweat."

"You surely don't mean to insinuate I've been overdriving the mare?"

"Well, surr, and since you mention it yourself, Allfred did say yesterday as 'ow you took 'er h'up ovurr Brandlebury 'Ill faster than 'er 'dd anny mind to go. The 'ills is steep 'ereabouts, surr, and cruel aard on the 'arses. An' 'tis naat the furst time neether. If you'll excuse me sayin' so, surr, them 'oove seen it do tell as 'ow you be raather a flash 'and with the reins."

"Well, upon my word, Jopson, this is something new! I drive for show? . . . I overwork a horse? Why, my man, where I come from, it used to be dinned into me on all sides that I was far too easy with them."

"Ca'an't say, surr, I'm sure." Jopson was perfectly civil, but equally non-committal.

"But I can!" gave back Mahony, with warmth. "I had two of my own there, let me tell you, and no beasts were ever better treated or cared for. They certainly hadn't to be walked up every slope for fear they'd lose their wind. They took their

honest share of the day's work. For where I come from——"
At the repetition of the phrase, he bit his lip.

"Aye, surr, ahl very well, I dessay, for such a country—
Australy, as I unnerstand," answered Jopson unmoved. "But
'twouldn't do 'ere, surr—in England. This's a civilised country."
And so on, to a somewhat acid wrangle, in which Mahony,
galled by the doubt cast on his compassion for dumb brutes,
was only restrained by the knowledge that, in this matter of
conveyance, he was wholly in Jopson's power.—

"Really, my dear, if it weren't that the fellow kept his hat
in his hand, and scattered his 'sirs' broadcast, it might just
have been old Billy de la Poer himself I was talking to. *Do*
you remember Billy? And how, in his palmy days, one had to
wheedle a mount out of him, if he wasn't in the vein to hire?
The very same uppish independence! I don't know, I'm sure,
what this country's coming to. Though I will say, with all
his shortcomings, Billy never had the impudence to tell me I
couldn't drive."

The woman who was waiting for him in the hall brought
a summons to one of the lonely little farms that dotted the
inland hills.

"Three miles out, and only shanks' ponies to get me there
—just my luck; imagine, Mary, a place with but a single horse
for hire! To-night, I must go thoroughly into the money question again. I shan't be satisfied now, my dear, till I am independent of Jopson and his great fat pampered quadruped.—
Stable with him? Not I! Not if I have to build on here myself!"

His first visit led him down the main street of Buddlecombe.
It was between nine and ten o'clock, the hour of day at
which the little town was liveliest. Shopkeepers had opened
their shutters, sawdusted and sprinkled their floors, picked over
their goods, unlocked their tills, and tied on clean white aprons.
They might now be seen sunning themselves in their doorways,
exchanging the time of day with their neighbours, or shooing
off the dogs which, loosed from chain and kennel, frolicked,
yapped and sprawled over the pavement. Mounted butcher-
boys trotted smartly to and fro. A fisherman, urging a sluggish
horse and laden cart uphill, cried mackerel at two a penny.
And, from big houses and little, women were emerging, on
foot, or driving in donkey and pony-chaises, to do their market-
ing, to chat with one another, and, in buying, to glean the

news that had accumulated overnight. For every one knew everybody else in Buddlecombe, and was almost more interested in his neighbour's business than in his own. You could not, vowed Mahony, enter a shop for a penn'orth of tin-tacks—the selling of which was conducted as if you had all eternity to spare for it, what with the hunting up of a small enough bit of paper, the economical unravelling of a tangled length of twine—without learning that Mr. Jones's brindled cow had calved at last, or that the carrier had delivered to Mr. Du Cane still another hogshead of brandy-wine. This, together with many a sly inquiry as to where you yourself might be bound for, or the trend of your own affairs. Alongside the rampart stood half a dozen ancient men of the sea, discussing, with vigour, God knew what. A bottle-nosed constable, stationed in the middle of the road to superintend a traffic that did not exist, gossiped with the best.

Down this street Mahony walked, in the surtout, light trousers and bell-topper, which he still preferred to the careless attire of a country doctor. He was greeted with bows and bobs and touched forelocks. But the fact of his appearing on foot brought him many a quizzing glance; and there were also shoppers who came at a trot to the door to see and stare after him. Or perhaps, he thought with a grimace, the more than common interest he roused this morning was due to his ill-treatment of Jopson's mare, the tale of which had no doubt already been buzzed abroad. He was really only now, after several months' residence in Buddlecombe, beginning to understand the seven days' wonder with which he must have provided the inhabitants by settling in their midst—he, who bore with him the exotic aroma of the Antipodes! At the time, being without experience of little English country towns, he had failed to appreciate it. Where he came from, people had been too busy trying to get rich, to devote three-quarters of their conscious life to the affairs of others.

His visits in the town paid, he chose to leave it by the sea-front, and climb the steeper hill at the farther end, rather than retrace his steps and present himself anew to all these curious and faintly hostile eyes.

Thus began for him a day of fatigue and discomfort. The promise of the early morning was not fulfilled: the sun failed; down came the mist again; and the tops of the hills and the high roads that ran along them were lost in a bank of cloud. He was for ever opening and shutting his umbrella, as he passed from rain to fog, and fog to rain. Not a breath of air stirred. His greatcoat hung a ton-weight on his shoulders.

He walked moodily. As a rule, on his country rounds, he had the distraction of the reins: his eye, too, could range delightedly over the shifting views of lovely pastoral country, fringed by the belt of blue sea. To-day, even had the weather allowed of it, he could have seen nothing, on foot between giant hedgerows that walled in the narrow lanes leading from one cottage and one village to the next. Plodding along, he first tried, without success, to visualise the pages of his pass-book; then fell back on the deeper, subtler worry that was in him. This, sitting perched hobgoblin-like on his neck, pricked and nudged his memory, and would not let him rest. So that, on coming out of a house, and starting his tramp anew, he would murmur to himself: "Where was I . . . what was it? Oh, yes, I know: just suppose this should turn out to be Leicester over again!"—

For the present was not his first bid for a practice in England. That had been made under very different circumstances.

[2]

IT WAS at another breakfast-table, something over a year previously, that Mary, having opened and read it, handed him a letter bearing the Leicester postmark.— "From my mother." This ran:

Now my darlings, I don't want to hurry you away from all the grandeurs and gaieties of the Metropolis, and have you grumbling oh botheration take that old mother of ours; but I do long to see you both, my children, and to get my arms round you. Your room is ready, the bed made and aired— Lisby has only to run the bedwarmer over the sheets for the last time. My home is small, as you know, Polly, but you shall have a royal welcome, my dears, and I hope will make it yours till you have one of your own again.

"A royal welcome indeed, Mary! . . . one may say our first genuine welcome to England," declared Mahony; and threw, in thought, a caustic side-glance at the letters he had received from his own people since landing: Irish letters, charming in phrase and sentiment, but—to his own Irish eyes—only partially cloaking the writers' anxiety lest, as a result of his long absence from the country, he should take Irish words at their face value, take what was but the warm idea of an invitation, for the thing itself, and descend, with his wife, to quarter himself upon them.— "Now what do you say, love? Shall we pack our traps and be off? Yes, yes, I suppose I shall have to gulp down another cup of these dregs . . . that masquerade as coffee."

"Ssh, Richard! . . . not so loud." Mary spoke huskily, being in the grip of a heavy cold and muffled to the chin. "I should like it, of course. But remember, in engaging these rooms, you mentioned a month—if not six weeks."

"I did, I know. But . . . Well, my dear, to speak frankly, the sooner I walk out of them for the last time, the better I'll be pleased. How the deuce that hotel we stopped at had the effrontery to recommend them staggers me!" And with aversion Mahony let his eyes skim the inseparable accompaniments of a second-class London lodging: the stained and frayed table linen, cracked, odd china, dingy hangings; the cheap, dusty coal, blind panes, smut-strewn sills. "Fitzroy Square, indeed! By hanging out of the window till I all but over-reach myself, I catch a glimpse of a single sooty tree branch. And the price we're asked to pay for the privilege! I assure you, Mary, though we had to fork out rent for the full six weeks, we should save, in the end, by going. The three we've been here have made a sad hole in my pocket."

"Yes. But of course we've done some rather extravagant things, dear. Cabs everywhere—because of your silly prejudice against me using the omnibus. Then that concert . . . the Nightingale, I forget her name . . . and the Italian Opera, and Adelina Patti. I said, at the time, you should have left me at home; you could have told me all about it afterwards. What with gloves and bouquet and head-dress, it must have cost us close on five pounds."

"And, pray, are we to be here at last, in the very heart of things, with twenty years' rust—oh, well! very nearly twenty—to rub off us, and yet go nowhere and hear nothing? No, wife, that's not the money I begrudge. All the same, just let me tell you what our stay in London has run to, so far—I totted it up at three A.M., when those accursed milk-wagons began to rattle by"; and here he did aloud, for Mary's benefit, a rapid sum in mental arithmetic. "Pray what do you say to that, madam? And not a single penny coming in . . . which I dare say helps to make me fidgety. For though, in the old days, the money ran away in great style, it flowed back at the same rate.— No, I know I haven't," he answered another objection on her part. "But on second thoughts, I've decided to postpone seeing over hospitals and medical schools till I'm settled in practice again, and have a fixed address on my pasteboards. I shall then get a good deal more deference shown me than I should at present, a jump-up, sprung from the dickens knows where."

He had lighted the after-breakfast pipe he could now allow himself, and, pacing the room with his hands in his dressing-gown pockets, went on: "This feeling of being a mere nobody and nothing regularly haunts me. I'm paying, I expect, for having lived so long in a town like Ballarat, where it was easy to imagine oneself a personage of importance. Here, all such vanity is soon crushed out of one. The truth of the matter is, London's too big for me; I don't feel equal to it—I believe one can lose the habit of great cities, just like any other. I've certainly never felt more solitary than I do here. Strange, isn't it, to complain of solitude in the most densely populated spot on earth? . . . and after my experience, too, of life in the bush. Yet so it is; and sometimes, especially since you've been laid up, Mary—for which I hold myself mainly responsible, my dear, running you off your legs as I did at first——"

"Still, we *can* say, Richard, can't we, we've seen all there is to be seen?" threw in Mary, with a kind of cheerful inattention. Risen meanwhile from the breakfast-table, she had opened the door of the chiffonier; and her thoughts were now divided between Richard's words, and the fresh depredations in her store of provisions that had taken place overnight.

Mahony snorted. "A fiftieth part of it would be nearer the mark!— Well, as I was saying . . . if you'll do me the kindness to listen . . . this last week or so, since I've been mooning about by myself— Gad! to think how I once looked forward to treading these dingy old streets again—half silly with the noise of the traffic . . . upon my word, wife, that begins to get on my nerves, too, and give me the headache: it goes on like a wave that never breaks; I find myself eternally waiting for a crash that doesn't come. Well, as I say, when I push my way along through all these hard, pale, dirty London faces—yes, my dear, even the best of 'em look as though they needed a thorough scrub with soap and water . . . (as for me, if I wash my hands once, I wash 'em twenty times a day; I defy any one to keep clean in such an atmosphere). All strange faces, too; never one you recognise in the whole bunch; while out there, of course, the problem was, to meet a person you did *not* know.— Well, there come times, if you'll believe me, when I've caught myself feeling I'd hail with pleasure even a sight of old What-was-his-name?—you know, Mary, that vulgar old jackanapes on board who was for ever buttonholing me . . . my particular *bête noire*—yes, or even sundry other specimens of the *omnium gatherum* we were blessed with."

"Well, I never! And me who thought you were only too glad to get rid of them."

"Faith and wasn't I! . . . at the time. Indeed, yes." And Mahony smiled; for, at Mary's words, a picture rose before him of his fellow-passengers as he had last seen them, in the dusk of an October day, standing huddled together like frightened sheep on the platform of the great railway-terminus: an outlandish, countrified, colonial-looking set, if ever there was one, with their over-bushy hair and whiskers, their over-loud shepherds'-plaids and massy watch-chains, the ladies' bonnets (yes, Mary's too!) seeming somehow all wrong. Even the most cocksure of the party had been stunned into a momentary silence by the murk of fog and steam that filled the space under the lofty roofing; by the racket of whistling, snorting, blowing engines; the hoarse shouts of cabbies and porters. But, the first shock over, spirits had risen in such crescendo that, with a hasty: "Come, love, let *us* get out of this!" he had torn Mary from voluminous embraces, bundled her into a four-wheeler and bidden the driver whip up. A parting glance through the peep-hole showed the group still gesticulating, still vociferating, while crowns and half-crowns rained on grinning porters, who bandied jokes about the givers with expectant Jehus and a growing ring of onlookers. Their very luggage, rough, makeshift, colonial, formed a butt for ridicule.

Lost in such recollections—they included the whole dirty, cold, cheerless reality of arrival; included the first breath drawn of an air that smells and tastes like no other in the world; the drive in a musty old growler, reeking of damp

straw, and pulled by something "God might once have meant
for a horse!" to an hotel, the address of which he had kept to
himself: "Or we should have the whole lot of 'em trapesing
after us!"—sunk in these memories, Mahony let a further remark of Mary's pass unheeded. But when, with a raucous cry,
a butcher's boy stumped down the area steps, bearing in his
wooden tray the very meat, red and raw, that was to be dished
up on their table later on, he swung abruptly round, turning
his back on a sight he could not learn to tolerate. "Was there
ever such a place for keeping the material needs of the body
before one? . . . meat, milk, bread! . . . they're at it all day
long.— My dear, I think I've heard you say your mother's
house is not cursed with a basement? Come, love, let us accept her invitation and go down into the country. The English
country, Mary! Change of air will soon put you right again,
and I could do, I assure you, with a few nights' uninterrupted
sleep. Besides, once I'm out of London, it will be easier to see
how the land lies with regard to that country practice I've set
my heart on."

This last reason would, he knew, appeal to Mary, whose
chief wish was to see him back at work. And sure enough,
she nodded and said, very well then, they would just arrange
to go.

For her part, Mary saw that Richard's mind was as good
as made up: to oppose him would only be to vex him. Of
course, it went against the grain in her to be so fickle: to take
lodgings for six weeks and abandon them at the end of three!
(Vainly had she tried, at the time, to persuade Richard to a
weekly arrangement. Richard had *bought* the smile on their
landlady's grim face; and she felt certain did not regret it.)
But though she hadn't shown it, she had been shocked to hear
the sum total of their expenses since landing. Nor was there
anything to keep them in London. They had fitted themselves
out from top to toe, in order to lose what Richard persisted in
calling "the diggers' brand"; and, say what he might to the
contrary, they had seen and heard enough of London to last
them for the rest of their lives. Museums, picture galleries,
famous buildings: all had been scampered through and they
themselves worn out, before the first week was over: her ship-
softened feet still burned at the remembrance.— Yes, for herself, she would be well pleased to get away. Privately, she

thought London not a patch on Ballarat; thought it cold, comfortless, dreary; a bewildering labyrinth of dirty streets. And the longer she stayed there, the more she regretted the bright, clean, sunny land of her adoption.

Thus it came about that, before the third week was over, they were in the train bound for Leicester.

It was a wet day. Rain set in at dawn, and continued to fall, hour after hour, in one of those steady, sullen, soulless downpours that mark the English autumn. Little could be seen by the two travellers, who, during the afternoon, sat huddled chillily in wraps and rugs, the soles of their feet burning or freezing on tin foot-warmers; seen, either of the cast-iron sky, over which drifted lower, looser bulges of cloud; or of the bare, flattish country through which the train ran. On the one side, the glass of the narrow window was criss-crossed with rain stripes; on the other, the flying puffs of steam, unwinding from the engine like fleecy cardings, wearisomely interposed between their eyes and the landscape. Now and then Mahony, peering disconsolately, caught a glimpse of a lowlying meadow, which, did a brook meander through it, was already half under water. Here and there, on a rise, he distinguished a melancholy spinney or copse: in its rainy darkness, trailed round by wreaths of mist, as by smoke, it looked fantastic as a drawing by Doré. On every station at which they halted stood rows of squat, ruddy-faced figures, dripping water from garments and umbrellas, the rich mud of the countryside plastered over boots and leggings. They made Mahony think of cattle, did these sturdy, phlegmatic country people— the soaked and stolid cattle that might be seen in whitepainted pens beside the railway, or herded in trucks along the line. And both men and beasts alike seemed insensitive to the surrounding gloom.

On the platform at Leicester, reached towards five o'clock, so many muddied feet had passed and repassed that, even under cover, not a clean or a dry spot was left. And still the rain fell, hissing and spitting off the edges of the roof, lying as chocolate-coloured puddles between the rails. In the stationyard the wet cabs and omnibuses glistened in the dusk; and every hollow of their leather aprons held its pool of water. The drivers, climbing down from their boxes, shook themselves

like dogs; the patient horses drooped their heads and stood
weak-kneed, their coats dark and shiny with moisture.

"Good Lord! . . . what weather!" grumbled Mahony, as,
having got Mary into the little private omnibus that was to
bear them to their destination, he watched a dripping, beery-
faced coachman drag and bump their trunks on to the roof of
the vehicle, and stack the inside full with carpet-bags and
hand-portmanteaux. "Yet I suppose this is what we have got
to expect for the rest of our days.— Keep your mouth well
covered, my dear."

Behind her mufflings, Mary vented the opinion that they
would have done better to time their landing in England for
earlier in the year.

"Yes; one forgets out there what an unspeakable climate
this is.— The dickens! Look at the mould on the floor! I declare to you the very cushions are damp." Having squeezed
into the narrow space left vacant for him, Mahony vehemently
shut the door against the intruding rain. And the top-heavy
vehicle set to trundling over the slippery cobbles.

But the discomforts of the journey were forgotten on
arrival.

The omnibus drew up in a side street, before a little red-
brick house—one of a terrace of six—standing the length of a
broom-handle back from the road. A diminutive leaden por-
tico overhung the door. Descending a step and going through
a narrow passage, they entered what Mahony thought would
be but a dingy sitting-room. But although small, and as yet
unlit by candles, this room seemed all alive with brightness.
A clear fire burned in a well-grate; a copper kettle on the hob
shone like a great orange; the mahogany of the furniture, polished to looking-glass splendour, caught and gave back the
flames, as did also, on the table spread for tea, a copper urn
and the old dented, fish-back silver. On the walls twinkled the
glass of the family portraits; even the horsehair had high
lights on it. A couple of armchairs faced the blaze. And to this
atmosphere of cosy comfort came in, chill and numb, two
sun-spoiled colonials, who were as much out of place in the
desolate rain-swept night, as would have been two lizards, but
lately basking on a sun-baked wall.

"Come, this is really *very* jolly, Mary!"

427

Thus Mahony, toasting his coat-tails before the fire, while their hosts were absent on the last ceremonies connected with tea. And went on, warmed through now, both in mind and body: "I fear you've had a shocking old grizzler at your side of late, love. But I've felt like a fish out of water. Idleness doesn't agree with me, Mary. I must get back to work, my dear. I want a house of my own again, too. When I see a snug little place like this, after those unspeakable lodgings, why, upon my word, it makes me feel inclined to jump at the first vacancy that offers."

"Oh, that would never do," said Mary, with a smile. And their hands, which had met, fell apart at the sound of footsteps.

It was also a cheerful evening; one that opened with jest and laughter. For barely were they seated at the tea-table when sister Lisby, who towered head and shoulders above her stout little dot of a mother—Lisby shamelessly betrayed a secret, telling how, while the travellers were upstairs removing their wraps, Mother had seized her and danced her round, exclaiming as she did: "Oh, my dear, aren't we grand? . . . aren't we grand?" "Which I may mention was not intended for you, Polly—I would say Mary! For I feel sure, if you could see inside my mother's heart, you would find yourself there no more than fourteen—the age you were when last she saw you."

They all laughed; and Mother covered her old confusion by picking up the sugar-tongs, and dropping an extra lump into Mahony's cup.

"Now give over, miss, will you!" she said affectionately. "Any one but such a pert young thing as you would make allowance for an old woman's pleasure at getting a son again. Ready-made, too—without any bother. Eight of 'em, Richard, my dear, have I brought into this world in my day—a baker's dozen, all told, boys and girls together—and not one is left to their poor old mother but this forward young party here. And she'd be off if she could."

"My mother," said Lisby—having filled and handed round the cups, she was now engaged in apportioning a pork pie, performing the task with a nicety that made Mahony think of Shylock and his bond; not a crumb was spilt or wasted— "My mother would have me sit all day at the parlour window, on the watch for some Prince Charming. To him she would

gladly resign me. But because I wish to go out into the world,
and stand on my own feet——"

"Lisby! Not woman's rights, I hope?" interposed Mary. And
reassured: "Then, mother, I should let her try it. Especially
now you've got me to look after you. Lisby, my dear, if you
had been in the colony with us, in the early days—" and here
Mary dilated on some of the hard and incongruous jobs she
had seen women put their hands to.

"Now, did you ever!" ejaculated Lisby—with force, but with
a divided mind. At present she was carving a cold chicken,
with the same precision as in the case of the pie. (Mahony
laughed afterwards, when, sunk deep in the feathers, he lay
watching the gigantic shadows flung by a single candle on the
white ceiling, and Mary braided her hair; laughed and said,
Lisby's carving made him think of a first-year medical performing on a frog.) "*Never* did I hear tell of such things! I
declare, my dear, I am reminded of Miss Delauncey of Dupew.
You will remember her, Polly—I would say Mary." ("I think
I do just remember the name," from Mary.) "Well, my dear,
what must she do but leave home—against her father's will—
to go and be a governess in Birmingham."— And now Lisby
in her turn held forth, on the surprising adventures of Miss
Delauncey, who, finding herself in a post that did not suit her,
was obliged to take another.

This kind of thing happened more than once during the
meal: the ball of talk, glancing aside from the guests' remoter
experiences, was continually coming back to Lisby and the
world she knew. Her old mother, it seemed to Mahony, was
shyer, more retiring. But though she did not say much, it was
she who peeped into cups to see if the bottoms were showing;
who put tidbits on Mary's plate when Mary was not looking;
pressed Mahony to a dish of cheesecakes with a smile that
would have won any heart. He returned the smile, accepted
the cakes; but, otherwise, finding no point of contact, sat
silent.— Mary, with an eye to him through all Lisby's chat,
feared her relatives would think him very stiff and dull.

But, tea over, chairs drawn to the fire, feet planted on the
fender, Mother turned her pretty old pink-and-white face,
framed in its lisse cap and bands, to Mahony, and seeing him
still sit meditative, laid her plump little hand over his long
thin one, which rested on the arm of his chair. And as he did

not resist, she made it a prisoner, and carried it to her shiny old black silk lap. Sitting in this way, hand in hand with him, she began to put gentle questions about the lives and fates of those dearest to her: John, John's two families of children, and his wives, neither of whom, not the lovely Emma, nor yet soft, brown-eyed Jinny—to whom, through her letters, Mother had grown deeply attached—could she now ever hope to know on earth. Next, Zara, whom she called Sarah: "For the name I chose for her at her baptism I still think good enough for her," —with a stingless laugh at her eldest daughter's elegancies. Steady Jerry, who would never set the Thames on fire. Ned, poor dear unfortunate Ned, who had been a source of anxiety to her since his birth— "Ah, but I was troubled when I carried him, Richard!"—from whom she had not heard directly for many a long day. Inquiring thus after her brood, and commenting on what she heard with a rare good sense, she gradually lured Mahony into a talking-fit that subdued even Lisby, and kept them all out of their beds till two o'clock in the morning. Once started, Richard proved regularly in the vein; and Mary no longer needed to fear lest he be thought dull or stand-off. Indeed, she found herself listening with interest. For he told things—gave reasons for throwing up his Ballarat practice, described sensations on the homeward voyage, and in London—which were new even to her. At some of them she rather opened her eyes. She didn't want to insinuate that Richard was inventing them on the spur of the moment; but she did think—and on similar occasions had thought before now—that certain ideas occurred to him only when he got fairly wound up: he was like a fisher, who didn't always know what he was going to catch.— Besides, there was this odd contradiction in Richard: he who was usually so reserved could, she had noticed, sometimes speak out more frankly, unbosom himself more easily, to people he was meeting for the first time, than to those he lived his life with. It was as if he said to himself, once didn't count.

[3]

THE next-door house, the first in the row, stood at right angles to the rest, and faced two diverging streets of shops and stores. Further, the little leaden rain-shield over the front door was supported by a pair of pillars, coloured to resemble marble, between which hung a red lamp. This lamp had burned there, night for night, for over half a century: the stone of the doorstep was worn to a hollow by the countless feet that had rubbed, and scraped, and shuffled, under its ruby glow. For the house belonged to old Mr. Brocklebank, the surgeon, who was one of the original landmarks of the neighbourhood. He had, in fact, lived there so long that none was old enough to remember his coming—with the possible exception, said Mother, of old Joe Dorgan, for sixty years past ostler at the "Saddlers' Arms." Joe was now in his dotage, and his word did not count for much; but, in earlier life, he had been heard to tell of the slim and elegant figure young Brocklebank had once cut, in redingote, choker, and flowered gilet; and of how people had thought twice before summoning him, owing to his extreme youth. This defect time had remedied; and so effectually that it soon passed belief to connect youth and slimness with the heavy and corpulent old man. When, for instance, Mother came there as a bride, he had seemed to her already elderly; the kind of doctor a young wife could with propriety consult.

The practice had flourished till it was second to none; and he was reported, being a bachelor and very thrifty, not to say close-fisted, to have laid by the thousands which, in this town, were commonly associated only with leather or hose. But now he had all but reached the eighties; and despite one of those marvellous country-bred English constitutions—founded on ruddy steaks, and ale, and golden cheddars—the infirmities of age began to vex him. For some time past, his patients had hesitated to call him out by night, or in bad weather, or for what he might consider too trifling a cause; though they remained his faithful adherents, preferring any day a bottle of Mr. B.'s good physic to treatment by a more modish doctor. Recently, however, he had let two comparatively simple cases slip through his fingers; while the habit was growing on him of suddenly nodding off at a bedside; what time the patient had to lie still until the old gentleman came to himself again. A blend, too, of increasing deafness and obstinacy led him to shout people down. So that, altogether, something like a sigh of relief went up when, one fine day, a great-nephew appeared, and the rumour ran that Mr. B. was retiring: was being carried off to end his honourable and useful career under another's tutelage; to be wheeled to the grave-brink in the humiliating bath-chair to which he had condemned many a sufferer.— And house and practice were for sale.

Lisby came primed with the news—brought by the milkman on his early round—to the breakfast-table. And Mother, her first shock over, and her eyes dried, fell into a reminiscent mood.

"Dear oh deary me! Old Mr. B. laid on the shelf! Why, it seems only like the other day I saw him for the first time . . . when Johnny was born. Yet it must be nigh on five-and-forty years; Johnny will be forty-five come March. In walks Mr. B.—I'd never needed a doctor till then—and says to me—me, poor young ignorant thing, lying thankful to have escaped with my life—in he comes: 'Here's a fine fish we've landed to-day, madam! Here's a new recruit for the Grenadier Guards! Twelve pounds, if an ounce, and a leg like a three-year-old!' I up on my elbow to see, and he quite gruffly: 'Lie down, you villainous young mother, you! Do you want to make an orphan of the brat?' He had always to have his joke, had Mr. B.; and we were good friends from the day. One after another he brought the whole batch of you into the world.— Deary me, I shall miss him. Many and many's the time he's stepped over the railing with his weekly news-sheet: 'Here's a murder case to make you ladies' blood run cold,' he would say. Or: 'Another great nugget found on the gold-fields!'—for he knew the ties I had with the colony. And the last sound I used to hear at night was him knocking out his pipe on the chimney-piece. It was such a comfort to me—after your father went, and the boys scattered—to know we'd a man so close. Especially in '59, when those dreadful burglaries took place."

"Now, mother, give over trying to make yourself engaging," was Lisby's comment on this. "You know, the truth is, no one troubled less about the burglars than you. Before my mother went to bed, she would lay out all the silver and plate, and her rings and brooches, in neat piles on the table, so as to save the robbers trouble, should they come."

"So as to save my own skin, you saucy girl!— Well, well! . . . what's past is past. To be sure, it wouldn't have done for him to go on doctoring till he lost his memory, and perhaps mixed his drugs and poisoned us all."

"It would not indeed. And for the rest, my dear mother, I tell you what: Mary and I will take up our abode next door and look after you," said Mahony.

At the moment, the words passed as the jest they were meant for. But they sowed their seed. Mahony ate his toast and drained his cup with an absent air; and as soon as breakfast was over he made Mary a private sign to follow him upstairs. There, while she sat on the edge of the bed, he fidgeted about the room, fingering objects and laying them down again, sticking pins in and out of the plump pincushion, in a manner that told of a strong, inner excitement.

"I spoke without reflection, but, upon my soul, it does look rather like the finger of Providence, Mary. An opening to crop up in this way at my very elbow! . . . one that's not to be despised, either, if report speaks true. Really, wife, I don't know what to think. It has quite unsettled me. Here have I been expecting to have to travel the country, visiting this place and that, answering advertisements that lead to nothing, or myself advertising and receiving no replies—all so much nerve and shoe wear—and a dreary business at the best of times. . . . You see, my dear, what I need, first of all, is English experience. I mean"—he made an airy gesture—"I must be able to say, when I find the perfectly suitable position I'm looking for: 'I've been practising in such and such a place, for so and so many years, and have had a first-class connection there.'— You notice, I hope, I have no intention—should I take the chance offered me, that is, and pop in here—of making it a permanency. It remains my ambition to live in the country. But if only half what they say of old Brocklebank's affairs is to be believed, a few years here wouldn't hurt me. There are *pots* of money to be made in these manufacturing towns, once a practice is set going—and this has existed for over half a century.— Besides, it might even improve under my hands . . . why not, indeed? Such a Methuselah must have been entirely out of date in medicine. Which also means I should have no difficulty in disposing of it again, when the time came. And might get more for it than I now have to give.— I confess, it isn't exactly the spot I would have chosen, even to start in, were money and time no object to me. But considering, Mary, what our expenses have been . . . the lateness of the season, too! Why, it's virtually winter already, and the worst possible time of year to travel in." And so on, with much more in the same strain, and a final bait of: "Another point we mustn't lose sight of is that here, you, love, would have the company of your dear mother and your sister. And I think I know what a pleasure that would be to you."

"Why, yes, of course, as far as that's concerned," said Mary, who had not interrupted by a word, while he was speaking.

"Well, and the rest?" he asked a trifle querulously. "Don't I convince you, love?"

"Why, yes," said Mary again, but slowly. "In one way. I agree it might be worth considering. But I wouldn't be in *too* great a hurry, Richard. Look about you. See some other places first."

"Yes, and while I hum and haw, and think myself too good for it, some one else snaps it up. The profession is in very different case here, my dear, from what it was in the colonies. It's overcrowded . . . worked to death. I can't afford to be too particular. I must just find a modest corner, slip into it, and be thankful.— And let me give you a piece of advice, Mary," he went on more warmly, with the waxing impatience of a man who longs to see his own hesitation overthrown. "It's no earthly use your comparing everything that turns up on this side of the globe, with Ballarat. A practice like that won't come my way again; or at least not in the meantime. *Try*, love, not to let yourself be influenced by the size of a house and the width of a street. I assure you, once more, you have no conception what these provincial concerns are worth. If I step into old Brocklebank's shoes, you may drive in your carriage yet, my dear!"

Mary had run through so many considerations in listening, that she had really listened more to herself than to him. Of course, much of what he said was sound. Did he settle here, it would save time and money—and one of her standing fears about the new venture had been that Richard would prove too hard to please. But for him now to rush to the other extreme!— Nor was she one to stand out for showiness and style; or rather, she would not be, were Richard a different man. But he, with his pernicketiness!— And it was all very well for him to say, don't draw comparisons; how could one help it? To have flung up a brilliant practice, a big house and garden, a host of congenial friends . . . for this: a miserable pokey house, in a small dull street, in a dull ugly dirty town!— As

434

for what *she* stood to gain by it, the living door by door with mother and sister, fond as she was of them, she could see, even here, drawbacks that were invisible to his man's eye.

However, since the one way to deal with Richard was to give him his head, and only by degrees deftly trickle in doubts and scruples, Mary smothered her own feelings for the time being.— Perhaps he was right, said she: the place might do for a start; and she was certainly against him going travelling in winter—with the objection he had to flannel. Mr. Brocklebank's advisers might, of course, ask a stiff price for the goodwill of the practice; still, if he got on well for two or three years, that would soon be covered. Thus Mary, trusting to a certain blind common sense that *did* exist in Richard, for all his flightiness, if he was neither badgered nor opposed. ("Just the Irish way of getting at a thing backwards!" was how he himself described it.) One point, though, she insisted on; and that was, he should take an outside opinion on the practice, before entering into negotiations.

Entirely pacified, Mahony kissed her, and together they went downstairs. According to Mother, who had now to be drawn into confidence, the person to consult would be Bealby, the chemist; he had dispensed for Mr. B. ever since the old man grew too comfortable to do it for himself. So Mahony on with his hat and off to Bealby's shop, well content to leave Mary to damp the exasperating flutter into which the news had thrown her relatives. Well, no, he wouldn't say that: in Mother even this was bearable. It was true, declaring you might knock her down with a feather, she had seated herself heavily in her chair by the fire, to think and talk over the plan in detail. But her cheery old mind saw only the bright side of it; while her kindly, humorous smile took the sting from fuss and curiosity. Lisby was harder to repress. She threw up her hands. "No! *never* did I hear tell of such a thing, Polly—I would say Mary! Going off to buy a practice, my dear, for all the world as if it were a tooth-brush or a cravat!"

—Richard safely out of the house, Mary felt constrained to come to his defence.

"You must remember, Lisby, it doesn't seem *quite* such an important affair to Richard as it does to you. With all his experience. Living in the colony, too, one learnt to make up one's mind quickly. You had to. Think of shares, for instance.

They might be all right when you went to bed, and by the morning have sunk below par; so that you had to decide there and then whether to sell out or risk holding on."— The mild amusement with which Richard's behaviour provided Lisby, was apt to jar on Mary.

From the chemist Mahony got all the information he wanted —and more. The object of his visit grasped, he was led into a dingy little parlour behind the shop, where, amid an overflow of jars and bottles and drawer-cases, Bealby carried on his ex-business life. And both doors noiselessly closed, to ensure their privacy, the chemist—a rubicund, paunchy old man, with snow-white hair and whiskers—himself grew so private that he spoke only in a whisper, and accompanied his words with a forefinger laid flat along his nose. This mysterious air gave the impression that he was divulging dark secrets; though he had no secret to tell, nor would his hearer have thanked him for any. Plainly, he was a rare old gossip, and as such made the most both of his subject and the occasion. Mahony could neither dam, nor escape from his flow of talk.— However, his account of the practice was so favourable that the rest had just to be swallowed—even disagreeable tittle-tattle about the old surgeon's mode of life. At the plum kept to the last—Brocklebank, it appeared, had actually been called in professionally to the great house of the district, Castle Bellevue—Mahony could not repress a smile; Bealby alluding to it with a reverence that would have befitted a religious rite. Of more practical importance was the information that there were already two candidates for the practice in the field; but that to these, he, Mahony, would no doubt be preferred; for both were young men, just about to start. And: "We want no fledglings, no young sawbones, in a position such as this, sir! Now, with an elderly man like yourself . . ."— Wincing, Mahony contrived soon after to let slip the fact that he was but a couple of years over forty.

"His eyes almost jumped out of his head when I said it, Mary. The fellow had evidently put me down for sixty or thereabouts," he came back on the incident that night. "It made me feel I must be beginning to look a very old man."

"Not old, Richard. Only rather delicate. And the people here are all so rosy and sturdy that they don't understand anyone being pale and thin."

"Well, I'm positive he thought me a contemporary, if not just of old B.'s, at least of his own."

What he did not mention to Mary was the impression he saw he left Bealby under, that lack of success had been the reason of his quitting Australia. Were he only more skilled at blowing his own trumpet! Actually, the old fool seemed to think he, Mahony, would be bettering himself by settling in Leicester!

"Well, sir, I can promise you you will find an old-established, first-class practice, such as this, a very different thing from those you have been used to. England, doctor, old England! There's no place like it. Home, home, sweet home!"— At which Mahony, who had himself, aloud and in secret, rung changes on this theme, regarded the speaker—his paunch, due to insufficient exercise; his sheeplike, inexperienced old face; his dark little living-room; and darker still, mysterious, provincial manner—looked, and knew that he did not, in the very least, mean the same thing any more.

    *   *   *   *   *

"Come, give over, Mary!" said Mother affectionately.

Mother sat by the fire in the twilight, her hands folded placidly in her lap. She was neither a sewer nor a knitter. If not nimbly trotting about the house, in aid of the rheumaticky old servant, she liked to sit still and do nothing; which Richard said made her a most soothing companion. Her words were addressed to Mary, who was rattling a sewing-machine as if her life depended on it. They also referred to a remark passed in a pause of her handle-twirling. This had constituted a criticism of Richard—or as much of a criticism as Mary could rise to. Which, here, she felt quite safe in making, so surely did she know Richard nested in Mother's heart.

That afternoon—it was December, and night now soon after three o'clock—he had—and not for the first time—stepped over the low railing that separated the garden-plots, to say: "Come, Lisby, let us go a-gallivanting!" Nothing loath, Lisby, also not for the first time, laid aside her needle, tied on bonnet and tippet, and off they went, arm-in-arm to prowl round the lighted shops of the town.

Mary's objection was: "But if he were wanted, Mother! I shouldn't know where to send for him."

"My dear, Eliza would find him for you, in less than half an hour.— Besides, Mary, it's very unlikely anyone would want him in such a hurry as all that."

"Yes, I suppose so. It's me that's silly. But you see, in Ballarat he never dreamt of going out without leaving word just where he was to be found. Indeed, he seldom went out for pleasure, at all. He was much too busy."

Mother did not put the question that would have leapt, under similar conditions, to Lisby's lips: "Then why, in the name of fortune, did he leave it?" She only said: "You must have patience, my dear."

"Oh, it's not me—it's him I'm afraid of. Patience is one of the things Richard hasn't got."

There was a brief silence. Then: "You have a very good husband, Mary. Value him, my dear, at his true worth.— Nay, child, let the lamp be. Can't you sit idle for half an hour?"

She stirred the fire to a blaze, which lit up their faces, and the many-folded drapery of their gowns.

"I know that, Mother. But he doesn't get easier to manage as he grows older. In some ways, Richard is most difficult— very, very queer."

"And pray, doesn't the old tree get knobby and gnarled? . . . Take a hint from your mother, my dear—for though, Mary, you've been so long away from me, I know my own flesh and blood as no one else can. Be glad, child, not sorry, if Richard has his little faults and failings—even if you can't understand 'em. They help to bind him. For his roots in this world don't go deep, Mary. He doesn't set proper store on the prizes other men hanker after—money, and position, and influence, and such like." She paused again, to add: "It's a real misfortune, my dear, you have no children."

"Yes, and me so fond of them, too. But I'm not sure about Richard. He's got used, now, to being without them, to having only himself to consider. I'm afraid he'd find them in the way."

"And yet it was of Richard I was thinking," said the old lady gently.

"You say he's hard to manage, Mary," she went on. "But la! child, what does that matter? He's kind, generous, straight as a die—I'm sure I'm right in thinking he's never done a mean action in his life?"

"Never! It isn't in him."

"Well, then!" said Mother: and her cheerful old tone was like a verbal poke in the ribs. "He might be easier to manage, Mary—and thoughtless . . . or stingy . . . or attentive to other women. You little know what you're spared, child, in not having that to endure. There are some poor wives would think you like the princess in the fairy-tale, who couldn't sleep for the pea." She fell into a reverie over this, sat looking into the heart of the fire. "Men?—ah, my dear! to me even the best of 'em seem only like so many children. We have to be mothers to 'em as well as wives, Mary; watch over them the same as over those we've borne; and feel thankful if their nature is sound, behind all the little surface tricks and naughtinesses. Men may err and stray, my dear, but they must always find us here, to come back to, and find us forgiving and unchanged.— But tut, tut, what a sermon your old mother's preaching you! As if you weren't the happiest of wives!" and she laid her soft old hand on Mary's. "I got led into it, I suppose, because of the strong tie between us: you're more like me, Mary, than any of the rest. Another thing, too: I'm a very old woman, my dear, and know I shan't live to see the end of the day's business. So always remember, love, Mother's advice to you was this: not to worry over small things—the big one will need all your strength. And you can't do Richard's experiencing for him, Mary, however much you'd like to spare him the knocks and jars of it.— But I do declare, here they come. Now what will they say to finding us two old cronies gossiping in the dark?"

The shoppers' steps echoed down the quiet street—really sounding like one rather heavy footfall—and turned in at the gate. And then there were voices and laughter and the sound of rustling paper and snipped string, in the little room, where Mary lit the lamp, and Lisby displayed her presents—sweetmeats, a piece of music she had coveted, a pair of puce-covered gloves, a new net for her chignon—while Mother tried to prevent the great round pork pie Mahony deposited on her lap, from sliding into the grate.

"You dear naughty spendthrift of a man! Why, the girl's head will be turned."

"Come, Mother, let me give her a little pleasure."

"You give yourself more, or I'm much mistaken."

"Pooh! Such trifles! I shouldn't otherwise know what to do

439

with my small change," retorted Mahony. And Mary laughed and said: "Wait, Mother, till the practice really begins to move, and then you'll see!"

This nudged Mahony's memory. "Has any one been?"

"They hadn't when I came over. And Mary Ann has not knocked at the wall.— Oh yes, the boy called with an account from Mr. Bealby."

The news of the blank afternoon, together with Mary's colonialism, grated on Mahony. "*Do* knight him, my dear, while you're about it," he said snappishly.

"Oh, well, Bealby, then. Though I really can't see what it matters. And out there, if I *hadn't* said Mr. Chambers, Mr. Tangye, you would have been the one to suffer."

"And I can assure you, my dears, Bealby won't think any the worse of you for turning him into a gentleman," soothed Mother.

"Oh! but Richard is very correct—aren't you, dear?"

Here Lisby had also to put in her spoke.

"And Bellvy Castle, pray?—what of Bellvy Castle? Has still no groom come riding post-haste to summon you?"

Heartily tired of this jest, which he himself had innocently started, Mahony picked up a book and stuck his nose in it. "No, nor ever will."

"Come, Lisby," said Mother, "the kettle's boiling its head off.— Richard, my dear, draw up your chair to me; you must be cold and famished.— Nay, Mary, I'll not let you go home. We're going to drink a cosy cup together. And afterwards Richard shall tell us more adventures of the early days. I've looked forward to it all the afternoon. It's as good as any book."

Mahony had more than once said to his wife: "Before I knew your mother, Mary, I used to think *you* the warmest-hearted creature under the sun. But now that I know her, love, and can draw comparisons, I declare you sometimes seem to me quite a hard and reasonable young woman!"

And then he would fall to musing on the subject of wisdom inborn and acquired. Here was this little old lady, who knew nothing of the world, had never, indeed, travelled fifty miles from her native place, and yet was richer in wisdom—intuitive wisdom, the wisdom of the heart—than any second mortal he had met. He could not picture to himself the situation, however tangled, that Mary's mother would fail to see through, and, seeing, to judge soundly and with loving-kindness.— Yes, his acquaintance with and affection for her was the one thing that helped him over the blank disappointment of these early weeks.

[4]

THE surgery was a small, darkish room on the ground floor, a step or two below street level; and the window behind which Mahony spent the greater part of his first English winter was screened from the curiosity of passers-by, by an attorney's brown gauze shade. Across this blind, he saw people move like shadows; or like bodies immersed in water, only the tops of whose crowns showed above the surface. There went the hooded tray and crooked arm of the tinkling muffin-man; and the wares of the buy-a-brooms. There, also, to the deep notes of his bigger bell, and his insistent: "To all whom it may concern!" passed the shiny black hat of the town crier. Regularly, too, at dusk, through fog or silvery rain, the lamp-lighter's ladder and torch rose into Mahony's field of vision, flicking alive the little gas flame that set his own brass plates a-glitter.

About this surgery hung a disagreeable, penetrating smell— a kind of blend of the countless drugs that had been housed and mixed there for over half a century—and, air as you might, it was not to be got rid of. It gave even Mary, who was not sensitive to smells, the headache. Otherwise, during Richard's absences, she might have used this room, which held a comfortable armchair. As it was, she found herself fairly crowded out. The passage was so narrow that two people were a tight fit in it; and, were more than two in waiting, they had to be furnished with seats in the little parlour to the back, pokier, this, than even the surgery, and very dark—Richard called it the "Black Hole"—giving as it did on a walled-in yard, no bigger than a roofless prison cell. Although, the accommodation was so cramped that it was like living in a mouse-trap. Still, it would have been folly, in the beginning, to separate house from practice, when the two had hung together for so long. Time enough later on, to make changes. Mary's own idea was to turn the first-floor bedroom into a drawing-room. Richard talked of moving; of knocking two houses into one; even of building for himself. In the meantime, he had taken the house on a short lease, preferring to pay a higher rent for a few years, than to bind himself for the mystic seven.— And so it was mainly in the bedroom that Mary spent *her* first winter; sewing, sheerly to kill time, garments she did not need, or which she might just as well have "given out." Sitting bent over her needle in the half daylight, she could sometimes almost have smiled, did she think of the sacrifices they had made—all for this. But for the most part she felt troubled and anxious. Richard had tied himself down for three years; but not a month had passed before her constant, nagging worry was: how long will he hold out?

Mahony, too, was offended by the atmosphere of his room: though not so much by the drugs, to which his nose was seasoned, as by the all-pervading reek of stale tobacco. This hung about and persisted—though a carpenter speedily prized open the hermetically sealed window—and only became bearable when a good fire burned, and the room was thoroughly warm. Cooled off, it had a cold, flat, stagnant smell that turned you sick. His old forerunner must have kept his pipe going like a furnace; have wadded it, too, with the rankest of weeds. Even had the practice been shaping satisfactorily, this smell might have ended by driving him from the room; which would also have meant from the house. As things stood, however, it was not worth his while to think of moving. Before a month was up, he suspected what two months showed, and three made plain as the nose on his face: the whole affair had been of the nature of a gross take-in.

There he sat, in his dingy, stuffy den, with the last numbers of the medical journals, new books on medicine, before him, and was too unsettled to read, or, if he did, to make sense of what he read. The mischief was not only that the practice didn't move properly: what came was of entirely the wrong sort. He had not had half a dozen calls to good houses since starting. The patients who had thus far consulted him were the servant-girls and petty tradesmen of the neighbourhood. And none too many of these either. Which, however, did not exactly surprise him. For with gentry of this persuasion he had never in his life been popular.

In fits of exasperation, he knew what it was to feel convinced that the entries in the books laid before him at purchase, the rosy tales of Brocklebank's receipts, had been in-

vented for his decoying. If not, *what,* in the name of fortune,
had become of the practice? In calmer moments, he absolved
those about him from the charge of wilful fraud: they had
acted according to their lights—that was all. That their way
of looking at things was not his, was constantly being brought
home to him anew.— And how, indeed, could he expect them,
who had passed their whole lives, fixed as vegetables, on the
selfsame spot, to know his touchstone for a practice? For example, the visit, famous in local history, paid by old Brocklebank to Bellevue Castle. On closer scrutiny, this dwindled
into the bandaging of a turned ankle, an ankle belonging to
one of the under-servants, who had slipped on a greasy cobble
while at market. Never had old B. set foot in the Castle: or,
at most—little more than a servant himself—had entered it but
by the back door. Chagrin was not the only feeling this incident roused in Mahony: he found insufferable the obsequious
attitude of mind it spoke of, in those concerned. Long residence in a land where every honest man was the equal of his
neighbour had unfitted him for the genuflexions of the English
middle-classes before the footstools of the great.— But he had
given up trying to make himself or his views intelligible. For
all that those about him understood, he might as well have
been speaking Chinese; while any reference to the position
and income he had turned his back on, called to their eyes a
look of doubt, and even disbelief. They considered him a
supremely lucky man to have stepped into old Brocklebank's
shoes; and at his door alone would the blame be laid, if he
failed to succeed.

And failing he was! So far, he had booked the magnificent sum of slightly over a couple of pounds weekly. Two
pounds! It reminded him of the first struggle-and-starve campaign he had waged, years ago, on taking up practice after his
marriage. Only under one condition could he have faced the
present situation with equanimity; and that, paradoxically
enough, was, if he had not seen the colour of the money, and
it had stood on account to some of the big houses round about.
As it was, it dribbled in, a few shillings here, a few there;
which meant that his spending had also to be done in driblets
—a habit it was easier to lose than to recapture. Yes! if the
handful of shares he had left invested in the colony were not
bringing in what they did, he and Mary would, at this

moment, have been reduced to living on their capital.

Talking of Mary: her position here was another bite he could not swallow. It had really not been fair of him, to foist this kind of thing on Mary. To begin with, the house—possibly the neighbourhood, too, dark, crowded, airless—did not suit her. She looked pale and thin, and had never quite lost the cough she had arrived with. How could she, indeed, when she sat, for hours at a stretch, stooped over her needle? She had no society worth the name—never a drive, a party, a bazaar. Her sole diversion was tending her mother; undertaking the countless odd jobs the old lady and her rheumaticky maidservant had need of. In one way, of course, this was right and proper; and he did not begrudge her to the mother from whom she had so long been parted. His grudge was aimed at another quarter. Soon after Christmas Lisby had made good her escape, and was now established as resident mistress at a Young Ladies' Seminary near Leeds. Which wormed, in spite of himself.

No complaint crossed Mary's lips; she sacrificed herself as cheerfully as usual. None the less, he owed one of his chief worries, during these weeks, to Mary. For he could *feel* that she did not expect him to hold out here, and that she lived in daily suspense lest he should throw up the sponge. The consciousness of this galled him—got on his nerves. Yet never had he felt so averse to breaking silence. It was not only self-annoyance at the foolishness he had been guilty of, in dumping himself down in such a hole; or anticipation of a resigned, I-told-you-so attitude on Mary's part—she *had* told him so, of course; but it wouldn't be Mary if, when the crisis came, she twitted him with it. No, what tied his tongue was his own disinclination to face the future.

The result was that Mary, too, grew fidgety: it was so odd, so unlike Richard to bottle himself up in this fashion. She began to be afraid he was afraid of her, and of what she might say. So, one evening, as they sat together over book and needle, she herself broke the ice, by asking him point-blank whether he regretted having settled in Leicester. "For I can see the practice is not doing much in the meantime. Still, of course . . . if you otherwise like the place——"

At her first word the torrent burst.

"Like it? I wish to God I'd never set foot in its hideous

444

red-brick streets! As for the practice not doing much . . . my dear, it has melted into thin air . . . and that's all there is to say about it! The great majority of that old horse-doctor's patients have given me the go-by—what on earth has become of the wealthy shoemakers, etc., whose names stood on his books, Heaven alone knows! It can't be that they disapprove of my treatment, for they've never even put it to the test. Upon my word, Mary, I sometimes think the whole thing was a fake and a swindle. But I can tell you this: if I stop here, I'm on the high road to becoming a sixpenny doctor for the masses. And I will confess to feeling myself a little too good for that."

"I should think so! It's really most unfortunate, Richard.— But what's to be done?"

"The only course *I* can see, is to get out of it. I've made a big mistake, my dear, and the shortest and cheapest way in the end will be to admit it, and tot up the balance. I could curse myself, now, for not having taken your advice. Over-hasty as always! The only excuse for me is, I honestly believed there was money to be made here. I think I was in a panic, too, at the rate at which our funds were running away."

"Well, it's no use crying over spilt milk. But since you own you did rush rather blindly into this, be warned and don't, for goodness sake, do the same thing in getting out of it. Give it at least a year's trial."

But the bare idea turned him cold. Now, too, that he had had his say, he felt doubly resolute. Aloud, he declared that another three months spent in these close dark quarters, among this stickiest provinciality, in the mud, wind and rain of this dirty, wet, dismal town, would drive him crazy. "The very smell of the place does for me. Leather and corn and horses —horses and leather and corn! A population of ostlers and grooms and commercial gentlemen, and cattle-dealers and bull-necked farmers. No, thank you, my dear! No more of it for me! Naturally, I shall sell at a loss; but the sooner the better, Mary, before the practice falls to pieces altogether."— And from this decision he was not to be moved.

The question of what next, brought them to another dead-lock. Mary had got it into her head that, if he went from here, it should only be to London—and was dumbfounded by the moody silence into which he fell at London's very name.— "It's society you've missed, dear. Even had you got on well, you couldn't have put up with the lack of that. But if you persist in sticking to your original plan, and going to live in some miserable little village, it will be worse than ever. You used to say you felt cut off in Ballarat. But since we've . . ."

"And you? . . . what about you, pray?"

"Oh, for me it's been different"—dear Mary!—"living next door to my mother, and all that."

"Well, I can tell you this, wife. I've grown more attached to your mother, her kind heart and sound sense, than I was to anyone in all Australia. And certainly more than I am to my own."

"Surely it's time you proved that? What must they be thinking of you?" ("They? Oh, they'll understand. You forget they're Irish, too, love!") "Well, Richard, my advice is . . . if you're quite determined to move from here . . . go and pay some visits, and travel about a bit, as you ought to have done at first."

Than this, no suggestion could have jumped better with Mahony's mood: his cramped soul longed to stretch its wings. Spring was at the door, too: that English spring, the marvels of which he had seen so often in imagination—and in imagination continued to catch his only glimpse of them, shut up between brick walls as he was. At Mary's words he had a sudden vision of all the loveliness—green downs rolling to the sea, orchards in blossom, dewy old bird-haunted gardens—that he had missed, in flinging himself hugger-mugger on the business of money-making, in this sordid town. And so, overthrowing, in his haste, his original plan of waiting till he was in more prosperous circumstances to present himself, he packed his carpet-bag, and went off to visit his relatives and to renew his acquaintance with his *alma mater,* putting the practice up for sale, and leaving a *locum* to hold together what remained of it. According to the innate perversity of things, he had no sooner done this, than it showed signs of betterment. His substitute was called in to one of the hosier kings, bespoken by the wife of a wealthy tanner. Mere chance, of course, but it did look as though fate had a special down on him.

* * * * * * *

446

Book II: *The Way Home*

The nominal goal of his journey was Dublin; and, after that, Edinburgh. But when he looked back on the weeks that followed, he saw them solely in the light of a journey into the past. And now, too, he grasped why he had so long postponed embarking on it. He was, he discovered, one of those who have a nervous aversion to returning on their traces.

Alighting from his car at a corner of the square, he stood, bag in hand, and gazed at his old home. It was very early on a gusty, grey, spring morning; and he himself was cold and unslept. Already, too, the spiritual depression that is Ireland's first gift to her homing sons was invading him: looking about him he saw only stagnation and decay.— Here now he stood, a worn and elderly wayfarer, over whose head thirty odd years had passed since, as a boy, he light-heartedly trod this pavement. Thirty years! Yet it might have been yesterday. For nothing was changed—or nothing but himself. And, as he moved towards the house, he had—in self-defence as it were—a moment of vision, in which the long trail of his life swept past the eye of his mind: his rich, motley life, with all its blanks and prizes, its joys, pains, and compensations, let alone the multitude of other lives with which it had come into touch.— And to think there had been moments when he counted it a failure!

In the bulging glass flower-case outside the ground-floor window, a familiar collection of ferns and green things pursued their morbid growth. Down in the area stood the empty saucer, placed there full, of a night, for any thirsty beast that passed. Here was the well-known dent in the brass knocker; the ugly crack in the stone coping. As of old, the balcony showed green and mildewed with the water that leaked from a pair of flower-tubs; just as he remembered it, the white carriage step was split asunder—a trap for delicate feet. With the difference, that the mould was thicker, the split wider, the cracks more pronounced.

It was the same with his relatives; they, too, had made giant strides along the road of decay: throats had sagged, eyes were grown smaller, knuckles bonier. Of the three, the older generation had worn best. His mother carried herself erectly, was slender—slender to emaciation—and, an inveterate enemy of crinoline, wore clinging, trailing black garments of a style all her own, she and his sisters moving like lank, heavily

447

draped maypoles, where other women bulged and billowed and swam. ("Good Lord, what frights!" was his verdict on this deviation from the norm.) With their ivory faces, long, finely pointed noses, straight Irish eyebrows, and pretty, insincere Irish mouths, the three of them looked like replicas of the one cameo (as did also he, could he but have seen himself); and since, in age, there was less than a score of years between the trio, the relationship might have been that of sisters, rather than mother and daughters.

Thus dispassionately, and Irishly, he viewed them. As they him.— "My beloved son, colony life is disastrous. It ruins the body . . . as it ruins the soul."— From the way they looked at him, as this was said, he saw that they found him unnaturally withered—very old for his age. Still, his greying temples and wrinkled brows touched them little, compared with the burning question whether he had come home in time to save this soul of his alive. For they were even more deeply rapt than of old, in the mysteries and ecstasies of religion. On its conduct they lavished their remaining vitality; while the mother faith, which flourished so abundantly around them, supplied them with an outlet for the bitter hatred which life's hardships had engendered in them. Popery was an invention of the Arch-Fiend; its priests were the "men of sin."— To Mahony, who had learnt to regard all sects and denominations as branches of the one great tree, such an attitude was intolerable.

He stayed with them but for three days; longer he could not have borne the lifeless atmosphere of his old home. But . . . seventeen years, and for three days! There was, however, another reason. Their poverty was such that it wrung his heart to have to watch their shifts and makeshifts. In this big house not a single servant moved; his sisters' thin, elderly hands were hard and seamy with work. The two women rose at daybreak, to clean the steps and polish the knocker. Themselves they washed and got up the finely darned damask; kept bright the massive bits of silver, than which there was little else on the oval surface of a dinner-table built to seat a score of people. They did their scanty shopping in distant neighbourhoods, where they were not known, creeping out with a basket early in the morning, while others of their class were still

between the sheets.— No! the food they set before him stuck
in his throat; it was so much taken from them, who looked
so bloodless. Yet, though he grudged himself each mouthful,
he did not dare either to refuse what was offered him, or to
add to it, by a gift of money or eatables—anything that might
have shown them he saw how matters stood. Banknotes
slipped, unmentioned, into a letter from far-off Australia had
been a different thing. These could be politely ignored—as,
indeed, they had always remained unacknowledged. He imagined the fine gesture with which his mother let them flutter
through her fingers, in saying airily to Sophy and Lucinda:
"Some nonsense of poor Richard's!" He ventured no more
than to bring her a bouquet of cut flowers, and a vellum-
bound book of devotions. Even hothouse grapes might have
exuded a utilitarian flavour. But all he felt went into his gift;
and he knew just the nerve in the proud old heart that would
be satisfied by it. For though he did not warm to them, yet
like spoke to like, blood to blood, directly they met again.
He could read their private thoughts, their secret feelings. At
a glance he saw through the inventions and excuses, the tricks
and stratagems, with which they bolstered up their lives; while
yet retaining their dignity as great ladies. Again, the flashes of
mordant humour, which not your godliest Irishman can ever
wholly subdue; or the sudden, caustic, thumb-nail sketch of
friend or foe: these were so familiar to him as to seem his
own: while the practical Irish habit of stripping things of
false sentiment was homely and refreshing. Thus, with regard
to Mary's childlessness, his mother queried briskly: "Has
fretted for lack of a family? Nonsense! In such a climate, she
was much better without." Again: "Her relatives will miss you.
No doubt they placed great faith in your skill. Besides, your
visits cost them nothing!" Or her description of a neighbour's
state as: "A demi-fortune—cab and one horse!"

Many were the inquiries made after Mary, the regrets expressed at her absence; but he, in his heart (as probably they
in theirs), felt relieved that she had not accompanied him. For
Mary would certainly have put her foot in it here. There
would have been no keeping out of her face the pity she
burned with; she would have made presents where presents
were an injury; have torn down veils that were sacred, even

449

between the women themselves; would, in short, have come hopelessly to grief amid the shoals and quicksands through which it was necessary to steer a course.— Whereas, to him, the task was second nature.

He took leave of them without regret. Once away, however, he was conscious of a feeling of something like guilt towards them. For he understood now, only too plainly, what the withdrawal of the ninety to a hundred pounds yearly, which, in his later, palmy days, he had been able to allow them—what the abrupt stoppage of this sum must have meant to them. It had no doubt made all the difference between comparative ease and their present dire poverty. Yet never by so much as a word had they hinted at this. There was surely something great about them, too—for all their oddity.

    ✻   ✻   ✻   ✻   ✻

Did this experience give him the sensation of a bad dream, in which he, who was alive, went down among those who had ceased to live, his return to Edinburgh and its well-known scenes had exactly the opposite effect: made *him* feel like a shade which is permitted to revisit the haunts of men. For here was life in all its pristine vigour, life bubbling hot from the source—and aeons divided him from it. Here he found again his own youth—eager, restless, passionate—though encased now in other forms. Other keen young spirits swept from hospital to theatre, and from theatre to lecture-room, as he once had done; and were filled to the brim, they, too, with high purpose and ambition. Never before had it been made so clear to him, of what small worth was the individual: of what little account the human moulds in which this life-energy was cast. Momentous alone was the presence of the great Breath: the eternal motor impulse. Each young soul had its hour, followed a starry trail, dreamed a kingship; then passed—vanishing in the ranks of the mediocre, the disillusioned, the conquered—to make room for the new company of aspirants thronging on behind. Many of these lads would, no doubt, in looking back, find as little in their lives to feel proud of as he found in his: nothing accomplished of all they now so surely anticipated. And one or other of them might also, when his time came, hover, an elderly ghost, eyed with a flagrant curiosity by this insolently young throng—how contemptuously would not he himself have stared at the apparition, in the old days!—hover round the precincts, the real old middle-aged hack, returned for a glimpse at the scenes of his youth.— Such were his feelings, the experience being one that drove his years home to him with a cruel stab. Whereas, otherwise, he sailed along, fondly nursing the belief that there was still some show of youthfulness left in him.

Over these reflections he fell into an elegiac mood; and, not having Mary at his elbow, to nudge him to attention over against the realities, he let day after day slip by, without calling on, or otherwise making himself known to distinguished members of the profession. He shirked the necessary explanations. The one attempt he did make, turned out poorly. Spelt, too, a good dose of patronage for this untrumpeted doctor from the backwoods.

To Mary he wrote: "I do not see much advancement in physick." But this was only half the truth. Where theory was concerned, there existed a certain feeling of newness in the air. The shining lights of his own day were now but a pair of crabbed old invalids, waiting each for his mortal release. The man of the hour—or so rumour had it—was a young surgeon in Glasgow; which "God-forsaken" city British and foreign physicians were actually travelling to and settling in, to see demonstrated a new means for hindering germ-putrefaction. At first, he, Mahony, inclined to side with his old chief, who turned a cold shoulder on young Lister and his experimenting. But after reading up the subject in the Medical Library, he changed his mind. Pasteur's theory of the existence of certain spores in the atmosphere might not yet be proved to every one's satisfaction; but the examples published by this Dr. Lister, illustrating the successful employment of the new method, could not but make a deep impression. In the end, he would, for two pins, have taken rail himself to Glasgow, where, it was claimed, in even the most insanitary hospital wards, pyaemia, erysipelas, and hospital gangrene had been well nigh stamped out.

It was while he still lingered, ruminating these things, that, in a medical journal, he saw advertised for sale a first-class practice on the south coast of England, in a locality which was described as lovely, sheltered, salubrious. Something in the wording of the paragraph took his fancy, and he wrote for particulars. The reply was so favourable that, instead of either travelling to Glasgow or going back to Leicester, he set out by way of Bristol for the south. To see the place was straightway to lose his heart to it; here, for once, was a dream come true. The advertiser turned out to be as young as Brocklebank had been old—a practitioner of but a year's standing. But to the hardy old surgeon as a reed to an oak. For even the soft air of this sheltered nook had not been mild enough for a congenital throat-weakness; and the young man was hieing him to the Cape, where he proposed to remain. Such was his eagerness to be gone, that he came a considerable way to meet Mahony in the matter of price.— And now letters passed and telegrams flew between husband and wife; till, even the electric wire proving too circumstantial for Richard's impatience, Mary was bidden to pack her bag and join him there. She came, and was herself charmed with the spot—as, indeed, how could she help being, cried Richard, who was as elated as a child. You might search England through, and not find its equal.

The chief difficulty was, to get a house. Young Philips, as a bachelor, had lived in furnished apartments; which, of course, was impossible for them. But it was literally a case of Hobson's choice. For most people owned their houses— had been born and would die in them, like their fathers before them—and in all the place only two were vacant. One was of a type that disfigures many a seaside town: a high, gloomy house—in a terrace of three—standing right on the pavement of a side street. With no garden of its own, it was darkened by the foliage of the big trees in the gardens opposite. Still worse, it turned its back on the sea. A lawyer had lived here; the ground-floor windows bore the hated shades. His widow, planning to move from the neighbourhood, was willing to let the house on lease. But Mahony took a furious dislike to it; and even Mary thought it dull, and rather large for the two of them. The second, much smaller, and older—some hundred and fifty years, said report—was, on the other hand, bright and cheerful, and had a charming old-world garden, with a magnificent view across the Bay. But it was for sale. Nor was the position it occupied so suitable as that of the lawyer's: it stood above the town, half-way up a steep hill. Still, distances were surely negligible, argued Mahony, in so

small a place; and whoever really needed a doctor would summon him, whether it meant fifty yards further or no.

None the less the decision cost him his sleep of a night.
Mary was patently in favour of the one to be rented; his
inclinations all leaned to the other. He walked past this a dozen
times a day, and went over it so often that the agent suggested his keeping the keys, until he had made up his mind.
It was ridiculous, he told himself, to think of buying a house,
before he had sampled the practice; yet seldom had he been
so torn. And, once again, Mary, pitying his distraction, came
to the rescue and said, well, after all, perhaps he should just
buy and be done with it. For she saw what would happen if
he didn't: he would never cease to bemoan his loss, and to find
fault with the house he was in. Better for his peace of mind
that he should take the monetary risk—and though this meant
using up the last remainder of their available ready money.
But there was also another unspoken thought at the back of
Mary's mind. The knowledge that he had thus involved himself might help him to sit firm, if—and with a person like
Richard the contingency *had* to be allowed for—he afterwards
tired of the place.

So he bought; and not for a second had he regretted it—
any more than he regretted having pitched his tent in this
loveliest of spots. On the contrary, he counted himself a remarkably lucky man.

❀   ❀   ❀   ❀   ❀

And thus to Buddlecombe.

[5]

The practice bore out its reputation. The huckster, the publican, and the ostler were in the minority here; Mahony's visit-
ing-list was studded with good names. This change for the
better, together with the pride he took in his pretty house and
garden, sent his spirits up sky-high. And, as was natural, he
read his own satisfaction into others.— "If I'm not much mistaken, Mary, people here are well pleased to have a medical
man of a reasonable age in their midst again."— It fell to Mary
to keep him gently damped; to prevent him skipping off the
earth altogether, in his new-found lightness of heart.

At first, though, even she had to admit there was nothing to complain of.

For if Mahony here felt himself restored to his own level professionally, on the social side—which was important, too—things also promised to run smoothly. Of course, English people were notoriously slow to take you to their hearts; and, even after they had found out all about you, would still go walking round you, looking you up and down. Once, however, these sticklers were sure with whom they had to deal, they made rich amends. And so, Mary had numerous callers of the right kind; and invitations followed the calls. The vicar's wife took her up—a due appearance at church having been made, and a pew hired—and she joined a circle that sat twice a week to sew for the heathen. Further, she was asked to help in visiting and distributing tracts among the lower orders; in getting up a Penny Reading to raise funds for the promulgation of the Gospel; to take a table at the annual Sunday School Feast: was, in short, made free of all the artless diversions of the parish.

In addition to this, the month was April; and the thousand and one beauties of an exceptionally fine spring unrolled before their eyes. Declared Mahony: to be present at this budding and bursting, this sprouting and flowering, more than made up for the disappointments he had suffered since landing in England. What a feast of tender green, of changing colours, was here spread for eyes sore with the harshness and aridity of the Australian landscape, the eternal grey-green of its skimpy foliage! When he first arrived, every sheltered slope and sunny bank was yellow with primroses; the lesser celandine bedecked the meadow-grass, violets were mauve and purple in the hedgerows; and no sooner did these show signs of fading than the ground became blue with myriads of bells, which, taken in the mass, looked like patches of sky dropped to earth. And the blue in its turn yielded to the ruby-pink of the red campion. Against a background of starry blackthorn blazed the golden gorse. The cliffs were covered with the comical little striped brown pokers of the horsetails, which soon branched out into bristly brooms; and, piercing the rust-red carpet of last year's growth, up sprang the straight nimble spears of the bracken. In the high hedges the ruddy cane of the willows was smothered by the succulent green tips of hawthorn and bramble;

while on the rolling countryside, that belle of trees, the larch, stood out among the copperish buds of the beeches and the first tightly folded leaves of the chestnuts, with a pale green feathery loveliness all its own.

But with the onset of summer, when gardeners were busy netting strawberry-beds and currant-bushes against the greedy thrush; and the blackbird, his wooing done, was omitting the top notes at the end of his call: by this time, in spite of Mahony's liking for the place, and for the moderate, but sympathetic practice, sly doubts had begun to invade him whether things were really at bottom as satisfactory as they seemed, or whether both in his professional and their twofold social life, there was not a fly in the ointment. In his own case, the suspicion soon deepened to a certainty.— Robinson was that fly.

Of the person who bore this name he had, of course, heard nothing, at the time of buying. Only by degrees did Robinson come within his ken. A surgeon, some years his own junior, the fellow had originally, it now turned out, held the whole practice of the place, and for miles round, in his hands. Then, three years previously, he had married a rich widow—report credited her with eight to ten thousand a year—bought a fine property, and retired. Since then—again according to rumour—he had spent more time than was fitting, in the company of the bottle. However that might be, his former wide professional connection, his wife's money and social standing, combined to make him *persona grata* in all the best houses; while among the townspeople and villagers, slow of wit, and opposed to change as only English country-people could be, the memory, or rather the habit of him, had persisted, to the tribulation, no doubt, of his successors. For there came moments when Mahony mistrusted the throat-weakness alleged by young Philips; or at least wondered whether this was his sole reason for quitting so promising a position, after a bare year's trial. And who had preceded Philips? At first, what he, Mahony, had to meet was no more than a casual mention of Robinson's name. "Mr. Robinson said this, or would have done that"; and, at the outset, he had been simple enough to believe it a slip of the tongue for Philips. He soon learned better. A question put, a scrap of gossip retailed by Mary, taught him that Robinson was still a power in the place. For yet a while, however, he ascribed what was going on to hard-dying custom, which might be overcome.

The first time he scented actual danger was, when one of two spinsters he was attending complained of her sister's slow progress, and said she would ask Mr. Robinson to look in, he understanding their constitutions better than anyone else.

"If you do that, my good woman, you see no more of me!" was Mahony's quick retort.— And so he lost a patient.

Thereafter, on his rounds, he himself began to catch glimpses of the bottle-nosed surgeon—sitting perched in a high gig beside a groom in livery; altogether a very smart turn-out—and this went on until, upon his word of honour, it positively looked as if the fellow intended taking up practice again . . . filching it back from under his very nose. A pretty thing that would be to happen, now he had staked his all on it! A shabby trick, and no mistake!—one, too, that ran counter to every known rule of medical etiquette.

And the mischief was—with a brain like his—let the door open to one such suspicion, and straightway a dozen others seized the chance of inserting themselves. He next fell to questioning the apparent ease with which Mary and he had entered the polite society of the place. For, the longer he lived there, the more plainly he saw just what a wasps' nest of caste and prejudice they had fallen into. Social life in Buddlecombe was the most complicated affair under the sun: was divided into innumerable grades; made up of a series of cliques, rising one above the other, and fitting as exactly as a set of Japanese boxes. No such simple matter, and that was a fact, for a pair of newcomers to find themselves to rights in it. But they, in their ignorance, had pranced boldly in, where those who knew better walked warily and with discretion.— The vicar's wife had taken Mary up: yes; but, by now, Mahony had come to see that she would be equally attentive to anyone who might prove useful in helping to run the parish, or in slaving for foreign missions. And he began to doubt whether, often as Mary went to the vicarage, she was invited to the really select parties there given. She had never, for instance, met the Blakeneys of "The Towers," people he knew to be hand-in-glove with the vicaress. Mary either did not notice or, noticing, heed such trivial details—she just laughed, and said cheerily: "Rubbish!" or "You *are* fanciful, Richard!"—but he most emphatically did, and thanked you for being put off with the second best. And besides her insensitiveness to slights, she was hopelessly obtuse when it came to observing the invisible but cast-iron barriers with which the various cliques hedged themselves round, to keep those a step lower in the scale from coming too near.

"Not shake hands with that nice old Mr. Dandy just because he was once in trade? I never heard such a thing!" In Ballarat, Mary had been used to feel flattered did her grocer—rich, influential, a trustee of the church, a member of the Horticultural Society—emerge from behind the counter, specially to chat with her. "I think we should just make a beginning."

"Indeed and you'll put your foot in it with a vengeance, my dear, if you try anything of that kind here . . . when I'm still struggling to get a stand."

"Oh, well, of course, if you look at it that way. . . . But all the same . . . when I remember . . ." Her sentence tailed off into a speaking silence.

He understood. "*Tempi passati,* love! Nowadays, we must do as Rome does.— Recollect, too, my dear, these things may seem trifling enough to you . . . and me . . . who have knocked about the world; but to people here they're the very A B C of good breeding—have been sucked in with their mother's milk. We mustn't appear ignoramuses of the first water."

"But I've *got* to be friendly with your patients, Richard, whoever they are."

"True. But even you must draw the line somewhere, you know."

"I'm afraid I don't; I'm not clever enough. It doesn't seem human either. For we're all the same flesh and blood."

Yes, for the countless niceties and distinctions of social etiquette, Mary had, as she confessed, little aptitude. It sometimes seemed that, if a mistake was possible, she made it.

The two chief houses in Buddlecombe, the "Hall" and the "Court," were closed when the Mahonys settled there, the families being respectively abroad on foreign travel, and in residence in London. During their absence, the temporary leader, who gave the sign and set the key, and to whom the vicar deferred with his treacliest smile, was the owner of "Toplands." This was a Mrs. Challoner, a widow with two sons, and a person of great wealth and importance—"Toplands" was really the biggest and most up-to-date place in the neighbourhood, both Hall and Court being cramped, by comparison, and mouldy with age. But let the Trehernes or the Saxeby-Corbetts

457

show so much as the tips of their noses, and this lady subsided with extraordinary swiftness, collapsed like a jack-in-the-box; for, though her husband's antecedents were irreproachable, there was, on her own side, some shadowy connection with "malt," which could never be forgotten, or forgiven her; or at least "only by the grace of God . . . or of the Saxeby-Corbetts."

Mrs. Challoner was a member of the vicarage sewing-circle; and here she met Mary, to whom she seemed to take a liking; for she called, asked her to "Toplands," and, as a special mark of favour, drove her out in her carriage; Mahony being simultaneously summoned to attend the younger of the two sons, a delicate lad of seventeen. Thus, when, in Mary's opinion, the time had come to return the various invitations they had received, by herself sending out cards for a party, she felt justified in including Mrs. Challoner. And, sure enough, had in reply a graceful note of acceptance. So far good. But now it was that Mary let her hospitable impulses outride her discretion. At the vicarage she had made a further acquaintance, in the shape of a Mrs. Johnston-Perkes, a very charming lady, who had been settled in Buddlecombe not much longer than they themselves. And having it from this person's own lips that she came of a good Oxfordshire family, besides meeting her where she did—Mrs. Dandy, for example, was not made free of the sewing-club—how was Mary to guess that the Johnston-Perkes were not "in the swim"? Nor could Richard have helped her. For the dark fact, unknown to either, was that, in his day, the husband's father had had some connection with a publishing firm; and though Mr. Perkes himself had never soiled his hands thus, but only spent the fortune accumulated for him, yet the business stigma—pray, did not the issuing of books imply the abhorred counter, over which goods passed?—clung to him, to his eternal detriment, his lady-wife suffering with him, and tracked them from place to place. What followed proved—according to Mahony—that, though good enough for God and His works—witness the lady's presence at the vicarage!—the Johnston-Perkes were not by any means good enough for the upper crust of Buddlecombe; and the consequence was, Mary's party was a failure. There was no open contretemps; Mrs. Challoner and her satellites behaved with perfect civility. But it was impossible, to Mahony's mind, to misread the crip-

pling surprise writ big on these people's faces; and the atmosphere of the drawing-room remained icy—would not thaw.

Another thing that sent people's eyebrows up was the supper
to which Mary sat them down, as the clock struck ten.— At this
date, she had not been long enough in Buddlecombe to know
it for an unalterable rule that, unless the invitation was to dinner, a heavy, stodgy dinner, of one solid course after another,
from which, if you happened to be a peckish eater, you rose
feeling as though you could never look on food again; except
in this case, the refreshment offered was of the lightest and
most genteel: a biscuit; a jug of barley-water for the gouty, or
lemon-water for the young—at most, a glass of inferior sherry,
cellars not being tapped to any extent on such occasions.— But
Mary had gone at her supper in good old style, giving of her
best. And Mahony was so used to leaving such matters entirely
to her, that it had never entered his head to interfere. Not until
the party was squeezed into the little dining-room, round a
lengthened dinner-table, on which jellies twinkled, cold fowls
lay trussed, sandwiches were piled loaf-high—not till then, and
till he saw the amazed glances flying between the ladies, did
he grasp how wrong Mary had gone. A laden supper-table was
an innovation: and who, pray, were these newcomers, hailing
from God only knew where, to attempt to improve on the customs of Buddlecombe? It was also a trap for the gouty—and all
were gouty, more or less. Thirdly, such profusion constituted a
cutting criticism on the meagre refreshments that were here
the rule.— He grew stiff with embarrassment; felt, if possible,
even more uncomfortable than did poor Mary at the refusals
and head-shakings that went down one side of the table and
up the other. For none broke more than the customary Abernethy, or crumbled a sandwich. Liver-wings and slices of
breast, ham patties and sausage-rolls, made the round, in vain.
Mrs. Challoner gave the cue; and even the vicar, a hearty
eater, followed her lead, the only person to indulge being the
worthy gentleman who had caused half the trouble—and *him*
Mahony caught being kicked by his wife under the table.

He felt so sore, on Mary's behalf, that, by the time he had
escorted the last guest through the sentry-box porch, he was
fairly boiling over. Flinging downstairs to the dining-room,
where he found his wife disconsolately regarding her table,

which looked almost as neat as when she first arranged it, he flashed out. "Well, you've done it now! What in heaven's name possessed you to sit people down to a spread like this?"

Mary had begun to collect her tartlets—dozens of them—on one large dish, and was too preoccupied to lend him more than half an ear. To herself she said: "What *shall* I do with them?"

"Do? Bury 'em, my dear, in a corner of the garden! Hide 'em away out of sight. I wish you could get the memory out of people's minds as easily. *Our* supper-party will be the talk of Buddlecombe for many a day to come!"

"Just because I tried to make it as nice as I knew how? I think you judge every one by yourself, Richard. Because you didn't enjoy it . . ."

"Then, pray, why was nothing touched?"

"Perhaps they didn't feel hungry. I oughtn't to have had it till an hour later."

"Nothing of the sort! Though you had given it to 'em at five in the morning, they would still have walked home on empty stomachs. This kind of thing isn't done here, my dear, and the sooner you get that into your head the better!"

"Never will I descend to their starvation-diet!" cried Mary warmly.

"Another thing: what in heaven's name induced you to mix those Perkeses up with Mrs. Challoner and her set? That was a *faux pas* of the first water."

"I do declare, I never seem to do anything right! But you said nothing: you didn't know. For if it comes to that, Richard, you make mistakes, too."

"Indeed and I should like to know how?"— Mahony was huffed, in a second.

"I didn't mean to say anything about it. But it appears the vicar took it very badly, the other Sunday, that you went to hear that London preacher at the Methodist Chapel. I overheard something that was said at the last sewing-party—about your perhaps being really a dissenter."

"Well, of all the . . . Object to my going to hear a well-known preacher, just because he belongs to another sect? Preposterous!"

"Yes, if it's anything to do with yourself, it's preposterous. But when it's me, it's mistakes, and *faux pas*, and all the rest of it.— Sometimes, I really feel quite confused. To remember I mustn't shake hands here, or even bow there! That in some quarters I must only say 'Good afternoon,' and not 'How do you do?'—and then the other way round as well. That nice Mrs. Perkes is not the thing and ought to be cold-shouldered; and when I have company, I'm not to give them anything to eat. Oh, Richard, it all seems to me such *fudge!* How grown-up people can spend their lives being so silly, I don't know. Out *there*, you had to *forget* what a person's outside was like— I mean his table-manners, and whether he could say his aitches —as long as he got on and was capable . . . or rich. But here, it's always: '*Who* is he? How far back can he trace his pedigree?'— And nothing else seems to matter a bit. I do believe you might be friends with a swindler, or a thief, as long as his family-tree was all right. And the disgrace trade seems to be! Why, looked at this way, there wasn't any one in Ballarat who was fit to know. Just think of dear Tilly and old Mr. Ocock! Here they would be put down as the vulgarest of the vulgar. One certainly wouldn't be able even to *bow* to them! And then remember all they were to us, and how fond I was of Tilly, and what a splendid character she had. No, this kind of thing goes against the grain in me. I'm afraid the truth is, I like them vulgar best. And I'm too old, now to change."

"You too old!" cried Mahony, amazed to hear this, his own dirge, on his wife's lips. "Why, Mary love,"—and from where he sat, he held out his hand to her across the table, over the creams and jellies standing like flowers in their cups. "You but a couple of months over thirty, and far and away the best-looking woman in the place! . . . Candidly, my dear, never did I set eyes on such a pack of scarecrows—from the vicaress, with her wolf's teeth, up the scale and down.

"You don't feel very happy or at home here, love—I see that," he went on. "And I sometimes doubt, my dear, whether I did right to uproot you from your adopted country."

"I certainly liked being there better than here. Still, I'm quite ready, as you know, to put up with things. Only you mustn't scold me, Richard, when I make mistakes. I do my best, dear, but . . ."

"We'll lay our heads together, love, and so avoid them. And, as a beginning, Mary, we'll stifle the natural feelings of friendliness and goodwill we have always had for our fellow-mortals —no matter what their rank in life. We'll forget that we're all,

461

as you say, the sons of Adam, and are placed on this earth-ball for a very brief period, in which it would certainly be to our advantage to love our neighbours as ourselves. And we'll learn to be narrow, and bigoted, and snobbish, and mean with our grub . . . eh, Mary? Joking apart, my dear, you see how it is. We've either got to adapt ourselves to the petty outlook of those about us, or be regarded as a pair of boors, who've brought home with them the manners and habits of the back-woods. And that means turning out again, love. For I won't stay here to be looked down on . . . when I'm conscious of feeling every whit as good as anybody else."

"Now when you talk like that, Richard . . . You know I'm willing to put up with any mortal thing, as long as I can feel *sure* you're happy and contented. But when I think, dear, of the down you used to have on narrowness and snobbishness . . . in the old days. And this is even worse."

"All the same, I felt I could stand no more of the rough diamonds we had to hobnob with, out there."

"Still, some were diamonds, weren't they?"

"What we need, you and I, Mary, is a society that would take the best from both sides. The warm-heartedness of our colonial friends, their generosity and hospitality; while we could do without the promiscuity, the worship of money, the general loudness and want of refinement.— You wonder if I shall be happy here? I like the place, love; it's an ideal spot. I like this solid old house, too: and, so far, the climate has suited me. I seem to be getting on fairly well with the people; and though the practice is still nothing extraordinary, it has possibilities."

"Yes; but——"

"But? Well, I undoubtedly miss the income I used to have; there's little or no money to be made; compared with Ballarat, it's the merest niggling. And besides that, there was a certain breadth of view—that we'd got used to, you and I. Here, things sometimes seem atrociously cramped and small and provincial. But we must remember good exists everywhere and in every one, wife, if we only take the trouble to look for it. And since the fates have pitched us here, here we must stay and work our vein, until we've laid the gold bare. We've got each other, love, and that's the chief thing."

"Of course it is."

And now they were up and doing, he helping her to stow away her feast, so that it should not meet Selina's eye in the morning. And over this there was a good deal of merriment: they had to eat up some of the more perishable things themselves, which they did to a confession from Mary, that she really had not meant to make *quite* so much, but had been lured on, from one thing to another, by the thought of how nice it would look on the table. They packed away a decent amount in the larder, for appearance sake; the rest in a cupboard in the surgery.

But afterwards, Mary as she took down her hair, Mahony as he went round the house locking up, each dedicated the matter a further and private reflection. She said to herself, astonished: "I do believe Richard is turning radical!" and then went on to muse, a little wryly, that the "fates," to which he so jauntily referred, were, after all, but another name for his own caprices. He, on the other hand, after justifying an omission to himself with: "No use worrying the poor little soul about that damn fool Robinson!" sent her a thought so warm that it resembled a caress. For, at heart, his whole sympathy was with Mary and Mary's ineradicable generosity. Alone, and his irritation cooled, he ranged himself staunchly on her side, against the stiff uncharitable little world on which they were fallen.

[6]

ENTERING the house late one summer afternoon, his pockets bulged with scraps of weed and wildflower—the country people still gaped at sight of their doctor, descended from his trap, and round glass in one eye, poking and prying in the hedgerows—Mahony was turning these specimens out on the hall table, when Mary called from the dining-room. "Richard! A great surprise!"

He went downstairs to her, pulling off his gloves. "What? . . . the mail in already? I calculated it wasn't due for another week, at least."

"And such a big one!"

Mary sat in an armchair, her lap full of envelopes, a closely written sheet of foreign note in her hand. Mahony picked up the several letters bearing his name, and ran his eye over the superscriptions. Their English post-bag was a lean one; but the

463

arrival of the Australian mail more than atoned for it; and the deciphering of the crossed and re-crossed pages, the discussing of the news from the old home, occupied the pair of them for days. Among his pile, Mahony found a letter from Chinnery of the London Chartered, another from Archdeacon Long, a third from an old fellow-practitioner; while a bulky envelope promised a full business statement from Simmonds, the agent he had left in charge of his money affairs.— Taking off his greatcoat, he blew his nose, and sat down to read at his ease.

First, though, he had to hear from Mary the gist of those of hers she had fleetly skimmed, prior to going back and reading them over again, word by word, with a brooding seriousness.

"Just fancy, Richard, John writes he's been forced to shut up his house and go and live at the Melbourne Club. *What* a state of things! That lovely house left to go to rack and ruin. It seems the last housekeeper turned out worst of all; she didn't set her cap at him, like Mrs. Perry, but he discovered that she carried on improperly with men. To think of a dreadful woman like that being in charge of poor Jinny's children! Now, John has put all three to boarding-school. And Josey still the merest baby. How he expects them to do well, I don't know—with never a proper home, or a mother's care. Then, here's Trotty . . . or Emma, as he will persist in calling her. It seems the reports she brings back from school are most unsatisfactory. Her mistress accuses her of being idle and flighty. Trotty flighty! If ever there was a dear, good-hearted little soul . . . easy to manage, and open as the day. But John still seems to have his old down on Emma's children . . . and poor Emma who thought nothing too good for them! *Do* you remember their beautiful little clothes when they first came to us?— And that brings me to a bit of real bad news. Johnny has run away —*bolted*—as John puts it. Just listen to this. *And now I pass to the doings of my son—my only son—and heir. After keeping the boy to his desk under my own eye, for the past twelve months, and endeavouring by precept and severity to make an honest man of him—in vain, Mary, for never a moment's gratification or satisfaction have I had from him; never a thank-you has he given me for all the money spent on him—he was lazy, deceptive, defiant, and frequented loose company . . . Richard! At seventeen! . . . neglected his duties, took more wine than was good for him, played cards for money, and in the end went*

so far as to abstract his losses from my private drawer.— Isn't
it dreadful?— *When I had him up before me, and taxed him
with it, and threatened him with exposure, he flouted my authority, as good as whistled in my face; then actually had the
audacity to assert he owed me no gratitude, since I had never
done anything for him; and the next morning was missing—his
bed had not been slept in. When, after the lapse of several
weeks, I contrived to track him, I learned, to my shame and
disgrace, that he had shipped before the mast to America—that
eldorado of thieves and scoundrels. Now he may shift for himself; I wash my hands of him. I have cut him out of my will;
and shall do the same by Emma, unless she mends her ways.
You will scarcely credit it, my dear Mary, but her schoolmistress writes me that the girl—not yet fifteen years of age, mark
you!—has had to be "publicly rebuked" for coquetting with
members of the other sex in a place of worship.—* Oh, stuff and
nonsense, John! Never will I believe such a thing of Trotty.
I know a great deal more about the child than you do. All she
needs is a firm, kind hand, and that she evidently hasn't got.
How well I remember her flinging her arms round my neck,
when I kissed her good-bye, and begged me to take her with
me. If only I could have! And if I were only there now, to find
out what all this means. John winds up with the usual: *Thank
God, Jane's children are of another disposition. I am confident
I shall never be disgraced by them.* No, my dear John, they
haven't the spirit. But . . . well, I never did!" and Mary let her
hand fall flop on the table. "Just listen to this! A postscript—
I didn't see it before. He says: *Your sister Zara seems about to
make a fool of the first water of herself. She is, I hear—for I
have seen nothing of her, I am thankful to say—contemplating
matrimony.—* Richard! And he doesn't even say who to. Isn't
that like a man? Can it . . . could it be . . . But there! I believe
I saw a letter from Zara herself."

Dropping John's, Mary sought among the envelopes in her
lap, picked on one, hastily slit it open, and began to fly the
lines. "Mm . . . a tirade against John, of course . . . how those
two do bicker! They seem to get worse and worse, the older
they grow. Now where can it be? Mm . . . *No one can put up
with him any longer . . . has had to close his house, thus providing——*"

"Hullo, my dear! . . . here's news," cried Mahony, and

slapped his thigh. He had waited patiently for John's Jeremiad
to end. In Zara's pursuit of matrimony he took no interest
whatever. "Well, upon my word! Who would have dreamt of
this? Those *Australia Felixes* . . . you remember, Mary, I
bought them rather as a pig in a poke; and they've done nothing but make calls ever since. Now, here they are, actually declaring a three-pound dividend. My highest expectations did
not exceed thirty shillings—and even that would have been
handsome. Think what it will be when they get in ten more
stamps. Fifty pounds a month, for certain! My dear! we shall
end by being moneyed people, after all."

"Don't I hope so!" said Mary; and resumed her search for
Zara's plum. "It looks as if she's not going to mention it. Then
it can't be as fixed as John thought. This is all about her pupils.
They dote on her, as usual, and she drives out every day in the
carriage with Mrs. Noot, and plays and sings in the drawing-
room all the evening. Zara is certainly lucky in her employers.—
Oh, here it is—tucked away in a postscript. *Other and fairer
prospects beckon, my dear Mary, than those of eternally improving the minds of other people's children. At present I can
say no more. But your cleverness will no doubt enable you to
divine what I leave unsaid.* And that's all. Now, I suppose, I
must wait another three months to hear who it is, and how it
happened. Oh dear, how *out* of everything we do seem here!"

"They've got the money together for the chancel at last,"
threw in Mahony. "I must write and congratulate Long on that.
Splendid work! They've had the laying ceremony, too, and
hope, twelve months hence, that the Bishop will be up conse-
crating. The last Fancy Bazaar did the job. Here's a message to
you with regard to that. Mrs. Long's warm love, and she missed
your help sadly at the refreshment-stall.— What? Well, I'm
glad! Old Higgins in my place as Trustee. Ha, ha! Listen to
this. *And now an item, doctor, after your own heart. We recently had with us a disciple and follower of Spurgeon—one
of the faithful, who seceded with the great men from the
Evangelical Alliance. He preached a first time in the Baptist
Chapel, but this proved too small to hold a quarter of those
who wished to hear him. And so the second time, on a Sunday
evening, he appeared on the platform of the new 'Alfred Hall'
—a very fine building, by the way, of which we are justly
proud. This was packed to the doors. The consequence was,*

466

*I preached to empty benches. Well! believing that the Word
of God remains the Word of God, no matter under what guise
it is presented, I cut my discourse short, doffed my cassock,
and went home to bed. The worthy fellow called on me next
day; wished to exchange Bibles—his, I am told, deeply under-
scored—but I did not feel justified in going so far as that.*"

"Oh, Polly's lost her baby, poor thing!" cried Mary, whom
the doings of Spurgeon's follower interested but mildly. "I do
feel sorry for her. Not but what she takes it very sensibly. And
if you think . . . six children, and that teeny-weeny house. Still,
it's rather sad. She says: *Of course nobody misses it, or cared
anything about it, but me. But it was rather a nice little kid,
Mary, and well formed. I had it at the breast for a day, and
felt its little fingers, and it had blue eyes.* Now fancy that!—
and the rest of them so dark. Polly would think it belonged all
the more to her, because of it. She says Ned's keeping a little
steadier—that will be good news for Mother. He's clerk in a
coal merchant's office now, and brings home his wages pretty
regularly. They've got the use of a paddock for the children to
play in, when they're not at school—the State School, of course.
Poor old Ned!" and Mary sighed.

But a message in Mr. Chinnery's made her smile. *Tell Mrs.
Mahony how much she is missed in society here. Those pleasant evenings we used to spend at your house, doctor, and her
famous suppers, are still talked of, and will long be remembered.*— "There, my dear! that's a feather in your cap, and
should console you for recent happenings."

With this, Mahony's budget was exhausted, and he rose to
go to the surgery, where he proposed to make a few calculations in connection with his little windfall. But Mary held him
back for yet a moment.

"I do declare, marrying's in the air. Now here's Jerry gone
and got engaged. Who to? He writes: *The prettiest girl in all
the world and the best as well.* Let us only hope that's true.
Dear old Jerry! He deserves a good wife, if ever anyone did.—
It seems to be somebody in Melbourne. But, oh dear me! she's
only sixteen—barely a year older than Trotty. That's too
young."

"Is it indeed? I know somebody who was once of a different
opinion."

"Ah, but I was old for my age.— Fanny her name is—Fanny

467

Jessop. Dear Jerry! He's so sensible in other things. If only he has not let his feelings run away with him here!"

"Poor old Mary wife! If only *you* were there to look after them all—eh? Better as it is, love. You'd have the burden of Atlas on your shoulders again."

"What atlas?" asked Mary absently, having passed on to her next correspondent.

But the letter she spent longest over was the one she kept till the last—till Richard had retired to his room. For only to Tilly did she write nowadays with anything approaching frankness; and in this reply, oddly written, indifferently spelt, there might be private references to things she had said, besides the plain truth about all and any it touched on. Afterwards, Richard would get, in her, Mary's, own words, what he needed to hear.

> *Beamish House,*
> *Lake Wendouree,*
> *Ballarat.*

My darling Mary,—Yours of 19th was a rare old treat. Job brought it when I wasn't at home— I'd driven out to have a look at the mare Zoe, who's in foal, and at grass in a paddock of Willy Urquhart's. Didn't I pounce on it when I found it, that's all. I read it through twice without stopping, my dear. And didn't know whether to be glad or sorry when I'd done it. You write cheery enough, Mary, but it doesn't seem to me you can be really happy in a place like you say Leicester is—all damp and dreary, and no garden or space, and no jollifications, and so little company. I'm glad it's not me—that's all. Australy, for ever, for this chicken. Your description of the rainy season over there gives me cold shivers down my spine. Gimme the sun, thank you, and horses, and a garden, and everything just as jolly as can be. Fine feathers and grand airs and blue blood aren't in my line anyhow.

Now for my budget. I'm still the gay old widder I was when you heard last, and haven't felt tempted to change my state. To tell the truth, Mary, though I gad about as usual and don't sit at home and pull a long face, I still miss dear old Pa. It was so homey to hear him say: "Now then, what's my girl been up to to-day?" whenever I came in: and the joy of my life to see him set his will against Monseer H.'s. Well, he can't say he's forgotten. I've put him up the grandest monument in all

468

the new cemetery. Pa in a sort of nightshirt, Mary, with wings
attached, flying off, and a female figure all bowed up and
weeping on the ground. This is all right for me, but sometimes
I think Pa would rather have been took just sitting on a log
and smoking his pipe. But Henry and the man as done it
wouldn't hear of such a thing, said it wouldn't be ideel.

The chief news of this establishment is that Tom and Johnny
has moved out. I was for keeping them on—we're none of us
chickens any more—but Henry was dead against it, and pecked
and nagged at me till I gave in for sheer peace sake. They're
boarded out, poor boys, and Tom comes over every morning
to see after the fowls. One of these days I shall have to put my
foot down and squash Henry—I see that. For it was the same
with the weeds. Pa used to say: "Wear no weepers for me,
Tilda!"—meaning veils and hangers and all that—"you've nothing to grieve for, old girl." And I to comfort him: "Right you
are, old Jo! If my memory lasts so long, that is, for you'll beat
Methuselah yet!" But when Henry heard of it, he all but stood
on his head—my dear, he has Agnes going round with a flounce
of crepe a yard wide on her skirts. And indeed, Mary, I don't
think I could ever have faced walking up the aisle of a Sunday,
without a black bonnet and all complete; though between ourselves it makes me feel a proper old crow. Don't tell, my dear,
but when I drive out into the bush, I stuff a shady old hat in a
basket under the seat, and as soon as I get far enough, I off
with the bonnet and on with the hat. The weepers do draw the
flies so. Aye, and flies of another colour, too, Mary, if you'll
believe me. But they come to the wrong shop here; none of
your long-nosed fortune-snuffers for me. And that reminds me
—what do you think Henry's latest is? Says I ought to have
some one to live with me—that it isn't commy faut for an attractive young widder-woman like me to live all by herself!
Ha ha! Do you see any green in this child's eye? I think I can
be trusted, don't you, Mary, to look after myself. But I enjoy
keeping Mossieu Henry on the quake. What he's afraid of is
that all I got from poor old Pa won't fall to his and Agnes's
kids when I hop the twig. Talking of Agnes, I don't see Miladi
once in a blue moon nowadays. I hear she's "not at all well."
It's my private belief something's wrong there, Mary. They've
changed doctors three times, tell your husband, since he left.
Louisa Urquhart's presented her husband with the eleventh.

How she keeps it up so regular beats me. But there's ructions in that family, I can tell you. Willy's been "unusual" gay. This time it was a governess, a real young spark, I hear, they had up to Yarangobilly to teach the eldest kids. She got bundled out double-quick at the end, and Willy's looked meek as a suckling-lamb ever since. I drop in to see Ned's Polly now and again—you've heard I suppose she lost her last. And a good thing too. She's got more than she can manage, as it is. I'd love to adopt one of her curly blacks, but if you so much as hint at such a thing she's up and at you like a wildcat. I hear from her, young Jerry's the newest candidate for the holy estate. They do say the bride elect still plays with dolls. Lor, Mary! what will these infants be up to next? Another piece of news is, that obstinate old brute in Melbourne has gone and put all poor Jinn's blessed little nippers to boarding-school. That does hit me hard, Mary. Though there's so little love lost between us, that I can't exactly feel surprised. But I get even with him in another way, my dear. I've won over the old vinaigrette, alias schoolmarm, here— I won't say just how; but she needed new globes etc. for her schoolhouse; and then I take a whole bundle of her silly old prospectuses, and scatter 'em broadcast. So we have a kind of agreement, all unbeknownst to the Honourable, that the kid Trotty can come home with me of a Saturday afternoon, instead of spending the rest of her day on the backboard. I swear not to let her out of my sight, that's all. She's a nice little kid, full of life, though young enough for her age, and I try to give her a good time. But she's easily satisfied. What she likes best is to make butter, so I just pin an apron on her and turn her into the dairy with Martha, among the milk-pans and churns. But let me tell you this, my dear. The Honourable John needn't indulge any fool ideas about economising in housekeepers and having her to do it for him, when her schooling's over—as old Prunes and Prisms tells me he does. You mark my words, Mary, some one a great deal younger and handsomer than him will soon pop up and whip her off. She's much too pretty for the single life.

I think that's all my news. We had great church festifications lately and look forward to more when the chancel's built. I say, the doctor had some "Australia Felixes," hadn't he? I hear they've struck the reef. But this is a fearful long scrawl, and yet not half so comfortable as even a quarter of an hour's good yarn would be, is it? When shall we have that again, Mary darling? I don't lose hopes for someday. And as you know I've sworn never to cross the water, it must mean the other way about. Yes, I still believe I shall see you back home again: and when you do come, you'll find you are not forgotten by your devoted old crony—Tilly.

[7]

THE end of September brought day after day of soft, steamy mists, which saturated everything with moisture, and by night dripped as a fine rain, turning low-lying parts of the garden to a fearsome bog. Did you mount to the roads on the high level, you were in the clouds themselves, which trailed past you like smoke. There was no horizon to seaward. At a little distance from the shore, the grey water became one with a bank of vapour; the yellow cliffs vanished; suns neither rose nor set.

It was exasperating weather. These eternal sea fogs, which never a puff of wind came to chase away, seemed literally to bury you alive. They brought out the sweat on the flagged floors and passages of the old, old house; a crop of mould sprang up in the corners of the dining-room; the bread mildewed in the bin. Did the back door stand open, frogs took advantage of it to hop in and secrete themselves; slugs squeezed through cracks and left their silvery trail over the carpets. Mary began to fear the house would prove but sorry winter quarters; and she had ample leisure to indulge such reflections, the bad weather confining her almost wholly within doors. Here was no kind friend, with buggy or shandrydan, to rout her out and take her driving; and ladies did not walk in Buddlecombe: the hilly roads were too steep, the flat roads too muddy. So, once more, she sat and sewed, and sewed; faced by the prospect of a long, dull, lonely winter. Calls and invitations had rather dropped off, of late . . . as was not unnatural; and she would have been for seeing nothing peculiar in it, had she not connected it, in some obscure way, with Richard and the practice. This had also declined; was failing, it was plain, to live up to its early promise.

She was unaware that no sooner had the "Court" reopened for the winter, than the tale—in a garbled version—of the innovations attempted by the "new doctor's wife" was carried to the ears of its mistress. And Mrs. Archibald Treherne pinched a pair of very thin lips and further arched already supercilious eyebrows. That was all; but it was enough. And, in consequence, from the choicest entertainments of the autumn the Mahonys found themselves conspicuously omitted.

Their only personal connection with the big house was due to one of those unhappy contretemps, such as were given to rankling for ever after Mahony's mind.

On learning of the family's arrival, both he and Mary privately thought it probable an exchange of courtesies would follow. Hence, when one day a footman was found to have handed in cards during Mary's absence—his mistress keeping her seat in her carriage at the foot of the hill—the visit did not take them by surprise. Within the week, Mary drove out in a hired vehicle to return it.

A bare half-hour later she was home again, looking flushed and disturbed.

"Richard! . . . . a most *awkward* thing has happened. Those cards were not meant for us at all. It was the footman's mistake. He ought to have left them at the next house down the road—that little thatched cottage at the corner. They were for a Mrs. Pigott, who's staying there."

"What? Well, upon my word!"

Leaning back in his chair, Mahony stared at his wife, while he took in the significance of her words. "And, pray, do you mean to say the woman doesn't intend to call on *you* . . . as well?"

"Evidently not." Mary was crestfallen.

"*What?* But will call on this Mrs. Pigott?—living in a farmer's thatched cottage?" And Mary not replying, he burst out: "You will never, my dear, with my consent, set foot in that house again!"

"Indeed, I don't want to!" said Mary, and sitting down she untied her bonnet-strings and threw them over her shoulders. "I don't know *when* I've felt so uncomfortable. I was ushered into the drawing-room—it seemed crowded with people— and there she sat, holding our cards between her thumb and finger, and looked from them to me and back again. I heard something about 'the new doctor's wife' as I went in. Then she asked to what she owed my visit, said she hadn't the pleasure, and so on—all in front of these other people—

the Brookes of 'Shirley,' I think they were—that retired old General . . . you met him once, you know, and thought him very stuck-up. I had to explain how it had happened; I felt my face getting as red as fire; I could have sunk through the floor. I didn't know whether to walk straight out again, or what, and she didn't help me—didn't get up, or shake hands, or anything. Fortunately, a very nice person—a sort of companion, I think—asked me to rest a little after my drive, and I thought it would make things less awkward for everybody if I did; so I just sat down for a minute, and said a word or two, and then got up and bowed and left. She came with me as far as the door—the companion, I mean."

White with anger, Mahony shuffled and re-shuffled the papers that lay before him on the writing-table; his hands shook. "We've never been treated like this in our lives before, Mary, and I for one won't put up with it!—or allow you to either. Damn the woman and her insolence! Talk about breeding and blue blood—give me ordinary decent feelings, and a little kindness, and you can keep the blood, thank you! I snap my fingers at it."— In imagination he saw his Mary, faced by a like predicament, doing her utmost to smooth over the embarrassment of the moment, and set the unfortunate intruder at ease.

And time did not lessen his resentment. On the contrary, the longer he nursed it, the sorer he grew. Rudeness to Mary —such a thing had never before come within the range of his experience—stung him, he found, almost more than rudeness to himself.— But was the thrust not actually aimed at him . . . through her? What had the object of it been but to drive home to him, once and for all, the galling fact that, on this side of the world, the medical profession carried with it no standing whatever? In the colonies, along with the Parson, the Police Magistrate, and so on, he had helped to constitute the upper ten of a township. Here, the doctor—and quite especially the country doctor—stood little higher in the social scale than did the vet., and the barber. Oh, those striped poles! Tradition died so hard a death in this slow-thinking, slow-moving country. Ingrained in people, not to be eradicated, was a memory of the day when the surgeon was but the servant, the attendant lackey, of the great house.

Grimly cogitating thus, he prepared in advance for further

snubs and slights, by going about with his chin in the air, looking, to the last degree, stiff and unapproachable. For, that
Mary's misadventure would remain a secret, he did not for
a moment believe. There were all too many mouths in Buddlecombe agape for gossip—it would be threshed out over
every Tabby's tea-table—and those already inclined to look
down their noses at him and Mary would have a fresh excuse
for so grimacing. Anything was possible in such a petty-
minded, tittle-tattling place. Hence, it did not surprise him
to hear that Robinson had been called to the "Court." The
trouble was, of course, that the townspeople and lesser folks
were faithful in imitation of their betters; and soon it began
to seem to him that he was, not occasionally, but everlastingly
getting out of Robinson's way. And as he sat at home over the
fire—Mary kept fires going, to drive the damp out; though,
in order to breathe, you had to leave the windows wide open
to mist and fog—his thoughts were anything but cheerful.
There was not work enough for two—or money either. As
it was, he was having to depend more than he cared for, on
his Australian dividends.

It was at this juncture that the report reached his ears
of illness at "Toplands," where the younger son lay prostrate
with gastric fever. But his services were not requisitioned.

Then came that morning when Mary, grave and worried,
broke the news to him that Robinson's gig had been seen at
the gates of "Toplands"; the morning when, unable to hire
a horse for his rounds, he was tormented, as he trudged the
country lanes, by the knowledge that, like the last, this practice, too, was threatening to peter out.

Late that evening, as he sat reading, there came a loud rat-
tatting at the front door. The doctor in him pricked up his
ears at the now unfamiliar sound: it was like an old-time
call to action—in the land of cruel accident and sudden death.
The visitor admitted, an excited voice was heard in the passage, and Mary's in reply; after which Mary herself entered
the surgery, shutting the door behind her, and looking, for
her, irresolute and uncomfortable. The elder of the two Challoner boys had, it seemed, come driving down post-haste from
"Toplands." His brother lay dying. Would Dr. Mahony come
back with him—the dogcart was at the door—and meet Mr.
Robinson?

"Meet *Robinson?* Not if *I* know it!"

"I told him I couldn't be sure. But, Richard, there's nobody else—unless he rides all the way to Brixeter. And there and back would take him at least four hours. His brother might be dead by then. Their mother is almost out of her mind, poor thing."

"Poor thing, indeed! After the way she's treated us. But you haven't a scrap of pride in you."

"Not when it's a case of life or death, I haven't. Dear, don't you think you could manage to overlook what's happened? . . . not stand on etiquette? If the boy should die, you'd reproach yourself bitterly for not having gone."

"You never *will* understand these things, Mary!—and though you live to be a hundred. Little did I dream," he said, with violence, as he slapped his book to, and ungraciously rose to his feet, "when I settled here, that I should ever come down to playing second fiddle in this ignominious fashion."

"It may be your chance to play first again—if you cure him."

Mahony pshawed.

Off he drove, though, as she had known all along he would; and did not get back till four in the morning. Then, half a glance was enough to show her—she wakened from a light sleep on his entry—that he was in a state of extreme nervous exasperation. So she asked only a single question: did the lad still live? But Richard could not contain himself; and, as he moved about the bedroom, winding up his watch and letting his collar fly, he burst out: "Nothing on earth will induce me to stop in this place, Mary, to be insulted as I have been to-night! This is worse—a hundred times worse!—than the colony."

From under her lashes, Mary shot him a swift look he did not see: a look full of motherly tenderness—and yet triumphant. Aloud, she merely said: "But think what a feather in your cap it will be if the boy recovers! . . . the prestige you will gain."

"Prestige? Pah! Robinson will say he did the curing, and I stepped in and took the credit. A fat lot of prestige to be got from that! Mary, there's been a dead set made against me here—I've felt it now for some time, though why, I knew no more than Adam. To-night, I believe I got a clue. It's

475

Australia, if you please!—the fact of my having practised in Australia is against me." And at Mary's vigorously expressed disbelief: "Well! just listen to this, my dear, and judge for yourself. First of all, they prefer Robinson *fuddled,* to me sober. Yes, it's the simple truth. When I get to 'Toplands,' I find him there tight—stupidly tight—standing by the bed, staring like an owl. Quite devoid of shame he evidently is not, though, for, no sooner did he see me, than off he bolted —leaving me as much in the dark as ever. I tried to get some information from the womenfolk about the earlier stages of the complaint; but not one was capable of giving a connected answer. . . . I'd sent the other young fellow off for the barber to shave his head, and leeches and lancets. Young Leonard lay convulsed and insensible. And yet, if you'll believe me, Robinson had been telling them it was gastric, and plying him with brandy. Inflammation of the membranes of the brain, Mary!—and the fool killing him with stimulants. While I was making mustard poultices for his feet and legs, back comes Robinson, and attempts to feel his pulse. I said: 'Now look here, my good man, if you don't give me some particulars of this case, I shall proceed to treat it without you.' He answered not a word. Then I turned to her. 'Now, madam,' said I, 'I'm not going to stand this. Either he or I must leave the room—or indeed the house—and until you decide which, I go downstairs.' She followed, all but clawing at my coat. He lurches after us, shouting abuse . . . for the whole house to hear. And what, pray, do you think he said? . . . amongst other scurrilous trash. 'Well and good! If you prefer the opinion of this old quack to mine, take it and abide by the consequences. Australia! We all know what *that* means. Ask him what other trades he's plied there. Make him turn out his credentials . . . and you'll open your eyes, I can tell you!' It was as much as I could do to keep from knocking him down. Only the thought of the lad upstairs restrained me. *She* was very humble and apologetic, of course; besought me to take no notice; almost grovelled to me to save her son, etc. etc. I made short work of her, though."

"Besides, you can surely afford to smile at such rubbish, Richard?" Mary strove to soothe him. "It would be beneath your dignity to take any notice of it. Especially as he wasn't himself."— Distressed though she felt at this return for Rich-

ard's kindness, Mary was also very unpleasantly worked on
by his interlarded "My good man!" and the general hoity-toity
air of his narration. What a peppery fellow he was! How could
he ever expect to succeed, and be popular? That kind of tone
would not go down here.

"I make allowance for his condition . . . of course I do! . . .
but all the same it does not incline me, my dear, to put up any
longer with such insulting behaviour," he said hotly. "There's
been too much of it lately, altogether: if not open abuse like
this, yet affronts of a more covert kind.— But if such are the
tales that are going the round about me, Mary—charlatan and
quack, a colonial ne'er-do-well trading on a faked diploma,
and so on; if it's a blot on my reputation to have lived and
practised in the colonies, instead of mouldering away in this
miserable hole—then much is explained that has been dark
to me.— Anyhow, it came over me with a rush to-night: I go
from here! They don't want me; I'm not good enough for
them—a man who has held a first-class practice in the second
city of Victoria, not good enough for the torpid livers of
Buddlecombe! Very well, then, let them get some one else . . .
I'm done with 'em.— Really, Mary, I sometimes feel too sick
and tired of the struggle that I fancy throwing up medicine
altogether. What would you say, love, to taking a small cottage somewhere, and living modestly on the little we have?"

Now, what *would* he say next? wondered Mary, with an
inward sigh. But the present was not the moment to combat
such vagaries. Richard was sore and smarting; and in this
mood he just tossed off suggestions without thinking; letting
his anger out in them as the hole in the lid of a kettle let out
steam. So she only said: "Let us first see what happens here.
Is there any chance of Lenny Challoner recovering?"

"Frankly, I don't think there is. I give him till the coming
midnight. He'll probably die between then and dawn."

But this prediction was not fulfilled. The boy weathered the
night; and, after sixty hours' unconsciousness, spoke to those
about him, though with wandering wits.

Buddlecombe was all a-twitter and agog: the affair was
discussed over counters by tradesmen and goodwives; at mahogany dinner-tables; in the oaken settles of inns. Every one
knew to a T everything that had happened . . . and a good deal
more: were for and against the two doctors in their feud.

"'Tis a'anyway little better'n boo'tchers a hoald t' lot of un,"
—thus Raby, the town crier, summed up the matter to his
cronies of the "Buddlecombe Arms." "Bu'ut if us was ca'alves,
'tis the ha'and us knows as us 'ud ra'ather die by."

Yes, chiefly against him, felt Mahony: and it screwed him
stiff as rod. The majority sided with the townsman who had
lived among them for years; who was rich enough to spend
freely in their shops, subscribe heavily to their charities; besides being an expert in the right admixture of joviality and
reserve, necessary to make his failings go down.

Mary fought this idea with all her might. Richard was just
reading his own feelings into other people, as usual. She herself clung to the belief that the sick boy would pull through,
now he had held out so long. Which would be a veritable
triumph for Richard.— If only he did not spoil things by his
uncompromising behaviour! For he was in a most relentless
frame of mind. More than one of Robinson's patients subsequently sent for him. But he, riding the high horse, declined
to touch a single other of the enemy's cases. They should
apply for relief, said he, to Mr. Jakes of Brixeter.

Meanwhile, of course, he did not spare himself over the
patient he had taken in hand. But, eventually, in spite of his
care, the boy died, killing Mary's hopes, and enabling Robinson to go about cockahoop, boasting that wrong treatment had
finished him off. It *had* been "gastric," after all!

And now, as he stalked his way or drove his gig about the
hilly roads and narrow streets, Mahony felt himself indeed a
marked man.

"Till Christmas . . . not a day longer! I was never built for
this."— And, as he said it, his thoughts flew back to a time
when the merest hint that his skill was doubted had shaken his
roots to their depths. Here, where he had as yet hardly put out
a sucker, the wrench was easier, and at the same time a
hundredfold more destructive.

[8]

BUT, before Christmas came, Mary's hope that things would
somehow right themselves burned up anew—if hope that
could be called, which ran so counter to her own inclinations,
and to the possible issue she now thought she desired.

478

Book II: *The Way Home*

With the onset of November, it was the turn of "Buddle-combe Hall" to reopen. And, thereupon, a wave of new life seemed to run through the sluggish little town. The Saxeby-Corbetts, returning, as it were took possession of the place; and they had this advantage over the Trehernes—a childless couple—that they counted a baker's dozen in family, all told. Their arrival was after the fashion of crowned heads. First came dragloads of servants, male and female, and of varying ages—from the silver-headed butler down to young scullery and laundry-maids—after which the windows of the great house were flung up, the chimneys belched smoke, hammerings and beatings resounded; while various elderly women in the town tied on rusty black and went off to give obsequious aid. Footmen in livery lounged about the inns; grooms rode swathed horses out to exercise. The trades-people well-nigh lost their wits with excitement. One heard of nothing, now, on entering a shop, but "the family," its needs and preferences.

"Never, in all my life, have I seen anything to equal it!" cried Mahony, exasperated. "The way these poor creatures burn to prostrate themselves."

The list of young people would not be full till the holidays began; but, meanwhile, donkey and pony-carts were met with, containing the smaller children, their attendant governesses and nursemaids. The squire himself, a ruddy-faced man in early middle age, mounted on a fine chestnut, might be observed confabbing with the farmers; and lastly came his lady, driving herself in a low chaise: a bony-jawed, high-nosed woman, whose skin told of careless exposure to all weathers. Dressed anyhow, too, said Mary, who had once seen her in the town with an old garden-hat perched on her head, a red flannel spencer thrown on over her bodice.

And now, at the sound of wheels, grocer and butcher would prick up their ears and pop from their respective doors, merely on the off chance of pulling their forelocks, and (as likely as not) receiving in return a snub from the lady of the "Hall." For, in spite of what Mahony called their "piteous desire" to please, she was never satisfied, and hurled at their heads, in vigorous language, her frank opinion of their wares.

"Now, Johnson, this will not do! That last meat you supplied to the servants' hall was tough as my boot. If the next is no better, I shall come and superintend the slaughtering

479

myself. It's my belief, my man, you don't know a heifer from a leather-gutted milch-cow!"

And Johnson, doubled in two with relish of her "Ladyship's" joke, could be heard right down the street vowing there should be no further ground for complaint; though a visit from her "Ladyship" to his humble establishment would at any time be reckoned as a honour: and so on and so on.

To mark his disapproval of this cringing and fawning, and for fear any hint of patronage or condescension might come his way, Mahony had all his armour on, all his spines out, when he was unexpectedly summoned to the "Hall," to attend one of the children sick of a feverish cold. Mary saw him go, with many misgivings; but it actually seemed as if, for once, his lordly manner went down. By his own account, he successfully faced the imperious dame: "Who, if you please, my dear, was for herself pronouncing on the ailment—it turns out to be chicken-pox—and had nurses and maids dancing like puppets to a string. I soon let her see that kind of thing wouldn't do with me, Mary. And she took the hint fast enough, changed her tone, and behaved like any other decently bred woman.— I had certainly rather, though," he added, "have her for a friend than an enemy."

Oh, if this could only be! thought Mary. It might alter everything. And it was here, with him daily at the "Hall," where the nursery in a body succumbed to the pox, that her confidence bloomed anew. For, in a way, Richard even became a kind of protégé of its mistress: she would keep him, after his professional visit was paid, to chat about the colonies, and hear his impressions of England. Even Mary herself received a call, and though it was one of a somewhat quizzing inspection, and Madam was "not at home" when she returned it, yet Richard was pleased, which was the main thing. He himself was twice bidden to dinner—a little informal dinner, at which only another man or two was present; a state of things that seemed to mark as true the report that the dame had small liking for the company of her own sex.

Yes, Richard's fortunes seemed at last to have taken a definite turn for the better, when, of a sudden, the blow fell which put an end to hopes and fears alike. What was behind it, Mary did not know, and never learned. But, one morning at breakfast, Richard blurted out in summary fashion that he had resolved, overnight, to shake the dust of Buddlecombe off his feet. And, actually, before she had recovered from the shock of this announcement, the house was up for sale, and she hard at work sorting and packing. Coming as it did on top of her renewed confidence, the decision hit Mary hard. It also gave a further push to her tottery faith in Richard's judgment. Of course, it was clear something unpleasant had happened at the dinner-party. But she could get nothing out of Richard— absolutely nothing—except that he was done "for all eternity" with place and people. In vain she reasoned, argued, pleaded . . . and even lost her temper. He remained obstinately silent, leaving her to her own conjectures—which led nowhere. Leicester? . . . yes, compared with this, his bolting from Leicester had been as easy to understand as an A B C—ugly town that it was, with no practice worth speaking of, and the little that did exist, of the wrong kind. But here, where she had thought his first irate "Till Christmas!" was gradually being overlaid; here, she could only put his abrupt determination down to one of his most freakish and wayward impulses.— And in the intervals of her work, Mary would let her hands drop to her lap, and look with anxious eyes into the future.

Mahony saw her trouble; saw, too, how rudely her trust in him was shaken. But he did not enlighten her—he would rather have cut his tongue out. For what had happened concerned Mary first of all; and though there was a chance she might have taken it less tragically than he—in real "Mary-ish" fashion—yet he felt as averse to bringing the words over his lips, as to letting her see how deeply they had mortified him.—

Another informal invitation to dine at the "Hall" had reached him—at least, he took it to be such, since Mary was not included. At the entrance to the great house, however—six o'clock of a frosty December evening—he ran into old Barker, a retired Anglo-Indian, just dismounting from his hired fly; and, to his amazement, he saw that, this time, Barker had his ladies with him. Becoming involved in their entrance, he was waiting with the Colonel for wife and daughters to rejoin them, when the old valetudinarian found that he had left his jujubes in the pocket of his greatcoat. Standing thus alone, close to the half-open drawing-room door, Mahony suddenly heard his own name spoken, in the harsh, grating voice of their hostess.— "Yes; and from the colonies. I can tell

481

you I *was* put out, when I came back and found what had happened. I wrote off at once to that sheep, young Philips, and gave him a sound rating for letting himself be frightened away, after the trouble I had been to, to get him here." At this, a gentler voice murmured a query; to which the answer rang shrill and clear: "Oh, well, *he* is quite presentable!"

This it was that stuck in Mahony's throat.— And, on getting home shortly after midnight, he did not go down the passage to the bedroom, but turned into the surgery, which faced the hall-door. No sound came from Mary! she was evidently asleep.

He did not strike a match: feeling his way to the window, he raised the blind and leaned his forehead on the glass. The sea lay still, and black as ink, under a starlit sky—as starlight went here. Presently the moon, now entered on her last quarter, would come up from behind the cliffs, and throw a lurid light—lurid, because the light of decay—over the cold sea and sleeping town, picking out the line of silvery shingle that edged the beach, and making the odd old curved breakwater look as though it was built of marble.

He had been at white heat all the evening. Again and again, amid the desultory talk, both at the dinner-table and afterwards in the drawing-room, the rasping voice had rung in his ears: "*He* is quite presentable!"—while he could imagine, though he had not seen, the impudent shrug which accompanied the stressing of the pronoun. Thus wantonly did mortals glance at, sum up, and dismiss one another. The jar to his pride was a rude one. For, ingrained in him, and not to be eradicated, was the conviction that he was gentleman first, doctor second: slights might be aimed at his profession, but not at him in person.— And yet, in comparison, the patronising "presentable" affixed to himself left him cold. It was the sneer at Mary that stung him to the quick. *That* was something he would never be able either to forget or forgive. Did he contemplate this great heart, full to the brim of charity, of human kindness; this mine of generous impulse; this swift begetter of excuse and explanation for everything in others that was not as fair and honest as in herself; did he consider that, to assist in their need any of these purblind souls who sat so lightly in judgment on her, she would have stripped the clothing from her back: then he burned with a wrath too deep for words. He did not know one of them worthy to tie up her shoe-lace.— And yet, such a worm for truth existed in him, so plaguy an instinct to get to the root of a matter, that, even as he burned, he found himself looking Mary up and down, viewing her from every angle, and with a purely objective eye. He saw her at home, in church, in the company of others; saw her gestures, her movements, her smile; heard her laughter, the tones of her voice, and her way of speaking: all these, for the first time, as things for themselves, detached from the true, sound core of her. And, as he did so, he was forced to own that, in a way, these people were justified of their criticism: she *was* different. But not as they meant it. Her manner had a naturalness, her gestures a spontaneity, which formed only too happy a contrast to their ruled and measured restraint.— And indeed, as he studied her, it began to seem to him that into all Mary did or said there had crept something large and free—a dash of the spaciousness belonging to the country that had become her true home. She needed elbowroom. Her voice was deeper, fuller, more resonant than theirs; she fixed a straight, simple gaze on people and things; walked with a freer step, was franker in her speech, readier with her tongue; she stood up to members of the other sex as women emphatically did *not* do here, and they did not belong to the class of "Madam of the Hall." No connection between Mary and the pursed-up mouth, the downcast, unroving, unintelligent eye, the hands primly folded at the waist, the short, sedate steps, of the professing English lady. For that, the net of her experience had been too widely cast. She had rubbed shoulders with all sorts; had been unable to afford the "lady's" privilege of shutting an eye to evil or wrong-doing, and pretending it did not exist. And if, in the process, she had come to be a shade too downright in her opinions, too blunt for the make-believe of antique conventions . . . well, he thought he might safely leave it to Him who had broken bread with publicans and sinners, to adjudge which was the worthier attitude of the two.

Thus he reasoned; but, ever and again, his mind veered back to the personal thrust. Mary vulgar! . . . Mary, of whom he had felt so fondly proud, having grown to middle age hearing on all sides that she had not her equal in those attributes that make a woman blessed. "Out there," he had seen

483

her courted, made much of; none had approached her in popularity. And from this happy state he had torn her away . . . for what? For the privilege of being looked down on as not quite a lady . . . had uprooted her from the country she loved best and fitted best into, to make her a stranger on the face of the earth.— So much for Mary. But did he himself feel any more at home here than she? Not a bit of it! Nor had he been a jot apter at adjusting himself. They stood out, the pair of them, like over-large figures on a miniature background. The truth was, they had utterly lost the knack of running in a groove; life, in its passage, had hammered them out into citizens of the world. So that, by now, an indelible stamp was on them. And, with this as their dower, cured for ever of an excessive insularity, they had come back to find an England that had not budged by an inch; where people's outlook, habits, opinions, were just what they had always been— inelastic, uninspired. Worse, these islanders seemed to preen themselves on their very rigidity, their narrow-mindedness, their ignorance of any life or country but their own; waving aside, with an elegant flutter of the hand, everything of which they themselves had no cognisance. And into this closed circle he and Mary—especially Mary—had come blundering, trampling on prejudice, surrounded by an aura of adventure . . . and unsuccessful adventure, at that! . . . was it indeed any wonder they found themselves outside the pale!

Well, this ended it! He could not picture himself going on living there with a nervous eye eternally cocked at Mary, to see how she was comporting herself, or how what she did struck the wretched group of snobs he had been fool enough to dump her down amongst; the while he winced at idiosyncrasies he yet grudged to admit. No, the wider the distance he could put between himself and Buddlecombe, the better he would be pleased. But where to go? . . . what next? Back to some sordid manufacturing town, with its black mud and slippery cobble-stones, to act as medical adviser to a handful of grooms and servant girls? Or to another country hole, to see exclusive country-folk turn up their noses at your wife, and watch the practice in which you had invested your hard-earned hundreds melting away, filched by one belonging to the inner circle, whose chief merit was never having been out of England? Not if he knew it!— There now remained only London

to consider—Mary would no doubt harp anew on the openings
to be found there. But at the mere thought of London he
shrank into himself, as he had shrunk under his first physical
impression of it. What he had then suspected he now felt
sure of. Great cities were not for him: he was too old to stand
the strain of their wear and tear. And therewith the list of
possibilities on this side of the globe was exhausted. Would he
had stayed on the other! *Civis Britannicus sum*—that knowledge should have been enough for him. Instead of which,
burning to prove his citizenship, he had chased back, with, in
his heart, the pent-up feelings of his long, long absence. He
laughed now, did he recall the exultation with which he had
descried the shadowy outlines of the English coast. "Out
there," he had seen this old country through the rose-red
spectacles of youthful memory. Now, he knew that the thrill
he had experienced on again beholding it—his pleasure in its
radiant greenness—was the sum total of the satisfaction he
was to get from it. No sooner ashore—and not even Mary had
fathomed his passionate desire to stand well here—than he
had felt himself outsider and alien. England had no welcome
for her homing sons, or any need of them: their places were
long since filled.

But hold! let him be frank with himself. Had he liked the
motherland any better than it liked him? He had not. Indeed,
his feelings were a great deal more active than any want of
liking. He hated it—yes! hate was not too strong a word—
and had done, from the first. His attempt at transplanting
himself had been a sad and sorry failure; but he had gone
about with bandaged eyes, refusing to face the truth, struggling to persuade himself that all was well. Now, in this
moment of clarity, the countless rebuffs he had had to endure,
since landing, rose before him. London had overwhelmed,
Leicester repelled him. In this country hole, he had been the
veriest square peg: there was no money to be made; no outlet
for his abilities. Returning, full of honours and repute, he
found people darkly suspicious of his colonial experience—
the mere fact of his having lived and practised in Australia a
slur on his good name. Again, he had come back on what he
believed to be but the threshold of middle age—and without
being greatly troubled by it; for, "out there," men of his own
years had kept pace, gone along with him—and everywhere

he had been made to feel himself well over his prime, if not indeed—thanks to Australian pallor and wrinkles—an old man: one of those broken-down adventurers who limp home, at long last, to eke out the remainder of a wasted life.

But what next?—what in all the world next? To this question he could find no answer. Nor was he helped by staring at the sea, or the golden, lemon-shaped moon that now came up on its back from behind the dark mass of the cliffs. The purchase of a third practice was beyond him: if he went from here, he went empty-handed. Possibly, he might get again for the house what he had given for it—though he had discovered that it was both damp, and in need of repair—but this sum would not suffice to set him up anew. No, the outlook was darker than, a moment before, the night had been; no moon rose for him.— And he lay long wakeful, grappling, in a cold sweat, with the many small practical details of the break —details which it is so easy to overlook in the taking of sweeping decisions, yet which afterwards rise up like mountains— and following the square of silver that flooded in through the uncurtained window, and slowly moved across the bed on its passage from wall to wall. With the glimmer of the material dawn, however—red behind those cliffs that had delivered up the moon, great Jupiter hanging like a globe of silver above them—there came to him, too, the dawning of a possible solution. But, at his first hint of it, he flung restlessly over on his side, unable to bear its weight. A bolder hand than his was needed, to sweep away the cobwebs of prejudice and nervous aversion in which he had spun himself. It took Mary to do it; and she did; though not till she had talked herself hoarse, in an attempt to make him see reason, begging him to hold the field and show fight; till her head swam with listening to his monotonous: "What now? Where can I go?" Then, abruptly determined, she cut the knot by facing him and answering squarely: "Why, home again!"—words which first made Mahony wince, then snort with contempt.— But he had no other suggestion to offer—or none but the fatuous one Mary had already smiled at, that, he having given up practice, they should retire to some tiny cottage, do without domestic help, see no company, and live on the slender sum that came to them from Australia. "I think we could be very happy and content, love, living so—just you and I?" If a soul can be said to laugh, then, in spite of her trouble, Mary's soul rocked with laughter, at this fresh sample of Richard's fantasy. Oh, was there ever such an unpractical old dreamer! . . . such an inability to see things as they were. No doubt he pictured a show cottage, wreathed in roses and honeysuckle, where they would pass idyllic days. The slow death-in-life of such an existence, the reaction of his haughty pride against the social position—or want of position—that would be forced upon them, was hidden from him. Perhaps mercifully hidden . . . and Mary sighed.

But she did not falter . . . either at his first disdainful sniff, or, later on, when his eyes came stealing back to hers; came tamed, all the scorn gone out of them. "Only do not call it home," was his unspoken request. Short of a miracle that name would never, he believed, cross his lips again. No place could now be "home" to him, as long as he lived. He was an outcast and a wanderer once more; he must go back, in humiliation, to the land that had eaten up his prime, and there make the best of the years that were left him.

As time wore on, however, and their preparations for departure advanced; as, too, the prospect of a change of scene hoisted its pirate flag again, this sense of bitterness subsided; the acute ache turned to a dull pain that was almost a relief. And worked on by this, as by the joy which, for all her anxieties, Mary could not quite conceal, the relief also imperceptibly changed its character, and grew to be a warm spot in his heart.

And one evening, when the supper dishes had been pushed aside, to make room for Mary's desk—she was methodically noting the contents of a tin trunk—Mahony, watching her, and thinking how the frequent coughs and colds she had suffered from, since being in England, had thinned her down, spoke his thought aloud.— "Well, love, whatever happens, *you* at least will grow fat and well again, and be the healthy woman you always were."

"Now, for goodness sake, don't start to worry about me. I'm all right," said Mary. "It takes time to get used to a strange climate." She entered a few more items, in her clear, pointed writing, then laid her pen down, and put her chin on her hand. "The thing I like to think of, Richard, is how soon I shall be seeing them all again—Ned, and Jerry, and Tilly, and the dear children. I can hardly believe it. I *have* missed them so."

"Poor little wife! And shall I tell you what *I* dwell most on? 'Pon my soul, Mary, it's of getting my teeth into a really sweet apple again—instead of a specimen that's red on one side only. I believe England will stick in my mind, for the rest of my days, as the land where the fruit doesn't ripen."

"And yet costs so much to buy."

"And if I know you, my dear, it's the Abernethy biscuit and thin lemon-water you won't forget. Well, well, madam! you'll soon be able to pamper your guests once more, to your heart's content."

"Perhaps. But I shall at least see who it is Jerry thinks of marrying."

"See? . . . yes. But don't hug the belief you'll be able to influence him in his choice."

"I may not want to.— And there's Johnny to try and find out about, poor boy, and what this nonsense is John writes about Trotty. And to keep Zara from making a goose of herself.— Oh! now that we're really going home at last, I feel how dreadfully cut off from them all, I have been here."

"And they'll every one hail you joyfully, my dear, rest assured of that! . . . be literally foaming with impatience to make use of you again. I should only like to know how they've got on without you."— Mahony had risen from his chair and was standing on the hearthrug, with his back to the fire. Having meditatively warmed his coat-tails for a moment, he added: "There's another thing, Poll, I don't mind telling you I look forward to, my dear, and that is, seeing a real sunrise and sunset again. On this side of the world . . . well, as often as not, the sun seems just to slip in or out of a bank of clouds. There's none of that sense of a coming miracle . . . that uplifting effect of space . . . of splendour of colouring. Why, I've still in my memory evenings when half the field of the sky was one pink flush—with a silver star twinkling through—or a stretch of unreal green deepening into yellow—or mauve. . . . The idea has come to me at times that it must have been from glories of this kind that the old Greek scribe drew his picture of the New Jerusalem, in the Book known as Revelation. . . . Yes, I must say, things here—colouring, landscape, horizon

488

—have all seemed very dull and cramped . . . like the souls of the people themselves."

Again he fell into thought. Then, warmed up by these confidences, he went further. "Mary, love, let me confess it to you: I realise I have made a sad fool of myself, over this whole business. And now must pay the piper. . . . My ever leaving Ballarat was a fatal mistake. If I had only had the sense to take your advice! I was run down—at the end of my tether—from years of overwork. A twelvemonth out of harness would have set me right again: a voyage to this side; fresh surroundings and associations—and no need to stint with the money either, for we should now have been going back to our old ample income. Instead of having to face another start on as good as nothing . . . eat humble pie before them all, too. For they will certainly grasp what has happened.— No, I see it now, my dear; I was too old for such a drastic break. One's habits stiffen with one's joints. You've noticed I've been hurt by people here implying I'm out-of-date, old-fashioned—good enough for the colonies, but not for the home-country—but, upon my word, Mary, I don't know if there isn't some truth in it. I stopped too long in the one place, my dear; with the result that I ought to have stopped there altogether.— Well, well! . . . there's only this about it: fiasco though it has proved, it has not hit me as hard as it might have done, considering the exaggerated expectations I came home with. Which, in itself, is enough to show me age is rendering me indifferent.— Actually, my dear, I believe much of the sting is taken from what has happened by the sight of your satisfaction at returning. Never should I have brought you here—never! I thought to find myself among a different set of people altogether. In memory I confused good breeding with tact and kindliness. Whereas, now, if it comes to a choice between blue blood and inborn goodness of heart, then what I say is: give me nature's gentlefolk all the time. There's as little likeness between them as between this eternal clammy drizzle and some of those cloudless winter days we knew on the Flat."

"Richard! Don't forget how you hated the climate there. And how poorly the sun made you feel."

"Nor do I. And in spite of the mizzle, and damp, and want

489

of sun, I've thriven in this country. But one can't live on climate alone. And when I let my mind dwell on the way I —we—have been treated here; how we've been looked down on and slighted; the stodgy lack of goodwill . . . animosity even . . . the backbiting and gossip! I tell you this, love: there's but one person I shall regret when I leave; one only, of whom I shall carry away a warm remembrance; and that's, as you know, your dear old mother. But can you guess why? Upon my word, I believe it's because there's something in her warm-heartedness and generosity, her overflowing hospitality, that reminds me of the people we lived among so long!"

"Well! it's late . . . we must to bed," he went on, after a silence which Mary did not break, there seeming really nothing left for her to say. "I've no plans, my dear, nor have I at present the spirit to make any. It seems best, at this moment, to leave the future in the lap of the gods. I know this much, though: I'm cured of castle-building for ever."

Mary nodded, and acquiesced; or at least again said nothing: and she kept to this attitude in the weeks that followed, when, as was only natural, Richard's mind, far too active and uneasy to rest, began to play round the plans he *might* have made, had he not forsworn the habit. These including settling somewhere by the sea; either near Melbourne, or at one of the watering-places on the Bay—such as Dromana, or Schnapper Point. Mary let him talk. She herself was persuaded that the only rational thing for him to do was to return to Ballarat. It was of no use his riding the high horse: feelings of pique and pride must yield to practical considerations. He was known from one end of Ballarat to the other; and the broken threads could there be picked up more swiftly and with greater ease than anywhere else. It would, of course, no longer be a case of Webster Street—unless the doctor to whom he had sold the practice had failed, or proved otherwise unsatisfactory. But Richard would find room somewhere; even if it had to be on the Redan, or at Sebastopol, or out at Buninyong. And though he could now never hope to reach the income he had wilfully abandoned—oh, the unspeakable folly of man!—never hope to give up general practice for that of consultant or specialist, yet, with care, something might still be salvaged from the wreck of the past.— And, nursing these schemes, Mary set her lips and frowned with determination.

490

Never again, in the years to come, should Richard be able to say he repented not having taken her advice. This time, she would set her will through, cost what it might.

PART II

[1]

THE good ship *Florabella*, eighty-four days out from Liverpool, made the Australian coast early one spring morning; and, therewith, the faint, new, spicy smell of land wafted across the water.

Coming up from below to catch a whiff of it, her passengers blinked dazzled eyes at the gaudy brilliancy of light and colouring. Here were no frail tints and misty trimmings; everything stood out hard, clear, emphatic. The water was a crude sapphire; the surf that frothed on the reefs white as milk. As for the sky, Mahony declared it made him think of a Reckitt's bluebag; while a single strip of pearly cloud to the east looked fixed, immovable—solid as those clouds on which, in old paintings, cherubs perch or lean.

Outside the "Rip" the vessel hove to, to take up the pilot; and every neck was craned to watch his arrival; for with him would come letters and news—the first to reach the travellers since their departure from England. Hungrily was the unsealing of the mail-bag awaited.

Mary's lap would hardly hold the envelopes that bore her name. They were carried to her by the grizzled old Captain himself, who dealt them out, one by one, cracking a joke to each. Mary laughed; but at the same time felt a touch of embarrassment. For her to receive so large a share of the good things—under the very noses, too, of those unfortunates who got none—seemed not in the best of taste. So, the tale told, she retired with her budget to the cabin; and Mahony, having seen her below, went back to read his own correspondence on deck.

But she had done no more than finish John's note of welcome and break the seal of Tilly's, when a foot came bounding through the saloon, off which the cabin opened, and there was Richard, again—Richard, with rumpled hair, eyes alight, red

491

of face, looking for all the world like a rowdy schoolboy. Seizing her by the hands, he pulled her to her feet, and would have twirled her round. But Mary, her letters strewing the floor, protested—stood firm.

"Richard! What *is* the matter?"

"Mary! Wife! Here's news for us! . . . here's news. A letter from ——" and he flourished a sheet of paper at her. "I give you three guesses, love. But nonsense!—you couldn't . . . not if you guessed till Doomsday. No more pinching and scraping for us, Mary! No more underpaid drudgery for me! My fortune's made. I am a rich man . . . at last!"

"Richard dear! What is it *now?*"

Mary spoke in the lightly damping tone Mahony was wont to grumble she reserved for him alone. But to-day it passed unnoticed.

"Here you are, Madam—read for yourself!"—and he pushed a crumpled letter into her hand. "It's those *Australia Felixes* we have to thank for it. What a glorious piece of luck, Mary, that I should have stuck to them, and gone on paying their wretched calls, when every one else let them lapse in despair! John will be green with envy.— And this is only the begining, my dear. There's no telling what they'll do when they get the new plant in—old Simmonds says so himself, and he's not given to superlatives as you know.— Yes, it's good-bye to poverty!"—and, forgetting in his excitement where he was, Mahony flung round to pace the floor. Baulked by the narrow wall of the cabin, he had just to turn to the right-about. "It means I can now pick and choose, Mary—put up my plate in Collins Street East—hold my head as high as the best."

"Oh, dear, how glad I am! . . . for your sake." The tears sprang to Mary's eyes; she had openly to wipe them away. "You know how dark the future has sometimes seemed, Richard.— But this is so sudden. I can hardly believe it. Are you sure it's *really* true?" And now she stroked the page smooth, to read for herself.

"You for my sake. . . . I for yours! What haven't *you* had to put up with, my poor love, through being tied to a rolling old stone like me? But now, I promise you, everything will be different. There's nothing you shall not have, my Mary— nothing will be too good for you. You shall ride in your own carriage . . . keep half a dozen servants. And when once you

are free of worries and troubles, you'll grow fat and rosy
again, and all these little lines on your forehead will disappear."

"And perhaps you won't dislike the colony so much . . . and
the people . . . if you can feel independent of them," said Mary
hopefully. Could he have promised her, from this day forth,
a tranquil and contented mind, it would have been the best
gift of any.

When he had danced out—danced was the word that
occurred to her to describe the new spring in his step, which
seemed intolerant of the floor—had gone to consult the steward about the purchase of a special dozen of champagne,
which that worthy was understood to hold in store for an
occasion such as this: when Mary sat down to collect her wits,
she indulged in a private reflection, which neither then nor
later did she share with Richard. It ran: "Oh, how thankful I
am we didn't get the letter till we were safely away from that
. . . from England. Or he might have taken it into his head to
stop there."—

Mahony felt the need of being alone, and sought out a
quiet spot to windward, where he was likely to be undisturbed. But news of the turn in his fortunes had run like wildfire through the ship, started by the steward, to whom, in the
first flush, he had garrulously communicated it. And now came
one after another of his fellow-passengers, to wring his hand
and wish him joy. It was well meant; he could not but answer
in kind. But then, they, too, had changed. From mere nonde-
scripts and undesirables they were metamorphosed into
kindly, hearty folk, generous enough, it seemed, to feel almost
as elated at a fellow-mortal's good luck as if it were their own.
His hedge of spines went down: he turned frank, affable, easy
of approach; though any remaining stand-offishness was like to
have been forgiven him, who, at a stroke, had become one of
the wealthiest men on board.

He could see these simple souls thought he took his windfall very coolly. Well! . . . in a way he did. Just for the moment
he had been carried off his feet—as indeed who could fail
to be, when, by a single lucky chance, one spin of fate's wheel,
all that had become his, which half a lifetime's toil had failed
to give him? Yet ingrained in him was so lively a relish, so
poignant a need for money, and the ease of mind and body

493

money would bring, that the stilling of the want had something almost natural about it: it resembled the payment of an overdue debt. Yes, affluence would fit him like a second skin. The beggardom of early days, the push and scramble for an income of later life—these had been the travesty.

Next came a sense of relief—relief unspeakable. Alone by now in his windy corner, he could afford to let his eyes grow moist with it; while the finger he passed round inside his collar trembled. From what a nightmare of black care, a horde of petty anxieties, did the miracle of this day not set him free! To take but a single instance: the prospect of having to explain away his undignified return to the colonies had cost him many a night's sleep. Now, he was the master of circumstance, not its playball.— And into the delights of this sensation he plunged as into a magic water; laved in it, swam, went under; and emerged a new man. The crust of indifference, the insidious tiredness, the ennui that comes of knowing the end of a thing before you have well begun it, and knowing it not worth while: all such marks of advancing age fell away. Youthfully he squared his shoulders; he was ready to live again, to live with zest. And under the influence of this revival there stirred in him, for the first time, a more gracious feeling towards the land for which he was heading. What he had undergone there in his day, none but himself knew; but, if his sufferings had been great, great, too, was the atonement now made him. Indeed, the bigness of the reward had in it something of the country's own immensity—its far-flung horizons.

"And perhaps, after all . . . who knows, who knows! . . . I myself . . . the worm that was in me . . . that ceaseless hankering for—why, for happiness of course! . . . the end of man's every wild-goose chase . . . the belief in one's *right* to it . . . the fixed idea that it must be waiting for you somewhere . . . remains but to go in search of it. So, is it not conceivable . . . thus made wiser . . . all fear for the future stilled, too— *how* fear lames and deadens!—independent, now . . . beholden to nobody"—such were some of the loose tags of thought that drifted through his brain.

Till one or other touched a secret spring, and straightway he was launched again on those dreams and schemes with which he believed his last unhappy experience had for ever put him out of conceit.— Oh, the house he would build! . . . the grounds he would lay out! . . . the books he would buy . . . and buy . . . till he had a substantial library of his own. All the rare and pretty things that should be Mary's. The gifts they would make her dear old mother. The competency that should rescue his own people from their obscure indigence. The deserving strugglers to whom he would lend a hand. Even individuals he disliked or was fretted by—Zara, Ned, Ned's encumbrances—sipped from his overflow. Indeed, he actually caught himself thinking of people—poor devils, mostly—who had done him a bad turn, and of how he could now requite them.

Over these imaginings the hours flew by—hours not divided off, each from the next, but fusing to form one single golden day: of a kind such as does not come twice in a lifetime.— Meanwhile, the vessel was well advanced up the great Bay; and familiar landmarks began to come into view. He had sometimes wondered, on the voyage out, what his feelings would be, when he saw these well-known places again, and knew that the pincer of the "Heads" had snapped behind him. Now, he contemplated them with a vacant eye; did not take up the thread of a personal relationship. Or once only: at sight of a bare old clump of hills behind Geelong. Then, he impulsively went below to fetch Mary—Mary was packing the cabin furniture, sewing up mattresses in the floor-carpeting, the mirror in the blankets—and she, good-naturedly rising from her knees, for to-day she had not the heart to refuse him anything, tied on her bonnet and accompanied him on deck. There, standing arm-in-arm, they thought and spoke of a certain unforgettable evening, now years deep in the past.

"What greenhorns we were then, love, to be sure! So mercifully ignorant of all the ups and downs in store for us."— But his tone was light, even merry; for to-day the ups had it.

"Yet, you seemed to me *very* old and wise, Richard. I suppose it came of you wearing that horrid beard."

"And what a little sprite you were!—so shy and elusive. There was no catching you . . . or getting a word in edgewise if one did—thanks to that poor old chattering Mother B., and her two bumpkins."

"Whom you couldn't tell apart . . . how that did make me laugh!" said Mary. To add with a sigh: "Poor Jinny! Little did we think, then, she would have to go so much sooner than the rest."

"My dear, a good half of that party is dust by now."

But no melancholy tinged the reflection. In his present mood, Mahony accepted life, and the doom life implied, with cheerfullest composure.

✻ ✻ ✻ ✻ ✻ ✻

Hardly a letter received by Mary that morning but had besought them to regard the writer's house as their own: they had now only to make their choice. "Yes, and give umbrage to all the rest. Nonsense, Mary! We'll just slip off quietly to a good hotel. We do not need now to consider expense, my dear, and we shall be much freer and more comfortable at an hotel, than if we tied ourselves down to stay with people."

But Mahony's plan miscarried.

What a home-coming that was! No sooner had the ship cast anchor than rowing-boats began to push off from the pier; while one that had been lying on its oars made for them with all speed. Mary, standing hatted and shawled for landing, looked again, rubbed her eyes, and exclaimed: "Why, I do declare if it isn't Tilly! Oh, *Richard,* what a difference the weeds make!" And sure enough, a few minutes later Tilly's head came bobbing up over the side, and the two women lay in each other's arms, half laughing, half crying, drawing back, first one, then the other, the better to fix her friend.— Certainly, Tilly had never shown to more advantage. In old days, her hats had been flagrant, her silks over-sumptuous, her jewellery too loud. Now, the neat widow's bonnet, with its white frill and black hangings, formed a becoming frame for her yellow-brown hair, tanned skin, and strong white teeth; the chains, lockets, and brooches of twenty-two-carat Ballarat gold had given way to decorous jet; the soft black stuff of the dress moulded and threw up every good point in the rich, full-bosomed figure. Silently, Mary noted and rejoiced. But Tilly, one glance snatched, blurted out: "Well, I must say England 'asn't done much for *you,* my dear! In all my born days, Mary, never did I see you look so peaked and pasty. Sea-sickness? Not it! It's that *horrible* climate you've 'ad to put up with. I declare your very letters—with their rain, rain, and fog, fog—used to gimme the blue devils. 'Ow you ever stood it beats me.

496

Well! you've come back 'ere, my dear, to the finest climate in the world. We'll 'ave you up to the mark again, in a brace o' shakes."

Further she did not get, for here now was John arriving—a somewhat greyer and leaner John than they had left him, but advancing upon one, thought Mahony, with the same old air of: *I* am here; all is well. Having cordially embraced his sister, John wrung his brother-in-law's hand: "It would be false to pretend surprise, my dear Mahony, at your decision to return to us." On his heels came none other than Jerry and his wife: a fair, fragile slip of a girl this—Australian-born and showing it, in a skin pale as a white flower. Mary put her arms round the child—she was scarcely more—and kissed her warmly: while in one breath the little wife, who was all a-flutter and a-tremble, confided to her how very, very much afraid she had felt of this meeting, knowing Mary to be dear "Harry's" favourite sister: and how she hoped dear Mary, please, wouldn't mind her calling him Harry, but she had once had a dog named Jerry, a white dog with a black patch over one eye; and it seemed so droll, didn't it? to call your husband by the same name as a dog, especially such a funny-looking dog; although if dear Mary wished it very, very much . . . all this gabbled off at top speed, like a lesson got by rote.— Mary promptly reassured her: it was her good right to call her husband by whatever name she chose, so long as *he* did not mind; and that—with a loving glance at Jerry—she would guarantee he didn't. Then she turned to her brother. The same steady old sober-sides, she felt sure; but, in addition, now grown quite the man: broad of shoulder, richly whiskered, and, as could be seen at a glance, the most devoted of husbands. Did his young wife speak to some one, he tried to overhear what she was saying; watched the effect of her words on the other; smiled in advance at her little jokes, to incite the listener to smile, too—for all the world after the fashion of a fond mother playing off her child. And when, sprite-like, the girl had run to the other side of the ship, he took the opportunity, before following her, to squeeze his sister's hand and murmur: "*What* do you say to my little Fanny, Mary? Isn't she perfect?"

"Dear, dear Jerry! If she's only half as good as she's pretty . . . and I can see she is," said Mary, returning the squeeze.

Meanwhile, quite a crowd had collected on the wharf, to which the party was rowed in a boat so laden that, at moments, the ladies instinctively held their breaths to lighten the load; while the little bride shrank into the crook of her husband's arm. Here stood Zara, fluttering a morsel of cambric: she had feared an attack of *mal de mer,* she whispered, did she embark on so choppy a sea.— ("We could hardly, I think, love, expect Zara to consider us worth the half-guinea the boatmen were charging!" was Mahony's postprandial comment.)— Here were Agnes Ocock and Amelia Grindle, with sundry of their children, and the old Devines, and Trotty, advanced to a hair-net, and John's three youngest in charge of their schoolmistress; besides many a lesser friend and acquaintance who had made light of the journey to the port. Hand after hand was thrust forth, with: "I trust I see you in prime health, ma'am?" "Dear, dearest Mary! *How* we have missed you!" or: "Thought you'd never hold it out over there, sir." "Delighted, doctor, I'm sure, to welcome you back to our little potato-patch!" And those who could not get near enough for more, along with a sprinkling of curious strangers, enjoyed just forming the fringe of the crowd. It was a pleasant break in the monotony of colonial life to catch a glimpse of arrivals from overseas; to note the latest fashion in hair and dress; to hear news and pick up gossip.

Mary had just stooped to the youngest of the children, marvelling at its growth, when her ear caught an oddly familiar sound, an uneven, thumping footfall, and, turning quickly, whom in all the world should she see but Purdy, out of breath and red in the face, but otherwise looking just the same as of old, or at least "not *very* different"—a phrase, this, with which Mary had already covered a marked change in more than one present. John's singular spareness of rib, Zara's greying front, Agnes's florid cheeks, the wizened-apple aspect of Amelia Grindle. In Purdy's case it cloaked a shining-through of the cranium, did he bare his head; more than a hint of coming stoutness; a cheap and flashy style of dress. First, though, she shot a lightning glance at Richard: how would he take this sudden apparition? The look reassured her: he was to-day uplifted above all ordinary prejudice. There was just an instant's hesitation, and then he himself stepped forward, both hands outheld, one to grasp Purdy's right, the other to clap on

his shoulder; while his: "Dickybird, my boy! How are you?
. . . how are you?" came simultaneously with Purdy's: "Dick,
old man, I heard your tub was in. I thought I must just trot
along and give you a pawshake."— And thus the old bond
was cemented anew.

Thought Mary: was there any end to the good things with
which this day was full?

Led to the group, Purdy came in for his share of the welcome. For he had not been back to Ballarat, it proved, since
his abrupt departure some years previously; and his former
friends and acquaintances hailed him with the lively interest
and curiosity peculiar to people who see but few fresh faces,
and never forget an old one.

He shook hands all around. When it came to Tilly: "I need
hardly introduce *you* two, I think!" said Mary slyly.

Tilly burst into a roar. "I should say not, indeed! Why, my
dear, I can remember 'im when 'e was only *so* 'igh,"—and
she measured a foot from the ground.

Purdy capped her fiction. "What? Is that all? Why, she
lisped her first prayer at my knee."

But the children grew peevish; it was time to make a move.
At the first breathing of the word hotel, however, such a
chorus of dissent broke out that Mahony's plan had there and
then to be let drop. Not a guest-chamber, it seemed, but had
been swept and dressed for them—John's excepted, John still
leading a bachelor life at the Melbourne Club. Even Jerry
and his bride had made ready their tiny weatherboard; and
now Jerry put his lips to Mary's ear to say how inconsolable
little Fanny would be, if they went elsewhere: she had sat
stitching till past midnight, at wonderful bows for bed- and
window-hangings—a performance which, in the young husband's eyes, far outweighed the fact of them living miles off,
at Heidelberg, to which place a coach ran but at ten of a
morning; so that the present night would have to be spent in
Melbourne, under the bride's father's roof. Had Mary been
free to please herself, she would have waived all other considerations, rather than disappoint the youthful pair. But
Richard! She could hear his amused and sarcastic ha-ha, at the
idea of "camping out" with utter strangers, for the pleasure
of next morning being "carted off" to Heidelberg. Meanwhile,
on her other side, Fanny was whispering: just fancy, Harry

hadn't been able to tell her what dear Mary's complexion was, whether blonde or brunette. She had chosen pink for her bows, because pink suited most people, and she had clapped her hands on finding she was right; but she thought she would have sunk through the floor, had she hit on blue. And when Mary laughingly declared that blue was one of her favourite colours, and that, even in yellow or green, the trimmings would have been equally appreciated, little Fanny bit her lip, and looked as though she was going to cry.— All this in a rapid aside.

The Devines won the day—after a heated discussion, in which everybody spoke at once. These good people had actually a carriage-and-pair in waiting, that the travellers might be spared the brief railway journey from port to town; as well as a spring-cart for the baggage. There was no standing out against Mrs. Devine's persuasions, seconded as they were by the M.L.C. himself, who, from a modest place in the background, threw in, whenever he got the chance: "My 'ouse is entirely at your disposal, sir. We beg you and your good lady will do us the *h*'onour."

"Indeed and I'll *not take no!*" declared his wife; and, under a pair of nodding, hearse-like plumes, her fat, rosy face beamed on those about her, after the manner of a big red sun. "'Tis a great h'empty barn, that's what it is, and I've looked to this day to fill it.— Why, dearie, so's not to 'ear quite so much of me own footsteps, I've been and taken in one o' Jake's sister's 'usband's sister's children."

Thus the Mahonys found themselves rolling townwards in the Devines' well-hung landau, on their knees a picnic-basket containing port wine and sandwiches, with which to refresh and sustain the inner man.

Mahony fell silent as the wheels revolved; a smile played round his lips. He was laughing at himself for having imagined it would be necessary to explain away his reappearance in these people's midst. One and all had followed John's lead, in finding his return to Australia—Australia *facile princeps!*— the most natural thing in the world.

At South Yarra they became the occupants of the largest guest-chamber in a brand-new mansion, which counted every comfort and luxury the upholsterers had known how to cram into it, and now only needed really to be lived in. Its stiff

formality reminded Mary, the homemaker, of the specimen
rooms set out in a great furniture warehouse; rooms in which
no living creature has ever left a trace. Her fingers itched to
break up the prim rows of chairs ranged against the walls;
lightly to disarrange albums; to leave on antimacassars the
impress of a head.

Here, Mrs. Devine having finally satisfied herself that they
had everything they required—down to a plump and well-
studded pincushion, on which the pins wrote "Welcome!"—
for: "I've no faith in them giddy girls, dearie,"—husband and
wife were at last alone together.

"Whew!" breathed Mahony, and sinking into an armchair,
he fanned himself with his handkerchief. "Well! I sincerely
hope you're satisfied, Mary. Royalty itself could not ask for a
warmer welcome than you have had, my dear." But again he
smiled as he spoke; and the usual edge of his words was
wanting.

"You, too," said Mary, who was fighting the lock of a
carpet-bag. Then she laughed. "As if royalty ever got hugged,
and kissed, and slapped on the back! But indeed, Richard, I
shall never, never forget the kindness that's been shown us
to-day.— And what a lovely house this is! . . . I mean, could
be made."

"My dear, you shall have as good—and better. Rather much
oilcloth here, for my taste. The grounds, too, struck me as
stiffish, what I saw of them." Rising to take another look
through a raised slat of the venetian, he turned and beckoned
his wife. "What do you say to this, Mary?" Peeping over his
shoulder, she saw their host, in comfortable corduroys, without his coat, his shirt-sleeves rolled up above his elbows,
trundling a loaded wheelbarrow. Said Mahony: "Seems to
have turned into a very decent sort of fellow indeed, does
our good Cincinnatus."

"Who? . . . Mr. Devine? Yes, hasn't he? I thought it most
tactful of him to be quiet in the carriage, when he saw you
didn't want to talk."

Below, on a dinner-table built to accommodate a score, a
veritable banquet was spread out. They sat down to it at six
o'clock, a large family party. For on the wharf, Mrs. Devine,
as winner, had scattered her invitations broadcast, even insisting on Tilly exchanging her hotel for the second-best spare

room. Zara was present, together with Jerry and his wife, and John, and Trotty, who hung on one of Aunt Mary's arms, as did pretty Fanny on the other; and the health of the home-comers, and the happy change in Mahony's fortunes, were drunk to in bumpers of champagne. By every one but the master of the house; before whose plate stood a jug of barley-water. In the intervals of signalling to the servants where to put the dishes, and whose glass or plate stood empty, Mrs. Devine, purply moist with gratification and excitement, drew Mahony's attention to this jug, with a nudge and a wink.

"Your doin', doctor . . . all thanks to you. Jake took the pledge that time you know of, and never 'as 'e broke it since, no matter where 'e is, or in 'oos company." She actually laid her pudgy hand on Mahony's and gave it a warm squeeze.

"Very creditable . . . very creditable indeed," murmured Mahony, stiff with embarrassment lest his host should overhear what was being said.

But Mrs. Devine had already telegraphed to her husband down the length of the table; and the good man smiled and nodded, and sipped his barley-water in Mahony's direction.

The ladies withdrawing, and Jerry sidling out soon after, the three men pulled their chairs closer; and now colonial affairs took the place of family gossip and perfunctory inquiries about "home." As fellow-members of the Legislative Council, John and Devine had become fast friends. It was also in the wind, it seemed, that Devine might be called on to form a ministry. Puzzled by the many changes, the new men and new names that had come up during his absence, Mahony acted chiefly the listener; but the interested listener: for it was gratifying to find himself once more at the fountain-head. His companions' talk, ranging over a great variety of topics, harked back yet and again to the great natural catastrophe, in the face of which legislation was powerless—the unprecedented drought, which, already in its fourth year, was ruining the squatters right and left, compelled, as they were, to part with their thousands on thousands of dying sheep, for the price of the skins alone.

In listening, Mahony eyed the two men up and down. His bearded host looked sound as a bell. But it was otherwise with John—"He's a shocking bad colour,"—and knowing his brother-in-law to be of temperate habits, he resolved, when an opportunity offered, to have a word with him in private.

It grew late; for over an hour John's horses had pawed the gravel of the drive. Finally, Mahony excused himself on grounds of fatigue, and ran upstairs. But he might have saved his haste. For Mary had taken her hairbrush and gone to Tilly's room. There, a fresh log having been thrown on the whitewashed hearth, the two women sat and talked far into the night.

[2]

MAHONY's first lightning plan of putting up his plate at the top of Collins Street, among the bigwigs of the profession, was not carried out. For when, the day after landing, he went to interview Simmonds, his man of business, he found his affairs in even more brilliant condition than Simmonds's letter—written a fortnight back, to await the ship's arrival—had led him to believe. That had put the sum lying to his credit at between ten and eleven thousand pounds. By now, however—a second company in which he was interested choosing the self-same moment to look up—combined dividends were flowing in at the rate of twelve to fifteen hundred pounds a month. And this, despite the enormous outlay incurred by the Australia Felix Company in sinking a fourth shaft, lighting the mine throughout with gas, erecting the heaviest plant yet seen on the goldfields.

In the conveyance that left Collins Street at midday for South Yarra, Mahony sat, feeling mildly stunned by the extent of his good fortune, as by Simmonds's confident prediction of still grander things to come; sat, with far-away eyes, absently noting the velvety black shadows that accompanied vehicles and pedestrians up and down the glaring white centre of the great street. He had already drawn attention to himself by smiling broadly, at thought of the news he was taking home to Mary. Now, as a fresh idea struck him, he uttered a smothered exclamation, and tried to slap his knee; a gesture that entangled him with a stout party whose crinoline overflowed him, and gave a pimply-faced youth sitting opposite, a chance to exercise his wit.

"Fy, matey, fy! What'ud our missis say?"

The vehicle—a kind of roofless omnibus—started with a lunge that sent the two rows of passengers toppling like ninepins one against another. Mahony alone raised his voice in apology: he had lain on the shoulder of the fat woman. The man on her farther side angrily bade her take her danged feathers out of his eye. The greater number recovered their balance by thrusting an elbow and lodging it firmly in a neighbour's rib.

Even in his present holiday mood this promiscuity was too much for Mahony. He regretted now not having accepted Devine's offer of a buggy; and half-way to his destination, dismounted, and covered the rest of the distance on foot.

This was better. In the outlying district where he found himself, no traffic moved. Roads and paths were sandy, and grass-edged. The scattered houses lay far back in large gardens, which were screened by rows of Scotch firs. He met no one; could think in peace; and, over a knotty point, he stopped short and dug with his stick in the sand.

The brilliant idea that had flashed through his mind in the omnibus was: why go back into harness at all? Retire! . . . retire, and live on his dividends . . . here was the solution. From now on be free to devote himself to the things that really mattered, in which he had hitherto had no share.

He threshed the scheme out as he went, and was plain-spoken with himself. I am now a middle-aged man: forty-three and a quarter, to be exact in point of time, but a good ten years older with regard to bodily health . . . and disillusionment: considerably more than half-way, that is, on my journey to the green sod. And what have I so far had of my life? It has been one long grind: firstly to keep my head above water, and then to live up to my neighbours; while every attempt to free myself has failed, the last great wild-goose chase most completely of any.— Yes, the real trouble has always been want of money—of money and time—or of money enough to have time. Now that I possess the one, should I not be a fool beyond compare if I failed to make myself master of the other also? Shall I start afresh to toil and moil—put my neck in the yoke, when I have the chance of running free? Think of all the wonders of this world I shall die without knowing—the books I shall not have read, the scientific discoveries, the intellectual achievements, I shall never even have heard of. Oh, the joy of

devoting my remaining years to a congenial occupation! One
cannot love one's work, the handle one grinds by—the notion
that such a thing is possible belongs to a man's green and salad
days. Though, perhaps, if one climbed to the top of the tree.
. . . But for the majority of us mortals, the fact that we labour
to earn our bread by a certain handiwork soon wears all liking for it threadbare. It becomes a habit—like the meals one
eats . . . the clothes one puts on of a morning.— Ambitions to
be sacrificed? But are there? I had them once; in plenty.
Where are they now? Blown into thin air—spent like smoke.
The fag of living was too much for me.— And so, in following
my bent, I sacrifice nothing—or nothing but the possibility of
fresh humiliations . . . and much unnecessary pother . . . an
infinitude of business.

Thus he reasoned, thus justified himself to himself, arriving
at the house with his arguments marshalled ready to be laid
before Mary. The walk, however, had taken longer than he
expected; the afternoon was now far advanced, and he footsore and hungry. But though he could hear the servants chattering in the kitchen, none came to offer him so much as a cup
of tea. They would, of course, suppose him to have lunched;
or else Madam D. had the keys of the larder in her petticoat
pocket. The big house yawned inhospitably still and empty—
but for a common-looking child in copper-toed boots and oilcloth apron, which he unexpectedly ran across: it fled from
him like a startled cat. Mary was out driving with her hostess,
and did not get back till close on dinner-time. There was another party that night; they sat down fifteen to table, and went
to bed only in the small hours. He could do no more than skim
the cream off his interview for her benefit, before retiring.

His chance came next morning.

Ten o'clock had struck, but Mary was still in bedgown and
slippers, her hair tied in its nightly bunch of half a dozen little
plaits on the crown of her head. This state of undress did not,
however, imply that she had newly risen—as a matter of fact,
she had been up and doing for a couple of hours. But it was
one of the rules of this extraordinary house that visitors did not
breakfast till after ten; the longer after, the better, but at any
moment *past* the hour, provided the servants did not know
beforehand what it would be: they must be kept up to the
mark, hover perpetually on the alert for the ringing of the

dining-room bell: and many and scathing were Richard's comments on the practice of using your guests as the stick with which to belabour your slaves. Mrs. Devine herself, clad in a voluminous paisley gown, her nightcap bound under her chin, was early astir: she gave her husband, who rose at dawn to work among his flowers—as he had once worked among his market produce—breakfast at eight, before he left for town. But if you belonged to the élite, were truly *du bon ton,* you did not descend till the morning was half over, and even then must appear "stifling elegant yawns, which betray the effort it has been to tear your high-born limbs from the feathers!"—so ran another of Richard's glosses. The first morning, he and Mary had blundered in this respect; on the second, they were wiser; and now loitered chilly and hungry above-stairs. Chafing at the absurdity of the thing, and fretting for his breakfast, Mahony grumbled: "Was there ever such fudge? As if the woman didn't know I used to have to be up at daybreak, if necessary . . . was in my consulting-room hours before this."

Mary, who had been writing letters and sewing, began to dress her hair. "Do try not to fuss so, dear. After all, it's only a little thing. It pleases her to imagine she's up in the ways of good society. She even means it flatteringly.— Besides, every house has its peculiarities."

"Then give me my own, thank you. But what absurd nonsense you do talk, Mary! I'm sure, when you had 'em, you never tyrannised over guests in this stark fashion. You were their drudge, my dear; danced to their tune. But I believe you'd sacrifice the last scrap of your personal comfort to pander to the foibles of other people."

"Nonsense!" said Mary stoutly; and with a thought that flitted half-way towards the pot and the kettle. "But we can't possibly let her see we don't like it."

She had unbound her hair: freed from its plaits, it hung all crinks and angles. Now, she set, with long, smooth sweeps, to brushing it to its customary high gloss.

Mahony pulled a chair to the window, threw up the sash, and leant his elbow on the sill. The morning was warm and balmy, after a bitterly cold night. By midday, the sun would have gained almost summer strength, gradually to fade through the autumn of the afternoon, till, with darkness, you were back in a wintry spring. The orange-blossom scent of the pittosporums, now everywhere in flower, filled the air. Sunning himself thus, he fell to informing Mary, yet once again, what he had made up his mind to, overnight; spoke shortly and impatiently, and with decision. For, this time at least, he knew that his planning involved his wife in no hardships: he was not asking her to shoulder fresh burdens for him.

Practised hand though she was at concealing surprise, and rightly attributing Richard's snappishness to the want of a good hot cup of coffee, Mary could not help echoing his words, her hairbrush suspended in the air. "Give up practice altogether?" And, at his emphatic affirmation: "But, Richard, you'd soon get tired of having nothing to do."

"Nothing to do, indeed! I, who all my life have longed for a little leisure to follow my own pursuits! Haven't I told you, Mary, again and again, that if I were to read from sunrise to sundown, for the rest of my days, I shouldn't get through a quarter of the books that are waiting for me?"

"Oh, dear, don't talk such rubbish. As if you could spend all the rest of your life reading! Why, I've often heard you say, after sitting with your head in a book for even a few hours running, it felt like a boiled turnip."

"But, good God! . . . I shall have a garden, I suppose? . . . and a decent horse to ride?"

"Now, Richard, it's no use mincing words: you do tire easily of things—much more easily than other people. And I'm sure you'd tire of idleness, as well. After working as hard as you have, for so many years."

"Oh, well, my dear . . . go on acting the brake on the coach. I suppose that, too, is a mission in life."

"How you do snap one up!— There's this about it, of course, you *could* go back into practice at any time, if you wanted to." ("Thank you, never again for me!") "Oh, Richard, you only say that now. In a couple of years, you may have completely changed your mind.— No, it's not a bit of good getting angry. If I can't agree, I can't. And I must say, I think it's a step that requires most careful consideration. Besides which, you promised, remember, not so *very* long ago, to be guided next time by what *I* thought."

"So I did. But here the case is different—entirely different. Not twopenceworth of risk is entailed. I have no intention of speculating further, as you ought to know—if you know any-

507

thing at all about me—and, well invested, this money that has fallen to us is enough to keep us in comfort till our lives' end."

But a dry: "I dare say," was all he could get out of Mary. She refused to be rushed into a decision.—

The long, elaborate breakfast over: they had to eat their way through chops and steaks, eggs and rissoles, barracouta and garfish, fruit, hot rolls, preserves, tea and coffee: breakfast coped with, Mary, dressed for driving, waited in the darkened drawing-room for the carriage to come round, and for her hostess to cease goading on her several maidservants, and tracking down their misdeeds: ("She was certainly happier in the old days with just one.") Propping her chin in her hand, and poking with the tip of her parasol at one of the fruit-and-flower baskets enworked in the maroon ground of the Brussels carpet, Mary wrestled with the problem of Richard's future. His present project called for a readjustment of all her private plans for his benefit. These had never wavered; remained those she had hatched on the morrow of the Buddlecombe fiasco; and, throughout the voyage, she had listened in silence to his fluid plannings and imaginings what he was going to do next— had just listened, and let him talk. Ballarat had seen his beginnings; seen his rise to one of its most popular medical men; it should also, she was resolved, learn to know him as the money-eyed consultant who could afford to see as few patients as he wished, be called in only to complicated cases. It was ridiculous for him to think of starting all over again, in a strange place, when there, in Ballarat, was his old reputation waiting ready-made for him. What was the point of success either, if it did not come to you among the friends of your less palmy days?

But the intention he now expressed of retiring into private life cut clean through these aspirations.— And yet, for the first time, Mary hesitated. The difference was, what he now proposed made a subtle appeal to her. For, to be nothing, to have neither trade nor profession, to fold one's hands and live on one's income—that was the *ne plus ultra* of colonial society, the ideal tirelessly to be striven after. Work brought neither honour nor glory here, where all too many had been manual labourers, the work itself of a low or disreputable kind. And the contingency of Richard ending as the private gentleman, the leisured man of means, had never been wholly absent from

Mary's mind—or wouldn't have been, had he not so quixotically cut his career in half.

There was another point, too: was anybody better fitted than Richard, by birth and breeding, to live as the gentleman? Where so many floundered like fish out of water, he would be entirely in his element. If *only* she could have felt surer of him! But thanks to Buddlecombe, she knew now that, no matter how fixed he seemed, at the first trifling unpleasantness—a hint, for example, that, medically, he was on the shelf—he would be up and off to prove the contrary; perhaps again, as on the last occasion, not even condescending to tell her where the trouble lay. Oh dear, it *would* be nice to have a husband who saw things sensibly and practically!—as one did oneself. How the two of them could then have put their heads together. Instead of her always having to make allowance for unreckonable impulses.

One comfort: there was no more talk on his part of going "home" with his fortune. The old foolish idea that he would be happier in England had been knocked on the head. At considerable expense, and much worry and trouble, poor old Richard! Still, if he *would* buy his experience in this costly fashion. . . . Here, however, Mary's musings were cut short by the entrance of Mrs. Devine, shawled and bonneted for driving, and struggling to button a magenta kid glove across a palm not built for such a covering: it bulged through the opening, creased and rolled with fat. The good lady was keyed up to a high pitch with domestic disasters—a chipped wineglass, a scrap of flue found under a bed— "Liars and deceivers every one, dearie!" But the great red face beamed with goodwill. No malice was in it; only the delights of the chase: so that the onlooker was reluctantly driven to conclude Mrs. Devine heartily enjoyed her slave-driving.

And, her private doubts and scruples notwithstanding, Mary could not but feel pleased and proud, for Richard's sake, at the stir caused by the announcement that he had no further need to practise medicine. Congratulations showered on him. Himself, he laughed, in his new, happy fashion.— "I declare, so much fuss they make, my dear, I might have discovered the North Pole"— And having got him safely away from the tyrannic rules Mrs. Devine considered essential to his comfort—or the comfort of his blue blood—and settled in a furnished house

near the Carlton Gardens, Mary prepared to guide him gently
and imperceptibly along the road she thought it for his good
he should go. In doing this, however, she found herself up
against a stone wall, in the shape of a hitherto unsuspected
trait in Richard: a violent aversion to returning on his traces.
When it dawned on him that she was still hankering after
Ballarat, he lost his temper, and vowed, with the utmost vehemence, that *when* he was done with a place, he was done, and
wild horses shouldn't drag him back to it.

"Good God, Mary! one's dead self would confront one at
every turn. Here one did this, there that. You don't stocktake,
my dear, when you are going on living in a place; but a break
—and even a brief one—forces you to it . . . in murderous fashion. I should thank you for the constant reminder how life is
flying, and how little one has made of it, and what a fool one
was in the past, and yet how full of hopes and aspirations."—
With cobwebby stuff such as this, there was no coming to
grips.

No, it was to be Melbourne this time. What was more, he
had resolved to build his own house. He was sick to death of
suiting his needs to those of other people.

Build? . . . well, yes, there was something to be said for it:
Mary hastily swallowed her dismay, seeing his feathers rise in
earnest. Build? . . . before he knew anything about a locality?
Why, a neighbour's fowls only needed to cackle or crow too
early of a morning, railway-whistles or church-bells sound too
plainly, and all his peace and pleasure would be gone. She was
not going to risk any such contingency as this, thank you! And
so, having wormed the information out of him that he leaned
to the district lying between St. Kilda and Brighton, she set to
work to make private inquiries. She took John into confidence,
and John and she laid their heads together, to circumvent
Richard in his harebrained scheme. A string or two was pulled;
and, one day, while Richard and she were driving round looking for a site, they happened, as if by chance, on the very
house to suit them. One, too, that was not yet in the public
market. As John had foreseen, Richard lost his heart to it on
the spot, and before the week was out had become its owner.—
Well! buying offhand was bad enough; but a good deal less
risky than building.

Houses in Melbourne were of two types: either spacious,

white, two-storied buildings, almost as broad as they were long, with balcony and verandah to the front, and needing but to stand in a sandy compound to advertise their origin; or low, sprawly villas, a single story high, covering much ground space, and wearing their circlet of verandah like a shady hat.— Mahony's purchase was of this latter kind.

Built some ten years previously by a wealthy squatter, who was now about to become a permanent absentee, it stood within half an hour's walk of the Brighton beach, on a quiet, sandy road, the edges of which were fringed with grass and capeweed. The grounds, running to between four and five acres, were all stocked and fully grown; and included kitchen-and flower-garden, a couple of croquet lawns, and a fair-sized orchard. From the gates, no glimpse of the house could be caught, so thick were the protecting shrubberies, so closely set the Scotch firs. These grounds turned the scales for Mahony. To get a garden—and such a garden—ready-made, instead of having to wait for it to grow! In the house itself the only alter-ation he planned was a large study to be thrown out on the orchard-side. Otherwise, it suited them to a nicety.

[3]

WHILE Richard haunted his new property and egged on the workmen, and sat drawing up a list of books for dispatch to an Edinburgh bookseller, Mary, in the intervals of choosing car-pets and curtains, fell to unravelling the knots and tangles into which the several members of her family had tied themselves. And after, for two years, having had to deal exclusively with a difficult, faddy person like Richard, she found this a com-paratively simple job. Those to whose aid she now came saw things from the same angle as herself, and they spoke a com-mon language.

Zara had first innings. Seated in the drawing-room of the Carlton house, Zara poured out her woes, with much drying of eyes, and the old, old recriminations against John. Never, she wept, had she met any one so hard, so self-centred as John. He was also too stingy to lift a finger to help you; and, in her opinion, richly deserved the misfortunes that had befallen him —Emma's untimely death, and the loss of Jinny; the disgrace of Johnny's flight, and Trotty's misdemeanours. Who could

wonder at it, indeed, if he had treated wives and children as
he was now treating her?

"But, Zara——"

Oh, John had the influence, could do it *easily*, if he chose.
But, of course, for that, he was too down on the match. As if
his own second marriage had been anything to boast of! Pray,
who was Jinny? A publican's daughter! . . . and, if the truth
was told, common as dirt. But my——

"I'm still utterly in the dark, Zara. Who is it John objects to
. . . that you want to marry?"

"Not *I* want to marry, if you please, Mary!" Zara's tone was
acid as a lemon. "It's *quite* the other way about. If it only
rested with *me*——"

"Yes, but *who?*"

"Haven't you wits enough to guess, my dear? Who is it that
has followed me and pestered—yes, *pestered!*—me with his attentions, ever since my first visit to Ballarat?"

Ballarat? Her first visit? . . . "Zara! You surely don't
mean——"

"My dear, I have not a heart of *stone*—like *some* people I
could mention: I can stand out no longer against his prayers
and persuasions. Year after year, year after year—not *many*
women, Mary, can boast of having inspired such devotion. He
worships the very ground I tread—and has done, ever since
those early days . . . though I was then little more than a child.
Of course, I am sensible he is not *quite* my equal——"

"Oh, good gracious, Zara, what does that matter, if you
really care for him? You know I've no patience with nonsense
of that kind."

Mary spoke with a robust heartiness; but her thoughts were
elsewhere, and travelled swiftly. In the two years that had
elapsed since last she saw her, Zara had crossed a subtle
boundary, and, from being a youngish person who looked a
trifle worn and tired, had turned into an elderly person who
looked young for her age: which made all the difference in
the world. For, alas! Zara's features were not of that well-
boned type, whose cameo outlines show up even better in the
middle years than under the plump padding of youth. Short,
irregular, piquant, they had depended wholly on freshness and
round contours for their charm. Now that the dimples had
run to lines, the cheeks hollowed, the skin sagged, Zara wore

512

the pathetic aspect of a faded child. When she drooped her
fine eyes, it was really sad, to one who loved her, to see how
haggard and old she looked. Poor Zara! All her choice offers
and good chances come to nothing. She had dangled them too
long; been over fastidious; and now it was too late. Mary
could read this out of what she said: this and more. Even the
posts open to her as finishing-governess were not, it appeared,
what they had once been. Younger women, competent to teach
the new-fangled "callisthenics," and dull, dry pieces by "Mo-
sar'," instead of the tuneful *morceaux* in which Zara excelled,
were now getting the plums. It did seem a shame, considering
Zara's talents, and her long experience; but so it was. Perhaps
she had grown a trifle "scratchy" with the years; and she
would no doubt be harder than ever to please. Her elegant
sprightliness was deserting her, too, giving place to a kind of
fixed pettishness.— And so, having thus rapidly turned the
matter over, Mary soothed her sister by promising to do her
best to further the marriage. She would beard John in his den,
and urge him to use his influence—according to Zara, he was
on friendly terms with a prominent member of the Baptist
Union—to procure for her intended, who was still, it leaked
out, but an unsalaried "helper," the pastorate that would enable them to wed.

"Meanwhile, you must bring Hemp . . . Mr. Hempel to
see us."

As visiting John at the Melbourne Club was, of course, out
of the question, Mary took the only slightly less bold step of
calling at the great warehouse in Flinders Lane. And having climbed a dark, steep stair to the first story, and passed
through various rooms, where clerks, perched on high stools,
stole curious glances at the apparition of a silk-and-velvet-clad
lady, whispered to be the senior partner's sister: this ordeal behind her, she arrived, a trifle pink and confused, at the door
of John's sanctum.

John himself emerged to meet her.

"Yes, John, quite alone. . . . I hope you won't mind. But I
wanted very much to see you."— And having regained breath
and composure, Mary lost no time in going straight to the core
of Zara's business.

John listened, with a patience he would have shown no one
else, his dark eyes, so like Mary's own, yet so much older in

513

worldly wisdom, turned intently on her.— "Objections to her
marrying? . . . she says so? My dear girl, as far as I, personally,
am concerned, my sister Zara may wed a navvy if she chooses
—I repeat, a navvy!—always provided, that is, he has the means
to support her, once the knot is tied. But this Methody-fellow,
now . . . have you seen him? No? Then, pray, do so without
delay, my dear, and Richard also. After which, let me hear, if
you please, if you are still of the same mind."

"Your sister Zara," he went on, "admits to having laid by,
in the course of her governessing, some five hundred pounds:
knowing Zara as we do, seven or eight hundred would, I make
no doubt, be nearer the mark. This sum, well invested, will ensure her yearly some eighty or ninety pounds—not a princely
income, I dare say, but, I think you will agree with me, sufficient for the requirements of a single female. Should she, however, fritter away her savings on this what's-his-name, it would,
in the event of his decease, fall to her relatives to support her.
Which I, for one, am not disposed to do."

Mary, in her turn, had refrained from interrupting. Now,
however, nothing daunted, she insisted on John viewing the
case from Zara's standpoint: the very natural desire of an
ageing woman for a home and a husband of her own; the
dreaded stigma of old-maidism; the weariness and monotony
of going on teaching other people's children year after year,
and year after year; the mortification of seeing younger women
chosen over your head, and your salary steadily decreasing as
you grew older. And, finally, by dint of what she afterwards
described to Richard as "this, that, and the other thing," she
got John so far as to promise that if, after seeing the bridegroom-elect, she still thought the marriage should go forward,
he would do what lay in his power to procure for Hempel the
pastorate in the little up-country township of Wangawatha, on
which Zara had set her heart.

This accomplished, Mary drew on her gloves, which she
had removed for the sherry and biscuits brought forth by John
from a cupboard with a: "Both dry unfortunately, my dear
girl, since I am not, as a rule, honoured by visits from the
sweet-toothed sex."

"And does business flourish, John?"

"It does, Mary. Yes, on that score I have nothing to complain of—nothing whatever. As you will have observed, we

have recently made considerable additions to the premises, and young MacDermott has been definitely taken into partnership.— Still, as far as I myself am concerned, I confess there come moments when, in spite of everything, I look round me and ask: *cui bono?* For whom do I build? . . . since there is no one to step into my shoes when I am gone."

John and *cui bono!* . . . John to talk of being "gone"! Mary's eyes widened and darkened. But she did not let the opportunity slip. "Look here, John, what I have always been meaning to say: I firmly intend to try and find out what has become of Johnny—and if possible get him home again. It seems dreadful to me that a boy of that age, and one I was so fond of, too, should just disappear, and perhaps never be heard of again. I feel convinced there was nothing radically wrong. He was just wilful, and headstrong, and got led astray by bad company. I can't help thinking, after this taste of hardship, he'd be ready to come back and settle down, and make you proud of him."

Was it fancy, or did a new expression flit over John's face at her words?—a kind of hope look out of his eyes? If so, it was gone again at once, drowned in the harsh expression he seemed to reserve for poor Emma's children. "Nay, I have washed my hands of him, Mary. He has publicly disgraced me.— And from all I hear, I fear his sister is about to follow the example he has set her."

At this Mary laughed outright. "Really, John! I'm surprised at you: letting yourself be imposed on by the tales of some prim old school-marm. You wait; I mean to have Trotty down to stay with me; and then I'll very soon find out the truth about her.— Besides, you know you *can't* wash your hands of your children, in this way; it's unnatural. I wish to goodness I could see you comfortably settled in your own house once more, with them all about you. This is very well, but it *isn't* home."— And Mary's glance swept the leaded windows, the cobwebbed corners, the white dust on books and papers, the dimness of the office furniture; to end with John himself. To her eye, he had a rather uncared-for appearance nowadays; he looked unbrushed, much less spruce than of old.

"Well, well!" John, his elbows on the arms of his chair, lightly met his ten fingers and tipped them, to a shrug of the shoulders. "Ah! had it pleased the Almighty to make women

515

other than they are—yourself excepted, my dear Mary, always excepted. But that reminds me. I have been intending, for some time past, to ask you to drive out and go over the house, and report to me on its condition. The last person I placed in charge proved as untrustworthy as the rest."

Stowing away the key in her petticoat pocket, Mary gladly undertook the commission. And, as she jogged homewards in a wagonette, she felt well satisfied with what she had achieved; and not on Zara's score alone.— "Poor old John! He doesn't *know* how lonely and uncomfortable he is. Or how, in his heart of hearts, he's fretting for that boy."

Meanwhile, after considerable shilly-shallying, Zara had introduced Hempel afresh, in what proved an exceedingly painful visit.

"I declare," said Mary afterwards, "every time I spoke, I seemed to put my foot in it."

To begin with, it was plain at once what John had meant by his: wait till you have seen him! Hempel was now but the shadow of his former self, shrunken, emaciated, with overbright eyes, and a dry cough that took him in paroxysms, at the end of which he withdrew a spotted handkerchief from his lips.

Zara looked so annoyed when this happened, that, for her sake, Mary tried to seem unobservant. But after one particularly violent explosion, the words: "Oh, what *do* you do for it?" escaped her, in spite of herself.

"It's *nothing* in the world but the dust, Mary," cut in Zara smartly, before Hempel could reply. "I vow Carlton to be the dustiest suburb in all Melbourne. How you came to select it amazes me—positively it does!"

"I look upon it as a righteous affliction, ma'am," said Hempel loudly and slowly, and as though Zara had not spoken. "Such things are sent to try us. 'Oom the Lord loveth 'e chasteneth."

"Besides, he is perfectly well able to control it, if he chooses."
— Zara was so caustic that Mary hurriedly made a diversion by inviting her upstairs. And curiosity to hear a detailed account of the interview with John, got the better of Zara's patent reluctance to leave the two men alone together.

"He looks dreadfully delicate, Zara," said Mary dubiously, when the bedroom door had shut behind them.

"My dear Mary, a change of climate is *all* that is necessary.

516

We have taken the very *best* medical advice. I truly hope Richard will not go putting any far-fetched notions into his head."— And overriding Mary's delicate inquiries with a dramatic: "The happiness of my life is at stake!" Zara declined a chair, swept her crinoline about the room, and, having greedily extracted the gist of John's promises, knew no peace till they returned to the parlour.

Hempel—he now wore a short, woolly beard round face and throat—had certainly improved in his way of speaking. Still, he did have lapses; and these, Zara accentuated and underlined in distressing fashion. Throughout the visit, she sat bolt upright on the extreme edge of her chair, almost prompting the words into Hempel's mouth; and, at every misplaced or unaccomplished "h," she half-closed her eyes and drew in her breath with a semi-audible groan, as if the aspirate were a missile that had struck her. Hempel alone remained undisturbed by her behaviour. Richard, Mary knew, would be fuming inwardly at such tactlessness; and her own discomfiture was so acute that she trebled the warmth of her manner towards the unfortunate man.

"And now, what are we to call you?" she asked, as Zara rose to go. "Mister sounds too stiff altogether for a relation."

Instantly she saw that, with this well-meant question, she had made another mistake. Zara turned a dark red, and, flashing a warning glance at Hempel, began a hurried babble of adieus. But Hempel was either too dense or too obstinate to see.

"My name, ma'am, is Ebenezer." ("Edgar, Mary, Edgar is what I call him!") "Yes, Miss Turn'am 'ere"—and, so saying, Hempel signified Zara, without looking at her, by an odd little outwark jerk of the elbow, and a smile that struck even Mary as malicious—"Miss Turn'am don't cotton to it, and wants to persuade me to fancy names. But I say the one as my parents chose for me in the name of the Lord is good enough for me. So I'll be ableeged by Ebenezer, if you please."

"It's in the Bible, too, isn't it?" threw in Mary, feeling, if she did not see, the silent laughter with which Richard was shaking. And to herself she thought: "Oh dear, won't he catch it when he gets outside!"

"Ha ha! Serves her right . . . serves her very well right. Mrs. Ebenezer! Why, of course, it comes back to me now." ("I felt

517

sure it was Edward—or I shouldn't have asked," said Mary ruefully. "And now I shan't know what to call him. It puts me in
a regular box.") "But I can tell you this, my dear: your sister
Zara is about to commit a monstrous folly. The fellow is far
gone in phthisis. If Zara wants a job as sick-nurse, she'll get it
—and, upon my word, Mary, I don't know that she won't be
better employed in seeing the poor chap decently and comfortably into his coffin, than in grafting her insincerities and
affectations on the young. A more lukewarm bridegroom,
though, it has seldom been my lot to meet."

"How hard on her you are! Yes, both you and John. Every
woman *naturally* wants a husband . . . and a good thing, too,
or where would the world be?— Besides, if she doesn't marry,
you men are the first to twit her with being an old maid. But
if she shows any inclination for it, it's considered matter for a
joke . . . or not quite nice."

"Hear, hear! Why, love, at this rate we shall soon have
you clad in bloomers and spouting on a platform for women's
rights."

"Richard! Don't speak to me of such horrors.— But we're
talking about Zara. I must say, after seeing Hempel, I agree
with John, it's a ridiculous match. He really doesn't seem to
care that much for her——"

"Which is but natural. At his stage of the disease, a man is
entirely occupied with his own health . . . and his God."

"And I thought Zara most cutting with him. No, I'm afraid
she's taking him just to be married."

But, even as she said it, Mary had a glimpse into depths that
were closed to her menkind. Just to be married! It meant that
solace of the woman who was getting on in years—the plain
gold band on the ring finger. It meant no longer being shut out
from the great Society of Matrons; no longer needing to look
the other way were certain subjects alluded to; or pretending
not to notice the nods and winks, the silently mouthed words,
that went on behind your back. It was all very well when you
were young; when your very youth and innocence made up
for it: as you grew older, it turned to a downright mortification—like that of going in to dinner after the bride of eighteen.

"Besides, we *can't* dictate to Zara as if she was still a child.
She has a right to buy her own experience . . . even if it's only
with a poor creature like Hempel."

Another unspoken thought that lurked comfortably at the back of Mary's mind, was of the more than liberal pin-money Richard was now giving her. He had said expressly, too, she need render no account of how she spent it. Thus, should the worst happen, she would be able to see to it that neither he nor John had to put hand to pocket.

A last attempt to bring Zara to reason, however, she made. And having only succeeded in fanning the flames—sister-wise, Zara took interference less well from her than from any one —Mary tilted her chin, and sighing: "Well, we must just make the best of it!" forthwith requested John to do his share.

One thing, though, she did not yield in: she went off by herself to town, and bought the stuff for Zara's wedding dress. For Zara, she could see, was meditating satin and orange-blossoms; and, against this, all Mary's common sense rose in arms.— "For a place like Wangawatha! And with not even a Bishop to entertain. . . . I mean, Hempel being a Baptist." So she chose Madras muslin—finest Madras, which cost a good deal more than satin—and a neat bonnet trimmed with lilac.

"For these you can wear to chur—to chapel, Zara, you know, when the hot weather comes."— But Zara was so angry that she forgot to thank Mary for the gift, and tried the texture of the muslin between the thumb and finger, as if it were a bit of print.

And so a quiet wedding was celebrated at the Carlton house, a ceremony in which the only hitch was a somewhat lengthy pause for the bridegroom to recover his breath, after a fit of coughing; a glass of champagne was drunk to the health of the newly wedded; and off they went in a shower of rice which Mary took care was thick enough to satisfy even Zara. Nor was a satin slipper forgotten, for the back of the carriage-and-pair, all flowered and favours, which Mahony had provided to drive the happy couple to the *Silver Crown*, the steamboat on which they would sail down the Bay to Sorrento.

The very last thing, upstairs in the bedroom, Mary pressed a small wad of notes into Zara's hand. "A bit of my wedding present to you, dear Zara. Now don't stint on your honeymoon. Put up at the best hotel, and enjoy yourselves. Remember, one is only married once."

"*Merci, ma bonne Marie, merci!*" said Zara: in the course of the past hour she had gradually taken on the allures of an

elder married woman towards her junior. "But I should have
done so, in any case."

❧   ❧   ❧   ❧   ❧   ❧

The rice swept up, the hundred and one boxes of wedding
cake dispatched, which should intimate to even the least of
Zara's acquaintances that she had quitted the single state,
Mary turned to her next job, and drove one morning to St.
Kilda to inspect John's house. She went by herself, for she
thought John would not thank you to have other eyes than hers
quizzing his neglected home. And she was glad indeed no one
else was present, when, the coachman having unlocked the
front door and drawn up the blinds for her, she was free to
wander through the deserted rooms. The house had stood
empty almost as long as she had been absent from the colony;
and, in such a climate as this, two years spelt ruin. No window
or door had fitted tightly enough, when hot winds and their
accompanying dust-storms swept the town. The dust crunched
gritty underfoot; lay in a dense white layer over all tables and
polished surfaces; made it impossible to look out of the windows. The cobwebs that hung from the corners of the ceilings,
and festooned the lustred chandeliers, were thick as string
with it. You could hardly see yourself in the mirrors for fly-
specks, or see the wax flowers under their shades. Everywhere,
in hundreds, flies and blowflies lay dead. Moths had ravaged
each single woollen article she laid hand on. The beautiful
Brussels carpets were eaten into holes, as were also curtains
and bed-hangings, table-covers, and the backs of wool-worked
chairs. It was truly a scene of desolation.

In John's bedroom she chanced to open a leaf of the great
triple-fronted mahogany wardrobe, to look if any clothes had
been left hanging to share in the general dilapidation; and
there, the first thing she lighted on was a shawl of "poor
Jinny's"—or what had once been a shawl, for it was now riddled like a colander, and all but fell to pieces as she touched
it. For a moment Mary stood lost to the present. What memories that shawl called up! Of softest white cashmere, with
a handsome floral border, it had been John's present to Jinny
on the birth of their first child: "And if the next's a boy, Jane,
I promise you one of richest India silk, my love!" But, even so,

this gift had filled Jinny's cup to the brim. Mary could only remember it wrapped in tissue paper, tied with bows of ribbon, and smelling of camphor to knock you down—Jinny had hardly dared to wear it, for fear the dust should discolour it, or the sun fade the bordering. There had been quite a quarrel one day, when John and she were staying with them in Ballarat, because Jinny had visited the Ococks in her second-best. "Far from me be it, Mary, to inculcate an extravagant spirit in Jane, or encourage her to run up bills at the milliner's. But she is now my wife, and it is her duty to dress accordingly," had been John's way of putting it. Well, poor Jinny! she might just as well have worn her finery and worn it out . . . as only have had it on her back some dozen times in all. She was gone where no shawls were needed.

"It's really a lesson not to hoard one's clothes, but to use and enjoy them while you can. Not to get anything too grand, either, which makes it seem a pity to wear.

"John ought to have given all such things away," she said to herself a few minutes later. For a nudge of memory had drawn her to a lumber-room, where four zinc-and-wood saratogas were lined up in a row. These held all that remained to mortal eyes of "poor Emma." For Jinny had once, soon after marriage, confessed to a wild fit of jealousy, in which she had packed away every scrap of her predecessor's belongings.— Fifteen years dead! The things were now, no doubt, mere rags and tatters, for the box-lid was not made that could keep out the moth. Some day, she, Mary, must make it her business to run through them, to see if no little enduring thing was left that could be handed on to Trotty, as a memento of her long-dead mother.——

"Regular Bluebeard's chambers!" was Richard's comment, when she told him of her discoveries.

But Mary had her thinking-cap on, and sat cogitating how she could best reduce John's affairs to order. The house must be opened up without loss of time, scrubbers and cleaners turned in, painters and upholsterers, and then . . .

A few days later, she came home radiant.

"I've got the very *person* for John!" and, undoing her bonnet-strings, she threw them back with an air of triumph.— It was a hot November afternoon.

"What? . . . yet again?" quoth Mahony, and having kissed her good-day, he laid his book face downward on his knee, and prepared to listen. "Tell me all about it."

"Quite one of the most sensible women I've ever met."

"Then, my dear, you do *not* mean pretty Fanny!"

For Mary had been out spending a couple of days with the young pair at Heidelberg, to pay her over-due respects to the cottage of which she had heard so much.

"It really is a dear little place. And kept in apple-pie order."

She had soon discovered, though, that the prevailing neatness and nicety were not the result of any brilliant housewifely qualities in the little bride. The good genius proved to be an aunt—"Auntie Julia"—who had had charge of the motherless girl since birth.

"One of those neat, brisk little women, Richard, who do everything they put their hands to, well, and without fuss. Her hair's grey, but she is not really old. What struck me first was when she said: 'Now please don't imagine I'm a fixture here, Mrs. Mahony. I just came to help my little Fan over her first troubles in setting up house. Believe me, I don't hold with old aunts—or mothers either—quartering themselves upon the newly wed. Young people should be left to their own devices—learn to look for aid to each other alone.— No! poor old Auntie Julia's job is done; she's permanently out of work.'"

It was here Mary thought she descried a light in John's darkness. Taking the bull by the horns, she there and then told Miss Julia the story of her brother's two marriages, and of his vain attempts to live in peace and harmony with Zara.

"Poor fellow, poor fellow! Dear Mrs. Mahony, I agree with you: relatives are not the easiest people in the world to get on with. They are either so much alike that each knows all the time just what the other is thinking—and that is fatal; for, if you won't mind my saying so, the private thoughts we indulge in, even of our nearest, are not of a fit kind to be made public." ("But with such a merry twinkle in her eye, Richard, that it took away anything that might have sounded sharp or biting.") "Or else brothers and sisters are so different and contrary that they might have been born on different planets."

Next, Mary enumerated the long line of housekeepers who had wandered in their day through John's establishment. "In at one door, and out at the next!"

"Aha! You needn't tell me where the shoe pinched there. I
see, I see. Each of 'em in turn set her cap at the fascinating
widower—thought she was *the* one chosen by fate to fill your
poor sister-in-law's place. Now, may I speak frankly? If *I* take
the post, you may make your mind perfectly easy on that
score. I'm not of the marrying sort. Some men are born to be
bachelors; some women, bless 'em, what's known as old maids.
I can assure you, my dear Mrs. Mahony, I am happiest in the
single life. Nor have I missed having a family of my own, for
my little Fan here has been as much mine as though I had
borne her."— Here, however, seeing Mary's rather dubious air,
she laid a hand on her arm, and added reassuringly: "But don't
be afraid, my dear. I do not noise these views abroad. They're
just between you, and me, and the tea-caddy."

"It was really said very nicely, Richard—not at all indeli-
cately."

"All the same, I should give her a hint that such radical ideas
would be fatal to her prospects with his lordship," said Mahony, who had recently smarted anew under his brother-in-
law's heavy-handed patronage.

"Nonsense! She won't talk like that to a *man*.— And I feel
sure I'm right; she's the very person."

And so she was. No sooner had John, on Mary's recommendation, made definite arrangements with Miss Julia, than
tangles seemed to straighten of themselves. Hers was a master
mind. In less than no time, the house was cleaned, renovated,
repaired; efficient servants were engaged; John was transferred
from his uncomfortable Club quarters to a comfortable do-
mesticity. And Miss Julia proved herself of an exquisite tact in
running the establishment, in meeting John's wishes, in agreeing with him without yielding a jot of her own convictions.
And thereafter, John—"He couldn't, of course, let the credit for
the changed state of affairs go out of the family!"—John went
about singing Mary's praises, and congratulating himself on
being the possessor of so capable a sister.

Next, Jinny's three mites were brought home from boarding-
school; and together Mary and Miss Julia stripped them of
their "uniforms," undid their meagre little rats'-tails, and freed
their little bodies from the stiff corsets in which even the infant
Josephine was encased. Three pleasant-faced, merry-eyed little
girls emerged, who soon learned to laugh and play again, and

filled the dead house with the life it needed. They adored Auntie Julia; and were adored by their father, as of old.

There remained only Trotty—or Emmy, as she was now called. Mary had confabbed with Miss Julia, and they had shaken their heads in unison over John's extraordinary attitude towards his first family. But, on meeting the girl, Miss Julia struck her palms together, and cried: "What! stand out against *that*? . . . my dear, have *no* fear! Just let your brother grow used to seeing such a daughter opposite him at breakfast, and he'll soon miss her if she chances to be absent. *Exactly* what he needs to preside over his dinner-table. It shall be my task to train her for the post."

In the meantime, however, Mary kept Emmy at her own side, in order to renew acquaintance with one she had known so well as a child.

[4]

EMMY also served to fill a gap.

As always, when forced to live at haphazard, without a fixed daily routine, Mahony was restless, and ill at ease. He had not even a comfortable room to retire to: his present den was the dull little back parlour of a town house. Books, too, he came very short in; it did not seem worth while unpacking those he had brought out with him; and the newly ordered volumes could not be expected to arrive for months to come. Nor did he even see much of Mary: what time she had to spare from her relatives was spent in endless discussions with decorators and upholsterers.

The company of his young niece was thus a real boon to him. Emmy had no obligations, was free to go with him when and where he chose. What was more, with neither the cares of a family nor of house-furnishing on her mind, her thoughts never strayed. And a sound friendship sprang up between the oddly matched pair. No longer afraid of her uncle, Emmy displayed a gentle, saucy, laughing humour. Mahony hired a little horse for her, and they rode out together, she pinned up in Mary's old habit; rode out early of a morning, while other people were still fast asleep. Their first destination was invariably the new house, to see what progress had been made since the day before: holding her habit high, Emmy would run from

room to room, exclaiming. Thence they followed quiet, sandy
tracks that led through stretches of heath and gorse to the sea.
Or they strolled on foot, Emmy hanging on her uncle's arm
and chattering merrily: a simple-hearted, unaffected girl, as
natural as she was pretty, which was saying a good deal, for
she promised, one of these days, to be a regular beauty. "Strawberries and cream" was Mahony's name for her. She had in-
herited her mother's ripe-corn fairness, and limpid, lash-swept
eyes; but the wild-rose complexion of the English-born woman
had here been damped to palest cream, in which, as a striking
contrast, stood out two lovely lips of a vivid carnation-red—
a daring touch on the part of nature, that already drew men's
eyes as she passed. In person, she was soft and round and
womanly. But the broad little hands, with their slyly bitten
nails, were still half a child's. She was childishly unconscious,
too, of her attractions, innocent in the use to which she put
them; and blushed helplessly, did anyone remark on her appearance—as the outspoken people who surrounded her were
only too apt to do. Without being in the least clever, she had
a bright, open mind, and drank in, with interest, all Mahony
could give her: tales of his travels, or of the early days; de-
scriptions of books and plays; little homilies on the wonders
of nature. If he had a fault to find with her, it was that she
seemed just as sweetly grateful for, say, "Auntie Julia's" en-
joinders how to hold her crochet-needle, or hints on dress and
deportment, as to him for his deeper lore. Yes, the child had
an artless and inborn desire to please, and dissipated her favours in a manner that belonged very surely to her age . . . *and*
her sex. For he might say "child," but let him remember that
his own little Polly-Mary had been but a couple of months
older, when he ran her off from among her playmates and
friends.

Altogether, there was much about John's daughter—no! not
thus would he put it—about Mary's niece, that reminded him
of Mary herself, as a little mouse of a bride, long years ago.
And not the least striking point of resemblance was this whole-
hearted surrender of attention. It would, of course, be unreasonable to expect the faculty to persist: life in its course
brought, to even the fondest of wives, distractions, cares, and
interests of her own. But there was no denying it, this lack
of preoccupation it was, this freedom—even emptiness, if you

would—of mind, into which oneself poured the contents, that rendered a very young woman so delightful a companion.

And when, at length, the move to the new house was made, and Mahony set about unpacking, arranging and cataloguing the books he had, and planning where those to come should be shelved, Emmy was still his right hand. Mary, busy with strange servants, with the stocking of kitchen and larder, could do no more than occasionally look in to see how the two of them were getting on, and keep them supplied with refreshment. Good-naturedly, she yielded Emmy entirely to Richard, who now passed to overhauling his minerals, plants, and butterflies, all of which collections had made the journey to England with him and back. And glass cases, stacks of blotting-paper, and sheets of cork were set up afresh in this big, pleasant room, the windows of which looked down a vista cut through spreading oleanders, to where, in the orchard, peach and almond-blossom vied in pinkness against a pale blue sky.

But, not very long now, and Emmy was spirited away to grace her father's table. Then, his own affairs in order, domestic appointments running smoothly, Mahony, before settling down to study, drove out with Mary in the neat brougham he had given her, to return some of the visits that had been paid them. Later on, too, he accompanied her to dinners, balls, and soirées; or played the host at his own table, which Mary soon surrounded with guests.

The society in which they here found themselves had a variety and a breadth about it that put it on a very different footing from either the narrow Ballarat circle of earlier years, or the mediaeval provincialism into which they had stumbled overseas. And moments came when, squarely facing the facts, Mahony admitted to himself he might go farther and fare worse: in other words, that he could now never hope to know anything better. The most diverse tastes were catered for. There was the ultra-fashionable set that revolved round Government House and the vice-regal entertainments; that covered the lawns at Flemington and Caulfield; drove out in splendid four and six-in-hands to champagne picnics at Yan Yean; overflowed the dress circle at the Theatre Royal, where Bandmann was appearing in his famous rôles; the ladies decked for all occasions—lawn, theatre, picnics, dusty streets alike—in the flimsiest and costliest of flowing robes. At the head of this

aristocracy of wealth stood those primitive settlers, the great
squatter-kings, owners of sheep-runs that counted up to a hundred thousand acres: men whose incomes were so vast that
they hardly knew how to dispense them, there existing here
no art treasures to empty the purse, nor any taste to buy them,
had they existed. Neither did travel tempt these old colonists,
often of humble origin, whose prime had been passed buried
in the bush; while it had not yet become the fashion to educate sons and daughters "at home." Since, however, fortunes
were still notoriously precarious—flood or fire could ruin a man
overnight—and since, too, the sense of uncertainty that characterised the early days had bitten too deep ever to be got out
of the blood, "spend while you may" remained the motto men
lived by. And this led to a reckless extravagance that had not
its equal anywhere in the world. Women lavished fortunes on
dress, which grew to be a passion in this fair climate; on jewellery with which to behang their persons; on fantastic entertainments; men drank, betted, gambled; while horse-racing
had already become, with both sexes, the obsession it was to
remain.— This stylish set—it also included fabulously lucky
speculators, as well as the great wool-buyers—Mahony did not
do much more than brush in passing. His sympathies inclined
rather to that which revolved round the trusty prelate who,
having guided the destinies of the Church through the ups and
downs of its infancy, now formed a pivot for the intellectual
interests of the day—albeit of a somewhat non-progressive,
anti-modern kind. Still, the atmosphere that prevailed in the
pleasant rooms at "Bishopscourt" was the nearest thing to be
found here to the urbane, unworldly air of English university
or cathedral life.— Next in order came the legal luminaries,
Irishmen for the most part, with keen, ugly faces and scath-
ingly witty tongues; men whose enormous experience made
them the best of good company. To which clique also belonged the well-known surgeons and physicians of the eastern
hill; the bankers, astutest of financiers; with, for spice, the
swiftly changing politicians of the moment, here one day, gone
the next, with nothing but their ideas or their energy to recommend them, and dragging with them wives married in their
working days . . . well, the less said of the wives the better.

Such was the society in which Mahony was now called on
to take his place. And the result was by so much the most vivid

expression of his personality he had yet succeeded in giving, that it became *the* one that imprinted itself on men's minds, to the confusion of what had gone before and was to come after: became the reality from which his mortal shadow was thrown.— "Mahony?" would be the query in later years. "Mahony? Ah yes, of course, you mean Townshend-Mahony of *Ultima Thule*,"—this being the name he had bestowed on his new house.— Mary regarded him fondly and with pride. Certain it was, no matter in what circles he moved, whose dinnertable he sat at, whose hearthrug he stood on, he was by far the most distinguished-looking man in the room. And not only this: a kind of mellowness now descended on him, a new tolerance with his fellow-men; while an inner peace seemed to shine through his eyes. The lines of work and worry disappeared; he filled out both in face and figure, and loved to tease Mary by declaring he was on the high road to growing fat. He brushed up his musical accomplishments, too; and his pleasant tenor, his skill as a flute-player, brought him into fresh demand. Miss Timms-Kelly, Judge Kelly's daughter, who had quite the finest amateur voice in Melbourne, was heard to say she preferred Richard's second in a duet, to any other; and many an elaborate aria, full of shakes and trills, did she warble to his obbligato on the flute.

How happy all this made Mary, she could not have told. To know Richard even moderately contented would have satisfied her; to see him actually taking pleasure in life caused her cup to run over. She had now not a care left, hardly a wish unfulfilled. And she showed it. The eclipse in health and good looks she had suffered by reason of her transplantation was past: never had she felt better than at present; while, in appearance, she bloomed anew—enjoyed a kind of Indian summer. At thirty-two, an age when, in the trying climate of the colony, a woman was, as often as not, hopelessly faded, Mary did not need to fear comparison with young ladies ten years her junior. Her skin was still flawless, her eye as brilliant, her hair as glossy as of old. In figure she inclined to the statuesque, without being either too tall or too full: arms and shoulders were unsurpassed in their rounded whiteness. A certain breadth of brow alone prevented her, at this stage of her life, from being classed among the acknowledged beauties of her sex: it lent her a thoughtful air, where she should have been merely pleasing.— But, after all, what did this matter? Her real beauty, as Richard often reflected, consisted in the warmth and loving-kindness that beamed from her eyes, illuminating a face which never a malicious thought had twisted or deformed. Her expression was, of course, no more one of utter unsuspicion—experience had seen to that—just as her mind was no longer afflicted with the adorable blindness that had been its leading trait in girlhood. Mary now knew very well that evil existed, and that mortals were prone to it. But she would not allow it could be inborn; held fast to her unconquerable belief in the innate goodness of every living soul; and was never at a loss to exonerate the sinner.— "No wonder he's what he is, after the life he has been forced to lead. We mightn't have turned out any better ourselves, with his temptations." Or: "She has never had a chance, poor thing! Circumstances have always been against her."

With her anxieties on Richard's behalf, Mary's ambitions for him—that he should climb the tree, make a name—also gradually sank to rest. Her mind was thus at liberty to follow its own bent. Now, fond though she was of her fellow-creatures, the formal round of social life had never made a very deep appeal to her: she liked to see people merry and enjoying themselves, but she herself needed something more active to engross her. Her house, well staffed, well run, claimed only a fraction of her attention. Hence, she had now plenty of time to devote herself to what Richard called her true mission in life: the care of others—especially of the poor and suffering, the unhappy and unsure. And many a heart was lightened by having Mary to lean on, her strong common sense for a guide. Her purse, too, was an unending solace. Even in the latter years in Ballarat, she had had to dispense her charities carefully, balancing one against another, saving something here, to give away there. Now, her income was equal to all the calls made on it . . . and more . . . Richard generously bidding her add to her own pin-money anything left over from the handsome cheque he gave her for housekeeping expenses. And since he, mindful of his promise, never inquired what she did with it, she was at last free to give as royally as she chose . . . in any direction.— But if he did not ask to see her passbook, neither did she see his: he would not have her troubling her head, he said, about their general expenditure. At first, she rather demurred at this: she

529

would have liked to know, say, how their outlay per month tallied with the sum at their disposal; and she missed the talks they had been used to have, over how best to portion out their income. But Richard said those days were over and done with: she would lose her way, he teased her, among sums of four figures—for, in a twinkling, his late-found affluence had thrown him back on the traditional idea, that money affairs were the man's province, not the woman's. For her comfort, he stressed once more the fact that he did not intend to speculate; also that at long last, he would, despite the enormous premium, be able to insure his life. In the event of anything happening to him, she would be well provided for, and thus might now spend what he gave her, freely and without scruple. So, yielding to these persuasions, Mary acquiesced in the new arrangement, and gradually slipped into the delightful habit of taking money for granted. After all, the confidence was mutual: he trusted her not to run up, on the sly, bills at milliner's or jeweller's; she, too, had to trust in her turn. She valued his faith in her, and was careful not to abuse it. Her own accounts were scrupulously kept: just as in the old days, she wrote down every shilling she spent, and knitted her brows over the half-pennies; with the result that she soon began to accumulate a tidy little nest-egg.

Her charities were her sole extravagance, her personal wants remaining few and simple.— Besides, Richard was for ever making her presents. For it could not, with truth, be said of him that his tastes did not expand with his purse—or the fact might be that he satisfied needs only too long repressed. At any rate, he put his men-servants into livery, stocked his cellars, bought silver table-appliances and egg-shell china, had his crest stamped wherever it could find a place. And the things he bought for Mary were of the same costly nature. In addition to the carriage, which, she had to admit, was both useful and necessary, his gifts included jewellery (which she wore more to please him than because she had any real liking for it)—rings and chains, brooches and bracelets—all things *his* wife ought to have, and never had had: curling ostrich feathers for hat and fan; gold-mounted mother-of-pearl opera-glasses; hand-painted fans; carved ivory card-cases; ivory-backed brushes and silver vinaigrettes: any fal-lal, in short, that struck his eye or caught his fancy.

There came a day on which he fairly outdid himself. Soon after inscribing their names in the visiting-book at Government House, they received invitations to a ball there, in honour of two men-of-war that were anchored in the Bay—a very select affair indeed: none of your promiscuous May Day crushes! As it would be their first appearance in style, Mahony —a trifle uncertain whether Mary would do the thing handsomely enough—insisted on fitting her out. The pale blue silk he chose for her gown was finest Lyons, the cost of which, without making, ran to thirty pounds: Mary had never seen a silk like it. It was got privatim, through John, who had it direct from the French factory. John, too, was responsible for the crowning glory of Mary's attire. For, after Richard had added a high, pearl-studded Spanish comb for her hair, John one day showed him a wonderful shawl that had just come into the warehouse, suggesting it would look well on Mary. For once Mahony found himself in agreement with his brother-in-law. Of softest cashmere, supple as silk—and even softer to the touch—the scarlet ground of the shawl was well-nigh hidden by a massive white Indian embroidery; so that the impression gained was one of sumptuous white silk, broken by flecks of red. It was peaked, burnous-like, to form a hood, and this and the corners were hung with heavy white silk tassels. So magnificent an affair was it that Mary had severe qualms about wearing it: in her heart she considered it far too showy and elaborate. But Richard had no doubt paid an enormous price for it, and would be hurt, into the bargain, if she said what she thought.

He himself was charmed with the effect, when she draped the cloak over the sky-blue of her gown.— "Upon my word, my dear, you'll put every other woman in the shade!"

But even he was not prepared for the stir that ran through the ballroom on their arrival. In among the puces and magentas the rose-budded pinks and forget-me-notted blues, came Mary, trailing a bit of oriental splendour, and wearing it, as only she could, with a queenly yet unconscious air.

Seated on a dais among the matrons—for, nowadays, she danced only an occasional "square," leaving round dances to the young—Mary drew the fire of all eyes.

And it was not the opera-cloak alone.

"A skin like old Florentine ivory!" declared an Englishman

531

fresh from "home." The guest of the Governor, he was wandering through this colonial assembly much as a musical connoisseur might wander through a cattle-yard. Till Mary caught his eye. . . . And when she dropped the cloak, for the honour of a quadrille with his Excellency, this same visitor was heard to dilate on the tints cast by the blue on the ivory . . . to murmur of Goya . . . Velasquez.

Subsequently he was introduced, and sat by her side for the better part of an hour.

At two o'clock, when Mahony handed her to the carriage, it was with something of the lover-like élan that even the least fond husband feels, on seeing his wife the centre of attraction. "Now, Madam! . . . wasn't I right? Who was the success of the evening, I should like to know?"

"Oh, Richard . . . Put up the window, dear; it's cold. If there can be any talk of a success . . . then it's the cloak you mean, not me."

"It took you to carry it off, love. Not another woman in the room could have done it. Made it seem very well worth the price I had to pay for it."

"Which reminds me: you haven't yet told me what that was."

"My business, sweetheart! Yours to play the belle, and get compared to the old masters by admiring strangers."

"*Really*, Richard!" Mary made the deprecating movement of the chin with which she was wont to rebuke extravagances. "Why, dear, he was so high-falutin I didn't know half the time what he was talking about." Then, fearing she had been too severe, she added: "Of course, I'm very glad you were pleased," —and hoped that was the end of it. Compliments, even from one's husband, were things to be evaded if possible. "Well, I must remember poor Jinny, and not hoard it up for the moths to get at." But there was more than a dash of doubt in Mary's tone, and she sighed. Not merely for Jinny. She did not know when another opportunity so splendid as this evening's would arise. For an ordinary one, such finery would certainly be out of place.

"Wear it or not, as you please, love. It has served its end . . . stamped itself on a moment of time," said Mahony, and fell therewith into a brown study.

But, as he helped her from the carriage, he stooped and

kissed her . . . which Mary was very much afraid the coachman saw.

[5]

THAN queening it at balls, she felt more in her element seated
in a rather dingily furnished drawing-room, holding poor
Agnes Ocock's hand.

Although it had struck five, and the worst heat of the day
was over, Agnes was still in her bedgown—she had been lying
down with the headache, she said—nor could Mary persuade
her to exchange this for bonnet and shawl, and drive out with
her in the brougham that stood at the door.

"Another time, dearest, if you do not mind. To-day I have
no fancy for it."

Mary was shocked by the change the past six months had
worked in her friend; and disagreeably impressed by the com-
mon-featured house in which she found her: it had no garden,
but stood right on the dusty St. Kilda Parade. Agnes was growing very stout; her fine skin looked creased—like her robe—her
cheek was netted with veins, her hair thin, under a cap set
awry. Mary knew the rumours that were current; and her heart
swelled with love and pity.

"Just as you like, dear. And how are the children? Are they
in? May I see them?"

"Oh, yes, the children . . . Why . . . the truth is, dearest
Mary, I haven't . . . they are not with me. Henry thought . . .
he thought——"

Agnes's voice broke, and after a painful struggle to compose
herself, she hid her face in her hands.

Leaning forward, Mary laid an arm around her shoulders.
"Dearest Agnes, won't you tell me your trouble? Is it the little
one you . . . you lost, you are fretting over?"

And now there was no sound in the room but that of
crying—and such crying! It seemed difficult to connect these
heavy, nerve-racking sobs with the lovely, happy little Agnes
of former days. Holding her close, Mary let her weep un-
stintedly.

"Oh, Mary, Mary! I am the most miserable creature alive."

Yes, it was the loss of the child that was breaking her heart
. . . or rather, the way in which she had lost it.

538

"It was the finest baby you ever saw, Mary—neither of the others could compare with it. They were all very well, as little things; but this one. . . . His tiny limbs were so round and smooth—it was like kissing velvet—and yet so firm. And dimples everywhere. And he was born with a head of golden hair—like spun glass—so fine. I never knew Henry so pleased and proud. He said such a child did me credit . . . and this used rather to make me wonder, Mary; for Baby wasn't a bit like Henry . . . or like the other two. He resembled my family; had blue eyes; we named him after my father, because of it. But do you know who he reminded me of most of all? I've never told anyone before; but I'll tell you. It was of Eddie, Mary . . . and, through Eddie, of Mr. Glendinning. When Eddie was born he used to lie in my lap, just as soft and fair . . . and sometimes I think I forgot, and imagined this baby *was* Eddie over again . . . and that made me still fonder of him; for one's first *is* one's first, love, no matter how many come after. And then . . . then . . . He was five months old, and trying to grasp things, and taking notice—oh, such a happy, happy babe! And then, one morning, I wasn't feeling well, Mary—the doctor said the nursing of such a hearty child was a great strain on me; it was so hard to keep my strength up: then a giddy fit took me—I had been giving him the breast, and got up to lay him down—nurse wasn't there. I must have been dizzy with sitting so long stooped over him— I even think I had dozed a little—and he was so heavy for his age. I got up, and came over faint all of a sudden— the doctor says so . . . and I tottered, Mary, and Baby fell— fell out of my arms . . . on his little head—I heard the thud— yes, the thud . . . but not a cry or a sound . . . nothing . . . nothing . . . he never cried again."

"Oh, my poor Agnes! Oh, you poor, poor thing!"

Mary was weeping, too; the tears ran down her cheeks as she sat and listened, and let Agnes sob her heart out. But she made no attempt to palliate or console; did not speak of an accident, for which it was impossible to blame yourself; or of God's will, mysterious, inscrutable: she just grieved, with an intensity of feeling that made her one with the bereft. Things of this kind went too deep for words; were hurts from which there could be no recovery. Time might grow its moss over them . . . hide them from mortal sight . . . that was all.

As she drove home, she reflected, pitifully, how strange it was that so soft and harmless a creature as Agnes should thus be singled out for some of life's hardest blows. Agnes had so surely been born for happiness—and to make others happy. Misfortunes such as these ought to be kept for people of stronger, harder natures, and with broader backs; who could suffer, and still carry their heads high. Agnes was merely crushed to earth by them . . . like a poor little trampled flower.

But before she reached the house, a fearful suspicion crossed her mind.

Tilly nodded confirmingly.

"The plain English of it is, she was squiffy."

And went on: "It was hushed up, my dear, you bet!—kept dark as the grave . . . doctor changed, etc. etc. They actually 'ad the face to put it down to the *nurse's* carelessness; said nurse being packed off at once, *handsomely remunerated,* mind you, to hold 'er tongue. An' a mercy the child died; the doctor seemed to think it might 'ave been soft, 'ad it lived— after such a knock on the pate—and *can* you see 'Enry dragging the village idiot at 'is heels? *Never* was a man in such a fury, Mary. Ugh! that white face with those little pitch-black eyes rolling round in it—it gave me the fair shakes to look at 'im. 'Pon my word, I believe, if 'e'd dared, 'e'd 'ave slaughtered Agnes there and then. *His* child, *his* son!—you know the tune of it. 'E'll never forgive 'er, you mark my words he won't! . . . the disgrace, and all that—for, of course, everybody knew all about it, and a good deal more. She was odd enough before- hand, never going anywhere. Now, she's taking the sea-air at St. Kilda, and, if you ask me, she'll go on taking it . . . till Doomsday."

"The very way to drive her to despair!" cried Mary; and burned.

Tilly shrugged. "It's six of one and 'alf a dozen of the other, to my mind. I'd almost rather be put away to rot like a poi- soned rat in an 'ole, than live under the whip of Mossieu Henry's tongue—not to mention 'is eye!"

"Agnes shall not die like a rat in a hole, if *I* can help it."

"Ah, but you can't, my dear! . . . don't make any mistake about that. You might as well try to bend a bar of iron as 'Enry.— And I must say, Mary, it does sometimes seem a good deal of fuss to make over one small kid. She can 'ave more for the asking."

"*Tilly!*" Mary looked up from her sewing—the two women sat on the verandah of Tilly's house in Ballarat, where Mary was visiting—in reproof and surprise, at a speech so unlike her friend. It was not the first, either; Tilly often wore a mopy, world-weary air nowadays, which did not sit naturally on her.— "Each child that lives is just itself," added Mary. "That's why one loves it so."

"Oh, well, I s'pose so. And as you know, love, I'd 'ave 'ad a dozen if I could. It wouldn't 'ave been one too many to fill this 'ouse."

Mary believed she read the answer to the riddle. "Look here, Tilly, you're lonely . . . that's what's the matter with you."

And Tilly nodded, dumpily—again unlike herself.

"Fact is, Mary, I want something to *do*. As long as dear old Pa lived, and I 'ad the boys to look after, it was all right— I never knew what it was to be dull. But now . . . P'r'aps if they'd let me keep Tom and Johnny . . . or if I could groom my own 'orses, or ride 'em at the stakes . . . No, no, of course, I know it wouldn't do—or be *commy faut*. It's only my gab."

"I wonder, Tilly," said Mary, "I wonder if . . . have you never thought, dear, at times like these, that . . . that perhaps you might some day marry again?" She put the question very tentatively, knowing Tilly's robust contempt for the other sex. But Tilly answered pat: "Why, that's just what I 'ave, Mary."

"Oh!" said Mary. Then, to cover up her amazement, she added: "I think it would be the very best thing that could happen."

There followed a pause of some length. Mary did not know what to make of it. Tilly was humming and hawing: she fidgeted, coloured, shifted her eyes.

"Yes, my dear," she said at length, in answer to Mary's invitation to speak out: "I *have* something on my chest . . . something I want to say to you, Mary, and yet don't quite know 'ow. Fact is, I want you to do me a good turn, my dear. No, now just you wait a jiff, till you 'ear what it is. Tell you what, Mary, I've found meself regularly down in the mouth of late—off me grub—and that sort of thing. No, Pa's death 'as nothing whatever to do with it. I was getting on famously—

536

right as a trivet—till . . . well, till I went to town—yes, that time, you know, to meet you and the doctor." And, as Mary still sat blank and uncomprehending, she blurted out: "Oh, well . . . till I saw . . . oh, *you* know!—till I met *a certain person* again."

"A certain person? Do you . . . Tilly! Oh, Tilly, do you *really? Purdy?*"

Tilly nodded, heavily, gloomily, without the ghost of a smile. "Yes, it's a fact—and not one I'm proud of either, as you can guess. And yet again, I ask meself, why not? I need *some* one to look after, Mary . . . and that's the fair truth. 'E's down on 'is luck, as always; can't get the money to stick; and I've more than I know what to do with. And to see 'im there, lookin' so poor and shabby, and yet keeping 'is pecker up as 'e did—why, I dunno, but it seemed some'ow to 'urt me *'ere!*" —and Tilly, her aitches scattering more wildly than usual under the stress of her emotion, laid her hands, one over the other, on her left breast.

"But, Tilly——"

"Oh! now don't go and but me, Poll, like the dear good soul you are, and always 'ave been. If you mean, am I going to let 'im make ducks and drakes of what poor old Pa left me, I can truly say no—no fear! Not this child. But . . . well . . . look 'ere, Mary, I 'aven't spit out the whole truth yet. You'll laugh at what I'm going to tell you, and well you may do; it *sounds* rum enough. But you know, they do say old folks fall to playing again with toys, cuddling dolls and whittling chips. Well, *a certain person* 'ad a bit of hair, Poll, that used to curl behind 'is ear—many and many's the time, in the old spoony days, I've sat and twiddled it round me finger. Now, 'is hair's wearing thin on top, but the curl's still there—and I . . . would you believe it? . . . yes, I'm blessed if my finger didn't itch to be at it again. And what's worse, *has* itched, ever since. 'Ere I go, properly in the dumps and the doldrums, and, 'pon me word, feeling as if nothing 'ull ever matter much any more, if I can't. Oh, there's no fool like an old fool, Mary, love! . . . and nobody knows that better than the old fool 'im—herself."

"Oh, come, Tilly, you're not quite so ancient as you try to make out! As to what you say . . . it's been the living alone and all that, it's come of."

But though she spoke in a reassuring tone, Mary was none

the less genuinely perturbed: her robust, sensible Tilly reduced to such a foolish state! Why, it was like seeing one's dearest friend collapse under a sudden illness.

"P'r'aps. And p'r'aps not. But what I want you to do for me, old girl, is this. Ask me down to stop for a bit, and ask *him* to the house, while I'm there. The rest I'll manage for meself. Only, you won't let on to the doctor, will you, love, what I've told you? I don't want the doctor to know. 'E'd look down 'is nose at me with that queer look of 'is—no, I couldn't stand it, Poll! Henry, too—I shall keep 'Enry in the dark, till it's too late. 'E'd raise Cain. For, of course 'e thinks what Pa left me's safe to come to *his* brats. While, if I fix things up as I want 'em"—she lowered her voice—"I may 'ave kids of my own yet."

"Indeed and I hope so . . . from the bottom of my heart."——

Tell Richard? No, indeed!— As, that same afternoon, Mary drove in Tilly's "double buggy" down the dusty slope of Sturt Street, and out over the Flat, she imagined to herself what Richard would say—and think—did she make him partner in Tilly's confidences. What? . . . try to trap a man, and an old friend to boot, into a loveless marriage, merely because you wanted to twist a bit of hair round your finger? Why, he would snort with disgust at such folly . . . besides thinking it highly indelicate, into the bargain. As she was afraid she, Mary, did a little, too. The difference was: she saw, as he never would, that loneliness was at the bottom of it; loneliness, and the want of some one to care for, or, as Tilly put it, of something to *do*. It might also be that the old girlish inclination had never quite died out, but only slumbered, through all these years.— Not that that would count with Richard; indeed, it might count in just the opposite way. For he was more than straitlaced where things of this kind were in question: had a constitutional horror of them: and he would not consider it at all nice for the seeds of an old attachment to stay alive in you, when you were happily married to some one else. Another point: if Purdy yielded to the temptation and took Tilly and her money, Richard might always think less well of him for doing so; which would be a thousand pities, now the first move towards a reconciliation had been made. Whereas, if the engagement seemed to come about naturally, of itself . . . And, in this respect, there was really something to be said for it. Purdy once married and settled, the foolish barrier that had grown up between the two men would fall away, and they again become the friends they had been of old.

Reasoning thus, Mary arrived at the row of mean little weatherboard houses, in one of which Ned lived. She did not knock, but stepped across the verandah, turned the door-knob, and went down the passage. It was a Monday, and washing day. The brick floor of the kitchen overflowed with water, in which the young fry played. Polly, turning from the tubs, ran her hands over her arms, to sluice off the lather, before extending them, all moist and crinkled, in an embrace. By the copper sat Ned—poor Ned!—convalescent from the attack of acute bronchitis which had brought Mary in hot haste to Ballarat, a few weeks previously. Ned's chest and shoulders were wrapped up in an old red flannel petticoat, pinned under the chin; his feet, well out of the damp's way on an upturned sugar-box, were clad in down-at-heel felt slippers. His thick ringletty hair and curly beard hung long and unkempt above the scarlet drapery, forming a jet-black aureole, from which his face, chastened to a new delicacy, looked out beautiful as a cameo.

Pouncing on Mary, he talked volubly, in the hoarse whisper that was all the voice his illness had left him. It was the same old Ned, holding forth in the same old fashion: on the luck that had always been dead against him, the fair chance he had never yet had: man and theme alike lit up the same unquenchable optimism. He had to-day a yarn to tell of the fortune he might have made, not three months back, had he only, at the critical moment, been able to lay hands on the necessary: men had gone in and won, who had not a quarter of his flair. How much of it was truth and how much imagination, Mary did not know, or greatly care—in this, unlike Polly, who, rasped beyond measure, clicked an angry tongue and lashed out at Ned's "atrocious lies." Ned let her accusations pass unheeded; or just used the pause, as it seemed, to take breath, unfore starting anew. Which naturally enough doubled Polly's ire.

"If one could only *get* at 'im somehow, Mary! . . . give 'im a good flick on the raw. But Ned's got a hide like a hippopotamus; you *can't* hurt 'im, no matter how hard you try. There's something wrong about the make of 'im . . . somewhere."

Meanwhile Mary sat striving to keep the peace by dropping

in soothing words, while she pondered how best these two poor souls were to be helped. Helped they must be—that was plain. Moreover, Richard had given Mother a promise, on their farewell visit, that he would henceforth hold a protective arm over her unlucky favourite. On the voyage out, Mary had seriously considered adopting one—perhaps even two—of the black-haired brood. But here again, as once before on the occasion of a like offer from Tilly, Polly made short work of the suggestion. Not even to Mary, whom she dearly loved, would she give up her children.

"They're me own, and I'll stick to 'em, come what may! For they're all I've got, dearie . . . all I ever got from the whole galumphing galoot."— With which of course Mary was fain to agree; and though seven lived, and a ninth was on the way.

Nor could Polly be induced to part from them even for the benefit of their education.

"Ta, Mary love, you mean it kindly, but I'll not have 'em brought up above their station. To look down on their pa and ma ever after! They're a working-man's kids, love; and such they'll remain. Besides, you may be sure there'll be *some* of Ned's blowfly notions in some of their heads. And the State School's the best place to knock any such windy nonsense out of 'em."— Which sentiments, duly reported by Mary, Richard declared to be a gross example of parental selfishness. What right, he would like to know, had a mother to stand in the way of her offspring's betterment? No child with any true filial affection in his heart would grow up to despise his parents. On the contrary, as he understood the sacrifice they had made for him, his love and reverence for them would deepen and increase.— But this was just Richard's high-flown way of looking at things. Herself, Mary did not by any means feel so sure.

The knowledge that what Ned and Polly wanted was money, and nothing but money, was a fact she early and squarely faced. It was accompanied, however, by so disagreeable a sensation, that she was thankful Richard was not there to share it. Not only were they ready to take every shilling offered . . . poor things! no one could blame them for that, pinched and straitened as they were . . . it was their manner of accepting that wounded Mary. They pocketed what Richard sent them almost as a matter of course, frankly inspecting the amount, and sometimes even going so far as to wrinkle their noses over

Book II: *The Way Home*

it. Which was really hardly fair; for Richard was being very,
very generous to them; considering they were no blood relations of his, and he felt they didn't like him. Nor did they:
there was no getting away from that; they showed it even to
the extent of begrudging him his good luck . . . without which,
too, he would have been unable to do anything for them! Poor
Ned's eye burnt hot with envy, whenever Richard's rise in the
world was mentioned. While Polly alluded to it with an open
sneer.

"I say, *infra dig.*, isn't it, and no mistake, for a heavy swell
like he is now, to have such low-down connections . . . folk
who take in other people's washing!"

Mary could not bring herself to sit in judgment on them:
for all his tall talk, Ned had never in his life harmed a fly;
Polly's was just a generous nature warped and twisted by
poverty and an imprudent marriage. All the same, she was
very careful not to let Richard know how the wind blew. Her
letters to him, on Ned and Polly's behalf, were full of the
warm gratitude she herself would have felt, had she stood in
their shoes.

[6]

FOR the first time in his life, Mahony found himself in possession of all the books he wanted: rare books hard to get; expensive books he had till now never felt justified in buying.—
And Mary, his social conscience, being absent, he fell into
depths of abstraction, from which there was nothing to rouse
him.

His two old arch-enemies, time and money—or rather the
lack of them—had definitely ceased to plague him. His leisure
was unbounded; the morrow well provided for. Besides which,
the material comfort of his present surroundings was such as
he had hitherto known only in dreams. No domestic sounds
rasped his ear, scattered his attention; his spacious study, book-
lined from ceiling to floor, stood apart from the rest of the
house, and was solidly built. Was cool and airy, too; even in
the heat of midday, he caught a whiff of the sea. The garden,
with its several shrubberies and buffalo-grass lawns, its spreading fig-trees and dark firs, rested and refreshed the eye. Traffic
there went little or none in this out-of-the-way part. His meals

541

appeared on the table as by clockwork, served as he liked them, cooked to a turn. And so greatly did the hermit's life he now led jump with his mood, that invitations to social functions grew fly-spotted on the chimney-shelf, or were swept up by the housemaid from the floor.

He first undertook to examine the great moderns: those world-famous scientists and their philosophic spokesmen who dominated the intellectual life of the day. Thus far, he had read their works only in snatches, and at random. He now re-read them systematically, from A to Z. And, in advancing, he glowed with the liveliest satisfaction, feeling himself swept into the very heart of the controversies that raged round the idea of evolution, the origin of species, the antiquity of man. Step by step he followed the presentment of their monumental theories, the constructive or subversive deductions therefrom; and, yet once again, just as when, of old, he had written at the head of his Commonplace Book:

> "None ever feared that the truth should be heard,
> But those whom the truth would indict!"

it staggered him to think intelligent beings existed who could turn a deaf ear to such evidence, or, hearing, remain unconvinced.

Weeks passed. At the end of this time—Mary being still from home—he emerged, heavy-eyed and a trifle dazed, from sittings protracted late into the night, and paused to take his bearings. And it was now, on looking back over what he had read, that he became aware of a feeling of dissatisfaction. Chiefly with regard to the mental attitude of the writers themselves. So sound were their agruments that they might well, he thought, have refrained from the pontifical airs they saw fit to adopt; have been a shade less intolerant of views and beliefs that did not dovetail with their own. Riding on the crest of the highest wave of materialism that had ever broken over the world, they themselves were satisfied that life and its properties could be explained, to the last iota, in terms of matter; and, dogmatically pronouncing *their* interpretation of the universe to be the only valid one, they laid a crushing veto on any suggestion of a possible spiritual agency. Here it was he parted company with them. In the first place, he wondered, what had become

of their comparative, their historical sense? For the same thing
had surely happened before, in the world's history, bodies of
learned men arising, at various epochs, in divers lands, and
claiming to have solved the great riddle once and for all? Over
and above this, did Huxley's inflamed outbursts against the
"cosmogony of the semi-barbarous Hebrew"; his sighs that
the "myths of Paganism, dead as Osiris or Zeus," had not been
followed to their graves by the "coeval imaginations current
among the rude inhabitants of Palestine"; his bald definition
of science as "trained and organised common sense"—*did* Huxley's type of prejudiced and uninspired mentality, or yet that
of another well-known savant, who declared that one should
make up one's mind, beforehand, what was possible and what
not, incline you to trust these men's verdict, where the spiritual issues of human existence were concerned? In his own
case, certainly not. He believed and would continue to believe
it impossible, wholly to account for life and its phenomena
in terms of physiology, chemistry, physics.

Another thing that baffled him was: why, having advanced
to a certain point, should they suddenly stop short, with a
kingly gesture of: "Thus far and no farther"? Devoting, as
they did, decades of laborious research to the *origin* of life on
this globe, its age, its evolution, why should they leave untouched two questions of still more vital import: life's ultimate goal, and the moral mysteries of the soul of man?— Yes,
the chief bone he had to pick with them was that they had no
will to fathom such deeps; instead, they plumed themselves
on cold-shouldering them; flaunted as their device: *ignoramus
et ignorabimus.* Arrogantly sure of themselves, carried away
by a passion for facts, they covered with ridicule those—the
seers, the poets, the childlike in heart—who, over and above
the rational and the knowable, caught glimpses of what was
assumed to be unknowable; declaring, with a fierce and intolerant unimaginativeness, that the assertion which outstripped
the evidence was not only a blunder, but a crime. Strange,
indeed, was it to watch these masters toiling as they did to
interpret human life, yet denying it all hope of a further development, any issue but that of eternal nothingness. For his
part, he could not see why the evolution-formula should be
held utterly to rule out the transcendental-formula. But so it
was; every line of their works confirmed it . . . confirmed, too,

the reader's opinion that, in their bigoted attitude of mind, they differed not so very markedly from those hard-and-fast champions of orthodoxy who showed the whites of their eyes at the mere mention of "evolution," shut them tight to facts and evidence, and, in the rising flood of enlightenment, remained perilously clinging to the vanishing rock of dogma and tradition. On the one hand, for all answer to the burning needs and questionings of the hour, the tale of Creation as told in Genesis, the Thirty-nine Articles, the intolerable Athanasian Creed; on the other, as bitterly stubborn an agnosticism—each surely, in the same degree, stones for bread. One would have liked to call to them: Fear not to turn the light of research on the conception of that immortality which you affirm . . . which you deny.

Thus it came about that, little by little, Mahony found himself drifting away from the barren conclusions of science: just as, in earlier years, he had cast loose from a too rigid orthodoxy. Occult subjects had always had a strong fascination for him, and he now turned back to them; read ancient screeds on alchemy and astrology; the writings of Paracelsus and Apollonius of Tyana. Thence, he dived into mysticism; studied the biographies of Saint Theresa, Joseph Glanvill, Giordano Bruno, and pondered anew the trance history of Swedenborg. Men and women such as these, living their lives as a kind of experiment, and an arduous and painful experiment at that, were yet supported and uplifted by the consciousness of a mighty power outside, and at the same time within, themselves: a bottomless well of spiritual strength. Out of this inspiration they taught confidently that all life emanated from God (no matter what form it assumed in its progress), to God would return, and in Him continue to exist. Yes, spirituality outstripped intellect; there were mysteries at once too deep and too simple for learned brains to fathom. Actually, the unlettered man who said: "God is, and I am of God!" came nearest to reading the riddle of the universe.— How cold and comfortless, too, the tenet that this one brief span of being ended all! Without faith in a life—it might be, more lives than one—to come, how endure, stoically, the ills that here confronted us? . . . the injustices of human existence, the evil men did, the cruelty of man to his brothers, of God to man? Postulate a Hereafter, and the hope arose that, some day, the

ultimate meaning of all these apparent contradictions would
be made plain: the endless groping, struggling, suffering, prove
but rungs in the ladder of humanity's upward climb towards
self-realisation.— Not for him, the Byzantine Heaven of the
churches, with its mental stagnation, its frozen immobility,
wherein a jealous God, poorer in charity than the feeble creatures built in His image, spent Eternity damning those who
had failed to propitiate Him. Nor yet the doctrine of the Fall
of a perfect man from grace. He, Mahony, held this present
life to be but a portal, an antechamber, where dwelt an im-
perfect, but wholly vital creation, which, growing more and
more passionately aware, with the passing of the ages, of its
self-contained divinity, would end by achieving, by being
reabsorbed in, the absolute consciousness of the Eternal.

Yes, old faiths lay supine, stunned by the hammer blows of
science; and science had nothing soul-satisfying to offer in
their place. Surely now, if ever, the age was ripe for a new
revelation: humanity, racked by doubts, or cut to the heart by
atheistic denial, cried aloud for a fresh proof of God's existence, and of God's concern with man.— Restlessly feeling his
way, Mahony set himself to take the measure, where he had
so far only dabbled in it, of the new movement, spiritualism,
which, from its rise in a tiny American hamlet, had run like
a wildfire over Europe. And the deeper he dug himself into
the subject, the more vastly was he interested and impressed.
If what its followers claimed for it was true—and there were
men of standing among them, whose words could not be dismissed lightly, with a shrug—if the spirits of those who had
crossed the bourne were really able . . . as in the days of
Moses and the prophets . . . to return and speak with the loved
ones they had left—then it meant that a new crisis had arisen
in man's relation to the Unseen, with which both science and
religion would eventually have to reckon. Unlike the majority,
he was not put off by the commonplace means of communication employed—the rappings and the tappings, the laborious
telling over of the alphabet—nor yet by the choice, as agents,
of the illiterate and immature. He recalled the early history of
Christianity: the Chaldean shepherds; the Judaean carpenter's
shop; the unlettered fishermen; the sneers and gibes of Roman
society. God's ways had never been, never would be, man's
ways. Why, even as it was, some found the practice of con-

ventional Christianity none too easy, thanks to the frailty of the human channels through which the great message had to pass. The deterrent effect, on some, of the supercilious drawl of a ritualistic parson; one's inability to admit that a bad priest might read a true Mass; the fact that the celebrant, from whom you received the Eucharist, was known to be, in his spare hours, drinker and gambler, or one of those who systematically hunted small animals to death.— Measured by such stumbling-blocks as these, the spiritualists' sincere faith and homely conduct of their seances did not need to shirk comparison. Indeed, there would sometimes seem to be more genuine piety at their meetings, which invariably opened with prayer, than at many an ordinary church service.— But, however one looked at it, the question to be answered remained: was it possible to draw from this new movement proofs of the knowledge one's soul craved—the continuity of existence; the nearness, the interwovenness, of the spiritual world to the material; the eternal and omnipotent presence of the Creator?

    ❋   ❋   ❋   ❋   ❋   ❋

Mary wrote: *What in all the world are you doing with yourself, Richard? The Carters quite expected you last Wednesday, and the Rentouls had a place laid at dinner for you on Friday evening. Both write me, hoping you were not kept away by illness. Didn't you get the invitations, or what? I think it's high time I came home to look after you.*

To which Mahony replied: *Nonsense, my dear; I am getting on capitally—servants most attentive, and Cook dishing me up all manner of good things. Do not hurry back on my account.*

Mary's next letter bore the heading "Yarangobilly," and ran: *You see where I am now. The Urquharts insisted on my coming out—and Tilly with me. There's a large party here, as usual, and picnics, dancing and play-acting, and music and singing go on all the time. Willy drove in himself to fetch us, and would take no refusal; though I was sorry to leave Ballarat, which is as lovely as ever, and every one just as kind. Willy is just the same; doesn't look a day older; and is so full of life and fun you really can't help liking him, however much you may disapprove. Both he and Louisa seem pleased to have us here, and make no end of a fuss over us. They are full of regrets that you are not with me. I think it a great pity you didn't take my advice and come, too. Ever so many people have inquired after you.*

Not I! was Richard's response. *They never wanted me, my dear, when I was among them; why on earth should they miss me now? . . . when they've had ample time to forget all about me. It's only your imagination. As usual you read your own kind feelings into others.*

And Mary: *What rubbish you do talk, dear! I believe you're growing odd and fanciful through being so much alone. Do go out more, and not coop yourself up so.— Well, we're still here. Louisa won't hear of our leaving; it's quite a change for her to have friends of her own in the house—the others are mostly Willy's. Poor Louisa through never getting away— I mean with all the babies, etc.—makes hardly any. I think our visit will do her good. In spite of there being so much company, she's often alone. I'm afraid it's not to be wondered at—in such a gay party. She looks far older than her age, and "very" dowdy. What she needs is some one to take her in hand and freshen her up. I've made her promise to spend at least a month with me after I get back—the last baby's well over a year now, and there are no fresh expectations in the meantime, thank goodness . . . twelve are surely enough. I intend to stitch a rose in her bonnet, and teach her how to do her hair. Also get her into one of the new bustles. Her dresses are made in the style of the year one. She would still be quite pretty if nicely dressed, and, privately, I think that would be much more effective than sitting moping and fretting, and not caring how she looks. Fretting about Willy, I mean. I'm afraid he's incurable. He's very much épris again at present. This time it's a fascinating widow who's stopping here—a very charming person, and interested, unfortunately, in everything Willy's interested in—horses, dogs, riding, driving, cattle and sheep—to cut it short, in everything Louisa isn't.*

A week later. I had a long talk with Mrs. Marriner—that's the widow-lady I mentioned in my last. She's really much attached to Louisa, and would be her good friend, if only Louisa would let her. (Now I'm not imagining this!) But L. is so jealous that she can hardly be civil. There was quite a scene last night. It ended by poor Louisa going to bed in floods of tears. Of course I can see it from her side, too. It must be very

*hard to know that another woman pleases your husband bet-
ter than you do. Still, Willy has had so many fancies in his
day: I think Louisa needn't take this one too seriously. Gracey
—Mrs. Marriner, that is—was quite upset about it herself. She
is really a very frank and warm-hearted person, and it isn't
exactly her fault: she can't help pleasing. And so sensible, too.
We had a talk, she and I, about poor Agnes and her failing—
she knows all about it—and she quite agrees with me, it's
really some one's duty to tackle Mr. Henry.*

*And again: Oh no, Richard, you've got quite a false idea of
her. She's anything but designing—not at all one of those
widows who go about setting their caps at men. But you'll be
able to see for yourself; for she talks of taking a house at
Brighton when she gets back to town. And I'm sure you'll like
her, and get on well with her—she's so clever. You should have
heard her yesterday evening discussing the reform of gaols
and penitentiaries with a gentleman who's staying here. We
other ladies felt our noses quite out of joint.*

*Back in Ballarat Mary wrote: Well! I've done the deed,
dear. I thought it best not to mention it beforehand, for I
knew you would write about minding one's own business,
not interfering between husband and wife, etc. Tilly and I
came back to "Beamish House" at the end of the week, and
on Wednesday off I went and paid a visit to Mr. Henry, at his
office. Well, he couldn't have received me more civilly. He
told his clerk he was engaged, and would see nobody else
while I was there. Had wine and biscuits fetched—I can tell
you, paid me every attention. He also asked most kindly after
you.— As you may guess, I approached the subject of Agnes
very gingerly. Just hinted I had seen her, and how sorry I was
to find her in such a poor state of health. He was rather reserved at first. But when I gave him to understand she had
confided in me, and how broken-hearted she was, and what
reproaches she was making herself, and when I sympathised
with him over the loss of such a beautiful child . . . why, then,
he quite thawed and came out of his shell. Indeed, all but
broke down. Think of that with Mr. Henry, who has always
been so cold and stern! I never liked him so well. You'll perhaps say it is chiefly his pride he has been hurt in: but don't
you think that's hard enough, for a man like him? Well, one
thing led to another, and before long we were talking quite*

freely about poor little Agnes and her terrible weakness. He admitted he was at his wits' end to know what to do with her. Had had some thoughts of putting her in a Home, under a doctor's care: but shrinks from the publicity and disgrace. Then he fears her bad example on the children—the boy, Gregory, is seven now, and sharp as a needle—and servants will talk. He would like to try the effects of a sea voyage, but can't get away from the office for so long. One thing I made him promise, and that was, to let Agnes leave that dreadful house she is in, come to us for a time, and have the children with her again. I'll take good care they don't disturb you, dear. Besides, now, you have your nice big study to retire to, when you want to be quiet. When I came away—I must have been there nearly an hour—he took both my hands in his, and shook them and said: "God bless you, my dear Mrs. Mahony! I shall never forget your great kindness in this matter. Nor do I know another soul—certainly not one of your sex—to whom I could have spoken as I have to you." Think of that from Mr. Henry! Tilly hasn't got over it yet. She says it all comes of my having worn my best bonnet (the gay one with the flower in, that you like). But of course that's only her nonsense. And I do feel so glad I went, and didn't let myself be persuaded not to.

I hope the silk vests are a great success, and that you remember the right day for changing them.

[7]

"My papéh dotes on music. Positively, I have known my papéh to say he would rather do without his port at dinner than his music after dinner. My papéh has heard all the most famous singers. In his opinion, no one could compare with Malibran." Thus Miss Timms-Kelly; and, at his cue, the chubby, white-haired old Judge, surreptitiously snatching forty winks in a dark corner of the drawing-room, would start, open his eyes, and like a well-trained parrot, echo his daughter's words.

"Malibran? . . . ah, now, there was a voice for you!— Pasta could not hold a candle to her. As a young man I never missed an opera when she sang. Great nights, great nights! The King's Theatre packed to suffocation. All of us young music-lovers burning with enthusiasm . . . our palms tingling from applause!" Here, however, at some private sign, the speaker abruptly switched off his reminiscences, which threatened to carry him away, and got to the matter in hand.— "My dear, give us, if you please, *casta diva!* Though I say so myself, there is something in my daughter's rendering of that divine air, that recalls Malibran in her prime."

A musical party at the Timms-Kellys' tempted even Mahony forth from his retirement. On such evenings, in company with other devotees, he would wander up Richmond Hill and through the wooden gates of Vaucluse, where a knot of houses stood sequestered in a grove. The French windows of the Timms-Kellys' drawing-room were invariably set wide open; and guests climbing the hill could hear, while some way off, the great voice peal out—like a siren-song that urged and cajoled.

Miss Timms-Kelly herself bore the brunt of the entertainment; occasionally mingling in a duo with some manly second, or with the strains of Mahony's flute; but chiefly in solo. For the thin little tones of the other ladies, or their tinkly performances of "Maiden's Prayers" and "Warblings at Eve"; or the rollicking strains of a sea ballad (which was mostly what the gentlemen were good for), stood none of them an earthly chance against a voice like hers. It was a contralto, with, in its middle and lower registers, tones of a strange, dark intensity which made of it a real *voix sombre;* yet, of such exceptional compass, that it was also equal to *Or sai chi l'onore* and *Non mi dir, bell' idol mio.* Mahony used to say there was something about it, especially in its lower notes, that got at you, "like fingers feeling round your heart." Ladies, while admitting its volume and beauty, were apt to be rendered rather uncomfortable by it; and, under its influence, would fall to fidgeting in their seats.

In person, Miss Timms-Kelly matched her voice: though not over tall, she was generously proportioned, with a superb bust and exquisitely sloping shoulders. Along with this handsome figure went piquantly small hands and feet—she boasted a number three shoe—white teeth, full lips, a fresh complexion. But her chief charm lay in her animation of manner: she was alive with verve and gesture; her every second word seemed spoken in italics. Amazing, thought and said all, that one so fascinating should have reached the brink of the thirties without marrying; society had known her now for twelve years, and, during this time, the marvellous voice had rung out night for night, her old father faithfully drawing attention to its merits, the while he grew ever whiter and sleepier in his corner of the drawing-room.

But the little court that surrounded Miss Timms-Kelly consisted in the main of married men; or, at any rate, of such bachelors as were well past marrying age: greybeards, who, in listening to the strains of *Norma* or *Semiramide*, re-lived their youth. Eligible men fought a little shy of the lady; and, after a couple of visits to the house, were prone to return no more. Happily, Miss Timms-Kelly did not take this greatly to heart. Indeed, she even confessed to a sense of relief at their truancy. "All my life, love, I have preferred the company of *elderly* gentlemen. They make one feel so *safe*."

Mary, in process of dressing for one such evening, remarked: "Of course, it's very nice of Lizzie to say that . . . and most sensible. But all the same it *is* odd—I mean the fact of her never having married. Not only because of her voice—one doesn't marry a voice. But she really is a dear, warm-hearted creature. And so generous." At which Mahony stopped shaving his chin to throw in: "That's precisely it. Your marriageable man instinctively fears not being able to live up to the fair singer's generosity."

"*Really*, Richard! . . . it takes you to say queer things. Now *I* believe it comes to Lizzie never having had a mother to go about with. She's been obliged to put herself too much forward."

But, for all his two-edged comments, let Miss Timms-Kelly but open her mouth to sing, and Mahony was hopelessly her slave. His natural instinct for music had outlived even the long years of starvation in this country, where neither taste nor performance was worth a straw. Under the present stimulus, his dormant feelings awoke to new life: when the great voice rang forth he would sit rapt . . . absorbed. And where others, but faintly responsive to the influence, listened with only half an ear, the while they followed their own trains of thought, musing, gently titillated: "How fine the moon to-night!" or "I shall certainly succeed, if I carry through that deal," or "Perhaps after all Julia will hear my suit," he, Mahony, surrendered thought for emotion, and climbed the ladder of sound to a world built wholly of sound, where he moved light-footedly and at ease.

"Upon my soul, I would walk ten miles to hear her rendering of an aria by Mozart or Verdi!"

This was all very well in its way—its musical way. But now something happened which brought him with a sudden bump to earth. And, ever after, he twitted and blamed himself with having been the innocent cause of a most unnecessary complication.——

Towards the close of her stay in Ballarat, Mary had a second meeting—a chance one, this time—with Mr. Henry Ocock. And Ocock, in his new rôle of friend and adviser, let fall a hint with regard to a certain mining company in which he believed Mahony held shares. This was not the case; but Mary rather thought John did, begged Richard to find out, and, if so, to let him know what was being said. As Mr. Henry's information had been *sub rosa*, Mahony thought it wise to pass it on by word of mouth, and wrote John saying he would drop in for a moment, the following evening, on his way to Richmond: he was bound with his flute for Vaucluse, to accompany Miss Timms-Kelly in an aria. In the morning, however, John's groom brought a note, asking him to take pot-luck with the family at six o'clock that evening. Such things were possible in John's house nowadays, under the fairy rule of Miss Julia. And so he found himself that night at John's dinner-table.

As usual at this stage, when he had not seen his brother-in-law for a time, Mahony's chief sensation on meeting John was one of discomfort. Without doubt, some great change was at work in John. Lean as a herring, yellow as a Chinaman, he had been for months past. But the change in his manner was even more striking. Gone was much of the high-handedness, the pompous arrogance, it had once been so hard to stomach; gone the opulent wordiness of his pronunciamentos. He was now actually in point of becoming a morose and taciturn sort of fellow; prone, too, to fits of blankness, in which, staring straight before him, he seemed to forget your very presence. So much at least was plain: John was not taking the universe by any means so much for granted, as of old.

Money troubles? . . . such was the first thought that leapt to

Book II: *The Way Home*

Mahony's mind. Then, however, he laughed at himself. John's
business flourished like the green bay-tree: you never heard of
it but it was putting forth a fresh shoot in some fresh direction. No lack of money there!—the notion was just a telling
example of how one instinctively tried to read what had been
one's own chief bogey into another person's mind. Besides,
the warning passed on by Mary left John cold: he waved it
aside with a gesture that said: a few thousands more or less
signified nothing to him. Could the wife's idea that he was
fretting over the loss of his boy be the right one? Again, no:
that was just a woman's interpretation: *he* jumped to money,
she to the emotional, the personal. Then, after all, it must be
John's health that was causing him anxiety. But a tactful question on this score called forth so curt a negative that he could
not press it.

Not till the nuts and port were on the table did John shake
off his abstraction. Then, his trio of little girls ran into the
room—with the playful antics of so many tame white mice—
ran in and rubbed their sleek little comb-ringed heads against
their father's, and climbed over him with their thin little white-
stockinged legs. And John became solely the fond parent,
gathering his children to him, taking the youngest on his knee
and holding her to his watered-silk waistcoat, letting them
play with the long gold chain from which depended his *pince-
nez*, count his studs with their little fingers, disarrange the
ends of his cravat. At the lower end of the table, Emmy, who
had presided over the meal a radiant vision in white muslin
and blue ribbons, flushed, drooped her head, and looked as
though she were going to cry. For though the lovely girl had,
throughout dinner, hung distractedly on her father's lips, he
had never so much as glanced in her direction.

Mahony, watching her, fell into a reverie, so vividly did she
remind him of her dead mother, and the one—the only—time
he had seen John's first wife. It was here, in this very room,
that the gracious Emma, the picture of all that was comely,
had dandled her babes. One of the two, like herself, had vanished from mortal eyes. The other, a full-grown woman in her
turn, was now ripe for her own fate.

When Emmy shepherded the little girls to their nursery, he
turned to John.— "Upon my soul, it makes a man realise his
age, to see the young ones come on as they do!"

Something in this reflection seemed to flick John. His response was more in his old style. "You say so? For my part, I cannot admit to feeling a day older than I did ten years back. I am not aware of any decrease of vigour. I still rise at six, take a cold shower-bath, and attend to business for a couple of hours before breakfast. I have needed neither to diet myself for a gouty constitution, nor to coddle myself in flannel.—Age? Bah! At forty-six a man is in his prime . . . the very prime of life!"

Now, what in all the world got at him so, in that innocent remark of mine? wondered Mahony, even while he smoothed John's ruffled feathers.— After this one outburst, however, John relapsed into his former moody silence: and they sat smoking, with scant speech, till Mahony rose to leave. Then it turned out that John had forgotten the existence of a previous engagement on Mahony's side; and he made a lame attempt to overthrow it. ("Looks as if he didn't want to be left to the companionship of his own thoughts!") This being impossible, Mahony suggested that John should accompany him: it would be well worth his while, to hear Miss Timms-Kelly sing: and he, Mahony, undertook to guarantee him a hearty welcome. At first, John pooh-poohed the suggestion; musical evenings were not in his line; and though, of course, he had knocked up against old Timms-Kelly at the Club, he had never met the daughter. However, Mahony persisted; it would do him good; take him out of himself. In the end, John allowed himself to be persuaded; and off they went, in company.

"And that, my dear, was how it came about, in the first place. *I* dragged him with me, like the fool I was. And once there, the game was up. From the moment John entered the drawing-room, your friend Lizzie made what I can only describe as a dead set at him. She never took her eyes off him. She talked to him, she talked at him; she sang for him; asked his opinion of her selections; and there sat John, who doesn't know doh from re, or a major key from a minor, tapping his foot to the tune, and looking as if he had been a judge of music all his life. On two occasions afterwards, I found him there. But, mind you! only two. Then came that unfortunate evening at *Ernani*. It's no use asking *me*, Mary, how the muddle occurred. I can't tell you: I had nothing to do with it. All I know is, after the opera Mrs. Vance had to be escorted back

to North Melbourne; and this job naturally fell to me, John
not being the man to shoulder unpleasant duties if he can,
with propriety, put them off on some one else. Well, we hired
a wagonette and drove away—in a violent thunder-shower—
leaving the other three outside the theatre. But it appears that,
somehow or other, what with the rain, and the crush, the two
of them lost sight of the old man. According to John's account,
they stood waiting for him to turn up, till Miss Lizzie's teeth
were chattering with the cold. There seemed nothing for it,
but for him to call a cab and drive her home. He did so, and
the next morning I'm hanged if he doesn't get a furious letter
from the father, accusing them of having slipped off alone on
purpose. John heads straight for Vaucluse, to apologise; and
when he gets there, the old man hammers the table, declares
his daughter has been compromised, and ends by demanding
to know John's intentions. Now I ask you, what could John—
what could any man with the feelings of a gentleman—do,
under such circumstances, but offer the only reparation in his
power, and at once propose for her hand? Therewith, of
course, the old boy cools down . . . becomes amiability itself.—
I don't know, my dear, whether John was really guilty of an
indiscretion—that's his affair. But if you want *my* candid opinion, Mary, I think the whole thing was a put-up job. Your
friend Lizzie is a veritable Leyden jar."

Mary, whom the news of John's engagement had brought
flying home from Ballarat, here uttered a disclaimer. "Tch!
There you go, Richard . . . jumping to conclusions . . . as usual.
Still, I must say . . . I'm confident, as far as John was concerned, he had no idea of marrying again. I really don't know
what to think."

"Ah! but such a dear, kind, generous creature . . ."

"Why, so she is. But——"

"But it's another story, eh, when John the Great comes in
question?"

"Don't be so sarcastic! You know quite well, I'm very fond
of Lizzie. But poor John was just so comfortably settled—
I mean with Miss Julia to look after him. It seemed as if he
was going to have peace at last.— And then, think of the upset
again for those poor dear children."

"Indeed and I do. Though, on the other hand . . . stepmother to two families! I shouldn't care, love, to take on the

job. But there's another thing, Mary. Your brother is decidedly queer just now—I mean in his manner . . . and appearance. He looks a *tired* man. My own opinion is, he's seen the best of his health. Of course, he's lived a strenuous life—like all the rest of us—and is no longer as young as he was. But that's not enough . . . doesn't account for everything. And makes what has happened very disturbing. If only I'd let well alone that evening, and not urged him to accompany me . . . he'd probably never have set eyes on the woman. It is certainly a lesson to mind one's own business in this world—even when it's a question of doing a kindness . . . or what one thinks a kindness."—

"My déhling Mary! So we are to be sisters, love—actually sisters! I cannot say how overjoyed I am.— Never have I had such a surprise in all my life, déhling, as when my papéh informed me your brother had declared himself. I said: 'Papéh, are you quite, quite *sure* you are not mistaken?' For never had I imagined, love, that such a clever and accomplished man as your brother would select *me*, from among all the ladies of his acquaintance. My heart still flutters when I think of it. I walk on air.— Yes, déhling! Though how I shall ever manage to leave my dear papéh, I do not know."

"Dear Lizzie! I, too, am very glad.— But what about the children? Have you considered if it will suit you to be a stepmother? Emmy is a grown girl now—turned seventeen."

"Mary! The déhlings! The poor neglected lambs! Why, I yearn, dearest, simply yearn, to show them a mother's love."

But, on Emmy being presented, Lizzie's fervour suffered a visible abatement. Even to Mary's eye. And, an embrace given and received, her stepmother-to-be looked the girl up and down, with a coolness which not even her extreme warmth of manner could conceal.

"My déhling! Why, Mary, love, I had no idea—positively I had not . . . I declare it will be like having a younger sister.— My déhling girl! And I will show you how to dress your hair, love—two puffs, one on each side of the parting—it will be a *great* improvement to your appearance. That will please papéh, won't it? His dear *pet*, I feel sure. Who will be able to tell me *all* his little ways."

Emmy wept.

"I *hate* the way she does her hair, Aunt Mary. I wouldn't wear mine like that—not for anything! And I'm *not* going to show her how papa likes things done.— Oh, *couldn't* I come and live with you and Uncle Richard? I shall never be happy here, any more. *Why* does papa want to get married? Auntie Julia always promised me I should keep house for him, and he would learn to like me, in time. And now . . . now . . ."

It was not for a daughter to sit in judgment on her father, and Mary gently rebuked Emmy, even while she reflected that the girl had really a great deal of John's own spirit in her. Lizzie would not find her new position a bed of roses. For neither did the little ones take to her. They clung to Auntie Julia's hands and skirts; although, to these children, who were without personal beauty, their future mother was still more gracious than to Emmy. At first, that was. Afterwards, remarked Mahony, who was present at the introduction: afterwards, when she saw that they were not to be cozened into friendliness, she made him think of a pretended animal lover, who, on a dog failing to respond to his advances, looks as though he will presently kick it on the sly.— But then, said Mary, Richard had flown to the other extreme, and become both prejudiced and unfair, not being able to get over the march that had been stolen on him.

But to such a bagatelle as the likes or dislikes of a parcel of children, Miss Timms-Kelly paid small heed. She had other and more important fish to fry. The engagement was to be as brief as propriety admitted; and she was hard put to it to get her trousseau bought in time, furniture chosen, the affairs of her maidenhood set in order. Through the apartments of her new home she swept like a whirlwind . . . like a whirlwind, too, overthrowing and destroying. Painters and paperhangers were already hard at work. For much company would be seen there after the wedding, great receptions held: as the Honourable Mrs. Turnham, she would move not only in musical circles, but in the wider world of politics. John's prospects were of the best: it was an open secret that, for his services in the Devine ministry, he would probably receive a knighthood.— And small wonder, thought Mary, that Lizzie found the house shabby and antiquated. Nothing had been done to it since the day on which John, in his first ardour, had dressed it for his first bride.

Now, drastic changes were in progress. The old mahogany four-poster, with its red rep curtains—"Jinny's bed," as it per-

sisted in Mary's mind—was to be replaced by one of the new
French testers, with canopy and curtains at the head only.
(A rather risky innovation for John, at his age!) Oval plate-
glass mirrors in gilt frames, with bunches of candelabra attached, were hung at intervals round the drawing-room walls;
a splendid Collard and Collard ousted the old piano; bouquets
of wax flowers and fruit, under glass shades, topped the what-
nots; horsehair gave way to leather. And the nursery, which
stood next John's own bedroom, was requisitioned by Lizzie
as a boudoir, the children being relegated to the back of the
house.

And John?— To the four eyes that watched him, with curiosity and a motherly anxiety, John's attitude came as a surprise
and a relief. He was regularly caught up in the whirl: and,
for once leaving both business and politics in the lurch, danced
attendance on his affianced from morning till night. Though
he still had a haggard air, and certainly nowadays looked
what he was, an elderly man, yet a wave of new life ran
through him. In his attire, he grew almost as dapper as of
old. It seemed as if he was determined to carry the affair off
with a high hand. He spared no expense, baulked at no alteration; and the ring that sparkled on Lizzie's plump finger was,
even in this land of showy jewellery, so costly and magnificent
as to draw all eyes. Nor could he have been human, had he
not at heart felt proud of the fine figure cut by his bride-elect.
He *was* proud, and showed it.— More: when he returned from
his wedding-trip to Sydney and the Blue Mountains, every
one could see that he was very much in love.

[8]

It was a promise of long standing that, once fairly settled in
her new house, Mary should wipe off old debts, and invite to
stay with her those of her friends to whom she lay under an
obligation. She had plenty of room for them, plenty of time:
all that remained to do was to fix the order of their coming.

First, though, she charged herself with Emmy and the children, to get them out of the workpeople's way, and, after the
wedding—it was celebrated at All Saints, Brighton, and proved
a very swell affair indeed, John's four daughters following the
bride up the aisle—to leave Miss Julia free to put the house

finally in order, and make ready to hand over the keys to its new mistress. Emmy cried bitterly when the time came to return home: all Mary's reasoning and persuading had not succeeded in plucking from the girl's heart the sting this third marriage of her father's had implanted there. A great hope had been dashed in Emmy; and she went back hot with resentment against the intruder. The young ones were easier to manage. The excitement of the wedding, new frocks, new dolls, helped them over the break. For them, too, this would not be so complete. Miss Julia proposed to open a select school for the daughters of gentlemen, at which the three little girls were to be day pupils.

Not a word had passed between Mary and Miss Julia in criticism of John's marriage. Their eyes just met for a moment in a look of complete understanding ("Oh, these men . . . these men!"): then, with a nod and a sigh, they set resolutely to making the best of things—a task, said Mahony, in which the wife had at last found her peer.

John's affairs having thus once more slipped from her grasp, Mary devoted herself to the long line of visitors who now crossed the threshold of *Ultima Thule.*

Louisa Urquhart headed the list.— Louisa arrived one afternoon at Spencer Street railway-station, and was drawn from the train, her bonnet askew, her cheeks scarlet with excitement at having undertaken, without an escort, the four-hour journey from Ballarat. And after Louisa, who far outstayed her welcome, came Agnes Ocock and her children, and her children's nurses; came Zara and her husband, in search of expert medical advice; Jerry and his Fanny, the latter in a delicate state of health; a couple of Ned's progeny; Amelia Grindle and a sickly babe; came Mrs. Tilly: not to speak of other, less intimate acquaintances.

Mahony groaned.— It was all very well for Mary to say that, if he wished to be alone, he had only to go into his study and shut the door. He could and did retire there. But, like other doors, this, too, had a handle; and, since Mary would never, it seemed, get it into her head that to be busy among your books was to be seriously busy, the petty interruptions he suffered were endless. Take, for example, the case of Louisa Urquhart. This was by no means exhausted with the stitching of a rose in a drab bonnet. Louisa had lived so long in semi-invalid retirement that she was little better than a cretin with regard to the small, practical affairs of life. She did not know how to stamp a letter, or tie up a newspaper for the post; could not buy a pair of gloves, or cross a crowded street, without assistance. They had to accompany her everywhere. She also lived in a perpetual nervous flutter lest some accident should happen at Yarangobilly while she was absent: the house catch fire, or one of the children take a fit.— "That Willy will not do a bolt with a less dismal party than she, it would be rash indeed to assume! Of all the woebegone wet-blankets . . ."— Mahony was disgruntled: it spoilt his appetite for breakfast to listen to Louisa's whining, did she learn, by the morning post, that one of her infants had the stomach-ache; or to look on at the heroic efforts made by Mary to disperse the gloom. (The wife's infinite patience with the noodles she gathered round her invariably staggered him afresh.) Then, parties must needs be given in Louisa's honour—and the honour of those who came after. The hours for meals were disarranged, too, put backwards or forwards to suit the home habits of the particular guest.

Even more disturbing was the visit of Mrs. Henry, which followed. Here, he could not but share Mary's apprehensions lest something untoward should happen which might give servants or acquaintances an inkling of how matters stood. As for poor Mary, she grew quite pale and peaked with the strain; she hardly dared let Agnes out of her sight. At dinner-parties —and, of course, the very best people had to be asked to meet the wife of so important a personage as Mr. Henry—her eye followed the decanters on their rounds with an anxiety painful to see. (Between-times, she kept the chiffonier strictly locked.) During this visit, too, the servants made difficulties by refusing to wait on the strange nursemaids, who gave themselves airs; while, to cap all, a pair of the rowdiest and worst-behaved children ever born romped in the passage, or trampled the flower-beds in the garden. No walls were thick enough to keep out their noise; any more than the fact of their being in a stranger's house could improve their manners. The walls were also powerless against Zara's high-pitched, querulous voice, or the good Ebenezer's fits of coughing, which shook the unfortunate man till his very bones seemed to rattle. Later on, for variety, they had the shrill screaming of Amelia Grindle's sick babe (with Mary up and down at night, preparing foods); had Ned's children to be tamed, and taught to blow their noses; pretty Fanny tumbling into faints half a dozen times a day.— Of course, there was no earthly reason why all these people should not make his home theirs—oh dear no! If Jerry got a fortnight's holiday, what more natural than that he should choose to spend it in his sister's comfortable, well-appointed house, rather than in his own poky weatherboard? If Mrs. Devine wanted to take sea-air ("And really, Richard, one *has* to remember how extraordinarily kind she was to us on landing!"): the least one could do was to beg her to exchange Toorak for Brighton-on-Beach. Certainly, only the fact of John's house being but a paltry half-hour's walk distant and the ozone both families breathed of the same brand, saved them from having John and Lizzie quartered on them as well.

Yes, Mary's hospitality was rampageous—no other word would describe it. He had given her *carte blanche*, and he kept to his bond; but, as time went on, his groans increased in volume, he was sarcastic at the expense of "Mrs. Mahony's Benevolent Asylum," and openly counted the days till he should have his house to himself again. A quiet evening was a thing of the past; he was naturally expected to escort the ladies to the various entertainments. Besides, he was "only reading." What selfishness, to shut yourself up with a book, when a visitor's amusement was in question! For, as usual, Mary's solicitude was all for others. Much less consideration was shown him, personally, than in the old Ballarat days. Then, he had been the breadwinner, the wage-earner, and any disturbance of his life's routine meant a corresponding disturbance in their income. Here, with money flowing in without effort and abundantly—as it continued to do—there was no such practical reason to respect his privacy. And so it was: "Richard, will you answer these cards for me?" "See to the decanting of the port?" "Leave an order at the fruiterer's?" "Book seats for *East Lynne,* or *Maritana?*"

In this hugger-mugger fashion week after week, month after month ran away. Then, however, things seemed to be tailing off, and he was just congratulating himself that he had bowed the last guest out, when Tilly arrived, and back they fell into the old atmosphere of fuss and flutter. Tilly had originally stood high on Mary's list. Then, for some reason which was not made clear to him, her visit had been postponed; and he had comfortably forgotten all about it.

Once she was there, though, it was impossible to forget Tilly, even for an hour. Her buxom, bouncing presence filled the house. There was no escape from her strident voice, her empty, noisy laugh. The very silk of her gowns seemed to rustle more loudly than other women's; and she had a foot like a grenadier.— The truth was, his old aversion to Tilly, and the type she represented, broke out anew directly she crossed his door-sill. And, three times a day, he was forced to sit next her at meals, attend to her wants, and listen, as civilly as he might, to her crude comments on people and things.

In vain did Mary harp on Tilly's sterling qualities. Before a week was out, Mahony swore he would prefer fewer virtues and more tact. Goodness of heart could be rated too highly. Why should not quick-wittedness, and sensitiveness to your neighbour's tender places, also be counted to your credit? Why must it always be the blunt-tongued, the hob-nailed of approach, who got all the praise?

It was at the dinner-table, where, in the course of talk, the burning question of spirits and spirit-phenomena had come up; and Mary—Mary, not he: it would never have occurred to him to dilate on the theme before such as Tilly!—had told of the raps and movements of furniture that were taking place at the house of a Mrs. Phayre, a prominent member of Melbourne society. Now, Tilly knew very well he did not belong to those who dismissed such happenings with a smile and a shrug. Yet the mere mention of them was enough to send her off into an unmannerly guffaw.

"Ha, ha! . . . ha, ha, ha! To see your furniture jumping about the room! *I'd* pretty soon nab the slavey—you take my word for it, Mary, it's the slavey—who played such tricks on me. *I'd* bundle 'er off with a flea in 'er ear. There's no green, my dear, in *this* child's eye."

A glance at Richard showed him black as thunder. Mary adroitly changed the subject. But, afterwards, she came back on it.

"It's all very well, Richard, but you can't expect a common-sense person like Tilly *not* to be amused by that sort of thing."

"And pray do you mean to imply that every one who does not mock and jeer is devoid of sense?"

"Of course not. Besides, I didn't say sense; I said common sense."

"Well, my dear, since you yourself bring in the 'common,' I'll quote you the dictum of a famous man. 'Commonplace minds usually condemn everything that is beyond the scope of their understanding.'"

"How sweeping! And so conceited.— But Tilly is *not* commonplace. In many ways, she's just as capable as her mother was before her.— But I don't think we ought to be discussing her. While she's our visitor."

"Good God! Is one to go blind and dumb because a fool is under one's roof?"

"Well, really! I do wonder what you'll say next." Mary was hurt, and showed it.

But Mahony did not try to conciliate her. He had a further ground for annoyance. Ever since Tilly had come to the house, that side of Mary's nature had prevailed, with which he was least in sympathy. Never had she seemed so deadly practical, and lacking in humour; so instinctively antagonistic to the imaginative and speculative sides of life. Her attitude, for example, to the subject under discussion! At bottom, this was no whit different from Tilly's *"That* sort of thing," said as Mary said it, put her opinion of the new movement in a nutshell.

Out of this irritation he now demanded: "Tell me: are we never in this world to have the house to ourselves again?"

"But, Richard, you know Tilly *had* to come! . . . after the time I stayed with her. And now she's here—even though you do despise her so—we've got to do all we can to make her visit a success. I should hate her to think we didn't consider her good enough to introduce to our friends."

"Among whom she fits about as well as a porpoise in a basin of goldfish."

"As if a porpoise could get inside a basin! How wildly you do talk! Besides, you don't mean it. For, if ever there was a particular person about paying debts, it's you."

Late one afternoon he entered the house from the garden, where he had been superintending the laying out of a new shrubbery. The day before, he had found, to his dismay, that a gap in the screening hedge of lauristinus pittosporums allowed of errand-boys and nursemaids spying on a privacy he had believed absolute. The thought was unbearable. But the change had cost him a fierce tussle with his gardener, a pig-headed Scot, who held there were already too many shrubs about the place. Mahony felt hot and tired.

As he crossed the verandah, Mary came rustling out of the dining-room. She looked mysterious, but also, if he knew his Mary, a trifle uncomfortable. "Richard! I've got a surprise for you. I want you in the drawing-room."

"Surprise? Well, I suppose it will keep till I've washed the dust off."— The drawing-room spelt visitors, and he had looked forward to pipe and book.

In course of making a hasty toilet, however, he pricked up his ears. Down the passage came the tones of a voice that seemed strangely familiar. And, sure enough, when he entered the room on Mary's heels, he found what he expected: the visitor Tilly was entertaining with such noisy gusto was no other than Purdy.

Purdy sat on the circular yellow-silk ottoman, in the easiest of attitudes. With one leg stuck straight out before him, he hugged the other to him by the knee, and rocked his body backwards and forwards as he told what was evidently a capital story—to judge by his own roars of laughter, and Tilly's purple face and moist eyes, at which she made feeble dabs with her pocket-handkerchief.

The shock of the encounter drove the semblance of a hearty greeting out of Mahony. But, with this, he had exhausted himself; Purdy and he could find no points of contact; and after a few halting remarks and awkward pauses, Purdy faced round to Tilly again, and took up the broken thread of his yarn. And, from now on, both there and at the high tea to which Mary presently led them, Mahony sat silent and constrained. For one thing, he disdained competition with Tilly, in her open touting for Purdy's notice. Again, as he looked and listened, he understood Mary's discomfort and embarrassment. On the occasion of their last meeting Purdy, both of them had been blind and dizzy with happiness. Now, the scales fell from his eyes. This, his former intimate and friend! This common, shoddy little man, already pot-bellied and bald; whose language was that of the tap-room and the stable; who sat there bragging of the shady knowledge he had harvested in dark corners, blowing to impress the women; one of life's failures and aware of it, and, just for this reason, cocksure, bitter, intolerant—a self-lover to the *n*th degree! In the extravagant fables they were asked to swallow, he, Purdy, had seen the best of everything, the worst of everything, had always been in the thick of a fray, and in at the finish.

Well! one person present seemed to enjoy the tasteless performance, and that was Tilly, who hung on his lips. More: she even urged him to repeat some of his tallest stories for the benefit of Mary, who had been out of the room.

"Oh, Mary, love, you *must* 'ear that yarn of the splitter and the goanna. I've laughed fit to burst my sides. Go on, Purd., tell it again. It was a regular corker."— And, belonging to the class of those who pre-indulge, Tilly heehawed at full lung-strength, in anticipation of the coming joke. After which Mahony had to listen, for the second time, to some witless anecdotes, the real point of which was to show Purdy in his rôle of top dog.

Was it possible that he had ever enjoyed, or even put up with, this kind of thing? Had Purdy always been a vainglorious braggart, or had the boasting habit grown on him, as he went downhill? Of course, he himself had not become more tolerant as the years went by; and he could afford to yield to his antipathies, now that no business reasons made civility incumbent.— But there was more in it than this. In earlier days, a dash of the old boyish affection had persisted, to blind him to Purdy's feelings; just as the memory of their boyhood's standing—he the senior, Purdy the junior—had caused Purdy to look up to him, and defer to his opinion. Now, nothing of this remained. On either side. Long-suffering, deference, affection, had alike been flung on time's scrap-heap—at least during the two distasteful hours now spent in Purdy's company, not even the ghosts of such feeling stirred.— Then what had brought him back? Mere tuft-hunting? Where, too, in the name of Christendom, had Mary fished him up, who would have been so much better left in obscurity? Had she really fancied she would give him, Mahony, a pleasure thereby? *Poor* Mary!

But the thin smile of amusement that curled his lips at the thought faded, when he heard her pressing Purdy to come again. And the first time he got her alone—it was not till bedtime—he took her soundly to task.

"Your surprise this afternoon was a surprise, indeed—in more ways than one. But what possessed you, Mary, to ask him to repeat the visit? My dear, you must surely see for yourself we cannot have the eyesore he has become, about this house?"

Mary paused in the act of slipping the rings off her fingers on to the branches of her ring-tree, and looked surprised. "*What*, Richard? Your *oldest* friend?" But Mahony, versed in every lightest expression that flitted across the candid face before him, felt the emphasis to be overdone. Like himself, it was plain Mary had suffered something of a shock.

So he swallowed a caustic rejoinder, and said drily: "Of course, I know your intentions were of the best. But . . . Well, frankly, my dear, I think it's bad enough if you fill the house with your old friends."

He was right. Her discomfiture showed in the way she now flared up. "Fill the house? . . . with one person at a time, and never more than two? Well I never! But—since you put it that way, Richard—I think it's rather a good thing I do. Otherwise we should never have a soul inside the doors."

"Give me books, and I don't want people."

"Oh, I've no patience with such a narrow, selfish standpoint. Why, whatever would be the good of all this—I mean the nice house, and our not needing to worry about expense—if we didn't ask other people to share it with us?"

"Pray, have I hindered you from doing so?"

"Well, not exactly. But why start to grumble now, when it's a question of your best friend?"

At the repetition, his patience in turn failed him. "Best friend! Oldest friend! Good heavens, Mary! *do* think what you are saying. How can one continue to be friends with a person one never sees or hears of? Surely the word implies somebody with whom one has at least *half* an idea in common? People don't stand still in this world. They're always growing and changing—up, or down, or off at a tangent. *Panta rei* is the eternal truth: *semper idem* the lie we long to see confirmed. And to hug a sentimental memory of what a mortal once was to you, and go on trying to bolster up an intimacy on the strength of it—why, that's to drag a dead carcase behind you, which impedes your own progress.— No, the real friend is one you pick up at certain points in your life, whose way runs along with yours—for a time. A time only. A milestone on your passage—no more. Few or none march together the whole way."

"Milestones? Why not tombstones, while you're about it?" cried Mary hotly, repudiating a theory that seemed to her wholly perverse. "Of course, you're able to use words I don't understand, but *I* say, once a friend, always a friend. I know *I'd* be sorry to forget anyone I had ever liked—even if I didn't find much to talk to them about.— But you must always have you own ideas. I declare, you're going on now about people just as you do about places, and about not wanting to see them again, once you've left."

"Yes, places and people—one as the other. Let me face forward—not back.— But to return to the matter in hand: I don't mind telling you, I'd gladly *pay* our visitor of this afternoon to stop away . . . and drink his tea elsewhere."

"I never heard such a thing!" Then, however, another thought struck her. "You're not letting that silly old affair in Ballarat still prejudice you against him?"

Mahony laughed out loud. "Good Lord, no! The grass has been green over that for what seems like half a century."

"Then, I know: it's because he drank his tea out of his saucer—and things like that."

"Tch!" On the verge of letting his temper get away with him altogether, Mahony pulled up. "Well, my dear . . . well, perhaps you're not altogether wrong. I'll put it even more plainly, though. Mary, it's because he spoke and looked like what I veritably believe him to be: an ostler in some stable. Horsey checks, dirty nails, sham brilliants; and a mind and tongue to match.— No, I stick to what I've said: I'd offer him a ten-pound note to stop away."

"I never knew anyone so hard on people as you."

"Pray, *do* I need to mix with ostlers, at my time of life? . . . and in my present position? It's not my fault that I have gone up in the world, and he down."

"No, but all the more reason not to turn your back on somebody who hasn't had your good luck."

"I deny that I'm a snob. I'd invite my butcher or my baker to the house any day, so long as he had decent manners, and took an interest in what interests me."

"My dear Richard, you only say that because you know

567

you'll never have to! And if you did, you wouldn't like them a bit better than you do Purdy.— But I'm sure I sometimes don't know what's coming over you. You used to be such a stickler for remembering old friends and old kindnesses, and hadn't had enough to say about people who didn't. I believe it was the going home that changed you.— Yet, when you were in England, how you railed at the people there, for letting themselves be influenced by a person's outside—how he ate peas, or drank his soup, and things like that."

"England had nothing whatever to do with it.— But it was a very different thing in Ballarat, Mary, where my practice brought me up against all sorts of people, to whom I was forced to be civil. Now there's no such obligation. And so I decline, once and for all, to exhibit the specimen we saw to-day, to our social circle. If you're absolutely bent on be-friending him—and I know doing good is, to you, the tempta-tion strong drink is to others; although in my opinion, my dear, you'll end by *over*doing it: you've not looked yourself for some weeks past. If you must have Purdy here, kindly let it be when no one else is present, and if possible, if you please, when I, too, am out of the way.— What you're to say about me? Anything you choose. It doesn't matter. He won't miss me, so long as your friend Tilly is at hand to drink in his words. You certainly hit the bull's-eye this time, my dear, in providing her with entertainment. Purdy's egregious lying was pabulum after her own heart."

With which Richard slung a towel round his neck and retired to the bathroom, leaving Mary to the reflection that, if ever there was a person who knew how to complicate the doing of a simple kindness, it was Richard. Here he went, detesting Tilly with all his old fervour, and dead set from the start against Purdy, and against his coming to the house. (It was true Purdy had got rather loud and bumptious; but a sensible woman like Tilly could be trusted soon to knock the nonsense out of him.) Meanwhile she, Mary, had somehow to propitiate all three; and, in particular, to hinder Richard from showing what he felt. For, if the match came off, Purdy would become a rich and important personage, to whom every door would open. And then Richard, too, would come round—would have to. If, that was, she could meanwhile contrive to keep him from making lifelong enemies of the happy pair.

[9]

TILLY said:

"My dear! the minute I set eyes on 'er, I knew she was a fraud. And I thinks to meself: 'Just you wait, milady, till the lights go out, and I'll cook your goose for you!' Well, sure enough, there we all sat, 'and-in-hand in the dark, like a party of kids playing 'unt-the-slipper. And by-and-by one and another squeals: 'I'm touched!' What do *I* do, Mary? Why, I gradually work the hand I'm 'olding in me right, closer to me left, till I'd got *them* joined, and me right 'and free. (It's as easy as Punch, if you know 'ow to do it.) And when the man next me—oh, 'e *was* a solemn old josser!—when 'e said, in a voice that seemed to come from 'is boots: 'The spirits 'ave deigned to touch me!'—as if 'e'd said: 'God Almighty 'as arrived and is present!'—I made one grab, and got 'old of—now what *do* you think? I'm danged if it wasn't 'er false chignon I found in me hand. I thought she was going to give me the slip then, Mary, after all: she wriggled like an eel. But I held on like grim death, and, luckily for me, she'd a few 'airs left still clinging to her cranium. She squeals like a pig. 'Up with the lights,' says I; 'I've got 'er!' 'Turn up the lights if you dare,' cries she: 'it'll kill me.' Over goes a chair in the scrimmage, and then they did turn 'em up, and there was she, squirming on the floor, bald like an egg, with I don't know how many false gloves, and feathers, and things besides, pinned on to 'er body!"

Tilly sat by the fire in Mary's bedroom, her black silk skirts turned back from the blaze. She was in high feather, exhilarated by her own acumen, as by the smartness with which she had conducted the exposure. Opposite her, Mary, her head tied up in red flannel, crippled by the heavy cold and the face-ache that had confined her to the house, listened with a sinking heart. It was all very well for Tilly to preen herself on what she had done: Richard would see it in a very different light. He had gone straight to his study on entering; and, hurrying out in her dressing-gown, to learn what had brought the two of them home so early, Mary had caught a glimpse of his face.

It was enough. When Richard looked like that, all was over: you might as well talk to a stone image. His hatred of scenes —of being made conspicuous in public—amounted to a mania. Never would he forgive Tilly the blunder she had this evening committed.

It was most discouraging. For a fortnight past, she had done every mortal thing a friend could do, to advance Tilly's suit; plotting and planning, always with an anxious ear to the study-door, in a twitter lest Richard should suddenly come out and complain about the noise. For the happy couple, to whom she had given up the drawing room, conversed in tones that were audible throughout the house: a louder courtship Mary had never heard; it seemed to consist chiefly of comic stories, divided, one from the next, by bursts of laughter. Personally, she thought the signs and portents would not be really favourable till the pair grew quieter: every wooing *she* had assisted at had been punctured by long, long silences, in which the listener puzzled his brains to imagine what the lovers could be doing. However, Tilly seemed satisfied. After an afternoon of this kind, she went into the seventh heaven, and leaning on Mary's neck, shed tears of joy: it *was* a case of middle-aged love-sickness, and no mistake. True, she also knew moments of uncertainty, when things seemed to hang fire, under the influence of which she would vehemently declare: "Upon my soul, Mary love, if *he* doesn't *I* shall! I feel it in my bones."— A state of mind which alarmed Mary, and made her exclaim: "Oh no, don't, Tilly!—don't do that. I'm sure you'd regret it afterwards. Besides, you know, dear, later on, he might cast it up at you."

And here now, Tilly had probably spoilt everything, by her hasty, ill-considered action.

Fortunately for her, she didn't realize how deeply she had sinned; though even she could see that Richard was angry.— "Of course, love, the doctor's in a bit of a taking, I warn you of that. I couldn't get a word out of 'im, all the way 'ome.— Lor', Mary, what geese men are, to be sure! . . . even the best of 'em. Not to speak of the cleverest. To see all those learned old mopokes sitting there to-night, solemn as hens on eggs! . . . It was enough to make a cat laugh. But even if 'e *does* bear me a bit of a grudge, love, it can't be 'elped. I'm not a one, Mary, to sit by and see a cheat, and keep me mouth shut. A fraud's a fraud, love, and even if it's the Queen 'erself."

"Of course it is. I feel just the same as you. It sometimes makes my blood boil to watch Richard, with all his brains, letting himself be duped by some dishonest creature who only wants to make money out of him. But . . . when he once gets an idea in his head, there's no doing anything with him. And he's not in the least *grateful* for having his eyes opened."—

Grateful, indeed! When, after an hour's solitude, which might really have been expected to cool him down, he came into the bedroom, his very first words were: "I've but one thing to say. Either that woman leaves the house, or I go myself!"

For all Mary's firm resolve to act the peacemaker, this was more than she could swallow. "Richard, don't be so absurd! We *can't* turn a visitor out of doors. Decency forbids."

"It's *my* house, and for me to say who I'll have in it."

"Tilly's *my* friend, and I'm not going to have her insulted." — Mary's tone was as dogged as his own.

"No! but she is at liberty to insult mine . . . and make me a laughing-stock, into the bargain. Such a scandalous scene as to-night's, it has never been my lot to witness."

"However did it happen that you held a seance? The invitation only said cards and music. I'd have kept her at home, if I'd guessed, knowing her opinion of that sort of thing."

"I wish to God you had! You talk of decency? You need hardly worry, I think, my dear, in the case of a person who has so few decent feelings of her own. *If* you could have heard her! 'I got 'er! Up with the gas! *I'm* 'olding 'er—by 'er false 'air!'"— Mahony gave the imitation with extravagant emphasis. "I leave it to you to imagine the rest. That voice . . . the scattered aitches . . . the gauche and vulgar manner . . . the medium weeping and protesting . . . your friend parleying and exclaiming—at the top of her lungs, too—glorying in what she had done, as if it was something to be proud of, and blind as a bat to the thunder-glances that were being thrown at her . . . no! I shall never forget it as long as I live. She has rendered me impossible, Mary—and in a house where, till now, I have been an honoured guest."

The exaggeration of this statement nettled Mary. She clicked her tongue. "Oh, *don't* be so silly, Richard! Surely you can write and explain? Mrs. Phayre will understand . . . that you had nothing to do with it."

"Who am I that I should have to explain and apologise?—

and for the behaviour of a person she did us the courtesy to invite."

"But considering the woman *was* a fraud? Tilly vows she had all sorts of contrivances pinned to her body."

"There you go! Ready, as usual, to believe anyone rather than me! She was no more a fraud than I am. She came to us well attested by circles of the highest standing. Yet, in spite of this, an ignorant outsider, who is present at a sitting for the first time in her life, has the insolence to set herself up as a judge.— Mary! I've put up with the job lot you call your friends, for more than a twelvemonth. But this is the last straw. Out she goes, and that's the end of it!"

But this flicked Mary on the raw. "You seem to forget *some* of the job lot were my own relations."

"Oh, now get touchy, do! When you know very well what I mean. But enough is enough. I can stand no more."

"You talk as if you were the sole person to be considered. As usual, think of nobody but yourself."

"Ha! I like that," cried Mahony, exasperated. "I think I've been possessed of the patience of Job, if you ask me. For there's never been a soul among them, with whom I had two ideas in common."

"No, you prefer these wretched mediums and the silly people who are taken in by them. I wish spiritualism had never been invented!"

"Don't talk about what you don't understand!"

"I *do. I* know nearly every time we go out now, I have to sit by and watch you letting yourself be humbugged. And then I'm not to open my mouth, or say what I see, or have any opinion of my own."

"No! I should leave that to the superior wits of your friend Tilly."

"I think it's abominable the way you sneer at Tilly! But if you do it just to get her out of the house, you're on the wrong track. She's *not* going away just now, and that's all about it. Anyone but you would understand what's happening. But you're so taken up with yourself that you never see a thing— not if it's under your very nose!"

"And pray what do you mean by that? *What* is happening?" Pierced by a sudden suspicion, Mahony swung round and faced her. Good Lord, Mary!" . . . his voice trailed off in a kind of incredulous disgust. "Good Lord! You don't want to tell me you're being fool enough to try to bolster up a match between this woman and . . . and Purdy?"

Mary tightened her lips and did not reply.

Mahony's irritation burst its bounds. "Well, upon my soul! . . . well, of all the monstrous pieces of folly!"— After which, however, he broke off to throw in caustically: "Of course, if it comes to that, I'll allow they're excellently matched . . . in manners and appearance.— But the fellow's an incorrigible waster. Anyone can see that with half an eye. He'll make ducks and drakes of old Ocock's hard-earned pile.— Besides, has he shown the least desire for matrimony? Are you not lending yourself to a vulgar intrigue on the woman's part? If so, let me tell you that it's beneath your dignity—your dignity as my wife—and I, for one, decline to permit anything so offensive to go on under my roof.— Not to speak of having to see you bear all the blame, should things go wrong."

"No, really, Richard! this is *too* much," cried Mary, and bounced up from her seat. "For *goodness'* sake, let me manage my own affairs! To hear you talk, anyone would think I was still a child, to be told what I may and mayn't do—instead of a middle-aged woman. I'm quite able to judge for myself; yes! and take the consequences, too. But you blow me up just as if I wasn't a person for myself at all, but only your wife. I think you might show a *little* confidence in me. I shan't disgrace you even if I am fool enough to bring two people together again, who were once so fond of each other. Which you actually seem to have forgotten.— Though I think your own common sense might tell you. Tilly's alone in the world, and has more money than she knows what to do with. And he has none. I think you can safely leave it to her to look after her own interests. She's a good deal sharper than any of us, you included. And Purdy, too! You sneer at him for an ostler and a ne'er-do-well. He's nothing of the sort. For six months now, he's worked hard as a traveller in jewellery." ("Ha! . . . *that* explains the sham diamonds, the rings, and the breastpins.") "There you go! . . . sneering again. And here am I, struggling and striving to keep the peace between you, till I don't know whether I'm standing on my head or my heels. And as far as you're concerned, it's not the least bit of good. I think you grow more selfish and perverse day by day. You ought to have lived on a desert

573

island, all by yourself. Oh, I'm tired . . . sick and tired . . . of it
and of everything!"—and, having said her say, passionately,
and at top speed, Mary suddenly broke down and burst out
crying.

Mahony's anger was laid on the instant. "Why, my dear! . . .
why, Mary . . . what's all this about? Come, come love!"—as
her sobs increased in violence—"this will never do. There, there
. . . there's nothing to upset yourself over. The fact is, as you
say, you're absolutely worn out. We shall be having you ill in
earnest, if this goes on. And small wonder, I'm sure. I declare,
as soon as you're rid of your cold, I shall shut this place up,
and take you away from everybody, on a trip to Sydney and
the Blue Mountains."

"I don't want to go to Sydney. I only want to be left alone,
and not have my friends insulted and turned out of the house."

"Good God, wife! . . . surely you can give me credit for
some small degree of tact? But now, enough. Just you lie still,
and go to sleep. Or, as I say, we shall have you really ill."

"Oh, leave me out of it, do! I shall be all right in the morning."

But this was not the case. Mary coughed, and tossed, and
went from hot to cold, and cold to hot, for the greater part
of the night. In the morning, her head felt a ton weight on the
pillow. It was no good chafing; in bed she had to stay.— Mahony and Tilly faced each other in glum silence across the
length of the breakfast-table.

The next few days bringing no improvement, Tilly had the
good sense to pack her trunks and return to Ballarat. And it
was one crumb of comfort to Mary that, thanks to her indis-
position, this departure was accomplished without further unpleasantness.

Leaning over the bed for a farewell embrace, Tilly answered her friend's hoarse whisper with a shake of the head.
— "But don't you bother, love. My dear, you'll see what you
do see! I'm no chicken, Mary, nor any mealy-mouthed school-
girl, to lose me chance for want of opening me mouth.— But
whatever happens, I'll never forget how you tried to pull it
off for me, old girl—never! . . . not so long as I live."

And now, the nervous strain she had been under, of lying
listening for sounds of strife and warfare—this removed, Mary
was left at peace in her dimity-white bed, and gave herself

up to the luxury of feeling thoroughly out of sorts. Richard found plenty to say in admonition, as the days went by and she continued low and languid, unable to shake off what seemed, after all, but a heavy cold. He also laid down many a stringent rule to safeguard her, in future, from the effects of her inexhaustible hospitality.

Then, however, the words died on his lips.

*　　*　　*　　*　　*　　*

When the truth dawned on them that Mary's illness could be ascribed to a purely natural cause, and that, at long last, she was to bear a child, husband and wife faced the fact as diversely as they now faced all vital issues. In Mahony's feelings, bewilderment and dismay had the upper hand. For though, at one time, Mary's childlessness had been a real grief to him, so many years had passed since then that he had long ceased either to hope or to regret.— And when you had bowed thus to the inevitable, and arranged your life accordingly, it was disquieting, to say the least of it, to see your careful structure turned upside down. Rudely disquieting.

And this sense of inexpediency persisted, long after Mary was up and about again, her old blithe self, and the two of them had more or less familiarised themselves with the idea of the drastic change that lay in store for them. The truth was: he no longer wished for children. One needed to be younger than he, still in the early years of married life, to accept their coming unconcernedly. (Nor was he enough of a self-lover to crave to see himself re-duplicated, and thus assured of an earthly immortality.) He felt old: *was* old: too late, now, to conjure up any of the dreams that belonged by rights to the coming of a child. His chief sensation was one of fear: he shrank from the responsibility that was being thrust upon him. A new soul to guide, and shield from harm, and make fit for life! . . . when he himself was so unsure. How establish the links that should bind it to the world around it?—as to the world unseen. How explain evil? . . . and sin? . . . the doctrine of reward and punishment?—and reconcile these with the idea of a tender, all-powerful Creator. For, though one might indulge in theory and speculation for one's own edification, one dare not risk them on a child. How, then, reduce to a single formula, intelligible to a young mind, the knotty problems of the universe, over which he had worn his own brains sore? Another more selfish point of view was that he looked forward with real apprehension to the upheaval of his little world: the inroads on, the destruction of, that peace and solitude with which he had fallen so deeply in love.

One bright side to the affair was, that they were now, for the first time in their united lives, really able to afford the outlay involved. They could make comfortable, even extravagant, preparations for the new arrival; and only too gladly did he bid Mary spend what she chose. For, though his own pleasure in the prospect of fatherhood was severely tempered, it warmed his heart to see her joy. "Radiant" was the only word that described Mary. No irksome thoughts of responsibility bore *her* down. She would have laughed at the notion, in regard to a child of her own. But then, never was less of a doubter than Mary: no hypercritical brooding over man's relation to God, or God's to the world, had ever robbed her of an hour's sleep. She accepted things as they were, with a kind of simple, untroubled faith. Or was it perhaps just the reverse—the absence of any religious spirit? Sometimes he half believed it; and that there existed in Mary more than a dash of the pagan.— Well, however that might be, the coming of a babe would set the crown on a life which, in spite of its happiness, had so far lacked the supreme gift. For women's arms, like their bodies, were built to cradle and enfold the young of the race.

Mary wrinkled her brow over none but the most practical considerations. Enough to occupy her was the burning question which rooms to take for nurseries, in a house where all rooms had long ago had their use allotted them.

Mahony laughed at her worried air. "Why, build 'em, my dear, and as many as you choose! I'll not grudge the expense, I promise you."

But this, of course, was just one of Richard's harebrained schemes. The house was amply big enough as it stood; and any additions would only spoil its shape. Time enough, too, to think of extra accommodation when all was happily over. Thus Mary: deciding, eventually, that the guest-rooms were those that must be sacrificed: they were large, cool, airy; and, once the baby was there, she would have scant leisure for entertaining. At least, in the beginning.— And so, with this reso-

lution, which was at once put into effect, Mary's overdone and
tiresome hospitality found its natural end.

Next came the question of furnishing; and, here, all was
not plain sailing. For Richard proved to have ultra-queer notions about what would be good for a child—his child!—and
what wouldn't. The nurse was not even to share a room with
it—and this, when most nurses slept with their charges in
the same bed! Then, he tabooed carpets, as dust-traps, so
that there was no question of just covering the floor with a
good Brussels; and curtains must be of the thinnest muslin—
not rep. In the end, Mary had the floors laid in polished wood,
on which were spread loose strips of bamboo matting; and
dark green sunblinds were affixed to the outsides of the windows. The walls were distempered a light blue. In place
of the usual heavy mahogany, the furniture was of a simple
style, and painted white. The little crib—it had to be made to
order, for Richard would have none of the prevalent rocking-
cradles, which, he declared, had rocked many a baby into
convulsions—was white, as well. When all was finished the
effect was quite fairylike, and so novel, that tales of the nurseries got abroad, and visitors invariably asked, before leaving,
if they might be allowed to peep at them.— Meanwhile, Mahony did his share by hunting up pictures on which the infant
eye might rest with pleasure. He also bought toys; and would
arrive home with his pockets bulging. Mary bore with him
as long as he confined his purchases to woolly balls and rag
dolls. But when it came to his ordering in an expensive rocking-horse, she put her foot down.

"*Really*, Richard! Just suppose anything . . . I mean it will
be more than time enough, dear, for things like these, a year
or two from now."

"Of course, the doctor expects *his* kid to come into the world
able to walk and talk . . . like a foal or a calf. Never will such
a miracle have trod this old earth before!"

And as Tilly—she had come down, on her own initiative,
solely to be near Mary over her confinement—as she drove
back to the "George" at St. Kilda, where she was putting up,
she hummed the popular refrain:

"Oh, la, la!
What fools men are!"

577

For, besides making a donkey of himself over his purchases, Mahony was haunted, now the end drew nigh, by the fear of some accident happening to Mary. He hardly trusted her out of his sight; hardly let her put one foot before another,—"As jumpy as a Persian cat! You'd never think, would you, love, the doctor 'ad brought hundreds of brats into the world, in 'is day?"

Mary sat in a rocking-chair on the shady side of the verandah, and waved a palm-leaf fan to keep the flies off. More often, though, she was surrounded by yards of frothy muslin, real India muslin, which she fashioned into robes and petticoats, on which she frilled, and tucked, and embroidered, sewing every stitch by hand.

"A regular trousseau!" said Tilly; and enviously fingered the piles of gossamer garments.

On the ordeal that was before her, Mary herself was not given to brooding: for one thing, she felt altogether stronger, nowadays, than she had felt as a girl. And the first discomforts of her state over, her health was well maintained. But when December, with its livid heat, had slipped into the greater heats of January, and her time came, she gave birth as hardly as on that first occasion, long years ago; all but paying with her own for the new life she was bringing into the world. Well-known specialists, hastily summoned, performed a critical operation, Mahony's trust in his own skill as usual deserting him, where Mary was in question. And though the operation was successful and the child was born alive, days of acutest anxiety followed, before it was known if Mary would pull through. Tilly and Mahony buried the hatchet, in the long hours they spent together in that darkened bedchamber, where Mahony moved a pale, distraught shadow, and Tilly sat weeping silently, her handkerchief to her eyes. In the dining-room, John and Jerry strayed aimlessly to and fro among the furniture; and outsiders like Mrs. Devine would drive up early, and remain sitting in their carriages, to hear the latest bulletin. In the end, Mary's sound constitution triumphed, and she was gradually won back to life; but over a week passed before she even asked to see her child. Then, however, in sudden impatience, she tried to raise herself on her elbow— a movement that sent Tilly and the nurse flying to lay her flat again. Tilly it was who, going to the crib, carried to her on a pillow one of the tiniest babies ever seen: a waxen doll, with black hair an inch long, and the large black eyes of Mary's own family.

It was a boy. At his baptism, where John, Jerry and Lizzie stood sponsors, he received the name of Cuthbert—in full was to be known as Cuthbert Hamilton Townshend-Mahony.

PART III

[1]

THESE unlooked-for children—the following year twin girls were born, thus rounding off a trio—came too late to form the bond between their parents they might once have done. For that, the attitudes adopted towards them by father and mother, themselves now branched so far apart, were too dissimilar. In Mahony's case, once his children were there, in the flesh before him, all his puny fears of personal upset and mental pother fell away. He had only to feel tiny soft fingers straying over his face, to become the tenderest of fathers, loving his babies wholeheartedly. Now, he feared only for them, in their frailty and helplessness. Did he wake in the night and think he heard a cry, he was out of bed in an instant; and the nurse, entering from the next room to make sure of her charges, would find her master there before her—a tall, dressing-gowned figure, shading a candle with his hand. Often, too, when wakeful, he would rise and steal into the night-nursery, to take a peep at his little ones, lying relaxed in sleep. Yes, he was passionately solicitous for them—and not for their bodily health alone. He would have wished to shield their little plastic minds from all impressions that might pain or harm; have had them look only at beautiful and pleasant things, hear soft voices and kind words: on no child of his might hand be laid in anger.— The result was, the children, dimly conscious of his perpetual uneasiness, were rendered uneasy by it in their turn, for all the deep affection from which it sprang, never really warmed towards their father.

Instead, they sunned themselves in their mother's love, which knew nothing of fears or apprehensions. Mary laughed at Richard's exaggerated anxiety; though she was rejoiced to see him so fond. A self-centred person like him might well have found children a nuisance, and in the way.

To her they were all in all; and on them she lavished that great hoard of mother-love, which, till now, she had spent on the world at large. Had they been born shortly after her marriage, she, who was then little more than a child herself, would have been a child along with them; and the four would have grown up together, in a delightful intimacy. Of this, there was now no question. Coming when they did, the children stood to her only for possessions—her most precious possessions—but still, something absolutely her own, to do with just as she thought good. Through them, too, she believed she would some day gratify those ambitions which, where Richard was concerned, had proved so stark a failure. He had had no desire to walk the high paths she had mapped out for him. Her children would—and should.— In the meantime, however, ambition lay fallow in love; and it was to their mother the babies ran with their pains and pleasures, their discoveries and attainments. She alone gave them that sense of warmth and security, in which very young things thrive.

Their devotion to her was the one feature the three had in common. The twins—they soon earned the nickname of the "Dumplings"—were mere rolypoly bundles of good-nature and jollity, who rarely cried, and were as seldom ill as naughty. Mary boasted: the most docile children in the world! Passionately attached to each other—said Mahony, it was as though a single soul had been divided between two bodies—they toddled through babyhood quite literally hand in hand; faithfully sharing all good things that came their way; sleeping in the same crib, face to face, each with an arm flung protectively about the other's neck. To look at, they were as like as two peas, blue-eyed, fair-haired, dimpled, lovely to handle in their baby plumpness, and the most satisfying of armfuls. Their development, too, kept equal pace: they walked late, owing to the burden of their little rotundities; and long remained content with inarticulate sounds for speech.

The boy was of quite another fibre: as hard to manage as they were easy; as quick as they were slow— Tilly early said of him: "Lor', Mary! the doctor 'imself, in frocks and petticoats." But this referred chiefly to little physical tricks and similarities: a certain faddiness about his food, his clothes, his

580

belongings. In him was a strain that had nothing to do with his father.— A naughty child he was not—especially at first. He, too, began life as a placid infant, who slept well, did not cry, and accepted, philosophically, the bottle-substitute that was put to his lips. This meant, of course, that, in spite of his midget-size at birth, he was quite sound and healthy—in a fragile, wiry way. He continued small, but was neatly formed. To his mother's colouring, he added his father's straight features; and, even in babyhood, he had the latter's trick of carrying his head well back, and a little to one side. He walked before he was a year old, talked soon after; and, to his parents' intense pride, was able to pick out a given letter from a play-alphabet, before he either walked or talked.

His precocity showed itself in other ways as well. For a year and a quarter he was King of the House, the pivot of his little world, sole occupant of his mother's knee. Then came the sudden apparition of his sisters. In the beginning, Cuffy—thus he named himself—did not pay much heed to this pair of animated dolls, who moved their legs and arms when bathed, and rode out in a carriage beside his, but for the most part lay fast asleep and negligible. Only gradually did it dawn on him that his privileges were being invaded; that not only, indeed, was his reign as sole ruler at an end, but that the greater favours were falling to the newcomers' share. And, one day, the full knowledge of what had happened burst through, with disastrous results, Cuffy being then something over two years old. Dressed for driving, Mary entered the nursery; and Cuffy clamoured to be set upon her knee.

"Not now, darling, I've no time. You must wait till Mamma comes back."

But the nurses appearing at this moment with the babies, all warm and fragrant from the afternoon nap, Mary was not able to resist holding out her arms for them. She even lingered, fondling them, after the carriage was announced.

Cuffy had docilely retreated to a corner, where he played with a stuff elephant. But, on seeing this—seeing his mother, who had been too busy to nurse him, sit there petting the twins, who had not even *asked* to be nursed—he came back, trailing his beast behind him, and planting himself before her, stood and regarded her, with his solemn black eyes.— ("I do declare, Master Cuffy seems to look right through you and out

581

behind, when he stands and stares so!" was a saying of Nannan's.)

Relinquishing her babies, Mary stooped to him. "Say goodbye to Mamma."

To her amazement, Cuffy, instead of putting up his face for a kiss, darted at her what she described to Richard as "a dreadfully naughty, rebellious look," and going over to his rocking-horse, which, though he was not yet allowed to mount it, was his dearest treasure, started to beat it with both hands, and with such force that the patient effigy swung violently to and fro.

Shocked at this fit of temper, Nannan and Mary exclaimed in chorus:

"Master Cuffy! Well, I never did! Such tantrums!"

"Cuffy! What *are* you doing? If you are so naughty, Mamma will never take you on her knee again."

The child's back being towards her, she did not see how, at these words, the little face flushed crimson, the eyes grew round with alarm. Cuffy at once left off hitting the horse; just stood stock-still, as if letting what his mother had said sink in. But he did not turn and come to her.

Mary told Richard of the incident, as she buttoned her gloves. And Richard had Cuffy brought to him. Laying aside his book, he lifted the child to his knee.

"Papa is sorry to hear Cuffy has been naughty. Will Cuffy tell Papa why?"

Unwinkingly the great eyes regarded him. But there was no response.

"Fy, fy! To hit poor horsey . . . when it had done nothing to deserve it."

"Cuffy's 'orsey—own norsey."

"But, just because it *is* Cuffy's—Cuffy's very own—he must be kind . . . all the kinder . . . to it.— Never wreak your temper or your vengeance, my little son, on a person or thing that is entirely in your power. It's ungenerous. And I want my Cuffy to grow up into a good, kind man. As careful of the feelings of others as he is of his own."

Something in his father's voice—grave, measured, tender—got at the baby, though the words went over his head. And then Mahony saw what he long remembered: a fight for self-control extraordinary in one so young. The black eyes filled;

the little mouth twitched and trembled. But the child swallowed hard, again and again, in an attempt to keep back his tears. And when, at last, they broke through, he turned and hid his face against his father's coat. Not, Mahony felt sure, seeking there either comfort or sympathy. Merely that his distress might be unobserved.— Taking in his own the two little hands, which were locked in each other, Mahony drew them apart. Both palms were red and sore-looking, and no doubt still tingled hotly. The child had hurt himself most of all.

But Cuffy's tears were soon dried. After a very few seconds he raised his face, and, this having been patted with his father's handkerchief, he slid to the floor and trotted back to the nursery. And then, said Nannan, what a to-do there was! Master Cuffy dragged his little chair up beside the horse, climbed on the chair, and put his arms round the animal's neck, talking to it for all the world as if it was a live creature, and could talk back.

"Wos 'oo 'urt, dea' 'orsey?—poor 'ickle 'orsey! Cuffy didn't mean to. Wot 'oo say, 'orsey? 'Orsey 'oves Cuffy double-much? Dea' 'orsey! Cuffy 'oves 'orsey, too—much more better zan Effalunt."

Thereupon, having deposited horsey's rival upside-down in a dark cupboard, he begged a lump of sugar from Eliza, the under-nurse, and rammed it in between the steed's blood-red jaws; where it remained, until a trail of white ants were discovered, making a straight line for it from the window.

To Mary, Mahony said: "If I were you, my dear, I should be careful to distribute my favours equally. Don't let the little fellow feel that his nose has been put out of joint. He's jealous —that's all."

"Jealous? Of the babies? Of his own sisters? Oh, Richard! . . . I don't think that augurs very well for him.— And surely he can't learn too soon that it's for him to give way to them —as little girls?"

For almost the first time in his knowledge of her, Mahony seemed to sense a streak of hardness in Mary; for the first time, she did not excuse a wrongdoer with a loving word. And this her own child!

"He's but a baby himself. Don't ask too much of him," he soothed her. And added: "Of course, though, I only give you my idea. Do as you think best."— For Mary had proved as

capable as a mother as at everything else: she solved problems
by sheer intuition, where he would have fretted and fumbled.
Even the children's early religious training had, when the time
came, fallen to her. Here, again, she had no bothersome theories: just the simplest practice. The question whether Cuffy
and his sisters should be taught to pray, or not to pray; to invoke a personal, or an impersonal Deity; never entered her
head. As soon as they could lisp their first syllables, they knelt
night and morning at her knee, to repeat their "Gentle Jesus!"
and "Jesus, tender Shepherd!"— And as long as the great First
Cause was set forth in this loving and protective guise, Mahony
saw no reason to interfere. He contented himself with forbidding the name of God ever to be used as a threat, or in connection with punishment: the children were taught that the
worst that could befall a sinner was a temporary withdrawal of
God's love. Nor would he have the *"Thou God seest me!"* fal-
lacy—this reduction of the Omnipotent and Eternal to the level
of spyer and peeper—instilled into their young minds: while
such a purely human invention as the Devil—"That scapegoat
on which man piles the blame for the lapses in his own nature!"—was never to be so much as mentioned in the nursery.

These few simple rules laid down, he retired into the background. The comfortable knowledge that his children were in
the best of hands left his mind free.

Until now, it had been plain sailing. Now . . . well, Mary
invariably dated the beginning of the real trouble with Cuffy
from the day on which he flew into such a naughty passion
with his horse.— Exactly an easy child to manage, he had never
been; he was too fanciful for that. In his case, there was no
need for Richard to fuss and fidget about keeping ugly things
from him. Cuffy himself would have none of them. Before he
was a twelvemonth old, did he, in looking at his "Queen of
Hearts" story-book, draw near the picture of the thieving knave,
you saw his eyes getting bigger and bigger. And if he could
not contrive, with his baby hands, to turn two pages at once—
and nobody else might do it for him!—he would avert his
eyes altogether, or lay his palm flat over the wretch's ugly face.
The Doré illustrations to his big fairy-book had a kind of horrid fascination for him. There he would sit, staring at these
dense and gloomy forests, these ruined, web-hung castles lying
in their stagnant moats—and then, when bedtime came, he

turned frightened. It was of no use trying to shame him with: "Well, I never! A great boy like you! Why, the Dumplings aren't a bit afraid." Or cheerily assuring him: "There are no such things, darling, as witches and giants. They're only made up to amuse little children."

Cuffy knew better—when the lamp was out, and Nannan had left the nursery. Then, the picture he feared most: Hop-o'-my-Thumb, a creature in petticoats, no bigger than himself, leading a long string of brothers and sisters into a forest black as ink: this picture *would* rise up before him. Not only so, but he himself must join the tail, fall in after Hop-o', and follow into that dreadful wood, where the ogre lived.— Since he could not resist its attraction, the book had to be locked away.

The eldest, and a boy, to be such a baby! Mary felt quite abashed for Cuffy, in the eyes of the nursery, and lost no chance of poking fun at his fears. But it did not help; and eventually she saw that she must leave it to time, to drive this nonsense out of him. There were other, more actively disturbing traits in his nature, on which time might have the opposite effect. For example, for such a little child, he was far too close and reserved; he kept his thoughts and feelings buttoned up inside himself. He had a passionate temper if roused —"Cuffy's temper," it was called, as though of a special brand that belonged to him alone—but he did not often give it play. Was he hurt, or offended, or angry, he would, as a rule, retire to a corner, and stay there by himself. If he had to cry, he cried in a corner; he did not want to be petted or comforted; and he would also, in nine cases out of ten, not say— Richard declared would perhaps not be able to say—why he cried. Mary saw him growing up very unfrank and secretive; which, to her, spelt deceitful.

Again, it wormed in her that he was not a friendly or a trusting child—one of those who indiscriminately hold out their arms, or present a cheek. Cuffy would not go to strangers, or always give his kiss when bidden. Nor was he generous; he did not willingly share his toys, or his picture-books, or his lollipops. The things that belonged to *him*, belonged absolutely. Really, he seemed to look upon them as bits of himself, and hence not to be parted with. His favourite animals—horse and elephant—might be touched by no one. Was there a children's party in the nursery, special playthings had to be provided, or only those used that were the Dumplings' property. To Mary, bound by but gossamer threads to all things material, her little son's attitude was something of a mystery; and many a time did she strive with him, over the head of it. His inability to share with others stood to her for sheer selfishness. She trembled, too, lest the Dumplings should learn to copy him in this, and cease to be the open-hearted, open-handed little mortals they were. For they looked up to Cuffy with adoring eyes—Cuffy, who walked while they still drove; was present at dessert in the evening, while they were put to bed; wore knickerbockers instead of skirts.— But, try as she might, by teaching and example, she could not influence the boy, let alone master him; while the usual nursery proceeding of making a child's naughty fit end with an expression of contrition, shattered on Cuffy's obstinacy. If he did not feel sorry, he would not say he was; and, in the battle royal that ensued, he generally came off victor.— The fact was, in the dark-eyed mite she had now to deal with, Mary ran up against more than a dash of her own resolute spirit; and, naturally enough, failed to recognise it.

"He's got a shocking will of his own. And what troubles me, Richard, is, if he's as set as all this when he's not much more than a baby, whatever will he be when he grows up?"

"Set? Nonsense, my dear! The child's got character. Give it scope to expand. Try to influence him, and work on his good feelings, instead of bullying him."

"It's all very well for you to talk. You don't have to deal with him a dozen times a day. I must say, I sometimes think you might help a little more than you do." It was a sore point with Mary that Richard would not rise to his responsibilities as a father, but went on leading the life of a bookworm, and a recluse. "Especially as the child takes more notice of you than of anyone else."

But Mahony was not to be bought. "My dear, you've the knack, and I haven't.— Now don't worry. As long as he's honest and truthful, he'll be all right."

Honest? . . . truthful? That went without saying! It was only that Mary wanted her first-born to be so much more: sunny, lovable, transparent, brave—and a hundred other things, besides.

He was Nurse's darling, though. You had only, said Nan-

nan, to beware of knocking up against any of his funny little
fads, such as undressing him before people, or asking him to
eat with any but his own silver fork and spoon.

"What Master Cuffy needs is just a bit of managing. I can
twist him round my little finger."— But it did not tally with
Mary's ideas that a child of that age should have to be "managed" at all.

Turning from these traits in her son of which she could
not approve, she dwelt with pleasure on his marked quickness
and cleverness. Cuffy had sure fingers and a retentive memory.
At an early age he could catch a ball, and trundle a hoop;
could say his prayers without prompting; learn nursery rhymes
at a single hearing; could eat nicely, keep himself clean, button
up those of his buttons which were within reach: in short, do
everything in this line that could possibly be expected of so
young a mortal.

And, in addition, he had one genuine talent. For some
reason or other—"a throwback to his grandmother," supposed
Mahony—Cuffy had been dowered with a natural gift for
music. He learnt tunes more easily than he learnt his letters;
could hum "Rock of Ages" and "Sun of my Soul," before he
uttered a word. His ear was extraordinarily good, his little
voice sweet and true. And, knowing that Mary's intonation
was but faulty, that of the nursery faultier still, Mahony here
put in his single spoke in Cuffy's education. He had the boy
brought to his dressing-room of a morning; and there, while
he dressed, Cuffy, with his elephant, would sit perched on a
corner of the table, singing songs old and new. Together Mahony and his son practised "Oft in the Stilly Night," and "The
Land o' the Leal," and with such success that, was there company to dinner, Cuffy, clad in his best velvet tunic, would be
stood on a chair at dessert, to perform to the guests. And as he
gave forth, in baby language, such ditties as:

> "A temple to friendship,
> Cried Laura, enchanted,
> I'll build in my garden,
> The thought is divine!"

the ladies uttered rapturous exclamations; while the gentlemen, mostly without a note of music in them, declared: " 'Pon

my word, very remarkable, very remarkable indeed!" And
Aunt Lizzie, from whom Cuffy had picked up this song by
ear, hailed him as an infant prodigy, and painted for him a
future that made Mary's heart swell with pride.

❖   ❖   ❖   ❖   ❖   ❖

Such were Mahony's children.

[2]

MRS. MARRINER, the youngish widow whose acquaintance Mary
had made while visiting on the Urquharts' station, was a person of character. In the matter of dress, for example, she de-
fied the prevailing fashion; wore her light brown hair straight
back from her brow (which was classic), and, employing
neither net nor comb, twisted it in a Grecian knot on the nape
of her neck. She also eschewed crinoline, and wandered a tall,
willowy figure, the eyed of all beholders.

"Out and away too conspicuous!" was Mahony's verdict.
"The woman must *want* people to stare at her.— Though, I will
say, Mary, it's something of a treat to behold the natural female figure again, after the unnatural bulgings we've put up
with.— And a very fine figure, too!"

For this he had to admit: there was nothing unfeminine or
forbidding—"bloomerish" was his word for it—about the lady.
She was as handsome as she was striking. A full eye, a Grecian
nose, a slim waist: such were her charms; to say nothing of a
white, dimpled hand and a well-turned ankle.— And yet, every
one who knew her was agreed that she captivated less by reason of her comeliness than by the ease and elegance of her
manner.

She was just as popular with her own as with the sterner
sex. Which said a good deal; for, wherever she went, she
was run after "by the gentlemen." And small wonder, too,
thought Mary. For Gracey was up in any subject, however dry;
had brains really equal to "gentlemen's conversation."

Richard said: "It's not the least piquant thing about her,
Mary, that after she has been holding forth, supremely well,
on one of those learned themes you ladies as a rule fight shy
of, she will suddenly lapse into some delightful feminine in-
consequence. That, my dear, gives us men back, for a finish,

the sense of superiority we need!"— But here you just had one of the satirical remarks Richard was so apt at making—especially in the early stages of an acquaintance. Afterwards, he generally had to eat his words; or at least to water them down.

Mrs. Marriner rented a villa within easy driving distance of *Ultima Thule.* This was in the early days of the nursery, while the twins were still babies in arms, and Mary could go out but little. It fell to the newcomer to pick up the threads; and this she did with a will, calling so frequently and entering so wholeheartedly into Mary's interests, that they were soon the best of friends. She was devoted to children; and sometimes, as they sat on the verandah, Nannan would bring Cuffy out to them. And then it was a pretty sight to see the tall, handsome woman on her knees before the little child, rolling his woolly ball to him, or playing at peek-a-bo.

The merry voices lured even Mahony forth from his den. And having tossed his son into the air, he lingered for a word with his wife's guest. This happened more than once; after which, as Mary had foreseen, his sarcasms died away. Mrs. Marriner had travelled widely, and owned a large collection of photographs of famous beauty-spots; and the first time Mahony went to her house was when he and Mary drove over, one evening, to view these through a stereoscope. Dotting the rooms, they found many another interesting memento of her travels. On the chimney-piece stood candelabra of Dresden china. Framed and coloured prints of Venice by night, and of the blue grotto of Capri, adorned the walls. A statuette of Christ, by a Danish sculptor, ornamented the top of the piano. She had a very fair assortment of books—serious works, too: essays, poetry, history—both old, and of the newest; and Mahony carried away with him a couple of volumes by a modern writer of verse named Browning.

In addition, she was musical. Not in sister Lizzie's superb, almost professional fashion; but singing in a clear, correct voice, and playing the pianoforte with neatness and skill. Her performance of Mendelssohn's *Songs without Words,* and some pretty ballads by Blockley, was most enjoyable. And now it was Mahony's turn to suggest inviting her; after which he went back to practise duets, and listen to her execution of a sonata by Haydn. He relished, too, a conversation that rose for once above the affairs of the nursery.

For, the piano closed, the lady and he dropped into talk. And having skimmed the surface of various subjects, on which they found themselves in marvellous accord, they came round to the one which still engrossed Mahony's attention. Of spiritualism, Mrs. Marriner was ignorant; she begged the doctor to enlighten her. And the rough sketch he gave her interested her so much that she expressed a strong wish to know more. He promised to bring her an armful of books about it; and then, if her interest still held, to procure her the entrée to a sitting at the house of that arch-spiritualist, Mrs. Phayre, where remarkable phenomena were taking place. Weird noises could be heard there at dead of night: the furniture was moved by unseen hands from its place against the wall.

The next day he carried over the books; and Mrs. Marriner read them with what seemed to him a rare and unfeminine insight: that is to say, she was neither alarmed, nor derisive, not stupidly obstinate: and, so far, except for members of the inner circle, he had known no woman whose state of mind towards the question was not one of these three. She also jumped at his offer of introducing her at a seance.— Later on, she went even further. Learning that he was eager to find an unprofessional medium, with whom he might experiment in private, and on whom no shadow of suspicion could be held to rest, she herself proposed sitting at a small table in her own drawing-room. And after a few fruitless hours, during which he had every reason to admire her patience, they met with success: the table tilted under their hands, and a pencil, delicately sustained by the lady's fingers, wrote words that could be read. It was plain she was possessed of the power.

He went home to Mary in high feather.

"Now, perhaps, you'll believe there's something in it!"

"I'm sure I never said there wasn't *something*. It's only that . . ."

"You can hardly suspect your friend of being an impostor?"

"Good gracious, no! The idea!"

And Mary meant it. Gracey was no more capable of downright fraud than she herself.— And yet . . . yet . . . you might say what you liked; there was a part of you that simply *would not* accept the conclusions you were asked to draw. To think, because a table stood on two legs, or a pencil wrote: "I am here!" that dead people—people who lay mouldering in their graves!—were speaking to you . . . no! that she would never be able to believe, not if she lived to be a hundred. Why, you might just be leaning a *little* too heavily on your side of the table, without knowing it. Or your hand write things down in a kind of dream, and you imagine somebody or something else was doing it. And still be the most truthful person alive. Like Richard. Who again and again allowed himself to be imposed on.— The fact of the matter was: if people wanted to believe such things, believe they would, and nothing would stop them: the wish was father to the thought.— Well, at any rate this new hobby of Richard's had one advantage: it gave him *something to do*. Which was just what he needed. Instead of always sitting humped up over his books.

Under the stimulus, he began to look more like his old self. He spruced up his dress for one thing; and the daily ride to Gracey's gave him beneficial exercise. As time went on, their sittings proved so satisfactory that he began to think of publishing a small pamphlet, embodying the results. And though Mary would rather it had been on a less outlandish subject, yet she hailed the idea, and encouraged it.— For looking after Richard became, year by year, more like minding a fidgety child, who had always to be kept on the go. He had been such a worker in his day. And the old, old fear could still wake in her that, without active employment, he might all of a sudden turn restless, and declare himself tired of their lovely home.

But then came that afternoon when Lizzie, in the course of a visit, let drop an item of news which successfully routed Mary's peace of mind.

They did not see much of Lizzie nowadays; she and John were always in society; out, night after night, at concerts, dinners, balls. Or entertaining lavishly in their own home. It was an open secret that, very soon now, the longed-for knighthood would set the crown on John's labours for the colony.

Stateliness in person, gauzes and laces floating from arms and shoulders, trinkets and chains a-jingle, Lizzie swept through the hall, a very fine figure indeed. No wonder John was said still to be unable to refuse her anything!

Then, just about to step into her carriage, she paused. "Mary, déhling . . . I vow I all but forgot it! I have something to tell you, love, that I think will interest you. Mary! I met a gentle-

man on Friday, who was once acquainted with our friend—
the charmin' Gracey. And *what* do you think? My dear! she is
not a widow at all."

Mary was thunderstruck. "*Not* a widow? Lizzie! Then——"

"My déhling, her husband is still alive. He left her, love—
deserted her for another woman . . . the lowest of the low! At
this very moment, he lives with the creature . . . in his lawful
wife's stead."

As always, Mary's first impulse was to protect . . . defend.
"Oh, *poor* Gracey! Oh, poor thing! . . . how terrible for her!"

"Well, love! . . . I thought you ought to know since dear
Richard is so friendly there. And considering the ultra-strict
views he holds . . ."

"Yes, yes, of course. But, Lizzie, it's not her *fault*, is it? *She*
can't help the man she married turning out a scoundrel."

But though she spoke up thus, Mary was deeply perturbed;
and her mind became a sea of doubts, where no doubts had
been. She found herself looking at Gracey with other eyes. The
fact was, a divorced or legally separated woman—even one who
was just living apart from her husband—was by no means the
same as a widow . . . and never could be. Gracey knew that
well enough; else why, to a close friend like herself, had she
made a mystery of her state? And though not a shadow of
blame should rest on her (and Mary was sure it didn't), it
meant, none the less, that she had been through all sorts of
unpleasant matrimonial experiences, which a properly married,
or widowed, woman would know nothing about. *Something*
of them might have remained clinging to her . . . the old saw
about touching pitch would not keep out of Mary's head. It
was really dreadful. Such a dear, nice woman as Gracey!—
And yet . . . deep down in Mary's heart there dwelt the obstinate conviction that once married was always married, and
that as long as your husband lived you belonged at his side.
Did you sit firm, and hold fast to your rights as a wife, it
seemed incredible that another woman could ever usurp your
place. Had Gracey perhaps gone off in a tantrum, leaving the
coast clear? Oh! doubts would up to-day.— One result was
she found herself considering, with a more critical eye, the
friendship that had sprung up between Richard and Grace,
over their table-tilting. Never before had she known Richard
so absorbed by anything or anyone outside his home. Now sup-

pose, just suppose Gracey, thanks to her wretched married life,
had come to regard things—serious things, sacred things—more
lightly than she ought? What if, because of her own unhappy
past, she should not hold the marriage-tie to be binding?—
Why was she so attractive to the gentlemen? Did they know
or suspect anything? . . . In reply to which there flashed
through Mary's mind a memory of her last visit to Yarangobilly: Willy Urquhart's infatuation, and the state into which
poor Louisa had worked herself. Of course, there was really
no comparison between the two cases—none whatever! Willy
was a notorious flirt: Richard, a gentleman. And poor Louisa's
morbid, distorted outlook would never be hers.

Richard. . . . The question that teased Mary was: should she
tell him what she had heard, or just keep it to herself? In
one way she agreed with Lizzie that he ought to know, he
being so fastidious in his views. Besides, if he heard it from
some other source, he might feel aggrieved that she had held
back.— On the other hand, his knowing would probably cur-
tail, if not put a stop altogether to his and Gracey's experi-
ments: he wouldn't want to give people more food for talk.
And that would really be a pity.— Would it be disloyal to
him to say nothing? Disloyal to Gracey to tell what she so
plainly wished to keep dark? But Richard came first. He was
the one to be studied, if she had to choose between them.—
And here again, unlike poor Louisa, Mary felt she could weigh
the matter very calmly; for in her was a feeling nothing could
shake: the happily married woman's comfortable sense of possession. It was not only the fact of Richard being what he was.
Their life together rested on the surest of foundations: the
experiences of many, how many, years; the trials and tribula-
tions they had been through together, the joys they had shared;
the laughs they had had over things and people; a complete
knowledge of each other's prejudices and antipathies—who
else could unlock, with half a word, the rich storehouse of
memories they had in common? Homelier things, too, there
were in plenty, which bound no less closely: the airing and
changing of your underlinen; how sweet or how strong you
drank your coffee; how you liked your bed made; your hatred
of the touch of steel on fruit; of a darn in a sock.— Deeper
down, though, pushed well below the top-most layer of her
consciousness, just one unspoken fear *did* lurk. If she told

Richard what she had heard, and he did not take it in the spirit he had hitherto invariably shown towards irregularities of this kind, Mary knew she would feel hurt and humiliated. Not for herself; but for him.

    *   *   *   *   *

The sitting at an end, the table was put back in its place against the wall.

"You will smoke, doctor? Nay, please do! I like it. Here are matches.— Down, Rover! Not yet, Fitz!"— For, at her movement, a red setter had sprung up from a corner, and now stood, his front paws on her knee, ingratiatingly wagging his tail; while, observing his comrade's advance, an immense black cat, which had been dozing in an arm-chair, rose and dropped a kind of bob-curtsey with its hind quarters. "Behold my two tyrants! They think it time for a run.— Oh, yes, Mr. Fitz comes too."

"You are very fond of animals."

"I should be lost without them. They are such dear companions, in their dumb way." As she spoke, Mrs. Marriner fondled a silky ear, letting it slip, time and again, through a pretty, dimpled hand.

"Well do I know it! In my bachelor days, living in a bark-hut the whole of which would have gone into this room, I kept no less than three." And casting the net of his memory, Mahony told of his long-forgotten pets, and of their several untimely ends.— "After which, I took no more."

"You had not the heart?"— Now, would any but a genuine animal-lover have put this question?

"It was not exactly that. But, as a hard-worked medico, with a growing practice . . . the burden of them, you see, would have fallen on my wife. And she does not greatly care for animals."

"Dear Mary. And now, of course, she has her babies."

"Yes, and all a mother's fears and tremors for them, with regard to the four-footed race."

"That is but natural. While they are so tiny."— In the kindly indulgence of her tone, the speaker seemed to take all mothers and their weaknesses under her wing. "And yet, doctor, if I had been blessed with little ones, I think I should have brought up babies, puppies, and kittens *en masse* . . . as one family party.— Correct me, though, if I speak foolishly. Perhaps, when children come, they are all in all."

"It *is* amazing how the little beggars twine themselves round one's heart.— Before my boy was born, my chief feeling was a dread of the coming responsibility. I can laugh at myself now. For my wife has shouldered everything of that sort . . . and as a matter of course, I leave the children entirely to her."

"I think dear Mary quite the most capable person I know."

What a handsome creature she was, to be sure, as she sat there, full-bosomed yet slender, her neat waist held by a silver girdle, her face alight with sympathy and understanding! Mahony felt himself glow and expand. He answered heartily: "There have, indeed, been few situations in life Mary has not proved equal to."

The words set a string of memories vibrating; and a silence fell. Unlike many of her sex, who would have babbled on, the lady just smiled and waited; and even her waiting was perfect in tact.

Mahony felt drawn to unbosom himself. "Talking of my children . . . it is sometimes a sorry thought to me that my acquaintance with them must necessarily be a brief one. I mean, the probability is, I shall see them but to the threshold of their real life—no further. And would like so well to know what they make of it. Influence them, too . . . if it were possible."

His meaning was grasped . . . and with ease. "I understand that. Indeed I do . . . especially in the case of such a gifted child as our sweet little Cuffy."

"Well, yes . . . I do sometimes think the boy is quick beyond the common run."

"Without doubt he is. Look at his genuine musical ability."

"Ah, but there you mention the one bit of his education I do take a hand in. For Mary has no ear for music. Nor even any particular liking for it."

"And it is so important, is it not, that the ear should be well trained from the first? The spadework done before the child is even aware of it." (Here, if ever, spoke your true musician!) "But, doctor, if our findings are correct, you may still have the joy of watching over your little brood from the other side . . . *n'est-ce pas?*"

"Ah, now . . . if that might be! If one could just be sure

of that!" And on the instant Mahony mounted his hobby-horse and was carried away. "With this, my dear lady, you put your finger on what seems to me one of the most vital points in the whole question. Have you ever, I wonder, reflected what a difference it would make, did we mortals *seriously* believe in a life to come? . . . I don't mean the Jewish-Byzantine state of petrified adoration, that the churches offer us. . . . I mean life such as we know it: a continuation of the best of this earthly existence—mental striving, spiritual aspiration, love for our neighbour. If we did so believe, our every perspective would alter. And the result be a marked increase in spirituality. For the orthodox Christian's point of view is too often grossly materialistic—and superstitious. The tenacity with which he clings to a resurrection of the flesh—this poor cankered flesh! . . . after countless years deep in its grave—that grave on which he dwells with so morbid a pleasure! Or his childish fear of death—despite the glories that are promised him on the other side . . . do these not remind you of the sugar-candy with which an infant is bribed to take its pill? Against all this, set the belief that, in dying, we pass but from one room to another of the house of life—the 'many mansions' of which Christ spoke. The belief that an invisible world exists around us—the spirit counterpart of this we know. That those we have lost still live, and love, and await us . . . on the other side of a veil which already a few, of rarer perceptions than the rest, have pierced.— But forgive me, pray! When once I get going on this subject, I know no measure.— And I confess . . . so few opportunities to talk of it arise. My wife, as you are aware, has scant sympathy with the movement; sees, I am afraid, only its shady side."

"Dearest Mary. She is so practically minded."

"And not in respect of this alone. She is often, for instance, rendered genuinely uneasy by my long hours of study. She would rather have me up and doing—and though it were but riding for pleasure along the seashore. Books to her represent only a means of killing time."

Mrs. Marriner turned the full weight of a grave, sweet smile upon him. "While we book-lovers . . . well! as far as I am concerned, doctor, my life would be a blank indeed, without the company of the printed page."

"And what of me? . . . whose dearest dream it was, the

596

while I slaved for a living, to be able to end my days in a library. I declare to you, it is still a disturbing thought to me that I shall die leaving so many books unread."

"Let me comfort you. My dear father, who lived to a ripe old age, was given to complaining, towards the end, that he had 'read all the books'—or at least all that were worth reading."

"Of course; as one grows older; and harder to please. . . . Myself, though, I seem still far from that. The lists I send my bookseller grow longer, not shorter.— But it's not the unread books only. While we're on these ghost-thoughts that haunt the back of our minds—we all have them, I suppose— let me confess to another; and that is that I shall probably need to go, having seen all too few of the grandeurs and beauties of this world. Pass on to the next, without knowing what the Alps or the Andes are like, or the torrents of the Rhine."

"But, doctor . . . what hinders you?— I don't mean the Andes,"—and Mahony was the recipient of a sheerly roguish smile. "But travel is so easy, nowadays. One packs one's trunks, books one's berth—*et voilà!* What hinders you?"

Ah, what? . . . what, indeed! Mahony hesitated for a moment, before replying. "The truth is, the years we spent in England were thoroughly uncongenial . . . to us both. We were glad, on getting back to the colony, to settle down. And having once settled . . ."

Yes, that was it; of his own free will he had saddled himself with a big, expensive house, and all that belonged to its upkeep: menservants and maidservants, horses and carriages. Mary had taken root immediately; and now the children . . . their tender age. . . . But, darker than all else, loomed Mary's attitude . . . or what this might be expected to be, if— "The truth is, my wife does not . . . I mean she has gone through so many upheavals already, on my account, that I should hardly feel justified . . . again . . . so soon . . . But there's no denying it: I do sometimes feel like an old hulk which lies stranded, while, out in the world, life goes on. But there! All my days I've been gnawed by the worm of change—change of any sort. As a struggling medico, I longed for leisure and books. Pinned to the colony, I would be satisfied with nothing but the old country. Now that I have ample time, and more books than I can read, I would wish to be up and out, seeing the world. And my dear wife naturally finds it difficult to keep pace with such a weathercock."

"I think it is with you as the German poet sings: 'There, where thou art not, there alone is bliss!'"

"Indeed and that hits my nail squarely on the head. For I can assure you, it's no mere spirit of discontent—as some suppose. It's more a kind of . . . well, it's like reaching out after—after, say, a dream one has had, and half forgotten, and struggles to recapture. That's badly put. But perhaps you will understand."

A lengthy silence followed. The clock ticked; the dog sighed gustily. Then, feeling the moment come, the lady rose from her chair and swept her skirts to the piano.— "Let me play to you," said she.

Mahony accepted, gratefully.

Once the music had begun, however, he fell back on his own reflections, which were quickened, rather than hampered, by the delicate tinkling of the piano. He felt strangely elated: not a doubt of it, a good talk was one of the best of medicines, particularly for such a dry, bottled-up old fogey as he was on the verge of becoming. Of course, did you open your heart, you must have, for listener, one who was in perfect tune with you; who could pick up your ideas as you dropped them; take your meaning at a word. And mortals of this type were all too rare; in respect of them, his own life had been a sandy waste. Which had told heavily against him. For, looking down the years, he saw that, all through, his most crying need had been for spiritual companionship; for the balm of tastes akin to his own. It was a crippling reflection that never yet had he found the person to whom he could have blurted out his thoughts without fear of being misunderstood . . . or disapproved . . . or smiled at for an oddity.— Here, now, having unexpectedly tapped a woman's quick perception, a lively womanly sympathy, he had a swift vision of what might have been—that misty picture that inhabits the background of most minds. To need but to turn, to know his idiosyncrasies accepted—even valued—his mental gropings accompanied, his roving spirit gauged, and condoned . . . not as any fault of his own, but as an innate factor in his blood!— Ah! but for that to come to pass, one would have to leave choosing one's fellow-traveller on the long life-journey, until one's own mind and character had formed and ripened. How could one tell, in the twenties, what one would be on nearing the fifties?—in which direction one would have branched out, and set, and stiffened? At twenty, all was glamour and romance; and it seemed, then, to matter little, whether or no a heart was open to the sufferings of the brute creation; whether the written word outweighed the spoken; in how far the spiritual mysteries made appeal—questions which gradually, with time, came to seem more vital than all else. In youth, one's nature cried aloud for companionship . . . one's blood ran hot . . . the mysteries played no part. And then, the years passed and passed, and one drifted . . . drifted . . . slowly, but very surely . . . until— Well, in many a case, he supposed, the fact that you had drifted never came to consciousness at all. But, should anything happen to pull you up with a jerk, force you to cast the plummet; should you get an inkling of something rarer and finer: then, yes, then, the early flames being sunk to a level glow, you stood confounded by your aloofness . . . by the distance you had travelled . . . the isolation of your state.— But had he, in good sooth, ever felt other than lonely, and alone? Mary was—had always been—dearest and best of wives . . . yet . . . yet . . . had they, he and she, between them, a single idea in common? . . . did they share an interest, a liking, a point of view?—with the one exception of an innate sobriety and honesty of purpose. No! for more years than he cared to count, Mary had done little, as far as he was concerned, but sit in judgment: she silently censured, mentally condemned, all those things in life which he held most worth while: his needs, his studies, his inclinations —down to his very dreams and hopes of a Hereafter.

✻   ✻   ✻   ✻   ✻   ✻

Lizzie said: "My dear, our lady friend is in *hoops* now, if you please! Nothing *extreme,* of course, considering from whom she takes her present cue. *Just* the desired *soupçon!*— Mary, love, she went about as a Slim Jane *only* because the *cavaliere* of the moment approved the simplicity of the human form divine. To-day, she is a rapping and tapping medium—as we very well know. To-morrow, love, the wind will shift to another quarter, and we shall hear of the fair lady running to matins and communicating on an empty stomach. Or visiting

599

in a prison cell, got up as a nursing sister, *à la* Elizabeth Fry."

Hoops . . . nothing extreme . . . considering from whom she takes her present cue.— At these words, and even while she was standing up for Gracey's sincerity, there leapt to Mary's mind, with a stab of real pain, Richard's nervous hatred of the exaggerated—the bizarre.— And whether it was hoops, or hooplessness.

[3]

THESE rather waspish comments—Lizzie never seemed able to resist having a thrust at Gracey—were made in the drawing-room at *Ultima Thule,* where the two wives sat waiting for their husbands to rejoin them. John and Lizzie were dining there quietly, at John's express request: the groom had ridden over after lunch with a line from John, asking if he and Lizzie might take pot-luck with them that evening. Richard said: "Wonders will never cease!" and of course a refusal was not to be thought of; but Cook had been very put out by the shortness of the notice; so much so indeed, that Mary had driven off to town, to fetch some delicacies; thinking, as she went, how in the old days *she* would have run up a dinner for four, and one well worth eating, too, in less than an hour. Her hands did sometimes itch to show such a fair-weather worker as Cook what *could* be done.

By this time, the evening was more than half gone, and still the gentlemen lingered: after sitting an interminable time over their port, they had betaken themselves to the study, and there they remained; though Lizzie had sung all Richard's favourite songs and pieces, some of them more than once. To pass the time, she had also sung to Cuffy; for—as had happened ere this, when she was dining there—Nannan had appeared at the drawing-room door to say Master Cuffy could not be got to sleep, thinking that his Auntie might sing to him. Cuffy as audience was better than none, so Lizzie begged for the child to be brought in; and thereupon Cuffy appeared on Nannan's arm in his little red flannel nightgown, his feet swathed in a crib-blanket, his eyes alight with expectation. Seated on his mother's knee, he drank in: "There was a Friar of Orders Grey," and the sad ditty of "Barbara Allan," himself rendering "Sun of my Soul" before, soundly kissed and cosseted by his aunt, who had a great liking for the little man, he was carried back to bed.

Towards ten o'clock, Lizzie could no longer conceal her yawns—used as she was to the society of gentlemen, she had plainly found it a very dull evening. Mary and she had talked themselves out: and, where she had first surreptitiously peeped, she now openly drew her watch from her belt. This, John's latest present to her, was a magnificent affair, crusted back and front with diamonds, while tiny brilliants sprinkled the long gold chain on which it hung. Unlike most women, Lizzie could wear any quantity of jewellery without looking overloaded. At the present moment, a little heap of rings and bracelets lay on the lid of the piano; for, in despair, she had re-seated herself at the keys and begun anew to sing.

At the best of times Mary found it hard to fix her mind on music for five minutes together; and on this evening she had had more than enough of it. She now let her thoughts stray in comfort. She wondered what could be keeping the two men . . . it was certainly rather impolite of Richard, considering Lizzie was his guest . . . wondered if the children were safely tucked in, and whether Nannan had at last got Cuffy to sleep: what an excitable child he was, compared with the babies!— The dinner had been very nice; she thought Richard would be pleased: Cook needn't have made quite so much fuss beforehand. But there! When they undertook anything of this kind, it usually went off well. The table had looked lovely: she flattered herself she knew how to arrange flowers with anyone; and both silver and china had shown to best advantage. The house, of course, had something to do with it. This drawing-room, for instance, how well it lighted up!—they had entertained so little, of late, that one was apt to forget what a pretty room it was. Richard declared he much preferred it to John's—it was in better taste, even though less costly—and Mary's eyes wandered lovingly round walls and furniture, lingering on the great gild-edged mirror, which reached to the ceiling; the lovely girandoles, a present from Richard; the lustred chandelier; the glass-shaded ormolu clock. The carpet, too, was of a most uncommon lemon colour; the suite, in a brocade to match, had a pattern of French lilies on it. She loved every inch of the place. *What* a happy ending to all their ups and downs! . . . to be settled at last in such a home as this. Sometimes, when she looked back on the 'Black Hole,' or the snails and damp of Buddlecombe, she thought she did not always fully appreciate her present good fortune.

But Lizzie here striking up a tune Mary knew well enough to be able to tap her foot to it, her thoughts came back with a jerk. She eyed the singer in listening, and: "Handsomer than ever!" was her mental comment; although, by now, Lizzie was embarked on that adventure which, more than any other, steals from a woman's good looks. What with her full, ex- quisitely sloping shoulders—they stood out of the low-cut bertha as out of a cup—her dimpled arms and hands, with the fingers elegantly curled on the notes of the piano; her rich red lips, opening to show the almond-white teeth; her massive throat, swelling and beating as she sang . . . yes, Lizzie had indeed thriven on matrimony! It was otherwise with John. One had grown gradually used, as time passed, to the loss of that air of radiant health, of masterful assertion, which had formerly distinguished him. But, since his mar- riage, he had turned almost into an old man. Thin as a lath, he walked with a slight stoop, and hair and beard were grey. His face seemed to have grown longer, too, more cadaverous; his eye had an absent, inturned expression. At dinner he had been very silent. He had just sat there listening to Lizzie, hanging on her lips—really, if he went on like this when the two of them were at a big party, or at a stranger's house, it would not be quite the thing.

Afterwards, in the drawing-room, Lizzie made open com- plaint of his inertia; discussing him in that barefaced way of hers, which plumed itself on calling a spade a spade.

"Yes, he is growing stodgy, déhling—stodgy and slow! I said to him the other day, I said: 'John, love! this will *never* do. *Where* is the man I married?'— Will you believe it, Mary, he actually wished to stop at home from Government House Ball, last night? While this evening, if you please, he throws up an important dinner-party at Sir Joshua Dent's, to come here.— Not but what it has been a *charmin'* evening, déhling! But a man in John's position has not the right to pick and choose."

"Are you sure he is quite well, Lizzie? He looks very thin to me."

"Oh dear, yes! Perfectly well. John was never made to be fat."

The laggards at length appearing, Lizzie crashed out a chord, and rose from the piano-stool to hail and reproach them. A pretty pair to be sure, cried she playfully, yet not without malice, the while she slid on rings and clicked the catches of bracelets; a pretty pair of husbands, to prefer the society of their pipes to that of their wives! She had been looking forward all the evening to a duo with Richard. It was evident she had reckoned without her host!— Richard made one feeble attempt to fall in with her tone; John none at all. He seemed only in haste to go; asked for the carriage to be brought round at once; himself rang the bell and gave the order.

Lizzie might be too full of her own grievances to notice how the wind blew; but Mary had eyes in her head. She saw that something was seriously amiss the moment the two men entered the room. Richard looked pale and distracted—and as for John! Whatever could be the matter? Had they quarrelled? . . . had a scene?

Then, in coming along the passage from the bedroom, with Lizzie enshawled at her side, she caught a murmured word of Richard's, that was evidently meant only for John's ear. And when she had seen her guests off she did not re-enter the house, but stood on the verandah, anxiously awaiting Richard, who had gone to open the gate.

At the crunch of his feet on the gravel, she moved forward, exclaiming impetuously, before she was level with him: "Richard! What's the matter? What was wrong with John to-night?"

"Matter? What on earth do you mean?" He stooped to pick up something; was exaggeratedly casual and indifferent.

"Now, dear, you needn't put on that tone to me. I saw directly you came into the drawing-room. . . . Have you and he fallen out?"

"Good God, no! What have you got in your head now?"

"Well, then, what is it? You can't deceive me, Richard . . . you don't look like that for nothing."

"Who wants to deceive you, I'd like to know?" He was very short and gruff.

"Is John ill?"

"My dear Mary, don't try and *pump* me, if you please! You know my aversion to that kind of thing."

"Richard, I heard with my own ears what you said to him in the hall . . . about a possible loophole. What did you mean? Oh, *don't* be so obstinate!— Very well, then! I shall go over and see John myself, the first thing in the morning."

"Indeed and you'll do nothing of the sort."

Mary set her lips. "He's my brother. I've a right to know what's happened."

"A confidence is a confidence; and I'm hanged if I'll be hectored into betraying it."

"Anyone would think I was asking out of mere curiosity," cried Mary; and tears of vexation rose to her eyes. "I know— I have the feeling—there's something very wrong. And you go on talking about confidences . . . and your own pride in not betraying them . . . when John looked to me as if he'd got his death sentence."

Richard's start did not escape her. He retorted, though less surely: "But it is at his own urgent request, Mary, that I hold my tongue!"

"Then he *did* come to consult you about his health? Oh, Richard. please! . . . don't keep me in suspense. What is it?"

"My dear, if you had gone through what I did to-night! I suppose I may as well out with it; for, as usual, with your wild shot you have hit the bull's-eye. The fact of the matter is, what I had to tell John *did* amount to a sentence of death."

"Then . . . then it is——"

"The worst. I examined him. A growth in the liver. No, no, too late now, for anything of that kind. My private opinion is, he hasn't more than six months to live."

"*Richard!* . . . Though I think I've been afraid of something like this . . . it's just as if, inside me, I had felt what was coming."

"And I suspected it. But you know, Mary, what your brother is . . . so unapproachable. I must say this, though: I was moved this evening to a profound admiration for him. He took the verdict like a man . . . without flinching."

"Yes, yes. But what does that matter now? The thing is, you've let him go home alone—with this on his mind—and only Lizzie beside him . . . who cares for no one but herself."

Mary had not known she thought this of Lizzie; it just popped out.

"A great spider! . . . that's what the woman is, if you want my opinion," cried Mahony angrily. "But what could I do?— Besides, at heart, I'm one with him. There are crises in a man's life that are best fought through alone."

"Not while I'm here.— Where I'm going? Why, to him, of course!"

"At this hour of night? Indeed, I advise you very strongly, Mary, to do nothing of the kind. Not only will he resent—and rightly too—my having broken my word, but he won't thank you either, for intruding.— Besides, he'll have gone to bed. How can you knock him up? What excuse have you?"

Mary reached for a wrap and threw it over her shoulders. "John won't be in bed. And I'll make it all right about you; don't be afraid.— No, no, I'll just walk over.— As for intruding . . . I've always understood John better than any of you. Besides, I don't see how people can care whether they do or not—at a time like this."

"Well, well! at least put on a pair of sound walking-boots and a proper shawl.— Of course I am. If you must go, I go with you."

Stepping out of the gate, they plodded through the sand of the road that led past, now a large garden, now a wild, open space covered with gorse and heath. Masses of firs stood out black and forbidding. In the distance could be heard the faint lapping of the sea.

They walked in silence. Once only did Mary exclaim aloud, out of the many conflicting thoughts that were going round and round in her head: "Lizzie, of course, must know nothing. The last thing John will want is for her to be worried or upset."

And Mahony: "It will not be long now, my dear, before she, and every one else, has to know."

"When I think, Richard, how . . . how proud she has been of it all—I mean, John's position . . . and their entertainments . . . and his future—how she has looked forward to the title coming . . . Oh dear, oh dear! If only Jinny were beside him now . . . or poor dear Emma!"

On reaching the house they unlatched the gate with care, and, like a pair of conspirators, crept over the grass, to avoid

605

the noise their steps would have made on the gravelled path. The venetian blinds were down, but bars of light filtered through them in Lizzie's bedroom on the one side, and in John's sanctum on the other.— Mary tiptoed round the verandah, and tapped on her brother's window-pane.

"It is I, John! . . . Mary."

There was a moment's pause, then the French window opened noiselessly, and she disappeared inside the room.

On the front verandah, a rocking-chair had been left standing. Mahony sat down in it, and waited . . . and waited. Time passed; an hour . . . two hours . . . and still Mary did not return. Lizzie's light had long ago gone out; not a sound came from the house; nor did any living thing move in garden or road. So absolute was the stillness that, more than once, as he sat there, he heard a petal drop from a camellia in the central bed. John had a fine show of these stiff, scentless flowers. They stood out, white and waxen, against the dark polish of their leaves.

It was spring, and a night warm enough to release the scents of freesia and boronia; though, as usual, the pittosporums outdid all else. There was no moon; but the stars made up for that; the sky was powdered white with them— was one vast field of glittering silver. Leaning back in his chair Mahony lay looking up at them, and thinking the old, well-worn thoughts that besiege a mortal at sight of the Creator's prodigality. Pigmy man's insignificance in face of these millions of worlds; the preposterousness of the claim that his tiny existence can engage the personal notice of Him who has strewn the Milky Way; and yet the bitter reality of his small, mad miseries, the bottomless depths of his mental anguish: pain, as the profoundest of life's truths, the link by which man is bound up with the Eternal . . . pain that bites so much deeper than pleasure, outlasting pleasure's froth and foam as granite outlasts thistledown.

And now John's link was being forged . . . his turn had come to taste pain's bitterness—John, who, all his days, had looked haughtily down on weakness and decay, as touching others, not himself. The material things of this world had been his pride and his concern. His soul, that poor soul which Mary, once more the comforter, was standing by in its black hour, had gone needy and untended. Now, he was being

abruptly called on to leave everything he prized: marriage
and happiness, wealth, a proud standing, ambition crowned.
Never, in his forward march, had John looked deeper; though,
in his own way, he had walked according to his lights: a man
of enterprise and energy, upright in business, grappling with
the hardships of a new country, a pathfinder for those who
were to come after.— Yet, for all this, a strangely unsympathetic nature! It was not alone the absence of the spiritual
in him. It was the cold, proud, narrow fashion in which he
had lived enclosed in his earthly shell, keeping the door
rigidly shut on intruders. No one had really known John—
known what manner of man housed within. Perhaps he had
acted thus out of fear; had been afraid of the strange fears
that might be found in him. Afraid of his fellows discovering
that he was hollow, a sham and a pretence, where they had
imagined wonderful strength and lovely virtues.

Well! . . . let that be as it might. The time was past for
probing and conjecturing. John's hour had struck; and the
phantom which had thus far borne his name, striding confident and alert through the world of men, would be blotted
out. However one looked at it, it was a melancholy business.
The swiftness of the blow made one realise, anew, on the
edge of what an abyss one walked. Life was like a procession
that trooped along this perilous margin, brimful of hope and
vigour, gay, superbly unthinking; and then, of a sudden, there
was a gap in the ranks, and one of the train had vanished,
had pitched headforemost into the depths, to be seen no
more—by mortal eyes, at least. Such a disaster must surely
say . . . to those who had pinned their hearts to this world,
with no more than a conventional faith in one to come (which
amounted to little or none)—must surely seem to say: take
all you can get, while there is still time! A little while, and it
may be too late. Even in himself, who had won through to the
belief that life was a kind of semi-sleep, death the great
awakening, it called up the old nervous fear of being snatched
away before he was ready to go. One lived on . . . *he* lived
on . . . inactive as a vegetable . . . and at any moment the
blow might fall, and his chance be gone for ever—of doing
what he had meant to do, of seeing what he had meant to
see.— And now, sitting there under the multitudinous stars,
Mahony let the smothered ache for movement, the acute

longing for change of scene that was smouldering in him, come to full consciousness. Yes, there was no denying it: the old restlessness was strong on him again; he was tired of everything he knew—tired of putting on his clothes in the morning and taking them off at night; tired of nursery talk, and the well-known noises about the house, and the faces he saw every day. Tired of his books, too, and of his own familiar company. He wanted fresh scenes and people; wanted to open his eyes on new surroundings; be on the move again—feel a deck under his feet, and the rigours of a good head wind—all this, while health and a semblance of youth were left him. Another few years, and he would be past enjoying it. Now was the time to make the break . . . to cut his bonds . . . front Mary's grief and displeasure.

Mary! . . . At her name, the inner stiffening, the resistance, with which his mind had approached her, yielded; and in its place came a warm uprush of feeling. Her behaviour on this very night—how surely and fearlessly she had come to the stricken man's aid, without a single hampering thought of self! There was nobody like Mary in a crisis such as the present: happy the mortal who, when his end came, had her great heart to lean on. That was worth all else. For, of what use, in one's last hour, would be the mental affinity, the ties of intellect, he had lately so pitied himself for having missed? One would see these things, then, for the earth-trimmings they were. A child, faced with the horrors of the dark, does not ask for his fears to be shared, or to have their origin explained to him. He cries for warm, enfolding arms, with which to keep his terrors at bay; or which alone, if met these must be, can help him through the ordeal. Man, on his death-bed, was little more than such a child; and it was for the mother-arms he craved, to which he clung in passing, till, again like a child, he had fallen to sleep. Hope, faith, and love, these three . . . yes, but needed was a love like Mary's, compounded of utter selflessness, and patience, and infinite forbearance—a love which it was impossible to sin against or overthrow . . . which had more than a touch of the divine in it: a dim image of that infinite tenderness God Himself might be assumed to bear towards the helpless creatures He had made.— Measured by it, all other human experience rang hollow.

[4]

MAMMA and Papa were going away; Master Cuffy would
need to be a *very* good boy, and do everything he was told;
so that Mamma would be pleased with him, when she came
back.— Thus Nannan, while Eliza and she gave the three
children their morning bath; and two pairs of blue eyes and
one of black were turned on her, in curiosity and wonder-
ment. Cuffy, extending his arm to have the raindrops rubbed
off it, echoed her words: "Mamma and Papa goin' away!"—
It sounded exciting.

After breakfast, he broke the news to Effalunt, who, though
now in his old age, hairless, and a leg short, was still one of
the best beloveds; for Cuffy had a faithful heart.

Going away? What would it be like? Hi-spy-hi in the
garden? . . . or a pitchnick? . . . or Mamma putting on a
pretty dress wif beads round her neck?

He played at it during the morning: he got under an
opossum-rug and was a bear to the Dumplings, and go'ed
away. Later on, he was allowed to crawl inside a leather
trunk that stood in Mamma's bedroom, and have the lid
nearly shut on him.

The carriage came round after lunch: the trunk was hoisted
to the roof; Mamma and Papa had their bonnets on.

There stood Nannan, a Dumpling's hand in each of hers.
The babies, though o-eyed, were serene; but Cuffy by now
was not so sure. He had watched Mamma's dresses being put
into the trunk, and Papa sitting on it, to make it shut; and
the thing that worried him was, how Mamma could get up
in the morning, if her clothes were locked inside the big box.
He began to feel uncomfortable. And so, now the moment
had come, he was busy being a horse, every inch of him,
capering up and down the verandah, stamping, tossing his head.

The Dumplings obediently put up their faces and offered
their bud-mouths. Cuffy had to be called to order.

Said Mary: "Why, darling, aren't you coming to kiss
Mamma and Papa good-bye? Or be a little sorry they're
going?"

Sorry? Why? He hadn't been naughty!— Perfunctorily
Cuffy did what was required of him, but his heart went on
being a horse.

609

It was not till night that the trouble broke through. Then, as often as Nannan entered the nursery, he was sitting bolt upright and wide-eyed in his crib, his little face looking each time wanner and whiter as he piped: "Is Cuffy's Mamma and Papa tum 'ome yet, Nannan?"

"There you have it!" said Nurse to Eliza. "This is what happens when gentlemen get to interfering in things they don't understand. If the doctor 'ud just 'ave let me say, as I wanted to, that they were gone to a party, there'd 'ave been none of this. Master Cuffy knows well enough what a party is, and though it 'ad lasted for weeks it wouldn't 'ave made any difference to him, bless 'is little heart! It's the things they *don't* understand that worries children.— This fad now, that they must 'ave nothing but the truth told 'em. Lord bless you! If we did that, there soon wouldn't be any more children at all . . . nothing but little old men and women."—

And, to mark her disapproval of Mahony's methods, Nannan kept the forbidden lamp alight, and sat by the crib-side with Cuffy's hand in hers, till he fell asleep.

❖   ❖   ❖   ❖   ❖   ❖

Meanwhile, Mary and Richard had taken the afternoon train to Ballarat. For the date set for Tilly's marriage had come right in the middle of the trouble about John.

Seated in a first-class saloon carriage, Mary undid her bonnet-strings and put her feet up on the cushions, with a sigh of relief. Off at last! And opposite her sat Richard—a most morose and unamiable Richard, it was true, who made it abundantly plain that he was being dragged to Ballarat against his will. Still, there he was, and that was the chief thing. Up to the last minute, she hadn't felt certain of him.

She had early determined it was his duty to be present at Tilly's wedding, and had spared no pains to win him over. Hadn't it to a certain extent been his fault that Tilly's plans had failed, the time she stayed with them before Cuffy was born? If he had not been so down on her, the plot she was hatching for Purdy's benefit might then and there have come to a head. As it was, one thing after another had happened to delay the issue. Purdy, evidently misunderstanding Tilly's abrupt departure, had disappeared up-country again, on his commercial rounds. Then, still up-country somewhere, he had

been in a frightful buggy-accident, pitching out headforemost,
and all but breaking his neck. For months nothing could be
heard of him, he lying at death's door, with concussion and
broken bones, in a little bush hospital. His jewellery was lost,
and of course his job with it. When Tilly did finally contrive
to run him to earth, he was literally at his last farthing, a sick
and broken man. Tilly had behaved like her own splendid
self: waiving any false pride, she had journeyed straight to
see him; and at their very first meeting the pair of them had
arrived at an understanding (Mary could make a shrewd guess
how!) the result of which was, they were now to be man and
wife.— An even more urgent reason why Richard should put
in an appearance at the wedding was that it would no doubt
greatly improve Purdy's social standing, if it became known
that Dr. Mahony had travelled all the way from Melbourne
to be present. And Purdy, poor fellow, could well do with
such a lift. Even she, Mary, who had seen him in so many a
tight fit, had felt shocked at his condition after this, his last
adventure.

Thus she reflected, as she watched the landscape slip past
the window: yellowish-grey flats, for the most part, or stone-
strewn paddocks, tufted with clumps of brown grass, and here
and there a shaggy blue-gum: all of which she had seen too
often before to pay much heed to it. Still, she never wanted
to read in a train. So unlike Richard, whose sole idea of a
journey was to bury himself in a book from start to finish. At
the present moment he was deep in a pamphlet entitled: "The
Unity, Duality, or Trinity of the Godhead?"— Tch! what
questions he did vex his head with! . . . he must always be
trying to settle the universe. If only he would sometimes give
his poor brains a rest!

He was looking pale and washed-out, too, not by any means
at his best . . . for re-introduction to all the old friends. But
what could you expect, if he *would* spend his life cooped up
indoors?—never leaving the house except to attend long, hot
seances; or sittings with Gracey. And these last had rather
fallen off, of late. Mary didn't know why, and he said nothing;
but Lizzie as usual was prolific in hints. Poor old Richard!—
She did hope things would go smoothly for him during the
next three days. She would feel relieved when they were
over.—

611

And then, even as she thought this, if one of those tricky little unforeseen incidents did not happen, which invariably threw him into a state of fuss!

They had drawn up at a small wayside station—a mere bark shed—from which, leading back to an invisible township, ran a long red road, straight as a ruled line, on which a moving cloud of red dust spoke to the presence of a single vehicle. In this shed, evidently just deposited there, sat a very young woman, with an infant that was screaming at the full pitch of its lungs, purple in the face with rage or pain. The young mother strove to pacify it: she shook and dumped it about; and at last, in desperation, as faces gathered at every carriage-window, soundly smacked it. This was more than Mary, fresh from the care of her own babies, could bear. Regardless of Richard's alarmed: "Now do, for goodness sake, Mary, mind your own business and not interfere!" she put her head out of the window, and cried: "Oh, *don't* do that! Turn it up and see if it hasn't got a pin running into it."

At this, a perfect fusillade of laughter ran along the train; even the guard pausing, flag in hand, to join in. Mary, not greatly abashed, laughed with the rest, while the girl, now as scarlet as her child, angrily turned the infant upside down for investigation.

But Richard was furious: "*How* you can make yourself so ridiculous God alone knows!"

"Fiddlesticks! Would you have me let the baby scream itself into a fit?"

"The story will be all over Ballarat by night. And you the butt of the place!"

"No, really, Richard! . . . you are *too* absurd!" cried Mary hotly; then, however, bit her lip and left it at that. It was no good irritating him still further. There would probably be enough in the coming days to do that, without her putting in her spoke.

Which was so: no sooner did they reach Ballarat than the trouble began. On the platform stood Tilly, wreathed in smiles, open-armed in welcome, but gone, alas! was the decent and becoming black to which, as "old Mrs. Ocock," she had been faithful for so long. In its stead . . . well, there was no mincing the fact: she looked fit for *Punch!* Her dress, of a

612

loud, bottle-green satin, was in the very latest mode, worn
entirely without crinoline, so that her full form was outlined
in unspeakable fashion; her big capable hands were squeezed
into lemon-coloured kid gloves, tight to bursting; and on her
head perched a monstrous white hat, turned up at the side,
and richly feathered.

"Oh dear, oh dear!"

For Mary knew very well: neither the genuine sincerity of
Tilly's greeting, nor her multitudinous arrangements for their
comfort, would suffice to blot from Richard's mind the figure
she cut this day.

Climbing to the driver's seat of an open buggy, all her
feathers afloat, Tilly trotted a pair of cream ponies in great
style up Sturt Street. Of course, everybody in Ballarat knew
her, so it didn't matter a scrap on her own account what she
looked like. It was Richard who was to be pitied.

The next thing to provoke him was her arbitrary disposal
of his personal liberty. For Tilly had it all fixed and settled
that, directly supper was over, he should go back to town, to
"Moberley's Hotel," and there spend the evening with the
bridegroom-elect.

"She wants the two of them to be seen in public together,"
thought Mary, as she helped Richard on with his overcoat
and muffled him up in a comforter; for the air on this tableland struck cold, after Melbourne's sea-level. "And, of course,
for that, there's no better place than Moberley's Coffee
Room."— Aloud, she said reprovingly: "Ssh! She'll hear you.—
Besides, you know, dear, you needn't stop long." But Richard,
chilly and tired from the railway journey, looked as though
he could cheerfully have consigned Tilly and her nuptials to
the flames.—

"And now you and I can 'ave a real cosy evening to ourselves, love, while the lords of creation smoke and jaw about
early days," said dear blind old Tilly. Or perhaps she was not
quite so blind as she seemed; and just wanted to be rid of
Richard and the atmosphere of glacial politeness that went
out from him. Anyhow, off he set, with a very bad grace, and
the two women retired to Tilly's bedroom. Here, a great log
fire burned on the whitewashed hearth; and Tilly kept the
poker in her hand with which to thump the logs, did the

blaze threaten to fail. This dyed the dimity-hangings of the four-poster; made ruddy pools in the great mahogany wardrobe.

Said Tilly: "Well, here we are again, Poll, you and me, like so often before . . . and the day after to-morrow's me wedding-day. 'Pon me word, it's hard to believe; and yet . . . I don't know, dearie, but somehow it seems no time since us three bits of girls used to sit over the fire, and gas about all the grand things that was going to happen to us. That's ages back, and yet, except that we're grown a bit bulkier, you and me, it might be only yesterday. I don't feel a day older, and that's the truth; which is odd, when you come to think of it . . . with pa, and ma, and Jinn, and poor old Pa all gone, these ever so many years!— I say, *do* you remember, Poll, how Purd used to ride down from Melbourne? And how, when 'e'd gone, I'd count the days off on me fingers till 'e'd come again?"

"I think you're a very lucky woman, Tilly, to get your heart's wish like this. I do hope it will bring you every happiness."

"I think it will, Poll. I'm not going into it with me eyes shut, or any of the flighty notions one has as a young girl— heaven on earth, and bunkum of that sort.— But now, listen to me, dearie, there's things I want to say to you. First of all, Mary, I've fixed, once we're spliced, for Tom and Johnny to come back to this house—which they never ought to 'ave left. I won't say it 'asn't taken a bit of managing; for it has. But my mind was quite made up. It's gone to me heart, all these years, to see how badly those poor lads 'ave been cared for. Enough to make poor old Pa turn in 'is grave."

But Mary had raised her eyebrows. For all its kindness, she thought the plan a most unwise one. Just suppose Purdy should turn nasty! In subtle connection the question sprang to her lips: "What about the money side of it—settlements, and all that?"

Tilly nodded. "Ah! I can see what you're thinking, love— writing me down a love-sick old fool, who's going to let Pa's good money be made ducks and drakes of. It's true, the most of what I've got *will* pass to Purd, to do as 'e likes with. But somehow I don't believe 'e'll be a waster. A man who's gone short as long as him . . . However, just in case, Poll"—here Tilly sank her voice to a mysterious hiss—"the fact is, love,

I've got a reserve fund of me own, a nest-egg, so to speak, which I don't mean to let on a word about . . . no, not to anybody. Except you. I've laid something by, my dear, in the last few years, made a bit at the races, sold out of *Blazing Diamonds* in the nick of time, etc., etc., and the long and the short of it is, Mary, I've between seven and eight thousand by me, at this very minute. What's more, I intend to keep it; just let it lie, have it to draw on, in case of trouble. One never knows. I've got a small tin box, my dear, and out in the dairy, going down the ladder into the cellar, a flag's come loose, which just leaves room for it. There's no chance, there, of fire, or thieves either—no one but meself even sets foot in the place. If anything happens to me, it's you'll find it. The boys are to have it, if I go first. For, as you can see, love, with no blood-tie between them and me, there wouldn't be much call on Purd, would there, to support 'em, after my death?"

Indeed, that was true; nor could Purdy be blamed, if he failed to recognise the obligation. It said a good deal for him that he was willing to accept, as inmates of his house, these two middle-aged men, one of whom was a confirmed drunkard, with lucid intervals, the other little more than an overgrown child.— As for Tilly's plan of keeping a large sum of money on the premises, risky though it seemed, Mary faltered in her criticism of it. For she knew too well the advantage of a private purse, into which you could dip at will. Instead of having to run to your husband with all the little extra expenses that *would* crop up, spare as you might. They were never kindly greeted. Richard, too, had been the most generous of husbands, and she a fairly good manager. Tilly, on the other hand, was lavish and lordly with money, Purdy still a dark horse in respect of it.

Another thing: as long as Purdy and Mr. Henry knew nothing, Tilly could neither be wheedled out of her savings, nor bullied into re-investing them.

When, at the end of an hour, the two women kissed goodnight, Tilly uttered her usual request: "Now, mind, not a word to the doctor, love!"

Oh dear no! (*How* Richard would have jeered!)— Besides, when he got home, some half-hour later, he was so full of a new grudge against Tilly that every word had to be weighed, for fear of fanning the flames anew. It seemed that, on reach-

ing Moberley's, he had found Purdy the centre of a rowdy
party, whose noise and laughter could be heard even before
he entered the hotel. More: his appearance was totally unexpected. Purdy looked as if he couldn't believe his eyes; ejaculated: "What, Dick? You here already?" and then turned back
to his companions—the motley collection of commercial travellers and bar-haunters he had gathered round him. Ten minutes of this were enough for Mahony; he slipped unobserved
from the room. Recognising, however, that the appointment
had been a ruse on Tilly's part, to get rid of him, he did not
come back to the house, but took a long walk round the lake
in the dark. There, at least, he could be sure of not running
into anyone he knew.

He seemed to have this idea, that of dodging familiar faces,
on the brain. Did ever anyone hear the like? . . . on his return,
for the first time, to the place where he had spent a third of
his life . . . where he had been so well known, and sought
after. But really *just* how odd Richard had become in the last
few years, while the children were monopolising her attention,
Mary had not grasped till now. And before the following
day was out, she was heartily sorry she had not left him at
home. One of his worst bad nights did not help to mend
matters. He vowed he had not missed the striking of a single
hour; but had tossed and turned on a too hard bed, in a too
light room, listening to the strange noises of a strange house,
and wakened for good and all, long before dawn, by the
crowing of "a thousand infernal roosters." Before anyone else
stirred, he was up and out, on a long tramp bushwards.

There was nothing to be done with him. Summoned to the
drawing-room to greet Amelia Grindle and Agnes Ocock, who
had driven over immediately after breakfast, "for a glimpse
of our darling Mary," he was so stiff, and found so little to
say, that poor Amelia, timid and fluttery as ever, hardly dared
to raise her eyes from her boots. Thereafter—and most of
Mary's old friends found their way to "Beamish House," that
morning—she left him in peace on the back verandah, and
sought to waylay Tilly, whose main idea of hospitality—poor
old Tilly!—was continually to be bothering him with something fresh to eat.

The person who did not look near was Purdy; and this was
an additional source of offence. The least he could have done,

said Richard, was to ride out and make up for his offensive
behaviour of the night before. Didn't the fellow grasp that he,
Mahony, was in Ballarat solely with the object of doing him
a good turn? Privately, Mary thought it very unlikely that
Purdy, or Tilly either, saw Richard's presence there in this
light. Aloud she observed that he must know it would not be
considered proper for the bridegroom to hang about the house,
the day before the wedding. But Richard said: propriety be
hanged!

He also flouted her suggestion that he should himself pay
some visits—look up the Archdeacon, or Chinnery of the
"National," or those colleagues on hospital or asylum, with
whom he had once been intimate.

"Not I! If they want to see me, let *them* make the overture!"

"Don't be silly. Of course they'd like to see you again."

"I know better."

"Then why, if you're so sure of it, feel hurt because they
don't come? For that's what you are," said Mary bluntly.—
She wore a large cooking-apron over her silk gown, and looked
tired, but content. She had helped to set the wedding-breakfast
on long trestle-tables running the length of the hall; had
helped to pack and strap the bride's trunks for the journey to
Sydney; baked some of her famous cakes, and laid the foun-
dation for the more elaborate cream dishes that were to be
whipped up the first thing next morning.

She went on: "Personally, I don't see how you can expect
people to run after you, when you've never bothered to keep
up with them . . . written a line or sent a message."— And
just because she herself thought *some* of Richard's old friends
might have done him the compliment of calling, Mary spoke
very warmly. Adding: "Well, at least you'll take a stroll round
the old place, now you're here, and see how it's grown."

"Indeed and I'll do nothing of the sort! . . . now don't start
badgering me, Mary. Why on earth should I go to the trouble
of soldering up old links, for the sake of a single day? I shall
never be here again."

"Tch, tch!" said Mary. "With you it's always yourself . . .
nothing but I, I, I!"—

"Well, upon my word! . . . I like that. After my dragging
all the way here . . . not to speak of being perched up

to-morrow before a churchful of people, for them to stare at and gossip about!"

At this Mary laughed aloud. "Oh, Richard! As if they would ever think of looking at anybody but the bride! . . . or bride-groom."

But Richard, it seemed, suffered from an intense nervous conviction that he would be a target for all eyes.

    ✸   ✸   ✸   ✸   ✸   ✸

Something before three o'clock the following afternoon, Mary stood on the front verandah, which was white and scrunchy with flowers and rice, and watched him, carpet-bag in hand, make a dash for gate, trap, and the train that was to carry him back to town.— Indoors, the guests still lingered: you could hear a buzz of talk, the clink of glasses, the rustle of silk; and she herself was not leaving till next day, having promised Tilly first to see the house restored to order. But nothing would persuade Richard to stop a moment longer than was necessary. He fled.—

Tossing hat and bag on the cushions of the railway carriage, Mahony fell into a seat and wiped his forehead. Doors slammed; a bell rang; they were off. Well, *that* was over, thank God! . . . and never, no, never! would he let himself be trapped into anything of the kind again. To begin with, he had been inveigled there on false pretences. It no doubt buttered Tilly's vanity, to see his name topping the list of her wedding-guests. But, as far as all else was concerned, he might have stayed comfortably at home. Purdy had not cared a three-penny-bit one way or the other. As for it ever dawning on the fellow that he was being given a leg-up . . . a social safe-conduct, so to speak—all such rubbish originated in Mary's confounded habit of reading her own ideas into other people. At his expense.

But while he could dismiss Tilly and her folly with a smile, Purdy's bovine indifference roused a cold resentment in him. Consciously, he had washed his hands of the connection long ago. And yet it seemed as if a part of him still looked for gratitude—or at least a show of gratitude—did he exert himself on Purdy's behalf. Which was absurd.— And anyhow Purdy had never been famous for delicacy of feeling—a graceless, thankless beggar from the start! In his heyday, a certain

debonair blitheness had cloaked his shortcomings. Now, time
having robbed him of every charm, he stood revealed in all
his crudity: obese, loose-mouthed, with an eye that was grown
shifty from overreaching his fellow-men: *how* he plumed
himself on his skill as a Jeremy Diddler! Oh, this insufferable
exaggeration!—this eternal bragging . . . even while they were
waiting in the church for the arrival of the bride, he had been
unable to refrain. Mary said: "Do have patience. Mark my
words, Tilly will soon knock him into shape." But Mahony
doubted it. Once a boaster, always a boaster!—besides which,
the fair fat Tilly was too far gone in love to wish to chip and
change her chosen. Her face had been oily with bliss, as she
stood with her groom before the altar, he in a check the
squares of which could have been counted from across the
road; draped in a watch-chain on which he might have hanged
himself; she, puce-clad, in a magenta bonnet topped with
roses the size of peonies, which sat crooked over one ear.
(Mary, at her side, cool and pale in silver grey, looked as
though sprung from a different branch of the human race.)

What a farce the whole thing had been! . . . from beginning
to end. The congratulations he had had to smirk a response
to, on "his friend's" marriage, "his friend's" good fortune.
Then, old Long's flowery periods, which would have well
befitted a dewy damsel of eighteen, but bordered on the ludicrous when applied to Tilly, who would never see forty-five
again, and had been through all this before. Henry Ocock
"giving away" his mature stepmother and her money-bags,
his father's money-bags, those bags that should by rights have
descended to *his* son: in spite of his sleek suavity, it was not
hard to imagine the wrath that burned behind Henry's chalky
face and boot-button eyes. He was aging, was Henry; white
hairs showed in his jetty beard; and the creasing of his lids
made him look foxier than ever. But so it was with all of
them. Those he had left young were now middle-aged; the
middle-aged had grown old. Like Henry's, their faces had not
improved in the process. Time seemed to show up the vacancy
that had once been overlaid by rounded cheeks and a smooth
forehead. Or else the ugly traits in a nature, ousting the good,
had been bitten in as by an etcher's acid. He wondered what
secrets his own phiz held, for those who had eyes to see. The
failures and defeats his prime had been spent in enduring . . .

had each left its special mark?—in the shape of hollow, or droop, or wrinkle. Oh, his return to this hated place called up bitter memories from their graves: raised one obscene ghost after another, for his haunting. Here, he was to have garnered the miraculous fortune that would lift him, for ever, out of the mud of poverty; here had dreamt the marriage that was to be like no other on earth; here turned back, with a high heart, to the profession that should ensure him ease and renown—even the cutting himself loose, when everything else had miscarried, was to have heralded the millennium.— No! one's past simply did not bear thinking about. Looking back was wormwood, and a wound. It meant remembering all the chances you had not taken; the gaudy soap-bubble schemes that had puffed out at a breath; meant an inward writhing at the toll of the years flown by, empty of achievement—at the way you had let time get the better of you. Time, which led down and down, with a descent ever steeper and more rapid, till it landed you . . . in who knew what Avernus?— Nervously Mahony unclasped his bag, and rummaged a book from its depths. To lose himself in another's thoughts was the one anodyne that was left him.

The train was racing now. They had passed Navigator, white and sweet with lucerne; and the discomforts and absurdities of the past forty-eight hours were well behind him.

❖   ❖   ❖   ❖   ❖   ❖

Cuffy, playing that evening on the front verandah, was surprised by the sudden advent of his father, who caught him up, tossed and soundly kissed him, with a: "And how is my little man? How is my darling?"— But, at three years old, even a short absence digs a breach. Cuffy had had time to grow shy. He coloured, hung his head, looked sideways along the floor; and, as soon as he was released, pattered off to Nannan and the nursery.

[5]

THE old mahogany four-poster with the red rep hangings had been brought out from among the lumber, and set up afresh in John's study. And soon after his interview with Mahony, John shifted his quarters to this room, on the pretence of

sleeping poorly and disturbing his wife. Lizzie raised fierce
objections to the change. It took Mary to mollify her, and to
insist that she must now place her own health and comfort
above everything.— Save in this one point, it was true, Lizzie
needed small persuasion. The household danced to her whims.

Emmy's room was only a trifle nearer the study than were
the other bedrooms: but, in everything that touched her father,
the girl's senses were preternaturally acute. And so it happened that she started out of her first sleep, wakened she did
not know by what, but conscious, even as she opened her eyes,
of sounds coming from her father's room—the strange, heart-
rending sounds of a man crying. Sitting up in bed, her hands
pressed to her breast, Emmy listened, all of a shake, till she
could bear it no longer: stealthily unlatching the door, she
crept down the passage to the study. And there, on this and
many another night, she lay crouched on the mat, her heart
bursting with love and pity; while within, John, believing
himself alone with his Maker, railed and rebelled, in blind
anguish. against his fate.— Yes, Emmy knew before anyone
else that some disaster had come upon her father. And in the
riot of emotion the knowledge stirred in her, there was one
drop of sweetness: she alone shared his secret.

The feeling of intimacy this engendered did much to help
her over the days of suspense that followed: when she waited
from hour to hour for the unknown blow to fall. She confided
in no one—not even her Aunt Mary. Her father himself she
dared not approach. Papa was so stern with her. Once, after
a night when she really thought her heart would break, she
ventured a timid: "Papa, if there is anything . . . I mean,
Papa . . . if I could . . ." But he stared so angrily at her that
she turned and ran from the room, for fear of bursting out
crying—as much at the sound of her own words, and the
feeling of self-pity they roused in her, as at his cold repulse.
She did not see the look he threw after her, as she went. "Her
mother's daughter!" was his muttered comment; and long past
days rose before him, when there had been one at his side
from whom nothing was hid.— Tatting and crocheting, crocheting and tatting, Emmy gave her imagination free play.
A failure in business, even bankruptcy, was the solution she
favoured—being still too young to face, of herself, the destructive thought of death. And did this happen, and Papa lose

all his money, then would come *her* chance. He would learn that he had one faithful soul at his side, one shoulder to lean on. Together they would go away, he and she, anywhere, right into the bush if necessary, and start life afresh.— But, again, there were moments when she indulged an even dearer hope: at last, perhaps, Papa was beginning to see what a dreadful mistake his marriage had been.

For Emmy hated her stepmother; hated her, and sat in judgment on her, with the harshness of the young creature who has been wounded in her tenderest susceptibilities. Thus, though, for the most part, she rejoiced to know Lizzie among the uninitiated, she could also burn with a furious, unreasoning anger against her, for living on, so blindly, so selfishly, without noticing that something was amiss. At sight of the big woman lying stretched on her *chaise longue,* idly fanning herself, book and vinaigrette at her elbow; or Papa bathing her temples for her with lavender-water, or running errands for her, like a servant—at things like these, Emmy clenched her fists, and averted her tell-tale eyes. She hated, too, Lizzie's vigorous exaggerated manner of speaking; hated the full red lips that went in and out, and up and down, when she talked; her affected languor . . . her unwieldy figure . . . the baby that was on the way.

But, with the crash, came also the chance of revenge. Then, it was Emmy's turn; and she could say in all good faith: "Oh, *don't* let her—don't let . . . Mamma go into him, Aunt Mary! She worries him so."— As always, there was just the suspicion of a pause—a kind of intake of the breath—before she got the "Mamma" out: a name here bestowed for the third time, and only after a severe inward struggle, because *he* had wished it.—

Meanwhile, though, John's serene and dignified existence had been shattered to its foundations; carrying with it, in its fall, the peace and security of those lesser lives that depended on it. For close on six months, he had kept his own counsel. With his once full lips pinched thin in his old, greying face, he went doggedly to and from the warehouse in Flinders Lane, as he had done every day for five-and-twenty years: driving off at nine of a morning, and returning as the clock struck six to escort Lizzie to any entertainment she still cared to patronise: and this, though his skin had gone the colour of dry clay, or a dingy plaster, and he was so wasted that his

clothes seemed to flap scarecrow-like on his bones. Mary's
heart bled for him; and even Richard was moved to remark
that what John must be suffering, both mentally and physically, God alone knew. But they could only pity in silence;
open compassion was not to be thought of—after the one
terrible night Mary had spent with John, the subject of his
illness was taboo, even to her. Alone, sheathed in his impenetrable reserve, he prepared for his departure; bade farewell,
behind locked doors, to a life of surpassing interest, now cut
short in mid-career. In politics, his place would not be hard
to fill. But of the great business he had built up, he was still
the mainspring; and, in a last spurt of his stiff pride, he
laboured to leave all that concerned it in perfect order.— And
yet, watching him with her heart in her eyes, Mary sometimes
wondered . . . wondered whether the unquenchable optimism
that had made him the man he was, had even yet wholly
deserted him. He had had so little experience of illness, and
was, she knew, still running privily from doctor to specialist;
giving even quacks and their remedies a trial. Did he nurse a
hope that medical opinion, right in ninety-nine cases, might
prove wrong in his, and he have the hundredth chance? One
thing at least she knew: he intended, if humanly possible,
to bear up till the child was born and Lizzie better able to
withstand the blow.

But this was not to be. The morning came when, in place
of rising and tapping at his wife's door, solicitously to inquire
how she had passed the night, John, beaten at last, lay prostrate in his bed . . . from which he never rose again.

A scene of the utmost confusion followed. Mary, summoned
just as she was sitting down to breakfast, found Lizzie in
hysterics, John writhing in an agony he could no longer conceal. The scared servants scuttled aimlessly to and fro; the
children, but half dressed, cried in a corner of the nursery.
Emmy alone had kept her wits about her—though she, too,
shook as with the ague.

Meeting Mary at the front door, she held out two clasped
hands, imploringly. "Oh . . . what *is* it? Aunt Mary! *what* is
the matter with Papa?"

"Emmy! . . . your poor, dear father—my darling, I look
to you to be brave and help me—he will need all our help
now."

Long prepared for some such emergency, Mary took control. Dispatching the groom at a gallop for the doctor, she mixed a soothing-draught for Lizzie ("See to her first," was John's whispered request) and gave John the strongest opiate she dared. The children were dressed, put in the carriage, and sent to *Ultima Thule*. Then, as Richard had directed, Mary cleared the sickroom of superfluous furniture; while Emmy bore a note to Miss Julia—Mary's sole confidante in the affair. And faithful to a promise, Miss Julia left her assistant in charge of the school, and was back with Emmy inside an hour. Without her aid—she at once saw to Lizzie, and brought the servants to their senses—without this sane, calm presence, Mary did not know how she would have managed, John, from the start, obstinately refusing to let her out of his sight.— Or, for that matter, without Emmy either . . . Emmy was her right hand. Nimble, yet light-footed as a cat; tireless; brave; Emmy now proved her mettle. Nothing was beneath her; she performed the most menial duties of the sickroom with a kind of fiery, inner gratitude. And, these done, would sit still as a mouse, a scrap of needlework in her hand, just waiting for the chance of springing up afresh. Her young face grew thin and peaked; and the life went out of her step; but she never complained, or sought to obtrude her own feelings. Only one person knew what she was suffering. It was on Auntie Julia's neck that she had had her single breakdown, had wept out her youthful passion of love and despair.

"What shall I do! Oh, what *shall* I do?"

And Auntie Julia, knowing everything, understanding everything, wisely let her cry and cry, till she could cry no more.— "There, there, my little one! There, there!"— But, after this, Emmy did not again give way. Indeed, thought Mary, there was something in her of John's own harsh self-mastery: a trait that sat oddly on her soft and lovely girlhood.

Lizzie was the sorest trial. But then, poor thing, was it to be wondered at, in her condition, and after the shock John had given her?— For when, that first morning, he failed to present himself at her bedside, Lizzie passed in a twinkling from a mood of pettish surprise to one of extreme ungraciousness. The housemaid was peremptorily bidden to go knock at the master's door and ask the reason of his negligence. Her confused stammerings throwing no light on this, Emmy was

loudly rung for. "Pray, my love, be so good as to find out if
your Papéh, who has evidently *forgotten* to wish me a good-
morning, does not even intend going to town to-day!" And
when Emmy, sick and trembling, yet with a kind of horrific
satisfaction, returned bearing John's brutal reply: "No, not
to-day, nor yet ever again!" Lizzie, now thoroughly roused,
threw on a wrapper and swept down the passage to her husband's room.

On discovering the true state of things, she dropped to the
floor in a swoon. Restored to consciousness and got back to
bed, she fell to screaming in hysterical abandonment—on his
arrival the doctor had more to do for her than for John, and
pulled a long face. And even when the danger of a premature
confinement was over, and the worst of the hysteria got under,
she would lie and sob and cry, breaking out, to whoever would
listen, in wild accusations.

"Oh, Mary, love! When I think *how* I have been deceived!
. . . the trick that has been played on me . . . me who ought to
have known before anyone else. John and his absurd secrecy!
—he has made a perfect fool of me, even in the eyes of the
servants."

"My poor, dear Lizzie! But, do believe me, he only wanted
to spare you . . . as long as he possibly could. Consider him,
now, and his sufferings, and don't make it harder for him than
you can help. Think, too, of your baby."

But she might as well have talked to a post: Lizzie continued stormily to weep and to rail. The two older women
bore patiently with her, even coming to consider it a good
thing that she was thus able to vent her emotion. It remained
for Emmy, Emmy with the hard and unyoung look her face
assumed when she spoke of her stepmother, to make the bitter
comment: "She's not really *sorry* for Papa—she's *savage*, Aunt
Mary, that's what she is!"—a point of view which Mary herself was so rigidly suppressing that it received but scant
quarter.— "Emmy, Emmy! You must *not* say such things of
your Mamma." But Richard declared the girl had hit the
nail on the head. It was herself, and herself alone, Lizzie
grieved for.

"And is it so unnatural? Has Fate not played her a shabby
trick? She took John, as we all knew, because he was by far
the best catch that had ever come her way. Now, after a few

625

brief years of glory, and when her main ambition was about to materialise, the Lady Turnham-to-be sees herself doomed to a widow's dreary existence: all weepers and seclusion: with, for sole diversion, the care of an unwanted infant. Not to speak of the posse of stepdaughters she has loaded herself up with!"

"It *does* sound harsh . . . the way you put it," said Mary; and re-tied her bonnet-strings: she had run over one evening for a peep at her children.

However, if he and Emmy were right about Lizzie and her feelings, then what a blessing it was that John, in his illness, made no demands on her, asking neither for nor after her. With his one request, on the morning of his collapse, that she should receive first attention, all his thought for her seemed exhausted: just as, in the brutal answer he returned her by Emmy, had evaporated his love and care. From the sound of her pitiless crying he turned with repugnance away. Did she enter his room, with a swish of the skirts, either forgetting to lower her voice, or hissing in a melodramatic whisper, he was restless till she withdrew. Except for Mary—and he fretted like a child if Mary was long absent—John asked only to be left alone.

On taking to his bed, he had severed, at one stroke, every link with the outside world: and soon he was to lie drug-sodden and mercifully indifferent even to the small world of his sickroom. But, before this happened, he expressed one wish—or, rather, gave a last order. The nature of his illness was not to be made known beyond the family circle.

"Trying to keep his Chinese Wall up to the end," said Mahony. "His death—like his life—is to be nobody's business but his own. Well, well . . . as a man lives so he shall die!"

But Mary was much perturbed. A dying man's whim!—and as such, of course, it had to be respected. But what *could* it hurt now, whether people knew what was the matter with John or not? Concealing the truth meant all sorts of awkward complications.— But Emmy, overhearing this, flushed sensitively, and looked distressed. "Oh, Aunt Mary, don't you *see?* Papa is . . . is *ashamed* of having a cancer."

Ashamed? . . . ashamed of an illness? Mary had never heard of such a thing, and was very severe on the idea. But Richard, struck afresh by Emmy's acumen, declared: "That's it! The

626

girl is right. *You* call it a sick man's fancy, I the exaggerated reserve of a lifetime; but Emmy knows better, sees deeper, than any of us." And added, a moment later: "It strikes me, my dear, that if, instead of hankering after that impossible scape-grace of a son, just because he *was* a son, your brother had had a little more eye for the quick wits and understanding of his daughter, he might have been a happier man."—

News of the serious illness of the Honourable John Milli-bank Turnham, M.L.C., brought an endless string of callers and inquirers to the door: the muffled knocker thudded un-ceasingly. People came in their carriages, on horseback, on foot; and included not merely John's distracted partners, and his colleagues on the Legislative Council, but many a lesser man and casual acquaintance—Mary herself marvelled to see how widely known and respected John had been. And those who could not come in person wrote letters of condolence, sent gifts of luscious fruit, and choice flowers, and out-of-season delicacies—anything, in short, of which kindly people could think, to prove their sympathy. It was one person's task to receive the visitors, answer the letters, acknowledge the gifts. Fortunately, this very person was at hand, in the shape of Zara. Zara's elegant manners, and her ease in expressing her-self on paper, were exactly what was wanted.

She and Hempel had put up in lodgings at Fitzroy, prior to setting out on the forlorn hope of a sea voyage. For, after numerous breakdowns, poor Hempel—he looked as if the first puff of wind would blow him overboard; Richard called him: "The next candidate for the Resurrection!"—had been obliged definitely to abandon his pastorate. In the meantime, he was resting in bed from the fatigues of the train journey, before undertaking the fresh fatigues to which Zara, in her wilful blindness, condemned him.

At John's, Zara received in the dining-room, among horse-hair and mahogany, as better befitting the occasion than the gilt and satin of the drawing-room. Lugubriously clad, she spoke with the pious and resigned air of one about to become a mourner. "My poor brother," "Our great grief," "God's will be done!"— But, of an evening, when the rush was over, she carried to Lizzie a list of names and gifts, and a sheaf of letters.

Her sibilant tones were audible through the half-closed

door. "Yes, Judge O'Connor—yes, yes, my dear, himself in person! . . . with his own and his lady's compliments . . . desires to be kept informed of our dear John's progress."

And Lizzie's rich, fruity tones: "Major Grenville, did you say? . . . on behalf of his Excellency? Very gratifying . . . oh, very gratifying, indeed!"

Mary was never one to jib at trifles. But Emmy, as often as she heard them at it, clenched her fists and ground her teeth. *How* she hated them! . . . hated them. To be able to care who called and who did not call, when Papa lay dying! In her passionate young egoism she demanded that there should be no room in any mind but for this single thought.

But, as week added itself to week, and John still lay prostrate; and since, too, the most heartfelt inquiries evoked none but the stereotyped response: "No improvement," the press of sympathisers visibly declined. People ceased to call daily; came but once a week; then, at still wider intervals. And at length, even the hardiest dropped off, and a great stillness settled round the dying man. John was forgotten; was reckoned to the dead before he was actually of them.— Only once more on earth would he, for a brief hour, play a leading part.

The flawless constitution that had been so great an asset to him in his life, stood him now in ill stead. His dying was arduous and protracted. Behind the red rep hangings there went on one of those bitter struggles with death that wring from even the least sensitive an amazed: "Wherefore? To what end?" Cried Mahony, watching John's fruitless efforts: "The day will come, I'm sure of it, when we shall agree to the incurable sufferer being put painlessly away. We need a lethal chamber, and not for dumb brutes alone."— At which Mary looked apprehensive, and wished he wouldn't. A good job, said she, he was no longer in practice. Or what *would* his patients have thought?

"Thank God, the muzzle of medical etiquette is off my jowl!"

Meanwhile, of course, he was in his element, and all tenderness and consideration for John—he went, for instance, to endless trouble in procuring for him the newest make of water-bed—which was just what one would expect of Richard. Nor would he have him teased about religious questions, or his approaching end. On the other hand, had John shown the least desire for religious consolation, Richard would have been the person to see that he got it.

But this, John did not do. At those rare moments when he was awake to his surroundings and tolerably free from pain, he lay exhausted and inert, his eyes closed, and with little to distinguish him from one already dead. What his innermost thoughts were, what his hopes and fears of a hereafter, remained his own secret.— The single wish that crossed his lips seemed to point to his mind still occupying itself with earthly things.

Mary, sewing beside the bed, looked up one day to find his sunken eyes open, and fastened on her.

She rose and leaned over him. "What is it, John? Do you want anything?"

He signified yes with his lids, sparing himself any superfluous word for fear of rousing up his enemy. Then, in a thick, raucous whisper: "I should like . . . to see . . . the boy. Yours."

Thus it came about—greatly against the wish of Mahony, who held that illness and suffering were evil sights for childish eyes—that Cuffy was one day lifted into the carriage beside Nannan, where he sat, his little legs a-dangle, clad in his best velvet tunic and with his Scotch cap on his head. He looked pale and solemn. Nannan and Eliza had made such funny faces at each other, and had whispered and whispered. And while she was dressing him, Nannan had talked about nothing but how good and quiet he must be, and what would happen to him if he wasn't. In consequence, directly he was set down from the carriage, Cuffy started walking on the tips of his toes; and, on tiptoe, holding fast to his nurse's hand, he crept laboriously up the gravel path to the house.

At the front door stood Cousin Emmy, who kissed him, and led him in. Like Nannan, she, too, said: "Now you must be a *very* good boy, Cuffy, and not make the least noise." Cuffy's heart began to thump with anxiety: he walked more gingerly than before. The house felt like the nursery when the Dumplings were asleep. Emmy opened a door into a room that was quite dark. It had also a very nasty smell. Some one was snoring. Cuffy tried to pull back.

"Now, be good, Cuffy!"

Then he was at his mother's knee, mechanically holding out

629

his hands to have his little gloves peeled off. But his thoughts were with his eyes—pinned to some one lying in a bed . . . a man with a dark yellow face, and a grey beard, who was asleep and snoring—like Nannan did. Cuffy did not associate this funny-looking person with his uncle; he just stood and stared stupidly. Nevertheless, something very disturbing began to go round inside him; and he swallowed hard.

Then two big black shiny eyes were awake and looking at him. They looked and looked. Cuffy stood transfixed, his lips apart, his breath coming unevenly, his own eyes round with a growing fear.

A yellow hand like a claw came over the bedclothes towards him, and some one tried to speak; and only made a funny sound—and tried again.

" . . . Does you credit. But . . . at his age . . . John . . . a finer . . . child."— After which, the eyes shut and the snoring began anew.

Then, though he had only just come, somebody said: "Kiss your uncle good-bye, Cuffy."

This was too much. As he was lifted up, Cuffy made protest, wildly working his arms and legs.— "No, no!"

But his lips had brushed something cold and clammy before, his clothes all twisted round him, he was put back on the floor. And, by then, the face on the bed had changed: the eyes were all wrinkles now; the mouth like a big black hole. Somebody screamed. And now people were scurrying about, and there came Aunt Lizzie running in her dressing-gown, and she was naughty, and cried, making the noise he had been told not to. His own tears flowed; but, true to his promise, he did not utter a sound.

Then, some one took his hand and ran him out of the room, to the dining-room, where, his eyes wiped and his nose blown, Cousin Emmy gave him a nectarine, which she peeled for him and cut up in quarters, because it was "nicer so." He was also allowed to eat it messily, and not scolded for letting the juice drip down his tunic.— But as he did this, and while his voice was still quavery and his nose sniffly, he asked curiously: "Why does your hands do so funny, Cousin Emmy?"— Cuffy always wanted to know why.

At home again, he felt the need of blowing out his shrunken self-esteem. It was a chance, too, of making himself big in

the eyes of his playfellow Josey, the youngest of his three
cousins, a long-legged girl of seven, who domineered over him,
smacked him, and used his toys without asking. There she
came along the verandah, dragging his best horse and cart—
with her nasty big black eyes, and the hair that stuck straight
out behind her round comb.

Under seal of secrecy, and with an odd sense of guilt, as if
he was doing something he ought not to, Cuffy confided to
her his discovery that big people cry, too. "I seed your
Mamma do it."

But Josey, in place of being impressed, was very angry:
grabbing the secretmonger's silky topknot, she shook him
soundly: "That's a storwy, Cuffy Mahony, and you're a
howwid storwy-teller! Gwown-up people *never* cwy!"— The
fact that she spoke with a strong lisp, while a baby like Cuffy
could talk plainly, always rendered Josey very emphatic.
Moreover, in the present case, she still burned with shame at
the disgraceful knowledge that not only Mamma could cry,
but Papa too.

John died five days later, at midnight.

The afternoon before, an odd thing happened. Mary and
Emmy were alone with him, he lying drugged and comatose,
and Mary had been fanning him, for it was very warm. Outside, from a copper-coloured sky, a scorching north wind blew;
the windows of the room were tight shut against swirling
clouds of dust. There was no sound but John's laboured
breathing, and, exhausted, Mary thought she must have
dropped into a doze. For when, warned by a kind of instinct,
she started up, she saw that John's eyes were open: he was
gazing, with a glassy stare, at the foot-end of the bed. And, as
he watched, an extraordinary change came over the shrunken,
jaundiced face. The eyes widened, the pin-hole pupils dilated;
while the poor, burst lips, on which were black sores that
would not heal, parted and drew back, disclosing the pallid
flesh of the gums.— John was trying to smile.

A second later, and the whole face was transfigured—lit
up by an expression of rapturous joy. John even made a violent effort to raise himself—to hold out his arms. His breath
came sobbingly.

"Emma! . . . Oh, *Emma! . . . wife!*"

631

At first sound of her name, Emmy sprang from her seat behind the curtains and threw herself on her knees at the bedside, close to John's groping hand. "Papa! . . . yes, oh yes? . . . oh, papa . . . *darling!*"

But John did not hear her. All the life left him was centred in his eyes, which hung, dazed with wonder, on something visible to them alone. Bending over the passionately weeping girl, Mary whispered: "Hush, hush, Emmy! Hush, my dear! . . . He sees . . . he thinks he sees your mother."——

Mahony knew nothing of this occurrence till long after. By the time he got there that evening, the death-agony had begun; and now the one thought of those gathered round John's bed was, to ease and speed his passing. It was a murderous business. For the drug that had thus far blunted the red-hot knives that hacked at his vitals suddenly lost its power: injections now gave relief but for a few moments on end; and, hour after hour, hour after hour, his heart-breaking cry for help beat the air. "Morphia . . . morphia! . . . for God's sake, morphia!"

But the kindly, bearded physician who sat with a finger on John's wrist remained impassive: the dose now necessary to reduce the paroxysms would be more than the weakened heart could bear. And so, livid, drenched in sweat, John fought his way to death through tortures indescribable.

At the end of the afternoon, those present felt that the limits of human endurance had been reached. All eyes hung on the doctor's, with the same mute appeal. The two men, Mahony and the other, exchanged a rapid glance. Then, bending over the writhing, anguished thing that had once been John Turnham, the doctor addressed it by name. "Mr. Turnham! you are in your right mind . . . and fully aware of what you are saying. Do you take the injection necessary to relieve you, of your own free will, and at your own risk?"

"For the love of God!"

A moment's stir and business, and the blessed sedative was running through the quivering veins, the last excruciating pangs were throbbing with hammer-strokes to their end: upwards, from the feet, crept the blissful numbness . . . rising higher . . . higher . . . higher. And, as peace descended, and the heavy lids fell to, Mahony stepped forward, and taking

one of the dying hands in his, said in a loud, clear voice:
"Have no fear of death, John!"

Already floating out on the great river, John yet heard these
words, and was arrested by them. Slowly the lids rolled back
once more, and, for the fraction of a second, the broken eyes
met Mahony's. In this, their last, living look, not a trace was
left of the man who had been. They were now those of one
who was about to be: fined and refined; rich in an experience
that transcended all mortal happenings; wise with an ageless
wisdom. And, as they closed for ever to this world, there came
an answer to Mahony's words, in ever so faint a flattening of
the lips, an almost imperceptible intake at the corners of the
mouth; which, on the sleeping face, had the effect of a smile:
that lurking smile, remote with peace, and yet touched with
the lightest suspicion of amused wonder, that sometimes
makes the faces of the dead so good to see.

John did not wake again. Towards midnight his breathing
grew more stertorous, the intervals between the breaths
longer. And finally the moment came when the watchers
waited for the next . . . and waited . . . in vain.

All was over; the poor weeping, shattered women were
led from the room. Mary, despite her grief, kept her presence
of mind; and Miss Julia with her. But Lizzie was convulsed;
and poor little Emmy, her long service ended, broke down
utterly, and had to be carried to bed, and chafed, and dosed
with restoratives. Zara was bidden see to the children, John's
three, who had been brought over during the afternoon in
case their father should ask for them: forgotten, hungry,
tired, they had cried themselves to sleep, and now lay huddled
in a tear-stained group on the dining-room sofa. Mahony and
the doctor busied themselves for yet a while in the death-
chamber; after which, decently composed and arranged, John
formed no more than a sheet-draped rising on the bed's
smooth plain. Mahony locked the door behind him and took
the key. The dogcart had come round, and Jerry, who was to
drive back to town with the doctor, stood, his collar turned
up, all of a fidget to get home to Fanny and the children.
Mahony went out with them, and, having watched them drive
off, paused to breathe in the night air, which was fresh and
welcome after the fetid odours of the sickroom. And standing

there under the stars, he sent, like an arrow of farewell, a
parting thought to the soul that might even now be winging
its way to freedom, and to whom soon all mysteries would be
plain. John had made a brave end. There had been no whining
for pity or pardon: on his own responsibility he had lived, and
he died by the same rule—the good Turnham blood had come
out in him to the last.— And, as he re-entered the house,
where, by now, the last exhausted watcher was sinking into
unconsciousness, Mahony murmured half-aloud to himself:
"Well done, John , , , well done!"

[6]

SOME six months later, the Mahonys undertook their second
voyage to England. They sailed by the clipper-ship *Atrata*,
and travelled in style, accompanied by a maid to attend to
Mary and both nurses.— And *Ultima Thule* passed into other
hands.

It had proved easier to persuade Mary to the break than
Mahony had dared to hope. John's illness and death paved the
way. For, by the time her long vigil at his bedside was over,
and Lizzie seen safely through a difficult confinement, Mary's
own health was beginning to suffer. A series of obstinate
coughs and colds plagued her; and the doctor who sounded
her considered a thorough change of air advisable. A change
of scene, too. For though Mary was not giving to moping, and,
at the time, had thankfully accepted John's release from pain,
yet when it came to taking up her ordinary life again, the full
sense of her loss came home to her.— And not to her alone,
but to everybody. John's had been such a vigorous personality.
Its withdrawal left a gap nothing could fill.

None the less, the sacrifice she was now called on to make
was a bitter one, and cost her much heartburning: when she
first grasped the *kind* of change Richard was tentatively proposing, she burst into heated exclamation.— What, break up
their home *again?* . . . their lovely home? Leave all the things
they had collected round them? Leave intimates and friends,
and their assured position? . . . to go off again no one knew
where . . . and where nobody knew them? Oh, he couldn't
possibly mean it!— And what about the children? . . . still
mere babies— "And though you talked till you were black

634

in the face, Richard, you would never get me to leave them behind!"—and the drawbacks of ship-life for them at their tender age? . . . the upset in their habits . . . not getting to sleep in good time, and improper feeding . . . not to speak of having to watch them grow spoilt and fractious—winding up with her dread of the sea, his antipathy to England and English life.

But Mahony, though he spoke soothingly, stuck to his guns. It was only to be a visit this time, he urged. It could hardly hurt the house to be let for a year or so? A good tenant would no doubt take good care of it; and it would be there, just as it stood, for them to come back to. Then, of course, both nurses would go with them, to look after the children; and as for the darlings being too young for a voyage, that was the sheerest nonsense: on the contrary, it would do them a world of good, and perhaps even turn Cuffy into a sturdy boy. The same could be said for her own ailments: there was nothing like the briny for laying coughs and colds; while the very best cabin on board would go far towards lessening the horrors of seasickness. Lastly, as for England, why, they would not know it for the same country, travelling as they did to-day. Lots of money, introductions to people, going everywhere, seeing everything; and ending up, if she felt disposed, with a jaunt to the Paris Exhibition and a tour of the Continent.— "It isn't every wife, my dear, has such an offer made her."

But his words fell flat: Mary only shrugged her shoulders in reply. Tours and exhibitions meant nothing to her. She hadn't the least desire to travel—or at any rate to go farther afield than Sydney or Tasmania. She had been so happy here . . . so perfectly happy! Why, oh why, could Richard not be content? And that he could forget so easily how he had hated England . . . and disliked the English. . . . Well, no: she must be fair to him. As he said, life over there would probably be a very different thing now they had money. (Though all the money in the world wouldn't stop it raining!) He might also be right about the voyage doing the chicks good: it would certainly give them, tiny tots though they were, just that something which colonial-bred children lacked. But oh, her home! . . . her beautiful home . . . it always came back to this. To have to turn out, hand it over to strangers, have strangers tramping about your best carpets, sleeping in your beds, using your egg-shell china—even the best of tenants would not care for the things as you did yourself. She had asked nothing better than to spend the rest of her life at *Ultima Thule,* in peace and happiness, seeing her children grow up well-known and respected; and here now came Richard, for whom even a few years of it had proved too many. Luxury and comfort, or poverty and hard work, it did not seem to matter which: the root of the evil lay in himself.— On the other hand, she mustn't forget how splendidly he had behaved over John's illness: never grumbling at her long, long absences, or at being left to the tender mercies of the servants. Many another husband, too, might have said: let them *hire* some one to do their nursing, and not wear out my wife over it! But Richard was not like that.

Hence, her first heat having cooled, wiser counsels prevailed; the end of which was a sturdy resolve to smother her own feelings and think of him. Two considerations finally turned the scale. One was that when, with Lizzie's convalescence, she was free to return home, she had got a nasty shock at the state in which she found Richard. Without her to nag at him, and rout him out, he had let himself go as never before. He had forgotten to change his things, or to have his hair cut; had neglected his meals, neglected the children— lost interest even in his beloved garden. And for this they had to thank that horrid spiritualism, and nothing in the world besides! During the last months, while she had been wrapped up in John, it had come to be a perfect obsession with him; and from a tolerably clear-headed person, he had turned into a bundle of credulous superstition. Why, he actually sat, for as long as an hour at a time, with a pencil in his hand, waiting for it to write by itself—write messages from the dead . . . and wasn't he angry when she laughed at him!

This was one thing—the chance for him of a complete break with all such nonsense. Another, that, coming back to him as it were with fresh eyes, she saw that he was beginning to look very elderly. He seemed to be growing downwards, losing his fine height, through always sitting crouched over books; and the fair silky hair at his temples was quite silvery now, did you peer closely at it. It was hard to think of Richard as old . . . and him still well under fifty! Yet the coming on of age might account for much. Elderly people did settle into ruts; and, once in them, were impossible to move. Perhaps his present morbid hankering after change was a kind of warning from something in him, to shake himself up and get out of his groove before it was too late. In which case, it would be folly and worse than folly, on her part, to try to prevent him.

For his sake, then, and for this alone. When it came to a question of Richard's bodily health and welfare, all other considerations must go by the board.— One condition, however, she did stand out for, and that was, that the house should not be let to anyone, no matter whom, for longer than a year. By then, she was positive, Richard would have had his fill of travelling, with the varied discomforts it implied, and be thankful to get back to his own dear home.

Thus it came that *Ultima Thule* was put into an agent's hands, and Mary fell to sorting and packing, and making her preparations for the long sea voyage.— Not the least of these was fitting the three children out anew from top to toe. Richard had forbidden them even an armband as mourning for their uncle—he was never done railing at Lizzie, for having turned John's three into little walking mountains of bombazine and crêpe. So Mary was free to indulge her love for dainty stuffs and pretty colours. And, thought she, if ever children paid for dressing, hers did. The Dumplings were by now lovely, fair-haired, blue-eyed three-year-olds, with serious red mouths, and firm chubby legs. They prattled the livelong day; loved and were loved by every one. Cuffy, dark, slim, retiring, formed just the right contrast. People often stopped Nurse to ask whose children they were. And, on this, their first excursion into the big world, nobody should be able to say they were not the best-dressed, best-cared-for children on the ship!

Before, however, a suitable tenant for the house had been found—Richard would not even *consider* the people who had so far looked over it: when it came to the point, he was the fastidious one of the two, and wailed over the invasion of his privacy—before anything further had been decided, a note arrived one morning from Tilly, saying she and Purdy had come down from Ballarat overnight and were putting up at "Scott's." So after breakfast, Mary on with her bonnet and drove to town.

She found Tilly established in a fine sitting-room on the first floor of the hotel, looking very, very prosperous . . . all silk and bugles. Purdy was out, on the business that had brought him to Melbourne: "So we two have got all the morning, love, to jaw in." As she spoke, Tilly whipped off Mary's bonnet and mantle, and carried them to the bedroom, supplying Mary meanwhile with one of her own caps, lest anyone should enter the room and find her with a bare pate. Then, a second chair having been drawn up for her to put her feet on, a table with cake and wine set at her elbow, they were free to fall to work. They had not met since Tilly's wedding; and Mary had now to tell the whole sad story of John's illness and death, starting from the night on which he had unexpectedly come to consult Richard, and not omitting his queer hallucination the day before he died (an incident she had religiously kept from Richard, as only too likely to encourage his present craze). Next they discussed Lizzie, her behaviour during John's illness, her attitude to the children, and the birth of her boy—a peevish, puny infant, to whom, much against her inclination, she thinking the world of her own family and little of any other, she had been induced to give John's name. And then John's will, "John's infamous will!" as Richard called it, by which Lizzie was left sole executrix, and trustee of Emmy and the little girls' money (five thousand apiece), with free use of the interest, so long as she provided a home for them under her roof.— "Which, as you can see, Tilly, is about as foolish a condition as the poor fellow could well have made."

Tilly nodded; but suppressed the: "Yes, but oh, how like 'im!" that jumped to her lips, on the principle of not picking holes in the dead.— "But what about if Madam marries again . . . eh, Mary? How then?"

Mary nodded ruefully. "Why, then it's the usual thing: she's cut off with a penny; most of the money goes to the boy; and Richard and Jerry become trustees in her stead." But, extenuating where Tilly had suppressed, Mary added: "You must remember, my dear, the will was drawn up directly after marriage, when John was still very much in love."

"Lor', Mary, *what* a picnic!" said Tilly, and sagely wagged her head. "My dear, can't you see 'em? Madam, gone sour as curds, clinging like grim death to 'er posse of old maids!—

638

Poor old Jinn! Poor little kids! Caught like fishes in a net."

"Yes, well, except that . . . as Richard says . . . it's very unlikely . . ."

Their eyes met.

"Why, yes, I suppose it is," said Tilly dryly.

Thence they passed to their own affairs; and Mary told of the fresh uprootal that was in store for her; and, in the telling, let out some of the exasperation that burned in her at the prospect. Tilly was the one person who would understand what it meant to her; to whom she could utter a word of complaint. To the world at large, Richard and she must, and would, always present a united front.

Said she: "Oh, I *did* think this time, Tilly, he would be satisfied; when he'd got everything he could possibly wish for. It was a different matter his leaving Ballarat—and I couldn't blame him myself, for not wanting to settle permanently in England. But here . . . our nice house . . . his library . . . the garden . . . And the stupid part of it is, I know he'll regret it . . . tire of being on the move long before we can get back into the house. I'm making up my mind to *that*, before I start."

"Poor old girl! You do have a tough time of it."

"Besides, there are the chicks to think of now, as well. Their father says the voyage will do them good, and he may be right. But the voyage isn't everything. What about the change of climate for them, while they're so small? It may be too much for Cuffy, going into the cold over there, as we shall do. Then, travelling isn't the thing for little children— you know what an excitable child Cuffy is—and they'll pick up bad manners from people they'd otherwise never meet. I *can't* have my children sacrificed.— And then, just think what it's going to cost us, taking three servants, renting a fur- nished house in London, making a tour of the Continent, and all the rest of it. Richard has such grand notions, nowadays. Economy's a word that has ceased to exist for him. The money's there, and it's to be spent, and that's all about it. But it does sometimes seem to me . . . I mean, I can't help feeling it would be better if I had some idea what we've got and how it goes."

Having, however, opened her heart thus, Mary came to a stop: there were things she drew the line at touching on, and though her hearer was only Tilly. You did not, even to your dearest friend, belabour the point that your husband was growing old and rusty, stiff in body and in mind. You locked the knowledge up, with a pang, inside your own heart. Again, Tilly had always made such game of spiritualism. Did she now hear that, from an interested inquirer, Richard had become an out-and-out adherent, bowing to the craze in all its aspects, accepting as gospel the rubbish its devotees talked, attending sittings which opened with prayers and hymns, just as if they were trying to take the place of going to church— why, at this, Tilly would certainly tap her forehead and make significant eyes, imagining goodness only knew what. So Mary kept a wifely silence.

Besides, it was now Tilly's turn to talk. Tilly had brought a rare budget of gossip with her from the old home; and no one could give this in racier, more entertaining fashion than she. Mary listened and laughed, throwing in a reproving: "Now, *really*, Tilly!" at some of the speaker's most daring shots; growing grave-eyed were the tragedies alluded to that underlay many a prosperous exterior.

Not till all the old friends had been inquired after, did she press nearer home. "And now, Tilly, how about yourself, my dear? Forgive my asking. But are you . . . has it been . . . Come! you know what I mean."

Tilly laughed out loud. "Indeed and it has, old girl!—and no apologies needed. Yes, love, the very *best* of husbands. But I was right as rain, Mary, in what I said beforehand— no spendthrift, as I'm alive! Why, 'e even goes to the other extreme, love, and holds the purse-strings a bit tighter than yours truly 'as been used to. Though it's not for me to complain, my dear, considering 'ow he handles money. I'm still a bit dazed by it, myself. A born knack with the shekels, and that's the truth! I declare to you, old Pa's leavings have almost *doubled*, in these six months. Purd's got a sort of second-sight, which tells 'im to the minute what o'clock it is. All that was wrong with him, Mary, was never having enough of the needful to show what 'e was made of."

"Well, I *am* glad to hear that—I am indeed!"

She went home full of the news. "We were both wrong, you see."

But it would not have been Richard, if he hadn't made ironical remarks about the bloom being still on the grapes, etc., etc. . . . Wait till a couple of years had passed, said he, and then see how the land lay. For, if Purdy had started speculating already . . .

"Ah, but Tilly says he has a kind of sixth sense for the ups and downs of the share market."

"Many a wife believes the same till the crash comes.— But you know *my* opinion of our national vice."

"Well, you'll be able to judge for yourself. They're coming to dinner this evening."

"Oh, botheration take it! Have we really got to have them here?"

"Now, Richard . . . when Tilly's in town for the first time since her wedding! Certainly we have. Besides, I'm sure you'll be interested to see what marriage has done for Purdy."

"Oh Lord, Mary! Am I not, even at my time of life, allowed to know what interests me and what doesn't?"

"Well, I shan't see Tilly again for ever and ever so long. I do beg you to be nice to her, dear . . . to both of them," said Mary.

And when the time came he was . . . of course he was: with the near prospect of escape from people, Richard invariably found it easy to be charming to them! Another thing, she had pandered to his weak side by preparing a very choice little dinner; while the table looked its best, and she wore one of his favourite dresses—a black velvet gown with jet trimmings, cut square at the neck.

But the main reason for his amiability was, without a doubt, the immense improvement that had taken place in Purdy: it was noticeable even as the latter entered the drawing-room. In appearance, he would, it was true, never be very much, what with his limp, and so on; and his lack of distinction was doubly remarkable when Richard was present, who was so slender and aristocratic-looking. But his aggressiveness had gone; he was no longer up in arms against the world. Gone, too, was the dreadful boasting that had so set Richard against him; and he had quite given over telling tiresome stories . . . thanks, thought Mary, to having married one of the most sensible of women. At the single threatened lapse into his old tone, she distinctly felt Tilly seek and find his foot beneath the table.—

"Didn't I say she'd pull him into shape?" and: "Upon my word, wife! if ever there was an exploded notion, it is that the possession of this world's goods makes for evil. Why! there was actually a touch of his old self about the fellow to-night."

The ormolu clock on the drawing-room mantelpiece had just chimed eleven. Mary was giving her toes a final toast before retiring, Richard securing the hasps and bolts of shutters and French windows.

"Yes, indeed, quite," agreed Mary; but with an absent air. She was thinking of Tilly—dear old Tilly!—in whom the change had been no less marked. Looking very buxom and rather handsome, in magenta velvet, Tilly had sat, smiling broadly, but with less to say for herself than ever in her life before. Instead of paying attention to Richard, as she ought to have done, she had all the time been listening to Purdy, drinking in his words, and signing to Mary to listen, too, by many a private nod, or aside, or meaning tilt of the brows. So palpably eager was she for him to shine, that more than once she had been unable to resist breaking in with a: "Oh, come now, Purd, take a *leetle* bit of the credit to yourself!—it was *his* doing really, Mary, and no one else's, though 'e tries now to make out it was Blake's." And at Purdy's "Forgive my old woman's dotage, you two . . . it's still kissing-time with us, you know!"—at this, Tilly had smirked and blushed like a sixteen-year-old.

Meanwhile, Richard was saying from the hearthrug, where he stood nursing his coat-tails: " . . . an interesting chat, after you had left the room, my dear. I was hearing all about the Mitcham case, from within—the big mining suit, you know, that has created such a scandal in Ballarat . . . you must remember old Grenville, of Canterbury Station, his deafness, and his expletives, and those enormous black cigars of his—he always had one stuck in the corner of his mouth, when he drove his four-in-hand into town."

"Of course I do. A very kind old gentleman I thought him."

"Yes . . . he had rather a way with the ladies.— Well, as I was saying, this fellow Blake, that Purdy swears by, was one of the partners in the company formed after old G. had sold his mine—at a dead loss, mind you, and on the express advice of his confidential manager, who, directly after, became a promoter of the new company. When the output suddenly redoubled, and the shares began to soar, old Grenville, naturally enough, thought he had been done, and sued them for fraud. The jury could not agree. Now, there's a rumour of a settlement. If it takes place, it is calculated that the shares will rise in value by two to three hundred per cent. Purdy stands to make his fortune—thanks to having some one at his elbow who is in the swim."

But Mary pursed her lips and looked dubious. "Well, I don't know, Richard . . . I must say, it sounds to me rather shady."

"Hm . . . well, yes, myself I prefer to keep clear of that sort of thing.— All the same, Mary, I couldn't help thinking what a terrible slowcoach old Simmonds is, compared with these modern brokers one hears of. One never gets any valuable inside information from him—for the very good reason that he doesn't know it himself."

"But so honest and trustworthy!"

"Oh, yes, there's that about it," said Richard, a trifle morosely, Mary thought.

"And what do you say to the house? Wasn't it a funny thing Purdy tumbling across some one like that?" she hastened to add, in an attempt to divert his mind from old Simmonds's shortcomings."

"A stroke of luck of the first order!"

For amongst other news, Purdy had had a tidbit for them. Only that very day, it seemed, in the coffee-room of the hotel, he had run up against a squatter from Darumbooli, who was on the look-out for a furnished house, standing in its own grounds and not too far from the sea, where he could settle wife and daughters while the latter attended a finishing school. Purdy had at once thought of *Ultima Thule*, and extolled its beauties: its lawns, and shrubberies, and fruit gardens, its proximity to the sea. The squatter had pricked up his ears; and, if they agreed, would come out to view the house early next morning.

Whereupon the last trace of Mahony's starchedness had melted, in a glow of gratitude and content.

"Upon my word, Mary, it sounds the very thing, at last!"

THAT night he could not sleep. To begin with, he had been unused, of late, to an evening's talk; bits and scraps of it went on buzzing round his brain, long after he lay abed. Then, something he had eaten had disagreed with him; Cook's shortcrust must have been too rich, or the pears over-ripe. He tossed and turned, to the disturbance of poor Mary; tried lying high, lying low, counting sheep, and other silly tricks; all to no purpose; before an hour was over, the black thoughts of the night—those sinister imaginings born of darkness and immobility—had him in their grip.

Their approach was stealthy. For he had gone to bed in high feather at the prospect of at length securing a tenant. Weeks had dragged by, and the house was still unlet. He fumed as often as he thought of it. To put a house such as his on the market, and get no offer for it! Sell? . . . yes. He could have sold three times over. But the idea of renting a place, ready furnished, seemed not to enter the colonial mind.— Now, however, if Purdy was to be trusted . . . A rich squatter, too . . . some one who would no doubt be willing to pay a good price for a good thing—though this condition was not, God be thanked, the *sine quâ non* it would once have been.— Still, money was money; you could not have too much of it . . . especially here, where it had retained all its pristine power. Give a man means, and you gave him friends and favours, and a rank second to none. To take a petty instance: what had money not done for the very person they had had before their eyes, that evening? From the seedy little down-at-heel of a year back, Purdy had been metamorphosed into . . . well, at least rendered presentable enough to bid to your table. Money had restored his shrunken self-respect. It had also brought out in him talents which not his oldest friends had guessed at. That Purdy, of all people, should prove a dabster in the share-market!—exchange, to such good purpose, bar-parlour for "Corner." No doubt, the years he had spent hobnobbing with every variety of doubtful individual had sharpened his wits. You saw something of that in the shrewd choice he had made of a broker. For, three parts of the game, did you enter the big gamble, depended on your having a wide-awake adviser at your elbow. And this man Blake, of whom they had heard so much that night, did actually seem to be one in a thousand.

One in a thousand . . . one in a thousand . . . a thousand . . .
Mahony was on the point of dropping off, to the rhythm of
these words, when a vague uneasiness began to stir in him; or,
more exactly, when he became abruptly aware that, deep
down in him, a nagging anxiety had for some time been at
work. Coming to, with a jerk, he sent his thoughts back over
the evening. What was it? . . . what had happened to prick
him, when all had seemed to go so smoothly? He groped, and
groped. Then . . . ha! . . . he had it. Simmonds. The name
whizzed into his mind like a dart; like a dart stuck there, and
was not to be got out. And no sooner had he found this clue
than, with a rush, a swarm of vexatious thoughts and impressions was upon him. First, he realised that his seeming good
spirits were all humbug; at heart he had been depressed by
the tale of Purdy's successes. They had made him feel out-of-
date—a back number, an old fossil, who had to learn from
some one he had always considered his inferior, what was actually happening in the world of mines and shares. And for
this, he held Simmonds to blame. What was the use of a confidential agent who did not keep you up to the mark in things?
— Not that he wanted to speculate; or, at least, not as the
word was understood here. But he wished to feel that he *could*
have done so, and with as much aplomb as anybody, did the
fit take him. And brooding over the chances he had no doubt
missed, and even at this moment might be missing: at a picture of himself lying high and dry, while one and another—
mere whipper-snappers like Purdy—floated easily out to fortune, an acute irritation mastered him: him lying helpless and
an easy prey.

He turned his pillow, and, even as he did so, told himself
that the fault had been not Simmonds's, but his own. Yes, the
truth was, he had not cared enough—had had no ambition.
Otherwise, why have laid his affairs in the hands of such a
humdrum?—and, what was worse, have left them there.
Honest?—yes: but so was many a noodle honest; and in these
new countries honesty alone, unbacked by any more worldly
qualities, stood not a mortal chance. And again a vision
danced before his closed lids. He saw the thousands he had
failed to make—thousands that grew to hundreds of thousands
as he watched—fluttering just beyond *his* grasp, though within

easy reach of others. And now, to sting him, the earlier bitterness returned ... in the form of a galling envy. To see Purdy, the foolish harum-scarum, the confessed failure, the mean little *commis voyageur!*—to see such a one about to pass, surpass him, in means and influence: this was one of the bitterest mouthfuls he had ever had to swallow.

And here, seizing its chance, a further fear insinuated itself. What if it should not end with this? Simmonds being what he was, might he not fail in other ways as well, and let what he already held slip through his fingers? ... not be sufficiently on the *qui vive?*—and he, Mahony, wake one morning to find himself a poor man. A shiver ran down his spine at the thought, and he made a feverish movement: he would have liked to throw off the bedclothes, spring up, and go hot-foot to call Simmonds to account. Since, however, he was condemned to lie like a log, his imagination did the work for him, running riot in a series of pictures—a panorama, in which he was gradually stripped of his possessions—reduced to ruin and its accompanying disgrace ... till cold drops stood out on his forehead.

Sitting up, he fumbled for a handkerchief. The change of position brought him a moment's calmness. Good Lord! what was he doing? ... working himself into such a state. It was like old times, when he had had to worry himself half to death about money ... or the lack of it.— He drank a glass of water, and rolled over on his other side.

Scarcely, however, had his head touched the pillow when he was off again, stabbed by yet another nightmare thought. What if it should be a case of fraud on Simmonds's part? ... deliberate fraud. Might not the lethargy, the stolid honesty, be but a pose?—the cloak to cover a rascally activity? Like the confidential agent whose double-dealing they had heard of that night, it would be child's play for Simmonds, just because he appeared so straight and aboveboard, to fleece his clients— or at least such among them as gave him the open chances that he, Mahony, had. Careless, distraught, interested in everything rather than in money, he had ambled along, unthinking as a babe, leaving Simmonds to his own devices for months, nay, years, at a time. Now, he could not wait for daylight, to get his affairs back into his own hands. If only he were not too late!— And thus on and on, ever deeper into the night, his suspicions growing steadily more sinister, till there was no crime of which he was not ready to suspect his man of business. A dozen times he had trapped him, unmasked him, brought him to justice, before he fell into a feverish doze, in which not Simmonds but himself was the fugitive, hunted by two monstrous shadow policemen, who believed him criminal before the law. Waking with a terrific start he pulled himself together, only at once to sink back in dream. This time, he was being led by Purdy and some one strangely resembling that bottle-nosed old schemer, Robinson, who had played him a dirty trick over an English practice, to a cemetery, where stood a tombstone bearing Simmonds's name. Why, good Lord! the fellow's dead . . . dead! . . . and what of me? "Who's got my money? Where is it? Where am I?" cried Mahony aloud—and woke at the sound of his own voice, to see pale lines of light creeping in at the sides of the windows. His pulse was bounding, Mary sleepily murmuring: "Oh dear, oh dear, what *is* the matter?"— Rising, he opened a window, and stuck his hot head out into the morning air.

At breakfast-time, he emerged pale and peevish, to a day that proved hardly less wearing than the night had been. One, too, that called for a clear brain and prompt decisions. For the owner of Darumbooli, Baillie by name, put in an appearance, as arranged. A smart whip, he drove himself: in person an elderly Scot, tanned, sun-wrinkled, grey-whiskered, with a bluff, yet urbane manner—a self-made man, it was plain, and wholly unlettered, but frank, generous, honourable: one of nature's gentlemen, in short, and a type Mahony invariably found it easy to do business with. Better still, he turned out to be one of your genuine garden-lovers: as the pair of them walked about the grounds of *Ultima Thule,* in spite of the talk running freely on other topics, none of the details and improvements Mahony felt proudest of, but was observed and bespoken: the white-strawberry bed, the oleander grove, the fernery, the exquisitely smooth buffalo-grass lawns, on which sprays were kept playing. A good garden was, it seemed, a desideratum with Baillie. And he fell in love with Mahony's at first sight.

But . . . yes, yes! now came the fly in the ointment . . . he wished to buy, not to rent: had never, he averred, had any idea of renting a house: it was entirely "that fellow Smith's mistake" ("all Purdy's muddle!"). The schooling proved another bit of fiction. His daughters were past their school years: of an age to be launched in society. Darumbooli—station and sheeprun—was up for sale: Baillie had already refused a bid of ninety thousand: and planned from now on to settle in Melbourne.

Having thus cleared the air, and added that, only the day before, he had seen a house at Toorak, which, though not a patch on this, would serve his purpose, he offered a sum for *Ultima Thule*, just as it stood, with all its contents, which sent Mahony's eyebrows half-way up his forehead.

Mary was speechless when she heard the upshot of the interview; when, too, she saw that Richard's mind—that mind which seemed unable to hold fast to any mortal thing for long together—was more than three parts made up to accept Baillie's offer. Anc too discomfited to meet this Irish fluidity with her usual wily caution, she no sooner found her voice than she cried: "Oh, Richard, *no!*— That we *can't* do . . . we really can't! Think of all the things we got specially out from home . . . the French tapestry . . . and the carpets . . . and . . . and everything!"

Tch! Now he had this to go through . . . on top of his bad night, and his own burning irresolution. His nerves felt like the frayed ends of a rope. But, as always, opposition spurred him on.

"But, my dear, with such a sum at our disposal, we shall be able to furnish our *next* house ten times as well. Look here, Mary, I tell you what we'll do. We'll bring every atom of stuff out with us, from London or Paris: the very newest style of thing—there won't be a drawing-room—or a house— in the colony like it."

"Oh, Richard! . . . Oh, I *do* think——" For an instant bitterness choked Mary. Then, she could not resist pricking him with a "And pray, have *you* decided to let all your books go, as well?"

"My books? Most certainly not! I made that clear on the spot.— But how absurd, Mary! What would a man whose whole life has been spent among sheep and cattle do with my volumes of physics and metaphysics?"

But Mary put on her obstinate face. "My things mean just as much to me as yours do to you."

"Now, for goodness sake, my dear, be reasonable!" cried

Richard, growing excessively heated. "I suppose even a squatter can use a chair or a sofa; needs a bed and a table; but what, I ask you, would he make of Lavater . . . or the Church Fathers?"

"It's always the same! I am expected to give up everything; you nothing.— But if my wishes and feelings can be set aside, don't you care about the children . . . I mean about them all having been born here?"

"Indeed and I do not! I would no more have them tie their feelings to the shell of a house than I'd have mourners hang round a grave."

"Oh! there's no talking to you nowadays, your head's so full of windy stuff.— But I tell you this, Richard, I refuse to have my children dragged from place to place . . . as I've been. It's not as if it's ever helped a bit either, our giving up home after home. You're always wild, at the moment, to get away, but afterwards you're no happier than you were before. And then, what makes me so angry: you let yourself be influenced by such silly, trivial things. I believe you're ready to sell this house, just because you *like* the man who wants to buy it, or because he's praised up the garden. But you'll be sorry for it, I know you will, before you've even landed in England. I haven't lived with you all these years for nothing."

"Oh, well, my dear," said Mahony darkly, "I'm an old man now, and you won't be troubled with me much longer. When I'm gone, you'll be able to do just as you please."

Mary's black eyes flashed, and she opened her lips to a sharp retort; then shut them tight, and said nothing. For, to this, there could be no real reply; and Richard knew it.

The bargain struck—for struck of course it was, as she had seen from the first it would be: "I've gone too far; I can't draw back now!" was Mahony's angry flare of self-defence. Thereafter, it only remained for Mary to apply her age-old remedy, and make the best of a very bad job. But the present was by so much the most unreasonable thing Richard had ever done, and she herself felt so sore and exasperated over it, that not for several days was she cool enough to discuss the matter with him. Then, however, each coming half-way to meet the other, they had a long talk, in the course of which Mahony sought to make amends by letting her into some of his money secrets, and she extracted a solemn promise that, except for a mere fringe—a couple of thousand, say, for travelling and other immediate expenses—the sum he was receiving from Baillie (it ran to five figures) should be reserved for the purpose of reestablishing themselves, when they came back to the colony. Never with her consent should he plunge into fresh extravagances, over the head of this extra capital. But Mahony bade her make her mind easy. They ought, he considered, to be able to live as comfortably in England on their dividends, as here; and the price of *Ultima Thule* should be faithfully laid by, for the purpose of building, on their return, the house that would form their permanent home.— "For my travelling days will be over by then, my dear. We'll plan it together, love, every inch of it; and it will be more our own than any house we've lived in."

"Yes, yes, I dare say."— But Mary's tone lacked warmth, was rich in incredulity.

And now for Simmonds!— As he made ready to go to town, Mahony recalled, with a smile, his grotesque imaginings of two nights back. What a little hell the mind could create for a man's undoing! But, none the less, though he now ridiculed them, his nightmares, both waking and sleeping, had left a kind of tingling disquietude in their train. He felt he would do well to have a straight talk with Simmonds, go carefully through his share-list, and arrange in detail for the conduct of his affairs during his absence.

He went off jauntily enough.— "Well, good-bye, my dear! Don't expect me till about six."

But not a couple of hours later, as Mary was on her knees before a drawer of her great wardrobe, which she was beginning to dismantle, she heard his foot on the verandah, and the next moment his voice, sharp, querulous, distracted, cried: "Mary! Mary, where are you?"

"Yes, dear? Yes, I'm coming.— Why, Richard, whatever is wrong now?" For, with a despairing gesture, Mahony had tossed his hat on the hall-table, and himself dropped heavily on a chair.

"You may well ask. Here's a pretty kettle of fish! It's all over now, with our getting away."

"What do you mean?— But not here. The servants . . . Come into the bedroom. Well, you do look hot and tired." She brought him a glass of home-brewed ginger-beer; and while he sat and sipped, she listened to his story; listened, and put two and two together. Arrived at his agents' office in Great Bourke Street—not in the best frame of mind to start with, owing to an altercation with a cabby—he had found to his surprise and annoyance that Simmonds was absent from business. Worse still, had been, for over two months. He was ill, bedridden— yes, yes, seriously ill.— "Confound the fellow! I believe he means to die, just to inconvenience me. Mary! my dream the other night . . . it flashed across me as I walked home. Depend upon it, one doesn't dream that kind of thing for nothing." Richard's tone was one of gloomiest foreboding.

"What nonsense, dear! How can you be so silly?"

In place of Simmonds, he had been met by a . . . well, by an individual, a sort of clerk, who was in charge—at least he presumed so: he had never set eyes on the fellow before, and never meant to again, if he could help it!— "To find a par to his behaviour, Mary, you would need to go back to the very early days, when every scoundrelly Tom, Dick, and Harry believed himself your equal!"

"Why? What did he say?"

Say? Well, first, it was plain to Mary, he had not known from Adam who Richard was. Without getting up from his chair, over the arm of which his legs dangled; and not trou- bling to take his head out of a newspaper, he had asked the intruder's pleasure, in the free-and-easy colonial fashion which, long as he had lived there, Richard had never learned to swal- low. Besides, not to be recognised in a place he honoured with his patronage was in itself a source of offence. Haughtily pre- senting his card (which, Mary could see, had lamentably failed to produce an effect), he demanded to speak to Simmonds, with whom he had important business to transact.

"Pray, what answer do you think I got? In a voice, my dear, the twang of which you could have cut with a knife, I was in- formed: 'Well, in that case, doc., I guess you'll have to keep it snug—locked up in your own bosom, so to say! For the boss lies sick abed, and all the business in the world—and not the Queen's 'erself—wouldn't get him up from it.' Whereupon I clapped on my hat, on with my gloves, and out of the place! In which, as long as Simmonds is away, I shall not set foot again.— But now, as you see, we're in a pretty fix. All our plans knocked on the head! The house sold, the agreement signed—

or as good as signed . . . it's utterly impossible to draw back. Why the deuce was I in such a hurry? We shall have to go into apartments, Mary—take the children into common lodgings. Good God! Such a thing is not to be contemplated for a moment!"— Thus Mahony, as, deeply agitated, he paced the room.

Mary let him talk; listened to this and much more before she threw in a mild: "But surely we can take a furnished house? There'd be nothing common about that.— All the same, Richard, I don't believe Simmonds, who has always been so straight and aboveboard, would put anyone in to look after things who wasn't honest, too—in spite of uncouth behaviour. And you can't refuse to deal with a person just because he has no manners . . . and doesn't know how to address you."

"My dear Mary, it has been a one-man show all these years; and the probability is, when the old fellow broke down he had no one to turn to. But I can assure you, if I left my investments in such hands, I shouldn't know a moment's peace all the time I was away. Besides, if he does die, the whole concern will probably go smash."

Oh, the fuss and the flutter! As if it wasn't bad enough to have your house sold over your head, without this fresh commotion on top of it! There must surely be something very slipshod and muddle-headed about the way Richard managed his affairs. She didn't say so, but, had she been in his shoes, she would have known long ago of Simmonds's illness. As it was, this clerk might have been cheating the clients right and left. But anything to do with money (except, of course, the spending of it!) had of late years become anathema to Richard.

Now, he went about with a hand pressed to an aching head; and after putting up with this for some days, and herself feeling wholly at a loss, Mary made a private journey to town, to visit Tilly. She would see what that practical, sagacious woman thought of the situation.

Tilly, of course, at once laid her finger on the weak spot, by asking bluntly: "But whyever doesn't the doctor take advice of some of 'is friends?—the big-bow-bow ones, I mean. They'd be able to tell 'im, sure enough."

"Why, Tilly, the fact is Richard hasn't got . . . I mean, his friends are not business men, any more than he is. If only John were alive! He'd have been the one."

"Well, look here, Poll, I can ask Purd about it, if you like. He may know, and if 'e doesn't, 'e can easily find out— I mean whether this old S. is really going to hop the twig, or what. Purd has strings 'e can pull. Don't worry; it'll be all right. Poor old girl, though, you *do* have a lot to put up with, don't you?— you who might be so happy and comfortable!"

Mary went home intending to keep silence about her inter-meddling—at any rate, till she saw what came of it. But Richard was regularly in the doldrums: he had to be comforted somehow. At first, of course, as she had expected, he was furi-ous; and abused her like a pickpocket for discussing his private affairs with an outsider.— "You *know* how I hate publicity! As for telling them in that quarter . . . why, I might as well go out and shout them from the housetop!"

"Richard . . . you can't afford . . . if you're really so set on getting away . . . to mind now who knows and who doesn't!"

But on this point, as always they joined issue. He accused her of being wanting in personal dignity; she said that his ridiculous secrecy over money matters would end by leading people to believe there was something fishy about them.

"Let them! What does it matter to me what they think?"

"Why, I don't know *anyone* who'd resent it more—so proud and touchy as you are!" And, since home truths were the order of the day, she added: "You know, dear, it's just this: you've only yourself to thank for the fix you're in. You've cut yourself off from every one, and now, when you need help, you haven't a soul to turn to. And because I have, and make use of them, then your pride's hurt."

Which was the very truth. He had let slip friends and ac-quaintances who might have been useful to him at this junc-ture; but . . . *could* one nurse people, the inner impulse to friendship lacking, solely from motives of opportunism? The idea revolted him.— True, also, was what she said about the damage to his pride. Not, however, because they were *her* friends, as she supposed, but because they were the friends they were.— Again, he shrank in advance from the silly figure he was going to cut, did the story get about town how he had sold his house and packed his portmanteaux, while, all un-known to him, the chief spoke in his wheel had collapsed. What a fool he would look!— Though, of course, the fact was,

Simmonds had handled his affairs without supervision for so long, that he had come to look on the fellow as a kind of fixture in his life.

And, in spite of everything, his determination to get away did not weaken. In mind, he had already started—was out on the high seas. Impossible, now, to call his thoughts home. And the feeling that such a course might be expected of him—that Mary would expect it—only served to throw him into a frenzy of impatience; make him more blackly intolerant of each fresh obstacle that appeared in his path.

Then Tilly appeared: he saw her from the window, all furbelows and flounces, and wearing an air at once important and mysterious. She and Mary retired to the drawing-room; and there he could hear them jabbering, discussing *him* and his concerns, as he sat pretending to read. This went on and on—would they never end? Even when plainer tones, and the opening and shutting of doors, seemed to herald Tilly's departure, all that followed was a sheerly endless conversation on the step of the verandah. By the time Mary came in to him, he was nervily a-shake. And her news was as bad as it could be. Old Simmonds was doomed; was in the last stages of Bright's disease; his place of business would know him no more. Most of his clients had already transferred to other agents; and Purdy's advice to Richard was, to lose no time in following their example.

"Huh! All very well . . . very easily said! But to whom am I to turn, I'd like to know? . . . when there isn't one honest broker in a thousand. Swindlers—damned swindlers!—that's what they are, every man-jack of 'em. And here am I, just going out of the colony, and with all this fresh money to invest."

Said Mary: "I've been thinking" (which, of course, meant tittle-tattling with Tilly), "why not write to Mr. Henry, and consult him? He's such a good business man; and knows so many people. He might be able to recommend some one to you."— But, with this suggestion, she only added fuel to the inordinate, unreasonable grudge Richard still bore every one connected with the old life. "Nothing would induce me! . . . to eat humble pie before that crew."

"Well, then, dear, *do* let us postpone our journey . . . if only for six months."

He was equally stubborn. "Sooner than that—if it comes to

654

that!— I'll sell right out, and take every penny I possess to the other side. And never set foot in the colony again."

"Now, for goodness sake, Richard! . . ." cried Mary; then bit her lip. He was quite capable of carrying out his threat, did she make the lightest show of opposition.

On this occasion, however, his rashness took another form. After spending the whole of the next day in town, where he had gone to visit his banker, to settle with his wine merchant, arrange for the storing of his books, and so on, he came home at six to dinner, looking a different man. On her, who had gone about all day with a crease between her brows, not knowing whether to pack for a voyage or for the removal to another house, he burst in, and catching her by the waist, kissed her and swung her round.— "Here's your bear come home! But cheer up, Mary, cheer up, my love, and make your mind easy! All will yet be well."

"What? Do you mean to say you've actually——?"

"Yes, thank the Lord, I have!"

Over the dinner-table, he gave her particulars. At the end of a bothersome, wasted morning, he had dropped into "Scott's," and there, in the coffee-room, had tumbled across Purdy. ("What!—*Purdy?*" was Mary's amazed inner comment, she being, as usual, hard at work drawing inferences.) Purdy had met him in friendliest fashion: "I've come to the conclusion, my dear, I have sometimes been rather hard on the boy, of late." They had lunched together, and, over a chop and a bottle of claret, had got talking; and there they had sat, for the better part of an hour. Naturally enough, the subject of Simmonds's collapse had come up, and the fix into which it put him, Mahony, over getting away. Purdy— " 'Pon my word, Mary, I saw to-day he's got his head screwed on the right way!"—had given him various useful tips how to deal with the modern broker, which an innocent old sheep like himself would never have dreamt of. And then, right at the end, just as they were making a move, Purdy had scratched his head and believed he perhaps knew some one who might——"

"*Not* Blake?"

"Blake? Absurd! Good Lord, no! Blake needs watching. With a man like that, you must be on the spot yourself." (Richard knew *all* about it, to-night.) No, no: this was no flashy daredevil, but a steady-going, cautious sort of a fellow, who could be trusted to "look after your interests during your absence, and transmit *the* interest . . . ha, ha!— Oh, and I must tell you this, Mary! When he said—Purdy, I mean— 'I believe I know some one who'd suit you, Dick!' where do you suppose my thoughts flew? They went back, love, to a day, more years ago than I care to count, when he used the self-same words. We were riding to Geelong together, he and I, two care-free young men—heigh-ho!—and not many hours after, I had the honour of meeting a certain young lady . . . ! Well, wife, if this introduction turns out but half as well as that, I shall have no cause to complain. Anyway, I took it as a good omen. We hadn't time, just then, to go further into the matter; but I am to meet Purdy again to-morrow, and then I shall hear all details."

He rattled on, in the highest of spirits, seeing everything fixed and settled; and Mary had not the heart to damp him by putting inconvenient, practical questions. And having said his say, and refilled her glass and his own, he sent for the children —they had been hushed back into the nursery for the past three days, while Papa had a headache. Now, setting his girlies on his knees, with Cuffy standing before him, he told the trio of the big ship that was coming to take them away, and on which they were to live—for weeks, and weeks, and weeks.

The Dumplings' eyes grew round. "An' s'all us 'ave bekspup on ze big s'ip?" asked Lallie, the elder of the twins.

"Bekspup on ze big s'ip?" echoed her sister.

"Breakfast, *and* dinner, *and* tea, and go to sleep in little beds like boxes, built on to the wall, and look out of little windows, just big enough for your little heads, and see nothing, wherever you look, but the great, wide sea."

"Ooo! Bekfast, *an'* dinner, *an'* tea!"— Cuffy had to cut a few capers about the room to let off steam, before he could listen to more.

Mary took no part in the merry chatter. She sat abstracted, tapping the tablecloth with a dessert-knife balanced between her first and second fingers. And when Nannan had taken away the children, she abruptly came back on the subject of her thoughts.— "Of course, you'll see this person Purdy speaks of, see what you think of him yourself, before finally deciding on anything?"

"Of *course*, my dear, of course!"

"It seems rather . . . I mean, it seems strange Purdy didn't . . . And as *he* is doing the recommending, I can't very well ask Tilly what she thinks about it."

"And who on earth wants you to? I'll be very much obliged if you *don't* interfere! Surely, Mary, I can be trusted to do some of my own business? I'm not quite on the shelf yet, I hope."

"Oh, come, Richard . . . After all, you know . . . I mean it's not so *very* long ago, and nothing would have induced you to take Purdy's advice."

"And pray who was it brought home glowing tales of how splendidly he had got on, thanks to his acuteness, and financial genius, etc., etc., etc.?"

"Yes, I know. But still . . ."

"But as soon as I come into it, or *because* I come into it, you lose every atom of faith. I wonder if all wives are as distrustful of their husbands' capabilities as you. A bad lookout for them if they are!"

Mary did not deny the charge. Doubtful she was, and doubtful she remained: an attitude of mind that severely tried Mahony's temper, he having more than one private scruple of his own.

For instance, his second meeting with Purdy, in which he had planned to be very cautious and to throw out wily feelers, was a failure. On getting to the hotel, he found that Purdy could spare him but a few moments, himself having an urgent appointment to keep. They did not sit down, and their talk was scampered through at lightning speed. However, the main thing was, Purdy supplied him with a list of people for whom this man Wilding had acted—and well-known names they were, too!—and himself undertook to put in a word on Mahony's behalf. In the meantime, it would be as well to write and summon Wilding to town.— Write? Yes; for now it turned out that the business was carried on, not in Melbourne, but in Ballarat. Purdy vowed he had mentioned this fact the day before; but, if so, Mahony had failed to hear him. Not that it mattered much, seeing that he himself was about to quit Melbourne. It might even, he agreed, the majority of his investments being in Ballarat mines, prove a benefit to have an agent who was on the spot.

Still, the conversation left him visibly less jubilant. While from the interview he had some days later with Wilding him-

self, he returned tired and headachy—always, Mary knew, a
bad sign, where Richard was concerned. Of course, he met
her with a: "Well, well, my dear, all our troubles are now
over!"—which was true, in so far as the business side of the
affair had gone off smoothly enough. The transfer had been
effected, power of attorney given, new investments arranged
for, his existing share-list overhauled and revised. But . . .
well, the fact of the matter was, he had not been very favourably impressed by the man himself. He could find no likeness
in him to the portrait drawn by Purdy—and probably amplified
by his own mind, which looked for a second Simmonds—of a
staid and dignified man of affairs. No, Wilding was again one
of your rough diamonds: over-familiar, slangy, a back-slapper,
and, like every one else here, in a tearing hurry: he hardly
bothered to listen to what you said, knew everything you were
going to say beforehand, and better than you. His appearance,
too, was against him—at least to one who set store by the
fleshly screen. Wilding had a small, oblique eye; fat, pursed
lips; fat, grubby fingers, on which flashy rings twinkled; a diamond pin that took your breath away. Also, from an injudicious word he let drop, the idea leapt at Mahony . . . well! it
might be pure fancy on his part . . . or owing to these unlovely
looks . . . besides, it was only a fleeting impression . . . vaguely
troubling . . . But come! it would not do to let a personal antipathy to the man's appearance prejudice you against him . . .
as Mary was never tired of preaching! What though Wilding
was no beauty? Whose hands here *were* impeccably clean?
Was this not just the type of your modern broker, as compared
with one of the old school? The main thing, the only thing that
really mattered, was that as a broker he should prove alert
and up-to-date. And in this respect, his credentials were excellent. What was more, it leaked out, in something he said, that
Purdy had also been in correspondence with him over the affair. Might one not safely assume a hint on Purdy's part that
he himself meant to keep an eye on things, during his friend's
absence from the colony?

And now, at last, nothing stood in the way of their departure; and preparations were rushed forward that they might
sail by the vessel of their choice. Mahony superintended the
sorting and packing of his books, and saw them carted to a
depository; then rearranged the furniture and bought fresh

pieces to fill the bare walls where the bookcases had stood. Next, he conveyed the luggage—it filled a lorry—to the wharf, saw it aboard and stowed away between hold and cabins. Of these, they had three of the largest amidships; and the best warehouse in Melbourne had carpeted, furnished, curtained them. No need, this time, for Mary to toil and slave. Like a queen, she had only to step aboard and take possession.

They spent the last couple of days at an hotel. And one morning, having received word overnight that the *Atrata* was ready to sail, they, the nurses, and the children, packed into two landaus and were driven to William's Town. There, early though it was, they found a pretty crowd assembled. Everybody they knew, or had ever met, had turned out to see them off, headed by dear old Sir Jake and Lady Devine, the Bishop and Mrs. Moreton, Baron von Krause, the famous botanist, old Judge Barmore, and many another, not to speak of Mary's intimate personal friends, Richard's spiritualist circle, and relatives and members of the family. For a full half-hour they were hard at it, shaking hands, and exchanging greetings and farewells. Richard, in his new travelling rig, spruce from top to toe, was urbanity itself: as, indeed, how should he fail to be, when, within cooee, rode the good ship that was to carry him off?— There was also a generous sprinkling of children present, the colonial youngster never being denied the chance of an outing. And to Cuffy, standing stiff and important in red gloves and a tasselled sash, came Cousin Josephine to hiss in his ear: "Ooo . . . aren't I glad *I'm* not going! Our servant, Mawy Ann, says you'll pwobably *all* go to the bottom of the sea!" and then to laugh maliciously at Cuffy's chalk-white face.

Rowed on board, they found the cabins hardly big enough to house the masses of flowers that had been deposited in them —great stately bouquets in lace or silver holders; lavish sprays; or purple and white arrangements shaped like anchors, "For remembrance." And beside the flowers were piled cases of fruit and delicacies, as well as other more endurable keepsakes: scent, and fans, and cushions, and books. Nor were the children forgotten. Over-excited, and the despair of their nurses, Cuffy and his sisters rushed to and fro, their arms full of wonderful new toys.

Said Mary, with tears in her eyes: "I think they're the dearest, kindest people in all the world."

The last to leave the ship were Jerry, Tilly, and Emmy. Emmy broke down over the parting, and cried bitterly, looking, none the less, lovely as ever, in her deep, becoming mourning. Mary—and Richard too—would much have liked to take the girl with them; both as a companion for Mary, and in order that foreign travel might give a fitting polish to John's eldest daughter. But Lizzie vehemently opposed the plan. Nor was Emmy's own heart in it. For, since John's death, she had taken upon herself the entire charge of her little brother, heaping on his infant head all the love that had once been her father's. Hence, she could not tear herself away.

Jerry, a bank manager now, the father of a family, and hailing from the township of Bummaroo, had stayed the night with them at their hotel; and, John being no more, Mary had seized the chance of unburdening herself, to this staid, younger brother, of some of the doubts that haunted her with regard to Richard's present flighty management of his money affairs. Bummaroo was not very far from Ballarat; and Jerry promised indirectly to find out, and keep her informed of, what was going on.— "Don't you worry, old girl. I can easily run over to the Flat from time to time, and see how the land lies."

Tilly, the last to go, sat on the edge of a bunk, and was very down in the mouth. "Upon my word, Poll, I seem to feel it more this time than last—which is just what a silly old Noah's-Ark like me *would* do, considering it was for always then, and here you'll be back before the kids 'ave cut their second teeth."

And now the last bell went; the ship was cleared, the ladder hauled up; and all the din and bustle of weighing anchor began. The wind being favourable, the Captain undertook to reach the "Heads" before night; and he was as good as his word. They made a record voyage down the great Bay; caught the tide before it turned; and headed straight for the Bight. Mahony, in his old sea-mood of rare expansiveness, went below to announce their whereabouts. But, by now, thanks to a freshening wind and the criss-cross motion of the ship, all was confusion in the cabins. The Dumplings, very sick, were being hurriedly undressed; Mary and the nurses staggered about, a hand to their dizzy heads. Cuffy alone was unconcerned: his father found him playing in the saloon, twirling to and fro on one of the revolving chairs. Here was a chip of the old block!

Wrapping the child in a rug he bore him aloft, to see the passage through the "Rip."

Perched on a capstan, Cuffy followed the proceedings with a lively interest, and to a running fire of questions. Why was the sea so white and bubbly? Where was it running away to? What were reefs? Why were lighthouses? Why was a pilot? *How* did he know? Why did he have such a big boat all to himself? Why didn't he have a staircase? Did he have his own skin on under the oil? When was the sea *shut?* . . . and many another. But gradually the little voice ceased its piping, and a silence fell—unnoticed by Mahony, who himself was carried away once more by a splendid inner exultation, at dancing in the open, leaving land behind. He stood lost in his own feelings, till suddenly he felt the little body his arm enclosed give a great shiver.

He looked down. "What is it, darling? Are you cold?"

But Cuffy just nestled closer into the crook of his father's arm, and did not reply. He had no words at his disposal to tell what he felt at sight of nightfall on these wild, grey, desolate seas. Nor did he dare to resolve the more actual fear of Cousin Josey's implanting, and put the question that burned on his lips: "How far is it to the bottom?" . . . For perhaps Papa did not know that was where they were all likely to go.

"Come then. It's long past bedtime."— And lifting the child from his perch, Mahony carried him below.

In the gloom of the cabin the hanging-lamp swayed from side to side, with a slow, rhythmical movement; timbers creaked and groaned; from the pantries came the noise of shifting, slithering china—sounds that were as music in Mahony's ears, telling as they did of a voyage begun.

Mary turned a feeble head.

"Oh, Richard! . . . where *have* you been? Why, the child will be perished. Well, you'll have to see to him yourself now. We're all much too ill."—

And thereafter, between convulsive fits of retching, she heard from the cabin opposite, where Mahony was undoing little buttons and untying tapes, the voices of father and son raised in unison, as they sang:

> *"Rocked in the Cradle of the Deep,*
> *I lay me down . . . in peace to sleep."*

[8]

THE house they took for the winter was in Kensington Gore, and the children walked every day with their nurses in Kensington Gardens. When they first arrived, the great trees, with branches that grew almost low enough to be pulled (if you jumped) were thick with leaves, and shady like houses. Then, the leaves tumbled off and lay on the ground, and, when Nannan didn't see you, you shuffled your feet through them, kicking up a dust, and making a noise like crackly paper. Afterwards, men brought brooms and swept the leaves into heaps along the paths, and burned them in little bonfires; and then what fun it was to run like blind men, with eyes tight shut, through the clouds of smoke. You trundled your hoop up and down these paths, but didn't go far away, because you couldn't see where they ended, for mist; and Nannan said you might get lost, or tumble into a round pond. And one day, a strange, thick, yellow mist came down, and hid even the path you were walking on, and made your throat tickle and your eyes sting; and Nannan and Eliza, talking about pea-soup, rushed for home, feeling frightened, big as they were, and having to be helped across the road by a policeman, who made light with what Eliza said was a "bull's-eye."

After this, Cuffy got a cough, and had to take tablespoonfuls of cod-liver oil, and to stay indoors while the Dumplings walked. It was dull work. The nursery was so high up that you couldn't see anybody but trees from the windows, which were barred; and you were not allowed to look out at all, if they were open. Nannan said looking over made her poor old head dizzy; and she lived in fear of seeing one of them "land on the pavement." So, left alone, Cuffy hammered with his knuckles on the panes, making tunes for himself, or beat them out on his drum and xylophone, till Nannan, sewing by the fire, said her poor old head was like to split.

Cuffy gave her his gravest attention. "Are you so *very* old, Nannan?"

"Why, no, not so very," said Nannan, with a queer laugh: she was buxom, and in her prime.

"How old?"

"As old as my tongue and a little older than my teeth," was the cryptic reply, which, far from ending the conversation, led on through a tangle of question and answer—why tongues grew before teeth, what made teeth, where they came from—to the eternal wonder: "Was I born, too?" and "How?"

"A caution, that child, if ever there was one!" said Nannan, in relating this "poser" and how she had queered it— "Only *naughty* little boys ask things like that, Master Cuffy!"—to Eliza and Ann over tea. This was drunk in a kind of cubby-hole off the night nursery, the three colonials having failed to fraternise with the posse of English servants who had been taken over with the house: a set of prim, starched pokers these, ran the verdict; and deceitful, too, with their "sirs" and "mad-ams" to your face, and all the sneery backbiting that went on below-stairs.—

In regard to Cuffy, however, Nannan's opinion was general: an awkward child to deal with. You never knew what fresh fad was going to get the whiphand of him. For instance, his first fear, of Cousin Josey's suggestion, that they would all be drowned, which had preyed on him during the voyage: this allayed, he was haunted by the dread of being lost, or at least overlooked—like a bag or an umbrella—in this great, strange, bewildering place. Even at the pantomime, at Drury Lane, he suffered torments lest, when it was over, Nannan and Eliza should suddenly forget that he and the Dumplings were there, and go home without them; so that, from the close of the first scene on, he inquired regularly every few minutes throughout the afternoon: "Is this the end?" till Nannan's patience gave way, and she roundly declared that never would she bring him to a theatre again. It was the same at Madame Tussaud's—the same, plus an antipathy that amounted to a horror of all these waxen people, with their fixed, glassy eyes; and a fan-tastic fear that he might be mistaken for one of them, and locked in among them, did he not keep perpetually on the move. His hot little hand tugged mercilessly at Eliza's baggy glove.— Yes! more bother than half a dozen other children put together. Just a walking bundle, said Nannan, of whims and crotchets.

Chief of these, and most tiresome of all, was the idea that he could not—or must not—sleep of a night, as long as his father and mother were out. Did they attend an evening party, he tossed restless till their return. And if, in spite of himself, he dozed off, it was only to start up with the cry: "Is my Papa

and Mamma come home yet?" Nannan was at her wits' end
what to do with him; and, more than once, boldly transgressed
her instructions about absolute truth in the nursery. For it was
not as if Master Cuffy really wanted his parents, or even
wanted to see them. No sooner did he know they were back,
under the same roof with him again, than he turned over and
slept like a top.

The mischief was: they were out almost every night. For, in
violent contrast to the hermit's life he had been leading, Mahony was now never happy unless he was on the go. An itch
for distraction plagued him; books and solitude had lost their
charm; and an evening spent in his own society, in this large,
dark, heavily furnished house, sent his spirits down to zero.
They had brought many an excellent letter of introduction
with them; a carriage-and-pair stood at their disposal; and so,
throughout that winter except for an occasional party of their
own, they went out night after night, to dinners, balls and
card-parties; to soirées, conversaziones and lectures; to concerts and operas. They heard Tietjens sing, and Nilsson, and
Ilma di Murska; Adelina Patti with Nicolini; and a host of
lesser stars. Richard said they must make the most of their
time; since it was unlikely they would ever be on this side of
the world again. To which, however, Mary now secretly demurred: or not till the children are grown up. For, though
foreign travel meant little to her, she was already determined
that her children should not miss it—it, or anything else in life
that was worth having.

In the beginning, she was heartily glad of the change in
Richard's habits, and followed him without a grumble wherever he wished: he wouldn't budge a step without her. But, as
week after week went by, she did occasionally long for an
hour to herself; to prowl round the shops; see something of
the children; write her letters in peace. As things stood, it was
a ceaseless rush from one entertainment to another, not to
mention all the dressing and re-dressing this implied. Done,
too, with Richard standing irritable and impatient in the hall,
watch in hand, calling: "Now *do* come along, Mary!—can't you
hear, my dear? We shall certainly be late."

"Really, Richard! you hardly give me time to do my hair.
I'm sure I don't know what I look like."— For he was dis-

pleased did she fail to make the best of herself. *His* wife must be as well turned out as anyone else's.

She comforted herself with the thought that it was not for long: they had taken this house only for a twelvemonth; and there was talk, as soon as the weather improved, of a trip to Ireland to see Richard's sisters, and to the Midlands to visit Lisby, now Headmistress of a Young Ladies' Seminary. So, in the meantime, she went without her tea to sit through interminable political debates; or struggled to keep her eyes open at meetings of learned societies, where old grey-beards droned on, by the hour, without your being able to hear the half of what they said.— "I suppose it does *somebody* some good!" thought she. Richard, for instance, who had read so many clever books, and enjoyed teasing his brains. Herself, she felt a very fish out of water.

Nowhere more so than at the spiritualist seances, which, for peace sake—and also because everybody was doing it—she now regularly attended.— London was permeated with spiritualism; you hardly met a person who was not a convert to the craze. The famous medium Home had already retired, on his marriage, into private life, much to Richard's disappointment; but he had left scores of imitators behind him, who were only too well versed in his tricks and stratagems. The miracles you could see performed! Through the ceiling came apports of fresh flowers with the dew on them, or roots with the soil still clinging; great dinner-tables rose from the floor; lights flitted; apparitions appeared, spoke to you, took you by the hand. But nothing that happened could shake Mary's convinced unbelief. She was of those who maintained that so-called "levitation" was achieved by standing on your toes; the "fire-test" by your having previously applied chemicals to the palm of your hand; while the spirits that walked about were just so much drapery on a broomstick. And it invariably irritated her anew, to see Richard sitting solemnly accepting all this nonsense as if it heralded a new revelation. Of course, many clever men besides him were the dupes of their own imaginations. Learning and common sense did not seem to go together. *She* preferred, thank you, to trust the evidence of her own eyes and ears.

However, she kept these thoughts to herself, patiently doing all that was required of her in the way of linking hands in dark rooms, hymn-singing, and the rest, with only an occasional silent chuckle at the antics of the believers. But then came an evening when circumstances forced her hand. Well, yes . . . that was partly true. They were at a sitting with the medium of whom she had long had her doubts; and, on this night, the evidence for fraud seemed to her so glaring that she determined to put it to the test. For once, Richard was not beside her. Instead, on her right, she had a lady who fell into raptures at each fresh proof of the "dear spirits'" presence. Stealthily bringing her two hands together (as Tilly had long ago instructed her), Mary freed one from this person's hold; and, when "spirit-touches" were again proclaimed by her neighbour (they never visited *her!*) she made a grab, and, just as she expected, found the medium—easily recognisable by her bulk—crouched on her knees inside the circle, with a long feather whisk in her hand. In the dark, and in utter silence, a struggle went on between them, she holding fast, the medium wriggling this way and that, and ultimately, by lying almost flat on the floor, contriving to wrench herself free. Not a word did Mary say. But at the end, when the lights were turned up, it was announced that the "spirits" complained of an unsympathetic presence in the circle; and after some hocus-pocus with slate-writing, etc., she, Mary, was designated, and asked to withdraw.

Richard, pale and extremely haughty, made the best of the situation in face of all these strangers, none of whom but eyed Mary as if she were a moral pariah. Inwardly, he was raging; and he freely vented his anger in the carriage going home.

"There you have it! Your mulish obstinacy . . . your intolerable lack of imagination . . . your narrow, preconceived notions of what can and what cannot happen!" Till Mary, too, lost her temper, and blurted out the plain facts of the case. "I knew her by her figure. What's more, I distinctly felt the big wart she has on the side of her chin."

But, with this, it seemed, she merely displayed her ignorance. For the spirit body, in manifestation, was but the ethereal shadow cast by the physical, and its perfect duplicate. Richard also went on to crush her with St. Paul's "terrestrial and celestial"; harangued her on the astounding knowledge of the occult possessed by the early Christians. It was no good talking. Everything she said could be turned against her.

As she brushed her hair for the night, however, she could not resist remarking, in a final tone: "Well! all I know is, if these really *are* spirits who come back, it doesn't make me think much of heaven. That the dead can still take an interest in such silly, footling things!"

"Quite so, my dear. You keep your traditional fancy picture of semi-birds and harps and crowns. It best suits a mind like yours to make its heaven as remote and unreal as possible. For the truth is, you no more believe in it than you do in the tale of Cinderella."— Richard was bitingly jocose.

"*Really*, Richard! . . . what next, I wonder!— Though I must say, I don't think there's much to choose between harps and things, and playing concertinas and tilting tables. One's as stupid as the other."

"And how else in all the world . . . can *you* perhaps suggest a better way for a discarnate being to make its presence known? Every beginning is crude—and always has been.— Though, for that matter, what is the Morse alphabet, in use on the electric telegraph, but a series of transmitted raps?"

"Well, I'm not clever enough to argue about these things. But I know this: if *I* go to heaven, I hope at least to find there'll be something—something really useful—*to do*."

But when the light was out, and they lay composing themselves for sleep, she heard Richard mutter to himself: "There may be . . . there possibly *is* . . . fraud. And why not? . . . do not rogues ofttimes preach the Gospel? But that there's truth in it—a truth greater than any yet dreamed of—on that I would stake my soul. Ours the spadework . . . only God knows what the end will be."

The result of this affair was that Mary no longer frequented seances. On such nights Richard went out alone, and she sat comfortably by the fire, her feet on the fender, her needlework or the children at hand.

But not for long. As suddenly as Richard had thrown himself into the whirl, so suddenly he tired of it; and at the first hint of spring—it was early February; birds had begun to twitter in the parks, the spikes of the golden crocus to push up through the grass, and Richard petulantly to discard his greatcoat—on one of these palely sunny days he came home restless to the finger-tips, and before the evening ended was proposing to start, then and there, for the Continent. Why should they not shut up the house, send the children to the seaside, and jaunt off by themselves, hampered by only the lightest of luggage, and moving from place to place as their fancy led them?

Why not? There was, nowadays, no practical reason why he should scruple to satisfy any and every whim. And so his roughly sketched plan was carried out.— With the sole difference that they took Cuffy with them. For, as soon as Nannan heard what was in the wind, she marched down stairs and said bluntly, she did not choose to shoulder the charge of Master Cuffy, all by herself. The child was anyhow but poorly, what with the colds and things he had had since getting here; a walking mass of the fidgets besides; and if now his papa and mamma were going away as well, she guaranteed he'd worry himself (and everybody else) into a nervous fever. Mahony cut short the argument that followed, by saying curtly: "We'll take the youngster with us!" and pooh-poohed Mary's notion that travelling would be bad for the child. Much less harmful, said he, than staying behind and fretting his heart out. Besides, Ann would be there, Ann could look after him.

And so it came about that Cuffy journeyed in foreign parts, bearing with him, snail-like, all that stood to him for home.

Of these early travels, the most vivid memory he retained was, oddly enough, the trivial one of being wrapped in an opossum-rug, and carried in some one's arms from a train to a ship, and back to a train. But in those buried depths of his mind to which he had normally no access, a whole galaxy of pictures lay stored; and, throughout his life, was the hidden spring that released them touched, one and another would abruptly flash into consciousness. As a small boy they put him in many an awkward fix; for he could never prove what he said, or even make it sound probable; and, at school, among companions whose horizon was bounded north, south, east, and west by the Bush, they harvested him a lively crop of ridicule and opprobrium. ("A tarnation liar . . . that young Cuffs Ma*hony!*") But there *were* houses built in water—somehow he knew it—and bridges with shops on them. Boats with hoods, too, and men who stood up in them to row with a single oar. There *was* a statue so big that you could climb into its nose and sit there, and look out of its eyes: rivers not red and muddy, but apple green; a tower that leaned right over to one

668

side; long-legged birds that built their nests on chimney-tops.—
But then again, on the heel of such bold assertions a sudden
doubt would invade the speaker; a doubt whether he had not,
after all, only *dreamt* these things. With no one to whom he
could turn for confirmation, with every object that related to
them lost or destroyed, Cuffy, throughout his later boyhood,
swung like a pendulum between fact and dream, and was
sadly torn in consequence.

❋   ❋   ❋   ❋   ❋   ❋

Travelling from Dover to Calais, and thence to Paris, the
party set off on what, in thought, Mary ever after dubbed:
"that mad race across Europe."

For, the Channel behind them, Richard's restlessness broke
out in a new form: it seemed impossible for him to be content
in any place they visited, for more than a day or two on end.
In vain did Mary protest: "But, Richard, we're not seeing *anything!*" Within a few hours of his arrival in a town, he had had
enough of it, sucked it dry; and was fidgeting to be off to the
next on their line of route.— Nor was this itch for movement
all. The strange food did not suit him: he either liked it too
well, and ate too heartily of it, or he turned from it altogether.
Then, the noisiness of foreign cities—the cobbled streets, the
rattling of the loosely hung vehicles, the loud foreign voices,
the singing, the tambourining—got on his nerves, and, together
with the unshaded windows of hotel bedrooms, kept him
awake half the night: him spoilt, for how many a year, by the
perfectly darkened sashes, the ordered silence of his sleeping-
room at *Ultima Thule.* And all the beauties in the world could
not make up to Richard for lack of sleep. Or, to turn it round:
rob him of his sleep, and you robbed him of his power to enjoy fine scenery, or handsome monuments.— And so, they
sometimes arrived at a place and left it again, without having
really seen very much more of it than the four walls of a room.

Before they had got any distance, it became clear to Mary
that Richard's travelling-days were . . . well, one could hardly
say "over," when they had only just begun. The truth was, they
had come too late. He was no longer able to enjoy them.

It was not the physical discomforts alone that defeated him.
The fancies he went in for, as soon as he set foot on foreign
soil, made his life a misery to him. In Paris, for instance, he

was seized by a nervous fear of the street traffic; actually felt afraid he was going to be run over. If he had to cross one of the vast squares, over which vehicles dashed from all directions, he would stand and hesitate on the kerb, looking from side to side, unable to resolve to take the plunge; and wasn't he angry with her, if she tried to make a dash for it! His own fears rendered him fussy about Cuffy and the maid's safety, too. He wouldn't hear of them going out alone; and insisted, of a morning, on shepherding them to their walk in the Public Gardens. If he was prevented, they must drive there in a *fiacre*. Which all helped to make the stay in Paris both troublesome and costly.— Then, there was that time in Strasbourg, when they set out to climb the tower of the cathedral. It was certainly a bad day to choose, for it had rained in the night and afterwards frozen over, and even the streets were slippery. But Richard was bent on seeing the Rhine, and the Vosges, and the Black Forest from the top of the steeple; so up they went. As far as the platform, it was plain sailing. But on the tower proper, when they were mounting the innumerable stone steps—all glassy with ice, and very tricky to keep a footing on—which led to the spire, he grew pale, and confessed to feeling giddy . . . you certainly did look through the wide-open stonework right down to the street below, where people crawled like ants. And after another bend in the stair, he clinging fast to the iron hand-rail, he had ignominiously to give in and descend again: backwards, too!— "I felt I should either fall through one of the openings, or throw myself out. Great heights are evidently not for me."

And this was not wholly due to imagination. For after going up the Leaning Tower at Pisa, and taking a peep over the crooked side, he felt so sick, on reaching the ground, that he had to go back to the hotel and lie down.

Again, a beautiful city like Munich was ruined for him, by the all-pervading smell of malt from its many breweries. The whole time they were there, he went about with his nose in the air, sniffing; and he never ceased to grumble. Next, as the Tyrolese mountains were so close, they took train and went in among them; but this didn't suit him either. The nearness of these drear, dark masses wakened in him, he said, an overpowering sense of oppression; made him feel as if he *must* climb them; get to their summits, in order to be able to breathe.— One moment abjuring heights, another hankering after them! . . . who could keep pace with such inconsistencies?

Of course, there were times when he smiled at himself; saw the humour of the situation; especially when he had just escaped from one of his bugbears. But then came the next (he was never prepared for them) and hit him equally hard. The thing he *couldn't* laugh at was his—their—"infernal ignorance of foreign lingos." Not to be able to express himself properly, make himself fully understood, riled and fretted him; though less, perhaps, than did her loud and unabashed efforts to say what she wanted to say. And because he couldn't argue, or expostulate, with porters, waiters, cabbies, and the like, he constantly suspected these people of trying to do him. The queer thing was, he preferred being diddled, putting up with it in gloomy silence, to trying, in broken German or Italian, to call the cheats to account. Many an extra franc and thaler and lira did this hypersensitiveness cost him. But his dread of being laughed at was stronger than himself.

Yes! there was always something. He never let himself have any real peace or enjoyment.— Or so thought Mary at the time. It was not till afterwards, when he fell to re-living his travels in memory, that she learned how great was the pleasure he had got out of them. Inconveniences and annoyances were by then sunk below the horizon. Above remained visions of white cities, and slender towers, and vine-clad hills; of olive groves bedded in violets; fine music heard in opera and oratorio; coffee-drinking in shady gardens on the banks of a lake; orchards of pink almond-blossom massed against the misty blue of far mountain valleys.

Of all the towns they touched, even including Naples and Rome, Venice suited him best; and this, she firmly believed, because he went there with the idea that, having neither streets nor wheeled traffic, it must of necessity be a quiet and restful place. Herself she noticed nothing of this. Dozens of people walked the narrow alleys—you could really go everywhere on foot—and the cries of the gondoliers, the singing and mandoline-playing, lasted far into the night. But Richard throve on it; though it was June now, and very hot, and alive with mosquitoes. He bathed daily on the Lido, and for the rest of the day kept cool in picture-galleries and churches, of which he never seemed to tire. Whereas she, after half an hour of screwing up her eyes and craning her neck at ceilings, had had more than enough.

They had been there for a whole fortnight, and there was still no talk of their moving on, when something happened which cut their stay through as with a knife. The smallest details of that July afternoon—it started with one of Cuffy's outbreaks—were burnt into Mary's brain.

Richard had gone after lunch to the British Consul's, to get their Australian mail: Mary was anxiously waiting for news of Tilly. She wrote at her own home budget while expecting his return, sitting in the cool hotel bedroom, with Cuffy playing on the floor beside her. Deep in her letter, she did not notice that the child had strayed to the balcony. How long he had been there, still as a mouse, she did not know; but she was suddenly startled by hearing him give a shrill cry.

"Oh, no . . . *no!*"

Laying down her pen, she stepped through the window. "And what's the matter with *you?*"

On the opposite side of the canal, some men were engaged in drowning a puppy. They had tied a weight to the little animal's neck, before throwing it into the water, but this was not heavy enough to keep it down; and again and again, in a desperate struggle for breath, it fought its way to the surface, only to be hit at with sticks, did it come within arm's reach. Finally, amid the laughter of the crowd, the flat side of an oar caught it full on its little panting snout and terrified eyes. With a shriek that was almost human, it sank, not to rise again.

"Run inside, Cuffy. Don't stay here watching those nasty cruel men," said Mary, and took him by the arm. But Cuffy tore it away and remained standing with dilated eyes and open lips, breathing rapidly. The last blow struck, he burst into a passion of tears, and turning, ran to a corner of the room, where he threw himself face downwards on the floor.

There followed one of those dreadful exhibitions of rage or temper, which Mary found it so hard to reconcile with her little son's usual docility. Cuffy kicked and screamed, and wouldn't be touched, like the naughtiest of children; and at the same time was shaken from head to foot by sobs about which there was nothing childish.

She was still bending over him, still remonstrating, when the door opened and Richard came in. One glance at his face

672

was enough to make her forget Cuffy and spring to her feet.

"Richard! Why, my dear . . . why what*ever* is the matter?"— For he had gone out, not an hour earlier, in the best of spirits; and here he came back white as a ghost, with dazed-looking eyes and shuffling feet. "My dear, what is it? Are you ill? Has the sun . . . ?"

Midway in a sob, Cuffy stopped to listen . . . held his breath.

Pouring himself out a glass of water, and spilling it as he poured, Richard drank, in a series of gulps. Then, from a bundle of newspapers and letters he was carrying, he drew forth a folded sheet and handed it to Mary.

"Read this."

In deep apprehension, she took the paper. As she read, she, too, went pale. It was a telegram from Jerry, forwarded by their London banker, and ran: *Return immediately. Most urgent. Wilding absconded America.*

Mary could not all at once take in the full sense of the words. "But how . . . what does it mean, Richard? I don't understand."

"Mean? Ruin, I suppose. In all probability I am a ruined man."— And dropping heavily on a chair, Mahony buried his face in his hands.

Cuffy sat up, and peeped furtively at his father and mother, with round eyes.

"Ruin? But how? Why? Oh dear, *can't* you speak?— No, no, Richard! What are you thinking of? Remember the child." For, from under his hands, tears were dripping on the table.— "Go to Ann, Cuffy. She shall take you out, or give you your tea. Run away, dear . . . quickly!— Now, Richard, pull yourself together! It's no good breaking down. *What* has happened? What do you intend to do?"

"Yes, what am I to do? Oh, help me, help me, Mary! . . . to know what's best."

"Of course, dear, of course I will."

Stifling her own alarm, Mary sat down at his side and took his hand in hers, to quieten him. It was evident he had had a severe shock. He admitted as much himself: the thing had come so suddenly. He told how, out of the dazzling sunshine, he had stepped into the cool office at the consulate, had passed the time of day with a clerk, had been chatting with the fellow when the telegram was handed him.

"This has just arrived for you, sir. I was about to send it on to your hotel."

Yes, he had not even stopped talking as he tore it open. The next moment the room had started to swing round him; he had been obliged to take a seat, every one staring at him, eyeing him askance. How he managed to get out of the place, and home, he didn't know. His mind seemed to have escaped control; felt like a child's puzzle that had been rudely jolted into hundreds of pieces, and had now all to be re-set.— "Which I don't feel equal to, Mary—and that's the truth. Something seems to have broken inside me."

Oh, how like a bad dream, the remainder of that day! For the practical side of the matter could not wait—not for a single hour. Richard half-way restored to composure, they had set to work in cold blood to discuss the situation. It was plain to them both that he must get back to Melbourne with the least possible delay. Till then, he would not know how he stood. Things might not, urged Mary, be quite so black as they looked at first glance, Wilding's absence yet prove capable of a rational explanation. But Richard, she could see, feared the worst . . . had no real hope of this. (And in her heart even she thought the tone of Jerry's message belied it. Oh, where *would* they have been, had she not had that private confab with Jerry the night before sailing!)— No, the conclusion Richard had jumped to at first reading, he still maintained: after the fashion of many a dishonest broker, Wilding had sold the scrip he held from his clients, and bolted with the proceeds. Now, the only question was: what was left; what could be saved from the wreck.— A mail steamer was due to leave Venice some time during the week; and on this, Richard must, if humanly possible, secure a berth. And the rest of the day passed in running from wharf to agent, from consul to banker. The money question had also to be gone into: what he still had in hand; how much remained on his letters of credit; what balance lay in the London bank. Then they had to think of the furniture, the curios and pictures, they had bought on their travels, and sent back to England. The London house would have to be got rid of; the servants paid off, etc., etc. Before evening, Mary's brain was reeling with all the details it was necessary to take in. But this rush and flurry was exactly what Richard needed. And she kept him at it, kept him on the go, till late at night, with the result that he went to bed dog-tired—too worn out to think.

But he had hardly dozed off when they were roused by Cuffy starting up in his sleep, screaming: "No, no! . . . don't hit him . . . oh, *doggy!*"

Hastily informed what had happened, Mahony struck a light and rose; and forgetting his own trouble over a need even more pressing than his own, he lifted Cuffy out of bed and set him on his knee. There he talked to him, as, thought Mary, only Richard could talk, when he chose. He recapitulated the scene of the afternoon, made the child, amid tears and frantic sobs, live through it afresh; then fell to work to dispel the brooding horror that lay over it. Such things as this were often to be met with in life; Cuffy must be a brave little man, and face them squarely. Somehow, they all fitted into a great scheme on God's part, which our poor brains were too puny to under-stand. To be pitied was not only poor doggy, whose struggles had soon ceased, but also the men who could act so cruelly towards their little brother—no less a brother because he had not the gift of speech. Cuffy must try to feel sorry for them, too, who had most likely never had anyone to teach them the difference between right and wrong. And he must make up for their want of love, by being doubly kind himself to all dumb creatures.— And so on and on, in a quiet, soothing voice, till the child's terror was allayed, and he slept, his arms clasped like a vice round his father's neck.

Forty-eight hours later Richard, with for luggage a single leather portmanteau, boarded the Overland Mail for Egypt—and thus ended a two days' nightmare, in which he had never ceased to torture himself with the bitterest reproaches.— "It is all my fault . . . my own fault . . . I alone am to blame. If *only* I had had patience . . . not been so headstrong . . . listened to you!"— The last glimpse Mary had of him, showed him stand-ing at the taffrail of the tender that carried passengers to the great steamer; standing very erect, and making a brave at-tempt to smile, as he waved his hat in farewell; for, when the time came, his chief thought was of her, and of how he could ease the parting.

Till now, Mary had kept up; had had, indeed, not a moment to think of herself, so busy had she been consoling, supporting, encouraging. But now that everything was over and she sat alone in the hotel bedroom, all she had gone through, all the conflicting emotions of these two past days—not the least of which were self-reproaches every whit as bitter as Richard's own—took toll of her. Behind locked doors, she broke down and wept bitterly.

The thought of her coming loneliness appalled her. For over twenty years, she had never been absent from Richard for more than a few weeks at a time . . . never been parted from him by more than a couple of hundred miles. Now, this violent and abrupt separation, with all the seas between, made her feel as if she had been roughly torn in two. For months and months to come, she would have no one to lean on, no one to consult—oh, *what* if one of the children should fall ill, and Richard not be there! She also shrank, with the timidity of unuse, from the prospect of having to emerge from her womanly seclusion and rub shoulders with the outside world. Her work had invariably lain in the background. When it came to a personal contact with business and business people, Richard had always been there, to step forward and bear the brunt. Now, she, who had travelled but the briefest of distances unescorted, was called on to undertake, by herself, not only the far journey across the Continent, but the infinitely more trying one of a two to three months' sea-voyage round the Cape. And until she got on board! To be faced, before that, were railway officials, porters, house-agents, shipping companies, bankers; the drawing of cheques and the paying of bills; the dismissing of servants; the packing and transport of baggage and furniture, the embarking, the long, long voyage with but one nurse for the children, and nobody to look after her—her, the worst of bad sailors!— But hardest of all was the knowledge that she would have to remain in her present state of ignorance and uncertainty, knowing nothing of what had actually happened, or of Richard—how he was bearing up, whether he was well or ill— until she herself landed in Melbourne, some six months hence.

But the barest hint of illness in connection with Richard was enough to make her mind swerve, with a sudden jerk, from herself and her own troubles to him. Desperately as she would miss him, and need him, yet she had small doubt—something within told her so—that, when she stood face to face with things, she would contrive to get on somehow. But he!—how was he ever going to manage without her? . . . to nerve him, and to soothe him, and to listen to his outpourings—away from her, he quite literally would not have a soul to speak to. She saw him on the outward voyage, eternally pacing the deck, a prey to blackest anxiety—and the last thought of self went under, in a fierce uprush of pity for him, so solitary, so self-centred, so self-tormented. Oh, that he might be spared the worst! He was old for his age; much too old to have to begin life afresh—life which, with every caprice satisfied, had yet become so hard for him, become an hourly tussle with flimsy, immaterial phantoms, whose existence other people never so much as dreamed of. And to know him pinched for money again, going short, denying himself, fretting over the straits to which he had brought her and the children . . . no! Mary felt there was nothing, absolutely nothing, she would not do, to help him, to spare him.

Well! . . . sitting crying wasn't the way to begin. That was a fool's job. She must just set her teeth and make the best of things—separation, uncertainty, responsibility—endeavouring, when it came to business, to stand her ground, even though she was but an inexperienced woman.— And, as a first step, she got up, dried her eyes, and bathed her face. After which she had trunks and saratogas brought out, and fell to packing.

But more and more, as the day wore on, did a single thought take possession of her—and, in this thought, Mary came as near as she ever would, to a conscious reflection on the aim and end of existence. It began with her suddenly becoming aware how she longed to hug her babies to her again, and how much she had missed them; a feeling until now resolutely repressed . . . for Richard's sake. Now, as, in imagination, she gathered her little ones to her heart—and gathered Richard with them, he, too, just an adored and absent child—it came over her like a flash that, amid life's ups and downs, to be able to keep one's little flock about one, to know one's dearest human relationships safe and unharmed, was, in good truth, all that signified. Compared with this, hardships and misfortune weighed no more than feathers in the balance.

"As long as we can be together . . . as long as I have Richard and my children . . . nothing else really matters. I can bear anything . . . put up with anything . . . if only they are spared me!"

BOOK III

ULTIMA THULE

"And some there be, which have no memorial . . ."

ECCLESIASTICUS, XLIV, 90

PART I

[1]

WHEN, for the third time in his life, Richard Mahony set foot in Australia, it was to find that the fortune with which that country a few years back had so airily invested him, no longer existed. Thanks in part to his own want of acumen, in part to the trickery of a scoundrel, he was a ruined man; and at the age of forty-nine, with a wife and children dependent on him, must needs start life over again. In surroundings to which foreign travel, a wider knowledge of the beauties of the old world, had rendered him doubly alien.

Twice, in the past, he had plucked up his roots from this soil. Each time, believing that the break was final. For no links of affection or gratitude bound him to the land of his adoption: he turned, in distaste, from the materialism of colonial life, the crude aspirations that dominated it; and, like many another bred to greenery and lushness on the farther side of the grey, dividing seas, could find no beauty in its dun and arid landscape. It was left to a later generation to discover this: to those who, with their mother's milk, drank in a love of sunlight and space; of inimitable blue distances and gentian-blue skies. To them, the country's very shortcomings were, in time, to grow dear: the scanty, ragged foliage; the unearthly stillness of the bush; the long, red roads, running inflexible as ruled lines towards a steadily receding horizon . . . and en-

678

gendering in him who travelled them a lifelong impatience with hedge-bound twists and turns. To their eyes, too, quickened by emotion, it was left to descry the colours in the apparent colourlessness: the upturned earth that shewed red, white, puce, gamboge; the blue in the grey of the new leafage; the geranium red of young scrub; the purple-blue depths of the shadows. To know, too, in exile, a rank nostalgia for the scent of the aromatic foliage; for the honey fragrance of the wattle; the perfume that rises hot and heavy as steam from vast paddocks of sweet, flowering lucerne—even for the sting and tang of countless miles of bush ablaze.

Of ties such as these, which end by drawing a man home, Richard Mahony knew nothing. He returned to the colony, at heart the stranger he had always been.

Landing in Melbourne one cold spring day in the early seventies, he tossed his belongings into a hansom, and, without pausing to reflect, drove straight to his old club at the top of Collins Street. But his stay there was short. For no sooner did he learn the full extent of his losses, his true financial situation, than he was ripe to detect a marked reserve, not to say coolness, in the manner of his former friends and acquaintances. More than one, he fancied, was deliberately shunning him. Bitterly he regretted his overhasty intrusion on this, the most exclusive club in the city; to which wealth was the passport. (He had forgotten, over his greater wanderings, how small a world he had here come back to. Within the narrow clique of Melbourne society, anything that happened to one of its members was quickly known to all; and the news of *his* crash had plainly preceded him.) Well! if this was a foretaste of what he had to expect—snubs and slights from men who would once have been honoured by his notice—the sooner he got out of people's way, the better. And bundling his clothes back into his trunk, he drove off again, choosing, characteristically enough, not a quiet hotel in a good neighbourhood, but a second-class boarding-house on the farther side of the Victoria Parade. Here, there was no chance whatever of his meeting any one he knew. Or, for that matter, of meeting any one at all! For these outlying streets, planned originally for a traffic without compare —the seething mob of men, horses, vehicles, that had once flowed, like a living river, to the goldfields—now lay as bare as they had been thronged. By day an occasional spindly buggy might amble along their vast width, or a solitary bullock-wagon take its tortoise way; but after dark, feebly lit by ill-trimmed lamps set at enormous distances one from another, they turned into mere desolate, wind-swept spaces. On which no creature moved but himself.

It was here that he took his decisions, laid his plans. His days resembled a blurred nightmare, in which he sped from one dingy office to the next, or sat through interviews with lawyers and bankers—humiliating interviews, in the course of which his unbusiness-like conduct, his want of *nous* in money-affairs was mercilessly dragged to light. But in the evening he was free: and then he would pace by the hour round these deserted streets, with the collar of his greatcoat turned up to his ears, his hands clasped at his back, his head bent against the icy south winds; or, caught by a stinging hail-shower, would seek shelter under the lee of an old, half dismantled "Horse, Cow and Pig-Market," of which the wild wind rattled and shook the loose timbers as if to carry them sky-high.

Of the large fortune he had amassed—the fortune so happily invested, so carefully husbanded—he had been able to recover a bare three thousand pounds. The unprincipled scoundrel in whose charge he had left it—on the advice of an equally unprincipled friend—had fleeced him of the rest. On this pitiful sum, and a handful of second-rate shares which might bring him in the equivalent of what he had formerly spent in a year on books, or his wife on her servants and the running of the nurseries, he had now to start life anew: to provide a home, to feed, clothe, educate his children, pay his way. One thing was clear: he must set up his plate again with all dispatch; resume the profession he had been so heartily glad to retire from, but a few years ago. Now, his first bitterness and resentment over, he felt only too thankful to have it to fall back on.

The moot question was, where to make the start; and in the course of the several anxious debates he had with himself on this subject, he became more and more relieved that Mary was not with him. Her absence undoubtedly gave him a freer hand. For, if he knew Mary, she would be all in favour of his settling up-country, and dead against his remaining in Melbourne. Now he was as ready as any man could be, to atone to her for the straits to which he had brought her. But—he must be allowed to meet the emergency in his own way. It might not be the wisest or the best way: but it was the only one he felt equal to.

Bury himself alive up-country, he could and would not! . . . not if she talked till all was blue. He saw her points, of course: they were like herself . . . entirely practical. There were, she would argue, for every opening in Melbourne ten to be found in the bush, where doctors were scarce, and twice and three times the money was to be made there. Living-expenses would be less, nor would they need to keep up any style. Which was true enough . . . as far as it went. What, womanlike, she would overlook, or treat as of slight importance, was the fact that he had also his professional pride to consider. He, condemn himself to the backwoods, who, in his day, had been one of the leading physicians on Ballarat? . . . who had contributed freely to medical journals, been noted for his sureness of diagnosis and the skill of his hand? Frankly, he thought he would be doing not only himself, but his children after him, an injury, did he consent to anything of the kind. No! he felt himself too good for the bush.

But the truth had still another facet. Constrained, at his age, and after several years of care-free leisure, to buckle to work again, he could only, he believed, find the necessary courage, under conditions that were not too direly repellent. And since, strive as he might, he could not break down Mary's imagined disapproval, he threw himself headlong into the attempt to get things settled—irrevocably settled—before she arrived; took to scouring the city and its environs, tramping the inner and outer suburbs, walking the soles off his boots and himself to the shadow, to find a likely place. Ruefully he turned his back on the sea at St. Kilda and Elsternwick, the pleasant spot of earth in which he once believed he had found his *ultima Thule;* gave the green gardens of Toorak a wide berth—no room there for an elderly interloper!—and, stifling his distaste, explored the outer darkness of Footscray, Essendon, Moonee Ponds. But it was always the same. If he found what he thought a suitable opening, there was certain not to be a house within cooee fit to live in.

What finally decided him on the pretty little suburb of Hawthorn—after, of course, he had thoroughly prowled and nosed about, to make sure he would have the field to himself—was not alone the good country air, but the fact that, at the junction of two main streets—or what would someday be main streets, the place being still in the making—he lit on a capital building lot, for sale dirt-cheap. For a doctor, no finer position could be imagined—and in fancy he ran up the house that was to stand there. Of brick, two stories high, towering above its neighbours, it would face both ways, be visible to all comers. The purchase of the land was easily effected—truth to tell, only too easily! He rather let himself be blarneyed into it. The house formed the stumbling-block. He sped from firm to firm; none would touch the job under a couple of thousand. In vain he tried to cut down his requirements. Less than two sitting-rooms they could not possibly do with; besides a surgery and waiting-room. Four bedrooms, a dressing-room or two, a couple of bathrooms, were equally necessary; while no house of this size but had verandah and balcony to keep the sun off, and to serve as an outdoor playroom for the children.

There was nothing for it, in the long run, but to put his pride in his pocket and take the advice given him on every hand: to build, as ninety-nine out of a hundred did here, through one of the numerous Building Societies that existed to aid those short of ready money. But it was a bitter pill for a man of his standing to swallow. Nor did it, on closer acquaintance, prove by any means the simple affair he had been led to believe. In the beginning, a thousand was the utmost he felt justified in laying down. But when he saw all that was involved, he contrived, after much anxious deliberation, to stretch the thousand to twelve hundred, taking out a mortgage at ten per cent, with regular repayment of capital.

It was at this crisis that he felt most thankful Mary was not with him. *How* she would have got on his nerves! . . . with her doubts and hesitations, her aversion to taking risks, her fears lest he should land them all in Queer Street. Women paid dearly for their inexperience: when it came to a matter of business even the most practical could not see beyond the tips of their noses. And, humiliating though the present step might be, there was absolutely no cause for alarm. These things were done—done on every hand—his eyes had been opened to that, in the course of his recent wanderings. By men, too, less favourably placed than he. But even suppose, for supposing's sake, that he did not succeed to the top of his expectations—get, that was, the mortgage paid off within a reasonable time

—where would be the hardship in treating the interest on a loan as a rental, in place of living rent-free? (And a very moderate rent, too, for a house of this size!) But Mary, being what she was, would never manage to forget the debt that lay behind. And it was here the temptation beset him to hold his tongue, to say nothing to her about the means he had been forced to employ. Let her believe he had built out of his own resources. For peace' sake, in the first place; to avoid the bother of explanation and recrimination. (What a drag, too, to know that somebody was eternally on the *qui vive* to see whether or no you were able to come up to the mark!) Yet again, by keeping his own counsel, he would spare her many an hour's anxiety—a sheerly needless anxiety. For any doubts he might have had himself, at the start, vanished like fog before a lifting breeze as he watched the house go up. Daily his conviction strengthened that he had done the right thing.

It became a matter of vital importance to him that the walls should be standing and the roof on, before Mary saw it: Mary was one of those who needed the evidence of their senses; could grasp only what she had before her eyes. Then, pleasure at getting so fine a house might help to reconcile her to his scheme . . . God alone knew what the poor soul would be expecting. And so, in the belief that his presence stimulated the workpeople, he spent many an hour in the months that followed watching brick laid to brick, and the hodmen lumber to and fro; or pottering about among clay and mortar heaps: an elderly gentleman in a long surtout, carrying gloves and a cane; with greyish hair and whiskers, and a thin, pointed face.

Again, he cooled his heels there because he had nothing else to do. Once bitten, twice shy, was his motto; and he continued rigidly to give friends and relatives the go-by: time enough to pick up the threads when he could step out once more in his true colours. Besides, the relatives were Mary's; the friends . . . well, even in his limber days, the social virtues had not been strong in him. The consequence was, he now fell into a solitariness beyond compare: got the habit of solitude, which is as easily acquired as any other; and neither missed nor needed the company of his fellows.

Since, however, every man who still stands upright needs some star to go by, he kept his eyes steadfastly fixed on the coming of wife and children. This was to be his panacea for every ill. And as the six months' separation drew to an end, he could hardly contain himself for anxiety and impatience. Everything was ready for them: he had taken a comfortably furnished house in which to install them till their own was built; had engaged a servant, moved in himself. Feverishly he scanned the shipping-lists. Other boats made port which had left England at the same time . . . and even later . . . despite gales, and calms, and contrary winds. But it was not till the middle of December that the good ship *Sobraon,* ninety odd days out, was sighted off Cape Otway; and he could take train to Queenscliffe for a surprise meeting with his dear ones, and to sail with them up the Bay.

In his hand he carried a basket of strawberries—the first to come on the market.

Standing pointing out to the children familiar landmarks on the shores of their new-old home, Mary suddenly stopped in what she was saying and rubbed her eyes.

"Why! I do declare . . . if it's not— Look, children, *look,* there's your Papa! He's waving his handkerchief to you. Wave back! Nod your heads! Throw him a kiss!"

"Papa! . . . dere's Papa!" the twins told each other, and obediently set to wagging like a pair of china mandarins; the while with their pudgy hands they wafted kisses in the direction of an approaching boat-load of men.

"Where's he? *I* don't see!" opposed Cuffy, in a spirit to which the oneness of his sisters—still more, of sisters and mother—often provoked him. But this time he had a grievance as well. Throughout the voyage, there had been ever such lots of laughing and talking and guessing, about who would reckernise Papa first: and he, as the eldest, had felt quite safe. Now, Mamma, who had joined in the game and guessed with them, had spoiled everything, not played fair.

But for once his mother did not heed his pouting. She was gazing, with heart in her eyes, at the Health Officer's boat, in which, by the side of the doctor coming to board the ship, sat Richard, in a set of borrowed oilskins, ducking his head to avoid the spray, and waving and shouting like an excited schoolboy. In a very few minutes now, the long, slow torture of the voyage would be over, and she would know the worst.

Here he came, scrambling up the ladder, leaping to the deck.

"Richard! . . . my dear! Is it really you? But *oh*, how thin you've got!"

"Yes, here I am, safe and sound! But you, wife? . . . how are you?— *And* the darlings? Come to Papa, who has missed you more than he can say!— Good day, good day, Eliza! I hope I see you well?— But *how* they've grown, Mary! Why, I hardly know them."

The Dumplings, pink and drooping with shyness, but docile as ever, dutifully held up their bud mouths to be kissed; then, smiling adorably, wriggled back to Mamma's side, crook'd finger to lip. But Cuffy did not smile as his father swung him aloft, and went pale instead of pink. For, at sight of the person who came jumping over to them, he had been seized by one of his panicky fears. The Dumplings, of course, didn't remember Papa, they couldn't, they were only four; but he did . . . and somehow he remembered him *diffrunt*. Could it be a mistake? Not that it wasn't him . . . he didn't mean that . . . he only meant . . . well, he wasn't sure what he did mean. But when this new-old Papa asked: "And how's my big boy?" a fresh spasm of distrust shot through him. Didn't he know then that everybody always said "small for his age"?

But, dumped down on the deck again, he was forgotten, while over his head the quick clipped voice went on: "Perfectly well! . . . and with nothing in the world to complain of, now I've got you again. I thought you'd *never* come. Yes, I've been through an infernally anxious time, but that's over now, and things aren't as bad as they might be. You've no need to worry. But let's go below where we can talk in peace." And with his arm round her shoulders, he made to draw Mary with him . . . followed by the extreme silent wonder of three pairs of eyes, whose owners were not used to seeing Mamma taken away like this, without asking. Or anybody's arm put round her either. When she belonged to them.

But at the head of the companion-way Mahony paused and slapped his brow.

"Ha! . . . but wait a minute! . . . Papa was forgetting. See here!" and from a side pocket of the capacious oilskins he drew out the basket of strawberries. These had suffered in the transit, were bruised and crushed.

"What, strawberries?—already?" exclaimed Mary, and eyed the berries dubiously. They were but faintly tinged.

685

"The very first to be had, my dear! I spied them on my way to the train.— Now then, children!"

But Mary barred the way . . . stretched out a preventing hand. "Not just now, Richard. Later on, perhaps . . . when they've had their dinners. Give them to me, dear!"

Jocularly he eluded her, holding the basket high, out of her reach. "No, this is *my* treat!— Come, who remembers the old game? 'Open your mouths and shut your eyes and see what Jacko will send you!'"

The children closed in, the twins displaying rosy throats, their eyes faithfully glued to.

But here Mary peremptorily interposed. "No, no, they mustn't! I should have them ill. The things are not half ripe."

"What? Not let them eat them? . . . after the trouble I've been to, to buy them and lug them here? Not to speak of what I paid for them!"

"I'm sorry, Richard, but— Ssh, dear! surely you must see . . ." Mary spoke in a low, persuasive voice, at the same time frowning and making other wifely signals to him, to lower his. (And thus engrossed, did not feel a pull at her sleeve, or hear Cuffy's thin pipe: "*I'll* eat them, Mamma. I'd *like* to!" Now, he knew it was Papa, all right.) For several of their fellow passengers were watching and listening, and there stood Richard, looking supremely foolish, holding aloft a single strawberry.

But he was too put out to care who saw or heard. "Well and good then, if they're not fit to eat—not even *after* dinner!— there's only one thing to be done with them. Overboard they go!" And picking up the basket he flung it and its contents into the sea. Before the children . . . Eliza . . . everybody!

With her arm through his, Mary got below, to the privacy and seclusion of the cabin. The same old Richard! touchy and irascible . . . wounded by any trifle. But she very well knew how to manage him; and, by appealing to his common sense and good feelings, soon talked him round. Besides, on this particular day, he was much too happy to see them all again, long to remain in dudgeon. Still, his first mood of pleasure and elation had fizzled out and was not to be recaptured. The result was, the account he finally gave her of the state of his finances, and their future prospects, was not the rose-coloured one he had intended and prepared. What she now got to hear bore more relation to sober fact.

[2]

A NEIGHBOUR's cocks and hens wakened him before daybreak. The insensate creatures crew and cackled, cackled and crew; and, did they pause for breath, the sparrows took up the tale. He could not sleep again. Lying stiff as a log, so as not to disturb Mary, he hailed each fresh streak of light that crept in at the sides of the blinds or over the tops of the valances; while any bagatelle was welcome that served to divert his thoughts and to bridge the gap till rising-time. The great mahogany wardrobe, for instance. This began as an integral part of the darkness, gradually to emerge, a shade heavier than the surrounding gloom, as a ponderous mass; only little by little, line by line, assuming its true shape. Faithfully the toilet-glass gave back each change in the room's visibility. Later on there were bars to count, formed by un-evennesses in the slats of the venetians, and falling golden on the whitewashed walls.

Yes, whitewash was, so far, the only covering the walls knew. The papering of them had had to be indefinitely post-poned. And gaunt indeed was the effect of their cold white-ness on eyes used to rich, dark hangings. This was one reason why he preferred the penance of immobility, to getting up and prowling about downstairs. Never did the house look more cheerless than of an early morning, before the blinds were raised, the rooms in order. One realized then, only too plainly, what a bare barn it was; and how the task of render-ing it cosy and homelike had baffled even Mary. He would not forget her consternation on first seeing it; her cry ·of: "But Richard! . . . how shall we *ever* fill it?" Himself he stood by dumbfounded, as he watched her busy with tape and meas-ure: truly, he had never thought of this. She had toiled, dear soul, for weeks on end, stitching at curtains and draperies to try to clothe the nakedness—in vain. If they had not had the books to fall back on, the place would have been uninhabit-able. But he had emptied the whole of his library into it, with the result that books were everywhere: on the stair-landings, in the bedrooms; wherever they could with decency stop a gap. Another incongruity was the collection of curios and bric-à-brac garnered on their travels. This included some rare and costly objects, which looked odd, to say the least of it, in a room where there were hardly chairs enough to go round. For he had had everything to buy, down to the last kitchen fork and spoon. And by the time he had paid for a sideboard that did not make too sorry a show in the big dining-room; a dinner-table that had some relation to the floor-space; a piano, a desk for his surgery, and so on, he was bled dry. Nor did he see the smallest prospect, in the meantime, of finishing the job. They had just to live on in this half-baked condition, which blazoned the fact that funds had given out; that he had put up a house it was beyond his means to furnish. How he writhed when strangers ran an appraising glance over the place!

No: unrested, and without so much as a cup of tea in him, he could not bring himself to descend and contemplate the evidences of his folly. Instead, the daylight by now being come, he lay and totted up pound to pound until, for sheer weariness, he was ready to drop asleep again. But eight o'clock had struck; there could be no lapsing back into unconsciousness. He rose and went down to breakfast.

They had the children with them at table now. And good as the little things were by nature, yet they rose from ten hours' sound sleep lively as the sparrows: their tongues wagged without a stop. And though he came down with the best intentions, he soon found his nerves jarred. Altering the position of his newspaper for the tenth time, he was pettishly moved to complain: "Impossible! *How* can I read in such a racket?"

"Oh, come, Richard!" said Mary cheerily. "You can't expect children to sit and never say a word."

But she hushed them, with frowns and headshakes, to a bout of whispering, or the loud, hissing noise children make in its stead; under fire of which it was still harder to fix his thoughts.

Retired to the surgery, he was no better off; for now the thrumming of five-finger exercises began to issue from the drawing-room, where the children were having their music-lessons. This was unavoidable. With the arrival of the patients, all noise had to cease; later on, Mary was too busy with domestic duties to sit by the piano; and that the youngsters must learn music went without saying. But the walls of the house had proved mere lath-and-plaster; and the tinkle of the piano, the sound of childish voices and Mary's deeper tones raised in one-two-threes, and one-two-three-fours, so distracted him that it took him all his time to look up, and make notes on, his cases for the day. By rights, this should have been his hour for reading, for keeping abreast of things medical. But not only silence failed him; equally essential was a quiet mind; and, as long as his affairs remained in their present uncertain state, that, too, was beyond his reach. Before he got to the foot of a page, he would find himself adding up columns of figures.

The truth was, his brain had reverted to its old, familiar employment with a kind of malicious glee. He was powerless to control it. Cark and care bestrode him; rode him to death; and yet got him nowhere; for all the calculations in the world would not change hard facts. Reckon as he might, he could not make his dividends for the past six months amount to more than a hundred and fifty pounds. A hundred and fifty! Nor was this wretched sum a certainty. It came from shares that were to the last degree unstable—in old days he had not given them a thought. And, against this, stood the sum of eight hundred pounds. Oh! he had grossly overestimated his faculty for self-deception. Now that he was in the thick of things, it went beyond him to get this debt out of his mind. Suppose anything should happen to him before he had paid it off! What a legacy to leave to Mary! Out and away his sorest regret was that, in the good old days now gone for ever, he had failed to insure his life. Thanks to his habitual dilatoriness, he had put it off from year to year; always nursing the intention, shirking the effort. Now, the premium demanded would be sheerly unpayable.

At present, everything depended on how the practice panned out. The practice . . . Truth to tell, after close on a six months' trial, he did not himself know what to make of it. Had he been less pressed, for time and money, he might have described it as not unpromising. As matters stood, he could only say that what there *was* of it was good: the patients of a superior class, and so on. But from the first it had been slow to move—there seemed no sickness about—the fees slower still to come in. If, by the end of the year, things did not look up, he would have to write down his settling there as a bad job.

It was an acute disappointment that he had only managed to secure two paltry lodges. Every general practitioner would know what *that* meant. He had built on lodge-work; not only for the income it assured, but also to give a fillip to the private practice. Again: not expecting what work there was to be so scattered, he had omitted to budget for horse hire, or the hire of a buggy. This made a real hole in his takings. He walked wherever he could; but calls came from places as far afield as Kew and Camberwell, which were not to be reached on foot. Besides, the last thing in the world he could afford to do was to knock himself up. Even as it was, he got back from his morning round tired out; and after lunch would find himself dozing in his chair. Of an evening, he was glad to turn in soon after ten o'clock; the one bright side to the general slackness being the absence of nightwork. Of course, such early hours meant giving the go-by to all social pleasures. But, truly, he was in no trim for company, either at home or abroad. How he was beginning to rue the day when he had burdened himself with this great house, merely that he might strut and make a show among his fellow-men! When the plain truth was, he would not turn a hair if he never saw one of them again.

Yes, his present feeling of unsociableness went deeper than mere fatigue: it was a kind of deliberate turning-in on himself. Mary no doubt hit the mark, when she blamed the months of morbid solitude to which he had condemned himself, on reaching Melbourne. He had, declared she, never been the same man since.

"I ought to have known better than to let you come out alone."

She spoke heartily; but doubts beset her. It was one thing to put your finger on the root of an ill; another to cure it. Yet a failure to do so might cost them dear. Here was Richard, with his way and his name to make, with a practice to build up, connections to form; and, instead of taking every hand that offered, he refused invitations, shirked introductions; and, shutting himself up, declined into this queer "let me alone and don't bother me" state, than which, for a doctor, she could imagine none more fatal.

Of course, having to start work again, at his age, was no light matter; and he undoubtedly felt the strain; found it hard, besides, after all the go-as-you-please later years, to nail himself down to fixed hours, and live by the clock. He complained, too, that his memory wasn't what it used to be. Names, now. If he didn't write down a name the moment he heard it, it was bound to escape him; and then he could waste the better part of a morning in struggling to recapture it.

"You're out of the way of it, dear, that's all!" she resolutely strove to cheer him, as she brushed his hat and hunted for his gloves. "Now have you your case-book? And is everything in your bag?" More than once he had been obliged to tramp the whole way home again, for a forgotten article.

The reminder annoyed him. "Yes, yes, of course! But my thermometer . . . now where the dickens have I put that?" And testily he tapped pocket after pocket.

"Here . . . you've left it lying. Oh, by the way, Richard, I wonder if you'd mind leaving an order at the butcher's, as you go past?"

But at this he flared up. "Now, Mary, *is* it fair to bother me with that kind of thing, when I've so much else to think of?"

"Well, it's only . . . the shop's so far off; and I can't spare cook. You've just to hand in a note as you pass the door."

"Yes, yes! A thousand and one reasons!"

"Oh, well, never mind! Eliza and the children must go that way for their walk—though it does take them down among the shops."

"And why not? Are the children everlastingly to be spared at my expense?"

He went off, banging the gate behind him. The latch did not hold; Mary stepped out to secure it. And the sight of him trudging down the road brought back her chief grievance against him. This was his obstinate refusal to keep a horse and trap. It stood to reason: if he would only consent to drive on his rounds, instead of walking, he would save himself much of the fatigue he now endured; and she be spared his perpetual grumbles. Besides, it was not the thing for a man of his age and appearance to be seen tramping the streets, bag in hand. But she might as well have talked to a post. The only answer she got was that he couldn't afford it. Now this was surely imagination. She flattered herself she knew something about practices by now, and could tell pretty well what the present one was likely to throw off . . . if properly nursed. To the approximate three hundred a year which Richard admitted to drawing from his dividends, it should add another three; and, on six, with her careful management, they could very well pull through, to begin with. It left no margin for extravagances, of course; but the husbanding of Richard's strength could hardly be put down under that head. Since, however, he continued obdurate, she went her own way to work, with the result that, out of the money he allowed her to keep house on, she contrived, at the end of three months, to hand him back a tidy sum.

"Now if you don't feel you want to *buy* a horse and buggy, you can at least give a three months' order at the livery-stable."

But not a bit of it! More, he was even angry. "Tch! *Do*, for goodness' sake, leave me to manage my own affairs! I don't want a horse and trap, I tell you. I prefer to go on as I am." And, with that, her economies just passed into, were swallowed up in, the general fund. She wouldn't do it again.

"Mamma!"

This was Cuffy, who had followed her out and climbed the gate at her side. He spoke in a coaxy voice; for, as likely as not, Mamma would say: "Run away, darling, and don't bother me. I've no time." But Cuffy badly wanted to know something. And, since Nannan left, there had never been any one he could ask his questions of: Mamma was always busy, Papa not at home.

"Mamma! Why does Papa poke his head out so when he walks?"

"That's stooping. People do it as they grow older." Even the child, it seemed, could see how tiresome Richard found walking.

"What's it mean growing old—really, truly?"

"Why, losing your hair, and your teeth, and not being able to get about as well as you used to."

"Does it hurt?"

"Of course not, little silly!"

"Does Papa lose his teeth? Does Eliza? And why has he always got a bag now?"

"*What* an inquisitive little boy! He carries things in it to make people well with."

692

"Why does he want to make them well?"

"To get money to buy you little folks pretty clothes and good things to eat. But come . . . jump down! And run and tell Eliza to get you ready for your walk."

"I don't *like* going walks with Eliza," said Cuffy, and, one hand in his mother's, reluctantly dragged and shuffled a foot in the gravel. "Oh, I *do* wis' I had my little pony again."

"So do I, my darling," said Mary heartily, and squeezed his hand. "I'm afraid you'll be forgetting how to ride. I must talk to Papa. Then, perhaps Santa Claus . . . or at your birthday party . . ."

"Ooh! Really, truly, Mamma?"

"We'll see."— At which Cuffy hopped from side to side up the length of the path.

And Mary meant what she said. It was unthinkable that *her* children should come short in any of the advantages other children enjoyed. And not to be able to ride, and ride well, too, in a country like this, might prove a real drawback to them in after life. Now she had pinched and screwed for Richard's sake, to no purpose whatever. The next lump sum she managed to get together should go to buy a pony.

But this was not all. Besides riding, the children ought to be having dancing-lessons. She did so want her chicks to move prettily and gracefully; to know what to do with their hands and feet; to be able to enter a room without awkwardness; and they were just at their most impressionable age: what they now took in, they would never forget, what they missed, never make good. But she could hope for no help from Richard; manlike, he expected graces and accomplishments to spring up of themselves, like wild flowers from the soil. Everything depended on her. And she did not spare herself. Thanks to her skill with her needle, they were still, did they go to a party, the best-dressed children in the room; and the best-mannered, too, Nannan's strict upbringing still bearing fruit. None of her three ever grabbed, or gobbled, or drank with a full mouth; nor were they either lumpishly shy or overforward, like the general ruck of colonial children.

But they were getting big; there would soon be more serious things to think of than manners and accomplishments. If only Richard did not prove too unreasonable! So far, except for music-lessons, they had had no teaching at all, one of his odd ideas being that a child's brain should lie fallow till it was seven or eight years old. This meant that she had sometimes to suffer the mortification of seeing children younger than Cuffy and his sisters able to answer quite nicely at spelling and geography, while hers stood mutely by. In the Dumplings' case it did not greatly matter: they were still just Dumplings in every sense of the word; fat and merry playbabies. But Cuffy was sharp for his age; he could read his own books, and knew long pieces of poetry by heart. It seemed little short of absurd to hold such a child back; and, after she had once or twice seen him put publicly to shame, Mary took, of a morning, when she was working up a flake-crust, or footing her treadle-machine, to setting him a copy to write, or giving him simple lessons in spelling and sums. (Which little incursions into knowledge were best, it was understood, not mentioned to Papa.)

Her thoughts were all for her children. Herself she needed little; and was really managing, without difficulty, to cut her coat to suit her cloth. In the matter of dress, for instance, she still had the rich furs, the sumptuous silks and satins she had brought with her from home—made over, these things would last her for years—had all her ivory and mother-o'-pearl ornaments and trifles. True, she walked where she had driven; hired less expensive servants, and rose betimes of a morning; but who shall say whether these changes were wholly drawbacks in Mary's eyes, or whether the return to a more active mode of life did not, in great measure, outweigh them? It certainly gave her a feeling of satisfaction, to which she had long been a stranger, to know that not a particle of waste was going on in her kitchen; that she was once more absolute monarch in her own domain. Minor pleasures consisted in seeing how far she could economise the ingredients of pudding or cake, and yet turn it out light and toothsome. Had Richard wished to entertain, she would have guaranteed to hold the floor with any one, at half the cost.

But there was no question of this. They lived like a pair of hermit crabs; and, in spite of the big house, might just as well have been buried in the bush. For, having talked herself hoarse in pointing out the harm such a mode of life would do the practice, she had given way and made the best of things; as long, that was, as Richard's dislike of company had only to do with the forming of new acquaintances. When, however, he began to grumble at the presence of her own intimate friends and relatives, it was more than she could stand. In the heated argument that followed her perplexed: "Not ask Lizzie? Put off the Devines?" she discovered, to her amazement, that it was not alone his morbid craving for solitude that actuated him: the house, if you please, formed the stumbling-block! Because this was still unpapered, and rather scantily furnished, he had got it into his head that it was not fit to ask people to; that he would be looked down on, because of it. Now, did *anyone* ever hear such nonsense? Why, half the houses in Melbourne were just as bare, and nobody thought the worse of them. People surely came to see you, not your furniture! But he had evidently chafed so long in silence over what he called the "poverty-stricken aspect of the place," that there was now no talking him out of the notion. So Mary shrugged and sighed; and, silently in her turn, took the sole way left her, which was an underground way; so contriving matters that her friends came to the house only when Richard was out of it . . . a little shift it was again wiser not to mention to Papa. She also grew adept at getting rid of people to the moment. By the time the gate clicked at Richard's return, all traces of the visit had been cleared away.

[3]

THUS she bought peace.— But when it came to putting up a guest in the house, of making use of the unused spare room, finesse did not avail; and a violent dispute broke out between them. To complicate matters, the guest in question was Richard's old bugbear, Tilly.

Tilly, whose dearest wish had been fulfilled some six months back, by the birth of a child, but who, since then, had remained strangely silent, now wrote, almost beside herself with grief and anxiety, that she was bringing her infant, which would not thrive, to town, to consult the doctors there. And Mary straightway forgot all her schemes and contrivances, forgot everything but a friend in need, and wrote off by return begging Tilly, with babe and nurse, to make their home her own.

Mahony was speechless when he heard of it. He just gave

695

her one look, then stalked out of the room and shut himself up in the surgery, where he stayed for the rest of the evening. While Mary sat bent over her needlework, with determined lips and stubborn eyes.

Later on, though, in the bedroom, his wrath exploded in bitter abuse of Purdy, ending with: "No one belonging to that fellow shall ever darken *my* doors again!"

At this, she, too, flared up. "Oh, of course! . . . put all the blame for what happened on somebody else. It never occurs to you to blame yourself, and your own rashness and impatience. Who but you would have trusted a man like Wilding? —but Tilly being Purdy's wife is nothing but an excuse. It's not only her. You won't let a soul inside the doors. You're getting perfectly impossible to live with."

"Why should my wishes alone be disregarded? The very children's likes and dislikes are taken more account of. You consider every one . . . only not me!"

"And you consider no one but yourself!"

"Well, this is my house, and I have the right to say who shall come into it."

"It's no more yours than mine. And Tilly's my oldest friend, and I'm not going to desert her now she's in trouble. I've asked her to come here, and come she shall!"

"Very well, then, if she does, I go!"— And so on, and on.

In the adjoining dressing-room, the door of which stood ajar, Cuffy sat up in his crib and listened. The loud voices had wakened him and he couldn't go to sleep again. He was frightened; his heart beat pit-a-pat, pit-a-pat. And when he heard somebody begin to cry, he just couldn't help it, he had to cry, too. Till a door went, and quick steps came running; and then there were Papa's hands to hold to, and Papa's arms round him; and quite a lot of Hambelin Town and Handover City to put him to sleep.

The knot was cut by Tilly choosing, with many, many thanks, to stay at a hotel in town. There Mary sought her out, one late autumn afternoon, when the white dust was swirling house-high through the white streets, and the south wind had come up so cold that she regretted not having worn her sealskin. Alighting from the train at Prince's Bridge, she turned a deaf ear to the shouts of: "Keb, Keb!" and leaving the region of warehouses—poor John's among them—made her way on foot up the rise to Collins Street. This was her invariable habit nowadays, if she hadn't the children with her: was one of the numerous little economies she felt justified in practising . . . and holding her tongue about. Richard, of course, would have snorted with disapproval. *His* wife to be tramping the streets! But latterly she had found her tolerance of his grandee notions about what she might, and might not do, wearing a little thin. Under the present circumstances they seemed, to say the least of it, out of place. She had legs of her own, and was every bit as well able to walk as he was. If people looked down on her for it . . . well, they would just have to, and that was all about it!

These brave thoughts notwithstanding, she could not but wish—as she sat waiting in a public coffee-room, the door of which opened and shut a dozen times to the minute, every one who entered fixing her with a hard and curious stare—wish that Tilly had picked on a quieter hotel, one more suitable to a lady travelling alone. She was glad when the waiter ushered her up the red-carpeted stairs to her friend's private sitting-room.

Tilly was so changed that she hardly knew her. Last seen in the first flush of wifehood, high-bosomed, high-coloured, high-spirited, she seemed to have shrunk together, fallen in. Her pale face was puffy; her eyes deeply ringed.

"You poor thing! What you must have suffered!"

Mary said this more than once, as she listened to Tilly's tale. It was that of a child born strong and healthy— "As fine a boy as ever you saw, Mary!"—with whom all had gone well, until, owing to an unfortunate accident, they had been forced to change the wet nurse. Since then they had tried one nurse after another; had tried hand-feeding, goat's milk, patent mixtures; but to no purpose. The child had just wasted away. Till he was now little more than a skeleton. Nor had he ever sat up, or taken notice. The whole day long he lay and wailed, till it nearly broke your heart to hear it.

"And me . . . who'd give my life's blood to help 'im!"

"Have you seen MacMullen? What does he say?"

Tilly answered with a hopeless lift of her shoulders. "'E calls it by a fine name, Mary—they all do. And 'as given us a new food to try. But the long and the short of it is, if the wasting isn't stopped, Baby will die." And the ominous word

697

spoken, Tilly's composure gave way: the tears came with a gush and streamed down her cheeks, dropping even into her lap, before she managed to fish a handkerchief from her petticoat pocket.

"There, there, you old fool!" she rebuked herself. "Sorry, love! It comes of seeing your dear old face again. For weeping and wailing doesn't help either, does it?"

"Poor old girl! it *is* hard on you . . . and when you've so wanted children."

"And'm never likely to 'ave another. Other people can get 'em by the dozen—and as 'ealthy as can be."

"Well, I shouldn't give up hope of pulling him through— no matter what the doctors say. You know, Tilly . . . it may seem an odd thing to come from me . . . but I really haven't *very* much faith in them, after all. I mean—well, you know, they're all right if you break your leg, or have something definite the matter with you, like mumps or scarlet fever—or if you want a tumor cut out. But otherwise, well, they never seem to allow enough . . . I mean, for *commonsense* things. Now, what I think is, as the child has held out so long, there must be a kind of toughness in him. And there's always just a chance you may still find the right thing."

But when, leaning over the cot, she saw the tiny, wizened creature that lay among its lace and ribbons: ("Hardly bigger than a rabbit, Richard! . . . with the face of an old, old man —no, more like a poor starved little monkey!") when, too, the featherweight burden was laid on her lap, proving hardly more substantial than a child's doll: then, Mary's own heart fell.

Sitting looking down at the little wrinkled face, her mother eyes full of pity, she asked: "What does Purdy say?"

"'Im?" Again Tilly raised her shoulders, but this time the gesture bespoke neither resignation nor despair. "Oh, Purd's sorry, of course!"

"I should think so, indeed!"

"*Sorry!* Does being sorry *help?*" And now her words came flying, her aitches scattering to the winds. "The plain truth is, Mary, there's not a man living who can go on 'earing a child cry, cry, cry, day and night, and night and day, and keep 'is patience and 'is temper. And Purd's no different to the rest. When it gets too bad, 'e just claps on 'is 'at, and flies out of the 'ouse—to get away from it. Men are like that. Only the rosy side of things for them! And, Purd, 'e must be *free*. The smallest jerk of the reins and it's all up. As for a sick child . . . and even though it's 'is own—oh, I've learnt *something* about men these three years, Mary! Purd's no good to lean on, not an 'apporth o' good! 'E's like an air-cushion —goes in when you lean, and puffs out somewhere else. And 'ow can 'e 'elp it?—when there isn't anything *but* air in 'im. No, 'e's nothing in the world but fizzle and talk . . . a bag of chaff—an 'ollow drum."

Mary heard her sadly and in silence. This, too! Oh, the gilt was off poor Tilly's gingerbread in earnest.

But, in listening, she had also cocked an attentive ear, and she now said: "Tilly, there's something about that child's cry . . . there's a tone in it—a . . ."

"'Ungry . . . !" said Tilly fiercely. "'E's starving—that's what it is."

"Of course, hungry, too. But I must say it sounds to me more *angry*. And then look how he beats the air with his little fists. He's not trying to suck them; or even to get them near his mouth. What I'm wondering is . . . Richard can't, of course, touch the case, now it's in MacMullen's hands. But I'm going home to tell him all about it. He used to have great luck with children, in the old days. There's no saying. He *might* be able to suggest something. In the meantime, my dear, keep a good heart! Nothing is gained by despairing."

"Bless you, Mary! If any one can put spunk into a mortal it's you"——

"Starving?" said Mahony on hearing the tale. "I shouldn't wonder if starving itself was not nearer the mark."

"But, Richard, such a *young* child . . . do you really think . . . Though I must say, when I sat there and heard that *exasperated* sort of cry . . ."

"Exactly. Who's to say where consciousness begins? . . . or ends. For all we know, the child in the womb may have its own dim sentience. Now I don't need to give *you* my opinion of the wet-nurse system. None the less, if the case were mine, I should urge the mother to leave no stone unturned to find the person who first had it at the breast. A woman of her class will still be nursing."

"Mary! I'll give 'er the 'alf of what I 'ave. I'll make a spectacle of meself!—go on me knees down Sturt Street, if need be; but back she comes!" were Tilly's parting words as she stepped into the train.

And sure enough, not a week later, a letter arrived to say that the woman, run to earth, had, by dint of fierce appeals to her motherhood, and unlimited promises ("What it's going to cost me, Purd will *never* know!") been induced to return. A further week brought a second communication to the breakfast-table, scrawled in a shaky hand, and scrappily put together, but containing the glad news that the child had actually gained a few ounces in weight, and, better still, had ceased its heartrending wail. Tilly's joy and gratitude were of such a nature that Mary did not dare to deliver the message she sent Richard, as it stood. She just translated the gist of it into sober English.

And a good job, too, that she had watered it down! For Richard proved to be in one of his worst, early-morning moods; and was loud in scorn of even the little she passed on.

He ended by thoroughly vexing her. "Never did I know such a man! Things have come to such a pass that people can't even feel grateful to you, without offending you. Your one desire is to hold them at arm's length. You ought to have been born a mole!"

In speaking she had hastily re-inserted Tilly's letter in its envelope. A second letter was lying by her plate. This she read with wrinkled brows, an occasional surreptitious glance at Richard, and more than one smothered: "Tch!" She also hesitated for some time before deciding to hand it, past three pair of inquisitive young eyes, over the table.

"Here! I wonder what you'll say to this? It's not my fault this time, remember!"

Mahony incuriously laid aside his newspaper, took the sheet, frowned at the writing, and tilted it to the correct angle for his eyes, which were "not what they used to be."

The letter ran:

My dear Mrs. Mahony,

My dear wife has been ordered a sea-voyage for the benefit of her health, and before sailing wishes, as ladies will, to visit the Melbourne emporiums to make some additions to her wardrobe. It is impossible for me to accompany her to town, though I shall hope to bid her "au revoir" before she sails, a fortnight hence. May I trespass upon your goodness, and request you to be Agnes's cicerone and escort, while in Melbourne for the above object? I need not dwell on her preference for you in this rôle, over every one else.

Give my due regards to your husband,

and, believe me,

very truly yours,

Henry Ocock

"In plain English, I presume, it's to be your duty to keep her off the bottle."

"*Richard!* . . . ssh! How *can* you?" expostulated Mary, with a warning frown; which was justified by Cuffy at once chiming in: "Do ladies have bottles, too, Mamma, as well as babies?" (Cuffy had been deeply interested in the sad story of Aunt Tilly's little one and its struggle for life.) "Now, you chicks, Lallie untie Lucie's bib, and all three run out and play.— *Not* before the children, Richard! That boy drinks in every word. You'll have him repeating what you say in front of Agnes. For I suppose what Mr. Henry really means is that we are to invite her here?"

"The hint is as plain as the nose on your face."

"Yes, I'm afraid it is," and Mary sighed. "I wonder what we should do. I'm very fond of Agnes; but I've got the children to think of. I shouldn't like *them* to get an inkling . . . On the other hand, we can't afford to offend an influential person like Mr. Henry."

"I know what I *can't* afford—and that's to have this house turned into a dumping-ground for all the halt and maimed of your acquaintance. The news of its size is rapidly spreading. And if people once get the idea they can use it in lieu of an hotel, God help us! There'll be nothing for it, but to move . . . into a four-roomed hut."

"Oh, Richard! if you would only tell me how we really stand, instead of making such a mystery of it. For we can't go on living without a soul ever entering our doors."

"We can be glad if we manage to live at all."

"There you go! One exaggeration after the other!"

"Well, well! I suppose if Ocock has set his mind on us drynursing his wife, we've got to truckle to him. Only don't ask me to meet *him* over the head of it. I've no intention of being patronised by men of his type, now that I've come down in the world."

"*Patronised?* When I think how ready people were to take us up when we first came here! But you can't expect them to go on asking and inviting for ever, and always being snubbed by a refusal."

Agnes. Sitting opposite her old friend in the wagonette that bore them from the railway station, watching the ugly tic that convulsed one side of her face, Mary thought sorrowfully of a day, many a year ago, when, standing at the door of her little house, she had seen approach a radiant vision, in riding-habit, curls and feathers. What a lovely creature Agnes had been! . . . how full of kindliness and charm! . . . and all to end in this: a poor little corpulent, shapeless, red-faced woman, close on fifty now, but with the timid uncertain bearing of a cowed child. Never should she have married Mr. Henry! With another man for a husband, everything might have turned out differently.

The first of a series of painful incidents occurred when, the cab having drawn up at the gate, the question of paying the driver's fare arose. In old days, the two of them would have had a playful quarrel over it, each disputing the privilege with the other. Now, Agnes only said: "If you will be so good, love? . . . my purse so hard to get at," in a tone that made Mary open her eyes. It soon came out that she had been shipped to Melbourne literally without a penny in her pocket. Wherever they went, Mary had to be purse-bearer, Agnes following meekly and shamelessly at her heels. An intolerable position for any man to put his wife in! It was true she had *carte blanche* at the big drapery stores; but all she bought—down to the last handkerchief—was entered on a bill for Mr. Henry's scrutiny. Did she wish to make a present—and she was just as generous as of old—she had so to contrive it (and she certainly showed a lamentable want of dignity, the skill of a practised hand, in arranging matters with the shopman) that, for instance, one entry on the bill should be a handsome mantle, which she never bought. The result was a sweet little ivory-handled parasol for "darling Mary"; a box of magnificent toys and books for the children, of whom she made much.

From her own she was completely divorced, both boy and girl having been put to boarding-school at a tender age. But Agnes was fond of children; and, of a morning, while Mary was shaking up beds or baking pastry, would sit on the balcony watching the three at play; occasionally running her fingers through the twins' fair curls, which were so like the goldilocks of the child she had lost.

She never referred to any of them; and had evidently long ago ceased to feel either grief or remorse at her baby's death. She just lived on, dully and stupidly, without pride, without shame—so long, that was, as she was not startled or made afraid. The company of the children held no alarms for her; but early in the visit Mary found it necessary to warn Richard: "Now whatever you do, dear, don't be short and snappy before her. It throws her into a perfect twitter."

And Richard, who, for all his violence of expression, would, she well knew, not have harmed a fly, was thereafter gentleness itself in Mrs. Henry's presence, attending to her wants at table, listening courteously to her few diffident opinions, till the little woman's eyes filled with tears, and she ceased to spill her tea or mess her front with her egg. "The doctor . . . so nice, love . . . so very, very kind!"

"She has evidently been bullied half out of her wits."

Throughout the fortnight she stayed with them, Mary was the faithfullest of guardians, putting her own concerns entirely on one side to dog her friend's footsteps. And yet, for all her vigilance, she could sometimes have sworn that Agnes's breath was tainted; while on the only two occasions on which she let her out of her sight . . . well! what happened then, made her look with more lenience than before on Mr. Henry's precautions. Once, Lucie had a touch of croup in the night and could not be left, so that Agnes must needs go alone to her dressmaker; and once came an invitation to a luncheon-party, in which Mary was not included. Each time, a wagonette was provided for Mrs. Henry from door to door, and paid to wait and bring her home; while Richard even condescended to give the driver a gentle hint and a substantial tip. And yet, both times, when she returned and tried to get out of the cab . . . oh, dear! there was nothing for it but to say, in a loud voice, for the servants' benefit: "I'm so sorry you don't feel well, dear. Lean on me!" to get the door of the spare room shut on her, and whip her into bed.

"Jus' like a *real* baby!" thought Cuffy, who had not forgotten the remark about the bottle. Running into the spare room in search of his mother, he had found Aunt Agnes sitting on the side of the bed, with only her chemise on and a very red face, while Mamma, looking funny, rummaged in a trunk. Going to bed in the daytime? Why? Had she been naughty? And was Mamma cross with her, too? She was with him. She said: "Go away at once!" and "Naughty boy!" before he was hardly inside. But Aunt Agnes was funny altogether. Cook and Eliza thought so, too. They laughed and whispered things he didn't ought to hear. But he did one. And that night at the supper-table, curiosity got the better of him and he asked out loud: "Where's Auntie Agnes too tight, Mamma?"

"Too tight? Now whatever do you mean by that?"

Mary's tone was jocosely belittling. But Cuffy was not deceived by it. Instinctively he recognised the fond pride that lurked beneath the depreciation—the amused interest in "what in all the world the child would say next!" He was also spurred on by the attention of the Dumplings, who, remembering sad affairs of too much cake and tight pinny-bands, sat eager and expectant, turning their eyes from Mamma to him and back again.

"Why, Eliza said . . . she said Auntie Agnes was tight—too tight."

Above his head the eyes of husband and wife met; and Mahony threw out his hands as if to imply: "There you have it!"

But Mamma was *drefully* angry. "How dare you repeat such a nasty, vulgar thing! I'm *ashamed* of you—you're a very naughty boy!"

Besides really "wanting to know," Cuffy had thought his question a funny one, which would call forth laughter and applause. He was dumbfounded, and went red to the roots of his hair. What had he said? Why was Mamma so cross? Why was it more wrong for Auntie Agnes to be tight than Lallie or Lucie?— And now he had made Mamma and Papa cross with each other again, too.

"It's not *repeating* kitchen talk that matters, Mary; but that the child should be in the way of hearing it at all."

704

"Pray, how can I help it? I do my best; but it's quite impossible for me never to let the children out of my sight. I've told you over and over again, what they need is a governess."

As the time approached for Mr. Henry's arrival, Agnes grew more and more ill at ease: her tic redoubled in violence; she could settle to nothing, and wandered aimlessly from room to room; while, on receipt of the letter fixing the day, she began openly to shake and tremble. "You won't mention to Henry, Mary . . . I mean . . . oh, love, you understand?" and all Mary's tactful assurances did not quieten her. Her fear of her husband was painful to see; almost equally painful her barefaced relief when, at the eleventh hour, important business cropped up which made it impossible for Mr. Henry to get away.

"Of course, if things have come to this pass between them, then it's much better they should be separated for a while. But that he can let *any* business interfere with seeing her off on so long a journey—well, all I can say is . . ." said Mary; and left the rest of her wrath to the imagination.

"Tut, tut! . . . when he's got some one here to do his dirty work for him. He probably never had any intention of being present."

So the two women drove to Sandridge, and boarded a sailing-vessel bound for the Cape. The best cabin amidships had been engaged for Agnes, and tastefully furnished. There were flowers in it, and several boxes of biscuits and oranges for the voyage. But Agnes did not so much as look round; she only cried and cried; and, when the time for parting came, threw her arms about Mary and clung to her as if she would never let go. It was, said Mary afterwards, just like seeing a doomed creature off for perdition.

"I don't believe she'll ever come back. Oh, it's a burning shame! Why *couldn't* he have put her in a Home?"

"My dear, that would publish his disgrace to the world. He has chosen the one polite and irreproachable way of getting rid of her . . . without a scandal."

"You mean she'll . . . ? But surely she won't be able to get it on board ship?"

"If you think that, Mary, you still know next to nothing of the tricks a tippler is up to!"— And how right he was, was

705

shewn when the cook, in turning out the spare room, came upon a regular nest of bottles—empty medicine bottles, the dregs of which bespoke their contents—tucked away inside the first bend of the chimney.

Mary wrote to Mr. Henry informing him of Agnes's departure; also that the visit had passed off *without contretemps:* and, shortly after, she received the gift of a photograph-album, bound in vellum, and stamped in gold with her initials. It was a handsome and costly present. But Mahony waxed bitterly sarcastic over the head of it.

"An album! . . . a photograph-album! . . . as sole return for the expense we've been put on—why, cab-hire alone must have run into pounds—over *his* wife, whom we did not invite and had no wish to see. Not to speak of the strain the visit has been on you, my dear."

"But Richard, you wouldn't have him send us money?—ask for our *bill!*" Mary spoke heatedly, to hide her own feelings, which were much the same as his. Richard singled out cab-fares; but these were but one item of many. In the course of a long day's shopping, Agnes and she had needed lunch and refreshment—manlike, he no doubt imagined them living on air!—and not infrequently Agnes had fancied some article in a shop where no account was run: none of which extras had been mentioned to him. The truth was, what with this, that and the other thing, Mary had been forced to make a sad hole in her savings.

"We certainly don't need Ocock's assistance in going down-hill," was Richard's parting shot.

It was true, a very hearty note accompanied the album; the pith of which was: "If at any time, my dear Mrs. Mahony, an opportunity to return your great kindness to my dear wife should arise, I trust you will let me hear of it."

[4]

TO-MORROW was the Dumplings' birthday, and they were having a big party. But it was his, Cuffy's party, too; for when he had first got six, they didn't have a house yet, and there was no room for a party. It was really *most* his, 'cos he was the oldest: his cake would be six stories high, and have six lighted candles round it, and his chair be trimmed with most green leaves. Mamma said he might cut the cake his very own self, and make the pieces big or little, just as he liked. She stopped in the kitchen all day, baking jam tarts and sausage-rolls, and men had taken the drawing-room carpet off, and sprinkled the floor with white dust, so's you could slide on it. All his cousins were coming, and Cousin Emmy, and lots and lots of other children. But it was not of these grandeurs Cuffy thought, as he sat on the edge of the verandah, and, for sheer agitation, rocked himself to and fro. The truth was, in spite of the glorious preparations, he felt anything but happy. Guiltily and surreptitiously he had paid at least a dozen visits to the outhouse at the bottom of the yard, to steal a peep inside. First, Mamma had said "soon," for the pony, and then "someday," and then his birthday: so to-morrow was his last hope. And this hope was growing littler and littler. If *only* he hadn't told! But he had, had whispered it in a secret to the Dumplings, and to that horrid tease, Cousin Josey, as well. And promised them rides, and let the twins draw lots, who should be first; and they'd guessed and guessed what colour it would be; all in a whisper so's Mamma shouldn't hear.

"*I* fink it'll be black," said Lallie; and Lucie nodded: "Me, too! An' wiv' a white tail."

"But I *know* it'll be brown!"

"He knows it'll be brown!" buzzed one fatty to the other.

"Huh! I wouldn't *have* a pony with a white tail."

But, peep as often as he might, no little horse appeared in the shed; and Cuffy went about with a strange, empty, sinking feeling inside him—a sense of having been tricked. Nor did the several handsome presents he found beside his bed make up to him for this bitter disappointment. He early kicked over a giraffe belonging to the giant Noah's Ark, and broke its neck; flew into a tantrum when rebuked; was obstreperous about being dressed, and snarly to his sisters; till Mary said, if he didn't behave, he'd go to bed instead. How he dreaded the display of the presents! Cousin Josey with her sneery laugh would be sure to blurt out in front of everybody: "He said he was going to get a pony! Ho! Where's your pony now?" The Dumplings were easier to deal with. In answer to their round-eyed wonder he just said, in airy fashion: "He says he can't come quite to-day. He didn't get born yet."

"Have you seed him?"

"Course I have!" Which left the twins more dazzled than would have done the animal's arrival.

But it proved a lively party. It lasted from three till past eleven, and the whole house, with the exception of the surgery, was turned upside down for it. Quite twenty children came, and nearly as many grown-ups. The drawing-room was stripped bare of its furniture, but for a line of chairs placed round the walls. Verandah and balcony were hung with Chinese lanterns, and dozens of coloured balloons. In the dining-room a long table, made up of several smaller tables put together, was laden with cakes and creams and jellies; and even the big people found the good things "simply delicious." And though, of course, Mary could not attempt to compete with some of the lavish entertainments here given for children—the Archie Whites had actually had a champagne supper for their five-year-old, the Boppins hired a *chef* from a caterer's—yet she had spared no pains to make her children's party unique in its way. And never for an instant did she allow the fun to flag. Even the quite little tots, who soon tired of games and dancing, were kept amused. For their benefit a padded see-saw had been set up on the verandah, as well as a safe nursery swing. On the stair-landings stood a bran pie and a lucky bag; while Emmy superintended the fishing for presents that went on, with rod and line, over the back of the drawing-room sofa.

In a pause between the games, Mary walked through the drawing-room, her black silk skirts trailing after her, the hands of the two of the smallest children in hers; one of them John's baby-boy, a bandy-legged mite, still hardly able to toddle. Mary was enjoying herself almost as much as the children; her cheeks were rose-pink with satisfaction; her eyes a-sparkle. At this moment, however, her objective was Cuffy, who, his black eyes not a whit less glittery than her own, his topknot all askew (he was really getting too big for a top-knot; but she found it hard to forgo the morning pleasure of winding the silky curl about her finger) Cuffy was utilizing the pause to skate up and down the slippery floor. He was in wild spirits: Cousin Josey had contented herself with making a hidjus face at him, and pinching him on the sly; the tidbit of the evening, the cutting of the cake, was still to come; and he had played his piece—"Home Sweet Home" "with runs"—which had earned him the usual crop of praise and applause. Now, there was no holding him.

"Cuffy! Cuffy *dear*, don't romp like that! You *must* behave, and set a good example to your visitors. Listen! I think I heard Papa. Run and tell him to slip on another coat, and come in and see the fun."

But Cuffy jerked his arm away: Mamma was not so easily forgiven. "Shan't! . . . don't want to!" and was off again like a flash.

"Tch! He's so excited.— Emmy, you go to your uncle; you can usually get round him. He really ought to put in an appearance. It will do him good, too . . . and amuse him."

Emmy hesitated. "Do you think so, Aunt Mary?"

"Why, of course."

"I'll take Baby, then. Perhaps Uncle will let me lay him down on his sofa. It's time he had a nap; he screams so at night, if he gets over-tired."

"You're wonderful with that child, Emmy," said Mary, watching the girl cuddle her little step-brother in her arms, where he curled up and shut his eyes, one little hand dangling limp and sleepy over her shoulder. "I'm sure Lizzie ought to be very grateful to you."

"I don't know what I'd do without him."

Emmy tapped at the surgery door. "May I come in?"

The blind was down; she could just make her uncle out, sitting hunched and relaxed in his armchair. He gave a violent start at her entrance, exclaiming: "Yes, yes? What is it?— Oh, you Emmy! Come in, my dear, come in. I think I must have dropped off." And passing a fumbly hand over his forehead, he crossed to the window and drew up the blind.

What! with all that noise? thought Emmy wonderingly. Aloud she said: "May I stay here a little with Jacky? I want him to have a nap."

"Surely." And Mahony cleared the end of the sofa that she might find a place with her burden. "And how is the little man to-day?"

"Oh, doing finely! He has hardly been afraid of anything this afternoon."

"We must examine him again," said Mahony kindly, laying

709

a finger on the child's sweat-damp hair, and noting the nervous pucker of the little brows.

There was a pause, Emmy gazing at her nursling, Mahony at her. Then: "How vividly you do remind me of your mother, my dear! The first time I ever saw her—she could have been little older than you are now—she held you on her lap . . . just as you hold Jacky."

"Did she?" Emmy played meditatively with a tassel on the child's shoe. "People are always saying that . . . that I'm like her. And sometimes, Uncle, I think it would be nicer just to be like oneself. Instead of a kind of copy."

To no one else would she have confided so heretical a sentiment. But Uncle Richard always understood.

And sure enough: "I can see your point, Emmy," said he. "You think: to a new soul, why not a brand-new covering? All the same, child, do not begrudge a poor wraith its sole chance of cheating oblivion."

"I only mean——"

"I can assure you, you've nothing to fear from the comparison, nothing at all!" And Mahony patted his niece's hand, looking fondly at her in her white, flounced tarlatan, a narrow blue ribbon round her narrow waist, a wreath of forget-me-nots in her ripe-corn hair. There was no danger to Emmy in letting her know what you thought of her, so free from vanity was she. Just a good, sweet, simple creature

But, now, the girl bethought herself of her errand. "Oh yes, Aunt Mary sent me to tell you . . . I mean she thought, Uncle, you might like to come and see what fun the children are having."

On the instant Mahony lost his warmth. "No, no. I'm not in the mood."

"Uncle, the Murdochs and the Archie Whites are here . . . people who'd very much like to see you," Emmy gently transposed Mary's words.

"Entirely your aunt's imagination, child! In reality, she knows as well as I do that it's not so. In the course of a fairly long life, my dear, I have always been able to count on the fingers of one hand, those people—my patients excepted, of course—who have cared a straw whether I was alive or dead. No, Emmy. The plain truth is: my fellow-men have little use for me—or I for them."

"Oh, Uncle . . ." Emmy was confused, and showed it. Talk of this kind made her feel very shy. She could not think of anything to say in response: how to refute ideas which she was sure were not true. Positively sure. For they opened up abysses into which, young girl-like, she was afraid to peer. An awkward pause ensued before she asked timidly: "Do you feel very tired to-night?"

"To the depths of my soul, child!" Then, fearing lest he had startled her with his violence, he added: "I've had—and still have—great worries, my dear . . . business worries."

"Is it the practice, Uncle? Doesn't it do well?"

"That, too. But I have made a sad fool of myself, Emmy—a sad fool! And now here I sit, seeking in vain to repair the mischief."

Alone again, he let himself fall back into the limp attitude in which she had surprised him. It was well-being to sit there, every muscle relaxed. He came home from tramping the streets dog-tired, and all of a sweat: as drained of strength as a squeezed lemon.

No one else appeared to disturb him. Emmy, bless her! had done her work well, and Mary might now reasonably be expected to leave him in peace. Let them jig and dance to the top of their bent, provided he was not asked to join in. He washed his hands of the whole affair. From the outset, the elaborate preparations for this party had put his back up. It was not that he wanted to act the wet-blanket on his children's enjoyment. But the way Mary went about things stood in absolutely no relation to his shrunken income She was striving to keep pace with people who could reckon theirs by the thousand. It was absurd. Of course, she had grown so used, in the latter years, to spending royally, that it was hard for her own to trim her sails. Just, too, when the bairns were coming to an age to appreciate the good things of life. And, again, reason nudged him with the reminder that any ultra-extravagance on her part was due, in the first place, to her ignorance of his embarrassments. He had not enlightened her . . . he never would. He felt more and more incapable of standing up to her incredulous dismay. In cold blood, it seemed impossible to face her with the tidings: "The house we live in is not our own. I have run myself—run you and the children, too—into debt—to the tune of hundreds of pounds!" At the mere thought

711

of it, he might have been a boy again, standing before his mother, and shaking in his shoes over the confession of some youthful peccadillo. A still further incentive to silence was the queer way his gall rose at the idea of interference. That, he could not endure! And it went beyond him to imagine Mary *not* interfering. If he knew her, she would at once want to take the reins: to manage him and his affairs as she managed house and children.— And to what was left of his freedom he clung as if his life depended on it.

Excuse enough for meddling she would have; he had regularly played into her hands. Had he only never built this accursed house! It, and it alone, was the root of all the trouble. Had he contented himself with a modest weatherboard, they might not have been led to entertain beyond their means—for the very good reason that she would not have had room for it—and he have enjoyed the fruits of a quiet mind. Instead of which, for the pleasure of sitting twirling his thumbs in a bleak and barren magnificence, he had condemned himself to one of the subtlest forms of torture invented by man: that of being under constraint to get together, by given dates, fixed sums of money. The past three months had been a nightmare. Twenty times a day he had asked himself: shall I be able to do it? And when, by the skin of his teeth, he had contrived to foot his bill and breathe more freely, behold! the next term was at the door, and the struggle had all to begin anew. And so it would go on, month after month; round and round in the same vicious circle. Or with, for sole variety, a steadily growing embarrassment. As it was, he could see the day coming when he would be able to pay no more than the bare interest on the loan. And the humiliation this spelt for him, only he knew. For, on taking up the mortgage, he had airily intimated that he intended, *for a start,* making quarterly re-payments of fifty pounds; while later on . . . well, only God knew what hints he had dropped for later on: his mind had been in haste to forget them. Did he now fall into arrears, his ignominious financial situation would be known to every one, and he a marked man.

Who could have thought this place would turn out so poorly? —become a jogtrot little suburban affair, that just held together, and no more! Such an experience was something new to him, and intolerable. In earlier days, it was always he who had given up his practices, not they him. He had abandoned them, one after the other, no matter how well they were doing. Here, the pages of his case-book remained but scantly filled. A preternaturally healthy neighbourhood! Or was that just a polite fiction of his own making? More than once, recently, it had flashed through his mind that, since putting up his plate, he had treated none but the simplest cases. Only the A B C of doctoring had been required of him. The fact was, specialists were all too easy to get at. But no! that wouldn't hold water either. Was it not rather he himself who, at first hint of a complication, was ready to refer a patient? . . . to shirk undue worry and responsibility? Yes, this was his own share in the failure; this, and the fact that his heart was not in the work. But, indeed, how should it be? When he recalled the relief with which, the moment he was able, he had forsaken medicine . . . where *could* the joy come in over taking it up again, an older, tireder man, and, as it were, at the point of the sword? And with the heart went the will, the inclination. Eaten up by money-troubles, he had but faint interest to spare for the physicking of petty ailments. Under the crushing dread lest he should find himself unable to pay his way, he had grown numb to all else. Numb . . . cold . . . indifferent.

What did *not* leave him cold, but, on the contrary, whipped him to a fury of impatience and aversion, was the thought of going on as he was: of continuing to sit, day after day, as it were nailed to the spot, while his brain, the only live part of him, burnt itself out in maddening anxieties and regrets. Oh, fool that he had been! . . . fool and blind. To have known himself so ill! *Never* was he the man to have got himself into this pitiable tangle . . . with its continual menace of humiliation . . . disgrace. What madness had possessed him? Even in his younger days, when life still seemed worth the pother, he had avoided debt like the plague. And to ask himself now, as an old man, and one grown weary of effort, to stand the imposition of so intolerable a strain, was nothing short of suicidal. Another half-year like the last, and he would not be answerable for himself.

He began to toy with the idea of flight. And over the mere imagining of a possible escape from his torments, he seemed to wake to life again, to throw off the deadly lethargy that paralysed him. Change . . . movement . . . action: this it was he panted after! It was the sitting inactive, harried by mur-

713

derous thoughts over which he had lost the mastery, that was killing him. If once he was rid of these, all might again be well.— And now insidious fancies stole upon him: fancies which, disregarding such accidents of the day as money and the lack of money, went straight to the heart of his most urgent need. To go away—go far away—from everything and every one he had known; so that what happened should happen to him only—be nobody's business but his own! Away from the crowd of familiar faces, these cunning, spying faces, *which knew all,* and which Mary could yet not persuade herself to forbid the house. Somewhere, where she would be out of reach of the temptations that here beset her, and he free to exist in the decent poverty that was now his true walk in life. Oh, for privacy! privacy and seclusion . . . and freedom from tongues. To be once more a stranger among strangers, and never see a face he knew again!

He had not yet found courage, however, for the pitched battle he foresaw, when something happened that fairly took his breath away. As it were overnight, he found himself the possessor of close on two hundred and fifty pounds. Among the scrip he still held were some shares called "Pitman's," which, until now, had been good for nothing but to make calls. Now, they took a sudden upward bound, and, at a timely hint from a grateful patient, who was in the swim, Mahony did a little shuffle—selling, buying, and promptly re-selling—with this result. True, a second venture, unaided, robbed him of the odd fifty. None the less, there he stood, with his next quarter's payments in his hand. He felt more amazed than anything else by this windfall. It certainly did not set his mind at rest; it came too late for that. Try as he would, he could not now face the idea of remaining at Hawthorn. He had dwelt too much, by this time, on the thought of change; taken too fixed an aversion to this room where he had spent so many black hours; to the house, the practice, the neighbourhood. Something within him, which would not be silenced, never ceased to urge: free yourself! . . . escape—while there is still time.

In these days Mary just sighed and shrugged her shoulders. Richard had hardly a word even for the children: on entering the house he retired at once to the surgery, and shut himself in. What he did there, goodness only knew. But it was not possible nowadays for her to sit and worry over him, or to take his moods as seriously as she would once have done. And any passing suspicion of something being more than ordinarily amiss was apt, even as it crossed her mind, to be overlaid by, say, the size of the baker's bill, or the fact that Cuffy had again outgrown his boots.— But she had also a further reason for turning a blind eye. Believing, as she truly did, that Richard's moroseness sprang mainly from pique at having to take up work again, she was not going to risk making matters worse by talking about them. Richard was as suggestible as a child. A word from her might stir up some fresh grievance, the existence of which he had so far not imagined.— But, when the crash came, it seemed as if a part of her had all along known and feared the worst.

None the less, it was a shattering blow: one of those that left you feeling ten years older than the moment before. And in the scene that followed his blunt announcement, and lasted far into the night, she strove with him as she had never yet striven, labouring to break down his determination, to bring him back to sanity. For more, much more than themselves and their own prosperity was now at stake. What happened to them happened equally to the three small creatures they had brought into the world.

"It's the children, Richard! Now they're there, you haven't the *right* to throw up a fixed position, as the fancy takes you . . . as you used to do. It didn't matter about me. But it's different now—everything's different. *Only* have patience! Oh! I can't believe you really mean it. It seems incredible . . . impossible!"

Mahony was indignant. "Pray, do you think no one considers the children but you? When their welfare is more to me than anything on earth?"

"But, if that's true, how can you even *think* of giving up this place? . . . the house—our comfortable home! You know quite well you're not a young man any more. The openings would be so few. You'd never get a place to suit you better."

"I tell you I *cannot* stop here!"

"But why? Give me a single convincing reason.— As to the idea of going up-country . . . that's madness pure and simple! How often did you vow you'd never again take a country practice, because of the distances . . . and the work? How will you be able to stand it now? . . . when you're getting on for fifty. You say there's nothing doing here; but, my opinion is, there's just as much as you're able for."

This was so exactly Mahony's own belief that he grew violently angry. "Good God, woman! is there no sympathy in you? . . . or only where your children are concerned? I tell you, if I stop here, I shall end by going demented!"

"I never heard such talk! The practice may be slow to move —I think a town-practice always would be—but it'll come right, I'm sure it will, if you'll *only* give it the chance!" Here, however, another thought struck her. "But what I don't understand is, *why* we're not able to get on. What becomes of the money you make? There must be something very wrong, somewhere. Hand over the accounts to me; let me look into your books. With no rent to pay, and three or four hundred coming in . . . besides the dividends . . . oh, would anyone else —anyone but you—want to throw up a certainty, and drag us off up-country, just when the children are getting big and need decent companions . . . and schooling—what about their education, pray?—have you thought of that? . . . or thought of anything but yourself, and your own likes and dislikes?" And as he did not reply, but maintained a stony silence, she broke out: "I think men are the most impossible creatures God ever made!" and pressing her face into the pillow, burst into tears.

Mahony set his teeth. If she could not see for herself that it was a case, for once, of putting him and his needs first, then he could not help her. To confide in her still went beyond him. Mary had such a heavy hand. He could hope for no tenderness of approach; no instinctive understanding meeting him half-way. She would pounce on his most intimate thoughts and feelings, drag them out into daylight and anatomise them; would put into words those phantom fears, and insidious evasions, which he had so far managed to keep in the twilight where they belonged.— He shuddered at the thought.

But Mary had not finished. Drying her eyes, she returned to the charge. "You say this place is a failure. I deny it, and always shall. But if it hasn't done as well as it might, there's a reason for it. It's because you haven't the way with you any longer. You've lost your manner—the good, doctor's manner you used to do so much with. You're too short with people nowadays; and they resent it, and go to some one who's pleas-

anter. I heard you just the other day with that lawyer's wife
who called . . . how you blew her up! *She'll* never come again!—
A morbid hypochondriac? I daresay. But in old days you'd
never have told a patient to her face that she was either sham-
ming or imagining."

"I'm too old to cozen and pander."

"Too old to care, you mean!— Oh, for God's sake, think
what you're doing! Try to stop on here a little longer, and if
it's only for six months. Listen! I've got an idea." She raised
herself on her elbow. "Why shouldn't we take in boarders? . . .
just to tide us over, till things get easier. This house is really
much too big for us. One nursery would be enough for the
children; and there's the spare room, and the breakfast-room.
. . . I could probably fill all three; and make enough that way
to cover our living expenses."

"Boarders? . . . *you?* Not while *I'm* above the sod!"—

The children wilted . . . oh, it was a dreadful week! Papa
never spoke, and slammed the doors and the gate whenever
he went out. Mamma sat in the bedroom and cried, hastily
blowing her nose and pretending she wasn't, if you happened
to look in. And Cook and Eliza made funny faces, and whispered behind their hands. Cuffy, mooning about the house
pale and dejected, was—as usual when Mamma and Papa
quarrelled—harassed by the feeling that, somehow or other, he
was the guilty person. He tried cosseting Mamma, hanging
round her: he tried talking big to the Dumplings, of what he
meant to do when he was a man; he even glanced at the idea
of running away. But none of these things lightened the weight
that lay on his chest. It felt just as it had done the night Lucie
had the croup and crowed like a cock.

And then, one afternoon, Mahony came home transfigured;
and all was changed. His very step, as it crunched the gravel,
told its own tale. He ran up the stairs two at a time, calling
for Mary; and, the door of the bedroom shut on them, broke
at once into excited talk. It appeared that, in a chance meeting
that day with a fellow-medico ("Pincock, that well-known
Richmond man!") he had heard of what seemed to him "an
opening in a thousand": a flourishing practice, to be had for
the asking, at a place called Barambogie in the Ovens District.

"A rising township, my dear, half mining, half agricultural
and where there has never been but one doctor. He's an old

717

friend of Pincock's, and is giving up—after ten years in the place—for purely personal reasons . . nothing to do with the practice. It arose through Pincock asking me if I knew of any one who would like to step into a really good thing. This Rummel wants to retire, but will wait on of course till he hears of a successor. Nor is he selling. Whoever goes there has only to walk in and settle down. Such a chance won't come my way again. I should be mad to let it slip."

This news rang the knell of any hopes Mary might still have nursed of bringing him to his senses. She eyed him sombrely as he stood before her, pale with excitement; and such a wave of bitterness ran through her that she quickly looked away again, unable to find any but bitter words to say. In this glance, how-ever, she had for once really seen him—had not just looked, without seeing, after the habit of those who spend their lives together—and the result was the amazed reflection: "But he's got the eyes of a child! . . . for all his wrinkles and grey hairs."

Mahony did not notice her silence. He continued to dilate on what *he* had said and the other had replied, till, in alarm, she burst out: "I hope to goodness you've not committed your-self in any way? . . . all in the dark as you are!"

"Come, come now, my dear!" he half cozened, half fell foul of her. "Give me credit for at least a ha'p'orth of sense! You surely don't imagine I showed Pincock my cards? I flatter my-self I was thoroughly off-hand with him . . . so much so, indeed, that before night he'll no doubt have cracked the place up to half a dozen others.— Come, Mary, come! I'm not quite the fool you imagine. Nor do I mean to be unreasonable. But I confess, my inclination is just to slip off, and see the place, and make a few confidential inquiries. There can surely be nothing against that—can there?"

There could not. Two days later, he took the early morning train to the north.

[5]

1

The Sun Hotel, Barambogie

My own dear Wife,

I hope you got my note announcing my safe arrival. I could not write more; the train was late and I tired out. The journey took eight hours and was most fatiguing It turned into an oppressively hot day. About noon, a north wind came up, with its usual effect on me of headache and lassitude. The carriage was like a baking-oven. As for the dust, I've never seen its equal. Ballarat in summer was nothing to it. It rose in whirl-winds, to the tops of the gums. We were simply smothered.— But what a country this of ours is for size! You have only to get away from the sea-board, and travel across it as I did, to be staggered by its vastness.— And emptiness. Mile after mile of bush, without the trace of a settlement. The railway stations mere bark sheds; the townships, when we could see them for dust, very small and mean. Of course, everything looks its worst, just now. There have been no rains here yet, and they are sadly needed. Grass burnt to a cinder, creeks bone-dry, and so on.— However, as it was all quite new to me, I found plenty to interest me. The landscape, too, improved as we got further north, grew hillier and more wooded; and beyond Benalla we had a fine view of the high ranges.

So much for the journey. As I mentioned, Rummel met me at the station, walked to the hotel with me, and stopped for a chat. He is a most affable fellow, well under forty I should say, tall and handsome, and quite the gentleman—I shall find considerable difficulty in coming after him. I was too tired that night to get much idea of the place, but now that I have had a couple of days to look about me, I can honestly say I am delighted with it. To begin with, I am most comfortably lodged; my bed is good, the table plentiful, landlady very attentive. It is a larger and more substantial township than those we passed on the way up; the houses are mostly of brick—for coolness in summer—and all have luxuriant gardens. There is a very pretty little lake, or lagoon, as they call it here, skirted by trees and pleasant paths; and we are surrounded by wooded ranges. Vineyards cover the plains.

As to the information I had from Pincock, it was rather under than above the mark. Barambogie is undoubtedly a rising place. For one thing, there's a great mine in the neighbourhood, that has only been partially worked. This is now about to be reorganised: and when started, will employ no fewer than a hundred and fifty men. Every one is sanguine of its paying.— I was out and about all yesterday, and again this morning, introducing myself to people. I have met with the

719

greatest courtesy and civility—the Bank Manager went so far as to say I should be a real acquisition. I think I can read between the lines that some will not be displeased to see the last of Rummel. He is by no means the universal favourite I should have imagined. Between ourselves, I fancy he takes a drop too much. He is still seeing patients, but intends leaving in a couple of days. The chemist says I shall have no difficulty in doing eight hundred to a thousand per annum. And Rummel himself told me he has had as many as a hundred midwifery cases in a year. There are three or four nice families, so you, my dear, will not be entirely cut off from society. It is said to be a splendid winter climate. Even now, in late autumn, we have clear blue skies, and bracing winds from the south. And we should certainly save. No one here keeps more than one servant, and grand entertainments are unknown. No clubs either, thank God! You know what a drawback they . . . or rather the lack of them has been to me at Hawthorn. They're all very well if you hold them yourself, but play the dickens with a practice if you don't. I should only be too glad to settle in a place where they're non-existent.

The difficulty is going to be to find a house. There are only two vacant in all Barambogie. One of these is in poor repair, and the owner—the leading draper—declines to do anything to it. Besides, he wants a rental of eighty pounds p.a., on a four years' lease—which, of course, puts it out of the question. The other is so small that none of our furniture would go into it. But where there's a will there's a way; and I have got an idea—and I think a brilliant one. There's a fine old Oddfellows' Hall here, which is in disuse and up for auction. It's of brick —looks like a chapel—and is sixty feet long by twenty broad. Well, my plan is, to buy this, and convert it into a dwelling-house. The body of the hall will give us six splendid rooms, with a passage down the middle, and we can add kitchen, scullery, outhouses, etc. I would also throw out a verandah. There's a fair piece of land, which we could turn into a garden. The alterations will be easy to make, and not cost much; and there we are with out and away the best house in the place!— I fear, though, even under the most favourable circumstances, we shall not be able to use all our furniture here. I haven't yet seen a room that would hold your wardrobe, or the dining-room sideboard.

If I decide to stay, I shall lose no time in consulting a builder. You for your part must at once see an agent, and put the Hawthorn house in his hands. I feel sure we shall have no difficulty in letting it.

And now I must bring this long scrawl—it has been written at various odd moments—to a close. I have appointed to see Rummel again this afternoon, to have another parley with him. Not that I shall definitely fix on anything, though, till I hear from you. From now on, I intend to take your advice. But I do trust that what I have told you will prove to you that this is no wildgoose-chase, but the very opening of which I am in search. It distresses me more than I can say, when you and I do not see eye to eye with each other.— Now take good care of your dear self, and kiss the chicks for me. Forgive me, too, all my irritability and bad temper of the past six months. I have had a very great deal to worry me—far more than you knew, or than I wanted you to know. It is enough for one of us to bear the burden. But this will pass and everything be as of old, if I can once see the prospect of earning a decent income again. Which I am perfectly sure I shall do here.

Your own

R.T.M.

2

The Sun Hotel, Barambogie

My dear Mary,

I must say you are the reverse of encouraging. Your letter threw me into such a fit of low spirits that I could not bring myself to answer it till to-day. It's bad enough being all alone, with never a soul to speak to, without you pouring cold water on everything I suggest. Of course, as you are so down on my scheme of rebuilding the Oddfellows' Hall, I will let this unique opportunity for a bargain slip, and dismiss the idea from my mind. Perhaps, though, you will tell me what we are to do— with not another house in the place vacant—or at least nothing big enough to swing a cat in. As you are so scathing about my poor plans, you had better evolve some of your own.

I had the news about the mine on reliable authority; it was not, as you try to make out, a mere wild rumour. Nor is what I said about people being glad to get rid of Rummel, a product of my own imagination. I received more than one plaint to that effect, in the course of my visits.

However, since I wrote last, I have begun to doubt the wisdom of settling here. It's not the house-question alone. I've seen Greatorex, the draper, again, and he has so far come around as to agree to re-floor the verandah and whitewash the rooms; if I take the house on his terms. I repeat once more, it is the best house in Barambogie. Six large rooms, all necessary outhouses, a shed fitted with a shower-bath, and a fine garden —we might indeed consider ourselves lucky to get it. Rummel lives in a regular hovel; the parson in a four-roomed hut with not a foot of ground to it, nor any verandah to keep off the sun. Greatorex's is a palace in comparison. Of course, though, as you express yourself so strongly against the four-years' lease, I shall give up all idea of coming to an agreement with him.

Besides, as I said above, I have practically decided not to remain. Your letter is chiefly responsible for this. I can see you have made up your mind, beforehand, not to like the place. And if you were unhappy, I should be wretched, too, and reproach myself for having dragged you and the children into so outlandish an exile. I quite agree, it would be hard work for you with but a single servant; but I can assure you, we should be eyed askance, if we tried to keep more. In a place like this, where there is only one standard of living, it would render us most unpopular. But even should you change your mind, my advice would be, not to come for at least three months. By that time, I should know better how the practice was shaping. Of course, things may look brighter for me when Rummel goes, and I begin to get something to do. I've been here nearly a fortnight now, and he shews no more signs of leaving than at first. He is still attending patients; the people run after him in the streets. He has been extraordinarily popular; as it is not to be wondered at, with his good looks and ingratiating manners. Only a few trifling cases have come my way. It is very disheartening. To add to this, I have been feeling anything but well. The change of water has upset me. Then, my bedroom is dark and airless; and the noise in the hotel is enough to drive one crazy. It goes on till long past midnight, and begins again before six.

Another thing that worries me is the fact that I should be alone of the profession here, if I stayed. I daresay I should get used to it in time; but just now, in my poor state, it would be an additional strain, never to have a second opinion to fall back on.— I don't need you to tell me, my dear, that a hundred confinements in the year would be stiff work. But they would also mean a princely income.— However, I have no intention of dragging you here against your will: and shall now cast about for something else. I heard to-day of a place called Turramungi, where there is only one doctor, and he a bit of a duffer. I will go over by coach one morning, and see how the land lies.

But do try and write more cheerfully. I am sure you have no need to be so depressed—in our pleasant home, and with the children to bear you company. I am sorry to hear you have heard of no likely tenants. We ought to get a rent of at least two hundred, without taxes. As I said before, your wardrobe and the sideboard will have to be sold. Perhaps the incoming tenant will take them.

The flies are very troublesome to-day. I have constantly to flap my handkerchief while I write.

Shall hope to send you better news of myself next time.

R.T.M.

3

The Sun Hotel, Barambogie

My dear Wife,

A line in great haste. I have just seen an advertisement in the "Argus," calling for applications for medical officer to the Boorandoora Lodge, and have made up my mind to apply. I have written off posthaste for further particulars, in order to get my application in before Friday. After spending close on three weeks here, I have decided once and for all that it would be infinitely more satisfactory to make an extra couple of hundred a year at Hawthorn, with our fine house behind us, than to bury ourselves in this wild bush. A third Lodge would give a tremendous fillip to the practice. And the more I see of this place, the less I like it.

Of course, my application may not be considered. Lambert, who had the Boorandoora last, held it at twenty-one shillings a head, and found medicine. I mean to tender seventeen-and-six, without physic. Graves, I know, won't look at them under

723

twenty. So I think I ought to stand a very good chance. Don't take any further steps about the house in the meanwhile.

Since I wrote last, I have had a little more to do. I was called out several miles yesterday. And the people I went to told me that if I had not been here, they would have sent for the man at Turramungi. So you see Rummel is not persona grata everywhere. He is still about, and as much in my way as ever; for, as long as he is on the spot, people won't consult anyone else. I wish to God I had not been in such a hurry to come. However, one thing makes me more hopeful: the date of his auction is fixed at last, for Monday next.

                                        In haste
                                        Your own
                                        R.T.M.

4

                              The Sun Hotel, Barambogie

My darling Mary,

So you approve, do you, of my idea of putting in for the Boorandoora? I got the information I wanted from the Secretary of the lodge; and if I resolve to offer my services, shall do so for the sum I named. It is all very well, my dear, to talk about it being beneath my dignity to underbid others, and to ask how I myself should once have characterised such a proceeding. (Personally, I think you might keep remarks of this kind to yourself.) What I do is done wholly for your sake. If I could get this third lodge, it might save you having to turn out and part with your furniture; and to make that possible, I am ready to sacrifice my professional pride. There are so many others, younger men than I, who are only too ready to step in. And I look on it as my sole remaining chance to earn a decent livelihood within reach of civilisation.

However, I must confess, I have again become somewhat undecided. The fact is, Rummel has gone at last: and he gave me his word, on leaving, that he would never come back. The auction took place as arranged; house and ground selling for a hundred and ninety pounds. Since he went, I have been genuinely busy. The parson is ill with inflammation of the liver; and I was called out yesterday a distance of five miles. The hire of a buggy costs seven-and-six—less than half, you see, what I had to pay in Hawthorn. This afternoon I go by train to Mirrawarra, and shall walk back. It becomes daily more evident to me that there is a very fine practice to be done here. And every one I meet implores me to stay. Some, indeed, grow quite plaintive at the idea of losing me.

I have also had a pleasant surprise about the house. Greatorex now says he is willing to let for three years instead of four, if I pay the first year's rent in advance. This seems to me an extremely fair offer. You see it would only be like paying a small sum down for the practice. I am going over the house with him again to-morrow, and will then let you know what I decide. The point at issue is, should I not do better to accept this certain opening, with all its drawbacks, than take the uncertain chance of Hawthorn with a third lodge . . . if I get it!

Your very own
R.T.M.

5

The Sun Hotel, Barambogie

My own dear Wife,

Well! the die is cast; I have finally made up my mind to remain in Barambogie. I did not put in for the lodge after all, but resolved to give this place a further ten days' trial. And well that I did! For the practice has looked up with a vengeance: it is now as plain as a pikestaff that I have capital prospects here, and should be a fool indeed to let them slide. If I had not popped in when I did, there would certainly have been others—and, for that matter, I am still not quite sure there may not be another settling. In the meantime, I am seeing fresh patients daily, and have not had my clothes off for the past two nights. The day before yesterday I was called ten miles out to attend a case which Guthrie of Coora has neglected: and I have been bespoken for three future events. This morning I drove seven miles into the bush: for which I shall charge five guineas. In the month I have been here—ten days without Rummel—I have taken fifteen pounds, and booked close on fifty. What do you think of that? I feel quite sure I shall easily touch a thousand a year. Of course, it will mean hard work, but the mere prospect of such a thing keys me up.

It was the doing nothing at Hawthorn that preyed so on my mind. If only I can earn a good income, and provide for you and the darlings in the style to which you are accustomed, I shall be a happy man once more!

The people here are overjoyed at the prospect of keeping me. They continue to declare I cannot fail to succeed. Everybody is most civil, and all invite me to drink with them. I have considerable difficulty in making them understand that I do not go in for that kind of thing. It sometimes needs a good deal of tact to put them off without giving offence: but so far I have managed pretty well. From all I now hear, Rummel must have been a seasoned drinker—a regular toper. I saw the Bank Manager to-day. He was very queer. Had evidently been taking nobblers. He has been in charge of the Bank here for over twenty years, and thinks there is no place like Barambogie. Vows I shall make my fortune.

Greatorex promises to set about the repairs without delay. My private opinion is, he's in high feather at securing such good and careful tenants. I went over the house with him again yesterday. The rooms are not quite as large as I thought— I will send you the exact measurements in a day or two—but all have French windows and are fitted with venetian blinds. The garden is well stocked with fruit, flowers, and vegetables. I shall keep a man to look after it. I think you had better try and induce one of the servants from home to accompany you. Perhaps Eliza would come; as the children are used to her. Here, there is little or nothing in that line to be had. Slipshod dollops demand ten shillings a week. The parson keeps none; has no room for any.

Archdeacon Coote of Taralga called on me yesterday, and made quite a fuss over me. I have also been introduced to the wife of one of the leading squatters. Like every one else, she says it will be a red-letter day for the place if we come, and looks eagerly forward to making your acquaintance.

Now, if only we can let the house! The mere possibility of this, and of our being all together once more, makes me wildly happy. Tell the chicks there is a splendid summerhouse in the new garden, and I will see to it that a swing is put up for them. They shall have everything they want here.

Your own old husband,

Richard Townshend Mahony

726

6

The Sun Hotel, Barambogie

My dear Mary,

I am sorry you write in such low spirits. I agree with you, it is most unfortunate that we are obliged to break up our home; but it was blackest folly on my part ever to build that house, and now I am punished for it. I cannot say how deeply I regret having to ask you and the little ones to put up with bush life; and you may rest assured I should not do so, if I saw any other way out. But it is this or nothing.

It doesn't mend matters to have you carping at the class of person we shall need to associate with. For goodness' sake, don't go putting ideas of that kind into the children's heads! We are all God's creatures; and the sooner we shake off the incubus of a false and snobbish pride, the better it will be for us. There are good and worthy people to be found in every walk of life.

You are utterly wrong in your suspicions that I am letting myself be flattered and bamboozled into staying. But there! . . . you never do think any one but yourself has a particle of judgment.

No, there's nothing in the way of a school—except, of course, the State School. You had better find out what a governess would cost. About the house, I am afraid it is really not very much bigger than our first cottage in Webster St.—the wooden one—before we made those additions to it. I enclose the measurements of the rooms. You will see that the drawing-room and chief bedroom are the same size—12 by 13—the others somewhat smaller. It will be as well to sell the pierglass and the drawing-room chiffonier. And it's no good bringing the dining-room table, or the big sofa . . . or the tall glass book-case. Or the three large wardrobes, either; they wouldn't go in at the doors. But do try and not fret too much over sacrificing these things. A few years here, and you will be able to replace them; and then we will pitch our tent somewhere more to your liking.

I reckon the move will cost us about a hundred pounds.

I am still busy. Barambogie is anything but the dead-and-alive hole you imagine. No less than six coaches a day draw up at this hotel. The weather continues fine. I have a good appetite: it suits me to be so much in the open air, instead of cooped up in that dull surgery. I wish I slept better, though. The noise in the hotel continues unabated. I have the utmost difficulty in getting to sleep, or in remaining asleep when I do. The least sound disturbs me—and then I am instantly wide awake.— The other night, though, I had a very different experience. Something very queer happened to me. I dropped off towards three, and had been asleep for about an hour—fast asleep—when some noise or other, I don't know what, wakened me with a terrific start . . . one of those fearful jerks awake which the nightbell used to give me, you remember. Except that, in those days, I was all there in an instant. Here, I couldn't for the life of me come back, and went through a few most awful seconds, absolutely incapable of recollection. There I sat, bolt upright, my heart beating like a sledge-hammer, powerless to remember who I was, where I was, and what I was doing. My brain seemed like an empty shell . . . or a watch with all the works gone out of it. Or if you can imagine a kind of mental suffocation, a horrid struggle for breath on the part of the brain. And when, by sheer force of will, I had succeeded in fighting back to a consciousness of my personal identity, I still could not locate myself, but imagined I was at home, and fumbled for the matches on the wrong side of the bed! It was most unpleasant—a real dissociation for the time being—and I did not sleep again, dreading a return. I think it came from worry—I have been much upset. Your letter . . . and all you said in it . . . your grief and disappointment. Add to this, that I had no proper rest the night before, having been up with a patient till three. I shall be more careful in future.

My love to the darlings,

Your own

R.T.M.

[6]

IT WAS nearing eleven and a chilly, cloudy night, when the little party, flanked by Eliza, alighted on the platform at Barambogie, where for nearly an hour Mahony had paced to and fro. They were the only passengers to leave the train; which straightway puffed off again; and since the man hired by Mahony to transport the baggage was late in arriving, there was nothing for it but to wait till he came. The stationmaster, having lingered for a time, turned out the solitary lamp and departed; and there they stood, a forlorn little group, round a tumulus of luggage. It was pitch dark: not a single homely light shone out, to tell of a human settlement; not the faintest sound broke the silence. To Mary, it seemed as if they had been dumped down in the very heart of nowhere.

But now came the man wheeling a truck; and straightway a wordy dispute broke out between him and Richard, in which she had to act as peacemaker. Boxes and portmanteaux were loaded up; carpet-bags, baskets, bundles counted and arranged: all by the light of a lantern. Richard, agog with excitement, had to be kept from waking the twins, who had dropped asleep again on top of the trunks. And all the while an overtired and captious Cuffy plucked at her sleeve. "Is this the bush, Mamma? . . . is *this* the bush? *Where?* I don't see it!"

The little procession started, headed by the man with truck and lantern, the Dumplings riding one in Richard's arms, one in Eliza's, Mary and Cuffy bringing up the rear. Leaving the station behind them, they walked on till they came to a broad road, flour-soft to the feet, Cuffy kicking and shuffling up the dust to the peevish whine of: "What *sort* of a bush, Mamma?" and passed in single file down a long narrow right-of-way, between two paling fences.

On emerging, they faced something flat and black and mysterious. Mary started. "Whatever's that?"

"The Lagoon, my dear, the Lagoon! The house fronts it, you know. Has the best outlook of any in the town."

(For the children to fall into! . . . *and* mosquitoes!)

Long after every one else was asleep Mary lay and listened . . . and listened. It was years since she had lived anywhere but in a town; and this house seemed so lonely, so open to intruders. The leaves rustling in the garden, each fresh flap of the venetians startled her afresh; and, in spite of the long, tiring journey, and the arduous days that had preceded it, she could not compose herself to sleep. And when, at last, she did fall into an uneasy doze, she was jerked back to consciousness in what seemed the minute after, by a shrill and piercing scream—a kind of prolonged shriek, that rent and tore at the air.

"Richard! . . . oh, Richard! what in the world is that?"

"Don't be alarmed, my dear. It's only the mill whistle."

"A mill? So close?"

"It's all right, Mary; you'll soon get used to it. Myself I hardly notice it now. And it doesn't last long. There! you see, it has stopped already."

His attempt to make light of the appalling din had something pathetic about it. Mary bit back her dismay.

And it was the same in the morning, when he led her round house and garden: he skimmed airily over the drawbacks—the distance of the kitchen from the house; the poor water-supply; the wretched little box of a surgery; the great heat of even this late autumn day—to belaud the house's privacy, separated as it was from the rest of the township by the width of the Lagoon; the thickness of the brick walls; the shade and coolness ensured by an all-round verandah. And though daylight, and what it showed up, only served to render Mary more and more dubious, she had not the heart, on this first morning, to damp him by saying what she really thought. Instead, her tour of inspection over, she buckled to her mammoth job of bringing comfort out of chaos: putting up beds and dressers; unpacking the crockery; cutting down curtains and carpets, and laying oilcloth; working dusty and dishevelled, by the light of a candle, till long past midnight for many a night. While Richard, his professional visits over, undertook to mind and amuse the children, who were sadly in her way, dashing about helter-skelter, pale with the excitement of the new.

For, oh! what a lovely house this was!— Long before anyone else was astir, Cuffy had pattered out barefoot to explore; and, all his life after, he loved an empty house for its sake. It had nothing but doors; which spelt freedom: even the windows were doors. There were no stairs. A passage went right down the middle, with a door at each end, which always stood open, and three room-doors on each side. You could run out of any of the windows and tear round the verandah, to play Hide-and-Seek or Hi-spy-hi. And not even Eliza was there to say: "Don't!" or "You mustn't!" She was in the faraway kitchen, scrubbing or washing up. They had breakfast off a packing-case, which was great fun; and Papa was so nice, too. The very first morning he explained what the bush meant, and took them all out walking to find it; and then Cuffy learnt that it was not *one* bush he had come to see, but lots of

730

bushes; with trees so high that, even if you almost broke your neck bending back, you couldn't see the end of them.

Dancing ahead of Papa, who held hands with the Dumplings, and sometimes walking backwards, to hear better, Cuffy fired question after question. How did the bush get there first? Why did nobody live in it? What were all the deep holes full of water? Why were they abandoned? Why did people dig for gold? How did they do it? Why was money?— a fusillade of questions, to which on this day, he got full and patient answers. Papa gave them each a three-penny bit, too, to spend as they liked. The twins carried theirs squeezed tight to show Mamma; but he put his in his pocket.

On the way home they went along a street, where there were lots of little shops, with verandahs. Men were leaning against the verandah posts, smoking and spitting; and other men came to the doors and stared, as they went by. Papa was very polite to them, and said "Good morning!" to everybody, with a little bow, and whether they did or not. And sometimes he said as well: "Yes, these are my youngsters! Don't you think I've reason to be proud of them?" . . . and as often as this happened, Cuffy felt uncomfortable. For these weren't the sort of men you stopped and talked to: you just said good morning, and went home. Besides, they didn't seem as if they *wanted* to speak to you. They didn't take their pipes out; and some of them looked as if they thought Papa was funny . . . or silly. Two winked at each other when they thought he wasn't looking—made eyes like Cook and Eliza used to do.

Then, at a hotel, they met a fat, red-faced man—the landlord, Papa said—who seemed at first to be going to be nicer. When Papa pushed them forward, and said: "My young fry arrived at last, you see!" he smiled back and said: "And a very jolly little set of nippers, too! Pleased to know you, missies! How do, sir, how do! Now what will yours be?"

"Cuthbert Hamilton Townshend-Mahony," replied Cuffy, lightning-quick and politely. He was dumbfounded by the roar of laughter that went up at his words; not only the landlord laughed, but lots of larrikins, too, who stood round the bar. Even Papa laughed a little, in a funny, tight way.

Mamma didn't, though. Cuffy heard them talking, and she sounded cross. "Surely, Richard, you needn't drag the children in as well?"

Papa was snappy. "I don't think, Mary, you quite realise how necessary it is for me to leave no stone unturned."

"I can't help it. I'm not going to have *my* children mixed up in the affair!" When Mamma was cross, she always said "*my* children."

Cuffy didn't wait to hear more. He ran down the garden, where he mooned about till dinner-time. He wouldn't ever—no, he wouldn't!—go down the street where those horrid men were again. And if he saw them, he'd stamp his feet at them, and call them nasty names. And he'd tell Papa not to, as well—he wouldn't let him; he'd hold on to his coat. For they didn't like Papa either.

"Ooo . . . tum on! Us'll dance, too!" cried the twins. And taking hands, they hopped and capered about the drawing-room, their little starched white petticoats flaring as they swung. For Papa was dancing with Mamma. He had seized her by the waist and polkaed her up the passage, and now was whirling her round, she trying to free herself and crying: "Stop, Richard, stop! You'll make me sick." But Papa just laughed and twirled on, the Dumplings faithfully imitating him, till, crash, bang! a vase of Parian marble on the big centre table lost its balance, toppled over and was smashed to atoms.

"There! . . . that's just what I expected. There's no room here for such goings-on," said Mary ruefully, as she stooped to the fragments.

It came of her having called Richard in to view the drawing-room, where, for over a week, she had stitched and hammered, or sat perched on the top rung of a step-ladder. Herself, she was not displeased with her work; though she mourned the absence of the inlaid secretaire, the card-table, the ottoman. These things were still in the outhouse, in their travelling-cases; and there they would have to remain. The Collard and Collard took up nearly the whole of one wall; the round rosewood table devoured the floor-space; everything was much too large. And the best bits, the Parisian gilt-legged tables and gilt-framed mirrors, made absolutely no show, huddled and cramped together as they were.

But Richard went into ecstasies. "They'll never have seen a room like it!—the people here. We'll show them what's what,

wife, eh? . . . make 'em open their eyes! Mary, I prophesy
you'll have the whole township come trooping over the
Lagoon to call. We shall need to charge 'em admission!"— And
therewith he had seized and swung her round. So undignified!
. . . before Eliza. Besides egging the children on to do likewise.

But there was no dampening Richard just now. Though a
fortnight had passed, he was still in the simmer of excitement
into which their coming had thrown him. While she stitched,
even while she turned the handle of the sewing-machine, he
would stand at her side and talk, and talk, in a voice that was
either pitched just a shade too high, or was husky and tremulous. The separation had plainly been too much for him. His
joy at getting them again was not to be kept within bounds.

"You're absolutely all I've got, you know . . . you and the
children."

Which was quite literally true: so true that, at times, Mary
would find herself haunted by the unpleasant vision of a
funeral at which it was not possible to fill a single coach with
mourners. Richard—to be followed to his grave by the doctor
who had attended him, the parson who was to bury him . . .
and not a soul besides! Her heart contracted at the disgrace
of the thing: the shame of letting the world know how little
he had cared for anyone, or been cared for in return.

Impatiently she shook her head, and turned to listen to
voices in the passage. They were those of Richard and a
patient; but chiefly Richard's. For he had carried his talkative
fit over to strangers as well . . . and Mary sometimes wondered
what they thought of him: these small shop-keepers and
farmers, and vinegrowers, and licensed publicans. Well, at
any rate, they wouldn't be able to bring the usual accusation
against him, of stiff-necked reserve. The truth was, they just
came in for their share of his all-pervading good humour. The
children, too. Had he always made so much of the children,
they would have felt more at home with him, and he have
had less cause for jealous grumbles. He even unearthed his old
flute, screwed the parts together, and to Cuffy's enchantment
played them his one-time show-piece: "The Minstrel Boy."—
And it was the same with everything. He vowed the Barambogie bread to be the best, the butter the sweetest he had
ever tasted: going so far as to compliment the astonished
tradespeople on their achievements. And Mary, watching in

silence, thought how pleasant all this was . . . and how unnatural . . . and waited for the moment to come when he would drop headlong from the skies.

In waiting, her head with its high Spanish comb bent low over her work, she gave the rein to various private worries of her own. For instance, she saw quite clearly that Eliza's stay with them would not be a long one. Forgetful of past favours, as of the expense they had been at in bringing her there, Eliza was already darkly hinting her opinion of the place; of the detached kitchen; the dust, the solitude. Again, the want of a proper waiting-room for patients was proving a great trial. The dining-room seemed never their own. More serious was the risk the children thereby ran of catching some infectious illness. Then, she sometimes felt very uneasy about Richard. In spite of his exuberance, he looked anything but well. The bout of dysentery he had suffered from, on first arriving, had evidently been graver than he cared to admit. His colour was bad, his appetite poor; while as for sleep, if he managed four consecutive hours of a night, he counted himself lucky. And even then it wasn't a restful sleep; for he had got the absurd idea in his head that he might not hear the nightbell—in this tiny house!—and at the least sound was awake and sitting up. Again, almost every day brought a long trudge into the bush, from which he came home too tired to eat. And Mary's old fear revived. Would he ever be able to stand the wear and tear of the work?—especially as the practice grew, and he became more widely known.

But, even as she asked herself the question, another doubt flew at her. Was there any real prospect of the practice growing, and of his retrieving his shattered fortunes? Or had he, in burying himself in this wild bush, committed the crowning folly of his life? And, of the two, this fear ate the deeper. For she thought he *might* have so husbanded his strength as to carry on for a few years; but, the more she saw of place and people, the slenderer grew her belief that there was money to be made there. How anybody in his five senses could have professed to see in Barambogie what Richard did—oh, *no* one but Richard could have so deceived himself! Of all the dead-and-alive holes she had ever known, this was the deadest. Only two trains a day called there, with eight hours between. The railway station was mostly closed and deserted, the stationmaster to be found playing euchre at the "Sun." Quite a quarter of the shops in the main street were boarded up; the shafts round the township had all been worked out, or abandoned. As for the tale of the big mine . . . well, she considered that had been just a bait with which to hook a simple fish! How she did wish she had somebody to talk to! Richard was no use at all . . . in his present mood. To the few feelers she threw out, he declared himself exaggeratedly well content. Though the number of patients was still not great, his calls into the bush were royally paid. It was five guineas here, ten there; as compared with the petty fees he had commanded at Hawthorn. "Surely, my dear, if money flows in at this rate, we can put up with a few slight drawbacks?"

Such as the flour mill, thought Mary grimly. This dreadful mill! Would any but a man so complacently have planked them down next door to it? It entirely spoilt the garden, with its noise and dust. Then, the mill-hands who passed to and fro, or sat about outside the fence, were a very rough lot; and five times a day you had to stop in what you were saying, and wait for the shriek of the steam-whistle to subside. Except for the railway station, their house and the mill stood alone on this side of the Lagoon, and were quite five minutes' walk from the township. Richard hugged himself with his privacy, and it certainly was nicer, for the children's sake, to be away from shops and public-houses. But, for the practice, their seclusion was a real disadvantage. Rummel had lived in the main street; and his surgery had been as handy for people to drop into for, say, a cut finger or a black eye, as was now the chemist's shop. Then, the Lagoon itself . . . this view, of which Richard had made so much! After the rains, when there was some water in it, it might be all right; but just now it was more than three parts dry, and most unsightly. You saw the bare cracked earth of its bottom, not to speak of the rubbish, the old tins and boots and broken china, that had been thrown into it when full. And the mosquitoes! She had been obliged to put netting round all their beds; and what it would be like in summer passed imagining. The summers here bore an evil name.

From such reflections, in the weeks and months that followed, she had nothing but work to distract her. The society airily promised her by Richard failed to materialise. She received just three callers. And only one of these—the Bank Manager's wife, a young thing, newly wed—was worth considering. The stationmaster's . . . the stationmaster himself was an educated man, with whom even Richard enjoyed a chat; but he had married beneath him . . . a dressmaker, if report spoke true. Mrs. Cameron, wife of the Clerk of the Court, had lived so long in Barambogie that she had gone queer from it. Nor was it feasible to ask the old couple over of an evening, for cards or music; for, by then, old Cameron was as a rule so fuddled that he couldn't tell a knave from a king. The parson was also an odd fish, and a widower without family; the Presbyterian minister unmarried. The poor children had no playfellows, no companions. Oh, not for herself, but for those who were more to her than herself, Mary's heart was often very hot and sore.

Nevertheless, she put her shoulder to the wheel with all her old spirit; rising betimes to bathe and dress the children, cutting out and making their clothes, superintending the washing and ironing, cooking the meals; and, when Eliza passed, and a young untrained servant took her place, doing the lion's share towards keeping the house in the spotless state Richard loved, and her own sense of nicety demanded. But the work told on her. And not alone because it was harder. In Hawthorn, she had laboured to some end; Richard had had to be re-established, connections formed, their own dear house tended. All of which had given her mind an upward lift. Here, where no future beckoned, it seemed just a matter of toiling for toil's sake. The consequence was, she tired much more readily; her legs ached, her feet throbbed, and the crow's feet began to gather round her eyes. She was paying, of course, so she told herself, for years of luxury and idleness, in which Richard had been against her lifting a finger. And it was no easy thing to buckle to again, now that she was "getting on," "going downhill": being come to within a twelvemonth of her fortieth year.

[7]

"Cousin Emmy, tell about little Jacky!"

"Little Jacky what died."

"No, *don't!* Tell what the gumtrees talk."

Cuffy hated the tale of Baby Jacky's illness and death; for

736

Cousin Emmy always cried when she told it. And to see a grown-up person cry wasn't proper.

The four of them were out for their morning walk, and sat resting on a fallen tree.

"Well, dears, poor little Jacky was so often ill that God thought he would be happier in heaven. His back teeth wouldn't come through; and he was so feverish and restless that I had to carry him about most of the night. The last time I walked him up and down, he put his little arms round my neck and said: 'Ting, Memmy!'—he couldn't say 'sing' or 'Emmy' properly, you know"—a detail which entranced the Dumplings, who had endless difficulties with their own speech. "And those were the very last words he said. In the middle of the night he took convulsions——"

"What *are* c'nvulshuns, Cousin Emmy?"— The question came simultaneously, none of the three being minded, often as they had heard the story, to let the narrator skip this, the raciest part of it.

"Why, poor darling, he shivered and shook, and squinted, and rolled his eyes, and went blue in the face, and his body got stiff, and he turned up his eyes till you could only see the whites. And then he died, and we dressed him in his best nightgown, and he lay there looking like a big wax doll—with white flowers in his hands. And his little coffin was lined with white satin, and trimmed with the most *beautiful* lace . . ." And here sure enough, at mention of her nursling's last costly bed, Emmy began to cry. The three children, reddening, smiled funny little embarrassed smiles, and averted their eyes; only occasionally taking a surreptitious peep, to see what Cousin Emmy looked like when she did it.

With the heel of his boot Cuffy hammered the ground. He knew something else . . . about Cousin Emmy . . . something naughty. He'd heard Mamma and Papa talking; and it was about running away, and Aunt Lizzie being most awfully furious. And then Cousin Emmy had come to stay with them. He was glad she had; he liked her. Her hair was yellow, like wattle; her mouth ever so red. And she told them stories, Mamma could only read stories. And never had time.

To-day, however, there would be no more. For round a bend of the bush track, by which they sat, came a figure which the children were growing used to see appearing on their walks.

It was the Reverend Mr. Angus. He wore a long black coat that reached below his knees, and a white tie. He had a red curly beard, and pink cheeks. (Just like a lady, thought Cuffy.) At sight of the lovely girl in deep mourning, bathed in tears, these grew still pinker. Advancing at a jog-trot, their owner seated himself on the tree, and took Emmy's hand in his.

The children were now supposed to "run away and play." The twins fell to building a little house, with pieces of bark and stones; but Cuffy determined to pick a *beeyutiful* nosegay, that Cousin Emmy would like ever so much, and say "How pretty!" to, and "How kind of you, Cuffy!" Mr. Angus had a face like a cow; and when he spoke he made hissing noises through his teeth. The first time he heard them, Cuffy hadn't been able to tear his eyes away, and had stood stockstill in front of the minister, till Cousin Emmy got quite cross. And Mr. Angus said, in *his* opinion, little people should not only be seen and not heard, but not even seen!

All right then! Whistling his loudest, Cuffy sauntered off. He would be good, and not go near any of the old, open shafts; quite specially not the one where the old dead donkey had tumbled in, and floated. You weren't allowed to look down this hole, not even if somebody held your hand . . . like Mr. Angus did Cousin Emmy's. (Why was he? She couldn't fall off a *log*.) It had a nasty smell, too. Cousin Emmy said only to think of it made her sick. And Mamma said they were to hold their noses as they passed. Why was the donkey so nasty because it was dead? What did a dead donkey *do?*

But first he would pick the flowers. It wouldn't take long, there were such lots of them. Papa said he must thank the rains for the flowers; and it had rained every day for nearly a month. The Lagoon was quite full, and the tank, too; which made Mamma glad.— And now Cuffy darted about, tearing up bits of running postman, and pulling snatches of the purple sarsaparilla that climbed the bushes and young trees, till he had a tight, close bunch in his hot little hand. As he picked, he sniffed the air, which smelt lovely . . . like honey. . . . Cousin Emmy said it was the wattle coming out. To feel it better, he shut his eyes, screwed them up to nothing, and kept them tight. And when he opened them again, everything looked *new* . . . as if he'd never seen it before . . . all the white trees, tall like poles, that went up and up, to where, right at the top, among whiskery branches, were bits of blue that were the sky.

With the elastic of his big upturned sailor-hat between his teeth—partly to keep it on; partly because he loved chewing things: elastic, or string, or the fingers of kid gloves—Cuffy ran at top speed to the donkey-hole. But a couple of yards from the shaft, his courage all but failed him. What was he going to see? And ooh! . . . it *did* smell. Laying his flowers on the ground, he went down on his hands and knees and crawled forward, till he could just peep over. And then, why, what a sell! It wasn't a donkey at all—just water—and in it a great lump that stuck out like a 'normous boiled pudding . . . oh, and a million, no, two million and a half blowflies—walking on it, and a smell like—ooh, yes! just exactly like . . .

But before he could put a name to the odour, there was a great shouting and cooee-ing, and it was him they were calling . . . and calling. In his guilty fright, Cuffy gave a great jerk, and off went his hat with its pulped elastic—went down, down, down, while the blowflies came up. He just managed to wriggle a little way back, but was still on all fours (squashing the flowers) when they found him, Mr. Angus panting and puffing, with tears on his forehead, Cousin Emmy pressing her hand to her chest, and saying, oh, dear, oh, dear! Then Mr. Angus took him by the shoulder and shook him. Little boys who ran away in the bush *always* got lost, and never saw their Mammas and Papas again. They had nothing to eat, and starved to death, and not till years afterwards were their skeletons found. Cuffy, who knew quite well where he was, and hadn't meant to run away, thought him very silly . . . and rude.

It was the loss of the hat that was the tragedy. This made ever so many things go wrong, and ended with Cousin Emmy having to go back to live with Aunt Lizzie again, and them getting a real *paid* governess to teach them.

Hatless, squeezed close up to Cousin Emmy to be under her parasol, Cuffy was hurried through the township. "Or people will think your Mamma is too poor to buy you a hat."

The children's hearts were heavy. It infected them with fear to see Cousin Emmy so afraid, and to hear her keep saying: "What *will* Aunt Mary say?"

Not only, it seemed, had the hat cost a lot of money—to get another like it Mamma would have to send all the way to Melbourne. But it also leaked out that not a word was to have been said about Mr. Angus meeting them, and sitting on the log, and talking.

"Why not? Is it naughty?"

"Of *course* not, Cuffy! How can you be so silly! But——"

But . . . well, Aunt Mary would certainly be dreadfully cross with her for not looking after him better. How *could* he be so dishonourable, the first moment she wasn't watching, to go where he had been strictly forbidden to . . . such a *dirty* place! . . . and where he might have fallen head-foremost down the shaft, and never have been seen again?

Yes, it was a very crestfallen, guilt-laden little party that entered the house.

Mamma came out of the dining-room, a needle in one hand, a long thread of cotton in the other. And she saw at once what had happened, and said: "Where's your hat?— *Lost* it? Your nice, new hat? How? Come in here to me."— The twins began to sniff, and then everything was up.

Yes, Mamma was very cross . . . and sorry, too; for poor Papa was working his hardest to keep them nice, and then a careless little boy just went and threw money into the street. But ever so much crosser when she heard where the hat had gone: she scolded and scolded. And then she put the question Cuffy dreaded most: "Pray, what were you doing there . . . by yourself?" In vain he shuffled, and prevaricated, and told about the nosegay. Mamma just fixed her eyes on him; and it was no good; Mr. Angus had to come out.— And now it was Cousin Emmy's turn. She went scarlet, but she answered Mamma back quite a lot, and was angry, too; and only when Mamma said she wouldn't have believed it of her, and it was the behaviour of a common nursegirl, and she would have to speak to her uncle about her—at that Cousin Emmy burst out crying, and ran away and shut herself in her room.

Then Mamma went into the surgery to tell Papa. She shut the door, but you could hear their voices through it; and merely the sound of them, though he didn't know what they were saying, threw Cuffy into a flutter. Retreating to the furthest corner of the verandah, he sat with his elbows on his knees, the palms of his hands pressed against his ears.

And while Emmy, face downwards on her pillow, wept: "I don't care . . . let them fall down mines if they want to! . . .

he's very nice . . . Aunt Mary isn't fair!" Mary was saying: "I did think she could be trusted with the children—considering the care she took of Jacky."

"Other people's children, my dear—other people's children! He might have been her own."

Mary was horrified. "Whatever you do, don't say a thing like that before Cuffy! It would mean the most awkward questions. And surely *we* are not 'other people'? If Emmy can't look after her own little cousins. . . . The child might have been killed, while she sat there flirting and amusing herself."

"It's not likely to happen again."

"Oh, I don't know. When I tackled her with it, she got on the high horse at once, and said it wasn't a very great crime to have a little chat with somebody: life was so dull here, and so on."

"Well, I'm sure that's true enough."

"*What* a weak spot you have for the girl!— But that's not all. It didn't take me long to discover she'd been trying to make the children deceive me. They were to have held their tongues about this Angus meeting them on their walks. . . . Cuffy went as near as he could to telling a fib over it. Now you must see I couldn't have that sort of thing going on . . . the children taught fibbing and deceiving!"

"No, that certainly wouldn't do."

"Then, imagine a girl of Emmy's birth and upbringing plotting to meet, on the sly, a man we don't even invite to the house! She'll be the talk of the place. And what if she got herself into some entanglement or other, while she's under our care? John's eldest daughter, and an insignificant little dissenter, poor as a church mouse, and years older than she is! *Think* what Lizzie would say!"

"My dear, Lizzie's sentiments would be the same, and were it Crœsus and Adonis rolled into one."

"Well, yes, I suppose they would.— But Emmy is far too extravagant to make a poor man's wife. Do you know, she changes her underclothing every day of the week! You should hear Maria grumble at the washing! Besides, she's everlastingly titivating, dressing her hair or something. She does none of the jobs one expects from a nursery-governess. And if I dare to find fault . . . I don't know, but she seems greatly changed. I think first her father's death, and then Jacky's, have thoroughly spoiled her."

741

"Well! to have the two mortals you've set your heart on snatched from you, one after the other, isn't it enough to dash the stoutest? . . . let alone an innocent young girl. Emmy has been through a great spiritual experience, and one result of it might very well be to mature her . . . turn her into a woman who feels her power. It will probably be the same wherever she goes, with a face like hers. In her father's house, she would of course have met more eligible men than we, in our poor circumstances, can offer her. Still, my advice would be, such as they are, ask 'em to the house. Let everything be open and aboveboard."

"What! invite that little Angus? Stuff and nonsense! It would only be encouraging him.— Besides, it's all very well for you to theorise; I have to look at it from the practical side. And it surely isn't what one has a governess for? . . . to smooth the way for her flirtations! I may as well tell you everything. When she first came, I used to send her running up to the station— if I needed stamps, or small change, or things like that—Mr. Pendrell is always so obliging. But I had to stop it. She took to staying away an unconscionable time, and his wife must have got wind of it, she began to look so queerly at Emmy, and to drop hints. Most uncomfortable. And then you've surely noticed how often old Thistlethwaite comes to see us now, compared with what he used to, and how he sits and stares at Emmy. He looks at her far too much, too, when he's preaching, and I've heard him pay her the most outrageous compliments. A clergyman and a widower, and old enough to be her *grand*father! But Emmy just drinks it in. Now, mind you, if there were any question of a decent match for her, I'd do what I could to help . . . for I don't believe Lizzie will ever let her say how-do-you-do to an eligible! But I *cannot* have her getting into mischief here—why, even the baker tries to snatch a word with her, when he delivers the bread!—and being branded as forward, and a common flirt. No, the truth is, she's just too pretty to be of the least practical use."

Mahony made no reply.

"Are you *listening*, Richard? . . . to what I say."

"Yes, I hear."

"I thought you were asleep. Well, now perhaps you'll rouse yourself, and tell me what I ought to do."

"I suppose there's nothing for it: Emmy must go."

"And then?"

"Then?"

"I mean about the children. Who's to give them their lessons, and their music-lessons? . . . and take them out walking?"

"My dear, *can* you not teach them yourself for a bit?"

"No, Richard, I *cannot!* At the age they're at now, they need one person's undivided attention. They've simply *got* to have a governess!"

"Oh, well! I suppose if you must, you must . . . and that's all about it."

The implication in these words exasperated Mary.

"If *I* must? I'm not asking anything for myself! You've never heard me utter a word of complaint. But I can't do more than I am doing. Anyone but you would see it. But you're as blind as a bat!"

"Not so blind as you think, my dear. One thing I see is that you never hesitate to load me up with a fresh expense."

"No, that's out-and-away unfair!" cried Mary, thoroughly roused. "I, who slave and toil . . . and when I'm not even convinced that it's necessary, either! For you're always saying you're satisfied with the practice, that the fees come in well, and so on; and yet to get anything out of you, nowadays, is like drawing blood from a stone. I don't care a rap about myself; I'll put up with whatever you like; but I can't and won't sit by and see my children run wild! I think that would break my heart. I shall fight for them to my last breath."

"Yes, for them! But, for me, never a trace of understanding or sympathy!"— And now the quarrel began in earnest.

Cuffy, sitting hunched up on the verandah, squeezed his ears until they sang.

[8]

THE day began at six . . . with the pestilential screech of the mill-whistle. This also started the children off. Bird-like sounds began to issue from their room across the passage: there was no muting these shrill, sweet trebles. And soon Miss Prestwick's thin voice made itself heard, capped by Mary's magisterial tones, and the dashing and splashing of bath-water, and small feet scampering, and Maria thudding up and down, clattering her brooms.

There was no more chance of sleep. He, too, rose.

The water of the shower-bath was tepid and unrefreshing.
It had also to be sparingly used. Then came breakfast—with
mushy butter, the pat collapsing on its way from the cellar,
with sticky flies crawling over everything, a soiled cloth, the
children's jabber, Miss Prestwick's mincing airs, and Mary
checking, apportioning, deciding. Mahony ate hastily, and,
there being here no morning paper or early post to engage
him, retired to the surgery. His cases written up, his visits for
the day arranged, he sat and waited, and listened. This was
the time when a walking-patient or two might call for treatment; and the footsteps of anyone nearing the house could be
heard a long way off, crunching the gravel of the path by the
Lagoon, coming up the right-of-way. And as he sat idly twirling his thumbs, it became a matter of interest to speculate
whether approaching steps would halt at his door, or move on
towards the railway station. In waiting, he could hear Cuffy's
voice proclaiming loudly and unnaturally: *Jer suise urn petty
garsong, de bun figoor.*

After a couple of false alarms, there was a knock at the
door; and Maria introduced a working-man, with a foreign
body in his eye. A grain of mortar extracted, and the eye
bathed, Mahony washed, stitched and bandaged a child's
gashed knee, and drew a tooth for a miner's wife. Mary's aid
was needed here, to hold the woman's hands. It was Mary, too,
who applied restoratives, and helped to clean up the patient.
After which, she brushed yesterday's dust from his wide-
awake, held a silk coat for him to slip his arms into, and
checked the contents of his bag.

He set off on his morning round, following the path that ran
alongside the Lagoon. Here and there the shadow of a fir-tree
fell across it, and, though the season was but late spring, the
shade was welcome. Emerging from the Lagoon enclosure, he
entered the single street that formed the township of Barambogie. This was empty but for a couple of buggies, their hoods
white with the dust of innumerable bush journeys, which
stood outside a public-house.

But the sound of his foot on the pavement, his shadow on
the glass of the shop-windows, made people dart to their doors,
to see who passed. Huh! it was only "the new doctor"; and out
of *him* nothing was to be got . . . in the shape of a yarn, or a
companionable drink.

One or two threw him a "Mornin'!" The rest contented themselves with a nod. But all alike regarded his raised hat and courteous "Good day to you!" "Good morning, sir!" with the colonial's inborn contempt for form and ceremony. By the Lord Harry! slapdash was good enough for them.

On this particular morning Mahony had three calls to pay.

Arrived at the Anglican parsonage—a shabby brick cottage, standing on a piece of ground that had never been fenced in —he took up the knocker, which, crudely repaired with a headless nail and a bit of twine, straightway came off in his hand. He rapped with his knuckles, and the Reverend Thistlethwaite, in nightshirt and trousers, and with bare feet, appeared from his back premises, where he had been feeding fowls. Reaffixing the knocker with a skill born of long practice, he opened the door of the parlour, into which there was just room to squeeze. On the table, writing-materials elbowed the remains of a mutton-chop breakfast. Blowflies crawled over the fatted plates.

An unsightly carbuncle lanced and dressed, the reverend gentleman—he was a fleshy, red-faced man, of whom unkind rumour had it that there were times when his tongue tripped over his own name—laid himself out to detain his visitor. He was spoiling for a chat.

"Yes, yes, doctor, hard at work . . . hard at work!"—with an airy wave of the hand at pens, ink and paper. "Must always get something fresh, you know, of a Sunday morning, to tickle 'em up with. Even the minor prophets are racked, I can assure you, in the search for a rousing heading."

Mahony replaced lancet and lint in silence. It was common knowledge that old Thistlethwaite had not written a fresh sermon for years; but had used his stale ones again and again, some even said reading them backwards, for the sake of variety. The implements littering the table were set permanently out on view.

Insensitive to Mahony's attitude, he ran on: "Talking of rummy texts now . . . did y'ever hear the story of the three curates, out to impress the Bishop with their skill at squeezing juice from a dry orange, who, each in turn, in the different places he visited on three successive Sundays, held forth on the theme: 'Now Peter's wife's mother lay sick of a fever?' You have? . . . capital, isn't it? But I'll warrant you don't know the yarn of old Minchin and the cow. It was at Bootajup, in the Western District, and his first up-country cure; and Minch, who was a townbird born and bred, was officiating for the first time at Harvest Festival. The farmers had given liberally, the church was full, Minch in the reading-desk with his back to a side door, that had been left open for coolness. All went well till the middle of the Psalms, when he saw the eyes of his congregation getting rounder and rounder. Old Minch, who was propriety in person, thought his collar had come undone, or that he'd shed a private button . . . ha, ha! Whereas, if you please, it was a cow who had strayed to the door, and was being agreeably attracted by the farm produce. Minch looked round just as the animal walked in, lost his head, dropped his book, and bolted; taking the altar rails at a leap, with cassock and surplice bunched up round him. Ha, ha! Capital . . . capital! It was Minchin, too, who was once preaching from the text: 'And God shall wipe away all tears from their eyes,' when he found himself forced to sneeze some dozen times running. Ha, ha, ha! His own eyes poured tears—ran with water. Out it came: a-tischoo, a-tischoo! The congregation rocked with laughter.— What? . . . you must be toddling? Well, well! we know you doctors are busy men. Hot?—call this hot? I wonder what you'll say to our summers! Well, good day, doctor, good day!"

" 'Except ye become as little children' . . . 'for such is the kingdom of heaven.' *My* God! . . . then give me earth."

Striking off on a bush track, Mahony trudged along, leaving a low trail of dust in his wake. His goal was a poor outlying wooden shanty, to treat a washerwoman's severely scalded leg and foot. The wound, some days old, was open, dirty, offensive; the woman, who sat propped up before her tubs, struggling to finish her week's work, loud-mouthed with pain.

"She don't half holler 'n screech if oner the kids knocks up against it," volunteered a foxy-looked girl who stood by, sucking her thumb, and watching, with an unholy interest, the sponging off of the foul rags, the laying bare of the raw flesh.

Mahony's impatient "Why on earth didn't you send for me sooner?" brought no coherent response; but his prescription of complete rest in a horizontal position effectually loosed the sufferer's tongue. "Didn't I know you'd be after orderin' me some such foolery? Who's to kape us? I've no man. I'm a poor lone widder . . ."

"Apply to your priest for aid."

"The praste? A fat lot o' good that 'ud be!—the great lazy louse! We cud all starve, afore *he'd* lift a finger."

"Well, I've warned you. I can do no more." And cutting further discussion short, Mahony put on his hat and walked out of the house.

As, however, the foxy child, thumb in mouth, lolloped after him, he took a sovereign from his pocket. "Here, my girl, here's something to tide you over. Now see that your mother lies up. You're old enough to lend a hand."

But before he had gone a hundred yards, he turned on his heel, recalling the low, cunning look that had leapt into the girl's eyes at sight of the gold piece. "Fool that I am! . . . the mother will never see it."

Caught in the act of secreting the coin in her stocking, the girl went livid with fury. "What d'you mean? D'you think I was goin' to pinch it? Ma! . . . d'you hear, Ma? . . . what he says? Ma! he's callin' me a thief."

"A thief, indeed! Me child a thief?— And you, you pesky young devil, you hand that chip over or I'll wring your neck!"

Thence to the shop of Ah Sing, the Chinese butcher, where a rachitic infant lay cramped with the colic. Mahony looked with pity on the little half-breed, slit of eye and yellow of skin, and was very short with the mother, a monstrously fat woman, who stood, her arms a-kimbo, answering his questions with an air of sulky defiance. No, she didn't know, not she, what had caused the colic: *she'd* done nothing. But here, espying an empty tin dish that had been thrust under the bed, Mahony picked it up and sniffed it. "Ha! here we have it. What filthy messes has your husband been feeding the child on now? Haven't I told you her stomach will not stand them?"

"Mrs. Ah Sing" bit back the abusive rejoinders that were given to escaping her, at any reference to her child's mixed origin: "Doctors" were Sing's best customers. But, the visit over, she flounced into the shop and seizing a knife, let loose her spleen in hacking down some chops, while she vociferated for all to hear: "Filthy mess, indeed . . . *I'll* mess him! Let him look to his own kids, say I! That boy brat of his is as white as a sheet and thin as a lizard.— Here, you Sing, weigh this, and look sharp about it, you crawling slug, you!"

"Malia! me give lil baby powder—you no sendee more for doctor-man, Malia!" said the soft-voiced, gentle Chinaman who owned her.

"Oh, hell take the kid!—and you along with it!" gave back Maria.—

On the way home Mahony overtook his children and the governess, returning from their morning walk. The twins' short fat legs were weary. Entrusting his bag to Cuffy, who forthwith became "the doctor," bowing graciously to imaginary patients, and only waggling the bag just the least little bit, to hear the things inside it rattle, their father took his little girls by the hand. Poor mites! They were losing their roses already. Somehow or other, he must make it possible to send them away when the real hot weather came. This was no place for children in summer; he heard it on every side. And his, reared to sea-breezes, would find it doubly hard to acclimatise themselves. Stung by these reflections, he unthinkingly quickened his pace, and strode ahead, a gaunt figure, dragging a small child at a trot on either hand. Miss Prestwick gave up the chase.

Dinner over, out he had to turn again. Back to the main street and the hotel, where a buggy should have been in waiting. It was not. He had to stand about in the sun while the vehicle was dragged out, the horse fetched, harnessed, and backed between the shafts. A strap broke in the buckling; the ostler, whistling between his teeth, leisurely repaired the damage with a bit of string.

Stiffly Mahony jerked himself up into the high vehicle and took the reins. He had a ten-mile drive before him, over the worst possible roads; it would be all he could do to reach home by dark. The horse, too, was unfresh. In vain he urged and cajoled; the animal's pace remained a dilatory amble, and the heat seemed to accumulate under the close black hood, which weighed on his shoulders like a giant hat. Yet, if he alighted to slip a rail, it was so much hotter outside that he was glad to clamber back beneath its covering. Still, he did not complain. These bush visits were what brought the shekels in: not the tinkering with rachitic infants or impecunious Irish, whom, as this morning, he sometimes paid for the privilege of attending. (Ha, ha! . . . capital! . . . as that fool Thistle-thwaite would have said.) And to-day promised to be more than ordinarily remunerative; for he had another long drive before him that evening, in an opposite direction. He could count on clearing a ten-pound note.

But when, towards six o'clock, he reached home, the summons he was expecting had not come. There was time for a bath, a change, a rest! and still the trap that should have fetched him had not appeared. He began to grow fidgety. The case was one of diphtheria. On the previous day he had given relief by opening the windpipe; it was essential for him to know the result of the operation. What could the people be thinking of? Or had the child died in the meantime? . . . the membrane spread downwards, causing obstruction below the tube? "Surely, in common decency, they would have let me know?"

He wandered from room to room, nervously snapping his fingers. Or sat down and beat a tattoo on chair-arm or table, only to spring up at an imaginary sound of wheels.

Mary dissuaded him from hiring a buggy and driving out to see what had happened. She also pooh-poohed his idea of an accident to the messenger. The father, a vinegrower, had several men, and more than one horse and buggy, at his disposal. The likelihood was, he would have come himself, had the child been worse. *Unless*, of course . . . well, it wasn't death *she* thought of! But the township of Mittagunga was not much farther than Barambogie from the patient's home; and there was another doctor at Mittagunga. She did not speak this thought aloud; but it haunted her; and, as the evening wore eventlessly away, the question escaped her in spite of herself: "Can you have offended them? . . . in any way?"

"*Offended* them? I?— Well, if it's offensive to leave one's bed in the middle of the night, for an eight-mile drive on these abominable roads, to perform a ticklish operation!" And very bitterly: "What extraordinary ideas you do have, Mary! What on earth do you mean now?"

But Mary, repenting her slip, was not prepared to stir up the heated discussion that would inevitably follow.

She went into the dining-room, and sat down to her sewing; while he fell to pacing the verandah. But though she, too, never ceased to keep her ears pricked for the noise of wheels,

749

no sound was to be heard, but that of Richard's feet tramping to and fro (*"How* tired he will be to-morrow!"*) and the peevish whine of a little nightwind round the corners of the house. But sorry as she felt for him, she did not again try to reason with him or console him. For when in one of his really black moods, he seemed to retire where words could not get at him. And these moods were growing on him. Nowadays, any small mishap sufficed to throw him into a state of excitement, the aftermath of which was bottomless depression. How would it all end?— Letting her work fall, Mary put her chin in her hand, and sat staring into the flame of the kerosene lamp. But she did not see it. She seemed to be looking through the light at something that lay beyond . . . something on the farther side, not only of the flame, but of all she had hitherto known of life; to be looking, in visionary fashion, out towards those shadowy to-morrows, for the first of which Richard was so surely incapacitating himself . . . an endless line of days that would come marching upon her, with never a break, never a respite, each fuller of anxiety than the one that went before.

Till, with a shiver, she resolutely shook herself free. "Tch! . . . it comes of listening to that silly, dismal wind."

Yet when, on the clock striking eleven, she stepped out on the verandah, her first words were: "Oh, what a lovely night!"

For the little wind whistled and piped out of a clear sky; and the moon, at full, drenched the earth with its radiance. Before the house, the Lagoon lay like a sheet of beaten silver. Trees and bushes, jet-black on one side, were white as if with hoar frost on the other. The distant hills ran together with the sky in a silver haze. All was peace . . . except for the thudding of Richard's feet.

"My dear, I'm sure it's no use waiting up any longer. They won't come now. Do go to bed."

"I'm too worried. I couldn't sleep."

"But at least it would rest you. As it is, you're wearing yourself out."

"Very easy for you to talk! But if anything should happen . . . the responsibility . . . my practice here—I can't afford it, Mary, and that's the truth! . . . not yet."

There was nothing to be done. With a sigh that was like a little prayer for patience, Mary turned away.

[9]

THE postman handed in a letter with a mourning border fully an inch wide; there was barely room for name and address, which were squeezed in anyhow. It was from Mr. Henry; and, in opening it in some trepidation, Mary read the sad news of Agnes's death. Mr. Henry was kind enough to give her full particulars. Agnes had, it seemed, stood the voyage out well. But on landing at the Cape she had met with an accident; had caught her foot in a rope and fallen heavily; and the shock had brought on an apoplexy, from which she never rallied. Mr. Henry wrote as one bereft of all he held dear; as the fond father, whose pious duty it would henceforth be to fill a mother's place to his orphaned children. In reading the letter aloud, Mary swallowed hard; then veiled her discomfort with an apologetic: "Oh, well, you know . . . poor man! . . . I dare-say—" by which she meant to imply that, with death's entry on the scene, the realities were apt to get overlaid. Mr. Henry saw himself and his situation, not as they were, but as he would have wished them to be.

Richard, of course, sniffed at Ocock's layman-ish account of his wife's end. And he was right. For Tilly's gloss on the affair ran: "Purd heard from a man who was on board the same ship. It's true she did trip over a rope and come a crop-per (and not the first time neither, as we know) and this brought on a violent attack of d.t.'s which carried her off. Henry hasn't looked the same man since. His relief is immense —simply immense."

But Mary's faithful, stubborn heart rebelled. For Agnes's own sake, her death was perhaps, pitifully enough, the best solution. But that, of all who had known her, none should mourn her passing; that even among her nearest it should only stir a sense of good riddance and relief: the tragedy of such a finish stirred Mary to the depths. Tenderly she laid away the keepsake Mr. Henry sent her for remembrance: a large cameo-brooch, at the back of which, under glass, was twined a golden curl, cut from the head of the little child whose untimely end had cost Agnes her bitterest tears.

A day or two later there came into her possession a still more pathetic memento: a letter from the dead, which had to be opened and read though the hand that wrote it was lying cold at the bottom of a grave. It had been found by Mr. Henry amongst his wife's belongings—found sealed and addressed, but never posted—a blotted and scrawled production, and more than a little confused, but full of love and kindness; though written with the firm conviction that they would never meet again. Poor thing, poor thing!— And having read, Mary hid it away at the back of a drawer, where no eyes but her own would ever see it. She could not have borne Richard's sarcastic comments on Agnes's poor spelling and poorer penmanship.

But there was nothing new in this secretiveness: she was falling more and more into the way of keeping Richard in the dark. A smash of china by the clumsy servant; Miss Prestwick's airs and insufficiencies; the exorbitant price of the children's new boots; disturbing gossip retailed by the girl: of vexations such as these, which were her daily portion, he heard not a word. It left her, of course, much freer to deal with things. But it also spared him the exhaustion of many a towering rage (under the influence of which he was quite capable, for instance, of writing to the bootmaker and calling him a thief), saved him, too, from going off into one of his fits of depression, when he imagined the whole world in league against him. The real truth was, he hadn't enough to occupy him; and not a soul to speak to . . . except his dreadful patients. Nor did he ever write or receive a letter. In coming here, he seemed to have had but the one desire: to forget and to be forgotten.

She it was who sat up at night, spinning out the letters necessary to make people remember you. And it fell to her to write the note of welcome, when Baron von Krause, the well-known botanist, proposed to break his journey from Sydney to Melbourne, solely to pay them a visit.— Though putting up a visitor nowadays meant considerable inconvenience: they had to turn out of their own room, she going in with the children, Richard making shift with the dining-room sofa. Still, in this case, she thought the upset worth while: for Richard's sake. He had been as friendly with the Baron as it was in his nature to be with anybody; and the latter had once spoken to her, in warm terms, of Richard's intimate knowledge of the native flora, and lamented the fact that he should not have found time to systematise his studies.

The next morning, while Richard was out, she climbed the step-ladder and unearthed the glass-cases that contained his collections of plants, minerals and butterflies: for the first time, on moving into a new house, he had not set them up in his room. But she wasn't going to let people think that, because he had come to live up-country, he was therefore running to seed. And having dusted and rubbed and polished, she ranged the cases along the walls of the passage and on the dining-room sideboard. To the delight of the children.

But she might have spared her pains. As far as Richard was concerned, the visit was a failure.

Baron von Krause arrived during the forenoon. Richard was on his rounds, and did not reach home till they were half through dinner. And, then, he tried to get out of coming to table! Going in search of him on his non-appearance, she found him sunk in his armchair, from which he vowed he was too tired to stir . . . let alone exert himself to entertain strangers.

"Strangers? There's only him! And he's just as nice as he always was. We're getting on capitally. The children, too."

The Baron was a short, sturdy little man, bronzed brown with the sun—beside him, Richard, who never tanned, looked almost transparent—dark of hair and beard, and with a pair of kindly blue eyes that beamed at you from behind large gold spectacles. Veteran colonist though he was, still he spoke a jargon all his own, coupled with a thick, foreign accent. He also expressed himself with extreme deliberation, using odd, archaic words ("Like the Bible," thought Cuffy), and, could he not at once find the word he sought, he paused in what he was saying and scoured his mind till he had captured it. This, added to the fact that he did things at table that were strictly forbidden them, made him an object of enormous interest to the children; and three pairs of eyes hung entranced on him, as he ate and spoke, to the detriment of their owners' own table-manners. In waiting, too, for him to be delivered of a word, three little faces went pink with a mixture of embarrassment and anticipation. In vain did Mary privately frown and shake her head. A knifeful of peas, "me*lan*choly" for melancholy, and all three were agog again. It was a real drawback, at a time like this, to have such *noticing* children.

But, with their father's entry, a change came over their behaviour. Cuffy kept his eyes fixed on his plate and minded what he was doing, and Lallie and Lucie faithfully followed suit. The fun was at an end. For it wasn't at all the same when Papa forgot, in the middle of a sentence, what he was going to say (because Mamma interrupted him with a potato) and tried and tried his hardest to remember, and couldn't, and got very cross with himself. Mamma thought it was funny, though, for she laughed and said she believed he'd forget his head, if it wasn't screwed on; and then she told a story about Papa nearly going out without his collar, and how she had rushed after him and saved him . . . which made Papa cross with her, as well.

It was too hot to go walking. And after dinner, Mahony having been called back to the surgery, the Baron strayed to the drawing-room, opened the piano, and put his hairy, knuckly hands on the keys. Mary thought this an excellent chance to slip away and "see to things"; but Richard, the patient gone, first set his door ajar, then came along the passage and sat down in an armchair by the drawing-room window. Cuffy, at ball on the verandah, also crept in, and took up his position close to the piano, leaning against it and staring fixedly at the player—listening, that is to say, after the fashion of children, as much with the eyes as with the ears (as if only by keeping the maker of the sounds in view can they grasp the sounds themselves)—the while he continued mechanically to tip his ball from hand to hand.

The Baron was playing something hard and ugly . . . like five-finger exercises, but with more notes, oh! *lots* of notes, in it . . . and to and fro went the ball, to and fro. This lasted a long time, and the Baron was hot when he'd finished, and had to wipe his neck, and clean his glasses. Then he did some more; and this time it was prettier, with a tune to it, and it danced in little squirts up the piano; and Cuffy was obliged to smile . . . he didn't know why; his mouth just smiled by itself. He also left off fiddling with the ball. By now the Baron had become aware of his small listener. Musician-wise had noted, too, the child's instinctive response to the tripping scherzo. Pausing, he peered at Cuffy through his large round spectacles; and, before putting his fingers in place for the third piece, leant over and patted the boy's cheek, murmuring as he did: "Let us see then . . . yet, let us see!" To Cuffy he said: "Hearken now, my little one . . . hearken well to this! Here

I shall give you food for the heart as well as for the head!"—
And then he began to play music that was quite, quite different to that before . . . and wasn't *like* music any more. It whispered in the bass, and while it whispered, it growled; but the
treble didn't growl: it cried.

And now something funny happened to Cuffy. He began
to feel as if he'd like to run away; he didn't *want* to listen
. . . and his heart started to beat fast. Like if he *had* run. The
Baron 'd said he was playing to it . . . perhaps that was why
. . . for it seemed to be getting bigger . . . till it was almost too
tight for his chest. Letting his ball fall, he pressed his fists
close to where he thought his heart must be. Something hurt
him in there . . . he didn't *like* this music, he wanted to call
out to it to stop. But the piano didn't care: it went on and on,
and though it tried once to be different, it always came back
and did the same thing over again . . . a dreadful thing . . . oh!
something *would* burst in him, if it didn't leave off . . . he felt
all swollen . . . yes, he was going to burst . . .

Then, without so much as taking his fingers off the keys, the
Baron began to make a lot of little notes that sounded just like
a wind, and throwing back his head, and opening his mouth
wide, he sang funny things . . . in ever such a funny voice.

> *Uber'm Garten durch die Lüfte*
> *Hört' ich Wandervögel zieh'n*
> *Das bedeutet Frühlingsdüfte,*
> *Unten fängt's schon an zu blüh'n!*

The relief, the ecstatic relief that surged through Cuffy at
these lovely sounds, was too much for him. His eyes ran over,
and tears ran down his cheeks; nor could he help it, or stop
them, when he found what they were doing.

Mamma—she had come back—made ever such big eyes at
him.

"*Cuffy!* What on earth . . . Is *this* how you say thank-you
for the pretty music?" (If only he was not going off, before
a visitor, into one of his tantrums!)

"Nay, chide him not!" said the Baron, and smiled as he
spoke: a very peculiar smile, indeed, to Mary's way of thinking. And then he took no more notice of her at all, but bent
over Cuffy and asked, in quite a *polite* voice: "Will you that I
play you again, my little one?"

755

"No . . . no!"— As rude as the Baron was polite, Cuffy gave a great gulp, and bolted from the room to the bottom of the garden; where he hid among the raspberry-bushes. He didn't know what the matter was; but he felt all sore; humiliated beyond telling.

When he went back, aggressively sheepish and ashamed, Papa had gone. But Mamma and the Baron were talking, and he heard Mamma say: ". . . without the least difficulty . . . ever since he was a tiny tot.— Oh, here we are, are we?— Now, Baron, he shall play to you."

Something turned over in Cuffy at these words. "*No!* I won't!"

But Mamma threw him a look which he knew better than to disobey. Besides, she already had his music-book on the rack, the stool screwed up, and herself stood behind it, to turn the pages. Ungraciously Cuffy climbed to the slippery leather top, from which his short legs dangled. Very well then, if he must play, he must, he didn't care; but he wouldn't look at his notes, or listen to what he did. Instead, he'd count how many flies he could see in front of him, on the wall and the ceiling. One . . . two . . .

The piece—it dated from Mary's own schooldays—at an end, his mother waited in vain for the customary panegyric.

But the Baron merely said: "H'm," and again: "H'm!" Adding, as a kind of afterthought: "Habile little fingers."

When he turned to Cuffy, however, it was with quite a different voice. "Well, and how many were then the flies on the *plafond,* my little one?"

Colouring to his hair-roots (*now* he was going to catch it!) Cuffy just managed to stammer out: "Twelve blowflies and seventeen little flies."

But the Baron only threw back his head, and laughed and laughed. "Ha-ha, ha-ha! Twelve big and seventeen little! That it good . . . that is very good!" To add mysteriously: "Surely this, too, is a sign . . . this capacity for to escape!— But now come hither, my son, and let us play the little game. The bad little boy who counts the flies, so long he plays the bad piece, shall stand so, with his face to the wall. I strike the notes—*so!* —and he is telling me their names—if Mr. G or Mrs. A—yes? List now, if you can hear what is this?"

"Huh, that's easy! That's C."

"And this fellow, so grey he?"

"A—E—B." Cuffy liked this: it was fun.

"And now how many I strike? D, F . . . right! B, D sharp . . . good! And here this—an ugly one, this fellow! He agree not with his neighbour."

"That's two together . . . close, I mean. G and A."

"*Ach Himmel!*" cried the Baron. "The ear, it, too, is perfect!" — And swiftly crossing the room, he took Cuffy's face in his hands and turned it up. For a moment he stood looking down at it; and his brown, bearded face was very solemn. Then, stooping, he kissed the boy on the forehead. "May the good God bless you, my child, and prosper His most precious gift!"— And this, just when Cuffy (after the fly episode) had begun to think him rather a nice old man!

Then he was free to run away and play; which he did with all his might. But later in the afternoon, when it was cool enough to go walking, it was Cuffy the Baron invited to accompany him.— "Nay, we leave the little sisters at home with the good Mamma, and make the promenade alone, just we both!"

Cuffy remembered the flies, forgave the kiss, and off they set. They walked a long way into the bush, farther than they were allowed to go with Miss Prestwick; and the Baron told him about the trees, and poked among the scrub, and used a spyglass like Papa, and showed him things through it. It *was* fun.

Then they sat down on a log to rest. And while they were there, the Baron suddenly picked up his right hand, and looked at it as if it was funny, and turned it over to the back, and stretched out the fingers, and felt the tips, and where the thumb joined on. And when he had done this, he didn't let it go, but kept hold of it; and putting his other hand on Cuffy's shoulders, said: "And now say, my little man, say me why you did weep when I have played?"

Cuffy, all boy again, blushed furiously. He didn't like having his hand held either. So he only looked away, and kicked his heels against the tree, so hard they hurt him. "I dunno."

Mamma would have said: "Oh, yes, you do!" But the Baron wasn't cross. He just gave the hand a little squeeze, and then he began to talk, and he talked and talked. It lasted so long that it was like being in church, and was very dull, all about things Cuffy didn't know. So he hardly listened. He was chiefly intent on politely wriggling his hand free.

But the Baron looked so nice and kind, even when he'd done this, that he plucked up courage to ask something he wanted very much to know; once before when he had tried it, everybody had laughed at him, and made fun.

"What does music *say?*"

But the Baron wasn't like that: He looked as solemn as church again, and nodded his head. "Aha! It commences to stir itself . . . the inward apperception.— The music, it says what is in the heart, my little one, to each interprets the own heart. That is, as you must comprehend, if the one who is making it is the *genie,* and has what in his *own* heart to say. That bad piece, now, you have played me have said nothing —nothing at all . . . oh, how wise, how wise, to count the little flies! But that what you have flowed tears for, my child, that were the sufferings of a so unhappy man—the fears that are coming by night to devour the peace—oh, I will not say them to one so tender! . . . but these, so great were they, so unhappy he, that at the last his brain has burst" (There! he *knew* he had been going to burst!) "and he have become mad. But then, see, at once I have given you the consolation. I have sung you of the nightingale, and moonshine, and first love . . . all, all, of which the youth is full. Our dear madman he has that made, too. His name was Schumann. Mark that, my little one . . . mark it well!"

"Shooh man.— What's mad?"

"*Ach!* break not the little head over such as this. Have no care. The knowledge will soon enough come of pain and suffering."

Cuffy's legs were getting *very* tired with sitting still. Sliding down from the log, he jumped and danced, feeling now somehow all glad inside. "*I* will say music, too, when I am big!"

"*Ja, ja,* but so easy is it not to shake the music out of the sleeve! Man must study hard. It belongs a whole lifetime thereto . . . and much, much courage. But this I will tell you, my little ambitious one! Here is lying"— and the Baron waved his arm all round him—"a great, new music hid. He who makes it, he will put into it the thousand feelings awoken in him by this emptiness and space, this desolation; with always the serene blue heaven above, and these pale, sad, so grotesque trees that weep and rave. He puts the golden wattle in it, when it blooms and reeks, and this melancholy bush, oh, so old, so old, and this silence as of death that nothing stirs. No, birdleins will sing in *his Musik*. But will you be that one, my son, you must first have given up all else for it . . . all the joys and pleasures that make the life glad. These will be for the others, not for you, my dear . . . you must only go wizout . . . renounce . . . look on!— But come, let us now home, and I will speak . . . yes, I shall speak of it to the good Mamma and Papa!"

"Preposterous, I call it!" said Mary warmly, and threw the letter on the table. The Baron's departure was three days old by now, and the letter she had just read written in his hand. "Only a man could propose such a thing! Why don't you say something, Richard? Surely you don't . . ."

"No, I can see it's out of the question."

"I should think so! At *his* age! . . . why, he's a mere baby. How the Baron could think for a moment we should let a tot like him leave home . . . to live among strangers—with these Hermanns or Germans, or whatever he calls them—why, it's almost too silly to discuss. As for his offer to defray all expenses out of his own pocket . . . no doubt he means it well . . . but it strikes me as very tactless. Does he think we can't afford to pay for our own children?"

"I'll warrant such an idea never entered his head. My dear, you don't understand."

"It's you I don't understand. As a rule you flare up at the mere mention of money. Yet you take this quite calmly."

"Good Lord, Mary! the man means it for a compliment. He not only took a liking to the boy, but he's a connoisseur in music, a thoroughly competent judge. Surely it ought to flatter you, my dear, to hear his high opinion of our child's gift."

"I don't need an outsider to tell me that. If anyone knows Cuffy is clever, it's me. I ought to: I've done everything for him."

"This has nothing to do with cleverness."

"Why not? What else is it?"

"It's music, my dear!" cried Mahony, waxing impatient. "Music, and the musical faculty . . . ear, instinct, inborn receptivity."

"Well?"

"Good God, Mary! . . . it sometimes seems as if we spoke a different language. The fact of the matter is, you haven't a note of music in you!"

Mary was deeply hurt. "I, who have taught the child everything he knows? He wouldn't even be able to read his notes yet, if it had been left to you! Haven't I stood over him, and drummed things into him, and kept him at the piano? And all the thanks I get for it is to hear that I'm not capable of judging . . . haven't a note of music in me! The truth is, I'm good enough to work and slave to make ends meet, and all the rest of it. But when it comes to anything else, anything *cleverer* . . . then the first outsider knows better than I do. Thank God, I've still got my children! They at least look up to me. And that brings me back to where I started. I've got them, and I mean to keep them. Nothing shall part me from them. If Cuffy goes, I go too!"

On the verandah the three in question played a game of their own devising. They poked at each other round a corner of the house, with sticks for swords, advancing and retreating to the cry of "Shooh, man!" from the army of the twins, to which Cuffy made vigorous response: "Shooh, woman!"

And this phrase, which remained in use long after its origin was forgotten, was the sole trace left on Cuffy's life by the Baron's visit.

[10]

THE almond-trees that grew in a clump at the bottom of the garden had shed their pink blossoms and began to form fruit. At first, did you slyly bite one of the funny long green things in two, you came to a messy jelly . . . bah! it *was* nasty . . . you spat it out again, as quick as you could. But a little later, though you could still get your teeth through the green shell, which was hairy on your tongue and sourer than ever, you found a delicious white slippery kernel inside. Cuffy made this discovery one afternoon, when Mamma had gone to the Bank to tea, and Miss Prestwick was busy writing letters. He ate freely of the delicacy; and his twin shadows demanded to eat, too. Their milk teeth being waggly, he bit the green casing

760

through for them; and they fished out the kernels for themselves.

That night, there were loud cries for Mamma. Hurrying to them, candle in hand, Mary found the children pale and distressed, their little bodies cramped with grinding, colicky pains.

Green almonds?— "Oh, you naughty, *naughty* children! Haven't I told you never to touch them? Where was Miss Prestwick?— There! I've always said it: she isn't *fit* to have charge of them. I shall pack her off first thing to-morrow."

Followed a time of much pain and discomfort for the almond-eaters; of worry and trouble for Mary, who for several nights was up and down. All three paid dearly for their indulgence; but recovery was not in order of merit. Cuffy, who had enjoyed the lion's share, was the first to improve: remarkable, agreed Richard, the power of recuperation possessed by this thin, pale child. The twins, for all their sturdiness, were harder to bring round.

However, at last they, too, were on their feet again, looking very white and pulled down, it was true; still, there they were, able to trot about; and their father celebrated the occasion by taking the trio for a walk by the Lagoon. The world was a new place to the little prisoners. They paused at every step to wonder and exclaim.

What happened, no one knew. At the time, it seemed to Mary that, for a first walk, Richard was keeping them out too long. However, she said nothing; for they came back in good spirits, ate their supper of bread and milk with appetite, and went cheerily to bed.

Then, shortly after midnight, Lallie roused the house with shrill cries. Running to her, Mary found the child doubled up with pain and wet with perspiration. By morning, she was as ill as before. There was nothing for it but to buckle down to a fresh bout of nursing.

Of the two lovely little blue-eyed, fair-haired girls, who were the joy of their parents' lives, as Cuffy was the pride: of these, Mahony's early whimsy, that a single soul had been parcelled out between two bodies, still held good. Not an act in their six short years but had, till now, been a joint one. Hand in hand, cheek to cheek, they faced their tiny experiences, turning to each other to share a tidbit, a secret, a smile. But if, in such oneness, there could be talk of a leader, then

761

it was Lallie who led. A quarter of an hour older, a fraction of an inch taller, half a pound heavier, she had always been a thought bolder than her sister, a hint quicker to take the proffered lollipop, to speak out her baby thoughts. Just as Cuffy was their common model, so Lucie patterned herself on Lallie; and, without Lallie, was less than half herself; even a temporary separation proving as rude a wrench as though they had been born with a fleshly bond.— And it was a real trial, in the days that followed, to hear the bereft Lucie's plaintive wail: "Where's Lallie? I want Lallie . . . I want Lallie."— "Surely, Cuffy, you can manage to keep her amused? Play with her, dear. Let her do just as she likes," said Mary—with a contorted face, in the act of wringing a flannel binder out of all but boiling water.

She spoke briskly; was cheerful, and of good heart.— For, in the beginning, no suspicion of anything being seriously amiss crossed her mind. It was just a relapse, and as such needed carefullest nursing and attention. In the course of the fifth day, however, one or two little things that happened stirred a vague uneasiness in her. Or, rather, she saw afterwards that this had been so: at the moment, she had let the uncomfortable impressions escape her with all speed. It struck her that the child's progress was very slow. Also she noticed that Richard tried another remedy. However, this change seemed to the good; towards evening Lallie fell into a refreshing sleep. But when, next morning, after a broken night she drew up the blind, something in the child's aspect brought back, with a rush, and intensified, her hazy disquiets of the previous day. Lallie was oddly dull. She would not open her eyes properly, or answer when spoken to; and she turned her face from the cooling drink that was held to her lips.

"She doesn't seem so well this morning."

Mary's voice was steady, as she uttered these words—this commonplace of the sickroom. But even as she spoke, she became aware of the cold fear that was laying itself round her heart. It seemed to sink, to grow strangely leaden, as she watched Richard make the necessary examination . . . ever so gently . . . she had never really known how gentle his hands were, till she saw them used on the shrinking body of his own child.— "Papa's darling . . . Papa's good little girl!"— But, the sheet drawn up again, he avoided meeting her eyes. As if that

would help him! She who could read his face as if it were a
book . . . how did he hope to deceive *her?*—and where one of
her own babies was concerned!

"Richard, what is it? Do you . . ."

"Now, my dear, don't get alarmed. There's bound to be a
certain amount of prostration . . . till the dysentery is checked.
I shall try ipecac."

But neither ipecacuanha, nor yet a compound mixture—administered in the small doses suited to so young a patient—had
any effect. The inflammation persisted, racking the child with
pain, steadily draining her of strength. It was a poor limp little
sweat-drenched body, with loosely bobbing head, that Mary,
had she to lift it, held in her arms. Throughout this day, too,
the sixth, she was forced to listen, sitting helplessly by, to a
sound that was half a wail and half a moan of utter lassitude.
And, towards evening, a more distressing symptom set in, in
the shape of a convulsive retching. On her knees beside the
bed, her right arm beneath Lallie's shoulders, Mary suffered,
in her own vitals, the struggle that contorted the little body
prior to the fit of sickness. Hers, too, the heart-rending task
of trying to still the child's terror—the frightened eyes, the
arms imploringly outheld, the cries of "Mamma, Mamma!" to
the person who had never yet failed to help—as the spasms
began anew.

"It's *all* right, my darling, my precious! Mamma's here—here,
close beside you. There, there! It'll soon be better now."— And
so it went on for the greater part of the night.

In the intervals between the attacks, when the exhausted
child dozed heavily, Mary, not venturing to move from her
knees, laid her face down on the bed, and wrestled with the
One she held responsible. "Oh, God, be merciful! She's such
a little child, God! . . . to have to suffer so. Oh, spare her! . . .
spare my baby."

By morning light, she was horrified to find that the little
tongue had turned brown. The shock of this discovery was
so great that it drove over her lips a thought that had come
to her in the night . . . had haunted her . . . only to be thrust
back, again and again, into the limbo where it belonged. What
if Richard . . . if perhaps some new remedy had been invented,
since last he was in practice, which he didn't know of?—he
had been out of the way of things so long.

763

Now, a wild fear for her child's life drowned all lesser considerations.— "What . . . what about getting a second opinion?"

Mahony looked sadly at her, and laid his hand on her shoulder. "Mary . . . dear wife—" he began; then broke off: too well he knew the agonies of self-reproach that might await her. "Yes, you're right. I tell you what I'll do. I'll run up to the station and get Pendrell to telegraph to Oakworth. There's a man there . . . I happen to know his name."

Never a moment's hesitation over the expense it would put him to: never a sign of hurt at the doubt cast on his own skill. God bless him! From where she sat Mary watched him go: he took a short-cut up the back yard, past kitchen and henhouse. Oh, but he had no hat on! . . . had gone out without one . . . had *forgotten* to put his hat on—he who was so afraid of the sun! As she grasped what the omission meant, at the lightning-flash it gave her into his own state of mind, she clenched her hands till her nails cut her palms.

At earliest, the doctor could not arrive before five o'clock. All through the long hours of that long, hot day, she sat and waited for his coming: pinning her faith to it—as one who is whirling down a precipitous slope snatches at any frail root or blade of grass that offers to his hand. Something—some miracle would . . . *must* . . . happen!—to save her child. She was quite alone. Richard had to attend his patients, and in the afternoon to drive into the bush: other people could not be put off, or neglected, because his own child lay ill. The wife of the Bank Manager, hearing of their trouble, came and took away the other children. And there Mary sat, heedless of food or rest, conscious only of the little tortured body on the bed before her; sat and fanned off the flies, and pulled up or turned down the sheet, according as fever or the rigors shook the child, noting each creeping change for the worse, snatching at fantastic changes for the better. Her lips were thin and dogged in her haggard face; her eyes burned like coals; it was as if, within her, she was engaged in concentrating a store of strength, with which to invest her child.— But on going out to the kitchen to prepare fresh rice-water, she became aware that, for all the broiling heat of the day, her hands were numb with cold.

Richard came rushing home, to meet the train. To warn, too,

the stranger to caution. "Not a word, I beg of you, before my wife. She is breaking her heart over it."

But one glimpse of the man who entered the room at Richard's side brought Mary's last hope crashing about her ears; and in this moment she faced the fact that Lallie must die. The newcomer was just an ordinary country doctor—well she knew the type!—rough, burly, uncouth. Into the ordered stillness of the sickroom he brought the first disturbance. He tripped over the mat, his boots creaked, his hands were clumsy —or seemed so, compared with Richard's. Oh, the madness of calling in a man like this, when she had Richard at her side! Fool, fool that she was! Now, her only desire was to be rid of him again. She turned away, unable to look on while he handled Lallie, disarranged—hurt—her, in pulling back the sheet and exposing the distended, drumlike little body. ("Um . . . just so!") His manner to Richard, too, was galling; his tone one of patronage. He no doubt regarded him as some old hack who had doddered his life away up-country, and could now not treat even a case of dysentery, without the aid of a younger man. And for this, which was all her doing, Richard would have to sit with him and listen to him, till the down train went at ten. It was too much for Mary. The tears that had obstinately refused to flow for the greater grief rose to her eyes, and were so hot and angry that they scorched the back of her lids.

That night, in the stillness that followed his departure, the last torment was inflicted on the dying child in the shape of a monstrous hiccough. It started from far, far down, shot out with the violence of an explosion, and seemed as if it would tear the little body in two. Under this new blow Mary's courage all but failed her. In vain did Mahony, his arm round her bent shoulders, try to soothe her. "My darling, it sounds worse than it is. We feel it more than she does . . . now." Each time it burst forth an irrepressible shudder ran through Mary, as if it were she herself who was being racked.— And on this night her passionate prayer ran: "Take her, God! . . . take her if you must! I give her back to you. But oh, let it be soon! . . . stop her suffering . . . give her peace." And as hour after hour dragged by, without respite, she rounded on Him and fiercely upbraided Him. "It is cruel of You . . . cruel! No earthly father would torture a child as You are doing. . . . You, all-powerful, and called Love!"

But, little by little, so stealthily that its coming was imperceptible, the ultimate peace fell: by daybreak there was nothing more to hope or to fear. Throughout the long day that followed—it seemed made of years, yet passed like an hour— Lallie lay in coma, drawing breaths that were part snores, part heavy sighs. Time and place ceased to exist for Mary, as she sat and watched her child die. Through noon and afternoon, and on into the dark, she tirelessly wiped the damp brow and matted curls, fanned off the greedy flies, one little inert hand held firmly in her own: perhaps somehow, on this, her darling's last, fearsome journey, the single journey in her short life that she had taken unattended, something would tell her that her mother was with her, her mother's love keeping and holding her.— On this day Richard did not leave the house. And their kind friend again fetched away the other children.

The *other* children? . . . what need now of this word! Henceforth, there would always and for ever be only two. Never again, if not by accident, would the proud words, "My three!" cross her lips.— There she sat, committing to oblivion her mother-store of fond and foolish dreams, the lovely fabric of hopes and plans that she had woven about this little dear one's future; sat bidding farewell to many a tiny endearing feature of which none but she knew: in this spun-glass hair the one rebellious curl that would not twist with the rest; secret dimples kneaded in the baby body; the tiny birthmark below the right shoulder; the chubby, dimpled hands—Richard's hands in miniature—all now destined to be shut away and hidden from sight. Oh, what was the use of creating so fair a thing, merely to destroy it! (They say He knows all, but never, never can He have known what it means to be a mother.)

Midnight had struck before Mahony, his arms about her, could half lead, half carry her from the room. For, her long agony of suspense over, she collapsed, broke utterly down, in a way that alarmed him. He ran for restoratives; bathed her forehead; himself undressed her and got her to bed. Only then came the saving tears, setting free the desperate and conflicting emotions, till now so rigorously held in check, in a storm of grief of which he had never known the like. There was something primitive about it, savage even. For, in it, Mary wept the passion of her life—her children. And over the sacrifice she was now called on to make, her heart bled, as raw, as lacerated, as once her body had lain in giving them birth.

For long Mahony made no attempt to soothe or restrain. Well for her that she could weep! A nature like Mary's would not be chastened by suffering: never would she know resignation; or forgive the injury that had been done her. This physical outlet was her sole means of relief.

But the moment came when he put out his hand and sought hers. "Wife . . . my own dearest! . . . it is not for ever. You . . . we . . . shall see our child again."

But Mary would have none of it. Vehemently she tore her hand away. "Oh, what does that help? . . . help *me!* I want her now . . . and here. I want to hold her in my arms . . . and feel her . . . and hear her speak. She will never speak to me again. Oh, my baby, my baby! . . . and I loved you so."

"She knew it well. She still does."

"How do *you* know? . . . how do you *know?* Those are only words. They may do for you. . . . But I was her mother. She was mine; my very own. And do you think she wanted to die . . . and leave me? They tore her away—and tortured her—and frightened her. They may be frightening her still . . . such a little child, alone and frightened . . . and me not able to get to her!— Oh, *why* should this just happen to us? Other people's children aren't taken . . . they grow up . . . grow old. And we are so few . . . why, *why* had it to be?"

Mea culpa, mea maxima culpa!— "If only I had never brought you to this accursed place!"

There was an instant's pause, a momentary cessation of her laboured breathing, as the bed shook under the shudders that stand to a man for sobs, before she flung round, and drew him to her.

"Mary, Mary! . . . I meant it for the best."

"I know you did, I know! I *won't* have you blame yourself. It might have happened anywhere." (Oh, my baby, my baby!)

Now they clung to each other, all the petty differences they laboured under obliterated by their common grief. Till suddenly a sound fell on their ears, driving them apart to listen: it was little Lucie, waking from sleep in an empty bed, and crying with fear. Rising, her father carried her over and laid her down in his own warm place; and Mary, recalled from her senseless weeping by a need greater than her own, held out her arms and gathered the child in. "It's all right, my darling! Mamma's here."

This, the ultimate remedy.— Half an hour later when he crept back to look, mother and child slept, tear-stained cheek to cheek.

His hand in his father's, Cuffy was led into the little room where Lallie lay.— "I want them to have no morbid fear of death."

On waking that morning—after a rather jolly day spent at the Bank . . . or what would have been jolly, if Lucie hadn't been such a cry-baby . . . where he had been allowed to try to lift a bar of gold, and to step inside the great safe: on waking, Cuffy heard the amazing news that Lallie had gone away: God had taken her to live with Him. His eyes all but dropped out of his head, a dozen questions jumped to his tongue; but he did not ask one of them; for Mamma never stopped crying, and Papa looked as he did when you didn't talk to him, but got away and tried not to remember. So Cuffy sat on the edge of the verandah and felt most awfully surprised. What had happened was too strange, too far removed from the range of his experience, too "int'resting," to let any other feeling come up in him. He wondered and wondered . . . why God had done it . . . and why He had just wanted Lallie. Now he himself . . . well, Luce *had* got so whiny!

But the darkened room and a sheet over the whole bed did something funny to him . . . inside. And as his father turned the slats of the venetian, so that a pale daylight filtered in, Cuffy asked—in a voice he meant to make whispery and small, but which came out hoarse like a crow: "What's she covered up like that for?"

For answer, Mahony drew back the double layer of mosquito-netting, and displayed the little sister's face.— "Don't be afraid, Cuffy. She's only asleep."— And indeed it might well have been so. Here were no rigidly trussed limbs, no stiffly folded arms: the heave of the breath alone was missing. Lallie lay with one little hand under her cheek, her curls tumbling naturally over her shoulder. The other hand held a nosegay, a bit of gaudy red geranium tied up with one of its own

768

leaves—the single poor flower Mahony had found still a-bloom in the garden.

"Kiss her, Cuffy."

Cuffy obeyed—and got a shock. "Why's she so cold?"

"Because her spirit is flown. This dear little body, that we have known and loved, was only the house of the spirit; and now is empty, and must fade. But though we shall not see her, our Lallie will go on living and growing . . . in a grace and beauty such as earth cannot show."— And more to himself than to the body beside him, Mahony murmured:

> Not as a child shall we again behold her,
> For when, with raptures wild,
> In our embraces we again enfold her,
> She will not be a child,
> But a fair maiden in her Father's mansions . . .

"Will she . . . do you mean . . . be grown up?" And Cuffy fixed wide, affrighted eyes on his father.— For, in listening to these words, he had a sudden vision of a Lallie who looked just like Miss Prestwick, or Cousin Emmy, with a little small waist, and bulgings, and tight, high, buttoned boots. And against this picture—especially the boots—something in him rose and screamed with repugnance. He wanted Lallie's fat little legs in socks and strapped shoes, as he had always known them. He *would* not have her different!

"Oh, no, no . . . *no!*"— And with this, his habitual defence against the things he was unwilling to face, Cuffy tore his hand away, and escaped to his sanctuary at the bottom of the garden.

Here, for the first time, a sense of loss came over him. (It was the boots had done it.) What, never see Lallie any more? . . . as his little fat sister? It couldn't be true . . . it couldn't! "I don't believe it . . . I *don't* believe it!" (Hadn't they told him that very morning that God had taken her away, when all the time she was in there lying on the bed?) And this attitude of doubt persisted; even though, when he got back the next after-noon from a long walk with Maria. God had kept His word and she was gone. But many and many a day passed before Cuffy gave up expecting his little sister to re-appear. Did he go into an empty room, or turn a corner of the verandah, it seemed to him that he *must* find Lallie there: suddenly she would have come back, and everything be as it was before. For since, by their father's care, all the sinister ceremonials and paraphernalia of death were kept from them, he was free to go on regarding it solely in the light of an abrupt disappearance . . . and if you could be spirited away in this fashion, who was to say if you mightn't just as easily pop up again? Also by Mahony's wish, neither he nor Lucie ever set foot in the outlying bush cemetery, where, in due time, a little cross rose to inform the curious that the small mound before them hid the mortal remains of Alicia Mary Townshend-Mahony, aged five and a half years.— Providing people, at the same time, with a puzzle to scratch their heads over. For, in place of the usual reference to lambs and tender shepherds, they found themselves confronted by the words: *Dans l'espoir*. And what the meaning of this heathenish term might be, none in Barambogie knew, but all were suspicious of.

"We've simply *got* to afford it," was Mary's grim reply.— There she stood, her gaunt eyes fixed on Richard, the embodiment of a mother-creature at bay to protect her young.

Christmas had come and gone, and the fierce northern summer was upon them in earnest. Creeks and water-holes were dry now, rivers shrunk to a trickling thread; while that was brown straw which had once been grass. And Mary, worn down by heat and mental suffering, was fretting her heart out over her remaining baby, little Lucie, now but the ghost of her former self. Coming on top of Lucie's own illness, her twin-sister's death had struck her a blow from which she did not seem able to recover. And to see the child droop and fade before her very eyes rendered Mary desperate. This was why, to Richard's procrastinating and undecided: "I must see if I can afford it," she had flung out her challenge: "We've *got* to!"

"I suppose you're right."

"I know I am!"——

Many and heartfelt had been the expressions of sympathy from those friends and acquaintances who had read the brief notice on the front page of the *Argus*. Outsiders, too, people Mary had almost forgotten, showed that they still remembered her, by condoling with her in her loss. But it was left to dear old Tilly to translate sentiment into practical aid.

"How I feel for you, my darling, words wouldn't tell. It's the cruellest thing ever happened. But, oh, the blessing, Mary, that you've still got your other two. You must just remember how much they need you, love, while they're so small, and how much you are to them.— And now hark to me, my dear. I'd been planning before this to take a shanty at Lorne, for the hot weather; and what I want is for you to come and share it with me—share expenses, if you like, me knowing what you are! But get the chicks away from that wicked heat you must! — Besides, helping to look after Baby'll be the best of medicines for that poor forlorn little mite, who it makes my heart ache even to think of."

Too great were the odds—in this case the welfare, perhaps the very life, of his remaining children—against him. Mahony bowed his head. And when Mary had gone, he unlocked a private drawer of his table and drew out a box in which lay several rolls of notes, carefully checked and numbered. Once more he counted them through. For weeks, nay, for months, he had been laboriously adding pound to pound. In all there were close on forty of them. He had fully intended to make it fifty by New Year. Now, there was no help: it would have to go. First, the doctor's fare from Oakworth; then the costs of the funeral . . . with a five-pound note to the parson. What was left after these things were paid must be sacrificed to Mary and the children. They would need every penny of it . . . and more, besides.

PART II

[1]

To come back to the empty house, having watched the train carry them off: ("Kiss papa good-bye! . . . good-bye . . . good-bye, my darlings! Come back with rosy cheeks.— Try to forget, Mary . . . my poor old wife!") to come back to the empty house was like facing death anew. All the doors, three on each side of the central passage, stood open, showing unnatural-looking rooms. Mary had done her best to leave things tidy, but she had not been able to avoid the last disorder inevitable on a journey. Odd sheets of newspaper lay about and lengths of twine; the floors were unswept, the beds unmade; one of

the children had dropped a glove . . . Mahony stooped to it
. . . Cuffy's, for a wager, seeing that the middle finger was
chewed to pulp. And as he stood holding it, it seemed as if
from out these yawning doors, these dismal rooms, one or
other of his little ones must surely dart and run to him, with
a cry of "Papa . . . Papa!" But not a sound broke the silence,
no shadow smudged the whitewash of the walls.

The first shock over, however, the litter cleared up, the
rooms dressed, he almost relished the hush and peace to which
the going of wife and children had left him. For one thing,
he could rest on the knowledge that he had done for them
all that was humanly possible. In return, he would, for several
weeks to come, be spared the mute reproach of two wan little
faces, and a mother's haggard eyes. Nor need he crack his
brains for a time over the problem of an education for the
children in this wilderness, or be chafed by Mary's silent but
pregnant glosses on the practice. In a word he was *free* . . .
free to exist unobserving and unobserved.

But his satisfaction was short-lived: by the end of the second
day, the deathlike stillness had begun to wear him down.
Maria was shut off in the detached kitchen; and, on getting
home of a late afternoon, he knew that, but for the final mill-
screech, and the distant rumble of the ten-o'clock train, no
mortal sound would reach his ears the long night through. The
silence gathered, descended, and settled upon him, like a fog
or a cloud. There was something ominous about it, and, instead of reading, he found himself listening . . . listening. Only
very gradually did the thought break through that he had
something to listen for. Dark having fallen, might not a tiny
ghost, a little spirit that had not yet found rest afar from those
it loved, flit from room to room in search of them? What more
likely, indeed? He strained his ears. But only his pulses buzzed
there. On the other hand, about eleven o'clock one night, on
coming out of the surgery to cross to the bedroom, he could
have sworn to catching a glimpse of a little shape . . . vague,
misty of outline, gone even as he saw it, and yet unmistakable
. . . vanishing in the doorway of the children's room. His heart
gave a great leap of joy and recognition. Swiftly following, he
called a name; but on the empty air: the room had no occupant. For two nights after he kept watch, to waylay the apparition, should it come; but, shy of human eyes, it did not show

itself again. Not to be baulked, he tried a fresh means: taking
a sheet of paper he let his hand lie lightly along the pencil.
And, lo and behold! at the second trial the pencil began to
move, seemed to strive to form words; while by the fourth
evening words were coming through. *Her Mamma . . . her
Luce . . . wants her Mamma.*

The kitchen clock had stopped: Maria, half undressed, stealing tiptoe into the house to see the time, a tin lamp with a
reflector in her hand, was pulled up short, half-way down the
passage, by the sound of voices. Hello! who was Doctor talking
to? A patient at this hour? But nobody had knocked at the
door. And what . . . oh, crikey! whatever was he saying? The
girl's eyes and mouth opened, and her cheeks went pale, as the
sense of what she heard broke on her. Pressing herself against
the wall, she threw a terrified glance over her shoulder, into
the inky shadows cast by the lamp.——

"Ma! I was fair skeered out of me senses. To hear 'im sitting
there a-talkin' to that pore little kid, what's been dead and
buried this month and more! An' him calling her by her name,
and saying her Ma would soon be back, and then she wouldn't
need to feel lonely any more—why, I tell yer, even this mornin'
in broad daylight, I found myself lookin' behind me the whole
time.— Go back? Stop another night there? Not me! I couldn't,
Ma! I'm *skeered.*"

"You great ninny, you! What could 'urt yer, I'd like to
know? . . . as long as you say yer prayers reg'lar, and tells the
troof. Ghosts, indeed! I'll ghost you!"— But Maria, more imagi-
natively fibred, was not to be won over.

Mahony listened to the excuses put forward by her mother
on his reaching home that evening; listened with the kindly
courtesy he kept for those beneath him who met him civilly
and with respect. Maria's plea of loneliness was duly weighed.
"Though, I must say, I think she has hardly given the new
conditions a fair trial. However, she has always been a good
girl, and the plan you propose, Mrs. Beetling, will no doubt
answer very well during my wife's absence."

It not only answered: it was an improvement. Breakfast was
perhaps served a little later than usual, and the cooking proved
rather coarser than Maria's who was Mary-trained. But it was
all to the good that, supper over, Mrs. Beetling put on her bonnet and went home, leaving the place clear. His beloved little

ghost was then free to flit as it would, without fear of surprise or disturbance. He continually felt its presence—though it did not again materialise—and message after message continued to come through. Written always by a third person, in an unfamiliar hand . . . as was only to be expected, considering that the twins still struggled with pothooks and hangers . . . they yet gave abundant proof of their authorship.

Such a proof, for instance, as the night when he found that his script ran: *Her baby . . . nose . . . kitchen fire.*

For a long time he could make nothing of this, though he twisted it this way and that. Then, however, it flashed upon him that the twins had nursed large waxen dolls, clad as infants; and straightway he rose to look for the one that had been Lallie's. After a lengthy search by the light of the single candle, in the course of which he ransacked various drawers and boxes, he found the object in question . . . tenderly wrapped and hidden away in Mary's wardrobe. He drew it forth in its white trappings, and, upon his soul, when he held it up to the candle to examine it, he found that one side of the effigy's nose had run together in a kind of blob . . . *melted* . . . no doubt through having been left lying in the sun, or—yes *or* held too close to a fire! Of a certainty he had known nothing of this: never a word had been said, in *his* hearing, of the accident to so expensive a plaything. At the time of purchase, he had been wroth with Mary over the needless outlay. Now . . . now . . . oh, there's a divinity that shapes our ends! . . . now it served him as an irrefragable proof.

In his jubilation he added a red-hot postscript to his daily letter. "I have great—great and joyful—news for you, my darling. But I shall keep it till you come back. It will be something for you to look forward to, on your return to this horrid place."

To which Mary replied: "You make me very curious, Richard. Can North Long Tunnels have struck the reef at last?"

And he: "Something far, far nearer our hearts, my dear, than money and shares. I refer to news compared with which everything earthly fades into insignificance."

Alas! he roused no answering enthusiasm. "Now Richard, don't delude yourself . . . or let yourself be deluded. Of course you knew about that doll's nose. Lallie cried and was so upset. I'm sure what's happening is all your own imagination. I do think one can grossly deceive oneself—especially now you're quite alone. But oh don't trifle with our great sorrow. I couldn't bear it. It's still too near and too bitter."

Of his little ghostly visitant he asked that night: "How shall we ever prove, love, to dear Mamma, that you are really and truly her lost darling?"

To which came the oddly disconcerting, matter-of-fact reply: "Useless. Other things to do. Comes natural to some. Not to her." But Mahony could not find it in his heart to let the matter rest there. So fond a mother, and to be unwilling . . . not to dare to *trust* herself . . . to believe!

And believe what, too? Why, merely that *their* little one, in place of becoming a kind of frozen image of the child they had known, and inhabiting remote, fantastic realms, to which they might some day laboriously attain: that she was still with them, close to them, loving and clinging, and as sportive as in her brief earthly span. It was no doubt this homely, *undignified* aspect of the life-to-come that formed the stumbling-block: for people like Mary, death was inconceivable apart from awfulness and majesty: in this guise alone had it been rung and sung into them. For him, the very lack of dignity was the immense, consoling gain. Firmly convinced of the persistence of human individuality subsequent to the great change, he had now been graciously permitted to see how thin were the walls between the two worlds, how interpenetrable the states. And he rose of a morning, and lay down at night, his heart warm with gratitude to the Giver of knowledge.

But a little child-ghost, no longer encased in the lovely, rounded body that had enhanced its baby prattle and, as it were, decked it out: a little ghost had, after all, not very much to say. A proof of identity given, assurances exchanged that it is still loved and was loved, and the talk trickled naturally to an end. You could not put your arms round it, and hold it to you, in a wordless content. Also, as time passed and Lallie grew easier in her new state, it was not to be denied that she turned a trifle freakish. She would not always come when called, and, pressed as to where she lingered, averred through her mentor, that she was "fossicking." An attempt to get at the meaning of this, involved Mahony in a long, rambling conversation with the elder ghost, that was dreary in the extreme. For it hinged mainly on herself and her own affairs. And, grateful though he was to her for her goodness to his child, he took no interest in her personally; and anything in the nature of a discussion proved disastrous. For she had been but a seamstress in her day, and a seamstress she remained; having, it would seem, gained nothing through her translation, either in knowledge or spirituality.

He flagged. To grip him, an occupation needed to be meaty —to give him something with which to tease his brains. And his present one, supplying none, began little by little to pall, leaving him to the melancholy reflection that, for all their aliveness, our lost ones were truly lost to us, because no longer entangled in the web called living. Impossible for those who had passed on to continue to grieve for a broken doll; to lay weight on the worldly triumphs and failures that meant so much to us; to concern themselves with the changing seasons, the rising up and lying down, the palaver, pother and ado that made up daily life. Though the roads to be followed started from a single point, they swiftly branched off at right angles, never to touch again while we inhabited our earthly shell . . . and, in this connection, he fell to thinking of people long dead, and of how out of place, how *in the way* they would be, did they now come back to earth. We mortals were, for worse or better, ever on the move. Impossible for us to return to the stage at which *they* had known us.

And so it came about that one evening when, with many a silent groan, he had for close on half an hour transcribed the seamstress's platitudes (if it was himself who wrote, as Mary averred, then God help him! . . . he was in, beyond question, for cerebral softening!) with never a word or a sign from Lallie: on this evening he abruptly threw the pencil from him, pushed back his chair, and strode out on the verandah. He needed air, fresh air; was ravenous for it . . . to feel his starved lungs fill and expand. But the December night was hotter even than the day had been; and what passed for air was stale and heavy with sunbaked dust. The effort of inhaling it, the repugnance this smell roused in him, brought him to. Like a man waking from a trance, he looked round him with dazed eyes, and ran a confused hand over his forehead. And in this moment the dreams and shadows of the past two weeks scattered, and he faced reality: it was near midnight, and he stood alone on the ramshackle verandah, with its three broken steps leading down to the path; with the drooping, dust-laden shrubs of the garden before him; the bed of dust that formed the road, beyond. He had come to earth again—and with a bump.

A boundless depression seized him: a sheerly intolerable flatness, after the mood of joyous elation that had gone before. He felt as though he had been sucked dry: what remained of him was but an empty shell. Empty as the house, which, but for a single lamp, lay dark, and tenantless, and silent as the grave. Since the first night of Mary's departure, he had not visualised it thus. Now, he was dismayed by it—and by his own solitude. To rehearse the bare facts: wife and children were a hundred and fifty miles away; his other little child lay under the earth; even the servant had deserted: with the result that there was now not a living creature anywhere within hail. This miserable Lagoon, this shrunken pool of stagnant water, effectually cut him off from human company. If anything should happen to him, if he should be taken ill, or break a limb, he might lie where he fell, till morning, his calls for help unheard. And the thought of his utter isolation, once admitted, swelled to alarming proportions. His brain raced madly— glancing at fire . . . murder . . . sudden death. Why, not a soul here would be able even to summon Mary back to him! . . . no one so much as knew her address. Till he could bear it no longer: jumping out of bed, he ran to the surgery and wrote her whereabouts in large letters on a sheet of paper, which he pinned up in a conspicuous place.

The first faint streaks of daylight, bringing relief on this score, delivered him up to a new—and anything but chimerical —anxiety. What was happening . . . what in the name of fortune was happening to the practice? Regarding, for the first time, the day and the day's business other than as something to be hurried through, that he might escape to his communion with the unseen, he was horrified to see how little was doing, how scanty the total of patients for the past fortnight.— And here was Mary writing that she would shortly need more money!

Nobody at all put in an appearance that morning—though he sat out his consulting-hour to the bitter end. By this time, he had succeeded in convincing himself that the newcomer, Mrs. Beetling, was to blame for the falling-off. Untrained to the job, she had very probably omitted to note, on the slate provided for the purpose, the names of those who called while he was absent. Either she had trusted to her memory and forgotten; or had been out when she ought to have kept the house; or had failed to hear the bell. The dickens! What would people think of him, for neglecting them like this?

By brooding over it, he worked himself into a state of nervous agitation; and, directly half-past ten struck, pushed back his chair and stalked out, to take the culprit to task.

Mrs. Beetling was scrubbing the verandah, her sleeves rolled up above her elbows, arms and hands newborn-looking from hot water and soda. At Mahony's approach, she sat back on her heels to let him by; then, seeing that he intended to speak to her, scrambled to her feet and dried her hands on her apron.

"I wish to have a word with you, Mrs. Beetling."

"Yes, sir?"

She was civil enough, he would say that for her. In looking up at him, too, she smiled with a will: a pleasant-faced woman, and ruddy of cheek . . . another anomaly in this pale country.

But he fronted her squarely for the first time: at their former interview, he had been concerned only to cut her wordiness short. And this broad smile of hers advertised the fact that she had gums bare almost as a babe's; was toothless, save for a few black and rotten stumps in the lower jaw.

Now Mahony was what Mary called a "fad of the first water" with regard to the care of the mouth. He never tired of fulminating against the colonial habit of suffering the untold agonies of toothache, letting the teeth rot in the head, rather than have them medically attended. And the sight here presented to him so exasperated him that he clean forgot what he had come out to say, his irritation hurling itself red-hot against this fresh object of offence.

As though he had a meek and timid patient before him, he now said sternly: "Open your mouth! . . . wide!"

"*Sir!*" Mrs. Beetling's smile faded in amazement. Instinctively pinching her lips, she blinked at Mahony, turned red, and fell to twiddling with a corner of her apron. (So far, she had turned a deaf ear to the tales that were going the round about "the ol' doctor." Now . . . she wondered.)

"Your mouth . . . open your mouth!" repeated Mahony, with the same unnecessary harshness. Then, becoming vaguely aware of the confusion he was causing, he trimmed his sails. "My good woman . . . I have only this moment noticed the disgraceful state of your teeth. Why, you have not a sound one left in your head! What have you been about? . . . never to consult a dentist?"

"Dentist, sir? Not me! Not if I was paid for it! No one'll never get me to any dentist."

"Tut, tut, you fool!" He snapped his fingers; and went on snapping them, to express what he thought of her. And Mrs. Beetling, growing steadily sulkier and more aggrieved, was now forced to stand and listen to a fierce tirade on the horrors of a foul mouth and foul breath, on the harm done to the digestive system, the ills awaiting her in later life. Red as a peony she stood, her apron all twisting in her fingers, her lips glued tight; once only venturing a protest. "I never bin ill in me life!" and, still more glumly: "I suppose me teeth's me own. I kin do what I like with 'em"— To and fro paced Mahony, his hands clasped behind his back, his face aflame; thus ridding himself, on his bewildered hearer, of his own distractedness, the over-stimulation of his nerves; and ending up by vowing that, if she had a grain of sense in her, she would come to the surgery and let him draw from her mouth such ruins as remained. At which Mrs. Beetling, reading this as a threat, went purplish, and backed away in real alarm.— Not till he was some distance off on his morning round, did it occur to him that he had forgotten his original reason in seeking her out. Never a word had he said of her carelessness in writing up the patients! The result was another wild bout of irritation—this time, with himself—and he had to resist an impulse to turn on his heel. What the deuce would he do next? What tricks might his failing memory not play him?

On her side, Mrs. Beetling also yielded to second thoughts. Her first inclination had been to empty her bucket on the garden-bed, let down her skirts, tie on her bonnet, and bang the gate behind her. But she bit it back. The place was a good one: it 'ud be lunatic not to keep it warm for Maria. No sooner, though, did she see Mahony safely away, than she let her indignation fly, and at the top of her voice. "Well, I'm blowed . . . blowed, that's what I am! Wants to pull out all me teef, does he? . . . the *butcher!* Blackguardin' me like that! Of all the lousy ol' ranters . . ."

"Eh, ma?" said a floury young mill-hand, and leant in passing over the garden gate. "What's up with *you?* Bin seein' one of the spooks?"

"You git along with you, Tom Dorrigan! And take yer arms off that gate!"

"They do say Maria seed one widout a head and all! Holy Mother o' God protect us!"—and the lad crossed himself fearfully, as he went.

While Mrs. Beetling, still blown with spite and anger, gathered her skirts in both hands, and charging at a brood of Brahmapootras that had invaded the garden to scratch up a bed, scuttled them back into the yard.

[2]

His way led him through the main street. The morning was drawing towards noon, and the overheated air, grown visible, quivered and flimmered in wavy lines. He wore nankeen trousers, which looked a world too wide for him, and flapped to and fro on his bony shanks. His coat, of tussore, was creased and unfresh, there being no Mary at hand daily to iron it out. On his head he had a sun hat, hung with puggaree and fly-veil: he also carried a sun-umbrella, green-lined; while a pair of dark goggles dimmed for him the intolerable whiteness of sky, road, iron roofs. Thus he went: an odd figure, a very figure of fun, in the eyes of the little township. And yet, for all his oddity, wearing an air . . . an air of hauteur, of touch-me-not aloofness, which set him still further apart. The small shopkeepers and publicans who made up the bulk of the population had never known his like; and were given vigorously to slapping their legs and exclaiming: "By the Lord Harry! . . . goes about with his head as high as if he owned the place."

On this day, though, he passed unnoticed. In the broad, sun-stricken street, none moved but himself. The heat, however, was not the sole reason for its emptiness. He who ran might read that the place was thinning out. With the abandonment of the project to reorganise the great mine—the fairy-tale of which had helped to settle *him* there—all hope of a fresh spurt of life for Barambogie was at an end. The new Bank that was to have been opened to receive the gold, the crew of miners and engineers who should have worked the reefs, had already faded into the *limbus fatuorum* where, for aught he knew, they had always belonged. What trade there was, languished: he counted no less than four little shops in a row, which had recently been boarded up.

Pluff went his feet in the smothery dust of the bush road— his black boots might have been made of white leather—the flies buzzed in chorus round his head. Of the two visits he had to pay, one was a couple of miles off. Two miles there, and two back . . . on a morning when even the little walk along the Lagoon had fagged him. Oh! he *ought* to have a buggy. A country practice without a horse and trap behind it was like trying to exist without bread . . . or water.— And now again, as if, on this particular day, there was to be no rest or peace for him, a single thought, flashing into his brain, took entire possession of it and whizzed madly round. He plodded along, bent of back, loose of knee, murmuring distractedly: "A buggy . . . yes, God knows, I ought to have a buggy!" But the prospect of ever again owning one seemed remote; at present, it was as much as he could do to afford the occasional hire of a conveyance. What must the townspeople think, to see him eternally on the tramp? For nobody walked here. A convey-ance stood at every door . . . but his. They would soon be beginning to suspect that something was wrong with him; and from that to believing him unable to pay his way was but a step. In fancy he saw himself refused credit, required to hand over cash for what he purchased . . . he, Richard Mahony! . . . till, in foretasting the shame of it, he groaned aloud.

And the case he had come all this way to attend would not profit him. His patient was a poor woman, lying very sick and quite alone in a bark hut, her menfolk having betaken themselves to work. He did what he could for her; left her more comfortable than he found her: he also promised medi-cines by the first cart that went by her door. But he knew the class: there was no money in it; his bill would have to be sent in time after time. And the older he grew, the more it went against the grain to badger patients for his fees. If they were too mean, or too dishonest, to pay for his services, he was too proud to dun them. And thus bad debts accumulated.

On the road home, the great heat and his own depression overcame him. Choosing a shady spot, he lowered himself to the burnt grass for a rest; or what might have been a rest, had not the sound of wheels almost immediately made him scramble to his feet again: it would never do for him to be caught sitting by the roadside. In his haste, he somehow pressed the catch of his bag, which forthwith opened and spilled its contents on the ground. He was on his knees, fumbling to replace these, when the trap hove in sight.

It was a single buggy, in which three persons, a young man and two young women, sat squeezed together on a seat built for two. None the less, the man jerked his horse to a stand, and, with true colonial neighbourliness, called across: "Like a lift?"—to receive, too late to stop him, a violent dig in the ribs from his wife's elbow.

"Thank you, thank you, my good man! But you are full already." Provoked at being caught in his undignified position, Mahony answered in a tone short to ungraciousness.

"Devil a bit! Bess 'ere can sit by the splashboard."

"*No*, sir! I should not dream of inconveniencing the lady on my account."

"O.K.!" said the man. "Ta-ta, then!" and drove on.

"The *lady!* Did you hear 'im? Oh, Jimminy Gig! . . . ain't he a cure?" cried Bess, and bellowed out a laugh that echoed back to where Mahony stood.

"Bill, you great *goff*, didn't you feel me poke you? Don't you know 'oo that was? We don't want him up here along of us . . . not for Joe!"

Bill spat. "Garn! It's a goodish step for th'ol' cove, and a regular roaster into the bargain."

"Garn yerself, y'ol' mopoke!— I say, what was 'e doin' there's what I'd like to know. Did you see him, kneelin' with all them things spread out around him? Up to some shady trick or other, I'll be bound!"

Bess nodded darkly. "Nobody 'ull go near the house any more after dark. Maria Beetling sor a black figger in the passage one night, with horns and all, and heard 'im talkin' to it. She tore home screamin' like mad for her ma."

"Ah, git along with yer bunkum! You wimmin's mouths is allers full o' some trash or other. I never *heard* such talk!"— and Bill ejected a fresh stream of juice over the side.

His wife made a noise of contempt. "It's gospel truth! I heard ol' Warnock the other day talkin' to Mrs. Ah Sing. An'

they both said it was a crying shame to have a doctor here
who went in for magic and such-like. Nor's that all. A fat lot
o' good his doctoring kin be. To go and let his own kid die!
If he couldn't cure it, what kin *we* hope for, 'oo he hates like
poison?"

"They do say, he *boiled* her," said Bess mysteriously. "Made
her sit in water that was too hot for her, till her skin all peeled
off and she was red and raw. She screeched like blue murder:
Maria heard her. They had to rush out and send for another
doctor from Oakworth. But it was too late. He couldn't save
her.— An' then just look at his pore wife! So pale an' woebegone! Shaking in her shoes, I guess, what he'll be doing to
her next."

"He ought to be had up for it. Instead of being let streel
round, with his highty-tighty airs!"

"No, gorblimey, you two! . . . of all the silly, clatterin' hens!"
and leaning forward Bill sliced his horse a sharp cut on the
belly. In the cloud of dust that rose as the buggy lurched
forward they vanished from sight.—

"Ha! didn't I know it? their butt—their laughing-stock!"
chafed Mahony, in answer to the girl's guffaw; and his hands
trembled so that he could hardly pick up his scattered belongings. In his agitation he forgot the rest he had intended to
allow himself, and plodded on anew, the sweat trickling in
runnels down his back, his mouth and nostrils caked dry.
Meanwhile venting his choler by exclaiming aloud, in the
brooding silence of the bush: "What next? . . . what next, I
wonder! Why, the likelihood is, they'll boggle at my diagnoses . . . doubt my ability to dose 'em for the d.t.'s or the
colic!"— And this idea, being a new one, started a new train
of thought, his hungry brain pouncing avidly upon it. Thereafter, he tortured himself by tracking it down to its last and
direst issues; and, thus engrossed, was callous even to his
passage along the main street, for which, after what had just
happened, he felt a shrinking distaste, picturing eyes in every
window, sneers behind every door.

Safe again within the four walls of his room, he tossed hat
and bag from him, and sank into the armchair, where he lay
supine, his taut muscles relaxed, his tired eyes closed to
remembrance. And in a very few minutes he was fast asleep:
a deep, sound sleep, such as night and darkness rarely brought

him. Dinner-time came and went; but he slept on; for Mrs. Beetling, still nursing her injuries, did not as usual put her head in at the door to say that dinner was ready; she just planked the dishes down on the dining-room table and left them there.— And soon the pair of chops, which dish she served up to him day after day, lay hard and sodden in their own fat.

Hunched in his chair, his head on his chest, his mouth open, Mahony drew breaths that were more than half snores. His carefully brushed hair had fallen into disarray, the lines on his forehead deepened to grooves; on his slender hands, one of which hung between his knees, the other over an arm of the chair, the veins stood out blue and bold.

No sound broke the stillness, but that of the clock striking the hours and half-hours. Only very gradually did the sleeper come up from those unfathomed depths, of which the waking brain keeps no memory, to where, on the fringe of his consciousness, a disturbing dream awaited him. It had to do with a buggy, a giant buggy, full of people; and, inverting the real event of the day on which it was modelled, he now longed with all his heart to be among them. For it seemed to him that, if he could succeed in getting into this buggy, he would hear something—some message or tidings—which it was important for him to know. But though he tried and tried again, he could not manage to swing himself up; either his foot missed the step, or the people, who sat laughing and grimacing at him, pushed him off. Finally, he fell and lay in the dust, which, filling eyes, nose, mouth, blinded and asphyxiated him. He was still on his back, struggling for air, when he heard a voice buzzing in his ear: "You're wanted! It's a patient come. Wake up, wake up!"—and there was Mrs. Beetling, leaning over him and shaking him by the arm, while a man stood in the doorway and gaped.

He was out of his chair and on his feet in a twinkling; but he could not as easily collect his wits, which were still dream-bound. His hands, too, felt numb, and as if they did not belong to him. It took him the space of several breaths to grasp that his caller, a farmer, was there to fetch him to attend his wife, and had a trap waiting at the gate. He thought the man looked at him very queerly. It was the fault of his old poor head, which was unequal to the strain of so sudden a waking. Proffering an excuse, he left the room to plunge

784

it in water. As he did this, it occurred to him that he had had
no dinner. But he was wholly without appetite; and one
glance at the fatty mess on the table was enough. Gulping
down a cup of tea, he ate a couple of biscuits, and then,
shouldering his dustcoat, declared himself ready. It was a
covered buggy: he leant far back beneath the hood as they
drove. This time, people should *not* have the malicious pleasure of eyeing him.

❊   ❊   ❊   ❊   ❊   ❊

I send you what I can, my dear, but I advise you to spin it
out and be careful of it, Mary, for it is impossible to say when
more will be forthcoming. Things are very, very slack here.
There is no sickness and no money. I could never have believed a practice would collapse like this, from over seventy
pounds a month to as good as nothing. In this past week I
have only had four patients . . . and they all poorish people.
I feel terribly worried, and sit here cudgelling my brains what
it will be best to do. The truth is, this place is fast dying out—
every one begins to see, now, that it has had its day, and will
never recover. Two of the tradespeople have become insolvent
since you left, and others totter on the brink.

The heat is unbelievable. The drought continues . . . no
sign yet of it breaking, and the thermometer eternally up
between 90 and 100. (And even so, no sickness!) I am getting
very anxious, too, about the water in the tank, which is low
and dirty. If rain does not soon come now, we shall be in a
pretty plight.

I sleep wretchedly; and time hangs very heavy. The peaches
are ripening, grapes twopence a pound; but butter is hard to
get, and unless it rains there will soon be none to be had.

I do not see, under these circumstances, that we can incur
the expense of another governess. The children will either have
to attend the State School, or you must teach them yourself.

I do not like your lined paper. I detest common notepaper.
Go to Bradley's when you are in town, and order some good
cream-laid. They have the die for the crest there.

"Oh dear, oh dear, he's at it again!" sighed Mary; and let
the letter fall to her knee.

"Whatever is it now?" asked Tilly.

785

In the shadow cast by the palings that separated a little weatherboard house from the great golden-sanded beach, the two women, in large, shady hats, sat and watched their children play. Lucie, at her mother's side, was contentedly sorting a heap of "grannies and cowries"; but Cuffy had deserted to the water's edge directly he spied the servant-girl bringing out the letter. He *hated* these letters from Papa; they always made Mamma cross . . . or sorry . . . which spoilt the day. And it was so lovely here! He wished the postman would never, never come.

"Oh, the usual Jeremiad!" said Mary; and dropped her voice to keep the child from hearing. "No sickness, weather awful, the water getting low, people going bankrupt—a regular rigmarole of grumbles and complaints."

"Determined to spoil your holiday for you, my dear! . . . or so it looks to me."

"I agree, it's a *dreadful* place; never should we have gone there! But he would have it, and now he's got to make the best of it. Why, the move cost us over a hundred! Besides, it would be just the same anywhere else."

"Well, look here, Mary, my advice is—now, Lucie, be a good child and run away and play with your brother, instead of sitting there drinking everything in! Feeling as you do about it, my dear, you must just be firm, and stick to your guns. You've given in to 'im, your whole life long, and a fat lot of thanks you've ever 'ad for it. It's made me *boil* to see you so meek! . . . though one never dared say much, you always standing up for him, loyal as loyal could be! But time's getting on, Mary; you aren't as young as you were; and you've got others now to think of, besides 'im. I just shouldn't stand any more of 'is nonsense."

"Yes, I daresay it *was* bad for him, always having his own way. But now he's got to learn that the children come first. They have all their lives before them, and I *won't* sit by and see him beggar them. He says we can't afford another governess; that they must either go to the State School—*my* children, Tilly!—or I teach them myself. When my hands are so full already that I could do with a day twice as long! And then he's so unreasonable. Finds fault with my notepaper and says I am to go to Bradley's and order some expensive cream-laid. Now I ask you!"

"Unreasonable?" flamed Tilly, and blew a gust from mouth

and nose. "There's *some* people, Mary, 'ud call it by another name, my dear!"

Mary sighed anew, and nodded. "I'm convinced, from past experience, that this idea of the practice failing is just his own imagination. He's lonely, and hasn't anyone to talk to, and so he sits and broods. But it keeps me on the fidget; for it's almost always been something imaginary that's turned him against a place, and made him want to leave it. And if he once gets an idea in his head, I might as well talk to the wind. Indeed, what I say only makes matters worse. Perhaps some one else might manage him better. Really, I can't help wondering sometimes, Tilly, if I've been the right wife for him, after all. No one could have been fonder of him. But there's always something in him that I can't get at; and when things go badly, and we argue and argue . . . why, then, the thought will keep cropping up that perhaps some one else . . . somebody cleverer than I am.— Do you remember Gracey Marriner, who he was so friendly with over that table-rapping business? She was so quick at seeing what he meant . . . and why he did things . . . and they found so much to talk about, and they read the same books, and played the piano together. Well, I've sometimes felt that perhaps she . . ." But here the tears that had gathered in Mary's eyes threatened to run over, and she had to grope for her handkerchief.

"*Her!* Lor, Mary! . . . he'd have tired of 'er and her la-di-da airs inside three months," ejaculated Tilly, and fiercely blew her own nose in sympathy. "If ever there's been a good wife, my dear, it's you! But a fig for all the soft sawder that's talked about marriage! The long and the short of it is, marriage is sent to *try* us women, and for nothin' on earth besides."

The children reacted in distinctive fashion to the sight of their mother crying. Little Lucie, who had heard, if not grasped, all that passed, hung her head like a dog scolded for some fault it does not understand. Cuffy, casting furtive backward glances, angrily stamped his feet, so that the water splashed high over his rolled-up knickerbockers. This not availing, he turned and deliberately waded out to sea.

Ah! then Mamma *had* to stop crying, and to notice him. "Cuffy! Come back!"

"*What* a naughty boy!" sermonised Aunt Tilly. "When his poor mother is so worried, too."—

"Yes, my great fear is, Richard's heading for another move. Really, after a letter like this, I feel I ought just to pack up and go home."

"What! After you come down 'ere looking like a ghost, and as thin as thin? . . . I *won't* hear of it, Mary!"

"You see, last time he took me completely by surprise. I'm resolved *that* shan't happen again!"

"Hush! hark! . . . was that Baby?" And Tilly bent an ardent ear towards the verandah, where her infant lay sleeping in a hammock.

"I heard nothing.— There's another reason, too, why I want to stay there, wretched place though it is. It's the . . . I don't feel I *can* go off and leave the . . . the little grave with nobody to care for it. It's all I've got left of her."

"The blessed little angel!"

"Later on . . . it may be different. But to go away now would tear me in two. Though it may and probably will mean row after row."

"Yes, till he wears you down. That's always been 'is way.— Ah! but that *is* Baby sure enough." And climbing to her feet, Tilly propelled her matronly form up the sandy path.

She returned in triumph bearing the child, which, but half awake, whined peevishly, ramming two puny fists into sleep-charged eyes; on her face the gloating, doting expression with which she was wont to follow its every movement. For her love, waxing fat on care and anxiety, had swelled to a consuming passion, the like of which had never before touched her easy-going life.

Mary rose and shook the sand from her skirts. "I must see what I can find to say to him, to cheer him up and keep him quiet."

"And our good little Lucie here, and Cuffy, too, shall mind darling Baby for Auntie, whilst she makes his pap."

But the children hung back. Minding Baby meant one long fight to hinder him from putting things—everything: sand, shells, your hand, your spade—in his mouth, and kicking and screaming if you said no; and Aunt Tilly rushing out crying: "What are they *doing* to my precious?"— Lucie had already a firm handful of her mother's dress in her grasp.

"Now, Mary! you can't possibly write with that child hanging round you."

"Oh, she won't bother . . . she never does," said Mary, who could not find it in her heart to drive her ewe-lamb from her.

"Oh, well, then!" said Tilly, with a loveless glance at the retreating Cuffy. "Muvver's jewel must just tum *wif* 'er, and see its doody-doody dinner cooked!"— And smothering the little sallow face, the overlarge head in kisses, she, too, sought the house.

("Really Tilly is *rather* absurd about that baby!")

("How Mary *does* spoil those children!")

With which private criticism, each of the other, Tilly fell to stirring a hasty-pudding, and Mary sat her down before pen and paper.— And thus ended what, little as they knew it, was to be the last of their many confidential talks on the subject of Richard, his frowardness and crabbedness, his innate inability to fit himself to life. From now on, Mary's lips were in loyalty sealed.

[3]

UNDER the heat-veiled January skies, Mahony saw his worst fears realised. His few remaining patients dropped off, no others appeared to take their places; and, with this, the practice in Barambogie virtually came to an end.

There he sat, with his head between his hands, cudgelling his brains. For it staggered credulity that every form of sickness, that the break-neck casualties inseparable from bush life, should one and all fade out in so preposterous a fashion. In the unhealthy season, too, compared with the winter months in which he had settled there. What were the people up to? What cabal had they formed against him? That some shady trick was being played him, he did not for a moment doubt. Suspiciously he eyed Mrs. Beetling when she came to her job of a morning. *She* knew what was going on, or he was much mistaken: she looked very queerly at him, and often gave him the impression of scuttling hurriedly away. But he had never been any hand at pumping people of her class: it took Mary to do that. And so he contented himself, did he chance upon the woman, with fixing her in silence; and otherwise treating her with the contempt she deserved. He had more important things to occupy him. These first days of blank, unbroken idleness were spent in fuming about the house like a caged animal: up the passage, out on the verandah, right round this, and back to the passage. Again and again he believed he heard the front gate click, and ran to seat himself in the surgery. But it was always a false alarm. And after a few seconds' prickling suspense, in which every nerve in his body wore ears, he would bound up from his seat, hardly master of himself for exasperation. These infamous people! Why, oh, why, had he ever set foot among them? . . . ever trodden the dust of this accursed place! A man of his skill, his experience, wilfully to put himself at the mercy of a pack of bush-dwellers . . . Chinese coolies . . . wretched half-castes!— And, striding ever more gauntly and intolerantly, he drove his thoughts back, and salved his bleeding pride with memories of the past. He saw himself in his heyday, one of the best-known physicians on Ballarat; famed alike for his diagnoses and sureness of hand; called in to perform the most delicate operations; robbed of his sleep by night, on the go the livelong day, until at last, incapable of meeting the claims made on him, there had been nothing left for it but to fly the place.— And spurred by the exhilaration of these memories, he quickened his steps till the sweat poured off him.

But he was not to be done. He'd shew these numskulls whom they had to deal with . . . make them bite the dust. Ha! he had it: that case of empyema and subsequent operation for *paracentesis thoracis,* which he had before now contemplated writing up for the *Australian Medical Journal.* Now was the time: he would set to work straightway, dash the article off, post it before the sun went down that night. It would appear in the March issue of the journal; and these fools would then learn, to their eternal confusion, that they had among them one whose opinions were of weight in the selectest medical circles. With unsteady hands he turned out a drawer containing old notes and papers, and, having found what he wanted, spread them on the table before him. But, with his pen inked and poised ready to begin, he hesitated. In searching, he had recalled another, rarer case: one of a hydatid cyst in the sub-cutaneous tissue of the thigh. This would be more telling; and going on his knees before a wooden chest, in which he stored old memoranda, he rummaged anew. Again, however, after a lengthy hunt, he found himself wavering. His notes were not as full as he had believed: there would be finicking details to verify, books to consult which he could no longer get at. So this scheme, too, had to be let drop. Ah! but now he had really hit it. What about that old bone of contention among the medical profession, homœopathy? Once on a time he had meant to bring out a pamphlet on the subject, and, if he remembered rightly, had made voluminous notes for it. Could he find these, he would be spared all brain-fag. And, again, he made his knees sore and his head dizzy over a mass of dusty, yellowing papers. After which, re-seating himself with an air of triumph, he ruled a line in red ink on a sheet of foolscap, and wrote above it, in his fine, flowing hand: Why I do not practice Homœopathy.

"If, as is so often asserted, the system of homœopathing as practised by Hahnemann and his followers . . ."

But having got thus far, he came to a standstill, re-dipped a pen that was already loaded, bit the end of it, wrinkled his brows. What next? . . . what did he want to say? . . . how to end the sentence? And when he did manage to catch a glimpse of his thought, he could not find words in which to clothe it . . . the right words. They would not come at his beck; or phrases either. He floundered, tried one, then another; nothing suited him; and he grew more and more impatient: apparently, even with his notes before him, it was going to be beyond him to make a decent job of the thing. He had been silent too long. Nor could he, he now found, work up the heat, the orthodox heat, with which he had once burnt: the points he had formerly made against this quack and his system now seemed flat or exaggerated. So indifferent had he grown with the years, that his present attitude of mind was almost one of: let those who choose, adopt Hahnemann's methods, those who will, be allopaths. And, as he sat there, struggling to bring his thoughts to heel, to re-kindle the old fire, the tardy impulse to express himself died out. He threw his pen from him. *Cui bono?* Fool, fool! to think of blistering his brains for the benefit of these savages among whom his present lot was cast. What would they understand of it, many of whom were forced to set crosses where their names should have stood? And when he was so tired, too, so dog-tired physically, with his feverish runnings to and fro, and exhausted mentally with fretting and fuming. Much too tired (and too rusty) to embark on a piece of work that demanded utmost care and discrimination . . . let alone cope with the labour of writing it down. Suddenly, quite suddenly, the idea of exertion, of any effort whatever, was become odious to him . . . odious and unthinkable. He put his arms on the table, and hid his face in them; and, lying there, knew that his chief desire was fulfilled: to sit with his eyes screened, darkness round him, and to think and feel just as little as he saw. But, a bundle of papers incommoding him, he raised his hand, and, with a last flash of the old heat, crumpled notes and jottings to balls, and tossed them to the floor. There they lay, till, next morning, Mrs. Beetling swept them up and threw them on the kitchen fire.

And now silence fell anew—a silence the more marked for the stormy trampling that had preceded it. Said Mrs. Beetling to her crony, the ostler's wife: "I do declare, 'e's that mousy quiet, you never c'd tell there was a livin' creatur' in the 'ouse—no more'n a triantelope nor a centipede!" No longer had she to spend time dodging her master: shrinking behind open doors to avoid crossing his path, waiting her opportunity to reach bedroom or dining-room unobserved. He never left the surgery; and she could work with a good grace, scrubbing floors that were not trodden on, cooking food the lion's share of which it fell to her to eat.—

Meanwhile, a burning February ran its course. To step off the verandah now was like stepping into a furnace. The sky was white with heat: across its vast pale expanse moved a small, copper-coloured sun. Or the hot winds streaked it with livid trails of wind-smitten cloud. The very air was white with dust. While did a windstorm rise, the dust-clouds were so dense that everything—trees, Lagoon, township, the very garden itself—was blotted out. Dust carpeted the boards of the verandah, drove into the passage, invaded the rooms. But never a drop of rain fell. And then the fires started: in all the country round, the bush was ablaze: the sky hung dark as with an overhead fog; the rank tang of burning wood smarted the lungs.

In the little oven of a house, the green blinds were lowered from early morning on. Behind them, in a bemusing twilight; behind the high paling-fence that defended house from road, Mahony sat isolate—sat shunned and forgotten. And, as day added itself to day, the very sound of his own voice grew

strange to him, there being no need for him ever to unclose
his lips. Even his old trick of muttering died out—went the
way of his pacing and haranguing. For something in him had
yielded, had broken, carrying with it, in its fall, the black
pride, the bitter resentment, the aggressive attitude of mind,
which had hitherto sustained him. And this wholesale collapse
of what he had believed to be his ruling traits made him feel
oddly humble . . . and humiliated . . . almost as if he had
shrivelled in stature. Hence, he never went out. For the single
road led through the street of malicious eyes: and, now,
nothing would have prevailed on him to expose himself to
their fire. More and more the four walls of his room began to
seem to him haven and refuge. And gradually he grew as
fearful of the sound of footsteps approaching the door as he
had formerly been eager for them. For they might mean a
summons to quit his lair.

But no steps came.

Had he had but a dog to lay its moist and kindly muzzle
on his knee, or a cat to arch its back under his hand, the
keenest edge might have been taken off his loneliness. But
for more years than he could count, he had been obliged to
deny himself the company of those dumb friends, who might
now have sought, in semi-human fashion, to relieve the inhuman silence that had settled round him. Nothing broke
this—or only what was worse than the silence itself: the awful
mill-whistle, which, five times a day, marked the passage of
the empty hours with its nerve-shattering shriek. He learnt to
hate this noise as if it had been a live and malignant thing;
yet was constrained to wait for it, to listen to it—even to count
the seconds that still divided him from its blast. His books
lay unopened, withdrawn into their primary state of so much
dead paper. And it was not books alone that lost their meaning, and grew to seem useless, and a burden. He could forget
to wind up his watch, to pare his nails; he ceased to care
whether or no his socks were worn into holes. The one task
to which he still whipped himself was the writing of the few
lines necessary to keep Mary from fretting. (To prepare her,
too. *Absolutely nothing doing . . . incredible . . . heart-
breaking.*) Otherwise, he would sit, for an hour at a time,
staring at some object on the table before him, till it, the
table, the room itself, swam in a grey mist. Or he followed,

with all the fixity of inattention, the movements of a fly . . . or the dance of dust motes laddering a beam.

But this inertia, this seemingly aimless drifting, was yet not wholly irrational. It formed a kind of attempt, a three-fold attempt, on the part of his inmost self, to recover from . . . to nerve himself anew for . . . to avoid rousing a whit sooner than need be . . . the black terrors that stalked those hours when he had not even the light of day to distract him.

To wake in the night, and to know that, on this side of your waking, lies no ray of light or hope . . . only darkness and fear. To wake in the night: be wide awake in an instant, with all your faculties on edge: to wake, and be under compulsion to set in, night for night, at the same point, knowing, from grim experience, that the demons awaiting you have each to be grappled with in turn, no single one of them left unthrown, before you can win through to the peace that is utter exhaustion.

Sometimes, he managed to get a couple of hours' rest beforehand. At others, he would start up from a profound sleep, believing the night far advanced; only to find that a bare ten or fifteen minutes had elapsed since he closed his eyes. But, however long or short the period of oblivion, what followed was always the same; and, after a very few nights, he learnt wisdom, and gave up struggling to escape the unescapable. Rising on his pillow, he drew a long breath, clenched his fists, and thrust off.

The order in which his thoughts swept at him was always the same. The future . . . what of the future? With the practice gone, with nothing saved on which to start afresh, with but the slenderest of sums in hand for living expenses, and the everlasting drain of the mortgage, he could see no way out of his present impasse but through the bankruptcy court. And in this country even an unmerited insolvency, one brought about by genuine misfortunes, spelt disgrace, spelt ruin. And not for oneself alone. To what was he condemning Mary . . . and the children? . . . his tenderly reared children. Poverty . . . charity . . . the rough and ready scramble of colonial life. Oh, a man should indeed take thought and consider, before he gave such hostages to fortune!— And here, as he tossed restlessly from side to side, there came into his mind words he had read somewhere, or heard some one say, about life and its ultimate meaning. Stripped of its claptrap, of the roses and false sentiment in which we loved to drape it, it had actually no object but this: to keep a roof over the heads and food in the mouths of the helpless beings who depended on us.— Burns, too . . . Bobbie Burns.— Oh, God! . . . there he went again! This accursed diminutive! Night for night he vowed he would not use it, and night for night his tongue slipped, and it was out before he could help himself. Had he then no longer the power to decide what he would or would not say? Preposterous! . . . preposterous, and infuriating! For the whole thing— both the slip and his exasperation—was but a ruse on the part of his mind, to switch him off the main issue. And to know this, and yet be constrained, night after night, to the mechanical repetition of so utter a futility . . . his cold rage was such that several minutes had invariably to pass, before he was calm enough to go on.

A way out! . . . there *must* be a way out. Hoisting himself on the pillow, till he all but sat erect, and boring into the dark with eyes hot in their sockets, he fell feverishly to telling over his affairs; though by now this, too, had become a sheerly automatic proceeding: his lips singsonging figures and sets of figures, while his brain roved elsewhere. What he could *not* avoid was the recital of them: this formed another of the obstacles he was compelled nightly to clamber over, on the road to sleep. Bills and bad debts, shares, and dividends, and calls, payments on the mortgage, redemption of the capital: these things danced a witches' sabbath in his head. To them must now be added the rent of the house they lived in. He had reckoned on covering this with the rental from the house at Hawthorn. But they had had no luck with tenants: were already at their second; and the house was said to be falling into bad repair. In the Bank in Barambogie there stood to his credit, stood between him and beggary, the sum of not quite one hundred pounds. When this was done, God help them!

Why had he ever left Melbourne? What evil spirit had entered into him and driven him forth? What *was* that in him, over which he had no power, which proved incapable of adhesion to any soil or fixed abode? For he might arm himself, each time anew, with another motive for plucking up his roots: it remained mere ratiocination, a sop flung to his reason, and in no wise got at the heart of the matter. Wherein lay the fault, the defect, that had made of him throughout his life a hunted man? . . . harried from place to place, from country to country. Other men set up a goal, achieved it, and remained content. He had always been in flight.— But from what? Who were his pursuers? From what shadows did he run?— And in these endless nights, when he lay and searched his heart as never before, he thought he read the answer to the riddle. Himself he was the hunter and the hunted: the merciless in pursuit and the panting prey. Within him, it would seem, lodged fears . . . strange fears. And, at a given moment, one of these, hitherto dormant and unsuspected, would suddenly begin to brew, and go on growing till he was all one senseless panic, and blind flight the only catholicon. No matter what form it took—whether a morbid anxiety about his health, or alarm at the swiftness with which his little day was passing— its aim was always the same: to beat him up and on. And never yet had he succeeded in defying it. With the result that, well on in years, and burdened by responsibilities, he stood face to face with ruin. Having dragged with him those who were dearer to him than his own life.— But stop! Was that true? . . . and not just one of those sleek phrases that dripped so smoothly off the tongue. *Were* they dearer? In this moment of greater clarity he could no longer affirm it. He believed that the instinct of self-preservation had, in his case, always been the primary one. And digging deeper still, he got, he thought, a further insight into his motives. If this was so, then what he fled must needs be the reverse of the security he ran to seek: in other words, annihilation. The plain truth was: the life-instinct had been too strong for him. Rather than face death and the death-fear, in an attempt to flee the unfleeable, he had thrown every other consideration to the winds, and ridden tantivy into the unknown.

But now all chance of flight was over. He sat here as fast a prisoner as though chained to a stake—an old and weary man, with his fiftieth birthday behind him.— *Old*, did he say? By God! not as a man's years were reckoned elsewhere. In this accursed country alone. Only here were those who touched middle age regarded as decrepit, and cumberers of the soil. Wisdom and experience availed a man nothing, where only brawn had value. As for the three-score years and ten— But no! . . . no use, no use! . . . words would not help him. Not thus could it be shirked! He had to fight through, to the last spasm, the paroxysm of terror which at this point shook him, as with a palsy, at the knowledge that he would never again get free; that he was caught, trapped, pinned down . . . to be torn asunder, devoured alive. His pulses raced, his breath came hard, the sweat that streamed off him ran cold. Night after night, he had the same thing to undergo; and from bitter experience he knew that the fit would gradually exhaust itself, leaving him spent, inert.— But this was all. With this, his compliance ceased, and there came a block. For, below the surface here, under a lid which he never lifted, which nothing would have induced him to raise by a hair's-breadth, lurked a darker fear than any, one he could not face and live; even though, with a part of his mind, a watchful part, a part that it was impossible to deceive, he *knew* what it was.

Swerving violently, he laid the onus of his terror on a side issue: the confession that stood before him, the confession to Mary, of his ruinous debt. As he pictured this, and as the borrowed emotion swelled it out, it turned to something horrible . . . monstrous . . . the performance of which surpassed his strength. How could he ever break the news to her, all unsuspecting, who shrank from debt as other women from fire or flood? What would she say? . . . hurl what bitter words at him, in her first wrath and distress? She being what she was, he believed the knowledge would well-nigh break her heart . . . as it almost broke his, to think of the anguish he must inflict on her.— And, once again, the years fell away, and he was a little velvet-suited lad, paling and quivering under the lash of a caustic Irish tongue. But there also came times when some such vividly recalled emotion proved the way out. Then, one or other episode from the forty-year-old past would rise before him with so amazing a reality that he re-lived it to its flimsiest details, hearing the ominous tick of the clock on the chimney-piece, smelling the scent of lavender that went out from his mother's garments. At others, the past failing in its grip, there was nothing for it but to fight to a finish. And so he would lie, and writhe, and moan, and beat the pillow with his hands, while tears that felt thick as blood scalded his cheeks.

But gradually, very gradually, this last convulsion spent

797

itself: and, as at the approach of soft music from a distance, he was aware of the coming end . . . of the peace advancing, at which all the labour of the night had been directed. Peace at last! . . . for his raw nerves, his lacerated brain. And along with it a delicious drowsiness, which stole over him from his finger-tips, and up from his feet, relaxing knotted muscles, loosening his hands, which now lay limp and free. He sank into it, letting himself go . . . as into a pond full of feathers . . . which enveloped him, closed downily about him . . . he sinking deeper . . . ever deeper . . .

Until, angry and menacing, shattering the heavenly inertia, a scream!— Who screamed? A child? What was it? Who was hurt?— Oh, God! the shock of it, the ice-cold shock! He fell back on the pillow, his heart thudding like a tom-tom. Would he *never* grow used to it? . . . this awful waking! . . . and though he endured it day after day. For . . . as always . . . the sun was up, the hour six of a red-hot morning, and the mill-whistle flayed the silence. In all he had slept for not quite three-quarters of an hour.

Thereafter he lay and stared into the dusty light as he had stared into the darkness. Needle-like pulses beat behind his lids; the muscles round eyes and mouth were a-twitch with fatigue. From the sight of food he turned with a sick man's disrelish. Swallowing a cup of milkless tea, he crossed to the surgery and shut himself in. But, on this particular day, his habit of drowsing through the empty hours was rudely broken through. Towards midday, he was disturbed by the door opening. It was Mrs. Beetling who, without so much as a knock, put her head in to say that the stationmaster had hurt his foot and wanted doctor to come and bandage it.

The stationmaster?— He had been far away, on high cliffs that sloped to the sea, gathering "horsetails" . . . and for still an instant his mind loitered over the Latin equivalent. Then he was on his feet, instinctively fingering the place where his collar should have been. But neither coat nor collar . . . and: "My boots, my good woman, my boots!" The dickens! Was that he who was shouting? Tut, tut! He must pull himself together, not let these spying eyes note his fluster. But there was another reason for the deliberateness with which he sought the bedroom. His knees felt weak, and he could hardly see for the tears that would keep gathering. Over three weeks now—close on a month—since anyone had sent for him. *All* were not dead against him then! Oh, a good fellow, this Pendrell! . . . a good fellow! . . . a man after his own heart, and a gentleman.— And throwing open drawers and cupboards, he made many an unnecessary movement, and movements that went wide of their mark.

In putting arnica and lint in his bag, he became aware that his hands were violently a-shake. This wouldn't do. Impossible to appear before a patient in such a state. He clenched his fists and stiffened his arms; but the tremor was stronger than his will, and persisted. As a last resource, he turned to the sideboard, poured some sherry into a tumbler, and gulped it down.

Quitting the house by the back door, he went past the kitchen, the woodstack, the rubbish-heap, a pile of emptied kerosene-tins, the pigsties (with never a pig in them), the fowls sitting moping in the shrinking shade. His eyes ran water anew at the brassy glare; and, phew! . . . the heat! In his haste he had forgotten to put a handful of vine-leaves in the crown of his wideawake. The sun bore down on him with an almost physical weight: he might have had a loaded sack lying across neck and shoulders. And as soon as he let the hasp of the gate fall, he was in the dust of the road; and then his feet were weighted, as well.

But his thoughts galloped. Oh, that this call might be the start of a new era for him! . . . the awful stagnation of the past month prove to have been but a temporary lull, a black patch, such as any practice was liable to; the plot he had believed hatched against him to have existed only in his own imagination; and everything be as before . . . he still able to make a living, pay his way.— "Mercy! . . . dear God, a little mercy!"— But if that were so, then he, too, would need to do his share. Yes, he would make a point, from now on, of meeting the people here on their own level. He would ask after their doings . . . their wives and children . . . gossip with them of the weather and the vines . . . hobnob—no, drink with them, he could and would not! But he knew another way of getting at them. And that was through their pockets. Fees! Quite likely he had set his too high. He would now come down a peg . . . have his charges. They'd see then that it was to their advantage to call him in, rather than send elsewhere for a stranger. It might also be policy on his part—in the mean-time, at any rate—to treat trivial injuries and ailments free of charge. (Once the practice was set going again, he'd make them pay through the nose for all the worry and trouble they had caused him!) If *only* he could get the name of being free-handed . . . easy-going—could ingratiate himself . . . become popular.

So rapt was he that though, at the level crossing, his feet paused of themselves, he could not immediately think why he had stopped, and gazed absently round. Ha! the trains, of course. But there *were* no trains at this hour of the day: the station was shut up, deserted. A pretty fool he would look was he seen standing there talking to himself! He must hurry in, too, out of the sun. The heat was beginning to induce giddi-ness; the crown of his head felt curiously contracted. But he had still some distance to go. He spurred himself on, more quickly than before; his feet keeping time with his wingy thoughts.

Mary was hard put to it not to alarm the children. Every few minutes her anxiety got the better of her, and dropping her work, she would post herself at a corner of the verandah, where she could see down the road. She had been on the watch ever since the postman handed in Richard's letter, that morning, for the telegram that was to follow. Her first impulse had been to start for home without delay; and, despite Tilly's reasonings and persuasions, she had begun to sort out the children's clothes. Then she wavered. It would be madness to go back before the heat broke. And, if the practice was dead as Richard averred, there was no saying when the poor mites would get another change of air.

Still . . . Richard needed her. His letter ran: "I am afraid what I have to tell you will be a great shock to you. I was up at the stationmaster's just now and found myself unable to articulate. I could not say what I wanted. I lay down, and they brought me water. I said I thought it was a faint—that I had been out too long in the sun. I fear it is something worse. I am very, very uneasy about myself. I have been so distressed about the practice. I think that must have upset me. Intense mental depression . . . and this awful heat—what with solitude and misfortunes I have been terribly put about. All the same

I should not worry you, if it were not for my dread of being taken ill alone. I am almost unwilling to bring you and the children back in the meantime. The heat baffles description. I should never spend another February here—it would be as much as my life is worth. Perhaps the best thing to do will be to wait and see how I am. I will telegraph you on Monday morning early. Take no steps till you hear."

But to this a postscript had been added, in a hand it was hard to recognize as Richard's: "Oh, Mary wife, come home, come home!—before I go quite mad.—"

Down by the water's edge, Cuffy played angrily. He didn't know what he loved best: the seaweed, or the shells, or the little cave, or the big pool on the reef, or the little pool, or bathing and lying on the sand, or the smell of the ti-trees. And now— Oh, *why* had Papa got to go and get ill, and spoil everything? *He'd* seen Mamma beginning to pack their things, and it had made him feel all hot inside. Why must just *his* clothes be packed? He might get ill, too. Perhaps he would, if he drank some sea. Aunt Tilly said it made you mad. (Like Shooh man.) All right then, he would get mad . . . and they could see how they liked it! And, so saying, he scooped up a palmful of water and put it to his mouth. It ran away so fast that there was hardly any left; but it was enough: eugh! wasn't it nasty? He spat it out again, making a 'normous noise, so that everybody should hear. But they didn't take a bit of notice. Then a better idea struck him. He'd give Mamma the very nicest things he had: the two great big shells he had found all by himself, which he kept hidden in a cave, so that Lucie shouldn't even touch them unless he said so. He'd give them to Mamma, and she'd like them so much that she'd want to stop here, and never go home—oh, well! not for a long, long time.— Off he raced, shuffling his bare feet through the hot, dry, shifty sand.

But it was no good: she didn't care. Though he made her shut her eyes tight and promise not to look, while he opened her hand and squeezed the shells into it, and shut it again, like you did with big surprises. She just said: "What's this? Your pretty shells? My dear, what should I do with them? No, no! . . . you keep them for yourself!"—and all the while she wasn't *really* thinking what she said. And he couldn't even tell her why, for now Aunt Tilly shouted that the telegram-boy was coming at last; and Mamma just pushed the shells back and ran out into the road, and tore open the telegram like anything, and smiled and waved it at Aunt Tilly, and they both laughed and talked and wiped their eyes. But then everything was all right again, for it was from Papa, and he had telegrammed: "Am better, do not hurry home."

[4]

IN SPITE, however, of this reassurance, Mary could not rest. And one fine morning not long after, the trunks were brought out again, and she and Tilly fell to packing in earnest.

Cuffy's resentment at being torn from the sea a whole fortnight too soon, did not stand before the excitement of a journey: first in a coach and then in a train. Besides, Mamma had given him a little box to himself, to pack his shells in. Importantly he carried this, while she and Aunt Tilly ran about counting the other luggage. There was so much—portmanteaux and bundles, and baskets and bonnet-boxes, and beds and mattresses, and buckets and spades, and the perambulator—that they were afraid there wouldn't be room for it in the coach. But there was: they had it all to themselves. And di*reck*ly the door was shut, the lunch-basket was opened; for one of the most 'squisite things about a journey was that you could eat as much as you liked and whenever you liked. Mamma was so nice, too, and didn't scold when you and Lucie rushed to look first out of one window and then the other. But Aunt Tilly said you trod on her feet, and knocked against Baby, and you were a perfect nuisance; in all her born days she'd never known such fidgets. But Mamma said it was only high spirits, and you couldn't be always carping at children, wait till Baby got big and she'd see! And Aunt Tilly said she'd take care he wasn't brought up to be a nuisance to his elders. Cuffy was afraid they were going to get cross, so he sat down again, and only waggled his legs. He didn't like Aunt Tilly much. He didn't like fat people. Besides, when Baby squawked she thought it was lovely, and gave him everything he wanted to put in his mouth. They were in the train now, and *wouldn't* it be fun to pinch his leg! But he couldn't, 'cos he wasn't sitting next him. But he stuck his boot out and pressed it as hard as ever he could against Baby's foot, and Aunt Tilly didn't see, but Baby did, and opened his eyes and looked at him . . . just horrid!

Then came Melbourne and a fat old lady in a carriage and two horses, who called Mamma my dearie! She lived in a *very* big house with a nice old gentleman with a white beard, who took his hand and walked him round "to see the grounds" (just as if he was grown up!) He was a very funny man, and said he owed (only he said it "h'owed") everything to Papa, which made Cuffy wonder why, if so, he didn't pay him back. For Papa was always saying he hadn't enough money. But Mamma had told them they must be specially good here, and not pass remarks about *anything*. So he didn't. One night they went to a Pantomime called *Goody Two-Shoes*—not Mamma, she was still too sorry about Lallie being dead—and once to hear music and singing in a theatre. The old Sir and Lady took them both times, and at the music Lucie was a donkey and went to sleep, and had to be laid down on a coat on the floor. He didn't! He sat on a chair in the front of a little room, like a balcony, and listened and listened to a gipsy singing in a voice that went up and up, and made you feel first hot and then cold all over. Afterwards people made a great noise clapping their hands, and he did it, too, and made more noise than anybody. And the gipsy came by herself and bowed her head to every one, and then she looked at him, and smiled and blew him a kiss. He didn't much care for that, because it made people laugh; and he didn't know her. They all laughed again when they got home, till he went red and felt more like crying. He didn't, though; he was too big to cry now; everybody said so. The funny thing was, lots of big people did cry here; there seemed always to be some one crying. Aunt Zara came to see them all dressed in black, with black cloths hanging from her bonnet, and a prickly dress that scratched—like Papa's chin when he hadn't shaved. This was because she was a widder. She had a black streak on her handkerchief, too, to cry on, and felt most awfully sorry about writing to Mamma on paper that hadn't a "morning border," but what with one thing and another . . . Cuffy hoped Mamma wouldn't mind, and asked what a morning border was, but was only told to run away and play. He didn't. He stopped at the window and pretended to catch flies, he wanted so much to hear. Aunt Zara said she lit'rally didn't know where to turn, and Mamma looked sorry, but said if you made beds you must lie on them. (That *was* rummy!) And Aunt Zara said she thought she had been punished enough. Mamma said as long as she had a roof over her head she wouldn't see anyone belonging to her come to want, and there *were* the children, of course, and she was at her wits' end what to do about them, but of course she'd have to consult Richard first, and Aunt Zara knew what he was, and Aunt Zara said, only too well, but there was nothing she wouldn't do, she'd even scrub floors and wash dishes.

"Maria always scrubs our floors!"

It just jumped out of him; he did so want her to know she wouldn't have to. But then she said the thing about little pitchers, and Mamma got cross as well, and told him to go out of the room at *once,* so he didn't hear any more.

Then Cousin Emmy came, and she cried too—like anything. He felt much sorrier for her than Aunt Zara. He had to sniffle himself. She was so nice and pretty, but when she cried her face got red and fat, and Mamma said if she went on like this she'd soon lose her good looks. But she said who'd she got to be good-looking for, only a pack of kids, which made him feel rather uncomfortable, and he thought she needn't have said that. But it was very int'resting. She told about somebody who spent all her time dressing in "averdi-poy," and was possessed by a devil (like the pigs in the Bible). He longed to ask what she meant, but this time was careful and didn't let anything hop out of him, for he was going to hear just *everything.* Mamma seemed cross with Cousin Emmy, and said she was only a very young girl and must put up with things, and one day Mister Right would come along, and it would be time enough, when that happened, to see what could be done. And Cousin Emmy got very fierce and said ther'd never be any Mister Right for her, for a man was never allowed to shew so much as his nose in the house. (Huh! *that* was funny. Why not his nose?) Mamma said she'd try and make *her* see reason, and Cousin Emmy said it'ud be like talking to a stone statue, and it would always be herself first and the rest nowhere, and the plain truth was, she was simply crazy to get married again and there'd never be any peace till she had found a husband. And Mamma said, then she'd have to look out for some one with lots of money, your

Papa's will being what it was. And Cousin Emmy said she was so sick and tired of everything that sometimes she thought she'd go away and drown herself. And then she cried again, and Mamma said she was a very wicked girl, even to *think* of such a thing. He had to wink his own eyes hard, when she said that, and went on getting sorrier. And when she was putting on her hat to say good-bye he ran and got his shells, and when he was allowed to go to the gate with her, he shewed her them and asked if she'd like to have them "for keeps." And Cousin Emmy thanked him most awfly, but couldn't think of robbing him of his beautiful shells . . . oh, well, then, if he wanted it *so* much, she would, but only one, and he should keep the other and it would be like a philippine, and they wouldn't tell anybody; it would just be their secret. Which it was.

Next day they went to see Aunt Lizzie, where Cousin Emmy lived with "John's cousins" . . . no, he meant "John's children." They couldn't see John, for he was dead. In the wagonette Mamma told him all about the 'squisite songs Aunt Lizzie used to sing him when he was quite a young child, and he hoped she would again; but when he asked her, when she had finished kissing, she clapped her hands and said law child, her singing days were over. It was Aunt Lizzie who was averdipoy—he knew now it meant fat, and not putting on something, for he had asked Mamma at dinner and Mamma had told him; but she had been cross, too, and said it was a nasty habit, and he *must* get out of it, to listen to what his elders said, especially if you repeated it afterwards. He didn't like Aunt Lizzie much. She had a great big mouth, to sing with, and she opened it so wide when she talked you could have put a whole mandarin in at once; and she had rings on her fingers that cut you, when she squeezed.

And then Mamma and her wanted to talk secrets, and they were told to go and play with their cousins. Cousin Emmy took them. Two of them were nearly grown-up, with their hair in plaits, and they didn't take much notice of them, but just said, what a funny little pair of kids to be sure, and whatever was their Mamma thinking of not to put them in mourning for their sister. They all had great big staring black eyes and it made him sorry he had. Cousin Josey was as horrid as ever. She said she guessed he was going to be a dwarf, and would have to be shown at an Easter Fair, and Lucie looked a reg'lar cry-baby. Cousin Emmy told her not to be so nasty, and she said her tongue was her own. Cousin Josey was only ten, but *ever* so big, with long thin legs in white stockings and black garters which she kept pulling up; and when she took off her round comb, and put it between her teeth, her hair came over her face till she looked like a gorilla. When she said that about the cry-baby he took hold of Lucie's hand to pertect her, and squeezed it hard, so's she shouldn't cry. But then Cousin Josey came and pinched Lucie's nose off between her fingers and showed it to her, and she pinched so hard that Luce got all red, and screwed up her eyes like she really was going to cry. Cousin Emmy said she was not to take any notice what such a rude girl did, and then Cousin Josey stuck out her tongue, and Cousin Emmy said she'd box her ears for her if she didn't take care. And then Cousin Josey put her fingers to her nose and waggled them—which was most awfly wicked—and Cousin Emmy said no it was too much and tried to catch her, and she ran away and Cousin Emmy ran too, and they chased and chased like mad round the table, and the big girls said, go it Jo, don't let her touch you, and first a chair fell over and then the tablecloth with the books on it and the inkstand, and it upset on the carpet and there was an awful noise and Aunt Lizzie and Mamma came running to see what was the matter. And Aunt Lizzie was furious and screamed and stamped her foot, and Cousin Josey had to come here, and then she boxed her ears on both sides fit to kill her. And Mamma said oh Lizzie don't and something about drums, and Aunt Lizzie said she was all of a shake, so she hardly knew what she was doing, but this was just a specimen, Mary, of what she had to put up with, they fought like turkey-cocks, and Cousin Emmy wasn't a bit of good at managing them but just as bad as any of them, and there was never a moment's peace, and she wished she'd seen their father at Jericho before she'd had anything to do with him or his spoilt brats. And the other two winked at each other, but Cousin Emmy got wild and said she couldn't wish it more than she did, and she wouldn't stand there and hear her father ubbused, and Aunt Lizzie said for two pins and if she'd any more of her sauce she'd box *her* ears as well, though she *did* think herself so grand. And Cousin Emmy said she dared her to touch her, and it was *dreadful*. He was ever so glad when Mamma said it was time to go home, and he put on his gloves in a hurry. And when they got home Mamma told the Lady about it and said it was a "tragedy" for everybody concerned. He didn't like Cousin Emmy quite so well after this. And that night in bed he told Luce all about the shells, and the philippine, and Luce said if he'd given it her she'd have given it him back and then he'd still have had two. And he was sorry he hadn't.

Uncle Jerry was a nice man . . . though he didn't have any whiskers. Mamma said he looked a perfect sketch, and he'd only cut them off to please Aunt Fanny who must always be ahlamode. Mamma said he had to work like a nigger to make money, she spent such a lot, but he gave him and Lucie each a shilling. At first it was only a penny, and first in one hand, then in the other, but at the end it was a shilling, to spend *exactly* as they liked.

And then they had to go home, and got up ever so early to catch the train. This time it wasn't so jolly. It was too hot: you could only lie on the seat and watch the sky run past. Mamma took off their shoes, and said, well, chicks, we shall soon be seeing dear Papa again now, won't that be lovely? And he said, oh yes, won't it. But inside him he didn't feel it a bit. Mamma had been so nice all the time at the seaside and now she'd soon be cross and sorry again . . . about Lallie and Papa. She looked out of the window, and wasn't thinking about them any more . . . thinking about Papa.— Well, he *was* glad he hadn't spent his shilling! He nearly had. Mamma said what fun it would be if he bought something for Papa with it. But he hadn't. For Papa wrote a letter and said for God's sake don't buy *me* anything, but Mamma did . . . a most beautiful silver fruit-knife. Luce had bought her doll new shoes . . . perhaps some day he'd buy a kite that 'ud fly up and up to the sky till you couldn't see a speck of it . . . much higher than a swing . . . high like a . . .

Good gracious! he must have gone to sleep, for Mamma was shaking his arm saying, come children, wake up. And they put on their shoes again and their hats and gloves and stood at the window to watch for Papa, but it was a long, long time, till they came to Barambogie. Papa was on the

platform and when he saw them he waved like anything
and ran along with the train. And then he suddenly felt
most awfly glad, and got out by himself di*reck*ly the door
was open, and Mamma got out too, but as soon as she did,
she said oh Richard, what *have* you been doing to yourself?
And Papa didn't say anything, but only kissed and kissed
them, and said how well they looked, and he was too tired
to jump them high, and while he was saying this he suddenly
began to cry. And the luggage-man stared like anything and
so did the stationmaster, and Mamma said, oh dear whatever is it, and not before everybody Richard, and please just
send the luggage after us, and then she took Papa's arm and
walked him away. And Luce and him had to go on in front
. . . so's not to see. But he did, and he went all hot inside,
and felt most awfly ashamed.

And Papa cried and cried . . . he could hear him through
the surgery door.

[5]

WHEN Mary came out of the surgery and shut the door behind
her, she leaned heavily up against it for a moment, pressing
her hand to her throat; then, with short steps and the blank
eyes of a sleep-walker, crossed the passage to the bedroom
and sat stiffly down. She was still in bonnet and mantle, just
as she had got out of the train: it had not occurred to her to
remove them. And she was glad of the extra covering, for,
in spite of the heat of the day, she felt very cold. Cold . . .
and old. The scene she had just been through with Richard
seemed, at a stroke, to have added years to her age. It had
been a dreadful experience. With his arms on the table, his
head on his arms, he had cried like a child, laying himself
bare to her, too, with a child's pitiful abandon. He told of
his distraction at the abrupt stoppage of the practice; of
his impression of being deliberately shunned; of his misery
and loneliness, his haunting dread of illness—and, on top of
this, blurted out pell-mell, as if he could keep nothing back,
as if, indeed, he got a wild satisfaction out of making it,
came the confession of his mad folly, the debt, the criminal
debt, in which he had entangled them, and under the shadow
of which, all unknown to her, they had lived for the past

year. Oh! well for him that he could not see her face as he spoke; or guess at the hideous pictures his words set circling in her brain; the waves of wrath and despair that ran through her. After her first spasmodic gasp of: *"Richard! Eight* hundred pounds!" the only outward sign of her inner commotion had been a sudden stiffening of her limbs, an involuntary withdrawal of the arm that had lain round his shoulders. Not for a moment could she afford to let her real feelings escape her: her single exclamation had led to a further bout of self-reproaches. Before everything, he had to be calmed, brought back to his senses, and an end put to this distressing scene. What would the children think, to hear their father behave like this? . . . his hysterical weeping . . . his loud, agitated tones. And so, without reflection, she snatched at any word of comfort that offered; repeated the old threadbare phrases about things not being as black as he painted them; of everything seeming worse if you were alone; of how they would meet this new misfortune side by side and shoulder to shoulder—they still had each other, which was surely half the battle? With never a hint of censure; till she had him composed.

But as she sat in the bedroom, with arms and legs like stone, resentment and bitterness overwhelmed her . . . oh a sheerly intolerable bitterness! Never! not to her dying day, would she forgive him the trick he had played on her . . . the deceit he had practised. On her . . . his own wife! So *this* was why he had left Hawthorn!—why he had not been able to wait to let the practice grow—*this* the cause of his feverish alarm here, did a single patient drop off! Now she understood—and many another thing besides. Oh, what had he done? . . . so recklessly done! . . . to her, to his children. For there had been no real need for this fresh load of misery: they could just as easily—more easily—have rented a house. His pride alone had barred the way. It wouldn't have been good enough for him; nothing ever *was* good enough; he was always trying to outshine others. No matter how she might suffer over it, who feared debt more than anything in the world. But with him it had always been self first. Look at the home-coming he had prepared for her! He had hardly let her step inside before he had sprung his mine.— Of course, he had lost his head with excitement at their arrival . . . had hardly known what he was saying. Yes! but no doubt he had also thought to himself: at the pass to which things were come, the sooner his confession was made, the better for him. *What* a home-coming!

Farther than this, however, she did not get. For the children, still in their travelling clothes, and hot, tired and hungry, were at the door, clamouring for attention. With fumbly hands she took off her bonnet, smoothed her hair, pinned on her cap, tied a little black satin apron round her waist; and went out to them with the pinched lips and haggard eyes it so nipped Cuffy's heart to see.—

Her pearl necklace would have to go: that was the first clear thought she struck from chaos. It was night now: the children had been fed and bathed and put to bed, the trunks unpacked, drawers and wardrobes straightened, the house— it was dirty and neglected—looked through, and Richard, pale as a ghost, but still pitifully garrulous, coaxed to bed in his turn. She sat alone in the little dining-room, her own eyes feeling as if they would never again need sleep. Her necklace . . . even as the thought came to her she started up, and, stealing on tiptoe into the bedroom, carried her dressing-case back with her . . . just to make sure: for an instant she had feared he might have been beforehand with her. But there the pearls lay, safe and sound.— Well! as jewellery, she would not regret them: she hadn't worn them for years, and had never greatly cared for being bedizened and behung. Bought in those palmy days when money slid like sand through Richard's fingers, they had cost him close on a hundred pounds. Surely she ought still to get enough for them— and for their companion brooches, rings, chains, ear-rings and bracelets—to make up the sums of money due for the coming months, which Richard admitted not having been able to get together. For, consent to let the mortgage lapse, she never would: not if she was forced to sell the clothes off her back, or to part, piece by piece, with the Paris ornaments, the table silver . . . Richard's books. It would be sheer madness; after having paid out hundreds and hundreds of pounds. Besides, the knowledge that you had this house behind you made all the difference. If the worst came to the worst, they could retire to Hawthorn, and she take in boarders. She didn't care a rap what she did, as long as they contrived to pay their way.

How to dispose of the necklace was the puzzle. To whom could she turn? She ran over various people, but dismissed them all. Even Tilly. When it came to making Richard's straits public, she was hedged on every side. Ah; but now she had it: *Zara!* If, as seemed probable, Zara came to take up her abode with them, to teach the children, she would soon see for herself how matters stood. (And at least she was one's own sister.) Zara . . . trailing her weeds—why, yes, even these might be turned to account! Widows did not wear jewellery; and were often left poorly off. People would pity her, perhaps give more, because of it.

And so, having fetched pen, ink and paper, Mary drew the kerosene lamp closer, and set to writing her letter.

It wasn't easy; she made more than one start. Not even to Zara could she tell the unvarnished truth. She shrank, for instance, from admitting that only now had she herself learnt of Richard's difficulties. Zara might think strange things . . . about him and her. So she put the step she was forced to take, down to the expenses of their seaside holiday. Adding, however, that jewellery was useless in a place like this, where you had no chance of wearing it; and even something of a risk, owing to the house standing by itself and having so many doors.

The letter written, she made a second stealthy journey, this time to the surgery, where she ferreted out Richard's case-books. She had a lurking hope that, yet once more, he might have been guilty of his usual exaggeration. But half a glance at the blank pages taught her better. Things were even worse than he had admitted. What *could* have happened during her absence? What had he done, to make people turn against him? Practices didn't die out like this in a single day!— somehow or other he must have been to blame. Well! it would be her job, henceforth, to put things straight again: somehow or other to re-capture the patients. And if Richard really laid himself out to conciliate people—he *could* be so taking, if he chose!—and not badger them . . . Let him only scrape together enough for them to live on, and she would do the rest: her thoughts leapt straightway to a score of petty economies. The expenses of food and clothing might be cut down all round; and they would certainly go on no more long and costly holidays: had she only known the true state of affairs before setting out this summer! But she had been so anxious about the children . . . oh! she was forgetting the children. And here, everything coming back to her with a rush, Mary felt her courage waver. Merciless to herself; with only a half-hearted pity for Richard, grown man that he was, and the author of all the trouble; she was at once a craven, and wrung with compassion where her children were concerned.

At the breakfast-table next morning she sat preoccupied; and directly the meal was over put the first of her schemes into action, by sending for the defaulting Maria and soundly rating her. But she could get no sensible reason from the girl for running away—or none but the muttered remark that it had been "too queer" in the house, with them all gone. After which, tying on her bonnet, Mary set out for the township, a child on either hand. Lucie trotted docilely; but Cuffy was restive at being buttoned into his Sunday suit on a week-day, and dragged back, and shuffled his feet in the dust till they were nearly smothered.— Instead of trying to help Mamma by being an extra good boy!

"But I don't *feel* good!"

Once out of sight of the house, Mary took two crêpe bands from her pocket, and slipped them over the children's white sleeves. Richard's ideas about mourning were bound to give . . . had perhaps already given offence. People of the class they were now dependent on thought so much of funerals and mourning. But he never stopped to consider the feelings of others. She remembered, for instance, how he had horrified Miss Prestwick, with his heathenish ideas about the children's prayers. All of a sudden one day, he had declared they were getting too big to kneel down and pray "into the void," or to "a glorified man"; and had had them taught a verse which said that loving all things big and little was the best kind of prayer, and so on; making a regular to-do about it when he discovered that Miss Prestwick was still letting them say their "Gentle Jesus" on the sly.

Here, she righted two hats, and took Cuffy's elastic out of his mouth; for they were entering the township; and, for once, the main street was not in its usual state of deserted-

ness, when it seemed as if the inhabitants must all lie dead
of the plague . . . or be gone *en masse* to a Fairing. The
butcher's cart drove briskly to and fro; a spring-cart had
come in from the bush; buggies stood before the Bank. The
police-sergeant touched his white helmet; horses were being
backed between the shafts of the coach in front of the "Sun."
Everybody of course eyed her and the children very curiously, and even emerged from their shops to stare after them.
It was the first time she had ever walked her children out,
and on top of that, she had been absent for over two months.
(Perhaps people imagined she had gone for good! Oh, could
that possibly be a reason? No, really . . . !) However, she
made the best of it: smiled, and nodded, and said good-day;
and, in spite of their inquisitive looks, every one she met
was very friendly. She went into the butcher's to choose
a joint, and took the opportunity of thanking the butcher
for having served the doctor so well during her absence.
The man beamed; and showed the children a whole dead
pig he had hanging in the shop. She gave an order to the
grocer, who leaned over the counter with two bunches of
raisins, remarking "A fine little pair of nippers you have
there, Mrs. Mahony!" To the baker she praised his bread,
comparing it favourably with what she had eaten in Melbourne; and the man's wife pressed sweets on the children.
At the draper's which she entered to buy some stuff for pina-
fores, the same fuss was made over them . . . till she bade
them run outside and wait for her there. For the drapery
woman began putting all sorts of questions about Lallie's
illness, and what they had done for her, and how they had
treated it . . . odd and prying questions, and asked with a
strange air. Still, there was kindliness behind the curiosity.
"We did all feel that sorry for *you*, Mrs. Mahony . . . losing
such a fine sturdy little girl!" And blinking her eyes to keep
the tears back, Mary began to think that Richard must have
gone *deliberately* out of his way, to make enemies of these
simple, well-meaning souls. Bravely she re-told the tale of
her loss, being iron in her resolve to win people round; but
she was thankful when the questionnaire ended, and she was
free to quit the shop. To see what the children were doing,
too. She could hear Cuffy chattering away to somebody.

This proved to be the Reverend Mr. Thistlethwaite, who

had engaged the pair in talk with the super-heartiness he reserved for what he called the "young or kitchen fry" of his parish. In his usual state of undress—collarless, with unbuttoned vest, his bare feet thrust in carpet slippers—he was so waggish that Mary could not help suspecting where his morning stroll had led him.

"Good morning, Madam, good morning to you! Back again, back again? *And* the little Turks! Capital . . . quite capital!"

He slouched along beside them, his paunch, under its grease spots, a-shake with laughter at his own jokes. The children of course were all ears; and she would soon have slipped into another shop and so have got rid of him—you never knew what he was going to say next—if a sudden bright idea had not flashed into her mind.

It came of Mr. Thistlethwaite mentioning that the Bishop was shortly expected to visit the district; and humorously bemoaning his own lot. For, should his Lordship decide to break his journey at Barambogie on his way home, he, Thistlethwaite, would be obliged to ask him to share his bachelor quarters. "Which are all very well for hens and self, Mrs. Mahony . . . hens and self! But for his Lordship? Oh dear, no!"

Privately Mary recognised the ruse. The piggery in which Thistlethwaite housed had stood him in good stead before now: never yet had the parsonage been in fit state to receive a brother cleric. At the present crisis, however, she jumped at the handle it offered her.

"But he must come to us!" cried she. "The doctor and I would be only too delighted. And for as long as he likes. Another thing: why not, while he *is* here, persuade him to give us a short lecture or address? We might even get up a little concert to follow, and devote the money to the fencing fund."— For the church still stood on open ground. In the course of the past year but a meagre couple of pounds had been raised towards enclosing it; and what had become of these nobody knew.

And now Mary's ideas came thick and fast; rising even to the supreme labour of a "Tea-meeting." And while Thistlethwaite hummed aloud in ever greater good humour, mentally cracking his fingers to the tune of: "That's the ticket . . . women for ever! The work for them, and the glory for us!"

Book III: *Ultima Thule*

Mary was telling herself that to secure the Bishop as their guest would go far towards restoring Richard's lost prestige. He would be reinstated as the leading person in the township; and the fact of his Lordship staying with them would bring people about the house again, who *might* turn to patients. At any rate Richard and he would be seen in the street together, and, at concert or lecture, it would naturally fall to Richard to take the chair.

Striking while the iron was hot, she offered her services to mend the altarcloth; to darn and "get up" a surplice; to over-sew the frayed edges of a cassock. She would also see, she promised, what could be done to hide a hole in the carpet before the lectern, in which his Lordship might catch his foot. For this purpose they entered the church. It was pleasantly cool there, after the blazing heat out of doors; and, having made her inspection, Mary was glad to rest for a moment. The children felt very proud at being allowed inside the church when it wasn't Sunday; and Thistlethwaite actually let Cuffy mount the pulpit-steps and repeat: "We are but little children weak," so that he could see what it felt like to preach a sermon. Cuffy spoke up well, and remembered his words, and Mr. Thistlethwaite said they'd see him in the cloth yet; but all the time he, Cuffy, wasn't *really* thinking what he was saying. For he spied a funny little cupboard under the ledge of the pulpit, and while he was doing his hymn, he managed to finger it open, and inside he saw a glass and a water-jug and a medicine-bottle. And next Sunday he watched the water Mr. Thistlethwaite drank before he preached and saw he put medicine in it first. But when he asked Mamma if he was ill, and if not, why he took it, she got cross, and said he was a very silly little boy, and he was to be sure and not say things like that, before people.

There was still Richard to talk over, on getting home. And he was in a bad temper at their prolonged absence. "All this time in the township? What for? Buying your own eatables? What on *earth* will people think of you?— Not to speak of dragging the children after you like any nursemaid!"

"Oh, do *not* interfere! Let me go my own way to work."

To reconcile him to the Bishop's visit was a tough job. Gloomily he admitted that it might serve a utilitarian end. But the upset . . . to think of the upset! "It means the sofa

815

for me again. While old M., who's as strong as a horse, snores on my pillow. The sofa's like a board; I never sleep a wink on it; it sets every bone in my body aching."

"But *only* for one night! . . . or at most two. Surely you can endure a few aches for the good that may come of it? Oh, Richard, *don't* go about thinking what obstacles you can put in my way! I'm quite sure I can help you, if you'll just give me a free hand."

And she was right . . . as usual. The mere rumour that so important a visitor was expected—and she took care it circulated freely—brought a trickle of people back to the house. By the end of the week, Richard had treated four patients.

[6]

THEY were at breakfast when the summons came—breakfast, the hardest meal of any to get through, without friction. Richard, for instance, ate at top speed, and with his eyes glued to his plate; in order, he said, not to be obliged to see Zara's dusty crêpe and bombazine, the mere sight of which, on these hot mornings, took away his appetite. But he also hoped, by example, to incite Zara to haste: now she was there, the meals dragged out to twice their usual length. For Zara had a patent habit of masticating each mouthful so-and-so many times before swallowing; and the children forgot to eat, in counting their aunt's bites. With their ears cocked, for the click at the finish. Mamma said it was her teeth that did it, and it was rude to listen. Aunt Zara called her teeth her *mashwar*. Why did she, and why did they click? But it was no good asking *her*. She never told you anything . . . except lessons.

Yes, Mary had got her way, and for a couple of weeks now, Zara had been installed as governess. As a teacher she had not her equal. She also made a very good impression in the township, looking so much the lady, speaking with such precision, and all that. But—well, it was a good job nothing had been said to Richard of her exaggerated offer to wash dishes and scrub floors. How he would have crowed! Apart from this, she had landed them in a real quandary by arriving with every stick of furniture she possessed; such as her bed, her mahogany chest of drawers, a night-commode. In the tiny bedroom, which was all they had to offer her, there was hardly room to stand; while still unpacked portmanteaux and gladstone-bags lined the passage; Zara having turned nasty at a hint of the outhouse. And directly lessons were over, she shut herself up among these things with a bottle of French polish.

Of course, poor soul! they were all that was left of her own home: you couldn't wonder at her liking to keep them nice. And the main thing was, the children were making headway. Reward enough for her, Mary, to hear them gabbling their French of a morning, or learning their steps to Zara's: "One, two, *chassez,* one!" Such considerations didn't weigh with Richard, though. Just as of old, everything Zara said or did exasperated him. He was furious with her, too, for grumbling at the size of her room.— But there! It wasn't only Zara who grated on his nerves. It was everybody and everything.

On this particular day, all her tact would be needed. For the message Maria had looked in during breakfast to deliver, was a summons to Brown's Plains; and if there was one thing he disliked more than another, it was the bush journeys he was being called on to face anew. "What! . . . *again?* Good God!" he looked up from his gobbling to ejaculate. Which expression made Zara pinch her lips and raise her eyebrows; besides being so bad for the children to hear. She, Mary, found his foot under the table and pressed it; but that irritated him, too, and he was nasty enough to say: "What are you kicking me for?" Breakfast over, she questioned Maria, and sent her to the "Sun" to bespeak a buggy; looked out his driving things, put likely requisites in his bag—as usual the people hadn't said what the matter was—and, her own work in the house done, changed her dress and tied on a shady hat. Now that Zara was there to mind the children, she frequently made a point of accompanying Richard on these drives.

The buggy came round: it was another of her innovations to have it brought right to the door; he had nothing to do but to step in. At the gate, however, they found Cuffy, who began teasing to be allowed to go, too. He had no one to play with; Lucie was asleep, and Maria was busy, and Aunt Zara shut up in her room; and he was *so* tired of reading! Thus he pouted, putting on his special unhappy baby face; and, as often as he did this, it got at something in his mother, which made her weak towards her first-born. So she said, oh, very well then, if he wanted to so much, he might; and sent him in to wash his hands and fetch his hat. Richard, of course, let loose a fresh string of grumbles: it would be hot enough, with just the pair of them, without having the child thrown in. But Mary, too, was cross and tired, and said she wasn't going to give way over every trifle; and so Cuffy, who had shrunk back at the sharp words, was hoisted up, and off they set.— And soon the three of them, a tight fit in the high, two-wheeled, hooded vehicle, had left the township behind them, and were out on bush tracks where the buggy rocked and pitched, like a ship on the broken waters of a rough sea.

Cuffy had never before been so far afield, and his spirits were irrepressible. He twisted this way and that, jerked his legs and bored with his elbows, flinging round to ask question after question. It fell to Mary to supply the answers; and she had scant patience with the curiosity of children, who hardly listened to what you told them, in their eagerness to ask anew. But her "I wonder!" "How do *I* know?" and "Don't bother me!" failed to damp Cuffy, who kept up his flow, till he startled her by exclaiming with a vigorous sigh: "Ugh, I *do* feel so hot and funny!" His small face was flushed and distressed.

"That's what comes of so much talking!" said Mary, and without more ado whisked off his sailor-hat, with its cribbing chin-elastic, undid his shoes, slid his feet out of his socks.

Thus much Cuffy permitted. But when it came to taking off his tunic, leaving him to sit exposed in his little vest, he fought with her unbuttoning hands.

"*Don't,* Mamma—I won't!"

"But there's nobody to see! And it wouldn't matter if they did—you're only a little boy. No, you *would* come! Now you must do as I tell you."

And when she knew quite well how he felt! Why, not even Lucie was allowed to see him undressed. Since they slept in the same room, she had always to go to bed first, and turn her face to the wall, and shut her eyes tight, while he flew out of his clothes and into his nightshirt. To have to sit in broad daylight with naked arms, and his neck too, and his braces showing! All his pleasure in the drive was spoiled. At each turn in the road he was on thorns lest somebody should be there who'd see him. Oh, *why* must Mamma be like this? Why didn't she take her own clothes off? His belonged to him. (He *hated* Mamma.)

Nursing this small agony, he could think of nothing else. And now there was silence in the buggy, which lurched and jolted, Richard taking as good as no pains to avoid the foot-deep, cast-iron ruts, the lumpy rocks and stones. Over they went sideways, then up in the air, and down again with a bump. "Oh, gently, dear! *Do* be careful!" He wasn't the driver for this kind of thing. She never felt really safe with him.— And here there came to her mind a memory of the very first time they had driven together: on their wedding journey from Geelong to Ballarat. How nervous she had been that day! . . . how home-sick and lonely, too! . . . beside some one who was little more than a stranger to her, behind a strange horse, on an unknown road, bound for a place of which she knew nothing. Ah well! it was perhaps a wise arrangement on the part of Providence that you *didn't* know what lay ahead . . . or you might never set out at all. Could *she* have foreseen all that marriage was to mean: how Richard would change, and the dance he would lead her; all the nagging worry and the bitter suffering; then, yes, then, poor young inexperienced thing that she was, full of romantic ideas, and expecting only happiness as her lot, she might have been excused for shrinking back in dismay.— Her chief objection to driving, nowadays, was the waste of time. To make up for having to sit there with her hands before her, she let her mind run free, and was deep in her usual reckonings—reducing grocer's and butcher's bills, making over her old dresses for the children—when a violent heave of the buggy all but threw her from her seat: she had just time to fling a protective arm in front of Cuffy, to save the child from pitching clean over the splashboard. Without warning, Richard had leant forward and dealt the horse a vicious cut on the neck. The beast, which had been ambling drearily, started, stumbled, and would have gone down, had he not tugged and sawed it by the mouth. For a few seconds they flew ahead, rocking and swaying, she holding to the child with one hand, to the rail with the other.— "Do you want to break our necks?"

Mahony made no reply.

Gradually the rough canter ceased, and the horse fell back on its former jog-trot. It was a very poor specimen, old and lean; and the likelihood was, had been in harness most of the morning.

Again they crawled forward. The midday heat blazed; the red dust enveloped them, dimming their eyes, furring their tongues; there was not an inch of shade anywhere. Except under the close black hood, where they sat as if glued together.

Then came another savage lash from Richard, another leap on the part of the horse, more snatching at any hold she could find, the buggy toppling this way and that. Cuffy was frightened, and clung to her dress, while she, outraged and alarmed, made indignant protest.

"Are you crazy? If you do that again, I shall get out!"

For all answer Richard said savagely: "Oh, hold your tongue, woman!" Before the child, too!

But her hurt and anger alike passed unheeded. Mahony saw nothing—nothing but the tremulous heat-lines which caused the whole landscape to quiver and swim before him. His head ached to bursting: it might have had a band of iron round it, the screws in which were tightened, with an agonising twist, at each lurch of the vehicle, at Cuffy's shrill pipe, Mary's loud, exasperated tones. Inside this circlet of pain his head felt swollen and top-heavy, an unnatural weight on his shoulders: the exact reverse of an unpleasant experience he had had the night before. Then, as he went to lay it on the pillow, it had seemed to lose its solidity, and, grown light as a puff-ball, had gone clean through pillow, bolster, mattress, drawing his shoulders after it, down and down, head-foremost, till he felt as if he were dropping like a stone through space. With the bed-curtain fast in one hand, a bedpost in the other, he had managed to hold on while the vertigo lasted, his teeth clenched to hinder himself from crying out and alarming Mary. But the fear of a recurrence had kept him awake half the night, and to-day he felt very poorly, and disinclined for exertion. He would certainly have jibbed at driving out all this distance, had it not been for

Mary and her hectoring ways. He was unable to face the fuss
and bother in which a refusal would involve him.

If only they could reach their destination! They seemed to
have been on the road for hours. But—with the horse that
had been fobbed off on him! . . . old, spiritless, and stubborn
as a mule . . . And there he had to sit, hunched up, crushed
in, with no room to stir . . . with hardly room to breathe.
One of Mary's utterly mistaken ideas of kindness, to dog his
steps as she did. To tack the child on, too . . . Because *she* liked
company . . . But his needs had never been hers. Solitude . . .
solitude was all he asked! . . . to be let alone the greatest
favour anyone could now do him. Privacy had become as
essential as air or water to the act of living. His brain refused its work were others present. Which reminded him,
there was something he had been going to think over on
this very drive: something vital, important. But though he
ransacked his mind from end to end, it remained blank. Or
mere disconnected thoughts and scraps of thought flitted
across it, none of which led anywhere. Enraged at his power-
lessness, he let the horse taste the whip; but the relief the
quickened speed afforded him was over almost as soon as
begun, and once more they ambled at a funeral pace. Damnation take the brute! Was he, because of it, to sit for ever on
this hard, narrow seat, chasing incoherencies round an empty
brain? . . . to drive for all eternity along these intolerable
roads? . . . through this accursed bush, where the very trees
grimaced at you in distorted attitudes, like stage ranters de-
claiming an exaggerated passion—or pointed at you with the
obscene gestures of the insane . . . obscene, because so wholly
without significance.— And again he snatched up the whip.

But the prolonged inaction was doing its work: a sense of
unreality began to invade him, his surroundings to take on
the blurred edges of a dream: one of those nightmare-dreams
in which the dreamer knows that he is bound to reach a
certain place in a given time, yet whose legs are weighed
down by invisible weights . . . or which feel as if they are
being dragged through water, tons of impeding water . . . or
yet again, the legs of elephantiasis . . . swollen, monstrous,
heavy as lead: all this, while time, the precious time that
remains *before* the event, is flying. Yes, somewhere . . . far
away, out in the world . . . life and time were rushing by:

he could hear the rhythm of their passing in the beat of his blood. He alone lay stranded—incapable of movement. And, as always at the thought of his lost freedom, madness seized him: dead to everything but his own need, he rose in his seat and began to rain down blows on the horse: to beat it mercilessly, hitting out wherever the lash found place—on head, neck, ears, the forelegs, the quivering undersides. In vain the wretched creature struggled to break free, to evade the cut of the thong: it backed, tried to rear, dragged itself from side to side, ducked its defenceless head, the white foam flying. But for it, too, strapped down, buckled in, there was no chance of escape. And the blows fell . . . and fell.

"*Richard!* Oh *don't*—don't beat the poor thing like that! How can you! What are you doing?" For, cruellest of all, he was holding the animal in, to belabour it, refusing to let it carry out its pitiful attempts to obey the lash. "You who pretend to be so fond of animals!" There was no anger now in Mary's voice: only entreaty, and a deep compassion.— And in the mad race that followed, when they tore along, in and out of ruts, on the track and off, skimming trees and bushes, always on the edge of capsizing, blind with dust: now, frightened though she was, she just set her teeth and held fast, and said never a word . . . though she saw it was all Richard could do to keep control: his lean wrists spanned like iron.

Brought up at length alongside a rail-and-post fence, the horse stood shaking and sweating, its red nostrils working like bellows, the marks of the lash on its lathered hide. And Richard was trembling too. His hand shook so that he could hardly replace the whip in its socket.

With an unspoken "Thank God!" Mary slid to the ground, dragging Cuffy after her. Her legs felt as if they were made of pulp.

"I think this must be the place. . . . I think I see a house. . . . No, no, you stop here! I'll go on and find out." (Impossible for him to face strangers, in the state he was in.) "Hush, Cuffy! It's all right now." Saying this, she made to draw the child under a bush; he was lying sobbing just as she had dropped him.

But Cuffy pushed her away.— "Leave me alone!" He only wanted to stop where he was. And cry. He felt so *dread*fully miserable. For the poor horse . . . it couldn't cry for itself . . .

and only run and run—and it hadn't *done* anything . . . 'cept be very old and tired . . . prayeth best who loveth best . . . oh! everything was turned all black inside him. But for Papa, too, because . . . he didn't know why . . . only . . . when Mamma had gone, and Papa thought nobody would see him, he went up to the horse's neck and stroked it. And that made him cry still more.

But when he came and sat down by him and said "Cuffy!" and put out his arms, then he went straight into them, and Papa held him tight, so that he could feel the hard sticking-out bone that was his shoulder. And they just sat, and never spoke a word, till they heard Mamma coming back; and then Papa let him go and he jumped up and pretended to be looking at something on the ground.

Mary carried a dipper of water.

"Yes, this is it, right enough. There's been an accident—the son—they're afraid he's broken his leg. Oh, *why* can't people send clearer messages! Can you rig up some splints? A man's bringing a bucket for the horse. Come, let me dust you down. No, I'll wait here . . . I'd rather."

Richard went off, bag in hand: she watched him displacing and replacing slip-rails, walking stiffly over the rough ground. Just before he vanished, he turned and waved, and she waved back. But, this last duty performed, she sat heavily down, and dropped her head in her hands. And there she sat, forgetful of where she was, of Cuffy, the heat, the return journey that had to be faced: just sat, limp and spent, thinking things from which she would once have shrunk in horror.—

All the way home Cuffy carried in his pocket half of one of the nicest sugar-biscuits the people had sent him out by Papa. It was a present for the horse. But when the moment came to give it, his courage failed him. Everybody else had forgotten; the horse, too: it was in a great hurry to get back to its stable. He didn't like to be the only one to remember, to make it look as if he was still sorry. So, having feebly fingered the biscuit—the sugary top had melted and stuck to his pocket—he ate it up himself.

[7]

FOR some time after this, Cuffy fought shy of his father; and tried never, if he could help it, to be alone with him. It wasn't only embarrassment at having been nursed and petted like a baby. The events of the drive left a kind of fear behind them: a fear not of his father, but for him: he was afraid of having to see what Papa was feeling. If he was with him, he didn't seem able not to. And he didn't *like* it. For he wanted so much to be happy—in this house that he loved, with the verandah, and the garden, and the fowls, and the Lagoon—and when he saw Papa miserable, he couldn't be. So he gave the end of the verandah on which the surgery opened a wide berth; avoiding the dining-room, too . . . when it wasn't just meals. For there was no sofa in the surgery, and if Papa had a headache he sometimes went and lay down in the dining-room.

But he couldn't *always* manage it.

There was that day Mamma sent him in to fetch her scissors, and Papa was on the sofa, with the blind down and his eyes shut, and his feet sticking over the end. Cuffy walked on the tips of his toes. But just when he thought he was safe, Papa was watching him. And put his hand out and said: "Come here to me, Cuffy. There's something I wish to say to you."

The words struck chill. With resistance in every limb, Cuffy obeyed.

"Pull up the hassock. Sit down." And there he was, alone in the dark with Papa, his heart going pit-a-pat.

Papa took his hand. And held on to it. "You're getting a big boy now; you'll soon be seven years old . . . when I was not much older than that, my dear, I was being thrashed because I could not turn French phrases into Latin."

"What's Latin?" (Oh, perhaps, after all, it was just going to be about when Papa was little.)

"Latin is one of the dead languages."

"How can it . . . be dead? It isn't a . . . a man."

"Things perish, too, child. A language dies when it is no longer in common use; when it ceases to be a means of communication between living people."

This was too much for Cuffy. He struggled with the idea for a moment, then gave it up, and asked: "Why did you have to? And why did your Mamma let you be thrashed?" (Lots and lots of questions. Papa always told.)

"Convention demanded it . . . convention and tradition . . .

the slavish tradition of a country that has always rated the
dead lion higher than the live dog. And thralls to this notion
were those in whose hand at that time lay the training of the
young. The torturing rather! A lifetime lies between, but I can
still feel something of the misery, the hopelessness, the inability to understand what was required of you, the dread of what
awaited you, was your task ill done or left undone. A forlorn
and frightened child . . . with no one to turn to, for help, for
advice. That most sensitive, most delicate of instruments—the
mind of a little child! Small wonder that I vowed to myself, if
ever I had children of my own . . . to let the young brain lie
fallow . . . not so much as the alphabet . . . the A B C . . .".—
Thus, forgetful of his little hearer, Mahony rambled on. And
Cuffy, listening to a lot more of such talk (nasty talk!) kept
still as a broody hen, not shuffling his feet, or sniffling, or doing
anything to interrupt, for fear of what might come next.

Then Papa stopped, and was so quiet he thought he'd gone
to sleep again. He hoped so. He'd stay there till he was *quite*
sure. But through his trying too hard not to make a noise, a
button squeaked, and Papa opened his eyes.

"But . . . this wasn't what I brought you here to say." He
looked fondly at the child and stroked his rough, little-boy
hand. "Listen, Cuffy. Papa hasn't felt at all well lately, and is
sometimes very troubled . . . about many things. And he wants
you, my dear, to promise him that if anything should . . . I
mean if I should"—he paused, seeking a euphemism.—"if I
should have to leave you, leave you all, then I want you to
promise me that you will look after Mamma for me, take care
of her in my place, and be a help to her in every way you can.
Will you?"

Cuffy nodded: his throat felt much too tight to speak. Dropping his head, he watched his toe draw something on the carpet. To hear Papa say things like this made him feel like he
did when he had to take his clothes off.

"Your little sister, too, of course, but Mamma most of all.
She has had so much to bear . . . so much care and trouble.
And I fear there's more to come. Be good to her, Cuffy!— And
one other thing. Whatever happens, my little son . . . and who
knows what life may have in store for you . . . I want you
never to forget that you are a gentleman—a gentleman first and

foremost—no matter what you do, or where you go, or who your companions may be. *Noblesse oblige*. With that for your motto, you cannot go far wrong."

"What a lot of little hairs you've got on your hand, Papa!"

Cuffy blurted this out, hardly knowing what he said. Nobody . . . not even Papa . . . had the right to speak such things to him. They *hurt*.

Free at last, he ran to the garden, where he fell to playing his wildest, merriest games. And Mahony, lying listening to the childish rout, thought sadly to himself: "No use . . . too young!"

That Papa might be going away stayed Cuffy's secret: he didn't even tell Lucie. Or at least not till she got a secret, too. He saw at once there was something up; and it didn't take him half a jiffy to worm it out of her. They sat on the other side of the fowl-house; but she whispered, all the same. "I fink Mamma's going away."

Cuffy, leaning over her with his arm round her neck, jerked upright, eyes and mouth wide open. *What?* . . . Mamma, too? Oh, but that couldn't be true . . . it couldn't! He laughed out loud, and was very stout and bold in denial, because of the fright it gave him.— "Besides if she did, she'd take us with her!"

But his little sister shook her head. "I heard her tell Papa yesterday, one of vese days she'd just pack her boxes an' walk outer the house an' leave bof him an' the child'en. An' then he could see how he liked it." And the chubby face wrinkled piteously.

"Hush, Luce! they'll hear you—don't cry, there's a good girl! I'll look after *you* . . . always! An' when I'm a big man I'll . . . I'll marry you. So there! Won't that be nice?"

But Cuffy's world tottered. Papa's going would be bad enough . . . though . . . yes . . . *he'd* take care of Mamma so well that she'd never be worried again. But that *she* should think of leaving them was not to be borne. Life without Mamma! The nearest he could get to it was when he had once had to stop alone at a big railway station, to mind the luggage, while Mamma and Luce went to buy the tickets. It had taken so long, and there were so many people, and he was sure the train would go without them . . . or else they might forget him, forget to come back . . . or get into a wrong train and he be left there . . . standing there for always. His heart had thumped and thumped . . . and he watched for them till his eyes got so big that they almost fell out . . . and the porters were running and shouting . . . and the doors banging . . . oh dear, oh dear!—

He knew what the row had been about—a picture Cousin Emmy had painted, quite by herself, and sent as a present to Mamma. Mamma thought it was a lovely picture, and so did he: all sea and rocks, with little men in red caps sitting on them. But Papa said it was a horrible dorb, and he wouldn't have it in *his* house. And Mamma said that was only because it was made by a relation of hers, and if it had been one of his, he would have liked it; and it was an oil painting, and oil paintings were ever so hard to do; and when she thought of the time it must have taken Emmy, and the work she had put into it . . . besides, she'd always believed he was fond of the girl. And Papa said, Good God, so he was, but what had that to do with "heart"? And Mamma said, well, he might talk himself hoarse, but she meant to hang the picture in the drawing-room, and Papa said he forbade it . . . and then he'd run away, so as not to hear any more, but Luce didn't, and it was then she heard.

He hated Aunt Zara. Aunt Zara said, with them quarrelling as they did, the house wasn't fit to live in. He went hot all over when she said this. And that night he got a big pin and stuck it in her bed with the point up, so as it would run into her, when she lay down. And it must have; because she showed it to Mamma next day, and was *simply furious*. And he had to say yes, he'd done it, and on purpose. But he wouldn't say he was sorry, because he wasn't; and he stopped naughty, and never did say it at all.

For then the Bishop came to stay, and every one was nice and smiley again.

The Bishop was the same genial, courtly gentleman as of old. Tactfulness itself, too: in the three days he was with them, never, by word or by look, did he show himself aware of their changed circumstances. He admired house and garden, complimented Mary on her cooking, and made much of the children. Especially Lucie. "I shall steal this little maid before I'm finished, Mrs. Mahony! Pop her in my pocket, and take her home as a present to my wife!" And the chicks were on their best behaviour—they had had it well dinned into them beforehand, not to comment on the Bishop's attire. But even if it had been left to his own discretion, Cuffy would in this case have held his tongue. For, truth to tell, he thought the Bishop's costume just a *little rude*. To wear your legs as if you were still a little boy, and then . . . to have something hanging down in front. Mamma said it was an apron, and all Bishops did—even a "sufferin'" Bishop like this one. But surely . . . surely . . . if you were a grown-up gentleman . . .

Zara, too, did her share. At table, for instance, what with looking after Maria and the dishes, keeping one eye on the children, the other on the Bishop's plate, Mary's own attention was fully occupied. Richard sat for the most part in the silence that was now his normal state; he was, besides, so out of things that he had little left to talk about. Hence it fell to Zara, who was a fluent conversationalist and very well read, to keep the ball rolling. The Bishop and she got on splendidly (Zara had by now, of course, returned to the true fold). Afterwards, he was loud in her praises. "A very charming woman, your sister, Mrs. Mahony . . . very charming, indeed!" And falling, man-like, under the spell of the widow's cap, he added: "How bravely she bears up, too! So sad, so *very* sad for her, losing her dear husband as she did! Still . . . God's ways are not our ways. His Will, not ours, be done!"

At which Mary winced. For he had used the self-same words about their own great grief; had worn the same sympathetic face; dispensed a like warm pressure of the hand. And this rankled. It was true she did not parade her loss in yards of crêpe. But that anyone who troubled to think could compare the two cases! A little child, cut prematurely off, and Hempel, poor old Hempel! Zara's *pis aller*, who had had one foot in the grave when she married him, whom she had badgered and bullied to the end. But these pious phrases evidently formed the Bishop's stock-in-trade, which he dealt out indiscriminately to whoever suffered loss or calamity. And now her mind jumped back to the afternoon of his arrival, when after tea Richard and he had withdrawn to the surgery. "A most delightful chat!" he subsequently described the hour spent in there; though she, listening at the door, knew that Richard had hardly opened his mouth. At the time, she had thought it most kind of the Bishop so to make the best of it. Now, however . . .

And when, later on, he returned from a visit to church and parsonage, and still professed himself well content, she began to see him with other eyes. It was not so much tact and civility, on his part, as a set determination not to scratch below the surface. He didn't want to spoil his own comfort by being forced to see things as they really were.

Of course, this turn of mind made him the pleasantest of guests. (Fancy, though, having to live perpetually in such a simmer of satisfaction!) And even here his wilful blindness had its drawbacks. Had he been different, the kind of man to say: "Your husband is not looking very well," or: "Does Dr. Mahony find the climate here try him?" or otherwise have given her an opening, she might have plucked up courage to confide in him, to unburden herself of some of her worries—oh! the relief it would have been, to speak freely to a person of their own class. As it was, he no doubt firmly refused to let himself become aware of the slightest change for the worse in Richard.

Well, at least her main object was achieved: if wanted, the Bishop had to be sought and found at "Doctor's." She also so contrived it that Richard and he were daily seen hobnobbing in public. Each morning she started them off together for the township: the short, thickset, animated figure, the tall, lean, bent one.

And now the crown was to be set on her labours by a public entertainment. First, a concert, of local talent; after which his Lordship promised to give them a short address.

Then, at the very last minute, if Richard didn't threaten to undo all her work! For, if he did not take the chair at this meeting, she would have laboured in vain. Just to think of seeing that fool Thistlethwaite in his place; or old Cameron, the Bank Manager, who as likely as not would be half-seas over.

But Richard was as obstinate as a mule. "I *can't*, Mary" . . . very peevishly . . . "and what's more, I won't! To be stuck up there for all those yokels to gape at! For God's sake, leave me alone!"

She could cheerfully have boxed his ears. But she kept her temper. "All you've got to do, dear, is to sit there . . . at most to say half-a-dozen words to introduce his Lordship. You, who're such a dab hand at that sort of thing!"— Until, by alternate wheedling and bullying, she had him worn down.

But when the evening came, she almost doubted her own wisdom. By then he had worked himself up into a sheerly ridiculous state of agitation: you might have thought he had to appear before the Queen! His coat was too shabby, his collar was frayed; he couldn't tie his cravat, or get his studs in— she had everything to do for him. She heard him, too, when he thought no one was listening, feverishly rehearsing the reading which the Bishop, at a hint from her, had duly persuaded him into giving. No, she very much feared Richard's day for this kind of thing was over.

The hall at the "Sun" was packed. From a long way round, from Brown's Plains and the Springs, farmers and vine-growers had driven in with their families: the street in front of the hotel was black with buggies, with wagonettes, spring-carts, shandrydans and drays. And the first part of the evening went off capitally. There was quite a fund of musical talent in the place: the native-born sons and daughters of tradesmen and publicans had many of them clear, sweet voices, and sang with ease. It was not till the turn came of the draperess, Miss Mundy, that the trouble began—they hadn't ventured to leave her out, for she was one of the main props of the church, and head teacher in the Sunday School. But she had no more voice than a peahen; and what there was of it was not in tune. Then, though elderly and very scraggy, she had dressed herself up to the nines. She sang "Comin' thro' the Rye" with what she meant to be a Scotch accent . . . said jin for gin, boody for buddy . . . and smirked and sidled like a nancified young girl. To the huge delight of the audience, who had her out again and again, shouting "Brave-o!" and "Enkor!"

And the poor silly old thing drank it all in, bowed with her hand on her heart, kissed the tips of her gloves—especially in the direction of the Bishop—then fluttered the pages with her lavender kids and prepared to repeat the song. This was too much for Richard, who was as sensitive to seeing another person made a butt of, as to being himself held up to ridicule. From his seat in the front row he hissed, so loudly that everybody sitting round could hear: "Go back, you fool, go back! Can't you see they're laughing at you?"

It was done out of sheer tenderheartedness; but . . . For one

thing, the Bishop had entered into the fun and applauded with
the rest; so it was a sort of snub for him, too. As for Miss
Mundy, though she shut her music-book and retired into the
wings, she glared at Richard as if she could have eaten him;
while the audience, defrauded of its amusement, turned nasty,
and started to boo and groan. There was an awkward pause
before the next item on the programme could be got going.
And when Richard's own turn came—he was reading selections
from "Out of the Hurly-Burly"—people weren't very well disposed towards him. Which he needed. For he was shockingly
nervous; you could see the book shaking in his hands. Then,
too, the light was poor, and though he rubbed and polished at
his spectacles, and held the pages up this way and that, he
couldn't see properly, and kept reading the wrong words, and
having to correct himself, or go h'm . . . h'm . . . while he tried
to decipher what came next. And through his stumbling so, the
jokes didn't carry. Nobody laughed; even though he had picked
out those excruciatingly funny bits about the patent combination step-ladder and table, that performed high jinks of itself
in the attic at night; and the young man who stuck to the
verandah steps when he went a-courting: things that usually
made people hold their sides.

If only he would just say he couldn't see, and apologise and
leave off . . . or at least cut it short. But he was too proud for
that; besides, he wouldn't think it fair, to fail in his share of
the entertainment. And so he laboured on, stuttering and
stumbling, and succeeding only in making a donkey of himself. Suppressed giggles were audible behind Mary: yes, people were laughing now, but not at the funny stories. Of course,
at the finish, the audience didn't dare not to clap; for the
Bishop led the way; but the next minute everybody broke out
into a hullabaloo of laughing and talking; in face of which the
Bishop's "Most humorous! Quite a treat!" sounded very thin.

The exertion had worn Richard out: you could see the perspiration trickling down his face. The result was, having immediately to get on his feet again, to introduce the Bishop, he
clean forgot what he had been going to say. Nothing came.
There was another most embarrassing pause, in which her own
throat went hot and dry, while he stood clearing his and looking helplessly round. But, once found, his words came with a
rush—too much of a rush: they tumbled over one another and

got all mixed up: he contradicted himself, couldn't find an end to his sentences, said to-morrow when he meant to-day, and *vice versa;* which made sad nonsense. The Bishop sat and picked his nose, or rather pinched the outside edge of one nostril between thumb and middle finger, looking, as far as a man of his nature could, decidedly uncomfortable. Behind her, a rude voice muttered something about somebody having had "one too many."

And things went from bad to worse: for Richard continued to ramble on, long after the Bishop should have been speaking. There was no one at hand to nudge him, or frown a hint. His subject had of course something to do with it. For the Bishop had elected to speak on "Our glorious country: Australia!" and that was too much for Richard. How could he sing a *Te Deum* to a land he so hated? The very effort to be fair made him unnecessarily wordy, for his real feelings kept cropping up and showing through. And then, unluckily, just when one thought he had finished, the words "glorious country" seized on his imagination; and now the fat was in the fire with a vengeance. For he went on to say that any country here, wonderful though it might be, was but the land of our temporary adoption; the true "glorious country" was the one for which we were bound hereafter: "That land, of which our honoured guest is one of the keepers of the keys!" Until recently this Paradise had been regarded as immeasurably distant . . . beyond earthly contact. Now, the barriers were breaking down.— "If you will bear with me a little, friends, I will tell you something of my own experiences, and of the proofs—the irrefragable proofs—which I myself have received, that those dear ones who have passed from mortal sight still live, and love us, and take an interest in our doings!"— And, here, if he didn't give them . . . didn't come out in front of all these scoffing people, with that foolish, ludicrous story of the doll . . . Lallie's doll! Mary wished the floor would open and swallow her up.

The giggling and tittering grew in volume. ("Sit down, Richard, oh, sit down!" she willed him. *"Can't* you see they're laughing at you?") People could really hardly be blamed for thinking he had had a glass too much; he standing there, staring with visionary eyes at the back of the hall. But by now he had worked himself into such a state of exaltation that he saw nothing . . . not even the Bishop's face, which was a study, his Lordship belonging to those who held spiritualism to be of the devil.

"Where's dolly?" "Want me mammy!" "Show us a nose!" began to be heard on all sides. The audience was getting out of hand. The Bishop could bear it no longer: rising from his seat on the platform, he tapped Richard sharply on the arm. Richard gave a kind of gasp, put his hand to his forehead, and breaking off in the middle of a sentence, sat heavily down.

Straightway the Bishop plunged into his prepared discourse; and in less than no time had his audience breathlessly engrossed in the splendid tale of Australia's progress.

[8]

WEPT Mary, his Lordship's visiting having ended in strain and coolness: "How could you! . . . how *could* you? Knowing what he thinks—and him a guest in the house! And then to hold our poor little darling up to derision—for them to laugh and mock at—oh! it was cruel of you . . . cruel. I shall never forget it."

"Pray, would you have me refuse, when the opportunity offers, to bear witness to the faith that is in me? Who am I to shrink from gibes and sneers? Where would Christianity itself be to-day, had its early followers not braved scorn and contumely?"

"But *we're* not early Christians! We're just ordinary people. And I think it's perfectly dreadful to hear you make such comparisons. Talk about blasphemy . . ."

"It's always the same. Try to tell a man that he has a chance of immortality . . . that he is not to be snuffed out, at death, like a candle . . . and all that is brutal and ribald in him comes to the surface."

"Leave it to the churches! . . . it's the churches' business. You only succeed in making an utter fool of yourself."

Immortality . . . and a doll's nose! Oh, to see a man of Richard's intelligence sunk so low! For fear of what she might say next, Mary flung out of the room, leaving him still haranguing, and put the length of the passage between them. At the verandah door she stood staring with smouldering eyes into the garden. Telling herself that, one day, it would not be the room only she quitted, but the house as well. She saw a picture of herself, marching, with defiant head, down the path and out of the gate, a child on either hand. (Yes! the children went, too: she'd take good care of that!) Richard should be left to the tender mercies of Zara: Zara who, at first sound of a raised voice, vanished behind a locked door! That might bring him to his senses. For things could not go on as they were. Never a plan did she lay for his benefit, but he somehow crossed and frustrated it. And as a result of her last effort, they were actually in a worse position than before. Not only was the practice as dead as a doornail again, but a new load of contempt rested on Richard's shoulders.

The first hint that something more than his spiritistic rantings might be at work, in frightening people off again, came from Maria. It was a couple of weeks later. Mary was in the kitchen making pastry, dabbing blobs of lard over a rolled-out sheet of paste, and tossing and twisting with a practised hand, when Maria, who stood slicing apples, having cast more than one furtive glance at her mistress, volunteered the remark: "Mrs. Mahony, you know that feller with the broke leg? Well, they do say his Pa's bin and fetched another doctor, orl the way from Oakworth."

"What boy?— Young Nankivell? Nonsense! He's out of splints by now."

"Mike Murphy told the grocer so."

"Now, Maria, you know I won't listen to gossip. Make haste with the fruit for this pie."

But it was not so easy to get the girl's words out of her head. Could there possibly be any truth in them? And if so, did Richard know? He wouldn't say a word to her, of course, unless his hand was forced.

At dinner, she eyed him closely; but could detect no sign of a fresh discomfiture.

That afternoon, however, as she sat stitching at warm clothing—with the end of March the rains had set in, bringing cooler weather—as she sat, there came a knock at the front door, and Maria admitted what really seemed to be a patient again at last, a man asking imperiously for the doctor. He was shown into the surgery, and, even above the whirring of her sewing-machine, Mary could hear his voice—and Richard's too —raised, as if in dispute, and growing more and more heated. She went into the passage and listened, holding her breath.

Then—oh! what was that? . . . who? . . . *what?* . . . *a horse-whipping?* Without hesitation she turned the knob of the surgery door and walked in.

"What is it? What's the matter?" With fearful eyes she looked from one to the other. In very fact the stranger, a great red-faced, burly fellow, held a riding-whip stretched between his hands.

And Richard was cowering in his chair, his grey head sunk between his shoulders. Richard . . . *cowering?* In an instant she was beside him, her arm about his neck. "Don't mind him! . . . don't take any notice of what he says."

Roughly Mahony shook himself free. "Go away! . . . go out of the room, Mary! This is none of your business."

"And have him speak to you like that? I'll do nothing of the sort! Why don't you turn him out?" And, as Richard did not answer, and her blood was up, she rounded on the man with: "How dare you come here and insult the doctor in his own house? You great bully, you!"

"*Mary!*—for God's sake! . . . don't make more trouble for me than I've got already."

"Now, now, madam, I'll trouble you to have a care what you're saying!"—and the network of veins on the speaker's cheeks ran together in a purplish patch. "None of your lip for me, if you please! As for insults, me good lady, you'll have something more to hear about the rights o' that! You've got a boy of your own, haven't you? What would you say, I'd like to know, if a bloody fraud calling himself a doctor, had been and made a cripple of him for life?"

(*That* hit. Cuffy? . . . a cripple! Oh, Richard, Richard, what *have* you done?)

"As fine a young chap as ever you see, tall and upstanding. And now 'tis said he'll never walk straight again, but 'll have to hobble on crutches, with one leg four inches shorter than the other, for the rest of his days.— But I'll settle you! I'll cork your chances for you! I'll put a stop to your going round maiming other people's children. I'll have the lor on you, that's what I'll do! I'll take it into court, by Jesus I will!"

"You'll ruin me."

"I'll never stop till I have . . . so help me, God! . . . as you've ruined me boy. You won't get the chance to butcher no one else—you damned, drunken old swine, you!"

Richard sat motionless, head in hand, and the two fingers that supported his temple, and the skin on which they lay, looked as though drained of every drop of blood. But he said not a word—let even the last infamous accusation pass unchallenged. Not so Mary. With eyes so fierce that the man involuntarily recoiled before them, she advanced upon him. "How dare you? . . . how *dare* you say a thing like that to my husband? You! . . . with a face which shows everybody what your habits are . . . to slander some one who's never in his life been the worse for drink! Go away! . . . we've had enough of you . . . go away, I say!"—and throwing open the door she drove him before her.— But on the garden path he turned, and shook his fist at the house.

Richard had not stirred; nor did he look up at her entry. And to her flood of passionate and bewildered questions he responded only by a toneless: "It's no use, Mary; what he says may be true. A case of malunion. Such things do happen. And surgery has never been one of my strong points."— Try as she would, there was nothing more to be got out of him.

In despair, she left him, and went to the bedroom. Her brain was spinning like a Catherine wheel. Yet something must be done. They could not—oh, they *could* not!—sit meekly there, waiting for this new and awful blow to fall. She must go out, track the man, follow him up; and snatching her bonnet from the drawer she tied it on—it had a red rose on a stalk, which nodded at her from the mirror. She would go on her knees to him, not to take proceedings. He had a wife. *She* might understand . . . being a woman, be merciful. But . . . Cuffy . . . a cripple . . . would *she* have had mercy? What would *her* feelings have been, had she had to see her own child go halt and lame? No, Richard was right, it was no good; there was nothing to be done. And tearing off her wraps she threw herself face downwards on the bed, and wept bitterly.

She did not hear the door open, or see the small face that peered in. And a single glimpse of the dark mass that was his mother, lying shaking and sobbing, was enough for Cuffy: he turned and fled. Frightened by the angry voices, the children had sought their usual refuge, up by the henhouse. But it got night, and nobody came to call them, or look for them, and nobody lit the lamps; and when they did come home the table wasn't spread for supper. Cuffy set to hunting for Mamma. But after his discovery his one desire was not to see anything else. In the dark drawing-room, he hid behind an armchair. Oh, *what* was the matter now? What *had* they done to her? It could only be Papa that hurt her so. *Why* did he have to do it? Why couldn't he be nice to her? Oh, if only Papa—yes, if . . . if only Papa *would* go away, as he said, and leave them and Mamma together! Oh, pray God, let Papa go away! . . . and never, never come back.—

But that night—after a sheerly destructive evening, in which Mary had never ceased to plead with, to throw herself on the mercy of, an invisible opponent: I give you my word for it, he wasn't himself that day . . . what with the awful heat . . . and the length of the drive . . . and the horse wouldn't go . . . he was so upset over it. And then, the loss of our little girl . . . that was a blow he has never properly got over. For he's not a young man any more. He's not what he was . . . *anyone* will tell you that! But they'll tell you, too, that he has never, never neglected a patient because of it. He's the most conscientious of men . . . has always worked to the last ounce of his strength, put himself and the state of his own health last of all. . . . I have known him tramp off of a morning, when anybody with half an eye could see that he himself ought to be in bed. And so kind-hearted! If a patient is poor, or has fallen on evil days, he will always treat him free of charge.— Oh, surely people would need to have hearts of stone, to stand out against pleas such as these?— Or she lived through, to the last detail, the horrors of a lawsuit: other doctors giving evidence against Richard, hundreds of pounds having to be paid as damages, the final crash to ruin of his career. And when it came to the heritage of shame and disgrace that he would thus hand on to his children, her heart turned cold as ice against him.— But that night, every warring feeling merged and melted in a burning compassion for the old, unhappy man who lay at her side; lay alarmingly still, staring with glassy eyes at the moonlit window. Feeling for his hand, she pressed it to her cheek. "Don't break your heart over it, my darling. Trust me, I'll win him round . . . *somehow!* And then we'll go away—far away from here—and start all over again. No one need ever know."

But she could not get at him, could not rouse him from the

torpor in which this last, unmerited misfortune had sunk him. And there they lay, side by side, hand in hand, but far as the poles apart.

The court, airless and fetid, was crowded to the last place. With difficulty he squeezed into a seat on a hard, backless bench . . . though he was too old and stiff, nowadays, to sit for long without a support. The judge—why, what was this? He knew that face . . . had surely met him somewhere? . . . had dined with him, perhaps, or tilted a table in his company—the judge held a large gold toothpick in his hand, and, in the course of the proceedings, must have picked in turn every tooth he had in his head. Foul teeth . . . a foul breath . . . out of such a mouth should judgment come? He felt in his pocket to see if, in a species of prevision, he had brought his forceps with him; and sharply withdrew his hand from a mess of melting jujubes. (The children, of course . . . oh, devil take the children! They were always in his way.) Believing himself unseen, he stealthily deposited the sticky conglomerate on the floor. But his neighbour, a brawny digger, with sleeves rolled high above the elbow, and arms behaired like an ape's, espied him, and made as if to call the attention of the usher to his misdeed. To escape detection, he rose and moved hurriedly to the other side of the court; where, oddly enough, there seemed after all to be plenty of room.

Here, he was seated to much better advantage; and pulling himself together, he prepared to follow the case. But . . . again he was baffled. Plaintiff's counsel was on his feet; and, once more, the striking likeness of the fellow to somebody he had known distracted him. Hang it all! It began to look as if every one present was more or less familiar to him. Secretly he ran his eye over the assembly, and found that it was so . . . though he could not have put a name to a single man-jack of them. However, since nobody seemed to recognise him, he cowered down and trusted to pass unobserved. But, from now on, he was aware of a sense of mystery and foreboding; the court and its occupants took on a sinister aspect. And, even as he felt this, he heard two rascally-looking men behind him muttering together. "Are you all right?" said one. To which the other made half-audible reply: "We are, if that bloody fool, our client——" Ha! there was shady work in hand; trouble brewing for somebody. But what was *he* doing there? What brought him to such a place?

Wild to solve the riddle, he made another desperate attempt to fix his thoughts. But these haunting resemblances had unnerved him; he could do nothing but worry the question where he had met plaintiff's counsel. The name hung on the very tip of his tongue; yet would not come out. A common, shoddy little man, prematurely bald, with a protruding paunch and a specious eye—he wouldn't have trusted a fellow with an eye like that farther than he could see him! Most improperly dressed, too; wearing neither wig nor gown, but a suit of a loud, horsey check, the squares of which could have been counted from across a road.

This get-up it was, which first made it plain to him that the case under trial had some secret connexion with himself. Somehow or other he was involved. But, each time, just as he thought he was nearing a clue, down would come a kind of fog and blot everything out.

Through it, he heard what sounded like a scuffle going on. It seemed that the plaintiff was drunk, not in a fit state to give evidence . . . though surely that was his voice protesting vehemently that he had never been the worse for drink in his life? The two cut-throats in the back seat muttered anew; others joined in; and soon the noise from these innumerable throats had risen to an ominous roar. He found himself shouting with the rest; though only later did he grasp what it was all about: they were calling for the defendant to enter the witness-box. Well, so much the better! Now, at last, he would discover the hidden meaning.

The defendant proved to be an oldish man, with straggly grey hair and whiskers, and a round back: he clambered up the steps to the witness-box, which stood high, like a pulpit, with a palpable effort. This bent back was all that could be seen of him at first, and a very humble back it looked, threadbare and shiny, though brushed meticulously free of dust and dandruff. Surely to goodness, though, he needn't have worn his oldest suit, the one with frayed cuffs? . . . his second-best would have been more the thing . . . even though the coat did sag at the shoulders. Edging forward in his seat, he craned his neck; then half rose, in his determination to see the fellow's face— and, having caught a single glimpse of it, all but lost his balance and fell, with difficulty restraining a shriek that would have pealed like the whistle of a railway-engine through the court, and have given him away . . . beyond repair. For it was himself he saw, himself who stood there, perched aloft before every eye, holding fast, with veined and wrinkled hands, to the ledge of the dock: himself who now suddenly turned and looked full at him, singling him out from all the rest. His flesh crawled, his hairs separated, while something cold and rapid as a ball of quicksilver ran from top to bottom of his spine.— Two of him? God in heaven! But this was madness. *Two* of him? The thing was an infamy . . . devilish . . . not to be borne. *Which was he?*

And yet, coeval with the horror of it, ran an obscene curiosity. So *this* was what he looked like! *This* was how he presented himself to his fellow-men. Smothering his first wild fear, he took in, coldly and cruelly, every detail of the perched-up figure, whose poverty-stricken, yet sorrily dandified appearance had been the signal of a burst of ribald mirth. He could hear himself laughing at the top of his lungs; especially when, after a painful effort to read a written slip that had been handed to him, his double produced a pair of horn-rimmed spectacles, and shakily balanced them on the top of his long thin nose. Ha, ha! This was good . . . was very good. Ha, ha! A regular owl! . . . exactly like an old owl. A zany. A figure of fun.

Then, abruptly, his laughter died in his throat. For, hark! . . . what was this? . . . what the . . . ! God above! he was pleading now—*pleading?* nay, grovelling!—begging abjectly for mercy. He whined: "Me Lud, if the case goes against me I'm a ruined man. And he has got his knife in me, me Lud! . . . he's made up his mind to ruin me. A hard man . . . a cruel man! . . . if ever there was one. Oh, spare me, me Lud! . . . take pity on my poor wife and my two little children!"— The blood surged to his head, and roared in neck and temples till he thought they would burst. *Never!* . . . no, never in all his days, had he sought either pity or mercy. And never, no matter what his plight, would he sink so low. The despicable sniveller! The unmanly craven! . . . he disowned him—loathed him —spat at him in spirit: his whole being swam in hatred. But even as, pale with fury, he joined in the hyæna-like howl against clemency that was being raised, a small voice whispered in his ear that his time was running short. He must get out of this place . . . must escape . . . save himself . . . from the wrath to come. Be up and away, head high, leaving his ghost to wring its hands . . . and wail . . . and implore. Long since he had lifted his hat to his face, where he held it as if murmuring a prayer. But it was no longer the broad-brimmed wideawake he had brought with him into court; it had turned into a tall beaver belltopper, of a mode at least twenty years old, and too narrow to conceal his face. He tossed it from him, as, frantic with the one desire, he pushed and struggled to get out, treading on people's feet, crushing past their knees—oh! was there no end to their number, or to the rows of seats through which he had to fight his way? . . . his legs growing heavier and heavier, more incapable of motion. And then . . . just when he thought he was safe . . . he heard his own name spoken: heard it said aloud, not once but many times, and, damnation take it! by none other than old Muir the laryngologist, that pitiful old fossil, that infernal old busybody, dead long since, who, it seemed, had been in court throughout the proceedings, and now recognised him, and stood pointing at him. Again a shout rose in unison, but this time it was his name they called, and therewith they were up and on his heels, and the hue and cry had begun in earnest. He fled down Little Bourke Street, and round and up Little Collins Street, running like a hare, but with steadily failing strength, drawing sobbing breaths that hurt like blows; but holding his left hand fast to his breastpocket, where he had the knife concealed. His ears rang with that most terrifying of mortal sounds: the wolf-like howl of a mob that chases human game and sees its prey escaping it. For he *was* escaping; he would have got clean away if, of a sudden, Mary and the children had not stood before him. In a row . . . a third child, too. He out with his knife . . . *now* he knew what it was for! But a shrill scream stayed his hand . . . who screamed? who screamed? . . . and with such stridency. Mary! . . . it could *only* be Mary, who would so deliberately foul his chances. For this one second's delay was his undoing. Some one dashed up behind and got him by the shoulder, and was bearing him down, and shaking, shaking, shaking . . . while a fierce voice shrieked in his ear: "Richard! . . . oh, *Richard,* do wake up. You'll terrify the children. Oh, what dreadful dream have you been having?"

And it was broad daylight, the mill-whistle in full blast, and he sitting up in bed, shouting, and drenched in sweat. The night was over, a new day begun, in which had to be faced, not the lurid phantasmagoria of a dream-world that faded at a touch, but the stern, bare horrors of reality, from which there was no awakening.

[9]

THE facts of the case, brought to light by vigorous action on Mary's part, were these. The boy had been removed to the Oakworth hospital, where he was to be examined. Only when this was done could the surgeon in charge say whether there was any possibility of correcting the malunion, by re-breaking and re-setting the limb; or whether the patient would have to remain in his present degree of shortness. He hoped to let them know in about three days' time.— It might, of course, be less.

"There's nothing for it; we must just have patience," said Mary grimly and with determination, as she re-folded the telegram and laid it back on the table.

Patience? Yes, yes; that went without saying; and Mahony continued to feign busyness with pencil and paper, till the door had shut behind her.

Alone, he fell limply back in his chair. So this was it . . . this was what it had come to! His fate had passed out of his own keeping. Another—a man his junior by several years—would sit in judgment on him, decide whether or no he was competent to continue practising the profession to which he had given up the best years of his life. In the course of the next three days.— Three days. What *were* three days? . . . in a lifetime of fifty years. A flea-bite; a single tick of time's clock. An infinitesimal fragment chipped off time's plenty, and for the most part squandered unthinkingly. In the ecstasy of happiness—cr to the prisoner condemned to mount the scaffold—a breath, a flash of light, gone even as it came.— *Three days!* To one on the rack to learn whether or no he was to be found guilty of professional negligence, with its concomitants of a court of law, publicity, disgrace; to such a one, three days were as unthinkable as infinity: a chain of hours of torture, each a lifetime in itself.

For long he sat motionless, wooden as the furniture around

him; sat and stared at the whitewashed walls, till he felt that, if he did not get out from between them, they might end by closing in on him and crushing him. Pushing back his chair, he rose and left the house, heading in the direction of the railway station: never again would he cross the Lagoon path to show his face in the township! From the station he struck off on a bush track. This was heavy with mud; for it had rained in torrents towards morning: the hammering of the downpour on the iron roof no doubt accounted for some of the sinister noises of which his dream had been full. Now, the day was fine: a cool breeze swung the drooping leaves; the cloudless sky had deepened to its rich winter blue. But to him the very freshness and beauty of the morning seemed a mockery, the blue sky cruel as a pall. For there was a blackness under his lids, which gave the lie to all he saw.

He trudged on, with the sole idea of somehow getting through the day . . . of killing time. And, as he went, he mused, ironically, on the shifts mortals were put to, the ruses they employed, to rid themselves of this precious commodity, which alone stood between them and an open grave.

Then, abruptly, he stopped, and uttering an exclamation, swung round and made for home. *It might, of course, be less.* Who knew, who knew? By this time it was just possible that another telegram had arrived, and he was tormenting himself needlessly. Was he not omitting to allow for the fellow-feeling of a brother medico, who, suspecting something of what he was enduring, might hasten to put him out of suspense? (How his own heart would have bled for such a one!) And so he pushed forward, covering the way back in half the time, and only dropping his speed as he neared the gate. For the children sat at lessons in the dining-room, and three pairs of eyes looked up on his approach. At the front door he paused to dry his forehead, before stepping into the passage, where the life-giving message might await him. But the tray on the hall-table was empty; empty, too, the table in the surgery. His heart, which had been palpitating wildly, sank to normal; and simultaneously an immense lassitude overcame him. But without a moment's hesitation he turned on his heel and went out again . . . with stealthy, cat-like tread. The last thing he wanted to do was to attract Mary's attention.

He retraced his steps. But now so tired was he that, every

hundred yards or so, he found himself obliged to sit down, in order to get strength to proceed. But not for long: there was a demon in him that would not let him rest; which drove him up and on till, in the end, he was seized and spun by a fit of the old vertigo, and had to throw his arms round a tree-trunk, to keep from falling. "Drunk again! . . . drunk again."

He was done for . . . played out. Home he dragged once more, sitting by the wayside when the giddy fits took him, or holding fast to the palings of a fence. It was one o'clock and dinner-time when he reached the house. Well! in any case, he would not have dared to absent himself from the table. (Oh, God, on such a day, to have been free and unobserved!)

But he had over-rated his powers of endurance. The children's prating, Mary's worried glances in his direction, the clatter of the dishes, Zara's megrims: all this, the ordinary humdrum of a meal, proved more than his sick nerves could bear. His usual weary boredom with the ritual of eating turned to loathing: of every word that was said, every movement of fork to mouth, of the very crockery on the table. Half-way through, he tossed his napkin from him, pushed his chair back, and broke from the room.

To go out again was beyond him. Entering the surgery, he took his courage in both hands; and, not with his nerves alone, but with every muscle at a strain, braced himself to meet the slow torture that awaited him, the refined torture of physical inaction; the trail of which may be as surely blood-streaked as that from an open wound. With his brain on fire, his body bound to the rack, he sat and watched the hands of the clock crawl from one to two, from two to three, and three to four; and the ticking of the pendulum, and the beat of his own pulses, combined to form a rhythm—a conflicting rhythm—which well-nigh drove him crazy. As the afternoon advanced, however, there came moments when, with his head bedded on his arms, he lapsed into a kind of coma; never so deeply, though, but that his mind leapt into awareness at the smallest sound without. And all through, whether he waked or slept, something in him, inarticulate as a banshee, never ceased to weep and lament . . . to wail without words, weep without tears.

Later on, a new torture threatened; and this was the coming blast of the mill-whistle. For a full hour beforehand he

sat anticipating it: sat with fingers stiffly interlocked, temples
a-hammer, waiting for the moment when it should set in. Nor
was this all. As the minute-hand ticked the last hour away,
stark terror seized him lest, when the screech began, he, too,
should not be able to help shrieking; but should be forced to
let out, along with it, in one harsh and piercing cry, the repressed, abominable agony of the afternoon. At two minutes
to the hour he was on his feet, going round the table like a
maddened animal, wringing his hands and moaning, under his
breath: it is too much . . . I am not strong enough . . . my God,
I implore thee, let this cup pass! And now, so sick and dazed
with fear was he that he could no longer distinguish between the murderous din that was about to break loose, and
the catastrophe that had befallen his life. When, finally, the
hour struck, the whistle discharged, and the air was all one
brazen clamour, he broke down and wept, the tears dripping
off his face. But no sound escaped him.

Supper time.— He wanted none; was not hungry; asked only
to be left in peace. And since Mary, desperate, too, after her
own fashion, could not make up her mind to this, but came
again and yet again, bringing the lamp, bringing food to tempt
him, he savagely turned the key in the lock.

Thereafter, all was still: the quiet of night descended on
the house. Here, in this blissful silence, he took his decision.
Numbed to the heart though he was—over the shrilling of the
siren something in him had cracked, had broken—he knew
what he had to do. Another day like this, and he would not be
answerable for himself. There was an end to everything . . .
and his end had come.

Mary, stealing back to remind him that it was close on midnight, found him stooped over a tableful of books and papers.
"Don't wait for me. I'm busy . . . shall be some time yet."

Relieved beyond the telling to find his door no longer shut
against her, and him thus normally employed, she put her arm
round his shoulders, and laid her head against his. "But not
too late, Richard. You must be so tired." Herself she felt sick
and dizzy with anxiety, with fatigue. It was not only what had
happened, but the way Richard was taking it . . . his secrecy . . . his morbid self-communing. God help him! . . . help
them all!

Desperately Mahony fought down the impulse to throw off

her hampering arm, to cry out, to her face, the truth: go away
. . . go away! I have done with you! And no sooner had the
bedroom door shut behind her than he brushed aside his
brazen pretence at work—it would have deceived no one but
Mary—and fell to making the few necessary preparations.
Chief of these was the detaching of a couple of keys from
his bunch of keys, and laying them in a conspicuous place.
After which he sat and waited, for what he thought a reasonable time, cold as a stone with fear lest she, somehow sensing
his intention, should come back to hinder him. But nothing
happened; and cautiously unlatching the door, he listened out
into the passage. Not a mouse stirred. Now was the time!
Opening the French window he stepped on to the verandah.
But it had begun to rain again; a soft, steady rain; and some
obscure instinct drove him back to get his greatcoat. This hung
in the passage; and had to be fetched in jerks—a series of jerks
and pauses. But at last he had it, and could creep up the yard,
and out of the back gate.

His idea was, to get as far from the house as possible . . .
perhaps even to follow the bush track he had been on that
morning. (That morning only? It seemed more like a century
ago.) But the night was pitch dark: more than once he caught
his foot, tripped and stumbled. So, groping his way along outside the palings of the fence, and the fence of the mill yard,
he skirted these, and doubled back on the Lagoon. To the right
of the pond stood a clump of fir-trees, shading the ruins of
what had once been an arbour. It was for these trees he made:
an instinctive urge for shelter again carrying the day.

Arrived there, he flung himself at full length on the wet and
slimy ground. (No need now, to take thought for tic or rheumatism, and the other bodily ills that had plagued him.) And
for a time he did no more than lie and exult in the relief this
knowledge brought him—this sense of freedom from all things
human. "Fear no more the heat of the sun," nor the strangle-
coils in which money and money-making had wound him, nor
Mary's inroads on his life, nor the deadening responsibilities
of fatherhood. Now, at long last, he was answerable to himself
alone.

Gradually, however, this feeling died away, and an extraordinary lucidity took its place. And in his new clearness of vision
he saw that his bloodiest struggle that day had been, not with

the thing itself, but with what hid it from him. Which was
Time. He had set up Time as his bugbear, made of it an implacable foe, solely to hinder his mind from reaching out to
what lay beyond. That, he could not face and live. He saw it
now, and was dying of it: dying of a mortal wound to the
most vital part of him—his pride . . . his black Irish pride.
That he, who had held himself so fastidiously aloof from men,
should be forced down into the market-place, there to suffer
an intolerable notoriety; to know his name on people's lips . . .
see it dragged through the mud of the daily press . . . himself
branded as a bungler, a botcher! God, no; the mere imagining
of it nauseated him. Dead, infinitely better dead, and out of
it all! Life and its savagery put off, like a garment that had
served its turn. Then, let tongues wag as they might, he would
not be there to hear. In comparison, his death by his own hand
would make small stir. A day's excitement, and he would pass
for ever into limbo; take his place among those pale ghosts of
whose earth-life every trace is lost. None would miss him, or
mourn his passing—thanks to his own *noli me tangere* attitude
towards the rest of mankind. For there had been no real love
in him: never a feeler thrown out to his fellow-men. Such sympathy as he felt, he had been too backward to show: had given
it only in thought, and from afar. Pride, again!—oh! rightly was
a pride like his reckoned among the seven capital sins. For
what *was* it, but an iron determination to live untouched and
untrammelled . . . to preserve one's liberty, of body and of
mind, at the expense of all human sentiment. To be sufficient
unto oneself, asking neither help nor regard, and spending
none. A fierce, Lucifer-like inhibition. Yes, this . . . but more
besides; Pride also meant the shuddering withdrawal of oneself, because of a rawness . . . a skinlessness . . . on which the
touch of any rough hand could cause agony; even the chance
contacts of every day prove a source of exquisite discomfort.

Thus he dug into himself. To those, on the contrary, whose
welfare had till now been his main solicitude, he gave not a
thought. For this was *his* hour; the hour between himself and
his God: the end of the old life, the dawn, so he surely believed, of the new. And now that release was in sight—port
and haven made, after the desolate, wind-swept seas—he marvelled at himself for having held out so long. At the best of
times small joy had been his: while, for many a year, never a

blink of hope or gladness had come his way. Weary and unslept, he had risen, day after day, to take up the struggle; the sole object of which was the grinding for bread. The goal of a savage: to one of his turn of mind, degradation unspeakable. A battle, too, with never a respite—interminable as time itself. (Why, the most famous Agony known to history had lasted but for three hours, and a sure Paradise awaited the great Martyr.) Even the common soldier knew that the hotter the skirmish, the sooner it would be over, with, did he escape with his life, stripes and glory for a finish. Ah! but with this difference, that the soldier was under duress to fight to the end: for those who flung down their muskets and ran, crying, hold! enough! the world had coined an evil name. And at this thought, and without warning, such a red-hot doubt ran through him, such a blazing host of doubts, that he fell to writhing, like one in the grip of insufferable physical anguish. These doubts brought confusion on every argument that he had used to bolster up his deed. What was he doing? . . . what was he about to do? He, a coward? . . . a deserter? . . . abandoning his post when the fire was hottest?—leaving others to bear the onus of his flight, his disgrace? . . . and those others the creatures he had loved best? Oh, where was here his pride!

Besides: no Lethe awaits me, but the judgment seat. How shall I face my Maker?— The phrasing was that of his day; the question at issue one with which men have tortured themselves since the world began. Have I the right to do this thing? Is my life my own to take?— And in the fierce conflict of which he now tossed the helpless prey, he dug his left hand into the earth until what it grasped was a compact mass of mud and gravel. (His right, containing the precious phial, was under him, held to his breast.) Only little by little, with pangs unspeakable, did the death-throes of his crucified pride cease, and he emerge from the struggle, spent and beaten, but seeing himself at last in his true colours. Too good . . . too proud to live? Then, let him also be too proud to die: in this ignominious fashion . . . this poltroon attempt to sneak out of life by a back door. Should it be said of him, who had watched by so many a deathbed, seen the humblest mortals rise superior to physical suffering, that, when his own turn came, he was too weak to endure?—solely because the torments he was called on to face were not of the body, but the mind? Pain . . . anguish ... of body or of mind ... individual pain ... the pangs of all humanity. Pain, a state of being so interwoven with existence that, without it, life was unthinkable. For, take suffering from life, and what remained? Surely, surely, what was so integral a part of creation could not spring from blind chance? ... be wholly evil? ... without value in the scheme of things? A test!—God's acid test ... failing to pass which, a man might not attain to full stature. And if this were so, what was *he* doing, to brush the cup from his lips, to turn his back on the chance here offered him? But oh! abhorrent to him was the pious Christian's self-abasement: the folded hands, the downcast eyes, the meek "God wills it!" that all too often cloaked a bitter and resentful spirit. Not thus, not thus! God would not be God, did He demand of men grovelling and humiliation. Not the denial of self was called for, but the affirmation: a proud joy (here, surely, was the bone for his own pride to gnaw at?) at being permitted to aid and abet in the great Work, at coupling, in full awareness, our will with His. So, then, let it be! And with a movement so precipitate that it seemed after all more than half involuntary, he lifted his hand and threw far from him the little bottle of chloroform, which he had clutched till his palm was cut and sore. It was gone: was lost, hopelessly lost, in rain and darkness. He might have groped till morning without finding it.

But such a thought did not cross his mind. For now a strange thing happened. In the moment of casting the poison from him, he became aware—but with a sense other than that of sight, for he was lying face downwards, with fast closed eyes, his forehead bedded on the sleeve of his greatcoat—became suddenly aware of the breaking over him of a great light: he was lying, he found, in a pool of light; a radiance thick as milk, unearthly as moonlight. And this suffused him, penetrated him, lapped him round. He breathed it in, drew deep breaths of it; and, as he did so, the last vestiges of his old self seemed to fall away. All sense of injury, of mortification, of futile sacrifice was wiped out. In its place there ran through him the beatific certainty that his pain, his sufferings—and how infinitesimal these were, he now saw for the first time—had their niche in God's Scheme (pain the bond that linked humanity: not in joy, in sorrow alone were we yoke-fellows) that all creation, down to the frailest protoplasmic thread, was one with God;

and he himself, and everything he had been and would ever
be, as surely contained in God, as a drop of water in a wave,
a note of music in a mighty cadence. More: he now yearned
as avidly for this submergedness, this unison of all things living, as he had hitherto shrunk from it. The mere thought of
separation became intolerable to him: his soul, ascending, sang
towards oneness as a lark sings its way upwards to the outer
air. For, while the light lasted, he *understood:* not through any
feat of conscious perception, but as a state—a state of being—
a white ecstasy, that left mere knowledge far behind. The import of existence, the mysteries hid from mortal eyes, the key
to the Ultimate Plan: all now were his. And, rapt out of himself, serene beyond imagining, he touched the hem of peace at
last . . . eternal peace . . . which passeth understanding.

Then, as suddenly as the light had broken over him, it was
gone, and again night wrapped him heavily round; him, by
reason of the miracle he had experienced, doubly dark, doubly
destitute. (But I have *known* . . . *nothing* can take it from
me!) And he had need of this solace to cling to, for his awakening found his brain of an icy clearness, in which no jot or
tittle of what awaited him was veiled from him. As if to test
him to the utmost, even the hideous spectre of his blackest
nights took visible form, and persisted, till, for the first time,
he dared to look it in the face.— And death seemed a trifle in
comparison.

But he struggled no more. Caked in mud, soaked to the skin,
he climbed to his feet and staggered home.

❖ ❖ ❖ ❖ ❖ ❖

What a funny noise! . . . lots of noises . . . people all talking
at once; and ever so loud. Cuffy sat up, rubbing his eyes, for
there were lights in them. Stars . . . no, *lanterns!* Huh! *Chinese*
lanterns? But it wasn't Christmas! He jumped out of bed and
ran to the door, opened it and looked out; and it was two
strange men with lanterns walking up and down the passage
and round the verandah. And Mamma was there as well, in
her red dressing-gown with the black spots on it, and her hair
done for going to bed, and she was crying, and Aunt Zara (oh!
she *did* look funny when she went to bed) was blowing her
nose and talking to the man. And when she saw him, she was
most awfully angry and said: "Go back to bed at once, you

naughty boy!" And Mamma said: "Be good, Cuffy . . . for I can bear no more." And so he only just peeped out, to see what it was. And it was Papa that was lost. *Papa . . . lost?* (How *could* grown-up people be lost?) in the middle of the night . . . it was dark as dark . . . and he might never come back. Oh no! it couldn't be true. Only to think of it made him make such a funny noise in his throat that Lucie woke up, and wanted to know, and cried, and said: "Oh dear Papa, come back!" and was ever so frightened. And they both stepped out of bed and sat on the floor and listened. And the men with the lanterns— it was the sergeant and the constable—went away with them, and you could only hear Mamma and Aunt Zara talking and crying. And he waited till it seemed nearly all night, and his toes were so cold he didn't feel them. Lucie went to sleep again, but he couldn't. And all the time his heart thumped like a drum.

Then he thought he saw a monkey in a wood, and was trying to catch it, when somebody shouted like anything; and first it was Maria on the verandah, and then Aunt Zara in the passage, and she called out: "It's all right, Mary! They've got him . . . he's coming!" And then Mamma came running out, and cried again, and kept on saying: "I must be brave . . . I must be brave." And then one's heart almost jumped itself dead, for there was Papa, and he couldn't walk, and the police were holding him up, and he had no hat on, and was wet, the water all running out of him, and so muddy, the mud sticking all over his greatcoat and in his face and hair—just like the picture of Tomfool in the "King of Lear." And Mamma began to say dreadfully: "Oh, *Richard!* How *could*—" and then she stopped. For as soon as Papa saw her he pulled himself away and ran to her, and put his arms round her neck and said: "Oh, Mary, my Mary! . . . I couldn't do it! . . . I couldn't do it." And then he nearly fell down, and they all ran to hold him up, and put him in the bedroom and shut the door. And he didn't see him again, but he saw Maria and Aunt Zara carrying in the bath, and hot water and flannels. And Papa was found. He tried to tell Lucie, but she was too sleepy, and just said: "I fought he would." But he was so cold he couldn't go to sleep again. And then something in him got too big and he had to cry, because Papa was found. But— What did it mean he said he *couldn't* be lost? Why not?

[10]

ON ONE of the numerous packing-cases that strewed the rooms —now just so much soiled whitewash and bare boards—Mary sat and waited for the dray that was to transport boxes and baggage to the railway station. Her heart was heavy: no matter how unhappy you had been in it, the dismantling of a home was a sorry business, and one to which she never grew accustomed. Besides, this time, when they left, one of them had to stay behind. As long as they lived here, her child had not seemed wholly gone; so full was the house of memories of her. To the next, to any other house they occupied, little Lallie would be a stranger.

Except for this, she was as thankful as Richard to turn her back on Barambogie—and he had fled like a hunted man, before he was fit to travel. For the first time in their lives, the decision to leave a place had come from her; she had made up her mind to it while he was still too ill to care what happened. By the next morning the tale of his doings was all over the town: he would never have been able to hold up his head there again. For it wasn't as if he had made a *genuine* attempt . . . at . . . well, yes, at suicide. To the people here, his going out to take his life and coming back without even having *tried* to, would have something comic about it . . . something contemptible. They would laugh in their sleeves; put it down to want of pluck. When what it really proved—fiercely she reassured herself—was his fondness for her, for his children. When the moment came, he couldn't find it in his heart to deal them such a blow.

For several days, however, she did no more than vehemently assert to herself: we go! . . . and if I have to beg the money to make it possible. Richard paid dearly for those hours of exposure: he lay in a high fever, moaning with pain, and muttering light-headedly. As soon, however, as his temperature fell and his cough grew easier, she made arrangements for a sale by auction, and had a board with "To let!" on it erected in the front garden.

Then, his keys lying temptingly at her disposal, she seized this unique opportunity, and, shutting herself up in the surgery, went for and by herself into his money-affairs; about which it was becoming more and more a point of honour with him, to keep her in the dark. There, toilfully, she grappled with the jargon of the law: premiums, transfers, conveyances, mortgager and mortgagee (oh, *which* was which?) the foreclosing of a mortgage, rights of redemption. Grappled, too, with the secrets of his pass-book. And it was these twin columns which gave her the knock-out blow. As far as ready money went, they were living quite literally from hand to mouth—from the receipt of one pound to the next. In comparison, the deciphering of his case and visiting-books was child's play. And, here, taking the bull by the horns, she again acted on her own initiative. Risking his anger, she sent out yet once more the several unpaid bills she came across, accompanying them by a more drastic demand for settlement than he would ever have stooped to.

For the first time, she faced the possibility that they might have to let the mortgage lapse. Already she had suspected Richard of leaning towards this, the easier solution. But so far she had pitted her will against his. And, even yet, something stubborn rose in her and rebelled at the idea. As long as the few shares he held continued to throw off dividends, at least the interest on the loan could be met. While the rent coming in from the house at Hawthorn (instead of being a source of income!) would have to cover the rent of the house they could no longer live in, but had still to pay for. Oh, it sounded like a bad dream!—or a jingle of the House-that-Jack-built order.

None the less, she did not waver in her resolution: somehow to cut Richard free from a place that had so nearly been his undoing. And, hedge and shrink as she might, fiercely as her native independence, her womanish principles—simple, but still the principles of a lifetime—kicked against it, she had gradually to become reconciled to the prospect of loading them up with a fresh burden of debt. The matter boiled down to this: was any sacrifice too great to make for Richard? Wasn't she really, at heart, one of those women she sometimes read of in the newspapers, who, rather than see their children starve, *stole* the bread with which to feed them?

Yet still she hesitated. Until one night, turning his poor old face to her, Richard said: "It's the sea I need, Mary. If I could just get to the sea, I should grow strong and well again, I know I should.— But there! ... what's the use of talking? As the tree falls, so it must lie!" On this night, casting her scruples to the winds, Mary sat down to pen the hated appeal.

"For Richard's sake, Tilly, and only because I'm desperate about him, I'm reduced to asking you if you could possibly see your way to lend me a hundred and fifty pounds. I say 'lend' and I mean it, though goodness knows when I shall be able to repay you. But Richard has been so ill, the practice has entirely failed, and if I can't get him away from here I don't know what will happen."

Tilly's answer, received by return, ran: "Oh Mary love, I feel that sorry for you, I can't say. But thanks be, I can 'do' my dear, and I needn't tell you the money is yours for the asking. As for 'lending'—why, if it makes your poor mind easier put it that way: but it won't worry me if I never see the colour of the oof again, remember that. All I hope is, you'll make tracks like one o'clock from that awful place, and that the doctor'll soon be on his legs again.— But Mary! aren't I glad I kept that nest-egg as you know of! You were a bit doubtful at the time, love, if you remember. But if I hadn't where should I be to-day? Something must have warned me, I think: sit up, you lovesick old fool, you, and take thought for the time when it'll be all calls and no dividends. Which, Mary, is now. The plain truth being, his lordship keeps me that tight, that if I didn't have what I do, I might be sitting in Pentridge. And, he, the great loon, imagines I come out on what he gives me!— Oh, men are fools, my dear, I'll say it and sing it to my dying day—and if it's not a fool, then you can take it from me it's a knave. There ought to be a board up warning us silly women off.— Except that I've got my blessed Babe. Which makes up for a lot. But oh! if one could just get children for the wishing, or pick 'em like fruit from the trees, without a third person having to be mixed up in it. (I do think the Lord might have managed things better.) And I won't deny, Mary, the thought has come to me now and then, just to take Baby and my bit of splosh, and vamoose to somewhere where a pair of trousers'll never darken my sight again."

Whereupon, for several mornings, the postman handed in a couple of newspapers, the inner sheets of which contained the separate halves of a twenty-pound note: this being Tilly's idea of the safest and quickest means of forwarding money.

"Just something I'd managed to lay past for a rainy day,"

Mary lied boldly, on handing Richard his fare to town and ten pounds over for expenses. And pride, scruples, humiliation, all faded into thin air before the relief, the burning gratitude, her gift let loose in him. "Wife! you don't . . . you *can't* know what this means to me!" And then he broke down and cried, clinging like a child to her hand.

Restored to composure, he burst into a diatribe against the place, the people. What it had done to him, what they had made of him . . . him, whose only crime was that of being a gentleman! "Because I wouldn't drink with them, descend to their level. Oh, these wretched publicans! . . . these mill-hands, and Chinese half-castes . . . these filthy Irish labourers! Mary, I would have done better to go to my grave, than ever to have come among them. And then the climate! . . . and the water-hole they call a Lagoon! . . . and the mill-whistle—that accursed whistle! It alone would have ended by driving me mad. But let me once shake the dust of the place off my feet, and Richard will be himself again! A kingdom for a horse? Mine— no kingdom, but a cesspool—for the sea! The sea! . . . elixir of life . . . to me and my kind. Positively, I begin to believe I'm one of those who should never live out of earshot of its waves."

This new elation held, up to the very end (when the thought of being recognised or addressed, on the station, by any of those he was fleeing from, threw him into a veritable fever). In such a mood he was unassailable: insensitive alike to pain or pleasure. Hence, the report that finally reached them from the Oakworth hospital didn't touch him as it ought to have done . . . considering the affair had all but killed him. He really took it very queerly. The surgeon wrote that the operation had been successful; there was now every hope that, the over-lapping corrected, perfect union would be obtained; which, as the lad's father also professed himself satisfied, would no doubt lift a weight from Dr. Mahony's mind. But Richard only waxed bitterly sarcastic. "Coming to their senses at last, are they? . . . now it's too late. Beginning to see how a gentleman ought to be treated!" Which somehow wasn't like him . . . to harp on the "gentleman."

He even came back on it, in a letter describing an acquaintance he had made (Richard and chance acquaintances!) in sailing down the Bay to Shortlands Bluff. This was a fellow medico: "Like myself, a gentleman who has had misfortunes, and is now obliged to resume practice." Still more disconcerting was it to read: "I told him about Barambogie, and mentioned the house being to let and the sale of the furniture, and said there was a practice ready to hand. Rather quiet just now, but certain to improve. If he took it, all I should ask would be a cheque for fifty pounds at the end of the year. I put our leaving down entirely to the climate. Should he write to you, be sure and do not put him off." At which Mary winced.—And yet . . . Another man might get on quite well here; some one who understood better how to deal with the people. So she answered guardedly: being loath to annoy him and spoil his holiday, which really seemed to be doing him good. He boasted of sound nights and improved appetite: *As usual the sea makes me ravenous.* And so it went on, until the time came when it was no longer possible to shirk the question: what next? Then, at once, they were at loggerheads again.

In passing through Melbourne, Mahony had seen an advertisement calling for tenders for a practice at a place named Narrong; and with her approval had written for particulars. To Mary this opening seemed just the thing. More than three times the size of Barambogie, Narrong stood in a rich, squatting district, not very far north of Ballarat. The practice included several clubs; the climate was temperate: if Richard could but get a footing there—the clubs alone represented a tidy income—the future might really begin to look more hopeful.

And at first he was all in favour of it. Then, overnight as it were, he changed his mind, and, without deigning to give her a single reason, wrote that he had abandoned the idea of applying. It was the sea that had done it; she could have sworn it was: this sea she so feared and hated! Besides, the usual thing was happening: no sooner did Richard get away from her than he allowed himself to be influenced by every fresh person he met. And taking advantage of his credulity, people were now, for some obscure purpose of their own, making him believe he could earn three or four hundred a year at Shortlands Bluff . . . though it was common knowledge that such seaside places lay dead and deserted for nine months out of the twelve. Besides, there was a doctor at Shortlands already; though now close on seventy, and unwilling to turn out at night.

The one valuable piece of information he gave her was that

the billet of Acting Health Officer, with a yearly retaining-fee and an additional couple of guineas for each boarding, was vacant. All else, she felt sure, was mere windy talk. Thus, people were advising him, if he settled there, not only to keep a horse and ride round the outlying districts, but also to cross twice or thrice weekly to the opposite side of the bay, and open consulting-rooms at some of the smaller places. "With my love of sailing this would be no toil to me . . . sheerly a pleasure." It was true, old Barker intended to hang on to the two clubs in the meanwhile; but by Christmas he hoped to have these in his own hands. He had found the very house for them—a great piece of good luck, this, for private houses were few. She would do well, however, to part with some of the heavier furniture; for the rooms were smaller than those they were leaving. Also to try to find a purchaser for the "Collard and Collard," since coming here he had learned that an "Aucher Frères" was better suited to withstand the sea air. The climate, of course, was superb—though very cold in winter—the bathing excellent: "In summer I shall go into the sea every day." Best of all they were within easy reach of Melbourne . . . and that meant, civilisation once more. "I feel very happy and hopeful, my dearest. Quite sure my luck is about to turn."

Angry and embittered, Mary made short work of his fallacies. And now high words passed between them: she believing their very existence to be at stake; he fighting, but with considerable shuffling and hedging (or so it seemed to her) to defend his present scheme. And neither would give way.

Till, one morning, she held the following letter in her hand:

I see it's no use my beating about the bush any longer—you force me, by writing as you do, to tell you what I did not mean to worry you with. The truth is, I have not been at all well again. My old enemy, for one thing—requiring the most careful dieting—the old headaches and fits of vertigo. I have also fallen back on very poor nights; no sleep till four or five . . . for which however, I must say, your letters are partly responsible. Feeling very low the other day, I went to Geelong and saw Bowes-Smith, who visits there; and it was his opinion that I should be totally unfit to cope with the work at Narrong. Which but confirms my own. Of course, as you are so set on it, I might try it for three months—alone. But I cannot do impossibilities, and I feel, more and more, that I am an old and broken man. (Another thing, I should again have no one to consult with—and . . . as you ought to know by now . . . I am not well up in surgery.) My poor head has never recovered the shock it got last summer . . . when you were away. No doubt I had a kind of fit. And though I have said nothing about it, I have been sensible of some unpleasant symptoms of a return of this, on more than one occasion since. My affection, which was aphasia, may come on again at any time. It may also end in . . . well, in my becoming a helpless burden . . . to you and every one. Nothing can be done; there is no treatment for it, but a total absence of worry and excitement. So, if you regret Narrong, you must forgive me; it was done for your sake.

One other thing. Every one here takes boarders during the season: there is no disgrace attached to it. You could probably fill the house . . . and in that way I should not feel that I was leaving you entirely unprovided for. There is no dust or dirt here either: whereas at Narrong I should need to keep two horses and a man and buggy.

Send me some warmer underclothing, the continual blow of the equinoctial gales.

There is sure to be plenty of sickness when the visitors come. Shortlands will lead to strength, Narrong to the Benevolent Asylum.

Your loving husband

R.T.M.

P.S. I am so worried I hardly know what I am writing for God's sake cheer up.

At which Mary threw the letter on the table and laughed aloud. Hear how ill I am, but be sure not to take it to heart! Oh, it wasn't fair of him . . . it wasn't fair! He had her down and beaten, and he knew it: to such a letter there could be but one reply. Picking it up she reread it, and for a moment alarm riddled her. Then, with a jerk, she pulled herself together. How often Richard had . . . yes! over and over again. Besides, you could just as easily deceive yourself with bad dreams as with rosy ones. *How much of what he wrote was true?* His health had certainly suffered; but that was all due to this place.

He said so himself. Let him once get away from here . . .
Places. And if she now insisted on his going to Narrong, even
on his definitely applying for the practice, there would be
more swords held over her head, more insidious hints and
threats. He complained of not being able to find his words:
well, would any one think that surprising, did they know the
life he had led here? . . . how he never went out, never spoke
to a soul, but sat, for days on end, gloomily sunk in himself.

His airy suggestion that she should open the house to boarders stung and aggrieved her . . . coming from him. The idea
was her own; she had mooted it long ago. *Then,* it had outraged his feelings. "Not as long as *I* live!" Which attitude, bereft of common sense though it was, had yet had something
very soothing in it. Now, without a word of excuse, he climbed
down from his perch and thrust the scheme upon her . . . as
his own! Blown into thin air was his pride, his thought for her
standing, his care for the children's future. Her heart felt dark
and heavy. Of course, if the worst *should* come to the worst
. . . but then she would be doing it for *them,* not for him . . .
or rather, not just in order that he might somehow get his own
way. Oh he had cried wolf too often! And a desperate bitterness; the sensation of being "had"; of him baulking at no
means to achieve his end, was upon her again, clouding her
judgment. She simply did not know what to think.

And this attitude of doubt accompanied her through all the
dreary weeks of uprootal; down to the day when the bellman
went up and down the main street, crying the sale; when the
auction-flag flew from the roof; and rough, curious, unfriendly
people swarmed the house, to walk off with her cherished belongings. And as she worked, watched, brooded, a phrase
from Tilly's letter kept ringing and buzzing through her head.
"Sometimes, the thought has come to me, just to take Baby and
me bit of splosh and go off somewhere where . . ."

For nothing in the world would she have her children defrauded of their piano. Every toy they possessed, too, went
with them; she saw to that. (*He* never thought of parting with
his books!) While the Paris ornaments were her share of the
spoils. (But, anyhow, it would have been casting pearls before swine to offer them for sale here.)— As, one by one, she
took apart the gilt-legged tables, the gilt candelabra, to lay the
pieces between soft layers of clothing, memories of the time

when they were bought came crowding in on her. She saw the Paris shops again, the salesman bowing and smirking, the monkey-like little courier who had acted as interpreter. But, most vividly of all, she saw Richard himself. The very clothes he had worn were plain to her: there he stood, erect and handsome, a fine and dignified figure. And then, in pitiful contrast, a vision of him as, a few weeks back, he had slunk up to the railway station: a shamed and humiliated old man. Dear God! . . . these passionate angers he roused in her, the unspeakable irritations she was capable of feeling with him, were things of the surface only. Dig deeper, and nothing mattered . . . *but* him. Aye, dig only deep enough, and her heart was raw with pity for him. Let what might, happen to her; let the children go short, run wild; let him drag them at his heels the whole world over: she would submit to everything, endure everything, if she could only see him—Richard, her own dear husband!—hold up his head once more, carry himself with the old confidence, fear to meet no one's eye, knowing that he had never yet wilfully done any man hurt or wrong.

PART III

[1]

"Papa, papa!—the flag! The flag's just *this* minnit gone up."

"The flag! Papa's this minnit gone up!"

The children came rushing in with the news, Lucie, in her zeal to echo Cuffy, bringing out her words the wrong way round. But *how* funny! Papa was fast asleep in his chair, and at first when he waked up couldn't tell where he was. He called out quite loud: "Where am I? Where the dickens am I?" and looked as if he didn't know them. But as soon as he did, he ran to the window. "Quite right! Splendid! So it is.— Now who saw it first?"

"Lucie," said Cuffy stoutly; for he had seen first *all* the times; Lucie never would, not if she was as old as old. And so Lucie received the hotly coveted penny, her little face, with the fatly hanging cheeks that made almost a square of it, pink with pleasure. But also with embarrassment. Would God be *very* angry with Cuffy for tellin' what wasn't true? (She thought God must look just like Papa when he was cross.)

Papa scuttled about. Shouting.

"Mary! Where are you? The flag's gone up. Quick! My greatcoat. My scarf."

"Yes, yes, I'm coming.— But . . . why . . . you haven't even got your boots on! Whatever have you been doing since breakfast?"

"Surely to goodness, I can call a little time my own? . . . for reading and study?"

"Oh, all right. But fancy you having to go out again to-day. With such a sea running! And when you got so wet yesterday."

"It's those second-hand oilskins. I told you I ought to have new ones.— Now where are my papers?— Oh! these confounded laces. They *would* choose just this moment to break. It's no good; I can't stoop; it sends the blood to my head."

"Here . . . put up your foot!" And going on her knees, Mary laced his boots. *Till* she got him off! The fuss—the commotion!

Standing in the doorway, Cuffy drank it all in. This *was* an exciting place to live. To have to rush like mad as soon as ever a flag went up! If only someday Papa would take him with him! To go down to the beach with Papa, and row off from the jetty—Papa's own jetty—and sit in the boat beside him, and be rowed out, by Papa's own sailors, to the big ship that was waiting for him. Waiting just for Papa. When he was a big man he'd be a doctor, too, and have a jetty and a boat of his own, and be rowed out to steamers and ships, and climb on board, and say if they were allowed to go to Melbourne.— But how *funny* Papa was, since being here. When his voice got loud it sounded like as if he was going to scream. And then . . . he'd said he was busy . . . when he was really asleep! He believed Papa was afraid . . . of Mamma. Knew she'd be cross with him for going to sleep again directly after breakfast. It made him want to say: Oh, *don't* be afraid, Papa, big men never do be . . . only little children like Lucie. (Specially not one's Papa.)—

Slamming the driving-gate behind him—with such force that it missed the latch and, swinging outwards, went to and fro like a pendulum—Mahony stepped on to the wide, sandy road, over which the golden-flowered capeweed had spread

till only a narrow track in the centre remained free. It was
half a mile to the beach, and he covered the ground at a jog-
trot; for his fear of being late was on a par with his fear that
he might fail to see the signal: either through a temporary
absence of mind, or from having dozed off (the sea air was
having an unholy effect upon him) at the wrong moment.
Hence his bribe to the children to be on the look-out.— Now
on, past neat, one-storied weatherboards, past Bank and
church and hotels he hurried, breathing heavily, and with a
watchful eye to his feet. For his left leg was decidedly stiffish;
and, to spare it, his pace had to be a long, springing step with
the right, followed by a shorter one with the left: a gait that
had already earned him the nickname in Shortlands of "Old
Dot-and-go-one."

Taking the Bluff, with its paths, seats and vivid grass-carpet,
in his stride, he scrambled down the loose sand of the cliff,
through the young scrub and the ragged, storm-bent ti-trees,
which were just bursting into pearly blossom. And the result
of this hurry-scurry was that he got to the beach too soon: his
men had only just begun to open up the boat-shed. Fool that
he was! But it was always the same . . . and would be to-
morrow, and the day after that: when his fears seized him,
he was powerless against them. Having irritably snapped his
fingers, and urged on the crew with an impatient: "Come,
come, my good men, a little more haste, if you please!" he
retired to the jetty, where he paced to and fro.

But at last the boat was launched, the sailors had grasped
their oars: he, too, might descend the steps and take his seat.—
And now he knew that all the press and fluster of the past
half-hour had been directed towards this one exquisite moment: in which they drew out to ride the waves. Of the few
pleasures left him, it was by far the keenest: he re-lived it in
fancy many a night when his head lay safe on the pillow.
To-day was a day, too, after his own heart. A high sea ran,
and the light boat dived, and soared, and fell again, dancing
like a cockleshell. The surface of the water was whipt by a
wind that blew the foam from the wave-crests in cloudlets of
steam or smoke. The salt spray was everywhere: in your eyes,
your mouth, your hair. Overhead, between great bales of
snowy cloud, the sky was gentian-blue; blue were the hills
behind the nestling white huts of the quarantine-station, on

the opposite side of the bay; indigo-blue the waters below. In-
toxicated by all this light and colour, at being one again with
his beloved element, he could have thrown back his head and
shouted for joy; have sent out cries to match the lovely commotion of wind and sea. But there was no question of thus
letting himself go: he had perforce to remain as dumb as the
men who rowed him. Above all, to remember to keep his eyes
lowered. For the one drawback to his pleasure was that he
was not alone. He had a crew of six before him, six pairs of
strange eyes to meet; and every time he half-closed his own
and expanded his nostrils, the better to drink in the savour of
the briny, or, at an unusually deep dip, let fly a gleeful exclamation, they fixed him stonily, one and all. There was no
escaping them, pinned to his seat as he was: nor any room for
his own eyes . . . nowhere to rest them . . . except on the bottom of the boat. Only so could he maintain his privacy.—
Eyes . . . human eyes. Eyes . . . *spies*, ferreting out one's
thoughts . . . watchdogs, on the *qui vive* for one's smallest
movement . . . spiders, sitting over their fly-victims, ready to
pounce. Eyes. Slits into the soul; through which you peered,
as in a twopenny peepshow, at clandestine and unedifying
happenings. A mortal's outside the *ne plus ultra* of dignity
and suavity . . . and then the eyes, disproving all! Oh! it ought
not to be possible, so to see into another's depths; it was
indecent, obscene: had he not more than once, in a woman's
comely countenance, met eyes that were hot, angry, malignant? . . . unconscious betrayers of an unregenerate soul.
None should outrage him in like fashion: he knew the trick,
and guarded against it, by keeping his own bent rigidly on
the boards at his feet . . . on the boot-soles of the man in front
of him. But smiles and chuckles were not so easily subdued:
they would out . . . and out they came!

As, however, the boat drew nearer the vessel that lay to,
awaiting them, a new anxiety got the upper hand. Wrinkling
his brows, he strained to see what was in store for him. Ha!
he might have known it: another of those infernal rope lad-
ders to be scaled. He trembled in advance. For you needed the
agility of an ape, to swing yourself from the tossing boat to
the bottom rung of the ladder; the strength of a navvy to
maintain your hold, once you were there, before starting on
the precarious job of hoisting yourself, rung by rung, up the

ship's steep side. And to-day, with this wild sea running, it was worse than ever—was all the men could do to bring the boat close enough, yet not too close, alongside, for him to get a grip on the rope. The seat he stood on was slippery, his oilskins encumbered him: he made one attempt after another. Each time, before he had succeeded in jerking himself across, the gulf opened anew. Finally, in most undignified fashion, he was laid hold of, and pushed and shoved from behind; and thereafter came a perilous moment when he hung over the trough of sea, not knowing whether his muscles would answer to the strain, or whether he would drop back into the water. Desperately he clung to the swaying rope; what seemed an eternity passed before he could even straighten himself, let alone climb out of reach of the waves.— Deuce take it! you needed to be at least twenty years younger for acrobatics of this kind.

Hanging over the side, the ship's crew followed his doings with the engrossed and childish interest of men fresh from the high seas. As he came within reach, however, willing hands were thrust forth to help him. But he was shattered by his exertions, the deck wet, and no sooner did he set foot on it than his legs shot from under him, and he fell heavily and awkwardly on his back. And this was too much for the onlookers, just suited their elephantine sense of humour, already tickled by his unseamanlike performance on the ladder: one and all burst into a loud guffaw. Bruised and dazed he scrambled to his feet, and, hat and bag having been restored him, was piloted by a grinning seaman to the captain's cabin.

There had been no single case of sickness on the outward voyage: the visit was a mere formality; and the whole affair could have been settled inside five minutes—had he not been forced to ask the captain's leave to rest a little, in order to recover before undertaking the descent: his hips ached and stung, his hand shook so that he had difficulty in affixing his signature. He thought the captain, a shrewd-eyed, eagle-nosed Highlander, whose conversation consisted of a series of dry "Aye, aye's!" looked very oddly at him, on his curt refusal of the proffered bottle. "Thank you, I never touch stimulants."

As he hobbled home, wet and chilled, his head aching from its contact with the deck, arm and shoulder rapidly stiffening: as he went, he had room in his mind for one thought only:

I've taken on more than I can manage. I'm not fit for the job—or shan't be . . . much longer. And then? . . . my God! . . . *and then?*— But hush! Not a word to Mary.

Entering the dining-room he pettishly snatched off the dish-cover. "*What?* . . . hash again? I declare, of late we seem to live on nothing else!"

Mary sighed. "If I serve the meat cold, you grumble; if I make it up, you grumble, too. I can't throw half a joint away! What am I to do?"

He suppressed the venomous: "Eat it yourself!" that rose to his lips. "I've surely a right to expect something fresh and appetising when I get back after a hard morning's work? You know I loathe twice-cooked meat!"

"I thought you'd bring such an appetite home with you that you'd be equal to anything. Other times you do. But you don't know your own mind from one day to the next."

"If that's all you have to say, I won't eat anything!"— And despite her expostulations and entreaties: "Richard! come back, dear, don't be so silly!" he banged out of the room.

Instantly Cuffy pushed his plate away. "I don't like it either, Mamma."

Glad of a scapegoat, Mary rounded on the child with a "Will *you* kindly hold your tongue, sir!" letting out not only her irritation with Richard, but also the exhaustion of a morning's governessing: a task for which she was wholly unfitted by nature. "You'll not leave the table till you've eaten every scrap on your plate."

And Cuffy, being really very hungry—he had only said like Papa to try and make Mamma think Papa wasn't *quite* so bad—obeyed without a further word.

Afterwards, he had to go to the butcher's with a basket to buy a chop—a big one and not too fat, Papa didn't eat fat—and then, when the whole house smelt good with frying, to go in and say to Papa that dinner was ready.

But Papa was asleep, and snoring; and he didn't like to wake him. He fidgeted about and made a noise for a bit, and then went out and said so.

But Mamma sent him back: the chop was cooked and had to be eaten. So he put his hand on Papa's arm and shook it. But Papa knocked it off, and jumped up, calling out: "What is it? . . . what is it now?" And very angry: "*Can't* you let me be?— Oh, it's you, my dear?— What? Not I! Tell your mother I want nothing."

And then Mamma came marching in herself, and was furious. "And when I've sent out specially to get it! I never heard such nonsense. Going the whole day without food just to spite me!"

She was quite close up to Papa when she talked this; and they were both dreadfully angry; and then . . . then Cuffy di*stink*ly saw Papa's foot fly out and hit her . . . on her knee. And she said: "*Ooh!*" and stooped down and put her hand to it, and looked at him, oh! so fierce . . . but she didn't say any more, not a word (and he knew it was because he was there), but turned her back and walked out of the room and slammed the door. And he felt frightened, and went away, too; but not before he'd seen Papa put his face in his hands, just as if he was going to cry.

They kept a goat now: it was chained up in the back yard, to eat the grass and things, which would have smothered them if it hadn't. Well, he went out to the goat—it was tied up and couldn't run away—and kicked it. It maa-ed and tore round like mad; but he just didn't care; he kicked again. Till Luce came out and saw him and made awful eyes, and said: "Oh, *Cuffy!* Oh, poor little Nanny! Oh, you bad, wicked boy! I'll go wight in and tell Mamma what you're doin'!"

But Mamma could not be got at. She was in the bedroom with the door locked; and she wouldn't come out, though you called and called, and rattled the handle. (But she wasn't dead, 'cos you could hear them talkin'.)—

With his arms round her, his face on her shoulder, Richard besought her: "Mary, Mary, what is it? What's the matter with me? Why am I like this?—oh, why?"

"God knows! You seem not to have an atom of self-control left. When it comes to kicking me . . . and in front of the children . . . " Her heart full to bursting, Mary just stood and bore his weight, but neither raised her arms nor comforted him.

"I know, I know. But it isn't only temper—God knows it isn't! It's like a whirlpool . . . a whirlwind . . . that rises in me. Forgive me, forgive me! I didn't mean it. I had a nasty fall on the deck this morning. I think that knocked the wits out of me."

866

"A fall? How? Were you hurt?" Mary asked quickly. At any hint of bodily injury, and was it but a bruise, she was all sympathy and protection.

Meekly now, but with only the ghost of an appetite, Mahony sat down to the congealed chop, which he sliced and ate, half-chewed, while Mary moved about the room, her lids red-rimmed and swollen. And the children, having snatched one look at her, crept away with sinking hearts. Oh, Mamma dear, dear, don't . . . *don't* be unhappy!

In telling of this fall, and making it answerable for his subsequent behaviour, Mahony failed to mention one thing: the uneasiness his leg was causing him. Some perverse spirit compelled him to store this trouble up for his own tormenting—that night, when he lay stiff as a corpse, so as not to deprive Mary of her well-earned rest. This numbness . . . this fatal numbness . . . He tried to view himself in the light of a patient: groped, experimented, investigated. What! cutaneous anæsthesia as well? For he now found he could maltreat the limb as he would; there was little or no answering sensation. Positively he believed he could have run a pin into it. Sick with apprehension, he put his hand down to try yet once more, by running his finger-nails into and along the flesh—and was aghast to hear a shrill scream from Mary. *"Richard!* What *are* you doing? Oh, how you have hurt me!"

He had drawn blood on her leg instead of his own.

[2]

MARY waited, as for the millennium, for the opening of the summer season. In the meantime, Shortlands lay dead to the rest of the world: the little steamer neither brought nor took off passengers; the big ships all went past. But on every hand she heard it said: let the season once begin, and there would be work for every one; the life of a year was crowded into three brief months. If only they could manage to hold out till then! For December was still two months off, and of private practice there was as good as none. The place was so healthy, for one thing (oh! there must surely be something very wrong about a world in which you had to feel *sorry* if people weren't ill) and the poorer classes all belonged to the clubs, which Richard hadn't got. His dreams of keeping a horse and riding round the district, of opening consulting-rooms on the other side, had, as she had known they would, ended in smoke: twice he had crossed the bay, he had not even covered his fare. She wondered, sometimes, if such sickness as there was did not still find its way to Dr. Barker, retired though the old man professed to be. It was certainly owing to him that nightwork had become extinct here. Through his refusing to leave his bed, the inhabitants had simply got out of the way of being taken ill at night!

And Richard did nothing to mend matters. On the contrary. At present, for instance, he was going about in such a simmer of indignation at what he called the trick that had been played on him—the misleading reports of the income to be made here—that he was apt to let it boil over on those who did approach him. Then, too, the dreadful habit he had fallen into, of talking to himself as he walked, put people off. (From something the servant-girl let drop, she could see that he was looked on as very odd.) But when she taxed him with it, he flared up, and vowed he never in his life had been guilty of such a thing; which just showed he didn't know he was doing it. If he had, he would have been more careful; for he liked the place (hardly a day passed on which he did not sigh: "If I can *only* make a living here!") in spite of its deadness . . . and also of the cold, which found out his weak spots. And, for once in their lives, they were in agreement: she liked it, too. There were people of their own class here, and she had been received by them with open arms. Though, as she could see, this very friendliness might have its drawbacks. For Richard had been quite wrong (as usual): the members of this little clique did not let lodgings, most emphatically not; they drew, indeed, a sharp line between those who did and those who didn't. Well! she would just have to see . . . when the time came. If, then, the practice did not look up— But oh! how she hoped and prayed it would: she could hardly trust herself to think what might happen if it didn't.

One afternoon as they sat at tea—it was six o'clock, on a blustery spring day—they heard the click of the gate, and looking out saw some one coming up the path: a short, stoutish man in a long-skirted greatcoat, who walked with a limp.

Mary rubbed her eyes. "Why . . . why, Richard!"

"What is it? . . . who is it?" cried Mahony, and made as if

to fly: he was in one of those moods when the thought of facing a stranger filled him with alarm.

"Why . . . I . . ."

"He's walking right in!" announced Cuffy.

"An' wavin' his hand, Mamma!"

Sure enough, the newcomer came up the verandah steps and unceremoniously tapped on the window-pane. "Hullo, good people all! . . . how are you?" And *then*, of course, he with his hat off, showing a head innocent of hair, there was no mistaking him.

With one eye on Richard, who was still capable of trying to do a bolt, one on the contents of her larder-shelves, Mary exclaimed in surprise. "Well, of all the . . . Purdy! Where have you sprung from? Is Tilly with you?"

"*Tilly?* Mrs. P. Smith? God bless my soul no! My dear, this wind 'ud give 'is Majesty the bellyache for a month; we'd hear tell of nothing else. Lord bless you, no! We never go out if it blows the least little tiddly-wink, or if there's a cloud in the sky, or if Old Sol's rays are too strong for us! We're a hothouse plant, *we* are!— What do you say to that, you brawny young nippers, you?"

It was the same old Purdy: words just bubbled out of him. And having taken off his coat and chucked the children under the chin—after first pretending not to know them because of their enormous size, and then to shake in his shoes at such a pair of giants—he drew in his chair and fell to, with appetite, on the toothsome remains of a rabbit-pie and the home-baked jam tarts that Mary somehow conjured up to set before him. "These sea-voyages are the very devil for makin' one peckish. I've a thirst on me, too . . . your largest cup, Polly, if you please, will just about suit my measure!"— As she listened to his endless flow, Mary suspected him of already having tried to quench this thirst, on the way there.

In eating, he told of the business that had brought him to Shortlands; and at greater length than was either necessary or desirable; for there was a lot in it about "doing" a person, in revenge for having been "done" by him, and the children of course drank it all in. Mary did her best to edge the conversation round, knowing how strongly Richard disapproved of their being initiated, before their time, into the coarse and sordid things of life. But what followed was even worse. For now Purdy started indulging in personalities: "I say, you two, isn't this just like old times . . . eh?" he said as he munched. "Just like old times . . . except of course that we're all a good bit thicker in the tummy and thinner on the thatch than we were, ha, ha! . . . your hum. serv. in partic.! *Also*"—and he winked his right eye at the room at large—"excepting for the presence of the young couple I observe sitting opper*site*, who were *not* on the tappis, or included in the programme, in those far-off days—eh, Poll! Young people who insisted on putting in an appearance at a later date, unwanted young noosances that they were!" (At which Cuffy, flaming scarlet, looked anxiously at his mother for a denial: she had told him over and over again, how enjoyed she and Papa had been to see him.) "Well, well! such little accidents will happen. But far from us was it to think of such . . . all those many . . . now *how* many years was it ago? Thirty—for a cert! Ah, no hidin' your age from me, Mrs. Poll! . . . after the manner of ladies when they come to the sere and yellow leaf. I've got you nailed, me dear!"

Colouring slightly (she thought talk of this kind in sorry taste before the children), Mary was just about to say she didn't mind who knew how old she was, when Richard, who, till now, had sat like a death's-head, brought his fist down on the table with a bang. "And I say, not a day over twenty-five!"— He did make them jump.

Purdy, so jovial was he, persisted in taking this to refer, not to the date, but to her age, and bantered harder than ever, accusing Richard of trying to put his wife's clock back. And what with Richard arguing at the top of his voice to set him right, and Purdy waggishly refusing to see what was meant, it looked for a moment as if it might come to an open quarrel between them.

"Richard! . . . hush, dear!" frowned Mary, and surreptitiously shook her head. "What can it matter? Oh, don't be so silly!" For he was agitatedly declaring that he would fetch out his old case-books, and prove the year, black on white. She turned to Purdy: "You've told me nothing at all yet about Tilly and the boy."

But Purdy had plainly no wish to talk of wife or child, and refused to let himself be diverted from the course of reminiscence on which he had embarked. To oblige her, he

870

dropped his mischievous baiting with a: "Well, well, then, so be it! I suppose I'm gettin' soft in the uppers!" but continued to draw on his memories of the old days, spinning yarns of things that had happened to him, and things she was quite sure hadn't, egged on by the saucer eyes of the children. "Remember this, Poll? . . . remember that?" she vainly endeavouring to choke him off with a dry: "I'm afraid I don't." She sat on pins and needles. If only he wouldn't work Richard up again! But it almost seemed as if this was his object; for he concluded his tale of the Stockade and his flight from Ballarat, with the words: "And so afeared for his own skin was our friend old Sawbones there, that he only ventured out of an evening after dark; and so the wound got mucky and wouldn't heal. And that's the true story, you kids, of how I came to be the limping-Jesus I am and ever shall be, world without end, amen!"

Of all the wicked falsehoods! (Or had he *really* gone about nursing this belief?) Such expressions, too! . . . before the children. Thank goodness, Richard hadn't seemed to hear: otherwise, she would have expected him to fly out of his chair. A stolen glance showed him sitting, head on chest, making patterns on the tablecloth with the point of his knife. And having failed thus to draw him, if Purdy didn't now dish up, with several unsavoury additions, the old, old story of the foolish bet taken between the two of them, as young men, that Richard wouldn't have the pluck to steal a kiss from her, at first meeting; and how, in the darkness of the summer-house, he had mistaken one girl for the other and embraced Jinny instead. "Putting his arms round her middle—plump as a partridge she was too, by gum!—and giving 'er a smack that could have been heard a mile off. Killing two birds with one stone I call it! . . . gettin' the feel of a second gal under his hands, free, gratis and for nothing."

At such indelicacy Mary held her breath. But what was this? Instead of the furious outburst for which she waited, she heard a . . . chuckle. Yes, Richard was laughing—his head still sunk, his eyes fixed on the tablecloth—laughing and nodding to himself, at the memory Purdy had called up. And then—oh, no! it was incredible: to her horror, Richard himself added a detail, the grossness of which sent the blood to her cheeks.

871

What was more, he was going on. "Run away and play, children! At once! Do you hear?" For Cuffy was listening open-mouthed, and laughing, too, in an odd, excited way. She had them off their chairs and out of the room in a twinkling. Herself she stood for a moment in the passage, one hand pressed to her face. Oh! by fair means or foul— "You're wanted. Yes, immediately!"— And after that it was not hard to get Purdy up from the table as well, and dispatched about his business.

But as soon as the children were in bed, she went into the surgery, and there, shutting fast the door, let out her smothered wrath, making a scene none the less heated because it had to be carried on under her breath. To her stupefaction, Richard flatly denied the charge. What was she talking about? No such words had ever crossed *his* lips! "Before my children? Whose every hair is precious to me?" He was as perturbed as she, at the bare idea. Oh! what was to be done with a person whose memory was capable of playing him such tricks? In face of his indignation, his patent honesty, you couldn't just rap out the word "liar!" and turn on your heel.

Yes! a disastrous visit from start to finish. The children alone got pleasure from it. Purdy took a great liking to them —he, who hadn't a word to say for his own child!—and on the verandah next morning, the trio were very merry together. Cuffy's laugh rang out again and again.

For Cuffy thought Mr. Purdy a *very* nice man . . . even if his head *was* shiny like an egg, and he was nearly as fat as that ol' Sankoh in the big book with the pictures. (Papa, he was like Donk Quick Shot, who tried to kill the windmills.) He had two be*aut*iful big diamond rings on his fingers, and a watch that struck like a clock, and a whole bunch of things, little guns and swords and seals, hanging on his chain. He gave them each half-a-crown and said not to tell Mamma, and rode Luce to market on his foot, and sang them a lovely song that went:

A man whose name was Johnny Sands
Had married Betty Hague,
And though she brought him gold and lands,
She proved a terrible plague;

Book III: *Ultima Thule*

For O she was a scolding wife,
Full of caprice and whim,
He said that he was tired of life,
And she was tired of him.

Ever so much of it, all about these people, till she fell into the river and asked him to pull her out, and Johnny Sands would have, but:

I can't, my dear, tho' much I wish,
For you have tied my hands!

He and Luce jumped about and sang it, too. Oh, wasn't it nice when somebody was happy and jolly and funny? instead of always being sorry, or cross. He thought he could *nearly* have asked Mr. Purdy what it meant when you said: the female nobleman obliges. It belonged to him, Papa had said it did; but he hadn't ever dared ask anybody about it; people like Aunt Zara laughed so, when you didn't understand. But he was going to . . . some day.—

The climax came next morning, when, the front door having closed behind the guest, the children came running out of the dining-room, crying gleefully: "Look, Mamma! Look what he's left on the table!" For an instant Richard stood and stared incredulously at the five-pound note Cuffy was holding aloft; the next, with a savage exclamation, he had snatched it from the child's hand, and was through the porch and down the path, shouting at the top of his voice: "Here you, sir, come back! How dare you! Come back, I say! Do you take my house for a hotel?"

But Purdy, already on the other side of the gate, and limping off as hard as he could go, only made a half-turn, waved one arm in a gesture that might have meant anything, and was out of sight. Short of running down the street in pursuit, or of mixing one of the children up in it . . . Beside himself with rage, Richard threw the note to the ground and stamped on it, then plucking it up, tore it to bits.

Taking him by the arm, Mary got him indoors. But for long she could not calm him. (Oh, was there *ever* such a tactless fool as Purdy? Or was this just another of those

873

spikey thrusts at Richard, which he seemed unable to resist?)

"Does he think because he's gone up in the world and I've come down, that it gives him the right to insult me in this way?—him, the common little ragamuffin I once picked out of the gutter? (Oh no, Richard!) To come here and offer me alms! . . . for that's what it amounts to . . . pay his few shillingsworth of food with a present of pounds? Why, I would rather rot in my grave than be beholden to him!" (Oh, how Richard did at heart despise him!) "*Charity!*—from *him* to *me!*"

"He shall never come again, dear." (Though how were you to help it, if he just walked in?)

Behind the locked door (she seemed always to be locking doors now) she sat, wide-lapped in her full skirts; and, when Richard had railed himself tired, he knelt down before her and laid his face on her dress. Her hands went to and fro over the grey beard, on which the hair was wearing so thin. What could she do for him? . . . what was to become of him? . . . when every small mischance so maddened, so exasperated him. That a stupid, boorish act like Purdy's could so shatter his self-control! Her heart wept over him; this heart which, since the evening before, had lain under the shadow of a new fear; a fear so ominous that she still did not dare to put it into words; but against which, for her children's sake, she might have to take up arms . . . to lock, so to speak, yet another door.

The upshot of the matter, of course, was that she had to replace the destroyed note from her jealously guarded store. This, Richard haughtily sealed up and posted back, without a single covering word.

There was, however, one bright side to the affair. And again it was the children who benefited.

In running them out after breakfast to buy some lollipops, Purdy had got permission from the postmaster, an old friend of his, to take them up the lighthouse; and so the three of them went up, and up, and up a staircase that twisted like a corkscrew, hundreds of steps, till they came to where the great lamp was that shone at night; and then, tightly holding hands, they walked round the little narrow platform outside, and looked down at the sea, all bubbly and frothy, and the white roofs of the houses. They found their own, and it didn't look

874

any bigger than a doll's-house. Afterwards, they were asked inside the post office—right inside!—and they peeped through the little window where the stamps were sold, and saw the holes where the letters were kept; and the two tel'graph machines that went click, click; and how tape ran away on wheels with little dots and dashes on it, that the postmaster said were words. And then he took them into his house behind, to see his Mamma and his four grown-up sisters, who were ever so nice, and asked their names, and said Cuffy *was* a big boy for his age, and Luce was a cuddly darling; and they cut a cake specially for them, and showed them a ship *their* Papa had made all by himself, even the little wooden men that stood on the decks. They laughed and joked with Mr. Purdy, and they had the most lovely teeth, and sang songs for them, till Cuffy was wild with delight.

Thus, through Purdy's agency, a house was opened to the children, the like of which they had never known: a home over which no shadow brooded; in which the key was set to laughter and high spirits, and the nonsensical gaiety that children love. Cuffy and Lucie, petted and made much of, completely lost their hearts to their new friends, and talked so much of them, teasing to be allowed to visit them, that Mary felt it incumbent on her to tie on her bonnet and pay a call in person. She came back entirely reassured. The daughters, one and all Australian-born, were charming and accomplished girls; while in old Mrs. Spence, the widow of an English university man who, in the early days, had turned from unprofitable gold-digging to Government service, she found one who, in kindliness and tolerance, in humour and common sense, reminded her vividly of her own mother, long since dead.

To the children this old lady early became "Granny"; and even Cuffy, who had begun to fight shy of his mother's knee, was not above sitting on hers. A Granny was diffrunt . . . didn't make you feel such a baby. And it was of her kind old face that he eventually succeeded in asking his famous question.

"Bless the child! . . . now what can he mean?" Then, noting the sensitive flush that mounted, Granny cried: "Pauline, come you here!— Pauline will know, my dear. She's ever so much cleverer than a silly old woman like me."

And pretty Pauline—they were all four so pretty and so nice that Cuffy couldn't tell which he liked best—knelt down before

875

him, he sitting on Granny's lap, and, with her dress bunching up round her and her hands on his knees, explained, *without laughing a bit. Noblesse oblige* didn't mean the obliging female nobleman at all: he had got it mixed up with poet and poetess. "What it says, Cuffy dear, is that people who are born to a high rank . . . like Kings and Queens . . . must always remember who they are, and act accordingly. Little gentlemen must always behave *like* gentlemen, and never do anything low or mean. Do you see?"

And Cuffy nodded . . . and nodded again. Yes, now he knew. And he never would!— But he knew something else, too. He loved Pauline more'n anybody in the world.

[3]

"There you go . . . tripping again! You keep one in a perfect fidget," sighed Mary.

"It's these confounded shoes. They're at least two sizes too big."

"I told you so! But you were bent on having them easy."

Entering the surgery Mahony kicked the inoffensive slippers from his feet, and drew on his boots. After which, having opened the door by a crack, to peer and listen, he stole into the passage to fetch hat and stick.

But Mary, in process of clearing the breakfast-table, caught him in the act. "What? . . . going out already! I declare your consulting hours become more of a farce every day.— Well, at least take the children with you."

"No, that I can't! They're such a drag."

And therewith he whipped out of the house and down the path, not slackening his pace till he had turned a corner. Mary was quite capable of coming after him and hauling him back. Escape he must!— from the prison cell that was his room; from the laming surveillance to which she subjected him. Only out of doors, with the wind sweeping through him, the wild expanse of sea tossing in the sunlight, could he for a little forget what threatened; forget her dogging and hounding; enjoy a fictitious peace . . . dream of safety . . . forget—forget!

He made for the Bluff, where, for an hour or more, he wandered to and fro: from the old grey lighthouse and flagstaff, at one end, to pier and township at the other. He carried

his hat in his hand, and the sea wind played with his fine,
longish hair, till it stood up like a halo of feathers round his
head. That no chance passer-by should use them as spy-holes,
he kept his eyes glued to the ground; but at the same time he
talked to himself without pause; no longer mumbling and muttering as of old, but in a clear voice, for any to hear, and
stressing his words with forcible gestures: throwing out an
open palm; thumping a closed fist in the air; silencing an
imaginary listener with a contemptuous outward fling of the
hand.

He was obliged to be energetic, for it was Mary he argued
with, Mary he laboured to convince; and this could only be
done by means of a tub-thumper's over-emphasis. Where he
was in question. She believed others readily enough. But he
never had her wholly with him; invariably she kept back some
thought or feeling; was very woman in her want of straightness and simplicity. Even here, while shouting her down with:
"I tell you once for all that it *is* so!" he felt that he was not
moving her.— But stay! What was it he sought to convince her
of? Confound the thing! it had slipped the leash and was gone
again: grope as he might, standing stockstill the while in middle of the path, and glaring seawards, he could not recapture
it. Not that this was anything new. Nowadays, his mind seemed
a mere receptacle for disjointed thoughts, which sprang into
it from nowhere, skimmed across it, and vanished . . . like
birds of the air. Birds. Of Paradise, Parrakeets . . . their sumptuous green and blue and rosy plumage. You caught one,
clasped it round, and, even as you held it, felt its soft shape
elude you, the slender tail-feathers glide past, till but the empty
hole of your curled hand remained. A wonderful flight of
parrakeets he had once seen at . . . at . . . now *what* was the
name of that place?—a Y and a K, a K and a Y. Damnation take
it! this, too, had flown; and though he scoured and searched,
working letter by letter through the alphabet: first the initial
consonants, then the companion vowels . . . fitting them together—mnemonics—artificial memory . . . failing powers . . .
proper names went first—gone, gone! . . . everything was gone
now, lost in a blistering haze.

Such a frenzied racking of his poor old brain invariably
ended thus . . . with a mind empty as a drum. And though he
crouched, balled like a spider, ready to pounce on the meagrest

image that showed, nothing came: the very tension he was at, held thought at bay. His senses on the other hand were strung to a morbid pitch; and, little by little, a clammy fear stole over him lest he should never again know connected thought; be condemned eternally to exist in this state of vacuity. Or the terror would shift, and resolve itself into an anticipation of what would, what *must* happen, to end the strain. For there was nothing final about it: the blood roared in his ears, his pulses thudded like a ship's engines, the while he waited: for a roar, fit to burst his eardrums; for the sky to topple and fall upon his head, with a crash like that of splitting beams. Thunder—thunder breaking amid high mountains . . . echoing and re-echoing . . . rolling to and fro. Or oneself, with closed eyes and a cavernous mouth, emitting a scream: a mad and horrid scream that had nothing human left in it, and the uttering of which would change the face of things for ever. This might escape him at any moment; here and now: wind and sea were powerless against it—he could feel it swelling . . . mounting in his throat. He fought it down: gritted his teeth, balled his fists, his breath escaping him in hoarse, short jerks. Help, help! . . . for God's sake, help!

And help approached . . . in the shape of a middle-aged woman who came trapesing along, dragging a small child by the hand.

Swaying round his stick which he dug into the gravel for a support, Mahony blocked her way, blurting out incoherencies; in a panic lest she should pass on, abandon him. "Good morn'g, my good woman! . . . good morn'g. A pleasant morn'g. Cool breeze. A nice lil girl you have there. A fine child. Know what I'm saying, speak from exp'rience . . . a father myself. Yes, yes, two little girls . . . golden curls, healthy, happy. Like criteks . . . chirking. A boy, too. Porridge for rickets . . . you've let yours walk too soon. Nothing like porridge for forming bone. The Highlanders . . . main sustenance . . . magnif'cent men.— Eh? What? Well, good day . . . good day!"

For, having edged round and past him, the woman grabbed her child and made off. Not till she had put a safe distance between them, did she stop to look round. "Well, I'm blowed! Of all the rum o' cusses!" There he went, without a hat, his hair standing up anyhow, and talking away nineteen to the dozen. The whole time he'd spoke to her, too, he'd never so much as took his eyes off the ground.

In his wake, Mahony left a trail of such open mouths. Espying a man digging a garden, he crossed the road to him and leaned over the fence. A painter was at work on the beach, re-painting a boat: he headed for him, wading ankle-deep through the loose, heavy sand.

Of these, the former spoke up sturdily. "Can't say as I understand what you're drivin' at, mister, with them sissyfass-stones you tork of. But this I do know: anyone who likes can have *my* job! An' to-day rather'n to-morrow."

The painter knew the "ol' doctor" by sight, and stopped his work to listen, not impolitely, to certain amazing confidences that were made him. After which, watching the departing figure, he thrust his fingers under his cap and vigorously scratched his head. "Crickey! So *that's* him, is it? Well, they do say . . . and dang me! I b'lieve they're not far wrong."

Dog-tired, footsore, Mahony limped home, his devils exorcised for the time being. At the gate a little figure was on the watch for him—his youngest, his lovely one, towards whom his heart never failed to warm: her little-girl eyes had nothing of the boy's harassing stare. Holding her to him, he walked up the path. Then: "Good God! but I said I had two. What . . . *what* came over me? The creature will think I was lying . . . boasting!" Where should he find her, to put things right? . . . by explaining that one of the two no longer wore bodily form; but had been snatched from them amid pain and distress, the memories of which, thus rudely awakened, he now—in the twenty odd yards that divided gate from door—re-lived to their last detail, and so acutely that he groaned aloud.

Hot with the old pity, he laid a tender hand on Mary's shoulder; and following her into the dining-room ate, meekly and submissively, what she set before him: without querulous carping, or fastidious demands for the best bits on the dish. And this chastened mood holding, he even offered, in the course of the afternoon, to walk the children out for her.

Bidden to dress himself, Cuffy obeyed with the worst possible grace. It was dull enough walking with Mamma, who couldn't tell stories because she was always thinking things;

but, when it came to going out with Papa . . . well, Mamma never did it herself, and so she didn't know what it was like. But he couldn't ask to be let stop at home, because of Luce. He *had* to be there to protect Luce, who was so little and so fat. Mamma was always saying take care of her.

Papa held their hands and they started quite nice; but soon he forgot about them, and walked so quick that they nearly had to run to keep up, and could look at each other across behind him. And they went round by the bay at the back, where the mussels were, and heaps of mud, and no waves at all. Luce got tired direckly. Her face hung down, very red. *Somehow* he'd got to make Papa go slower.

"Tell us a story!"— He said it twice before Papa heard.

"A story? Child! I've no stories left in me."

("You ask him, Luce.")

"Tell 'bout when you was a little boy, Papa," piped Lucie, and trotted a few steps to draw level.

"No, tell 'bout when you first saw Mamma." Luce, she loved to hear how Papa's big sisters had smacked him and put him to bed without his supper; but he liked best the story of how Papa had seen nothing, only Mamma's leg, in a white stocking and a funny black boot, when he saw her first; and it was jumping out of a window. He'd jumped out, too, and chased her; but then he let her go and went away; but as soon as he got home he slapped his leg and called himself a donkey, and hired a horse and galloped ever and ever so many miles back again, to ask her if she'd like to marry him. And first she said she was too young, and then she did. He'd heard it a million times; but it was still exciting to listen to . . . how in a hurry Papa had been!

But to-day everything went wrong. Papa began all right; but so loud that everybody who was passing could hear. But then he got mixed, and left out the best part, and said the same thing over again. And then he couldn't remember Aunt Tilly's name, and didn't listen when they told him, and got furious—with himself. He said he'd be forgetting his own name next, and that *would* be the end of everything. And then he jumped on to the funny bit in the arbour that Mr. Purdy had teased him about, where he'd kissed somebody called Miss Jinny instead of Mamma . . . and this really truly *was* funny, because Mamma was so little and spindly and Miss Jinny was fat. But when he came to this he forgot to go on, and that he was telling them a story, and that they were there, and everything. He said: "My God! how could I have done such an idiotic thing? . . . have made such an unspeakable fool of myself! Took her in my arms and kissed her—the wrong girl . . . the wrong girl! I can hear them still—their ribald laughter, their jeers and guffaws . . . their rough horseplay! And how she shrank before them . . . my shy little Polly! . . . my little grey dove! I to make her the butt of their vulgar mirth!" And then he made a noise as if something hurt him, and talked about pain-spots one shouldn't ever uncover, but shut up and hide from everybody. And then some more, in a dreadful hoarse voice, about a scream, and somebody who'd soon have to scream out loud, if he didn't keep a hold on himself.

Cuffy couldn't bear it any longer; he pulled his hand out (Papa didn't notice) and let Papa and Luce go on alone. He stayed behind, and kicked the yellow road-flowers till all their heads fell off. But then Luce looked back, and he could see she was crying. So he had to gallop up and take her hand. And then he called out—he simply shouted: "Papa! Lucie's tired. She wants to go home to Mamma."

"Tired? . . . my poor little lamb? Such short leggykins! See . . . Papa will carry her." And he tried to lift her up, and first he couldn't she was so heavy, and when he did, he only staggered a few steps and then put her down again. Luce had to walk home with their hands, and all the way back he made haste and asked questions hard, about the yellow flowers, and why they grew on the road, and why the wind always sang in the treble and never in the bass, and always the same tune; till they got to the gate. But you didn't tell how Papa had been . . . not a word! You were too ashamed.

Shame and fear.

If you were coming home from Granny's, walking nicely, holding Luce's hand and taking care of her, and if you met a lot of big, rough, rude boys and girls coming from the State School, what did you do? Once, you would have walked past them on the other side of the road, sticking your chin up, and not taking any notice. Now, you still kept on the other side (if you didn't run like mad as soon as you saw them), but you looked down instead of up, and your face got so red it hurt you.

For always now what these children shouted after you was: "Who'd have a cranky doctor for a father? . . . who'd have a cranky doctor for a father!" and they sang it like a song, over and over, till you had gone too far to hear. And you couldn't run away; you *wouldn't* have! You squeezed Luce's hand till you nearly squeezed it off, and whispered: "*Don't* cry, Luce . . . don't let them see you cry!" And Luce sniffed and sniffed, trying not to.

You didn't tell this either; nor even speak to Luce about it. You just tried to pretend to yourself you didn't know. Like once, when Miss Prestwick was new and had taken them too long a walk at Barambogie, and Luce hadn't liked to ask, and had had an accident: he'd been ever so partic'lar then not to look at her; he'd kept his head turned right round the other way. That was "being a gentleman." But this about Papa . . . though you tried your hardest to be one here, too, you couldn't help it; it was always there. Like as if you'd cut your finger, and a little clock ticked inside. And being good didn't help either; for it wasn't your *fault,* you hadn't *done* anything. And yet were ever so ashamed . . . about somebody . . . who wasn't you . . . yet belonged to you. Somebody people thought silly, and had to laugh at . . . for his funny walk . . . and the way he talked.— Oh, *why* had one's Papa got to be like this? Other children's Papas weren't. They walked about . . . properly . . . and if they met you they said: "Hullo!" or "How do you do?"

Something else wormed in him. Once in Barambogie he had seen a dreadful-looking boy, with his mouth open and his tongue hanging out, and bulgy eyes like a fish. And when he'd asked Maria she said, oh, he was just cranky, and an idjut. But Papa wasn't like *that!* The thought that anyone could think he was, was too awful to bear.

"What's it really mean, Bridget, cranky?" he asked, out of this pain, of the small servant-girl.

And Bridget, who was little more than a child herself, first looked round, to make sure that her mistress was not within hearing, then mysteriously put her mouth to his ear and whispered: "It means . . . *what your Pa is.*"—

Granny, on whose knee he sat, held him from her for an instant, then snatched him close. "Why bother your little head with such things?"

"I just want to know."

As usual Granny turned to Pauline for aid; and Pauline came over to them and asked: "Who's been saying things to you, my dear? Take no notice, Cuffy! Oh, well, it just means . . . different—yes, that's what it means: different from other people." But he saw her look at Granny and Granny at her; and his piece of cake was extra big that day, and had more currants in it than Luce's.

But a "diffrunt doctor" didn't mean anything at all.

But now you and Luce never stopped running all the way home, and you went a long way round, so as not to have to go down the street where the State School was. And when Papa took you for a walk, you *chose* the hidjus way at the back. When all the time you might have gone on the real beach, by the real sea.

For what a lovely place this would have been, if it hadn't been for Papa! There wasn't any wattle here to shut your eyes and smell and smell at, and you couldn't smell the sun either, like in Barambogie. But the beach and the sea made up for everything. You could have played on the beach till you died. The sand was hot and yellow, and so soft that it felt like a silk dress running through your fingers; and there were big shells with the noise of the sea in them, and little ones with edges like teeth; and brown and green and red and pink sea-weed; and pools to paddle in; and caves to explore when the tide went out. And soon lots of little boys and girls—*nice* ones! —who you could have played with, if you had been allowed, came to the seaside, too. But Mamma always said: keep to yourselves. Which meant there was only him and Luce. And then you learned to swim. The bathing-woman said you were a born fish; and you wished you were: then you could have stopped in the water for ever—and never have needed to go home again—or for walks with Papa.—

Fear. All sorts of fears.

One was, when he lay in bed at night and listened to the wind, which never stopped crying. Mamma said it was because the room was at a corner of the house, and the corner caught the wind; but Bridget said it was dead people: the noise people made when they were dead. "But my little sister Lallie's dead!" "Well, then, it's her you hear." (But Lallie had never cried like that!) But Bridget said it was the voice of her soul in torment, hot in hell; and though he *knew* this wasn't true, because

Lallie was in heaven, he couldn't help thinking about it at night, when he was awake in the dark. Then it did sound like a voice—lots of voices—and as if they were crying and sobbing because they were being hurt. Other times it seemed as if the wind was screeching just at him, very angry, and getting angrier and angrier, till he had to sit up in bed and call out (not too loud because of Luce): "Oh! *what's* the matter?" But it didn't stop: it just went on. And even if you stuffed your fingers in both your ears, you couldn't shut it out; it was too treble. Till you couldn't stand it any longer, and jumped out of your own bed and went to Luce's, and lifted the blankets and got in beside her—she was always fast asleep—and held on to her little fat back. And then you went to sleep, too.

But Mamma was cross in the morning when she came in and found you: she said it wasn't nice to sleep two in one bed.

"But you and Papa do!"

"That's quite different. A big double bed."

"Couldn't Luce and me have a double bed, too?"

"Certainly not," said Mamma; and was ashamed of him for being afraid of the dark. Which he wasn't.

Worse still were those nights when he had to lie and think about what was going to happen to them, when all their money was done. Mamma didn't know; she often said: "What *is* to become of us!" And it was Papa's fault. They never ought to have come to live here; they ought to have gone to a place called Narrong, where there was plenty of money; but Papa wouldn't; so now they hadn't enough, and quite soon mightn't have any at all. Perhaps not anything to eat either! His mind threw up a picture of Luce crying for bread, which so moved him that he had to hurry on. Maria's mother had taken in washing. But you couldn't think of Mamma doing that: standing at the tubs, and mangling and ironing, and getting scolded if the buttons came off. No, he wouldn't ever let her! He'd hold her hands, so that she couldn't use the soap. Or else he'd pour the water out of the tubs.

But *quite* the most frightening thing was that when no more money was left, Mamma and Papa might have to go to prison. Once, when he was little, he'd heard them talking about somebody who couldn't pay his debts, and so had cheated people, and been put in gaol. And this dim memory returning now to torture him, he rolled and writhed, in one of childhood's hellish agonies. *What* would he and Luce do? How could they get up in the morning, and have breakfast, and know what to put on, or what they were to practise, without Mamma and—no! *just* without Mamma. And though he might talk big and say he wouldn't let her be a washerwoman, yet inside him he knew quite well he was only a little boy, and not a bit of use, *really*. If the sergeant came and said she had to go to prison, nothing he could do would stop her. Oh, Mamma . . . Mamma! She alone, her dear, substantial presence, stood guard between him and his shadowy throng of fears. And now, when he and Lucie raced home hand in hand of an afternoon, their first joint impulse was to make sure of Mamma: to see that she was still there . . . hadn't gone out, or . . . been taken away. Only close up to where she stood, radiating love and safety, a very pillar of strength, was it possible for their fragile minds to sustain, uninjured, the grim tragedy that overhung their home, darkening the air, blotting out the sun, shattering to ruin all accustomed things, in a fashion at once monstrous and incredible.

[4]

As IF struck by a beneficent blindness, Mary, alone unseeing, alone unsuspecting, held to her way. And, in excuse of her wilful ignoring of many a half-thought and passing impression, her care to keep these from coming to consciousness, there was this to be said: she knew Richard so well. Who but she had endured, for the better part of a lifetime, his whimsies, his crotchets? When had she ever thought of him, or spoken of him, but as queer, freakish, eccentric? Hence, was it now to be wondered at that, as age crept on and added its quota, his peculiarities should wax rather than wane? The older, the odder seemed but natural to her, who had never looked for anything else.

Meanwhile, October passed into November, November into December; and one day—overnight, as it seemed—the season was upon them. The houses on either side ran over with new faces; there was hardly a spare seat in church on Sunday; you had to wait your turn for a cabin at the baths. And the deck of the little steamer, which came daily, was crowded with lively, white-clad people. Now was the time . . . if ever . . . for Richard's fortunes to turn.

But the day dragged by in the old monotony; not a single new patient knocked at the door. Instead, by the end of the week Mary had definite information that old Barker was being called out again. Yes, people were actually preferring this antediluvian old man to Richard! And could one altogether blame them? Who would want to consult a doctor who went about talking to himself, and without a hat? . . . who omitted to brush his hair, or brush the fluff off his coat-collar, and thought nothing of appearing in public with a two-days' growth on his chin! She could imagine landladies and hotel-keepers advising their guests: "Oh, I shouldn't have *him,* if I were you! Extremely queer! Goes nowhere."

Boarders. It was boarders or nothing now . . . and not a moment to lose either, with a season that lasted for a bare three months. Like the majority of people in Shortlands, she would have to seize the chance and make money while she could, by throwing open her house to strangers. Grimly she tied on her bonnet and went down into the township, to hang out her name and her terms as a boarding-house keeper; to face the curious looks, the whispers and raised eyebrows: what? . . . the grand Mrs. Mahony? . . . reduced to taking in lodgers? Not till she got home again did she know how high she had carried her head, how rigidly set her jaw, over the taking of this step which would once have seemed like the end of the world to her. But, true to herself, she refused to allow her strength to be sapped by vain regrets. Instead, she turned with stubborn energy to the re-arrangement of her house. If Richard and she moved into the children's bedroom, and the children slept in the small inner room, lit by a skylight, she would have two good-sized bedrooms to let, in which she could put up as many as four to five people. At two guineas a head this would bring in ten a week. Ten guineas a week for three months! . . . of which not a penny should pass out of her hands.

On the day this happened—and in the swiftness and secrecy of her final decision there was something that resembled a dash of revenge—on this day, Richard was out as usual all the morning, strolling about on cliffs or beach. And though he came home to dinner, he was in one of his most vacant moods, when he just sat and ate—ravenously—noticing nothing of what went on around him.— But, anyhow, she would not, at this eleventh hour, have started to thresh the matter out with him. Better, first to get everything irrevocably fixed and settled.

Perhaps, though, she had a dim foreboding of what awaited her. For, the next time he came back, he was wider awake, and took in the situation at a glance. And then there was a scene the like of which she had never known. He behaved like a madman, stamping and shouting about the house, abusing her, and frightening the poor children out of their wits. In vain she followed him, reasoning, arguing, throwing his own words in his teeth: had the idea not been his, originally? Besides, what else was there left for her to do, with no patients, no money coming in, and old Barker resuming practice? He would not listen. Frenzy seized him at the thought of his threatened privacy: strangers to occupy his bedroom, hang their hats in the passage, go in and out of his front door! Not as long as *he* lived! "My mother . . . my sisters . . . the old home in Dublin—*they* would sooner have starved!" And as he spoke, he sent his hat and stick flying across the hall table, and the brass card-tray clattering to the floor. He kicked it to one side, and with an equally rough push past Mary, who had stooped to recover it, banged into the surgery and locked the door. And there he remained. She could neither get at him, nor get a word out of him.

Late that night, the children, their parents' neighbours now, sat miserably huddled up together. Lucie had been fast asleep; but Cuffy had so far only managed to doze uneasily, in this funny room where the window was in the roof instead of the wall: he was quite sure something would look in at him through it, or else fall down on his head. Now, they sat and clung to each other, listening . . . listening . . . their little hearts pounding in their chests. "Oh, *don't*, Papa! Oh, what's he doing to her?" To which Cuffy gave back sturdily: "*I* don't hear anything, Luce, truly I don't!" "Oh, yes, you do! And now I know she'll go away . . . Mamma will . . . and leave us!" "No, she won't! She told me so yesterday—promised she wouldn't ever!" Though his teeth were chattering with fear.

For Mary had at last reached what seemed the limits of human endurance. After pleading and imploring; after reasoning, as with a little child: after stabbing him with bitter words, and achieving nothing but to tear and wound her own heart, she gave it up, and, turning bodily from him, as she had

already turned in mind and deed, she crushed her face into
the pillow and gave way, weeping till she could weep no
more; as she had not wept since the death of her child. But
on this night no loving arms reached out to her, to soothe and
console. Richard might have been made of stone: he lay stock-
still, unmoved, staring with glassy eyes into the moonlight.

From sheer exhaustion, she thought she must have sunk into
a momentary unconsciousness; for, coming to with a start, she
found the place beside her empty. Throwing back the sheet,
she jumped to the floor, her temples a-throb, and ran into the
hall. There, among the lines and squares of greenish moonshine that filtered through the open doors of the rooms, stood
Richard, a tall white figure, just as he had got out of bed. He
was at the front door, fingering the lock, plainly on the point
of leaving the house. Abominably frightened, but still mindful of the sleeping children, she called to him under her
breath: "*Richard!* What are you doing?"

He did not answer: she had to go up to him and shake his
arm. "What's the matter? Where are you going?"

"To find peace."

So gaunt and old! . . . the ribbed neck and stooping shoulders . . . the poor thin shanks: and once, he, too, had been
young, and handsome, and upstanding! As always, did she
compare present with past, an immense compassion swept
through Mary, driving every smaller, meaner feeling before it.
She put out her arms, put them round him, to hold, to protect.
"Oh, but not like this . . . and at this hour! Wait till morning.
Come back and try to sleep. Come, my dear, come!"

But he resisted her. Only by dint of half pushing, half pulling, did she manage to get him back to bed. He seemed dazed;
as if he were moving in a dream. And though, during the
hours that followed, she sometimes believed he slept, she herself did not dare to close her eyes, so great was the fright he
had given her.

But Mahony slept as little as she did. With his back to her,
withdrawn from any chance contact, he merely put into practice an art learned in scores of wakeful nights: that of lying
taut as the dead, while the long hours ticked away. Let her
think what she chose! . . . think him asleep—*or* dead . . . as
long as she held her cruel tongue. His hatred of her passed

imagining: his mind was a seething cauldron of hate and fury.
Fury with himself. For he had been within an ace of deliver-
ance, of getting through that door; beyond which lay everything his heart desired: space . . . freedom . . . peace. One and
all drenched in the moon's serene light. This light it was that
drew him; affecting him as do certain scenes or people, which,
on seeing them for the first time, you feel you have known
long since . . . in dreams, in a dream life. The sea, too, lay
without. Seas . . . silvered masses . . . leaping and tumbling
under a great round moon. And then, at the last moment, he
had been baulked of his freedom by the knowledge that he
was grown too tall for the doorway. To pass through it, he
would have needed to risk knocking his head against the door-
post, or to stoop; and, to-night, either alternative was beyond
him. His poor head felt so queer . . . so queer. Top-heavy, yet
weightless as a toy balloon. Already, on first laying it down, he
had had the old sensation of sinking through the pillow; of
falling, headforemost, into nothingness. Hence, he dared not
risk a blow; or the dizzy fit stooping would entail. And so
he had been caught and dragged back; made a prisoner of . . .
yet once more. But this time should be the last! Revenge!
. . . revenge is sweet. Vengeance is mine, saith the Lord: I will
repay! Fill the house with strangers, would she?—*his* house!
Cut the ground from under his feet?—deprive him of his only
haven? . . . why! even a rabbit had its burrow. To be without
covert; to know no place to creep to, for hiding, when the fit,
the burning need of escape seized him?— And then his eyes!
What in God's name should he do with his eyes? Strangers
at his table? On your p's and q's with strangers; aye, and on
the watch, too, lest they should find you out. And for all this
he had only Mary to thank—Mary, who might have been expected to show mercy. She? As well as blood of a stone!— And
now such a paroxysm of hatred shook him: the outcome, solid-
ified, intensified, of thousands of conflicts; of the ceaseless
clash and war of their opposing temperaments: that it was all
he could do to master the itch his fingers felt to close round
her throat. But he would be even with her yet! . . . somehow
. . . somehow . . . though he did not yet know how. *But . . . it
would have to do with money!* For it was money she was
after: with her it had always been money, from first to last.

What new tricks was she hatching this time? Was it going to *cost* money to take these lodgers in? Or was she doing it to *make* money? He was so confused to-night; his poor brain seemed smothered in cobwebs. But it didn't matter: either way would do. As long as he remembered that *it had to do with money.* And surely, surely, the long night would now soon end, and day break, and he be free to get up and set about what had to be done. (His home, his poor home, his sole refuge . . . eyes . . . greenish eyes in the moonlight, coming towards him, and, most horribly, without any accompanying face!) First, though, he would have to pull himself together, to endure in silence, without an answering shriek, the blast of the mill-whistle—that thrice-accursed, infernal din! Not much more than an hour now, till it was due to sound.

At breakfast he sat silent, seemed lost in thought. And Mary, to whom the dark hours had brought no clearness—every way she turned seemed barred to her—watched him, the passion of pity that had been wakened by the sight of his poor old scraggy form at the door in the moonlight, trying to escape from her—from *her!*—still hot in her.

But the meal over, he roused to a kind of life. Taking his little favourite on his knee, he caressed her. And then, of a sudden, he grew solicitous about the children: their morning walk, their daily dip in the sea. "Or"—to Lucie this, as he rocked her to and fro—"we shall not have them growing up tall and sturdy!" (If only he could hold on to the fact that *it had to do with money.*)

"Trust me to look after them," said Mary shortly, at a third repetition. Her own thoughts ran: If I can't talk to some one I shall go crazy. Something will have to be done. I know. There's old Mrs. Spence. She is so wise.

Would he never be rid of them? It seemed this morning as if Mary deliberately invented jobs to detain them. He fell to pacing the dining-room, his arms a-swing . . . and each time he came to the window he lifted his eyes in alarm, lest the flag should have run up the flagstaff. A ship at this moment would ruin everything.

But . . . softly! Mary was growing suspicious. "Are you stopping at home, then?"

"Yes, yes, I'm staying in. I'll look after the house." (Ha, ha!)

And at last gowns and towels, spades and buckets were

collected, the children's hats and her bonnet tied on, and off they went. It was a radiant summer morning, with a light breeze playing, but Mary saw nothing of it: her brain continued its feverish work, in the hope of finding some way out. Suppose I induced him to leave home for a time?—to go away for a holiday? . . . and so get the house to myself. Or even persuaded him to put up at a hotel. But before she had gone any distance she became aware of such a strange inner excitement, that it was only with difficulty she mastered an impulse to turn and go back to the house. Why had he been so anxious to get rid of them? Why this sudden odd concern for the children?— And here there leapt into her mind a story she had once read, or heard, of somebody who had sent his wife and his children out for a walk, and then deliberately hanged himself on a nail behind the scullery-door. But, this half-born apprehension spoken out, she fell righteously foul of herself: her reason, her common sense, that part of her which had waged a life-long war with the fantastic, the incorporeal, rose in arms. Such *nonsense!* Really . . . if one began to let oneself go. . . . (Besides, wasn't Bridget constantly in and out of the scullery?) Imaginings like these came solely from want of sleep. How angry Richard would be, too, if she reappeared!

So she went on, as usual making Cuffy the scapegoat for her nervous perplexity. "Don't eat your bathing-dress, you naughty boy! How often am I to tell you . . ."

"I'm *not* eating it! Only smelling."— He did though, sometimes. (And his sponge, too.)

"Well, that's not nice either."

"It *is!* It's scrumptious," cried Cuffy warmly. How did Mamma know? . . . she never bathed. The salty smell—and the taste—of damp blue serge when it was hot with the sun—ooh! too lovely for words. If he put it to his nose, he could hardly keep his legs from running: it made him shiver all over, simply not able to *wait,* to be in the water. And directly they came to the Bluff, he bolted: shot along the narrow wooden bridge that ran out from the beach, past the counter where gowns and towels were for hire, and into the Baths, where nothing but gowns and towels were hanging on the rails to dry, all one big salty smell. And you poked your nose into every empty cabin, to find a dry one; and then, hi! off with your clothes,

before Luce and Mamma got there, and into your gown, hot
with the sun, and all prickly and tickly; and then you galloped
round the platforms and out on the springboard, which
bounced you ever so high in the air, into water they said was
fifteen feet deep, but you didn't know, only if you jumped
straight, and made yourself quite stiff, you went down and
down, and took ever such a time to come up. Then you swam
back to the steps—all slimy, and with seaweed washing round
them, for they weren't ever out of the water—and up and off
the board again, again and again, till it was time to fetch
Luce, who was afraid to jump springboard.

"If I'm not back in an hour, make them come out," Mary
instructed the fat bathing-woman, who knew what young
water-rats the chicks were, and could be trusted to use force
if necessary.— And with this she turned to go.

But she had done no more than set foot on the wooden
causeway, when she saw some one dash on to it from the
other end, push rudely past a group of people, a servant it was
. . . and it was *Bridget,* with her hair half down, in her dirty
morning apron . . . and she came rushing up to her and seized
her hand, and pulled her by it, and sobbed and cried, for
everyone to hear: "Oh, Mrs. Mahony, come home! . . . come
home quick! The doctor's bin and lighted a fire on the surgery
table. He's burning the house down!"

"Bridget!"

Her heart, which had begun to hammer at first sight of
the girl, gave a gigantic bound, then seemed to stop beating:
she had to lean against the wooden railing and press both
hands to it, to get it to re-start. But, even so, she heard her
own voice saying: "Be quiet! Don't make such noise. There
are people . . . I'm coming, I'm coming!"

Home! Uphill, through loose, clogging sand; a short cut
over the grass of the gardens; along one reddish street and
into another, and round into a third; hampered at every step
by her long, heavy woman's clothing; not daring to run, for
fear of exciting comment, struggling even yet, for Richard's
sake, to keep up appearances; the perspiration glistening below her bonnet, her breath coming stormily; but with only one
thought: that of being in time to save him. At her side, Bridget,
gasping out her story. If it hadn't bin that he hadn't had no
matches, she'd never have known. But he'd had to come to the

kitchen for some, and she'd seen at once there was something in the wind. He'd looked at her, oh, ever so queer! And first he'd tried to take 'em without her seeing him . . . and when she had, he'd laughed, and had went up the passage laughing away to himself. She'd gone after him on tiptoe to see what he was up to, and she'd peeped through the crack of the door, and he'd got that black tin box of his open, and was taking papers and tied-up things out of it, piling 'em on the table, and striking matches, and setting fire to 'em. Holy Mother o' God, *how* she'd run!

There was smoke in the passage. The surgery was full of it; full of bits of flying ash and burnt papers. Through this she saw Richard. He stood at the table, the deal top of which was scorched and blackened, his dispatch-box open and empty before him, his hands in a heap of ashes which he was strewing about the room. He laughed and shouted. She heard her own name.

"*Richard!* My God! What have you done?"

Mary? . . . Mary's voice? Recoiling, he threw up his arms as if to ward off a blow, looking round at her with a face that was wry and contorted. At the sight of her standing in the doorway, he tried to shake his fist at her; but his arm crumpled up, refused to obey; tried to hurl a scurrilous word . . . to spit at her: in vain. What did happen was the thing against which, waking and sleeping, he had battled with every atom of his failing self-control: there escaped him, at long last, the scream, the insane scream, which signified the crossing of the Rubicon. And, as it broke loose, ringing in his ears like the bestial cry of a wounded, maddened animal, everything turned black before his eyes. He lost his balance, staggered, caught at a chair and went down, with the chair on top of him, like an ox felled by a single blow of the pole-axe. And there he lay, in a confused and crumpled heap on the floor.

And Mary, whom no audible sound had reached, who had read into the outward fling of his arm towards her only an appeal for help, for support, was on her knees beside him, her bonnet awry, her dress in disarray, crushing the poor old head to her breast, and crying: "Richard! *My darling!* What is it, oh, what is it?"

But to these words, with which she had so often sought enlightenment, sought understanding, there was now no reply.

[5]

His stertorous breathing could be heard through the house. Except for this, he might have been dead . . . behind the snow-white dimity and muslin hangings which she had put up in honour of those strangers who would now never cross the threshold. For Bowes-Smith, the well-known Melbourne physician, whom she had called in on the advice of Dr. Barker—yes! with Richard lying senseless at her feet, she had forgotten everything but his need, and had sent Bridget flying for the old man whom she had borne so bitter a grudge; and he had come at once, and been kindness itself. So active, too: it was hard to believe that he was between twenty and thirty years Richard's senior—oh, how *did* some people manage to live so long and be so healthy! But in spite of his consoling words, she could see that he took a very grave view of Richard's case. And Bowes-Smith and he had had a sheerly endless consultation—from which, of course, they shut her out—after which the former had broken it to her that, even if he recovered from the present fit, Richard would remain more or less of a sick man for the rest of his life.

The utmost care was essential; an entire absence of excitement. "For I cannot conceal from you that such apoplecti-form attacks, which—as in this case—differ little or not at all from true apoplexy, will be liable to recur."

He stood on the dining-room hearthrug, tall, lugubrious, sandy-whiskered, holding his gold-rimmed pince-nez in his hand, and tapping the air with it, while he cast about for his words, which came laboriously. They had known him well in the old days, and she remembered this habit; it had always made him seem something of a bore. Now, it maddened her. For she was keyed up to hear the truth, learn the worst; and, to be obliged to sit there, listening to him stumbling and fumbling! He was so bland, too, so non-committal; how differently he would have talked to Richard, had she lain ill! But she was only a woman; and, doctors being what they were . . . oh, she knew something about them from the inside! Usen't Richard to say that it was etiquette in the profession to treat a patient's relatives, and particularly his womenfolk, as so many cretins?

Ignoring her blunt question: "But if it isn't true apoplexy,

then what is it?" Bowes-Smith proceeded deliberately to cate-
chise her.

"I don't know, Mrs. Mahony, whether you are . . . h'm . . .
whether it is . . . er . . . news to you that I saw your husband,
some two or three months back? He . . . er . . . consulted me,
at the time, with regard to . . . h'm . . . to an attack . . . nay,
to recurring attacks of vertigo. I found him then under no . . .
h'm . . . no delusion as to his own state. He said nothing to
you? Did not take you into his confidence?"

"No, nothing," said Mary dully: and inconsequently remembered the letter she had had from him when she was trying to
induce him to settle in Narrong. She hadn't known then what
to believe; had more than half suspected him of writing as he
did, to further his own ends.

"And you have not noticed anything . . . h'm . . . out of the
way? There has been no marked change in his habits? No . . .
er . . . oddness, or eccentricity?" The questions lumbered
along, she sitting the while fiercely knotting her fingers.

"Nothing," she said again. Adding, however, in spite of herself: "But then he has always been peculiar. If he did seem a
little odder, of late, I merely put it down to his growing old."

"Quite so . . . er . . . most natural!" (She was keeping things
back, of course; wives always did. He remembered her well:
a handsome creature she had been, when last he saw her. The
eyes were still very striking.) "And how . . . er . . . with regard
to the present attack. Are you aware of anything having happened to . . . er . . . cause him undue excitement . . . or agitation?"

"No," said Mary staunchly. How could it matter now, what
had brought the fit on? Wild horses would not have dragged
from her any allusion to their bitter quarrel of the night before. That would have meant turning out, to this stranger, the
dark side of their married life. However, she again glossed
over the bluntness of her denial with: "But he was always one
to work himself up over trifles."

"Well, well! My colleague here . . . and if, at any time, you
would care to see me again, I am entirely at your disposal."
(No need to trouble the poor creature with more, at present.
Yes, truly, a magnificent pair of optics!) "Do not be . . . h'm
. . . alarmed at any slight . . . er . . . stiffness or rigidity of the
limbs that may ensue. That will pass."

And I a doctor's wife! thought Mary hotly. Aloud she said: "Oh, I'm not afraid—of paralysis or anything—as long as he is spared." And while the two men confabbed anew, she went to the bedroom and stood looking down at Richard. Her own husband! . . . and she could not even be told frankly what was the matter with him. For twenty-five years and more, she had had him at her side, to give her the truth if she asked for it. She had never known, till now, how much this meant to her.

Meanwhile, however, she spilt no jot of her strength in brooding or repining: every act, every thought, was concentrated on him alone. And not till the first signs of betterment appeared: when the dreadful snoring ceased, and his temperature fell to normal; when his eyes began to follow her about the room; when he was able to move one hand to point to what he wanted: not till then did she sit down, cold and grim, to face the future.

"My God! what's to become of us?"

A pitiful forty-odd pounds that stood to his credit in a Melbourne bank, and her own poor remnant of Tilly's loan, was literally all they had in the world. In that last mad holocaust everything else had gone: deeds and mortgages, letters and securities, down to the last atom of scrip. He had piled and burnt, till the dispatch-box was empty. Who would now be able to prove what shares he had held? Or how much had been paid off on the mortgage? The house at Barambogie was still on their hands; and almost the whole of their lease at Shortlands had still to run. How were these rents to be met? . . . and what would happen if they weren't? She would need expert advice, probably have to employ a lawyer—a thought that made her shiver. For she had the natural woman's fear of the law and its followers: thought of these only in terms of bills of costs . . . and sharp, dishonest practices.

But that must all come later. The burning question was where to turn for ready money. The little she had would go nowhere: Richard's illness . . . presents to the doctors, the servant's wages—nor could they live on air. Boarders were out of the question, now: for Richard's sake. *What* could she do? What did other women do, who were left in her plight, with little children dependent on them?— Driving her mind back, she saw that, as a rule, these "widows and things" were content to live at somebody else's expense, to become the limpets known as "poor relations," leaving the education of their children to a male relative. But she had not been Richard's wife for nothing. At the mere thought of such a thing, her back stiffened. Never! Not as long as she had a leg to stand on! . . . mere woman though she was.

"It's not money I want this time, Tilly," she wrote: and Tilly was but one of many, who, the news of Richard's breakdown having spread abroad as on an invisible telegraph, came forward with offers of help. "It's work. I don't care what; if only I can earn enough to keep us together." But here, even Tilly's ingenuity failed her: women of Mary's standing (let alone her advanced age, her inexperience) did not turn out of their sheltered homes and come to grips with the world. Impossible, utterly impossible, was to be read between the lines of her reply.

And, as day after day went by, without enlightenment, it began to look as if Tilly was right. Beat her brains as she would, Mary could find no way out.

To old Mrs. Spence, who, in this crisis, had proved a friend indeed, she finally made a clean breast of her despair.

"There seems literally nothing a woman *can* do. Except teach—and I'm too old for that. Nor have I the brains. I was married so young. And had so little schooling myself. No, the plain truth is, I'm fit for nothing. Really, there come moments when I can see us all ending in the Benevolent Asylum."

It was here that Mrs. Spence, nodding her sage, white-capped head in sympathy, made the tentative suggestion: "I wonder, my dear . . . has it never occurred to you to try to enter Government service?"

Mary winced . . . she hoped not too perceptibly. "Oh, I'm afraid that, again, would need more brains than I've got." It was well meant, of course, but . . . *so* to cut oneself adrift!

Undaunted, the old lady went on. "Plenty of women before you have done it. As a postmistress, you would have a house rent-free, with free lighting and firing, all sorts of perquisites, and a fixed salary. And I think, my dear, with the many friends you have at court, it would be easy for you to skip preliminaries. My son, I know, would be only too happy to help you in any way he could."

"You're very kind. But I feel sure I'm too old . . . and too stupid."

But that night, as she tossed wakeful on the hard little bed she had set up beside Richard's, her friend's words came back to her, and rang in her ears till they had effectually chased away all chance of sleep: so spurred and pricked her, in fact, that she sat up in bed and, hunching her knees, propped her elbows on them and dug her clenched fists into her chin. A house rent-free . . . nothing to pay for light and firing . . . a fixed salary!—she didn't know how much, of course, but it would need to be enough to support a family on, so many post-masters were married men. It would also mean that she could keep Richard and the children with her; and the fear of having to part from them was the worst she knew. And then those rents, those dreadful rents, which hung round her neck like millstones . . . might she not perhaps . . . But, oh, the come-down! . . . the indignity . . . the *publicity* of the thing!—in this colony where she had been so well known. A postmistress . . . she a postmistress! . . . forced to step out into the open, be-come a kind of public woman. To see her name—*Richard's* name—in printed lists, in official communications. (She might even have to tell her age.) Men—strange men—would be over her, she their subordinate, answerable to them for what she did. Worse still, she herself would have men under her, young men, of a class with which she had never come in contact. What would her friends and acquaintances say, to see her sink like this in the social scale? (At which, however, her native plain-dealing jogged her elbow, with the reflection that it would soon show who were true friends, and who not.) Oh, it was easy to *say* you didn't mind what you turned your hand to. But when it came to doing it!— And then, too, suppose she wasn't equal to the work? As she had said, and truly, she had no faith in her own abilities. Directly it came to book or head-learning, she thought of herself as dull and slow. Though here, oddly enough, the thought perked up and declined to be quenched, that, if Richard had only let her have a say, how-ever small, in the management of his affairs, these might never have got into the muddle they had. Figures didn't come hard to her.

Thus was she tossed and torn, between a womanly repug-nance, her innate self-distrust, and her sound common sense. And she got up in the morning still having failed to reconcile the combatants. It was the sight of Richard that determined her. When she saw him sitting propped up among his pillows, his lower jaw on the shake; when she heard his pitiful attempts to say what he wanted—like a little child he was having to be taught the names of things all over again—when she looked at this wreck, every other consideration fell away. What did she matter? . . . what did anything or anybody matter?—if only she could restore to health, and contrive to keep, in something of the comfort he had been used to, this poor old comrade of the years!

Henry Ocock held office in the present ministry; and it was to Mr. Henry she turned; for she considered that they had a common bond in the memory of poor Agnes. She wrote, without hedging, of Richard's utter physical collapse; of the loss—through fire—of his papers and securities; the urgent necessity she was under of finding employment. It had been suggested to her that she might try to enter Government service. Would he, for the sake of their old friendship, do her the great kindness to use his influence, on her behalf, with the present Postmaster General? Mr. Spence, in charge of the local office, had offered her the preliminary training. Had this not been so . . . "for I tell you plainly, I could never go in for an examination —try to pass the Civil Service, or anything of that sort. It would be quite beyond me."

Almost by return she held a page-long telegram in her hand, in which, making no attempt (as she had half feared he would) to press a loan on her. Mr. Henry said that he was only too happy to be able to help her. Her request came in the nick of time. An up-country vacancy was on the point of occurring. Did she think she could be ready, with Spence's aid, to take over charge there, say, in six weeks' time? If so, the P.M.G. would put in a relieving officer for that period. The rush and hurry of the thing cut the ground from under her feet. Hardly knowing whether she stood on her head or her heels, she straightway telegraphed acceptance.— And so the die was cast.

Henceforward, she was a member of the working classes. To begin with, she spent every afternoon, from two till six, at the Shortlands post office, learning her job.

The calvary this was to her, none but she knew. She would never have believed she was so sensitive, so touchy. A host of prejudices (many of them no doubt imbibed from Richard) which she hadn't even been aware of possessing, woke to life in her. The very fact of being tied down to leave home at a set hour, like any clerk or shopman, seemed to humiliate her, who had never come and gone but at her own sweet will. Then, every one in the township knew, of course, where she was bound for. People eyed her, and whispered about her, and pointed her out to one another as she passed: in her full silk skirts flounced to the waist, her dolman of silk velvet, her feathered bonnet: yes, there she went, Mrs. Dr. Mahony, off to learn to be a postmistress! The half-mile seemed unending; before she reached her destination her pale cheeks were dyed rose-pink.

In the office she stood, a middle-aged lady (close on two-and-forty years old) bonnetless and capless, amid a posse of young clerks: the telegraph operator, the messenger, the indoor clerk, the postman: to whom she was an object of unending curiosity. All of whom, too, could do in a twinkling the things that came so hard to her. And then their manners! They jostled her, failed to apologise, kept their hats on in her presence, lolled and lounged, bandied private jokes, laughed and talked openly in disregard of her, did Mr. Spence quit the office. Her courage might sometimes have failed her, had it not been that the money side of the business gave her so little trouble: she learnt in no time how to issue a money-order, to enter up a savings-book deposit, to handle postage stamps and registered letters; even to draw up the financial "statement" that was forwarded daily and monthly to Head Office. The telegraph it was that baffled her. Oh, this awful Morse code! It was like going to school again, to learn one's alphabet. Her memory was weak and undeveloped: she floundered and was hopelessly at sea amid the array of dots and dashes that stood for letters. The little paper handbook containing the code grew as shabby and dog's-eared as a child's lesson book. For she carried it with her everywhere she went, and slept with it under her pillow; of a night often starting up and striking a match to see if it was B that had three dots after its dash, or K more than one between its two. *Never* would she be able to "take by ear"! How she marvelled at these young clerks, who could jot down a whole telegram without so much as a glance at the tape. Whereas she had painfully to puzzle the message out, letter by letter. And the "sending" was harder still: with her lips pinched thin, her head thrown back, her black eyes fixed, in desperate concentration, on the empty air, laboriously she hammered out dash and dot, dot and dash.

All this, too, with one anxious ear turned towards home, where things grew worse instead of better. She had hoped that, once the physical effects of the stroke had worn off, and Richard was able to walk and talk again, his mind, too, would clear. Now, she began to doubt whether he would ever again be *quite* himself. Days came when he sat and brooded from morning till night: sat with his head on one thin hand, staring before him with eyes so sorrowful that it hurt you to look at them . . . though what he was thinking or remembering, she could never get him to say. At other times, he was unable to be still, or to stay in the same room for a minute on end; and then it took all her influence and persuasion to keep him indoors. The children, poor mites, in whose charge she was forced to leave him while she worked, could do nothing with him, and her first question of the forlorn little pair who ran to meet her, of an evening, was invariably: "Where's Papa?" To which more often than not the answer came: "Gone out. He *would* go, Mamma . . . we couldn't stop him. He went to look for you."

And then it was always: "Run, Cuffy, run quick! . . . and find him."

Once Cuffy had said: "Oh, can't Bridget go instead of me?" but Mamma had looked so funny at him that he'd never done it again. He went; his hands cold like frogs. For he was so ashamed. Papa would be standing on the green in front of the blacksmith's, and the blacksmith had stopped work, and a whole lot of larrikins were there as well, and they were all listening to Papa . . . who was sort of play-acting to himself, with his hands . . . and laughing at him and making fun. And Papa didn't see them; but *he* did. And then he wished Papa was dead, and that he didn't ever need to come and fetch him again. But he took his hand and said, quite small: "Papa, come home! Mamma wants you." And then he left off acting direckly, and was most awfully glad and said: "Where is she? Where *is* Mamma?" and came away, holding on to his hand like a little girl, and nearly running to get there.

That was one thing he hated. The other was, every afternoon Mamma went out and left him and Luce quite alone . . . with Papa. (And you didn't *like* to be with Papa, since he couldn't speak right: when you heard him say a spoon and he meant a chair, it made you feel sick inside, like when you saw a snake.) You were supposed to practise while Mamma was out, and you did; but your thoughts went on thinking and thinking; and it was always the same: suppose she *never* came back! Luce cried all the time. And then Papa came and was almost crying, too, and said: "Oh, *where* is Mamma? Will she never come home?" and he must go out and look for her. And it got tea-time, and nearly bedtime, and still she didn't come; and every time you looked at the clock only five minutes had gone, and it seemed like an hour. And at last it got so bad you went and stood down at the gate, or a little way in the road, and waited for the first bit of her to come round the corner.— And then, oh, how they ran! At least Luce did. He just whistled. For each time, once he saw Mamma safe again, he didn't seem to care a bit any more.

The day she told them they'd got to go away and live where there wasn't any sea, he'd been naughty. He'd cried and stamped, and pushed people when they tried to comfort him. But it wasn't a *real* "naughty": it was just something inside him and he couldn't stop it happening. No more springboard, no more lovely blue water to jump down into, no more hot salty smells. In his prayers at night, and in secret prayers offered up in corners of the garden, he begged and prayed God to let them stop there, or at least to let there be another sea where they were going. But God just didn't seem to hear.

They weren't to take their toys with them either, their great big best toys. They had to be sold. Mamma was sorry; but they simply hadn't got enough money for what it would cost to take the rocking-horse . . . or the doll's-house . . . or Cuffy's big grocer's-shop . . . or Luce's huge doll's-p'rambulator. Each of them would have needed a packing-case to itself.

Both he and Luce prayed about this, kneeling down in the long thick grass that grew behind the closet, with their eyes tight shut, and their hands put properly together; and he told Luce what to say. But it was no good. God wasn't there.

Or if He was, He liked Luce best. For by-and-bye she was allowed to take her doll with her, the big, baby one. Mamma said it was because she could carry it; but he b'lieved it was because Luce had cried so much. Of course you couldn't carry Dobbin, or the shop; but, my! it *did* hurt to think of anybody else sitting on the saddle, or using the scales. He took a pencil and wrote "My horse" in big letters under Dobbin's stomach, and cut a bunch of hairs out of his tail for a keepsake. And then, as God still didn't do anything, he *stole* something; took away a little bag of sugar and a tiny wee tin of biscuits out of the shop, and hid them; and when he told Luce, she did, too, and took a little sofa from the doll's-house drawing-room. But afterwards a man came with a pencil and book, and Mamma said he was going to write down the name of every single thing that was for sale, and then Luce got afraid, and told, and asked Mamma if she might keep it, and Mamma said no, it wouldn't be honest; and so she put it back. But he didn't; he stayed a thief; and said if Luce told on him, he'd put out both her doll's eyes.

Mamma, she didn't leave things behind . . . what *she* wanted. When Bridget fetched down from the top of the wardrobe those dirty old cork-boards, with butterflies pinned to them—most of them had got their wings knocked off them now—and old glass boxes with bits of stone in them, and dead flowers, and asked Mamma what to do with all this rubbish, Mamma said, give them here, and how she wouldn't part with them, not for anything in the world. And he said, then he didn't see why he couldn't take his horse; and Mamma was cross, and said little boys didn't know everything, but when he was as old as she was, he'd understand. But he did now: it was because they were Papa's. And when he said so, she sat back on her legs and went very red, and looked angry at him, and said: "What in the name of fortune is all this fuss for about that wretched animal? You know you hardly ever ride it now! It's too small."

"I don't care . . . it's mine!"

"Well, *I* think that's a very selfish way of looking at it.—Besides, where we're going, if we arrive with big, expensive toys, people will think we've come there under false pretences."

"And then?"

"Then we might be turned out."

Cuffy paled. "Is that because it's going to be a post office?"

"Yes. And now I hope you'll leave off pestering."

The day the oxshun was, millions of people walked about the house just as if it was theirs. He and Luce went to Granny's;

and Pauline took them for a bathe and let him stop in till his teeth trembled. But a few days after, they had to get up again in the middle of the night, and a buggy came to the door, and Mamma and Papa got in, and all their trunks and portmanteaux, and droved to the pier. A funny little steamer was there, and it was pitch dark; they had to go on board with a lantern. And they sat in a teeny-weeny saloon that was the shape of a heart, with one lamp hanging in the middle; and it was so dark you could hardly see your faces. And there was nobody else. Luce went to sleep; and Mamma was sick; but in between, when she felt better, she tried to pull the rug up round Papa—it would slip off . . . she was always very kind to Papa now. But Papa was angry. He said: "I don't *like* this, Mary; it's not what I've been accustomed to. There's something hole-and-corner about it." And she patted his hand: "But so nice and private, dear. We've got it all to ourselves." But Papa went on talking about who he was, and the kind of ships he'd travelled in, till Mamma told him how cheap it was, and what a lot of money it was going to save her. And then he began to cry, and cried and cried—and the captain (Mamma said) came in and looked at him—till he went to sleep. But *he* couldn't sleep. He'd always thought, even if they had to go away, there would be the beautiful steamer to sail on, with a big deck, and lots of people, and the band playing. Now he knew, because of Papa, they weren't good enough for big steamers any more. And it seemed just hours he lay and watched the lamp swing, and listened to Mamma being sick, and the waves making a noise on the sides; and always more strange men—sailors and things—came in and pretended to be busy. But he believed just so they could take a good look at Papa, who was asleep now, with his head hanging down and his mouth wide open, making funny noises . . . not like a grown-up gentleman any more.

[6]

THEIR destination was a place called Gymgurra, in the Western District, some two hundred miles from Melbourne; to be reached either by a night's sea voyage—round Cape Otway, and along the wild coast—or by a combined train and coach journey. With the ordeal of "taking over charge" before her,

Mary dared not risk the physical upset of a voyage. So, at Colac she got out of the train and into the mail coach, to lumber, the night through, over the ruts and jolts of bush roads, Lucie a dead weight on her lap, Cuffy lying heavily up against her.

There were only the three of them; Richard had had to be left behind. It had torn her heart to part from him, to hand him over to strangers; but not only Bowes-Smith, every one she consulted had advised against the fatigues of the journey for him, in his present state. So she had yielded—and not for his sake alone. In the beginning she would need to give her whole mind to her new work. Richard would be better looked after where he was. Thanks to Bowes-Smith she had managed to get him into a kind of private hospital, where he would live in comfort, under a doctor's eye.

At Toorak, the place was, standing in its own beautiful grounds: there were shrubberies and summer-houses, a croquet-lawn, a bowling-green, fruit and flower-gardens; the mere sight of which had a good effect on Richard. He brightened up, carried himself more erectly—even gave himself proprietary airs, as they walked together through the gardens. None the less, when the time for parting came, he wept bitterly, clinging like a child to her skirts. She had to romance about how soon she was coming back to fetch him—all the doctor thought it wise for him to be told, in the meanwhile, was that she was travelling on ahead to set the new house in order: he surely remembered how he had hated the bother and confusion of moving? And by now he was too deeply sunk in himself to put awkward questions. Not once, since his attack, had he troubled his head about ways and means, of where to-morrow's dinner was to come from. It was pitiable to see; and yet . . . she couldn't find it in her heart to grudge him the peace and content this indifference brought him. The doctors called it euphobia.

The one thing he did ask, again like a timid child, was: "Mary, it's not that place . . . that other place, Mary . . . the one with the whistle . . . and the . . . the . . . the canal, we're going back to, is it?"

"No, no, dear, indeed it's not! It's somewhere quite new; where there'll be all sorts of fresh things for you to see and do. And till then, Richard, think how comfortable you're going

to be here! Your own room, your own books; and this armchair by the window, so that you can sit and look out at the
flowers, and watch the croquet, and see all that happens."

But something else still wormed in him. "Who will—Mary,
will you . . . will they let me . . . clean . . . clean collars, Mary
. . . and those other things . . . hankchiefs?"

Here one had a glimpse of the old Richard, with his fastidious bodily habits. Mary got a frog in her throat over it. But
she answered sturdily enough: "Of course, they will! As many
as you like. And be sure, my darling, if there's anything you
don't feel quite happy about, to let me know, and I'll have it
put right at once."

As indeed there should be no difficulty in doing, considering
what she was paying. Though this, again thanks to Bowes-
Smith—and the fact of Richard being a medical man—was
only the half of what was charged an ordinary patient: five
guineas a week instead of ten. Even so, it was a desperately
heavy drain. She had put by as much as she dared towards
it—seventy pounds—from the sale of the furniture, so in the
meantime he was safe. When this was gone, she could but
hope and pray he would be well enough to come home.

Out of what remained of the auction money, together with
Richard's deposit and her own small savings, she had at once
paid off a quarter's rent on each of the houses. Neither was
yet due . . . and when Sir Jake heard what she had done, he
rather called her over the coals for so unbusiness-like a proceeding. But he didn't know—how could he?—the load it took
from her mind to know these things settled. With her, in the
coach, she carried three little packets of notes, two of which,
screwed up in old pieces of newspaper, and tied securely and
privately to her body, were towards the next quarter again.
The third lay in her sealskin handbag, and was for the expenses of the journey, and the purchasing of a few sticks of
furniture. It had been a sad blow to learn that the salary
attached to the Gymgurra post office was only eighty pounds
a year. Eighty pounds! Could she and the children possibly
live on that? And what, when Richard came, too? Of course
there was always a chance the house at Shortlands might find
a tenant—houses were so scarce there—even though the summer was by now half over. In which case, she would be some
pounds to the good. Jerry, too, in whose hands she had left

the affair of the perished documents, did not despair of retrieving *something* from the general ruin. But herself add a penny to her income she could not: as a Government servant her hands were tied.

Over these reckonings, the night wore away. (It would be money, always money now, she supposed, to the bitter end.) Still, she did not fail to send a warm thought back to the dear friends who had stood by her in her trouble. The Devines had not only housed them all, but had called in their own medical man to Richard, had helped her to make arrangements at the hospital, to interview doctor and matron. Lady Devine, too—notwithstanding her corpulence—had promised to visit Richard weekly and report on his progress. Old Sir Jake, with her hand in both of his, had gone as near as he dared towards offering her a substantial loan. Mr. Henry had driven out to tell her that Mr. Vibert, the Deputy P.M.G., was in receipt of special instructions with regard to her case; while the postmaster at the nearest town of any size to Gymgurra had orders to give her what help she needed. More, said he, the house at Gymgurra had been enlarged by three rooms. Then, dear old Tilly had travelled down from Ballarat to see her; Jerry came all the way from Wangaratta. Not to speak of many a kindness shewn her by less intimate acquaintances.— And yet, in spite of this, Mary felt that she was seeing more than one of them for the last time. Still was she Mrs. Townshend-Mahony, the one-time member of Melbourne society. From now on, as plain Mrs. Mahony, postmistress, she would sink below their ken: she read it in their eyes when she announced what she was going to do; announced it bluntly, even truculently; for she was determined not to sail under false colours.

It was the same with her relatives. Lizzie, for instance: Lizzie, who still traded on past glories—and also, alas! went on hoarding up poor John's children—was loud in praise of her courage and independence. But a blind man could have seen her relief when she learnt that these virtues were to be practised at a distance. Jerry, of course, like the sensible fellow he was, ranged himself on her side—if he did seem a trifle unsure of Fanny—but Zara made no bones of her horrification.

"Have you really thought *seriously*, Mary, of what you are about to do? Of the publicity, the notoriety it will entail? For, no matter what has happened, you are still our poor, dear Richard's wife. And my one fear is, the odium may redound on him."

"Zara, I've thought till I could think no more. But it's either this, or the workhouse. People who are too good to know me any longer must please themselves. To tell the truth, I don't very much care.— But as for what I'm doing reflecting on *Richard* . . . no, that's too absurd!"

It wasn't really Richard, it was herself Zara was concerned for; and in how far having a postmistress for a sister would damage her prospects. Besides, never again, poor thing, would she be able to give Richard's name as a reference.— Ah, had Zara only been different! Then, the two of them, sisters, and bound by one of nature's closest ties, might have combined forces; Zara have managed the house, taught the children, even perhaps have augmented their slender joint incomes by opening a little school.

Thinking these things, Mary found she must have dozed off; for when, feeling extremely cold, she opened her eyes again, it was broad daylight. Daylight: and all around her what seemed to her the flattest, barest, ugliest country she had ever had the misfortune to see. Not a tree, not a bit of scrub, hardly so much as a bush, broke the monotony of these plains, these immeasurable, grassy plains: here, flat as pancake, there rolling a little up and down, or rising to a few knobbly hillocks, but always bare as a shorn head—except for lumps of blackish rock that stuck up through the soil. You could see for miles on every side, to where the earth met the sky. Another ugly feature was the extreme darkness of the soil; the long, straight road they drove was as black as all the other roads she had known had been white or red. A cloudy sky, black roads, bare earth: to Mary, lover of towns, of her kind, of convivial intercourse, the scene struck home as the last word in loneliness and desolation.

Even the children felt it. "Why are there no trees?" demanded Cuffy aggressively, the crosspatch he always was after a broken night. "I don't *like* it without."

And Lucie's echoing pipe: "Why are there no trees, Mamma?"

And then the place itself.

"Is *this* it! Is this *all?*" more resentfully still. "Then I think it's simply hidjus!"

"Oh, come! Don't judge so hastily."

But her own courage was at zero when, having clambered down from the coach, with legs so stiff that they would hardly carry her, she stood, a child on either hand, and looked about her.— Gymgurra! Two wide, ludicrously wide cross-roads, at the corners of which were clustered three or four shops, a bank, an hotel, the post office, the lock-up; one and all built of an iron-grey stone that was almost as dark as the earth itself. There were no footpaths, no gardens, no trees: indeed, as she soon learnt, in Gymgurra the saying ran that you must walk three miles to see a tree; which, however, was not quite literally true; for, on the skyline, adjoining a farm, there rose a solitary specimen . . . a unicum.

Their new home, the "Post and Telegraph Office," with, on its front, the large round clock by which the township told the time, stood at one of the corners of the cross-roads. Facing it was a piece of waste ground used for the dumping of rubbish: thousands of tins lay scattered about, together with old boots, old pots, broken crockery: its next-door neighbour was the corrugated-iron lock-up. Until now, it had consisted only of an office and two small living-rooms. For her benefit a three-roomed-weatherboard cottage had been tacked on behind. This poor little dingy exterior was bad enough; but, inside, it was even worse. The former postmaster had been a bachelor; and before she and the children could live in the rooms he had left, these would have to be cleaned from top to bottom, and the walls given a fresh coat of whitewash, to rid them of greasy smears and finger-marks, of the stains of flies and squashed spiders. In the wooden portion—two small bedrooms and a kitchen—all the workmen's sawdust and shavings still lay about. From the back door three crude wooden steps led to a yard which, except for the water tank, held only rubbish: bottles galore, whole and broken; old boxes; boots and crockery again; with, she thought, every kerosene-tin that had been emptied since the house was first built. Never a spadeful of earth had been turned.

Thank God, she had not brought Richard with her! The mere sight of such a place might have done him harm. By the time he came, poverty-stricken though it was, she would engage to have it looking very different. And this thought gave her the necessary fillip. Mastering her dismay, throwing off her discouragement with bonnet and mantle, she pinned back her skirts and fell to work. With the help of an old, half-blind woman—women seemed very scarce here—she swept and scrubbed and polished, in an effort to make the little house clean and sweet; to free it of a dirty man's traces. Then, perched cn top of a step-ladder, with her own hands she whitewashed walls and ceilings. After which, taking coach to the neighbouring coast town, she bought the few simple articles of furniture they needed.— And, for all her preoccupation over trying to make one pound go as far as two, she could not help smiling at Cuffy's dismay as he watched her purchase of a kitchen-table for use in the dining-room. "But we can't eat our dinner off *that*, Mamma!" he nudged her, politely under his breath, lest the shopman should hear, but with his small face one wrinkle of perplexity.

And her whispered assurance that a cloth would hide the deal top didn't help. Cuffy continued sore and ashamed. It wasn't only this table. There was the dressing-table, too; and the washstand: they were both *really* only empty packing-cases, stood on their sides and covered over with pink s'lesha and book-muslin, to look nice. And for long he lived in dread of some inquisitive person lifting up cloth or curtain to peep underneath. It would be like seeing Mamma found out in a story. (If he were there he would tell that one of the legs had come off the real things and they were away being mended. It didn't matter about *him*. But to think of Mamma turning cheat gave him a funny stiff ache in his chest.)

He wasn't, he knew, being very good just now; he didn't seem able to help it. It was so dull here; there was nothing to do—not even a piano to play your pieces on. Out of chips and a block of wood left by the builders, he cut little boats, which he and Luce sailed in the wash-tubs by the back door . . . with matches for masts, and bits of paper for sails. But you couldn't go on doing that always. And Luce soon got tired, and went to see that Mamma hadn't run away. You weren't allowed in the office, where there would have been the machine to look at, and letters in the pigeon-boxes (had somebody once kept pigeons in them?) and to see how stamps were sold. And the yard had palings round it so high that you couldn't see over them, only peep through the cracks. You weren't supposed to go out in the street. You did. But there wasn't anything there either. The streets were all just bare.

This was the first time they hadn't had a garden; and fiercely Cuffy hated the gaunt, untidy yard; the unfinished back to the house. There hadn't been much at Shortlands either, only pear-trees and grass; but he liked grass; especially if it nearly covered you when you sat down in it. At Barambogie there had been flowers, and the verandah, and lots of paths . . . and heaps and heaps of trees and wattle to go out and walk in. He could remember it quite well. And in a kind of vague way, he remembered other things, too. Somewhere, there had been straight black trees like steeples, that swept their tops about when the wind blew; lawns with water spraying on them; hairy white strawberries that somebody made you open your mouth to have popped into. And, vague and faint as these memories were, as little to be caught and held as old dreams, they had yet left him a kind of heritage, in the shape of an insurmountable aversion to the crude makeshifts and rough slovenliness of colonial life. His little sister, on the other hand, carried with her, as the sole legacy of her short years, only a wild fear lest, one sure prop having given way, the other should now also fail her. Except at her mother's side, little Lucie knew no rest. She had, as it were, eternally to stand guard over the parent who was left. And, to her baby mind, the one good thing about this poor, ugly place was that Mamma never went out. Not even to church: a state of things that threw Cuffy who, ever since he could toddle, had been walked to church on his mother's hand, into fresh confusion. What would God think? It wouldn't do for Him not to *like* Mamma any more, now she was so poor. And He'd said as plain as plain, Remember the Sabbath Day to keep it holy. Oh dear! he was only a little boy, and nobody took any notice of him; but what with boxes dressed up as tables, and a table that pretended to be mahogany, and now none of them going to church, he felt as if his world was turning upside down. And that it was one's *Mamma* who did it . . . who ought to know better; be perfect, without sin. . . .

Mary was unaware of these vicarious sufferings on her behalf: had neither time nor thought to spare for a child's

911

imaginary torments. She was never off her feet—from seven in the morning till long past midnight. For when the office closed, she had still the main part of her work to do: food to prepare for the next day; to wash and iron and sew: whatever happened, her children must be spotlessly turned out.

Very soon after arriving, she had given the relieving officer his congé. The man's manners were intolerable. It also came to her ears that he was going about the township saying: "By the Lord Harry, there's a pair of eyes for you!" Which explained why he and the boy who was her sole assistant sat stolidly by, not budging to help, while she answered knocks at the little window: to dole out a single penny stamp, sell a postcard, repeat, till she was tired: "Nothing to-day," to inquiries for letters. She thought every man in the place must have come rapping at the wooden shutter . . . to take a look at her! Once alone with the lad, however, she had small difficulty in keeping him in his place. He was a heavy, lumpish youth; clerk, operator, telegraph-messenger rolled in one. The trouble was, he was so often absent. For though no letters were carried out, yet had a telegram to be delivered, what with the long distances to be covered on foot, and the lad's incurable propensity for gossip, she would find herself deserted for hours at a time, on the run between "key" and window, getting her "statement" made up at any odd moment. Luckily enough, the money side of the business continued to come easy to her. The figures seemed just to fall into line and to add up of themselves.

Had there been the day's work only to contend with, she would not have complained. It was the nights that wore her down. The nights were cruel. On every one of them, without exception, between half-past one and a quarter to two, there came a knocking like thunder at the front door. This was the coach arriving with the night mail: she had to open up the office, drag a heavy mail-bag in, haul another out. Not until this was over, could there be any question of sleep for her.

Almost at once it became a nervous obsession (she, who had had such small patience with Richard's night fancies!) that, did she even doze off, she might fail to hear the knocking—calculated though this was to wake the dead!—fail in her duty, lose her post, bring them all to ruin. Hence, she made a point of sitting up till she could sit no longer, then of lying down fully dressed, watching the shadows thrown by the candle on walls and ceiling, listening to the children's steady breathing, the wind that soughed round the corners of the house.

But when the coach had rumbled off, the sound of wheels and hoofs died away, and she might have slept, she could not. The effort of rising, of pulling the bags about and exchanging words with the driver, had too effectually roused her. Also, the glimpse caught through the open door of the black darkness and loneliness without alarmed her each time afresh. For the country was anything but safe. The notorious Kellys had recently been at work in the district, and not so very far from Gymgurra, either; the township still rang with tales of their exploits. And after the Bank, the post office was the likeliest place to be stuck up, if not *the* likeliest; for the Bank Manager had a strong-room, and no doubt a revolver, too . . . besides being a man. While she was only a defenceless woman, with no companions but two small children. If the bushrangers should appear one night and order her to "bail up," while they rifled the office, she would be utterly at their mercy.

The result of letting her mind dwell on such things was that she grew steadily more awake; and till dawn would lie listening to every sound. Never did the cheering fall of a human foot pass the house. Unlit, unpatrolled, the township slept the sleep of the dead. Only the dingoes snarled and howled; at first a long way off, and then, more shrilly, near at hand. Or the old volcano that stood in its lake some three miles away— it was said to be extinct, but really one didn't know—would suddenly give vent to loud, unearthly rumblings; which sometimes became so violent that the jugs on the washstand danced and rattled. And then the children, who had learned to sleep through the bustle of the coach, would wake up, too, and be frightened; and she would have to light the candle again and talk to them, and give them drinks, and re-arrange their pillows.

"It's all right, chicks. There's nothing to be afraid of. Mamma's here."

This satisfied them: Mamma was there, hence all was well . . . as though she were a kind of demigod, who controlled even the eruptions of volcanoes! With Lucie cuddled tight in her arms, all the fragrance of the child's warm body mounting to her, she lay and thought of her children with a pity that left mere love far behind. They trusted her so blindly; and she, what could she do for them? Except for this imagined security, she had nothing to give. And should anything happen to her, while they were still too young to fend for themselves—no! that simply did not bear thinking of. She had seen too much of the fates of motherless children in this country. Bandied from one to another, tossed from pillar to post . . . like so much unclaimed baggage. Rather than know hers exposed to such a lot . . . yes, there came moments when she could understand and condone the madness of the mother who, about to be torn away, refused to leave her little ones behind. For, to these small creatures, bone of her bone, and flesh of her flesh, links bound Mary that must, she felt, outlast life itself. Through her love for them, she caught her one real glimpse of immortality.

[7]

But these were night thoughts. By day, when the children were their very human selves—high-spirited, quarrelsome, up to endless mischief—the question of Richard and Richard's welfare again took first place in her mind.

The improvement she had so hoped for him, in his pleasant care-free surroundings, did not come to pass. She saw this, not so much from what the doctors wrote—they were painfully guarded—as from his own letters to her. Week by week these grew more incoherent; not words only, whole sentences were now being left out. They were written, too, in a large, unformed, childish hand, which bore no likeness to his fine, small writing; were smudged and ill-spelt. She felt them as shameful, and, directly she had deciphered them, hid them away: no eye but hers should see to what depths he had sunk.

And the doctors kept up their non-committal attitude to the end: the end, that was, of the three months for which she had their fees laid by. Then, they were forced to come out of their shell; and, to her letter saying that she could no longer afford to leave her husband in their charge, and asking for a frank opinion on his case, they wrote her what she had feared and foreseen: there was no hope of recovery for Richard. His mental deterioration, since coming under their notice, had been marked; signs of arterial degeneration were now to be ob-

served, as well. Did she seriously contemplate removing him,
they could only advise his further restraint in one of the public
institutions. They trusted, however, that she would reconsider
her decision. On all points it would be to the patient's advantage.

In her distress, Mary crushed the letter to a ball in her hand.
To re-read it, she had to stroke and smooth it flat again. For
the step they were urging upon her meant the end of everything: meant certification; an asylum for the insane. (The
children's father a certified lunatic!) Yet, just because of the
children . . . This was an objection the doctors had raised, in
telling her that Richard might last for years—in his present
state—when she first proposed keeping him with her. They
would be doubly against it now. And for days she went irresolute, torn between pity for Richard and fear for the children. In the end it was once more Bowes-Smith who got the
better of her. He pointed out how little, for all her devotion,
she could do, to ameliorate her husband's lot, compared with
the skilled nursing he would receive from properly trained
attendants. Besides, Richard was, he assured her, by now too
far gone in inattention really to miss her or to need her. There
seemed nothing for it but gratefully to accept his offer, himself to take the affair in hand. Thanks to his influence, Richard
had a chance of being lodged in one of the separate cottages
at the asylum, apart from the crowd: he would be under a
special warder, have a bedroom more or less to himself. And
so, with a heavy heart, Mary gave her consent; the various
legal and medical formalities were set in motion; and, soon
after, the news came that the change had been made and Richard installed in his new quarters. His books and clothing were
being returned to her. (Prisoners—no, she meant patients
—were not allowed any superfluous belongings. Nor, bitter
thought! need she now rack her brains where the new suit was
to come from, for which his late nurse had pressed, because
of his growing habit of spilling his food. From now on, he
would wear the garb of his kind.) But, after this, she heard no
more: with the shutting of the gates behind him silence fell—
a horrible, deathlike silence. Never again did one of his pitiful
little letters reach her; and the authorities blankly ignored her
requests for information. Finally, in response to a more vigorous demand than usual, she received a printed form, stating

that reports were issued quarterly, and hers would reach her in due course. Grimly she set her teeth and waited; meanwhile laying shilling to shilling for the journey to Melbourne, which she could see lay before her.— But, when the time came, she had to part with a little brooch, to which she had clung because it had been Richard's first gift to her, after marriage. Mr. Rucker, the clergyman, bought it of her for his wife.

Her story was, of course, common property in Gymgurra by now; and it was just an example of people's kindness when, the very next day, Mrs. Rucker brought the brooch back and, with her own hands, pinned it on again, saying things that made it impossible to take offence. Yes, Mary never ceased to marvel at the way in which friends sprang up around her, in her need, and put themselves out to help her. These Ruckers, for instance—they had no family of their own—were constantly taking the children off her hands. Hence, when the week's leave of absence for which she had applied was granted, she could part from Cuffy and Lucie with an easy mind.

And one cold spring night, towards two o'clock, she put on her warmest travelling clothes, and climbed into the coach for Colac. She had bespoken a seat . . . and a good job, too! For an election had taken place in the district, and the coach was crammed with men, some coming from the polling, others on their way to a cattle market. She sat, the night through, jammed in among them, her arms pinned to her sides, half suffocated with smoke, and deafened by their talk. Not till daybreak was she joined by one of her own sex. Then, on stopping at a wayside public-house, they found a thinly clad, elderly woman waiting for the coach, a little bundle in her hand. But there was not room for a mouse in among them, let alone an old woman: one rude voice after another bawled the information. At which the poor thing began to cry, and so heartbrokenly that Mary was touched. Elbowing her way to the window, she leaned out and questioned the woman. At what she heard, and at the continued crude joking of her fellow-travellers, she lost her temper, and rounding on them cried: "Do you mean to say there isn't one of you who's man enough to give up his seat?" And as, though the laughter ceased, none offered, she said hotly: "Very well then, if you won't, I will! I'm on my way, too, to see a sick person, but I'll take my chance of getting a lift later in the day.— I'm glad I'm not a man . . . that's all!"

"Now then, missis, keep your hair on!" And a lanky young fellow, with hands like ploughshares, and a face confusion-red at his own good deed, gawkily detached himself and stepped out. "Here y'are, ma, in you get! I'll toddle along on Shank's p's."

The two women made the rest of the journey in company, Mary even treading underfoot the prejudice of a lifetime and going second-class in the train. (There was no Richard now, to cast up his eyes in horror.) The poor soul at her side told a sad story: one's own troubles shrank as one heard it. She was bound for the Melbourne Hospital, where her son, her only child, lay dying: he had got "the water" on his chest, and the doctors had telegraphed she must come at once, if she wanted to see him alive. Her husband had been killed at tree-felling, only a few months back; and, her son gone, she would be alone in the world. Mary, feeling rich in comparison, shared with her her travelling-rug, her packet of sandwiches, her bottle of cold tea; and, at Spencer Street station, having saved considerably on her fare, was able to put the poor mother in a wagonette and pay for her to be driven straight to the hospital. For she could see the bushdweller's alarm at the noise and bustle of the city.

On parting, the woman kissed her hand. "God bless you, ma'am . . . God bless and keep you, the kindest lady ever I met!—and may He restore your poor gentleman to his right mind! I shan't never forget what you've done for me this day. And if ever there come a time when I c'ld do su'thing for you . . . but there! not likely—only, Bowman's me name —Mrs. Bowman, at Sayer's Thack, near Mortlake."

For Mary, the Devines' carriage and pair was in waiting. The old coachman smiled and touched his hat and said: "Very glad to see you again, ma'am!" tucked the black opossum-rug round her, and off they rolled, she lying back on the springy cushions. And all the time she was in Melbourne this convey-ance stood freely at her disposal, Lady Devine being by now grown too comfortable even for "carriage exercise." "By the time I've buttoned me boots, dearie, and put on me plumes, I'm dead beat. An' there are the 'orses eatin' their 'eads off

in the stable. You can't do Jake and me a greater kindness 'n
to use 'em."

Without this mechanical aid: to expedite her hither and
thither, to wait for her while she kept appointments, to carry
her on anew, Mary could impossibly have got through what
she did in the days that followed: looked back on, they resembled the whirligig horrors of a nightmare. She had come
to Melbourne tired, sad, and anxious enough, in all conscience.
But in the hard-faced, unscrupulous woman with which, at the
end of the time, her glass presented her, she hardly recognised
herself. Never in her life had she fought for anything as now
for Richard's freedom.

The morning after her arrival, she drove out to the asylum.
The way led through lovely Toorak, with its green lawns and
white houses, up Richmond Hill, and down into the unattrac-
tive purlieus of Collingwood. The carriage came to a standstill on a stretch of waste land, a kind of vast, unfenced paddock, where hobbled horses grazed. It could go no farther,
for, between them and the complex of houses, cottages, huts,
which formed the asylum, flowed the unbridged river. Rain
had fallen during the night, and the reddish, muddy stream,
which here turned and twisted like a serpent, ran so high that
the weeping willows (Richard's favourite *Salix Babylonica*)
which lined the bank, dragged their branches deep in the flood.
The houses, overhung by the ragged, melancholy gums, looked
shabby and neglected; one and all in need of a coat of paint.
Mary's heart fell.

Seating herself in the ferry, she was conveyed across the
water.

She had not announced her visit. Her intention was to see
for herself how Richard was lodged and cared for, at those
times when the place was closed to the public. Had the authorities known beforehand that she was coming, they might have
dressed and dolled him up for her. (Yes! she was fast turning
into a thoroughly suspicious and distrustful woman.) For passport, she had armed herself with a letter to the head doctor
from Sir Jake Devine.

And well that she had! Great its virtue was not, but, without it, she would hardly have got over the threshold. And,
once inside the front door, she had to fight her way forward,
step by step: it needed all her native obstinacy, her newly ac-

quired aggressiveness, not to allow herself to be bowed out by
the several assistants and attendants who blocked her path.
But having vowed to herself that she would see some one in
authority, she did; though in the end they fobbed her off with
a youngish fellow, to whom—he had cod's eyes and a domineering manner—she took an instant and violent dislike.

By this time, too, her blood was up; and the incivility of
her reception seemed the last straw. A good log-fire burnt in
the fireplace—the rest of the building struck her as very damp
and chill—a comfortable armchair was suitably placed, but he
did not invite her to approach the fire, or to take a seat. He
stood while he spoke . . . and kept her standing. She had, he
presumed, already been informed that this was not a visiting-
day—and certainly not an hour for visitors. As, however, he
understood that she had made a special journey from up-
country, they had stretched a point. What did she want?

"To know how my husband is."

His fish eyes bulged still more. Was that all? When the report would have been so shortly in her hands?

"I preferred to come myself. I wish to speak to my husband."

"For that, ma'am, you will need to present yourself at the
proper time." (Then it was as she thought. They were *not*
going to let her see Richard unprepared.)

As, however, she made no movement to withdraw, but stood
her ground, with, for all her shabby dress and black gloves
shewing white at the finger-tips, the air of a duchess, and an
answer for everything (danged if he knew how to treat such
a bold, bouncing woman!), he crossed the room, took a ledger
from a rack, and asked in tones of exasperation. "Well, what
in thunder is it, then? . . . your husband's name?"

"Quite so . . . exactly!" he cut her reply short. "If you think,
madam, with the dozens of patients we have on our hands . . .
it is possible to remember . . . the details and antecedents of
each individual case . . ." As he spoke, he was running a fat
first finger down column after column. "Ha! here we have it."
Transporting the book to the central table, he laid it flat, and
faced her over it. "Here it is; and I regret to inform you that
the report we should presently have sent you, would have been
of a highly unsatisfactory nature."

"Why? Is he so much worse?" With difficulty her dry lips
framed the words.

"I refer not to his state of health—the disease is running a normal course—but to his conduct. Ever since being admitted to the asylum, your husband has proved to the last degree obstreperous and unruly."

"Well, that I cannot understand!" gave back Mary hotly. "Where he was—before he came here—they had only good to say of him."

"No doubt, no doubt! A patient worth his eight or ten guineas a week——"

"*Five*, if you please! He received special terms . . . as a medical man."

"All of which is beside the point. The fact remains that, here, he is a constant source of trouble. We have been obliged more than once to place him in solitary confinement. His behaviour is such as to corrupt the other patients."

"*Corrupt?*"

"Corrupt."

"Well, all I can say is . . . there must be something very wrong in the way he's being treated. He would never willingly give trouble. By nature he's one of the gentlest and politest of men."

"Perhaps you would like to hear his warder on the subject?" And going to the fireplace, the young man rang a bell and instructed a servant: "Send 97B's keeper here to me."

(97B? Why B? why not A? Mary's mind seized on the trivial detail and held fast to it, so as not to have to face the . . . the degradation the numbering implied.)

The warder entered, touching his forelock: a coarse, strongly built man, with a low forehead and the under-jaw of a prize-fighter. Her heart seemed to shrivel at thought of Richard . . . Richard! . . . in the power of such a man.

She hung her head, holding tight, as if for support, to the clasp of her sealskin bag, while the warder told the tale of Richard's misdeeds. 97B was, he declared, not only disobedient and disorderly; he was extremely abusive, dirty in his habits (here the catch of the hand bag snapped and broke), would neither sleep himself at night, nor let other people sleep; also he refused to wash himself, or to eat his food. "It's always the same ol' story. No sooner I bring him his grub than he up and pitches the dishes at me head."

She thought she had the fellow there. "Do you mean to tell

me he . . . that you give him fresh crockery to break, every day?"

"Crockery? Ho, no fear! The plates and cups is all of tin."

At this Mary laughed, but very bitterly. "Ah, now I see! That explains it! For I know my husband. Never would you get him . . . nothing would induce him . . . to eat off tin!"

"Needs Sèvres, no doubt!"

"No! All he needs is to be treated like a gentleman . . . by gentlemen!"

But she had to keep a grip on her mind to hinder it from following the picture up: Richard, forced by this burly brute to grope on the floor for his spilt food, scrape it together, and either eat it, or have it thrust down his throat. So she shut her ears, made herself deaf to their further talk, stood as it were looking through the speakers and out beyond—at her ripening purpose.

When, however, at the end of the interview she made a last, passionate appeal to be allowed to see her husband, she was not too absorbed to catch the glance, alive with significance, that passed between the men. Sorry, said the keeper, but the patient was in bed resting, after a very bad night; he couldn't on any account have him woke up again. At which excuse, things (old things) that she had heard from Richard, about the means used to quell and break the spirits of refractory lunatics, jumped into her mind. There was not only feeding by force, the strait-jacket, the padded cell. There were drugs and injections, given to keep a patient quiet and ensure his warders their freedom: doses of castor oil so powerful that the unhappy wretch into whom they were poured was rendered bedridden, griped, thoroughly ill.

But she saw plainly, here was nothing to be done. Her fight to get him back would have to be carried on outside the walls of the asylum. Buttoning her gloves with shaky, fumbling fingers, she confronted her opponents in a last bout of defiance. "I find it hard to believe a word of what you've said. But I know this: my husband shall not stay here. I'll take him home and look after him myself. He shall never leave my side again."

They all but laughed in her face. The idea was a very woman's! No alienist would ever be got to revoke this particular patient's certificate . . . or advise his release. In his fits of mania, 97B was dangerous, and not merely to those about him; he needed protection against himself, which could only be given him by those trained to the job. Impossible! . . . utterly impossible.

She left them at it, turned her back and marched out of the room and down the corridor, through innumerable doors, not one of which she could afterwards remember having opened or shut (they were insubstantial as the people she met on her passage) made her way to the ferry and up the other side, where she was helped into the carriage. And even while she bowled forward again, she continued to sit rigid and insensible, her sole movement being to pull off her gloves—they incommoded her—that she might lock her fingers . . . in an iron grip. The skin of her face felt stretched: like a mask that was too tight for it. But she shed not a tear, either here or when, having reached home, she paced the floor of the room and told her story. Something stronger than herself had control of her: she was all one purpose, one flame. Her old friend it was who wept. "Oh, just to *think* of 'im being come to this! . . . 'im, the 'andsomest man I ever saw, and the best, as well!"

But she too, said: "Impossible! oh no, my dear, it *couldn't* be done!" when she heard of Mary's determination. "Your children—you 'ave your children to consider."

"Oh, I can take care of them. But should I ever again know a moment's peace, do you think, if I left him in that awful place? Richard? . . . my poor old husband! As it is, he'll believe I've deserted him . . . forgotten him . . . left off caring. No: I mean to get him out, or die in the attempt!"

And when the old lady saw the blazing eyes, the dilated nostrils, the set jaw with which this was said, she bowed before the iron will made manifest, and went over heart and soul to Mary's side. "Well, then, my love and my dearie, if nothing else will do—and, oh my dear, I feel in the bottom of my 'eart you're right!—then what I say is, we—Jake and me—'ull do everything that lies in our power to 'elp you. *I'll* manage Jake; you go on to the rest. Get 'old of 'em somehow, and give 'em no quarter! . . . and though they talk till all's blue about their laws and certificates. What's laws for, I'd like to know, if not to be got round!"

But this was the sole word of encouragement Mary heard. The rest of the world combined to iterate and reiterate the doctor's verdict of impossible, utterly impossible.

She battered at every likely door. All sense of pride having left her, any influential or well-known person who had once, in former years, broken bread at her table, or whom she had casually met at another's, she now waylaid or ran to earth. For along with her pride went also the retiring modesty, the shrinking from prominence, that had hall-marked her years of wifehood. She was no longer the "lady," watchful of her steps. She was a tiger fighting for her young—did not Richard, in his present state, stand for the youngest and most helpless of her children?—and she now found, to her astonishment, that she was quite capable of standing up to men, of arguing with them, of talking them down, and, if necessary, of telling them what she thought of them.

The medical profession, of course, furnished her with her most implacable opponents. The doctors to whom she turned acted as if *she* were the crazed one; or else they smiled good-humoredly at her, as at a child . . . or a woman. But, if she stood firm, refusing to be browbeaten or cajoled, they gave her short shrift. To remove an insane person with notedly violent periods—a perfectly proper subject for detention—from medical safe-keeping, in order to place him in inexperienced lay-hands: such an act would be a criminal proceeding on the part of any medical man found to sanction it. Her ignorance of matters medical alone acquitted her. Nor could she get them to credit the ill-treatment to which Richard was being subjected. Again, it was sheer ignorance on her part that made her take this view. The asylum authorities were doubtless fully justified in what they did: you could not *reason* with the deranged. And so on . . . and on.— How she came to hate and dread the words. Certification, Lunacy Laws, Lunacy Authorities! Their very sound seemed to shut away, for ever, from the rest of humanity, from every human feeling, those unfortunates who had fallen beneath the ban.

Giving the doctors up as a bad job, she turned her attention to other influential people she had known: members of parliament, bankers, the clergy. And here she was received with the utmost consideration, no one of these old friends and acquaintances reminding her, by so much as a look, that she was now but a poor up-country postmistress. All alike deplored Richard's fate, and offered her their heartfelt sympathy; but from none of them could she wring a promise of help or in-

terference. Their concern was entirely for her, her personal
safety, and that of her children. While the Bishop and his
brethren spoke in muted voices of God's Will, this mysterious
Will to which it was one's duty to submit—till she could have
flung her bag at their heads. A stone for bread, indeed, when
her only cry was: "Give me back my husband!"

Sir Jake, who had been won over—though rather half-heart-
edly, and solely as a result of endless, nagging curtain-lectures
—did what he could; but he no longer held office and his influence was slight. And the person on whom Mary had built
most, the one member of the present ministry she knew inti-
mately, Henry Ocock, was not to be got at. Though she called
every day, and sometimes twice a day, at his chambers, it was
always to learn that business still detained him in Ballarat.

She applied for a second week's leave of absence—and got
it. And when but forty-eight hours of this remained, and she
had still achieved as good as nothing, she sent Mr. Henry a
page-long telegram, imploring him, in the name of their old
friendship, to grant her an interview.

He travelled to Melbourne by the next train. She met him
one cold, dusty autumn afternoon, in a private sitting-room
at Scott's Hotel.

He came towards her with outstretched hands, but was so
shocked at her appearance that he would not let her say a
word before she was thoroughly rested and refreshed. Then,
the waiter having withdrawn, he drew up his chair and begged
her to tell him what he could do for her.

To this old friend, whose mottled hair she had known when
it was sleekest, jettiest raven, she now opened her heart; beginning from the time when, almost against her will, and
certainly against her better judgment, she had yielded to the
specious assurances of Bowes-Smith and his kind, and had consented to Richard becoming the inmate of a public lunatic
asylum. ("Never should I have let him get into their clutches!")
But so much had been made of the treatment, the individual
nursing he would receive there, and the beneficial effect this
would have on him, that she had sunk her scruples. Afterwards had come the stoppage of his letters, the dead silence of
his imprisonment, and her growing doubts; followed by her
journey to town, her tragic discovery of his true state, the insolence she had had to put up with from the young assistant—

"Hardly more than a medical student!"—the beggar's calvary she had since been through. Not a living soul, it seemed, was willing to break a lance for Richard: once certified, a man might just as well be under the soil. On all sides she had been bidden to go home and live in peace. Knowing what she knew? Would other women have done it? If so, they were made of different stuff from her. She would think herself a traitor, if she did not fight for Richard's release as long as she had a breath left in her body.

Ocock let her talk: heard her out in a lawyer's cogitative silence, the while thoughtfully pulling at and stroking his chin. Even after she had ceased speaking, he sat meditative—and so used was Mary, by now, to being instantly downed and dismissed, that this very silence fed her hopes. Hence, when at last he broke it, his words had the force of a blow. For all he did was to bring to her notice a point which he very much feared she had overlooked. And this was that she was no longer a private individual, but a public servant, in Government employ. Difficulties would certainly be raised from this side, too, did she apply—as she was bound to do—for permission to receive a certified lunatic in her home. The Department would hold that the efficient discharge of her duties, and the care, at the same time, of so sick a man, would be irreconcilable . . . impossible.

At this repetition of the word that had dogged her every step, something tipped over in Mary. Passionately flinging up her head, she looked full and squarely at Ocock: pinned with her own what Richard had been used to call "those shifty little black boot-buttons of eyes!" And then, almost before she knew it, words began to pour from her lips, things she could not have believed herself capable of saying—to any one, let alone Henry Ocock, now so far above her. (In after years, of a sleepless night, she would suddenly feel her face begin to burn in the darkness, at the mere remembrance of them. Spiritual blackmail, would have been Richard's name for it.)

It was of herself and Richard that she had meant to speak; of the tie between them which no living creature had the right to break. But Ocock's presence seemed to bring the whole past alive before her, and the past brought Agnes, and memories of Agnes: "The dearest, truest little soul that ever lived!" and of the murk and misery in which the poor thing's days had ended. And under the influence of this emotion everything came out. Not only, lost to shame, did she throw in her listener's teeth all she had done for Agnes: the expense she had been put to when she could ill afford it; the pains she had been at to save Agnes from herself: she also stripped the veneer off his own conduct, laying bare his heartlessness, his egoism, his cruelty, yes, even brutality: how, in order to keep up his dignity, save his own face, he had wantonly sacrificed his wife, abandoning her when she most needed love, pity, companionship; shutting her up to drink herself to death—even barbarously shipping her off to die alone, among strangers, in a strange land. Not a shred of self-respect did she leave on him: he should see himself, for once, as others saw him: and she went on, pouring out scorn on his hypocrisy and pretence, till she had him standing there as morally naked as he had come physically naked into the world, and would one day go out of it. Before she finished, the tears were running down her cheeks . . . for Agnes; her own troubles completely forgotten, for the moment, over the other's tragedy.

Her voice failing her, she came to a stop: just sat and stared before her, feeling, now the fit was over, cold and queer and shaky. But nothing would have made her take back a word of what she had said; not even though—as was only too likely —she had ruined her own chances for good and all.

As, however, the silence that followed seemed to be going to last for ever, she plucked up courage to glance at Mr. Henry. And she had the surprise of her life. For he was sitting gazing at her with a look such as she had never seen on his face; a kindly, indulgent, almost *fond* look; and—oh, was it possible?—with his eyes full of tears. More, these eyes were now as steady as her own: had quite ceased furtively to dart and run. And the crowning touch was put to this strange reception of her tirade by his nodding his head, slowly, several times in succession, and saying: "A staunch and loyal advocate, indeed!— My friend, a great fighter has been lost in you!"

Then he got up and went to the window, where he stood looking down into the street. Mary sat motionless, but odd thoughts and scraps of thoughts were whizzing round her brain. This then was how . . . stand up to him, *bully* him . . . if Agnes had only . . . but would never have had the spirit. And then his eyes! . . . the shiftiness more than half fear . . .

fear of discovery . . . and, once found out— But, oh! not praise
for her eloquence. If she hadn't touched him . . . or had
touched him solely in this way.

Coming back to her, he took her hands. "What you are
asking of me, Mrs. Mahony, means difficulties, of which you,
as a woman, do not realise the quarter . . . the half. I will
make you no fixed promises; which I might be unable to keep.
All I will say is, that for your sake—your sake alone!—I will
see what can be done."

And with this single straw to cling to, Mary travelled home.

[8]

HE HAD enjoined her to patience and patient she was—though
week ran into week, and month to month, in all of which time
she knew nothing of what was happening behind the scenes,
or what strings Ocock was pulling to upset the cumbrous machinery of medical law. She just dragged on from day to day,
as well as she could, in ignorance and suspense. But her nerves
often got the better of her, and then the children felt her
heavy, hasty hand. While in her official capacity, so set did
she become on her "rights," so unblushing in making her voice
heard, that her name grew to be a by-word in the service.
"That tartar at G.G.!" (which was the Morse call for Gymgurra) was how she was familiarly spoken of.

In this dreary time, when her narrow walls oppressed her
to breathlessness, but from which there was no possible escape
for her, one piece of good fortune came her way. The house
at Shortlands found a tenant; and so the money which she
had laboriously scraped together for the following quarter's
rent would not be needed. Hence, when at last the tide began
to turn, with the substitution of "highly dangerous," and "a
most risky experiment," for the maddening "impossible," she
actually had a small sum in hand, with which to make her
preparations. And she set about these forthwith; building on
her recently acquired knowledge of men and their ways. She
could look for no complete *volte face* on their part. Only in
this grudging, half-hearted fashion would their consent be
given.

Help in the house she must have, was she to be free to
devote what time she could spare from her office-work to

Richard. Her first thought was naturally of her poor old ageing sister, and she wrote to Zara, offering her houseroom in exchange for her services. But though, in her last situation little more than a nursemaid, Zara declined the proposal as stiffly and uncompromisingly as if she were rolling in money: dubbing Mary mad as a March hare to think of removing "our poor dear Richard" from safe control; madder still, to imagine that she, Zara, with her delicate nerves, would be able to live for a single day under the same roof as a lunatic. Emmy, unasked, wrote begging to be allowed to help care for "poor darling Uncle." But quite apart from the mixed motives that underlay the offer, this was out of the question. You could not so take the bloom off a young girl's life. There would be things to do for Richard—unfit things . . . And it was here that Mary bethought herself of the woman she had befriended on her journey to town, whose son had died soon after. So, in the same terms as to Zara, she wrote to "Mrs. Bowman at Sayer's Thack"— though it did seem rather like posting a letter into the void. Almost by return, however, came an ill-spelt scrawl, joyfully accepting the job; and a little later Mrs. Bowman herself got out of the coach, with all her worldly goods tied up in one small cardboard-box, but carrying with her, as a gift, a stringy old hen (fit only for the soup-pot) and half a pound of dairy butter. And in this poor, lone soul, Mary found yet another of those devoted, leech-like friends, who had starred her path through life.

The final surrender came in the form of a lengthy screed from Mr. Henry, in which he informed her that, after surmounting difficulties and obstacles greater even than he had anticipated, he had at last succeeded in bringing the various authorities involved—medical, legal, postal—to agree to the plan of Dr. Mahony's removal from control being given a provisional trial. That was to say, the patient would be accompanied to Gymgurra by two warders, who would remain there while the experiment was made. In the event of its failing, they would immediately escort the patient back to the asylum. Followed, this, by four pages in which Mr. Henry begged her once more seriously to consider what she was doing. It was still not too late to draw back. Should she, however, decide to go forward, he trusted she would further show her friendship for him, by regarding him as her banker, if the expenses of the undertaking proved too heavy for her purse. He would be only too happy to assist her.— Well, thank goodness! owing to her little windfall, she need be beholden to nobody; although, at this pass, she would not have hesitated to borrow freely. But, Bowey's expenses settled, she had still enough in hand to cover the three fares up from town, and those of the warders back; as well their board and lodging while in Gymgurra.

Only the day of arrival now remained to be fixed. But now, too, in the small hours when she lay waiting for the night mail, Mary was assailed by her first fears and apprehensions. It was not her ability to cope with, and control, and nurse Richard that she doubted. No, her fears concerned herself. Her own strength was already sorely taxed, she on the brink of those years when a woman most needed rest and care and a quiet life. Suppose *she* should fall ill! . . . need nursing herself? Or that she should die before him . . . be forced to leave him? him, and the children. This was the thought that haunted her nights; and though she drove it from her, fought it valiantly, it was often not to be got under till she had risen and paced the house.

When Cuffy heard that Papa was coming home, his black eyes opened till they seemed to fill his face.

"Do you mean he . . . he's coming back here? *Now?*"

"Yes. And you chicks must try your best to help me. I shall have more than ever to do."

"But is he . . . isn't he still . . ." It was no use; his mouth was full of tongue; the "mad" simply wouldn't come out. To which half-asked question Mamma said firmly: "Run away and play!"

But they were moving his bed, and he saw them: saw, too, a new bed being carried into Mamma's room. "What's that for? And where's my bed going?" And at the news that from now on he was to sleep in Bowey's room, the dismay he had so far bitten back broke through. "Oh, no, I *can't*, Mamma! I won't! . . . sleep in the same room as her."

"And why not, indeed?"

"She's . . . she's a *lady*."

"Really, Cuffy! I wonder where you get your ideas from? Pray, haven't you been sleeping all this time with Lucie and me? Are we not ladies, too?"

No, of course not!—they were only just their two selves. But, as usual, he didn't try to explain. It was never a bit of good.

With Lucie, whose chubby face wore a harassed look, beside him, he sat on the back steps, with his elbows on his knees, his chin hunched in his hands. The yard was mostly potatoes now—the floury sort that were so good to have for dinner, but left hardly any room to play. For you hadn't got to tread on them.— Oh, *why* did Papa need to come back? They had been so happy without him . . . even though they had to keep a post office, and weren't *real* ladies and gentlemen any more. But nobody had once laughed at them—at him and Lucie— since they came here, and they had had nothing to be ashamed of. Now, it was all going to begin over again. Oh, if only there had been anywhere to run to, he would have run away! But there wasn't, only just long, straight roads.

Here Lucie put her mouth inside his ear and whispered guiltily: "I don't b'lieve you're a bit glad!"

"Are *you?*"

Lucie nodded hard. Mamma was glad, so she was too; or she'd thought she was, till now. But Cuffy looked so funny that her little soul began to be torn afresh, between these two arbiters of her fate.

Cuffy wrinkled his lips up and his nose down. "You're not *true!* I don't believe it."

"I am!" But her face puckered.

"Well, I'm *not* . . . not a scrap! So there! And if you want to, you can go and tell."

But she didn't; she only cried. Cuffy was always making her cry. He couldn't ever be nice and think the same as Mamma and her. He always had to be diffrunt.—

It certainly *was* hard, though, to keep on being sorry when you saw how glad Mamma was. She smiled much more now, and sewed shirts, and got them ready for Papa; and she bought a new rocking-chair, specially for him to sit and rock in. And every day was most dreadfully anxious to know if there wasn't a letter in the mail-bag, to say when he was coming. And then she told them about how unhappy Papa had been since he went away, and how he had to eat his dinner off tin plates; and how they must try with all their mights to make up to him for it. And then she went back and told

them all over again about when they were quite little, and
how fond Papa had been of them, and how he thought there
were no children in the world like his; and how, now he was
old, and ill, and not himself, they must love him much more
than ever before. It made you feel *horrid!* But it didn't help;
you *just couldn't* be glad. It was like a stone you'd swallowed,
which stuck in you, and wouldn't go down.

And, at length, the suspense in which Mary had lived was
ended by a letter definitely fixing a date for the arrival of
Richard and his keepers. They would land at the neighbouring
seaport, between eight and nine in the morning. It was on her
advice, Richard being so excellent a sailor, that the sea route
had been chosen, for its greater privacy, few people, even at
this time of year, choosing to undergo a buffeting round the
wild coast. Now, all she had to do was to send word over the
road to Mr. Cadwallader Evans of the Bank. Long since, this
kind friend had placed his buggy and pair at her disposal, for
the occasion.

She rose at six when the morning came, and was busy brushing and shaking out her clothes: she had not been over the
threshold since her return from Melbourne. Not wishing to
disgrace Richard by too shabby an appearance, she put on her
one remaining silk dress, with its many flounces, her jet-
trimmed mantle, her best bonnet . . . in which still nodded the
red rose he had been used to fancy her in. But her hands were
cold and stupid as she hooked and buttoned and tied strings;
and, having climbed into the buggy and taken her seat, she
sat with a throat too dry for speech.

And after one or two well-meant efforts at encouragement,
the chatty little man who was her companion respected her
mood. He considered her "a dam fine woman for her age,"
and "a dam plucky one, too," but held the errand they were
out on for "a dam unpleasant job," and one he had undertaken solely to please his wife, who thought the world of Mrs.
Mahony. He didn't even dare to hum or to whistle, and so,
except for a passing flip or chirrup to the ponies, they drove
mile after mile in silence; neither casting so much as a glance
at the landscape, which both thought ugly and dull: once past
the volcano—a knobbly bunch of island-hills, set in the middle

of a shallow, weed-grown lake—it consisted of unbroken grassy downs, which sloped to a sandy shore on which the surf broke and thundered.

The wide streets of the little port were deserted; but at the jetty quite a crowd had gathered. There stood passengers who had already been landed, several idle girls and women, a goodly sprinkling of larrikins. One and all had their eyes fixed on a small rowing-boat that was making for the shore from the steamer, which lay at anchor some way out.

Having dismounted from the buggy and joined the throng, Mary asked of a young girl standing by: "What is it? What's the matter?"

"Ooo! . . . such fun!" said the girl, and tittered. "See that boat? There's a madman in it. He's being put off here. They've had to tie his arms up."

"Don't you think you should let me see to things? . . . and you wait in the buggy?" asked Mr. Evans, in concern. But Mary shook her head.

As the boat drew near, riding the surf, they saw that it contained, beside the oarsmen, two burly men who sat stooped over something lying prostrate on the floor of the boat. Mary hung back, keeping on the outskirts of the crowd, the members of which now pushed and pressed forward. But though the boat was alongside, its oars shipped, nothing happened—or nothing but a series of cries and shouts and angry exclamations, several men's voices going at once.

"They can't make him get up, that's what it is!" volunteered the girl, her pretty face distorted with excitement. "I bet they'll have to tie his legs as well, and then just haul him out. What fun if he falls in the water."

"I can't bear this," said Mary in an undertone; she believed she could hear, as well, the sound of cuffs and blows. "I must see what *I* can do." And in spite of her companion's demur, she stepped forward. Bravely tossing her head, she said to those around her: "Will you please let me pass? It's my husband."

They almost jumped aside to make way for her; open-mouthed, embarrassed, or flushed a dark red, like the pretty girl. Mary felt, rather than saw, the nudging elbows, the pointing and whispering, as, herself now the gazing-stock, she walked through the opening they left. Outwardly erect and composed, inwardly all a-quake, she advanced to the edge of the jetty, and went down three shallow steps to the landing-place.

The rough voices ceased at her approach, and the warders desisted from their efforts to shift a heavy body that struggled desperately to oppose them.

"Please, stand back, and let me try!" As she spoke, she caught a glimpse, at the bottom of the boat, of disordered clothing, dishevelled strands of white hair, a pair of roped hands working violently. Leaning as far over as she dared, she said in a low, but clear voice: "Richard dear, it's me—Mary! Don't you know me?"

On the instant the contortions ceased, and a kind of listening silence ensued. Then came a palpable attempt on the part of the prostrate form to raise itself; while a thin, cracked voice, which she would never have recognised as Richard's, said in a tone of extreme bewilderment: "Why, it's . . . it's Mrs. Mahony!"

"Yes, it's me; I've come to take you home. Get up, Richard—but at once, dear! . . . and don't lie there like that. The buggy's waiting." Again he made, she saw, a genuine effort to obey; but once more fell back.

"Take that rope off his hands!" And disregarding a warder's: "Well, at your own risk, lady!" she added: "And help him up."

But this was easier said than done. No sooner did the man approach him than his struggles began anew. He would not be touched by them. It was left to Mr. Evans and one of the sailors, who had not made off like the rest, to untie his wrists; after which, seizing him under the armpits, they hoisted him on to the quay. ("Mrs. Mahony . . . why, it's Mrs. Mahony!" piped the thin voice.)

"And now take my arm and come quietly . . . as quietly as you can! There are people watching. Show them how nicely you can walk."

("Mrs. Mahony . . . Mrs. Mahony!")

With him a dead weight on her right arm, Mr. Evans at his other side, pushing and supporting, they got his poor old shambling legs up the steps and through the crowd. He was so cold and stiff from exposure that it was all he could do to set one foot before the other. He had no boots on, no hat, no greatcoat. Of the carpet-slippers in which they had let him travel, one had been lost or had fallen off in the boat; his sock was full of holes. In his struggles, the right-hand sleeve of his coat had been almost wrenched from its armhole, his dirty shirt was collarless, his grey hair, long uncut, hung down his neck.

And the fear he was in was pitiful to see: he turned his head continually from side to side, trying to look back. "Where are they? Oh, don't let them get the doctor! . . . *don't* let them get him!"

"No, no, my darling! . . . don't be afraid. You're quite safe now . . . with me." And as soon as he had been half shoved, half dragged into the buggy, she sent her companion to warn the warders to keep out of sight. If follow they must, it would have to be in a separate vehicle.

On the drive home, she took Richard's poor benumbed hands in hers and chafed them; she spread her skirts over his knees to keep the wind off, unhooked her mantle and bound it round his chest. His teeth chattered; his face was grey with cold. Then, opening the little bottle of wine and water, and the packet of sandwiches which she had brought with her, she fed him, sip by sip and bit by bit; for he was ravenous with hunger and thirst. And though he quieted down somewhat, under the shelter of the hood, she did not cease to croon to him and comfort him. "It's all right, my dear, quite all right now. Those horrid men are far away; you'll never, never see them again. You're with me, your own Mary, who will look after you and care for you." Until, his hunger stilled, his worst fears allayed, exhausted, utterly weary, he put his head on her shoulder, and, with her arm laid round him to lessen the jolts of the road, fell asleep, slumbering as peacefully as a child on its mother's breast.

And so Richard Mahony came home.

[9]

A WEEK later Mary paid the warders off and dispatched them back to Melbourne. Not once had she needed them; there had been absolutely nothing for them to do—but hang about the hotel, eating and drinking at her expense. She went, besides, in mortal fear of Richard seeing them from the window, did they show themselves in the street, and of the shock this sight might be, undoing all the good she had done. So she handed out their return-fares and paid their bill, gladly . . . even though this came to a good deal more than she had expected, coarse brutes that they were! For their part, they could hardly believe their ears when they heard her report on Richard's behaviour since getting home; and they remained pessimistic to the end. "Ah! you'll have trouble with him yet, lady . . . for sure you will!" were their final words.

But she laughed in their faces. Richard was a lamb in her hands, a little child, whom she could twist round her finger. Just now, he spent his time weeping from sheer happiness, as he strayed from room to room of the little house . . . so wretchedly poor and mean compared with any he had known. But he was blind to its shortcomings. "And all this belongs to the doctor? . . . it's *his* house? . . . he'll never have to go away from it again? And these cups and plates—do they belong to the doctor, too? . . . and may he drink out of them and eat off them? And is this the doctor's own chair?" Again and again, she had to assure him and re-assure him: he might sit where he pleased, do what he liked, use everything. With difficulty, he took in his good fortune: at first, any unexpected knock at the door made him shake and try to hide.

Gradually, however—along with the marks and bruises that stained his poor old body—his alarms died out, and his eyes lost their hunted look. As long, that is to say, as Mary was with him, or he knew her close at hand: her presence alone spelt complete safety. It had been hard to make him understand that he was not to follow her into the office; he couldn't grasp this, and would often be found prowling round the office door, muttering confusedly. Even after he had learnt his lesson, she—hammering away at the key, or sitting stooped over her desk—would sometimes see the door open by a crack, and Richard's eyes and nose appear behind it . . . just to make sure. Then, if she nodded and smiled, and said: "It's all right, dear, I'm here!" he would go away content. His devotion to her, his submissive dependence on her, knew no bounds: a word of praise from her made him happy, a reproof bewildered him to tears. And was he really troublesome, she had only to warn him: "Richard, if you're not good, I shan't be able to keep you!" for him instantly to weep and promise betterment. No one, not even the children, might, in his presence, handle any object that he looked on as her peculiar property: the teapot, her scissors, her brush and comb. "Put that down! . . . put it down at once. It belongs to Mrs. Mahony."

Fortunately, he took quite a fancy to Mrs. Bowman, and had no objection to being waited on by her—when the monthly "statement" occupied Mary, or a visit from the Inspector impended. But then Bowey was capital with him, hit just the right tone, and never tried to order him about. She was a good cook, too, and, since he was prescribed frequent small quantities of nourishing food, she was for ever popping in from the kitchen, with a: "Now, sir, I've got a nice little cup of soup here, made specially for you . . . something I *know* you'll enjoy!" And he would let her bind his table-napkin round his neck, and even, in default of Mary, feed him with a spoon, to avoid the pitiful dropping and spilling that otherwise went on. He invariably addressed her as "the Cook," and spoke to her, and of her, as if she stood at the head of a large staff of servants. (Whose non-existence, oddly enough, he did not seem to remark.) For it was just as if a sponge had been passed over a large part of his brain, mercifully wiping out every memory of the terrible later years. He re-lived the period of his greatest prosperity; was once more, in imagination, either the well-to-do property-owner, or the distinguished physician. And since only those images persisted which had to do with one or other of these periods, his late-born children meant little to him: if he thought or spoke of them, it was as though they were still in their infancy. Sometimes, seeing them stand so tall and sturdy before him—a well-grown girl and boy of seven and eight—he grew quite confused. While, asked by Mary if he remembered his little lost daughter, he looked at her with stupid, darkened eyes, and could not think what she meant.

By seven, of a morning, he was washed and dressed and fed. Eight o'clock, when the office opened, saw him comfortably settled in the rocking-chair. Here, his day was spent. The chair stood by the window, which gave on the cross-roads and the main street; from it, he could see all that went on in the township. But his chief occupation was "reading." For his sake, Mary subscribed to a Melbourne newspaper—though this was a day and a half old before it reached them. But, for anything it mattered to him, it might have borne the date of a month back. As often as not, he read it upside down; his spectacles perched at an impossible angle on the extreme tip of his long, thin nose. In this position, he loved to proclaim the news to whoever had time to listen: Mary, slipping in and out; Mrs. Bowman, come to see that he wanted for nothing. And his information was invariably of some long past event: the death of Prince Albert, the siege of Sebastopol, the Indian Mutiny. And there good old Bowey would stand, her hands clasped under her apron, exclaiming: "What doings, sir, what awful doings you do tell of!"—for, to throw his hearer into a state of surprise, even of consternation, was one of the things that pleased him best.

Tired of reading, he would talk to himself by the hour together; his clear voice, with its light Irish slur, ringing through the house. And, hampered no longer by those shackles of pride and reserve which had made him the most modest of men, his theme was now always, and blatantly, himself. This self—to whom, as to every one else, he referred only in the third person—was the pivot round which his thoughts revolved, he passionately asserting and reasserting its identity, in a singsong that was not unlike a chant. "Richard Townshend-Mahony, F.R.C.S., M.D., Edinburgh; R. T. Mahony, M.D. and Accoucheur; Specialist for the Diseases of Women; Consulting Physician to the Ballarat Hospital!" and so on: only, the list having been sung through, to begin afresh, untiringly.

In appearance, now that he was once more clean and well cared-for, he remained a striking-looking man, with his straight, delicate features, his cloven chin, the silver hair smoothed back from his high forehead; and often, on coming into the room, and catching him seated and in profile—his gait, of course, was lamentable; he had never recovered the proper use of his legs—Mary had a passing, ghostlike glimpse of the man who had been. It was his eyes that gave him away. There had been a time when these blue-grey eyes had looked out on life with the expression of a wantonly hurt animal. Still later, a day when they had seldom lifted, but had brooded before them, turned inward on torments visible to them alone. Now, they met yours again, but as it were shrilly and blindly, all the soul gone out of them; nor ever a trace remaining of their

937

former puzzlement over life the destroyer. He was now the least troubled of men. Content and happiness had come to him at last, in full measure. No more doubts, or questionings, or wrestlings with the dark powers in himself: no anxiety over ways and means (Mary was there, Mary would provide); never a twinge of the old passionate ache for change and renewal . . . for flight from all familiar things. He desired to be nowhere but here: had, at long last, found rest and peace, within the four walls of a room measuring but a few feet square; that peace for which he had sought, desperately and vainly, throughout the whole of his conscious life; to which he would otherwise have attained only through death's gates.

To see him thus was Mary's reward: Mary, grown so thin that she could count her ribs; with black rings round her eyes, "salt-cellars" above and below her collar-bones; with enlarged, knobby knuckles, and feet that grew daily flatter. But she had no time to think of herself—to think at all, in fact!—nor did she linger regretfully over what had been, or grieve, in advance, for what was bound to come. And Richard's condition ceased to sadden her: valiantly she accepted the inevitable.

It was another matter with the children, who had in them a goodly share of Mahony's own thin-skinnedness. Cuffy and Lucie never grew used or resigned to the state of things: their father's imbecile presence lay a dead weight on their young lives. And violently conflicting feelings swung them to and fro. If, at dinner, Papa was scolded for spilling his food, or for gobbling—and he was most *dreadfly* greedy—Luce's eyes would shut so tight that almost you couldn't see she had any: while he, Cuffy, red as a turkey-cock, would start to eat just like Papa, from being made so sorry and uncomfortable to hear a big man scolded like a baby. They kept out of his way as much as possible, being also subtly hurt by his lack of recognition of them, when he knew Mamma so well: they were just as much belonging to him as Mamma! And, home from their morning lessons at the parsonage, they withdrew to the bottom of the yard, where Mamma couldn't so easily find them. For she was always trying to make Papa notice them . . . when you knew quite well he didn't care. It would be: "Show Papa your copybook . . . how nicely you can write now!" or: "Let him see your new boots!" At which something naughty would get up in Cuffy, and make him say nastily: "What for?

... what's the good? He doesn't *really* look!" But then Mamma would look so sorry that it hurt, and say: "Oh, you must be kind to him, Cuffy! And try not to let him feel it."

A doctor drove over once a week from Burrabool to write medicines for Papa, and he said Papa ought to take exercise, and it would be a good thing for him to go a short walk . . . every single day. And of course he and Luce had to do this, to help Mamma. For half an hour. The thought of it spoiled the whole morning—like whipping.

"Does it matter which way we go?"

Cuffy never failed to ask this, as a sop to his conscience. But really they always went the same road, the one that led straight out of the township. For, if you got past the lock-up, where the constable's little girl might be swinging on the gate, you were quite certain not to meet anybody. To make sure she wasn't, you first sent Luce out to look, then fetched Papa and hurried him by. After that, though, you had to walk as slow as slow, because he couldn't hardly walk at all: his knees bent and stuck out at every step. You each held his hand, and went on, counting the minutes till it was time to turn back. And to find when this was, you had to get his watch out of his pocket yourself, and look at it—which he didn't like, for he thought you were going to take it away from him. But it was no use asking him the time, because he said such funny things. Like: "The time is out of joint!" or: "A time to be born and a time to die!"

But when you said it was far enough, and they could go home, and turned him round, he was glad, too; and the whole way back he talked about nothing but his tea, and what there was going to be for it. And when Mamma came to the door, she didn't say what she would have said to *them*, that it was greedy and piggy to think about your meals so long beforehand. She just said: "Tea's all ready, dear; and Bowey has made you some delicious scones." He and Luce only had bread and butter, and didn't want it. They liked best to go and play like mad, because the walk was done, and they didn't have to do it again till next day.

But then came that awful afternoon when . . . ugh! he didn't like even to *think* about it . . . ever afterwards.

They had gone out as usual and walked along the road, and nobody saw them. And he was just going to fetch Papa's watch to look at the time . . . or had he *tried* to, and it wouldn't come, and he had pulled at it? He could never feel quite, quite sure: it remained a horrible doubt. And then, all of a sudden, quite suddenly Papa fell down: "His legs just seemed to shut up, Mamma, really truly they did!" (when she accused them of having hurried him). They couldn't stop him. . . . Luce nearly tumbled down, too . . . and Papa fell flat on his face and lay there; and it had rained, and the road was dirty, and he lay in it, so that his clothes and his face were full of mud. And he called out, and so did Luce: "Get up, Papa, you'll be all wet and dirty!" and again: "Mamma will be so cross if you don't!" and despairingly: "Oh, dear Papa, *do* get up and don't just lie there!" And then he did try, but couldn't seem to make his legs work properly, and went on lying with his face and hair in the dirt—quite flat. And they tugged and tugged at him, at his arms, and his coat, but couldn't move him, he was so big and heavy; and Luce began to cry; and he felt such a bone come in his own throat that he thought he'd have to cry, too. He began to be afraid the mud would choke Papa, and what would Mamma say then? And Papa kept on asking: "What is it? What's the doctor doing?" And then he shouted out, like as if he was deaf: "You've fallen down, Papa—oh, *do* get up! *What* shall we do if you don't!" And he said to Luce to run home and fetch Mamma, but she was frightened too; and she was frightened to stay there while he went; and so he felt his heart would burst, for they couldn't leave Papa alone. But just then a man came driving in a spring-cart, and when he saw them he stopped and said: "Hullo, you kids, what's up?" And "Whoa!" to his horse, and got out. And first he laughed a little, and winked at them, for he thought Papa was tipsy; but when they told him, and said it was their Papa, who couldn't walk any more because his legs were wrong, he stopped laughing, and was kind. He took hold of Papa till he made him stand up, and then he let down a flap of the cart and helped him in, and lifted them up, too, and they drove home that way, their legs hanging out at the back. And when they got to the post office Mamma came running to the door, and had a most awful fright when she saw Papa so wet and dirty, with mud on his face and hair, and scratched with stones where they had pulled him; and she sort of screamed out: "Oh, *what's* the matter? What have

you done to him?" (and they hadn't done anything at all).
But she was so sorry for Papa, and so busy washing him clean
and telling him not to cry, that she didn't have any time to
think about them, or how upset they were. They went away
and were together by themselves, at the bottom of the yard.

After this, though, they didn't have to take Papa walking
any more. He never went out.— But the memory of the accident persisted, and was entangled in their dreams for many a
night to come. Especially Cuffy's. Cuffy would start up, his
nightclothes damp with sweat, from a dream that Papa had
fallen dead in the road and that he had killed him. And, all
his life long, the sight of a heavy body lying prostrate and
unable to rise—a horse down in its traces, even a drunkard
stretched oblivious by the roadside—had the power to throw
him into the old childish panic, and make him want blindly to
turn and run . . . and run . . . till he could run no more.

[10]

THUS the shadows deepened. For still some time Mahony contrived to cover, unaided, the few yards that separated bedroom
from sitting-room. Then, he took to shouldering his way along
the walls, supporting himself by the furniture. And soon, even
this mode of progression proving beyond him, he needed the
firm prop of an arm on either side, was he to reach his seat by
the window. Finally, his chair was brought to the bedside,
and, with him in it, was pushed and pulled by the two women
to the adjoining room.

He never set foot to the ground again; was very prisoner
to this chair. Nor could he stoop, or bend his body sideways;
and did he now drop his spectacles, or let his paper flutter to
the floor, the house resounded with cries of "Mrs. Mahony,
Mrs. Mahony!" or "the Cook, the Cook!" Dead from the waist
down, he sat wooden and rigid; and the light of the poor
clouded brain that topped this moribund trunk grew daily
feebler. His newspaper ceased to interest him; he no longer
hymned his own praises: he just sat and stared before him, in
mournful vacancy.

Oh, what a work it was to die!—to shake off a body that
had no more worth left in it than a snake's cast skin, Mary
could imagine him saying of himself.— Not so she. She clung

jealously to each day on which she still had him with her; plodding to and fro on hot, swollen feet; gladly performing the last, sordid duties of the sick-room.

Then, gangrene setting in, he became bedridden; and she and Bowey united their strength to turn him from side to side, or to raise him the few necessary inches on his pillow. He was grown quite silent now, and indifferent to every one; the sight of food alone called up a flicker of interest in his dull eyes. But the day came when even to swallow soft jellies and custards was beyond him, and a few teaspoonfuls of liquid formed his sole nourishment. And at length his throat refusing even this office, there was nothing to be done but to sit and watch him die.

For three days he lay in coma. On the third, the doctor gave it as his opinion that he would not outlive the night.

Beside the low trestle-bed in which, for greater convenience, they had laid him, and on which his motionless body formed a long, straight hummock under the blankets, Mary sat and looked her last on the familiar face, now so soon to be hidden from her . . . it might be forever. For who knew, who could *really* know, if they would meet again? In health, in the bustle of living, it was easy to believe in heaven and a life to come. But when the blow fell, and those you loved passed into the great Silence, where you could not get at them, or they at you, then doubts, aching doubts took possession of one. She had sunk under them when her child died; she knew them now, still more fiercely. Death might quite well be the end of everything; just so many bones rotting in a grave.— And even if it was not, if there *was* more to come, how could it ever be quite the same again?—the same Richard to look at, and with all his weaknesses, who had belonged to her for nearly thirty years. She didn't believe it. If heaven existed, and was what people said it was, then it would certainly turn him into something different: a stranger . . . an angel!—and what had she to do with angels? She wanted the man himself, the dear warm incompetent human creature, at whose side she had been through so much. Who had so tried, so harassed her, made her suffer so.— Oh, as if that mattered now! What was life, but care and suffering?—for every one alike. His had never been much else. Even though his troubles were mostly of his own making. For he had always asked more of life than it could give: and if, for once, he got what he wanted, he had not known how to sit fast and hold it: so the end was the poor old wreck on the bed before her. Now, death was best. Death alone could wipe out the shame and disgrace that had befallen him—the shame of failure, the degradation of his illness. Best for the children, too; his passing would lift a shadow from their lives . . . they were so young still, they would soon forget. Yes, best for every one . . . only not for her. With Richard, the most vital part of herself—a part compounded of shared experience, and mutual endeavour, and the common memories of a lifetime—would go down into the grave.— Burying her face in her hands, Mary wept.

By day, for the children's, for her work's sake, she was forced to bear up. Now, there was nobody to see or hear her. The office was closed, the children slept: old Bowey dozed over the lamp in the kitchen. She could weep, without fear of surprise, alone with him who had passed beyond the sound of human grief; in this little back room where, by the light of a single candle, monstrous shadows splashed walls and ceiling; shadows that stirred and seemed to have a life of their own; for it was winter now, and the wild Australian wind shrilled round the house, and found its way in through the loosely fitting sashes.

How long she sat thus she did not know: she had lost count of time. But, of a sudden, something . . . a something felt not heard, and felt only by a quickening of her pulses . . . made her catch her breath, pause in her crying, strain her ears, look up. And as she did so her heart gave a great bound, then seemed to leave off beating. *He had come back.* His lids were raised, his eyes half open. And in the breathless silence that followed, when each tick of the little clock on the chest of drawers was separately audible, she saw his lips, too, move. He was trying to speak. She bent over him, hardly daring to breathe, and caught, or thought she caught the words: "Not grieve . . . for me. I'm going . . . into Eternity."

Whether they were actually meant for her, or whether a mere instinctive response to the sound of her weeping, she could not tell. But dropping on her knees by the bedside, she took his half-cold hand in her warm, live one, and kissed and

fondled it. And his lids, which had fallen to again, made one
last supreme effort to rise, and this time there was no mistaking the whisper that came over his lips. "Dear wife!"

He was gone again, even as he said it, but it was enough
. . . more than enough! Laying her head down beside his, she
pressed her face against the linen of the pillow, paying back
to this inanimate object the burning thankfulness with which
she no longer dared to trouble him. Eternity was something
vast, cold, impersonal. But this little phrase, from the long past
days of love and comradeship, these homely, familiar words,
fell like balsam on her heart. All his love for her, his gratitude
to her, was in them: they were her reward, and a full and
ample one, for a lifetime of unwearied sacrifice.

Dear wife! . . . dear wife.

He died at dawn, his faint breaths fluttering to rest.

Close on two days had to elapse before relative or friend
could get to her side: by the time Jerry and Tilly reached
Gymgurra, she herself had made all arrangements for the last
rites, and Richard was washed and dressed and in his coffin,
which stood on a pair of trestles just outside the kitchen door,
the doorways of the rooms having proved too small to admit
it. There he lay, with a large bunch of white violets in his
folded hands, looking very calm and peaceful, but also inex-
pressibly remote—from them all, from everything. Never again
would the clatter of crockery or the odours of cooking flay his
nerves.

The children, feeling oddly shy, sought their usual refuge.
And when strange men came with the coffin, and there was
a great walking about and tramping, they were told to keep
out of the way. But afterwards, Mamma called them in, and
took their hands, and took them to see Papa, who was all put
into his coffin now, with a bunch of flowers in front of him,
and his head on a most *beautiful* satin pillow trimmed with
lace. And Mamma kissed him and stroked his hair, and said
how young and handsome he looked, with the wrinkles gone
away from his face; but Cuffy only thought he looked most
frightfully asleep.

Luce had to have her hand held, every time she went by;
but he didn't; he didn't care. And all the time Papa had lain
in bed and was so ill, he hadn't either. Even when he heard

he was dead, and saw him with a sheet pulled over his face
it didn't seem to make any difference. Or wouldn't have, if
other people hadn't been so sorry for him. To see them sorry
gradually made him sorry, too. For himself. And that night,
when a great fat moon was on the sky, he went away and
stood and looked up at it, and then something that was just
like a line of poetry came into his head, and he said it over
and over, and it went: "Now the moon looked down on a
fatherless child!"

Next day though, when Papa was put in, and you couldn't
help seeing him every time you went along the passage, it was
different. And when Mamma got a large pocket-handkerchief
and spread it over his face and hands (when you were dead,
you couldn't shooh the flies away, and they liked to walk on
you), then he suddenly felt he wanted to see Papa again, most
awfully much. So when nobody was about, he went and pulled
the handkerchief off, and had a good long look at him: much
longer than when he was alive; for then Papa wouldn't have
liked it; besides him being too shy. Now he could stare and
stare; and he did; till he saw a secret: Papa had a little black
mole at the side of his nose, which he had never seen before.
This, and what Bowey said: that they would soon come now
and screw the lid down (just as he was, with the little mole,
and his eyelashes, and everything) gave him a very queer
feeling inside, and made his knees seem as if they weren't
going to hold him up much longer. He had to look away . . .
quickly . . . look at the violets, which had been sent as a
present: Papa was holding them just as if he was still alive.
And when he saw them, he suddenly felt he would like to
give him something, too. But only potatoes grew in the yard.
Potatoes had quite pretty little flowers when they did have,
white and purple, only they weren't come yet. But that afternoon, when he was at the parsonage with a note and was
coming away again, he *stole* a flower (a *lovely* little "polyanthers") his heart beating nearly to choke him, from having
to step on the flower bed, which was all raked in lines, and
in case he should be seen from the window. It got rather
crushed being in his pocket, but it was *very* pretty, red and
yellow, with bevelledy edges, and soft like velvet. And when
Mamma was in the office, and Bowey washing sheets, he went
on tiptoe to Papa to put his flower in. He meant to hide it

under the violets, where nobody but him would know; but, doing this, his own hand touched Papa's—and that was the end of everything. The mere feel of it, colder—much, much colder than a glass, or a plate, or a frog's back—filled him with horror . . . he nearly screamed out loud . . . and just dropped the flower anywhere, and the handkerchief all rumpled up, and ran for his life. And tore and tore, out of the house and down the yard . . . to the only quite private place he knew . . . where no one but him ever went: the space between the closet and the fence, so narrow that you had to squeeze in sideways. And he was only just in time. Before he quite got there, he'd begun to cry—as he'd never cried before. It came jumping out of him, in great big sobs.— He was *glad* Papa was dead—yes, ever so glad!—he told himself so, over and over. He'd never, never, never need to take him for walks again. And nobody would ever laugh, or point their fingers at them, or make fun of them, any more. For if you were once dead, you stopped dead—he knew that now. Not like when Lallie died, and he had gone on waiting for her to come back. Papa would never come back . . . or walk about . . . or speak to them again. He was going down into the ground, just like he was, with the shiny pillow, and the violets, and . . . and everything.— Oh, no, *no!* he couldn't bear it . . . he couldn't—even to think of it nearly killed him. And he stamped his feet, and stamped them, in a frenzy of rebellious rage. Oh, he *would* be good, and not care about anything, if only—if only . . . he'd take him for walks—anywhere!—yes, he would—if only . . . Oh, Papa! . . . dear, darling Papa! . . . come back, come back!

Afterwards, he had to go out of the gate and hang about the road, till his eyes got un-red again: not for anything would he have let Mamma or Luce or Bowey know he had had to cry.— And it made him feel hot and prickly all over, when he went indoors, to see that somebody (Mamma most likely) had found the little tumbled polyanthers and picked it up and put it right in the middle of the bunch of violets. *That* hurt more than anything.

At the last moment, the doctor, who was to have attended the funeral, telegraphed that he was unavoidably detained. This left an empty place in the single mourning coach; and Tilly, scandalised as it was by the paucity of mourners, straightway fell to work to drape a streamer round Cuffy's sailor-hat and sew a band on his left sleeve—she had arrived laden with gifts of crêpe and other black stuffs. Open-mouthed, aghast, Cuffy heard his doom. But, though quaking inwardly, he clenched his teeth and said not a word; just stood and let her sew him. Because of Mamma.

It was Mary, suddenly grown aware of his silent agony, who came out of her own grief to say: "No, Tilly, let the child be! . . . I won't have him forced. Richard would have been the last to wish it."

But scarcely had Cuffy breathed again, when he was plunged into a fresh confusion. Men came to shut down the coffin; and then, while Mamma was saying good-bye to Papa, she suddenly burst out crying—oh, simply *dreadfully!* He felt himself blush over his whole body, to hear her—*his* Mamma!—going on like this in front of these strange people, so fierce and don't-carish, and with her face all red and wrinkled up, like a baby's. But she didn't seem to mind, and didn't take a bit of notice when he poked her with his elbow and said: "Oh, hush, Mamma! They'll hear you!" Or of Uncle Jerry either, who put his hand on her shoulder and said: "It's all for the best, old girl—believe me, it is!" Aunt Tilly blew her nose so loud it hurt your ears, and winked and blinked with her eyes; but what *she* said was: "Remember, love, you're not left quite alone; you've got your children. *They'll* be your comfort! From now on they'll put aside their naughty ways and be as good as gold—I know they will!" (Huh!)

The hearse stood at the door, its double row of fantastic, feathered plumes, more brown than sable from long usage and the strong sunlight, nodding in the breeze. Brownish, too, were the antique, funereal draperies that hung almost to the ground from the backs of the two lean horses. The blinds in the neighbouring houses went down with a rush; and the narrow box, containing all that remained of the medley of hopes and fears, joys and sorrows and untold struggles, that had been Richard Mahony, was shouldered and carried out. The mourners—Jerry, the parson, the bank manager—took their seats in the carriage, and the little procession got under way.

Rounding the corner, and passing, in turn, the fire-bell, the Rechabites' Hall and the flour-mill, hearse and coach, resembling two black smudges on empty space, set to crawling up the slope that led out of the township. From the top of this

947

rise the road could be seen for miles, running without curve or turn through the grassy plains. About midway, in a slight dip, was visible the little fenced-in square of the cemetery, its sprinkling of white headstones forming a landmark in the bare, undulating country.

Amid these wavy downs Mahony was laid to rest.— It would have been after his own heart that his last bed was within sound of what he had perhaps loved best on earth—the open sea. A quarter of a mile off, behind a ridge of dunes, the surf, driving in from the Bight, breaks and booms eternally on the barren shore. Thence, too, come the fierce winds which, in stormy weather, hurl themselves over the land, where not a tree, not a bush, nor even a fence stands to break their force.— Or to limit the outlook. On all sides the eye can range, unhindered, to where the vast earth meets the infinitely vaster sky. And, under blazing summer suns, or when a full moon floods the night, no shadow falls on the sun-baked or moon-blanched plains, but those cast by the few little stones set up in human remembrance.

All that was mortal of Richard Mahony has long since crumbled to dust. For a time, fond hands tended his grave, on which in due course a small cross rose, bearing his name, and marking the days and years of his earthly pilgrimage. But, those who had known and loved him passing, scattering, forgetting, rude weeds choked the flowers, the cross toppled over, fell to pieces and was removed, the ivy that entwined it uprooted. And, thereafter, his resting-place was indistinguishable from the common ground. The rich and kindly earth of his adopted country absorbed his perishable body, as the country itself had never contrived to make its own, his wayward, vagrant spirit.

A NOTE ON THE
MANUFACTURE OF THIS BOOK

This book has been designed for the members of The Readers Club by W. A. Dwiggins, whose studio is in Hingham, Massachusetts; in planning the book, it was his interesting task to compress a vast number of words [three whole novels!] into one handsome and handy volume. The type in which the words are set is called Caledonia, and it was designed by Mr. Dwiggins himself: it is a comparatively new type, but is already in wide use for the setting of newspapers, magazines and books. The composition of the type, the printing and the binding were all done at the plant of The American Book–Stratford Press in New York. The drawings for the binding were of course made by Mr. Dwiggins. The paper was especially made for this book by the West Virginia Pulp and Paper Company.